BUSINESS STATISTICS

BUSINESS STATISTICS

(For B.Com. (Pass and Honours); B.A. (Economics Honours); M.B.A./M.M.S. of Indian Universities)

S.C. GUPTA

M.A. (Statistics); M.A. (Mathematics); M.S. (U.S.A.)

Associate Professor in Statistics (Retired)

Hindu College, University of Delhi

Delhi-110007.

Mrs. INDRA GUPTA

Himalaya Publishing House

ISO 9001:2015 CERTIFIED

First Edition : 1988
Second Thoroughly Revised and Enlarged Edition : 2013
Edition : 2015, 2016, 2018, 2019
Edition : 2020, 2021, 2023, 2024
Edition : 2025

Published by : Mrs. Meena Pandey
for **HIMALAYA PUBLISHING HOUSE PVT. LTD.,**
"Ramdoot", Dr. Bhalerao Marg, Girgaon, Mumbai - 400 004.
Phone: 022-23860170, 23863863; **Fax:** 022-23877178
E-mail: himpub@bharatmail.co.in ; **Website:** www.himpub.com

Branch Offices :

New Delhi : "Pooja Apartments", 4-B, Murari Lal Street, Ansari Road, Darya Ganj, New Delhi - 110 002. Phone: 011-23270392, 23278631; Fax: 011-23256286

Nagpur : Kundanlal Chandak Industrial Estate, Ghat Road, Nagpur - 440 018. Phone: 0712-2738731, 2721216

Bengaluru : Plot No. 91-33, 2nd Main Road, Seshadripuram, Behind Nataraja Theatre, Bengaluru - 560 020. Phone: 080-41138821; Mobile: 09379847017, 09379847005

Hyderabad : No. 3-4-184, Lingampally, Besides Raghavendra Swamy Matham, Kachiguda, Hyderabad - 500 027. Phone: 040-27560041, 27550139

Chennai : No. 34/44, Motilal Street, T. Nagar, Chennai - 600 017. Mobile: 09380460419

Pune : First Floor, "Laksha" Apartment, No. 527, Mehunpura, Shaniwarpeth (Near Prabhat Theatre), Pune - 411 030. Phone: 020-24496323, 24496333; Mobile: 09370579333

Cuttack : Plot No. 5F-755/4, Sector-9, CDA Market Nagar, Cuttack - 753 014, Odisha. Mobile: 09338746007

Kolkata : 3, S.M. Bose Road, Near Gate No. 5, Agarpara Railway Station, North 24 Parganas, West Bengal - 700109. Mobile: 09674536325

Printed by : Geetanjali Press Pvt. Ltd., Nagpur. On behalf of HPH.

Dedicated to

Our Parents

Preface

TO THE SIXTH EDITION

The book originally written over 20 years ago has been revised and reprinted several times during the intervening period. It is very heartening to note that there has been an increasing response for the book from the students of B.A. (Economics Honours), B.Com. (Pass and Honours); M.B.A./M.M.S. and other management courses, in spite of the fact that the book has not been revised for quite a long time. I take great pleasure in presenting to the readers, the **sixth thoroughly revised and enlarged edition** of the book. The book has been revised in the light of the valuable criticism, suggestions and the feedback received from the teachers, students and other readers of the book from all over the country.

Some salient features of the new edition are **:**

- The theoretical discussion throughout has been refined, restructured, rewritten and updated. During the course of rewriting, a sincere attempt has been made to retain the basic features of the earlier editions *viz.*, the simplicity of presentation, lucidity of style and the analytical approach, which have been appreciated by the teachers and the students all over India.
- Several new topics have been added at appropriate places to make the treatment of the subject matter more exhaustive and up-to-date. Some of the additions are given below :

Remark , page 5·57 : Effect of Change of Scale on Harmonic Mean.
Remark 4 , page 6·3 : Effect of Change of Origin and Scale on Range.
Remark 6 , page 6·10 : Effect of Change of Origin and Scale on Mean Deviation about Mean.
Remark 6 , page 7·3 : X_{max} and X_{min} in terms of Mean and Range.
Remark 2 , page 8·12 : Some Results on Covariance.
§ 8·10 , page 8·45 : Lag and Lead Correlation.
Remark 1 and Theorem , page 9·4 : Necessary and Sufficient Condition for Minima of E.
Remark , page 9·24 : Limits for r.
§ 11·9 , page 11·54 : Time Series Analysis in Forecasting.
§ 13·9 , page 13·9 : Covariance In Terms of Expectation.
§ 13·10 and **Remark** , page 13·14 : $\text{Var}(ax + by) = a^2 \text{Var}(x) + b^2 \text{Var}(y) + 2ab \text{Cov}(x, y)$
Equations (14·29*e*) and (14·29*f*) , page 14·31 : Distribution of the Mean $(\overline{X})$ of n *i.i.d.* $N(\mu, \sigma^2)$ variates.
§ 15·11·2 , page 15·18 – 15·19 : Sampling Distribution of Mean.

- A number of solved examples, selected from the latest examination papers of various universities and professional institutes, have been added. These are bound to assist understanding and provide greater variety.

- Exercise sets containing questions and unsolved problems at the end of each Chapter have been substantially reorganised and rewritten by deleting old problems and adding new problems, selected from the latest examination papers of various universities, C.A., I.C.W.A., and other management courses. All the problems have been very carefully graded and answers to the problems are given at the end of each problem.
- An attempt has been made to rectify the errors in the last edition.

It is hoped that all these changes, additions and improvements will enhance the value of the book. We are confident, that the book in its present form, will prove to be of much greater utility to the students as well as teachers of the subject.

We express our deep sense of thanks and gratitude to our publishers M/s Himalaya Publishing House and Type-setters, M/s Times Printographics, Darya Ganj, New Delhi, for their untiring efforts, unfailing courtesy, and co-operation in bringing out the book in such an elegant form.

We strongly believe that the road to improvement is never-ending. Suggestions and criticism for further improvement of the book will be very much appreciated and most gratefully acknowledged.

January, 2013

S.C. GUPTA
INDRA GUPTA

Preface

TO THE FIRST EDITION

In the ancient times Statistics was regarded only as the science of statecraft and was used to collect information relating to crimes, military strength, population, wealth, etc., for devising military and fiscal policies. But today, Statistics is not merely a by-product of the administrative set-up of the State but it embraces all sciences-social, physical and natural, and is finding numerous applications in various diversified fields such as agriculture, industry, sociology, biometry, planning, economics, business, management, insurance, accountancy and auditing, and so on. Statistics (theory and methods) is used extensively by the government or business or management organisations in planning future programmes and formulating policy decisions. It is rather impossible to think of any sphere of human activity where Statistics does not creep in. The subject of Statistics has acquired tremendous progress in the recent past so much so that an elementary knowledge of statistical methods has become a part of the general education in the curricula of many academic and professional courses.

This book is a modest though determined bid to serve as a text-book, for B.Com. (Pass and Hons.); B.A. Economics (Hons.) courses of Indian Universities. The main aim in writing this book is to present a clear, simple, systematic and comprehensive exposition of the principles, methods and techniques of Statistics in various disciplines with special reference to Economics and Business. The stress is on the applications of techniques and methods most commonly used by statisticians. The lucidity of style and simplicity of expression have been our twin objectives in preparing this text. Mathematical complexity has been avoided as far as possible. Wherever desirable, the notations and terminology have been clearly explained and then all the mathematical steps have been explained in detail.

An attempt has been made to start with the explanation of the elementaries of a topic and then the complexities and the intricacies of the advanced problems have been explained and solved in a lucid manner. A number of typical problems mostly from various university examination papers have been solved as illustrations so as to expose the students to different techniques of tackling the problems and enable them to have a better and throughful understanding of the basic concepts of the theory and its various applications. At many places explanatory remarks have been given to widen readers' horizon. Moreover, in order to enable the readers to have a proper appreciation of the subject-matter and to fortify their confidence in the understanding and application of methods, a large number of carefully graded problems, mostly drawn from various university examination papers, have been given as exercise sets in each chapter. Answers to all the problems in the exercise sets are given at the end of each problem.

The book contains 16 Chapters. We will not enumerate the topics discussed in the text since an idea of these can be obtained from a cursory glance at the table of contents. Chapters 1 to 11 are devoted to 'Descriptive Statistics' which consists in describing some characteristics like averages, dispersion, skewness, kurtosis, correlation, etc., of the numerical data. In spite of many latest developments in statistical techniques, the old topics like 'Classification and Tabulation' (Chapter 3) and 'Diagrammatic and Graphic Representation' (Chapter 4) have been discussed in details, since they still constitute the bulk of statistical work in government and business organisations. The use of statistical methods as scientific tools in the analysis of economic and business data has been explained in Chapter 10 (Index Numbers) and Chapter 11 (Times Series Analysis). Chapters 12 to 14 relate to advanced topics like Probability, Random

Variable, Mathematical Expectation and Theoretical Distributions. An attempt has been made to give a detailed discussion of these topics on modern lines through the concepts of 'Sample Space' and 'Axiomatic Approach' in a very simple and lucid manner. Chapter 15 (Sampling and Design of Sample Surveys), explains the various techniques of planning and executing statistical enquiries so as to arrive at valid conclusions about the population. Chapter 16 (Interpolation and Extrapolation) deals with the techniques of estimating the value of a function $y = f(x)$ for any given intermediate value of the variable x.

We must unreservedly acknowledge our deep debt of gratitude we owe to the numerous authors whose great and masterly works we have consulted during the preparation of the manuscript.

We take this opportunity to express our sincere gratitude to Prof. Kanwar Sen, Shri V.K. Kapoor and a number of students for their valuable help and suggestions in the preparation of this book.

Last but not least, we express our deep sense of gratitude to our Publishers M/s Himalaya Publishing House for their untiring efforts and unfailing courtesy and co-operation in bringing out the book in time in such an elegant form.

Every effort has been made to avoid printing errors though some might have crept in inadvertently. We shall be obliged if any such errors are brought to our notice. Valuable suggestions and criticism for the improvement of the book from our colleagues (who are teaching this course) and students will be highly appreciated and duly incorporated in subsequent editions.

June, 1988

S.C. GUPTA
Mrs. INDRA GUPTA

Contents

1 Introduction — Meaning & Scope

1·1. ORIGIN AND DEVELOPMENT OF STATISTICS

The subject of Statistics, as it seems, is not a new discipline but it is as old as the human society itself. It has been used right from the existence of life on this earth, although the sphere of its utility was very much restricted. In the old days, Statistics was regarded as the 'Science of Statecraft' and was the by-product of the administrative activity of the State. The word Statistics seems to have been derived from the Latin word '*status*' or the Italian word '*statista*' or the German word '*statistik*' or the French word '*statistique*', each of which means a political state. In the ancient times the scope of Statistics was primarily limited to the collection of the following data by the governments for framing military and fiscal policies :

(*i*) Age and sex-wise population of the country ;

(*ii*) Property and wealth of the country ;

the former enabling the government to have an idea of the manpower of the country (in order to safeguard itself against any outside aggression) and the latter providing it with information for the introduction of new taxes and levies.

Perhaps one of the earliest censuses of population and wealth was conducted by the Pharaohs (Emperors) of Egypt in connection with the construction of famous 'Pyramids'. Such censuses were later held in England, Germany and other western countries in the middle ages. In India, an efficient system of collecting official and administrative statistics existed even 2000 years ago - in particular during the reign of Chandragupta Maurya (324 – 300 B.C.). Historical evidences about the prevalence of a very good system of collecting vital statistics and registration of births and deaths even before 300 B.C. are available in Kautilya's '*Arthashastra*'. The records of land, agriculture and wealth statistics were maintained by Todermal, the land and revenue minister in the reign of Akbar (1556 – 1605 A.D.). A detailed account of the administrative and statistical surveys conducted during Akbar's reign is available in the book '*Ain-e-Akbari*' written by Abul Fazl (in 1596 – 97), one of the nine gems of Akbar.

In Germany, the systematic collection of official statistics originated towards the end of the 18th century when, in order to have an idea of the relative strength of different German States, information regarding population and output—industrial and agricultural—was collected. In England, statistics were the outcome of Napoleonic wars. The wars necessitated the systematic collection of numerical data to enable the government to assess the revenues and expenditure with greater precision and then to levy new taxes in order to meet the cost of war.

Sixteenth century saw the applications of Statistics for the collection of the data relating to the movements of heavenly bodies – stars and planets – to know about their position and for the prediction of eclipses. J. Kepler made a detailed study of the information collected by Tycko Brave (1554 – 1601) regarding the movements of the planets and formulated his famous three laws relating to the movements of heavenly bodies. These laws paved the way for the discovery of Newton's law of gravitation.

Seventeenth century witnessed the origin of *Vital Statistics.* Captain John Graunt of London (1620 – 1674), known as the Father of Vital Statistics, was the first man to make a systematic study of the birth and death statistics. Important contributions in this field were also made by prominent persons like Casper Newman (in 1691), Sir William Petty (1623 – 1687), James Dodson, Thomas Simpson and Dr. Price. The computation of mortality tables and the calculation of expectation of life at different ages by these persons led to the idea of '*Life Insurance*' and Life Insurance Institution was founded in London in 1698. William Petty wrote the book '*Essay on Political Arithmetic*'. In those days Statistics was regarded as Political Arithmetic. This concept of Statistics as Political Arithmetic continued even in early 18th century when J.P. Sussmilch (1707 – 1767), a Prussian Clergyman, formulated his doctrine that the ratio of births and deaths more or less remains constant and gave statistical explanation to the theory of '*Natural Order of Physiocratic School*'.

The backbone of the so-called modern theory of Statistics is the '*Theory of Probability*' or the '*Theory of Games and Chance*' which was developed in the mid-seventeenth century. Theory of probability is the outcome of the prevalence of gambling among the nobles of England and France while estimating the chances of winning or losing in the gamble, the chief contributors being the mathematicians and gamblers of France, Germany and England. Two French mathematicians Pascal (1623 – 1662) and P. Fermat (1601 – 1665), after a lengthy correspondence between themselves ultimately succeeded in solving the famous '*Problem of Points*' posed by the French gambler Chevalier de-Mere and this correspondence laid the foundation stone of the science of probability. Next stalwart in this field was, J. Bernoulli (1654 – 1705) whose great treatise on probability '*Ars Conjectandi*' was published posthumously in 1713, eight years after his death by his nephew Daniel Bernoulli (1700 – 1782). This contained the famous '*Law of Large Numbers*' which was later discussed by Poisson, Khinchine and Kolmogorov. De-Moivre (1667 – 1754) also contributed a lot in this field and published his famous '*Doctrine of Chance*' in 1718 and also discovered the Normal probability curve which is one of the most important contributions in Statistics. Other important contributors in this field are Pierra Simon de Laplace (1749 – 1827) who published his monumental work '*Theoric Analytique de's of Probabilities*', on probability in 1782; Gauss (1777 – 1855) who gave the principle of *Least Squares* and established the '*Normal Law of Errors*' independently of De-Moivre; L.A.J. Quetlet (1798 – 1874) discovered the principle of '*Constancy of Great Numbers*' which forms the basis of sampling; Euler, Lagrange, Bayes, etc. Russian mathematicians also have made very outstanding contributions to the modern theory of probability, the main contributors to mention only a few of them are : Chebychev (1821 – 1894), who founded the Russian School of Statisticians ; A. Markov (Markov Chains) ; Liapounoff (Central Limit Theorem); A. Khinchine (Law of Large Numbers) ; A Kolmogorov (who axiomised the calculus of probability) ; Smirnov, Gnedenko and so on.

Modern stalwarts in the development of the subject of Statistics are Englishmen who did pioneering work in the application of Statistics to different disciplines. Francis Galton (1822 – 1921) pioneered the study of '*Regression Analysis*' in Biometry; Karl Pearson (1857 – 1936) who founded the greatest statistical laboratory in England pioneered the study of '*Correlation Analysis*'. His Chi-Square test (χ^2-test) of Goodness of Fit is the first and most important of the tests of significance in Statistics ; W.S. Gosset with his *t*-test ushered in an era of exact (small) sample tests. Perhaps most of the work in the statistical theory during the past few decades can be attributed to a single person Sir Ronald A. Fisher (1890 – 1962) who applied Statistics to a variety of diversified fields such as genetics, biometry, psychology and education, agriculture, etc., and who is rightly termed as the Father of Statistics. In addition to enhancing the existing statistical theory he is the pioneer in *Estimation Theory* (Point Estimation and Fiducial Inference); *Exact* (small) *Sampling Distributions* ; *Analysis of Variance* and *Design of Experiments.* His contributions to the subject of Statistics are described by one writer in the following words :

"*R.A. Fisher is the real giant in the development of the theory of Statistics.*"

It is only the varied and outstanding contributions of R.A. Fisher that put the subject of Statistics on a very firm footing and earned for it the status of a full-fledged science.

Indian statisticians also did not lag behind in making significant contributions to the development of Statistics in various diversified fields. The valuable contributions of C.R. Rao (Statistical Inference); Parthasarathy (Theory of Probability); P.C. Mahalanobis and P.V. Sukhatme (Sample Surveys) ; S.N. Roy (Multivariate Analysis) ; R.C. Bose, K.R. Nair, J.N. Srivastava (Design of Experiments), to mention only a few, have placed India's name in the world map of Statistics.

1·2. DEFINITION OF STATISTICS

Statistics has been defined differently by different writers from time to time so much so that scholarly articles have collected together hundreds of definitions, emphasizing precisely the meaning, scope and limitations of the subject. The reasons for such a variety of definitions may be broadly classified as follows :

(*i*) The field of utility of Statistics has been increasing steadily and thus different people defined it differently according to the developments of the subject. In old days, Statistics was regarded as the 'science of statecraft' but today it embraces almost every sphere of natural and human activity. Accordingly, the old definitions which were confined to a very limited and narrow field of enquiry were replaced by the new definitions which are more exhaustive and elaborate in approach.

(*ii*) The word Statistics has been used to convey different meanings in singular and plural sense. *When used as plural, statistics means numerical set of data and when used in singular sense it means the science of statistical methods embodying the theory and techniques used for collecting, analysing and drawing inferences from the numerical data.*

It is practically impossible to enumerate all the definitions given to Statistics both as 'Numerical Data' and 'Statistical Methods' due to limitations of space. However, we give below some selected definitions.

WHAT THEY SAY ABOUT STATISTICS — SOME DEFINITIONS
"STATISTICS AS NUMERICAL DATA"

1. *"Statistics are the classified facts representing the conditions of the people in a State...specially those facts which can be stated in number or in tables of numbers or in any tabular or classified arrangement."*—**Webster.**
2. *"Statistics are numerical statements of facts in any department of enquiry placed in relation to each other."*— **Bowley.**
3. *"By statistics we mean quantitative data affected to a marked extent by multiplicity of causes".*—**Yule and Kendall.**
4. *"Statistics may be defined as the aggregate of facts affected to a marked extent by multiplicity of causes, numerically expressed, enumerated or estimated according to a reasonable standard of accuracy, collected in a systematic manner, for a predetermined purpose and placed in relation to each other."*—**Prof. Horace Secrist.**

Remarks and Comments. 1. According to Webster's definition only numerical facts can be termed Statistics. Moreover, it restricts the domain of Statistics to the affairs of a State *i.e.,* to social sciences. This is a very old and narrow definition and is inadequate for modern times since today, Statistics embraces all sciences – social, physical and natural.

2. Bowley's definition is more general than Webster's since it is related to numerical data in any department of enquiry. Moreover it also provides for comparative study of the figures as against mere classification and tabulation of Webster's definition.

3. Yule and Kendall's definition refers to numerical data affected by a multiplicity of causes. This is usually the case in social, economic and business phenomenon. For example, the prices of a particular commodity are affected by a number of factors *viz.*, supply, demand, imports, exports, money in circulation, competitive products in the market and so on. Similarly, the yield of a particular crop depends upon multiplicity of factors like quality of seed, fertility of soil, method of cultivation, irrigation facilities, weather conditions, fertilizer used and so on.

4. Secrist's definition seems to be the most exhaustive of all the four. Let us try to examine it in details.

(*i*) **Aggregate of Facts.** Simple or isolated items cannot be termed as Statistics unless they are a part of aggregate of facts relating to any particular field of enquiry. For instance, the height of an individual or the price of a particular commodity do not form Statistics as such figures are unrelated and uncomparable. However, aggregate of the figures of births, deaths, sales, purchase, production, profits, etc., over different times, places, etc., will constitute Statistics.

(*ii*) **Affected by Multiplicity of Causes.** Numerical figures should be affected by multiplicity of factors. This point has already been elaborated in remark 3 above. In physical sciences, it is possible to isolate the effect of various factors on a single item but it is very difficult to do so in social sciences, particularly when the effect of some of the factors cannot be measured quantitatively. However, statistical techniques have been devised to study the joint effect of a number of a factors on a single item (Multiple Correlation) or the isolated effect of a single factor on the given item (Partial Correlation) provided the effect of each of the factors can be measured quantitatively.

(*iii*) **Numerically Expressed.** Only numerical data constitute Statistics. Thus the statements like 'the standard of living of the people in Delhi has improved' or 'the production of a particular commodity is increasing' do not constitute Statistics. In particular, the qualitative characteristics which cannot be measured quantitatively such as intelligence, beauty, honesty, etc., cannot be termed as Statistics unless they are numerically expressed by assigning particular scores as quantitative standards. For example, intelligence is not Statistics but the intelligence quotients which may be interpreted as the quantitative measure of the intelligence of individuals could be regarded as Statistics.

(*iv*) **Enumerated or Estimated According to Reasonable Standard of Accuracy.** The numerical data pertaining to any field of enquiry can be obtained by completely enumerating the underlying population. In such a case data will be exact and accurate (but for the errors of measurement, personal bias, etc.). However, if complete enumeration of the underlying population is not possible (*e.g.*, if population is infinite, or if testing is destructive *i.e.*, if the item is destroyed in the course of inspection just like in testing explosives, light bulbs, etc.), and even if possible it may not be practicable due to certain reasons (such as population being very large, high cost of enumeration per unit and our resources being limited in terms of time and money, etc.), then the data are estimated by using the powerful techniques of *Sampling* and *Estimation* theory. However, the estimated values will not be as precise and accurate as the actual values. The degree of accuracy of the estimated values largely depends on the nature and purpose of the enquiry. For example, while measuring the heights of individuals accuracy will be aimed in terms of fractions of an inch whereas while measuring distance between two places it may be in terms of metres and if the places are very distant, *e.g.*, say Delhi and London, the difference of few kilometres may be ignored. However, certain standards of accuracy must be maintained for drawing meaningful conclusions.

(*v*) **Collected in a Systematic Manner.** The data must be collected in a very systematic manner. Thus, for any socio-economic survey, a proper schedule depending on the object of enquiry should be prepared and trained personnel (investigators) should be used to collect the data by interviewing the persons. An attempt should be made to reduce the personal bias to the minimum. Obviously, the data collected in a haphazard way will not conform to the reasonable standards of accuracy and the conclusions based on them might lead to wrong or misleading decisions.

(*vi*) **Collected for a Pre-determined Purpose.** It is of utmost importance to define in clear and concrete terms the objectives or the purpose of the enquiry and the data should be collected keeping in view these objectives. An attempt should not be made to collect too many data some of which are never examined or analysed *i.e.*, we should not waste time in collecting the information which is irrelevant for our enquiry. Also it should be ensured that no essential data are omitted. For example, if the purpose of enquiry is to measure the cost of living index for low income group people, we should select only those commodities or items which are consumed or utilised by persons belonging to this group. Thus for such an index, the collection of the data on the commodities like scooters, cars, refrigerators, television sets, high quality cosmetics, etc., will be absolutely useless.

(*vii*) **Comparable.** From practical point of view, for statistical analysis the data should be comparable. They may be compared with respect to some unit, generally time (period) or place. For example, the data relating to the population of a country for different years or the population of different countries in some fixed year constitute Statistics, since they are comparable. However, the data relating to the size of the shoe of an individual and his intelligence quotient (I.Q.) do not constitute Statistics as they are not comparable. In order to make valid comparisons the data should be homogeneous *i.e.*, they should relate to the same phenomenon or subject.

5. From the definition of Horace Secrist and its discussion in remark 4 above, we may conclude that :

"All Statistics are numerical statements of facts but all numerical statements of facts are not Statistics".

6. We give below the definitions of Statistics used in singular sense *i.e.*, Statistics as Statistical Methods.

WHAT THEY SAY ABOUT STATISTICS — SOME DEFINITIONS
"STATISTICS AS STATISTICAL METHODS"

1. *Statistics may be called the science of counting.* —Bowley A.L.
2. *Statistics may rightly be called the science of averages.* —Bowley A.L.

3. *Statistics is the science of the measurement of social organism, regarded as a whole in all its manifestations.* —**Bowley A.L.**
4. *"Statistics is the science of estimates and probabilities."* —**Boddington**
5. *"The science of Statistics is the method of judging collective, natural or social phenomenon from the results obtained from the analysis or enumeration or collection of estimates."* —**King**
6. *Statistics is the science which deals with classification and tabulation of numerical facts as the basis for explanation, description and comparison of phenomenon."*—**Lovin**
7. *"Statistics is the science which deals with the methods of collecting, classifying, presenting, comparing and interpreting numerical data collected to throw some light on any sphere of enquiry."*—**Selligman**
8. *"Statistics may be defined as the science of collection, presentation, analysis and interpretation of numerical data."* —**Croxton and Cowden**
9. *"Statistics may be regarded as a body of methods for making wise decisions in the face of uncertainty."*—**Wallis and Roberts**
10. *"Statistics is a method of decision making in the face of uncertainty on the basis of numerical data and calculated risks."*—**Prof. Ya-Lun-Chou**
11. *"The science and art of handling aggregate of facts—observing, enumeration, recording, classifying and otherwise systematically treating them."*—**Harlow**

Some Comments and Remarks. 1. The first three definitions due to Bowley are inadequate.

2. Boddington's definition also fails to describe the meaning and functions of Statistics since it is confined to only probabilities and estimates which form only a part of the modern statistical tools and do not describe the science of Statistics in all its manifestations.

3. King's definition is also inadequate since it confines Statistics only to social sciences. Lovitt's definition is fairly satisfactory, though incomplete. Selligman's definition, though very short and simple is quite comprehensive. However, the best of all the above definitions seems to be one given by Croxton and Cowden.

4. Wallis and Roberts' definition is quite modern since statistical methods enable us to arrive at valid decisions. Prof. Chou's definition in number 10 is a modified form of this definition.

5. Harlow's definition describes Statistics both as a science and an art—science, since it provides tools and laws for the analysis of the numerical information collected from the source of enquiry and art, since it undeniably has its basis upon numerical data collected with a view to maintain a particular balance and consistency leading to perfect or nearly perfect conclusions. A statistician like an artist will fail in his job if he does not possess the requisite skill, experience and patience while using statistical tools for any problem.

1·3. IMPORTANCE AND SCOPE OF STATISTICS

In the ancient times Statistics was regarded only as the science of Statecraft and was used to collect information relating to crimes, military strength, population, wealth, etc., for devising military and fiscal policies. But with the concept of *Welfare State* taking roots almost all over the world, the scope of Statistics has widened to social and economic phenomenon. Moreover, with the developments in the statistical techniques during the last few decades, today, Statistics is viewed not only as a mere device for collecting numerical data but as a means of sound techniques for their handling and analysis and drawing valid inferences from them. Accordingly, it is not merely a by-product of the administrative set up of the State but it embraces all sciences—social, physical, and natural, and is finding numerous applications in various diversified fields such as agriculture, industry, sociology, biometry, planning, economics, business, management, psychometry, insurance, accountancy and auditing, and so on. It is rather impossible to think of any sphere of human activity where Statistics does not creep in. It will not be exaggeration to say that Statistics has assumed unprecedented dimensions these days and statistical thinking is becoming more and more indispensable every day for an able citizenship. In fact to a very striking degree, the modern culture has become a statistical culture and the subject of Statistics has acquired tremendous progress in the recent past so much so that an elementary knowledge of statistical methods has become a part of the general education in the curricula of many universities all over the world. The importance of Statistics is amply explained in the following words of Carrol D. Wright (1887), United States Commissioner of the Bureau of Labour :

"To a very striking degree our culture has become a Statistical culture. Even a person who may never have heard of an index number is affected...by ... of those index numbers which describe the cost of living. It is impossible to understand Psychology, Sociology, Economics, Finance or a Physical Science without some general idea of the meaning of an average, of variation, of concomitance, of sampling, of how to interpret charts and tables."

There is no ground for misgivings regarding the practical realisation of the dream of H.G. Wells *viz.*, *"Statistical thinking will one day be as necessary for effective citizenship as the ability to read and write."* Statistics has become so much indispensable in all phases of human endeavour that it is often remarked, *"Statistics is what statisticians do"* and it appears that Bowley was right when he said, *"A knowledge of Statistics is like a knowledge of foreign language or of algebra; it may prove of use at any time under any circumstances."*

Let us now discuss briefly the importance of Statistics in some different disciplines.

Statistics in Planning. Statistics is imdispensable in planning – may it be in business, economics or government level. The modern age is termed as the 'age of planning' and almost all organisations in the government or business or management are resorting to planning for efficient working and for formulating policy decisions. To achieve this end, the statistical data relating to production, consumption, prices, investment, income, expenditure and so on and the advanced statistical techniques such as index numbers, time series analysis, demand analysis and forecasting techniques for handling such data are of paramount importance. Today efficient planning is a must for almost all countries, particularly the developing economies for their economic development and in order that planning is successful, it must be based on a correct and sound analysis of complex statistical data. For instance, in formulating a five-year plan, the government must have an idea of the age and sex-wise break up of the population projections of the country for the next five years in order to develop its various sectors like agriculture, industry, textiles, education and so on. This is achieved through the powerful statistical tool of forecasting by making use of the population data for the previous years. Even for making decisions concerning the day to day policy of the country, an accurate statistical knowledge of the age and sex-wise composition of the population is imperative for the government. In India, the use of Statistics in planning was well visualised long back and the National Sample Survey (N.S.S.) was primarily set up in 1950 for the collection of statistical data for planning in India.

Statistics in State. As has already been pointed out, in the old days Statistics was the science of State-craft and its objective was to collect data relating to manpower, crimes, income and wealth, etc., for formulating suitable military and fiscal policies. With the inception of the idea of Welfare State and its taking deep roots in almost all the countries, today statistical data relating to prices, production, consumption, income and expenditure, investments and profits, etc., and statistical tools of index numbers, time series analysis, demand analysis, forecasting, etc., are extensively used by the governments in formulating economic policies. (For details see Statistics in Economics). Moreover as pointed out earlier (Statistics in planning), statistical data and techniques are indispensable to the government for planning future economic programmes. The study of population movement *i.e.*, population estimates, population projections and other allied studies together with birth and death statistics according to age and sex distribution provide any administration with fundamental tools which are indispensable for overall planning and evaluation of economic and social development programmes. The facts and figures relating to births, deaths and marriages are of extreme importance to various official agencies for a variety of administrative purposes. Mortality (death) statistics serve as a guide to the health authorities for sanitary improvements, improved medical facilities and public cleanliness. The data on the incidence of diseases together with the number of deaths by age and nature of diseases are of paramount importance to health authorities in taking appropriate remedial action to prevent or control the spread of the disease. The use of statistical data and statistical techniques is so wide in government functioning that today, almost all ministries and the departments in the government have a separate statistical unit. In fact, today, in most countries the State (government) is the single unit which is the biggest collector and user of statistical data. In addition to the various statistical bureaux in all the ministries and the government departments in the Centre and the States, the main Statistical Agencies in India are Central Statistical Organisation (C.S.O.) ; National Sample Survey (N.S.S.), now called National Sample Survey Organisation (N.S.S.O.) and the Registrar General of India (R.G.I.).

Statistics in Economics. In old days, Economic Theories were based on deductive logic only. Moreover, the statistical techniques were not that much advanced for applications in other disciplines. It gradually dawned upon economists of the Deductive School to use Statistics effectively by making empirical studies.

In 1871, W.S. Jevons, wrote that :

"The deductive science of economy must be verified and rendered useful from the purely inductive science of Statistics. Theory must be invested with the reality of life and fact."

These views were supported by Roscher, Kines and Hildebrand of the Historical School (1843 – 1883), Alfred Marshall, Pareto, Lord Keynes. The following quotation due to Prof. Alfred Marshall in 1890 amply illustrates the role of Statistics in Economics :

"Statistics are the straws out of which I, like every other economist, have to make bricks."

Statistics plays a very vital role in Economics so much so that in 1926, Prof. R.A. Fisher complained of *"the painful misapprehension that Statistics is a branch of Economics."*

Statistical data and advanced techniques of statistical analysis have proved immensely useful in the solution of a variety of economic problems such as production, consumption, distribution of income and wealth, wages, prices, profits, savings, expenditure, investment, unemployment, poverty, etc. For example, the studies of consumption statistics reveal the pattern of the consumption of the various commodities by different sections of the society and also enable us to have some idea about their purchasing capacity and their standard of living. The studies of production statistics enable us to strike a balance between supply and demand which is provided by the laws of supply and demand. The income and wealth statistics are mainly helpful in reducing the disparities of income. The statistics of prices are needed to study the price theories and the general problem of inflation through the construction of the cost of living and wholesale price index numbers. The statistics of market prices, costs and profits of different individual concerns are needed for the studies of competition and monopoly. Statistics pertaining to some macro-variables like production, income, expenditure, savings, investments, etc., are used for the compilation of National Income Accounts which are indispensable for economic planning of a country. Exchange statistics reflect upon the commercial development of a nation and tell us about the money in circulation and the volume of business done in the country. Statistical techniques have also been used in determining the measures of Gross National Product and Input-Output Analysis. The advanced and sound statistical techniques have been used successfully in the analysis of cost functions, production functions and consumption functions.

Use of Statistics in Economics has led to the formulation of many economic laws some of which are mentioned below for illustration :

A detailed and systematic study of the family budget data which gives a detailed account of the family budgets showing expenditure on the main items of family consumption together with family structure and composition, family income and various other social, economic and demographic characteristics led to the famous *Engel's Law of Consumption* in 1895. Vilfredo Pareto in 19th-20th century propounded his famous *Law of Distribution of Income* by making an empirical study of the income data of various countries of the world at different times. The study of the data pertaining to the actual observation of the behaviour of buyers in the market resulted in the *Revealed Preference Analysis* of Prof. Samuelson.

Time Series Analysis, Index Numbers, Forecasting Techniques and Demand Analysis are some of the very powerful statistical tools which are used immensely in the analysis of economic data and also for economic planning. For instance, time series analysis is extremely used in Business and Economic Statistics for the study of the series relating to prices, production and consumption of commodities, money in circulation, bank deposits and bank clearings, sales in a departmental store, etc.,

(*i*) to identify the forces or components at work, the net effect of whose interaction is exhibited by the movement of the time series;

(*ii*) to isolate, study, analyse and measure them independently.

The index numbers which are also termed as '*economic barometers*' are the numbers which reflect the changes over specified period of time in (*i*) prices of different commodities, (*ii*) industrial/agricultural production, (*iii*) sales, (*iv*) imports and exports, (*v*) cost of living, etc., and are extremely useful in economic planning. For instance, the cost of living index numbers are used for (*i*) the calculation of real wages and for determining the purchasing power of the money; (*ii*) the deflation of income and value series in national accounts; (*iii*) grant of dearness allowance (D.A.) or bonus to the workers in order to enable them to meet the increased cost of living and so on.

The demand analysis consists in making an economic study of the market data to determine the relation between :

(*i*) the prices of a given commodity and its absorption capacity for the market *i.e.*, demand; and

(*ii*) the price of a commodity and its output *i.e.*, supply.

Forecasting techniques based on the method of curve fitting by the principle of least squares and exponential smoothing are indispensable tools for economic planning.

The increasing interaction of mathematics and statistics with economics led to the development of a new discipline called *Econometrics*—and the first Econometric Society was founded in U.S.A. in 1930 for "*the advancement of economic theory in its relation to mathematics and statistics...*" Econometrics aimed at making Economics a more realistic, precise, logical and practical science. Econometric models based on sound statistical analysis are used for maximum exploitation of the available resources. In other words, an attempt is made to obtain optimum results subject to a number of constraints on the resources at our disposal, say, of production capacity, capital, technology, precision, etc., which are determined statistically.

Statistics in Business and Management. Prior to the Industrial Revolution, when the production was at the handicraft stage, the business activities were very much limited and were confined only to small units operating in their own areas. The owner of the concern personally looked after all the departments of business activity like sales, purchase, production, marketing, finance and so on. But after the Industrial Revolution, the developments in business activities have taken such unprecedented dimensions both in the size and the competition in the market that the activities of most of the business enterprises and firms are confined not only to one particular locality, town or place but to larger areas. Some of the leading houses have the network of their business activities in almost all the leading towns and cities of the country and even abroad. Accordingly it is impossible for a single person (the owner of the concern) to look after its activities and management has become a specialised job. The manager and a team of management executives is imperative for the efficient handling of the various operations like sales, purchase, production, marketing, control, finance, etc., of the business house. It is here that statistical data and the powerful statistical tools of probability, expectation, sampling techniques, tests of significance, estimation theory, forecasting techniques and so on play an indispensable role. According to Wallis and Roberts : "*Statistics may be regarded as a body of methods for making wise decisions in the face of uncertainty.*" A refinement over this definition is provided by Prof. Ya-Lun-Chou as follows : "*Statistics is a method of decision making in the face of uncertainty on the basis of numerical data and calculated risks.*" These definitions reflect the applications of Statistics in business since modern business has its roots in the accuracy and precision of the estimates and statistical forecasting regarding the future demand for the product, market trends and so on. Business forecasting techniques which are based on the compilation of useful statistical information on lead and lag indicators are very useful for obtaining estimates which serve as a guide to future economic events. Wrong expectations which might be the result of faulty and inaccurate analysis of various factors affecting a particular phenomenon might lead to his disaster. The time series analysis is a very important statistical tool which is used in business for the study of :

(*i*) Trend (by method of curve fitting by the principle of least squares) in order to obtain the estimates of the probable demand of the goods; and

(*ii*) Seasonal and Cyclical movements in the phenomenon, for determining the '*Business Cycle*' which may also be termed as the four-phase cycle composed of prosperity (period of boom), recession, depression and recovery. The upswings and downswings in business depend on the cumulative nature of the economic forces (affecting the equilibrium of supply and demand) and the interaction between them. Most of the business and commercial series *e.g.*, series relating to prices, production, consumption, profits, investments, wages, etc., are affected to a great extent by business cycles. Thus the study of business cycles is of paramount importance in business and a businessman who ignores the effects of booms and depression is bound to fail since his estimates and forecasts will definitely be faulty.

The studies of *Economic Barometers* (Index Numbers of Prices) enable the businessman to have an idea about the purchasing power of money. The statistical tools of demand analysis enable the businessman to strike a balance between supply and demand. [For details, see Statistics in Economics].

The technique of Statistical Quality Control, through the powerful tools of 'Control Charts' and 'Inspection Plans' is indispensable to any business organisation for ensuring that the quality of the manufactured product is in conformity with the consumer's specifications. (For details see Statistics in Industry).

Statistical tools are used widely by business enterprises for the promotion of new business. Before embarking upon any production process, the business house must have an idea about the quantum of the product to be manufactured, the amount of the raw material and labour needed for it, the quality of the finished product, marketing avenues for the product, the competitive products in the market and so on. Thus the formulation of a production plan is a must and this cannot be achieved without collecting the statistical information on the above items without resorting to the powerful technique of '*Sample Surveys*'. As such, most of the leading business and industrial concerns have full-fledged statistical units with trained and efficient statisticians for formulating such plans and arriving at valid decisions in the face of uncertainty with calculated risks. These units also carry on research and development programmes for the improvement of the quality of the existing products (in the light of the competitive products in the market), introduction of new products and optimisation of the profits with existing resources at their disposal.

Statistical tools of probability and expectation are extremely useful in *Life Insurance* which is one of the pioneer branches of Business and Commerce to use Statistics since the end of the seventeenth century.

Statistical techniques have also been used very widely by business organisations in :

(*i*) *Marketing Decisions* (based on the statistical analysis of consumer preference studies – demand analysis).

(*ii*) *Investment* (based on sound study of individual shares and debentures).

(*iii*) *Personnel Administration* (for the study of statistical data relating to wages, cost of living, incentive plans, effect of labour dispute/unrest on the production, performance standards, etc.).

(*iv*) *Credit policy.*

(*v*) *Inventory Control* (for co-ordination between production and sales).

(*vi*) *Accounting* (for evaluation of the assets of the business concerns). (For details see Statistics in Accountancy and Auditing).

(*vii*) *Sales Control* (through the statistical data pertaining to market studies, consumer preference studies, trade channel studies and readership surveys, etc.), and so on.

From the above discussion it is obvious that the use of statistical data and techniques is indispensable in almost all the branches of business activity.

Statistics in Accountancy and Auditing. Today, the science of Statistics has assumed such unprecedented dimensions that even the subjects like Accountancy and Auditing have not escaped its domain. The ever-increasing applications of the statistical data and the advanced statistical techniques in Accountancy and Auditing are well supported by the inclusion of a compulsory paper on Statistics both in the Chartered Accountants (Foundation) and Cost and Works Accountants (Intermediate) examinations curriculum. Statistics has innumerable applications in accountancy and auditing. For example the statistical data on some macro-variables like income, expenditure, investment, profits, production, savings, etc., are used for the compilation of National Income Accounts which provide information on the value added by different sectors of economy and are very helpful in formulating economic policies. The statistical study (Correlation Analysis) of profit and dividend statistics enables one to predict the probable dividends for the future years. Further, in Accountancy, the statistics of assets and liabilities, and income and expenditure are helpful to ascertain the financial results of various operations.

A very important application of Statistics in accountancy is in the '*Method of Inflation Accounting*' which consists in revaluating the accounting records based on historical costs of assets after adjusting for the changes in the purchasing power of money. This is achieved through the powerful statistical tools of Price Index Numbers and Price Deflators.

The Regression Analysis theory is of immense help in Cost Accounting in forecasting cost or price for any given value of the dependent variable. Suppose there exists a functional relation between cost of production (c) and the price of the product (p), of the form :

$$c = f(p)$$

Then with the statistical tools of regression analysis we can predict the effect of changes in future prices on the cost of production. Statistical techniques are also greatly used in forecasting profits, determination of trend, computation of financial and other ratios, cost-volume-profit analysis and so on. The efficacy of the implementation of a new investment plan can be tested by using the statistical tests of significance.

In Auditing, sampling techniques are used widely for test checking. The business transactions and the volumes of the various items comprising balances in various accounts are so heavy (voluminous) that it is practically impossible to resort to 100% examination and analysis of the records because of limitations of time, money and staff at our disposal. Accordingly, sampling techniques based on sound statistical and scientific reasoning are used effectively to examine thoroughly only a sample (fraction – 2% or 5%) of the transactions or the items comprising a balance and drawing inferences about the whole lot (data) by using statistical techniques of Estimation and Inference.

Statistics in Industry. In industry, Statistics is extensively used in '*Quality Control*'. The main objective in any production process it to control the quality of the manufactured product so that it conforms to specifications. This is called process control and is achieved through the powerful technique of control charts and inspection plans. The discovery of the control charts was made by a young physicist Dr. W.A. Shewhart of the Bell Telephone Laboratories (U.S.A.) in 1924 and the following years and is based on setting the 3σ (3 – sigma) control limits which has its basis on the theory of probability and normal distribution. Inspection plans are based on special kind of sampling techniques which are a very important aspect of statistical theory.

Statistics in Physical Sciences. The applications of Statistics in Astronomy, which is a physical science, have already been discussed above. In physical sciences, a large number of measurements are taken on the same item. There is bound to be variation in these measurements. In order to have an idea about the degree of accuracy achieved, the statistical techniques (Interval Estimation – confidence intervals and confidence limits) are used to assign certain limits within which the true value of the phenomenon may be expected to lie. The desire for precision was first felt in physical sciences and this led the science to express the facts under study in quantitative form. The statistical theory with the powerful tools of sampling, estimation (point and interval), design of experiments, etc., is most effective for the analysis of the quantitative expression of all fields of study. Today, there is an increasing use of Statistics in most of the physical sciences such as astronomy, geology, engineering, physics and meteorology.

Statistics in Social Sciences. According to Bowley, "Statistics is the science of the measurement of social organism, regarded as a whole in all its manifestations." In the words of W.I. King, "The science of Statistics is the method of judging collective, natural or social phenomenon from the results obtained from the analysis or enumeration or collection of estimates." These words of Bowley and King amply reflect upon the importance of Statistics in social sciences.

Every social phenomenon is affected to a marked extent by a multiplicity of factors which bring out the variation in observations from time to time, place to place and object to object. Statistical tools of Regression and Correlation Analysis can be used to study and isolate the effect of each of these factors on the given observation. Sampling Techniques and Estimation Theory are very powerful and indispensable tools for conducting any social survey, pertaining to any strata of society and then analysing the results and drawing valid inferences. The most important application of statistics in sociology is in the field of *Demography* for studying mortality (death rates), fertility (birth rates), marriages, population growth and so on. In fact statistical data and statistical techniques have been used so frequently and in so many problems in social sciences that Croxton and Cowden have remarked :

"*Without an adequate understanding of the statistical methods, the investigator in the social sciences may be like the blind man groping in a dark room for a black cat that is not there. The methods of Statistics are useful in an over-widening range of human activities in any field of thought in which numerical data may be had.*"

Statistics in Biology and Medical Sciences. Sir Francis Galton (1822 – 1911), a British Biometrician pioneered the use of statistical methods with his work on '*Regression*' in connection with the inheritance of stature. According to Prof. Karl Pearson (1857 – 1936) who pioneered the study of '*Correlation Analysis*', the whole theory of heredity rests on statistical basis. In his Grammar of Sciences he says, "*The whole problem of evolution is a problem of vital statistics, a problem of longevity, of fertility, of health, of disease and it is impossible for the evolutionist to proceed without statistics as it would be for the Registrar General to discuss the rational mortality without an enumeration of the population, a classification of deaths and a knowledge of statistical theory.*"

In medical sciences also, the statistical tools for the collection, presentation and analysis of observed factual data relating to the causes and incidence of diseases are of paramount importance. For example, the factual data relating to pulse rate, body temperature, blood pressure, heart beats, weight, etc., of the patient greatly help the doctor for the proper diagnosis of the disease; statistical papers are used to study heart beats through electro-cardiogram (E.C.G.). Perhaps the most important application of Statistics in medical sciences lies in using the tests of significance (more precisely Student's t-test) for testing the efficacy of a manufacturing drug, injection or medicine for controlling/curing specific ailments. The testing of the effectiveness of a medicine by the manufacturing concern is a must, since only after the effectiveness of the medicine is established by the sound statistical techniques that it will venture to manufacture it on a large scale and bring it out in the market. Comparative studies for the effectiveness of different medicines by different concerns can also be made by statistical techniques.

Statistics in Psychology and Education. Statistics has been used very widely in education and psychology too *e.g.*, in the scaling of mental tests and other psychological data; for measuring the reliability and validity of test scrores ; for determing the Intelligence Quotient (I.Q.) ; in Item Analysis and Factor Analysis. The vast applications of statistical data and statistical theories have given rise to a new discipline called '*Psychometry*'.

1·4. LIMITATIONS OF STATISTICS

Although Statistics is indispensable to almost all sciences—social, physical and natural, and is very widely used in almost all spheres of human activity, it is not without limitations which restrict its scope and utility.

1. *Statistics does not study qualitative phenomenon.* 'Statistics are numerical statements in any department of enquiry placed in relation to each other'. Since Statistics is a science dealing with a set of numerical data, it can be applied to the study of only those phenomena which can be measured quantitatively. Thus the statements like 'population of India has increased considerably during the last few years' or 'the standard of living of the people in Delhi has gone up as compared with last year', do not constitute Statistics. As such Statistics cannot be used directly for the study of quality characteristics like health, beauty, honesty, welfare, poverty, etc., which cannot be measured quantitatively. However, the techniques of statistical analysis can be applied to qualitative phenomena indirectly by expressing them numerically after assigning particular scores or quantitative standards. For instance, attribute of intelligence in a group of individuals can be studied on the basis of their intelligence quotients (I.Q.'s) which may be regarded as the quantitative measure of the individuals' intelligence.

2. *Statistics does not study individuals.* According to Prof. Horace Secrist, "By Statistics we mean aggregate of facts affected to a marked extent by multiplicity of factors...and placed in relation to each other." Thus a single or isolated figure cannot be regarded as Statistics unless it is a part of the aggregate of facts relating to any particular field of enquiry. Thus statistical methods do not give any recognition to an object or a person or an event in isolation. This is a serious limitation of Statistics. For instance, the price of a single commodity, the profit of a particular concern or the production of a particular business house do not constitute statistics since these figures are unrelated and uncomparable. However, the aggregate of figures relating to prices and consumption of various commodities, the sales and profits of a business house, the income, expenditure, production, etc., over different periods of time, places, etc., will be Statistics. Thus from statistical point of view the figure of the population of a particular country in some given year is useless unless we are also given the figures of the population of the country for different years or of different countries for the same year for comparative studies. Hence Statistics is confined only to those problems where group characteristics are to be studied.

3. *Statistical laws are not exact.* Since the statistical laws are probabilistic in nature, inferences based on them are only approximate and not exact like the inferences based on mathematical or scientific (physical and natural sciences) laws. Statistical laws are true only on the average. If the probability of getting a head in a single throw of a coin is $\frac{1}{2}$, it does not imply that if we toss a coin 10 times, we shall get five heads and five tails. In 10 throws of a coin we may get 8 heads, 9 heads or all the 10 heads, or we may not get even a single head. By this we mean that if the experiment of throwing the coin is carried on indefinitely (very large number of times), then we should expect on the average 50% heads and 50% tails.

4. *Statistics is liable to be misused.* Perhaps the most significant limitation of Statistics is that it must be used by experts. According to Bowley, "Statistics only furnishes a tool though imperfect which is dangerous in the hands of those who do not know its use and deficiencies." Statistical methods are the most dangerous tools in the hands of the inexperts. Statistics is one of those sciences whose adepts must exercise the self-restraint of an artist. The greatest limitation of Statistics is that it deals with figures which are innocent in themselves and do not bear on their face the label of their quality and can be easily distorted, manipulated or moulded by politicians, dishonest or unskilled workers, unscrupulous people for personal selfish motives. Statistics neither proves nor disproves anything. It is merely a tool which, if rightly used may prove extremely useful but if misused by inexperienced, unskilled and dishonest statisticians might lead to very fallacious conclusions and even prove to be disastrous. In the words of W.I. King, "Statistics are like clay of which you can make a God or a Devil as you please." At another place he remarks, "Science of Statistics is the useful servant but only of great value to those who understand its proper use."

Thus the use of Statistics by the experts who are well experienced and skilled in the analysis and interpretation of statistical data for drawing correct and valid inferences very much reduces the chances of mass popularity of this important science.

1·5. DISTRUST OF STATISTICS

The improper use of statistical tools by unscrupulous people with an improper statistical bend of mind has led to the public distrust in Statistics. By this we mean that public loses its belief, faith and confidence in the science of Statistics and starts condemning it. Such irresponsible, inexperienced and dishonest persons who use statistical data and statistical techniques to fulfill their selfish motives have discredited the science of Statistics with some very interesting comments, some of which are stated below :

(*i*) An ounce of truth will produce tons of Statistics.
(*ii*) Statistics can prove anything.
(*iii*) Figures do not lie. Liars figure.
(*iv*) Statistics is an unreliable science.
(*v*) There are three types of lies – lies, damned lies and Statistics, wicked in the order of their naming ; and so on.

Some of the reasons for the above remarks may be enumerated as follows :

(*a*) Figures are innocent and believable, and the facts based on them are psychologically more convincing. But it is a pity that figures do not have the label of quality on their face.

(*b*) Arguments are put forward to establish certain results which are not true by making use of inaccurate figures or by using incomplete data, thus distorting the truth.

(*c*) Though accurate, the figures might be moulded and manipulated by dishonest and unscrupulous persons to conceal the truth and present a working and distorted picture of the facts to the public for personal and selfish motives.

Hence, if Statistics and its tools are misused, the fault does not lie with the science of Statistics. Rather, it is the people who misuse it, are to be blamed.

Utmost care and precautions should be taken for the interpretation of statistical data in all its manifestations. "Statistics should not be used as a blind man uses a lamp-post for support instead of illumination." However, there are misapprehensions about the argument that Statistics can be used effectively by expert statisticians, as is given in the following remark due to Wallis and Roberts:

"He who accepts statistics indiscriminately will often be duped unnecessarily. But he who distrusts statistics indiscriminately will often be ignorant unnecessarily. There is an accessible alternative between blind gullibility and blind distrust. It is possible to interpret statistics skillfully. The art of interpretation need not be monopolized by statisticians, though, of course, technical statistical knowledge helps. Many important ideas of technical statistics can be conveyed to the non-statistician without distortion or dilution. Statistical interpretation depends not only on statistical ideas but also on ordinary clear thinking. Clear thinking is not only indispensable in interpreting statistics but is often sufficient even in the absence of specific statistical knowledge. For the statistician not only death and taxes but also statistical fallacies are unavoidable. With skill, common sense, patience and above all objectivity, their frequency can be reduced and their effects minimised. But eternal vigilance is the price of freedom from serious statistical blunders."

We give below some illustrations regarding the mis-interpretation of statistical data.

1. "The number of car accidents committed in a city in a particular year by women drivers is 10 while those committed by men drivers is 40. Hence women are safe drivers". The statement is obviously wrong since nothing is said about the total number of men and women drivers in the city in the given year. Some valid conclusions can be drawn if we are given the proportion of the accidents committed by male and female drivers.

2. "It has been found that the 25% of the surgical operations by a particular surgeon are successful. If he is to operate on four persons on any day and three of the operations have proved unsuccessful, the fourth must be a success." The given conclusion is not true since statistical laws are probabilistic in nature and not exact. The conclusion that if three operations on a particular day are unsuccessful, the fourth must be a success, is not true. It may happen that the fourth operation is also unsuccessful. It may also happen that on any day two or three or even all the four operations may be successful. The statement means that as the number of operations becomes larger and larger, we should expect, on the average, 25% of the operations to be successful.

3. A report : "The number of traffic accidents is lower in foggy weather than on clear weather days. Hence it is safer to drive in fog."

The statement again is obviously wrong. To arrive at any valid conclusions we must take into account the difference between the rush of traffic under the two weather conditions and also the extra cautiousness observed when driving in bad weather.

4. "80% of the people who drink alcohol die before attaining the age of 70 years. Hence drinking is harmful for longevity of life." This statement is also fallacious since no information is given about the number of persons who do not drink alcohol and die before attaining the age of 70 years. In the absence of the information about the proportion of such persons we cannot draw any valid conclusions.

5. Incomplete data usually leads us to fallacious conclusions. Let us consider the scores of two students Ram and Shyam in three tests during a year.

	1st test	2nd test	3rd test	Average Score
Ram's Score	50%	60%	70%	60%
Shyam's Score	70%	60%	50%	60%

If we are given the average score which is 60% in each case, we will conclude that the level of intelligence of the two students at the end of the year is same. But this conclusion is false and misleading since a careful study of the detailed marks over the three tests reveals that Ram has improved consistently while Shyam has deteriorated consistently.

Remark. Numerous such examples can be constructed to illustrate the misuse of statistical methods and this is all due to their unjudicious applications and interpretations for which the science of Statistics cannot be blamed.

EXERCISE 1·1

1. (*a*) Write a short essay on the origin and development of the science of Statistics.

(*b*) Give the names of some of the veterans in the development of Statistics, along with their contributions.

2. (*a*) Discuss the utility of Statistics to the state, the economist, the industrialist and the social worker.

(*b*) Define "Statistics" and discuss the importance of Statistics in a planned economy.

3. (*a*) Define the term "Statistics" and discuss its use in business and trade. Also point out its limitations.

[*Punjab Univ. B.Com., April 1999*]

(*b*) Define the term "Statistics" and discuss its functions and limitations. [*C.S. (Foundation), June 2001*]

(*c*) Explain the importance of Statistics with respect to business and industry.

[*Delhi Univ. B.Com. (Pass), 2000*]

4. Explain critically a few of the definitions of Statistics and state the one which you think to be the best.

5. (*a*) "Statistics is a method of decision-making in the face of uncertainty on the basis of numerical data and calculated risks." Explain with suitable illustrations.

(*b*) Discuss the scope of Statistics. [*Punjab Univ. B.Com., Oct. 1998*]

6. Discuss briefly the importance of Statistics in the following disciplines :

(*i*) Economics	(*i*) Business and Management	(*iii*) Planning
(*iv*) Accountancy and Auditing	(*v*) Physical Sciences	(*vi*) Industry
(*vii*) Biology and Medical Sciences	(*viii*) Social Sciences	

7. Comment briefly on the following statements :

(*a*) "Statistics is the science of human welfare."

(*b*) "To a very striking degree our culture has become a statistical culture."

(*c*) "Statistical thinking will one day be as necessary for efficient citizenship as the ability to read and write."

8. (*a*) Comment briefly on the following statements :

(*i*) "Statistics can prove anything".

(*ii*) "Statistics affects everybody and touches life at many points. It is both a science and an art".

(*b*) "He who accepts statistics indiscriminately will often be duped unnecessarily, but he who distrusts statistics indiscriminately will often be ignorant indiscriminately." Comment on the above statement.

(*c*) "Sciences without statistics bear no fruit, statistics without sciences have no root." Explain the above statement with necessary comments.

9. Comment on the following statements illustrating your view point with suitable examples :

(*a*) "Knowledge of Statistics is like a knowledge of foreign language or of algebra. It may prove of use at any time under any circumstances." (*Bowley*)

(*b*) "Statistics is what statisticians do."

(*c*) "There are lies, damned lies and Statistics – wicked in the order of their naming."

(*d*) "By Statistics we mean aggregate of facts affected to a marked extent by multiplicity of causes, numerically expressed, enumerated or estimated according to reasonable standards of accuracy, collected in a systematic manner for a pre-determined purpose and placed in relation to each other'. (*Horace Secrist*)

(*e*) Statistics are the straws out of which I, like every other economist, have to make the bricks." (*Marshall*)

(*f*) "Statistics conceals more than it reveals." [*C.S. (Foundation), June 2002*]

(*g*) "Statistics are like bikinis : they reveal what is interesting and conceal what is vital."

10. (*a*) What do you understand by distrust of Statistics ? Is the science of Statistics to be blamed for it ?

(*b*) Write a critical note on the limitations and distrust of Statistics. Discuss the important causes of distrust and show how Statistics could be made reliable.

(*c*) Define 'Statistics' and discuss its uses and limitations. [*Punjab Univ. B.Com., 1998*]

(*d*) Discuss the use of Statistics in the fields of economics, trade and commerce. What are the limitations of Statistics.

(*e*) Explain : "Distrust and misuse of Statistics." [*C.S. (Foundation), June 2001*]

(*f*) "Statistics widens the field of knowledge." Elucidate the statement. [*C.S. (Foundation), June 2000*]

11. (*a*) "Statistical methods are most dangerous tools in the hands of the inexperts." Discuss and explain the limitation of Statistics.

(*b*) "The science of Statistics, then, is a most useful servant but only of great value to those who understand its proper use"–King.

Comment on the above statement and discuss the limitations of Statistics.

(*c*) "Statistics are like clay of which you can make a God or Devil, as you please."

In the light of this statement, discuss the uses and limitations of Statistics.

(*d*) "All statistics are numerical statements but all numerical statements are not statistics." Examine.

[*C.S. (Foundation), Dec. 2000*]

12. Comment on the following statements :

(*a*) "Statistics are like clay of which you make a God or Devil, as you please."

(*b*) "Statistics is the science of estimates and probabilities."

(*c*) "Statistics is the science of counting."

(*d*) "Statistics should not be used as a blind man uses a lamp post for support, instead of for illumination."

[*C.S. (Foundation), Dec. 2001*]

13. Comment on the following statistical statements, bringing out in details the fallacies, if any :

(*i*) "A survey revealed that the children of engineers, doctors and lawyers have high intelligence quotients (I.Q.). It further revealed that the grandfathers of these children were also highly intelligent. Hence the inference is that intelligence is hereditary."

(*ii*) "The number of deaths in military in a recent war in a country was 15 out of 1,000 while the number of deaths in the capital of the country during the same period was 22 per thousand. Hence it is safe to join military service than to live in the capital city of the country."

(*iii*) "The number of accidents taking place in the middle of the road is much less than the number of accidents taking place on its sides. Hence it is safer to walk in the middle of the road."

(*iv*) "The frequency of divorce for couples with the children is only about $\frac{1}{2}$ of that for childless couples; therefore producing children is an effective check on divorce."

(*v*) "The increase in the price of a commodity was 20%. Then the price decreased by 15% and again increased by 10%. So the resultant increase in the price was 20 – 15 + 10 = 15%."

(*vi*) "Nutritious Bread Company, a private manufacturing concern, charges a lower rate per loaf than that charged by a Government of India Undertaking 'Modern Bread.' Thus private ownership is more efficient than public ownership."

(*vii*) According to the estimate of an economist, the per capita national income of India for 1931-32 was Rs. 65. The National Income Committee estimated the corresponding figure for 1948-49 as Rs. 225. Hence in 1948-49, Indians were nearly four times as prosperous as in 1931-32 ?

14. Point out the ambiguity or mistakes found in the following statements which are made on the basis of the facts given :

(*a*) 80% of the people who die of cancer are found to be smokers and so it may be concluded that smoking causes cancer.

(*b*) The gross profit to sales ratio of a company was 15% in the year 1994 and was 10% in 1995. Hence the stock must have been undervalued.

(*c*) The average output in a factory was 2,500 units in January 1991 and 2,400 units in February 1991. So workers were more efficient in January 1991.

(*d*) The rate of increase in the number of buffalloes in India is greater than that of the population. Hence the people of India are now getting more milk per head.

15. Comment on the following :

(*a*) 50 boys and 50 girls took an examination. 30 boys and 40 girls got through the examination. Hence girls are more intelligent than boys.

(*b*) The average monthly incomes in two cities of Hyderabad and Chennai were found to be Rs. 330. Hence, the people of both the cities have the same standard of living.

(*c*) A tutorial college advertised that there was 100 per cent success of the candidates who took the coaching in their institute. Hence the college has got good faculty.

16. Fill in the blanks :

(*i*) The word Statistics has been derived from the Latin word ...... or the German word ......

(*ii*) The word Statistics is used to convey different meanings in ...... and ...... sense.

(*iii*) Statistics is an ...... and also a ....

(*iv*) ...... defined statistics as 'numerical statement of facts'.

(*v*) In singular sense, Statistics means ....

(*vi*) In plural sense, Statistics means ......

(*vii*) Prof. Ya-Lun-Chou defined Statistics as 'a method of .....

(*viii*) Bowley A.L. defined Statistics as ...... counting.

(*ix*) Statistics are of ...... help in human welfare.

(*x*) Prof. ...... is the real giant in the development of the theory of Statistics.

(*xi*) "Statistics are the ...... out of which I, like every other economist, have to make......" Alfred Marshall.

(*xii*) Two Indian statisticians who have made significant contribution in the development of statistics are ...... and ....

Ans. (*i*) status, statistik; (*ii*) singular, plural; (*iii*) art, science; (*iv*) A.L. Bowley; (*v*) statistical methods used for collecting analysing and drawing inferences from the numerical data; (*vi*) numerical set of data; (*vii*) decision making in the face of uncertainty on the basis of numerical data and calculated risks. (*viii*) science of (*ix*) great (immense); (*x*) R.A. Fisher; (*xi*) straws, bricks; (*xii*) P.C. Mahalanobis, C.R. Rao.

17. Indicate if the following statements are true (T) or false (F).

(*i*) The subject of statistics is a century old.

(*ii*) The word statistics seems to have been derived from Latin word status.

(*iii*) Statistics is of no use to humanity.

(*iv*) 'To a very striking degree, our culture has become a statistical culture'.

(*v*) Statistics can prove anything.

Ans. (*i*) F; (*ii*) T; (*iii*) F; (*iv*) T; (*v*) F.

2 Collection of Data

2·1. INTRODUCTION

As pointed out in Chapter 1, Statistics are a set of numerical data. (See definitions of Secrist, Croxton and Cowden, etc.). In fact only numerical data constitute Statistics. This means that the phenomenon under study must be capable of quantitative measurement. Thus the raw material of Statistics always originates from the operation of counting (enumeration) or measurement. For any statistical enquiry, whether it is in business, economics or social sciences, the basic problem is to collect facts and figures relating to particular phenomenon under study. The person who conducts the statistical enquiry *i.e.,* counts or measures the characteristics under study for further statistical analysis is known as *investigator.* Ideally, (though a costly presumption), the investigator should be trained and efficient statistician. But in practice, this is not always or even usually so. The persons from whom the information is collected are known as *respondents* and the items on which the measurements are taken are called the *statistical units.* [For details see § 2·1·2]. The process of counting or enumeration or measurement together with the systematic recording of results is called the collection of statistical data. The entire structure of the statistical analysis for any enquiry is based upon systematic collection of data.

On the face of it, it might appear that the collection of data is the first step for any statistical investigation. But in a scientifically prepared (efficient and well-planned) statistical enquiry, the collection of data is by no means the first step. Before we embark upon the collection of data for a given statistical enquiry, it is imperative to examine carefully the following points which may be termed as preliminaries to data collection :

(*i*) Objectives and scope of the enquiry.
(*ii*) Statistical units to be used.
(*iii*) Sources of information (data).
(*iv*) Method of data collection.
(*v*) Degree of accuracy aimed at in the final results.
(*vi*) Type of enquiry.

We shall discuss these points briefly in the following sections.

2·1·1. Objectives and Scope of the Enquiry. The first and foremost step in organising any statistical enquiry is to define in clear and concrete terms the objectives of the enquiry. This is very essential for determining the nature of the statistics (data) to be collected and also the statistical techniques to be employed for the analysis of the data. The objectives of the enquiry would help in eliminating the collection of irrelevant information which is never used subsequently and also reflect upon the uses to which such information can be put. In the absence of the purpose of the enquiry being explicitly specified, we are bound to collect irrelevant information and also omit some important information which will ultimately lead to fallacious conclusions and wastage of resources.

Further, the scope of the enquiry will also have a great bearing upon the data to be collected and also the techniques to be used for its collection and analysis. Scope of the enquiry relates to the coverage with respect to the type of information, subject matter and geographical area. For instance, if we want to study the cost of living index numbers, it must be specified if they relate to a particular city or state or whole of

India. Further, the class of people (such as a low-income group, middle-income group, labour class, etc.), for which they are intended should also be specified clearly. Thus, if the investigation is to be on a very large scale, the sample method of enumeration and collection will have to be used. However, if the enquiry is confined only to a small group, we may undertake 100% enumeration (census method). Thus if the scope of the enquiry is very wide, it has to be of one nature and if the scope of enquiry is narrow, it has to be of a totally different nature.

Thus the decision about the type of enquiry to be conducted depends largely on the objectives and scope of the enquiry However, the organisers of the enquiry should take care that these objectives and scope are commensurate with the available resources in terms of money, manpower and time limit required for the availability of the results of the enquiry.

2·1·2. Statistical Units to be Used. A well-defined and identifiable object or a group of objects with which the measurements or counts in any statistical investigation are associated is called a *statistical unit.* For example, in a socio-economic survey the unit may be an individual person, a family, a household or a block of locality. A very important step before the collection of data begins is to define clearly the statistical units on which the data are to be collected. In a number of situations the units are conventionally fixed like the *physical units* of measurement such as metres, kilometres, kilograms, quintals, hours, days, weeks, etc., which are well defined and do not need any elaboration or explanation. However in many statistical investigations, particularly relating to socio-economic studies, *arbitrary units* are used which must be clearly defined. This is imperative since in the absence of a clear-cut and precise definition of the statistical units, serious errors in the data collection may be committed in the sense that we may collect irrelevant data on the items, which should have, in fact, been excluded and omit data on certain items which should have been included. This will ultimately lead to fallacious conclusions.

REQUISITES OF A STATISTICAL UNIT

The following points might serve as guidelines for deciding about the unit in any statistical enquiry.

1. *It should be unambiguous.* A statistical unit should be rigidly defined so that it does not lead to any ambiguity in its interpretation. The units must cover the entire population and they should be distinct and non-overlapping in the sense that every element of the population belongs to one and only one statistical unit.

2. *It should be specific.* The statistical unit must be precise and specific leaving no chance to the investigators. Quite often, in most of the socio-economic surveys the various concepts/characteristics can be interpreted in different variant forms and accordingly the variable used to measure it may be defined in several different ways. For example, in an enquiry relating to the wage level of workers in an industrial concern the wages might by weekly wages, monthly wages or might refer to those of skilled labour only or of day workers only or might include bonus payments also. Similarly prices in an enquiry might refer to cost prices, selling prices, retail prices, wholesale prices or contract prices. Thus in a statistical enquiry it is important to distinguish between the *conventional* and the *arbitrary* definitions of the characteristics/variables, the former being the one prevalent in common use and shall always remain same (fixed) for every enquiry while the latter is the one which is used in a specific sense and refers to the working or operational definition which will keep on changing from one enquiry to another enquiry.

3. *It should be stable.* The unit selected should be stable over a long period of time and also *w.r.t.* places *i.e.*, there should not be significant fluctuations in the value of a unit at different intervals of time or at different places because in the contrary case, the data collected at different times or places will not be comparable and this would mar their utility to a great extent. The fluctuations in the value of money at different times (due to inflation) or in the measurement of weights at different places (due to height above sea level) might render the comparisons useless. Thus, the unit selected should imply, as far as possible, the same characteristics at different times or at different places.

4. *It should be appropriate to the enquiry.* As already pointed out, the concept and definition of arbitrary statistical units keep on changing from enquiry to enquiry. The unit selected must be relevant to the given enquiry. Thus, for studying the changes in the general price level, the appropriate unit is the wholesale prices while for constructing the cost of living indices (or consumer price indices) the appropriate unit is the retail prices.

5. *It should be uniform.* It is essential that the unit adopted should be homogeneous (uniform) throughout the investigation so that the measurements obtained are comparable. For example, in measuring length if we use a yard on some occasions and metre on other occasions in an investigation, the observations obtained would be confusing and misleading.

TYPES OF STATISTICAL UNITS

The statistical units may be broadly classified as follows :

(*i*) Units of collection.

(*ii*) Units of analysis and interpretation.

(*i*) **Units of Collection.** The units of collection may further be sub-divided into the following two classes :

(*a*) *Units of Enumeration.* In any statistical enquiry, whether it is conducted by 'sample' method or 'census' method, unit of enumeration is the basic unit on which the observations are to be made and this unit is to be decided in advance before conducting the enquiry keeping in view the objectives of the enquiry. The unit of enumeration may be a person, a household, a family, a farm (in land experiments), a shop, a livestock, a firm, etc. As has been pointed out earlier, this unit should be very clearly defined in terms of shape, size, etc. For instance, for the construction of cost of living index number, the proper unit of enumeration is household. It should be explained in clear terms whether a household consists of a family comprising blood relations only or people taking food in a common kitchen or all the persons living in the house or the persons enlisted in the ration card only. The concept of the household (to be used in the enquiry) is to be decided in advance and explained clearly to the enumerators so that there are no essential omissions or irrelevant inclusions.

(*b*) *Units of Recording.* The units of recording are the units in terms of which the data are recorded or in other words they are the units of quantification. For instance, in the construction of cost of living index number (consumer price index) the data to be collected from each household, among other things, include the retail prices of various commodities together with the quantities consumed by the class of people for whom the index is meant. The units of recording for quantity may be weight (in case of foodgrains), say, in kilograms, quintals, tons, etc., in case of clothing the unit of recording may be metres; the prices may be recorded in terms of rupees and so on.

Units of measurement (recording) may be *simple* or *composite*. The units which represent only one condition without any qualification (adjective) are called *simple units* such as metre, rupee, ton, kilogram, pound, bale of cloth, hour, week, year, etc. Such units are generally *conventional* and not at all difficult to define. However, sometimes care has to be taken in their actual usage. For example, the bale of cloth must be defined in terms of length, say, 20 metres, 50 metres or 100 metres. Similarly, in case of weight it should be clearly specified whether it is net weight or gross weight.

A simple unit with some qualifying words is called a *composite unit.* A simple unit with only one qualifying word is called a *compound unit.* Examples of such units are skilled worker, employed person, ton–kilometre, kilowatt hour, man hours, retail prices, monthly wages, passenger kilometres. For instance ton–kilometre means the number of tons multiplied by the number of kilometres carried; man hours implies the total number of workers multiplied by the number of hours that each worker has put in and so on. If two or more qualifying words are added to a simple unit, it is called a *complex unit* such as production per machine hour, output per man hour and so on. Thus as compared to simple units, composite (compound and complex) units are much more restrictive in scope and difficult to define. Such units should be defined properly and clearly as they need explanation about the unit used and also about the qualifying words.

(*ii*) **Units of Analysis and Interpretation.** As the name implies, the units of analysis and interpretation are those units in the form of which the statistical data are ultimately analysed and interpreted. It should be decided whether the results would be expressed in absolute figures or relative figures. The units of analysis and interpretation facilitate comparisons between different sets of data with respect to time, place or environment (conditions). Generally, the units of analysis are rates, ratios and percentages, and coefficients.

Rates involve the comparison between two heterogeneous quantities *i.e.*, when the numerator and denominator are not of the same kind *e.g.*, the mortality (death) rates, the fertility (birth) rates and so on. Rates are usually expressed per thousand. For instance, the Crude Birth Rate (C.B.R.) is the ratio of total number of live births in the given region or locality during a given period to the total population of that region or locality during the same period, multiplied by 1,000. Rate per unit is called coefficient. However, ratios and percentages are used for comparing homogeneous quantities *e.g.,* when the numerator and denominator are of the same kind. For example, "the ratio of smokers to non-smokers in a particular locality is 1 : 3" implies that 25% of the population are smokers.

From practical point of view for comparing data relating to different series, usually the unit of analysis is one which gives relative figures which are pure numbers independent of units of measurement. For instance, if we want to compare two series for variability (disperson) the appropriate unit of analysis is Coefficient of Variation [See Chapter 6] and for comparing symmetry of two distributions, we study the Coefficient of Skewness [See Chapter 7].

2·1·3. Sources of Information (Data). Having decided about the objectives and scope of the enquiry and the statistical units to be used, the next problem is to decide about the sources from which the information (data) can be obtained or collected. For any statistical enquiry, the investigator may collect the data first hand or he may use the data from other published sources such as the publications of the government/semi-government organisations, periodicals, magazines, newspapers, research journals, etc. If the data are collected originally by the investigator for the given enquiry it is termed as *primary data* and if he makes use of the data which had been earlier collected by some one else, it is termed as *secondary data.* For example, the vital rates *i.e.,* the rates of fertility and mortality in India prepared by the office of Registrar-General of India, New Delhi, are primary data but if the same data are reproduced in the U.N. Statistical Abstract (a publication of the United Nations Organisation), it becomes a secondary data. Obviously the type of enquiry needed for primary data is bound to be of a totally different nature than the type of enquiry needed for the use of secondary data. In case of primary data, the type of enquiry requires laying down the definitions of the various terms and the statistical units used in the enquiry, keeping in mind the objectives and scope of the enquiry. However, in the use of secondary data there are no such problems since the data have already been collected under a given set of definitions of various terms and units used. However, before using secondary data for statistical investigation under study, it must be subjected to careful editing and scrutiny with respect to their reliability, suitability and adequacy. [For details see § 2·6 in this Chapter]. For a given enquiry, the use of either primary or secondary data or both may be made, depending upon the purpose and scope of the enquiry.

2·1·4. Method of Data Collection. The problem does not arise if secondary data are to be used. However, if primary data are to be collected a decision has to be taken whether (*i*) *census method* or (*ii*) *sample technique*, is to be used for data collection. In the census method, we resort to 100% inspection of the population and enumerate each and every unit of the population. In the sample technique we inspect or study only a selected representative and adequate fraction (finite subset) of the population and after analysing the results of the sample data we draw conclusions about the characteristics of the population. In some situations such as population being infinite or very large, census method fails. Moreover, it is not practicable if the enumeration or testing of the units (objects) is destructive *e.g.,* for testing the breaking strength of chalk, testing the life of electric bulbs or tubes, testing of crackers and explosives, etc. Even, if practicable, it may not be feasible from considerations of time and money. Thus a choice between the sample method and census method is to be made depending upon the objectives and scope of the survey, the limitations of resources in terms of time, money, manpower, etc., and the degree of accuracy desired. In case of sample method the size of the sample and the technique of sampling like simple random sampling, stratified random sampling, systematic sampling, etc., are to be decided. [For detailed discussion, see Chapter 15 – Sampling Theory and Design of Sample Surveys].

2·1·5. Degree of Accuracy Aimed at in the Final Results. A decision regarding the degree of accuracy or precision desired by the investigator in his estimates or results is essential before starting any statistical enquiry. An idea about the precision aimed at is extremely helpful in deciding about the method of data collection and the size of the sample (if the enquiry is to be on the basis of a sample study). The information gained from any previous completed sample study on the subject in the form of precision achieved for a given sample size may serve as a useful guide in this matter provided there is no fundamental reason to change this empirical basis. In any statistical enquiry perfect accuracy in final results is practically impossible to achieve because of the errors in measurement, collection of data, its analysis and interpretation of the results. However, even if it were attainable, it is not generally desirable in terms of time and money likely to be spent in attaining it and a reasonable degree of precision is enough to draw valid inferences.

A decision regarding the precision of the results very much depends upon the objectives and scope of the enquiry. For example, if we are measuring the length of cloth for shirting or pant, a difference of centimetres is going to make substantial impact. But if we are measuring the distances between two places, say, Delhi and Mumbai, a difference of few metres may be immaterial and while measuring the distance between two distant places, say Delhi and New York (U.S.A.) a difference of few kilometres may be immaterial. Likewise in measuring cereals (rice, wheat etc.) a difference of few grams may not matter at all whereas in measuring gold even 1/15th or 1/20th part of a gram is going to make lot of difference. In the words of Riggleman and Frisbee, "*the necessary degree of accuracy in counting or measuring depends upon the practical value of accuracy in relation to its cost.*" However it should not be misunderstood to imply that one should sacrifice accuracy to conduct the enquiry at low costs.

2·1·6. Types of Enquiry. Another important point one has to bear in mind before embarking upon the process of collection of data is to decide about the type of enquiry. The statistical enquiries may be of different types as outlined below :

(*i*) Official, Semi-official or Un-official.
(*ii*) Initial or Repetitive.
(*iii*) Confidential or Non-confidential.
(*iv*) Direct or Indirect.
(*v*) Regular or Ad-hoc.
(*vi*) Census or Sample.
(*vii*) Primary or Secondary.

(*i*) **Official, Semi-official or Un-official Enquiry.** A very important factor in the collection of data is 'the sponsoring agency of the survey or enquiry'. If an enquiry is conducted by or on behalf of the central, state or local governments it is termed as official enquiry. A semi-official enquiry is one that is conducted by organisations enjoying government patronage like the Indian Council of Agricultural Research (I.C.A.R.), New Delhi; Indian Agricultural Statistics Research Institute (I.A.S.R.I.), New Delhi; Indian Statistical Institute (I.S.I.), Calcutta and New Delhi; and so on. An un-official enquiry is one which is sponsored by private institutions like the F.I.C.C.I., trade unions, universities or the individuals. Obviously the facilities available for each type of the above enquiries differ considerably. In an official enquiry, legal or statutory compulsions can be exercised asking the public or respondents to furnish the requisite information in time and that too at their own cost. In semi-official type enquiries also, the necessary information may be obtained without much difficulty. However, in un-official enquiries the investigator is faced with serious problems in getting information from the respondents. He can only pursuade and request them for information. In such enquiries there is only moral obligation and no legal compulsion on the respondents. Things are still worse if the enquiry is conducted by an individual who, at stages, has even to beg for information. Moreover, there are lot of differences in the financial positions of these three sponsoring agencies. Obviously, the state or central governments can afford to spend much more on an enquiry as compared with private institutions, which in turn, can generally spend more than an individual. Consequently, there is bound to be difference in the types of enquiries depending upon the sponsoring agency and also its financial implications.

(*ii*) **Initial or Repetitive Enquiry.** As the name suggests, an *initial* or *original* enquiry is one which is conducted for the first time while a *repetitive* enquiry is one which is carried on in continuation or repetition of some previously conducted enquiry (enquiries). In conducting an original enquiry the entire scheme of the plan starting with definitions of various terms, the units, the method of collection, etc., has to be formulated afresh whereas in repetitive enquiry there is no such problem as such a plan already exists and only the original enquiry is to be modified to suit the current situation and on the basis of the experience gained in the past enquiry. However, for making valid conclusions in a repetitive enquiry, it should be ascertained that there is not any material change in the definitions of various terms used in the original enquiry.

(*iii*) **Confidential or Non-confidential Enquiry.** In a confidential enquiry, the information collected and the results obtained are kept confidential and they are not made known to the public. The findings of such enquiries are meant only for the personal records of the sponsoring agency. The enquiries conducted by private organisations like trade unions, manufacturers' associations, private business concerns, are usually of confidential nature. On the other hand, the types of enquiries whose results are published and made known to the general public are termed as non-confidential enquiries. Most of the enquiries conducted by the state, private bodies or even individuals are of this type.

(*iv*) **Direct or Indirect Enquiry.** An enquiry is termed as *direct* if the phenomenon under study is capable of quantitative measurement such as age, weight, income, prices, quantities consumed and so on. However, if the phenomenon under study is of a qualitative nature which is not capable of quantitative measurement like honesty, beauty, intelligence, etc., the corresponding enquiry is termed as *indirect* one. In such an enquiry, the qualitative characteristic is converted into quantitative phenomenon by assigning appropriate standard which may represent the given attribute (qualitative phenomenon) indirectly. For example, the study of the attribute of intelligence may be made through the Intelligence Quotient (I.Q.) score of a group of individuals in a given test.

(*v*) **Regular or Ad-hoc Enquiry.** If the enquiry is conducted periodically at equal intervals of time (monthly, quarterly, yearly, etc.), it is said to be *regular* enquiry. For example, the census is conducted in India periodically every 10 years. Similarly a number of enquiries are conducted by the Central Statistical Organisation (C.S.O.) and their results are published periodically such as Monthly Abstract of Statistics, Monthly Statistics of Production of Selected Industries of India, Statistical Abstract, India (Annually) ; Statistical Pocket Book, India (Annually). On the other hand, if an enquiry is conducted as and when necessary without any regularity or periodicity, it is termed as *ad-hoc*. For instance C.S.O. and N.S.S.O. (National Sample Survey Organisation) conduct a number of ad-hoc enquiries.

(*vi*) and (*vii*). Enquiries of type (*vi*) *viz.*, **Census or Sample*** and (*vii*) **Primary or Secondary** have been discussed later in this chapter.

In any statistical enquiry, after deciding about the factors or problems enumerated above from § 2·1·1. § 2·1·6, we are now all set for the process of actual collection of data relating to the given enquiry. In the following sections, we will discuss the methods of data collection.

2·2. PRIMARY AND SECONDARY DATA

After going through the preliminaries discussed in the above section, we come to the problem of data collection. The most important factor in any statistical enquiry is that the original collection of data is correct and proper. If there are inadequacies, shortcomings or pitfalls at the very source of the data, no useful and valid conclusions can be drawn even after applying the best and sophisticated techniques of data analysis and presentation of the results. In this context, it may be interesting to quote the remarks made by a judge on Indian Statistics. "Cox, when you are bit older you will not quote Indian statistics with that assurance. The governments are very keen on amassing statistics—they collect them, add them, raise them to the *n*th power, take the cube root and prepare wonderful diagrams. But what you must never forget is that every one of those figures comes in the first instance from the 'Chowkidar' (*i.e.*, the village watchman) who just puts down what he damn pleases."**

It may be remarked that this quotation applies to India of very old days when no definite statistical set up existed in India. Today in India, we have a fairly sound and systematic method of data collection on almost all problems relating to various diversified fields such as economics, business, industry, demography, social, physical and natural sciences. As already pointed out the data may be obtained from the following two sources :

(*i*) The investigator or the organising agency may conduct the enquiry originally or

(*ii*) He may obtain the necessary data for his enquiry from some other sources (or agencies) who had already collected the data on that subject.

The data which are originally collected by an investigator or agency for the first time for any statistical investigation and used by them in the statistical analysis are termed as *primary* data. On the other hand, the

---

* For details see § 2·1·4 and Chapter 15.

** The earlierst use of this story seems to have been made in Sir Josiah Stamp, '*Some Economic Factors in Modern Life*', P.S. King and Son, London, 1929, p. 258-259.

data (published or unpublished) which have already been collected and processed by some agency or person and taken over from there and used by any other agency for their statistical work are termed as *secondary* data as far as second agency is concerned. The second agency if and when it publishes and files such data becomes the *secondary source* to any one who later uses these data. In other words secondary source is the agency who publishes or releases for use by others the data which was not originally collected and processed by it.

It may be observed that the distinction between primary and secondary data is a matter of degree or relativity only. The same set of data may be secondary in the hands of one and primary in the hands of others. In general, the data are primary to the source who collects and processes them for the first time and are secondary for all sources who later use such data. For instance, the data relating to mortality (death rates) and fertility (birth rates) in India published by the Office of Registrar General of India, New Delhi are primary whereas the same reproduced by the United Nations Organisation (U.N.O.) in its U.N. Statistical Abstract become secondary in a far as later agency (U.N.O.) is concerned. For this data, the office of Registrar General of India, is the primary source while U.N.O. is the secondary source. Likewise, the data collected by C.S.O. and N.S.S.O. for various surveys are primary as far as these departments are concerned but they become secondary if such data are used by other departments or organisations.

2·2·1. Choice Between Primary and Secondary Data. Obviously, there is lot of difference in the method of collection of primary and secondary data. In the case of primary data which is to be collected originally, the entire scheme of the plan starting with the definitions of various terms used, units to be employed, type of enquiry to be conducted, extent of accuracy aimed at, etc., is to be formulated whereas the collection of secondary data is in the form of mere compilation of the existing data. A proper choice between the type of data (primary or secondary) needed for any particular statistical investigation is to be made after taking into consideration the nature, objective and scope of the enquiry; the time and finances (money) at the disposal of the agency; the degree of precision aimed at and the status of the agency (whether government – state or central – or private institution or an individual).

Remarks 1. In using the secondary data it is best to obtain the data from the primary source as far as possible. By doing so, we would at least save ourselves from the errors of transcription (if any) which might have inadvertently crept in the secondary source. Moreover, the primary source will also provide us with detailed discussion about the terminology used, statistical units employed, size of the sample and the technique of sampling (if the sample method was used), methods of data collection and analysis of results and we can ascertain ourselves if these suit our purpose.

2. It may be pointed out that today, in a large number of statistical enquiries secondary data are generally used because fairly reliable published data on a large number of diverse fields are now available in publications of the governments (state or centre), private organisations and research institutions, international agencies, periodicals and magazines, etc. In fact primary data are collected only if there do not exist any secondary data suited to the investigation under study. In some of the investigations both primary as well as secondary data may be used.

3. **Internal and External Data.** Some statisticians differentiate between primary and secondary data in the form of internal or external data. Internal data of an organisation (of business or economic concern or firm) are those which are collected by the organisation from its own internal operations like production, sales, profits, loans, imports and exports, capital employed, etc., and used by it for its own purposes. On the other hand, external data are those which are obtained from the publications of some other agencies like governments (central or state), international bodies, private research institutions, etc., for use by the given organisation.

2·3. METHODS OF COLLECTING PRIMARY DATA

The methods commonly used for the collection of primary data are enumerated below :

(*i*) Direct personal investigation.

(*ii*) Indirect oral interviews.

(*iii*) Information received through local agencies.

(*iv*) Mailed questionnaire method.

(*v*) Schedules sent through enumerators.

2·3·1. Direct Personal Investigation. This method consists in the collection of data personally by the investigator (organising agency) from the sources concerned. In other words, the investigator has to go to the field personally for making enquiries and soliciting information from the informants or respondents. This nature of investigation very much restricts the scope of the enquiry. Obviously this technique is suited only if the enquiry is intensive rather than extensive. In other words, this method should be used only if the investigation is generally local – confined to a single locality, region or area. Since such investigations require the personal attention of the investigator, they are not suitable for extensive studies where the scope of investigation is very wide. Obviously, the information gathered from such investigation is original in nature.

Merits. (*i*) The first hand information obtained by the investigator himself is bound to be more reliable and accurate since the investigator can extract the correct information by removing the doubts, if any, in the minds of the respondents regarding certain questions. In case, the investigator suspects foul play on the part of respondent(s) in supplying wrong information on certain items he can check it by some intelligent cross-questioning.

(*ii*) The data obtained from such investigation is generally reliable if the type of enquiry is intensive in nature and if time and money do not pose any problems for the investigator.

(*iii*) When the audience is approached personally by the investigator, the response is likely to be more encouraging.

(*iv*) Different persons have their own ideas, likes and dislikes and their opinions on some of the questions may be coloured by their own prejudices and vision and as such some of them might react very sharply to certain sensitive questions posed to them. The investigator, being on the spot, can handle such a delicate situation creditably and effectively by his skill, intelligence and insight either by changing the topic or if need be, by explaining to the respondent in polite words the objectives of the survey in detail.

(*v*) The investigator can extract proper information from the respondents by talking to them at their educational level and if need be ask them questions in their language of communication and using local connotations, if any, for the words used.

Demerits. (*i*) As already pointed out this type of investigation is restrictive in nature and is suited only for intensive studies and not for extensive enquiries. This method is thus not suitable if the field of investigation is too wide in terms of the number of persons to be interviewed or the area to be covered.

(*ii*) This type of investigation is handicapped due to lack of time, money and manpower (labour). It is particularly time consuming since the informants can be approached only at their convenience and in case of working class, this restricts the contact of the investigator with the informants only in the evenings or at the week ends and consequently the investigation is to be spanned over a long period.

(*iii*) The greatest drawback of this enquiry is that it is absolutely subjective in nature. The success of the investigation largely depends upon the intelligence, skill, tact, insight, diplomacy and courage of the investigator. If the investigator lacks these qualities and is not properly trained, the results of the enquiry cannot be taken as satisfactory or reliable. Moreover the personal biases, prejudices and whims of the investigator may, in certain cases, adversely affect the findings of the enquiry.

(*iv*) Further, if the investigator is not intelligent, tactful or skillful enough to understand the psychologies and customs of the interviewing audience, the results obtained from such an investigation will not be reliable.

2·3·2. Indirect Oral Investigation. When the 'direct personal investigation' is not practicable either because of the unwillingness or reluctance of the persons to furnish the requisite information or due to the extensive nature of the enquiry or due to the fact that direct sources of information do not exist or are unreliable, an indirect oral investigation is carried out. For example, if we want to solicit information on certain social evils like if a person is addicted to drinking, gambling or smoking, etc., the person will be reluctant to furnish correct information or he may give wrong information. The information on the gambling, drinking or smoking habits of an individual can best be obtained by interviewing his personal friends, relatives or neighbours who know him thoroughly well. In these types of enquiries factual data on different problems are collected by interviewing persons who are directly or indirectly concerned with the subject matter of the enquiry and who are in possession of the requisite information. The method consists in collection of the data through enumerators appointed for this purpose. A small list of questions pertaining to the subject matter of the enquiry is prepared. These questions are then put to the persons, known as witnesses or informants, who are in possession of such information and their replies are recorded. Such a procedure for the collection of factual data on different problems is usually adopted by the Enquiry Committees or Commissions appointed by the government—State or Central.

Merits. (*i*) Since the enumerators contact the informants personally, as discussed in the first method, they can exercise their intelligence, skill, tact, etc., to extract correct and relevant information by cross examination of the informants, if necessary.

(*ii*) As compared with the method of "direct personal investigation", this method is less expensive and requires less time for conducting the enquiry.

(*iii*) If necessary, the expert views and suggestions of the specialists on the given problem can be obtained in order to formulate and conduct the enquiry more effectively and efficiently.

Demerits. (*i*) Due to lack of direct supervision and personal touch the investigator (sponsoring agency) has to rely entirely on the information supplied by the enumerators. The success of the method lies in the intelligence, skill, insight and efficiency of the enumerators and also on the fact that they are honest persons with high integrity and without any selfish motives. It should be ascertained that the enumerators are properly trained and tactful enough to elicit proper and correct response from the informants. Moreover, it should be seen that the personal biases due to the prejudices, and whims of the enumerators do not enter or at least they are minimised.

(*ii*) The accuracy of the data collected and the inferences drawn, depend to a large extent on the nature and quality of the witnesses from whom the information is obtained. A wrong and improper choice of the witnesses will give biased results which may adversely affect the findings of the enquiry. It is, therefore, imperative :

(*a*) To ascertain the reliability and integrity of the persons (witnesses) selected for interrogation. In other words, it should be ascertained that the witnesses are unbiased persons without any selfish motives and that they are not prejudiced in favour of or against a particular view point.

(*b*) That the findings of the enquiry are not based on the information supplied by a single person alone. Rather, a sufficient number of persons should be interviewed to find out the real position.

(*c*) That the witnesses really possess the knowledge about the problem under study *i.e.*, they are aware of the full factors of the problem under investigation and are in a position to give a clear, detailed and correct account of the problem.

(*d*) That a proper allowance about the pessimism or optimism of the witnesses depending upon their inherent psychology should be made.

2·3·3. Information Received Through Local Agencies. In this method the information is not collected formally by the investigator or the enumerators. This method consists in the appointment of *local agents* (commonly called *correspondents*) by the investigator in different parts of field of enquiry. These correspondents or agencies in different regions collect the information according to their own ways, fashions, likings and decisions and then submit their reports periodically to the central or head office where the data are processed for final analysis. This technique of data collection is usually employed by newspaper or periodical agencies who require information in different fields like sports, riots, strikes, accidents, economic trend, business stock and share market, policies and so on. This method is also used by the various departments of the government (state or central) where the information is desired periodically (at regular intervals of time) from a wide area. This method is particularly useful in obtaining the estimates of agricultural crops which may be submitted to the government by the village school teachers. A more refined and sophisticated way of the use of this technique is the *registration method* in which any event, say, birth, death, incidence of disease, etc., is to be reported to the appropriate authority appointed by the government like Sarpanch or Patwari in the village; or Block Development Officers (B.D.O.'s), civil hospitals or the health departments in the district headquarters, etc., as and when or immediately after it occurs. Vital statistics *i.e.*, the data relating to mortality (deaths) and fertility (births) are usually collected in India through the registration technique.

Merits. This method works out to be very cheap and economical for extensive investigations particularly if the data are obtained through part-time correspondents or agents. Moreover, the required information can be obtained expeditiously since only rough estimates are required.

Demerits. Since the different correspondents collect the information in their own fashion and style, the results are bound to be biased due to the personal prejudices and whims of the correspondents in different fields of the enquiry and consequently the data so obtained will not be very reliable. Hence, this technique of data collection is suited if the purpose of investigation is to obtain rough and approximate estimates only and where a high degree of accuracy is not desired.

In particular, the registration method suffers from the drawback that many persons do not report and thus neglect to register. This usually results in under-estimation. For an effective and efficient system of registration there should be legal compulsions for registration of events and also there should be sanctions for the enforcement of the obligation.

2·3·4. Mailed Questionnaire Method. This method consists in preparing a *questionnaire* (a list of questions relating to the field of enquiry and providing space for the answers to be filled by the respondents) which is mailed to the respondents with a request for quick response within the specified time. A very polite covering note, explaining in detail the aims and objectives of collecting the information and also the operational definitions of various terms and concepts used in the questionnaire is attached. Respondents are also requested to extend their full co-operation by furnishing the correct replies and returning the questionnaire duly filled in time. Respondents are also taken into confidence by ensuring them that the information supplied by them in the questionnaire will be kept strictly confidential and secret. In order to ensure quick and better response the return postage expenses are usually borne by the investigator by sending a self-addressed stamped envelope. This method is usually used by the research workers, private individuals, non-official agencies and sometimes even by government (central or state).

In this method, the questionnaire is the only media of communication between the investigator and the respondents. Consequently, the most important factor for the success of the 'mailed questionnaire method', is the skill, efficiency, care and the wisdom with which the questionnaire is framed. The questions asked should be clear, brief, corroborative, non-offending, courteous in tone, unambiguous and to the point so that not much scope of guessing is left on the part of the respondent. Moreover, while framing the questions the knowledge, understanding and the general educational level of the respondents should be taken into consideration.

Remark. "Drafting or framing the questionnaire", is of paramount importance and is discussed in detail in § 2·4 after 'Schedules sent through enumerators'.

Merits. (*i*) Of all the methods of collecting information, the 'mailed questionnaire method' is by far the most economical method in terms of time, money and manpower (labour) provided the respondents supply the information in time.

(*ii*) This method is used for extensive enquiries covering a very wide area.

(*iii*) Errors due to the personal biases of the investigators or enumerators are completely eliminated as the information is supplied directly by the person concerned in his own handwriting. The information so obtained is original and much more authentic.

Demerits. (*i*) The most serious drawback of this method is that it can be used effectively with advantage only if the audience (people) is (are) educated (literate) and can understand the questions well and reply them in their own handwriting. Obviously, this method is not practicable if the people are illiterate. Even if they are educated, there may be a number of persons who are not interested in the particular enquiry being conducted and as such they adopt an attitude of indifference towards the enquiry which results in their questionnaires finding place in the waste paper baskets. In the case of those who return the questionnaires after filling, a number of them supply haphazard, vague, incomplete and unintelligible information which does not serve much purpose. Thus, this method generally suffers from the high degree (*i.e.*, very large proportion) of non-response and consequently the results based on the information supplied by a very small proportion of the selected individuals cannot be regarded as reliable.

(*ii*) Quite often people might suppress correct information and furnish wrong replies. We cannot verify the accuracy and reliability of the information received. In general, this method also suffers from the low degree of reliability of the information supplied by the respondents.

(*iii*) Another limitation of this method is that at times, informants are not willing to give written information in their own handwriting on certain personal questions like income, property, personal habits and so on.

(*iv*) Since the questionnaires are filled by the respondents personally, there is no scope for asking supplementary questions for cross checking of the information supplied by them. Moreover, the doubts in the minds of the informants, if any, on certain questions cannot be dispelled.

2·3·5. Schedules Sent Through Enumerators. Before discussing this method it is desirable to make a distinction between a questionnaire and a schedule. As already explained, questionnaire in a list of questions which are answered by the respondent himself in this own handwriting while schedule is the device of obtaining answers to the questions in a form which is filled by the interviewers or enumerators (the field agents who put these questions) in a face to face situation with the respondents. The most widely used method of collection of primary data is the 'schedules sent through the enumerators'. This is so because this method is free from certain shortcomings inherent in the earlier methods discussed so far. In this method the enumerators go to the respondents personally with the schedule (list of questions), ask them the questions there in and record their replies. This method is generally used by big business houses, large public enterprises and research institutions like National Council of Applied Economic Research (NCAER), Federation of Indian Chambers of Commerce and Industries (FICCI) and so on and even by the governments – state or central – for certain projects and investigations where high degree of response is desired. Population census, all over the world is conducted by this technique.

Merits. (*i*) The enumerators can explain in detail the objectives and aims of the enquiry to the informants and impress upon them the need and utility of furnishing the correct information. Being on the spot, the enumerators can dispel the doubts, if any, of certain people to certain questions by explaining to them the implications of certain definitions and concepts used in the questionnaire.

(*ii*) This technique is very useful in extensive enquiries and generally yields fairly dependable and reliable results due to the fact that the information is recorded by highly trained and educated enumerators. Moreover, since the enumerators personally call on the respondents to obtain information there is very little non-response which occurs if it is not possible to contact the respondents even after repeated calls or if the respondent is unwilling to furnish the requisite information. Thus, this method removes both the drawbacks of the 'mailed questionnaire method', *viz.*, very large proportion of non-response and fairly low degree of reliability of the information.

(*iii*) Unlike the 'mailed questionnaire method', this technique can be used with advantage even if the respondents are illiterate.

(*iv*) As already pointed out in the 'direct personal investigation', due to personal likes and dislikes, different people react differently to different questions and as such some people might react very sharply to certain sensitive and personal questions. In that case the enumerators, by their tact, skill, wisdom and calibre can handle the situation very effectively by changing the topic of discussion, if need be. Moreover, the enumerators can effectively check the accuracy of the information supplied by some intelligent cross-questioning by asking some supplementary questions.

Demerits. (*i*) It is fairly expensive method since the team of enumerators is to be paid for their services and as such can be used by only those bodies or institutions which are financially sound.

(*ii*) It is also more time consuming as compared with the 'mailed questionnaire method'.

(*iii*) The success of the method largely depends upon the efficiency and skill of the enumerators who collect the information. Thus the choice of enumerators is of paramount importance. The enumerators have to be trained properly in the art of collecting correct information by their intelligence, insight, patience and perseverence, diplomacy and courage. They should clearly understand the aims and objectives of the enquiry and also the implications of the various terms, definitions and concepts used in the questionnaire. They should be provided with adequate guidelines so that their personal biases do not enter the final results of the enquiry. They should be honest persons with high integrity and should not have any personal axe to grind. They should be well versed in the local language, customs and traditions. If the enumerators are biased they may suppress or even twist the information supplied by the respondents. Inefficiency on the part of the enumerators coupled with personal biases due to their prejudices and whims will lead to false conclusions and may even adversely affect the results of the enquiry.

(*iv*) Due to inherent variation in the individual personalities of the enumerators there is bound to be variation, though not so obvious, in the information recorded by different enumerators. An attempt should be made to minimise this variation.

(*v*) The success of this method also lies to a great extent on the efficiency and wisdom with which the schedule is prepared or drafted. If the schedule is framed haphazardly and incompetently, the enumerators will find it very difficult to get the complete and correct desired information from the respondents.

Remarks. 1. In the last two methods *viz.*, 'mailed questionnaire method' and the 'schedules sent through enumerators', it is desirable to scrutinise the questionnaires or schedules duly filled in for detecting any apparent inconsistency in the information supplied by the respondents or recorded by the enumerators.

2. If resources (time, money and manpower) permit, two sets of enumerators may be used for recording information for the enquiry under investigation and their findings may be compared. This will, incidentally, provide a check on the honesty and integrity of the enumerators and will also reflect upon personal bias due to the prejudices and whims of the individual personalities (of the enumerators). However, this technique is not practicable in the case of interviewing individuals, who might get irritated, annoyed or confused when approached for the second time.

2·4. DRAFTING OR FRAMING THE QUESTIONNAIRE

As has been pointed out earlier, the questionnaire is the only media of communication between the investigator and the respondents and as such the questionnaire should be designed or drafted with utmost care and caution so that all the relevant and essential information for the enquiry may be collected without any difficulty, ambiguity and vagueness. Drafting of a good questionnaire is a highly specialised job and requires great care, skill, wisdom, efficiency and experience. No hard and fast rules can be laid down for designing or framing a questionnaire. However, in this connection, the following general points may be borne in mind :

1. *The size of the questionnaire should be as small as possible.* The number of questions should be restricted to the minimum, keeping in view the nature, objectives and scope of the enquiry. In other words, the questionnaire should be concise and should contain only those questions which would furnish all the necessary information relevant for the purpose. Respondents' time should not be wasted by asking irrelevant and unimportant questions. A large number of questions would involve more work for the investigator and thus result in delay on his part in collecting and submitting the information. These may, in addition, also unnecessarily annoy or tire the respondents. A reasonable questionnaire should contain from 15 to 20-25 questions. If a still larger number of questions is a must in any enquiry, then the questionnaire should be divided into various sections or parts.

2. The questions should be clear, brief, unambiguous, non-offending, courteous in tone, corroborative in nature and to the point so that not much scope of guessing is left on the part of the respondents.

3. *The questions should be arranged in a natural logical sequence.* For example, to find if a person owns a refrigerator the logical order of questions would be : "Do you own a refrigerator"? When did you buy it ? What is its make ? How much did it cost you ? Is its performance satisfactory ? Have you ever got it serviced ? The logical arrangement of questions in addition to facilitating tabulation work, would leave no chance for omissions or duplication.

4. *The usage of vague and 'multiple meaning' words should be avoided.* The vague works like good, bad, efficient, sufficient, prosperity, rarely, frequently, reasonable, poor, rich, etc., should not be used since these may be interpreted differently by different persons and as such might give unreliable and misleading information. Similarly the use of words with multiple meanings like price, assets, capital, income, household, democracy, socialism, etc., should not be used unless a clarification to these terms is given in the questionnaire.

5. Questions should be so designed that they are *readily comprehensible and easy to answer* for the respondents. They should not be tedious nor should they tax the respondents' memory. Further, questions involving mathematical calculations like percentages, ratios, etc., should not be asked.

6. *Questions of a sensitive and personal nature should be avoided.* Questions like 'How much money you owe to private parties ?' or 'Do you clean your utensils yourself ?' which might hurt the sentiments, pride or prestige of an individual should not be asked, as far as possible. It is also advisable to avoid questions on which the respondent may be reluctant or unwilling to furnish information. For example, the questions pertaining to income, savings, habits, addiction to social evils, age (particularly, in case of ladies), etc., should be asked very tactfully.

7. *Typed of Questions.* Under this head, the questions in the questionnaire may be broadly classified as follows :

(*a*) **Shut Questions.** In such questions possible answers are suggested by the framers of the questionnaire and the respondent is required to tick one of them. Shut questions can further be sub-divided into the following forms :

(*i*) **Simple Alternate Questions.** In such questions, the respondent has to choose between two clear cut alternatives like 'Yes or No' ; 'Right or Wrong' ; 'Either, Or' and so on. For instance, Do you own a refrigerator ?—Yes or No. Such questions are also called *dichotomous questions*. This technique can be applied with elegance to situations where two clear cut alternatives exist.

(*ii*) **Multiple Choice Questions.** Quite often, it is not possible to define a clear cut alternative and accordingly in such a situation either the first method (Alternate Questions) is not used or additional answers between Yes and No like Do not know, No opinion, Occasionally, Casually, Seldom, etc., are added. For instance to find if a person smokes or drinks, the following multiple choice answers may be used :

Do you smoke ?

Yes (Regularly)	□	No (Never)	□
Occasionally	□	Seldom	□

Similarly, to get information regarding the mode of cooking in a household, the following multiple choice answers may be suggested.

Which of the following modes of cooking you use ?

Gas	□	Coal (Coke)	□
Power (Electricity)	□	Wood	□
Stove (Kerosene)	□		

As another illustration, to find what conveyance an individual uses to go from his house to the place of his duty, the following question with multiple answers may be framed :

How do you go to your place of duty ?

By bus	□	By three wheeler scooter	□
By your own cycle	□	By taxi	□
By your own scooter/Motor cycle	□	On foot	□
By your own car	□	Any other	□

Multiple choice questions are very easy and convenient for the respondents to answer. Such questions save time and also facilitate tabulation. This method should be used if only a selected few alternative answers exist to a particular question. Sometimes, a last alternative under the category 'Others' or 'Any other' may be added. However, multiple answer questions cannot be used with advantage if it is possible to construct a fairly large number of alternative answers of relatively equal importance to a given question.

(*b*) **Open Questions.** Open questions are those in which no alternative answers are suggested and the respondents are at liberty to express their frank and independent opinions on the problem in their own words. For instance, 'What are the drawbacks in our examination system' ? ; 'What solution do you suggest to the housing problem in Delhi' ? ; 'Which programme in the Delhi TV do you like best' ? ; are some of the open questions. Since the views of the respondents in the open questions might differ widely, it is very difficult to tabulate the diverse opinions and responses.

Remark. Sometimes a combination of both shut questions and open questions might be used. For instance an open question : 'When did you buy the car' ?, may be followed by a multiple choice question as to whether its performance is (*i*) extremely good, (*ii*) satisfactory, (*iii*) poor, (*iv*) needs improvement.

8. *Leading questions should be avoided.* For example, the question 'Why do you use a particular brand of blades, say, Erasmic blades' should preferably be framed into two questions.

(*i*) Which blade do you use ?

(*ii*) Why do you prefer it ?

Gives a smooth shave	☐	Readily available in the market	☐
Gives more shaves	☐	Any other	☐
Price is less (Cheaper)	☐		

9. *Cross Checks.* The questionnaire should be so designed as to provide internal checks on the accuracy of the information supplied by the respondents by including some connected questions at least with respect to matters which are fundamental to the enquiry. For example in a social survey for finding the age of the mother the question 'What is your age' ?, can be supplemented by additional questions 'What is your date of birth' or 'What is the age of your eldest child ?' Similarly, the question, 'Age at marriage' can be supplemented by the question 'The age of the first child'.

10. *Pre-testing the Questionnaire.* From practical point of view it is desirable to try out the questionnaire on a small scale (*i.e.*, on a small cross-section of the population for which the enquiry is intended) before using it for the given enquiry on a large scale. This testing on a small scale (called *pre-test*) has been found to be extremely useful in practice. The given questionnaire can be improved or modified in the light of the drawbacks, shortcomings and problems faced by the investigator in the pre-test. Pre-testing also helps to decide upon the effective methods of asking questions for soliciting the requisite information.

11. *A Covering Letter.* A covering letter from the organisers of the enquiry should be enclosed along with the questionnaire for the following purposes :

(*i*) It should clearly explain in brief the objectives and scope of the survey to evoke the interest of the respondents and impress upon them to render their full co-operation by returning the schedule/questionnaire duly filled in within the specified period.

(*ii*) It should contain a note regarding the operational definitions to the various terms and the concepts used in the questionnaire; units of measurements to be used and the degree of accuracy aimed at.

(*iii*) It should take the respondents in confidence and ensure them that the information furnished by them will be kept completely secret and they will not be harassed in any way later.

(*iv*) In the case of mailed questionnaire method a self-addressed stamped envelope should be enclosed for enabling the respondents to return the questionnaire after completing it.

(*v*) To ensure quick and better response the respondents may be offered awards/incentives in the form of free gifts, coupons, etc.

(*vi*) A copy of the survey report may be promised to the interested respondents.

12. Mode of tabulation and analysis *viz.*, hand operated, machine tabulation or computerisation should also be kept in mind while designing the questionnaire.

13. Lastly, the questionnaire should be made attractive by proper layout and appealing get up.

We give below two specimen questionnaires for illustration.

MODEL I

Questionnaire for Collecting Information (Covering Production, Employment etc.) Relating to an Industrial concern

1. Name of the concern . . . . . .
2. (*a*) Name of the Proprietor/Managing Director . . . . . .

   (*b*) Qualifications : (*i*) Academic . . . . . (*ii*) Technical/Professional . . . . .
3. (*a*) Location (*b*) Telephone Number (*c*) e-mail Address

   (*i*) Factory . . . . . . (*i*) Factory . . . . . . (*i*) Factory . . . . .

   (*ii*) Office . . . . . (*ii*) Office . . . . . (*ii*) Office . . . . .
4. Factory Registration Number (with date) . . . . . .
5. Total Capital employed/Assets (approximately) . . . . . .
6. Number of Shifts . . . . . .

7. Whether the machinery used is indigenous ?
   Yes ☐ No ☐ Other ☐
8. What is the approximate value of the imported machinery ? ......
9. Whether the raw material used is available in domestic market ?
   Yes ☐ No ☐
10. From which country is the raw material imported ? ......
11. What is the approximate annual consumption of the raw material ? ......
12. Expenditure in foreign currency :
    (*i*) Foreign Travel ......; (*ii*) Technical know-how ......; (*iii*) Material and goods .....
13. Employment (Pay-roll) :

S. No.	*Categories*	*Working hours per week*	*No. employed*		*Salaries paid in '000 Rs.*	
			2001	*2002*	*2001*	*2002*
(*i*)	Management					
(*ii*)	Supervisory/Technical Personnel					
(*iii*)	Skilled workers					
(*iv*)	Unskilled workers					
(*v*)	Non-technical office staff					

14. Production :

S. No.	*Items (Production)*	*Installed Capacity*	*Actual Production*	
			2001	*2002*

15. Market 2001 2002
    (*a*) Gross value of sales ('000 Rs.) ....
    (*b*) Who are : (*i*) Immediate purchasers ...... (*ii*) End users ......
    (*c*) The extent of market is
    Local ☐ National ☐ International ☐
    (*d*) If the extent of the market is international
    (*i*) What are the approximate foreign exchange earnings (annually) ?
    (*ii*) Which countries are the chief importers of the product ?
    (*e*) Total Sales ('000 Rs.) :
    National market : ...... ; International market : ......
    (*f*) Are the present conditions of the market satisfactory/not satisfactory/poor ? ......
16. Financial Highlights

Items	*(Rupees '000s)*	
	2001	*2002*
Sales		
Profits		
Dividends		
Capital expenditure		
Fixed assets		
Shareholders' funds		

MODEL II

We give below the 1971 Census – Individual Slip which was used for a general purpose survey to collect :

(i) Social and cultural data like nationality, religion, literacy, mother tongue, etc.;

(ii) Exhaustive economic data like occupation, industry, class of worker and activity, if not working ;

(iii) Demographic data like relation to the head of the house, sex, age, marital status, birth place, births and deaths and the fertility of women to assess in particular the performance of the family planning programme.

1971 CENSUS – INDIVIDUAL SLIP

1. Name..
2. Relationship to the head of the family..
3. Sex............................ ; 4. Age.......................... ; 5. Marital status..............................
6. For currently married women only :
   (a) Age at marriage........... (b) Any child born in the last one year..............
7. Birth place :
   (i) Place of birth............ (ii) Rural or urban.................
   (iii) District....................... (iv) State/country...................
8. Last Residence :
   (i) Place of last residence............. (ii) Rural/urban................
   (iii) District.................. (iv) State/country.............
9. Duration of present residence............ 10. Religion.......................
11. Scheduled Caste or Tribe............. 12. Literacy.......................
13. Educational level............. 14. Mother tongue................
15. Other languages, if any...............
16. Main activity :
   (a) Broad category : (i) Worker (C, AL, HHI, OW)* (ii) Non-worker (H, ST, R, D.B.I.O.)**
   (b) Place of work (Name of Village/Town)
   (c) Name of establishment... (d) Name of Industry, Trade, Profession or Service . . . . . .
   (e) Description of work . . . . . . (f) Class of worker . . . . . .
17. Secondary work :
   (a) Broad category (C, AL, HHI, OW) (b) Place of work . . . . . .
   (c) Name of establishment . . . . . . (d) Nature of Industry, Trade, Profession or Service . . .
   (e) Description of work . . . . . . (f) Class of worker . . . . . .

2·5. SOURCES OF SECONDARY DATA

The chief sources of secondary data may be broadly classified into the following two groups :

(i) Published sources. (ii) Unpublished sources.

2·5·1. Published Sources. There are a number of national (government, semi-government and private) organisations and also international agencies which collect statistical data relating to business, trade, labour, prices, consumption, production, industries, agriculture, income, currency and exchange, health, population

---

* C : Cultivator
AL : Agriculture Labour
HHI : House Hold Industries
OW : Other Works

**H : Household Duties
ST : Student
R : Retired person or Renteer
DBIO : Dependent, Beggar, Institutions, Others

and a number of socio-economic phenomena and publish their findings in statistical reports on a regular basis (monthly, quarterly, annually, ad-hoc). These publications of the various organisations serve as a very powerful source of secondary data. We give below a brief summary of these sources.

1. *Official Publications of Central Government.* The following are various government organisations along with the year of their establishment [given in bracket ( )] which collect, compile and publish statistical data on a number of topics of current interest – prices, wages, population, production and consumption, labour, trade, army, etc.

(1) Office of the Registrar General and Census Commissioner of India, New Delhi (1949).***

(2) Directorate-General of Commercial Intelligence and Statistics – Ministry of Commerce (1895).

(3) Labour Bureau – Ministry of Labour (1946).

(4) Directorate of Economics and Statistics – Ministry of Agriculture and Irrigation (1948).

(5) The Indian Army Statistical Organisation (I.A.S.O.) – Ministry of Defence (1947).

(6) National Sample Survey Organisation (N.S.S.O.), Department of Statistics, Ministry of Planning (1950).****

(7) Central Statistical Organisation (C.S.O.) – Department of Statistics, Ministry of Planning (1951).

Some of the main publications of the above government agencies are :

(*a*) Monthly Abstract of Statistics ; Monthly Statistics of Production of Selected Industries in India ; Statistical Pocket Book, India ; Annual Survey of Industries – General Review ; Sample Surveys of Current Interest in India (all published annually) ; Statistical Systems of India ; National Income Statistics – Estimates of Savings in India (1960-61 to 1965-66) ; National Income Statistics – Estimates of Capital Formation in India (1960-61 to 1965-66) (Ad-hoc publications) ; all published by the Central Statistical Organisation (C.S.O.), New Delhi.

(*b*) Census data in various census reports ; Vital Statistics of India (Annual), Indian Population Bulletin (Biennial) – all published by Registrar-General of India (R.G.I.).

(*c*) Various statistical reports on phenomenon relating to socio-economic and demographic conditions, prices, area and yield of different crops, as a result of the various surveys conducted in different rounds by National Sample Survey Organisation (N.S.S.O.).

In addition to the above organisations a number of departments in the State and Central Governments like Income Tax Department, Directorate General of Supplies and Disposals, Railways, Post and Telegraphs, Central Board of Revenues, Textile Commissioner's Office, Central Excise Commissioner's Office, Iron and Steel Controller's Office and so on, publish statistical reports on current problems and the information supplied by them is, in general, more authentic and reliable than that obtained from other sources on the same subject.

2. *Publications of Semi-Government Statistical Organisations.* Very useful information is provided by the publications of the semi-government statistical organisations some of which are enumerated below :

(*i*) Statistics department of the Reserve Bank of India (Mumbai), which brings out an Annual Report of the Bank, Currency and Finance ; Reserve Bank of India Bulletin (monthly) and various monthly and quarterly reports.

(*ii*) Economic department of Reserve Bank of India ; (*iii*) The Institute of Economic Growth, Delhi.

(*iv*) Gokhale Institute of Politics and Economics, Poona ; (*v*) The Institute of Foreign Trade, New Delhi.

Moreover, the statistical material published by the institutions like Municipal and District Boards, Corporations, Block and Panchayat Samitis on Vital Statistics (births and deaths), health, sanitation and other related subjects provides a fairly reliable and useful information.

3. *Publications of Research Institutions.* Individual research scholars, the different departments in the various universities of India and various research organisations and institutes like Indian Statistical Institute

*** In India census has been carried out every ten years since 1881. Prior to the establishment of this organisation, the census was conducted by a temporary cell in the Ministry of Home Affairs.

**** National Sample Survey (N.S.S.) was set up in 1950 in Ministry of Finance. In 1957, N.S.S. was transferred to the Cabinet Secretariate and named National Sample Survey Organisation (N.S.S.O.).

(I.S.I.), Kolkata and Delhi ; Indian Council of Agricultural Research (I.C.A.R.), New Delhi ; Indian Agricultural Statistics Research Institute (I.A.S.R.I.), New Delhi ; National Council of Educational Research and Training (N.C.E.R.T.), New Delhi ; National Council of Applied Economic Research, New Delhi ; The Institute of Applied Man Power Research, New Delhi ; The Institute of Labour Research, Mumbai ; Indian Standards Institute, New Delhi ; and so on publish the findings of their research programmes in the form of research papers, or monographs or journals which are a constant source of secondary data on the subjects concerned.

4. *Publications of Commercial and Financial Institutions.* A number of private commercial and trade institutions like Federation of Indian Chamber of Commerce and Industries (FICCI), Institute of Chartered Accountants of India, Trade Unions, Stock Exchanges, Bank Bodies, Co-operative Societies, etc., publish reports and statistical material on current economic, business and other phenomena.

5. *Reports of Various Committees and Commissions appointed by the Government.* The report of the survey and enquiry commissions and committees of the Central and State Governments to find their expert views on some important matters relating to economic and social phenomena like wages, dearness allowance, prices, national income, taxation, land, education, etc., are invaluable source of secondary information. For instance Simon-Kuznet Committee report on National Income in India, Wanchoo Commission report on Taxation, Kothari Commission report on Educational Reforms, Pay Commissions Reports, Land Reforms Committee report, Gupta Commission report on Maruti Affairs, etc., are invaluable sources of secondary data.

6. *Newspapers and Periodicals.* Statistical material on a number of important current socio-economic problems can be obtained from the numerical data collected and published by some reputed magazines, periodicals and newspapers like Eastern Economist, Economic Times, The Financial Express, Indian Journal of Economics, Commerce, Capital, Transport, Statesman's Year Book and The Times of India Year Book, etc.

7. *International Publications.* The publications of a number of foreign governments or international agencies provide invaluable statistical information on a variety of important economic and current topics. The publications of the United Nations Organisation (U.N.O.) like U.N.O. Statistical Year Book, U.N. Statistical Abstract, Demographic Year Book, etc., and its subsidiaries like World Health Organisation (W.H.O.) on contagious diseases ; annual reports of International Labour Organisation (I.L.O.) ; International Monetary Fund (I.M.F.) ; World Bank ; Economic and Social Commission for Asia and Pacific (ESCAP) ; International Finance Corporation (I.F.C.) ; International Statistical Education Institute and so on are very valued publications of secondary data.

Remark. It may be pointed out that the various publications enumerated above vary as regards the periodicity of their publications. Some are published periodically at regular intervals of time (such as weekly, monthly, quarterly or annually) whereas others are ad-hoc publications which do not have any specific periodicity of publications.

2·5·2. Unpublished Sources. The statistical data need not always be published. There are various sources of unpublished statistical material such as the records maintained by private firms or business enterprises who may not like to release their data to any outside agency ; the various departments and offices of the Central and State Governments ; the researches carried out by the individual research scholars in the universities or research institutes.

Remark. In some of the socio-economic surveys the information is gathered from the respondents with the promise that it is exclusively meant for research programmes and will be kept strictly confidential. Such data are not published. In case it is published, it is done with a brief note namely, "Source : Confidential."

2·6. PRECAUTIONS IN THE USE OF SECONDARY DATA

Secondary data should be used with extra caution. Before using such data, the investigator must be satisfied regarding the reliability, accuracy, adequacy and suitability of the data to the given problem under investigation.

Proper care should be taken to edit it so that it is free from inconsistencies, errors and omissions. In the words of L.R. Connor "Statistics, especially other peoples' statistics, are full of pitfalls for the user" and therefore, secondary data should not be used before subjecting it to a thorough and careful scrutiny.

Prof. A.L. Bowley also remarks, "It is never safe to take the published statistics at their face value without knowing their meaning and limitations and it is always necessary to criticise the arguments that can be based upon them." In using secondary data we should take a special note of the following factors.

1. *The Reliability of Data.* In order to know about the reliability of the data, we should satisfy ourselves about :

(*i*) the reliability, integrity and experience of the collecting organistion.

(*ii*) the reliability of source of information and

(*iii*) the methods used for the collection and analysis of the data.

It should be ascertained that the collecting agency was unbiased in the sense that it had no personal motives and right from the collection and compilation of the data to the presentation of results in the final form in the selected source, the data was thoroughly scrutinised and edited so as to make it free from errors as far as possible. Moreover, it should also be verified that the data relates to normal times free from periods of economic boom or depression or natural calamities like famines, floods, earthquakes, wars, etc., and is still relevant for the purpose in hand.

If the data were collected on the basis of a sample we should satisfy ourselves that :

(*i*) The sample was adequate (not too small).

(*ii*) It was representative of the characteristics of the population, *i.e.,* it was selected by proper sampling technique.

(*iii*) The data were collected by trained, experienced and unbiased investigators under the proper supervisory checks on the field work so that sampling errors were minimised.

(*iv*) Proper estimation techniques were used for estimating the parameters of the population.

(*v*) The desired degree of accuracy was achieved by the compiler.

Remark. A source note, giving in details the sources from which data were obtained is imperative for the validity of the secondary data since to the learned users of statistics the reputations of the sources may vary greatly from one agency to another.

2. *The Suitability of Data.* Even if the data are reliable in the sense as discussed above it should not be used without confirming that it is suitable for the purpose of enquiry under investigation. For this, it is important :

(*i*) To observe and compare the objectives, nature and scope of the given enquiry with the original investigation.

(*ii*) To confirm that the various terms and units were clearly defined and uniform throughout the earlier investigation and these definitions are suitable for the present enquiry also. For instance, a unit like household, wages, prices, farm, etc., may be defined in many different ways. If the units are defined differently in the original investigation than what we want, the secondary data will be termed as unsuitable for the present enquiry. For example, if we want to construct the cost of living indices, it must be ensured that the original data relating to prices was obtained from retail shops, co-operative stores or super bazars and not from the wholesale market.

(*iii*) To take into account the difference in the timings of collection and homogeneity of conditions for the original enquiry and the investigation in hand.

3. *Adequacy of Data.* Even if the secondary data are reliable and suitable in terms of the discussion above, it may not be adequate enough for the purpose of the given enquiry. This happens when the coverage given in the original enquiry was too narrow or too wide than what is desired in the current enquiry or in other words when the original data refers to an area or a period which is much larger or smaller than the required one. For instance, if the original data relate to the consumption pattern of the various commodities by the people of a particular State, say, Maharashtra then it will be inadequate if we want to study the consumption pattern of the people for the whole country. Similarly if the original data relate to yearly figures of a particular phenomenon, it will be inadequate if we are interested in the monthly study. This is so because of the fluctuations in the phenomenon in different regions or periods.

Another important factor to decide about the adequacy of the available data for the given investigation is the time period for which the data are available. For example, if we are given the values of a particular phenomenon (say, profits of a business concern or production of a particular commodity) for the last 3-4 years, it will be inadequate for studying the trend pattern for which the values for the last 8-10 years will be required.

Hence, in order to arrive at conclusions free from limitations and inaccuracies, the published data *i.e.*, the secondary data must be subjected to thorough scrutiny and editing before it is accepted for use.

EXERCISE 2·1.

1. (*a*) What do you mean by a statistical enquiry ? Describe the main stages in a statistical enquiry.

(*b*) Describe the process of planning a statistical enquiry, with special reference to its scope and purpose, choice between sample and census approaches, accuracy and analysis of data.

2. If you are appointed to conduct a statistical enquiry, describe in general, what steps will you be taking from the stage of appointment till the presentation of your report.

3. (*a*) Distinguish between (*i*) primary and secondary data (*ii*) sampling and census method.

(*b*) Distinguish between primary data and secondary data and discuss the various methods of collecting primary data. [*C.S. (Foundation), Dec. 2000*]

(*c*) Explain the different methods of collecting primary data. (*Punjab Univ. B.Com., 1996*)

4. (*a*) What are the various methods of collecting statistical data ? Which of these is most reliable and why ?

(*b*) Describe the methods generally employed in the collection of statistical data, stating briefly their merits and demerits.

5. (*a*) Distinguish between Primary and Secondary data. Give a brief account of the chief methods of collecting Primary Data and bring out their merits and defects.

(*b*) Discuss the various methods of collecting 'primary data'. State the methods you would employ to collect information about utilisation of plant capacity in small-scale sector in the Union Territory of Delhi.

6. Distinguish between 'Primary Data' and 'Secondary Data'. State the chief sources of Secondary Data. What precautions are to be observed when such data are to be used for any investigation ?

7. A firm's own records are internal data. What is meant by external data, a primary data, a primary source and secondary source ? Which is preferred, primary sources or secondary sources, and why ? Why do you suppose secondary sources are so often used ?

8. (*a*) What are consumer primary and secondary data ? State those factors which should be kept in mind while using secondary data for the investigation.

(*b*) Distinguish between primary and secondary data. What precautions should be taken in the use of secondary data ?

(*c*) "Statistics, especially other people's statistics are full of pitfalls for the user unless used with caution." Elucidate the statement and mention what are the sources of the secondary data. [*Delhi Univ. B.Com. (Pass), 2001*]

9. (*a*) "In collection of statistical data common sense is the chief requisite and experience the chief teacher". Discuss the above statement with comments.

(*b*) "It is never safe to take published statistics at their face value without knowing their meanings and limitations and it is always necessary to criticise the arguments that can be based on them." (Bowley). Elucidate.

10. (*a*) Define a statistical unit and explain what should be the essential requirements of a good statistical unit.

(*b*) What are the essential points to be remembered in the choice of statistical units ?

(*c*) What is a statistical unit ? What do you mean by units of collection and units of analysis ? Discuss their relative uses.

(*d*) Giving appropriate reasons, state what units can be used for the following :

(*i*) Production of cotton in textile industry.
(*ii*) Labour employed in industry.
(*iii*) Consumption of electricity.

11. What are the essentials of a questionnaire ? Draft a questionnaire not exceeding ten questions to study the views on educational programmes of television and indicate an outline of the design of the survey.

12. What do you mean by a questionnaire ? What is the difference between a questionnaire and a schedule ? State the essential points to be remembered in drafting a questionnaire.

13. Discuss the essentials of a good questionnaire. "It is proposed to conduct a sample survey to obtain information on the study habits of University students in Chandigarh and the facilities available to them". Explain how you will plan the survey. Draft a suitable questionnaire for this purpose.

14. What are the different methods of collection of data ? Why are personal interviews usually preferred to questionnaire ? Under what conditions may a questionnaire prove as satisfactory as a personal interview ?

15. You are the Sales Promotion Officer of Delta Cosmetics Co. Ltd. Your company is about to market a new product. Design a suitable questionnaire to conduct a consumer survey before the product is launched. State the various types of persons that may be approached for replying to the questionnaire.

16. It is required to collect information on the economic conditions of textile mill workers in Mumbai. Suggest a suitable method for collection of primary data. Draft a suitable questionnaire of about ten questions for collecting this information. Also suggest how you will proceed to carry out statistical analysis of the information collected.

17. What are the essentials of a good questionnaire ? Draft a suitable questionnaire to enable you to study the effects of super markets on prices of essential consumer goods.

18. What are the chief features of a good questionnaire ? What precautions do you take while drafting a questionnaire ?

19. How would you organise an enquiry into the cost of living of the student community in a city ? Draw up a blank form to obtain the required information.

20. Fill in the blanks :

(*i*) There are ...... methods of collecting primary data.

(*ii*) Data are classified into ...... and ......

(*iii*) ...... is a suitable method of collecting data in cases where the informants are literate and spread over a vast area.

(*iv*) Data originally collected for any investigation is called ......

(*v*) The ...... data should be used after careful scrutiny.

Ans. (*i*) Four ; (*ii*) Primary and Secondary ; (*iii*) Mailed questionnaire method; (*iv*) Primary data; (*v*) Secondary.

21. What methods would you employ in collection of data considering accuracy, time and cost involved when the field of enquiry is :

(*i*) small; (*ii*) fairly large; (*iii*) very large.

Ans. (*i*) Direct personal interview ; (*ii*) and (*iii*) Mailed questionnaire method.

22. Assume that you employ the following data while conducting a statistical investigation :

(*i*) Estimate of personal income taken from R.B.I. bulletin.

(*ii*) Financial data of Indian companies taken from the annual reports of the Ministry of Law and Company Affairs.

(*iii*) Tabulation from schedules used in interviews that you yourself conducted.

(*iv*) Data collected by the National Sample Survey.

Which of the above is Primary Data ?

Ans. Only (*iii*).

23. Explain the necessity of editing primary and secondary data and briefly discuss points to be considered while editing such data.

3 Classification and Tabulation

3·1. INTRODUCTION — ORGANISATION OF DATA

In the last chapter we described the various methods of collecting data for any enquiry. Unfortunately the data collected in any statistical investigation, known as *raw data*, are so voluminous and huge that they are unwieldy and uncomprehensible. So, having collected and edited the data, the next important step is to organise it *i.e.,* to present it in a readily comprehensible condensed form which will highlight the important characteristics of the data, facilitate comparisons and render it suitable for further processing (statistical analysis) and interpretations.

The presentation of the data is broadly classified into the following two categories:

(*i*) Tabular Presentation.

(*ii*) Diagrammatic or Graphic Presentation.

A statistical table is an orderly and logical arrangement of data into rows and columns and it attempts to present the voluminous and heterogeneous data in a condensed and homogeneous form. But before tabulating the data, generally, systematic arrangement of the raw data into different homogeneous classes is necessary to sort out the relevant and significant features (details) from the irrelevant and insignificant ones.

This process of arranging the data into groups or classes according to resemblances and similarities is technically called *classification*. Thus, classification of the data is preliminary to its tabulation. It is thus the first step in tabulation because the items with similarities must be brought together before the data are presented in the form of a '*table*'.

On the other hand, the diagrams and graphs are pictorial devices for presenting the statistical data. However, in this chapter, we shall discuss only 'Classification and Tabulation' of the data while 'Diagrammatic and Graphic Presentation' of the data will be discussed in next chapter (Chapter 4).

3·2. CLASSIFICATION

It is of interest to give below the following definitions of Classification :

"*Classification is the process of arranging data into sequences and groups according to their common characteristics, or separating them into different but related parts.*"—**Secrist.**

"*A classification is a scheme for breaking a category into a set of parts, called classes, according to some precisely defined differing characteristics possessed by all the elements of the category.*"

—Tuttle A.M.

Thus classification impresses upon the 'arrangement of the data into different classes, which are to be determined depending upon the nature, objectives and scope of the enquiry. For instances the number of students registered in Delhi University during the academic year 2002-03 may be classified on the basis of any of the following criterion :

(*i*) Sex

(*ii*) Age

(*iii*) The state to which they belong

(*iv*) Religion

(*v*) Different faculties, like Arts, Science, Humanities, Law, Commerce, etc.

(*vi*) Heights or weights

(*vii*) Institutions (Colleges) and so on.

Thus the same set of data can be classified into different groups or classes in a number of ways based on any recognisable physical, social or mental characteristic which exhibits variation among the different elements of the given data. The facts in one class will differ from those of another class *w.r.t.* some characteristic called the *basis* or *criterion* of classification.

As an illustration, the data relating to socio-economic enquiry *e.g.*, the family budget data relating to nature, quality and quantity of the commodities consumed by the group of people together with expenditure on different items of consumption may be classified under the following major heads :

(*i*) Food

(*ii*) Clothing

(*iii*) Fuel and Lighting

(*iv*) House rent

(*v*) Miscellaneous (including items like education, recreation, medical expenses, gifts, newspaper, washerman, etc.).

Each of the above groups or classes may further be divided into sub-groups or sub-classes. For example, 'Food' may be sub-divided into Cereals (rice, wheat, maize, pulses, etc.); Vegetables; Milk and milk products ; Oil and ghee ; Fruits and Miscellaneous.

Thus it may be understood that to analyse any statistical data, classification may not be limited to one criterion or basis only. We might classify the given data *w.r.t.* two or more criteria or bases simultaneously. This technique of dividing the given data into different classes *w.r.t.* more than one basis simultaneously is called *cross-classification* and this process of further classification may be carried on as long as there are possible bases for classification. For instance, the students in the university may be simultaneously classified *w.r.t.* sex and faculty or *w.r.t.* age, sex and religion (three criteria) simultaneously and so on.

3·2·1. Functions of Classification. The functions of classification may be briefly summarised as follows :

(*i*) *It condenses the data.* Classification presents the huge unwieldy raw data in a condensed form which is readily comprehensible to the mind and attempts to highlight the significant features contained in the data.

(*ii*) *It facilitates comparisons.* Classification enables us to make meaningful comparisons depending on the basis or criterion of classification. For instance, the classification of the students in the university according to sex enables us to make a comparative study of the prevalence of university education among males and females.

(*iii*) *It helps to study the relationships.* The classification of the given data *w.r.t.* two or more criteria, say, the sex of the students and the faculty they join in the university will enable us to study the relationship between these two criteria.

(*iv*) *It facilitates the statistical treatment of the data.* The arrangement of the voluminous heterogeneous data into relatively homogeneous groups or classes according to their points of similarities introduces homogeneity or uniformity amidst diversity and makes it more intelligible, useful and readily amenable for further processing like tabulation, analysis and interpretation of the data.

3·2·2. Rules for Classification. Although classification is one of the most important techniques for the statistical treatment and analysis of numerical data, no hard and fast rules can be laid down for it. Obviously, a technically sound classification of the data in any statistical investigation will primarily depend on the nature of the data and the objectives of the enquiry. However, consistent with the nature and objectives of the enquiry, the following general guiding principles may be observed for good classification :

(*i*) *It should be unambiguous.* The classes should be rigidly defined so that they should not lead to any ambiguity. In other words, there should not be any room for doubt or confusion regarding the placement of the observations in the given classes. For example, if we have to classify a group of individuals as 'employed' and 'un-employed' : or 'literate' and 'illiterate' it is imperative to define in clear cut terms as to what we mean by an employed person and unemployed person ; by a literate person and illiterate person.

(*ii*) *It should be exhaustive and mutually exclusive.* The classification must be exhaustive in the sense that each and every item in the data must belong to one of the classes. A good classification should be free from the *residual class* like 'others' or 'miscellaneous' because such classes do not reveal the characteristics of the data completely. However, if the classes are very large in number as is the case in classifying various commodities consumed by people in a certain locality, it becomes necessary to introduce this 'residual class' otherwise the purpose of classification *viz*., condensation of the data will be defeated.

Further, the various classes should be mutually disjoint or non-overlapping so that an observed value belongs to one and only one of the classes. For instance, if we classify the students in a college by sex *i.e.*, as males and females, the two classes are mutually exclusive. But if the same group is classified as males, females and addicts to a particular drug then the classification is faulty because the group "addicts to a particular drug" includes both males and females. However, in such a case, a proper classification will be *w.r.t.* two criteria *viz*., *w.r.t.* sex (males and females) and further dividing the students in each of these two classes into 'addicts' and 'non-addicts' to the given drug.

(*iii*) *It should be stable.* In order to have meaningful comparisons of the results, an ideal classification must be stable *i.e.*, the same pattern of classification should be adopted throughout the analysis and also for further enquiries on the same subject. For instance, in the 1961 census, the population was classified w.r.t. profession in the four classes *viz*. (*i*) working as cultivator, (*ii*) working as agricultural labourer, (*iii*) working as household industry, and (*iv*) others. However, in 1971 census, the classification *w.r.t.* profession was as under :

(*a*) *Main Activity* : (*i*) Worker [Cultivator (*C*), Agricultural labourer (*AL*), Household industries (*HHI*), Other works (*OW*)].

(*b*) *Broad Category*. Non-worker [Household duties (*H*) ; Student (*ST*) ; Renteer or Retired person (*R*); Dependent, Beggers, Institutions and Others (*DBIO*)].

Consequently the results obtained in the two censuses cannot be compared meaningfully. Hence, having decided about the basis of classification in an enquiry, we should stick to it for other related matters in order to have meaningful comparisons.

(*iv*) *It should be suitable for the purpose.* The classification must be in keeping with the objectives of the enquiry. For instance, if we want to study the relationship between the university education and sex, it will be futile to classify the students *w.r.t.* to age and religion.

(*v*) *It should be flexible.* A good classification should be flexible in that it should be adjustable to the new and changed situations and conditions. No classification is good enough to be used for ever ; changes here and there become necessary with the changes in time and changed circumstances. However, flexibility should not be interpreted as instability of classification. The classification can be kept flexible by classifying the given population into some *major groups* which more or less remain stable and allowing for adjustment due to changed circumstances or conditions by sub-dividing these major groups into *sub-groups* or *sub-classes* which can be made flexible. Hence, the classification can maintain the character of flexibility along with stability.

Also see § 3·4·2 (Number of Classes) and § 3·4·3 (Size of Class Intervals).

3·2·3. Bases of Classification. The bases or the criteria *w.r.t.* which the data are classified primarily depend on the objectives and the purpose of the enquiry. Generally, the data can be classified on the following four bases :

(*i*) Geographical *i.e.*, Area-wise or Regional.

(*ii*) Chronological *i.e.*, *w.r.t.* occurrence of time.

(*iii*) Qualitative *i.e.*, *w.r.t.* some character or attribute.

(*iv*) Quantitative *i.e.*, *w.r.t.* numerical values or magnitudes.

In the following section we shall briefly discuss them one by one.

(*i*) Geographical Classification. As the name suggests, in this classification the basis of classification is the geographical or locational differences between the various items in the data like States, Cities,

Regions, Zones, Areas, etc. For example, the yield of agricultural output per hectare for different countries in some given period or the density of the population (per square km) in different cities of India, is given in the following tables.

TABLE 3·1
AGRICULTURAL OUTPUT OF DIFFERENT COUNTRIES
(In Kg Per Hectare)

Country	*Average Output*
India	123·7
USA	581·0
Pakistan	257·5
USSR	733·5
China	269·2
Syria	615·2
Sudan	339·8
UAR	747·5

Source : Yojana; Vol. XV, No. 18. 19th Sept. 1971, page 22.

TABLE 3·2
DENSITY OF POPULATION IN DIFFERENT CITIES OF INDIA
(Per Square Kilometre)

City	*Density of Population*
Kolkata	685
Mumbai	654
Delhi	423
Chennai	205
Chandigarh	48

Geographical classifications are usually presented either in an alphabetical order (which is generally the case in *reference tables**) or according to size or values to lay more emphasis on the important area or region as is done in Table 3·2 (and this is generally the case in *summary table**)

(*ii*) **Chronological Classification.** Chronological classification is one in which the data are classified on the basis of differences in time, *e.g.*, the production of an industrial concern for different periods ; the profits of a big business house over different years ; the population of any country for different years. We give in Table 3·3, the population of India for different decades.

TABLE 3·3
POPULATION OF INDIA (In Crores)

Year	*Population*
1901	23·8
1911	25·0
1921	25·2
1931	27·9
1941	31·9
1951	36·1
1961	43·9
1971	54·8
1981	68·3
1991	84·4

The time series data, which are quite frequent in Economic and Business Statistics are generally classified chronologically, usually starting with the first period of occurrence.

(*iii*) **Qualitative Classification.** When the data are classified according to some qualitative phenomena which are not capable of quantitative measurement like honesty, beauty, employment, intelligence, occupation, sex, literacy, etc., the classification is termed as *qualitative* or *descriptive* or *w.r.t. attributes*. In qualitative classification the data are classified according to the presence or absence of the attributes in the given units. If the data are classified into only two classes *w.r.t.* an attribute like its presence or absence among the various units, the classification is termed as *simple* or *dichotomous*. Examples of such classification are classifying a given population of individuals as honest or dishonest ; male or female ; employed or unemployed ; beautiful or not beautiful and so on. However, if the given population is classified into more than two classes *w.r.t.* a given attribute, it is said to be *manifold classification*. For example, for the attribute intelligence the various classes may be, say, genius, very intelligent, average intelligent, below average and dull as given below :

Population
↓
↓ Genius | ↓ Highly Intelligent | ↓ Average Intelligent | ↓ Below Average | ↓ Dull

* For detailed discussion on reference tables and summary tables, see § 3.7.3, on Types of Tabulation in this chapter.

Moreover, if the given population is divided into classes on the basis of simultaneous study of more than one attribute at a time, the classification is again termed as *manifold classification*. As an illustration, suppose we classify the population by sex into two classes, males and females and each of these two classes is further divided into two classes *w.r.t.* another attribute, say, smoking *i.e.,* smoker's and non-smokers, thus giving us four classes in all. Each of these four classes may further be divided *w.r.t.* a third attribute, say, religion into two classes Hindu, Non-Hindu and so on. The scheme is explained below.

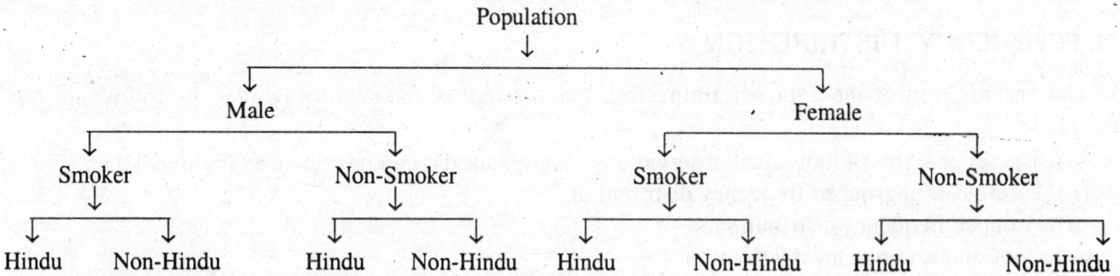

(*iv*) **Quantitative Classification**. If the data are classified on the basis of phenomenon which is capable of quantitative measurement like age, height, weight, prices, production, income, expenditure, sales, profits, etc., it is termed as quantitative classification. The quantitative phenomenon under study is known as *variable* and hence this classification is also sometimes called *classification by variables.* For example, the earnings of different stores may be classified as given in Table 3·4.

TABLE 3·4

DAILY EARNINGS (IN '00 RUPEES) OF 60 DEPARTMENTAL STORES

Daily earnings	*Number of stores*
Up to 100	6
101—200	14
201—300	8
301—400	10
401—500	8
501—600	6
601—700	4
701—800	4

In the above classification, the daily earnings of the stores are termed as *variable* and the number of stores in each class as the *frequency*. The above classification is termed as *grouped frequency distribution.*

Variable. As already pointed out, the quantitative phenomenon under study, like marks in a test, heights or weights of the students in a class, wages of workers in a factory, sales in a departmental store, etc., is termed a *variable* or a *variate*. It may be noted that different variables are measured in different units *e.g.,* age is measured in years, height in inches or cms ; weight in lbs or kgs, income in rupees and so on.

Variables are of two kinds :

(*i*) Continuous variable.

(*ii*) Discrete variable (Discontinuous variable).

Those variables which can take all the possible values (integral as well as fractional) in a given specified range are termed as continuous variables. For example, the *age* of students in a school (Nursery to Higher Secondary) is a continuous variable because age can take all possible values (as it can be measured to the nearest fraction of time : years, months, days, minutes, seconds, etc.), in a certain range, say, from 3 years to 20 years. Some other examples of continuous variable are height (in cms), weight (in lbs), distance (in kms). More precisely a variable is said to be continuous if it is capable of passing from any given value to the next value by infinitely small gradations.

On the other hand those variables which cannot take all the possible values within a given specified range are termed as discrete (discontinuous) variables. For example, the marks in a test (out of 100) of a group of students is a discrete variable since in this case marks can take only integral values from 0 to 100 (or it may take halves or quarters also if such fractional marks are given. Usually, fractional marks, if any, are rounded to the nearest integer). It cannot take all the values (integral as well as fractional) from 0 to 100. Some other examples of discrete variable are family size (members in a family), the population of a city, the number of accidents on the road, the number of typing mistakes per page and so on. A discrete variable is, thus, characterised by jumps and gaps between the one value and the next. Usually, it takes integral values in a given range which depends on the variable under study. A detailed discussion of the quantitative classification of a series or set of observations is given in § 3·3, "Frequency Distributions".

Remark. Values of the variable in a 'given specified range' are determined by the nature of the phenomenon under study. In case of heights of students in a college the range may be 4′ 6″ (*i.e.,* 137 cms) to 6′ 3″ (*i.e.,* 190 cms) ; in case of weights, it may be from 100 lbs to 200 lbs, say ; in case of marks in a test out of 25, it will be from 0 to 25 and so on.

3·3. FREQUENCY DISTRIBUTION

The organisation of the data pertaining to a *quantitative phenomenon* involves the following four stages :

(*i*) The set or series of individual observations - unorganised (*raw*) or organised (*arrayed*) data.
(*ii*) Discrete or ungrouped frequency distribution.
(*iii*) Grouped frequency distribution.
(*iv*) Continuous frequency distribution.

We shall explain the various stages by means of a numerical illustration.

Let us consider the following distribution of marks of 200 students in an examination, arranged serially in order of their roll numbers.

TABLE 3·5 **MARKS OF 200 STUDENTS**

70	45	33	64	50	25	65	75	30	20	41	53	48	21	28
55	60	65	58	52	36	45	42	35	40	30	33	37	35	29
51	47	39	61	53	59	49	41	15	53	43	32	24	38	38
42	63	78	65	45	63	54	52	48	46	46	50	26	15	23
57	53	55	42	45	39	64	35	26	18	41	38	40	37	40
49	42	36	41	29	46	40	32	34	44	54	35	39	31	48
37	38	40	32	49	48	50	43	55	43	39	41	48	53	34
22	41	50	17	46	32	31	42	34	34	32	33	24	43	39
42	25	52	38	46	40	50	27	47	34	44	34	33	47	42
48	45	30	28	31	17	42	57	35	38	17	33	46	36	23
42	21	51	37	42	37	38	42	49	52	38	53	57	47	59
61	33	17	71	39	44	42	39	16	17	27	19	54	51	39
43	42	16	37	67	62	39	51	53	41	53	59	37	27	29
33	34	42	22	31										

The data in the above form is called the *raw* or *disorganised data.* In the raw form the data are so unwieldy and scattered that even after a very careful perusal, the various details contained in them remain unfollowed and uncomprehensive. The above presentation of the data in its raw form does not give us any useful information and is rather confusing to the mind. Our objective will be to express the huge mass of data in a suitable condensed form which will highlight the significant facts and comparisons and furnish more useful information without sacrificing any information of interest about the important characteristics of the distribution.

3·3·1. Array. A better presentation of the above raw data would be to arrange them in an ascending or descending order of magnitude which is called the '*arraying*' of the data. However, this presentation (arraying), though better than the raw data does not reduce the volume of the data.

3·3·2. Discrete or Ungrouped Frequency Distribution. A much better way of the representation of the data is to express it in the form of a *discrete* or *ungrouped frequency-distribution* where we count the number of times each value of the variable (marks in the above illustration) occurs in the above data. This is facilitated through the technique of *Tally Marks* or *Tally Bars* as explained below :

In the first column we place all the possible values of the variable (marks in the above case). In the second column a vertical bar (|) called the *Tally Mark* is put against the number (value of the variable) whenever it occurs. After a particular value has occurred four times, for the fifth occurrence we put a cross tally mark (/) on the first four tally marks like 卌 to give us a block of 5. When it occurs for the 6th time we put another tally mark against it (after leaving some space from the first block of 5) and for the 10th occurrence we again put a cross tally mark (/) on the 6th to 9th tally marks to get another block of 5 and so on. This technique of putting cross tally marks at every 5th repetition (giving groups of 5 each) facilitates the counting of the number of occurrences of the value at the end. In the absence of such cross tally marks we shall get continuous tally bars like ǀǀǀǀǀǀǀǀ...and there may be confusion in counting and we are liable to commit mistakes also. Thus, the 2nd column consists of tally marks or tally bars. After putting tally marks for all the values in the data, we count the number of times each value is repeated and write it against the corresponding number (value of the variable) in the third column, entitled *frequency*. This type of representation of the data is called *discrete* or *ungrouped frequency distribution*. The marks (which vary from student to student) are called the *variable* under study and the number of students against the corresponding marks (which tell us how frequently the marks occur) is called the *frequency* (*f*) of the variable. The Table 3·6 below gives the ungrouped frequency distribution of the data in Table 3·5, along with the tally marks.

TABLE 3·6 FREQUENCY DISTRIBUTION OF MARKS OF 200 STUDENTS

Marks	*Tally Bars*	*Frequency*	*Marks*	*Tally Bars*	*Frequency*	*Marks*	*Tally Bars*	*Frequency*
15	ǀǀ	2	33	卌 ǀǀ	7	51	ǀǀǀǀ	4
16	ǀǀ	2	34	卌 ǀǀ	7	52	ǀǀǀǀ	4
17	卌	5	35	卌	5	53	卌 ǀǀǀ	8
18	ǀ	1	36	ǀǀǀ	3	54	ǀǀǀ	3
19	ǀ	1	37	卌 ǀǀ	7	55	ǀǀǀ	3
20	ǀ	1	38	卌 ǀǀǀ	8	57	ǀǀǀ	3
21	ǀǀ	2	39	卌 ǀǀǀǀ	9	58	ǀ	1
22	ǀǀ	2	40	卌 ǀ	6	59	ǀǀǀ	3
23	ǀǀ	2	41	卌 ǀǀ	7	60	ǀ	1
24	ǀǀ	2	42	卌 卌 ǀǀǀǀ	14	61	ǀǀ	2
25	ǀǀ	2	43	卌	5	62	ǀ	1
26	ǀǀ	2	44	ǀǀǀ	3	63	ǀǀ	2
27	ǀǀǀ	3	45	卌	5	64	ǀǀ	2
28	ǀǀ	2	46	卌 ǀ	6	65	ǀǀǀ	3
29	ǀǀǀ	3	47	ǀǀǀǀ	4	67	ǀ	1
30	ǀǀǀ	3	48	卌 ǀ	6	70	ǀǀ	2
31	ǀǀǀǀ	4	49	ǀǀǀǀ	4	75	ǀ	1
32	卌	5	50	卌	5	78	ǀ	1

From the frequency table given above, we observe that there are 8 students getting 38 marks, 14 students getting 42 marks, only 1 student getting 75 marks and so on. The presentation of the data in the form of an ungrouped frequency distribution as given above is better way than 'arraying' but still it does not condense the data much and is quite cumbersome to grasp and comprehend. The ungrouped frequency distribution is quite handy (*i*) if the values of the variable are largely repeated otherwise there will be hardly any condensation or (*ii*) if the variable (X) under consideration takes only a few values, say, if X were the marks out of 10 in a test given to 200 students, then X is a variable taking the values in the range 0 to 10 and can be conveniently represented by an ungrouped frequency distribution. However, if the variable takes the values in a wide (large) range as in the above illustration in Table 3·6, the data still remain unwieldy and need further processing for statistical analysis.

3·3·3. Grouped Frequency Distribution. If the identity of the units (students in our example) about whom a particular information is collected (marks in the above illustration) is not relevant, nor is the order in which the observations occur, then the first real step of condensation consists in classifying the data into different classes (or class intervals) by dividing the entire range of the values of the variable into a *suitable* number of groups called *classes* and then recording the number of observations in each group (or *class*). Thus, in the above data of Table 3·6, if we divide the total range of the values of the variable *viz.*, 78 – 15 = 63 into groups of size 5 each, then we shall get (63/5) = 13 groups and the distribution of marks is then given by the following *grouped frequency* distribution.

TABLE 3·7 DISTRIBUTION OF MARKS OF 200 STUDENTS

Marks (X)	*No. of Students (f)*	*Marks (X)*	*No. of Students (f)*
15—19	11	50—54	24
20—24	9	55—59	10
25—29	12	60—64	8
30—34	26	65—69	4
35—39	32	70—74	2
40—44	35	75—79	2
45—49	25		

The various groups into which the values of the variable are classified are known as *classes* or *class intervals* ; the length of the class interval (which is 5 in the above case) is called the *width* or *magnitude* of the classes. The two values specifying the class are called the *class limits* ; the larger value is called the *upper class limit* and the smaller value is called the *lower class limit.*

3·3·4. Continuous Frequency Distribution. While dealing with a continuous variable it is not desirable to present the data into a grouped frequency distribution of the type given in Table 3·7. For example, if we consider the ages of a group of students in a school, then the grouped frequency distribution into the classes 4—6, 7—9, 10—12, 13—15, etc., will not be correct, because this classification does not take into consideration the students with ages between 6 and 7 years *i.e.*, $6 < X < 7$; between 9 and 10 years *i.e.*, $9 < X < 10$ and so on. In such situations we form continuous class intervals, (without any gaps), of the following type :

Age in years :
Below 6
6 or more but less than 9
9 or more but less than 12
12 or more but less than 15

and so on, which takes care of all the students with any fractions of age.

The presentation of the data into continuous classes of the above type along with the corresponding frequencies is known as *continuous frequency distribution.* [For further detailed discussion, see Types of Classes—Inclusive and Exclusive—§ 3·4·4, page 3.11].

3·4. BASIC PRINCIPLES FOR FORMING A GROUPED FREQUENCY DISTRIBUTION

In spite of the great importance of classification in statistical analysis, no hard and fast rules can be laid down for it. A statistician uses his discretion for classifying a frequency distribution, and sound experience, wisdom, skill and aptness are required for an appropriate classification of the data. However, the following general guidelines may be borne in mind for a good classification of the frequency data.

3·4·1. Types of Classes. The classes should be clearly defined and should not lead to any ambiguity. Further; they should be exhaustive and mutually exclusive (*i.e.*, non-overlapping) so that any value of the variable corresponds to one and only one of the classes. In other words, there is one to one correspondence between the value of the variable and the class.

3·4·2. Number of Classes. Although no hard and fast rule exists, a choice about the number of classes (class intervals) into which a given frequency distribution can be divided primarily depends upon :

(*i*) The total frequency (*i.e.*, total number of observations in the distribution),
(*ii*) The nature of the data *i.e.*, the size or magnitude of the values of the variable,
(*iii*) The accuracy aimed at, and

(*iv*) The ease of computation of the various descriptive measures of the frequency distribution such as mean, variance, etc., for further processing of the data.

However, from practical point of view the number of classes should neither be too small nor too large. If too few classes are used, the classification becomes very broad and rough in the sense that too many frequencies will be concentrated or crowded in a single class. This might obscure some important features and characteristics of the data, thereby resulting in loss of information. Moreover, with too few classes the basic assumption that class marks (*i.e.*, mid-values of the classes) are representative of the class for computation of further descriptive measures of distribution like mean, variance, etc., will not be valid, and the so-called *grouping error* will be larger in such cases. Consequently, in general, the accuracy of the results decreases as the number of classes becomes smaller and smaller. On the other hand, too many classes *i.e.*, large number of classes will result in too few frequencies in each class. This might give irregular pattern of frequencies in different classes thus making the frequency distribution (frequency polygon) irregular. Moreover a large number of classes will render the distribution too unwieldy to handle, thus defeating the very purpose (or aim *viz*., summarisation of the data) of classification. Further the computational work for further processing of the data will unnecessarily become quite tedious and time consuming without any proportionate gain in the accuracy of the results. However, a balance should be struck between these two factors *viz*., the loss of information in the first case (*i.e.*, too few classes) and irregularity of frequency distribution in the second case (*i.e.*, too many classes) to arrive at a pleasing compromise, giving the optimum number of classes in the view of the statistician. Ordinarily, the number of classes should not be greater than 20 and should not be less than 5, of course keeping in view the points (*i*) to (*iv*) given above together with the magnitude of class interval, since the number of classes is inversely proportional to the magnitude of the class interval.

A number of rules of the thumb have been proposed for calculating the proper number of classes. However, an elegant, though approximate formula seems to be one given by Prof. Sturges known as *Sturges' rule*, according to which

$$k = 1 + 3{\cdot}322 \log_{10} N \qquad \ldots(3{\cdot}1)$$

where k is the number of class intervals (classes) and N is the total frequency *i.e.*, total number of observations in the data. The value obtained in (3·1) is rounded to the next higher integer.

Since log of one digited number is 0· (...) ; log of two digited number is 1· (...) ; log of three digited number is 2· (...) and log of four digited number is 3· (...), the use of formula (3·1) restricts the value of k, the number of classes, to be fairly reasonable. For example :

If $N = 10$, $k = 1 + 3{\cdot}322 \log_{10} 10 = 4{\cdot}322 \simeq 4$ $[\because \log_a a = 1]$
If $N = 100$, $k = 1 + 3{\cdot}322 \log_{10} 100 = 1 + 3{\cdot}322 \times 2 \log_{10} 10 = 1 + 6{\cdot}644 = 7{\cdot}644 \simeq 8$
If $N = 500$, $k = 1 + 3{\cdot}322 \log_{10} 500 = 1 + 3{\cdot}322 \times 2{\cdot}6990 = 1 + 8{\cdot}966 = 9{\cdot}966 \simeq 10$
If $N = 1000$, $k = 1 + 3{\cdot}322 \log_{10} 1000 = 1 + 3{\cdot}322 \times 3 \log_{10} 10 = 1 + 9{\cdot}966 = 10{\cdot}966 \simeq 11$
If $N = 10000$, $k = 1 + 3{\cdot}322 \times 4 = 1 + 13{\cdot}288 = 14{\cdot}288 \simeq 14$

Accordingly, the Sturges' formula (3·1) very ingeniously restricts the number of classes between 4 and 20, which is a fairly reasonable number from practical point of view.

The rule, however, fails if the number of observations is very large or very small.

Remarks. 1. The number of class intervals should be such that they usually give uniform and unimodal distribution in the sense that the frequencies in the given classes first increase steadily, reach a maximum and then decrease steadily. There should not be any sudden jumps or falls which result in the so-called *irregular* distribution. The maximum frequency should not occur in the very beginning or at the end of the distribution nor should it (maximum frequency) be repeated in which cases we shall get an irregular distribution.

2. The number of classes should be a whole number (integer) preferably 5 or some multiple of 5 viz., 10, 15, 20, 25, etc., which are readily perceptible to the mind and are quite convenient for numerical computations in the further processing (statistical analysis) of the data. Uncommon figures like 3, 7, 11, etc., should be avoided as far as possible.

3·4·3. Size of Class Intervals. Since the size of the class interval is inversely proportional to the number of classes (class intervals) in a given distribution, from the above discussion it is obvious that a choice about the size of the class interval will also largely depend on the sound subjective judgement of the statistician keeping in mind other considerations like N (total frequency), nature of the data, accuracy of the results and computational ease for further processing of the data. Here an approximate value of the magnitude (or width) of the class interval, say, 'i' can be obtained by using Sturges' rule (3.1) which gives :

$$i = \frac{\text{Range}}{\text{Number of Classes}} = \frac{\text{Range}}{1 + 3{\cdot}322\ \log_{10}^{N}} \qquad \text{[Using (3·1)]}$$

where Range of the distribution is given by the difference between the largest (L) and the smallest (S) value in the distribution.

i.e.,
$$\text{Range} = X_{max} - X_{min} = L - S \qquad \ldots(3{\cdot}2)$$

$$\therefore \qquad i = \frac{L - S}{1 + 3{\cdot}322\ \log_{10}^{N}} = \frac{\text{Range}}{k} \qquad \ldots(3{\cdot}3)$$

Another 'rule of the thumb' for determining the size of the class interval is that : "*The length of the class interval should not be greater than* $\frac{1}{4}$ *th of the estimated population standard deviation.*"* Thus, if $\hat{\sigma}$ is the estimate of the population standard deviation then the length of class interval is given by

$$i \leq \hat{\sigma}/4 = A, \text{ (say)}. \qquad \ldots(3{\cdot}4)$$

Remarks 1. From (3·3), we get :

$$k = \frac{\text{Range}}{i} \geq \frac{\text{Range}}{A} \qquad \left[\because i \leq A \Rightarrow \frac{1}{i} \geq \frac{1}{A}\right] \qquad \ldots(3{\cdot}5)$$

Thus, (3·4) also enables us to have an idea about the *minimum number of classes (k)* which will be given by :

$$k = \frac{\text{Range}}{A} \qquad \ldots(3{\cdot}5)$$

where range is defined in (3·2) and $A = \hat{\sigma}/4$.

If we consider a hypothetical frequency distribution of the life time of 400 radio bulbs tested at a certain company with the result that minimum life time is 340 hours and maximum life time is 1300 hours such that, in usual notations :

$N = 400$, $L = 1300$ hrs, $S = 340$ hrs, then using (3·3), we get

$$i = \frac{1300 - 340}{1 + 3{\cdot}322 \log_{10} 400} = \frac{960}{1 + 3{\cdot}322 \times 2{\cdot}6021} = \frac{960}{1 + 8{\cdot}644} = \frac{960}{9{\cdot}644} = 99{\cdot}54 \simeq 100 \qquad \ldots(*)$$

If the magnitude of the class interval is taken as 100, then the number of classes will be 10 [which is nothing but the value $9{\cdot}644 \simeq 10$ in the denominator of (*)].

2. Like the number of classes, as far as possible, the size of class intervals should also be taken as 5 or some multiple of 5 *viz*., 10, 15, 20, etc., for facilitating computations of the various descriptive measures of the frequency distribution like mean ($\bar{x}$), standard deviation (σ), moments, etc.

3. Class intervals should be so fixed that each class has a convenient *mid-point* about which all the observations in the class cluster or concentrate. In other words, this amounts to saying that *the entire frequency of the class is concentrated at the mid-value of the class. This assumption will be true only if the frequencies of the different classes are uniformly distributed in the respective class intervals.* This is a very fundamental assumption in the statistical theory for the computation of various statistical measures, like mean, standard deviation, etc.

4. From the point of view of practical convenience, as far as possible, it is desirable to take the class intervals of equal or uniform magnitude throughout the frequency distribution. This will facilitate the

* For detailed discussion on "Standard Deviation" see Chapter 6.

computations of various statistical measures and also result in meaningful comparisons between different classes and different frequency distributions. Further, frequency distributions with equal classes can be represented diagrammatically with greater ease and utility whereas in the case of classes with unequal widths the diagrammatic representation might give a distorted picture and thus lead to fallacious interpretations. However, it may not be practicable nor desirable to keep the magnitudes of the class intervals equal if there are very wide gaps in the observed data *e.g.*, in the frequency distribution of incomes, wages, profits, savings, etc., For example, in the frequency distribution of income, larger class intervals would (obscure) sacrifice all the details about the smaller incomes and smaller classes would give quite an unwieldy frequency distribution. Such distributions are quite common in many economic and medical data, where we have to be content with classes of unequal width.

3·4·4. Types of Class Intervals. As already stated, each class is specified by two extreme values called the class limits, the smaller one being termed as the lower limit and the larger one the upper limit of the class. The classification of a frequency distribution into various classes is of the following types :

(*a*) **Inclusive Type Classes.** The classes of the type 30—39, 40—49, 50—59, 60—69, etc., in which both the upper and lower limits are included in the class are called "*inclusive classes*". For instance, the class interval 40—49 includes all the values from 40 to 49, both inclusive. The next value *viz.*, 50 is included in the next class 50—59 and so on. However, the fractional values between 49 and 50 cannot be accounted for in such a classification. Hence, 'Inclusive Type' of classification may be used for a grouped frequency distribution for discrete variables like marks in a test, number of accidents on the road, etc., where the variable takes only integral values. It cannot be used with advantage for the frequency distribution of continuous variables like age, height, weight, etc., where all values (integral as well as fractional) are permissible.

(*b*) **Exclusive Type Classes.** Let us consider the distribution of ages of a group of persons into classes 15—19, 20—24, 25—29, etc., each of magnitude 5. This classification of 'inclusive type' for ages is defective in the sense that it does not account for the individuals with ages more than 19 years but less than 20 years. In such a situation (where the variable is continuous), the classes have to be made without any gaps as given below :

$$\left.\begin{array}{l}\text{15 years and over but under 20}\\\text{20 years and over but under 25}\\\text{25 years and over but under 30}\end{array}\right\}\qquad\ldots(*)$$

and so on ; each class in this case also being of magnitude 5. More precisely the above classes can be written as :

$$\begin{array}{lll}15\text{—}20 & \textit{i.e.,} & 15 \le X < 20\\ 20\text{—}25 & \textit{i.e.,} & 20 \le X < 25\\ 25\text{—}30 & \textit{i.e.,} & 25 \le X < 30\end{array}\Bigg\}\qquad\ldots(**)$$

and so on, where it should be clearly understood that in the above classes, the upper limits of each class are excluded from the respective classes. Such classes in which upper limits are excluded from the respective classes and are included in the immediate next class are termed as '*exclusive classes*'.

Remarks 1. For 'exclusive classes' the presentation given in (*) is preferred since it does not lead to any confusion. However, if presentation (**) is used, there is slight confusion about the overlapping values *viz.*, 20, 25, 30, etc., but whenever such presentation is used (which is extensively done in practice) it should be clearly understood that the upper limit of the class is to be excluded from that class. From the above discussion it is also clear that a choice between the 'inclusive method' or 'exclusive method' of classification will depend on the nature of the variable under study. For a discrete variable, the 'inclusive classes' may be used while for continuous variable the 'exclusive classes' are to be used.

TABLE 3·8

Age (on last birthday)	*No. of persons (f)*
20—24	6
25—29	10
30—34	14
35—39	9
40—44	6
45—49	5

2. However, sometimes, even for a continuous random variable the classification may be given to be of 'inclusive type'. As an illustration, let us consider the frequency distribution of age of a group of 50 individuals given in Table 3·8.

Although the variable (age) X is a continuous variable, here inclusive type of classes are used since we are recording the age as on late birthday and consequently it becomes a discrete variable taking only integral values. Since age is a continuous variable, we might like to convert this 'inclusive type' classification into 'exclusive type' classification. Since the ages are recorded as on last birthday, they are recorded almost one year younger (prior). For example, in the age group 20—24, there may be a person (or many persons) with ages 24·1, 24·2,...........up to 24·99. Thus all these persons who have not yet completed 25 years will be taken in the age group 20—24. Hence for obtaining 'exclusive classes' we can make a correction in the above distribution by converting 24 to 25. Accordingly for continuous representation of data (exclusive type), all the upper class limits in Table 3·8 will have to be increased by 1, thereby giving the (exclusive type) distribution, as given in Table 3·9.

TABLE 3·9

Age (on last birthday) (X)	*No. of persons* (f)
20—25	6
25—30	10
30—35	14
35—40	9
40—45	6
45—50	5

However, if the variable X is taken to denote the 'age on next birthday', then it would imply that the ages are recorded one year advance (*i.e.,* one year older than existing one). This will mean that the class 20—25 may include person(s) with ages just higher than 19 also. As such for continuity of the data the lower limit will have to be reduced by 1. Hence to obtain the 'exclusive type' classification for this case (X -age on next birthday *i.e.,* coming birthday), we shall have to subtract 1 from the lower limit of each class in Table 3·8 to get the distribution as given in Table 3·10.

TABLE 3·10

Age (on next birthday) (X)	*No. of persons* (f)
19—24	6
24—29	10
29—34	14
34—39	9
39—44	6
44—49	5

3. As far as possible the class limits should start with zero or some convenient multiple of 5. As an illustration if we want to form a frequency distribution of wages in a factory with class interval of 10 and the lowest value of wages (per week) is given to be Rs. 43, then instead of having classes 43—53, 53—63,...etc., a proper classification should be 40—50, 50—60, etc.

4. Class Boundaries. If in a grouped frequency distribution there are gaps between the upper limit of any class and lower limit of the succeeding class (as in the case of inclusive type of classification), there is need to convert the data into a continuous distribution by applying a correction for continuity for determining new classes of exclusive type. The upper and lower class limits of the new 'exclusive type' classes as called *class boundaries.*

If d is the gap between the upper limit of any class and lower limit of the succeeding class, the class boundaries for any class are then given by :

$$\left.\begin{aligned}\text{Upper class boundary} &= \text{Upper class limit} + \tfrac{1}{2}d \\ \text{Lower class boundary} &= \text{Lower class limit} - \tfrac{1}{2}d\end{aligned}\right\} \quad \ldots(3\cdot6)$$

$d/2$ is called the *correction factor.*

As an illustration, consider the following distribution of marks :

TABLE 3·11

Marks	*Class Boundary*
20—24	20 − 0·5, 24 + 0·5 *i.e.,* 19·5, 24·5
25—29	25 − 0·5, 29 + 0·5 *i.e.,* 24·5, 29·5
30—34	30 − 0·5, 34 + 0·5 *i.e.,* 29·5, 34·5
35—39	35 − 0·5, 39 + 0·5 *i.e.,* 34·5, 39·5
40—44	40 − 0·5, 44 + 0·5 *i.e.,* 39·5, 44·5

Here, $d = 25 - 24 = 30 - 29 = 35 - 34 = 1 \quad \Rightarrow \quad \dfrac{d}{2} = 0\cdot5$

This technique enables us to convert a grouped frequency distribution (inclusive type) into continuous frequency distribution and is extensively helpful in computing certain statistical measures like mode, median, etc., [See Chapter 5] which require the distribution to be continuous.

Thus, in Table 3·11, the lower class limits are 20, 25, 30, ..., 40 and the upper class limits are 24, 29,..., 44, while the lower class boundaries are 19·5, 24·5,..., 39·5 and the upper class boundaries are 24·5, 29·5,..., 44·5.

5. Mid-value or Class Mark. As the name suggests, the mid-value or the class-mark is the value of the variable which is exactly at the middle of the class. The mid-value of any class is obtained on dividing the sum of the upper and lower class limits (or class boundaries) by 2. In other words :

$$\left.\begin{aligned}\text{Mid-value of a class} &= \tfrac{1}{2}\,[\text{Lower class limit} + \text{Upper class limit}]\\ &= \tfrac{1}{2}\,[\text{Lower class boundary} + \text{Upper class boundary}]\end{aligned}\right\} \qquad \ldots(3\cdot7)$$

In the Table 3.11 of remark 4, it may be seen that the mid-values of various classes are : 22, 27, 32, 37, 42 respectively as given below :

$$\left.\begin{aligned}\tfrac{1}{2}(20+24)&=22\\ \tfrac{1}{2}(25+29)&=27\\ \tfrac{1}{2}(30+34)&=32\\ \tfrac{1}{2}(35+39)&=37\\ \tfrac{1}{2}(40+44)&=42\end{aligned}\right\} \quad \text{or} \quad \left\{\begin{aligned}\tfrac{1}{2}(19\cdot5+24\cdot5)&=22\\ \tfrac{1}{2}(24\cdot5+29\cdot5)&=27\\ \tfrac{1}{2}(29\cdot5+34\cdot5)&=32\\ \tfrac{1}{2}(34\cdot5+39\cdot5)&=37\\ \tfrac{1}{2}(39\cdot5+44\cdot5)&=42\end{aligned}\right.$$

It may be noted that whether we use class limits or class boundaries, the mid-values remain same.

Important Note. For fixing the class limits the most important factor to be kept in mind is as given below:

"***The class limits should be chosen in such a manner that the observations in any class are evenly distributed throughout the class interval so that the actual average of the observations in any class is very close to the mid-value of the class. In other words, this amounts to saying that the observations are*** *concentrated at the mid points of the classes.*"

This is a very fundamental assumption in preparing a grouped or continuous frequency distribution for computation of various statistical measures like mean, variance, moments, etc. [See Chapters 5, 6, 7] for further analysis of the data. If this assumption is not true then the classification will not reveal the main characteristics and thus give a distorted picture of the distribution. The deviation from this assumption introduces the so-called '*grouping error*'.

(*c*) **Open End Classes.** The classification is termed as '*open end classification*' if the lower limit of the first class or the upper limit of the last class are not specified and such classes in which one of the limits is missing are called '*open end classes*'. For example, the classes like the marks less than 20; age above 60 years, salary not exceeding Rupees 100 or salaries over Rupees 200, etc., are 'open end classes' since one of the class limits (lower or upper) is not specified in them. As far as possible, open end classes should be avoided since in such classes the mid-value or class-mark cannot be accurately obtained and this poses problems in the computation of various statistical measures for further processing of the data. Moreover, open end classes present problems in graphic presentation of the data also.

However, the use of open end classes is inevitable or unavoidable in a number of practical situations, particularly relating to economic and medical data where there are a few observations with extremely small or large values while most of the other observations are more or less concentrated in a narrower range. Thus, we have to resort to open end classes for the frequency distribution of income, wages, profits, payment of income-tax, savings, etc.

Remark. In case of open end classes, it is customary to estimate the class-mark or mid-value for the first class with reference to the succeeding class (*i.e.,* 2nd class). In other words, we assume that the magnitude of the first class is same as that of second class. Similarly, the mid-value of the last class is determined with reference to the preceding class *i.e.,* last but one class. This assumption will, of course, introduce some error in the calculation of further statistical measures (averages, dispersion, etc.—See Chapters 5, 6). However, if only a few items fall in the open end classes then :

(*i*) there won't be much loss in information in further processing of data as a consequence of open end classes, and

(*ii*) the open end classes will not seriously reduce the utility of graphic presentation of the data.

Example 3·1. *Form a frequency distribution from the following data by Inclusive Method, taking 4 as the magnitude of class-intervals :*

10, 17, 15, 22, 11, 16, 19, 24, 29, 18, 25, 26, 32, 14,
17, 20, 23, 27, 30, 12, 15, 18, 24, 36, 18, 15, 21, 28,
33, 38, 34, 13, 10, 16, 20, 22, 29, 19, 23, 31.

Solution. Since the minimum value of the variable is 10 which is a very convenient figure for taking the lower limit of the first class and the magnitude of the class intervals is given to be 4, the classes for preparing frequency distribution by the 'Inclusive Method' will be 10—13, 14—17, 18—21, 22—25,..., 34—37, 38—41, the last class being 38—41, because the maximum value in the distribution is 38.

To prepare the frequency distribution, since the first value 10 occurs in class 10—13 we put a tally mark against it, for the value 17 we put a tally mark against the class 14—17 ; for the value 15 we put a tally mark against the class 14—17 and so on. The final frequency distribution along with the tally marks is given in Table 3·12.

TABLE 3·12
FREQUENCY DISTRIBUTION

Class Interval	*Tally Marks*	*Frequency (f)*
10—13	卌	5
14—17	卌 III	8
18—21	卌 III	8
22—25	卌 II	7
26—29	卌	5
30—33	IIII	4
34—37	II	2
38—41	I	1
		Total 40

Example 3·2. *Following figures relate to the weekly wages of workers in a factory.*

Wages (in '00 Rs.)

100	*100*	*101*	*102*	*106*	*86*	*82*	*87*	*109*	*104*
75	*89*	*99*	*96*	*94*	*93*	*92*	*90*	*86*	*78*
79	*84*	*83*	*87*	*88*	*89*	*75*	*76*	*76*	*79*
80	*81*	*89*	*99*	*104*	*100*	*103*	*104*	*107*	*110*
110	*106*	*102*	*107*	*103*	*101*	*101*	*101*	*86*	*94*
93	*96*	*97*	*99*	*100*	*102*	*103*	*107*	*107*	*108*
109	*94*	*93*	*97*	*98*	*99*	*100*	*97*	*88*	*86*
84	*83*	*82*	*80*	*84*	*86*	*88*	*91*	*93*	*95*
95	*95*	*97*	*98*	*100*	*105*	*106*	*103*	*85*	*84*
77	*78*	*80*	*93*	*96*	*97*	*98*	*98*	*98*	*87*

Prepare a frequency table by taking a class interval of 5.

Solution. In the above distribution, the minimum value of the variable *X* (wages in '00 Rupees) is 75 and the maximum value is 110. Moreover, the magnitude of the class intervals is given to be 5. Since 'wages' is a continuous variable, the frequency distribution with 'Exclusive Method' would be appropriate. Since the minimum value 75 is a convenient figure to be taken as the lower limit of the first class, the class intervals may be taken as 75—80, 80—85, 85—90,..., 110—115, the upper limit of each class being included in the next class. The frequency distribution is given in Table 3·13.

TABLE 3·13
FREQUENCY DISTRIBUTION OF WAGES OF WORKERS IN A FACTORY

Weekly Wages (in '00 Rs.) (X)	*Tally Marks*	*No. of Workers (f)*
75—80	卌 IIII	9
80—85	卌 卌 II	12
85—90	卌 卌 卌	15
90—95	卌 卌 I	11
95—100	卌 卌 卌 卌	20
100—105	卌 卌 卌 卌	20
105—110	卌 卌 I	11
110—115	II	2
		Total = 100

Example 3·3. *Prepare a frequency distribution of the number of letters in a word from the following excerpt (ignore punctuation marks).*

"In the beginning", said a Persian Poet, "Allah took a rose, a lily, a dove, a serpent, a little honey, a Dead Sea Apple and a handful of clay. When he looked at the amalgam – it was a woman."

Also obtain (i) the number of words with 6 letters or more, (ii) the proportion of words with 5 letters or less, and (iii) the percentage of words with number of letters between 2 and 8 (i.e., more than 2 but less than 8).

Solution. Let X denote the number of letters in each word in the excerpt given above. We note that in the above excerpt there are words with number of letters ranging from 1 to 9. Hence X takes the values from 1 to 9. For example, in the first word 'In' there are 2 letters ; in the second world 'the' there are 3 letters ; in the third word 'beginning' there are 9 letters and so on. Thus, the corresponding values of the variable X in the above excerpt are as given below :

2, 3, 9, 4, 1, 7, 4, 5, 4, 1, 4, 1, 4
1, 4, 1, 7, 1, 6, 5, 1, 4, 3, 5, 3, 1
7, 2, 4, 4, 2, 6, 2, 3, 7, 2, 3, 1, 5

The frequency distribution along with the tally marks is given in the Table 3·14.

TABLE 3·14
FREQUENCY DISTRIBUTION OF NUMBER OF LETTERS IN A WORD

Number of letters in a word (X)	*Tally Marks*	*Frequency (f)*
1	卌 ||||	9
2	卌	5
3	卌	5
4	卌 ||||	9
5	||||	4
6	||	2
7	||||	4
8	—	0
9	|	1
		Total 39

(*i*) The number of words with 6 letters or more

$= 2 + 4 + 1 = 7$

(*ii*) The proportion of words with 5 letters or less is given by :

$$\frac{39-7}{39} = \frac{32}{39} = 0·82 \left(\text{or } \frac{9+5+5+9+4}{39} = \frac{32}{39} = 0·82 \right)$$

(*iii*) The percentage of words with the number of letters between 2 and 8 is :

$$\frac{5+9+4+2+4}{39} \times 100 \frac{24}{39} \times 100 = 61·45$$

Example 3·4. *In a survey, it was found that 64 families bought milk in the following quantities (litres) in a particular week.*

19	*16*	*22*	*9*	*22*	*12*	*39*	*19*	*14*	*23*
6	*24*	*16*	*18*	*7*	*17*	*20*	*25*	*28*	*18*
10	*24*	*20*	*21*	*10*	*7*	*18*	*28*	*24*	*20*
14	*23*	*25*	*34*	*22*	*5*	*33*	*23*	*26*	*29*
13	*36*	*11*	*26*	*11*	*37*	*30*	*13*	*8*	*15*
22	*21*	*32*	*21*	*31*	*17*	*16*	*23*	*12*	*9*
15	*27*	*17*	*21*						

Using Sturges' rule, convert the above data into a frequency distribution by 'Inclusive Method'.

Solution. Here the total frequency is $N = 64$. By Sturges' rule, the number of classes (k) is given by :

$$k = 1 + 3·322 \log_{10} 64 = 1 + 3·322 \times 1·8062 = 1 + 6·0002 = 7$$

Range = Maximum value – Minimum value = 39 – 5 = 34

Hence, the magnitude (i) of the class is given by
$$i = \frac{\text{Range}}{\text{Number of classes } (k)} = \frac{34}{7} = 4{\cdot}857 \simeq 5.$$

Hence taking the magnitude of each class interval as 5, we shall get 7 classes. Since the lowest value is 5, which is quite a convenient figure for being taken as the lower limit of the first class, the various classes by the inclusive method would be

5—9, 10—14, 15—19, 20—24, 25—29,
30—34, 35—39

Using tally marks, the required frequency distribution is obtained and is given in the Table 3·15.

TABLE 3·15

FREQUENCY DISTRIBUTION OF THE MILK PER WEEK AMONG 64 FAMILIES

Milk quantity (litres) (C.I.)	*Tally Marks*	*Number of families (f)*
5—9	~~IIII~~ II	7
10—14	~~IIII~~ ~~IIII~~	10
15—19	~~IIII~~ ~~IIII~~ III	13
20—24	~~IIII~~ ~~IIII~~ ~~IIII~~ III	18
25—29	~~IIII~~ III	8
30—34	~~IIII~~	5
35—39	III	3
		Total 64

Example 3·5. *A college management wanted to give scholarships to B. Com. students securing 60 per cent and above marks in the following manner :*

The marks of 25 students who were eligible for scholarship are given below :

74, 62, 84, 72, 61, 83, 72, 81, 64,
71, 63, 61, 60, 67, 74, 66, 64, 79,
73, 75, 76, 69, 68, 78 and 67.

Calculate the monthly scholarship paid to the students.

Percentage of Marks	*Monthly Scholarship In Rs.*
60—65	*250*
65—70	*300*
70—75	*350*
75—80	*400*
80—85	*450*

Solution. As we are given the amount of scholarships according to the percentage of marks of the students within classes 60—65, 65—70,..., 80—85, we shall convert the given distribution of marks into frequency distribution with these classes as obtained in Table 3·16.

TABLE 3·16

FREQUENCY DISTRIBUTION OF MARKS OF 25 STUDENTS

Percentage of marks	*Tally Marks*	*No. of Students (f)*	*Scholarship (in Rs.) (X)*	*Total Amount (f X)*
60—65	~~IIII~~ II	7	250	1750
65—70	~~IIII~~	5	300	1500
70—75	~~IIII~~ I	6	350	2100
75—80	IIII	4	400	1600
80—85	III	3	450	1350
Total		$\Sigma f = 25$		$\Sigma fX = 8{,}300$

Total monthly scholarship paid to the students is : $\Sigma fX =$ Rs. 8,300.

Example 3·6. *If the class mid-points in a frequency distribution of age of a group of persons are 25, 32, 39, 46, 53 and 60, find :*

(*a*) *the size of the class interval,* (*b*) *the class boundaries, and*

(*c*) *the class limits, assuming that the age quoted is the age completed last birthday.*

Solution. (*a*) The size (i) of the class interval is given by :

i = Difference between the mid-values of any two consecutive classes

= 7 [Since $32 - 25 = 39 - 32 = \ldots = 60 - 53 = 7$]

(*b*) Since the magnitude of the class is 7 and the mid-values of the classes are 25, 32,..., 60, the corresponding class boundaries for different classes are obtained on adding (for upper class boundaries) and subtracting (for lower class boundaries) half the magnitude of the class interval *viz.*, (7/2) = 3·5, from the mid-value respectively. For example the class boundaries for the first class will be (25 – 3·5, 25 + 3·5) *i.e.*, (21·5, 28·5) ; for the second class will be (32 – 3·5, 32 + 3·5) *i.e.*, (28·5, 35·5) and so on. Thus the various classes (Eclusive Type) with class boundaries are as given in Table 3·17.

TABLE 3·17

Class	*Mid-value*
21·5—28·5	25
28·5—35·5	32
35·5—42·5	39
42·5—49·5	46
49·5—56·5	53
56·5—63·5	60

(*c*) Assuming the age quoted (X) is the age completed on last birthday then X will be a discrete variable which can take only integral values. Hence the given distribution can be expressed in an 'inclusive type' of classes with class interval of magnitude 7, as given in Table 3·18.

(For details see Remark 2 § 3·4·4).

TABLE 3·18

Age (on last birthday)	*Mid-point*
22—28	25
29—35	32
36—42	39
43—49	46
50—56	53
57—63	60

Example 3·7. *The following table shows the distribution of the life time of 350 radio tubes.*

Lifetime (in hours) :	300—400	400—500	500—600	600—700	700—800	800—900	900—1000
Number of tubes :	6	18	73	165	62	22	4

Stating clearly the assumptions involved, obtain the percentage of tubes that have life time:

(*a*) *Greater than 760 hours* ; (*b*) *Between 650 and 850 hours;* and (*c*) *Less than 530 hours.*

Solution. Under the assumption that the class frequencies are uniformly distributed within the corresponding classes, we obtain by simple interpolation technique :

(*a*) Number of tubes with the lifetime over 760 hours

$$= 4 + 2 + \left(\frac{62}{100} \times 40\right) = 26 + 24{\cdot}8 = 50{\cdot}8 \simeq 51,$$ since number of tubes cannot be fractional.

Hence, required percentage of tubes $= \frac{51}{350} \times 100 = 14{\cdot}57.$

(*b*) Number of tubes with lifetime over 650 hours

$$= 4 + 22 + 62 + \frac{165}{100} \times 50 = 88 + 82{\cdot}5 = 170{\cdot}5 \simeq 171$$

Number of tubes with lifetime over 850 hours $= 4 + \left(\frac{22}{100} \times 50\right) = 15$

Hence the number of tubes with lifetime between 650 hours and 850 hours is 171 – 15 = 156.

The required percentage of tubes $= \frac{156}{350} \times 100 = 44{\cdot}57$

(*c*) Number of tubes with life less than 530 hours $= 6 + 18 + \frac{73}{100} \times 30 = 6 + 18 + 21{\cdot}9 = 45{\cdot}9 \simeq 46$

Hence required percentage of tubes $= \frac{46}{350} \times 100 = 13{\cdot}14.$

3·5. CUMULATIVE FREQUENCY DISTRIBUTION

A frequency distribution simply tells us how frequently a particular value of the variable (class) is occurring. However, if we want to know the total number of observations getting a value 'less than' or 'more than' a particular value of the variable (class), this frequency table fails to furnish the information as such. This information can be obtained very conveniently from the '*cumulative frequency distribution*', which is a modification of the given frequency distribution and is obtained on successively adding the frequencies of the values of the variable (or classes) according to a certain law. The frequencies so obtained are called the *cumulative frequencies* abbreviated as *c.f.* The laws used are of 'less than' and ' more than' type giving rise '*less than cumulative frequency distribution*' and '*more than cumulative frequency distribution*'. We shall explain the construction of such distributions by means of a numerical illustration.

3·5·1. Less Than Cumulative Frequency. Let us consider the distribution of marks of 70 students in a test as given in Table 3·19.

TABLE 3·19

Marks	*No. of students*
30—35	5
35—40	10
40—45	15
45—50	30
50—55	5
55—60	5
Total	70

Less than cumulative frequency for any value of the variable (or class) is obtained on adding successively the frequencies of all the previous values (or classes), including the frequency of variable (class) against which the totals are written, provided the values (classes) are arranged in ascending order of magnitude. For instance, in the above illustration, the total number of students with marks less than, say, 40 is 5 + 10 = 15; 'less than 50' is the sum of all the previous frequencies upto and including the class 45—50 *i.e.,* 5 + 10 + 15 + 30 = 60 and so on. The final distribution is given in Table 3·20.

TABLE 3·20
'LESS THAN' CUMULATIVE FREQUENCY DISTRIBUTION OF MARKS OF 70 STUDENTS

Marks	*Frequency (f)*	*'Less than' c.f.*
30—35	5	5
35—40	10	5 + 10 = 15
40—45	15	15 + 15 = 30
45—50	30	30 + 30 = 60
50—55	5	60 + 5 = 65
55—60	5	65 + 5 = 70

TABLE 3·20 (*a*)
LESS THAN *c. f.* DISTRIBUTION

Marks	*Frequency*
Less than 30	0
" " 35	5
" " 40	15
" " 45	30
" " 50	60
" " 55	65
" " 60	70

The 'less than' cumulative frequency distribution of Table 3·20 can also be written as given in Table 3·20(*a*).

3·5·2. More Than Cumulative Frequency. The 'more than cumulative frequency' is obtained similarly by finding the cumulative totals of frequencies starting from the highest value of the variable (class) to the lowest value (class). Thus in the above illustration the number of students with marks 'more than 50' is 5 + 5 = 10, and 'more than 40' is 15 + 30 + 5 + 5 = 55 and so on. The complete 'more than' type cumulative frequency distribution for this data is given in Table 3·21.

TABLE 3·21
'MORE THAN' CUMULATIVE FREQUENCY DISTRIBUTION OF MARKS OF 70 STUDENTS

Marks	*Frequency (f)*	*'More than' cumulative frequency (c.f.)*
30—35	5	65 + 5 = 70
35—40	10	55 + 10 = 65
40—45	15	40 + 15 = 55
45—50	30	10 + 30 = 40
50—55	5	5 + 5 = 10
55—60	5	5

TABLE 3·21 (*a*)
MORE THAN FREQUENCY DISTRIBUTION

Marks	*No. of students*
More than 30	70
" " 35	65
" " 40	55
" " 45	40
" " 50	10
" " 55	5
" " 60	0

The 'more than' *c.f.* distribution of Table 3·21 can also be expressed as given in Table 3·21 (*a*).

Remarks 1. In fact 'less than' and 'more than' words also include the equality sign *i.e.,* 'less than a given value' means 'less than or equal to that value' and 'more than a given value' means 'more than or equal to that value'.

2. Cumulative frequency distribution is of particular importance in the computation of median, quartiles and other partition values of a given frequency distribution. [For details See Chapter 5—Averages].

3. In 'less than' cumulative frequency distribution, the *c.f.* refers to the upper limit of the corresponding class and in 'more than' cumulative frequency distribution, the *c.f.* refers to the lower limit of the corresponding class.

Example 3·8. *Convert the following distribution into 'more than' frequency distribution.*

Weekly wages (less than '00 Rs.)	:	*20*	*40*	*60*	*80*	*100*
Number of workers	:	*41*	*92*	*156*	*194*	*201*

Solution. Here we are given, 'less than' cumulative frequency distribution. To obtain the 'more than' cumulative frequency distribution, we shall first convert it into continuous frequency distribution as shown in Table 3·22.

TABLE 3·22
MORE THAN c.f. DISTRIBUTION

Weekly wages (in '00 Rs.)	*No. of workers (f)*	*'More than' c.f.*
0—20	41	160 + 41 = 201
20—40	92 − 41 = 51	109 + 51 = 160
40—60	156 − 92 = 64	45 + 64 = 109
60—80	194 − 156 = 38	7 + 38 = 45
80—100	201 − 194 = 7	7

TABLE 3·22 (*a*)
'MORE THAN' FREQUENCY DISTRIBUTION

Weekly wages more than ('00 Rs.)	*No. of workers*
0	201
20	160
40	109
60	45
80	7
100	0

From Table 3·22, we obtain the 'more than' frequency distribution as given in Table 3·22 (*a*).

Example 3·9. *The credit office of a departmental store gave the following statements for payment due to 40 customers. Construct a frequency table of the balances due taking the class intervals as Rs. 50 and under Rs. 200, Rs. 200 and under Rs. 350, etc. Also find the percentage cumulative frequencies and interpret these values.*

Balances due in Rs.

337,	*570,*	*99,*	*759,*	*487,*	*352,*	*115,*	*60,*	*521,*	*95*
563,	*399,*	*625,*	*215,*	*360,*	*178,*	*827,*	*301,*	*501,*	*199*
110,	*501,*	*201,*	*99,*	*637,*	*328,*	*539,*	*150,*	*417,*	*250*
451,	*595,*	*422,*	*344,*	*186,*	*681,*	*397,*	*790,*	*272,*	*514*

Solution. Taking the class intervals as 50—200, 200—350, … …, and using tally marks, we obtain the following distribution of the balance due (in Rs.) from 40 customers.

TABLE 3·23
FREQUENCY TABLE OF BALANCE DUE (IN RUPEES) TO 40 CUSTOMERS

Balance due (in Rs.)	*Tally Marks*	*No. of customers (f)*	*Less than c.f.*	*Percentage c.f.**
50—200	~~IIII~~ ~~IIII~~	10	10	25·0
200—350	~~IIII~~ III	8	10 + 8 = 18	45·0
350—500	~~IIII~~ III	8	18 + 8 = 26	65·0
500—650	~~IIII~~ ~~IIII~~	10	26 + 10 = 36	90·0
650—800	III	3	36 + 3 = 39	97·5
800—950	I	1	39 + 1 = 40	100·0
Total		$N = \Sigma f = 40$		

* Percentage $c.f. = \frac{\text{Less than } c.f.}{N} \times 100$

The last column of the percentage cumulative frequencies shows that 25% of the customers have to pay less than Rs. 200, 45% of customers have to pay less than Rs. 350 ; 65% of the customers have to pay less than Rs. 500 ; 90% of the customers have to pay less than Rs. 650 ; 97·5% of the customers have to pay less than Rs. 800 and the balance due is less than Rs. 950 from each of the 40 customers *i.e.*, no customer has to pay more than Rs. 950.

3·6. BIVARIATE FREQUENCY DISTRIBUTION

So far our study was confined to frequency distribution of a single variable only. Such frequency distributions are also called *univariate frequency distributions*. Quite often we are interested in simultaneous study of two variables for the same population. This amounts to classifying the given population *w.r.t.* two bases or criteria simultaneously. For example, we may study the weights and heights of a group of individuals, the marks obtained by a group of individuals on two different tests or subjects, income and expenditure of a group of individuals, ages of husbands and wives for a group of couples, etc. The data so obtained as a result of this cross classification give rise to the so-called *bivariate frequency distribution* and it can be summarised in the form of *two-way* table called the *bivariate frequency table* or commonly called the *correlation table*. Here also the values of each variable are grouped into various classes (not necessarily the same for each variable) keeping in view the same considerations of classification as for a univariate distribution. If the data corresponding to one variable, say, X is grouped into m classes and the data corresponding to the other variable, say, Y is grouped into n classes then the bivariate table will consist of $m \times n$ cells. By going through the different pairs of the values (x, y) of the variables and using tally marks we can find the frequency for each cell and thus obtain the bivariate frequency table. The format of a bivariate frequency table is given in Table 3.24.

TABLE 3·24

BIVARIATE FREQUENCY TABLE

X Series → / Y Series ↓		Classes / Mid Points: x_1	x_2	...	x	...	x_m	Total of frequencies of Y
Classes	Mid Points							
	y_1							
	y_2							
	y				$f(x, y)$			f_y
	⋮							
	y_n							
Total of frequencies of X					f_x			Total $\Sigma f_x = \Sigma f_y = N$

Here $f(x, y)$ is the frequency of the pair (x, y).

Remarks 1. The bivariate frequency table gives a general visual picture of the relationship between the two variables under consideration. However, a quantitative measure of the linear relationship between the variables is given by the correlation coefficient (See Chapter 8, Correlation Analysis).

2. Marginal Distributions of X and Y. The frequency distribution of the values of the variable X together with their frequency totals as given by f_x in the above table is called the *marginal frequency distribution of* X. Similarly, the frequency distribution of the values of the variable Y together with the total frequencies f_y in the above table, is known as the *marginal frequency distribution of* Y.

3. Conditional Distributions of X and Y. The conditional frequency distribution of X for a given value of Y is obtained by the values of X together with their frequencies corresponding to the fixed values of Y. Similarly, we may obtain the conditional frequency distribution of Y for given values of X.

We shall now explain the technique of constructing bivariate frequency table and obtaining the marginal and conditional distributions of X and Y by means of numerical illustrations.

Example 3·10. (*a*) *Prepare a bivariate frequency distribution for the following data for 20 students :*

Marks in Law	*10*	*11*	*10*	*11*	*11*	*14*	*12*	*12*	*13*	*10*
Marks in Statistics	*29*	*21*	*22*	*21*	*23*	*23*	*22*	*21*	*24*	*23*
Marks in Law	*13*	*12*	*11*	*12*	*10*	*14*	*14*	*12*	*13*	*10*
Marks in Statistics	*24*	*23*	*22*	*23*	*22*	*22*	*24*	*20*	*24*	*23*

(*b*) *Also obtain the marginal frequency distributions of the marks in Law and marks in Statistics and the conditional frequency distribution of marks in Law when marks in Statistics are 23 and the conditional distribution of marks in Statistics when marks in Law are 12.*

Solution. (*a*) Let us denote the marks in Law by the variable X and the marks in Statistics by the variable Y. Then X takes the values from 10 to 14 *i.e.*, 5 values in all, and Y takes the values from 20 to 24 *i.e.*, 5 values in all. Thus the two-way table will consist of $5 \times 5 = 25$ cells.

To prepare the bivariate frequency table, we observe that the first student gets 10 marks in Law and 20 marks in Statistics. Therefore, we put a tally mark in the cell where the column corresponding to $X = 10$ intersects the row corresponding to $Y = 20$. Proceeding similarly we put tally marks for each pair of values (x, y) for all the 20 candidates. The total frequency for each cell is given in small brackets ( ), after the tally marks. Now count all the frequencies in each row and write at extreme right column. Similarly count all the frequencies in each column and write at the bottom row. The bivariate frequency distribution so obtained is given in Table 3·25.

TABLE 3·25
BIVARIATE FREQUENCY TABLE SHOWING MARKS OF 20 STUDENTS IN LAW AND STATISTICS

<table>
<tr><th>Marks in Law (X) →
Marks in Statistics (Y) ↓</th><th>10</th><th>11</th><th>12</th><th>13</th><th>14</th><th>Total (f_y)</th></tr>
<tr><td>20</td><td>| (1)</td><td></td><td>| (1)</td><td></td><td></td><td>2</td></tr>
<tr><td>21</td><td></td><td>|| (2)</td><td>| (1)</td><td></td><td></td><td>3</td></tr>
<tr><td>22</td><td>|| (2)</td><td>| (1)</td><td>| (1)</td><td></td><td>| (1)</td><td>5</td></tr>
<tr><td>23</td><td>|| (2)</td><td>| (1)</td><td>|| (2)</td><td></td><td>| (1)</td><td>6</td></tr>
<tr><td>24</td><td></td><td></td><td></td><td>||| (3)</td><td>| (1)</td><td>4</td></tr>
<tr><td>Total (f_x)</td><td>5</td><td>4</td><td>5</td><td>3</td><td>3</td><td>20</td></tr>
</table>

(*b*) The marginal frequency distributions of X and Y are given in Table 3·25(*a*).

TABLE 3·25 (*a*)
MARGINAL DISTRIBUTIONS

Marginal Distribution of X		*Marginal Distribution of Y*	
X	*f*	*Y*	*f*
10	5	20	2
11	4	21	3
12	5	22	5
13	3	23	6
14	3	24	4
Total	**20**	**Total**	**20**

TABLE 3·25 (*b*)
CONDITIONAL DISTRIBUTIONS

Conditional Distribution of X when Y = 23		*Conditional Distribution of Y when X = 12*	
X	*Frequency*	*Y*	*Frequency*
10	2	20	1
11	1	21	1
12	2	22	1
13	0	23	2
14	1	24	0
Total	6	Total	5

The conditional distributions of marks in Law (X) when marks in Statistics *i.e.*, $Y = 23$ and the conditional distribution of marks in Statistics (Y) when marks in Law, *i.e.*, $X = 12$, are given in Table. 3·25(*b*).

Example 3·11. *Following figures give the ages in years of newly married husbands and wives. Represent the data by a frequency distribution.*

Age of Husband	:	24	26	27	25	28	24	27	28	25	26
Age of Wife	:	17	18	19	17	20	18	18	19	18	19
Age of Husband	:	25	26	27	25	27	26	25	26	26	26
Age of Wife	:	17	18	19	19	20	19	17	20	17	18

[*Delhi Univ. B.Com. (Hons.), 1975*]

Solution. Let us denote the age (in years) of the husbands by the variable X and the age (in years) of wives by the variable Y. Then we observe that the variable X takes the values from 24 to 28 and Y takes the values from 17 to 20. Proceeding exactly as in Example 3·10, we obtain the bivariate frequency distribution given in Table 3·26.

TABLE 3·26

FREQUENCY DISTRIBUTION OF THE AGES (IN YEARS) OF NEWLY MARRIED HUSBANDS AND WIVES

Age of Wife (Y) ↓ \ *Age of Husband* (X) →	24	25	26	27	28	*Total* (f_y)
17	| (1)	||| (3)	| (1)			5
18	| (1)	| (1)	||| (3)	| (1)		6
19		| (1)	|| (2)	|| (2)	| (1)	6
20			| (1)	| (1)	| (1)	3
Total (f_x)	2	5	7	4	2	20

EXERCISE 3·1.

1. (*a*) What do you mean by classification of data ? Discuss in brief the modes of classification. [*Delhi Univ. B.Com. (Pass), 1996*]

(*b*) Briefly explain the principles of Classification. [*Delhi Univ. B.Com. (Pass), 2000*]

(*c*) What do you understand by classification of data ? What are its objectives ?

(*d*) What are different types of classification ? Illustrate by suitable examples.

2. "Classification is the process of arranging things (either actually or notionally) in groups or classes according to their resemblances and affinities giving expression to the unity of attributes that may subsist amongst a diversity of individuals".

Elucidate the above statement.

3. (*a*) What is meant by 'classification'? State its important objectives. Briefly explain the different methods of classifying statistical data. [*C.A. (Foundation), June 1993*]

(*b*) What are the purposes of *classification of data* ? State the primary rules to be observed in classification. [*C.A. (Foundation), Nov. 1995*]

4. (*a*) What are the advantages of data classification? What primary rules should ordinarily be followed for classification ? [*C.A. (Foundation), Nov. 1997*]

(*b*) What are different kinds of *classification* ? State, how the classification of data is useful. [*C.A. (Foundation), Nov. 2000*]

(*c*) State the principles underlying classification of data.

5. (*a*) What are grouped and ungrouped frequency distributions ? What are their uses ? What are the considerations that one has to bear in mind while forming the frequency distribution ?

(*b*) Discuss the problems in the construction of a frequency distribution from raw data, with particular reference to the choice of number of classes and the class limits.

6. (*a*) What are the principles governing the choice of :

(*i*) Number of class intervals. (*ii*) The length of the class interval. (*iii*) The mid point of class interval ?

(*b*) What are the general rules of forming a frequency distribution with particular reference to the choice of class-interval and number of classes ? Illustrate with examples. [*Calicut Univ., B.Com., 1999*]

7. What do you mean by an inclusive series ? How can an inclusive series be converted to an exclusive series ? Illustrate with the help of an example. [*Delhi Univ. B.Com. (Pass), 2002*]

8. Prepare a frequency distribution from the following figures relating to bonus paid to factory workers :

BONUS PAID TO WORKERS (in Rs.)

86	62	58	73	101	90	84	90	76	61
84	63	56	72	102	56	83	92	87	60
83	69	57	71	103	57	87	93	88	59
76	70	54	70	104	58	88	94	89	57
74	86	55	60	105	59	89	84	90	74
67	84	82	70	60	60	90	81	91	76
60	83	78	80	65	61	96	82	93	102
60	91	76	90	70	63	94	83	94	101
70	100	74	101	80	67	92	85	96	92

Take a class-interval of 5.

Ans. Frequencies of classes 50—54, 55—59,..., 100—104, 105—109 are respectively 1, 10, 11, 4, 11, 5, 13, 9, 15, 2, 8 and 1.

9. Describe in brief the practical problems of frequency distribution in classification of data on a variable according to class intervals, giving the definition of frequency distribution. [*C.A. (Foundation), Nov. 2001*]

10. (*a*) For the following raw data prepare a *frequency distribution* with the starting class as 5—9 and all classes with the same width 5.

Marks in English

12	36	40	16	10	10	19	20	28	30
19	27	15	21	33	45	7	19	20	26
26	37	6	5	20	30	37	17	11	20

Ans.

Marks :	5—9	10—14	15—19	20—24	25—29	30—34	35—39	40—44	45—49
Frequency :	3	4	6	5	4	3	3	1	1

(*b*) Classify the following data by taking class intervals such that their mid-values are 17, 22, 27, 32, and so on.

30	42	30	54	40	48	15	17	51	42	25	41
30	27	42	36	28	26	37	54	44	31	36	40
36	22	30	31	19	48	16	42	32	21	22	46
33	41	21									

[*Madurai-Kamaraj Univ. B.Com., 1995*]

Ans.

15—19	20—24	25—29	30—34	35—39	40—44	45—49	50—54
4	4	4	8	4	9	3	3

11. (*a*) The following are the weights in kilograms of a group of 55 students.

42	74	40	60	82	115	41	61	75	83	63
53	110	76	84	50	67	78	77	63	65	95
68	69	104	80	79	79	54	73	59	81	100
66	49	77	90	84	76	42	64	69	70	80
72	50	79	52	103	96	51	86	78	94	71

Prepare a frequency table taking the magnitude of each class interval as 10 kg. and the first class-interval as equal to 40 and less than 50.

Ans. Frequencies of classes 40—50, 50—60,...,110—120 are 5, 7, 11, 15, 8, 4, 3, 2 respectively.

(*b*) Prepare a statistical table from the following data taking the class width as 7 by inclusive method.

24	26	28	32	37	5	1	7	9	11	15
13	14	18	29	31	32	6	4	2	9	18
27	36	3	9	15	21	27	33	4	8	12
16	20	5	10	3	8	1	6	4	9	2
7	12	18	27	23	21	29	22	15	17	28

Ans. Frequencies of classes 1—7, 8—14, 15—21,..., 36—42 are respectively 15, 12, 11, 9, 6, 2.

12. Using Sturges' Rule $k = 1 + 3{\cdot}322 \log N$, where k is the number of class intervals, N is the total number of observations, classify in equal intervals, the following data of hours worked by 50 piece rate workers for a period of a month in a certain factory :

110, 175, 161, 157, 155, 108, 164, 128, 114, 178, 165, 133, 195, 151, 71, 94, 97,
42, 30, 62, 138, 156, 167, 124, 164, 146, 116, 149, 104, 141, 103, 150, 162, 149,
79, 113, 69, 121, 93, 143, 140, 144, 187, 184, 197, 87, 40, 122, 203, 148.

Ans. Using Sturges' rule we get k (No. of classes) = 7, Magnitude of class = (Range/k) = (174/7) ≃ 25.

Classes are 30—55, 55—80, 80—105,...,180—205. The corresponding frequencies are 3, 4, 6, 9, 12, 11, 5.

13. Two dice are thrown at random. Obtain the frequency distribution of the sum of the numbers which appear on them.

Hint and Ans. Total possible pairs of numbers on the two dice are as given below :

(1, 1), (1, 2),..., (1, 6) ; (2, 1), (2, 2),..., (2, 6) ; ... ..., (6, 1), (6, 2_,..., (6, 6)

If X denotes the sum of the numbers on the two dice then X is a discrete variable which can take the values 2, 3,..., 12.

Sum (X) :	2	3	4	5	6	7	8	9	10	11	12
Frequency :	1	2	3	4	5	6	5	4	3	2	1

14. If the class mid-points in a frequency distribution of a group of persons are : 125, 132, 139, 146, 153, 160, 167, 174, 181 pounds, find (*i*) size of the class intervals, (*ii*) the class boundaries, and (*iii*) the class limits, assuming that the weights are measured to the nearest pound. [*Delhi Univ. B.Com. (Hons.), 2007*]

Ans. (*i*) 7 (*ii*) 121·5—128·5, 128·5—135·5,...,177·5—184·5
(*iii*) 122—128, 129—135,..., 178—184.

15. With the help of suitable examples, distinguish between :

(*i*) Continuous and Discrete variable. (*ii*) Exclusive and Inclusive class intervals.
(*iii*) 'More than' and 'Less than' frequency tables. (*iv*) Simple and Bivariate frequency tables.

16. What do you mean by cumulative frequency (*c.f.*) distribution ; 'More than' and 'Less than' type *c.f.* distribution. Illustrate by an example.

17. The weekly observations on cost of living index in a certain city for the year 2000-01 are given below :

Cost of living index :	140—150	150—160	160—170	170—180	180—190	190—200
No. of workers :	5	10	20	9	6	2

Prepare 'less than' and 'more than' cumulative frequency distributions.

18. (*a*) Convert the following into an ordinary frequency distribution :

5 students get less than 3 marks ; 12 students get less than 6 marks;
25 students get less than 9 marks ; 33 students get less than 12 marks. [*Delhi Univ. B.Com. (Pass), 2001*]

Ans.	0—3	3—6	6—9	9—12
	5	7	13	8

(*b*) Following is a cumulative frequency table showing the number of packages and the number of times a given number of packages was received by a post office in 60 days :

No. of packages below :	10	20	30	40	50	60
No. of times received in 60 days :	17	22	29	37	50	60

Obtain the frequency table from it. Also prepare 'more than' cumulative frequency table.

19. (*a*) What is the difference between continuous and discrete variables ?

(*b*) Are the following variables discrete or continuous ? Give your answer with reason.

(*i*) Age on last birthday. ; (*ii*) Temperature of the patient.
(*iii*) Length of a room. ; (*iv*) Number of shareholders in a company.

Ans. (*ii*) and (*iii*) continuous ; (*i*) and (*iv*) discrete.

(*c*) State with reasons which of the following represent discrete data and which represent continuous data :

(*i*) Number of table fans sold each day at a Departmental Store.
(*ii*) Temperature recorded every half an hour of a patient in a hospital.
(*iii*) Life of television tubes produced by Electronics Ltd.
(*iv*) Yearly income of school teachers.
(*v*) Lengths of 1,000 bolts produced in a factory.

20. Complete the table showing the frequencies with which words of different number of letters occur in the extract reproduced below (omitting punctuation marks) treating as the variable the number of letters in each word :

"Her eyes were blue ; blue as autumn distance—blue as the blue we see between the retreating mouldings of hills and woody slopes on a sunny September morning : a misty and shady blue, that had no beginning or surface, and was looked into rather than at."

Ans. X:	1	2	3	4	5	6	7	8	9	10
f:	2	8	9	10	5	4	3	1	3	1

21. Prepare a frequency distribution of the words in the following extract according to their length (number of letters) omitting punctuation marks. Also give (*i*) the number of words with 7 letters or less ; (*ii*) the proportion of words with 5 letters or more ; (*iii*) the percentage of words with not less than 4 and not more than 7 letters.

"Success in the examination confers no absolute right to appointment, unless Government is satisfied, after such enquiry as may be considered necessary, that the candidate is suitable in all respects for appointment to the public service."

Ans. X:	2	3	4	5	6	7	8	9	10	11
f:	9	6	2	2	2	4	3	3	2	3

(*i*) 25, (*ii*) (19/36) = 0·5278, (*iii*) (10/36) × 100 = 27·28.

22. A company wants to pay daily bonus to its employees. The bonus is to be paid us under :

Daily Salary (Rs.) :	100—200	200—300	300—400	400—500	500—600	600—700
Daily Bonus (Rs.) :	10	20	30	40	50	60

Actual daily salaries of the employees, in Rupees, are as under :

175, 225, 375, 478, 525, 650, 570, 451, 382, 280
375, 465, 530, 480, 320, 515, 225, 345, 471, 450

Find out the total daily bonus paid to the employees.

Ans. Total daily bonus paid to the employees = Rs. 720.

23. From the following data construct a bivariate frequency distribution :

Age of husbands (in years) (x)	*Age of wives (in years)* (y)	*Age of husbands (in years)* (x)	*Age of wives (in years)* (y)	*Age of husbands (in years)* (x)	*Age of wives (in years)* (y)
28	22	28	21	27	21
26	21	27	21	26	19
27	21	27	20	25	19
25	20	26	20	26	20
28	22	27	19	27	21

Ans. x:	25	26	27	28	y:	19	20	21	22
f_x:	2	4	6	3	f_y:	3	4	6	2

24. The data given below relates to the heights and weights of 20 persons. You are required to form a two-way frequency table with class 62" to 64", 64" to 66" and so on, and 115 to 125 lbs, 125 to 135 lbs. and so on.

S. No.	*Weight*	*Height*	*S. No.*	*Weight*	*Height*	*S. No.*	*Weight*	*Height*
1.	170	70	8.	128	70	15.	140	67
2.	135	65	9.	143	71	16.	132	69
3.	136	65	10.	129	62	17.	120	66
4.	137	64	11.	163	70	18.	148	68
5.	148	69	12.	139	67	19.	129	67
6.	124	63	13.	122	63	20.	152	67
7.	117	65	14.	134	68			

Ans. [Frequencies: (W) = 4, 5, 6, 3, 1, 1 ; (H) = 3, 4, 5, 4, 4.]

25. The following figures are income (x) and percentage expenditure on food (y) in 25 families. Construct a bivariate frequency table classifying x into intervals 200—300, 300—400, ..., and y into 10—15, 15—20, ...

Write down the marginal distributions of x and y and the conditional distribution of x when y lies between 15 and 20.

x	*y*	*x*	*y*	*x*	*y*	*x*	*y*	*x*	*y*
550	12	225	25	680	13	202	29	689	11
623	14	310	26	330	25	255	27	523	12
310	18	640	20	425	16	492	18	317	18
420	16	512	18	555	15	587	21	384	17
600	15	690	12	325	23	643	19	400	19

26. What is meant by a bi-variate series? Taking 15 imaginary figures, construct a series of this type on discrete pattern. [*Delhi Univ. B.Com. (Pass), 1998*]

27. 30 pairs of values of two variables *X* and *Y* are given below. Form a two-way table :

X	14	20	33	25	41	18	24	29	38	45	23	32	37	19	28
Y	148	242	296	312	518	196	214	340	492	568	282	400	288	292	431
X	34	38	29	44	40	22	39	43	44	12	27	39	38	17	26
Y	440	500	512	415	514	282	481	516	598	122	200	451	387	245	413

Take class intervals of X as 10 to 20, 20 to 30 etc., and that of Y as 100 to 200, 200 to 300, etc.

[*Osmania Univ. B.Com., 1996*]

28. Following are the marks obtained by 24 students in English (*X*) and Economics (*Y*) in a test.

(15, 13), (0, 1), (1, 2), (3, 7), (16, 8), (2, 9), (18, 12), (5, 9), (4, 17), (17, 16), (6, 6), (19, 18)
(14, 11), (9, 3), (8, 5), (13, 4), (10, 10), (13, 11), (11, 14), (11, 7), (12, 18), (18, 15), (9, 15), (17, 3).

Taking class-intervals as 0—4, 5—9, etc., for X and Y both, construct—

(*i*) Bivariate frequency table. (*ii*) Marginal frequency tables of *X* and *Y*.

29. Fill in the blanks :

(*i*) Variables are of two kinds … … and … …

(*ii*) … … is the process of arranging data into groups according to their common characteristics.

(*iii*) In chronological classification, the data are classified on the basis of … …

(*iv*) … … classification means the classification of data according to location.

(*v*) Class-mark (mid-point) is the value lying half-way between … …

(*vi*) According to Sturges' rule, the number of classes (*k*) is given by : *k* = … …

(*vii*) The magnitude of the class (*i*) is given by : *i* = … …

(*viii*) … … of data is a function very similar to that of sorting letters in a post office.

(*ix*) Different bases of classification of data are … …

(*x*) The data can be classified into … … and … … type classes.

(*xi*) While forming a grouped frequency distribution, the number of classes should usually be between … …

(*xii*) In exclusive type classes, the upper limit of the class is … …

(*xiii*) In the continuous classes 0—5, 5—10, 10—15, 15—20 and so on, the class 15—20 means that the variable *X* takes the values … …

(*xiv*) Two examples of discrete variable are … … and … … and continuous variable are … … and … …

(*xv*) The classes in which the lower limit or the upper limit are not specified, are known as … …

(*xvi*) The difference between the upper and the lower limits of a class gives … … of the class.

(*xvii*) The number of observations in a particular class is called the … … of the class.

(*xviii*) If the data values are classified into the classes 0—9, 10—19, 20—29, and so on and the frequency of the class 20—29 is 12, it means that … … .

(*xix*) If the mid-points of the classes are 16, 24, 32, 40, and so on, then the magnitude of the class intervals is … … .

(*xx*) In (*xix*), the class boundaries are … … .

Ans. (*i*) discrete, continuous, (*ii*) classification. (*iii*) time. (*iv*) geographical. (*v*) the upper and the lower limits of the class. (*vi*) $k = 1 + 3{\cdot}322 \log_{10} N$; *N* is total frequency. (*vii*) *i* = (upper limit – lower limit) of the class. (*viii*) classification. (*ix*) geographical, chronological, qualitative and quantitative. (*x*) inclusive, exclusive. (*xi*) 5 and 15. (*xii*) is not included in the class. (*xiii*) 15 and more but less than 20 *i.e.*, $15 \le X < 20$. (*xiv*) marks in a test, number of accidents; height in inches, weight in kgs. (*xv*) open end classes. (*xvi*) the width or the magnitude. (*xvii*) frequency. (*xviii*) there are 12 observations taking values between 20 and 29, both inclusive *i.e.*, $20 \le X \le 29$. (*xix*) 8. (*xx*) 12—20, 20—28, 28—36, 36—44 and so on.

3·7. TABULATION – MEANING AND IMPORTANCE

By tabulation we mean the systematic presentation of the information contained in the data, in rows and columns in accordance with some salient features or characteristics. Rows are horizontal arrangements and columns are vertical arrangements. In the words of A.M. Tuttle :

"A statistical table is the logical listing of related quantitative data in vertical columns and horizontal rows of numbers with sufficient explanatory and qualifying words, phrases and statements in the form of titles, headings and notes to make clear the full meaning of data and their origin."

Professor Bowley in his manual of Statistics refers to tabulation as *"the intermediate process between the accumulation of data in whatever form they are obtained, and the final reasoned account of the result shown by the statistics."*

Tabulation is one of the most important and ingenious device of presenting the data in a condensed and readily comprehensible form and attempts to furnish the maximum information contained in the data in the minimum possible space, without sacrificing the quality and usefulness of the data. It is an intermediate process between the collection of the data on one hand and statistical analysis on the other hand. *In fact, tabulation is the final stage in collection and compilation of the data and forms the gateway for further statistical analysis and interpretations.* Tabulation makes the data comprehensible and facilitates comparisons (by classifying data into suitable groups), and the work of further statistical analysis, averaging, correlation, etc. It makes the data suitable for further Diagrammatic and Graphic representation.

If the information contained in the data is expressed as a running text using language paragraphs, it is quite time-consuming to comprehend it because in order to understand every minute details of the text, one has to go through all the paragraphs ; which usually contain very large amount of repetitions. Tabulation overcomes the drawback of the repetition of explanatory phrases and headings and presents the data in a neat, readily comprehensible and true perspective, thus highlighting the significant and relevant details and information. Tabulated data have attractive get up and leave a lasting impression on the mind as compared to the data in the textual form. Tabulation also facilitates the detection of the errors and the omissions in the data. Tabulation enables us to draw the attention of the observer to specific items by means of comparisons, emphasis and arrangement of the layout.

No hard and fast rules can be laid down for tabulating the statistical data. To prepare a first class table one must have a clear idea about the facts to be presented and stressed, the points on which emphasis is to be laid and familiarity with technique of preparation of the table. The arrangement of data tabulation requires considerable thought to ensure showing the relationship between the data of one or more series, as well as the significance of all the figures given in the classification adopted. The facts, comparisons and contrasts, and emphasis vary from one table to another table. Accordingly a good table (the requirements of which are given below) can only be obtained through the skill, expertise, experience and common sense of the tabulator, keeping in view the nature, scope and objectives of the enquiry. This bears testimony to the following words of A.L. Bowley :

"In the tabulation of the data common sense is the chief requisite and experience is the chief teacher."

3·7·1. Parts of a Table. The various parts of a table vary from problem to problem depending upon the nature of the data and the purpose of the investigation. However, the following are a must in a good statistical table :

(*i*) Table number
(*ii*) Title
(*iii*) Head notes or Prefatory notes
(*iv*) Captions and Stubs
(*v*) Body of the table
(*vi*) Foot-note
(*vii*) Source note

1. Table Number. If a book or an article or a report contains more than one table then all the tables should be numbered in a logical sequence for proper identification and easy and ready reference for future. The table number may be placed at the top of the table either in the centre above the title or in the side of the title.

2. Title. Every table must be given a suitable title, which usually appears at the top of the table (below the table number or next to the table number). A title is meant to describe in brief and concise form the contents of the table and should be self-explanatory. It should precisely describe the nature of the data (criteria of classification, if any) ; the place (*i.e.*, the geographical or political region or area to which the data relate) ; the time (*i.e.*, period to which the data relate) and the source of the data. The title should be brief but not an incomplete one and not at the cost of clarity. It should be un-ambiguous and properly worded and punctuated. Sometimes it becomes desirable to use long titles for the sake of clarity. In such a situation a 'catch title' may be given above the 'main title'. Of all the parts of the table, title should be most prominently lettered.

3. Head Notes (or Prefatory Notes). If need be, head note is given just below the title in a prominent type usually centred and enclosed in brackets for further description of the contents of the table. It is a sort of a supplement to the title and provides an explanation concerning the entire table or its major parts-like captions or stubs. For instance, the units of measurements are usually expressed as head such as 'in hectares', 'in millions', 'in quintals', 'in Rupees', etc.

4. Captions and Stubs. *Captions are the headings or designations for vertical columns and stubs are the headings or designations for the horizontal rows*. They should be brief, concise and self-explanatory. Captions are usually written in the middle of the columns in small letters to economise space. If the same unit is used for all the entries in the table then it may be given as a head note along with the title. However, if the items in different columns or rows are measured or expressed in different units, then the corresponding units should also be indicated in the columns or rows. Relative units like ratios, percentages, etc., if any, should also be specified in the respective rows or columns. For instance, the columns may constitute the population (in millions) of different countries and rows may indicate the different periods (years).

Quite often two or more columns or rows corresponding to similar classifications (or with same headings) may be grouped together under a common heading to avoid repetitions and may be given what are called *sub-captions* or *sub-stubs*. It is also desirable to number each column and row for reference and to facilitate comparisons.

5. Body of the Table. The arrangement of the data according to the descriptions given in the captions (columns) and stubs (rows) forms the body of the table. It contains the numerical information which is to be presented to the readers and forms the most important part of the table. Undesirable and irrelevant (to the enquiry) information should be avoided. To increase the usefulness of the table, totals must be given for each separate class/category immediately below the columns or against the rows. In addition, the grand totals for all the classes for rows/columns should also be given.

6. Foot Note. When some characteristic or feature or item of the table has not been adequately explained and needs further elaboration or when some additional or extra information is required for its complete description, foot-notes are used for this purpose. As the name suggests, footnotes, if any, are placed at the bottom of the table directly below the body of the table. Foot-notes may be attached to the title, captions, stubs or any part of the body of the table. Foot-notes are identified by the symbols *, **, ***, €€†, @, etc.

7. Source Note. If the source of the table is not explicitly contained in the title, it must be given at the bottom of the table, below the footnote, if any. The source note is required if the secondary data are used. If the data are taken from a research journal or periodical, then the source note should give the name of the journal or periodical along with the date of publication, its volume number, table number (if any), page number, etc., so that anybody who uses this data may satisfy himself, (if need be), about the accuracy of the figures given in the table by referring to the original source. Source note will also enable the user to decide about the reliability of the data since to the learned users of Statistics the reputations of the sources may vary greatly from one agency to another.

The format of a blank table is given in Table 3·27.

TABLE 3·27 FORMAT OF A BLANK TABLE

TITLE

[Head Note or Prefatory Note (if any)]

<table>
<tr><td rowspan="3">Stub Heading ↓</td><td colspan="5">Caption</td><td rowspan="3">Total</td></tr>
<tr><td colspan="2">Sub-Heads</td><td colspan="3">Sub-Heads</td></tr>
<tr><td>Column Head</td><td>Column Head</td><td>Column Head</td><td>Column Head</td><td>Column Head</td></tr>
<tr><td></td><td colspan="5">Body</td><td></td></tr>
<tr><td>Total</td><td></td><td></td><td></td><td></td><td></td><td></td></tr>
</table>

Foot Note :
Source Note :

Remarks 1. A table should be so designed that it is neither too long and narrow nor too short and broad. It should be of reasonable size adjusted to the space at our disposal and should have an attractive get up. If the data are very large they should not be crowded in a single table which would become unwieldy and difficult to comprehend. In such a situation it is desirable to split the large table into a number of tables of reasonable size and shape. Each table should be complete in itself.

2. If the figures corresponding to certain items in the table are not available due to certain reasons, then the gaps arising therefrom should be filled by writing N.A. which is used as an abbreviation for 'not available'.

3·7·2. Requisites of a Good Table. As pointed out earlier, no hard and fast rules can be laid down for preparing a statistical table. Preparation of a good statistical table is a specialised job and requires great skill, experience and common sense on the part of the tabulator. However, commensurate with the objectives and scope of the enquiry, the following points may be borne in mind while preparing a good statistical table.

(*i*) The table should be simple and compact so that it is readily comprehensible. It should be free from all sorts of overlappings and ambiguities.

(*ii*) The classification in the table should be so arranged as to focus attention on the main comparisons and exhibit the relationship between various related items and facilitate statistical analysis. It should highlight the relevant and desired information needed for further statistical investigation and emphasise the important points in a compact and concise way. Different modes of lettering (in italics, bold or antique type, capital letters or small letters of the alphabet, etc.), may be used to distinguish points of special emphasis.

(*iii*) A table should be complete and self-explanatory. It should have a suitable title, head note (if necessary), captions and stubs, and footnote (if necessary). If the data are secondary, the source note should also be given. [For details see § 3·7·1]. The use of dash (—) and ditto marks („) should be avoided. Only accepted common abbreviations should be used.

(*iv*) A table should have an attractive get up which is appealing to the eye and the mind so that the reader may grasp it without any strain. This necessitates special attention to the size of the table and proper spacings of rows and columns.

(*v*) Since a statistical table forms the basis for statistical analysis and computation of various statistical measures like averages, dispersion, skewness, etc., it should be accurate and free from all sorts of errors. This necessitates checking and re-checking of the entries in the table at each stage because even a minor error of tabulation may lead to very fallacious conclusions and misleading interpretations of the results.

(*vi*) The classification of the data in the table should be in alphabetical, geographical or chronological order or in order of magnitude or importance to facilitate comparisons.

(*vii*) A summary table [See § 3·7·3] should have adequate interpretative figures like totals, ratios, percentages, averages, etc.

3·7·3. Types of Tabulation. Statistical tables are constructed in many ways. Their choice basically depends upon :

(*i*) Objectives and scope of the enquiry.
(*ii*) Nature of the enquiry (primary or secondary).
(*iii*) Extent of coverage given in the enquiry.

The following diagrammatic scheme elegantly displays the various forms of tables commonly used in practice.

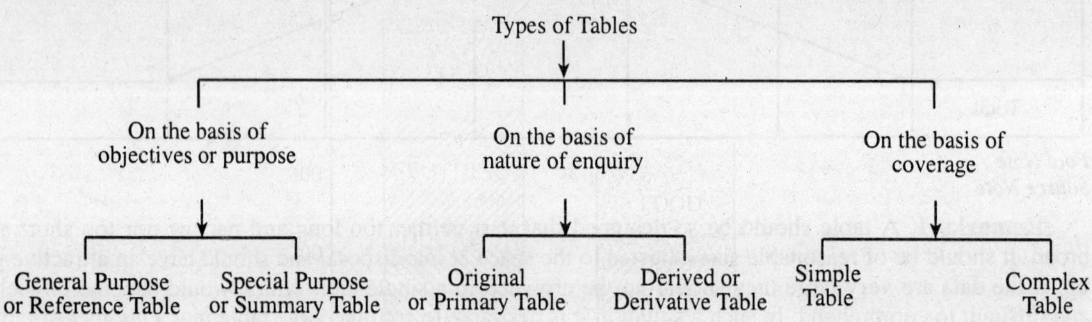

General Purpose (or Reference) and Special Purpose (or Summary) Tables. General purpose tables, which are also known as *reference tables* or sometimes *informative tables* provide a convenient way of compiling and presenting a systematically arranged data, usually in chronological order, in a form which is suitable for ready reference and record without any intentions of comparative studies, relationship or significance of figures. Most of the tables prepared by government agencies *e.g.,* the detailed tables in the census reports, are of this kind. These tables are of repository nature and mainly designed for use by research workers, statisticians and are generally given at the end of the report in the form of an appendix. Examples of such tables are : age and sexwise distribution of the population of a particular region, community or country ; payrolls of a business house ; sales orders for different products manufactured by a concern ; the distribution of students in a university according to age, sex and the faculty they join ; and so on.

As distinct from the general purpose or reference tables, the *special purpose* or *summary* tables (also sometimes called *interpretative* tables) are of analytical nature and are prepared with the idea of making comparative studies and studying the relationship and the significance of the figures provided by the data. These are generally constructed to emphasise some facts or relationships pertaining to a particular or specific purpose. In such tables interpretative figures like ratios, percentages, etc., are used in order to facilitate comparisons. Summary tables are sometimes called *derived* or *derivative* tables (discussed below) as they are generally derived from the general purpose tables.

Original and Derived Tables. On the basis of the nature or originality of the data, the tables may be classified into two classes :

(*i*) Primary tables (*ii*) Derived or Derivative tables.

In a primary table, the statistical facts are expressed in the original form. It, therefore, contains absolute and actual figures and not rounded numbers or percentages. On the other hand, derived or derivative table is one which contains figures and results derived from the original or primary data. It expresses the information in terms of ratios, percentages, aggregates or statistical measures like average, dispersion, skewness, etc. For instance, the time series data is expressed in a primary table but a table expressing the trend values and seasonal and cyclic variations is a derived table. In practice, mixtures of primary and derived tables are generally used, an illustration being given below :

TABLE 3·28. **LOAD CARRIED BY RAILWAYS AND ROAD TRANSPORT FOR DIFFERENT YEARS**
(In Billion Tonne Km)

Year	*Railways*	*Road Transport*	*Percentage Share*	
			Railways	*Road Transport*
1960-61	88	17	83·8	16·2
1965-66	117	34	77·5	22·5
1968-69	125	40	75·8	24·2
1973-74	122	65	65·2	34·8
1974-75	134	80	62·6	37·4
1975-76	148	81	64·6	35·4

Simple and Complex Tables. In a simple table the data are classified *w.r.t.* a single characteristic and accordingly it is also termed as *one-way* table. On the other hand, if the data are grouped into different classes *w.r.t.* two or more characteristics or criteria simultaneously, then we get a *complex* or *manifold* table. In particular, if the data are classified *w.r.t.* two (three) characteristics simultaneously we get a two-way (three-way) table.

Simple Table. As already stated, a simple table furnishes information about only one single characteristic of the data. For instance, Table 3·1 (*on page 3·4*) relating to agricultural output of different countries (in kg per hectare) ; Table 3·2 (*on page 3·4*) giving the density of population (per square kilometre) in different cities of India ; Table 3·3 (*on page 3·4*) giving the population of India (in crores) for different years, are all simple tables. As another illustration, the Table 3·29 giving the imports from principal countries (by sea, air and land) for the year 1975-76 is a simple table.

TABLE 3·29
IMPORTS FROM PRINCIPAL COUNTRIES BY SEA, AIR AND LAND FOR 1975-76
(Rupees in lakhs)

Country	*Imports*
Australia	10,167
Canada	23,201
France	19,653
(West) Germany	36,996
Japan	36,118
UK	28,400
USA	1,28,522
USSR	30,978

Two-way Table. However, if the caption or stub is classified into two sub-groups, which means that the data are classified *w.r.t.* two characteristics, we get a two-way table. Thus a two-way table furnishes information about two inter-related characteristics of a particular phenomenon. For example, the distribution of the number of students in a college *w.r.t.* age (1st characteristic) and sex (2nd characteristic) gives a two-way table. As another illustration, Table 3·30 which gives the load/distance by Railways and Road Transport for different years, is a two-way table.

TABLE 3·30. **LOAD CARRIED BY RAILWAYS AND ROAD TRANSPORT FOR DIFFERENT YEARS**
(In Billion Tonne Km)

Years	*Railways*	*Road Transport*
1960-61	88	17
1965-66	117	34
1968-69	125	40
1973-74	122	65
1974-75	134	80
1975-76	148	81

Three-way Tables. If the data are classified simultaneously *w.r.t.* three characteristics, we get a three-way table. Thus a three-way table gives us information regarding three inter-related characteristics of a particular phenomenon. For example, the classification of a given population *w.r.t.* age, sex and literacy, or the classification of the students in a university *w.r.t.* sex, faculty (Arts, Sciences, Commerce) and the class (Ist year, 2nd year, 3rd year of the under-graduate courses) will give rise to three-way tables. The tables given in Examples 3·12 to 3·19 are three-way tables. As another illustration, the following Table 3·31 representing the distribution of population of a city according to different age-groups (say, five age groups from 0 to 100 years), sex and literacy is a three-way table.

TABLE 3·31. **DISTRIBUTION OF POPULATION (IN '000) OF A CITY *w.r.t* AGE, SEX AND LITERACY**

Age Group	*Literates*			*Illiterates*			*Total*		
	Males	*Females*	*Sub-totals*	*Males*	*Females*	*Sub-totals*	*Males*	*Females*	*Row-totals*
0—20									
20—40									
40—60									
60—80									
80—100									
Column Totals									

Higher Order or Manifold Tables. These tables give the information on a large number of inter-related problems or characteristics of a given phenomenon. For example, the distribution of students in a college according to faculty, class, sex and year (Example 3·20) or the distribution of employees in a business concern according to sex, age-groups, years and grades of salary (Example 3·21) gives rise to manifold tables. Manifold or higher order tables are commonly used in presenting population census data.

Remark. It may be pointed out that as the order of the table goes on increasing, the table becomes more and more difficult to comprehend and might even become confusing. In practice, in a single table only upto three or sometimes four characteristics are represented simultaneously. If the study is confined to more than four characteristics at a time then it is desirable to represent the data in more than one table for depicting the relationship between different characteristics.

Example 3·12. *Present the following information in a suitable tabular form, supplying the figures not directly given :*

In 1995 out of total 2000 workers in a factory, 1550 were members of a trade union. The number of women workers employed was 250, out of which 200 did not belong to any trade union.

In 2000, the number of union workers was 1725 of which 1600 were men. The number of non-union workers was 380, among which 155 were women.

Solution.

TABLE 3·32. **COMPARATIVE STUDY OF THE MEMBERSHIP OF TRADE UNION IN A FACTORY IN 1995 AND 2000.**

Year →	*1995*			*2000*		
Trade Union ↓	*Males*	*Females*	*Total*	*Males*	*Females*	*Total*
Members	1550 – 50 = 1,500	250 – 200 = 50	**1,550**	**1,600**	1,725 – 1600 = 125	**1,725**
Non-members	1,750 – 1500 = 250	**200**	2000 – 1550 = 450	380 – 155 = 225	**155**	**380**
Total	2,000 – 250 = 1,750	**250**	**2,000**	1,600 + 225 = 1,825	125 + 155 = 280	1,725 + 380 = 2,105

Note. The bold figures are the given figures. The other values are obtained on appropriate additions or subtractions, since the totals are fixed.

Example 3·13. *In a sample study about coffee habit in two towns, the following information was received :*

Town A : *Females were 40% ; Total coffee drinkers were 45% and Males non-coffee drinkers were 20%.*

Town B : *Males were 55% ; Males non-coffee drinkers were 30% and Females coffee drinkers were 15%.*

Present the above data in a tabular form. [C.A. (Foundation), May 1997]

Solution.

TABLE 3·33

	Town A		
	Males	*Females*	*Total*
Coffee drinkers	60 – 20 = 40	45 – 40 = 5	**45**
Non-coffee drinkers	**20**	40 – 5 = 35	100 – 45 = 55
Total	100 – 40 = 60	**40**	**100**

Note. The figures in bold are the given figures.

TABLE 3·33(*a*)

	Town B		
	Males	*Females*	*Total*
Coffee drinkers	55 – 30 = 25	**15**	25 + 15 = 40
Non-coffee drinkers	**30**	60 – 30 = 30	100 – 40 = 60
Total	**55**	100 – 55 = 45	**100**

Note. The figures in the bold are the given figures.

The information in Tables 3·33 and 3·33(*a*) can be expressed in a single table as given in Table 3·33(*b*).

TABLE 3·33(*b*). **SEX-WISE PERCENTAGE OF COFFEE DRINKERS IN TOWNS A AND B**

	Town A			*Town B*		
	Males	*Females*	*Total*	*Males*	*Females*	*Total*
Coffee drinkers	40	5	45	25	15	40
Non-coffee drinkers	20	35	55	30	30	60
Total	60	40	100	55	45	100

Example 3·14. *Tabulate the following :*

Out of a total number of 10,000 candidates who applied for jobs in a government department, 6,854 were males, 3,146 were graduates and others, non-graduates. The number of candidates with some experience was 2,623 of whom 1,860 were males. The number of male graduates was 2,012. The number of graduates with experience was 1,093 that includes 323 females.

Solution. We are given that the total number of :

Applicants = 10,000 ; Males = 6,854 ; Graduates = 3,146 ; Experienced = 2,623.

Total number of Females = 10,000 – 6,854 = 3,146

Total number of Non-graduates = 10,000 – 3,146 = 6,854

Total number of In-experienced persons = 10,000 - 2,623 = 7,377

The above and the remaining given information can be summarised in the following Table 3·34.

TABLE 3·34 **DISTRIBUTION OF CANDIDATES FOR GOVERNMENT JOBS SEX-WISE EDUCATION-WISE AND EXPERIENCE-WISE**

Sex ↓	*Graduates*			*Non-graduates*			*Total*		
	Experi-enced	*In-experi-enced*	*Total*	*Experi-enced*	*In-experi-enced*	*Total*	*Experi-enced*	*In-experi-enced*	*Total*
Male	770	1242	**2012**	1090	3752	4842	**1860**	4994	**6854**
Female	**323**	811	1134	440	1572	2012	763	2383	3146
Total	**1093**	2053	**3146**	1530	5324	6854	**2623**	7377	**10000**

The figures in 'bold' are the given figures. The remaining values have been obtained by minor calculations (additions or subtractions), as the totals are fixed.

Example 3·15. *A survey of 370 students from Commerce Faculty and 130 students from Science Faculty revealed that 180 students were studying for only C.A. Examinations, 140 for only Costing Examinations and 80 for both C.A. and Costing Examinations.*

The rest had offered part-time Management Courses. Of those studying for Costing only, 13 were girls and 90 boys belonged to Commerce Faculty. Out of 80 studying for both C.A. and Costing, 72 were from Commerce Faculty amongst which 70 were boys. Amongst those who offered part-time Management Courses, 50 boys were from Science Faculty and 30 boys and 10 girls from Commerce Faculty. In all there were 110 boys in Science Faculty.

Present the above information in a tabular form. Find the number of students from Science Faculty studying for part-time Management Courses.

Solution. We are given that :

Total number of Commerce students = 370

Total number of Science students = 130

∴ Total number of all the students = 370 + 130 = 500

We are also given that out of these 500 students, the number of students studying :

For C.A. only = 180 ; For Costing only = 140 ; For both Costing and C.A. = 80

∴ Number of students studying for part-time Management courses = 500 – (180 + 140 + 80) = 100.

The above information and the remaining given information is summarised in the Table 3·35. The figures in 'bold' are the given figures.

TABLE 3·35. **FACULTY, SEX AND COURSE-WISE DISTRIBUTION OF STUDENTS**

Faculty	*Commerce*			*Science*			*Total*		
Courses	*Boys*	*Girls*	*Total*	*Boys*	*Girls*	*Total*	*Boys*	*Girls*	*Total*
Part-time Management	**30**	**10**	30 + 10 = 40	**50**	10	100 – 40 = 60	30 + 50 = 80	10 + 10 = 20	100
C.A. only									**180**
Costing only	**90**							**13**	**140**
C.A. and Costing	**70**	72 – 70 = 2	**72**			80 – 72 = 8			**80**
Total			**370**	**110**	130 – 110 = 20	**130**			500

Number of students from Science Faculty studying part-time Management courses is 60.

Example 3·16. *In 1990, out of a total of 2,000 students in a college 1,400 were for Graduation and the rest for Post-Graduation (P.G.). Out of 1,400 Graduate students 100 were girls. However, in all there were 600 girls in the college. In 1995, number of graduate students increased to 1,700, out of which 250 were girls, but the number of P.G. students fell to 500 of which only 50 were boys. In 2000, out of 800 girls, 650 were for Graduation, whereas the total number of graduates was 2,200. The number of boys and girls in P.G. classes was equal.*

Represent the above information in tabular form. Also calculate the percentage increase in the number of graduate students in 2000 as compared to 1990. [*C.A. (Foundation), Nov. 2001*]

Solution. The distribution of the number of students with respect to level of education and sex is obtained as follows :

Year 1990	*Graduation*	*Post-Graduation*	*Total*
Girls	**100**	600 – 100 = 500	**600**
Boys	1400 – 100 = 1300	600 – 500 = 100	2000 – 600 = 1400
Total	**1400**	2000 – 1400 = 600	**2000**

Note. The figures in bold are the given figures.

Year 1995	*Graduation*	*Post-Graduation*	*Total*
Girls	**250**	500 – 50 = 450	250 + 450 = 700
Boys	1,700 – 250 = 1450	**50**	1450 + 50 = 1500
Total	**1700**	**500**	1700 + 500 = 2200

	Year 2000		
	Graduation	*Post-Graduation*	*Total*
Girls	**650**	800 – 650 = 150	**800**
Boys	2200 – 650 = 1550	**150**	1550 + 150 = 1700
Total	**2200**	150 + 150 = 300	**2500**

The information in the above three tables can be expressed in single table as given in Table 3·36.

TABLE 3·36. **DISTRIBUTION OF STUDENTS ACCORDING TO DEGREE AND SEX FOR YEARS 1990 TO 2000.**

Degrees →	*Graduation*			*Post-graduation*			*Total*
Year ↓	*Boys*	*Girls*	*Total* (*a*)	*Boys*	*Girls*	*Total* (*b*)	(*a*) + (*b*)
1990	1300	100	1400	100	500	600	2000
1995	1450	250	1700	50	450	500	2200
2000	1550	650	2200	150	150	300	2500
Total	4300	1000	5300	300	1100	1400	6700

Percentage increase in the number of graduate students in 2000 as compared to 1990 is :

$$\frac{(2200-1400)}{1400} \times 100 = 57{\cdot}14\%.$$

Example 3·17. *Out of a total number of 1,807 women who were interviewed for employment in a textile factory of Mumbai; 512 were from textile areas and the rest from the non-textile areas. Amongst the married women who belonged to textile areas, 247 were experienced and 73 inexperienced, while for non-textile areas, the corresponding figures were 49 and 520. The total number of inexperienced women was 1,341 of whom 111 resided in textile areas. Of the total number of women, 918 were unmarried and of these the number of experienced women in the textile and non-textile areas was 154 and 16 respectively. Tabulate.*

Solution. Total number of women interviewed = 1,807

No. of women from textile areas = 512

∴ Number of women from non-textile areas = 1,807 – 512 = 1,295

Total number of married women in textile areas = 247 + 73 = 320

Total number of married women in non-textile areas = 49 + 520 = 569

Total number of inexperienced women = 1,341

∴ Total number of experienced women = 1,807 – 1,341 = 466

Total number of unmarried women = 918

∴ Total number of married women = 1,807 – 918 = 889

Total number of unmarried experienced women in textile areas = 154

and Total number of unmarried experienced women in non-textile areas = 16

After filling this information in the table, the remaining entries in the table of the experience, marital status and area-wise distribution of the number of women can now be completed by subtraction/addition, wherever necessary and is given in Table 3·37.

TABLE 3·37. **TABLE SHOWING THE NUMBER OF WOMEN INTERVIEWED FOR EMPLOYMENT IN A TEXTILE FACTORY ACCORDING TO THEIR MARITAL STATUS, EXPERIENCE AND AREA THEY BELONG**

	Textile Areas			*Non-textile Areas*			*Total*		
	Experienced	*Inexperienced*	*Total*	*Experienced*	*Inexperienced*	*Total*	*Experienced*	*Inexperienced*	*Total*
Married	247	73	320	49	520	569	296	593	889
Unmarried	154	38	192	16	710	726	170	748	918
Total	401	111	512	65	1,230	1,295	466	1,341	1,807

Example 3·18. *Draw up a blank table to show the number of candidates sex-wise, appearing in the Pre-university, First Year, Second Year and Third Year examinations of a university in the faculties of Art, Science and Commerce in the year 2002.*

Solution.

TABLE 3·38. **DISTRIBUTION OF CANDIDATES APPEARING IN THE UNIVERSITY EXAMINATIONS *w.r.t.* FACULTY, SEX AND EXAMINATION IN 2002**

Faculty →	*Arts*			*Science*			*Commerce*			*Total*		
Sex → *Examination ↓*	*M*	*F*	*Sub-Total*	*M*	*F*	*Sub-Total*	*M*	*F*	*Sub-Total*	*M*	*F*	*Row Totals*
Pre-university First Year Second Year Third Year												
Column Totals												

Note. *M* indicates Male ; *F* indicates Female.

Example 3·19. *Prepare a blank table to show the exports of three companies A, B, C to five countries U.K, U.S.A., U.S.S.R., France and West Germany, in each of the years 1995 to 1999.*

Solution.

TABLE 3·39. **EXPORTS OF THE COMPANIES A, B AND C TO FIVE COUNTRIES FROM 1995 TO 1999 (IN MILLION RUPEES)**

Year →	*1995*			*1996*			*1997*			*1998*			*1999*			*Total*		
Company → *Countries ↓*	A	B	C	A	B	C	A	B	C	A	B	C	A	B	C	A	B	C
UK USA USSR France West Germany																		
Total																		

Example 3·20. *Draw a blank table to present the following information regarding the college students according to :*

(*a*) *Faculty : Social Sciences, Commercial Sciences.*

(*b*) *Class : Under-graduate and Post-graduate classes.*

(*c*) *Sex : Male and Female.*

(*d*) *Years : 1998 to 2002.*

Solution. Please see Table 3·40, on page 3·37.

Example 3·21. *Prepare a blank table showing the number of employees in a big business concern according to :*

(*a*) *Sex : Males and Females.*

(*b*) *Five age-groups: Below 25 years, 25 to 35 years, 35 to 45 years, 45 to 55 years, 55 years and over.*

(*c*) *Two years: 2000 and 2001.*

(*d*) *Three grades of weekly salary: Below Rs. 4000; Rs. 4000 to 7000 ; Rs. 7000 and above.*

Solution. Please see Table 3·41, on page 3·37.

TABLE 3·40. DISTRIBUTION OF COLLEGE STUDENTS ACCORDING TO SEX, CLASS AND FACULTY FOR 1998 TO 2002

Faculty →	*Social Sciences*									*Commercial Sciences*								
Class →	*Under-Graduate*			*Post-Graduate*			*Total*			*Under-Graduate*			*Post-Graduate*			*Total*		
Sex → *Years* ↓	*M* (*i*)	*F* (*ii*)	*S.T.* (*iii*) = (*i*) + (*ii*)	*M* (*iv*)	*F* (*v*)	*S.T.* (*vi*) = (*iv*) + (*v*)	*M* (*i*) + (*iv*)	*F* (*ii*) + (*v*)	*S.T.* (*iii*) + (*vi*)	*M* (*vii*)	*F* (*viii*)	*S.T.* (*ix*) = (*vii*) + (*viii*)	*M* (*x*)	*F* (*xi*)	*S.T.* (*xii*) = (*x*) + (*xi*)	*M* (*vii*) + (*x*)	*F* (*viii*) + (*xi*)	*S.T.* (*ix*) + (*xii*)
1998																		
1999																		
2000																		
2001																		
2002																		

Note : *M* indicates Males ; *F* Indicates Females ; *S.T.* indicates sub-totals.
Remark : In the caption, we may have another sub-group named 'Total' of Social Sciences and Commercial Sciences as in Example 3·22.

TABLE 3·41. DISTRIBUTION OF THE NUMBER OF EMPLOYEES OF A BUSINESS HOUSE ACCORDING TO SEX, AGE AND SALARY FOR 2000 AND 2001.

Years ↓	*Sex* →	*Male*				*Female*				*Total*			
	Likely salary ('00 Rs.) → *Age in years* ↓	0—40	40—70	70 and over	Sub-total	0—40	40—70	70 and over	Sub-total	0—40	40—70	70 and over	Total
2000	0—25												
	25—35												
	35—45												
	45—55												
	55 and over												
	Sub-total												
2001	0—25												
	25—35												
	35—45												
	45—55												
	55 and over												
	Sub-total												

EXERCISE 3·2.

1. (*a*) Explain the terms 'classification' and 'tabulation' and point out their importance in a statistical investigation. What precautions would you take in tabulating statistical data ?

(*b*) What are the chief functions of tabulation ? What precautions would you take in tabulating statistical data ?

(*c*) Explain the purpose of classification and tabulation of data. State the rules that serve as a guide in tabulation of data.

2. (*a*) What do you mean by tabulation of data ? What precautions would you take while tabulating data ?

(*b*) Distinguish between classification and tabulation of statistical data. Mention the requisites of a good statistical table. [*Himachal Pradesh Univ. B.Com., 1998*]

(*c*) Distinguish between classification and tabulation. What precautions would you take in tabulating data ?

3. (*a*) What do you understand by tabulation ? State any six points that should be kept in mind while tabulating the data. [*CA (Foundation), May 1995*]

(*b*) Which important points should be kept in mind while preparing a good statistical table ?

[*C.A. (Foundation), May 1999*]

(*c*) What are the rules to be followed in preparing a statistical table ?

4. (*a*) Briefly discuss the essential parts of a statistical table. [*C.A. (Foundation), May 2001*]

(*b*) Draw a specimen table showing the various parts of a table. [*Osmania Univ. B.Com., 1997*]

5. Comment on the statement : "In collection and tabulation of data common sense is the chief requisite and experience the chief teacher".

6. "The statistical table is a systematic arrangement of numerical data presented in columns and rows for purposes of comparison." Explain and discuss the various types of tables used in statistical investigation after the data have been collected.

7. In a trip organised by a college there were 80 persons each of whom paid Rs. 15·50 on an average. There were 60 students each of whom paid Rs. 16. Members of the teaching staff were charged at a higher rate. The number of servants was 6 (all males) and they were not charged anything. The number of ladies was 24% of the total of which one was a lady staff member.

Tabulate the above information.

8. Tabulate the following data :

A survey was conducted amongst one lakh spectators visiting on a particular day cinema houses showing criminal, social, historical, comic and mythological films. The proportion of male to female spectators under survey was three to two. It indicated that while the respective percentages of spectators seeing criminal, social and historical films was sixteen, twenty-six and eighteen, the actual number of female viewers seeing these types was four thousand six hundred, twelve thousand two hundred, and seven thousand eight hundred respectively. The remaining two types of films, namely, comic and mythological, were seen by forty per cent and one per cent of the male spectators. The number of female spectators seeing mythological films was four thousand four hundred.

9. Present the following information in a suitable tabular form.

"In 1990, out of a total of 1750 workers of a factory, 1200 were members of a trade union. The number of women employees was 200 of which 175 did not belong to a trade union. In 1995, the number of union workers increased to 1580 of which 1290 were men. On the other hand, the number of non-union workers fell to 208, of which 180 were men.

In 2000, there were 1800 employees who belonged to a trade union and 50 who did not belong to a trade union. Of all the employees in 2000, 300 were women, of whom only 8 did not belong to a trade union".

10. Present the following information in a tabular form :

In 2001, out of a total of 4,000 workers in a factory, 3,300 were members of a trade union. The number of women workers employed was 500 out of which 400 did not belong to the union. In 2000, the number of workers in the union was 3,450 of which 3,200 were men. The number of non-union workers was 760 of which 330 were women.

11. A classification of the population of India by livelihood categories (agricultural and non-agricultural) according to the 1951 census showed that out of total of 356,628 thousand persons, 249,075 thousand persons belonged to agricultural category. In the agricultural category 71,049 thousand persons were self-supporting, 31,069 thousand were earning dependents and the rest were non-earning. The number of non-earning persons and self-supporting persons in the non-agricultural category were 67,335 thousand and 33,350 thousand respectively. The others were earning dependents.

Tabulate the above information expressing all figures in millions (1 million = 1,000 thousand).

12. A survey was conducted among 1,00,000 music listeners who were asked to indicate their preference for classical music, light music, folk songs, film songs and pop varieties of music. The male listeners interviewed were as many as female listeners. The survey indicated that while the percentage of listeners who preferred classical music, light music and folk songs were eight, thirteen and four respectively; the actual number of females for each of the first two kinds were six thousand. Of the listeners who liked folk songs, the number of male listeners was same as that of female listeners. While film songs were liked by number one and half times that for all other varieties put together, the number for pop music were only a fourth of the number of film song listeners. Sixty per cent of the listeners of pop music were females.

Prepare a table showing the distribution of music listeners according to sex and type of music.

13. What are different parts of a table ? What points should be borne in mind while arranging the items in a table ?

An investigation conducted by the education department in a public library revealed the following facts. You are required to tabulate the information as neatly and clearly as you can :

"In 1990, the total number of readers was 46,000 and they borrowed some 16,000 volumes. In 2000, the number of books borrowed increased by 4,000 and the borrowers by 5%.

The classification was on the basis of three sections : literature, fiction and illustrated news. There were 10,000 and 30,000 readers in the sections literature and fiction respectively in the year 1990. In the same year 2,000 and 10,000 books were lent in the sections illustrated news and fiction respectively. Marked changes were seen in 2000. There were 7,000 and 42,000 readers in the literature and fiction sections respectivley. So also 4,000 and 13,000 books were lent in the sections illustrated news and fiction respectively."

14. What is tabulation ? What are its uses ? Mention the items that a good statistical table should contain.

[*C.A. (Foundation), Nov. 1996*]

15. Out of total number of 2,807 women, who were interviewed for employment in a textile factory, 912 were from textile areas and the rest from non-textile areas. Amongst the married women, who belonged to textile areas, 347 were having some work experience and 173 did not have work experience, while for non-textile areas the corresponding figures were 199 and 670 respectively. The total number of women having no experience was 1,841 of whom 311 resided in textile areas. Of the total number of women, 1,418 were unmarried and of these the number of women having experience in the textile and non-textile areas was 254 and 166 respectively.

Tabulate the above information. [*C.A. (Foundation), May 1998*]

16. In 1995 out of a total of 4,000 workers in a factory 3,300 were members of a trade union. The number of women workers was 500 out of which 400 did not belong to the union. In 1994, the number of workers in the union was 3,450 of which 3,200 were men. The number of workers not belonging to the union was 760 of which 300 were women. Present data in a suitable tabular form. [*C.A. (Foundation), May 2000*]

17. What are the considerations to be taken into account in the construction of a table ? Construct a table for showing the profits of a company for a period of 5 years with imaginary figures. [*Madras Univ. B.Com., 1998*]

18. (*a*) What are the components of a good table.

(*b*) Construct a blank table in which could be shown, at two different dates and in five industries, the average wages of the four groups, males and females, eighteen years and over, and under eighteen years. Suggest a suitable title.

19. State briefly the requirements of a good statistical table.

Prepare a blank table to show the distribution of population of various States and Union Territories of India according to sex and literacy.

20. Draft a blank table to show the distribution of personnel working in an office according to (*i*) sex, (*ii*) three grades of monthly salary - below Rs. 10,000 ; Rs. 10,000 to Rs. 20,000 ; above Rs. 20,000, (*iii*) age groups : below 25 years, 25—40 and 40—60 and (*iv*) 3 years : 1995-96, 1996-97, 1997-98.

21. Draw up a blank table to show five categories of skilled and unskilled workers *i.e.*, regular, seasonal, casual, clerical and supervisory; further divided into family members and paid workers with monthly/daily rate and piece rate.

22. Draw up in detail, with proper attention to spacing, double lines, etc., and showing all sub-totals, a blank table in which could be entered the numbers occupied in six industries on two dates, distinguishing males from females, and among the latter single, married and widowed.

23. Draft a blank table to show the following information for the country *A* to cover the years 1974, 1989, 1999 and 2002.

(*a*) Population ; (*b*) Income-tax collected ; (*c*) Tobacco duties collected

(*d*) Spirits and beer duties collected ; (*e*) Other taxation.

Arrange for suitable columns to show also the "per capita" figures for (*b*), (*c*), (*d*), (*e*). Suggest a suitable title.

24. Fill in the blanks :

(*i*) … … is the first step in tabulation.

(*ii*) A … … is the systematic arrangement of data in rows and columns.

(*iii*) The numerical information in a statistical table is called the …… of the table.

(*iv*) In a statistical table, …… refer to the row headings and …… refer to column headings.

(*v*) In the collection and tabulation, …… is the chief requisite and …… is the chief teacher.

(*vi*) In a statistical table, the principal basis for the arrangement of captions and stubs in a systematic order are … … , … … , and … …

(*vii*) Classification is the … … step in … …

(*viii*) In a statistical table, captions refer to the … … headings and stubs refer to the … … headings.

(*ix*) In a statistical table, the data are arranged in … … and … …

(*x*) In a statistical table, ……should be avoided, especially in titles and headings.

Ans. (*i*) classification ; (*ii*) table ; (*iii*) body ; (*iv*) stubs, captions ; (*v*) commonsense, experience.
(*vi*) alphabetical, chronological and geographical; (*vii*) first, tabulation ;
(*viii*) column, row ; (*ix*) rows and columns ; (*x*) abbreviations.

4 Diagrammatic and Graphic Representation

4·1. INTRODUCTION

In Chapter 3, we discussed that classification and tabulation are the devices of presenting the statistical data in neat, concise, systematic and readily comprehensible and intelligible form, thus highlighting the salient features. Another important, convincing, appealing and easily understood method of presenting the statistical data is the use of diagrams and graphs. They are nothing but geometrical figures like points, lines, bars, squares, rectangles, circles, cubes, etc., pictures, maps or charts.

Diagrammatic and graphic presentation has a number of advantages, some of which are enumerated below :

(*i*) Diagrams and graphs are visual aids which give a bird's eye view of a given set of numerical data. They present the data in simple, readily comprehensible form.

(*ii*) Diagrams are generally more attractive, fascinating and impressive than the set of numerical data. They are more appealing to the eye and leave a much lasting impression on the mind as compared to the dry and uninteresting statistical figures. Even a layman, who has no statistical background can understand them easily.

(*iii*) They are more catching and as such are extensively used to present statistical figures and facts in most of the exhibitions, trade or industrial fairs, public functions, statistical reports, etc. Human mind has a natural craving and love for beautiful pictures and this psychology of the human mind is extensively exploited by the modern advertising agencies who give their advertisements in the shape of attractive and beautiful pictures. Accordingly diagrams and graphs have universal applicability.

(*iv*) They register a meaningful impression on the mind almost before we think. They also save lot of time as very little effort is required to grasp them and draw meaningful inferences from them. An individual may not like to go through a set of numerical figures but he may pause for a while to have a glance at the diagrams or pictures. It is for this reason that diagrams, graphs and charts find a place almost daily in financial/business columns of the newspapers, economic and business journals, annual reports of the business houses, etc.

(*v*) When properly constructed, diagrams and graphs readily show information that might otherwise be lost amid the details of numerical tabulations. They highlight the salient features of the collected data, facilitate comparisons among two or more sets of data and enable us to study the relationship between them more readily.

(*vi*) Graphs reveal the trends, if any present in the data more vividly than the tabulated numerical figures and also exhibit the way in which the trends change. Although this information is inherent in a table, it may be quite difficult and time-consuming (and sometimes may be impossible) to determine the existence and nature of trends from a tabulation of data.

4·2. DIFFERENCE BETWEEN DIAGRAMS AND GRAPHS

No hard and fast rules exist to distinguish between diagrams and graphs but the following points of difference may be observed :

(*i*) In the construction of a graph, generally graph paper is used which helps us to study the mathematical relationship (though not necessarily functional) between the two variables. On the other hand, diagrams are generally constructed on a plane paper and are used for comparisons only and not for studying the relationship between the variables. In diagrams data are presented by devices such as bars, rectangles, squares, circles, cubes, etc., while in graphic mode of presentation points or lines of different kinds (dots, dashes, dot-dash, etc.), are used to present the data.

(*ii*) Diagrams furnish only approximate information. They do not add anything to the meaning of the data and, therefore, are not of much use to a statistician or research worker for further mathematical treatment or statistical analysis. On the other hand, graphs are more obvious, precise and accurate than the diagrams and are quite helpful to the statistician for the study of slopes, rates of change and estimation, (interpolation and extrapolation), wherever possible. In fact, today, graphic work is almost a must in any research work pertaining to the analysis of economic, business or social data.

(*iii*) Diagrams are useful in depicting categorical and geographical data but they fail to present data relating to time series and frequency distributions. In fact, graphs are used for the study of time series and frequency distributions.

(*iv*) Construction of graphs is easier as compared to the construction of diagrams.

In the following sections we shall first discuss the various types of diagrams and then the different modes of graphic presentation.

4·3. DIAGRAMMATIC PRESENTATION

4·3·1. General Rules for Constructing Diagrams

1. Neatness. As already pointed out, diagrams are visual aids for presentation of statistical data and are more appealing and fascinating to the eye and leave a lasting impression on the mind. It is, therefore, imperative that they are made very neat, clean and attractive by proper size and lettering; and the use of appropriate devices like different colours, different shades (light and dark), dots, dashes, dotted lines, broken lines, dots and dash lines, etc., for filling the in between space of the bars, rectangles, circles, etc., and their components. Some of the commonly used devices are given below :

Fig. 4·1.

2. Title and Footnotes. As in the case of a good statistical table, each diagram should be given a suitable title to indicate the subject-matter and the various facts depicted in the diagram. The title should be brief, self explanatory, clear and non-ambiguous. However, brevity should not be attempted at the cost of clarity. The title should be neatly displayed either at the top of the diagram or at its bottom.

If necessary the footnotes may be given at the left hand bottom of the diagram to explain certain points or facts, not otherwise covered in the title.

3. Selection of Scale. One of the most important factors in the construction of diagrams is the choice of an appropriate scale. The same set of numerical data if plotted on different scales may give the diagrams differing widely in size and at times might lead to wrong and misleading interpretations. Hence, the scale should be selected with great caution. Unfortunately, no hard and fast rules are laid down for the choice of scale. As a guiding principle the scale should be selected consistent with the size of the paper and the size of the observations to be displayed so that the diagram obtained is neither too small nor too big. The size of the diagram should be reasonable so as to focus attention on the salient features and important characteristics of the data. The scale showing the values should be in even numbers or multiples of 5 or 10. The scale(s) used on both the horizontal and vertical axes should be clearly indicated. For comparative study of two or more diagrams, the same scale should be adopted to draw valid conclusions.

4. Proportion Between Width and Height. A proper proportion between the dimensions (height and width) of the diagram should be maintained, consistent with the space available. Here again no hard and fast rules are laid down. In this regard Lutz in his book *Graphic Presentation* has suggested a rule called '*root two*' rule, *viz*., the ratio 1 to $\sqrt{2}$ or 1 to 1·414 between the smaller side and the larger side respectively. The diagram should be generally displayed in the middle (centre) of the page.

5. Choice of a Diagram. A large number of diagrams (discussed below) are used to present statistical data. The choice of a particular diagram to present a given set of numerical data is not an easy one. It primarily depends on the nature of the data, magnitude of the observations and the type of people for whom the diagrams are meant and requires great amount of expertise, skill and intelligence. An inappropriate choice of the diagram for the given set of data might give a distorted picture of the phenomenon under study and might lead to wrong and fallacious interpretations and conclusions. Hence, the choice of a diagram to present the given data should be made with utmost caution and care.

6. Source Note and Number. As in the case of tables, source note, wherever possible should be appended at the bottom of the diagram. This is necessary as, to the learned audience of Statistics, the reliability of the information varies from source to source. Each diagram should also be given a number for ready reference and comparative study.

7. Index. A brief index explaining various types of shades, colours, lines and designs used in the construction of the diagram should be given for clear understanding of the diagram.

8. Simplicity. Lastly, diagrams should be as simple as possible so that they are easily understood even by a layman who does not have any mathematical or statistical background. If too much information is presented in a single complex diagram it will be difficult to grasp and might even become confusing to the mind. Hence, it is advisable to draw more simple diagrams than one or two complex diagrams.

4·3·2. Types of Diagrams. A large variety of diagrammatic devices are used in practice to present statistical data. However, we shall discuss here only some of the most commonly used diagrams which may be broadly classified as follows :

(1) One-dimensional diagrams *viz*., line diagrams and bar diagrams.

(2) Two-dimensional diagrams such as rectangles, squares, and circles or pie diagrams.

(3) Three-dimensional diagrams such as cubes, spheres, prisms, cylinders and blocks.

(4) Pictograms.

(5) Cartograms.

4·3·3. One-dimensional Diagrams

A. LINE DIAGRAM

This is the simplest of all the diagrams. It consists in drawing vertical lines, each vertical line being equal to the frequency. The variate (x) values are presented on a suitable scale along the X-axis and the corresponding frequencies are presented on a suitable scale along Y-axis. Line diagrams facilitate comparisons though they are not attractive or appealing to the eye.

Remark. Even a time series data may be presented by a line diagram, by taking time factors along X-axis and the variate values along Y-axis.

Example. 4·1. *The following data shows the number of accidents sustained by 314 drivers of a public utility company over a period of five years.*

Number of accidents:											
0	*1*	*2*	*3*	*4*	*5*	*6*	*7*	*8*	*9*	*10*	*11*
Number of drivers :											
82	*44*	*68*	*41*	*25*	*20*	*13*	*7*	*5*	*4*	*3*	*2*

Represent the data by a line diagram.

Solution.

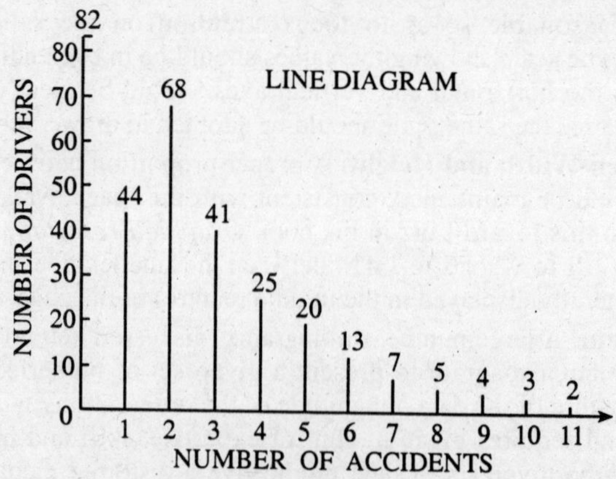

Fig. 4·2.

B. BAR DIAGRAM

Bar diagrams are one of the easiest and the most commonly used devices of presenting most of the business and economic data. These are especially satisfactory for categorical data or series. They consist of a group of equidistant rectangles, one for each group or category of the data in which the values or the magnitudes are represented by the length or height of the rectangles, the width of the rectangles being arbitrary and immaterial. These diagrams are called one-dimensional because in such diagrams only one dimension *viz.*, height (or length) of the rectangles is taken into account to present the given values. The following points may be borne in mind to draw bar diagrams.

(*i*) All the bars drawn in a single study should be of uniform (though arbitrary) width depending on the number of bars to be drawn and the space available.

(*ii*) Proper but uniform spacing should be given between different bars to make the diagram look more attractive and elegant.

(*iii*) The height (length) of the rectangles or bars are taken proportional to magnitude of the observations, the scale being selected keeping in view the magnitude of the largest observation.

(*iv*) All the bars should be constructed on the same base line.

(*v*) It is desirable to write the figures (magnitudes) represented by the bars at the top of the bars to enable the reader to have a precise idea of the value without looking at the scale.

(*vi*) Bars may be drawn vertically or horizontally. However, in practice, vertical bars are generally used because they give an attractive and appealing get up.

(*vii*) Wherever possible the bars should be arranged from left to right (from top to bottom in case of horizontal bars) in order of magnitude to give a pleasing effect.

Types of Bar Diagrams. The following are the various types of bar diagrams in common use :

(*a*) Simple bar diagram.
(*b*) Sub-divided or component bar diagram.
(*c*) Percentage bar diagram.
(*d*) Multiple bar diagram.
(*e*) Deviation or Bilateral bar diagram.

(*a*) SIMPLE BAR DIAGRAM

Simple bar diagram is the simplest of the bar diagrams and is used frequently in practice for the comparative study of two or more items or values of a single variable or a single classification or category of data. For example, the data relating to sales, profits, production, population, etc., for different periods may be presented by bar diagrams. As already pointed out the magnitudes of the observations are represented by the heights of the rectangles.

Remark. If there are a large number of items or values of the variable under study, then instead of bar diagram, line diagram may be drawn.

Example 4·2. *The following data relating to the strength of the Indian Merchant Shipping Fleet gives the Gross Registered Tonnage (GRT) as on 31st December, for different years.*

Year :	*1961*	*1966*	*1971*	*1975*	*1976*
GRT in '000 :	*901*	*1,792*	*2,500*	*4,464*	*5,115*

Source : Ministry of Shipping and Transport.

Represent the data by suitable bar diagram.

Solution.

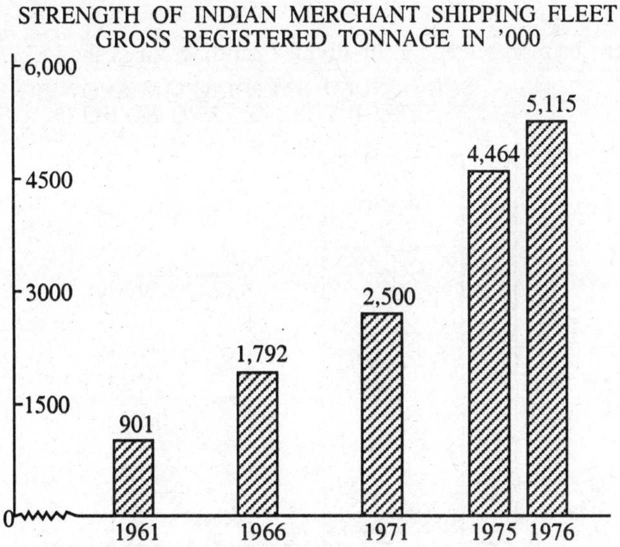

Fig. 4·3.

(b) SUB-DIVIDED OR COMPONENT BAR DIAGRAM

A very serious limitation of the bar diagram is that it studies only one characteristic or classification at a time. For example, the total number of students in a college for the last 5 years can be conveniently expressed by simple bar diagrams but it cannot be used if we have also to depict the faculty-wise or sex-wise distribution of students. In such a situation, sub-divided or component bar diagram is used. Sub-divided bar-diagrams are useful not only for presenting several items of a variable or a category graphically but also enable us to make comparative study of different parts or components among themselves and also to study the relationship between each component and the whole.

In general sub-divided or component bar diagrams are to be used if the total magnitude of the given variable is to be divided into various parts or sub-classes or components. First of all a bar representing the total is drawn. Then it is divided into various segments, each segment representing a given component of the total. Different shades or colours, crossing or dotting, or designs are used to distinguish the various components and a key or index is given along with the diagram to explain these differences.

In addition to the general rules for constructing bar diagrams, the following points may be kept in mind while constructing sub-divided or component bar diagrams :

(*i*) To facilitate comparisons the order of the various components in different bars should be same. It is customary to show the largest component at the base of the bar and the smallest component at the top so that the various components appear in the order of their magnitude.

(*ii*) As already pointed, an index or key showing the various components represented by different shades, dottings, colours, etc., should be given.

(*iii*) The use of sub-divided bar diagram is not suggested if the number of components exceeds 10, because in that case the diagram is loaded with too much information and is not easy to understand and interpret. Pie or circle diagram (discussed later) is appropriate in such a situation. The comparison of the various components in different bars is quite tedious as they do not have a common base and requires great skill and expertise.

Example 4·3. *Represent the following data by a suitable diagram :*

Items of Expenditure	*Family A (Income Rs. 500)*	*Family B (Income Rs. 300)*
Food	*150*	*150*
Clothing	*125*	*60*
Education	*25*	*50*
Miscellaneous	*190*	*70*
Saving or Deficit	*+10*	*–30*

Solution. The data can be represented by sub-divided bar diagram as shown below :

SUB-DIVIDED BAR DIAGRAM SHOWING EXPENDITURE OF TWO FAMILIES

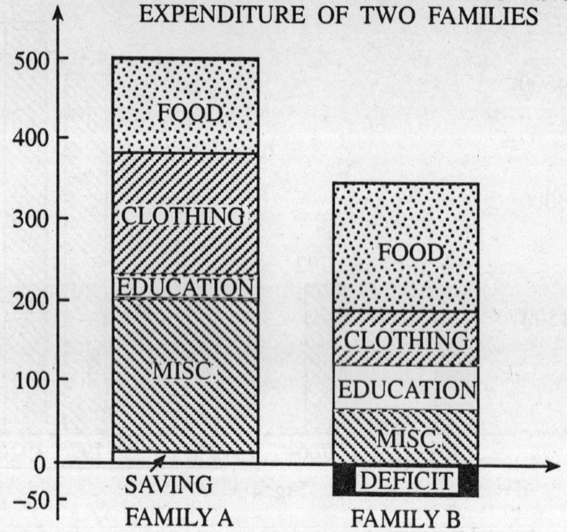

Fig. 4·4.

(*c*) PERCENTAGE BAR DIAGRAM

Sub-divided or component bar diagrams presented graphically on percentage basis give percentage bar diagrams. They are specially useful for the diagrammatic portrayal of the *relative changes* in the data. Percentage bar diagram is used to highlight the relative importance of the various component parts to the whole. The total for each bar is taken as 100 and the value of each component or part is expressed, as percentage of the respective totals. Thus, in a percentage bar diagram, all the bars will be of the same height, *viz.*, 100, while the various segments of the bar representing the different components will vary in height depending on their percentage values to the total. Percentage bars are quite convenient and useful for comparing two or more sets of data.

Example 4·4. *The adjoining table gives the break-up of the expenditure of a family on different items of consumption. Draw percentage bar diagram to represent the data.*

Item	*Expenditure (Rs.)*
Food	240
Clothing	66
Rent	125
Fuel and Lighting	57
Education	42
Miscellaneous	190

Solution. First of all we convert the given figures into percentages of the total expenditure as detailed below.

Item	*Rs.*	*Expenditure %*	*Cumulative %*
Food	240	$\frac{240}{720} \times 100 = 33{\cdot}33$	33·33
Clothing	66	$\frac{66}{720} \times 100 = 9{\cdot}17$	42·50
Rent	125	$\frac{125}{720} \times 100 = 17{\cdot}36$	59·86
Fuel and lighting	57	$\frac{57}{720} \times 100 = 7{\cdot}92$	67·78
Education	42	$\frac{42}{720} \times 100 = 5{\cdot}83$	73·61
Miscellaneous	190	$\frac{190}{720} \times 100 = 26{\cdot}39$	100·00
Total	720	100	

The percentage bar diagram is given in Fig. 4·5.

DIAGRAM SHOWING EXPENDITURE OF FAMILY ON DIFFERENT ITEMS OF CONSUMPTION

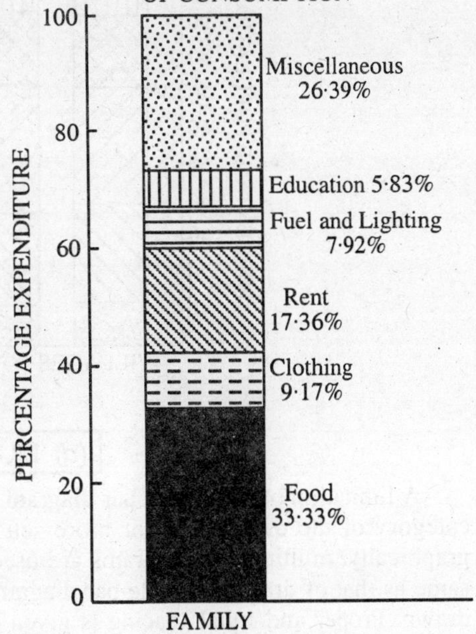

Fig. 4·5.

Example 4·5. *Draw a bar chart for the following data showing the percentage of total population in villages and towns:*

	Percentage of total population in	
	Villages	*Towns*
Infants and young children	*13·7*	*12·9*
Boys and girls	*25·1*	*23·2*
Young men and women	*32·3*	*36·5*
Middle-aged men and women	*20·4*	*20·1*
Elderly persons	*8·5*	*7·3*

Solution.

CALCULATIONS FOR PERCENTAGE BAR DIAGRAMS

Category	*Villages*		*Towns*	
	%	*Cumulative %*	*%*	*Cumulative %*
Infants and young children	13·7	13·7	12·9	12·9
Boys and girls	25·1	38·8	23·2	36·1
Young men and women	32·3	71·1	36·5	72·6
Middle aged men and women	20·4	91·5	20·1	92·7
Elderly persons	8·5	100·0	7·3	100·0
	100		100	

PERCENTAGE BAR DIAGRAM SHOWING TOTAL POPULATION IN VILLAGES AND TOWNS BY DIFFERENT CATEGORIES

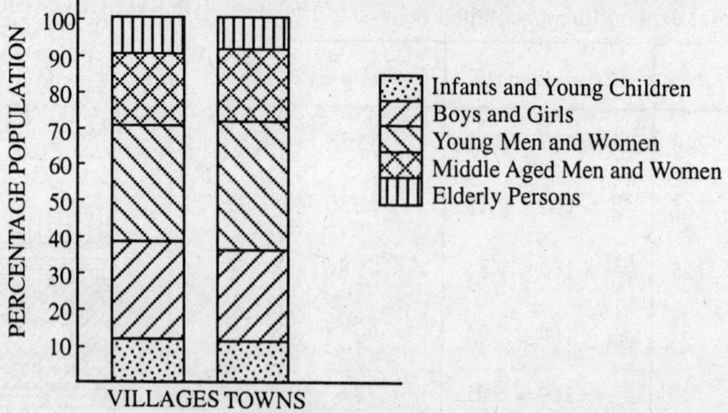

Fig. 4·6.

(*d*) MULTIPLE BAR DIAGRAM

A limitation of the simple bar diagram was that it can be used to portray only a single characteristic or category of the data. If two or more sets of inter-related phenomena or variables are to be presented graphically, multiple bar diagrams are used. The technique of drawing multiple bar diagram is basically same as that of drawing simple bar diagram. In this case, a set of adjacent bars (one for each variable) is drawn. Proper and equal spacing is given between different sets of the bars. To distinguish between the different bars in a set, different colours, shades, dottings or crossings may be used and key or index to this effect may be given.

Example 4·6. *The data below give the yearly profits (in thousand of rupees) of two companies A and B.*

Year	*Profits in ('000 rupees)*	
	Company A	*Company B*
1994-95	120	90
1995-96	135	95
1996-97	140	108
1997-98	160	120
1998-99	175	130

Represent the data by means of a suitable diagram.

Solution. The data can be suitably represented by a multiple bar diagram as shown below.

YEARLY PROFITS IN '000 RUPEES

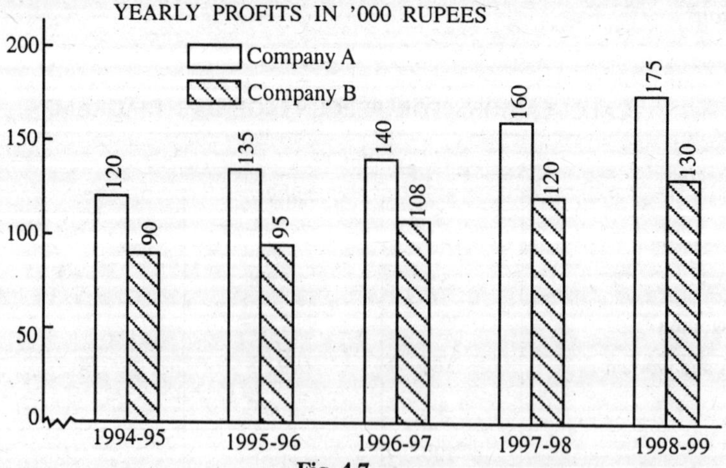

Fig. 4·7.

Remark. A careful examination of the above figures of profits for the two companies A and B reveals that in all the years from 1994-95 to 1998-99, company A shows higher profits than the company B. In such a situation when the values of one concern or unit show an increase over the values of the other concern or unit for all the periods under consideration, the data can be elegantly represented by a special type of sub-divided bar diagram, in which total refers to the values of the concern or unit with higher values and the lower portion (shaded) of the bar shows the values of other concern. The remaining portion (blank) shows the balance (excess) of the two concerns or units. We represent in Fig. 4.8 the above data in this manner.

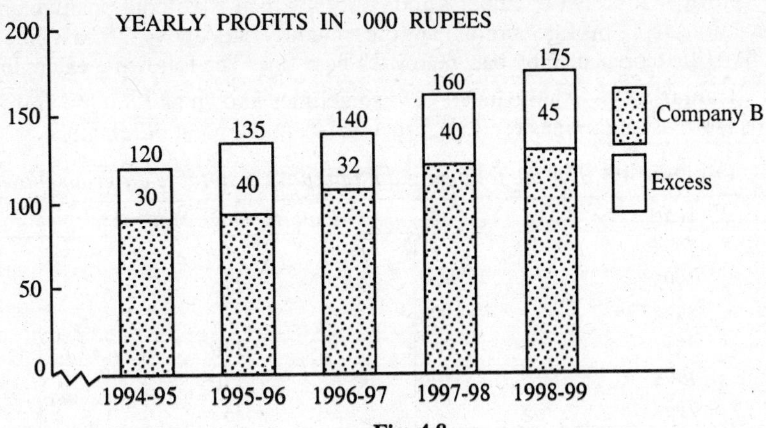

Fig. 4·8.

Example 4·7. *The following data shows the students in millions on rolls at school/university stage in India according to different class groups and sex for the year 1970-71 as on 31st March.*

Stage	*Boys*	*Girls*	*Total*
Class I to V	*35·74*	*21·31*	*57·05*
Class VI to VIII	*9·43*	*3·89*	*13·32*
Class IX to XI	*4·87*	*1·71*	*6·58*
University/College	*2·17*	*0·64*	*2·81*

Represent the data by (i) Component bar diagram and (ii) Multiple bar diagram.

Solution.

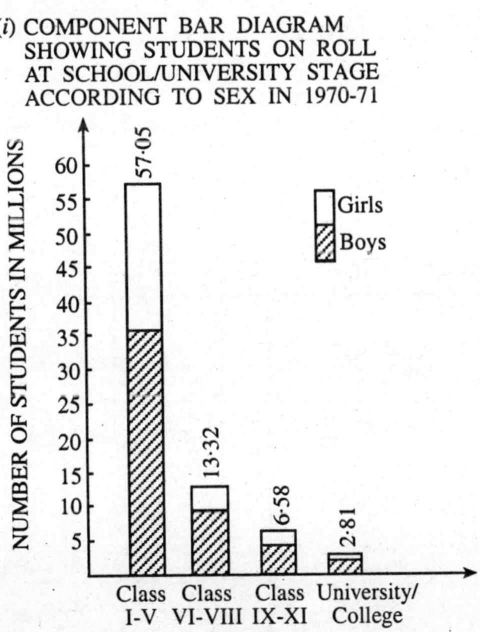

Fig. 4·9.

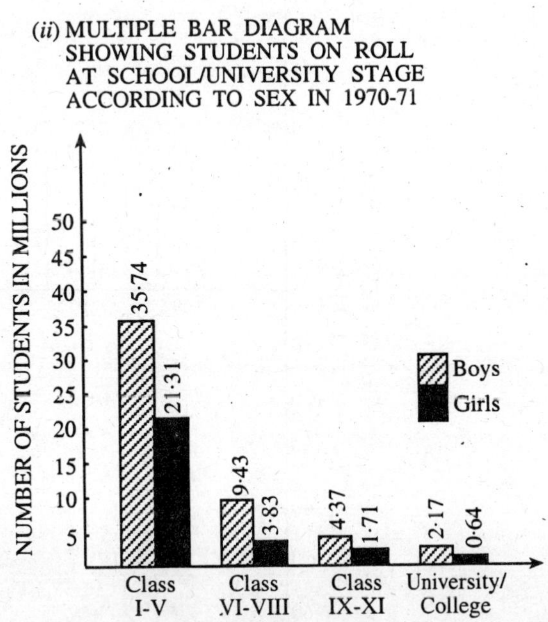

Fig. 4·10.

(e) DEVIATION BARS

Deviation bars are specially useful for graphic presentation of net quantities *viz.*, surplus or deficit, *e.g.*, net profit or loss, net of imports and exports which have both positive and negative values. The positive deviations (*e.g.*, profits, surplus) are presented by bars above the base line while negative deviations (loss, deficit) are represented by bars below the base line. The following example will illustrate the points.

Remark. Deviation bars are also sometimes known as *Bilateral Bar Diagrams* and are used to depict plus (surplus) and minus (deficit) directions from the point of reference.

Example 4·8. *For the following data prepare a suitable diagram showing Balance of Trade :*

Years	*Exports (In Rs. Million)*	*Inports (In Rs. Million)*
1994	*24*	*9*
1995	*115*	*92*
1996	*84*	*92*
1997	*110*	*120*
1998	*130*	*183*
1999	*162*	*187*

[*Delhi Univ. B.Com. (Pass), 2001*]

Solution.

Year	*Exports (In Rs. Million)*	*Imports (In Rs. Million)*	*Balance of Trade (In Million Rs.)*
1994	24	9	24 – 9 = 15
1995	115	92	115 – 92 = 23
1996	84	92	84 – 92 = – 8
1997	110	120	110 – 120 = –10
1998	130	183	130 – 183 = –53
1999	162	187	162 – 187 = –25

Deviation bar diagram showing balance of trade is given in Fig. 4·11 :

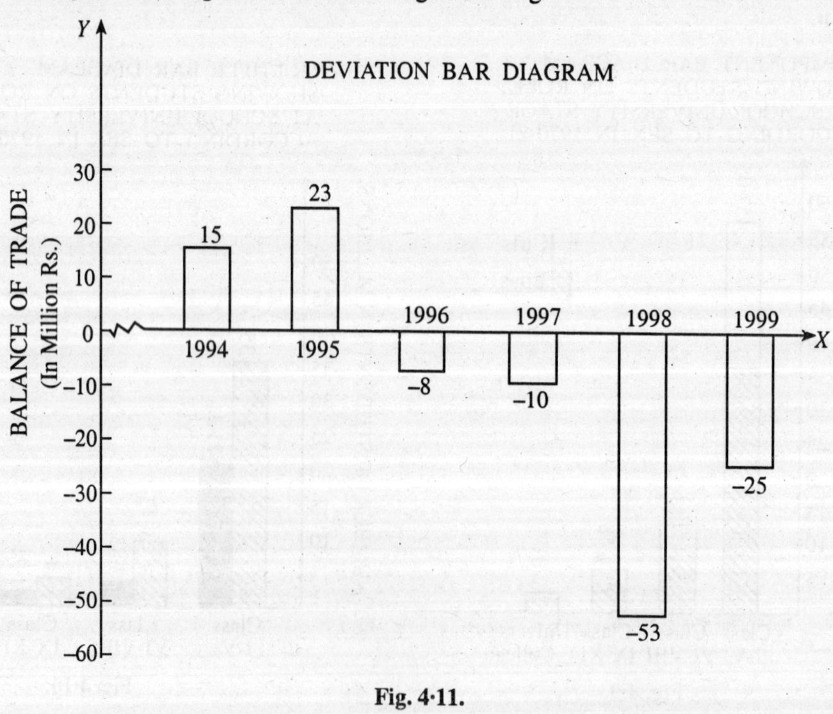

Fig. 4·11.

For more illustrations, see Examples 4·13 and 4·14

(f) BROKEN BARS

Broken bars are used for graphic presentation of the data which contain very wide variations in the values *i.e.,* the data which contain very large observations along with small observations. In this case the squeezing of the vertical scale will not be of much help because it will make the small bars to look too small and clumsy and thus will not reveal the true characteristics of the data. In order to provide adequate and reasonable shape for smaller bars, the larger (or largest) bar(s) may be broken at the top, as illustrated in Examples 4·9 and 4·10.

Remark. However, if all the observations are fairly large so that all the bars have a broken vertical axis, then instead they can be drawn with a *false base line* for the vertical axis. [For false base line, see § 4·4·2—Graphic Presentation.]

Example 4·9. *The following data relates to the imports of foreign merchandise and exports (including re-exports) of Indian merchandise (in million rupees) for some countries for the year 1975-76.*

Country	*Imports*	*Exports*	*Country*	*Imports*	*Exports*
Burma	53	89	*Germany (F.R.)*	3,566	1,173
Czechoslovakia	522	343	*Iran*	4,593	2,708
Canada	2,278	424	*United Kingdom*	2,683	4,020
Australia	1,015	477	*USSR*	2,958	4,128
Italy	799	785	*Japan*	3,548	4,263
France	1,852	835	*USA*	12,699	5,054

Represent the data by suitable diagram.

Solution. The above data is represented by bar-diagrams as shown below.

FOREIGN TRADE BY COUNTRIES
1975-76

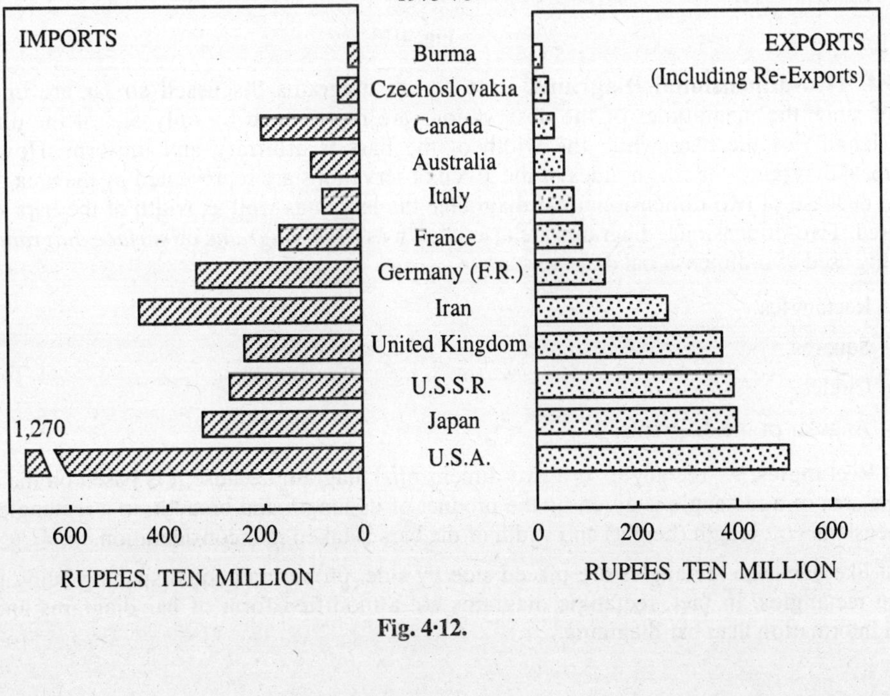

Fig. 4·12.

Example 4·10. *Represent the following data relating to the military statistics at the border during the war between the two countries A and B in 1999 by multiple bar diagram.*

Category	*Country A*	*Country B*
Army Divisions	*4*	*20*
Semi-Army Units	*50*	—
Fighter Planes	*75*	*700*
Tanks	*50*	*300*
Total Troops	*100,000*	*170,000*

Solution.

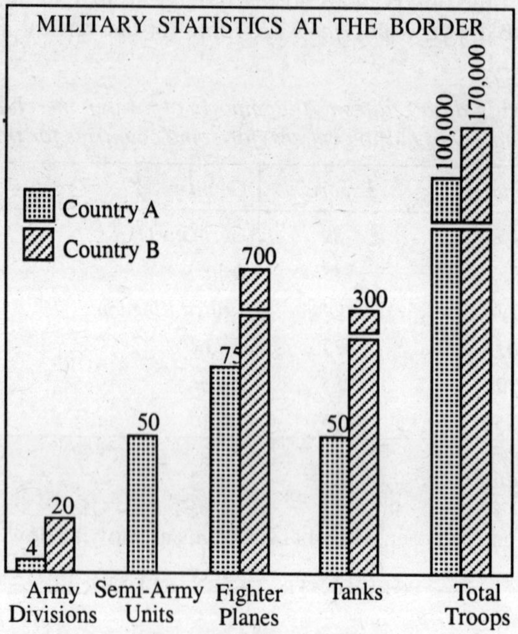

Fig. 4·13.

4·3·4. Two-dimensional Diagrams. Line or bar diagrams discussed so far are one-dimensional diagrams since the magnitudes of the observations are represented by only one of the dimensions *viz.*, height (length) of the bars while the width of the bars is arbitrary and uniform. However, in two-dimensional diagrams, the magnitudes of the given observations are represented by the area of the diagram. Thus, in the case of two-dimensional bar diagrams, the length as well as width of the bars will have to be considered. Two-dimensional diagrams are also known as *area diagrams* or *surface diagrams*. Some of the commonly used two-dimensional diagrams are :

(*A*) Rectangles.

(*B*) Squares.

(*C*) Circles.

(*D*) Angular or pie diagrams.

(A) Rectangles. A "rectangle" is a two-dimensional diagram because it is based on the area principle. Since the area of a rectangle is given by the product of its length and breadth, in a rectangle diagram both the dimensions *viz.*, length (height) and width of the bars is taken into consideration.

Just like bars, the rectangles are placed side by side, proper and equal spacing being given between different rectangles. In fact, rectangle diagrams are a modified form of bar diagrams and give a more detailed information than bar diagrams.

Like sub-divided bars, we have also *sub-divided rectangles* for depicting the total and its break-up into various components. Likewise *percentage rectangle* diagram may be used to portray the relative magnitudes of two or more sets of data and their components making up the total. We give below a few illustrations.

Example 4·11. *Prepare a rectangular diagram from the following particulars relating to the production of a commodity in a factory.*

Units produced	*1,000*
Cost of raw materials	*Rs. 5,000*
Direct expenses	*Rs. 2,000*
Indirect expenses	*Rs. 1,000*
Profit	*Rs. 1,000*

Solution. First of all we will find the cost of material, expenses and profits per unit as given below :

Cost of raw material per unit $= \text{Rs.} \frac{5000}{1000} = \text{Rs. } 5$

Direct expenses per unit $= \text{Rs.} \frac{2000}{1000} = \text{Rs. } 2$

Indirect expenses per unit $= \text{Rs.} \frac{1000}{1000} = \text{Re. } 1$

Profit per unit $= \text{Rs.} \frac{1000}{1000} = \text{Re. } 1$

DIAGRAM SHOWING COST AND PROFIT FOR A COMMODITY IN A FACTORY

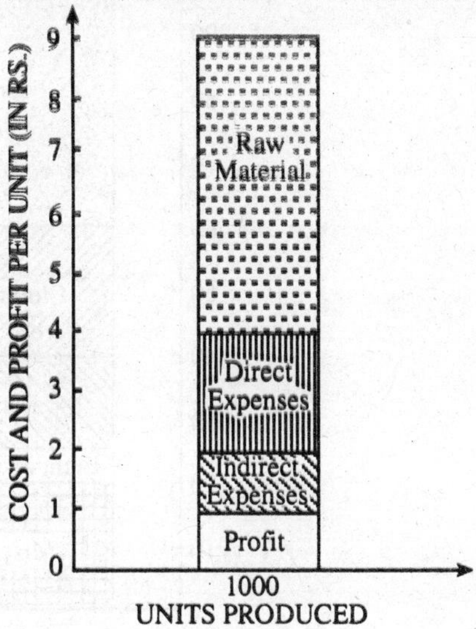

Fig. 4·14.

Example 4·12. *The following data relates to the monthly expenditure (in Rs.) of two families A and B.*

Item of Expenditure	*Expenditure (in Rs.)*	
	Family A	*Family B*
Food	*160*	*120*
Clothing	*80*	*32*
Rent	*60*	*48*
Light and fuel	*20*	*16*
Miscellaneous	*80*	*24*
Total	*400*	*240*

Represent it by a suitable percentage diagram.

Solution. Since the total expenses of the two families are different, an appropriate percentage diagram for the above data will be rectangular diagram on percentage basis. The percentage bar diagram will not be able to reflect the inherent differences in the total expenditures of the two families.

The widths of the rectangles will be taken in the ratio of the total expenses of the two families *viz.*, 400 : 240 *i.e.*, 5 : 3.

CALCULATIONS FOR PERCENTAGE RECTANGULAR DIAGRAM

	Family A			*Family B*		
Item of Expenditure	*Rs.*	*%*	*Cumulative %*	*Rs.*	*%*	*Cumulative %*
Food	160	40	40	120	50	50
Clothing	80	20	60	32	13·33	63·33
Rent	60	15	75	48	20	83·33
Light and fuel	20	5	80	16	6·67	90
Miscellaneous	80	20	100	24	10	100
Total	400	100		240	100	

PERCENTAGE RECTANGLE DIAGRAM SHOWING
MONTHLY EXPENDITURE OF TWO FAMILIES *A* AND *B*

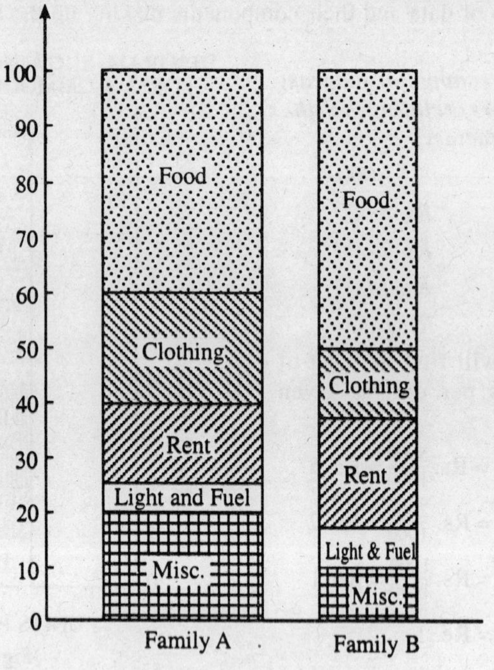

Fig. 4·15.

Example 4·13. *Represent the following data by a percentage sub-divided bar diagram.*

Item of Expenditure	*Family A*	*Family B*
	Income Rs. 500	*Income Rs. 300*
Food	*150*	*150*
Clothes	*125*	*60*
Education	*25*	*50*
Miscellaneous	*190*	*70*
Savings or Deficit	*+10*	*–30*

Solution. Since the total incomes of the two families are different, an appropriate percentage bar diagram for the above data will be rectangular diagram on percentage basis. The percentage bar diagram will not be able to reflect the inherent differences in the total incomes in the two families.

The widths of the rectangles will be taken in the ratio of the total incomes of the families *viz.*, 500 : 300 *i.e.*, 5 : 3.

CALCULATIONS FOR PERCENTAGE RECTANGULAR DIAGRAM

Item of Expenditure	*Family A* Expenditure (Rs.)	%	Cumulative %	*Family B* Expenditure (Rs.)	%	Cumulative %
Food	150	30	30	150	50	50
Clothes	125	25	55	60	20	70
Education	25	5	60	50	16.7	86.7
Miscellaneous	190	38	98	70	23.3	110.0
Savings or Deficit	+ 10	2	10	– 30	– 10	100
Total	500			300		

PERCENTAGE DIAGRAM SHOWING MONTHLY INCOME AND EXPENDITURE OF TWO FAMILIES *A* AND *B*

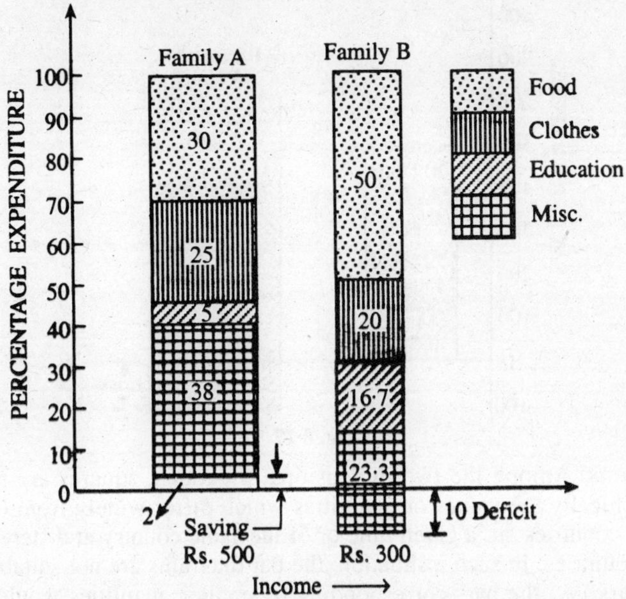

Fig. 4·16.

Example 4·14. *Draw a suitable diagram to represent the following information.*

	Selling price per unit (in Rs.)	*Quantity sold*	*Total Cost (in Rs.)*			
			Wages	*Materials*	*Misc.*	*Total*
Factory X	*400*	*20*	*3,200*	*2,400*	*1,600*	*7,200*
Factory Y	*600*	*30*	*6,000*	*6,000*	*9,000*	*21,000*

Show also the profit or loss as the case may be.

Solution. First of all we shall calculate the cost (wages, materials, misc.) and profit per unit as given in the following table.

	Selling price per unit (in Rs.)	*Quantity sold*	*Cost per unit (in Rs.)*				*Profit per unit (in Rs.)*
			Wages	*Materials*	*Misc.*	*Total*	
Factory X	400	20	160	120	80	360	400 – 360 = 40
Factory Y	600	30	200	200	300	700	600 – 700 = 100

Note. Negative profit is regarded as loss.

An appropriate diagram for representing this data would be the 'Rectangles' whose widths are in the ratio of the quantities sold *i.e.,* 20 : 30 *i.e.,* 2 : 3. Selling prices would be represented by the corresponding heights of the rectangles with various factors of cost (wages, materials, misc.) and profit or loss represented by the various divisions of the rectangles as shown in the following diagram (Fig. 4.17).

Remark. In the case of profit *i.e.,* when selling price (S.P.) is greater than cost price (C.P.), the entire rectangle will lie above the X-axis, the segment just above the X-axis showing profit. But in case of loss *i.e.,* when S.P. is less than C.P., we will have the rectangle with a portion lying below the X-axis which will reflect the loss incurred *i.e.,* the cost not recovered through sales. The values of each component are given by the product of the base with the corresponding height of the component (rectangle). For example, for the factory X, the area of the component for wages is $20 \times 160 = 3200$, which is the given cost.

SUB-DIVIDED RECTANGLE SHOWING COST, SALES AND PROFIT OR LOSS PER UNIT

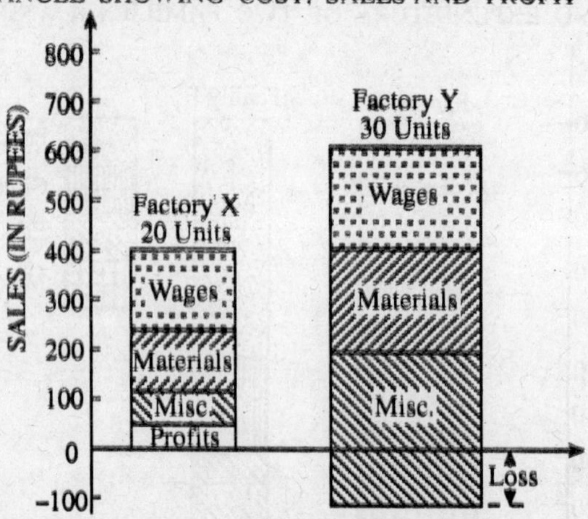

Fig. 4·17.

(B) Square Diagrams. Among the two-dimensional diagrams, squares are specially useful if it is desired to compare graphically the values or quantities which differ widely from one another as *e.g.*, the population of different countries at a given time or of the same country at different times or the imports or exports of different countries. In such a situation, the bar diagrams are not suitable, since they will give very disproportionate bars *i.e.*, the bars corresponding to smaller quantities would be comparatively too small and those corresponding to bigger values would be too big. In particular, if two values are in the proportion of 1 : 25 and if we draw bar diagram, one (bigger) will be 25 times (in height) than that of the other (smaller). In such a situation, square diagrams give a better presentation.

Like rectangle diagram, square diagram is a two-dimensional diagram in which the given values are represented by the area of the square. Since the area of the square is given by the square of its side, the side of the square diagram will be in proportion to the square root of the given observations. Thus if the two observations are in the ratio of 1 : 25, the sides of the squares will be in the ratio of their square roots *viz.*, 1 : 5.

Construction of the square diagrams is quite simple. First of all we obtain the square roots of the given observations and then squares are drawn with sides proportional to these square roots, on an appropriate scale which must be specified.

Remarks 1. The square may be drawn horizontally (on the same base line) or vertically one below the other to facilitate comparisons. However, in practice, the first method *viz.*, horizontal presentation is generally used since it economises space.

2. Although square diagram is a two-dimensional diagram, it is used to depict only a single magnitude or value.

Example 4·15. *Draw a square diagram to represent the following data.*

Country	*A*	*B*	*C*
Yield in (kg.) per hectare	*350*	*647*	*1,120*

Solution. The square roots of the given yields in (kg) per hectare give the proportion of the sides of the corresponding squares. The calculations are shown in the following table :

Country	*A*	*B*	*C*
Yield in (kg.) per hectare	350	647	1,120
Square root	18·7083	25·4362	33·4664
Ratio of the sides of the squares	1	1·36	1·79

The square diagram is given in Fig. 4·18.

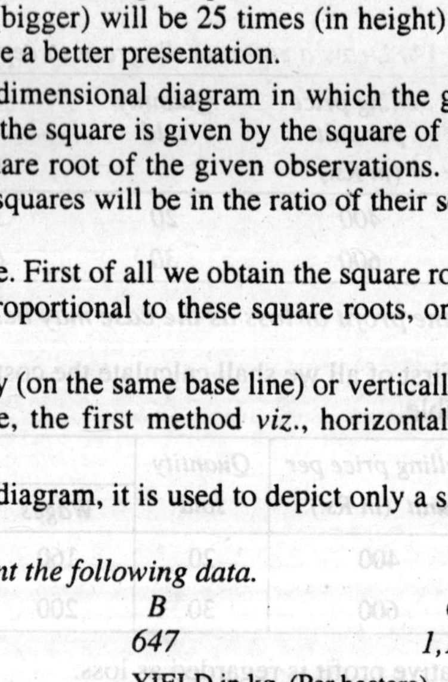

Fig. 4·18.

Remark. In the above table, the ratio of the sides of the squares has been obtained on dividing the square roots of the values for B and C by the square root of the value for A. This is easy to do on a calculator but without a calculator it is quite time-consuming. However, the things can be simplified to a great extent by dividing the square roots of the values of A, B and C by a whole number, say, 15 or 18. Division by, say, 15, gives the ratio of the sides of squares for A, B and C as 1·25, 1·70, 2·23 respectively. Squares can now be constructed by taking appropriate scale which must be specified in the diagram.

If we construct squares with sides 1·25 cms., 1·70 cms., and 2·23 cms., the scale will be obtained as follows :

Area of square for A is $(1·25)^2 = 1·5625$ square cms. This area represents the value 350 kg. Thus,

$$1·5625 \text{ sq. cms.} = 350 \text{ kg.} \quad \Rightarrow \quad 1 \text{ sq. cm.} = \frac{350}{1·5625} = 224 \text{ kg.}$$

(C) Circle Diagrams. Circle diagrams are alternative to square diagrams and are used for the same purpose, *viz.*, for diagrammatic presentation of the values differing widely in their magnitude. The area of the circle, which represents the given values is given by πr^2, where $\pi = 22/7$ and r is the radius of circle. In other words, the area of the circle is proportional to the square of its radius and consequently, in the construction of the circle diagram the radius of the circle is a value proportional to the square root of the given magnitude. Accordingly, the lengths which were taken as the sides of the square may also be taken as the radii of the circles representing the given magnitudes.

Remarks 1. Circle diagrams are more attractive and appealing than square diagrams and since both require more or less the same amount of work, *viz.*, computing the square roots of the given magnitudes (rather circles are easy to draw), circle diagrams are generally preferred to square diagrams.

2. Since square and circle diagrams are to be compared on an area basis, it is difficult to judge the relative magnitudes with precision, particularly by a layman without any mathematical or statistical background. Accordingly, proper care should be taken to interpret them. They are also more difficult to construct than the rectangle diagrams.

3. Scale. The scale to be used for constructing circle diagrams can be calculated as follows :

For a given magnitude 'a' we have

$$\text{Area} = \pi r^2 \text{ square units} = a \quad \Rightarrow \quad 1 \text{ square unit} = \frac{a}{\pi r^2}.$$

Example 4·16. *Represent the data of Example 4·15 by a circular diagram.*

Solution. The data of Example 4·15 can be represented by a circular diagram on taking the lengths of the sides of the squares which were taken in Example 4·15, as the radii of the corresponding circles. However, in this case, the scale will be modified accordingly.

$$\textbf{Scale :} \ 1 \text{ sq. cm.} = \frac{350}{\pi} = \frac{2450}{22} = 111·36 \text{ kg.}$$

YIELD IN KG (PER HECTARE)

SCALE : 1 sq. cm. = 111·36 kg.

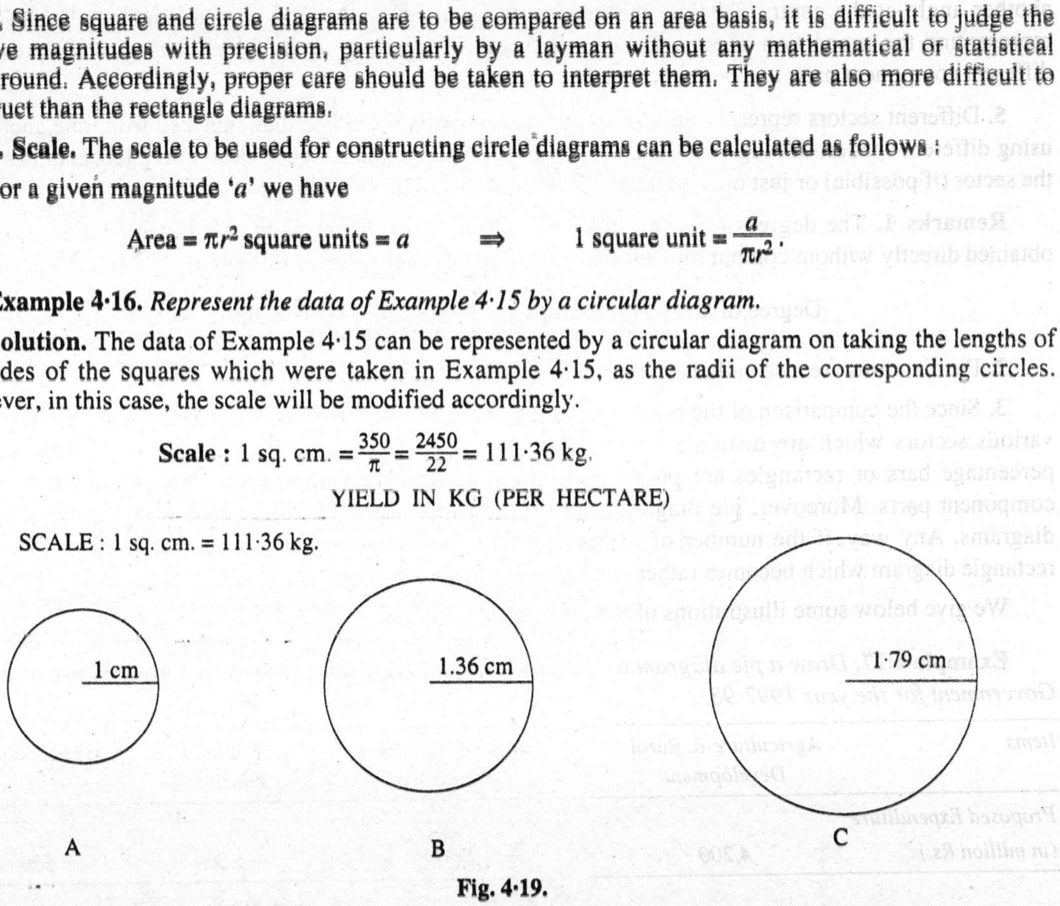

Fig. 4·19.

(D) Angular or Pie Diagram. Just as sub-divided and percentage bars or rectangles are used to represent the total magnitude and its various components, the circle (representing the total) may be divided into various sections or segments *viz.*, sectors representing certain proportion or percentage of the various component parts to the total. Such a sub-divided circle diagram is known as an **angular or pie diagram,** named so because the various segments resemble slices cut from a pie.

Steps for Construction of Pie Diagram

1. Express each of the component values as a percentage of the respective total.

2. Since the angle at the centre of the circle is 360°, the total magnitude of the various components is taken to be equal to 360° and each component part is to be expressed proportionately in degrees. Since 1 per cent of the total value is equal to 360/100 = 3·6°, the percentage of the component parts obtained in step 1 can be converted to degrees by multiplying each of them by 3·6.

3. Draw a circle of appropriate radius using an appropriate scale depending on the space available. If only one category or characteristic is to be used, the circle may be drawn of any radius. However, if two or more sets of data are to be presented simultaneously for comparative studies, then the radii of the corresponding circles are to be proportional to the square roots of their total magnitudes.

4. Having drawn the circle, draw any radius (preferably horizontal). Now with this radius as the base line draw an angle at the centre [with the help of protractor (D)] equal to the degree represented by the first component, the new line drawn at the centre to form this angle will touch the circumference. The sector so obtained will represent the proportion of the first component. From this second line as base, now draw another angle at the centre equal to the degree represented by the 2nd component, to give the sector representing the proportion of the second component. Proceeding similarly, all the sectors representing different component parts can be constructed.

5. Different sectors representing various component parts should be distinguished from one another by using different shades, dottings, colours, etc., or giving them explanatory or descriptive labels either inside the sector (if possible) or just outside the circle with proper identification.

Remarks 1. The degrees represented by the various component parts of a given magnitude can be obtained directly without computing their percentage to the total value as follows :

$$\text{Degree of any component part} = \frac{\text{Component value}}{\text{Total value}} \times 360°.$$

2. Pie diagrams are also called *circular* diagrams.

3. Since the comparison of the pie diagrams is to be made on the basis of the areas of the circles and of various sectors which are difficult to be ascertained visually with precision, generally sub-divided or percentage bars or rectangles are preferred to pie diagrams for studying the changes in the total and component parts. Moreover, pie diagrams are difficult to construct as compared with bars or rectangle diagrams. Any way, if the number of component parts is more than 10, pie chart is preferred to bar or rectangle diagram which becomes rather confusing in such a situation.

We give below some illustrations of pie diagrams.

Example 4·17. *Draw a pie diagram to represent the following data of proposed expenditure by a State Government for the year 1997-98.*

Items	*Agriculture & Rural Development*	*Industries & Urban Development*	*Health & Education*	*Miscellaneous*
Proposed Expenditure (in million Rs.)	*4,200*	*1,500*	*1,000*	*500*

[*Delhi Univ. B.Com. (Pass), 1997*]

Solution.

CALCULATIONS FOR PIE CHART

Items	*Proposed expenditure (in million Rs.)*	*Angle at the centre*
(1)	(2)	$(3) = \frac{(2)}{7200} \times 360°$
Agriculture and Rural Development	4,200	$\frac{42}{72} \times 360° = 210°$
Industries and Urban Development	1,500	$\frac{15}{72} \times 360° = 75°$
Health and Education	1,000	$\frac{10}{72} \times 360° = 50°$
Miscellaneous	500	$\frac{5}{72} \times 360° = 25°$
Total	7,200	360°

PIE DIAGRAM REPRESENTING PROPOSED EXPENDITURE BY STATE GOVERNMENT ON DIFFERENT ITEMS FOR 1997-98

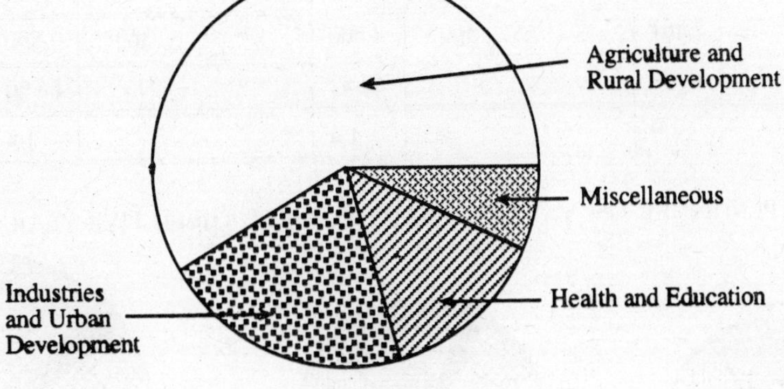

Fig. 4·20.

Example 4·18. *The following data shows the expenditure on various heads in the first three five-year plans (in crores of rupees).*

Subject	*Expenditure (in crores Rs.)*		
	First Plan	*Second Plan*	*Third Plan*
Agriculture and C.D.	361	529	1068
Irrigation and Power	561	865	1662
Village and Small Industries	173	176	264
Industry and Minerals	292	900	1520
Transport and Communications	497	1300	1486
Social Services and Miscellaneous	477	830	1500
Total	2361	4600	7500

Represent the data by angular (pie) diagrams.

Solution.

CALCULATIONS FOR PIE DIAGRAMS

Items of Expenditure	*Expenditure (in crores Rupees)*					
	First Plan		*Second Plan*		*Third Plan*	
	Rs.	*Degrees*	*Rs.*	*Degrees*	*Rs.*	*Degrees*
Agriculture and C.D.	361	$\frac{361}{2361} \times 360° = 55{\cdot}1°$	529	$\frac{529}{4600} \times 360° = 41{\cdot}4°$	1,068	$\frac{1068}{7500} \times 360° = 51{\cdot}2°$
Irrigation and Power	561	$\frac{561}{2361} \times 360° = 85{\cdot}5°$	865	$\frac{865}{4600} \times 360° = 67.7°$	1,662	$\frac{1662}{7500} \times 360° = 79{\cdot}8°$
Village and Small Industries	173	$\frac{173}{2361} \times 360° = 26{\cdot}4°$	176	$\frac{176}{4600} \times 360° = 13{\cdot}8°$	264	$\frac{264}{7500} \times 360° = 12{\cdot}7°$
Industry and Minerals	292	$\frac{292}{2361} \times 360° = 44{\cdot}5°$	900	$\frac{900}{4600} \times 360° = 70{\cdot}4°$	1,520	$\frac{1520}{7500} \times 360° = 73{\cdot}0°$
Transport and Communications	497	$\frac{497}{2361} \times 360° = 75{\cdot}8°$	1300	$\frac{1300}{4600} \times 360° = 101{\cdot}7°$	1,486	$\frac{1486}{7500} \times 360° = 71{\cdot}3°$
Social Services and Miscellaneous	477	$\frac{477}{2361} \times 360° = 72{\cdot}7°$	830	$\frac{830}{4600} \times 360° = 65{\cdot}0°$	1,500	$\frac{1500}{7500} \times 360° = 72{\cdot}0°$
Total	2,361	360°	4,600	360°	7,500	360°
Square Root	48·59		67·82		86·60	
Radii of circles	1·0		1·4		1·8	

EXPENDITURE ON VARIOUS HEADS IN FIRST THREE FIVE-YEAR PLANS

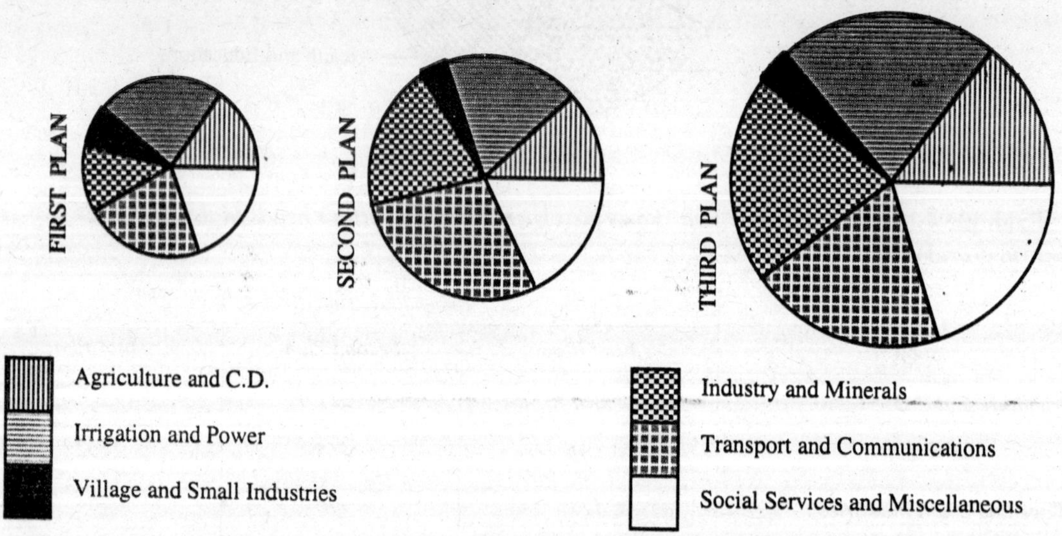

Fig. 4·21.

4·3·5. Three-Dimensional Diagrams. Three-dimensional diagrams, also termed as *volume* diagrams are those in which three dimensions, *viz.*, length, breadth and height are taken into account. They are constructed so that the given magnitudes are represented by the volumes of the corresponding diagrams. The common forms of such diagrams are cubes, spheres, cylinders, blocks, etc. These diagrams are specially useful if there are very wide variations between the smallest and the largest magnitudes to be represented. Of the various three-dimensional diagrams, '*cubes*' are the simplest and most commonly used devices of diagrammatic presentation of the data.

Cubes. For instance, if the smallest and the largest magnitudes to be presented are in the ratio of 1 : 1000, the bar diagrams cannot be used because the height of the biggest bar would be 1000 times the height of the smallest bar and thus they would look very disproportionate and clumsy. On the other hand, if square or circle diagrams are used then the sides (radii) of the squares (circles) will be in the ratio of the square roots *viz.*, $1 : \sqrt{1000}$ *i.e.*, 1 : 31·63 *i.e.*, 1 : 32 (approx.), which will again give quite disproportionate diagrams. However, if cubes are used to present this data, then since the volume of cube of side x is x^3, the sides of the cubes will be in the ratio of their cube roots *viz.*, $1 : \sqrt[3]{1000}$ *i.e.*, 1 : 10, which will give reasonably proportionate diagrams as compared to one-dimensional or two-dimensional diagrams.

Construction of a Cube of Side 'x'. The various steps are outlined below :

1. Construct a square ABCD of side x.

2. Draw EF as right bisector *i.e.*, perpendicular bisector of AB, [This is done by finding the mid-point of AB and then drawing perpendicular at that point to the line AB] such that EF = AB and half of it is above AB and half of it is below AB.

(*iii*) Join AE, CF and EF.

(*iv*) Through B draw a line BG parallel to AE (*i.e.*, BG || AE) such that BG = AE.

(*v*) Join EG and through G draw a line GH || EF such that GH = EF.

(*vi*) Join D and H.

(*vii*) Rub off the lines CF, EF and FH. Now CDHGEAC is the required cube.

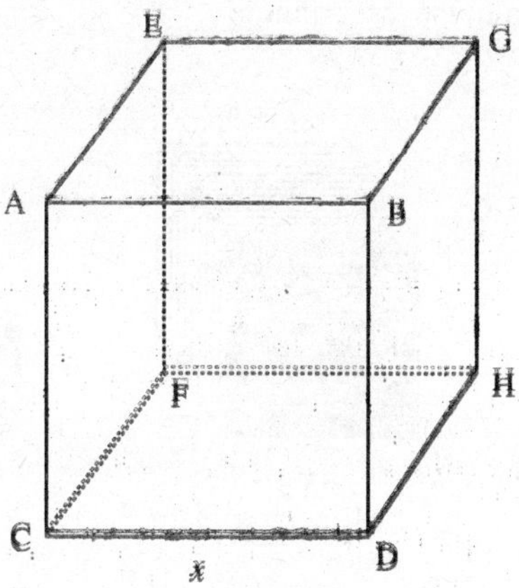

Fig. 4·22

Remarks 1. As already discussed, three-dimensional diagrams are used with advantage over one or two-dimensional diagrams if the range *i.e.*, the gap between the smallest and the largest observation to be presented, is very large. Moreover, they are more beautiful and appealing to the eye than bars, rectangles, squares or circles. However, since three-dimensional diagrams are quite difficult to construct and comprehend as compared to one-or two-dimensional diagrams, they are not very popular. Further, as the magnitudes are represented by the volumes of the cubes (volumes of the three-dimensional diagrams, in general), it is very difficult to visualise and hence interpret them with precision.

2. Cylinders, spheres and blocks are quite difficult to construct and are, therefore, not discussed here.

3. It is worthwhile pointing out here that now-a-days projection techniques are used to represent even one-dimensional diagrams as three-dimensional diagrams for giving them a beautiful and attractive get up.

Example 4·19. *The following table gives the population of India on the basis of religion.*

Religion	*Hinduism*	*Islam*	*Christianity*	*Sikhism*	*Others*
Number (in lakhs)	*2031·9*	*354·0*	*81·6*	*62·2*	*36·3*

Represent the data by cubes.

Solution. The sides of the cubes will be proportional to the cube roots of the magnitudes they represent.

Note. To compute cube root of a, *viz.*, $\sqrt[3]{a}$ or $a^{1/3}$, let $y = \sqrt[3]{a} = a^{1/3}$

Taking logarithm of both sides : $\log y = \frac{1}{3} \log_{10} a \Rightarrow y = \text{Antilog}\left[\frac{1}{3} \log_{10} a\right]$

COMPUTATION OF CUBE ROOTS

a	$log_{10}\,a$	$\frac{1}{3}log_{10}\,a$	Anti-log $[\frac{1}{3}\,log_{10}a]$	Ratio of sides
2031·9	3·3079	1·1026	12·67	3·83 ≃ 3·8
354·0	2·5441	0·8480	7·047	2·13 ≃ 2·1
81·6	1·9117	0·6372	4·337	1·31 ≃ 1·3
62·2	1·7938	0·5979	3·962	1·19 ≃ 1·2
36·3	1·5599	0·5199	3·311	1

Now we can express the data diagrammatically by drawing cubes with sides proportional to the values given in the last column.

Scale : $\frac{1}{8}$ cms^3 = 36·3 lakhs

Fig. 4·23.

4·3·6. Pictograms. Pictograms is the technique of presenting statistical data through appropriate pictures and is one of the very popular devices particularly when the statistical facts are to be presented to a layman without any mathematical background. In this, the magnitudes of the particular phenomenon under study are presented through appropriate pictures, the number of pictures drawn or the size of the pictures being proportional to the values of the different magnitudes to be presented. Pictures are more attractive and appealing to the eye and have a lasting impression on the mind. Accordingly they are extensively used by government and private institutions for diagrammatic presentation of the data relating to a variety of social, business or economic phenomena primarily for display to the general public or common masses in fairs and exhibitions.

Remark. Pictograms have their limitations also. They are difficult and time-consuming to construct. In pictogram, each pictorial symbol represents a fixed number of units like thousands, millions or crores, etc. For instance, in Example 4·20 which displays the number of vessels in the Indian Merchant Shipping fleet, one ship symbol represents 50 vessels and it is really a problem to represent and read fractions of 50. For example, 174 vessels will be represented in pictograms by 3 ships and about a half more ; 231 vessels will be represented in pictogram by 4 ships and a proportionate fraction of the 5th. This proportionate representation introduces error and is quite difficult to visualise with precision. We give below some illustrations of pictograms.

The following table gives the number of students studying in schools/colleges for different years in India.

STUDENTS ON ROLL AT THE SCHOOL / UNIVERSITY STAGE
(As on 31st March) *(In Million)*

Stage ↓	*1960-61*	*1965-66*	*1970-71*	*1974-75*	*1975-76*
Class I to XI	44·73	66·29	76·95	87·30	89·46
University/College	0·73	1·24	2·81	2·94	3·21

Source : Ministry of Education and Social Welfare.

The data can be represented in the diagrammatic form by pictogram (pictures) as given below :

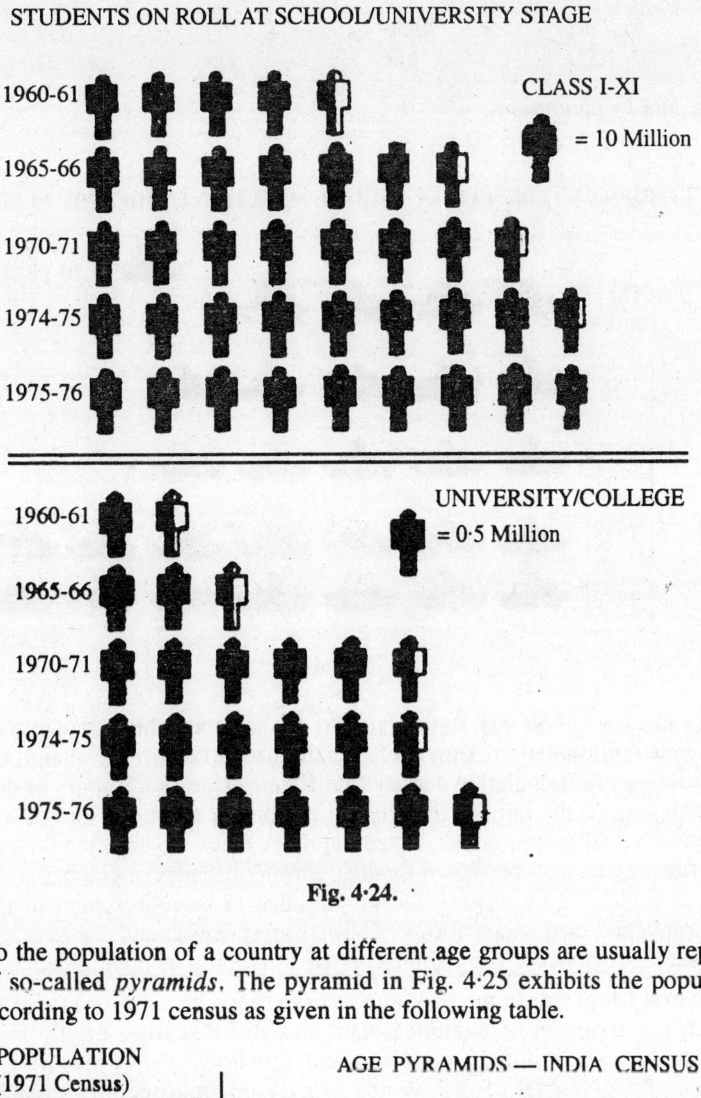

Fig. 4·24.

Data pertaining to the population of a country at different age groups are usually represented through pictures by means of so-called *pyramids*. The pyramid in Fig. 4·25 exhibits the population of India at various age-groups according to 1971 census as given in the following table.

DISTRIBUTION OF POPULATION BY AGE GROUPS (1971 Census)

Age-group	*Population (in '000)*
Under 1	16,519
1— 4	63,040
5—14	1,50,776
15—24	90,569
25—34	77,010
35—44	61,186
45—54	43,416
55—64	27,202
65—74	12,880
75 and over	5,446

Source : Registrar General of India.

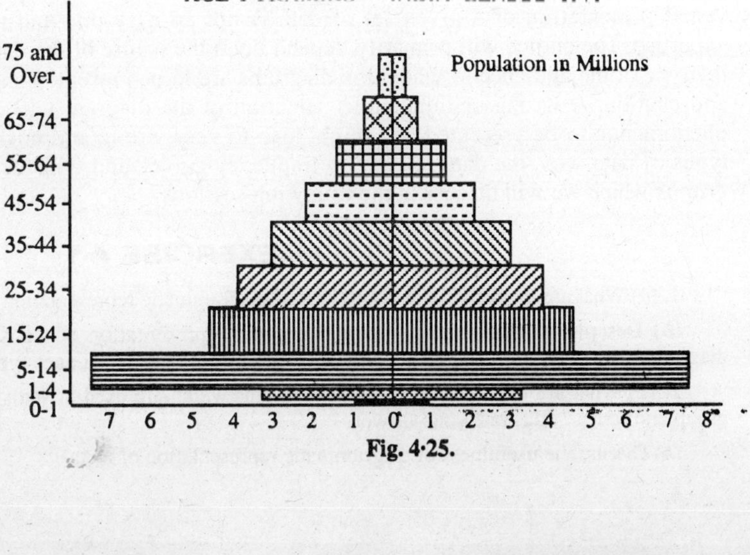

Fig. 4·25.

Example 4·20. *The following table gives the number of vessels as on 31st December, in Indian Merchant Shipping fleet for different years.*

Year	*1961*	*1966*	*1971*	*1975*	*1976*
No. of vessels	*174*	*231*	*255*	*330*	*359*

Represent the data by pictogram.

Solution.

NUMBER OF VESSELS IN INDIAN MERCHANT SHIPPING FLEET

Fig. 4·26.

4·3·7. Cartograms. In cartograms, statistical facts are presented through maps accompanied by various types of diagrammatic representation. They are specially used to depict the quantitative facts on a regional or geographical basis *e.g.*, the population density of different states in a country or different countries in the world, or the distribution of the rainfall in different regions of a country can be shown with the help of maps or cartograms. The different regions or geographical zones are depicted on a map and the quantities or magnitudes in the regions may be shown by dots, different shades or colours etc., or by placing bars or pictograms in each region or by writing the magnitudes to be represented in the respective regions. Cartograms are simple and elementary forms of visual presentation and are easy to understand. They are generally used when the regional or geographic comparisons are to be highlighted.

4·3·8. Choice of a Diagram. In the previous sections we have described types of diagrams which can be used to present the given set of numerical data and also discussed briefly their relative merits and demerits. No single diagram is suited for all practical situations. The choice of a particular diagram for visual presentation of a given set of data is not an easy one and requires great skill, intelligence and expertise. The choice will primarily depend upon the nature of the data and the object of presentation, *i.e.*, the type of the audience to whom the diagrams are to be presented and it should be made with utmost care and caution. A wrong or injudicious selection of the diagram will distort the true characteristics of the phenomenon to be presented and might lead to very wrong and misleading interpretations. Some special types of data, *viz.*, the data relating to frequency curves and time series are best represented by means of *graphs* which we will discuss in the following sections.

EXERCISE 4·1

1. (*a*) What are the merits and limitations of diagrammatic representation of statistical data ?

(*b*) Describe the advantages of diagrammatic representation of statistical data. Name the different types of diagrams commonly used and mention the situations where the use of each type of diagram would be appropriate.

2. (*a*) What are the different types of diagrams which are used in statistics to show the salient characteristics of group and series ? Illustrate your answer.

(*b*) Discuss the usefulness of diagrammatic representation of facts.

3. "Diagrams do not add anything to the meaning of Statistics but when drawn and studied intelligently, they bring to view the salient characteristics of the data". Explain.

4. "Diagrams help us visualize the whole meaning of a numerical complex data at a single glance." Explain the statement. [*Delhi Univ. B.Com. (Pass), 1999*]

5. The merits of diagrammatic presentation of data are classified under three heads : attraction, effective impression and comparison. Explain and illustrate these points.

6. (*a*) State the different methods used for diagrammatic representation of statistical data and indicate briefly the advantages and disadvantages of each one of them.

(*b*) Point out the usefulness of diagrammatic representation of facts and explain the construction of any of the different forms of diagrams you know.

(*c*) A Bar diagram and a Rectangular diagram have the same appearance. Do they belong to the same category of diagrams ? Explain. [*Delhi Univ. B.Com. (Pass), 1998*]

7. What types of mistakes are commonly committed in the construction of diagrams ? What precautions are necessary in this connection ?

8. (*a*) Draw a bar chart to represent the following information :

Year	1952	1957	1962	1967	1972	1977
No. of women M.P.'s	22	27	34	31	22	19

(*b*) In a recent study on causes of strikes in mills, an experimenter collected the following data.

Causes :	*Economic*	*Personal*	*Political*	*Rivalry*	*Others*
Occurrences (in percentage) :	58	16	10	6	10

Represent the data by bar chart.

9. Represent the following data by a percentage sub-divided bar-diagram :

Item of Expenditure	*Family A (Income Rs. 500)*	*Family B (Income Rs. 300)*
Food	150	150
Clothes	125	60
Education	25	50
Miscellaneous	190	70
Saving or Deficit	+10	–30

10. (*a*) Construct a multiple bar graph to represent Imports and Exports of a country for the following years :

Year	*1992-93*	*1993-94*	*1994-95*	*1995-96*	*1996-97*
Imports (In billion rupees)	19	30	45	53	51
Exports (In billion rupees)	20	25	33	40	51

(*b*) Draw a suitable diagram to present the following data :

	I Division	*II Division*	*III Division*	*Failures*	*Total No. of candidates*
1998	16	40	60	44	160
1999	12	44	72	34	162

11. Represent the following data by a sub-divided bar diagram :

College	*No. of Students*				
	Arts	*Science*	*Commerce*	*Agriculture*	*Total*
A	1200	800	600	400	3000
B	750	500	300	450	2000

12. Draw a rectangular diagram to represent the following information :

	Factory A	*Factory B*
Price per unit	Rs. 15·00	Rs. 12·00
Units produced	1000 Nos.	1200 Nos.
Raw material/unit	Rs. 5·00	Rs. 5·00
Other expenses/unit	Rs. 4·00	Rs. 3·00
Profit/unit	Rs. 6·00	Rs. 4·00

13. Represent the following data by a deviation bar diagram :

	Years					
	1994	*1995*	*1996*	*1997*	*1998*	*1999*
Income *(in crores of Rs.)*	15	16	17	18	19	20
Expenditure *(in crores of Rs.)*	18	17	16	20	17	18

[Delhi Univ. B.Com. (Pass), 2002]

14. (*a*) What do you mean by two-dimensional diagrams ? Under what situations they are preferred to one-dimensional diagrams ?

(*b*) Describe the (*i*) square and (*ii*) circle diagrams. Discuss their merits and demerits.

(*c*) What do you understand by Pie diagrams. Discuss the technique of constructing such diagrams.

15. The following table gives the average approximate yield of rice in kg. per acre in three different countries. Draw square diagrams to represent the data :

Country	A	B	C
Yield in (kg.) per acre	350	647	1120

16. Represent the following data on production of Tea, Cocoa and Coffee by means of a pie diagram.

Tea	Cocoa	Coffee	Total
3,260 tons	1,850 tons	900 tons	6,010 tons

17. (*a*) Point out the usefulness of diagrammatic representation of facts and explain the construction of volume and pie diagrams.

(*b*) A Rupee spent on 'Khadi' is distributed as follows :

	Paise
Farmer	19
Carder and Spinner	35
Weaver	28
Washerman, Dyer and Printer	8
Administrative Agency	10
Total	100

Present the data in the form of a pie diagram.

(*c*) Draw a pie diagram for the following data of Sixth Five-Year Plan Public Sector outlays:

Agriculture and Rural Development	12·9%
Irrigation, etc.	12·5%
Energy	27·2%
Industry and Minerals	15·4%
Transport, Communication, etc.	15·9%
Social Services and Others	16·1%

(Bangalore Univ. B.Com., 1997)

18. Draw a Pie diagram to represent the distribution of a certain blood group 'O' among Gypsies, Indians and Hungarians.

	Frequency			
Blood group	*Gypsies*	*Indians*	*Hungarians*	*Total*
'O'	343	313	344	1000

19. (*a*) Represent the following data by means of circular diagrams.

	No. of Employed			
Year	*Men*	*Women*	*Children*	*Total*
1951	1,80,000	1,10,000	70,000	3,60,000
1961	3,50,000	2,10,000	1,60,000	7,20,000

(*b*) Represent the following data by Pie diagram.

Items of Expenditure	*Expenditure (in Rs.)*	
	Family A	*Family B*
Food	150	120
Clothing	100	80
Rent and Education	120	80
Fuel and Electricity	80	40
Others	90	40

20. The areas of the various continents of the world in millions of square miles are presented below :

AREAS OF CONTINENTS OF THE WORLD

Continent :	Africa	Asia	Europe	North America	Oceania	South America	U.S.S.R	Total
Area (Millions of square miles) :	11·7	10·4	1·9	9·4	3·3	6·9	7·9	51·5

Represent the data by a Pie diagram.

4·4. GRAPHIC REPRESENTATION OF DATA

The difference between the diagrams and graphs has been discussed in §4·2. To summarise, diagrams are useful for visual presentation of categorical and geographical data while the data relating to time series and frequency distributions is best represented through graphs. Diagrams are primarily used for comparative studies and can't be used to study the relationship, (not necessarily functional), between the variables under study. This is done through graphs. Diagrams furnish only approximate information and are not of much utility to a statistician from analysis point of view. On the other hand, graphs are more obvious, precise and accurate than diagrams and can be effectively used for further statistical analysis, *viz.*, to study slopes, rates of change and for forecasting wherever possible. Graphs are drawn on a special type of paper, known as *graph paper*. The advantages of graphic representation of a set of numerical data have also been discussed in § 4·1.

Like diagrams, a large number of graphs are used in practice. But they can be broadly classified under the following two heads :

(*i*) Graphs of Frequency Distributions.

(*ii*) Graphs of Time Series.

Before discussing these graphs we shall briefly describe the technique of constructing graphs and the general rules for drawing graphs.

4·4·1. Technique of Construction of Graphs. Graphs are drawn on a special type of paper known as graph paper which has a fine net work of horizontal and vertical lines; the thick lines for each division of a centimetre or an inch measure and thin lines for small parts of the same. In a graph of any size, two simple lines are drawn at right angle to each other, intersecting at point 'O' which is known as *origin* or *zero of reference*. The two lines are known as *co-ordinate axes*. The horizontal line is called the *X-axis* and is denoted by X′OX. The vertical line is called the *Y-axis* and is usually denoted by YOY′. Thus, the graph is divided into four sections, known as the four *quadrants*, but in practice only the first quadrant is generally used unless negative magnitudes are to be displayed. Along the X-axis, the distances measured towards right of the origin *i.e.*, towards right of the line YOY′, are positive and the distances measured towards left of origin *i.e.*, towards left of the line YOY′ are negative, the origin showing

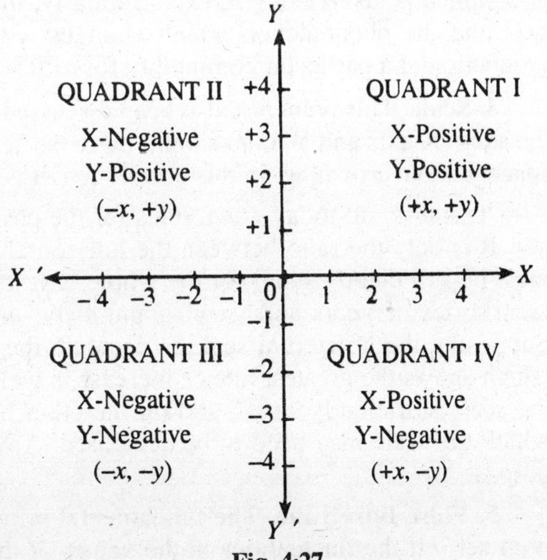

Fig. 4·27.

the value zero. Along the Y-axis, the distances above the origin *i.e.*, above the line X'OX are positive and the distances below the origin *i.e.*, below the line X'OX are negative. Any pair of the values of the variables is represented by a point (x, y), x usually represents the value of the independent variable and is shown along the X-axis and y represents the value of the dependent variable and is shown along the Y-axis. The four quadrants along the position of x and y values are shown in the Fig. 4·27.

In any pair (a, b), first coordinate, *viz.*, 'a' always refers to the ***X-coordinate*** which is also known as ***abscissa*** and the second coordinate, *viz.*, 'b' always refers to the ***Y-coordinate*** which is also known as ***ordinate***. As an illustration the points $P(4, 2)$, $Q(-3, 4)$, $R(3, -2)$ and $S(-2, -3)$ are displayed in the Fig. 4·28.

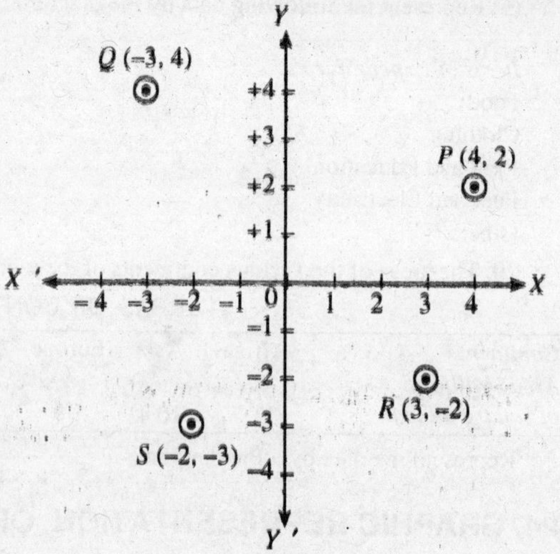

Fig. 4·28.

In the graph on a natural or arithmetic scale, the equal magnitudes of the values of the variables are represented by equal distances along both the axes, though the scales along X-axis and Y-axis may be different depending on the nature of the phenomenon under consideration.

4·4·2. General Rules for Graphing. The following guidelines (some of which have already been discussed in § 4·3·1 for diagrammatic representation of data), may be kept in mind for drawing effective and accurate graphs :

1. Neatness. (For details see § 4·3·1 page 4.2).

2. Title and Footnote (For details see § 4·3·1 page 4.2).

3. Structural Framework. The position of the axes should be so chosen that the graph gives an attractive and proportionate get up. It should be kept in mind that for each and every value of the independent variable, there is a corresponding value of the dependent variable. In drawing the graph it is customary to plot the independent variable along the X-axis and the dependent variable along the Y-axis. For instance, if the data pertaining to the prices of the commodity and the quantity demanded or supplied at different prices is to be plotted, then the dependent variable, *viz.*, price (which depends on independent forces of supply and demand) is taken along Y-axis while the independent variable *viz.*, quantity demanded or supplied is taken along X-axis. Similarly, in case of time series data, the time factor is taken along X-axis and the phenomenon which changes with time *e.g.*, population of a country in different years, production of a particular commodity for different periods, etc., is taken along Y-axis.

4. Scale. This point has also been discussed in § 4·3·1. It may further be added that the scale along both the axes (X-axis and Y-axis) should be so chosen that the entire data can be accommodated in the available space without crowding. In this connection, it is worthwhile to quote the words of A. L. Bowley :

"It is difficult to lay down rules for the proper choice of scales by which the figures should be plotted out. It is only the ratio between the horizontal and vertical scales that need to be considered. The figure must be sufficiently small for the whole of it to be visible at once : if the figure is complicated, related to long series of years and varying numbers, minute accuracy must be sacrificed to this consideration. Supposing the horizontal scale is decided, the vertical scale must be chosen so that the part of the line which shows the greatest rate of increase is well inclined to the vertical which can be managed by making the scale sufficiently small; and on the other hand, all important fluctuations must be clearly visible for which the scale may need to be decreased. Any scale which satisfies both these conditions will fulfill its purpose."

5. False Base Line. The fundamental principle of drawing graph is that the vertical scale must start with zero. If the fluctuations in the values of the dependent variable (to be shown along Y-axis) are very small relative to their magnitudes, and if the minimum of these values is very distant (far greater) from zero, the point of origin, then for an effective portrayal of these fluctuations the vertical scale is stretched by using *false base line*. In such a situation the vertical scale is broken and the space between the origin 'O' and the minimum value (or some convenient value near that) of the dependent variable is omitted by drawing two zig-zag horizontal lines above the base line. The scale along Y-axis is then framed accordingly. False base line technique is quite extensively used for magnifying the minor fluctuations in a time series data. It also economises space because if such data are graphed without using false base line, then the plotted data will lie on the top of the graph. This will give a very clumsy look and also result in wastage of space. However, proper care should be taken to interpret graphs in which false base line is used. As illustrations, see Examples 4·31 and 4·32 in § 4·4·4.

6. Ratio or Logarithmic Scale. In order to display proportional or relative changes in the magnitudes, the ratio or logarithmic scale should be used instead of natural or arithmetic scale which is used to display absolute changes. Ratio scale is discussed in detail in § 4·4·5.

7. Line Designs. If more than one variable is to be depicted on the same graph, the different graphs so obtained should be distinguished from each other by the use of different lines, *viz.*, dotted lines, broken lines, dash-dot lines, thin or thick lines, etc., and an index to identify them should be given. [See Examples 4·31 and 4·32].

8. Sources Note and Number. For details see § 4·3·1.

9. Index. For details see § 4·3·1.

10. Simplicity. For details, see § 4·3·1.

Remark. For detailed discussion on items 1, 2, 4, 8, 9 and 10, see § 4·3·1 replacing the word 'diagram' by 'graphs'.

4·4·3. Graphs of Frequency Distributions. The reasons and the guiding principles for the graphic representation of the frequency distributions are precisely the same as for the diagrammatic and graphic representation of other types of data. The so-called *frequency graphs* are designed to reveal clearly the characteristic features of a frequency data. Such graphs are more appealing to the eye than the tabulated data and are readily perceptible to the mind. They facilitate comparative study of two or more frequency distributions regarding their shape and pattern. The most commonly used graphs for charting a frequency distribution for the general understanding of the details of the data are :

(*A*) Histogram. (*B*) Frequency Polygon.

(*C*) Frequency Curve. (*D*) "Ogive" or Cumulative Frequency Curve.

The choice of a particular graph for a given frequency distribution largely depends on the nature of the frequency distribution, *viz.*, discrete or continuous. In the following sections we shall discuss them in details, one by one.

A. HISTOGRAM

It is one of the most popular and commonly used devices for charting *continuous* frequency distribution. It consists in erecting a series of adjacent vertical rectangles on the sections of the horizontal axis (X-axis), with bases (sections) equal to the width of the corresponding class intervals and heights are so taken that the areas of the rectangles are equal to the frequencies of the corresponding classes.

Construction of Histogram. The variate values are taken along the X-axis and the frequencies along the Y-axis.

Case (*i*) *Histogram with equal classes*. In the case, if classes are of equal magnitude throughout, each class interval is drawn on the X-axis by a section or base (of the rectangle) which is equal (or proportional) to the magnitude of the class interval. On each class interval (as base) erect a rectangle with the height proportional to the corresponding frequency of the class. The series of adjacent rectangles (one for each class), so formed gives the histogram of the frequency distribution and its area represents the total frequency of the distribution as distributed throughout the different classes. The procedure is explained in Example 4.21.

Case (*ii*) *Histogram with unequal classes*. If all the classes are not uniform throughout; as in case (*i*) the different classes are represented on the X-axis by sections or bases which are equal (or proportional) to the magnitudes of the corresponding classes and the heights of the corresponding rectangles are to be adjusted so that the area of the rectangle is equal to the frequency of the corresponding class. This adjustment can be done by taking the height of each rectangle proportional (equal) to the corresponding *frequency density* of each class which is obtained on dividing the frequency of the class by its magnitude, *viz.*,

$$\text{Frequency Density (of a class)} = \frac{\text{Frequency of the class}}{\text{Magnitude of the class}}.$$

Instead of finding the frequency density a more convenient way (from the practical point of view) is to make all the class intervals equal and then adjust the corresponding frequency by using the basic assumption that all the frequencies are distributed uniformly throughout the class. This consists in taking the lowest class interval as standard one with unit length on the X-axis. The adjusted frequencies of the different classes are obtained on dividing the frequency of the given class by the corresponding Adjustment Factor (A.F.) which is given by :

$$\text{A.F. for any class} = \frac{\text{Magnitude of the class}}{\text{Lowest class interval}}.$$

Thus, if the magnitude of any class interval is twice (three) the lowest class interval, the adjustment factor is 2(3) and the height of the rectangle which is represented by the adjusted frequency will be $\frac{1}{2}\left(\frac{1}{3}\text{rd}\right)$ of the corresponding class frequency and so on. This is illustrated in Example 4·22. This adjustment gives the rectangles whose areas are equal to the frequencies of the corresponding classes.

Remarks 1. *Grouped (Not Continuous) Frequency Distribution.* It should be clearly understood that histogram can be drawn only if the frequency distribution is continuous. In case of grouped frequency distribution, if classes are not continuous, they should be made continuous by changing the class limits into class boundaries and then rectangles should be erected on the continuous classes so obtained. As an illustration, see Example 4·24.

2. *Mid-points given.* Sometimes, only the mid-values of different classes are given. In such a case, the given distribution is converted into continuous frequency distribution with exclusive type classes by ascertaining the upper and lower limits of the various classes under the assumption that the class frequencies are uniformly distributed throughout each class. (See Example 4·25.)

3. *Discrete Frequency Distribution.* Histograms, may sometimes also be used to represent discrete frequency distribution by regarding the given values of the variable as the mid-points of continuous classes and then proceeding as explained in Remark 2 above.

4. *Difference between Histogram and Bar Diagram.* (*i*) A histogram is a two-dimensional (area) diagram where both the width (base) and the length (height of the rectangle) are important whereas bar diagram is one-dimensional diagram in which only length (height of the bar) matters while width is arbitrary.

(*ii*) In a histogram, the bars (rectangles) are adjacent to each other whereas in bar diagram proper spacing is given between different bars.

(*iii*) In a histogram, the class frequencies are represented by the area of the rectangles while in a bar diagram they are represented by the heights of the corresponding bars.

5. *Open-end classes.* Histograms can't be constructed for frequency distributions with open end classes unless we assume that the magnitude of the first open class is same as that of the succeeding (second) class and the magnitude of the last open class is same as that of the preceding (*i.e.*, last but one) class.

6. Histogram may be used for the graphic location of the value of Mode (See Chapter 5).

Example 4·21. *Draw histogram for the following frequency distribution.*

Variable :	*10—20*	*20—30*	*30—40*	*40—50*	*50—60*	*60—70*	*70—80*
Frequency :	12	30	35	65	45	25	18

Solution.

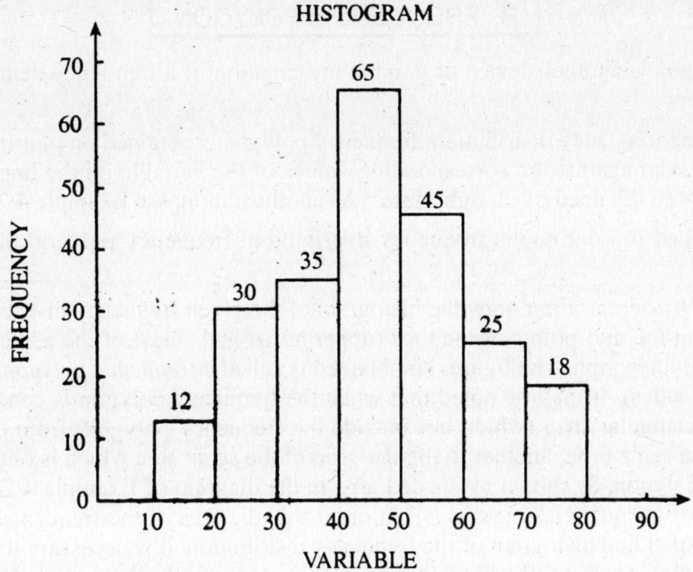

Fig. 4·29.

Example 4·22. *Represent the following data by means of a histogram.*

Weekly Wages ('00 Rs.) :	*10—15*	*15—20*	*20—25*	*25—30*	*30—40*	*40—60*	*60—80*
No. of Workers :	*7*	*19*	*27*	*15*	*12*	*12*	*8*

Solution. Since the class intervals are of unequal magnitude, the corresponding frequencies have to be adjusted to obtain the so-called '*frequency density*' so that the area of the rectangle erected on the class interval is equal to the class frequency. We observe that first four classes are of magnitude 5, the class 30—40 is of magnitude 10 and the last two classes 40—60 and 60—80 are of magnitude 20. Since 5 is the minimum class interval, the frequency of the class 30—40 is divided by 2 and the frequencies of classes 40—60 and 60—80 are to be divided by 4 as shown in the adjoining table.

Weekly Wages ('00 Rs.)	*No. of Workers (f)*	*Magnitude of Class*	*Height of Rectangle*
10—15	7	5	7
15—20	19	5	19
20—25	27	5	27
25—30	15	5	15
30—40	12	10	(12/2) = 6
40—60	12	20	(12/4) = 3
60—80	8	20	(8/4) = 2

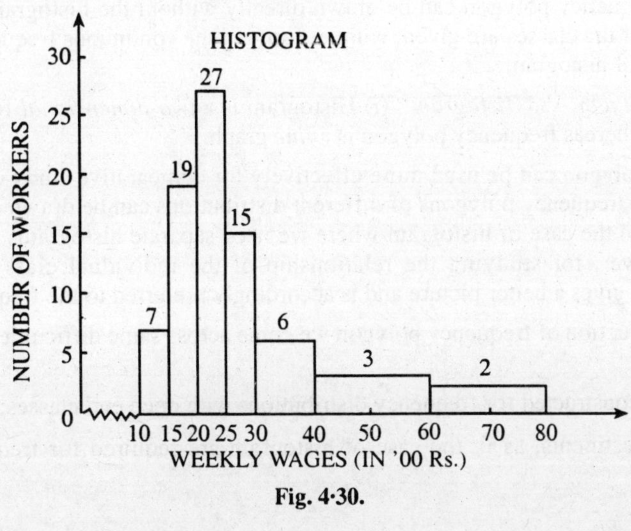

Fig. 4·30.

B. FREQUENCY POLYGON

Frequency polygon is another device of graphic presentation of a frequency distribution (continuous, grouped or discrete).

In case of discrete frequency distribution, frequency polygon is obtained on plotting the frequencies on the vertical axis (Y-axis) against the corresponding values of the variable on the horizontal axis (X-axis) and joining the points so obtained by straight lines. [As an illustration, see Example 4·23.]

In case of grouped or continuous frequency distribution, frequency polygon may be drawn in two ways.

Case (*i*) *From Histogram.* First draw the histogram of the given frequency distribution as explained in § 4·4·3 (A). Now join the mid-points of the tops (upper horizontal sides) of the adjacent rectangles of the histogram by straight line graph. The figures so obtained is called a *frequency polygon.* (Polygon is a figure with more than four sides). It may be noted that when the frequency polygon is constructed as explained above it cuts off a triangular strip (which lies outside the frequency polygon) from each rectangle of the histogram. But, at the same time, another triangular strip of the same area which is outside the histogram is included under the polygon, as shown by shaded area in the diagram of Example 4·28. [This, however, is not true in the case of unequal class intervals]. In order that the area of the frequency polygon is equal to the area of the corresponding histogram of the frequency distribution, it is necessary to close the polygon at both ends by extending them to the base line such that it meets the X-axis at the mid-points of two hypothetical classes, *viz.*, the class before the first class and the class after the last class, at both the ends each with frequency zero [See Examples 4·24 and 4·25].

Case (*ii*) *Without Constructing Histogram.* Frequency polygon of a grouped or continuous frequency distribution is a straight line graph which can also be constructed directly without drawing the histogram. This consists in plotting the frequencies of different classes (along Y-axis) against the mid-values of the corresponding classes (along X-axis). The points so obtained are joined by straight lines to obtain the frequency polygon. As in Case (*i*), the frequency polygon so obtained should be extended to the base at both ends by joining the extreme points (first and last point) to the mid-points of the two hypothetical classes (before the first class and after the last class) assumed to have zero frequencies. The figure of the frequency polygon so obtained would be exactly same as in Case (*i*) except for the histogram.

This point can be elaborated mathematically as follows. Let $x_1, x_2, \ldots, x_n$ be the mid-values of n classes with frequencies $f_1, f_2, \ldots, f_n$ respectively. We plot the points $(x_1, f_1), (x_2, f_2), \ldots, (x_n, f_n)$ on the co-ordinate axes, taking mid-values along X-axis and frequencies along Y-axis and join them by straight lines. The first point (x_1, f_1) is joined to the point $(x_0, 0)$ and the last point (x_n, f_n) to the point $(x_{n+1}, 0)$ by straight lines and the required frequency polygon is obtained.

Remarks 1. Frequency polygon can be drawn directly without the histogram (as explained above) if only the mid-points of the classes are given; without forming the continuous frequency distribution which is desirable in the case of histogram.

2. *Frequency Polygon Vs. Histogram* : (*i*) Histogram is a *two-dimensional* figure, *viz.*, a collection of adjacent rectangles whereas frequency polygon is a *line* graph.

(*ii*) Frequency polygon can be used more effectively for comparative study of two or more frequency distributions because frequency polygons of different distributions can be drawn on the same single graph. This is not possible in the case of histogram where we need separate histograms for each of the frequency distributions. However, for studying the relationship of the individual class frequencies to the total frequency, histogram gives a better picture and is accordingly preferred to the frequency polygon.

(*iii*) In the construction of frequency polygon we come across same difficulties as in the construction of histograms, *viz.*,

(*a*) It cannot be constructed for frequency distributions with open end classes; and

(*b*) Suitable adjustments, as in the case of histogram are required for frequency distributions with unequal classes.

(*iv*) Unlike histogram, frequency polygon is a continuous curve and therefore possesses all the distinct advantages of graphic representation, *viz.*, it may be used to determine the slope, rate of change, estimates (interpolation and extrapolation), etc., wherever admissible.

Example 4·23. *The following data show the number of accidents sustained by 313 drivers of a public utility company over a period of 5 years.*

Number of accidents :	*0*	*1*	*2*	*3*	*4*	*5*	*6*	*7*	*8*	*9*	*10*	*11*
Number of drivers	*80*	*44*	*68*	*41*	*25*	*20*	*13*	*7*	*5*	*4*	*3*	*2*

Draw the frequency polygon.

Solution. See Fig. 4·31

FREQUENCY POLYGON OF NUMBER OF ACCIDENTS

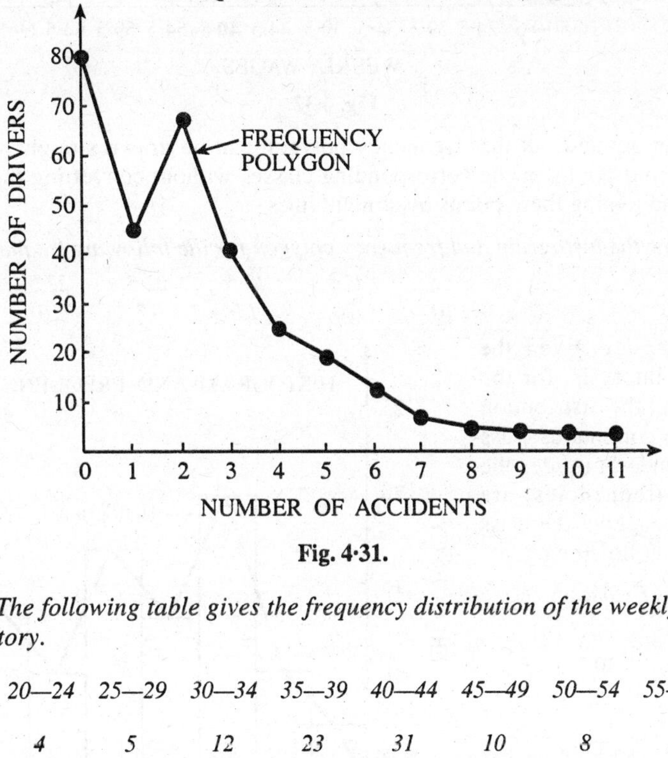

Fig. 4·31.

Example 4·24. *The following table gives the frequency distribution of the weekly wages (in '00 Rs.) of 100 workers in a factory.*

Weekly Wages ('00 Rs.)	*20—24*	*25—29*	*30—34*	*35—39*	*40—44*	*45—49*	*50—54*	*55—59*	*60—64*	*Total*
Number of Workers	*4*	*5*	*12*	*23*	*31*	*10*	*8*	*5*	*2*	*100*

Draw the histogram and frequency polygon of the distribution.

Solution. Since all the classes are of equal magnitude *i.e.,* 5, for the construction of the histogram, the heights of the rectangles to be erected on the classes will be proportional to their respective frequencies. However, since the classes are not continuous, the given distribution is to be converted into a continuous frequency distribution, with exclusive type classes before erecting the rectangles, as given in the following table.

Weekly Wages ('00 Rs.)	*19·5—24·5*	*24·5—29·5*	*29·5—34·5*	*34·5—39·5*	*39·5—44·5*	*44·5—49·5*	*49·5—54·5*	*54·5—59·5*	*59·5—64·5*
Number of Workers (f)	*4*	*5*	*12*	*23*	*31*	*10*	*8*	*5*	*2*

As usual, frequency polygon is obtained from histogram by joining the mid-points of the rectangles by straight lines, and extended both ways to the classes 14·5—19·5 and 64·5—69·5 on the X-axis, as shown in the Fig. 4·32.

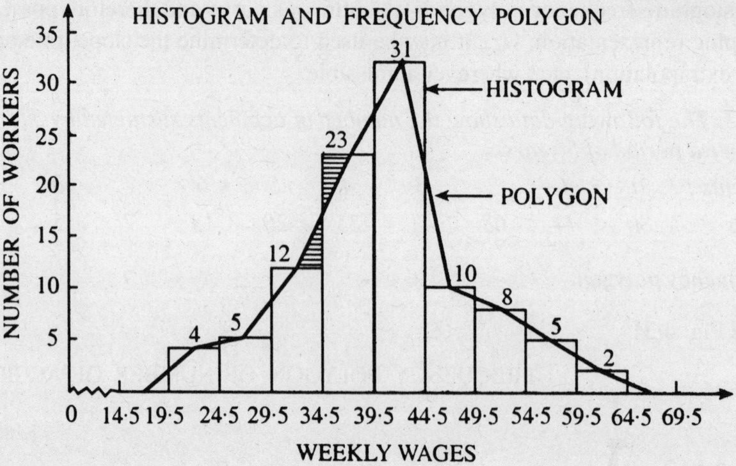

Fig. 4·32.

Remark. It may be pointed out that frequency polygon can be drawn straight way by plotting the frequencies against the mid-points of the corresponding classes without converting the given distribution into a continuous one and joining these points by straight lines.

Example 4·25. *Draw the histogram and frequency polygon for the following frequency distribution.*

Mid-value of class interval	:	*2·5*	*7·5*	*12·5*	*17·5*	*22·5*	*27·5*	*32·5*	*37·5*
Frequency	:	*7*	*10*	*20*	*13*	*17*	*10*	*14*	*9*

Solution. Since we are given the mid-values of the class intervals, for the construction of histogram, the distribution is to be transformed into continuous class intervals each of magnitude 5, (under the assumption that the frequencies are uniformly distributed throughout the class intervals), as given in the following table.

Class	*Frequency*
0—5	7
5—10	10
10—15	20
15—20	13
20—25	17
25—30	10
30—35	14
35—40	9

The histogram and frequency polygon are shown in the Fig. 4·33.

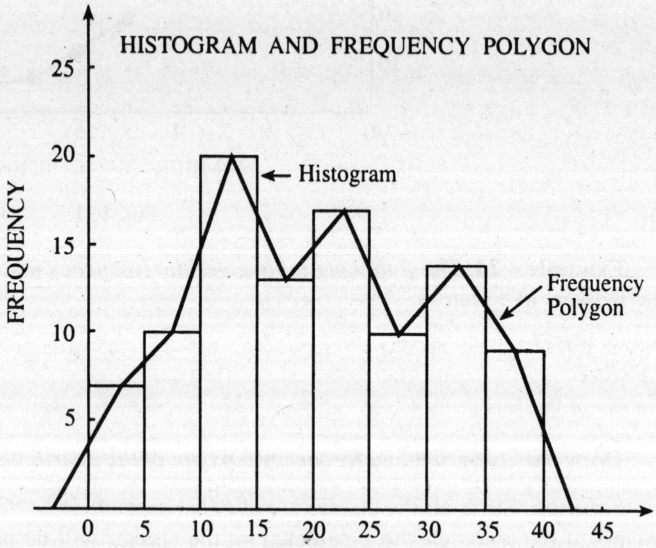

Fig. 4·33.

Remark. It may be noted that frequency polygon can be drawn even without converting the given distribution into classes. The frequencies are plotted against the corresponding mid-points (given) and joined by straight lines.

C. FREQUENCY CURVE

A frequency curve is a smooth free hand curve drawn through the vertices of a frequency polygon. The object of smoothing of the frequency polygon is to eliminate, as far as possible, the random or erratic fluctuations that might be present in the data. The area enclosed by the frequency curve is same as that of the histogram or frequency polygon but its shape is smooth one and not with sharp edges. Frequency curve may be regarded as a limiting form of the frequency polygon as the number of observations (total frequency) becomes very large and the class intervals are made smaller and smaller.

Remarks 1. Smoothing should be done very carefully so that the curve looks as regular as possible and sudden and sharp turns should be avoided. In case of the data pertaining to natural phenomenon like tossing of a coin or throwing of a dice the smoothing can be conveniently done because such data generally give rise to symmetrical curves. However, for the data relating to social, economic or business phenomenon, smoothing cannot be done effectively as such data usually give rise to skewed (asymmetrical) curves. [For details see § 4·4·3 C (*b*) page 4·36]. In fact, it is desirable to attempt a frequency curve if we have sufficient reasons to believe that the frequency distribution under study is fairly regular. It is futile to attempt a frequency curve for an irregular distribution. In general, frequency curves should be attempted

(*i*) for frequency distribution based on the samples, and

(*ii*) when the distribution is continuous.

2. We have already seen that a frequency polygon can be drawn with or without a histogram. However, to obtain an ideal frequency curve for a given frequency distribution, it is desirable to proceed in a logical sequence, *viz*., first draw a histogram, then a frequency polygon and finally a frequency curve, because in the absence of a histogram the smoothing of the frequency polygon cannot be done properly. As discussed in frequency polygon, the frequency curve should also be extended to the base on both sides of the histogram so that the area under the frequency curve represents the total frequency of the distribution.

3. A frequency curve can be used with advantage for interpolation [*i.e.*, estimating the frequencies for given value of the variable or in a given interval (within the given range of the variable)], provided it rises gradually to the highest point and then falls more or less in the same manner. It can also be used to determine the rates of increase or decrease in the frequencies. It also enables us to have an idea about the Skewness and Kurtosis of the distribution [See Chapter 7].

Example 4·26. *Draw a frequency curve for the following distribution :*

Age (Yrs.) :	*17—19*	*19—21*	*21—23*	*23—25*	*25—27*	*27—29*	*29—31*
No. of Students :	*7*	*13*	*24*	*30*	*22*	*15*	*6*

Solution. *See Fig. 4·34.*

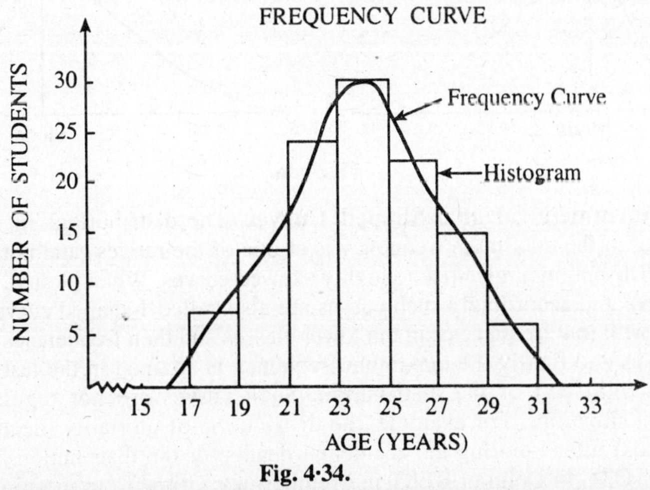

Fig. 4·34.

Types of Frequency Curves. Though different types of data may give rise to a variety of frequency curves, we shall discuss below only some of the important curves which, in general, describe most of the data observed in practice, *viz*., the data relating to natural, social, economic and business phenomena.

(*a*) **Curves of Symmetrical Distributions.** In a symmetrical distribution, the class frequencies first rise steadily, reach a maximum and then diminish in the same identical manner.

If a curve is folded symmetrically about a vertical line (corresponding to the maximum frequency), so that the two halves of the figures coincide, it is called a symmetrical curve. It has a single smooth hump in the middle and tapers off gradually at either end and is bell-shaped.

The following hypothetical distribution of marks in a test will give a symmetrical frequency distribution.

Marks	:	0—10	10—20	20—30	30—40	40—50	50—60	60—70	70—80	80—90
Frequency	:	40	70	120	160	180	160	120	70	40

If the data are presented graphically, we shall obtain a frequency curve which is symmetrical.

The most commonly and widely used symmetrical curve in Statistics is the Normal frequency curve which is given in Fig. 4·35. (For details, see Chapter 14 on Theoretical Probability Distributions).

Normal curve, generally describes the data relating to natural phenomenon like tossing of a coin, throwing of a dice, etc. Most of the data relating to psychological and educational statistics also give rise to normal curve. However, the data relating to social, business and economic phenomena do not conform to normal curve. They always give moderately asymmetrical (slightly skewed) curves discussed below.

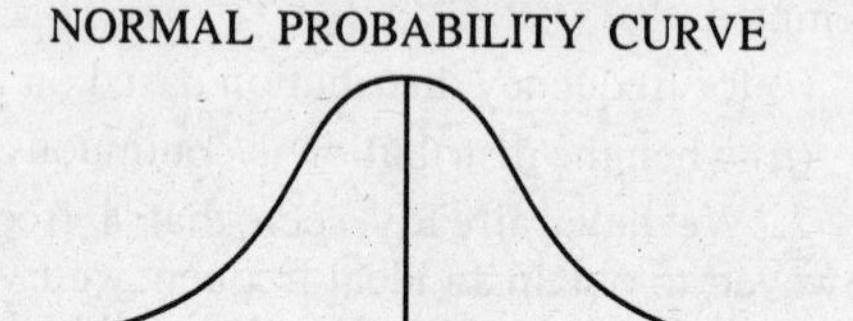

Fig. 4·35.

(*b*) **Moderately Asymmetrical (Skewed) Frequency Curves.** A frequency curve is said to be skewed (asymmetrical) if it is not symmetrical. Moderately asymmetrical curves are commonly observed in social, economic and business phenomena. Such curves are stretched more to one side than to the other. If the curve is stretched more to the right (*i.e.*, it has a longer tail towards the right), it is said to be *positively skewed* and if it is stretched more to the left (*i.e.*, has a longer tail towards the left), it is said to be *negatively skewed.* Thus, in a positively skewed distribution, most of the frequencies are associated with smaller values of the variable and in a negatively skewed distribution most of the frequencies are associated with larger values of the variable. The following figures show positively skewed and negatively skewed distributions.

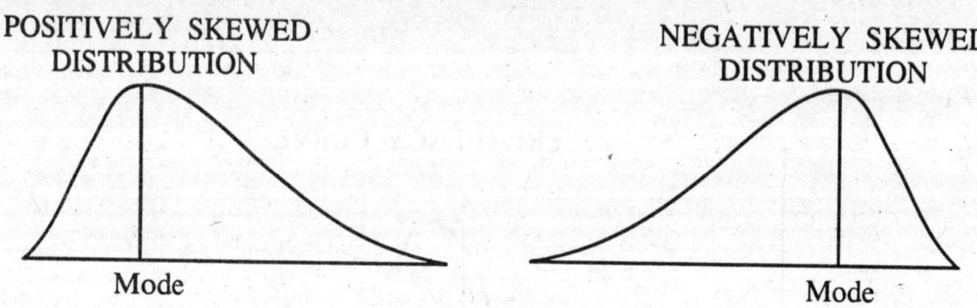

Fig. 4·36.

(*c*) **Extremely Asymmetrical or J-Shaped Curves.** The distributions in which the value of the variable corresponding to the maximum frequency is at one of the ranges (and not in the middle as in the case of symmetrical distributions), give rise to highly skewed curves. When plotted, they give a J-shaped or inverted J-shaped curve and accordingly such curves are also called J-shaped curves. In a J-shaped curve, the distribution starts with low frequencies in the lower classes and then frequencies increase steadily as the variable value increases and finally the maximum frequency is attained in the last class thus exhibiting a peak at the extreme right end of the distribution. Such curves are not regular curves but become unavoidable in certain situations. For example, the distribution of mortality (death) rates (along Y-axis) *w.r.t.* age (along X-axis) after ignoring the accidental deaths; or the distribution of persons travelling in local state buses, (*e.g.*, DTC in Delhi or BEST in Mumbai) *w.r.t.* time from morning hours, say, 7 A.M. to peak traffic hours, say, 10 A.M. will give rise to a J-shaped distribution [Fig. 4·37(*a*)]. Similarly in an inverted J-shaped curve the frequency decreases continuously with the increase in the variate values, the maximum frequency being attained in the beginning of the distribution. For example, the distribution of the quantity demanded *w.r.t.* the price; or the number of depositors *w.r.t.* their saving in a bank, or the number of persons *w.r.t.* their wages or incomes in a city, will give a reverse J-shaped curve [Fig. 4·37(*b*)].

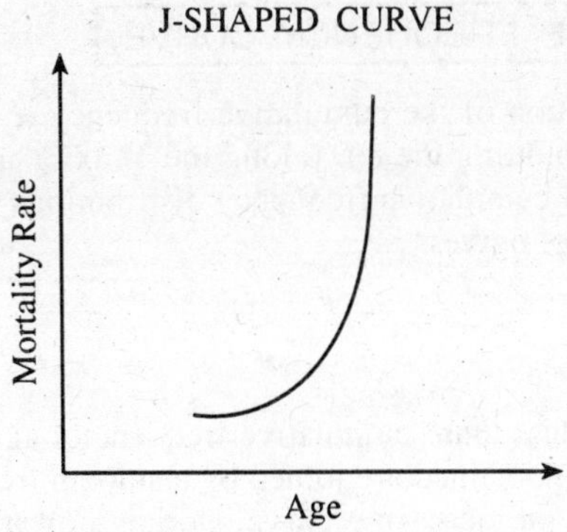

Fig. 4·37(*a*).

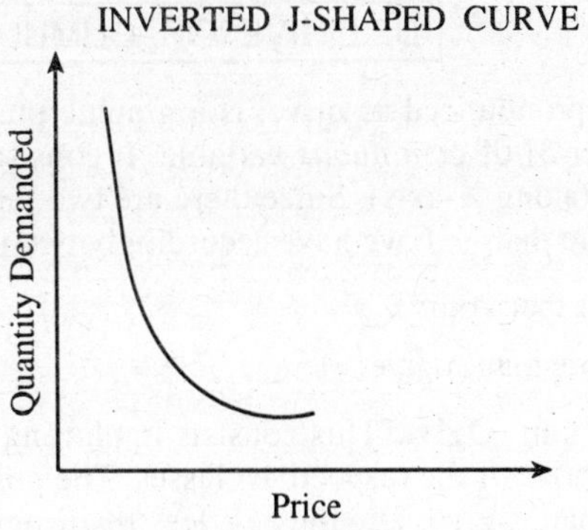

Fig. 4·37(*b*).

(*d*) **U-Curve.** The frequency distributions in which the maximum frequency occurs at the extremes (*i.e.*, both ends) of the range and the frequency keeps on falling symmetrically (about the middle), the minimum frequency being attained at the centre give rise to a U-shaped curve. In this type of distribution, most of values are associated with the values of the variable at the extremes *i.e.*, with smaller and larger values whereas smaller frequencies are associated with the intermediate values, the central value having the minimum frequency. Such distributions are generally observed in the behaviour of total costs where the curve initially falls steadily and after attaining the optimum level (in the middle), it starts rising steadily again. As another illustration, the distribution of persons travelling in local state buses between morning and evening peak hours will give, more or less, a U-shaped curve shown in Fig. 4·38.

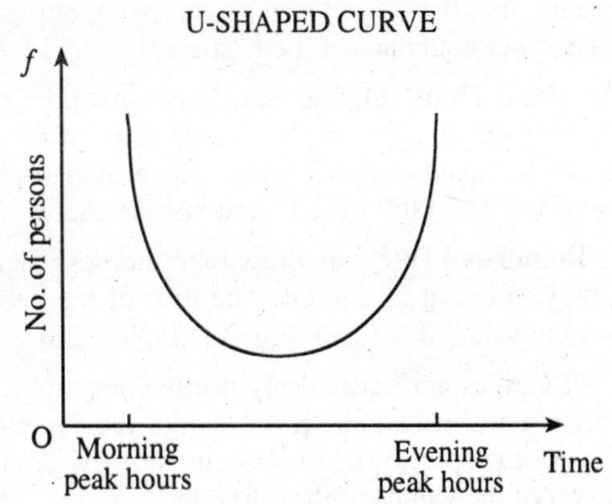

Fig. 4·38.

(*e*) **Mixed Curves.** In the curves discussed so far, we have seen that the highest concentration of the values lies at the centre (symmetrical curve), or near around the centre (moderately asymmetrical curve), or at the extremes (J-shaped and U-shaped curves). But sometimes, though very rarely, we come across certain distributions in which maximum frequency is attained at two or more points in an irregular manner as shown in Fig. 4·39.

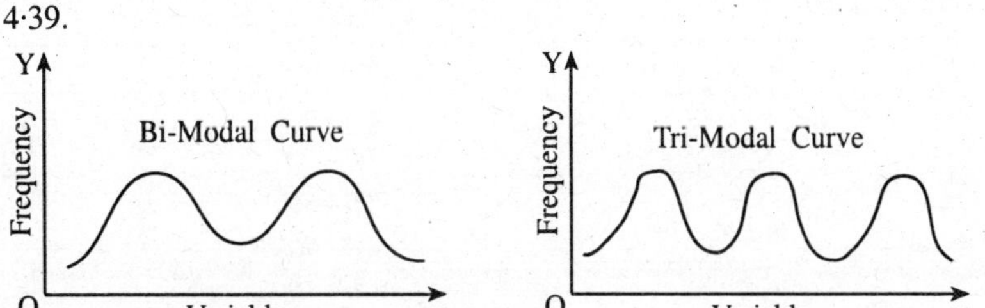

Fig. 4·39.

Such curves are obtained in a distribution where as the value of the variable increases, the frequencies increase and decrease, then again increase and decrease in an irregular manner; the phenomenon may be repeated twice or thrice as shown in the above diagrams or even more than that. The distributions with two humps are called bi-modal distributions and those with three humps are called tri-modal distributions while those with more than three humps are termed as multi-modal distributions. Such distributions are rarely observed in practice and should be avoided as far as possible because they cannot be usefully employed for the computation of various statistical measures and for statistical analysis.

D. OGIVE OR CUMULATIVE FREQUENCY CURVE

Ogive, pronounced as ojive, is a graphic presentation of the cumulative frequency (*c.f.*) distribution [See Chapter 3] of *continuous* variable. It consists in plotting the *c.f.* (along the Y-axis) against the class boundaries (along X-axis). Since there are two types of cumulative frequency distributions *viz.*, 'less than' *c.f.* and 'more than' *c.f.* we have accordingly two types of ogives, *viz.*,

(*i*) 'Less than' ogive.

(*ii*) 'More than' ogive.

'Less Than' Ogive. This consists in plotting the 'less than' cumulative frequencies against the *upper* class boundaries of the respective classes. The points so obtained are joined by a smooth freehand curve to give 'less than' ogive. Obviously, 'less than' ogive is an increasing curve, sloping upwards from left to right and has the shape of an elongated S.

Remark. Since the frequency below the lower limit of the first class (*i.e.*, upper limit of the class preceding the first class) is zero, the ogive curve should start on the left with a cumulative frequency zero at the lower boundary of the first class.

'More Than' Ogive. Similarly, in 'more than' ogive, the 'more than' cumulative frequencies are plotted against the *lower* class boundaries of the respective classes. The points so obtained are joined by a smooth freehand curve to give 'more than' ogive. 'More than' ogive is a decreasing curve and slopes downwards from left to right and has the shape of an elongated S, upside down.

Remarks 1. We may draw both the 'less than' ogive and 'more than' ogive on the same graph. If done so, they intersect at a point. The foot of the perpendicular from their point of intersection on the X-axis gives the value of median. [See Example 4·28].

2. Ogives are particularly useful for graphic computation of *partition values, viz.*, Median, Quartiles, Deciles, Percentiles, etc. [For details, see Chapter 5]. They can also be used to determine graphically the number or proportion of observations below or above a given value of the variable or lying between certain interval of the values of the variable.

3. Ogives can be used with advantage over frequency curves for comparative study of two or more distributions because like frequency curves, for each of the distributions different ogives can be constructed on the same graph and they are generally less overlapping than the corresponding frequency curves.

4. If the class frequencies are large, they can be expressed as percentages of the total frequency. The graph of the *cumulative percentage frequency* is called '*percentile curve*'.

Example 4·27. *Draw a less than cumulative frequency curve for the following data and find from the graph the value of seventh decile.*

Monthly income	*No. of workers*	*Monthly income*	*No. of workers*
0—100	*12*	*500—600*	*20*
100—200	*28*	*600—700*	*20*
200—300	*35*	*700—800*	*17*
300—400	*65*	*800—900*	*13*
400—500	*30*	*900—1000*	*10*

Solution. Less than cumulative frequency curve is obtained on plotting the 'less than' *c.f.* against the upper limit of the corresponding class and joining the points so obtained by a smooth free hand curve as shown in Fig. 4·40.

To obtain the value of seventh decile from the graph, at frequency $\frac{7N}{10} = \frac{7}{10} \times 250 = 175$, draw a line parallel to the X-axis meeting the 'less than' *c.f.* curve at point P. From P draw PM perpendicular to X-axis meeting it at M. Then the value of seventh decile is (Fig. 4.40) :

$$D_7 = OM = \text{Rs. } 545 \text{ [From the graph]}$$

'LESS THAN' CUMULATIVE FREQUENCY TABLE

Monthly Income	*No. of workers (f)*	*Less than c.f.*
0—100	12	12
100—200	28	40
200—300	35	75
300—400	65	140
400—500	30	170
500—600	20	190
600—700	20	210
700—800	17	227
800—900	13	240
900—1000	10	250
Total	$\Sigma f = 250$	

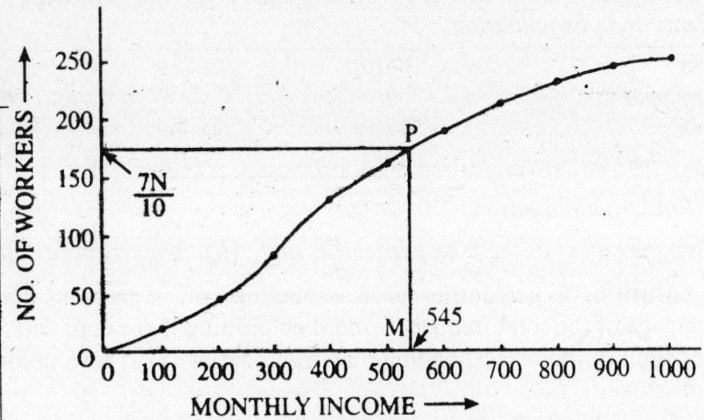

Fig. 4·40.

Example 4·28. *The following table gives the distribution of monthly income of 600 families in a certain city.*

Monthly Income ('00 Rs.)	*Below 75*	*75—150*	*150—225*	*225—300*	*300—375*	*375—450*	*450 and over*
No. of Families	*60*	*170*	*200*	*60*	*50*	*40*	*20*

Draw a 'less than' and a 'more than' ogive curve for the above data on the same graph and from these read the median income.

Solution. For drawing the 'less than' and 'more than' ogive we convert the given distribution into 'less than' and 'more than' cumulative frequencies (*c.f.*) as given in the following table.

Monthly Income ('00Rs.)	*No. of Families (f)*	*Less than c.f.*	*More than c.f.*
Below 75	60	60	600
75—150	170	230	540
150—225	200	430	370
225—300	60	490	170
300—375	50	540	110
375—450	40	580	60
450 and over	20	600	20

As already explained, for drawing 'less than' ogive, we plot 'less than' *c.f.* against the *upper limit* of the corresponding class intervals and join the points so obtained by smooth freehand curve. Similarly, 'more than' ogive is obtained on joining the points obtained on plotting the 'more than' *c.f.* against the lower limit of the corresponding class by smooth freehand curve.

From the point of intersection of these two ogives, draw a line perpendicular to the X-axis (monthly incomes). The abscissa (*x*-coordinate) of the point where this perpendicular meets the X-axis gives the value of median.

The 'more than' and 'less than' ogives and the value of median are shown in the Fig. 4·41.

From Fig. 4·41, Median = OM = 176 (approximately)

Hence, the median monthly income is Rs. 17,600.

'LESS THAN' AND 'MORE THAN' OGIVE

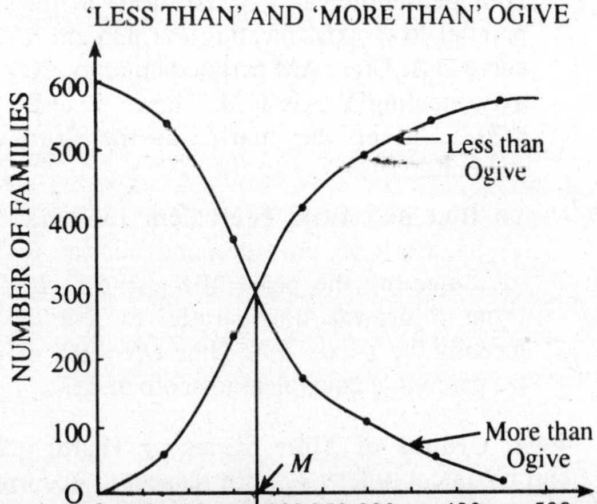

Fig. 4·41.

Example 4·29. *Draw a percentile curve for the following distribution of marks obtained by 700 students at an examination.*

Marks	*0—10*	*10—19*	*20—29*	*30—39*	*40—49*
No. of Students	*9*	*42*	*61*	*140*	*250*
Marks	*50—59*	*60—69*	*70—79*	*80—89*	
No. of Students	*102*	*71*	*23*	*2*	

Find from the graph

(i) the marks at the 20th percentile, and (ii) the percentile equivalent to a mark of 65.

Solution. A percentile curve is obtained on expressing the 'less than' cumulative frequencies as percentage of the total frequency and then plotting these cumulative percentage frequencies (*P*) against the upper limit of the corresponding class boundaries (*x*). These points are then joined by a smooth freehand curve.

COMPUTATION OF CUMULATIVE PERCENTAGE FREQUENCY DISTRIBUTION

Marks	*Frequency (f)*	*'Less than' c.f.*	*Percentage 'less than' c.f. (P)*
— 9·5	9	9	1·3
9·5—19·5	42	51	7·3
19·5—29·5	61	112	16·0
29·5—39·5	140	252	36·0
39·5—49·5	250	502	71·7
49·5—59·5	102	604	86·3
59·5—69·5	71	675	96·4
69·5—79·5	23	698	99·7
79·5—89·5	2	700	100·0

Percentage 'less than' *c.f.*

$$= \frac{\text{'Less than' } c.f.}{\text{Total frequency}} \times 100$$

$$= \frac{c.f.}{700} \times 100 = \frac{c.f.}{7}$$

(*i*) To find marks (*x*) corresponding to the 20th percentile, at *P* = 20, draw a line parallel to *X*-axis, meeting the percentile curve at *A*. Draw AM perpendicular to X-axis, meeting *X*-axis at *M*. Then *OM* = 31·5, gives the marks at the 20th percentile.

(*ii*) To find percentile equivalent to mark *x* = 65, at *x* = 65, draw perpendicular to *X-axis* meeting the percentile curve at *B*. From *B* draw a line parallel to X-axis meeting the *Y*-axis at *N*. Then *ON* = 92, is the percentile equivalent to score of 65.

PERCENTILE CURVE

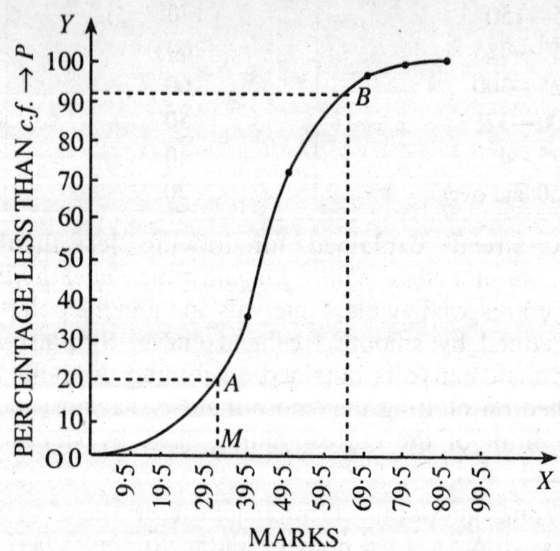

Fig. 4·42.

4·4·4. Graphs of Time Series or Historigrams. A time series is an arrangement of statistical data in a chronological order *i.e.,* with respect to occurrence of time. The time period may be a year, quarter, month, week, days, hours and so on. Most of the series relating to economic and business data are time series such as population of a country, money in circulation, bank deposits and clearings, production and price of commodities, sales and profits of a departmental store, imports and exports of a country, etc. Thus in a time series data there are two variables; one of them, the independent variable being time and the other (dependent) variable being the phenomenon under study.

The time series data are represented geometrically by means of *Time Series Graph* which is also known as *Historigram*. The independent variable *viz*., time is taken along the X-axis and the dependent variable is taken along the Y-axis. The various points so obtained are joined by straight lines to get the time series graph. If the actual time series data are graphed, the historigram is called *Absolute Historigram.* However, the graph obtained on plotting the index number of the given values is called *Index Historigram* and it depicts the percentage changes in the values of the phenomenon as compared to some fixed base period. Historigrams are extensively used in practice. They are easy to draw and understand and do not require much skill and expertise to construct and interpret them.

Remark. Time series graphs can be drawn on a natural (arithmetic scale) or on a ratio (semi-logarithmic or logarithmic) scale, the former reflecting the absolute changes from one period to another and the latter depicting the relative changes or rates of change. In the following sections we shall study the time series graphs on a natural scale. Ratio scale graphs are discussed in § 4·4·5.

The various types of time series graphs are :

(*i*) Horizontal Line Graphs or Historigrams (*ii*) Silhouette or Net Balance Graphs

(*iii*) Range or Variation Graphs (*iv*) Components or Band Graphs

Now we shall discuss them briefly, one by one.

A. HORIZONTAL LINE GRAPHS OR HISTORIGRAMS

In such a graph only one variable is to be represented graphically. As already explained, the desired graph (*historigram*) is obtained on plotting the time variable along the X-axis and the other variable *viz*., the magnitudes of the phenomenon under consideration along the Y-axis on a suitable scale and joining the points so obtained by straight lines. An illustration is given in Example 4·37.

Example 4·30. *Draw the graph of the following* :

Year	*1990*	*1991*	*1992*	*1993*	*1994*	*1995*	*1996*	*1997*
Yield (in million tons)	*12·8*	*13·9*	*12·8*	*13·9*	*13·4*	*6·5*	*2·9*	*14·8*

Solution. Taking the scale along X-axis as 1 cm = 1 year and along Y-axis as 1 cm = 2 million tons, the required graph is as shown in Fig. 4·43.

YIELD (IN MILLION TONS) FOR DIFFERENT YEARS

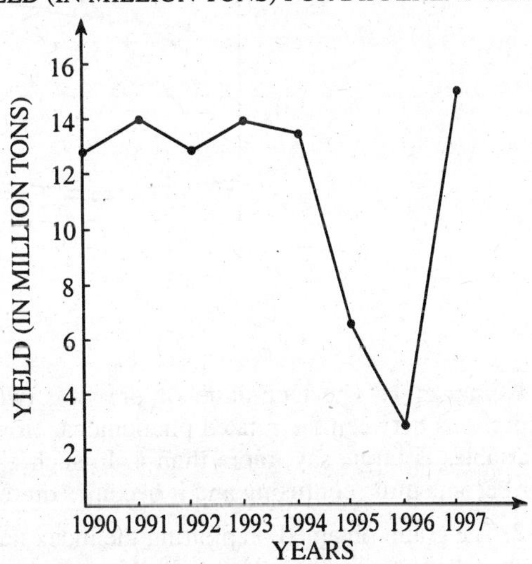

Fig. 4·43.

FALSE BASE LINE. As already explained [§ 4·4·2 (Item 5)], if the fluctuations in the values of the variable (to be shown along the Y-axis) are small as compared to their magnitudes and if the minimum value of the variable is very distant from origin *i.e.,* zero, then the technique of false base line is used to highlight these fluctuations. Illustrations are given in Examples 4·31 and 4·32.

HISTORIGRAM — TWO OR MORE VARIABLES

The time series data relating to two or more related variables *i.e.*, phenomena measured in the same unit and belonging to the same time period can be displayed together in the same graph using the same scales for all the variables along the vertical axis and the same scale for time along X-axis for each variable. The method for drawing such graphs is same as that of historigram for one variable. Thus we shall get a number of curves, one for each variable. They should be distinguished from each other by the use of different types of lines *viz.*, thin and thick lines, dotted lines, dash lines, dash-dot lines, etc., and an index to this effect should be given for proper identification of the curves. The following illustration will clarify the point.

Example 4·31. *The following table gives the index numbers of industrial production for India.*

INDEX NUMBER OF INDUSTRIAL PRODUCTION

Base : 1970 = 100

Item	*1971*	*1972*	*1973*	*1974*	*1975*	*1976*
Cement	*107·0*	*113·1*	*107·6*	*102·6*	*116·7*	*133·9*
Iron and steel	*100·6*	*112·0*	*96·1*	*100·2*	*121·3*	*145·0*
General Index	*104·2*	*110·2*	*112·0*	*114·3*	*119·3*	*131·2*

Represent them on the same graph paper.

Ans. As usual, we take time (years) along X-axis and the index numbers along Y-axis. Using false base line (for vertical axis) at 95, the graph is shown in Fig. 4·44.

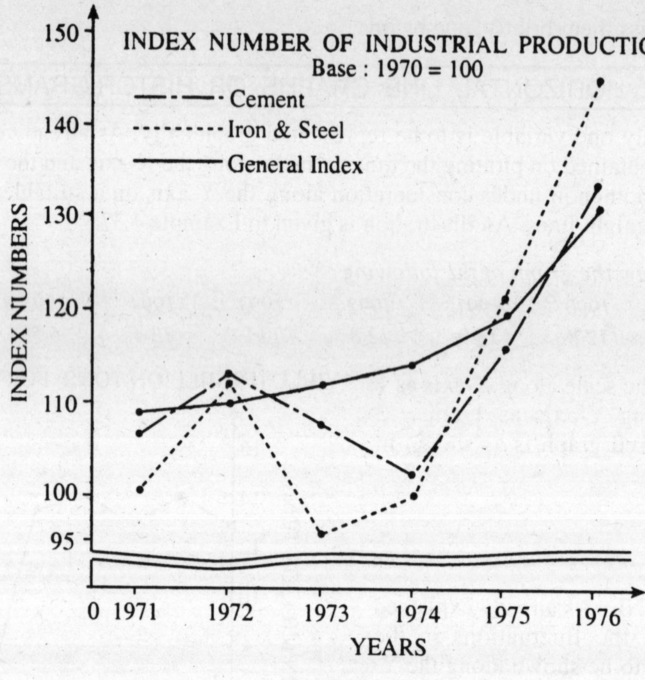

Fig. 4·44.

Remarks 1. The technique of drawing two or more historigrams on the same graph facilitates comparisons between the related phenomena. However, its use should not be recommended if the number of variables is large, say, more than 4. In such a case the different line graphs which may intersect each other become quite confusing and it becomes quite difficult to understand and interpret them.

2. The graph obtained on plotting the index number is known as *index historigram* and it represents the relative changes in the values of the variables under consideration. Two or more variable index historigrams on the same graph obviously facilitate comparisons. However, in order to arrive at any valid conclusion, the index numbers for all the variables should be computed with respect to the same base period.

3. *Graphs of two variables measured in different units.* The time series data relating to two related phenomena which are measured in different units *e.g.,* imports (quantity in million tons) and imports (values in crores Rupees) but pertaining to the same time period can also be displayed on the same graph. This is done by using two different vertical scales (one for each variable), one on the left and the other on the right; the scales for each variable being so selected that the two historigrams so obtained are close to each other. This objective can be achieved by taking the scales for each variable proportional to its average value *i.e.*, the average value of each variable is kept in or near about the middle of the vertical scale in the graph and the scale for each is selected accordingly. We explain this point by the following illustration.

Example 4·32. *Plot a graph to represent the following data in a suitable manner.*

Year	*1990*	*1991*	*1992*	*1993*	*1994*	*1995*	*1996*	*1997*
Imports (million tons)	*400*	*450*	*560*	*620*	*580*	*460*	*500*	*540*
Imports (million Rs.)	*220*	*235*	*385*	*420*	*420*	*380*	*360*	*400*

Solution. The time variable (Year) is recorded along the X-axis with scale 1 cm = 1 year and the variate values, imports (volume in tons) and imports (value in Rs.) are recorded along the Y-axis with scales :

1 cm = 20,000 tons (for imports-quantity)

1 cm = 20,000 Rs. (for imports-value)

and false base line is selected at 400,000 tons (for quantity) and Rs. 220,000 (for value). The graph is shown in Fig. 4·45.

VOLUME AND VALUE OF IMPORTS
(1990—1997)

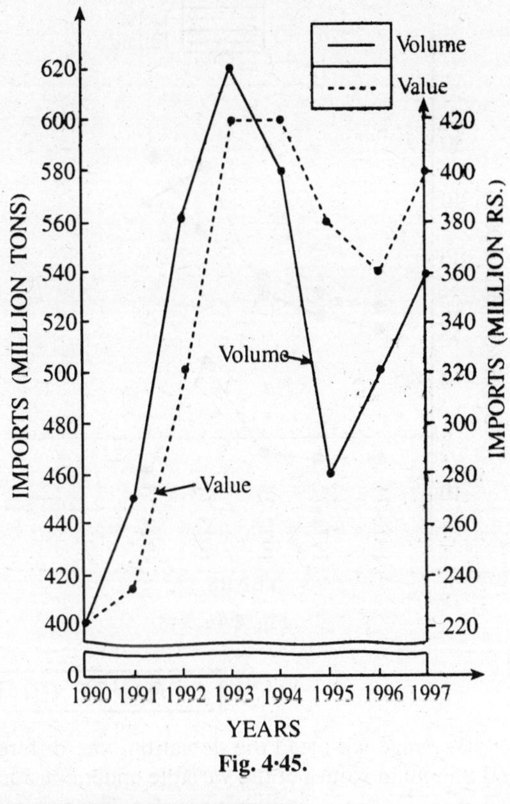

Fig. 4·45.

B. SILHOUETTE OR NET BALANCE GRAPH

This graph is specially used to highlight the difference or the net balance between the values of two variables along the vertical axis *e.g.*, the difference between imports and exports of a country in different years, sales and purchase of a business concern for different periods, the income and expenditure of a family in different months and so on. This can be done in any one of the following two ways :

Method 1. Obtain the net balance *viz.*, the difference between two sets of the values of the phenomena (variables) for different periods. Some of these differences may be negative also. Now, in addition to the two historigrams, one for each variable, draw a third historigram for the net balance on the same graph. A portion of this graph, (corresponding to the negative values of the net balance) will be below the X-axis.

Method 2. Draw two historigrams, one for each phenomenon (variable), on the same graph. The net balance between the variables is depicted by proper filling or shading of the space between the two historigrams, depicting clearly the positive and negative balance.

Both these methods are explained in the following illustration.

Example 4·33. *India's overall balance of payment situation (Billions of Rupees) is given below :*

Years :	*1970—71*	*1971—72*	*1972—73*	*1973—74*	*1974—75*
Credits	*18·9*	*20·9*	*24·2*	*46·1*	*40·7*
Debits	*22·2*	*24·9*	*26·7*	*33·0*	*47·2*
Balance (Credit – Debit)	*–3·3*	*– 4·0*	*– 2·5*	*13·1*	*–6·5*

Represent the above data on the same graph.

Solution. The above data can best be represented by the Silhouette or Net Balance Graph. The graphs obtained on using both the methods are given a below.

Method 1

INDIA'S OVERALL BALANCE OF PAYMENTS

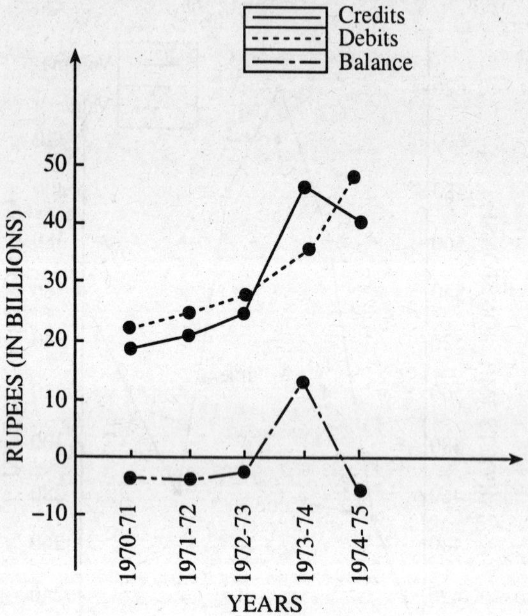

Fig. 4·46.

Method 2

CREDITS AND DEBITS DURING 1970—1975 (ALONG WITH BALANCE OF PAYMENTS)

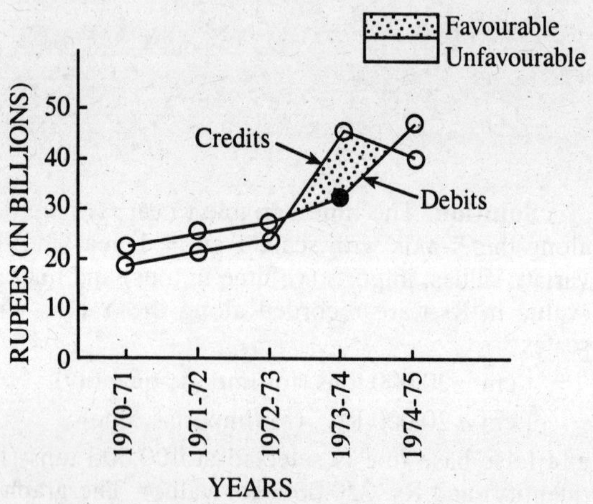

Fig. 4·47.

C. RANGE GRAPH OR ZONE GRAPH

By range we mean the deviation, *i.e.,* difference between the two extreme values *viz.,* the maximum and minimum values of the variable under consideration.

Range graph, also sometimes known as *zone graph,* is used to depict and emphasize the range of variation of a phenomenon for each period. For instance, for highlighting the range of variation of :

(*i*) the temperature on different days,

(*ii*) the blood pressure readings of an individual on different days,

(*iii*) price of a commodity on different periods of time, etc.,

the range or zone graph is the most appropriate and helps us to have an idea of the likely fluctuations in the magnitudes of the phenomenon under study. The range chart can be drawn in any of the following ways.

Method 1. For each time period, plot the maximum and minimum values of the variable and join them by straight lines to get the range lines. Plot the mid-point (average value of the variable) for each period. Join these points by straight lines to get the range graph. The range graph thus depicts the maximum, the minimum and the average value of the phenomenon for each period.

Method 2. This method consists in plotting two historigrams, one corresponding to the maximum values of the phenomenon for different periods and the other corresponding to the minimum values. The space between the two historigrams depicts the range of the variation and is prominently displayed by proper filling or shading it.

Both these methods are explained in the following illustration.

Example 4·34. *The following are the share price quotations of a firm for five consecutive weeks. Present the data by an appropriate diagram.*

Week	*1*	*2*	*3*	*4*	*5*
High	*102*	*103*	*107*	*106*	*105*
Low	*100*	*101*	*103*	*105*	*104*

Solution. Since the maximum and minimum price quotations of a firm for 5 consecutive weeks are given, the most appropriate graph for it is the zone or the range graph.

Taking weeks along X-axis and share price quotations along Y-axis and using the false base line at 100 for the vertical scale, the range chart as obtained by Method 1 is drawn in Fig. 4·48.

RANGE CHART FOR SHARE PRICE QUOTATIONS OF A FIRM

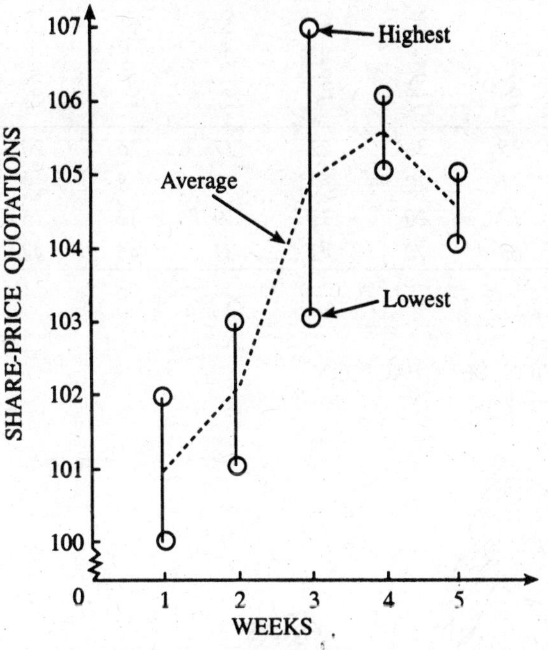

Fig. 4·48.

RANGE CHART FOR SHARE PRICE QUOTATIONS OF A FIRM

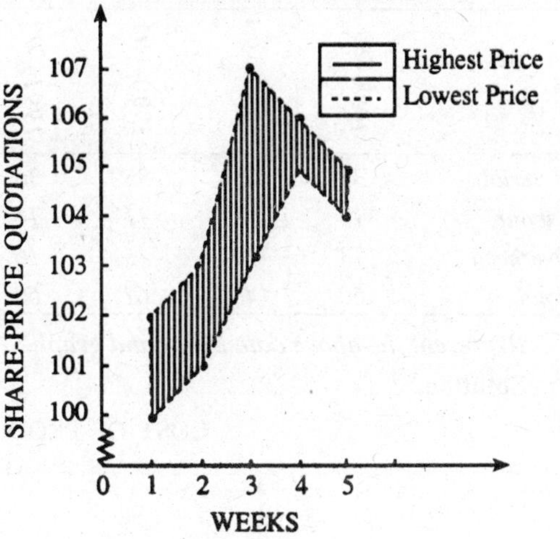

Fig. 4·49.

The range chart may also be drawn as in Figure 4·49 : (*c.f.*, Method 2).

D. BAND GRAPH

Like sub-divided bar diagram or pie diagram, the *band graph*, also known as *component part* line chart, is a line graph used to display the total value or the magnitude of a variable and its break up into different components for each period. The construction of such a chart which is used only for time series is quite simple and involves the following steps :

(*i*) For each period, arrange the break up of the value of the variable into various components in the same order.

(*ii*) Draw historigram for the first component.

(*iii*) Over this historigram draw another historigram for the 2nd component. This is done by drawing the 2nd historigram for the cumulative totals of the first two components.

(*iv*) Over the 2nd historigram draw another historigram for the third component. This is done by drawing the historigram for the cumulative totals of the first three components. This technique of drawing historigrams, one over the other is continued till all the components are exhausted. The last historigram, thus corresponds to the total value of the variable.

The space between different historigrams in the form of different bands or belts, one for each component, is prominently displayed by different types of lines *viz*., dash lines, dot lines, dash-dot lines, etc. This chart is specially useful to display the division of the total costs, total sales, total production, etc., into various component parts for different periods.

Remark. Just like percentage bar diagram or percentage rectangular diagram, band chart can also be used for time series where data are expressed in percentage form. In such a situation, the total value of the variable for each period is taken as 100 and bands will depict the percentage that different components bear to the total.

Example 4·35. *The following table gives the cost of production (in arbitrary units) of a factory in biennial averages* :

Items	*1988—89*	*1989—90*	*1990—91*	*1991—92*	*1992—93*	*1993—94*	*1994—95*	*1995—96*	*1996—97*	*1997—98*
Material	*37*	*25*	*35*	*36*	*35*	*38*	*22*	*17*	*26*	*20*
Labour	*10*	*8*	*11*	*11*	*11*	*12*	*7*	*5*	*8*	*9*
Overhead	*13*	*10*	*15*	*16*	*17*	*20*	*12*	*9*	*12*	*15*
Total	*60*	*43*	*61*	*63*	*63*	*70*	*41*	*31*	*46*	*44*

Represent the above data by a band graph.

Solution.

COST OF PRODUCTION OF A FACTORY
(1988—1998)

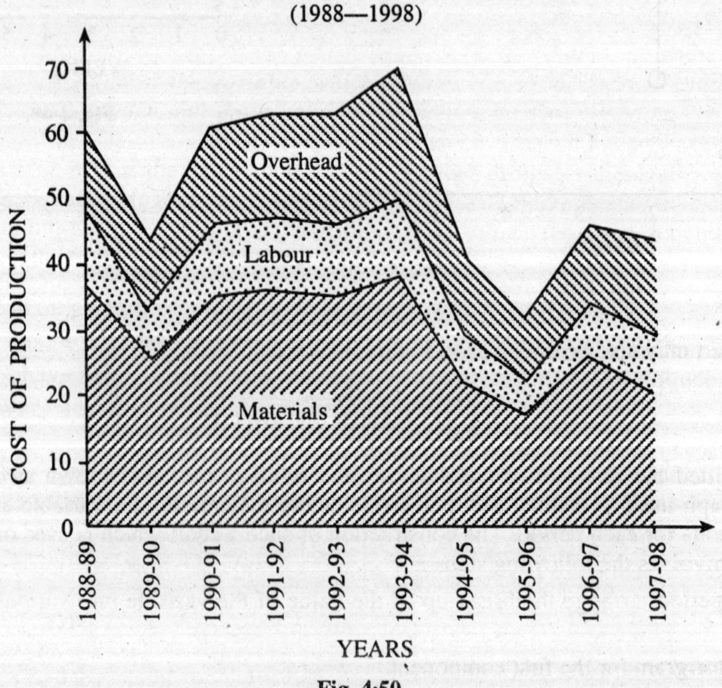

Fig. 4·50

4·4·5. Semi-Logarithmic Line Graphs or Ratio Charts. In the graphs discussed so far, we have used arithmetic *i.e.,* natural scale in which equal distances represent equal absolute magnitudes on both the axes. Such graphs can be used with advantage if we are interested in displaying the absolute changes in the value of a phenomenon and the variations in the magnitudes are such that they can be plotted in the available space in the graph paper. But quite often, particularly in the case of phenomena pertaining to growth like population, production, sales, profits, etc., the increase or decrease in the value of the variable is very rapid. In such a situation we are primarily interested to study the relative changes rather than the absolute changes in the value of the phenomenon and the arithmetic scale is not of much use. In such cases we use *semi-logarithmic* or *logarithmic* or *ratio scale* which is basically used to highlight or emphasize relative or proportionate or percentage changes in the values of a phenomenon over different periods of time.

Since $$\log\left(\frac{a}{b}\right) = \log a - \log b,$$

on a logarithmic scale, equal distances will represent equal proportionate changes.

There are two ways of using logarithmic scale :

Semi-logarithmic Line Graph. In such a graph, the time variable along X-axis is expressed on a natural scale and the logarithms of the values of the phenomenon under study for different periods of time are plotted on the vertical axis on a natural scale. The points so obtained are joined by straight lines to give the desired curve. Since, in this type of curve the logarithms are taken along only one axis, it is known as *semi-logarithmic graph* and it is specially useful for studying the rates of change in the dependent variable (phenomenon under study) for different periods of time in a time series.

Logarithmic Line Graph. In this graph, both the variables along horizontal and vertical axis are plotted on a logarithmic scale. For instance, for a time series data, the logarithms of the time values are plotted along horizontal axis and the logarithms of the values of the variable are plotted along the *vertical axis,* each on a natural scale. The required graph is obtained on joining the points so obtained by straight lines. However, it is very difficult to interpret such a graph and in practice, mostly semi-logarithmic graph is used.

Remarks 1. In a semi-logarithmic graph, almost always, the vertical scale or *Y*-scale is a logarithmic scale. Since a semi-logarithmic graph is useful for studying the relative changes or rates and ratios of increase or decrease over different periods of time, it is also called a *Ratio Graph* or *Ratio Chart* and the logarithmic scale is also called *ratio scale.*

2. For practical purposes, semi-logarithmic graph papers (in which vertical scale is logarithmic scale *i.e.,* log Y is marked along Y-axis and horizontal scale is natural *i.e.,* the values of X are marked in arithmetical scale), analogous to ordinary graph paper are available. The use of such a semi-logarithmic graph paper relieves us of the problem of looking up and plotting the logarithms of the values of a variable on a natural scale. The specimen of a semi logarithmic graph paper is given below.

SEMI-LOGARITHMIC GRAPH PAPER

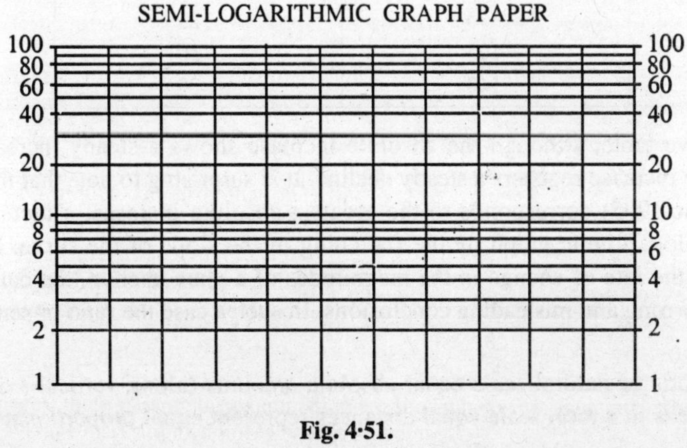

Fig. 4·51.

3. The following diagram (Fig. 4.52) displays the arithmetic and logarithmic scales.

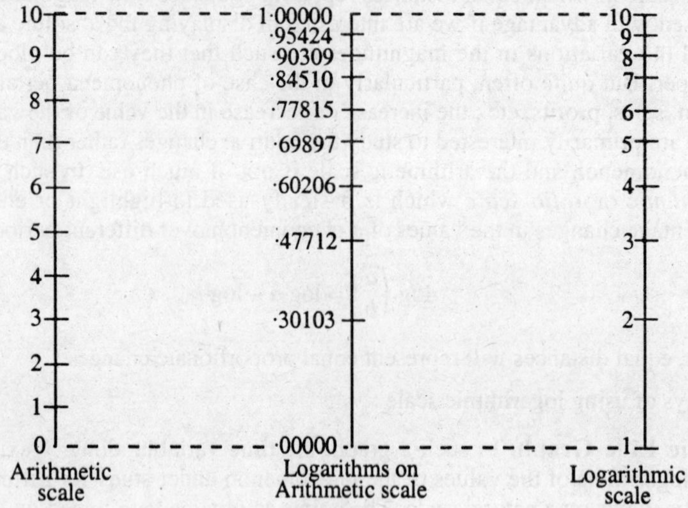

Fig. 4·52.

The reason why the logarithmic scale shows lower and lower distances as we move towards higher and higher magnitudes from 1 to 10 is that the series which is increasing by equal absolute amounts (on an arithmetic scale) is increasing at a diminishing rate.

Arithmetic Scale Graphs Vs. Ratio Scale Graphs

1. A line graph on an arithmetic scale depicts the absolute changes from one period to another whereas on a ratio scale it reflects the rate of change between any two points of time. Thus the graph drawn on natural scale will not be able to reflect the relative or percentage changes or the rate of change of the phenomenon for any two points of time. In most of the problems of growth, *e.g.,* data relating to population, production, sales or profits of a business concern, national income, etc., absolute changes if shown on the graph on a natural scale, are often misleading. As an illustration, let us consider the following hypothetical figures relating to the profits of a business concern.

Year	*Profits*	*Increase over profits of preceding year*	
	(Rs. in lacs)	*Absolute (Rs.. in lacs)*	*Percentage*
1990	15	—	—
1991	30	15	100·0
1992	50	20	66·7
1993	75	25	50·0
1994	105	30	40·0
1995	140	35	33·3

Thus in the above table, although the absolute increase shows a steady increase in the profits, the percentage or relative increase registers a steady decline. It is surprising to note that the smallest percentage increase (for the year 1995) corresponds to the greatest absolute increase, a fact which is prominently displayed on a semi-logarithmic graph by the flattening of the slope of the curve. Hence, if the primary objective is to study the rate of change in the magnitudes of a phenomenon, the data plotted on a natural scale will give quite wrong and misleading conclusions. In such a case the ratio or semi-logarithmic scale is the appropriate one.

2 On an arithmetic or natural scale equal absolute amounts (along vertical axis) are represented by equal distances whereas in a ratio scale equal distances represent equal proportionate movements or equal

relative rates of change or equal percentage changes. Thus in a natural scale, the readings are in arithmetical progression while in a ratio scale they are in geometric progression as exhibited in the Fig. 4·53.

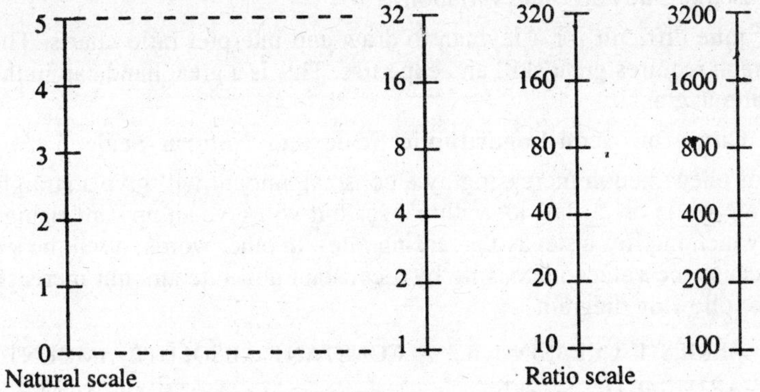

Fig. 4·53.

Thus on a logarithmic scale, the distances between the points on the vertical scale represent the distances of the logarithms of the numbers and not the distances of the numbers themselves.

3. On a natural or arithmetic scale, the vertical scale must start with zero. Since the logarithm of zero is minus infinity, *i.e.*, since log (0) = – ∞, in a ratio graph there is no zero base line. Thus, in a ratio graph, the vertical scale starts with a positive number. Further, since log (1) = 0, the value 1 is placed at a zero distance from the origin *i.e.*, at the origin itself. Hence, in a ratio chart, the origin along the vertical scale is at 1.

4. In case the magnitudes of the phenomenon under consideration have a very wide range, *i.e.*, the values differ widely in magnitudes, then ratio graph is more appropriate than the graph on an arithmetic scale.

5. In interpreting the graphs drawn on a natural scale, the relative position of the curve on the graph is very significant. But, in interpreting a ratio graph it is the shape, direction and degree of steepness of the graph (*i.e.*, straight line or a curve sloping upwards or downwards) that matters and not its position. Accordingly, on a semi-logarithmic scale, the different graphs can be moved up and down without changing their meaning (interpretation). Hence ratio graph can be effectively used to graph, for purposes of comparisons, two or more phenomena (variables) which differ widely in their magnitudes or which are measured even in different units. For instance, for charting the data relating to the population growth, agricultural or industrial output, prices, profits, sales, etc., the ratio graph or semi-logarithmic graph is more appropriate. Such comparison, however, might be misleading on a natural scale.

Uses of Semi-Logarithmic Scale or Ratio Scale. From the above discussion, the uses of ratio or semi-logarithmic scale may be summarised as follows :

1. For studying the rates of change (increase or decrease) or the relative or percentage changes in the values of a phenomenon like population, production, sales, profit, income, etc.

2. For charting two or more phenomena differing very widely in their magnitudes.

3. For charting and comparative study of two or more phenomena measured in different units.

4. When we are interested in proportionate or percentage changes rather than absolute changes.

Limitations of Semi-Logarithmic Scale or Ratio Scale

1. Since log (0) = – ∞ and the logarithm of a negative quantity is not defined, the ratio scale cannot be used to plot zero or negative values. Accordingly, it cannot be used to represent the 'Net Balance' or 'Balance of Trade' on the graph.

2. Another limitation of the ratio scale is that it cannot be used to study the total magnitude and its break up into component parts of any given phenomenon.

3. It cannot be used to study absolute variations.

4. Lastly, it is quite difficult for a layman to draw and interpret ratio charts. The interpretation of a semi-logarithmic graph requires great skill and expertise. This is a great handicap in the mass popularity of ratio or semi-logarithmic graphs.

Shape of the Curve on Semi-Logarithmic Scale and Natural Scale

1. The values of phenomenon increasing by a constant amount will give a straight line rising upward on an arithmetic scale while on a semi-logarithmic scale it will give an upward rising curve with its slope steadily declining (which implies a steady decreasing rate). In other words, it will be a curve concave to the base. This is so because the values increasing by a constant absolute amount increase at a declining rate. This is shown in the following diagram.

SERIES INCREASING BY A CONSTANT ABSOLUTE AMOUNT

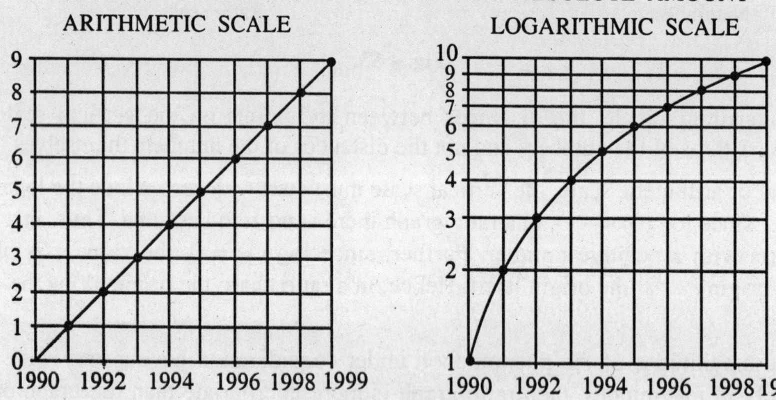

Fig. 4·54.

2. A time series increasing at a constant rate will give a curve convex to the base (*i.e.*, a curve rising upwards towards the right with its slope gradually increasing), on a natural scale. However, on a ratio scale, it will give an upward rising straight line graph as shown in the following diagram.

SERIES INCREASING AT A CONSTANT RATE

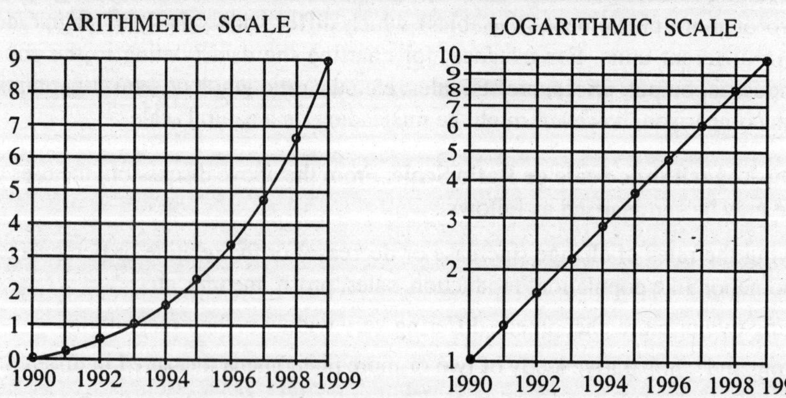

Fig. 4·55.

3. If the time series values decrease by a constant absolute amount the graphs on the two scales will be like the mirror images of the graphs in case 1, in the reverse order (as shown in the Fig. 4·64) *i.e.*, on a natural scale it will give a straight line moving downwards (rapidly declining) and on a ratio scale it will give a curve falling to the right with its slope increasing.

SERIES DECREASING BY CONSTANT ABSOLUTE AMOUNT

ARITHMETIC SCALE LOGARITHMIC SCALE

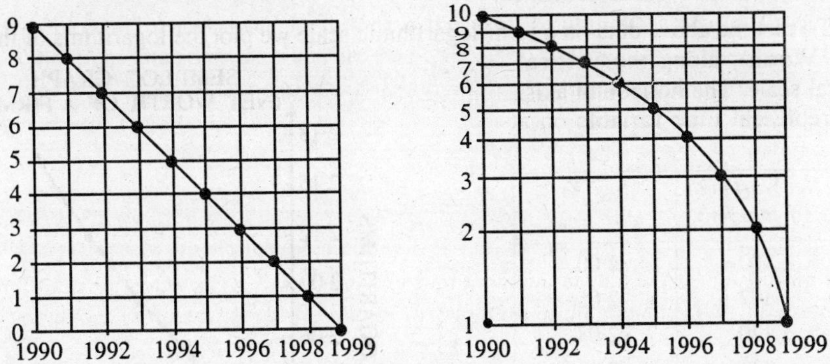

Fig. 4·56.

4. Similarly, for a time series decreasing at a constant rate, the graphs on the two scales will be the mirror images of the graphs in case 2, in the reverse order (as shown in the following diagram) *i.e.*, on an arithmetic scale, we shall get a curve moving downwards with a declining slope and on a semi-logarithmic scale we shall get a straight line moving downwards.

SERIES DECREASING BY CONSTANT RATE

ARITHMETIC SCALE LOGARITHMIC SCALE

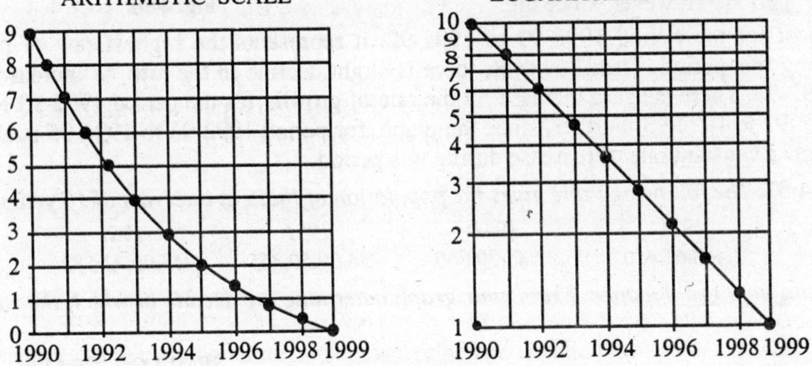

Fig. 4·57.

Interpretation of Semi-Logarithmic or Ratio Curves

1. If the curve is rising upwards, the rate of growth or increase is positive and a curve falling downwards indicates a decreasing rate.

2. If the curve is nearly a straight line which is ascending, it represents the series increasing, more or less, at a constant rate. Similarly, a nearly straight line curve which is descending *i.e.,* moving downwards, represents a series which is decreasing, more or less, at a uniform rate.

3. If the curve rises (falls) steeply at one point of time than at another, it depicts rapid rate of increase (decrease) at that point than at the other point.

4. If two curves on the same semi-logarithmic graph are parallel to each other, they represent equal percentage rates of change for each phenomenon.

5. If one curve is steeper than the other on the same ratio-chart, it implies that the first is changing at a faster rate than the second.

We now give below, some illustrations of the use of ratio or semi-logarithmic graphs.

Example 4·36. *A firm reported that its net worth (in lacs Rs.) in the years 1990-91 to 1994-95 was as follows :*

Year	*1990-91*	*1991-92*	*1992-93*	*1993-94*	*1994-95*
Net worth	*100*	*112*	*120*	*133*	*147*

Plot the above data in the form of a semi-logarithmic graph. Can you say anything about the approximate rate of growth of its net worth ?

Solution. To plot the above data on a semi-logarithmic scale we plot the logarithms of the dependent variable, (Net Worth), along the vertical axis on a natural scale. The horizontal axis, as usual, will represent time variable on a natural scale.

Year	*Net Worth (Y) (in lacs Rs.)*	*log (Y)*
1990-91	100	2·00
1991-92	112	2·05
1992-93	120	2·08
1993-94	133	2·12
1994-95	147	2·17

The graph is shown in Fig. 4·66.

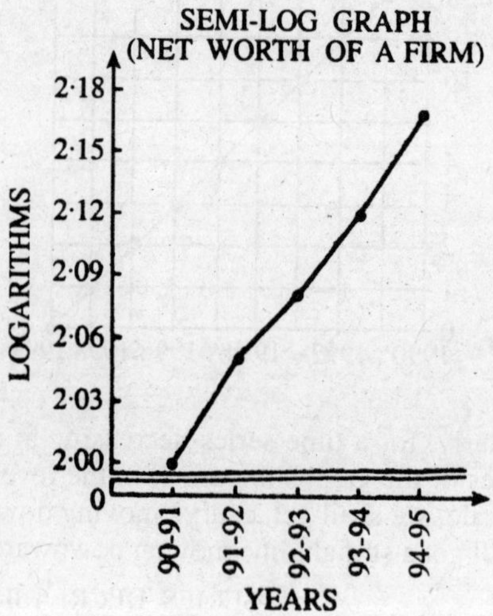

Fig. 4·58.

Comments. Since the graph is ascending throughout, it reflects the increasing rate of growth of the net worth for the entire period. However, since the graph is steepest for the period 1990-91 to 1991-92, it represents the highest rate of positive growth (increase) during this period. Then however, there is slight decline in the rate of increase for the period 1991-92 to 1992-93. There is again increase in the rate of growth for the period 1992-93 to 1994-95 over the period 1991-92 to 1992-93. Further, since the graph for period 1992-93 to 1994-95 is almost a straight line, it represents a constant rate of increase during this period.

Example 4·37. *The following table gives the population of India at intervals of 10 years :*

Year	*1931*	*1941*	*1951*	*1961*	*1971*
Population	*27,88,67,430*	*31,85,39,060*	*36,09,50,365*	*43,90,72,582*	*54,79,49,809*

Plot the data on a graph paper. From your graph determine the decade in which the rate of growth of population was,

(i) the slowest.

(ii) the fastest.

Solution. Since we are interested in determining the rate of growth for different decades, the appropriate graph will be obtained on plotting the data on a semi-logarithmic or ratio scale. Logarithms of the population values are plotted along the vertical axis on a natural scale and time variable (decades) are plotted along the horizontal axis on a natural scale.

Year	*Population (Y) (in lakhs)*	*log (Y)*
1931	2789	3·45
1941	3185	3·50
1951	3610	3·56
1961	4391	3·64
1971	5479	3·74

The graph is shown in figure 4·59

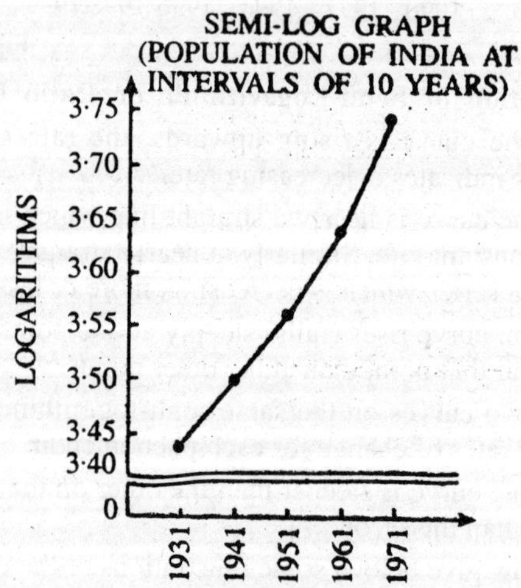

Fig. 4·59.

Comments. Since the graph is ascending throughout, it reflects an increasing rate of population growth throughout the entire period. Further, since the graph has a maximum steep during the period 1961—1971, the rate of growth is maximum during this decade. Again, since the graph has minimum steep for the period 1941—1951, the rate of growth is minimum during this decade.

4·5. LIMITATIONS OF DIAGRAMS AND GRAPHS

Diagrams and graphs are very powerful and effective visual statistical aids for presenting the set of numerical data but they have their limitations some of which are outlined below :

(*i*) Diagrams and graphs help in simplifying the textual and tabulated facts and thus may be regarded as supplementary to statistical tables. They should not be regarded as substitutes for classification, tabulation and some other forms of presentation of a set of numerical data under all circumstances and for all purposes. Julin has very elegantly stated this limitation in the following words :

"Graphic statistic has a role to play of its own ; it is not the servant of numerical statistics but it cannot pretend, on the other hand, to precede or displace it".

(*ii*) They give only general idea of data so as to make it readily intelligible and thus furnish only limited and approximate information. For detailed and precise information we have to refer back to the original statistical tables. Accordingly, diagrams and graphs should be used to explain and impress the significance of statistical facts to the general public who find it difficult to understand and follow the numerical figures. They are, therefore, appealing to a layman who does not have any statistical background but not to a statistician because they are not amenable to further mathematical treatment and hence are not of much use to him from analysis point of view.

(*iii*) They are subjective in character and therefore, may be interpreted differently by different people. If the same set of data are presented diagrammatically (graphically) on two different scales, the sizes of the diagrams (graphs) so obtained might differ widely and thus generally, might create wrong and misleading impressions on the minds of the people. Hence, they are likely to be mis-used by unscrupulous and dishonest people to serve their selfish motives during advertisements, publicity, etc. Hence, they should not be accepted on their face value without proper scrutiny and caution.

(*iv*) All the diagrams and graphs are not easy to construct. Two and three-dimensional diagrams, and ratio graphs require more time and great amount of expertise and skill for their construction and interpretation and are not readily perceptible to non-mathematical person.

(*v*) In case of large figures (observations), such a presentation fails to reveal small differences in them.

(*vi*) The choice of a particular diagram or graph to present a given set of data requires great expertise, skill and intelligence on the part of the statistician or the concerned agency engaged in the work. A wrong type of diagram/graph may lead to very fallacious and misleading conclusions. In this context C.W. Lowe writes :

"The important point that must be borne in mind at all times is that the pictorial presentation, chosen for any situation, must depict the true relationship and point out the proper conclusion. Use of an inappropriate chart may distort the facts and mislead the reader. Above all, the chart must be honest."

(*vii*) Diagrammatic presentation should be used only for comparison of different sets of data which relate either to the same phenomenon or different phenomena which are capable of measurement in the same unit. They are not useful, if absolute information is to be represented.

EXERCISE 4·2

1. (*a*) Discuss the utility and limitations of graphic method of presenting statistical data.

   (*b*) Discuss the advantages and limitations of representing statistical data by diagrams (including graphs).

   (*c*) What are the general rules of graphical presentation of data ? [*C.S. (Foundation), June 2001*]

   (*d*) Explain the advantages of graphic representation of statistical data.

2. (*a*) What are various types of graphs used for presenting a frequency distribution. Discuss briefly their (*i*) construction and (*ii*) relative merits and demerits.

   (*b*) Explain briefly the various methods that are used for graphical representation of frequency distribution.

3. Give an illustration each of the type of data for which you would expect the frequency curve to be :

(*i*) fairly symmetrical, (*ii*) positively skewed, (*iii*) negatively skewed, (*iv*) J-shaped, (*v*) U-shaped.

4. Comment on the following :

(*a*) "The wandering of a line is more powerful in its effect on the mind than a tabulated statement; it shows what is happening and what is likely to take place just as quickly as the eye is capable of working." —*Boddington*

(*b*) "Graphs are dynamic, dramatic. They may epitomise an epoch, each dot a fact, each slope an event, each curve a history ; wherever there are data to record, inferences to draw, or facts to tell, graphs furnish the unrivalled means whose power we are just beginning to realise and apply." —*Hubbard*

5. Explain clearly the distinctions between "*natural scale*" and "*semi-logarithmic scale*" used in the graphical presentation of data.

6. (*a*) What do you mean by a false base line ? Explain its utility in graphic representation of statistical data.

(*b*) "A false base line of a graph is a wrong base line." Comment.

(*c*) What is false base line ? Under what circumstances should it be used ?

7. Describe briefly the construction of histogram and frequency polygon of a frequency distribution and state their uses.

Prepare a Histogram and a Frequency Polygon from the following data :

Class :	0—6	6—12	12—18	18—24	24—30	30—36
f :	4	8	15	20	12	6

8. Draw a histogram of the following distribution :

Life of Electric Lamp (in hours) (Mid-values) :	1010	1030	1050	1070	1090
Firm A (No. of lamps) :	10	130	482	360	18

9. From the following data draw (*i*) *Histogram*, (*ii*) *Frequency polygon* and (*iii*) *Frequency curve*:

Class	0—10	10—20	20—30	30—40	40—50	50—60	60—70	70—80	80—90
Frequency	4	6	7	14	16	14	8	6	5

[*C.S. (Foundation), June 2000*]

10. Draw a histogram from the following data :

Daily wages (Rs.) :	10—20	20—30	30—40	40—60	60—80	80—110
No. of employees :	5	10	12	28	20	24

[*C.S. (Foundation), June 2002*]

11. Draw a histogram to represent the following distribution :

Monthly income	*No. of families*	*Monthly income*	*No. of families*
0— 750	15	3000— 5000	309
750—1000	51	5000 — 7500	162
1000—1500	199	7500—10000	66
1500—2000	240	10000—15000	50
2000—3000	324	15000—25000	27
		Total	1443

How many families can be expected to have monthly income between 3500 and 4250 rupees.

Hint : $\frac{4250-3500}{2000} \times 309 = 115{\cdot}88 \simeq 116.$

12. (*a*) What are cumulative frequencies ? How do you present them diagrammatically for discrete and continuous distributions ?

(*b*) What is a cumulative frequency curve ? Mention its kinds. Take an example to illustrate them.

(*c*) Explain the difference between a histogram and frequency polygon. What is an ogive curve ? State the purpose for which it is used.

13. Draw the 'less than' and 'more than' ogive curves from the data given below :

Weekly Wages ('00 Rs.) :	0—20	20—40	40—60	60—80	80—100
No. of Workers :	10	20	40	20	10

[*C.S. (Foundation), Dec. 2000*]

14. For the following distribution of wages, draw ogive and hence find the value of median.

Monthly Wages	*Frequency*	*Monthly Wages*	*Frequency*
12·5—17·5	2	37·5—42·5	4
17·5—22·5	22	42·5—47·5	6
22·5—27·5	10	47·5—52·5	1
27·5—32·5	14	52·5—57·5	1
32·5—37·5	3	Total	63

Ans. Md. = 26 (approx.)

15. Age distribution of 200 employees of a firm is given below. Construct a less than ogive curve and hence or otherwise calculate semi-inter-quartile range $(Q_3 - Q_1) / 2$ of the distribution.

Age in years (less than) :	25	30	35	40	45	50	55
No. of employees :	10	25	75	130	170	189	200

16. The following table gives the distribution of the wages of 65 employees in a factory :

Wages in Rs. (Equal to or more than)	50	60	70	80	90	100	110	120
Number of Employees	65	57	47	31	17	7	2	0

Draw a 'less than' ogive curve from the above data, and estimate the number of employees earning at least Rs. 63 but less than Rs. 75.

Ans. 15

17. Draw a less than cumulative frequency curve of the following distribution and find the limits for the central 60% of the distribution from the graph.

x (less than) :	5	10	15	20	25	30	35	40	45
Frequency :	2	11	29	45	69	83	90	96	100

Ans. 13 to 29·8.

18. Draw a less than ogive from the following data :

Weekly Income (Rs.) (equal to or more than)	12,000	11,000	10,000	8,000	6,000	4,000	3,000	2,000	1,000
No. of Families	0	6	14	26	42	54	62	70	80

From the graph estimate the number of families in the income range of Rs. 2,400 and Rs. 10,500. Also find maximum income of the lowest 25% of the families. *[Delhi Univ., B.Com,. (Hons.), 2006]*

Ans.

Income (in Rs. '000)	10—20	20—30	30—40	40—60	60—80	80—100	100—110	110—120
No. of families	10	8	8	12	16	12	8	6

57 (Approximately); Q_1 = Rs. 3,250.

19. The monthly profits (Rs. lakhs) earned by 100 companies during the financial year 2002-03 are given in the table below :

Monthly Profit (Rs. lakhs) :	20—30	30–40	40–50	50—60	60—70	70—80	80—90	90—100
Number of companies :	4	8	18	30	15	10	8	7

Draw the OGIVE by "less than method" and "more than method." *[Delhi Univ., (FMS), M.B.A., March 2004]*

20. Construct a frequency table for the following data regarding annual profits, in thousands of rupees in 50 firms, taking 25—34, 35—44, etc., as class intervals.

28	35	61	29	36	48	57	67	69	50
48	40	47	42	41	37	51	62	63	33
31	32	35	40	38	37	60	51	54	56
37	46	42	38	61	59	58	44	39	57
38	44	45	45	47	38	44	47	47	64

Construct a less than ogive and find :

(*i*) Number of firms having profit between Rs. 37,000 and Rs. 58,000.

(*ii*) Profit above which 10% of the firms will have their profits.

(*iii*) Middle 50% profit group.

Ans. (*i*) 30, (*ii*) Rs. 62,000, (*iii*) Rs. 39,000 to Rs. 56,000.

21. What do you mean by a historigram ? How does it differ from histogram ?

22. (*a*) What are different types of graphs commonly used to present a time series data ? Bring out their salient features.

(*b*) Describe briefly :

(*i*) Historigram, (*ii*) Silhouette or Net Balance Graph, (*iii*) Range Graph, (*iv*) Band Graph,

for presenting time series data.

23. Represent the data relating to consolidated budgetary position of states in India as given below, on a graph paper. (*Rs. crore*)

Year	*Revenue*	*Expenditure*	*Surplus or Deficit*
1955-56	560·1	626·4	–66·3
1956-57	577·0	654·3	–77·3
1957-58	705·6	677·3	+28·3
1958-59	742·1	745·8	–3·7
1959-60	833·9	829·9	+4·0

Also depict graphically, the net balance of trade.

24. Represent the following data by means of a time series graph.

Year	1990	1991	1992	1993	1994	1995	1996	1997	1998	1999
Export (Rs. '000)	267	269	263	275	270	280	282	272	265	266
Import (Rs. '000)	307	310	280	260	275	271	280	280	260	265

Show also the net balance of trade.

25. (*a*) What is a false base line? When is it used on an arithmetic line graph ? [*Delhi Univ. B.Com. (Pass), 2001*]

(*b*) Prepare a graph of the following data by using a false base line.

Consumer Price Index Numbers (1960 = 100)

Centre	Years					
	1969	1970	1971	1972	1973	1974
All India	177	186	192	207	250	360
Delhi	185	199	211	222	265	337

26. Present the following hypothetical data graphically.

AREA AND PRODUCTION OF RICE IN INDIA

Year	:	1987	1988	1989	1990	1991	1992
Area (Million Acres)	:	174·1	177·3	176·1	177·9	179·3	179·1
Production (Million Tonnes)	:	72·5	77·8	74·8	77·2	78·0	74·8

27. Marks obtained by 100 students in Economics are given below. Draw an appropriate graph to represent them :

Marks	*Males*	*Females*	*Total*
30—40	8	6	14
40—50	6	10	16
50—60	14	6	20
60—70	13	12	25
70—80	12	13	25
Total	53	47	100

[*C.S. (Foundation). Dec. 1999*]

Hint: Draw three graphs for males, females and total on the same graph paper.

28. Present the following data about India by a suitable graph :

PRODUCTION IN MILLION TONS

Year	*Rice*	*Wheat*	*Pulses*	*Other Cereals*	*Total*
1962	30	10	10	14	64
1963	32	11	8	18	69
1964	33	8·5	11·5	20	73
1965	35	12	11	20	78
1966	36	10	10	22	78
1967	38	11	9	23	81

Hint: Band Graph

29. Present the following data by a suitable graph :

MINIMUM AND MAXIMUM PRICE OF GOLD FOR 10 GMS. FOR THE YEAR 1967

Months	*Highest Price*	*Lowest Price*	*Months*	*Highest Price*	*Lowest Price*
	(*Rs.*)	(*Rs.*)		(*Rs.*)	(*Rs.*)
January	160·0	152·0	July	175·0	163·2
February	162·2	156·0	August	175·8	160·0
March	165·0	160·3	September	172·2	165·0
April	166·5	162·4	October	178·0	168·0
May	168·2	160·5	November	171·0	165·0
June	170·0	161·9	December	175·5	167·0

Hint: Range Graph.

30. (*a*) Differentiate between the natural scale and logarithmic scale used in graphic presentation of data. In which cases should the latter scale be used ?

(*b*) Explain what is meant by semi-logarithmic diagram and discuss its advantages over the natural scale diagram.

(*c*) Explain briefly how you will interpret the graphs drawn on a semi-logarithmic scale.

(*d*) What do you understand by a ratio-scale ? Under what situations ratio charts should be drawn ?

31. The following table shows the total sales of Gold Bonds by the Reserve Bank of India :

Month	*Year*	*Rs. ('000)*	*Month*	*Year*	*Rs. ('000)*
October	1965	15,560	April	1966	3,250
November	1965	13,170	May	1966	3,570
December	1965	18,740	June	1966	3,620
January	1966	12,450	July	1966	3,140
February	1966	8,320	August	1966	2,580
March	1966	7,540	September	1966	2,540

Represent the data graphically on the logarithmic scale

32. Plot the following data graphically on the logarithmic scale.

Year	*Total notes issued* (*in crores Rs.*)	*Total notes in circulation* (*in crores Rs.*)
1965—66	2890	2866
1966—67	3065	3020
1967—68	3242	3194
1968—69	3536	3497
1969—70	3866	3843

33. Present the following data graphically and comment on the features thus revealed :

Year	*Production of steel plates* (*in thousand tons*)	
	Unit A	*Unit B*
1990	30	40
1992	29	20
1994	31	10
1996	30	20
1998	30	30
2000	30	40
2002	30	60

How will the graph look like if the data are plotted on semi-logarithmic scale ?

5 Averages or Measures of Central Tendency

5·1. INTRODUCTION

One of the important objectives of statistical analysis is to determine various numerical measures which describe the inherent characteristics of a frequency distribution. The first of such measures is *average*. The averages are the measures which condense a huge unwieldy set of numerical data into single numerical values which are representative of the entire distribution. In the words of Prof. R.A. Fisher, "*The inherent inability of the human mind to grasp in its entirety a large body of numerical data compels us to seek relatively few constants that will adequately describe the data*". Averages are one of such few constants. Averages provide us the gist and give a bird's eye view of the huge mass of unwieldy numerical data.

Averages are the typical values around which other items of the distribution congregate. They are the values which lie between the two extreme observations, (*i.e.,* the smallest and the largest observations), of the distribution and give us an idea about the concentration of the values in the central part of the distribution. Accordingly they are also sometimes referred to as the *Measures of Central Tendency.* Averages are very much useful :

(*i*) For describing the distribution in concise manner.
(*ii*) For comparative study of different distributions.
(*iii*) For computing various other statistical measures such as dispersion, skewness, kurtosis and various other basic characteristics of a mass of data.

Remark. Averages are also sometimes referred to as *Measures of Location* since they enable us to locate the position or place of the distribution in question.

We give below some definitions of an average as given by different statisticians from time to time.

WHAT THEY SAY ABOUT AVERAGES — SOME DEFINITIONS

"*Averages are statistical constants which enable us to comprehend in a single effort the significance of the whole.*"—**A.L. Bowley**

"*An average is a single value selected from a group of values to represent them in some way, a value which is supposed to stand for whole group of which it is part, as typical of all the values in the group.*"—**A.E. Waugh**

"*An average value is a single value within the range of the data that is used to represent all of the values in the series. Since an average is somewhere within the range of the data, it is sometimes called a measure of central value.*"—**Croxton and Cowden**

"*An average is sometimes called a measure of central tendency because individual values of the variable usually cluster around it. Averages are useful, however, for certain types of data in which there is little or no central tendency.*"—**Crum and Smith**

"*Statistical analysis seeks to develop concise summary figures which describe a large body of quantitative data. One of the most widely used set of summary figures is known as measures of location, which are often referred to as averages, measures of central tendency or central location. The purpose for computing an average value for a set of observations is to obtain a single value which is representative of all the items and which the mind can grasp simply and quickly. The single value is the point or location around which the individual items cluster.*"

—**Lawrence J. Kaplan**

5·2. REQUISITES OF A GOOD AVERAGE OR MEASURE OF CENTRAL TENDENCY

According to Prof. Yule, the following are the desideratta (requirements) to be satisfied by an *ideal* average or measure of central tendency :

(*i*) *It should be rigidly defined i.e.,* the definition should be clear and unambiguous so that it leads to one and only one interpretation by different persons. In other words, the definition should not leave anything to the discretion of the investigator or the observer. If it is not rigidly defined then the bias introduced by the investigator will make its value unstable and render it unrepresentative of the distribution.

(*ii*) *It should be easy to understand and calculate* even for a non-mathematical person. In other words, it should be readily comprehensible and should be computed with sufficient ease and rapidity and should not involve heavy arithmetical calculations. However, this should not be accomplished at the expense of accuracy or some other advantages which an average may possess.

(*iii*) *It should be based on all the observations.* Thus, in the computation of an ideal average the entire set of data at our disposal should be used and there should not be any loss of information resulting from not using the available data. Obviously, if the whole data is not used in computing the average, it will be unrepresentative of the distribution.

(*iv*) *It should be suitable for further mathematical treatment.* In other words, the average should possess some important and interesting mathematical properties so that its use in further statistical theory is enhanced. For example, if we are given the averages and sizes (frequencies) of a number of different groups then for an ideal average we should be in a position to compute the average of the combined group. If an average is not amenable to further algebraic manipulation, then obviously its use will be very much limited for further applications in statistical theory.

(*v*) *It should be affected as little as possible by fluctuations of sampling.* By this we mean that if we take independent random samples of the same size from a given population and compute the average for each of these samples then, for an ideal average, the values so obtained from different samples should not vary much from one another. The difference in the values of the average for different samples is attributed to the so-called *fluctuations of sampling*. This property is also explained by saying that *an ideal average should possess sampling stability.*

(*vi*) *It should not be affected much by extreme observations.* By extreme observations we mean very small or very large observations. Thus a few very small or very large observations should not unduly affect the value of a good average.

5·3. VARIOUS MEASURES OF CENTRAL TENDENCY

The following are the five measures of central tendency or measures of location which are commonly used in practice.

(*i*) Arithmetic Mean or simply Mean
(*ii*) Median
(*iii*) Mode
(*iv*) Geometric Mean
(*v*) Harmonic Mean

In the following sections we shall discuss them in detail one by one.

5·4. ARITHMETIC MEAN

Arithmetic mean of a given set of observations is their sum divided by the number of observations. For example, the arithmetic mean of 5, 8, 10, 15, 24 and 28 is

$$\frac{5+8+10+15+24+28}{6} = \frac{90}{6} = 15$$

In general, if $X_1, X_2, \ldots, X_n$ are the given n observations, then their arithmetic mean, usually denoted by $\bar{X}$ is given by :

$$\bar{X} = \frac{X_1 + X_2 + \ldots + X_n}{n} = \frac{\Sigma X}{n} \qquad \ldots(5{\cdot}1)$$

where ΣX is the sum of the observations.

In case of frequency distribution :

X	X_1	X_2	X_2	...	X_n
f	f_1	f_2	f_3	...	f_n

the arithmetic mean $\bar{X}$ is given by :

$$\bar{X} = \frac{(X_1 + X_1 + \ldots f_1 \text{ times}) + (X_2 + X_2 + \ldots f_2 \text{ times}) + . + (X_n + X_n + \ldots f_n \text{ times.})}{f_1 + f_2 + \ldots + f_n}$$

$$= \frac{f_1X_1 + f_2X_2 + \ldots + f_nX_n}{f_1 + f_2 + \ldots + f_n} = \frac{\Sigma fX}{\Sigma f} = \frac{\Sigma fX}{N} \qquad \ldots(5·2)$$

where $N = \Sigma f$, is the total frequency.

In case of continuous or grouped frequency distribution, the value of X is taken as the mid-value of the corresponding class.

Remark. The symbol Σ is the letter capital sigma of the Greek alphabet and is used in mathematics to denote the sum of values.

Steps for the Computation of Arithmetic Mean

1. Multiply each value of X or the mid-value of the class (in case of grouped or continuous frequency distribution) by the corresponding frequency f.

2. Obtain the total of the products obtained in step 1 above to get ΣfX.

3. Divide the total obtained in step 2 by $N = \Sigma f$, the total frequency.

The resulting value gives the arithmetic mean.

Example 5·1. *The intelligence quotients (IQ's) of 10 boys in a class are given below :*

70, 120, 110, 101, 88, 83, 95, 98, 107, 100

Find the mean I.Q.

Solution. Mean I.Q. ($\bar{X}$) of the 10 boys is given by :

$$\bar{X} = \frac{\Sigma X}{n} = \frac{1}{10}(70 + 120 + 110 + 101 + 88 + 83 + 95 + 98 + 107 + 100) = \frac{972}{10} = 97·2$$

Example 5·2. *The following is the frequency distribution of the number of telephone calls received in 245 successive one-minute intervals at an exchange :*

Number of Calls	:	0	1	2	3	4	5	6	7
Frequency	:	14	21	25	43	51	40	39	12

Obtain the mean number of calls per minute.

Solution. Let the variable X denote the number of calls received per minute at the exchange.

COMPUTATION OF MEAN NUMBER OF CALLS

No. of Calls (X)	0	1	2	3	4	5	6	7	Total
Frequency (f)	14	21	25	43	51	40	39	12	$N = 245$
fX	0	21	50	129	204	200	234	84	$\Sigma fX = 922$

Mean number of calls per minute at the exchange is given by :

$$\bar{X} = \frac{\Sigma fX}{N} = \frac{922}{245} = 3·763$$

5·4·1. Step Deviation Method for Computing Arithmetic Mean. It may be pointed out that the formula (5·2) can be used conveniently if the values of X or/and f are small. However, if the values of X or/and f are large, the calculation of mean by the formula (5·2) is quite tedious and time consuming. In such a case the calculations can be reduced to a great extent by using the step deviation method which consists in taking the deviations (differences) of the given observations from any arbitrary value A.

Let $$d = X - A \qquad \ldots(5\cdot3)$$

then, $$\bar{X} = A + \frac{\Sigma fd}{N} \qquad \ldots(5\cdot4)$$

This formula is much more convenient to use for numerical problems than the formula (5·2).

In case of grouped or continuous frequency distribution, with class intervals of equal magnitude, the calculations are further simplified by taking :

$$d = \frac{X - A}{h} \qquad \ldots(5\cdot5)$$

where X is the mid-value of the class and h is the common magnitude of the class intervals. Then

$$\bar{X} = A + h\frac{\Sigma fd}{N} \qquad \ldots(5\cdot6)$$

Steps for Computation of Mean by Step Deviation Method in (5·6)

Step 1. Compute $d = (X - A)/h$, A being any arbitrary number and h is the common magnitude of the classes. Algebraic signs + or – are to be taken with the deviations.

Step 2. Multiply d by the corresponding frequency f to get fd.

Step 3. Find the sum of the products obtained in step 2 to get Σfd.

Step 4. Divide the sum obtained in step 3 by N, the total frequency.

Step 5. Multiply the value obtained in step 4 by h.

Step 6. Add A to the value obtained in step (5).

The resulting value gives the arithmetic mean of the given distribution.

Remarks 1. If we take $h = 1$, then formula (5·6) reduces to formula (5·4).

2. Any number can serve the purpose of the arbitrary constant 'A' used in (5·4) and (5·6) but generally the value of X corresponding to the middle part of the distribution will be more convenient. In fact, 'A' need not necessarily be one of the values of X.

Example 5·3. *Calculate the mean for the following frequency distribution :*

Marks :	*0—10*	*10—20*	*20—30*	*30—40*	*40—50*	*50—60*	*60—70*
Number of students :	*6*	*5*	*8*	*15*	*7*	*6*	*3*

(i) By the direct formula. ; *(ii) By the step deviation method.*

Solution.

COMPUTATION OF ARITHMETIC MEAN

Marks	*Mid-value (X)*	*Number of Students (f)*	*fX*	$d = \frac{X-35}{10}$	*fd*
0—10	5	6	30	–3	–18
10—20	15	5	75	–2	–10
20—30	25	8	200	–1	–8
30—40	35	15	525	0	0
40—50	45	7	315	1	7
50—60	55	6	330	2	12
60—70	65	3	195	3	9
		$N = \Sigma f = 50$	$\Sigma fX = 1670$		$\Sigma fd = -8$

***(i)* Direct Formula** : Mean $(\bar{X}) = \frac{\Sigma fX}{\Sigma f} = \frac{1670}{50} = 33\cdot4$ marks.

***(ii)* Step Deviation Method** : In the usual notations we have $A = 35$ and $h = 10$.

$$\therefore \quad \bar{X} = A + \frac{h\Sigma fd}{N} = 35 + \frac{10 \times (-8)}{50} = 35 - 1\cdot6 = 33\cdot4 \text{ marks.}$$

5·4·2. Mathematical Properties of Arithmetic Mean. Arithmetic mean possesses some very interesting and important mathematical properties as given below :

Property 1. *The algebraic sum of the deviations of the given set of observations from their arithmetic mean is zero.*

Mathematically, $\Sigma(X - \overline{X}) = 0,$ ...(5·7)

or for a frequency distribution : $\Sigma f(X - \overline{X}) = 0$ ...(5·7*a*)

Proof. $\Sigma f(X - \overline{X}) = \Sigma(fX - f\overline{X}) = \Sigma fX - \Sigma f\overline{X}$

$= \Sigma fX - \overline{X}\,\Sigma f = \Sigma fX - \overline{X}.N$ [$\because$ $\overline{X}$ is a constant and $\Sigma f = N$]

$\therefore$ $\Sigma f(X - \overline{X}) = N\overline{X} - \overline{X}.N = 0$ [$\because$ $\overline{X} = \frac{1}{N}\Sigma fX \Rightarrow \Sigma fX = N\overline{X}$]

Remarks 1. In computing *algebraic* sum of deviations, we take into consideration the plus and minus sign of the deviations $(X - \overline{X})$ as against the *absolute* deviations (*c.f.* Mean Deviation in Chapter 6) where we ignore the signs of the deviations.

2. Verification of Property 1 from the data of Example 5·3.

ALGEBRAIC SUM OF DEVIATIONS FROM MEAN

Marks	X	f	$X - \overline{X} = X - 33{\cdot}4$	$f(X - \overline{X})$
0—10	5	6	−28·4	−170·4
10—20	15	5	−18·4	− 92·0
20—30	25	8	− 8·4	− 67·2
30—40	35	15	1·6	24·0
40—50	45	7	11·6	81·2
50—60	55	6	21·6	129·6
60—70	65	3	31·6	94·8
				$\Sigma f(X - \overline{X}) = 0$

Thus $\Sigma f(X - \overline{X}) = 0$, as required.

It should be kept in mind that in case of the values of the variable when no frequencies are given, we will get $\Sigma(X - \overline{X}) = 0$.

As a simple illustration, let us consider the following case.

X	1	2	3	4	5	6	7	$\Sigma X = 28$
$X - \overline{X} = X - 4$	−3	−2	−1	0	1	2	3	$\Sigma(X - \overline{X}) = 0$

$$\overline{X} = \frac{\Sigma X}{n} = \frac{28}{7} = 4$$

Hence $\Sigma(X - \overline{X}) = 0$.

Property 2. Mean of the Combined Series. If we know the sizes and means of two component series, then we can find the mean of the resultant series obtained on combining the given series.

If n_1 and n_2 are the sizes and $\overline{X}_1$, $\overline{X}_2$ are the respective means of two groups then the mean $\overline{X}$ of the combined group of size $n_1 + n_2$ is given by :

$$\overline{X} = \frac{n_1\overline{X}_1 + n_2\overline{X}_2}{n_1 + n_2} \qquad \text{...(5·8)}$$

Proof. We know that if $\overline{X}$ is the mean of n observations

then $\overline{X} = \frac{\Sigma X}{n} \Rightarrow \Sigma X = n\overline{X}$

i.e., Sum of n observations $= n \times$ Arithmetic Mean ...(*)

If $\bar{X}_1$ is the mean of n_1 observations of the first group and $\bar{X}_2$ is the mean of n_2 observations of the second group, then on using (*), we get

The sum of n_1 observations of the first group $= n_1 \times \bar{X}_1 = n_1\bar{X}_1$

The sum of other n_2 observations of the second group $= n_2 \times \bar{X}_2 = n_2\bar{X}_2$

$\therefore$ The sum of $(n_1 + n_2)$ observations of the combined group $= n_1\bar{X}_1 + n_2\bar{X}_2$ ...(**)

Hence, the mean $\bar{X}$ of the combined group $n_1 + n_2$ observations is given by :

$$\bar{X} = \frac{\text{Sum of } (n_1 + n_2) \text{ observations}}{n_1 + n_2} = \frac{n_1\bar{X}_1 + n_2\bar{X}_2}{n_1 + n_2} \qquad \text{[From (**)]}$$

Remarks 1. Some writers use the notation $\bar{X}_{12}$ for the combined mean of two groups and thus we may write :

$$\bar{X}_{12} = \frac{n_1\bar{X}_1 + n_2\bar{X}_2}{n_1 + n_2} \qquad \text{...(5·8}a\text{)}$$

2. Generalisation. In general, if $\bar{X}_1, \bar{X}_2, ..., \bar{X}_k$ are the arithmetic means of k groups with $n_1, n_2, ..., n_k$ observations respectively then we can similarly prove that the mean $\bar{X}$ of the combined group of size $n_1 + n_2 + ... + n_k$ is given by :

$$\bar{X} = \frac{n_1\bar{X}_1 + n_2\bar{X}_2 + ... + n_k\bar{X}_k}{n_1 + n_2 + ... + n_k} \qquad \text{...(5·8}b\text{)}$$

Property 3. *The sum of the squares of deviations of the given set of observations is minimum when taken from the arithmetic mean.*

Mathematically, for a given frequency distribution, the sum

$$S = \Sigma f(X - A)^2, \qquad \text{... (5·9)}$$

which represents the sum of the squares of deviations of given observations from any arbitrary value 'A' is minimum when $A = \bar{X}$.

This means that, if for any set of data, we compute :

S_1 = Sum of squared deviations from mean $= \Sigma (X - \bar{X})^2$, and

S = Sum of squared deviations from any arbitrary point A

$= \Sigma (X - A)^2 \ ; \ A \neq \bar{X}$,

then S_1 is always less than S *i.e.,* $S_1 < S$.

Illustration of Property 3. Let us consider the values of the variable X as 1, 2, 3, 4, 5, 6, 7.

TABLE 1. **SUM OF SQUARED DEVIATIONS FROM MEAN**

X	$X - \bar{X} = X - 4$	$(X - \bar{X})^2$
1	−3	9
2	−2	4
3	−1	1
4	0	0
5	1	1
6	2	4
7	3	9
Total 28	$\Sigma(X - \bar{X}) = 0$	$\Sigma(X - \bar{X})^2 = 28$

TABLE 2. **SUM OF SQUARED DEVIATIONS ABOUT ARBITRARY POINT A = 5**

X	$X - A = X - 5$	$(X - A)^2$
1	−4	16
2	−3	9
3	−2	4
4	−1	1
5	0	0
6	1	1
7	2	4
Total		$\Sigma(X - A)^2 = 35$

$$\text{Mean } (\bar{X}) = \frac{\Sigma X}{7} = \frac{28}{7} = 4$$

The sum of the squared deviations of given observations from their mean, in this case is

$$\Sigma(X - \bar{X})^2 = 28. \text{ (From Table 1)}$$

For the above case we take the deviations of the values X from any arbitrary point A, ($A \neq \bar{X}$) and then compute the sum of squared deviations about A *viz.*, $\Sigma(X - A)^2$, $A \neq \bar{X}$; then this sum will be greater than 28 for all values of A. Let us in particular take $A = 5$, (not equal to mean $\bar{X} = 4$).

Thus $\quad \Sigma(X - A)^2 = \Sigma(X - 5)^2 = 35, \quad$ (From Table 2)

which is greater than the sum of squared deviations about mean *viz.*, 28.

Property 4. We have : $\quad \bar{X} = \frac{\Sigma fX}{N} \quad \Rightarrow \quad \Sigma fX = N\bar{X} \quad$ ...(5·10)

Result (5·10) is quite useful in the following problems :

(*a*) If we are given the mean wages ($\bar{X}$) of a number of workers (N) in a factory, then using (5·10) we can determine the total wage bill of the factory.

(*b*) Wrong Observations. Suppose we compute the mean $\bar{X}$ of N observations and later on it is found that one, two or more of the observations were wrongly copied down. It is now required to compute the corrected mean by replacing the wrong observations by the correct ones. By using (5·10), we can obtain the uncorrected sum of the observations which is given by $N\bar{X}$. From this, if we subtract the wrong observations, say, X_1' and X_2' and add the corresponding correct observations, say, X_1 and X_2 we can obtain the corrected sum of the observations which will be given by

$$N\bar{X} - (X_1' + X_2') + X_1 + X_2$$

Dividing this by N, we get the corrected mean.

In general, if r observations are misread as $X_1', X_2', \ldots, X_r'$ while correct observations are $X_1, X_2, \ldots, X_r$, then the corrected sum of observations is given by

$$N\bar{X} - (X_1' + X_2' + \ldots + X_r') + (X_1 + X_2 + \ldots + X_r)$$

Dividing this sum by N, we get the corrected mean.

For numerical illustration see Example **5·11**.

Remark. *If all the observations of a series are added, subtracted, multiplied or divided by a constant* β, *the mean is also added, subtracted, multiplied or divided by the same constant.*

Let the given observations of the series be $x_1, x_2, \ldots, x_n$ with mean $\bar{x}$, given by

$$\bar{x} = \frac{1}{n}\left(x_1 + x_2 + \ldots + x_n\right) \quad \ldots(*)$$

Let the new series obtained on adding, subtracting, multiplying and dividing each observation of the given x-series by a constant β be denoted by the variables U, V, W and Z respectively so that :

$$U = X + \beta, \qquad V = X - \beta, \qquad W = \beta X, \qquad Z = \frac{X}{\beta}$$

Then

$$\bar{U} = \bar{x} + \beta, \qquad \bar{V} = \bar{x} - \beta, \qquad \bar{W} = \beta \, . \, \bar{x}, \qquad \text{and} \quad \bar{Z} = \frac{1}{\beta} \cdot \bar{x}$$

Illustration. Let the mean of 10 observations be 35. If each observation is increased by 5, then the new mean is also increased by 5, *i.e.*, it becomes 35 + 5 = 40. Similarly, if each observation is decreased by 5, the new mean will be 35 – 5 = 30. Further, if each observation is multiplied by 2, the new mean will be $2 \times 35 = 70$.

5·4·3. Merits and Demerits of Arithmetic Mean

Merits. In the light of the properties laid down by Prof. Yule for an ideal measure of central tendency, arithmetic mean possesses the following merits :

(*i*) It is rigidly defined.

(*ii*) It is easy to calculate and understand

(*iii*) It is based on all the observations.

(*iv*) It is suitable for further mathematical treatment. The mean of the combined series is given by (5·8) or (5·8*a*). Moreover, it possesses many important mathematical properties (Properties 1 to 4 as discussed earlier) because of which it has very wide applications in statistical theory.

(*v*) Of all the averages, arithmetic mean is affected least by fluctuations of sampling. This property is explained by saying that arithmetic mean is a *stable* average.

Demerits. (*i*) The strongest drawback of arithmetic mean is that it is very much affected by extreme observations. Two or three very large values of the variable may unduly affect the value of the arithmetic mean. Let us consider an industrial complex which houses the workers and some big officials like general manager, chief engineer, architect etc. The average salary of the workers (skilled and unskilled) is, say, Rs. 8,000 per month. If the salaries of the few big bosses (who draw very high salaries) are also included, the average wage per worker comes out to be Rs. 12,000 say. Thus, if we say that the average salary of the workers in the factory is Rs. 12,000 p.m. it gives a very good impression and one is tempted to think that the workers are well paid and their standard of living is good. But the real picture is entirely different. Thus, in the case of extreme observations, the arithmetic mean gives a distorted picture and is no longer representative of the distribution and quite often leads to very misleading conclusions. Thus, while dealing with extreme observations, arithmetic mean should be used with caution.

(*ii*) Arithmetic mean cannot be used in the case of open end classes such as less than 10, more than 70, etc., since for such classes we cannot determine the mid-value X of the class intervals unless (*i*) we estimate the end intervals or (*ii*) we are given the total value of the variable in the open end classes. In such cases mode or median (discussed latter) may be used.

(*iii*) It cannot be determined by inspection nor can it be located graphically.

(*iv*) Arithmetic mean cannot be used if we are dealing with qualitative characteristics which cannot be measured quantitatively such as intelligence, honesty, beauty, etc. In such cases median (discussed later) is the only average to be used.

(*v*) Arithmetic mean cannot be obtained if a single observation is missing or lost or is illegible unless we drop it out and compute the arithmetic mean of the remaining values.

(*vi*) In extremely asymmetrical (skewed) distribution, usually arithmetic mean is not representative of the distribution and hence is not a suitable measure of location.

(*vii*) Arithmetic mean may lead to wrong conclusions if the details of the data from which it is obtained are not available. In this connection it is worthwhile to quote the words of H. Secrist :

"*If an average is taken as a substitute for the details, then the arithmetic mean, in spite of the simplicity and ease of calculation, has little to recommand when series are non-homogeneous.*"

The following example will illustrate this view point.

Let us consider the following marks obtained by two students A and B in three tests, *viz*., terminal test, half-yearly examination and annual examination respectively.

Marks in :	I Test	II Test	III Test	Average marks
Student A	55%	60%	65%	60%
Student B	65%	60%	55%	60%

The average marks obtained by each of the two students at the end of year are 60%. If we are given the average marks alone we conclude that the level of intelligence of both the students at the end of the year is same. This is a fallacious conclusion since we find from the data that student A has improved consistently while student B has deteriorated consistently.

(*viii*) Arithmetic mean may not be one of the values which the variable actually takes and is termed as a *fictitious* average. Sometimes, it may give meaningless results. In this context it is interesting to quote the remarks of the 'Punch' journal :

"*The figure of 2·2 children per adult female was felt to be in some respects absurd, and a Royal Commission suggested that middle classes be paid money to increase the average to a sounder and more convenient number*".

Example 5·4. *The numbers 3·2, 5·8, 7·9 and 4·5, have frequencies x, (x + 2), (x − 3) and (x + 6) respectively. If the arithmetic mean is 4·876, find the value of x.*

Solution.

COMPUTATION OF MEAN

Number (X)	*Frequency (f)*	*fX*
3·2	x	$3{\cdot}2x$
5·8	$x+2$	$5{\cdot}8\,(x+2)$
7·9	$x-3$	$7{\cdot}9\,(x-3)$
4·5	$x+6$	$4{\cdot}5\,(x+6)$

we have :

$$\Sigma f = x + (x+2) + (x-3) + (x+6) = 4x + 5$$

$$\Sigma fX = 3{\cdot}2x + 5{\cdot}8(x+2) + 7{\cdot}9(x-3) + 4{\cdot}5(x+6)$$

$$= (3{\cdot}2 + 5{\cdot}8 + 7{\cdot}9 + 4{\cdot}5)x + 11{\cdot}6 - 23{\cdot}7 + 27{\cdot}0$$

$$= 21{\cdot}4x + 14{\cdot}9$$

$$\therefore \quad \text{Mean} = \frac{\Sigma fX}{\Sigma f} = \frac{21{\cdot}4x + 14{\cdot}9}{4x+5} = 4{\cdot}876 \text{ (Given)}$$

$$\Rightarrow \quad 21{\cdot}4x + 14{\cdot}9 = 4{\cdot}876\,(4x+5)$$

$$\Rightarrow \quad 21{\cdot}4x + 14{\cdot}9 = 19{\cdot}504x = 24{\cdot}380$$

$$\Rightarrow \quad (21{\cdot}400 - 19{\cdot}504)x = 24{\cdot}380 - 14{\cdot}900$$

$$\Rightarrow \quad 1{\cdot}896x = 9{\cdot}480 \quad \Rightarrow \quad x = \frac{9{\cdot}480}{1{\cdot}896} = 5$$

Example 5·5. *In the following grouped data, X are the mid-values of the class intervals and c is a constant. If the arithmetics mean of the original distribution is 35·84, find its class intervals.*

X–c :	*–21*	*–14*	*–7*	*0*	*7*	*14*	*21*	*Total*
f :	2	12	19	29	20	13	5	100

[*Delhi Univ. B.Com. (Hons.) External), 2007*]

Solution. Here $X - c$ is the deviation d from arbitrary point c *i.e.*, $d = X - c$. Hence, the mean of the distribution is given by :

$$\bar{X} = c + \frac{\Sigma fd}{N} = c + \frac{\Sigma f(X-c)}{N} \qquad \ldots(*)$$

where $N = \Sigma f$.

COMPUTATION OF MEAN AND CLASS INTERVALS

$(X-c)$	f	$f(X-c)$	X	*Class interval*
–21	2	– 42	14	10·5—17·5
–14	12	–168	21	17·5—24·5
–7	19	–133	28	24·5—31·5
0	29	0	35	31·5—38·5
7	20	140	42	38·5—45·5
14	13	182	49	45·5—52·5
21	5	105	56	52·5—59·5
Total	$N = 100$	$\Sigma f(X-c) = 84$		

Using (*) we get

$$\bar{X} = c + \frac{\Sigma f(X-c)}{N} = 35{\cdot}84 \text{ (Given)} \Rightarrow c + \frac{84}{100} = 35{\cdot}84 \Rightarrow c = 35{\cdot}84 - 0{\cdot}84 = 35$$

$$\therefore \quad X - c = 0 \Rightarrow X = c = 35$$

Thus the mid-value of the class corresponding to the value $X - c = 0$ is $X = 35$. Further, since the magnitude of the class interval is 7, the corresponding class interval is obtained on adding and subtracting $(7/2) = 3{\cdot}5$ from 35 and is given by $(35 - 3{\cdot}5, 35 + 3{\cdot}5)$ *i.e.*, 31·5—38·5. The class intervals are given in the last column of the above table.

Example 5·6. *Find the class intervals if the arithmetic mean of the following distribution is 33 and assumed mean 35 :*

Step deviation	−3	−2	−1	0	+1	+2
Frequency	5	10	25	30	20	10

Solution. Here the given step deviation is the deviation d, where $d = (X - A)/h$.

Hence $\bar{X} = A + \frac{h\Sigma fd}{N};\ N = \Sigma f, \quad A = 35 \text{ (given)}$ ...(*)

COMPUTATION OF CLASS INTERVALS

Step deviation (d)	*Frequency (f)*	*fd*	*X*	*Class Interval*
−3	5	−15	5	0—10
−2	10	−20	15	10—20
−1	25	−25	25	20—30
0	30	0	35	30—40
1	20	20	45	40—50
2	10	20	55	50—60
Total	$N = 100$	$\Sigma fd = -20$		

Using (*), $\bar{X} = A + \frac{h\Sigma fd}{N} = 33 \text{ (Given)}$

$\Rightarrow \quad 33 = 35 - \frac{20h}{100} = 35 - 0{\cdot}2h$

$\Rightarrow \quad 0{\cdot}2h = 2 \Rightarrow h = 10$

Also $d = \frac{(X-A)}{h} \Rightarrow X = A + hd = 35 + 10d$

Hence, we can calculate different values of X corresponding to the given values of d. Further, since the magnitude of each class interval is $h = 10$, we obtain the required C.I.'s by adding $\frac{10}{2} = 5$, to and subtracting 5 from each mid-value (X), as shown in the last column of the above table.

Example 5·7. *From the following data of income distribution calculate the arithmetic mean. It is given that (i) the total income of persons in the highest group is Rs. 435, and (ii) none is earning less than Rs. 20.*

Income (Rs.)	*No. of persons*	*Income (Rs.)*	*No. of persons*
Below 30	*16*	*Below 70*	*87*
" 40	*36*	*" 80*	*95*
" 50	*61*	*80 and over*	*5*
" 60	*76*		

Solution. The open class "Income below 30" includes the persons with income less than Rs. 30. But since we are given that none is earning less than Rs. 20, this class will be 20—30. Moreover, we are given the cumulative frequency distribution which has to be converted into the ordinary frequency distribution as given in the following table :

COMPUTATION OF ARITHMETIC MEAN

Income	*Mid-value (X)*	*No. of persons (f)*	*fX*
20—30	25	16	400
30—40	35	36 – 16 = 20	700
40–50	45	61 – 36 = 25	1125
50—60	55	76 – 61 = 15	825
60—70	65	87 – 76 = 11	715
70—80	75	95 – 87 = 8	600
80 and over	—	5	435*
		$\Sigma f = 100$	$\Sigma fX = 4{,}800$

**It is given that total income in the highest group is Rs. 435.*

$\therefore$ Arithmetic Mean $= \dfrac{\Sigma fX}{\Sigma f} = \dfrac{4{,}800}{100} =$ Rs. 48.

Example 5·8. *An investor buys Rs. 1,200 worth of shares in a company each month. During the first 5 months he bought the shares at a price of Rs. 10, Rs. 12, Rs. 15, Rs. 20 and Rs. 24 per share. After 5 months what is the average price paid for the shares by him ?*

Solution. Let X denote the price (in Rupees) of a share. Then the distribution of shares purchased during the first five months is as follows :

Month	*Price per share (X)*	*Total Cost (fX Rs.)*	*No. of shares bought (f)*
1st	10	1200	$\frac{1200}{10} = 120$
2nd	12	1200	$\frac{1200}{12} = 100$
3rd	15	1200	$\frac{1200}{15} = 80$
4th	20	1200	$\frac{1200}{20} = 60$
5th	24	1200	$\frac{1200}{24} = 50$
Total		$\Sigma fX =$ Rs. 6000	$\Sigma f = 410$

Hence, the average price paid per share for the first five months is

$$\bar{X} = \frac{\Sigma fX}{\Sigma f} = \frac{6000}{410} = \text{Rs. } 14{\cdot}63.$$

Remark. For an alternative solution of this problem see Harmonic Mean, Example 5·58.

Example 5·9. *For a certain frequency table which has only been partly reproduced here, the mean was found to be 1·46.*

No. of accidents	:	*0*	*1*	*2*	*3*	*4*	*5*	*Total*
Frequency (No. of days)	:	*46*	*?*	*?*	*25*	*10*	*5*	*200*

Calculate the missing frequencies.

Solution. Let X denote the number of accidents and let the missing frequencies corresponding to $X = 1$ and $X = 2$ be f_1 and f_2 respectively.

We have

$$200 = 86 + f_1 + f_2$$

$$\Rightarrow \quad f_1 + f_2 = 200 - 86 = 114 \qquad \ldots(*)$$

$$\bar{X} = \frac{\Sigma fX}{\Sigma f} = \frac{f_1 + 2f_2 + 140}{200} = 1{\cdot}46 \text{ (Given)}$$

$$\Rightarrow \quad f_1 + 2f_2 + 140 = 1{\cdot}46 \times 200 = 292$$

$$\Rightarrow \quad f_1 + 2f_2 = 292 - 140 = 152 \qquad \ldots(**)$$

Subtracting (*) from (**), we get

$$f_2 = 152 - 114 = 38$$

COMPUTATION OF ARITHMETIC MEAN

No. of accidents (X)	*Frequency (f)*	*fX*
0	46	0
1	f_1	f_1
2	f_2	$2f_2$
3	25	75
4	10	40
5	5	25
Total	$86 + f_1 + f_2 = 200$	$f_1 + 2f_2 + 140$

Substituting in (*), we get

$$f_1 = 114 - f_2 = 114 - 38 = 76$$

Example 5·10. *The following are the hourly salaries in rupees of 20 employees of a firm :*

130	*62*	*145*	*118*	*125*	*76*	*151*	*142*	*110*	*98*
65	*116*	*100*	*103*	*71*	*85*	*80*	*122*	*132*	*95*

The firm gives bonuses of Rs. 10,15, 20, 25 and 30 for individuals in the respective salary groups exceeding Rs. 60 but not exceeding Rs. 80, exceeding Rs. 80 but not exceeding Rs. 100, and so on up to exceeding Rs. 140 but not exceeding Rs. 160. Find the average hourly bonus paid per employee.

Solution. First we shall express the given data in the form of a grouped frequency distribution with salaries (in Rupees) in the class intervals 61—80, 81—100, 101—120, 121—140 and 141—160. The first value in the above distribution is 130, so we put a tally mark against the class interval 121—140; next value is 62, so we put a tally mark against the class 61—80 and so on. Thus the grouped frequency distribution is as follows :

COMPUTATION OF AVERAGE HOURLY BONUS PER EMPLOYEE

Salary (in Rs.)	*Tally Marks*	*Frequency (f)*	*Bonus (in Rs.) (X)*	*fX*
61—80	||||/	5	10	50
81—100	||||	4	15	60
101—120	||||	4	20	80
121—140	||||	4	25	100
141—160	|||	3	30	90
Total		$\Sigma f = 20$		$\Sigma fX = 380$

$\therefore$ Average hourly bonus paid per employee $= \dfrac{\Sigma fX}{\Sigma f} = \dfrac{380}{20} =$ Rs. 19.

Example 5·11. *The mean salary paid to 1,000 employees of an establishment was found to be Rs. 180·40. Later on, after disbursement of salary, it was discovered that the salary of two employees was wrongly entered as Rs. 297 and 165. Their correct salaries were Rs. 197 and Rs. 185. Find the correct Arithmetic Mean.*

Solution. Let the variable X denote the salary (in rupees) of an employee. Then we are given :

$$\bar{X} = \frac{\Sigma X}{1000} = 180{\cdot}40 \quad \Rightarrow \quad \Sigma X = 180400 \quad \ldots(*)$$

Thus the total salary disbursed to all the employees in the establishment is Rs. 1,80,400. After incorporating the corrections we have :

Corrected ΣX = 180400 – (sum of wrong salaries) + (sum of correct salaries)

$$= 180400 - (297 + 165) + (197 + 185)$$

$$= 180400 - 462 + 382 = 180320$$

$\therefore$ Corrected mean salary $= \dfrac{180320}{1000} =$ Rs. 180·32.

Example 5·12. *The table below shows the number of skilled and unskilled workers in two small communities, together with their average hourly wages :*

Worker category	*Ram Nagar*		*Shyam Nagar*	
	Number	*Wage per hour*	*Number*	*Wage per hour*
Skilled	*150*	*Rs. 180*	*350*	*Rs. 175*
Unskilled	*850*	*Rs. 130*	*650*	*Rs. 125*

Determine the average hourly wage for each community. Also give reasons why the results show that the average hourly wage in Shyam Nagar exceeds the hourly wage in Ram Nagar even though in Shyam Nagar the average hourly wage of both categories of workers is lower.

Solution. Let n_1 and n_2 denote the number, and $\overline{X}_1$ and $\overline{X}_2$ denote the wages (in rupees) per hour of the skilled and unskilled workers respectively in the community. Let $\overline{X}$ be the mean wages of all the workers in the community.

Ram Nagar. We have :

$$n_1 = 150, \qquad \overline{X}_1 = \text{Rs. } 180$$

$$n_2 = 850, \qquad \overline{X}_2 = \text{Rs. } 130$$

$$\therefore \quad \overline{X} = \frac{n_1 \overline{X}_1 + n_2 \overline{X}_2}{n_1 + n_2} = \frac{150 \times 180 + 850 \times 130}{150 + 850}$$

$$= \frac{27000 + 110500}{1000} = \frac{137500}{1000} = \text{Rs. } 137{\cdot}50$$

Shyam Nagar. We have :

$$n_1 = 350, \qquad \overline{X}_1 = 175$$

$$n_2 = 650, \qquad \overline{X}_2 = 125$$

$$\therefore \quad \overline{X} = \frac{n_1 \overline{X}_1 + n_2 \overline{X}_2}{n_1 + n_2} = \frac{350 \times 175 + 650 \times 125}{350 + 650}$$

$$= \frac{61250 + 81250}{1000} = \frac{142500}{1000} = \text{Rs. } 142{\cdot}50$$

Thus, we see that the average wage per hour for all the workers combined is higher in Shyam Nagar than in Ram Nagar, although the average hourly wages of both types of workers are lower in Shyam Nagar. The reasons for this somewhat strange looking result may be assigned as follows :

The difference in the average hourly wages in Ram Nagar and Shyam Nagar :

(*a*) For skilled workers is Rs. (180 – 175) = Rs. 5

(*b*) For unskilled workers is Rs. (130 – 125) = Rs. 5

Thus, although the difference in the wages of skilled and unskilled workers in both the communities is same *viz.*, Rs. 5, the number of skilled workers getting relatively higher wages than the unskilled workers is much more in Shyam Nagar than in Ram Nagar and the number of unskilled workers getting relatively less wages is much less in Shyam Nagar than in Ram Nagar. In fact, the ratio of skilled workers to unskilled workers in Ram Nagar is 150 : 850 *i.e.*, 3 : 17 while in Shyam Nagar, it is 350 : 650 *i.e.*, 7 :13.

Example 5·13. *The mean of marks in Statistics of 100 students in a class was 72. The mean of marks of boys was 75, while their number was 70. Find out the mean marks of girls in the class.*

Solution. In the usual notations we are given :

$$n_1 = 70, \quad \overline{x}_1 = 75 \; ; \quad n_1 + n_2 = 100, \quad \overline{x} = 72 \; ; \quad \therefore \; n_2 = 100 - 70 = 30. \quad \text{We want } \overline{x}_2.$$

We have
$$\overline{x} = \frac{n_1 \overline{x}_1 + n_2 \overline{x}_2}{n_1 + n_2} \quad \Rightarrow \quad 72 = \frac{70 \times 75 + 30\overline{x}_2}{100}$$

$$\therefore \quad 72 \times 100 = 5250 + 30\,\overline{x}_2 \quad \Rightarrow \quad \overline{x}_2 = \frac{7200 - 5250}{30} = \frac{1950}{30} = 65$$

Hence, the mean of marks of girls in the class is 65.

Example 5·14. *The average daily wage of all workers in a factory is Rs. 444. If the average daily wages paid to male and female workers are Rs. 480 and Rs. 360 respectively, find the percentage of male and female workers employed by the factory.*

Solution. Let n_1 and n_2 denote respectively the number of male and female workers in the factory and $\overline{X}_1$ and $\overline{X}_2$ denote respectively their average daily salary (in Rupees). Let $\overline{X}$ denote the average salary of all the workers in the factory. Then we are given that :

$$\overline{X}_1 = 480, \qquad \overline{X}_2 = 360 \qquad \text{and} \qquad \overline{X} = 444$$

We have
$$\overline{X} = \frac{n_1 \overline{X}_1 + n_2 \overline{X}_2}{n_1 + n_2} \quad \Rightarrow \quad (n_1 + n_2)\,\overline{X} = n_1 \overline{X}_1 + n_2 \overline{X}_2$$

$$\Rightarrow \quad 444\,(n_1 + n_2) = 480 n_1 + 360 n_2 \quad \Rightarrow \quad (480 - 444) n_1 = (444 - 360) n_2$$

$\therefore \quad 36n_1 = 84n_2 \quad \Rightarrow \quad \dfrac{n_1}{n_2} = \dfrac{84}{36} = \dfrac{7}{3}$

Hence, the male workers in the factory are : $\dfrac{7}{7+3} \times 100 = \dfrac{7}{10} \times 100 = 70\%$

and the female workers in the factory are : $\dfrac{3}{7+3} \times 100 = \dfrac{3}{10} \times 100 = 30\%$.

Example 5·15. *The arithmetic mean height of 50 students of a college is 5′—8″. The height of 30 of these is given in the frequency distribution below. Find the arithmetic mean height of the remaining 20 students.*

Height in inches :	*5′—4″*	*5′—6″*	*5′—8″*	*5′—10″*	*6′—0″*
Frequency :	*4*	*12*	*4*	*8*	*2*

Solution. Let the variable X denote the height of the students in inches.

COMPUTATION OF MEAN HEIGHT OF 30 STUDENTS

Height in inches (X)	*Frequency* (f)	$d = \frac{X-68}{2}$	*fd*
64	4	−2	−8
66	12	−1	−12
68	4	0	0
70	8	1	8
72	2	2	4
	$\Sigma f = 30$		$\Sigma fd = -8$

$\bar{X}_1$ = Mean height (in inches) of $n_1 = 30$ students

$= A + \dfrac{h\Sigma fd}{\Sigma f} = 68 + \dfrac{2 \times (-8)}{30}$

$= \dfrac{2040 - 16}{30} = \dfrac{2024}{30}$ inches ...(*)

Let $\bar{X}_2$ denote the mean height of the remaining $n_2 = 50 - 30 = 20$ students. If $\bar{X}$ is the mean height of the 50 students, then we are given that :

$$\bar{X} = 5'\text{—}8'' = 68''$$

$$\bar{X} = \frac{n_1 \bar{X}_1 + n_2 \bar{X}_2}{n_1 + n_2} \quad \Rightarrow \quad 68 = \frac{30 \times \left(\frac{2024}{30}\right) + 20\,\bar{X}_2}{50} \qquad \text{[Using (*)]}$$

$\therefore \quad 2024 + 20\,\bar{X}_2 = 68 \times 50 = 3400 \Rightarrow \quad \bar{X}_2 = \dfrac{3400 - 2024}{20} = \dfrac{1376}{20} = 68{\cdot}8'' = 5'\text{—}8{\cdot}8''$.

5·5. WEIGHTED ARITHMETIC MEAN

The formulae discussed so far in (5·1) to (5·6) for computing the arithmetic mean are based on the assumption that all the items in the distribution are of equal importance. However, in practice, we might come across situations where the relative importance of all the items of the distribution is not same. If some items in a distribution are more important than others, then this point must be borne in mind, in order that average computed is representative of the distribution. In such cases, proper weightage is to be given to various items - the weights attached to each item being proportional to the importance of the item in the distribution. For example, if we want to have an idea of the change in cost of living of a certain group of people, then the simple mean of the prices of the commodities consumed by them will not do, since all the commodities are not equally important, *e.g.,* wheat, rice, pulses, housing, fuel and lighting are more important than cigarettes, tea, confectionery, cosmetics, etc.

Let $W_1, W_2, \ldots, W_n$ be the weights attached to variable values $X_1, X_2, \ldots, X_n$ respectively. Then the weighted arithmetic mean, usually denoted by $\bar{X}_w$ is given by :

$$\bar{X}_w = \frac{W_1X_1 + W_2X_2 + \ldots + W_nX_n}{W_1 + W_2 + \ldots + W_n} = \frac{\Sigma WX}{\Sigma W} \qquad \ldots(5{\cdot}11)$$

This is precisely same as formula (5·2) with f replaced by W.

In case of frequency distribution, if $f_1, f_2, \ldots, f_n$ are the frequencies of the variable values $X_1, X_2, \ldots, X_n$ respectively then the weighted arithmetic mean is given by :

$$\bar{X}_w = \frac{W_1(f_1X_1) + W_2(f_2X_2) + \ldots + W_n(f_nX_n)}{W_1 + W_2 + \ldots + W_n} = \frac{\Sigma W(f\,X)}{\Sigma W} \qquad \ldots(5{\cdot}12)$$

where $W_1, W_2, \ldots, W_n$ are the respective weights of $X_1, X_2, \ldots, X_n$.

Example 5·16. *A candidate obtained the following percentages of marks in an examination : English 60; Hindi 75; Mathematics 63; Physics 59 ; Chemistry 55. Find the candidate's weighted arithmetic mean if weights 1, 2, 1, 3, 3 respectively are allotted to the subjects.*

Solution. Let the variable X denote the percentage of marks in the examination.

COMPUTATION OF WEIGHTED MEAN

Subject	*Marks (%) (X)*	*Weight (W)*	*WX*
English	60	1	60
Hindi	75	2	150
Mathematics	63	1	63
Physics	59	3	177
Chemistry	55	3	165
		$\Sigma W = 10$	$\Sigma WX = 615$

$\therefore$ Weighted Arithmetic Mean (in%) $= \frac{\Sigma WX}{\Sigma W} = \frac{615}{10} = 61{\cdot}5.$

Example 5·17. *Comment on the performance of the students in three universities given below, using simple and weighted averages :*

University	*Bombay*		*Calcutta*		*Madras*	
Course of study	*% of pass*	*No. of students (in '00s)*	*% of pass*	*No. of students (in '00s)*	*% of pass*	*No. of students (in '00s)*
M.A.	*71*	*3*	*82*	*2*	*81*	*2*
M. Com.	*83*	*4*	*76*	*3*	*76*	*3·5*
B.A.	*73*	*5*	*73*	*6*	*74*	*4·5*
B.Com.	*74*	*2*	*76*	*7*	*58*	*2*
B.Sc.	*65*	*3*	*65*	*3*	*70*	*7*
M.Sc.	*66*	*3*	*60*	*7*	*73*	*2*

Solution.

COMPUTATION OF SIMPLE AND WEIGHTED AVERAGES

University →	*Bombay*			*Calcutta*			*Madras*		
Course of study	*Pass % age* (X_1)	*No. of students (in '00s)* (W_1)	W_1X_1	*Pass % age* (X_2)	*No. of students (in '00s)* (W_2)	W_2X_2	*Pass % age* (X_3)	*No. of students (in '00s)* (W_3)	W_3X_3
M.A.	71	3	213	82	2	164	81	2	162
M.Com.	83	4	332	76	3	228	76	3·5	266
B.A.	73	5	365	73	6	438	74	4·5	333
B.Com,	74	2	148	76	7	532	58	2	116
B.Sc.	65	3	195	65	3	195	70	7	490
M.Sc.	66	3	198	60	7	420	73	2	146
Total	432	20	1451	432	28	1977	432	21	1513

University	*Simple Average*	*Weighted Average*
Bombay	$\frac{\Sigma X_1}{6} = \frac{432}{6} = 72$	$\frac{\Sigma W_1 X_1}{\Sigma W_1} = \frac{1451}{20} = 72{\cdot}55$
Calcutta	$\frac{\Sigma X_2}{6} = \frac{432}{6} = 72$	$\frac{\Sigma W_2 X_2}{\Sigma W_2} = \frac{1977}{28} = 70{\cdot}61$
Madras	$\frac{\Sigma X_3}{6} = \frac{432}{6} = 72$	$\frac{\Sigma W_3 X_3}{\Sigma W_3} = \frac{1513}{21} = 72{\cdot}05$

On the basis of the simple arithmetic mean which comes out to be same for each University *viz.*, 72, we cannot distinguish between the pass percentage of the students in the three Universities. However, the weighted averages show that the results are the best in Bombay University (which has highest weighted average of 72·55), followed by Madras University (which has the weighted average 72·05), while Calcutta University shows the lowest performance.

Example 5·18. *From the results of two colleges A and B below state which of them is better and why ?*

Name of Examination	*College A*		*College B*	
	Appeared	*Passed*	*Appeared*	*Passed*
M.A.	*300*	*250*	*1000*	*800*
M. Com.	*500*	*450*	*1200*	*950*
B.A.	*2000*	*1500*	*1000*	*700*
B.Com.	*1200*	*750*	*800*	*500*
Total	*4000*	*2950*	*4000*	*2950*

Solution.

Name of Examination	*College A*			*College B*		
	Appeared (W_A)	*Passed*	*Pass % age* (X_A)	*Appeared* (W_B)	*Passed*	*Pass % age* (X_B)
M.A.	300	250	$\frac{250}{300} \times 100 = 83{\cdot}33$	1000	800	$\frac{800}{1000} \times 100 = 80$
M.Com.	500	450	$\frac{450}{500} \times 100 = 90$	1200	950	$\frac{950}{1200} \times 100 = 79{\cdot}17$
B.A.	2000	1500	$\frac{1500}{2000} \times 100 = 75$	1000	700	$\frac{700}{1000} \times 100 = 70$
B.Com.	1200	750	$\frac{750}{1200} \times 100 = 62{\cdot}5$	800	500	$\frac{500}{800} \times 100 = 62{\cdot}5$
Total	4000	2950	$\frac{2950}{4000} \times 100 = 73{\cdot}75$	4000	2950	$\frac{2950}{4000} \times 100 = 73{\cdot}75$

On the basis of the given information, it is not possible to decide which college is better, since the criterion for 'better college' is not defined. Let us try to solve this problem by taking the 'Higher Pass Percentage' as criterion for 'better college'.

From the calculation table, we find that the pass percentage in M.A., M.Com. and B.A. is better in college *A* than in college *B* and in B.Com. the pass percentage is same in both the colleges. The simple arithmetic mean of pass percentages in all the four courses is :

$$\overline{X}_A = \frac{83{\cdot}33 + 90 + 75 + 62{\cdot}50}{4} = \frac{310{\cdot}83}{4} = 77{\cdot}71 \quad ; \quad \overline{X}_B = \frac{80 + 79{\cdot}17 + 70 + 62{\cdot}50}{4} = \frac{291{\cdot}67}{4} = 72{\cdot}92$$

Since the mean pass percentage is higher for college *A* than for college *B*, we are tempted to conclude that college *A* is better than college *B*. However, this conclusion is not valid since the average pass percentage is affected by the number of students appearing in the examination in different courses. An appropriate average would be the weighted average of these pass percentages in different courses, the corresponding weights being the number of students appearing in the examination. The weighted means are :

$$\overline{X}_W(A) = \frac{\Sigma W_A X_A}{\Sigma W_A} = \frac{\text{Total number of students passed in college } A}{\text{Total number of students appeared in college } A} \times 100 = \frac{2950}{4000} \times 100 = 73{\cdot}75$$

$$\bar{X}_W(B) = \frac{\Sigma W_B X_B}{\Sigma W_B} = \frac{\text{Total number of students passed in college } B}{\text{Total number of students appeared in college } B} \times 100 = \frac{2950}{4000} \times 100 = 73{\cdot}75$$

On comparing the weighted means, we conclude that both the colleges *A* and *B* are equally good on the basis of the criterion of higher pass percentage for all the students taken together.

Example 5·19. (*a*). *Show that the weighted arithmetic mean of first n natural numbers whose weights are equal to the corresponding numbers is equal to* $(2n + 1)/3$.

(*b*) *Also obtain simple arithmetic mean.*

Solution. The first *n* natural numbers are 1, 2, 3, ..., *n*.

We know that :

$$\left.\begin{aligned} 1 + 2 + 3 + \ldots + n &= \frac{n(n+1)}{2} \\ 1^2 + 2^2 + 3^2 + \ldots + n^2 &= \frac{n(n+1)(2n+1)}{6} \end{aligned}\right\} \quad \ldots(*)$$

COMPUTATION OF WEIGHTED A.M.

X	W	WX
1	1	1^2
2	2	2^2
3	3	3^2
⋮	⋮	⋮
n	n	n^2

(*a*) Weighted arithmetic mean is given by :

$$\bar{X}_w = \frac{\Sigma WX}{\Sigma W} = \frac{1^2 + 2^2 + 3^3 + \ldots + n^2}{1 + 2 + 3 + \ldots + n} \qquad \text{[From above Table]}$$

$$= \frac{n(n+1)(2n+1)}{6} \cdot \frac{2}{n(n+1)} = \frac{2n+1}{3} \qquad \text{[From (*)]}$$

(*b*) Simple A.M. of first *n* natural numbers is

$$\bar{X} = \frac{\Sigma X}{n} = \frac{1 + 2 + 3 + \ldots + n}{n} = \frac{n(n+1)}{2n} = \frac{n+1}{2} \qquad \text{[From (*)]}$$

EXERCISE 5·1

1. (*a*) What is a statistical average ? What are the desirable properties for an average to possess ? Mention different types of averages and state why the arithmetic mean is the most commonly used amongst them. [*Delhi Univ. B.Com. (Pass), 1997*]

(*b*) State *two* important objects of measures of central value.

Hint. (*i*) To obtain a single figure which is representative of the distribution.

(*ii*) To facilitate comparisons.

2. What are 'measures of location' ? In what circumstances would you consider them as the most suitable measures for describing the central tendency of a frequency distribution ?

3. (*a*) Explain the properties of a good average. In the light of these properties which average do you think is the best and why ?

(*b*) What are the criteria of a satisfactory measure of the central tendency ? Discuss the standard measures of central tendency and say which of these satisfy your criteria.

(*c*) What do you mean by an 'Average' in Statistics. Mention the essentials of a good average.

4. What do you understand by arithmetic mean ? Discuss its merits and demerits. Also state its important properties.

5. "The figure of 2·2 children per adult female was felt to be in some respects absurd and the Royal Commission suggested that the middle class be paid money to increase the average to a rounder and more convenient number." (*Punch*)

Commenting on the above statement, discuss the limitations of the arithmetic average. Also point out the characteristics of a good measure of central tendency.

6. Calculate the average bonus paid per member from the following data :

Bonus (in Rs.) :	50	60	70	80	90	100	110
No. of persons :	1	3	5	7	6	2	1

Ans. Rs. 79.60.

7. (*a*) Peter travelled by car for 4 days. He drove 10 hours each day. He drove : first day at the rate of 45 km. per hour, second day at the rate of 40 km. per hour, third day at the rate of 38 km. per hour and fourth day at the rate of 37 km. per hour. What was his average speed ?

Ans. 40 km. p.h.

(*b*) Typist *A* can type a letter in 5 minutes, typist *B* in 10 minutes and typist *C* in 15 minutes. What is the average number of letters typed per hour per typist ?

Ans. Required average = (12 + 6 + 4)/3 = 7·33.

8. (*a*) A taxi ride in a city costs one rupee for the first kilometre and sixty paise for each additional kilometre. The cost for each kilometre is incurred at the beginning of the kilometre, so that the rider pays for a whole kilometre. What is the average cost for $2\frac{3}{4}$ kilometres ?

Ans. Average cost for $2\frac{3}{4}$ kms = (100 + 60 + 60) × $\frac{4}{11}$ Paise = 80 Paise.

(*b*) The mean weight of a student in a group of 6 students is 119 lbs. The individual weights of five of them are 115, 109, 129, 117 and 114 lbs. What is the weight of the sixth student ?

Ans. 130 lbs.

9. (*a*) Average marks in Statistics of 10 students of a class was 68. A new student took admission with 72 marks whereas two existing students left the college. If the marks of these students were 40 and 39, find the average marks of the remaining students. *[Delhi Univ.. B.Com. (Pass), 2000]*

Hint. $\bar{x} = \frac{(68 \times 10) + 72 - 40 - 39}{10 + 1 - 2} = 74·78$ marks (approx.).

(*b*) Shri Narendra Kumar has invested his capital in three securities, namely RELIANCE Ltd., TISCO and SATYAM : Rs. 40,000; Rs. 50,000 and Rs. 80,000 respectively. If he collects dividends of Rs. 10,000 from each company, compute his average return from three securities. *[Delhi Univ. B.Com. (Pass), 2000]*

Hint. Average rate of return = $\frac{\text{Total return}}{\text{Total tnvestment}} = \frac{3 \times 10{,}000}{40{,}000 + 50{,}000 + 80{,}000}$

Ans. 17·65%.

10. (*a*) Twelve persons gambled on a certain night. Seven of them lost at an average rate of Rs. 10·50 while the remaining five gained at an average of Rs. 13·00. Is the information given above correct ? If not, why ?

Ans. Information is incorrect.

(*b*) Goals scored by a hockey team in successive matches are 5, 7, 4, 2, 4, 0, 5, 5 and 3. What is the number of goals, the team must score in 10th match in order that the average comes to 4 goals per match.

Ans. 5.

(*c*) The sum of deviations of a certain number of observations measured from 4 is 72 and the sum of the deviations of the same value from 7 is –3. Find the number of observations and their mean. *[Delhi Univ. B.Com. (Hons.), 1997]*

Hint. Let *n* be the number of observations.

If $d = X - A$, then $\bar{X} = A + \frac{\Sigma d}{n}$; $\therefore \bar{X} = 4 + \frac{72}{n} = 7 + \frac{(-3)}{n}$. Solving, we get $n = 25$, $\bar{X} = 6·88$.

(*d*) The daily average sales of a store were Rs. 2,750 for the month of Feb. 1996. During the month, the highest and the lowest sales were Rs. 8,950 and Rs. 580 respectively. Find the average daily sales if the highest and the lowest sales are not taken into account. *[Delhi Univ. B.Com. (Hons.), 1997]*

Hint and Ans. *n* = No. of days in month of February of 1996 (Leap Year) = 29

Revised mean = Rs. $\frac{1}{27}[\Sigma X - 8{,}950 - 580]$ = Rs. $\frac{1}{27}[29 \times 2{,}750 - 8{,}950 - 580]$ = Rs. 2,600.74

Ans. Rs. 2,600.74

(*e*) Two variables *x* and *y* are related by : $y = (x - 5)/10$ and each of them has 5 observations. If the mean of *x* is 45, find the mean of *y*. *[I.C.W.A. (Foundation), Dec. 2006]*

Ans. $\bar{y} = [\bar{x} - 5)/10] = 4$.

11. (*a*) The following are the daily salaries in rupees of 30 employees of a firm :

91,	139,	126,	119,	100,	87,	65,	77,	99,	95,	108,	127,	86,	148,	116,
76,	69,	88,	112,	118,	89,	116,	97,	105,	95,	80,	86,	106,	93,	135.

The firm gave bonus of Rs. 10, 15, 20, 25, 30, 35, 40, 45 and 50 to employees in the respective salary groups : exceeding 60 but not exceeding 70, exceeding 70 but not exceeding 80 and so on up to exceeding 140 but not exceeding 150. Construct a frequency distribution and find out the total daily bonus paid per employee.

Ans. Average daily bonus = Rs. 27·50.

(*b*) The management of a college decides to give scholarship to the students who have scored marks 70 and above 70 in Business Statistics. The following are the marks scored by II B.Com. students :

71	73	74	85	86	88	91	94	96	99
74	74	76	93	91	94	96	98	88	94

The scholarship payable is given below :

Marks :	70—75	75—80	80—85	85—90	90—95	95—100
Scholarship amount (Rs.) :	100	200	300	400	500	600

Estimate the total scholarship payable and the average scholarship payable. *(Bangalore Univ. B.Com., 1999)*

12. A certain number of salesmen were appointed in different territories and the following data were compiled from their sales reports :

Sales ('000 Rs.) :	4—8	8—12	12—16	16—20	20—24	24—28	28—32	32—36	36—40
No. of salesmen :	11	13	16	14	—	9	17	6	4

If the average sales is believed to be Rs. 19,920, find the missing information.

Ans. Missing Frequency = 10.

13. The mean of the following frequency distribution is 50. But the frequencies f_1 and f_2 in classes 20—40 and 60—80 are missing. Find the missing frequencies.

Class :	0—20	20—40	40—60	60—80	80—100	
Frequency :	17	f_1	32	f_2	19	Total 120

[Delhi Univ. B.Com. (Pass), 1997]

Ans. $f_1 = 28, f_2 = 24$.

14. (*a*) The average salary of 49 out of 50 employees in a firm is Rs. 100. The salary of the 50th employee is Rs. 97·50 more than the average salary of all the 50 workers. Find the mean salary of all the employees in the firm.

(*b*) The mean of 99 items is 55. The value of 100th item is 99 more than the mean of 100 items. What is the value of 100th item. *[Delhi Univ. B.Com (Hons.), 2001]*

Ans. (*a*) Rs. 101·99, (*b*) 155.

15. (*a*) The mean of 200 items was 50. Later on it was discovered that two items were wrongly read as 92 and 8 instead of 192 and 88. Find out the correct mean.

Ans. 50·9.

(*b*) The average daily income for a group of 50 persons working in a factory was calculated to be Rs. 169. It was later discovered that one figure was mis-read as 134 instead of the correct value 143. Calculate the correct average income.

Ans. Rs. 169·18.

(*c*) The average marks of 80 students were found to be 40. Later, it was discovered that a score of 54 was misread as 84. Find the correct mean of 80 students. *[C.S. (Foundation), June 2001]*

Ans. 39·625.

16. 100 students appeared for an examination. The results of those who failed are given below :

Marks	5	10	15	20	25	30	*Total*
No. of Students	4	6	8	7	3	2	*30*

If the average marks of all students were 68.6, find out average marks of those who passed.

[Delhi Univ. B.Com. (Hons.), 2008]

Ans. $n_1 + n_2 = 100, n_1 = 30 \Rightarrow n_2 = 70$; $\overline{X}_1$ = Mean marks of failed students $= \dfrac{\Sigma fX}{\Sigma f} = \dfrac{475}{30}$.

$$\overline{X}_{12} = \frac{n_1 \overline{X}_1 + n_2 \overline{X}_2}{n_1 + n_2} = \frac{475 + 70\,\overline{X}_2}{100} = 68.6 \Rightarrow \overline{X}_2 = 91.21$$

17. Fifty students appeared in an examination. The results of the passed students in given in the adjoining table.

The average marks of all the students is 52. Find the average marks of the students who failed in the examination.

[I.C.W.A. (Foundation), Dec. 2006]

Ans. 21.

Marks	*No. of students*
40	6
50	14
60	7
70	5
80	4
90	4

18. Out of 50 examinees, those passing the examination are shown below. If average marks of all the examinees is 5·16, what would be the average marks of examinees having failed in it ?

Marks obtained	:	4	5	6	7	8	9
No. of students passing the Exam.	:	8	10	9	6	4	3

[*C.S. (Foundation), June 2002*]

Ans. 2·1.

19. (*a*) The mean age of a combined group of men and women is 30 years. If the mean age of the group of men is 32 and that of the group of women is 27, find out the percentage of the men and women in the group.

Ans. Men = 60%, Women = 40%.

(*b*) The mean annual salary of all employees in a company is Rs. 25,000. The mean salary of male and female employees is Rs. 27,000 and Rs. 17,000 respectively. Find the percentage of males and females employed by the company. [*C.A. (Foundation), Nov. 1995*]

Ans. Males = 80%, Females = 20%.

(*c*) If the means of two groups of m and n observations are 40 and 50 respectively, and the combined mean of two groups is 42, find the ratio $m : n$. [*I.C.W.A. (Foundation), June 2007*]

Ans. $m : n = 4 : 1$.

20. (*a*) The mean marks obtained by 300 students in the subject of Statistics are 45. The mean of the top 100 of them was found to be 70 and the mean of the last 100 was known to be 20. What is the mean of the remaining 100 students ?

Ans. 45.

(*b*) The mean hourly wage of 100 labourers working in a factory, running two shifts of 60 and 40 workers respectively, is Rs. 38. The mean hourly wage of 60 labourers working in the morning shift is Rs. 40. Find the mean hourly wage of 40 labourers working in the evening shift. [*Delhi Univ. B.Com. (Pass), 1996*]

Ans. Rs. 35.

21. (*a*) There are there sections in B.Com. 1st year in a certain college. The number of students in each section and the average marks obtained by them in the Statistics paper in the annual examination are as follows :

Section	*Average marks in Statistics*	*No. of Students*
A	75	50
B	60	60
C	55	50

Find the average marks obtained by the students of all the sections taken together.

Ans. 63·125.

(*b*) B.Com. (Pass) III year has three Sections *A*, *B* and *C* with 50, 40, 60 students respectively. The mean marks for the three sections were determined as 85, 60 and 65 respectively. However, marks of a student of section *A* were wrongly recorded as 50 instead of zero. Determine the mean marks of all the three sections put together.

[*Delhi Univ. B.Com. (Pass), 1995*]

Hint. Corrected $\overline{X}_A = \frac{50 \times 85 - 50 + 0}{50} = 84$; $\therefore$ Combined mean $(\overline{x}) = \frac{50 \times 84 + 40 \times 60 + 60 \times 65}{50 + 40 + 60} = 70$

22. The mean monthly salary paid to 77 employees in a company was Rs. 78. The mean salary of 32 of them was Rs. 75 and that of other 25 was Rs. 82. What was the mean salary of the remaining ?

Ans. Rs. 77·80.

23. Define the weighted arithmetic mean of a set of numbers. Show that it is unaffected if all the weights are multiplied by some common factor.

24. A contractor employs three types of workers-male, female and children. To a male worker he pays Rs. 16 per hour, to a female worker Rs. 13 per hour and to a child worker Rs. 10 per hour. What is the average wage per hour paid by the contractor if the number of males, females and children is 20, 15 and 5 respectively ?

Ans. Rs. 14·12.

25. Define a 'weighted mean'. Under what circumstances would you prefer it to an unweighted mean ?

Calculate the weighted mean price of a table from the following data, assuming that weights are proportional to the number of tables sold :

Price per table (Rs.)	:	3600	4000	4400	4800
No. of tables sold	:	14	11	9	6

Ans. Rs. 4070.

26. Compute the weighted arithmetic mean of the index number from the data below :

	Group				
	Food	*Clothing*	*Fuel and Light*	*House Rent*	*Miscellaneous*
Index No.	125	133	141	173	182
Weight	7	5	4	1	3

Ans. 141·15.

27. The following table gives the distribution of 100 accidents during seven days of the week of a given month. During the particular month there are 5 Mondays, Tuesdays and Wednesdays and only four each of the other days. Calculate the average numbr of accidents per day.

Days	*No. of Accidents*	*Days*	*No. of Accidents*
Sunday	26	Thursday	8
Monday	16	Friday	10
Tuesday	12	Saturday	18
Wednesday	10		

Ans. 14·13 ≃ 14.

28. To produce a scooter of a certain make, labour of different kinds is required in quantities as follows :

Skilled labour	:	50 hours
Semi-skilled labour	:	100 hours
Unskilled labour	:	300 hours

If hourly wage rates for these three kinds of labour are Rs. 100, Rs. 70 and Rs. 20 respectively, what is the average labour cost per hour in producing the scooter ? [*Delhi Univ. B.A. (Econ. Hons.), 1990*]

Hint. Use weighted arithmetic mean.

Ans. Rs. 40 per hour.

29. A candidate obtained the following percentages of marks in different subjects in the Half-Yearly Examination :

English	Statistics	Cost Accountancy	Economics	Income Tax
46%	67%	72%	58%	53%

It is agreed to give double weights to marks in English and Statistics as compared to other subjects. What is the simple and weighted arithmetic mean ? [*Delhi Univ. B.Com. (Pass), 2002*]

Ans. $\overline{X} = 59{\cdot}2\%$ and $\overline{X}_w = 58{\cdot}43\%$

30. Calculate simple and weighted arithmetic averages from the following data and comment on them :

Designation	*Daily salary (in Rs.)*	*Strength of the cadre*
Class I Officers	1,500	10
Class II Officers	800	20
Subordinate staff	500	70
Clerical staff	250	100
Lower staff	100	150

Ans. Simple Arithmetic Mean = Rs. 630. ; Weighted Arithmetic Mean = Rs. 302·86.

31. Comment on the performance of the students of three Universities given below using an appropriate average :

University →	*A*		*B*		*C*	
Course of Study ↓	*% of Pass*	*No. of students in hundreds*	*% of Pass*	*No. of students in hundreds*	*% of Pass*	*No. of students in hundreds*
M.A.	81	2	82	2	71	3
M.Com.	76	3·5	76	3	83	4
M.Sc.	73	2	60	7	66	3
B.Com.	58	2	76	7	74	2
B.Sc.	70	7	65	3	65	3
B.A.	74	4·5	73	6	73	5

Ans. Simple average (A.M.) of pass percentage is 72% in each case; we are unable to distinguish between the performance of students in the three universities.

However, on the basis of weighted average of pass percentage, University *C* (72·55%) is the best followed by University *A* (72·05%) and University *B* (70·61%).

32. From the results of two colleges *A* and *B* given below, state which of them is better and why ?

Name of Examination	*College A*		*College B*	
	Appeared	*Passed*	*Appeared*	*Passed*
M.A.	60	50	200	160
M.Com.	100	90	240	190
B.A.	400	300	200	140
B.Com.	240	150	160	100
Total	800	590	800	590

Hint and Ans. Find the weighted average of percentage of passed students (*X*), the corresponding weights (*W*) being the number of students appeared.

$$\bar{X}_W(A) = \frac{\Sigma W_A X_A}{\Sigma W_A} = \frac{590}{800} \times 100 = 73{\cdot}75\ ; \quad \bar{X}_W(B) = \frac{\Sigma W_B X_B}{\Sigma W_B} = \frac{590}{800} \times 100 = 73{\cdot}75$$

Taking 'higher pass percentage' as the criterion for better college, both the colleges *A* and *B* are equally good.

33. A travelling salesman made five trips in two months. The record of sales is given below :

The sales manager criticised the salesman's performance as not very good since his mean daily sales were only Rs. 54,000 (2,70,000/5). The salesman called this an unfair statement for his daily mean sales were as high as Rs. 55,200 (13,80,000/25). What does each average mean here ? Which average seems to be more appropriate in this case ?

Trip	*No. of days*	*Value of sales (in '00 Rs.)*	*Sales per day (in '00 Rs.)*
1	5	3,000	600
2	4	1,600	400
3	3	1,500	500
4	7	3,500	500
5	6	4,200	700
	25	13,800	2,700

Ans. The Manager obtained the simple arithmetic mean of the sales per day, while the salesman obtained the weighted arithmetic mean. The latter (weighted average) seems to be more appropriate.

5·6. MEDIAN

In the words of L.R. Connor :

"*The median is that value of the variable which divides the group in two equal parts, one part comprising all the values greater and the other, all the values less than median*". Thus median of a distribution may be defined as that value of the variable which exceeds and is exceeded by the same number of observations *i.e.,* it is the value such that the number of observations above it is equal to the number of observations below it. Thus, we see that as against arithmetic mean which is based on all the items of the distribution, the median is only *positional* average *i.e.,* its value depends on the position occupied by a value in the frequency distribution.

5·6·1. Calculation of Median.

Case (I) : Ungrouped Data. If the number of observations is odd, then the median is the *middle value* after the observations have been arranged in ascending or descending order of magnitude. For example, the median of 5 observations 35, 12, 40, 8, 60 *i.e.,* 8, 12, 35, 40, 60, is 35.

In case of even number of observations median is obtained as the arithmetic mean of the two middle observations after they are arranged in ascending or descending order of magnitude. Thus, if one more observation, say, 50 is added to the above five observations then the six observations in ascending order of magnitude are : 8, 12, 35, 40, 50, 60. Thus,

$$\text{Median} = \text{Arithmetic mean of two middle terms} = \tfrac{1}{2}(35 + 40) = 37{\cdot}5.$$

Remark. It should be clearly understood that in case of even number of observations, in fact, any value lying between the two middle values can serve as a median but it is a convention to estimate median by taking the arithmetic mean of the two middle values.

Case (II) : Frequency Distribution. In case of frequency distribution where the variable takes the values $X_1, X_2, \ldots, X_n$ with respective frequencies $f_1, f_2, \ldots, f_n$ with $\Sigma f = N$, total frequency, median is the size of the $(N + 1)/2$th item or observation. In this case the use of cumulative frequency (*c.f.*) distribution facilitates the calculations. The steps involved are :

(*i*) Prepare the '*less than*' cumulative frequency (*c.f.*) distribution.

(*ii*) Find *N*/2.

(*iii*) See the *c.f., just greater than N*/2.

(*iv*) The corresponding value of the variable gives median.

The example given below illustrates the method.

Example 5·20. *Eight coins were tossed together and the number of heads (X) resulting was noted. The operation was repeated 256 times and the frequency distribution of the number of heads is given below :*

No. of heads (X) :	*0*	*1*	*2*	*3*	*4*	*5*	*6*	*7*	*8*
Frequency (f) :	*1*	*9*	*26*	*59*	*72*	*52*	*29*	*7*	*1*

Calculate median.

Solution.

COMPUTATION OF MEDIAN

X	*f*	*Less than c.f.*
0	1	1
1	9	1 + 9 = 10
2	26	10 + 26 = 36
3	59	36 + 59 = 95
4	72	95 + 72 = 167
5	52	167 + 52 = 219
6	29	219 + 29 = 248
7	7	248 + 7 = 255
8	1	255 + 1 = 256

Here $N = \sum f = 256, \quad \Rightarrow \quad \frac{N}{2} = 128$

The cumulative frequency (*c.f.*) just greater than 128 is 167 and the value of *X* corresponding to 167 is 4. Hence, median number of heads is 4.

Case (III) : Continuous Frequency Distribution. As before, median is the size (value) of the $(N + 1)/2$th observation. Steps involved for its computation are :

(*i*) Prepare '*less than*' cumulative frequency (*c.f.*) distribution.

(*ii*) Find *N*/2.

(*iii*) See *c.f.* just greater than *N*/2.

(*iv*) The corresponding class contains the median value and is called the *median class.*

The value of median is now obtained by using the interpolation formula :

$$\text{Median} = l + \frac{h}{f}\left(\frac{N}{2} - C\right) \qquad \ldots(5·13)$$

where l is the lower limit of the median class,

f is the frequency of the median class,

h is the magnitude or width of the median class,

$N = \sum f$, is the total frequency,

and C is the cumulative frequency of the class *preceding* the median class.

Remarks 1. The interpolation formula (5·13) is based on the following assumptions :

(*i*) The distribution of the variable under consideration is continuous with exclusive type classes without any gaps.

(*ii*) There is an orderly and even distribution of observations within each class.

However, if the data are given as a grouped frequency distribution where classes are not continuous, then it must be converted into a continuous frequency distribution before applying the formula. This adjustment will affect only the value of l in (5·13).

2. Median will be abbreviated by the symbol *Md.*

3. *The sum of absolute deviations of a given set of observations is minimum when taken from median.* By absolute deviation we mean the deviation after ignoring the algebraic sign. Thus, if we take the deviation of the given values of the variable X from an assumed mean A, then $X - A$ may be positive or negative but its absolute value denoted by $| X - A |$, read as $(X - A)$ modulus or $(X - A)$ mod is always positive and we have

$$\Sigma f|X-A| > \Sigma d|X-Md| \quad \text{or} \quad \Sigma f|X-Md| < \Sigma f|X-A|; A \neq Md.$$

i.e., the sum of the *absolute deviations* about any arbitrary point A is always greater than the sum of the absolute deviations about the median. For further discussion, see Mean Deviation in Chapter 6 on Dispersion.

5·6·2. Merits and Demerits of Median.

Merits. (*i*) It is rigidly defined.

(*ii*) Median is easy to understand and easy to calculate for a non-mathematical person.

(*iii*) Since median is a *positional* average, it is not affected at all by extreme observations and as such is very useful in the case of skewed distributions (*c.f.* Chapter 7), *J*-shaped or inverted *J*-shaped distributions (*c.f.* Chapter 4) such as the distribution of wages, incomes and wealth. So in case of extreme observations, median is a better average to use than the arithmetic mean since the later gives a distorted picture of the distribution.

(*iv*) Median can be computed while dealing with a distribution with open end classes.

(*v*) Median can sometimes be located by simple inspection and can also be computed graphically. (See Ogive discussed in § 5·6·4.)

(*vi*) Median is the only average to be used while dealing with qualitative characteristics which cannot be measured quantitatively but can still be arranged in ascending or descending order of magnitude *e.g.*, to find the average intelligence, average beauty, average honesty, etc., among a group of people.

Demerits. (*i*) In case of even number of observations for an ungrouped data, median cannot be determined exactly. We merely estimate it as the arithmetic mean of the two middle terms. In fact any value lying between the two middle observations can serve the purpose of median.

(*ii*) Median, being a positional average, is not based on each and every item of the distribution. It depends on all the observations only to the extent whether they are smaller than or greater than it ; the exact magnitude of the observations being immaterial. Let us consider a simple example. The median value of

35, 12, 8, 40 and 60 *i.e.*, 8, 12, 35, 40, 60

is 35. Now if we replace the values 8 and 12 by any two values which are less than 35 and the values 40 and 60 by any two values greater than 35 the median is unaffected. This property is sometimes described by saying that median is *sensitive*.

(*iii*) Median is not suitable for further mathematical treatment *i.e.*, given the sizes and the median values of different groups, we cannot compute the median of the combined group.

(*iv*) Median is relatively less stable than mean, particularly for small samples since it is affected more by fluctuations of sampling as compared with arithmetic mean.

Example 5·21. *(a) In a batch of 15 students, 5 students failed in a test. The marks of 10 students who passed were 9, 6, 7, 8, 8, 9, 6, 5, 4, 7. What was the median of all the 15 students ?*

(b) If the relation between two variables x and y is 2x + 3y = 7, and the median of y is 2, find the median of x. [*I.C.W.A. (Foundation), Dec. 2005*]

Solution. (*a*) The marks of 10 students who passed when arranged in ascending order of magnitude are :

4, 5, 6, 6, 7, 7, 8, 8, 9, 9.

Since the five students who failed must have scored less than 4 marks, the marks of 15 students when arranged in ascending order are :

„ „ „ „ „ 4, 5, 6, 6, 7, 7, 8, 8, 9, 9. (1)

Here $N = 15$. Hence, the median value is the middle value *viz.*, 8th value in the series (1). Hence, median is 6.

(*b*) We are given :

$$\text{Median } (y) = 2 \quad ...(*) \quad \text{and} \quad 2x + 3y = 7 \quad \Rightarrow \quad x = \frac{1}{2}(7 - 3y) \quad ...(**)$$

Since the change of origin and the scale in the observations does not result in any change in the order (rank) of the observations, get from (**) and (*),

$$\text{Median } (x) = \frac{1}{2}[7 - 3 \text{ Median } (y)] = \frac{1}{2}(7 - 3 \times 2) = \frac{1}{2}.$$

Example 5·22. *The following table shows the age distribution of persons in a particular region.*

Age (years)	*No. of persons (in thousands)*	*Age (years)*	*No. of persons (in thousands)*
Below 10	2	*Below 50*	*14*
" 20	5	" 60	*15*
" 30	9	" 70	*15·5*
" 40	12	*70 and over*	*15·6*

(*i*) *Find the median age.*

(*ii*) *Why is the median a more suitable measure of central tendency than the mean in this case ?*

Solution.

(*i*) First of all we shall convert the given distribution into the continuous frequency distribution as given in the adjoining table and then compute the median.

COMPUTATION OF MEDIAN

Age (in years)	*Number of persons in '000 (f)*	*c.f. (less than)*
0—10	2	2
10—20	5 − 2 = 3	5
20—30	9 − 5 = 4	9
30—40	12 − 9 = 3	12
40—50	14 − 12 = 2	14
50—60	15 − 14 = 1	15
60—70	15·5 − 15 = 0·5	15·5
70 and over	15·6 − 15·5 = 0·1	15·6
	$N = \sum f = 15{\cdot}6$	

Here $\frac{N}{2} = \frac{15{\cdot}6}{2} = 7{\cdot}8$. Cumulative frequency (*c.f.*) greater than 7·8 is 9. Thus the corresponding class 20—30 is the median class. Hence, using the median formula (5·13), we get

$$\text{Median} = 20 + \frac{10}{4}(7{\cdot}8 - 5) = 20 + \frac{5}{2} \times 2{\cdot}8$$
$$= 20 + 5 \times 1{\cdot}4 = 27$$

Hence, median age is 27 years.

(*ii*) In this case median is a more suitable measure of central tendency than mean because the last class *viz.*, 70 and over is open end class and as such we cannot obtain the class mark for this class and hence arithmetic mean cannot be computed.

Example 5·23. *The frequency distribution of weight in grams of mangoes of a given variety is given below. Calculate the arithmetic mean and the median.*

Weight in grams :	*410—419*	*420—429*	*430—439*	*440—449*	*450—459*	*460—469*	*470—479*
Number of mangoes :	*14*	*20*	*42*	*54*	*45*	*18*	*7*

Solution. Since the interpolation formula for median is based on continuous frequency distribution we shall first convert the given inclusive class interval series into exclusive class interval series.

CALCULATIONS FOR MEAN AND MEDIAN

Weight in grams (Class boundaries)	*No. of Mangoes (f)*	*Mid-value (X)*	$d = \frac{X - 444{\cdot}5}{10}$	*fd*	*(Less than) c.f.*
409·5—419·5	14	414·5	−3	−42	14
419·5—429·5	20	424·5	−2	−40	34
429·5—439·5	42	434·5	−1	−42	76
439·5—449·5	54	444·5	0	0	130
449·5—459·5	45	454·5	1	45	175
459·5—469·5	18	464·5	2	36	193
469·5—479·5	7	474·5	3	21	200
Total	$\sum f = 200 = N$			$\sum fd = -22$	

$$\text{Mean }(\bar{X}) = A + \frac{h\Sigma fd}{N} = 444\cdot5 + \frac{10\times(-22)}{200} = 444\cdot5 - 1\cdot1 = 443\cdot4 \text{ gms.}$$

$N/2 = 100$. The *c.f.* just greater than 100 is 130.

Hence, the corresponding class 439·5— 449·5 is the median class. Using the median formula, we get

$$Md = l + \frac{h}{f}\left(\frac{N}{2} - C\right) = 439\cdot5 + \frac{10}{54}(100 - 76)$$

$$= 439\cdot5 + \frac{10\times24}{54} = 439\cdot50 + 4\cdot44 = 443\cdot94 \text{ gms.}$$

Example 5·24. *Find the missing frequency from the following distribution of daily sales of shops, given that the median sale of shops is Rs. 2,400.*

Sale in hundred Rs. :	0—10	10—20	20—30	30—40	40—50
No. of shops :	5	25	—	18	7

Solution. Let the missing frequency be '*a*'.

CALCULATIONS FOR MEDIAN

Sales in hundred Rs.	*No. of shops (f)*	*Cumulative frequency (c.f.)*
0—10	5	5
10—20	25	30
20—30	*a*	30 + *a*
30—40	18	48 + *a*
40—50	7	*N* = 55 + *a*

Since median sales is Rs. 2,400 (24 hundred), 20—30 is the median class. Using median formula, we get

$$24 = 20 + \frac{10}{a}\left(\frac{55+a}{2} - 30\right) \Rightarrow 4 = \frac{10}{a}\left(\frac{55+a-60}{2}\right) = \frac{5(a-5)}{a}$$

$$\therefore \quad 4a = 5a - 25 \quad \Rightarrow \quad a = 25.$$

Hence, the missing frequency is 25.

Example 5·25. *In the frequency distribution of 100 families given below, the number of families corresponding to expenditure groups 20—40 and 60—80 are missing from the table. However, the median is known to be 50. Find the missing frequencies.*

Expenditure :	*0—20*	*20—40*	*40—60*	*60—80*	*80—100*
No. of families :	*14*	*?*	*27*	*?*	*15*

Solution. Let the missing frequencies for the classes 20—40 and 60—80 be f_1 and f_2 respectively.

COMPUTATION OF MEDIAN

Expenditure (in Rupees)	*No. of families (f)*	*c.f. (Less than)*
0—20	14	14
20—40	f_1	$14 + f_1$
40—60	27	$41 + f_1$
60—80	f_2	$41 + f_1 + f_2$
80—100	15	$56 + f_1 + f_2$
	$N = 100 = 56 + f_1 + f_2$	

From the adjoining table, we have

$$\Sigma f = 56 + f_1 + f_2 = 100 \quad \text{(Given)}$$

$$\Rightarrow \quad f_1 + f_2 = 100 - 56 = 44 \quad \ldots(*)$$

Since median is given to be 50, which lies in the class 40—60, therefore, 40—60 is the median class. Using the median formula, we get :

$$50 = 40 + \frac{20}{27}[50 - (14 + f_1)] \quad \Rightarrow \quad 50 - 40 = \frac{20}{27}[36 - f_1]$$

$$\therefore \quad 10 = \frac{20}{27}(36 - f_1)$$

$$\Rightarrow \quad 27 = 2(36 - f_1) = 72 - 2f_1 \quad \Rightarrow \quad 2f_1 = 72 - 27 = 45 \quad \Rightarrow \quad f_1 = \frac{45}{2} = 22\cdot5 \simeq 23.$$

[Since frequency can't be fractional]

Substituting in (*), we get $f_2 = 44 - f_1 = 44 - 23 = 21$.

5·6·3. Partition Values. The values which divide the series into a number of equal parts are called the *partition values*. Thus median may be regarded as a particular partition value which divides the given data into two equal parts.

Quartiles. The values which divide the given data into four equal parts are known as *quartiles*. Obviously there will be three such points Q_1, Q_2 and Q_3 such that $Q_1 \le Q_2 \le Q_3$, termed as the three quartiles. Q_1, known as the *lower* or *first* quartile is the value which has 25% of the items of the distribution below it and consequently 75% of the items are greater than it. Incidentally Q_2, the *second* quartile, coincides with the median and has an equal number of observations above it and below it. Q_3, known as the *upper* or *third* quartile, has 75% of the observations below it and consequently 25% of the observations above it.

The working principle for computing the quartiles is basically the same as that of computing the median.

To compute Q_1, the following steps are required :

(*i*) Find $N/4$, where $N = \Sigma f$ is the total frequency.

(*ii*) See the (less than) cumulative frequency (*c.f.*) just greater than $N/4$.

(*iii*) The corresponding value of X gives the value of Q_1. In case of continuous frequency distribution, the corresponding class contains Q_1 and the value of Q_1 is obtained by the interpolation formula :

$$Q_1 = l + \frac{h}{f}\left(\frac{N}{4} - C\right) \qquad \ldots(5·14)$$

where l is the lower limit, f is the frequency, and h is the magnitude of the class containing Q_1,

and C is the cumulative frequency (*c.f.*) of the class preceding the class containing Q_1.

Similarly to compute Q_3, see the (less than) *c.f.*, just greater than $3N/4$. The corresponding value of X gives Q_3. In case of continuous frequency distribution, the corresponding class contains Q_3 and the value of Q_3 is given by the formula :

$$Q_3 = l + \frac{h}{f}\left(\frac{3N}{4} - C\right) \qquad \ldots(5·15)$$

where l is the lower limit, h is the magnitude, and f is the frequency of the class containing Q_3,

and C is the *c.f.* of the class preceding the class containing Q_3.

Deciles. Deciles are the values which divide the series into ten equal parts. Obviously there are nine deciles $D_1, D_2, D_3, \ldots, D_9$, (say), such that $D_1 \le D_2 \le \ldots \le D_9$. Incidentally D_5 coincides with the median.

The method of computing the deciles D_i, $(i = 1, 2, \ldots, 9)$ is the same as discussed for Q_1 and Q_3. To compute the ith decile D_i, $(i = 1, 2, \ldots, 9)$ see the *c.f.* just greater than $\frac{i \times N}{10}$. The corresponding value of X is D_i. In case of continuous frequency distribution the corresponding class contains D_i and its value is obtained by the formula :

$$D_i = l + \frac{h}{f}\left(\frac{i \times N}{10} - C\right), (i = 1, 2, \ldots, 9) \qquad \ldots(5·16)$$

where l is the lower limit, f is the frequency and h is the magnitude of the class containing D_i,

and C is the c.f. of the class preceding the class containing D_i

Percentiles. Percentiles are the values which divide the series into 100 equal parts. Obviously, there are 99 percentiles $P_1, P_2, \ldots, P_{99}$ such that $P_1 \le P_2 \le \ldots \le P_{99}$. The ith percentile P_i, $(i = 1, 2, \ldots, 99)$ is the value of X corresponding to *c.f.* just greater than $\frac{i \times N}{100}$. In case of continuous frequency distribution, the corresponding class contains P_i and its value is obtained by the interpolation formula :

$$P_i = l + \frac{h}{f}\left(\frac{i \times N}{100} - C\right), (i = 1, 2, \ldots, 99) \qquad \ldots(5·17)$$

where l is the lower limit, f is the frequency and h is the magnitude of the class containing P_i,

and C is the *c.f.* of the class preceding the class containing P_i.

In particular, we shall have :

$$P_{25} = Q_1, \qquad P_{50} = D_5 = Q_2, \qquad P_{75} = Q_3,$$
$$D_1 = P_{10}, \qquad D_2 = P_{20}, \qquad D_3 = P_{30}, \ldots, \qquad D_9 = P_{90}.$$

Remark. *Importance of partition values.* Partition values, particularly the percentiles are specially useful in the scaling and ranking of test scores in psychological and educational statistics. In the data relating to business and economic statistics, these partition values, specially quartiles, are useful in personnel work and productivity ratings.

5·6·4. Graphic Method of Locating Partition Values. The various partition values *viz.*, quartiles, deciles and percentiles can be easily located graphically with the help of a curve called the *cumulative frequency curve* or *Ogive.* The procedure involves the following steps :

Less Than Ogive

Steps 1. Represent the given distribution in the form of a less than cumulative frequency distribution.

2. Take the values of the variable (in the case of frequency distribution) and the class intervals (in the case of continuous frequency distribution) along the horizontal scale (X-axis) and the cumulative frequency along the vertical scale (Y-axis).

3. Plot the *c.f.* against the corresponding value of the variable (in the case of frequency distribution) and against the *upper limit* of the corresponding class (in the case of continuous frequency distribution).

4. The smooth curve obtained by joining the points so obtained by means of a free-hand drawing is called '*less than*' cumulative frequency curve or '*less than*' *ogive*.

The various partition values can be easily obtained from this ogive as illustrated in Example 5·32.

More Than Ogive. In this case we form the '*more than*' cumulative frequency distribution and plot it against the corresponding value of the variable or against the *lower limit* of the corresponding class (in case of continuous frequency distribution). The curve obtained on joining the points so obtained by smooth free-hand drawing is called 'more than' cumulative frequency curve or 'more than' ogive.

Remark. If we draw a perpendicular from the point of intersection of the two ogives on the x-axis, the foot of the perpendicular gives the value of *median.*

Example 5·26. *The following data gives the distribution of marks of 100 students. Calculate the most suitable average, giving the reason for your choice. Also obtain the values of quartiles, 6th decile and 70th percentile from the following data.*

Marks	*No. of students*	*Marks*	*No. of students*
Less than 10	*5*	*Less than 50*	*60*
" *20*	*13*	" *60*	*80*
" *30*	*20*	" *70*	*90*
" *40*	*32*	" *80*	*100*

Solution. We are given 'less than' cumulative frequency distribution. We shall first convert it into a grouped frequency distribution. Since 'marks' is a discrete random variable taking only integral values, the classes are : Less than 10, 10—19,..., 70—79. Further, since the formulae for median, quartiles and percentiles are based on continuous frequency distribution, we convert the distribution into exclusive type classes with class boundaries below 9·5, 9·5—19·5,..., 69·5—79·5 as given in the adjoining table.

COMPUTATIONS FOR MEDIAN, QUARTILES AND PERCENTILES

Class	*Frequency (f)*	*Less than c.f.*	*Class Boundaries*
Less than 10	5	5	Below 9·5
10—19	13 − 5 = 8	13	9·5—19·5
20—29	20 − 13 = 7	20	19·5—29·5
30—39	32 − 20 = 12	32	29·5—39·5
40—49	60 − 32 = 28	60	39·5—49·5
50—59	80 − 60 = 20	80	49·5—59·5
60—69	90 − 80 = 10	90	59·5—69·5
70—79	100 − 90 = 10	100 = N	69·5—79·5

Since the first class 'less than 10' is an open end class, we cannot compute any of the mathematical averages like mean, geometric mean or harmonic mean. The only averages we can compute in this case are median and mode. We compute below the median of the above distribution.

Median. $\frac{N}{2} = \frac{100}{2} = 50$. The *c.f.* just greater than 50 is 60. Hence, the corresponding class 39·5—49·5 is the median class.

$$\therefore \quad \text{Median} = 39{\cdot}5 + \frac{10}{28}\left(50 - 32\right) = 39{\cdot}5 + \frac{10 \times 18}{28} = 39{\cdot}50 + 6{\cdot}43 = 45{\cdot}93$$

Hence, median marks are 45·93.

Quartiles. $\frac{N}{4} = \frac{100}{4} = 25$ and $\frac{3N}{4} = \frac{3 \times 100}{4} = 75$. The *c.f.* just greater than *N*/4 is 32. Hence, the corresponding class 29·5—39·5 contains Q_1 which is given by :

$$Q_1 = 29 \cdot 5 + \frac{10}{12}\left(25 - 20\right) = 29 \cdot 5 + \frac{10 \times 5}{12} = 29 \cdot 50 + 4 \cdot 17 = 33 \cdot 67$$

The *c.f.* just greater than 3*N*/4 = 75 is 80. Hence, the corresponding class 49·5—59·5 contains Q_3 which is given by :

$$Q_3 = 49 \cdot 5 + \frac{10}{20}\left(75 - 60\right) = 49 \cdot 50 + \frac{10 \times 15}{20} = 49 \cdot 5 + 7 \cdot 5 = 57 \cdot 0.$$

6th Decile. $\frac{6N}{10} = \frac{6 \times 100}{10} = 60$. The *c.f.* just greater than 60 is 80. Hence, the corresponding class 49·5—59·5 contains D_6 which is given by :

$$D_6 = 49 \cdot 5 + \frac{10}{20}\left(60 - 60\right) = 49 \cdot 5$$

70th Percentile. $\frac{70N}{100} = \frac{70 \times 100}{100} = 70$. The *c.f.* just greater than 70 is 80. Hence, the corresponding class 49·5—59·5 contains P_{70} which is given by :

$$P_{70} = 49 \cdot 5 + \frac{10}{20}\left(70 - 60\right) = 49 \cdot 5 + \frac{10 \times 10}{20} = 49 \cdot 5 + 5 = 54 \cdot 5.$$

Example 5·27. *Comment on the following statement :*

"The median of a distribution is N/2, the lower quartile is N/4 and the upper quartile in 3N/4". (Here N denotes the total frequency.)

Solution. The statement is wrong. The median of a distribution is not *N*/2 but it is the value of the variable *X* which divides the distribution into two equal parts *i.e.*, median is the value of the variable *X* such that *N*/2 (*i.e.*, 50%) of the observations are less than it and *N*/2 observations exceed it. The lower quartile Q_1 is not *N*/4 but it is the value of the variable such that *N*/4 (*i.e.*, 25%) of the observations are less than Q_1. Similarly the upper quartile Q_3 is not 3*N*/4 but it is the value of the variable such that 3*N*/4 (*i.e.*, 75%) of the observations are less than it.

Example 5·32. *The following are the marks obtained by the students in Statistics :*

Marks	*Number of students*	*Marks*	*Number of students*
10 marks or less	4	*40 marks or less*	40
20 " "	10	*50 " "*	47
30 " "	30	*60 " "*	50

Draw a 'less than' ogive curve on the graph paper and show therein :

(i) The range of marks obtained by middle 80% of the students.

(ii) The median.

Also verify your results by direct formula calculations.

Solution. The above data can be arranged in the form of a continuous frequency distribution as given in the adjoining table.

Marks	*Frequency (f)*	*(Less than) c.f.*
0—10	4	4
10—20	10 – 4 = 6	10
20—30	30 – 10 = 20	30
30—40	40 – 30 = 10	40
40—50	47 – 40 = 7	47
50—60	50 – 47 = 3	$N = \Sigma f = 50$

Less Than Ogive. Plot the less than *c.f.* against the corresponding value of the variable in the original table (or against the upper limit of the corresponding class in the adjoining table) and join these points by a smooth free hand curve to obtain ogive. [See Fig. 5·1]

(*i*) At the frequency $\frac{N}{2} = 25$, (along the *Y*-axis) draw a line parallel to *x*-axis meeting the ogive at point *P*. Draw *PM* perpendicular to the *x*-axis. Then *OM* = 27·5, is the median marks.

(*ii*) The range of the marks obtained by the middle 80% of the students is given by $P_{90} - P_{10}$. To find P_{90} and P_{10} graphically, at the frequency $\frac{90}{100}N = 45$ and $\frac{10}{100}N = 5$, draw lines parallel to the x-axis meeting the (less than) ogive at Q and R respectively. Draw QN and RL perpendicular to the x-axis. Then

$$P_{90} = ON = 47 \text{ (app.) and } P_{10} = OL = 11{\cdot}7 \text{ (app.)}$$

$\therefore$ Required range of marks

$$= P_{90} - P_{10} = 47 - 11{\cdot}7 = 35{\cdot}3.$$

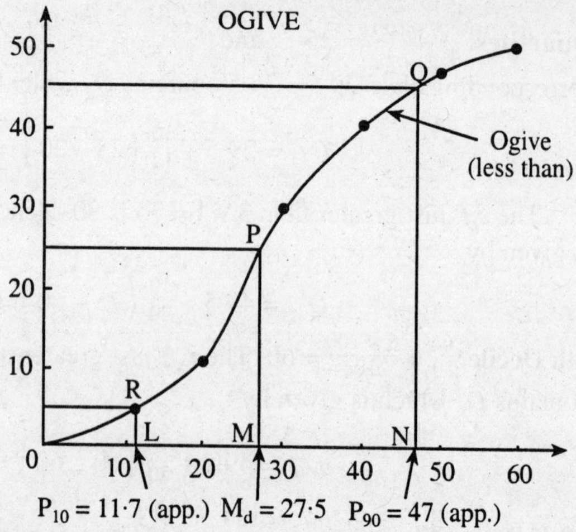

Fig. 5·1.

Values by Direct Calculations

Median. Here $\frac{N}{2} = 25$. The *c.f.* just greater than 25 is 30. Thus the corresponding class 20—30 is the median class. Using median formula, we get

$$\text{Median} = 20 + \frac{10}{20}\left(\frac{50}{2} - 10\right) = 20 + \frac{1}{2} \times 15 = 20 + 7{\cdot}5 = 27{\cdot}5$$

P_{10} **and** P_{90}. $\quad \frac{10}{100}N = \frac{10}{100} \times 50 = 5$

The *c.f.* greater than 5 is 10. Hence, P_{10} lies in the corresponding class 10—20.

$$\therefore \quad P_{10} = 10 + \frac{10}{6}(5 - 4) = 10 + \frac{10}{6} = 10 + 1{\cdot}67 = 11{\cdot}67$$

$\frac{90}{100}N = \frac{90}{100} \times 50 = 45$. The *c.f.* greater than 45 is 47.

Hence, the corresponding class 40—50 contains P_{90} and

$$P_{90} = 40 + \frac{10}{7}(45 - 40) = 40 + \frac{10 \times 5}{7} = 40 + 7{\cdot}14 = 47{\cdot}14$$

Hence, the range of the marks obtained by the middle 80% of the students is

$$P_{90} - P_{10} = 47{\cdot}14 - 11{\cdot}67 = 35{\cdot}47.$$

Example 5·28. *For a group of 5000 workers, the hourly wages vary from Rs. 20 to Rs. 80. The wages of 4 per cent of the workers are under Rs. 25 and those of 10 per cent are under 30; 15 per cent of the workers earn Rs. 60 and over, and 5 per cent of them get Rs. 70 and over. The quartile wages are Rs. 40 and Rs. 54, and the sixth decile is Rs. 50. Put this information in the form of a frequency table.*

Solution. We are given : $N = 5000$.

(*a*) $Q_1 = 40$ Rs. $\Rightarrow$ 25% *i.e.,* $\frac{25}{100} \times 5000 = 1250$ workers earn less than Rs. 40.

(*b*) $D_6 = 50$ Rs. $\Rightarrow$ 60% *i.e.,* $\frac{60}{100} \times 5000 = 3000$ workers earn below Rs. 50.

(*c*) $Q_3 = 54$ Rs. $\Rightarrow$ 75% *i.e.,* $\frac{75}{100} \times 5000 = 3750$ workers earn below Rs. 54.

Further, we are given that :

(*i*) 4% *i.e.,* $\frac{4}{100} \times 5000 = 200$ workers earn under Rs. 25.

(*ii*) 10% *i.e.,* $\frac{10}{100} \times 5000 = 500$ workers earn under Rs. 30.

(*iii*) 15% *i.e.,* $\frac{15}{100} \times 5000 = 750$ workers earn Rs. 60 and over and

(*iv*) 5% *i.e.,* $\frac{5}{100} \times 5000 = 250$ workers earn over Rs. 70.

Using the above information, we can compute the frequencies for the following class intervals :

Wages in Rs. : Under 25, 25—30, 30—40, 40—50, 50—54, 54—60, 60—70, 70 and over, as given in the following table :

Hourly Wages (in Rs.)	*No. of workers*	*Less than c.f.*
Under 25	200	200
25—30	500 – 200 = 300	500
30—40	1250 – 500 = 750	1250
40—50	3000 – 1250 = 1750	3000
50—54	3750 – 3000 = 750	3750
54—60	4250 – 3750 = 500	5000 – 750 = 4250
60—70	750 – 250 = 500	—
70 and over	250	—

Since the number of workers with wages under Rs. 25 is 200 and further, since it is given that the wages vary from Rs. 20 to Rs. 80, the first class *viz.*, under 25 can be taken as 20—25 and the last class, *viz.*, 70 and over can be taken as 70—80. In the above table, the various classes are of unequal widths. Rearranging and combining them to have classes with equal magnitude of 10 each, the final frequency distribution of wages of 5000 workers is as shown in the adjoining Table.

FREQUENCY DISTRIBUTION OF WAGES OF WORKERS

Hourly wages (in Rs.)	*No. of workers (f)*
20—30	200 + 300 = 500
30—40	750
40—50	1750
50—60	750 + 500 = 1250
60—70	500
70—80	250

EXERCISE 5·2

1. Define median and discuss its relative merits and demerits.

2. The mean is the most common measure of central tendency of the data. It satisfies almost all the requirements of a good average. The median is also an average, but it does not satisfy all the requirements of a good average. However, it carries certain merits and hence is useful in particular fields. Critically examine both the averages.

3. What do you understand by central tendency ? Under what conditions is median more suitable than other measures of central tendency ?

4. In each of the following cases, explain whether the description applies to mean, median or both :

(*i*) Can be calculated from a frequency distribution with open end classes.
(*ii*) The values of all items are taken into consideration in the calculation.
(*iii*) The values of extreme items do not influence the average.
(*iv*) In a distribution with a single peak and moderate skewness to the right, it is closer to the concentration of the distribution.

Ans. (*i*) median, (*ii*) mean, (*iii*) median (*iv*) median.

5. Find the medians of the following two series :

(*i*)	38	34	39	35	32	31	37	30	41
(*ii*)	30	31	36	33	29	28	35	36	

Ans. (*i*) 35, (*ii*) 32.

6. What are the properties of median ?

Following are the marks obtained by a batch of 10 students in a certain class test in Statistics (X) and Accountancy (Y).

Roll No. :	1	2	3	4	5	6	7	8	9	10
X :	63	64	62	32	30	60	47	46	35	28
Y :	68	66	35	42	26	85	44	80	33	72

In which subject is the level of knowledge of the students higher ?

Ans. Md (X) = 46·5, Md. (Y) = 55. Level of knowledge of students is higher in Accountancy.

7. Find mean and median from the data given below :

Marks obtained :	0—10	10—20	20—30	30—40	40—50	50—60
No. of students :	12	18	27	20	17	6

Ans. Mean = 28, Median = 27·41

8. Calculate arithmetic mean and median from the following series :

Income (Rs.) :	0—5	5—10	10—15	15—20	20—25	25—30
Frequency :	5	7	10	8	6	4

[*C.S. (Foundation), Dec. 2000*]

Ans. Arithmetic mean = 14·375 ; Median = 14.

9. For the data given below, find the missing freqeuncy if the Arithmetic Mean is Rs. 33. Also find the median of the series :

Loss per shop (Rs.) :	0—10	10—20	20—30	30—40	40—50	50—60
No. of shops :	10	15	30	—	25	20

[*C.A. (Foundation), Nov. 2000*]

Ans. Missing frequency = 25 ; Median = 33

10. Given below is the distribution of marks obtained by 140 students in an examination.

Marks :	10—19	20—29	30—39	40—49	50—59	60—69	70—79	80—89	90—99
No. of students :	7	15	18	25	30	20	16	7	2

Find the median of the distribution. [*C.A. PEE-1, May 2004*]

Ans. 51.167.

11. Compute median from the following data :

Mid-value :	115	125	135	145	155	165	175	185	195
Frequency :	6	25	48	72	116	60	38	22	3

Hint. The class intervals are : 110—120, 120—130,……, 190—200

Ans. Median = 153·79.

12. You are given below a certain statistical distribution :

Value :	Less than 100	100—200	200—300	300—400	400 and above	Total
Frequency :	40	89	148	64	39	380

Calculate the most suitable average giving reasons for your choice.

Ans. *Md* = 241·22.

13. The following table gives the distribution of marks secured by some students in a certain examination :

Marks :	0—20	21—30	31—40	41—50	51—60	61—70	71—80
No. of Students :	42	38	120	84	48	36	31

Find : (*i*) Median marks.

(*ii*) The percentage of failure if minimum for a pass is 35 marks.

Ans. (*i*) *Md* = 40·46 (*ii*) 31·58%.

14. Calculate the median from the following data :

Weight (in gms.) :	410—419	420—429	430—439	440—449	450—459	460—469	470—479
No. of Apples :	14	20	42	54	45	18	7

[*Andhra Pradesh Univ. B.Com., 1999*]

Ans. Median = 443·94 gms

15. Given below is the distribution of 140 candidates obtaining marks *X* or higher in a certain examination (all marks are given in whole numbers)

Marks (More than) :	10	20	30	40	50	60	70	80	90	100
Freqeuncy :	140	133	118	100	75	45	25	9	2	0

Calculate the mean and median marks obtained by the candidates.

Ans. Mean = 50·714, Median = 51·167.

16. The following table gives the weekly wages in rupees in a certain commercial organisation.

Weekly wages ('00 Rs.) :	30—	32—	34—	36—	38—	40—	42—	44—	46—	48—50
Frequency :	3	8	24	31	50	61	38	21	12	2

Find : (*i*) the median and the first quartile, (*ii*) the number of wage earners receiving between Rs. 3700 and Rs. 4700 per week.

Ans. (*i*) *Md* = Rs. 4029.51; Q_1 = Rs. 3777.42; (*ii*) 191.

17. Define a percentile. Find the 45th and 57th percentiles for the following data on marks obtained by 100 students :

Marks	20—25	25—30	30—35	35—40	40—45	45—50
No. of Students	10	20	20	15	15	20

[*C.A. (Foundation), May 1996*]

Ans. $P_{45} = 33{\cdot}75$; $P_{57} = 37{\cdot}33$.

18. Find :

(*a*) the 2nd decile, (*b*) the 4th decile. (*c*) the 90th percentile, and (*d*) the 68th percentile

for the data given below, interpreting clearly the significance of each.

Age of Head of Family (years)	*Number (in millions)*	*Age of Head of Family (years)*	*Number (in millions)*
Under 25	2·22	55—64	6·63
25—29	4·05	65—74	4·16
30—34	5·08	75 and over	1·66
35—44	10·45	Total	43·72
45—54	9·47		

Ans. $D_2 = 31{\cdot}94$ years, $D_4 = 40{\cdot}38$ years , $P_{90} = 67{\cdot}98$ years, $P_{68} = 52{\cdot}87$ years.

19. Find the (*i*) Lower quartile, (*ii*) Upper quartile, (*iii*) 7th decile, and (*iv*) 60th percentile, for the following frequency distribution :

Wages (Rs.) :	30—40	40—50	50—60	60—70	70—80	80—90	90—100
No. of Persons :	1	3	11	21	43	32	9

Ans. (*i*) Rs. 67·14, (*ii*) Rs. 83·44, (*iii*) Rs. 81·56, (*iv*) Rs. 78·37.

20. Draw an ogive for the data given below and show how can the value of median be read off from this graph. Verify your result.

Class Interval :	0—5	5—10	10—15	15—20	20—25	25—30
Frequency :	5	10	15	8	7	5

Ans. Median = 13·5 (approx.); By formula, Md = 13·33.

21. Draw a 'less than ogive' from the following data and hence find out the value of lower quartile.

Class Interval :	0—5	5—10	10—20	20—30	30—40	40—50
Frequency :	5	7	15	20	8	5

Ans. $Q_1 = 12$.

22. The frequency distribution of heights of 100 college students is as follows :

Height (cms.) :	141—150	151—160	161—170	171—180	181—190	Total
Frequency :	5	16	56	19	4	100

Draw an ogive (less than or more than type) of this distribution and from the ogive find

(*i*) the first quartile, (*ii*) the median, (*iii*) the third quartile, and (*iv*) Inter-quartile Range.

Ans. $Q_1 = 161{\cdot}2$ cms, $Q_3 = 170{\cdot}1$ cms, Median = 165·7 cms, I.Q. Range = 8.9 cm.

23. The monthly salary distribution of 250 families in a certain locality in Agra is given below :

Monthly Salary (Rs.)	*No. of Families*	*Monthly Salary (Rs.)*	*No. of Families*
More than 0	250	More than 2,000	55
More than 500	200	More than 2,500	30
More than 1,000	120	More than 3,000	15
More than 1,500	80	More than 3,500	5

Draw a 'less than' ogive for the data given above and hence find out :

(*i*) Limits of the income of middle 50% of the families ; and

(*ii*) If income-tax is to be levied on families whose income exceeds Rs. 1,800 p.m., calculate the percentage of families, which will be paying income-tax. [*Delhi Univ. B.Com. (Hons.), 2007*]

Ans. (*i*) Q_1 = Rs. 578 (*approx.*); Q_3 = Rs. 1850

(*ii*) $\frac{25}{(2000-1500)} \times (2000-1800) + 25 + 15 + 10 + 5 = 65$

$\therefore$ Percentage of families paying income tax $= \frac{65}{250} \times 100 = 26\%$.

24. Draw a 'less than' and 'more than' ogive curve for the following data and find median value :

No. of Children	0	1	2	3	4	5	6
No. of Families	150	72	50	28	12	8	5

[*Delhi Univ. B.Com. (Pass), 1999*]

Hint. Since the number of children is a discrete random variable which can take only positive integer values, the given frequency distribution can be expressed as grouped frequency distribution with exclusive type classes as given below.

Variable	0—1	1—2	2—3	3—4	4—5	5—6	6—7
Frequency	150	72	50	28	12	8	5

Ans. Median from ogive = 1·1 (*approx.*).

25. With the help of given data, find :

(*i*) Value of middle 50% items; (*ii*) Value of exactly 50% item; (*iii*) The value of P_{40} and D_6;

(*iv*) Graphically with the help of ogive curve, the values of Q_1, Q_3, median, P_{40} and D_6 :

Class Interval	10—14	15—19	20—24	25—29	30—34	35—39	Total
Frequencies	5	10	15	20	10	5	65

[*Delhi Univ. B.Com. (Hons.), 2008*]

Ans. (*i*) $Q_3 - Q_1 = 29.19 - 19.92 = 9.27$; (*ii*) $Md = Q_2 = 25.13$; (*iii*) $P_{40} = 23.17$, $D_6 = 26.75$

26. One hundred and twenty students appeared for a certain test and the following marks distribution was obtained:

Marks	:	0—20	20—40	40—60	60—80	80—100
Students	:	10	30	36	30	14

Find : (*i*) The limits of marks of middle 30% students.

(*ii*) The percentage of students getting marks more than 75.

(*iii*) The number of students who fail, if 35 marks are required for passing.

Ans. (*i*) $P_{35} = 41{\cdot}1$; $P_{65} = 61{\cdot}3$; (*ii*) $\frac{100}{120}\left[\left(\frac{30}{20}\times 5\right) + 14\right] = 17{\cdot}9\ \%$; (*iii*) $10 + \frac{15}{20} \times 30 = 32{\cdot}5 \simeq 33$.

27. The expenditure of 1,000 families is given as under :

Expenditure (in Rs.)	:	40—59	60—79	80—99	100—119	120—139
No. of families	:	50	?	500	?	50

The median for the distribution is Rs. 87. Calculate the missing frequencies.

Ans. 262·5, 137·5 ≃ 263, 137.

28. An incomplete frequency distribution is given as follows :

Variable :	10—20	20—30	30—40	40—50	50-60	60—70	70—80	Total
Frequency :	12	30	?	65	?	25	19	230

You are given that median value is 46.

(*a*) Using the median formula, fill up the missing frequencies.

(*b*) Calculate the Arithmetic Mean of the completed table.

Ans. (*a*) 34, 45 (*b*) 45·96

29. An incomplete distribution is given below :

Variable :	0—10	10—20	20—30	30—40	40—50	50—60	60—70
Frequency :	10	20	?	40	?	25	15

(*i*) You are given that the median value is 35. Find out missing frequency (given the total frequency = 170).

(*ii*) Calculate the arithmetic mean of the completed table.

[*Himachal Pradesh Univ. B.Com., 1999; Kerala Univ. B.Com., 1999*]

Ans. (*i*) 35,25 (*ii*) 35·88.

30. The data in the adjoining table represent travel expenses (other than transportation) for 7 trips made during November by a salesman for a small firm :

Trip	*Days*	*Expenses (Rs.)*	*Expenses per day (Rs.)*
1	0·5	13·50	27
2	2·0	12·00	6
3	3·5	17·50	5
4	1·0	9·00	9
5	9·0	27·00	3
6	0·5	9·00	18
7	8·5	17·00	2
Total	25·0	105·00	70

An auditor criticised these expenses as excessive, asserting that the average expense per day is Rs. 10 (Rs. 70 divided by 7). The salesman replied that the average is only Rs. 4·20 (Rs. 105 divided by 25) and that in any event the median is the appropriate measure and is only Rs. 3. The auditor rejoined that the arithmetic mean is the appropriate measure, but that the median is Rs. 6.

You are required to :

(*i*) Explain the proper interpretation of each of the four averages mentioned.

(*ii*) Which average seems appropriate to you ?

31. For a certain class of workers, numbering 700, hourly wages vary between Rs. 30 and Rs. 75. 12% of the workers are earning less than Rs. 35 while 13% are getting equal to or more than Rs. 60, out of which 6% are earning between Rs. 70 and Rs. 75. The first quartile and median wages are, respectively, Rs. 40 and Rs. 47. The 40th and 65th percentiles are Rs. 43 and Rs. 53 respectively. You are required to put the above information in the form of a frequency distribution and estimate the mean wages of the workers.

Ans. *Hourly wages (Rs.)* :	30—35	35—	40—	43—	47—	53—	60—
No. of workers :	84	91	105	70	105	91	49

$\overline{X}$ = Rs. 48·33.

32. For a certain group of saree weavers of Varanasi, the median and quartile earnings per hour are Rs. 44·3, Rs. 43·0 and Rs. 45·9 respectively. The earnings for the group range between Rs. 40 and Rs. 50. Ten per cent of the group earn under Rs. 42; 13% earn Rs. 47 and over, and 6% Rs. 48 and over. Put these data in the form of a frequency distribution and obtain the value of the mean wage.

Ans. *Hourly Wages (Rs.)* :	40—42	42—	43—	44·3—	45·9—	47—	48—50
No. of workers :	10	15	25	25	12	7	6

Mean = Rs. 44·50.

5·7. MODE

Mode is the value which occurs most frequently in a set of observations and around which the other items *of the set* cluster densely. In other words, mode is the value of a series which is predominant in it. In the words of Croxton and Cowden, "*The mode of a distribution is value at the point around which the items tend to be most heavily concentrated. It may be regarded as the most typical of a series of values.*"

According to A.M. Tuttle, '*Mode is the value which has the greatest frequency density in its immediate neighbourhood*'. Accordingly mode may also be termed as the *fashionable value* (a derivation of the French word 'la Mode') of the distribution.

In the following statements :

(*i*) average size of the shoe sold in a shop is 7,

(*ii*) average height of an Indian (male) is *5 feet 6 inches* (1·68 metres *approx.*),

(*iii*) average collar size of the shirt sold in a ready-made garment shop is 35 cms,

(*iv*) average student in a professional college spends Rs. 2,500 per month;

the average referred to is neither mean nor median but mode, the most frequent value in the distribution. For example, by the first statement we mean that there is maximum demand for the shoe of size No. 7.

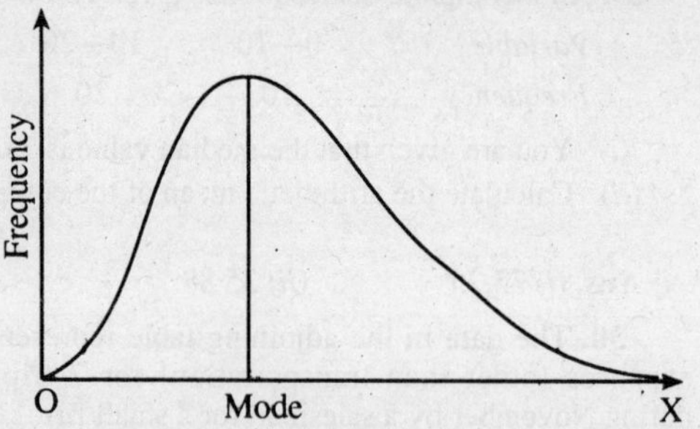

Fig. 5·2.

5·7·1. Computation of Mode. In case of a frequency distribution, mode is the value of the variable corresponding to the maximum frequency. This method can be applied with ease and simplicity if the distribution is '*unimodal*', *i.e.,* if it has only one mode. In other words, this method can be used with convenience if there is only one value with highest concentration of observations. For example, in the distribution :

X :	1	2	3	4	5	6	7	8	9
f :	3	1	18	25	40	30	22	10	6

the maximum frequency is 40 and therefore, the corresponding value of X *viz.,* 5 gives the value of mode. In case of a frequency curve (see Fig. 5.2) mode corresponds to the peak of the curve.

In the case of continuous frequency distribution, the class corresponding to the maximum frequency is called the *modal class* and the value of mode is obtained by the interpolation formula :

$$\text{Mode } = l + \frac{h\,(f_1 - f_0)}{(f_1 - f_0) - (f_2 - f_1)} = l + \frac{h\,(f_1 - f_0)}{2f_1 - f_0 - f_2} \qquad \ldots(5\cdot18)$$

where l is the lower limit of the modal class,

f_1 is the frequency of the modal class,

f_0 is the frequency of the class preceding the modal class,

f_2 in the frequency of the class succeeding the modal class,

and h is the magnitude of the modal class.

The symbols f_0, f_1 and f_2 can be explained easily as follows :

f_0 : Frequency of preceding class,

f_1 : Maximum frequency (Frequency of Modal class),

f_2 : Frequency of succeeding class.

Remarks 1. It may be pointed out that the formula (5·18) for computing mode is based on the following assumptions :

(*i*) The frequency distribution must be continuous with exclusive type classes without any gaps. If the data are not given in the form of continuous classes, it must first be converted into continuous classes before applying formula (5·18).

(*ii*) The class intervals must be uniform throughout *i.e.,* the width of all the class intervals must be the same. In case of the distribution with unequal class intervals, they should be made equal under the assumption that the frequencies are uniformly distributed over all the classes, otherwise the value of mode computed from (5·18) will give misleading results.

2. However, the above technique of locating mode is not practicable in the following situations :

(*i*) If the maximum frequency is repeated or approximately equal concentration is found in two or more neighbouring values.

(*ii*) If the maximum frequency occurs either in the very beginning or at the end of the distribution.

(*iii*) If there are irregularities in the distribution *i.e.,* the frequencies of the variable increase or decrease in a haphazard way.

In the above situations mode (or modal class in the case of continuous frequency distribution) is located by the *method of grouping* as discussed in Examples 5·31 and 5·32.

3. If the method of grouping gives the modal class which does not correspond to the maximum frequency f_1 *i.e.*, the frequency of modal class is not the maximum frequency, then in some situations we may get $2f_1 - f_0 - f_2 = 0$. [This will not be possible if f_1 is maximum and f_0 and f_2 are less than f_1]. In such a situation *viz.*, $2f_1 - f_0 - f_2 = 0$, the value of mode cannot be computed by the formula.

$$\text{Mode } = l + \frac{h\,(f_1 - f_0)}{2f_1 - f_0 - f_2}$$

as it gives $\quad \text{Mode } = l + \infty = \infty. \qquad [\because 2f_1 - f_0 - f_2 = 0]$

In such cases, the value of mode can be obtained by the formula :

$$\text{Mode } = l + \frac{h\,|f_1 - f_0|}{|f_1 - f_0| + |f_1 - f_2|} \qquad \ldots(5{\cdot}18a)$$

where $|A|$ represents the absolute (positive) value of A.

Formula (5·18*a*) is only an approximate formula and does not give very correct result because further grouping of classes, say, 4 at a time may give different value of the modal class and as such a different result.

As an illustration, for the following data :

X :	10—20	20—30	30—40	40—50	50—60	60—70	70—80	80—90	90—100	100—110
f :	4	6	5	10	20	22	24	6	2	1

the usual method of grouping (up to 3 classes at a time) will give 60—70 as the modal class such that : $f_1 = 22, f_0 = 20, f_2 = 24$ and therefore, $2f_1 - f_0 - f_2 = 44 - 20 - 24 = 0$. Hence, usual formula for mode cannot be applied. Using (5·18*a*), an approximate value of mode may be obtained as :

$$Mo = 60 + \frac{10\,|22 - 20|}{|22 - 20| + |22 - 24|} = 60 + \frac{10 \times 2}{2 + 2} = 60 + 5 = 65$$

5·7·2. Merits and Demerits of Mode.

Merits. (*i*) Mode is easy to calculate and understand. In some cases it can be located merely by inspection. It can also be estimated graphically from a histogram (*c.f.* § 5·7·3).

(*ii*) Mode is not at all affected by extreme observations and as such is preferred to arithmetic mean while dealing with extreme observations.

(*iii*) It can be conveniently obtained in the case of open end classes which do not pose any problems here.

Demerits. (*i*) Mode is not rigidly defined. It is ill-defined if the maximum frequency is repeated or if the maximum frequency occurs either, in the very beginning or at the end of the distribution; or if the distribution is irregular. In these cases, its value is located by the *method of grouping* (*c.f.* Examples, 5·31). If the grouping method also gives two values of mode, then the distribution is called *bi-modal* distribution (*c.f. Example 5·32*). We may also come across distributions with more than two modes, in which case it is called ***multimodal*** distribution. In case of bimodal or multimodal distributions, mode is not a representative measure of location and its estimate is obtained by the empirical relation :

$$\text{Mode} = 3 \text{ Median} - 2 \text{ Mean, discussed in § 5·8.}$$

(*ii*) Since mode is the value of X corresponding to the maximum frequency, it is not based on all the observations of the series. Even in the case of the continuous frequency distribution [*c.f.* Formula (5·18)], mode depends on the frequencies of modal class and the classes preceding and succeeding it.

(*iii*) Mode is not suitable for further mathematical treatment. For example, from the modal values and the sizes of two or more series, we cannot find the mode of the combined series.

(*iv*) As compared with mean, mode is affected to a greater extent by the fluctuations of sampling.

Uses. Being the point of maximum density, mode is specially useful in finding the most popular size in studies relating to marketing, trade, business and industry. It is the appropriate average to be used to find the ideal size *e.g.*, in business forecasting, in the manufacture of shoes or readymade garments, in sales, in production, etc.

5·7·3. Graphic Location of Mode. Mode can be located graphically from the histogram of frequency distribution by making use of the rectangles erected on the modal, pre-modal and postmodal classes. The method consists of the following steps :

(*i*) Join the top right corner of the rectangle erected on the modal class with the top right corner of the rectangle erected on the preceding class by means of a straight line.

(*ii*) Join the top left corner of the rectangle erected on the modal class with the top left corner of the rectangle erected on the succeeding class by a straight line.

(*iii*) From the point of intersection of the lines in steps (*i*) and (*ii*) above, draw a perpendicular to the *X*-axis (the horizontal scale). The abscissa (*X*-coordinate) of the point where this perpendicular meets the *X*-axis gives the modal value.

5·8. EMPIRICAL RELATION BETWEEN MEAN (M), MEDIAN (Md) AND MODE (Mo)

In case of a *symmetrical* distribution mean, median and mode coincide *i.e.*, Mean = Median = Mode (*c.f.* Chapter 7 on Skewness). However, for a *moderately* asymmetrical (non-symmetrical or skewed) distribution, mean and mode usually lie on the two ends and median lies in between them and they obey the following important *empirical* relationship, given by Prof. Karl Pearson.

$$\text{Mode} = \text{Mean} - 3\,(\text{Mean} - \text{Median}) \qquad \ldots(5{\cdot}19)$$

$$\Rightarrow \quad \text{Mean} - \text{Mode} = 3\,(\text{Mean} - \text{Median})$$

$$\Rightarrow \quad \text{Mean} - \text{Median} = \tfrac{1}{3}\,(\text{Mean} - \text{Mode}) \qquad \ldots(5{\cdot}19a)$$

Thus we see that the difference between mean and mode is three times the difference between mean and median. In other words, median is closer to mean than mode. The above relation between mean (*M*), median (*Md*) and mode (*Mo*) can be exhibited diagrammatically as follows (Fig. 5.3) :

Remarks. 1. Equation (5·19) may be rewritten to give :

$$\text{Mode} = \text{Mean} - 3\ \text{Mean} + 3\ \text{Median}$$

$$\Rightarrow \quad \text{Mode} = 3\ \text{Median} - 2\ \text{Mean} \qquad \ldots(5{\cdot}20)$$

This formula is specially useful to determine the value of mode in case it is ill-defined, *e.g.*, in the case of biomodal or multimodal distributions [*c.f.* Example 5·39].

2. If we know any two of the three values *M, Md* and *Mo*, the third can be estimated by using (5·20). The value so computed will be more or less same as obtained by using the exact formula provided the distribution is moderately asymmetrical.

3. For a positively skewed distribution [*c.f.* Chapter 7], mean will be greater than median and median will be greater than mode *i.e.*,

RELATIONSHIP BETWEEN ARITHMETIC MEAN, MEDIAN AND MODE

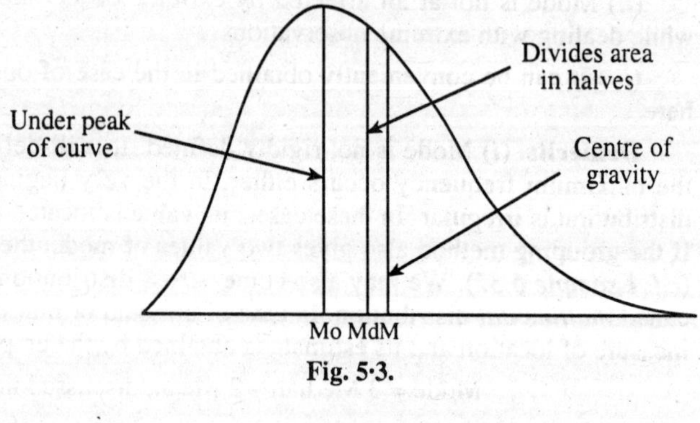

Fig. 5·3.

$$M > Md > Mo \quad \Rightarrow \quad Mo < Md < M$$

However, in a negatively skewed distribution the order of the magnitudes of the three averages will be reversed *i.e.*, for *negatively skewed distribution*, we have

$$Mo > Md > M \quad \Rightarrow \quad M < Md < Mo$$

Example 5.29. *(a) Find the mode of the following distribution :*

7, 4, 3, 5, 6, 3, 3, 2, 4, 3, 4, 3, 3, 4, 4, 2, 3

[*I.C.W.A. (Foundation), June 2005*]

(b) If the relation between two variables x and y be 2x + 5y = 24 and mode of y be 4, find the mode of x.

[*I.C.W.A. (Foundation), June 2006*]

Solution. (*a*) The frequency distribution of the variable (x) is obtained as given below.

x	2	3	4	5	6	7
Tally Marks	||	~~||||~~ ||	~~||||~~	|	|	|
Frequency (f)	2	7	5	1	1	1

Since the maximum frequency (7) corresponds to $x = 3$, the value of mode is 3.

(*b*) We are given :

$$\text{Mode } (y) = 4 \quad \ldots(*) \qquad \text{and} \qquad 2x + 5y = 24 \quad \Rightarrow \quad x = \frac{1}{2}(24 - 5y) \ldots (**)$$

If x and y are corrected by the relation $y = ax + b$, then the frequencies of the variable y are the same as the frequencies of the corresponding values of the variable x. Hence, the modes of the variables x and y are also connected by the same equation, *i.e.*,

$$y = ax + b \quad \Rightarrow \quad \text{Mode } (y) = \text{Mode } (ax + b) = a \text{ [Mode } (x)] + b \qquad \ldots(***)$$

Hence on using (***), we get from (**),

$$\text{Mode } (x) = \text{Mode}\left[\frac{1}{2}(24 - 5y)\right] = 12 - \frac{5}{2} \cdot \text{Mode } (y) = 12 - \frac{5}{2} \times 4 = 2 \qquad \text{[From (*)]}$$

Example 5·30. *Find the value of mean , mode and median from the data given below :*

Weight (in kg.) :	93—97	98—102	103—107	108—112	113—117	118—122	123—127	128—132
No. of students :	3	5	12	17	14	6	3	1

Solution. Since the formula for mode requires the distribution to be continuous with 'exclusive type' classes we first convert the classes into class bounderies as given in the following table :

COMPUTATION OF MEAN, MODE AND MEDIAN

Weight (in kg)	*Class boundaries*	*Mid-value (X)*	*No. of students (f)*	$d = \frac{X - 110}{5}$	*fd*	*Less than c.f.*
93—97	92·5—97·5	95	3	–3	–9	3
98—102	97·5—102·5	100	5	–2	–10	8
103—107	102·5—107·5	105	12	–1	–12	20
108—112	107·5—112·5	110	17	0	0	37
113—117	112·5—117·5	115	14	1	14	51
118—122	117·5—122·5	120	6	2	12	57
123—127	122·5—127·5	125	3	3	9	60
128—132	127·5—132·5	130	1	4	4	61
			$N = \Sigma f = 61$		$\Sigma fd = 8$	

Mean. Mean $= A + \frac{h\Sigma fd}{N} = 110 + \frac{5 \times 8}{61} = 110{\cdot}66$ kgs.

Mode. Here maximum frequency is 17. The corresponding class 107·5—112·5 is the modal class. Using the mode formula, we get

$$\text{Mode} = l + \frac{h(f_1 - f_0)}{2f_1 - f_0 - f_2} = 107{\cdot}5 + \frac{5 \times (17 - 12)}{2 \times 17 - 12 - 14}$$

$$= 107{\cdot}5 + \frac{25}{8} = 107{\cdot}5 + 3{\cdot}125 = 110{\cdot}625 \text{ kgs.}$$

Median. ($N/2$) = (61/2) = 30·5. The *c.f.* just greater than 30·5 is 37. Hence, the corresponding class 107·5—112·5 is the median class. Using the median formula, we get

$$Md = 107{\cdot}5 + \frac{5}{17}(30{\cdot}5 - 20) = 107{\cdot}5 + \frac{5 \times 10{\cdot}5}{17}$$

$$= 107{\cdot}50 + 3{\cdot}09 = 110{\cdot}59 \text{ kg.}$$

Example 5·31. *Construct a frequency distribution showing the frequencies with which words of different number of letters occur in the extract reproduced below (omitting punctuation marks, treating as the variable the number of letters in each word) and obtain the median and the mode of the distribution.*

A candidate at the time of applying for registration as a student of the institute should be not less than eighteen years of age and have passed the intermediate examination of a university constituted by law in India or an examination recognized by Central Government as equivalent thereto, or the National Diploma in Commerce Examination or the Diploma in Rural Service Examination conducted by the National Council of Rural Higher Education.

Solution. Here the variable X represents the number of letters in each word. For example, in the word 'candidate' there are 9 letters *c, a, n, d, i, d, a, t* and *e*. Hence X, corresponding to the word 'candidate' is 9. Thus replacing each word by the number of letters in it, the distribution of the number of letters in each word in the given paragraph is as follows :

1, 9, 2, 3, 4, 2, 8, 3, 12, 2, 1, 7, 2, 3, 9, 6, 2, 3,
4, 4, 8, 5, 2, 3, 3, 4, 6, 3, 12, 11, 2, 1, 10, 11, 2, 3,
2, 5, 2, 2, 11, 10, 2, 3, 7, 10, 2, 10, 7, 2, 3, 8, 7, 2,
8, 11, 2, 3, 7, 2, 5, 7, 11, 8, 2, 3, 8, 7, 2, 5, 6, 9

The above data can be arranged in the form of a frequency distribution as given in the adjoining table .

Median. Here $\frac{N}{2} = \frac{72}{2} = 36$. Since *c.f.* just greater than 36 is 38, the corresponding value of X is median, which is 4.

Mode : Since the above frequency distribution is not regular, the value of mode is located by the method of grouping.

As the distribution is not regular we cannot say that the value of mode is 2, which corresponds to the maximum frequency is 19. Here we try to locate mode by the method of grouping as explained in table below.

COMPUTATION OF MEDIAN

No. of letters in a word (X)	*Tally Marks*	*Frequency (f)*	*(Less than) c.f.*
1	|||	3	3
2	𝍸 𝍸 𝍸 ||||	19	22
3	𝍸 𝍸 ||	12	34
4	||||	4	38
5	||||	4	42
6	|||	3	45
7	𝍸 ||	7	52
8	𝍸 |	6	58
9	|||	3	61
10	||||	4	65
11	𝍸	5	70
12	||	2	72

COMPUTATION OF MODE : GROUPING TABLE

X	Frequencies (1)	(2)	(3)	(4)	(5)	(6)
1	3	22		34		
2	**19**		31		35	
3	12	16				20
4	4		8	11		
5	4	7			14	
6	3		10			16
7	7	13		16		
8	6		9		13	
9	3	7				12
10	4		9	11		
11	5	7				
12	2					

The frequencies in column (1) are the original frequencies. Column (2) is obtained by combining the frequencies two by two in column (1). Column (3) is obtained on combining the frequencies two by two in column (1) after leaving the first frequency. If we leave the first two frequencies and combine the frequencies two by two in column (1), we shall get a repetition of values obtained in column (2). Hence, we proceed to combine the frequencies in column (1) three by three to get column (4). The combination of frequencies three by three after leaving the first frequency and first two frequencies in column (1) results in columns (5) and (6) respectively. If we combine the frequencies three by three after leaving the first three frequencies in column (1), we get a repetition of values obtained in column (4). The maximum frequency in each column is represented by "bold type'.

For computing the value of mode we prepare the following analysis table :

ANALYSIS TABLE

Column No. in above Table (I)	*Maximum frequency (II)*	*Value or combination of values of X corresponding to maximum frequency in column (II) (III)*				
(1)	19		2			
(2)	22	1	2			
(3)	31		2	3		
(4)	34	1	2	3		
(5)	35		2	3	4	
(6)	20			3	4	5
Frequency of the variable (*X*)		2	5	4	2	1

Since the value 2 is repeated maximum number (5) of times, the mode is 2.

Example 5·32. *Calculate mode from the following data :*

Marks	*No. of Students*	*Marks*	*No. of Students*
Below 10	*4*	*Below 60*	*86*
" *20*	*6*	" *70*	*96*
" *30*	*24*	" *80*	*99*
" *40*	*46*	" *90*	*100*
" *50*	*67*		

Solution. Since we are given the cumulative frequency distribution of marks, first we shall convert it into the frequency distribution as given in the adjoining table.

Further, since the frequencies first decrease, then increase and again decrease, the distribution is irregular and hence the modal class is located by the method of grouping as explained in the table given below.

Marks	*Frequency (f)*
0—10	4
10—20	6 – 4 = 2
20—30	24 – 6 = 18
30—40	46 – 24 = 22
40—50	67 – 46 = 21
50—60	86 – 67 = 19
60—70	96 – 86 = 10
70—80	99 – 96 = 3
80—90	100 – 99 = 1

GROUPING TABLE

Marks	*Frequencies* (1)	(2)	(3)	(4)	(5)	(6)
0—10	4	6 (0—20)		24 (0—30)		
10—20	2		20 (10—30)		42 (10—40)	
20—30	18	**40** (20—40)				**61** (20—50)
30—40	**22**		**43** (30—50)	**62** (30—60)		
40—50	21	**40** (40—60)			**50** (40—70)	
50—60	19		29 (50—70)			32 (50—80)
60—70	10	13 (60—80)		14 (60—90)		
70—80	3		4 (70—90)			
80—90	1					

For computing modal class, we prepare the analysis table as given below :

ANALYSIS TABLE

Column No. in above Table (I)	Maximum frequency (II)	Class (es) corresponding to maximum frequency in (II) (III)				
(1)	22		30—40			
(2)	40	20—30	30—40	40—50	50—60	
(3)	43		30—40	40—50		
(4)	62		30—40	40—50	50—60	
(5)	50			40—50	50—60	60—70
(6)	61	20—30	30—40	40—50		
Number of times the class occurs		2	5	5	3	1

In the above table there are two classes *viz.*, 30—40 and 40—50 which are repeated maximum number (5) of times and as such we cannot decide about the modal class. Thus, even the method of grouping fails to give the modal class.

We say that in the above example mode is ill-defined and we locate it by the empirical formula :

$$Mo = 3Md - 2M \qquad \ldots(*)$$

For computation of Mean (M) and Median (Md), see calculation Table on page 5.52

$$\text{Mean} = A + \frac{h\Sigma fd}{N} = 45 + \frac{10 \times (-28)}{100} = 45 - 2{\cdot}8 = 42{\cdot}2.$$

Here $\frac{N}{2} = \frac{100}{2} = 50$. Since *c.f.* just greater than 50 is 67, the corresponding class 40—50 is the median class. Hence, using the median formula, we get

$$\text{Median} = 40 + \frac{10}{21}\left(\frac{100}{2} - 46\right) = 40 + \frac{10 \times 4}{21} = 40 + 1{\cdot}9 = 41{\cdot}9.$$

COMPUTATION OF ARITHMETIC MEAN AND MEDIAN

Marks	*Mid-value* (X)	*Frequency* (f)	*Less than c.f.*	$d = \frac{X-45}{10}$	*fd*
0—10	5	4	4	– 4	–16
10—20	15	2	6	–3	– 6
20—30	25	18	24	–2	–36
30—40	35	22	46	–1	–22
40—50	45	21	67	0	0
50—60	55	19	86	1	19
60—70	65	10	96	2	20
70—80	75	3	99	3	9
80—90	85	1	100	4	4
		$\Sigma f = 100$			$\Sigma fd = -28$

Substituting the values of M and Md in (*), we get

$$\text{Mode} = 3 \times 41{\cdot}9 - 2 \times 42{\cdot}2 = 125{\cdot}7 - 84{\cdot}4 = 41{\cdot}3.$$

Example 5.33. *In 500 small scale units, the return on investment ranged from 0 to 30 per cent, no unit sustaining any loss. Five per cent of the units had returns ranging from zero per cent to 5 per cent, 15 per cent of the units earned returns between 5 per cent and 10 per cent. The median rate of return was 15 per cent and the upper quartile was 20 per cent. The uppermost layer of returns of 25—30 per cent was earned by 50 units. Put this information in the form of a frequency table and find the rate of return around which there is maximum concentration of units.* [Delhi Unit. B.Com. (Hons.) (External), 2007]

Solution. On the basis of the given information we have : N = Total number of units = 500

(1) Number of units with returns ranging from 0 to 5% = 5% of 500 = $\frac{5}{100} \times 500 = 25$

(2) Number of units with returns between 5% and 10% = 15% of 500 = $\frac{15}{100} \times 500 = 75$

(3) Median rate of return = 15% $\Rightarrow$ 50% of $N = \frac{500}{2} = 250$ units have return $\leq 15\%$ ...(*i*)

$\therefore$ Number of units with return exceeding 10% but not exceeding 15% = 250 – (25 + 75) = 150

Upper Quartile (Q_3) = 20% $\Rightarrow$ $\frac{3N}{4} = \frac{3 \times 500}{4} = 375$ units have returns $\leq 20\%$

$\therefore$ Number of units with returns exceeding 15% but $\leq$ 20% = 375 – 250 = 125 [using (*i*)]

Number of units with returns between 25% to 30% = 50 (Given)

Hence, by the residual balance, the number of units with returns between 20% to 25%

$$= 500 - [25 + 75 + 150 + 125 + 50] = 500 - 425 = 75$$

Thus, the given information can be summarised in the form of a frequency distribution as given in the adjoining table.

The rate of return about which there is maximum concentration of units is given by the Mode of the rate of returns.

Since maximum frequency is 150, the modal class is 10—15.

Return in %	*No. of units (f)*	
0—5	25	
5—10	75 (f_0)	
10—15	150 (f_1)	Modal Class
15—20	125 (f_2)	
20—25	75	
25—30	50	

$$\therefore \text{ Mode} = l + \frac{h\,(f_1 - f_0)}{2f_1 - f_0 - f_2} = 10 + \frac{5\,(150 - 75)}{300 - 75 - 125} = 10 + \frac{5 \times 75}{100} = 10 + 3.75 = 13.75$$

Hence, the rate of return around which there is maximum concentration of units is 13.75%.

Example 5·34. *Below is given the frequency distribution of weights of a group of 60 students of a class in a school :*

Weight in kg.	*Number of students*	*Weight in kg.*	*Number of students*
30—34	*3*	*50—54*	*14*
35—39	*5*	*55—59*	*6*
40—44	*12*	*60—64*	*2*
45—49	*18*		

(*a*) *Draw histogram for this distribution and find the modal value.*

(*b*) (*i*) *Prepare the cumulative frequency (both less than and more than types) distribution, and* (*ii*) *represent them graphically on the same graph paper. Hence, find the (iii) median, and* (*iv*) *co-efficient of quartile deviation.*

(*c*) *With the modal and the median values as obtained in* (*a*) *and* (*b*), *use an appropriate empirical formula to find the arithmetic mean of this distribution.*

(*d*) *If students with weight below 40 kg. are eliminated from the frequency distribution, what will be the revised mean ? [Calculate the mean of the two rejected classes only and use the result obtained in* (*c*).]

Solution. (*a*) To draw the histogram and cumulative frequency curves (both less than and more than types) we first convert the distribution into continuous class intervals as given in the adjoining table.

Weight in kgs.	*Number of students (f)*	*Less than c.f.*	*More than c.f.*
29·5—34·5	3	3	60
34·5—39·5	5	8	57
39·5—44·5	12	20	52
44·5—49·5	18	38	40
49·5—54·5	14	52	22
54·5—59·5	6	58	8
59·5—64·5	2	60	2

(*a*) *Histogram*. Histogram is obtained on erecting rectangles on the class intervals with heights proportional to the corresponding class frequencies. [See Fig. 5·4.] Mode = OA = 48.

(*b*) (*i*) The 'less than' and 'more than' cumulative frequency distributions are given in the Table in Part (*a*).

(*ii*) The 'less than' and 'more than' (ogives) are drawn in the Fig. 5·5.

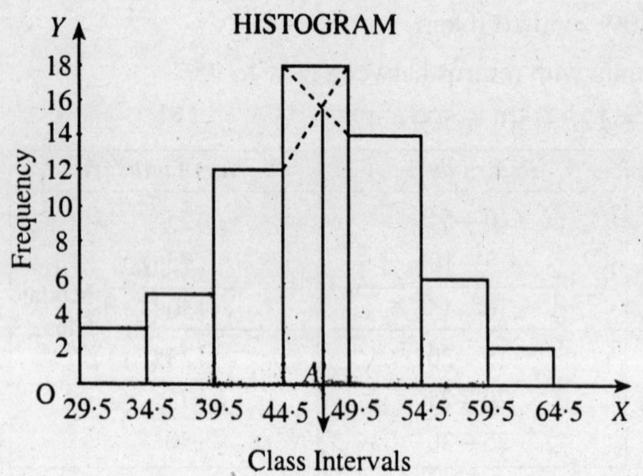

Fig. 5·4.

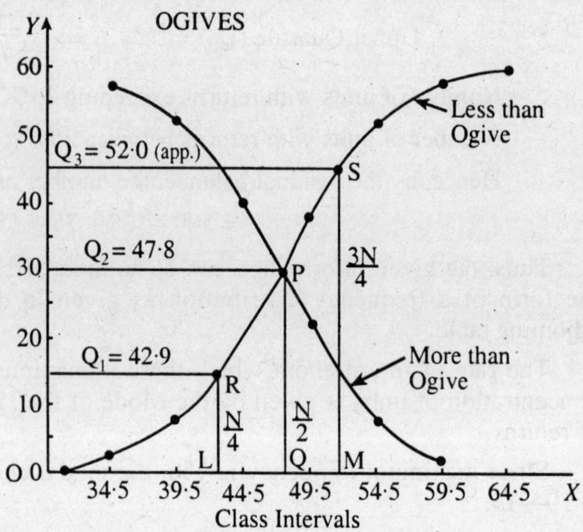

Fig. 5·5.

(*iii*) From the point of intersection P of the two curves (ogives), draw perpendicular on X-axis meeting X-axis at Q. Then OQ = 47·8 kgs. gives the median weight.

(*iv*) Draw lines parallel to X-axis at frequency equal to $N/4$ and $3N/4$ meeting the less than ogive at points R & S respectively. From R & S draw perpendiculars to X-axis meeting OX at L, M respectively. Then $Q_1 = OL = 42{\cdot}9$ kgs. and $Q_3 = OM = 51{\cdot}75$ kgs. The Coefficient of Quartile Deviation is given by :

$$\text{Coefficient of } Q.D. = \frac{Q_3 - Q_1}{Q_3 + Q_1} = \frac{51{\cdot}75 - 42{\cdot}90}{51{\cdot}75 + 42{\cdot}90} = \frac{8{\cdot}85}{94{\cdot}65} = 0{\cdot}0935$$

(*c*) The empirical relation between mean, median and mode is given by : $Mo = 3Md - 2M$

$$\therefore \quad \text{Mean } (M) = \frac{3Md - Mo}{2} = \frac{3 \times 47{\cdot}8 - 48}{2} = \frac{143{\cdot}4 - 48}{2} = \frac{95{\cdot}4}{2} = 47{\cdot}700 \text{ kgs.}$$

(*d*) Let $\bar{X}_1$ be the mean of the two classes with weight below 40 kgs.

$$\therefore \quad \bar{X}_1 = \frac{\Sigma fX}{\Sigma f} = \frac{281}{8} = 35{\cdot}125 \text{ kgs.}$$

Weight in kgs.	*Mid-value (X)*	*(f)*	*fX*
30—34	32	3	96
35—39	37	5	185
		$\Sigma f = 8 = n_1$, (say)	$\Sigma fX = 281$

Let $\bar{X}_2$ be the mean of the distribution obtained on eliminating the first two classes (*i.e.*, classes with weight below 40 kgs.). Then in the usual notations, we have

$$n_1 = 8,\ \bar{X}_1 = 35{\cdot}125;\ n_2 = 60 - 8 = 52,\quad \bar{X}_2 = ?,\quad \bar{X} = 47{\cdot}700 \qquad \text{[From Part (c)]}$$

Using the formula, $\bar{X} = \dfrac{n_1 \bar{X}_1 + n_2 \bar{X}_2}{n_1 + n_2}$, *we get*

$$60 \times 47{\cdot}700 = 8 \times 35{\cdot}125 + 52\,\bar{X}_2 \quad \Rightarrow \quad \bar{X}_2 = \frac{2862 - 281}{52} = \frac{2581}{52} = 49{\cdot}635 \text{ kgs.}$$

EXERCISE 5·3

1. What do you understand by mode ? Discuss its relative merits and demerits as a measure of central tendency. Also give two practical situations where you will recommend the use of mode.

2. What are the desideratta of a good average ? Compare the mean, the median and the mode in the light of these desideratta. Why are averages called measures of central tendency ?

3. How would you account for the predominant choice of arithmetic mean of statistical data as a measure of central tendency ? Under what circumstances would it be appropriate to use mode or median ?

4. Point out the merits and demerits of the mean the median, and the mode as measure of central tendency of numerical data.

5. Compare, giving illustrations, the arithmetic mean, the median and the mode in regard to :

(*a*) the effect of extreme items in computation,

(*b*) ease in computation,

(*c*) stability in sampling situations,

(*d*) existence of the average as an actual case, and

(*e*) popular use.

6. (*a*) Define mode. When is mode said to be ill-defined ? [*Delhi Univ. B.Com. (Pass), 1997*]

(*b*) A stockist of readymade garments should follow which type of average and why ?

[*Delhi Univ. B.Com. (Pass), 2001*]

7. The Bharat Ball Bearings Ltd., has collected the following data.

12, 19, 21, 30, 13, 19, 22, 31, 17, 20, 24, 31, 18, 21, 27, 31.

(*i*) Compute the arithmetic mean, the median and the mode using the sixteen observations given.

(*ii*) Why is the mode said to be an erratic measure of central tendency ?

(*iii*) Why is the median called a position average ?

Ans. *A.M.* = 22·25, *Md* = 21, *Mo* = 31

8. Calculate mean, median and mode from the following data of the heights in inches of a group of students :

61, 62, 63, 61, 63, 64, 64, 60, 65, 63, 64, 65, 66, 64

Now suppose that a group of students whose heights are 60, 66, 59, 68, 67, and 70 inches, is added to the original group. Find mean, median and mode of the combined group.

Ans. First group : $M = 63{\cdot}2$, $Md = 63{\cdot}5$, $Mo = 64$

Combined group : $M = 63{\cdot}75$, $Md = 64$, $Mo = 64$.

9. Atul gets a pocket money allowance of Rs. 12 per day. Thinking that this was rather less, he asked his friends about their allowances and obtained the following data which includes his allowance also — (amounts in Rs.)

12, 18, 10, 5, 25, 20, 20, 22, 15, 10, 10, 15, 13, 20, 18, 10, 15, 10, 18, 15, 12, 15, 10, 15, 10, 12, 18, 20, 5, 8.

He presented these data to his father and asked for an increase in his allowance as he was getting less than average amount. His father, a statistician, countered pointing out that Atul's allowance was actually more than the average amount.

Reconcile these statements.

Ans. Atul computed A.M. and his father computed Mode.

10. The number of fully formed apples on 100 plants were counted with following results :

No. of apples	0	1	2	3	4	5	6	7	8	9	10
No. of plants	2	5	7	11	18	24	12	8	6	4	3

(*i*) How many apples were there in all ?

(*ii*) What was the average of number of apples per plant ?

(*iii*) What was the modal number of apples ? [*Delhi Univ., B.Com., 1989, Allahabad Univ. B.Com., 1996*]

Ans. (*i*) 486 (*ii*) $\bar{X} = 4{\cdot}86$, (*iii*) $Mo = 5$.

11. Given below is the frequency distribution of marks obtained by 90 students. Compute the arithmetic mean, median and mode.

Marks	*No. of students*	*Marls*	*No. of students*
15—19	6	45—49	9
20—24	14	50—54	10
25—29	12	55—59	5
30—34	10	60—64	4
35—39	10	65—69	1
40—44	9		

Ans. Mean = 37·17, *Md* = 36, *Mo* = 23·5.

12. Find out the median and mode from the following table :

No. of days absent	*No. of students*	*No. of days absent*	*No. of students*
Less than 5	29	Less than 30	644
Less than 10	224	Less than 35	650
Less than 15	465	Less than 40	653
Less than 20	582	Less than 45	655
Less than 25	634		

Ans. *Md* =12·75, *Mo* = 11·35.

13. Find out the Mean, Median and the Mode in the following series—

Size (below) :	5	10	15	20	25	30	35
Frequency :	1	3	13	17	27	36	38

(Andhra Pradesh Univ. B.Com., 1998)

Ans. Mean = 19·74, *Md* = 21, *Mo* = 24·3.

14. In 500 small scale industrial units, the return on investment ranged from 0 to 30%, no unit sustaining any loss. 5% of industrial units had returns exceeding 0% but not exceeding 5%. 15% of units had returns exceeding 5% but not exceeding 10%. Median and upper quartile rate of return was 15% and 20% respectively. The uppermost layer of returns exceeding 25% but not exceeding 30% was earned by 25%. Present this information in the form of frequency table with intervals as follows :

Exceeding 0% but not exceeding 5% ; Exceeding 5% but not exceeding 10%

Exceeding 10% but not exceeding 15% ; Exceeding 15% but not exceeding 20%

Exceeding 20% but not exceeding 25% ; Exceeding 25% but not exceeding 30%.

Use *N*/4, 2*N*/4, 3*N*/4 as ranks of lower, middle and upper quartiles respectively. Find the rate of return around which there is maximum concentration of units. *[Delhi Univ. B.Com. (Hons.), 2008]*

Return in %	0—5	5–10	10—15	15—20	20–25	25—30
No. of units	25	75	150	125	0	125

Mode = 13.75; Rate of return around which there is maximum concentration of units is 13.75%.

15. Calculate the arithmetic mean and the median of the frequency distribution given below. Hence calculate the mode using the empirical relation between the three.

Class limits :	130—134	135—139	140—144	145—149	150—154	155—159	160—164
Frequency :	5	15	28	24	17	10	1

Ans. *M* = 145·35, *Md* = 144·92, *Mo* = 144·06.

16. (*a*) Briefly explain the role of grouping and analysis table in calculation of mode.

[Delhi Univ. B.Com. (Pass), 1999]

(*b*) From the following data of weight of 122 persons determine the modal weight by the method of grouping.

Weight (in lbs.)	100—110	110—120	120—130	130—140	140—150	150—160	160—170	170—180
No. of persons	4	6	20	32	33	17	8	2

[Osmania Univ. B.Com. 1998]

Hint. Method of grouping gives two modal classes 130—140 and 140—150 *i.e.*, the distribution is bimodal. Locate the value of mode by using the empirical relation $Mo = 3Md - 2M$.

Ans. Mean (*M*) = 139·51 ; Median (*Md*) = 139·69; Mode (*Mo*) = 140·05.

17. Calculate the Mode, Median and Arithmetic average from the following data.

Class	*f*	*Class*	*f*
0—2	8	25—30	45
2—4	12	30—40	60
4—10	20	40—50	20
10—15	10	50—60	13
15—20	16	60—80	15
20—25	25	80—100	4

Hint. Rewrite the frequency distribution with classes of equal magnitude 10.

Ans. $Mo = 28{\cdot}15$, $Md = 28{\cdot}29$, $Mean = 30{\cdot}08$.

18. In the following data, two class frequencies are missing.

Class	*Frequency*	*Class*	*Frequency*
100—110	4	150—160	?
110—120	7	160—170	16
120—130	15	170—180	10
130—140	?	180—190	6
140—150	40	190—200	3

However, it was possible to ascertain that the total number of frequencies was 150 and that the median has been correctly found to be 146·25.

You are required to find out with the help of the information given :

(*i*) Two missing frequencies.
(*ii*) Having found the missing frequencies, calculate arithmetic mean.
(*iii*) Without using the direct formula, find the value of the mode.

Ans. (*i*) 24, 25 ; (*ii*) $\overline{X} = 147{\cdot}33$; (*iii*) Mode = 144·08

19. The median and mode of the following hourly wage distribution are known to be Rs. 33·5 and Rs. 34 respectively. Three frequency values from the table are, however, missing. You are required to find out those values.

Wages in Rs. :	0—10	10—20	20—30	30—40	40-50	50—60	60—70	Total
No. of persons :	4	16	?	?	?	6	4	230

Ans. 60, 100, 40.

20. You are given the following incomplete frequency distribution. It is known that the total frequency is 1000 and that the median is 413·11. Estimate by calculation the missing frequencies and find the value of the mode.

Value (X)	*Frequency (f)*	*Value (X)*	*Frequency (f)*
300—325	5	400—425	326
325—350	17	425—450	?
350—375	80	450—475	88
375—400	?	475—500	9

Ans. Missing frequencies are 227 and 248 respectively. $Mo = 413{\cdot}98$.

21. "Hari put the jar of water and the packet of sweets on the ground and sat down in the shade of the tree and waited."

Prepare a frequency distribution for the words in the above sentence taking the number of letters in words as the variable. Calculate the mean, median and mode.

Ans. Mean = 3·56, Median = Mode = 3.

22. Treating the number of letters in each word in the following passage as the variable *x*, prepare the frequency distribution table and obtain its mean, median, mode.

"The reliability of data must always be examined before any attempt is made to base conclusions upon them. This is true of all data, but particularly so of numerical data, which do not carry their quality written large on them. It is a waste of time to apply the refined theoretical methods of Statistics to data which are suspect from the beginning."

Ans. Mean = 4·565, Median = 4, Mode = 3.

23. The frequency distribution of marks obtained by 60 students of a class in a college is given below :

Marks :	30—34	35—39	40—44	45—49	50—54	55—59	60—64
No. of Students :	3	5	12	18	14	6	2

(*i*) Draw Histogram for this distribution and find the modal value.
(*ii*) Draw a cumulative frequency curve and find the marks limits of the middle 50% students.

[Delhi Univ. B.Com. (Hons.), 1991]

Ans. (*i*) Mode = 47·5 marks, (*ii*) Q_1 = 42·5 marks, Q_3 = 52 marks.

24. Determine the values of Median and Mode of the following distribution graphically. Verify the results by actual calculations. After verifying, calculate the value of Mean and sketch a curve indicating the general shape of the distribution and comment.

Size	10—19	20—29	30—39	40—49	50—59	60—69	70—79	80—89	90—99
Frequency	11	19	21	16	10	8	6	3	1

[Delhi Univ. B.Com. (Hons.), 2009]

Hint. Change classes into class boundaries for *Md* and Mode. Use Ogive for *Md* and Histogram for Mode graphically.

Using Formula; $Md = 37.83$, $Mo = 32.35$; Mean = $[(3Md - Mo)/2] = 40.57$

$M > Md > Mo$ ⇒ Distribution is positively skewed.

25. In a moderately skewed distribution :

(*a*) Arithmetic mean = 24·6 and the mode = 26·1. Find the value of the median and explain the reason for the method employed.

(*b*) In a moderately asymmetrical distribution the value of median is 42·8 and the value of mode is 40. Find the mean.

(*c*) In a moderately asymmetrical distribution the value of mean is 75 and value of mode is 60. Find the value of median. *[Delhi Univ. B.Com. (Pass), 1996]*

Ans. (*a*) Median = 25·1, (*b*) Mean = 44·2, (*c*) Median = 70.

26. Find out the missing figures :

(*a*) Mean = ? (3 Median – Mode) ; (*b*) Mean – Mode = ? (Mean – Median)

(*c*) Median = Mode + ? (Mean – Mode) ; (*d*) Mode = Mean – ? (Mean – Median).

Ans. (*a*) 1/2, (*b*) 3, (*c*) 2/3, (*d*) 3.

27. (*a*) Which average would you use in the following situations :

(*i*) Sale of shirts : 16″, $15\frac{1}{2}$″, 15″, 15″, 14″, 13″, 15″.

(*ii*) Marks obtained : 10, 8, 12, 4, 7, 11 and X, (X < 5). Justify your answer.

Ans. (*i*) Mode, (*ii*) Median

(*b*) A.M. and Median of 50 items are 100 and 95 respectively. At the time of calculations two items 180 and 90 were wrongly taken as 100 and 10. What are the correct values of Mean and Median ?

Ans. Mean = 103·2; Median is same *viz.*, 95.

(*c*) Can the values of mean, mode and median be same ? If yes, state the situation.

Ans. $M = Md = Mo$, for symmetrical distribution.

28. (*a*) Find out the missing figure ; Mean = ? (3 Median – Mode)

Ans. 1/2.

(*b*) In a moderately asymmetrical distribution, the values of mode and median are 20 and 24 respectively. Locate the value of mean.

Ans. 25.

29. Fill in the blanks :

(*i*) ...... can be calculated from a frequency distribution with open end classes.

(*ii*) In the calculation of ...... , all the observations are taken into consideration.

(*iii*) ...... is not affected by extreme observations.

(*iv*) Average rainfall of a city from Monday to Saturday is 0·3 inch. Due to heavy rainfall on Sunday, the average rainfall for the week increases to 0·5 inch. The rainfall on Sunday was ... ...

(*v*) The sum of squared deviations is minimum when taken from ......

(*vi*) The sum of absolute deviations is minimum when taken from ......

(*vii*) Median = ... Quartile.

(*viii*) Mean is ...... by extreme observations.

(*ix*) Median is the average suited for ...... classes.

(*x*) For studying phenomenon like intelligence and honesty ...... is a better average to be used while for phenomenon like size of shoes or readymade garments the average to be preferred is ....

(*xi*) Typist *A* can type a sheet in 5 minutes, typist *B* in 6 minutes and typist *C* in 8 minutes. The average number of sheets typed per hour per typist is ......

(*xii*) The mean of 10 observations is 20 and median is 15. If 5 is added to each observation, the new mean is ...... and median is ......

(*xiii*) A distribution with two modes is called ...... and with more than two modes is called ....

(*xiv*) Average suited for a qualitative phenomenon is ....

(*xv*) If 25% of the observations lie above 80, 40% of the observations are less than 50 and 70% are greater than 40, then.

...... = 80 ; ...... = 50 ; ...... = 40

(*xvi*) Relationship between Md, Q_1, Q_2 and Q_3 is ......

(*xvii*) D_5, P_{80}, Md, D_7 and P_{50} are related by ......

(*xviii*) Relationship between D_4, Q_2, P_{60}, P_{75} and Q_3 is ......

(*xix*) The empirical relationship between mean, median and mode for a moderately asymmetrical distribution is ......

(*xx*) If the maximum frequency is repeated then mode is located by the method of ......

Ans. (*i*) *Md* or *Mo* (*ii*) Mean (*iii*) *Md* or *Mo* (*iv*) 1·7″ (*v*) Mean (*vi*) Median (*vii*) Second (*viii*) Very much affected (*ix*) Open end (*x*) Median, Mode (*xi*) 9·47 (*xii*) 25, 20 (*xiii*) Bi-modal, Multi-modal (*xiv*) Median (*xv*) $Q_3 = 80, P_{40} = D_4 = 50, P_{30} = 40$ (*xvi*) $Q_1 \leq Q_2 = Md \leq Q_3$ (*xvii*) $D_5 = P_{50} = Md \leq D_7 \leq P_{80}$ (*xviii*) $D_4 \leq Q_2 \leq P_{60} \leq P_{75} = Q_3$ (*xix*) $Mo = 3Md - 2M$. (*xx*) Grouping.

30. State, giving reasons, the average to be used in the following situations :

(*i*) To determine the average size of the shoe sold in a shop.

(*ii*) To determine the size of agricultural holdings.

(*iii*) To determine the average wages in an industrial concern.

(*iv*) To find the per capita income in different cities.

(*v*) To find the average beauty among a group of students in a class.

Ans. (*i*) Mode; (*ii*), (*iii*) and (*v*) Median ; (*iv*) Mean.

5·9. GEOMETRIC MEAN

The geometric mean, usually abbreviated as G.M.) of a set of *n* observations is the nth root of their product. Thus if $X_1, X_2, \ldots, X_n$ are the given *n* observations then their G.M. is given by

$$\text{G.M.} = \sqrt[n]{X_1 \times X_2 \times X_3 \times \ldots \times X_n} = (X_1 . X_2 \ldots X_n)^{1/n} \qquad \ldots(5\cdot21)$$

If $n = 2$ *i.e.*, if we are dealing with two observations only then G.M. can be computed by taking the square root of their product. For example, G.M. of 4 and 16 is $\sqrt{4 \times 16} = \sqrt{64} = 8$.

But if *n*, the number of observations is greater than 2, then the computation of the nth root is very tedious. In such a case the calculations are facilitated by making use of the logarithms. Taking logarithm of both sides in (5·21), we get

$$\log(\text{G.M.}) = \frac{1}{n} \log (X_1 X_2 \ldots X_n)$$

$$= \frac{1}{n} (\log X_1 + \log X_2 + \ldots + \log X_n)$$

$$= \frac{1}{n} \Sigma \log X \qquad \ldots(5\cdot21a)$$

Thus we see *that the logarithm of the G.M. of a set observations is the arithmetic mean of their logarithms*.

Taking Antilog of both sides in (5·21*a*), we finally obtain,

$$\text{G.M.} = \text{Antilog}\left[\frac{1}{n}\Sigma \log X\right] \qquad \ldots(5\cdot21b)$$

In case of frequency distribution (X_i, f_i); $i = 1, 2, \ldots, n$, where the total number of observations is $N = \Sigma f$,

$$\text{G.M.} = \left[(X_1 \times X_1 \times \ldots f_1 \text{ times}) \times (X_2 \times X_2 \times \ldots f_2 \text{ times}) \times \ldots \times (X_n \times X_n \times \ldots f_n \text{ times}\right]^{1/N}$$

$$= (X_1^{f_1} \times X_2^{f_2} \times \ldots \times X_n^{f_n})^{1/N} \qquad \ldots(5\cdot22)$$

Taking logarithm of both sides in (5·22), we get

$$\log \text{G.M.} = \frac{1}{N}\left[\log\left(X_1^{f_1} . X_2^{f_2} \ldots X_n^{f_n}\right)\right]$$

$$= \frac{1}{N}\left[\log X_1^{f_1} + \log X_2^{f_2} + \ldots + \log X_n^{f_n}\right]$$

$$= \frac{1}{N}\left[f_1 \log X_1 + f_2 \log X_2 + \ldots + f_n \log X_n\right]$$

$$= \frac{1}{N}\Sigma f \log X \qquad \ldots(5\cdot22a)$$

$$\Rightarrow \quad \text{G.M.} = \text{Antilog}\left[\frac{1}{N}\Sigma f \log X\right] \qquad \ldots(5\cdot22b)$$

In the case of grouped or continuous frequency distributions, the values of X are the mid-values of the corresponding classes.

Steps for the Computation of G.M. in (5·22*b*)

1. Find log X, where X is the value of the variable or the mid-value of the class (in case of grouped or continuous frequency distribution).

2. Compute $f \times \log X$ *i.e.*, multiply the values of log X obtained in step 1 by the corresponding frequencies.

3. Obtain the sum of the products $f \log X$ obtained in step 2 to get $\Sigma f \log X$.

4. Divide the sum obtained in step 3 by N, the total frequency.

5. Take the Antilog of the value obtained in step 4. The resulting figure gives the value of G.M.

5·9·1. Merits and Demerits of Geometric Mean.

Merits : (*i*) Geometric mean is rigidly defined.

(*ii*) It is based on all the observations.

(*iii*) It is suitable for further mathematical treatment. If G_1 and G_2 are the geometric means of two groups of sizes n_1 and n_2 respectively, then the geometric mean G of the combined group of size $n_1 + n_2$ is given by

$$\log G = \frac{n_1 \log G_1 + n_2 \log G_2}{n_1 + n_2} \qquad \ldots(5\cdot23)$$

Remark. The result in (5·23) can be easily generalised to the case of k groups as follows :

If $G_1, G_2, \ldots, G_k$ are the geometric means of the k groups of sizes $n_1, n_2, \ldots, n_k$ respectively, then the geometric mean G of the combined group of size $n_1 + n_2 + \ldots + n_k$ is given by :

$$\log G = \frac{n_1 \log G_1 + n_2 \log G_2 + \ldots + n_k \log G_k}{n_1 + n_2 + \ldots + n_k} \qquad \ldots(5\cdot23a)$$

(*iv*) Unlike arithmetic mean which has a bias for higher values, geometric mean has bias for smaller observations and as such is quite useful in phenomenon (such as prices) which has a lower limit (prices cannot go below zero) but has no such upper limit.

(*v*) As compared with mean, G.M. is affected to a lesser extent by extreme observations.

(*vi*) It is not affected much by fluctuations of sampling.

Demerits. (*i*) Because of its abstract mathematical character, geometric mean is not easy to understand and to calculate for a non-mathematical person.

(*ii*) If any one of the observations is zero, geometric mean becomes zero and if any one of the observations is negative, geometric mean becomes imaginary regardless of the magnitude of the other items.

Uses. In spite of its merits and limitations, *geometric mean is specially useful in averaging ratios, percentages, and rates of increase between two periods.* For example, G.M. is the appropriate average to be used for computing the average rate of growth of population or average increase in the rate of profits, sales, production, etc., or the rate of money.

Geometric mean is used in the construction of Index Numbers. Irving Fisher's ideal index number is based on geometric mean [See Chapter 10 on Index Numbers].

While dealing with data pertaining to economic and social sciences, we usually come across the situations where it is desired to give more weightage to smaller items and small weightage to larger items. G.M. is the most appropriate average to be used in such cases.

5·9·2. Compound Interest Formula. Let us suppose that P_0 is the initial value of the variable (*i.e.*, the value of the variable in the beginning and P_n be its value at the end of the period n and let r be the rate of growth per unit per period.

Since r is the rate of growth per unit per period, growth for period 1 is $P_0\, r$ and thus the value of the variate at the end of period 1 is $r\, P_0 + P_0 = P_0\,(1 + r)$. For the 2nd period the initial value of the variable becomes $P_0\,(1 + r)$. The growth for the 2nd period is $P_0\,(1 + r)\, r$ and consequently the value of the variable at the end of 2nd period is

$$P_2 = P_0\,(1 + r) + P_0\,(1 + r)r = P_0\,(1 + r)\,[1 + r] = P_0\,(1 + r)^2$$

Similarly proceeding, the value of the variable at the end of period 3 is

$$P_3 = P_0\,(1 + r)^2 + P_0\,(1 + r)^2 r = P_0\,(1 + r)^2[1 + r] = P_0\,(1 + r)^3$$

and finally, its value at the end of period n will be given

$$P_n = P_0\,(1 + r)^n, \qquad \ldots(5\cdot24)$$

which is the compound interest formula for money.

Equation (5·24) involves four unknown quantities :

P_n : The value at the end of period n ; P_0 : The value in the beginning ;

n : The length of the period ; r : The rate per unit per period.

If we are given P_0, r and n we can compute P_n by using (5·24) directly. However, (5·24) can be used to obtain any one of the four values when the remaining three values are given. For example, for given P_n, r and n we have :

$$P_0 = \frac{P_n}{(1 + r)^n} \qquad \ldots(5\cdot24a)$$

5·9·3. Average Rate of a Variable Which Increases by Different Rates at Different Periods. Let us suppose that instead of the values of the variable increasing at a constant rate in each period, the rate per unit per period is different, say, $r_1, r_2, \ldots, r_n$ for the 1st, 2nd,...and nth period respectively. Then, as discussed in the previous section we shall get :

P_1 = The value at the end of 1st period $= P_0\,(1 + r_1)$

P_2 = The value at the end of 2nd period $= P_0\,(1 + r_1)\,(1 + r_2)$

P_n = The value at the end of period $n = P_0(1 + r_1)\,(1 + r_2)\ldots(1 + r_n)$ ...(*)

If r is assumed to be the constant rate of growth per unit per period, then we get, [From (*)],

$$P_n = P_0\,(1 + r)^n \qquad \ldots(**)$$

Hence, equating the values of P_n in (*) and (**), the average rate of growth over the period n is given by :

$$(1+r)^n = (1+r_1)(1+r_2)...(1+r_n)$$

$$\Rightarrow \quad 1+r = \left[(1+r_1)(1+r_2)...(1+r_n)\right]^{1/n} \qquad ...(5\cdot25)$$

If $r_1, r_2, ..., r_n$ denote the *percentage* growth per unit per period for the n periods respectively then we have

$$1+\frac{r}{100} = \left[\left(1+\frac{r_1}{100}\right)\left(1+\frac{r_2}{100}\right)...\left(1+\frac{r_n}{100}\right)\right]^{1/n} \qquad ...(5\cdot26)$$

where r is the *average* percentage growth rate over n periods.

$$\therefore \quad 100+r = \left[(100+r_1)(100+r_2)...(100+r_n)\right]^{1/n}$$

$$\Rightarrow \quad r = \left[(100+r_1)(100+r_2)...(100+r_n)\right]^{1/n} - 100 \qquad ...(5\cdot26a)$$

Thus we see that *if rates are given as percentages, then the average percentage growth rate can be obtained on subtracting 100 from the G.M. of* $(100+r_1), (100+r_2), ..., (100+r_n)$.

Remark. It should be clearly understood that average percentage growth rate is given by (5·26) and not by the geometric mean of $r_1, r_2, ..., r_n$.

5·9·4. Wrong Observations and Geometric Mean. Let us suppose that the value of the geometric mean computed from n observations, say, $X_1, X_2, ..., X_n$ is G. On checking, it is found that some of the observations, say, X_1, X_2 and X_3 were wrongly copied instead of the correct observations X_1', X_2' and X_3'. We are interested in computing the correct value of the geometric mean.

$$G = \text{Geometric Mean of } X_1, X_2, ..., X_n = (X_1 . X_2 . X_3 ... X_n)^{1/n} \qquad ...(***)$$

On replacing the wrong observations X_1, X_2 and X_3 by the correct values, the corrected value of the geometric mean, say, G' is given by :

$$G' = (X_1' X_2' X_3' ... X_n)^{1/n} = \left(\frac{X_1'}{X_1}\cdot\frac{X_2'}{X_2}\cdot\frac{X_3'}{X_3}\cdot X_1 X_2 X_3 ... X_n\right)^{1/n}$$

$$= (X_1 X_2 X_3 ... X_n)^{1/n}\left(\frac{X_1' X_2' X_3'}{X_1 X_1 X_3}\right)^{1/n} = G.\left(\frac{X_1'}{X_1}\cdot\frac{X_2'}{X_2}\frac{X_3'}{X_3}\right)^{1/n} \quad \text{[From (***)]} \qquad (5\cdot26b)$$

The result in (5·26*b*), can be generalised to the case of more than three observations. For illustration, see Example 5·37.

Example 5·35. (*a*) *Find the Geometric Mean of 2, 4, 8, 12, 16 and 24.*

(*b*) *If the observations 2, 4, 8 and 16 occur with frequencies 4, 3, 2 and 1 respectively, find their geometric mean.* [*I.C.W.A. (Foundation), Dec. 2005*]

Solution. (*a*)

X	2	4	8	12	16	24	Total
log X	0·3010	0·6021	0·9031	1·0792	1·2041	1·3802	5·4697

$$\log(\text{G.M.}) = \frac{1}{n}\Sigma \log X = \frac{5\cdot4697}{6} = 0\cdot9116 \qquad \text{[Using (5·21 a)]}$$

$$\therefore \quad \text{G.M.} = \text{Antilog}(0\cdot9116) = 8\cdot158$$

Aliter $\quad \text{G.M.} = (2\times4\times8\times12\times16\times24)^{1/6} = (294912)^{1/6}$

$$\therefore \quad \log \text{G.M.} = \frac{1}{6}\log 294912 = \frac{5\cdot4698}{6} = 0\cdot9116 \quad \Rightarrow \quad \text{G.M.} = \text{Antilog}(0\cdot9116) = 8\cdot158.$$

(*b*) We are given :

x	2	4	8	16	
f	4	3	2	1	$N = \Sigma f = 10$

$$\text{G.M.} = (2^4 \times 4^3 \times 8^2 \times 16^1)^{1/10} = [2^4 \times (2^2)^3 \times (2^3)^2 \times 2^4]^{1/10}$$

$$= [2^4 \times 2^6 \times 2^6 \times 2^4]^{1/10} = [2^{4+6+6+4}]^{1/10} = 2^{\left(20 \times \frac{1}{10}\right)} = 2^2 = 4$$

Example 5·36. *Find the geometric mean for the following distribution :*

Marks	:	*0—10*	*10—20*	*20—30*	*30—40*	*40—50*
No. of students	:	*5*	*7*	*15*	*25*	*8*

Solution.

Marks	*Mid-Point (X)*	*No. of Students (f)*	*log X*	*f. log X*
0—10	5	5	0·6990	3·4950
10—20	15	7	1·1761	8·2327
20—30	25	15	1·3979	20·9685
30—40	35	25	1·5441	38·6025
40—50	45	8	1·6532	13·2256
		N = 60		84·5243

$$\text{Geometric mean} = \text{Antilog}\left[\frac{\Sigma f \log X}{N}\right] = \text{Antilog}\left[\frac{84{\cdot}5243}{60}\right] = \text{Antilog}\,[1{\cdot}40874] = 25{\cdot}64 \text{ marks.}$$

Example 5·37. *The geometric mean of 10 observations on a certain variable was calculated as 16·2. It was later discovered that one of the observations was wrongly recorded as 12·9; in fact it was 21·9. Apply appropriate correction and calculate the correct geometric mean.*

Solution. Geometric mean G of n observations is given by :

$$G = (X_1\, X_2, \ldots, X_n)^{1/n} \quad \Rightarrow \quad G^n = X_1\, X_2 \ldots X_n \qquad \ldots(*)$$

Thus the product of the numbers is given by :

$$X_1 X_2 \ldots X_n = G^n = (16{\cdot}2)^{10} \qquad [\text{Given } n = 10,\ G = 16{\cdot}2] \qquad \ldots(**)$$

If the wrong observation 12·9 is replaced by the correct values 21·9, then the corrected value of the product of 10 numbers is obtained on dividing the expression in (**) by wrong observation and multiplying by the correct observation. Thus,

$$\text{Corrected product } (X_1 X_2 \ldots X_n) = \frac{(16{\cdot}2)^{10} \times 21{\cdot}9}{12{\cdot}9}$$

Hence, corrected value of the geometric mean G', (say), is given by :

$$G' = \left[\frac{(16{\cdot}2)^{10} \times 21{\cdot}9}{12{\cdot}9}\right]^{1/10}$$

$$\Rightarrow \quad \log G' = \frac{1}{10}\left[\log (16{\cdot}2)^{10} + \log 21{\cdot}9 - \log 12{\cdot}9\right] = \frac{1}{10}\left[10 \log 16{\cdot}2 + \log 21{\cdot}9 - \log 12{\cdot}9\right]$$

$$= \frac{1}{10}\left[10 \times 1{\cdot}2095 + 1{\cdot}3404 - 1{\cdot}1106\right] = \frac{1}{10}\left[12{\cdot}0950 + 1{\cdot}3404 - 1{\cdot}1106\right] = \frac{12{\cdot}3248}{10} = 1{\cdot}2325$$

$$\Rightarrow \quad G' = \text{Antilog}\,(1{\cdot}2325) = 17{\cdot}08$$

Aliter. Using (5·26*b*) directly, we get : $G' = G \cdot \left(\frac{X_1'}{X_1}\right)^{1/10} = 16.2 \times \left(\frac{21{\cdot}9}{12{\cdot}9}\right)^{1/10}$

Example 5·38. *Three groups of observations contain 8, 7 and 5 observations. Their geometric means are 8·52, 10·12 and 7·75 respectively. Find the geometric mean of the 20 observations in the single group formed by pooling the three groups.*

Solution. In the usual notations, we are given that :

$$n_1 = 8, \quad n_2 = 7, \quad n_3 = 5; \quad G_1 = 8{\cdot}52, \quad G_2 = 10{\cdot}12, \quad G_3 = 7{\cdot}75$$

The geometric mean G of the combined group of size $N = n_1 + n_2 + n_3 = 8 + 7 + 5 = 20$, is given by :

$$\log G = \frac{1}{N}\left[n_1 \log G_1 + n_2 \log G_2 + n_3 \log G_3\right] = \frac{1}{20}\left[8 \log 8{\cdot}52 + 7 \log 10{\cdot}12 + 5 \log 7{\cdot}75\right]$$

$$= \frac{1}{20}\left[8 \times 0{\cdot}9304 + 7 \times 1{\cdot}0052 + 5 \times 0{\cdot}8893\right] = \frac{1}{20}\left[7{\cdot}4432 + 7{\cdot}0364 + 4{\cdot}4465\right] = \frac{18{\cdot}9261}{20} = 0{\cdot}9463$$

$\therefore \quad G = \text{Antilog}\,(0{\cdot}9463) = 8{\cdot}837$

Example 5·39. *Find the missing information in the following table :*

	Groups			
	A	*B*	*C*	*Combined*
Number	*10*	*8*	—	*24*
Mean	*20*	—	*6*	*15*
Geometric Mean	*10*	*7*	—	*8·397.*

[*Delhi Univ. B.Com, (Hons.), 1998*]

Solution. Taking the groups *A*, *B* and *C* as groups 1, 2 and 3 respectively, in the usual notations, we are given :

	Group A	Group B	Group C	Combined	
Number :	$n_1 = 10$	$n_2 = 8$	$n_3 = ?$	$n_1 + n_2 + n_3 = 24$	...(*i*)
Mean :	$\bar{x}_1 = 20$	$\bar{x}_2 = ?$	$\bar{x}_3 = 6$	$\bar{x} = 15$	...(*ii*)
Geometric Mean :	$G_1 = 10$	$G_2 = 7$	$G_3 = ?$	$G = 8{\cdot}397$	...(*iii*)

From (*i*), we get $\quad n_3 = 24 - n_1 - n_2 = 24 - 10 - 8 = 6 \quad$ ...(*iv*)

$$\bar{x} = \frac{n_1\bar{x}_1 + n_2\bar{x}_2 + n_3\bar{x}_3}{n_1 + n_2 + n_3} = \frac{10 \times 20 + 8\bar{x}_2 + 6 \times 6}{24} = 15 \text{ (Given)}$$

$$\Rightarrow \quad 8\,\bar{x}_2 = 15 \times 24 - 200 - 36 = 124 \quad \Rightarrow \quad \bar{x}_2 = \frac{124}{8} = 15{\cdot}5 \qquad \ldots(v)$$

$$\log G = \frac{n_1 \log G_1 + n_2 \log G_2 + n_3 \log G_3}{n_1 + n_2 + n_3} \quad \Rightarrow \quad \frac{10 \log 10 + 8 \log 7 + 6 \log G_3}{24} = \log\,(8{\cdot}397)$$

$$\therefore \quad 10 \times 1 + 8 \times 0{\cdot}8451 + 6 \log G_3 = 24 \times 0{\cdot}9242$$

$$\Rightarrow \quad G_3 = \text{Antilog}\left(\frac{22{\cdot}1808 - 10 - 6{\cdot}7608}{6}\right) = \text{Antilog}\left(\frac{5{\cdot}42}{6}\right) = \text{Antilog}\,(0{\cdot}9033) = 8{\cdot}004 \simeq 8 \; (\textit{approx.}).$$

Example 5·40. *Find the average rate of increase in population which in the first decade had increased by 20%, in the next by 30% and in the third by 40%.*

Solution. Since we are dealing with rate of increase in population, the appropriate average to be computed is the geometric mean and not the arithmetic mean.

CALCULATIONS FOR GEOMETRIC MEAN

Decade	*Rate of growth of population*	*Population at the end of the decade (X)*	*log X*
1	20%	120	2·0792
2	30%	130	2·1139
3	40%	140	2·1461
Total			$\Sigma \log X = 6{\cdot}3392$

$$\text{G.M.} = \text{Antilog}\left(\frac{1}{n}\Sigma \log X\right)$$

$$= \text{Antilog}\left(\frac{6{\cdot}3392}{3}\right) = \text{Antilog}\,(2{\cdot}1131)$$

$$= 129{\cdot}7$$

Hence, the average percentage rate of increase in the population per decade over the entire period is :

$$129{\cdot}7 - 100 = 29{\cdot}7.$$

Example 5·41. *Under what condition is geometric mean indeterminate ?*

If the price of a commodity doubles in a period of 4 years, what is the average annual percentage increase ?

Solution. Geometric mean is indeterminate if any one of the given observations is negative. In this case G.M. becomes imaginary. In general, G.M. is indeterminate (imaginary) if *odd number* of given observations are negative.

Also, if any one of the given observations is zero, G.M. becomes zero irrespective of the size of the other observations.

In the usual notations we are given :

$$P_0 = \text{Rs. } x, \text{ (say)} ; \quad P_n = \text{Rs. } 2x ; \quad n = 4.$$

If r is the average annual percentage increase in price over this period then we have :

$$P_n = P_0 (1 + r)^n \quad \Rightarrow \quad 2x = x(1 + r)^4$$

$$(1 + r)^4 = 2 \quad \Rightarrow \quad (1 + r) = 2^{1/4}$$

$$\Rightarrow \quad 1 + r = \text{Antilog}\left(\tfrac{1}{4}\log 2\right) = \text{Antilog}\left(\frac{0·3010}{4}\right) = \text{Antilog}\,(0·07525) = 1·190$$

$$\therefore \quad r = 1·190 - 1 = 0·19$$

Hence, the average annual percentage increase is 0·19 *i.e.*, 19%.

Example 5·42. *An assessee depreciated the machinery of his factory by 10% each in the first two years and by 40% in the third year and thereby claimed 21% average depreciation relief from taxation department, but the I.T.O. objected and allowed only 20%. Show which of the two is right.*

Solution.

COMPUTATION OF A.M. AND G.M.

Year	*Rate of depreciation*	*Value at the end of the year* (*X*)	*log X*
1	10%	90	1·9542
2	10%	90	1·9542
3	40%	60	1·7782
		$\Sigma X = 240$	$\Sigma \log X = 5·6866$

The average value (arithmetic mean) at the end of three years is :

$$\bar{X} = \frac{\Sigma X}{3} = \frac{240}{3} = 80$$

Hence, the average rate of depreciation per annum for the entire period of 3 years is 100 – 80 = 20%.

This can be computed otherwise by taking the average of 10%, 10%, 40% which is :

$$\frac{10 + 10 + 40}{3} = \frac{60}{3} = 20\%$$

The geometric mean is given by :

$$\text{G.M.} = \text{Antilog}\left(\tfrac{1}{3}\Sigma \log X\right) = \text{Antilog}\left(\frac{5·6866}{3}\right) = \text{Antilog}\,(1·8955) = 78·61$$

Hence, the average (geometric mean) rate of depreciation per annum for the entire period of three years is 100 – 78·61 = 21·39% ≃ 21%.

The assessee had claimed 21% depreciation using G.M. while the I.T.O. objected and allowed 20% depreciation using A.M.

Since we are dealing with rates, the arithmetic mean does not depict the average depreciation correctly. Geometric mean is the correct average to be used. Hence, I.T.O. was wrong in not allowing 21% depreciation as claimed by the assesse.

Example 5·43. (*a*) *Show that in finding the A.M. of a set of readings on a thermometer, it does not matter whether we measure the temperature in Centigrade (C) or Fahrenheit (F)* degrees.

[*Delhi Univ. B.A. (Econ. Hons.) 2000*]

(*b*) *However, in computing Geometric Mean, it does matter which readings we use.*

Solution. If F and C be the readings in Fahrenheit and Centigrade respectively then we have the relation :

$$\frac{F - 32}{180} = \frac{C}{100} \quad \Rightarrow \quad F = 32 + \frac{9}{5}C$$

Thus the Fahrenheit equivalents of $C_1, C_2, \ldots, C_n$ are

$$32 + \tfrac{9}{5}C_1, \; 32 + \tfrac{9}{5}C_2, \; \ldots, \; 32 + \tfrac{9}{5}C_n \text{ respectively.}$$

Hence, the arithmetic mean of the readings in Fahrenheit is

$$=\frac{1}{n}\left\{\left(32+\frac{9}{5}C_1\right)+\left(32+\frac{9}{5}C_2\right)+\ldots+\left(32+\frac{9}{5}C_n\right)\right\}$$

$$=\frac{1}{n}\left\{32n+\frac{9}{5}(C_1+C_2+\ldots+C_n)\right\}=32+\frac{9}{5}\left(\frac{C_1+C_2+\ldots+C_n}{n}\right)$$

$$=32+\frac{9}{5}\bar{C}\text{, which is the Fahrenheit equivalent of }\bar{C}.$$

Hence, in finding the arithmetic mean of a set of n readings on a thermometer, it is immaterial whether we measure temperature in Centigrade or Fahrenheit.

Geometric mean G, of n readings in Centigrade is : $G=(C_1\ C_2 \ldots C_n)^{1/n}$

Geometric mean G_1, (say), of Fahrenheit equivalents of $C_1, C_2, \ldots, C_n$ is

$$G_1=\left\{\left(32+\frac{9}{5}C_1\right)\left(32+\frac{9}{5}C_2\right)\ldots\left(32+\frac{9}{5}C_n\right)\right\}^{1/n}$$

which is not equal to the Fahrenheit equivalent of G *viz.*, $\left\{\frac{9}{5}\left(C_1 \cdot C_2 \ldots C_n\right)^{1/n}+32\right\}$.

Hence, in finding the geometric mean of the n readings on a thermometer, the scale (Centigrade or Fahrenheit) is important.

Example 5.44. *If the arithmetic mean of two unequal positive real number 'a' and 'b', (a > b), be twice as great as their geometric mean, show that*

$$a:b=(2+\sqrt{3}):(2-\sqrt{3})$$

[*I.C.W.A. (Foundation), June 2001*]

Solution. The arithmetic mean (A.M.) and the geometric mean (G.M.) of two unequal positive real numbers a and b, $(a > b)$, are given by :

$$\text{A.M.}=\frac{a+b}{2}\quad\text{and}\quad\text{G.M.}=\sqrt{ab}.$$

We are given :

$$\text{A.M.}=2\text{ G.M.}\quad\Rightarrow\quad\frac{a+b}{2}=2\sqrt{ab}\quad\Rightarrow\quad a+b=4\sqrt{ab}\qquad\ldots(i)$$

Also $(a-b)^2=(a+b)^2-4ab=16\,ab-4\,ab=12\,ab$ [From (i)]

$$\Rightarrow\quad(a-b)=\pm 2\sqrt{3}\sqrt{ab}\quad\Rightarrow\quad a-b=2\sqrt{3}\sqrt{ab}\quad(\because\ a>b)\qquad\ldots(ii)$$

Adding and subtracting (i) and (ii), we get respectively :

$$2a=2\sqrt{ab}\,(2+\sqrt{3})\quad\ldots(iii)\qquad\text{and}\qquad 2b=2\sqrt{ab}\,(2-\sqrt{3})\qquad\ldots(iv)$$

Dividing (iii) by (iv), we get :

$$\frac{a}{b}=\frac{2+\sqrt{3}}{2-\sqrt{3}}\quad\Rightarrow\quad a:b=(2+\sqrt{3}):(2-\sqrt{3})$$

5·9·5. Weighted Geometric Mean. If the different values $X_1, X_2, \ldots, X_n$ of the variable are not of equal importance and are assigned different weights, say, $W_1, W_2, \ldots, W_n$ respectively according to their degree of importance then their weighted geometric mean G.M. (W) is given by

$$\text{G.M.}(W)=(X_1^{W_1}\times X_2^{W_2}\times\ldots\times X_n^{W_n})^{1/N}\qquad\ldots(5\cdot27)$$

where $N=W_1+W_2+\ldots+W_n=\Sigma W$, is the sum of weights.

Taking logarithm of both sides in (5·27), we get

$$\log[\text{G.M.}(W)]=\frac{1}{N}\left[W_1\log X_1+W_2\log X_2+\ldots+W_n\log X_n\right]=\frac{1}{N}\Sigma W\log X$$

$$\Rightarrow\quad\text{G.M.}(W)=\text{Antilog}\left[\frac{1}{N}\Sigma\,W\log X\right]=\text{Antilog}\left[\frac{\Sigma W\log X}{\Sigma W}\right]\qquad\ldots(5\cdot27a)$$

Example 5·45. *The weighted geometric mean of the four numbers 8, 25, 19 and 28 is 22·15. If the weights of the first three numbers are 3, 5, 7 respectively, find the weight (positive integer) of the fourth number.*

Solution. Let the weight of the fourth number be w.

Weighted Geometric Mean (G) = 22·15 (*Given*)

Also $\log G = \dfrac{\Sigma W \log X}{\Sigma W} \quad \Rightarrow \quad \log 22{\cdot}15 = \dfrac{\Sigma W \log X}{\Sigma W}$

COMPUTATION OF WEIGHTED G.M.

X	$\log X$	W	$W \log X$
8	0·9031	3	2·7093
25	1·3979	5	6·9895
19	1·2788	7	8·9516
28	1·4472	w	1·4472w
Total		15 + w	18·6504 + 1·4472w

$$\Rightarrow \quad \log(22{\cdot}15) = \frac{18{\cdot}6504 + 1{\cdot}4472w}{15 + w}$$

$$\Rightarrow \quad (15 + w) \times 1{\cdot}3454 = 18{\cdot}6504 + 1{\cdot}4472w$$

$$\Rightarrow \quad 15 \times 1{\cdot}3454 + 1{\cdot}3454w = 18{\cdot}6504 + 1{\cdot}4472\,w$$

$$\Rightarrow \quad 20{\cdot}1810 + 1{\cdot}3454w = 18{\cdot}6504 + 1{\cdot}4472w$$

$$\Rightarrow \quad 1{\cdot}4472w - 1{\cdot}3454w = 20{\cdot}1810 - 18{\cdot}6504$$

$$\Rightarrow \quad 0{\cdot}1018w = 1{\cdot}5306$$

$$\Rightarrow \quad w = \frac{1{\cdot}5306}{1{\cdot}1018} = 15 \text{ approx.}$$

5·10. HARMONIC MEAN

If $X_1, X_2, \ldots, X_n$ is a given set of n observations, then their harmonic mean, abbreviated as H.M. or simply H is given by :

$$H = \frac{1}{\frac{1}{n}\left[\frac{1}{X_1} + \frac{1}{X_2} + \ldots + \frac{1}{X_n}\right]} = \frac{1}{\frac{1}{n}\Sigma\left(\frac{1}{X}\right)} = \frac{n}{\Sigma\left(\frac{1}{X}\right)} \qquad \ldots(5{\cdot}28)$$

In other words, *Harmonic Mean is the reciprocal of the arithmetic mean of the reciprocals of the given observations.*

In case of frequency distribution, we have

$$\frac{1}{H} = \frac{1}{N}\left[\frac{f_1}{X_1} + \frac{f_2}{X_2} + \ldots + \frac{f_n}{X_n}\right] = \frac{1}{N}\Sigma\left(\frac{f}{X}\right) \quad \Rightarrow \quad H = \frac{N}{\Sigma\,(f/X)} \qquad \ldots(5{\cdot}28a)$$

where $N = \Sigma f$, is the total frequency, X is the value of the variable or the mid-value of the class (in case of grouped or continuous frequency distribution) and f is the corresponding frequency of X.

Remark. Effect of Change of Scale on Harmonic Mean. Let $x_1, x_2, \ldots, x_n$ be the given set of n observations. If the variable x is transformed to the new variable u by change of scale : $u = kx, k \neq 0$ ...(*)
then, by definition

$$\frac{1}{\text{H.M. }(u)} = \frac{1}{n}\left[\frac{1}{u_1} + \frac{1}{u_2} + \ldots + \frac{1}{u_n}\right] = \frac{1}{n}\left[\frac{1}{kx_1} + \frac{1}{kx_2} + \ldots + \frac{1}{kx_n}\right] \qquad \text{[Using (*)]}$$

$$= \frac{1}{k}\cdot\frac{1}{n}\left[\frac{1}{x_1} + \frac{1}{x_2} + \ldots + \frac{1}{x_n}\right] = \frac{1}{k}\cdot\frac{1}{\text{H.M. }(x)}$$

$$\Rightarrow \quad \text{H.M.}(u) = k \times \text{H.M. }(x)$$

Hence, we have the following result :

$$\textit{If } u = kx,\ k \neq 0, \quad \textit{then} \quad \textit{H.M. }(u) = k \times \textit{H.M. }(x) \qquad \ldots[5{\cdot}28b]$$

5·10·1. Merits and Demerits of Harmonic Mean.

Merits : (*i*) Harmonic mean is rigidly defined.

(*ii*) It is based on all the observations.

(*iii*) It is suitable for further mathematical treatment.

If H_1 and H_2 are the harmonic means of two groups of sizes N_1 and N_2 respectively, then the harmonic mean H of the combined group of size $N_1 + N_2$ is given by :

$$\frac{1}{H} = \frac{1}{N_1 + N_2}\left[\frac{N_1}{H_1} + \frac{N_2}{H_2}\right] \quad ...(5·28c)$$

(*iv*) Since the reciprocals of the values of the variable are involved, it gives greater weightage to smaller observations and as such is not very much affected by one or two big observations.

(*v*) It is not affected very much by fluctuations of sampling.

(*vi*) It is particularly useful in averaging special types of rates and ratios where time factor is variable and the act being performed remains constant.

Demerits. (*i*) It is not easy to understand and calculate.

(*ii*) Its value cannot be obtained if any one of the observations is zero.

(*iii*) It is not a representative figure of the distribution unless the phenomenon requires greater weightage to be given to smaller items. As such, it is hardly used in business problems.

Uses. As has been pointed out in merit (*vi*) , harmonic mean is specially useful in averaging rates and ratios where time factor is variable and the act being performed *e.g.*, distance is constant. The following examples will clarify the point.

Example 5·46. *The following table gives the weights of 31 persons in a sample enquiry. Calculate the mean weight using (i) Geometric mean and (ii) Harmonic mean.*

Weight (lbs.) :	130	135	140	145	146	148	149	150	157
No. of persons :	3	4	6	6	3	5	2	1	1

Solution.

COMPUTATION OF G.M. AND H.M.

Weight (lbs.) (*X*)	*No. of persons* (*f*)	*log X*	*f log X*	$\frac{1}{X}$	$\frac{f}{X}$
130	3	2·1139	6·3417	0·00769	0·02307
135	4	2·1303	8·5212	0·00741	0·02964
140	6	2·1461	12·8766	0·00714	0·04284
145	6	2·1614	12·9684	0·00690	0·04140
146	3	2·1644	6·4932	0·00685	0·02055
148	5	2·1703	10·8515	0·00676	0·03380
149	2	2·1732	4·3464	0·00671	0·01342
150	1	2·1761	2·1761	0·00667	0·00667
157	1	2·1959	2·1959	0·00637	0·00637
	$\Sigma f = N = 31$		$\Sigma f \log X = 66·7710$		$\Sigma(f/X) = 0·21776$

$$\text{G.M.} = \text{Antilog}\left(\frac{1}{N}\Sigma f \log X\right) = \text{Antilog}\left(\frac{66·7710}{31}\right) = \text{Antilog}\,(2·1539) = 142·5$$

$$\text{H.M.} = \frac{N}{\Sigma(f/X)} = \frac{31}{0·21776} = 142·36$$

Hence, the mean weight of 31 persons using (*i*) geometric mean is 142·5 lbs. and (*ii*) harmonic mean is 142·36 lbs.

Example 5.47. *If $2u = 5x$, is the relation beween two variables u and x, and harmonic mean of x is 0·4, find the harmonic mean of u.* [*I.C.W.A. (Foundation), June 2005*]

Solution. $2u = 5x \quad \Rightarrow \quad u = \frac{5}{2}x \quad ...(*)$

Also H.M. $(x) = 0.4$ (Given) ...(**)

If $u_1, u_2, \ldots, u_n$ are n observations corresponding to $x_1, x_2, \ldots, x_n$ respectively, obtained by the transformation (*) so that

$$u_i = \frac{5}{2} x_i, \ (i = 1, 2, \ldots, n), \qquad \ldots(***)$$

then, by definition

$$\text{H.M.}(u) = \frac{1}{\frac{1}{n}\left[\frac{1}{u_1}+\frac{1}{u_2}+\cdots+\frac{1}{u_n}\right]} = \frac{1}{\frac{1}{n}\left[\frac{2}{5}\frac{1}{x_1}+\frac{2}{5}\cdot\frac{1}{x_2}+\cdots+\frac{2}{5}\frac{1}{x_n}\right]} \qquad \text{[From (***)]}$$

$$= \frac{5}{2}\left[\frac{1}{\frac{1}{n}\left[\frac{1}{x_1}+\frac{1}{x_2}+\cdots+\frac{1}{x_n}\right]}\right] = \frac{5}{2}\text{H.M.}(x) = \frac{5}{2}\times 0{\cdot}4 = 1 \qquad \text{[From (**)]}$$

Remark. We may state and use the result (5·28*b*) directly, to get from (*)

$$\text{H.M.}(u) = \frac{5}{2}\text{H.M.}(x) = \frac{5}{2}\times 0.4 = 1$$

Example 5.48. *Find the harmonic mean of* $\frac{1}{2}, \frac{2}{3}, \frac{3}{4}, \ldots, \frac{n}{n+1}$ *occurring with frequencies 1, 2, 3, ... , n respectively.* [*I.C.W.A. (Foundation), June 2006*]

Solution. The harmonic mean (H) is given by :

x	f	$\frac{1}{x}$	$\frac{f}{x}$
(1)	(2)	(3)	(4) = (2) × (3)
1/2	1	2	2
2/3	2	3/2	3
3/4	3	4/3	4
⋮	⋮		
$(n-1)/n$	$n-1$	$n/(n-1)$	n
$n/(n+1)$	n	$(n+1)/n$	$n+1$

$$\frac{1}{H} = \frac{\Sigma(f/x)}{\Sigma f} = \frac{2+3+4+\ldots+n+(n+1)}{1+2+3+\ldots+n}$$

$$= \frac{(1+2+3+\ldots+n)+n}{(1+2+3+\ldots+n)}$$

$$= 1 + \frac{n}{1+2+3+\ldots+n}$$

$$= 1 + \frac{n}{n(n+1)/2} = 1 + \frac{2}{n+1} = \frac{n+3}{n+1}$$

$$\therefore \quad H = (n+1)/(n+3)$$

Example 5·49. *A cyclist pedals from his house to his college at a speed of 10 km. p.h. and back from the college to his house at 15 km. p.h. Find the average speed.*

Solution. Let the distance from the house to the college be x kms.

In going from house to college, the distance (x kms) is covered in $x/10$ hours, while in coming from college to house, the distance is covered in $x/15$ hours. Thus a total distance of $2x$ kms is covered in $\left(\frac{x}{10}+\frac{x}{15}\right)$ hours.

$$\text{Hence, average speed} = \frac{\text{Total distance travelled}}{\text{Total time taken}} = \frac{2x}{\left(\frac{x}{10}+\frac{x}{15}\right)} = \frac{2}{\left(\frac{1}{10}+\frac{1}{15}\right)} = 12 \text{ km. p.h.}$$

Remarks. 1. In this case the average speed is given by the harmonic mean of 10 and 15 and not by the arithmetic mean.

2. If equal distances are covered (travelled) per unit of time with speeds equal to $V_1, V_2, \ldots, V_n$, say, then the average speed is given by the harmonic mean of $V_1, V_2, \ldots, V_n$ *i.e.*,

$$\text{Average speed} = \frac{n}{\left(\frac{1}{V_1} + \frac{1}{V_2} + \ldots + \frac{1}{V_n}\right)} = \frac{n}{\Sigma\left(\frac{1}{V}\right)}$$

Example 5·50. *A vehicle when climbing up a gradient, consumes petrol at the rate of 1 litre per 8 kms. while coming down it gives 12 kms. per litre. Find its average consumption for to and fro travel between two places situated at the two ends of a 25 km. long gradient. Verify your answer.*

[*Delhi Univ. B.A.* (*Econ. Hons.*), *1994*]

Solution. Since the consumption of petrol is different for upward and downward journeys (at a constant distance of 25 km.), the appropriate average consumption for to and fro journey is given by the harmonic mean of 8 km. and 12 km.

∴ Average consumption for to and fro journey

$$= \frac{1}{\frac{1}{2}\left(\frac{1}{8} + \frac{1}{12}\right)} = \frac{2}{\left(\frac{3+2}{24}\right)} = \frac{48}{5} = 9\cdot6 \text{ km. per litre} \qquad \ldots(*)$$

Verification. Consumption of petrol for upward journey of 25 km. @ 1 litre per 8 kms. $= \frac{25}{8}$ litres.

Consumption of petrol for downward journey of 25 km @ 1 litre per 12 kms. $= \frac{25}{12}$ litres.

∴ Total petrol consumed for total journey of 25 + 25 = 50 km. is

$$\left(\frac{25}{8} + \frac{25}{12}\right) \text{ litres} = 25\left(\frac{1}{8} + \frac{1}{12}\right) \text{ litres} = \frac{25}{24}(3+2) \text{ litres} = \frac{125}{24} \text{ litres}$$

∴ Average consumption for to and fro journey

$$= \frac{\text{Total distance}}{\text{Total petrol used}} = \frac{50 \times 24}{125} = \frac{48}{5} = 9\cdot6 \text{ km. per litre, which is same as in } (*).$$

Example 5·51. *In a certain office, a letter is typed by A in 4 minutes. The same letter is typed by B, C and D in 5, 6, 10 minutes respectively. What is the average time taken in completing one letter ? How many letters do you expect to be typed in one day comprising of 8 working hours ?*

[*Delhi Univ. B.A.* (*Econ. Hons.*), *1996; 1995*]

Solution. The average time (in minutes) taken by *each* of *A, B, C* and *D* in completing one letter is the harmonic mean of 4, 5, 6 and 10 given by :

$$\frac{4}{\frac{1}{4} + \frac{1}{5} + \frac{1}{6} + \frac{1}{10}} = \frac{4}{\left(\frac{15+12+10+6}{60}\right)} = \frac{240}{43} = 5\cdot5814 \text{ minutes per letter.}$$

Hence, expected number of letters typed by each of *A, B, C* and *D* is $\frac{43}{240}$ letters per minute.

Hence, in a day comprising of 8 hours = 8 × 60 minutes, the total number of letters typed by all of them (*A, B, C* and *D*) is :

$$\frac{43}{240} \times 4 \times 8 \times 60 = 344.$$

Example 5·52. *An investor buys Rs. 1,200 worth of shares in a company each month. During the first 5 months he bought the shares at a price of Rs. 10, Rs. 12, Rs. 15, Rs. 20, and Rs. 24 per share. After 5 months what is the average price paid for the shares by him ?*

Solution. Since the share value is changing after a fixed unit time (1 month), the required average price per share is the harmonic mean of 10, 12, 15, 20 and 24 and is given by :

$$\frac{5}{\left(\frac{1}{10} + \frac{1}{12} + \frac{1}{15} + \frac{1}{20} + \frac{1}{24}\right)} = \frac{5}{\left(\frac{12+10+8+6+5}{120}\right)} = \frac{5 \times 120}{41} = \text{Rs. } 14\cdot63.$$

Note. For an alternate solution, see Example 5·8.

5·10·2. Weighted Harmonic Mean. Instead of fixed (constant) distance being travelled with varying speeds (*c.f.* Remark 2, Example 5·49), let us now suppose that different distances are travelled with corresponding different speeds. In that case what is going to be the average speed ?

Let us suppose that distances $s_1, s_2, \ldots, s_n$, are travelled with speed $v_1, v_2, \ldots, v_n$ per unit of time. If $t_1, t_2, \ldots, t_n$ are the respective times taken to cover these distances then we have :

$$t_1 = \frac{s_1}{v_1}, \qquad t_2 = \frac{s_2}{v_2}, \qquad \ldots, \qquad t_n = \frac{s_n}{v_n} \qquad \ldots(*)$$

$$\therefore \quad \text{Average speed} = \frac{\text{Total distance travelled}}{\text{Total time taken}} = \frac{s_1 + s_2 + \ldots + s_n}{t_1 + t_2 + \ldots + t_n}$$

$$= \frac{s_1 + s_2 + \ldots + s_n}{\left[\dfrac{s_1}{v_1} + \dfrac{s_2}{v_2} + \ldots + \dfrac{s_n}{v_n}\right]} \qquad \text{[From (*)]}$$

$$= \frac{\Sigma s}{\Sigma\left(\dfrac{s}{v}\right)} = \frac{1}{\left(\dfrac{1}{\Sigma s}\right)\Sigma\left(\dfrac{s}{v}\right)} \qquad \ldots(5·30)$$

which is the weighted harmonic mean of the speeds, the corresponding weights being the distances covered.

Hence, *if different distances are travelled with corresponding different speeds, then the average speed is given by the weighted harmonic mean of the speeds, the corresponding weights beings the distances covered.*

Example 5·53. *You make a trip which entails travelling 900 kms. by train at an average speed of 60 km. p.h.; 3000 kms. by boat at an average of 25 km. p.h.; 400 kms. by plane at 350 km. p.h., and finally, 15 kms by taxi at 25 km. p.h. What is your average speed for the entire distance ?*

Solution. Since different distances are covered with varying speeds, the required average speed is given by the weighted harmonic mean of the speeds (in km. p.h) 60, 25, 350 and 25; the corresponding weights being the distances covered (in kms.) *viz.*, 900, 3000, 400 and 15 respectively.

COMPUTATION OF WEIGHTED H.M.

X	W	W/X
60	900	15
25	3000	120
350	400	1·43
25	15	0·60
	$\Sigma W = 4315$	$\Sigma(W/X) = 137·03$

$$\therefore \quad \text{Average Speed} = \frac{\Sigma W}{\Sigma(W/X)} = \frac{4315}{137·03} = 31·49 \text{ km. p.h.}$$

5·11. RELATION BETWEEN ARITHMETIC MEAN, GEOMETRIC MEAN AND HARMONIC MEAN

The arithmetic mean (A.M.), the geometric mean (G.M.) and the harmonic mean (H.M.) of a series of n observations are connected by the relation :

$$\text{A.M.} \geq \text{G.M.} \geq \text{H.M.} \qquad \ldots(5·31)$$

the sign of equality holding if and only if all the n observations are equal.

Remark. For two numbers we also have

$$G^2 = A \times H \qquad \ldots(5·32)$$

where A, G and H represent arithmetic mean, geometric mean and harmonic mean respectively.

Proof : Let a and b be two real positive numbers *i.e.*, $a > 0, b > 0$.

$$\text{Then} \quad \text{A.M.} = \frac{a+b}{2} \quad ; \quad \text{G.M.} = \sqrt{ab} \quad ; \quad \text{H.M.} = \frac{1}{\dfrac{1}{2}\left(\dfrac{1}{a} + \dfrac{1}{b}\right)} = \frac{2ab}{a+b} \qquad \ldots(*)$$

$$\therefore \quad A \times H = \frac{a+b}{2} \cdot \frac{2ab}{a+b} = ab = G^2$$

Example 5·54. *H.M., A.M. and G.M. of a set of 5 observations are 10·2, 16 and 14 respectively." Comment.*

Solution. We are given : $n = 5$; A.M. = 16 ; G.M. = 14 and H.M. = 10·2. Since A.M. > G.M. > H.M., the above statement is correct.

Example 5·55. *The arithmetic mean of two observations is 127·5 and their geometric mean is 60. Find (i) their harmonic mean and (ii) the two observations.*

[*Delhi Univ. B.Com. (Hons.), (External), 2007*]

Solution. (*i*) Let the two observations be a and b. Then we are given :

$$\text{Arithmetic Mean } = \frac{a+b}{2} = 127{\cdot}5 \quad \Rightarrow \quad a + b = 255 \qquad \ldots(*)$$

$$\text{G.M. } = \sqrt{a \times b} = 60 \quad \Rightarrow \quad ab = 3600 \qquad \ldots(**)$$

Harmonic mean of two numbers a and b is given by :

$$\text{H.M. } = \frac{2ab}{a+b} = \frac{2 \times 3600}{255} = \frac{480}{17} = 28{\cdot}24 \qquad \text{[From (*) and (**)]}$$

Aliter. For two numbers, we have :

$$G^2 = AH \quad \Rightarrow \quad H = \frac{G^2}{A} = \frac{60^2}{127{\cdot}5} = \frac{480}{17} = 28{\cdot}24$$

(*ii*) We have

$$(a-b)^2 = (a+b)^2 - 4ab = (255)^2 - 4 \times 3600 \qquad \text{[From (*) and (**)]}$$
$$= 65025 - 14400 = 50625$$

$$\therefore \quad a - b = \pm \sqrt{50625} = \pm 225$$

$a + b = 255$ and $a - b = 225$	$a + b = 225$ and $a - b = -225$
Adding, we get	Adding, we get
$2a = 480 \Rightarrow a = \frac{480}{2} = 240$	$2a = 30 \Rightarrow a = \frac{30}{2} = 15$
$\therefore\ b = 255 - a$ [From (*)]	$\therefore\ b = 255 - a$ [From (*)]
$= 255 - 240 = 15$	$= 255 - 15 = 240$

Hence, the two observations are 240 and 15

5·12. SELECTION OF AN AVERAGE

From the discussion of the merits and demerits of the various measures of central tendency in the preceding sections, it is obvious that no single average is suitable for all practical problems. Each of the averages has its own merits and demerits and consequently its own field of importance and utility. For example, arithmetic mean is not to be recommended while dealing with frequency distribution with extreme observations or open end classes. Median and mode are the averages to be used while dealing with open end classes. In case of qualitative data which cannot be measured quantitatively (*e.g.*, for finding average intelligence, honesty, beauty, etc.), median is the only average to be used. Mode is particularly used in business and geometric mean is to be used while dealing with rates and ratios. Harmonic mean is to be used in computing special types of average rates or ratios where time factor is variable and the act being performed *e.g.*, distance, is constant.

Hence, the averages cannot be used indiscriminately. For sound statistical analysis, a judicious selection of the average depends upon :

(*i*) the nature and availability of the data,
(*ii*) the nature of the variable involved,
(*iii*) the purpose of the enquiry.

(iv) the system of classification adopted, and

(v) the use of the average for further statistical computations required for the enquiry in mind.

However, since arithmetic mean :

(i) satisfies almost all the properties of an ideal average as laid down by Prof. Yule,

(ii) is quite familiar to a layman, and

(iii) has very wide applications in statistical theory at large,

it may be regarded as the best of all the averages.

5·13. LIMITATIONS OF AVERAGES

In spite of its very wide applications in statistical analysis, the averages have the following limitations :

1. Since average is a single numerical figure representing the characteristics of a given distribution, proper care should be taken in interpreting its value otherwise it might lead to very misleading conclusions. In this context, it might be appropriate to quote a classical joke regarding average about a village school teacher who had to cross a river along with his family. On enquiry he was given to understand that the average depth of the river was 3 feet. He measured the heights of the members of the family (himself, his wife, 2 daughters and 3 sons) and found that their average (mean) height was $3\frac{1}{2}$ feet. Since the average height of the family came out to be higher than the average depth of the river, he ordered his family to cross the river. But when he reached the other side of the river, three of his children were missing. He again checked his arithmetical calculations which still gave the same result and was wondering as to what and where was the mistake. He wrote a couplet in Urdu, reading :

'Arba jyon ka tyon
Kunba dooba kyon'

(Arba means arithmetic or calculations and Kunba means family). In fact, the teacher had the misconception about the average depth of the river which he mistook for uniform depth but in fact the river was very shallow in the beginning but became deeper and deeper and in the middle it was as deep as 4 feet or so. Accordingly, the members of the family with height bellow 4 feet were drowned.

2. A proper and judicious choice of an average for a particular problem is very important. A wrong choice of the average might give wrong and fallacious conclusions.

3. An average fails to give the complete picture of a distribution. We might come across a number of distributions having the same average but differing widely in their structure and constitution. To form a complete idea about the distribution, the measures of central tendency are to be supplemented by some more measures such as dispersion, skewness and kurtosis.

4. In certain types of distributions like U-shaped or J-shaped distributions, an average (which is only a single point of concentration) fails to represent the entire series [*c.f.* Chapter 4].

5. Sometimes an average might give very absurd results. For instance, the average of a family might come out in fractions which is obviously absurd. In this context we might quote the following :

"The figure of 2·2 children per adult female is felt in some respects to be absurd and the Royal Commission suggested that the middle classes be paid money to increase the average to a rounder and more convenient number".

EXERCISE 5·4

1. Define Geometric Mean and discuss its merits and demerits. Give two practical situations where you will recommend its use.

2. (*a*) "It is said that the choice of an average depends on the particular problem in hand".

Examine the above statement and give at least one instance each for the use of Mode and Geometric Mean.

(*b*) Discuss the strong and weak points of various measures of central tendency.

3. (*a*) What are the advantages and disadvantages of the chief averages used in Statistics ? Indicate their special uses if any.

(*b*) What are the desideratta for a satisfactory average ? Examine the geometric mean in the light of these desideratta and bring out the special properties of this average which lend to its use in intercensal population counts and in the construction of index numbers.

4. (*a*) "Each average has its own special features and it is difficult to say which one is the best". Explain and illustrate.

(*b*) Why is arithmetic mean generally preferred over median as the measure of central tendency ? What is the relation between arithmetic mean and geometric mean ? When is the latter preferred over the former ?

5. Explain the relative merits of geometric mean over other measures of central tendency.

6. Give a specific example of an instance in which :

(*a*) The median would be used in preference to arithmetic mean,

(*b*) The arithmetic mean would not be as satisfactory as the geometric mean, and

(*c*) Mode would be used in preference to the median.

7. (*a*) Find the G.M. of 1, 2, 3, $\frac{1}{2}$, $\frac{1}{3}$. What will be the geometric mean if '0' is added to this set of values ? *[I.C.W.A. (Foundation), June 2003]*

Ans. $G = \left(1 \times 2 \times 3 \times \frac{1}{2} \times \frac{1}{3}\right)^{1/5} = 1^{1/5} = 1 \;;\; G = 0$

(*b*) Find the geometric mean of : 1, 7, 18, 65, 91 and 103.

Ans. 20·62.

(*c*) Calculate geometric mean of the data : 1, 7, 29, 92, 115 and 375.

Ans. 30·50

8. *Calculate arithmetic mean and geometric mean of the following distribution*

x	:	*2*	*3*	*4*	*5*	*6*	*7*	*8*
f	:	*2*	*4*	*6*	*2*	*3*	*2*	*1*

Ans. A.M. = 4·5 ; G.M. 4·192.

9. If the population has doubled itself in twenty years, is it correct to say that the rate of growth has been 5% per annum ?

Ans. No. $r = 3{\cdot}5\%$.

10. The population of a city was 1,00,000 in 1975 and 1,44,000 a decade later. Estimate the population at the middle of the decade. *[Delhi Univ. B.A. (Econ. Hons.) 1996]*

Hint and Ans. r : Percentage rate of growth per annum.

Then $1{,}44{,}000 = 1{,}00{,}000\,(1+r)^{10} \Rightarrow (1+r)^{10} = \frac{144}{100} = \left(\frac{12}{10}\right)^2 \Rightarrow (1+r)^5 = \frac{12}{10} = 1.2.$

Estimated population at the middle of the decade = $1{,}00{,}000\,(1+r)^5 = 1{,}00{,}000 \times 1{\cdot}2 = 1{,}20{,}000.$

11. The population of India in 1951 and 1961 were 361 and 439 million respectively.

(*i*) What was the average percentage increase per year during the period ?

(*ii*) If the average rate of increase from 1961 to 1971 remains the same, what would be the population in 1971 ?

Ans. (*i*) 2%, (*ii*) 533·85 million.

12. The population of a country increased by 20 per cent in the first decade and by 30 per cent in the second decade and by 45 per cent in the third decade. Determine the average decennial growth rate of population.

Ans. 31·3%

13. A machine depreciates by 40% in the first year, by 25% in the second year and by 10% per annum for the next three years, each percentage being calculated on the diminishing value. What is the average percentage of depreciation for the entire period ? *[Delhi Univ. B.Com. (Hons.), 1994]*

Ans. 20%.

14. (*a*) An income-tax assessee depreciated the machinery of his factory by 20 per cent in each of the first two years and 40 per cent in the third year. How much average depreciation relief should he claim from the taxation department ? *[Delhi Univ. B.A. (Econ. Hons.), 1999; Bangalore Univ. B.Com., 1998]*

Ans. 27·32%.

(*b*) A businessman depreciated the machinery of his factory by 20% in the first two years and 40% in the third year. What is the average depreciation for the three years ? *[Delhi Univ. B.A. (Econ. Hons.), 2004]*

Ans. G.M. = 27.32%.

15. (*a*) An economy grows at the rate of 2% in the first year, 2·5% in the second year, 3% in the third, 4% in the fourth,...and 10% in the tenth year. What is the average rate of growth of the economy ?

Ans. 5·6% p.a. *(Nagarjuna Univ. B.Com., 1996)*

(*b*) The annual rates of growth achieved by a nation for 5 years are 5%, 7·5%, 2·5%, 5% and 10% respectively. What in the compound rate of growth for the 5 year period ? [*Delhi Univ. B.A. (Eco. Hons.), 1993*]

Ans. 5·9%.

16. The number of divorces per 1,000 marriages in a big city in India increased from 96 in 1980 to 120 in 1990. Find the annual rate of increase of the divorce rate for the period 1980 to 1990. [*Delhi Univ. B.Com. (Hons.), 1994*]

Hint. $120 = 96\left(1 + \frac{r}{100}\right)^{10} \quad \Rightarrow \quad 1 + \frac{r}{100} = \left(\frac{120}{96}\right)^{1/10}$

Ans. $r = 2{\cdot}26\%$.

17. If arithmetic mean and geometric mean of two values are 10 and 8 respectively, find the values.

Ans. 16, 4.

18. A man gets three successive annual rises in salary of 20%, 30% and 25% respectively, each percentage being reckoned in his salary at the end of the previous year. How much better or worse would he have been if he had been given three annual rises of 25% each, reckoned in the same way. [*Delhi Univ. B.A. (Econ. Hons.), 2006*]

Ans. The man would be better in the second case by 0·31% of his starting salary in the 1st year.

19. The geometric mean of 4 items is 100 and of another 8 items is 3·162. Find the geometric mean of the 12 items.

Ans. 10.

20. (*a*) Geometric mean of *n* observations is found to be *G*. How will you find the correct value of the Geometric Mean if some of the values used in its calculation are found to be wrong and should be replaced by correct values ?

(*b*) Geometric mean of 2 numbers is 15. If by mistake one figure is taken as 5, instead of 3, find correct geometric mean. [*Delhi Univ. B.Com. (Hons.) 1993*]

Hint. Let the two numbers be *a* and *b*. $\sqrt{ab} = 15 \quad \Rightarrow \quad ab = 225$

Wrong observation, (say), $a = 5 \qquad \therefore \quad b = \frac{225}{a} = \frac{225}{5} = 45$

Correct value of $a = 3$ (Given)

$\therefore$ Correct G.M. $= \sqrt{3 \times 45} = 11{\cdot}62$ *Or* Use Formula (5·26*b*)

(*c*) The geometric mean of four values was calculated as 16. It was later discovered that one of the value was recorded wrongly as 32 when, in fact, it was 162. Calculate the correct geometric mean.

[*Delhi Univ. B.Com. (Hons.), 2004*]

Ans. Correct G.M. $= (16) \times \left(\frac{162}{32}\right)^{1/4} = 16 \times \frac{3}{2} = 24$ [Using (5·26*b*)]

21. (*a*) Define simple and weighted geometric mean of a given distribution.

The weighted geometric mean of three numbers 229, 275 and 125 is 203. The weights for 1st and 2nd numbers are 2 and 4 respectively. Find the weight of the third.

Ans. 3.

(*b*) The weighted geometric mean of the four numbers 9, 25, 17 and 30 is 15·3. If the weights of the first three numbers are 5, 3 and 4 respectively, find the weight of the fourth number.

Ans. 2 (*approx.*).

22. (*a*) Define Harmonic Mean and discuss its merits and demerits. Under what situations would you recommend its use.

(*b*) Find the geometric and harmonic mean from the following data.

Items	:	1	2	3	4	5	6	7	8	9	10
Value	:	15	250	15·7	157	1·57	105·7	105	1·06	25·7	0·257

Ans. GM = 16·04; HM = 1·7637.

23. (*a*) Find the harmonic mean of the numbers $\frac{1}{5}, \frac{1}{4}, \frac{1}{3}, \frac{1}{2}$, 1. [*I.C.W.A. (Foundation), June 2004, Dec. 2002*]

Hint. $\frac{1}{H} = \frac{1}{5}\Sigma\left(\frac{1}{x}\right) = \frac{1}{5}(5 + 4 + 3 + 2 + 1) \quad \Rightarrow \quad H = \frac{1}{3}$

(*b*) If each of 3, 48 and 96 occurs once and 6 occurs thrice, verify that geometric mean is greater than harmonic mean. [*I.C.W.A. (Foundation), Dec., June 2004*]

Ans. G.M. = 12 ; H.M. = 6.94 ; G.M. > H.M.

24. What do you mean by Weighted Harmonic Mean ? When will you use it instead of Simple Harmonic Mean ? Explain by a practical situation.

25. It is said that "Choice of an average depends on the particular problem in hand." Examine the statement and give at least one instance each for the use of mode, geometric mean and harmonic mean. *[Delhi B.Com. (Hons.), 2007]*

26. From the following statements select any two which are correct and any three which are incorrect. In respect of each of such statements selected by you, give your comments explaining briefly why you consider the statement correct or incorrect :

(*i*) The median may be considered more typical than the mean because the median is not affected by the size of the extremes ;

(*ii*) In a frequency distribution the true value of the mode cannot be calculated exactly ;

(*iii*) The Geometric Mean cannot be used in the averaging of index numbers because it gives undue importance to small numbers ;

(*iv*) The Harmonic Mean of a series of fractions is the same as the reciprocal of the arithmetic mean of the series.

Ans. *(i) T, (ii) T, (iii) F, (iv) F.*

27. Show that the weighted harmonic mean of the first n natural numbers, where the weights are equal to the corresponding numbers, is given by $(n + 1)/2$. *[Delhi Univ. B.A. (Econ. Hons.), 2003]*

28. (*a*) An aeroplane flies around a square the sides of which measure 100 km. each. The aeroplane covers at a speed of 100 km. per hour first side, at 200 km. per hour the second side, at 300 km. per hour the third side and at 400 km. per hour the fourth side. Use the correct mean to find the average speed around the square.

Ans. 192 km. p.h.

(*b*) Four factories emit a kilogram of pollutant each in 4, 5, 8 and 12 days respectively. What is the average rate of pollutant discharge ? Use your answer to calculate the total pollutant discharged by the four factories in one week.

[Delhi Univ. B.A. (Econ. Hons.), 2005]

Hint. Find H.M. of 4, 5, 8, 12.

Ans. 1 kg. pollutant in $\frac{480}{79}$ days per factory.

Total pollutant discharged by four factories per week $= \frac{79}{480} \times 4 \times 7 = \frac{553}{120} = 4.608$ kg.

29. (*a*) A railway train runs for 30 minutes at a speed of 40 miles an hour and then, because of repairs of the track runs for 10 minutes at a speed of 8 miles an hour, after which it resumes its previous speed and runs for 20 minutes except for a period of 2 minutes when it had to run over a bridge with a speed of 30 miles per hour. What is the average speed ? *[Delhi Univ. B.Com. (Hons.), 2009]*

Hint. Average Speed = (Total Distance covered) ÷ (Total time taken)

$$= \left[\left(\frac{40}{60} \times 30 + \frac{8}{60} \times 10 + \frac{40}{60} \times 18 + \frac{30}{60} \times 2\right) \div (30 + 10 + 20)\right] \text{ m.p.h.}$$

Ans. 34·33 m.p.h.

(*b*) A train runs 25 miles at a speed of 30 m.p.h.; another 50 miles at a speed of 40 m.p.h.; then due to repairs of the track runs for 6 minutes at a speed of 10 m.p.h. and finally covers the remaining distance of 24 miles at a speed of 24 m.p.h. What is the average speed in miles per hour ? *[Punjab Univ. B.Com., 1994]*

Ans. 31·41 m.p.h.

30. (*a*) A cyclist covers his first three kilometres at an average speed of 8 kms. per hour, another 2 kms. at 9 kms. per hour and the last 2 kms. at 4 kms. per hour. Find the average speed for the entire journey.

Ans. 6·38 kms. per hour.

(*b*) If X travels 8 km. at 4 km. per hour; 6 km. at 3 km. per hour and 4 km. at 2 km. per hour, what would be the average rate per hour at which he travelled ? *[Delhi Univ. B.Com. (Pass), 1998]*

Ans. Weighted H.M. = 3 km. p.h.

31. (*a*) A man travelled by car for 3 days. He covered 480 km. each day. On the first day he drove for 10 hours at 48 km. an hour on the second day he drove for 12 hours at 40 km. an hour and on last day he drove for 15 hours at 32 km. an hour. What was his average speed ? *[Bombay Univ. B.Com., 1996]*

Ans. 38·919 km. p.h.

(*b*) Kishore travels 900 kms. by train at an average speed of 60 kms. per hour; 3,000 kms. by steamship at an average of 25 kms. per hour; 400 kms. by aeroplane at 350 kms. per hour; and finally 15 kms. by bus at 25 kms. per hour. Calculate his average speed for the entire journey. [*C.S.* (*Foundation*), *Dec. 2001*]

Ans. 31·556 km. p.h.

32. A man travels from Agra to Dehradun covering 204 miles at a mileage rate of 10 miles per gallon of petrol and via Ghaziabad with an additional journey of 40 miles at the rate of 15 miles per gallon. Find the average mileage per gallon.

Ans. 10·58 miles per gallon.

33. The consumption of petrol by a motor was a gallon for 20 miles while going up from plains to hill station and a gallon for 24 miles while coming down. What particular average would you consider appropriate for finding the average consumption in miles per gallon for up and down journey, and why ?

Ans. Harmonic Mean = 21·82 m.p. gallon.

34. A man having to drive 90 kilometres wishes to achieve an average speed of 30 kilometres per hour. For the first half of the journey he averages only 20 km. p.h. What must be his average for the second half of the journey if his overall average is to be 30 km. p.h.

Ans. 60 km. p.h.

35. An aeroplane travels distances of d_1, d_2 and d_3 kms. at speeds V_1, V_2 and V_3 km. per hour respectively. Show that the average speed (V) is given by :

$$\frac{d_1 + d_2 + d_3}{V} = \frac{d_1}{V_1} + \frac{d_2}{V_2} + \frac{d_3}{V_3}$$ [*Delhi Univ. B.A.* (*Econ. Hons.*), 1993]

36. (*a*) A person purchases one kilogram of cabbage from each of the four places at the rate of 20 kg., 16 kg., 12 kg. and 10 kg. per 100 rupee respectively. On the average how many kg. of cabbage has he purchased per 100 rupees ? [*Delhi Univ. B.Com.* (*Pass*), *2001*]

(*b*) If you spend Rs. 100 per week on apples and the price of apples for three weeks is Rs. 25, Rs. 20 and Rs. 10 per kilogram, what is the average price of apples for you ? [*Delhi Univ. B.A.* (*Econ. Hons.*), *2002*]

Ans. Rs. 15·79 per kg.

37. In a certain office a letter is typed by *A* in 4 minutes. The same letter is typed by *B*, *C* and *D* in 5, 6, 10 minutes respectively. What is the average time taken in completing one letter ? How many letters do you expect to be typed in one day comprising of 8 working hours.

Ans. H.M. = 5·58 minutes per letter ; Letters typed in 8 hours (480 minutes) = $\frac{480}{5\cdot58} \simeq 86$.

38. A scooterist purchased petrol at the rate of Rs. 24, Rs. 29.50 and Rs. 36.85 per litre during three successive years. Calculate the average price of petrol,

(*i*) If he purchased 150, 180 and 195 litres of petrol in the respective years and

(*ii*) If he spent Rs. 3,850, Rs. 4,675 and Rs. 5,825 in three years.

Give support to your answer. [*Delhi Univ. B.Com.* (*Hons.*), *2005*]

Hint. Average price of petrol/litre = $\frac{\text{Total money spent on petrol}}{\text{Total petrol consumed in litres}}$

(*i*) Weighted A.M. of prices the weights being the quantities of petrol purchased

(*ii*) Weighted H.M. of prices, the weights being the money spent on petrol.

Ans. (*i*) Rs. 30·65/litre, (*ii*) Rs. 30/litre (approx.)

39. (*a*) Define Arithmetic Mean, Harmonic Mean and Geometric Mean for a set of *n* observations and state the relationship between them.

Ans. $A \geq G \geq H$; the sign of equality holds if and only if all the observations are equal.

(*b*) Show the relationship between arithmetic mean and harmonic mean for the variable *X*, which can take the values *a* and *b* such that *a*, *b* are non-negative integers. [*Delhi Univ. B.A. (Econ. Hons.), 2007*]

Ans. $A \times H = \left(\frac{a+b}{2}\right) \cdot \left(\frac{2ab}{a+b}\right) = ab = G^2$

(*c*) If for two numbers, the arithmetic mean is 25 and the harmonic mean is 9, what is the geometric mean of the series ? [*C.A.* (*Foundation*), *May 2001*]

Ans. *G.M.* = 15.

(*d*) If A.M. of two numbers is 17 and G.M. is 15, find the H.M. of these numbers.

[*Delhi Univ. B.A. (Econ. Hons.), 2000*]

Ans. 13·24

40. (*a*) Comment on the following : "The G.M. and A.M. of a distribution are 27 and 30. Then H.M. is 26."

[*Delhi Univ. B.Com. (Hons.), 2009*]

Ans. Since A.M. ≥ G.M. ≥ H.M., the statement is correct.

(*b*) State giving reasons which average will be more appropriate in the following cases :

(*i*) The distribution has open-end classes.

(*ii*) The distribution has wide range of variations.

(*iii*) When depreciation is charged by diminishing balance method and an average rate of depreciation is to be calculated.

(*iv*) The distance covered is fixed but speeds are varying and an average speed is to be calculated.

[*Delhi. Univ. B.Com.* (*Pass*), *1999*]

Ans. (*i*) *Md* or *Mo,* (*ii*) *Md,* (*iii*) *G.M.*, (*iv*) *H.M.*

6 Measures of Dispersion

6·1. INTRODUCTION AND MEANING

Averages or the measures of central tendency give us an idea of the concentration of the observations about the central part of the distribution. In spite of their great utility in statistical analysis, they have their own limitations. If we are given only the average of a series of observations, we cannot form complete idea about the distribution since there may exist a number of distributions whose averages are same but which may differ widely from each other in a number of ways. The following example will illustrate this viewpoint.

Let us consider the following three series A, B and C of 9 items each.

Series										*Total*	*Mean*
A	15,	15,	15,	15,	15,	15,	15,	15,	15	135	15
B	11,	12,	13,	14,	15,	16,	17,	18,	19,	135	15
C	3,	6,	9,	12,	15,	18,	21,	24,	27	135	15

All the three series A, B and C, have the same size ($n = 9$) and same mean *viz.*, 15. Thus, if we are given that the mean of a series of 9 observations is 15, we cannot determine if we are talking of the series A, B or C. In fact, any series of 9 items with total 135 will give mean 15. Thus, we may have a large number of series with entirely different structures and compositions but having the same mean.

From the above illustration it is obvious that the measures of central tendency are inadequate to describe the distribution completely. In the words of George Simpson and Fritz Kafka :

"*An average does not tell the full story. It is hardly fully representative of a mass unless we know the manner in which the individual items scatter around it. A further description of the series is necessary if we are to gauge how representative the average is.*"

Thus the measures of central tendency must be supported and supplemented by some other measures. One such measure is *Dispersion*.

Literal meaning of dispersion is "*Scatteredness.*" We study dispersion to have an idea of the homogeneity (compactness) or heterogeneity (scatter) of the distribution. In the above illustration, we say that the series A is *stationary, i.e.*, it is constant and shows no variability. Series B is slightly dispersed and series C is relatively more dispersed. We say that series B is more homogeneous (or uniform) as compared with series C or the series C is more heterogeneous than series B.

We give below some definitions of dispersion as given by different statisticians from time to time.

WHAT THEY SAY ABOUT DISPERSION — SOME DEFINITIONS

"*Dispersion is the measure of the variation of the items.*"—**A.L. Bowley**

"*Dispersion is a measure of the extent to which the individual items vary.*"—**L.R. Connor**

"*Dispersion or spread is the degree of the scatter or variation of the variables about a central value.*" —**B.C. Brooks and W.F.L. Dick**

"*The degree to which numerical data tend to spread about an average value is called the variation or dispersion of the data.*"—**Spiegel**

"*The term dispersion is used to indicate the facts that within a given group, the items differ from one another in size or in other words, there is lack of uniformity in their sizes.*"—**W.I. King**

6·1·1. Objectives or Significance of the Measures of Dispersion. The main objectives of studying dispersion may be summarised as follows :

1. *To find out the reliability of an average.* The measures of variation enable us to find out if the average is representative of the data. As stated earlier, dispersion gives us an idea about the spread of the observations about an average value. If the dispersion is small, it means that the given data values are closer to the central value (average) and hence the average may be regarded as reliable in the sense that it provides a fairly good estimate of the corresponding population average. If the dispersion is large, then the data values are more deviated from the central value, thereby implying that the average is not representative of the data and hence not quite reliable.

2. *To control the variation of the data from the central value.* The measures of variation help us to determine the causes and the nature of variation, so as to control the variation itself.

It helps to measure the extent of variation from the standard quality of various works carried in industries. For example, we use 3-sigma (3-σ) control limits to determine if a manufacturing process is in control or not. This helps us to identify the causes of variation in the manufactured product and accordingly take corrective and remedial measures. [For detailed discussion, see Chapter 21, Statistical Quality Control.] The Government can also take suitable policy decisions to remove the inequalities in the distribution of income and wealth, after careful study of the dispersion of the income and wealth.

3. *To compare two or more sets of data regarding their variability.* The relative measures of dispersion may be used to compare two or more distributions, even if they are measured in different units, as regards their variability or uniformity. For detailed discussion, see § 6·12 Coefficient of Variation.

4. *To obtain other statistical measures for further analysis of data.* The measures of variation are used for computing other statistical measures which are used extensively in Correlation Analysis (Chapter 8), Regression Analysis (Chapter 9), Theory of Estimation and Testing of Hypothesis (Chapter 16), Statistical Quality Control (Chapter 21) and so on.

6·2. CHARACTERISTICS FOR AN IDEAL MEASURE OF DISPERSION

The desideratta for an ideal measure of dispersion are the same as those for an ideal measure of central tendency, *viz.* :

(*i*) It should be rigidly defined.
(*ii*) It should be easy to calculate and easy to understand.
(*iii*) It should be based on all the observations.
(*iv*) It should be amenable to further mathematical treatment.
(*v*) It should be affected as little as possible by fluctuations of sampling.
(*vi*) It should not be affected much by extreme observations.

All these properties have been explained in Chapter 5 on Measures of Central Tendency.

6·3. ABSOLUTE AND RELATIVE MEASURES OF DISPERSION

The measures of dispersion which are expressed in terms of the original units of a series are termed as *Absolute Measures*. Such measures are not suitable for comparing the variability of the two distributions which are expressed in different units of measurement. On the other hand, *Relative Measures* of dispersion are obtained as ratios or percentages and are thus pure numbers independent of the units of measurement. For comparing the variability of the two distributions (even if they are measured in the same units), we compute the relative measures of dispersion instead of the absolute measures of dispersion.

6·4. MEASURES OF DISPERSION

The various measures of dispersion are :

(*i*) Range.
(*ii*) Quartile deviation or Semi-Interquartile range.
(*iii*) Mean deviation.

(iv) Standard deviation.

(v) Lorenz curve.

The first two measures *viz.*, Range and Quartile deviation are termed as positional measures since they depend upon the values of the variable at particular position of the distribution. The last measure *viz.*, Lorenz curve is a graphic method of studying variability. In the following sections we shall discuss these measures in detail one by one.

6·5. RANGE

The range is the simplest of all the measures of dispersion. It is defined as the difference between the two extreme observations of the distribution. In other words, range is the difference between the greatest (maximum) and the smallest (minimum) observation of the distribution. Thus

$$\text{Range} = X_{max} - X_{min} \quad (6·1)$$

where $X_{max} = L$, is the greatest observation and $X_{min} = S$, is the smallest observation of the variable values.

In case of the grouped frequency distribution (for discrete values) or the continuous frequency distribution, range is defined as the difference between the upper limit of the highest class and the lower limit of the smallest class.

Remarks 1. In case of a frequency distribution, the frequencies of the various values of the variable (or classes) are immaterial since range depends only on the two extreme observations.

2. *Absolute and Relative Measures of Range.* Range as defined in (6·1) is an absolute measure of dispersion and depends upon the units of measurement. Thus, if we want to compare the variability of two or more distributions with the same units of measurement, we may use (6·1). However, to compare the variability of the distributions given in different units of measurement, we cannot use (6·1) but we need a relative measure which is independent of the units of measurement. This relative measure, called the *coefficient of range*, is defined as follows :

$$\text{Coefficient of Range} = \frac{X_{max} - X_{min}}{X_{max} + X_{min}} \quad \ldots(6·2)$$

where the symbols have already been explained. In other words, *coefficient of range is the ratio of the difference between two extreme observations (the biggest and the smallest) of the distribution to their sum.*

It is a common practice to use coefficient of range even for the comparison of variability of distributions given in the same units of measurement.

3. *Effect of Change of Origin and Scale on Range.*

Let the given variable X be transformed to the new variable U by changing the origin and scale in X as follows :

$$U = AX + B \quad \ldots(6.3)$$

$$\Rightarrow \quad U_{max} = A \,.\, X_{max} + B \quad \text{and} \quad U_{min} = A \,.\, X_{min} + B$$

$$\therefore \quad \text{Range}\,(U) = U_{max} - U_{min} = A\,(X_{max} - X_{min})$$

$$\Rightarrow \quad \text{Range}\,(U) = A \,.\, \text{Range}\,(X) \quad \ldots(6.3a)$$

Hence, *range is independent of change of origin but not of scale.*

4. *When is dispersion (variation) zero ?*

A crude measure of dispersion is :

Range = Largest sample observation – Smallest sample observation.

Range = 0, if Largest sample observation = Smallest sample observation

This is possible only if the variable takes a constant value *i.e.*, if all the observations in the sample have the same value.

For example, if a variable takes 5 values 8, 8, 8, 8, 8, then :

Largest value $(L) = 8$ and Smallest value $(S) = 8$

$$\therefore \quad \text{Range} = L - S = 8 - 8 = 0.$$

6·5·1. Merits and Demerits of Range. Range is the simplest though crude measure of dispersion. It is rigidly defined, readily comprehensible and is perhaps the easiest to compute, requiring very little calculations. However, it does not satisfy the properties (*iii*) to (*vi*) for an ideal measure of dispersion. We give below its limitations and drawbacks.

(*i*) Range is not based on the entire set of data. It is based only on two extreme observations, which themselves are subject to change fluctuations. As such, range cannot be regarded as a reliable measure of variability.

(*ii*) Range is very much affected by fluctuations of sampling. Its value varies very widely from sample to sample.

(*iii*) If the smallest and the largest observations of a distribution are unaltered and all other values are replaced by a set of observations within these values *i.e.*, X_{max} and X_{min}, the range of the distribution remains same. Moreover if any item is added or deleted on either side of the extreme value, the value of the range is changed considerably, though its effect is not so pronounced if we use the coefficient of range. Thus range does not take into account the composition of the series or the distribution of the observations within the extreme values. Consequently, it is fairly unreliable as a measure of dispersion of the values within the distribution.

(*iv*) Range cannot be used if we are dealing with open end classes.

(*v*) Range is not suitable for mathematical treatment.

(*vi*) Another shortcoming of the range, though less important is that it is very sensitive to the size of the sample. As the sample size increases, the range tends to increase though not proportionately.

(*vii*) In the words of W.I. King "*Range is too indefinite to be used as a practical measure of dispersion*."

6·5·2. Uses. (1) In spite of the above limitations and shortcomings range, as a measure of dispersion, has its applications in a number of fields where the data have small variations like the stock market fluctuations. the variations in money rates and rate of exchange.

(2) Range is used in industry for the statistical quality control of the manufactured product by the construction of R-chart *i.e.*, the control chart for range.

(3) Range is by far the most widely used measure of variability in our day-to-day life. For example, the answer to problems like, 'daily sales in a departmental store'; 'monthly wages of workers in a factory' or 'the expected return of fruits from an orchard', is usually provided by the probable limits - in the form of a range.

(4) Range is also used as a very convenient measure by meteorological department for weather forecasts since the public is primarily interested to know the limits within which the temperature is likely to vary on a particular day.

Example 6·1. *Calculate the range and the coefficient of range of A's monthly earnings for a year.*

Month	*Monthly earnings (In '00 Rs.)*	*Month*	*Monthly earnings (In '00 Rs.)*	*Month*	*Monthly earnings (In '00 Rs.)*
1	*139*	*5*	*157*	*9*	*162*
2	*150*	*6*	*158*	*10*	*162*
3	*151*	*7*	*160*	*11*	*173*
4	*151*	*8*	*161*	*12*	*175*

Solution.

Largest earning (L) = Rs. 17,500 ; Smallest earnings (S) = Rs. 13,900

$\therefore$ Range $= L - S = 17{,}500 - 13{,}900 =$ Rs. 3,600.

$$\text{Coefficient of range} = \frac{L-S}{L+S} = \frac{17{,}500 - 13{,}900}{17{,}500 + 13{,}900} = \frac{36}{314} = 0{\cdot}115$$

Example 6·2(*a*). *The following table gives the age distribution of a group of 50 individuals.*

Age (in years) :	*16 – 20*	*21 – 25*	*26 – 30*	*31 – 36*
No. of persons :	*10*	*15*	*17*	*8*

Calculate range and the coefficient of range.

(*b*). ∵ the variables x and y are related by $3x - 2y + 5 = 0$ and the range of x is 8, find the range of y.

[*I.C.W.A. (Foundation), Dec. 2005*]

Solution. (*a*) Since age is a continuous variable we should first convert the given classes into continuous classes. The first class will then become 15·5—20·5 and the last class will become 30·5—35·5.

$$\text{Largest value} = 35{\cdot}5 \;;\; \text{Smallest value} = 15{\cdot}5$$

$$\therefore \quad \text{Range} = 35{\cdot}5 - 15{\cdot}5 = 20 \text{ years}$$

$$\text{Coefficient of range} = \frac{35{\cdot}5 - 15{\cdot}5}{35{\cdot}5 + 15{\cdot}5} = \frac{20}{51} = 0{\cdot}39.$$

(*b*) We are given : $\quad \text{Range } (x) = 8 \quad \ldots(1)$

and $\quad 3x - 2y + 5 = 0 \quad \Rightarrow \quad y = \frac{1}{2}(3x + 5) = \frac{3}{2}x + \frac{5}{2}$

Hence, using (6.3*a*), we get

$$\text{Range } (y) = \frac{3}{2}\text{Range } (x) = \frac{3}{2} \times 8 = 12 \qquad \text{[From (1)]}$$

6·6. QUARTILE DEVIATION OR SEMI INTER-QUARTILE RANGE

It is a measure of dispersion based on the upper quartile Q_3 and the lower quartile Q_1.

$$\text{Inter-quartile Range} = Q_3 - Q_1 \qquad \ldots(6{\cdot}4)$$

Quartile deviation is obtained from inter-quartile range on dividing by 2 and hence is also known as *semi inter-quartile range*. Thus

$$\text{Quartile Deviation (Q.D.)} = \frac{Q_3 - Q_1}{2} \qquad \ldots(6{\cdot}5)$$

Q.D. as defined in (6·5) is only an absolute measure of dispersion. For comparative studies of variability of two distributions we need a relative measure which is known as Coefficient of Quartile Deviation and is given by :

$$\text{Coefficient of Q.D.} = \frac{(Q_3 - Q_1)/2}{(Q_3 + Q_1)/2} = \frac{Q_3 - Q_1}{Q_3 + Q_1} \qquad \ldots(6{\cdot}6)$$

Remarks 1. The quartile deviation gives the average amount by which the two quartiles differ from median. For a *symmetrical distribution* we have (*c.f.* Chapter 7).

$$Q_3 - Md = Md - Q_1 \quad \Rightarrow \quad Md = \frac{Q_1 + Q_3}{2} \qquad \ldots(*)$$

i.e., median lies half way on the scale from Q_1 to Q_3. Thus for a symmetrical distribution we have :

$$\text{Q.D.} + Q_1 = \frac{Q_3 - Q_1}{2} + Q_1 = \frac{Q_3 + Q_1}{2} = Md \qquad \text{[From (*)]}$$

and

$$Q_3 - \text{Q.D.} = Q_3 - \frac{Q_3 - Q_1}{2} = \frac{Q_3 + Q_1}{2} = Md \qquad \text{[From (*)]}$$

In other words, for a symmetrical distribution we have :

$$Q_1 = Md - \text{Q.D.} \quad \text{and} \quad Q_3 = Md + \text{Q.D.} \qquad \ldots(**)$$

Since in a distribution, 25% of the observations lie below Q_1 and 25% observations lie above Q_3, 50% of the observations lie between Q_1 and Q_3. Therefore, using (**) we conclude that for a symmetrical distribution $Md \pm$ Q.D. covers exactly 50% of the observations.

2. Rigorously speaking quartile deviation is only a positional average and does not exhibit any scatter around an average. As such some statisticians prefer to call it a measure of partition rather than a measure of dispersion.

6·6·1. Merits and Demerits of Quartile Deviation. *Merits.* Quartile deviation is quite easy to understand and calculate. It has a number of obvious advantages over range as a measure of dispersion. For example :

(*a*) As against range which was based on two observations only, Q.D. makes use of 50% of the data and as such is obviously a better measure than range.

(*b*) Since Q.D. ignores 25% of the data from the beginning of the distribution and another 25% of the data from the top end, it is not affected at all by extreme observations.

(*c*) Q.D. can be computed from the frequency distribution with open end classes. In fact, Q.D. is the only measure of dispersion which can be obtained while dealing with a distribution having open end classes.

Demerits. (*i*) Q.D. is not based on all the observations since it ignores 25% of the data at the lower end and 25% of the data at the upper end of the distribution. Hence, it cannot be regarded as a reliable measure of variability.

(*ii*) Q.D. is affected considerably by fluctuations of sampling.

(*iii*) Q.D. is not suitable for further mathematical treatment.

Thus quartile deviation is not a reliable measure of variability, particularly for distributions in which the variation is considerable.

6·7. PERCENTILE RANGE

This is a measure of dispersion based on the difference between certain percentiles. If P_i is the ith percentile and P_j is the jth percentile then the so-called *i-j* percentile range is given by :

$$i\text{-}j \text{ Percentile Range} = P_j - P_i, \ (i < j) \qquad \ldots(6{\cdot}7)$$

Thus *i -j Semi-percentile Range* is given by :

$$(P_j - P_i)/2, \ (i < j) \qquad \ldots(6{\cdot}7a)$$

The commonly used percentile range is the one which corresponds to the 10th and 90th percentiles. Thus taking $i = 10$ and $j = 90$ in (6·7), we get

$$\text{10-90 Percentile Range} = P_{90} - P_{10} \qquad \ldots(6{\cdot}8)$$

and

$$\text{10-90 Semi-percentile Range} = (P_{90} - P_{10})/2 \qquad \ldots(6{\cdot}8a)$$

The above measures are absolute measures only. The relative measure of variability based on percentiles is given by :

$$\text{Coefficient of 10-90 percentile} = \frac{(P_{90} - P_{10})/2}{(P_{90} + P_{10})/2} = \frac{P_{90} - P_{10}}{P_{90} + P_{10}} \qquad \ldots(6{\cdot}9)$$

Theoretically, 10-90 percentile range should serve as a better measure of dispersion than Q.D. since it is based on 80% of the data. However, in practice it is not commonly used.

Example 6·3. *Find :*

(*i*) *Inter-quartile Range;* (*ii*) *Quartile Deviation;* (*iii*) *Coefficient of Quartile Deviation, for the following distribution :*

Class Interval :	*0—15*	*15—30*	*30—45*	*45—60*	*60—75*	*75—90*	*90—105*
f :	*8*	*26*	*30*	*45*	*20*	*17*	*4*

Solution.

COMPUTATION OF QUARTILES

Class Interval	*f*	*(Less than) c.f.*
0—15	8	8
15—30	26	34
30—45	30	64
45—60	45	109
60—75	20	129
75—90	17	146
90—105	4	150
Total	$N = 150$	

Here $N/4 = 37{\cdot}5$. The *c.f.* just greater than 37·5 is 64. Hence, Q_1 lies in the corresponding class 30—45.

$$\therefore \quad Q_1 = l + \frac{h}{f}\left(\frac{N}{4} - C\right) = 30 + \frac{15}{30}\left(37{\cdot}5 - 34\right)$$

$$= 30 + \frac{3{\cdot}5}{2} = 30 + 1{\cdot}75 = 31{\cdot}75$$

$3N/4 = 112{\cdot}5$. The *c.f.* just greater than 112·5 is 129. Hence, Q_3 lies in the corresponding class 60—75.

$$\therefore \quad Q_3 = l + \frac{h}{f}\left(\frac{3N}{4} - C\right) = 60 + \frac{15}{20}\left(112{\cdot}5 - 109\right)$$

$$= 60 + \frac{3 \times 3{\cdot}5}{4} = 60 + 2{\cdot}625 = 62{\cdot}625$$

(*i*) Inter-quartile Range $= Q_3 - Q_1 = 62{\cdot}625 - 31{\cdot}750 = 30{\cdot}875$

(*ii*) Quartile Deviation $= \dfrac{Q_3 - Q_1}{2} = \dfrac{30{\cdot}875}{2} = 15{\cdot}44$ [From Pat (*i*)]

(*iii*) Using the results in Part (*i*), we get :

$$\text{Coefficient of Q.D.} = \frac{Q_3 - Q_1}{Q_3 + Q_1} = \frac{62{\cdot}63 - 31{\cdot}75}{62{\cdot}63 + 31{\cdot}75} = \frac{30{\cdot}88}{94{\cdot}38} = 0{\cdot}33.$$

Example 6·4(*a*). *Evaluate an appropriate measure of dispersion for the following data :*

Income (in Rs.) :	*Less than 50*	*50—70*	*70—90*	*90—110*	*110—130*	*130—150*	*Above 150*
No. of persons :	*54*	*100*	*140*	*300*	*230*	*125*	*51*

(*b*) *Comment on the following :*

If the coefficient of quartile deviation (Q.D) is 0.6 and Q.D. = 15, then $Q_1 = 10$ and $Q_3 = 40$.

[*Delhi Univ. B.Com (Hons.), 2009*]

Solution. (*a*) Since we are given the classes with open end intervals, the only measure of dispersion that we can compute is the quartile deviation.

COMPUTATION OF QUARTILE DEVIATION

Income (in Rs.)	*No. of persons (f)*	*Less than c.f.*
Less than 50	54	54
50—70	100	154
70—90	140	294
90—110	300	594
110—130	230	824
130—150	125	949
Above 150	51	1000

Here $N = 1000$, $\dfrac{N}{4} = \dfrac{1000}{4} = 250$, $\dfrac{3N}{4} = 750$

Since *c.f* just greater than 250 is 294, Q_1 (first quartile) lies in the corresponding class 70—90. Similarly, since *c.f.* just greater than 750 is 824, the corresponding class 110—130 contains Q_3. Hence,

$$Q_1 = 70 + \frac{20}{140}(250 - 154) = 70 + \frac{96}{7}$$
$$= 70 + 13{\cdot}714 = 83{\cdot}714$$

$$Q_3 = 110 + \frac{20}{230}(750 - 594) = 110 + \frac{2 \times 156}{23} = 110 + 13{\cdot}565 = 123{\cdot}565$$

$$\therefore \quad \text{Quartile deviation (Q.D.)} = \frac{Q_3 - Q_1}{2} = \frac{123{\cdot}565 - 83{\cdot}714}{2} = \frac{39{\cdot}851}{2} = 19{\cdot}925.$$

(*b*) $\text{Q.D.} = \dfrac{(Q_3 - Q_1)}{2} = 15 \text{ (Given)} \Rightarrow Q_3 - Q_1 = 30$ ...(1)

$\text{Coefficient of Q.D.} = \dfrac{Q_3 - Q_1}{Q_3 + Q_1} = 0.6 \Rightarrow Q_3 + Q_1 = \dfrac{30}{0.6} = \dfrac{30 \times 10}{6} = 50$ ...(2)

Adding (1) and (2), we get $2Q_3 = 80 \Rightarrow Q_3 = 40$

Subtracting (1) from (2), we get $2Q_1 = 20 \Rightarrow Q_1 = 10$

Hence, the given statement is true.

EXERCISE 6·1

1. (*a*) "Frequency distributions may either differ in the numerical size of their averages though not necessarily in their formations or they may have the same values of their averages yet differ in their respective formations."

Explain and illustrate how the measures of dispersion afford a supplement to the information about the frequency distributions given by the averages.

(*b*) Discuss the validity of the statement : "An average, when published, should be accompanied by a measure of dispersion, for significant interpretation."

2(*a*) Find the range and the coefficient of range for the following observations.

65, 70, 82, 59, 81, 76, 57, 60, 55 and 50. [*C.A. PEE-1, Nov. 2003*]

Ans. 32 ; 0.2424

(*b*) From the monthly income of 10 families given below, calculate

(*a*) the median, (*b*) the geometric mean, (*c*) the coefficient of range.

S. No.	:	1	2	3	4	5	6	7	8	9	10
Income in Rs.	:	145	367	268	73	185	619	280	115	870	315

Ans. (*a*) Md = Rs. 274 (*b*) G = Rs. 252·4, (*c*) Coefficient of Range = 0·84.

3. The index numbers of prices of cotton shares (I_1) and coal shares (I_2) in a given year are as under—

Month :	Jan.	Feb.	March	April	May	June	July	August	Sept.	Oct.	Nov.	Dec.
I_1 :	188	178	173	164	172	183	184	185	211	217	232	240
I_2 :	131	130	130	129	129	120	127	127	130	137	140	142

Calculate range for each share. Hence, discuss which share do you consider more variable in price.

Ans. Range (I_1) = 76, Coefficient of Range (I_1) = 0·19 ; Range (I_2) = 22, Coefficient of Range (I_2) = 0·084.
Cotton shares are more variable in prices.

4. Find the value of third quartile if the values of first quartile and quartile deviation are 104 and 18 respectively.
[*Delhi Univ. B.Com.* (*Pass*), *2002*]

Ans. $Q_3 = 140$.

5. Age distribution of 200 employees of a firm is given below : Construct a 'less than ogive curve, and hence or otherwise calculate semi-interquartile range $\frac{Q_3 - Q_1}{2}$ of the distribution :

Age in years (less than) :	25	30	35	40	45	50	55
No. of employees :	10	25	75	130	170	189	200

Ans. Q_1 = 33·5 years, Q_3 = 43 years, $\frac{Q_3 - Q_1}{2}$ = 4·75 years

6. Find the mode, median, lower quartile (Q_1) and upper quartile (Q_3) and Coeff. of Q.D. from the following data :

Wages :	0—10	10—20	20—30	30—40	40—50
No. of workers :	22	38	46	35	20

[*Maharishi Dayanand Univ. B.Com., 1997*]

Ans. Mode = 24·21 : Median = 24·46, Q_1 = 14·803, Q_3 = 24·21 ; Coeff. of Q.D. = 0·396.

7. Compute the Coefficient of Quartile Deviation of the following data :

Size	*Frequency*	*Size*	*Frequency*
4—8	6	24—28	12
8—12	10	28—32	10
12—16	18	32—36	6
16—20	30	36—40	2
20—24	15		

Ans. Q_1 = 14·5, Q_3 = 24·92, Coefficint of Q.D. = 0·2643

8. Find (*i*) Inter-quartile range, (*ii*) Semi-inter-quartile range, and (*iii*) Coefficient of quartile deviation, from the following frequency distribution :

Marks :	10—20	20—30	30—40	40—50	50—60	60—70	70—80	80—90
No. of students :	60	45	120	25	90	80	120	60

[*C.A. (Foundation), Dec. 1993*]

Ans. (*i*) 38·75, (*ii*) 19·375, (*iii*) 0·3647

9. From the following data,
(*i*) Calculate the 'percentage' of workers getting wages : (*a*) more than Rs. 44 ; (*b*) between Rs. 22 and Rs. 58.
(*ii*) Find the quartile deviation.

Wages (Rs.) :	0—10	10—20	20—30	30—40	40—50	50—60	60—70	70—80
No. of workers :	20	45	85	160	70	55	35	30

Ans. (*i*) (*a*) 32·4%, (*b*) 68·4%; (*ii*) Q_1 = 27·06, Q_3 = 49·29, Q.D. = 11·115.

10. Calculate the appropriate measure of dispersion from the following data :

Wages in Rs. per week :	Less than 35	35—37	38—40	41—43	Over 43
No. of wage earners :	14	62	99	18	7

Ans. Coefficient of Q.D. = 0·046.

11. Find out middle 50%, middle 80% and coefficient of Q.D. from the following table :

Size of items :	2	4	6	8	10	12
Frequency :	3	5	10	12	6	4

Ans. Quartile range = 4 ; Percentile range = 8, Coefficient of Q.D. = 0·25.

6·8. MEAN DEVIATION OR AVERAGE DEVIATION

As already pointed out, the two measures of dispersion discussed so far *viz.*, range and quartile deviation are not based on all the observations and also they do not exhibit any scatter of the observations from an average and thus completely ignore the composition of the series. *Mean Deviation* or the *Average Deviation* overcomes both these drawbacks. As the name suggests, this measure of dispersion is obtained on taking the average (arithmetic mean) of the deviations of the given values from a measure of central tendency. According to Clark and Schkade :

"Average deviation is the average amount of scatter of the items in a distribution from either the mean or the median, ignoring the signs of the deviations. The average that is taken of the scatter is an arithmetic mean, which accounts for the fact that this measure is often called the mean deviation."

6·8·1. Computation of Mean Deviation. If $X_1, X_2, \ldots, X_n$ are n given observations then the mean deviation (M.D.) about an average A, say, is given by :

$$\text{M.D. (about an average } A) = \frac{1}{n}\Sigma\,|X - A| = \frac{1}{n}\Sigma\,|d| \qquad \ldots(6{\cdot}10)$$

where $|d| = |X - A|$ read as mod $(X - A)$, is the *modulus value* or *absolute value* of the deviation (after ignoring the negative sign) $d = X - A$ and $\Sigma\,|d|$ is the sum of these absolute deviations and A is any one of the averages Mean (M), Median (Md) and Mode (Mo).

Steps for Computation of Mean Deviation

1. Calculate the average A of the distribution by the usual methods.

2. Take the deviation $d = X - A$ of each observation from the average A.

3. Ignore the negative signs of the deviations, taking all the deviations to be positive to obtain the absolute deviations, $|d| = |X - A|$.

4. Obtain the sum of the absolute deviations obtained in step 3.

5. Divide the total obtained in step 4 by n, the number of observations.

The result gives the value of the mean deviation about the average A.

In the case of frequency distribution or grouped or continuous frequency distribution, mean deviation about an average A is given by :

$$\text{M.D. (about the average } A) = \frac{1}{N}\Sigma f\,|X - A| = \frac{1}{N}\Sigma f\,|d| \qquad \ldots(6{\cdot}11)$$

where X is the value of the variable or it is the mid-value of the class interval (in the case of grouped or continuous frequency distribution), f is the corresponding frequency, $N = \Sigma f$, is the total frequency and $|X - A|$ is the absolute value of the deviation $d = (X - A)$ of the given values of X from the average A (Mean, Median or Mode).

Steps for Computation of Mean Deviation for Frequency Distribution

Steps **1, 2** and **3** are same as given above

4. Multiply the absolute deviations $|d| = |X - A|$ by the corresponding frequency f to get $f\,|d|$.

5. Take the total of products in step 4 to obtain $\Sigma f\,|d|$.

6. Divide the total in step 5 by N, the total frequency.

The resulting value is the mean deviation about the average A.

Remarks 1. Usually, we obtain the mean deviation (M.D.) about any one of the three averages mean (M), median (Md) or mode (Mo). Thus

$$\left.\begin{aligned} \text{M.D. (about mean)} &= \frac{1}{N}\Sigma f\,|X - M| \\ \text{M.D. (about median)} &= \frac{1}{N}\Sigma f\,|X - Md| \\ \text{M.D. (about mode)} &= \frac{1}{N}\Sigma f\,|X - Mo| \end{aligned}\right\} \qquad \ldots(6{\cdot}11a)$$

2. The sum of the absolute deviations (after ignoring the signs) of a given set of observations is minimum when taken about median. Hence *mean deviation is minimum when it is calculated from median.*

In other words, *mean deviation calculated about median will be less than mean deviation about mean or mode.*

3. As already pointed out in Remark 1, usually, we compute the mean deviation about any one of the three averages mean, median or mode. But since mode is generally ill-defined, in practice M.D. is computed about mean or median. Further, as a choice between mean and median, theoretically, median should be preferred since M.D. is minimum when calculated about median (c.f. Remark 2). But because of wide applications of mean in Statistics as a measure of central tendency, in practice mean deviation is generally computed from mean.

4. For a symmetrical distribution the range Mean ± M.D. (about mean) or Md ± M.D. (about median), [$\because$ $M = Md$ for a symmetrical distribution] covers 57·5% of the observations of the distribution. If the distribution is moderately (skewed), the range will cover approximately 57·5% of the observations.

5. Effect of Change of Origin and Scale on Mean Deviation About Mean.

Let $X_1, X_2, \ldots, X_n$ be n observations on the variable X. Let the variable X be transformed to the new variable Y by changing the origin and scale in X, by the transformation :

$$Y = AX + B \quad \Rightarrow \quad \overline{Y} = A\overline{X} + B \quad \Rightarrow \quad Y - \overline{Y} = A\,(X - \overline{X}) \qquad \ldots(6.12)$$

By definition,

$$\text{M.D. } (Y) \text{ about mean } = \frac{1}{n}\sum_{i=1}^{n} |(Y_i - \overline{Y})| = \frac{1}{n}\sum_{i=1}^{n} |A\ (X_i - \overline{X})| \qquad \text{[From (6.12)]}$$

$$= |A| \,.\, \frac{1}{n}\sum_{i=1}^{n} |X_i - \overline{X}| = |A| \,.\, [\text{M.D. } (X) \text{ about mean}]$$

Hence, we have the following result.

$$Y = AX + B \quad \Rightarrow \quad \text{M.D. } (Y) \text{ about mean} = |A| \times [\text{M.D. } (X) \text{ about mean}] \qquad \ldots(6.12a)$$

6·8·2. Short-cut Method of Computing Mean Deviation. For computing the mean deviation, first of all we have to calculate the average about which we want the mean deviation, by the methods discussed in the previous chapter. In case the average is a whole number, the method of computing mean deviation by formulae (6·10), (6·11) or (6·12) is quite convenient. But if the average comes out in fractions, this method becomes fairly tedious and time-consuming and requires lot of algebraic calculations. In such a case we compute the mean deviation by taking the deviations from an arbitrary point 'a', near the average value and applying some corrections as given below :

$$\text{M.D. (about Mean)} = \frac{1}{N}\left[\sum f\,|X - a| + (M - a)\left(\sum f_B - \sum f_A\right)\right] \qquad \ldots(6\cdot13)$$

where

M is the mean,

a is the arbitrary constant near the mean,

$\sum f_B$ is the sum of all the class frequencies before and including the mean value,

and $\sum f_A$ is the sum of all the class frequencies after the mean value.

Similarly, using the short cut method,

$$\text{M.D. (about median)} = \frac{1}{N}\left[\sum f|X - a| + (Md - a)\left(\sum f_B' - \sum f_A'\right)\right] \qquad \ldots(6\cdot13a)$$

where now, Md is the median, a is some arbitrary constant near the median, $\sum f_B'$ is the sum of the class frequencies before and including the median value, and $\sum f_A'$ is the sum of the class frequencies after the median value.

Remarks 1. Obviously,

$$\sum f_A + \sum f_B = N \qquad \ldots(6\cdot14)$$

$$\Rightarrow \quad \sum f_B = N - \sum f_A$$

$$\text{or} \quad \sum f_A = N - \sum f_B$$

$$\text{Similarly} \quad \sum f_B' = N - \sum f_A' \qquad \ldots(6\cdot14a)$$

2. The above formulae (6·13) and (6·13a) are true provided all the values of the variable which are above the average (M or Md) are also above 'a' and those which are below the average are also below 'a'.

The arbitrary constant '*a*' should be taken some arbitrary integral value near the average value, *i.e.*, it should be a value in the average class. ***The short cut method will not yield correct result if 'a' is taken outside the average class.***

6·8·3. Merits and Demerits of Mean Deviation

Merits : (*i*) Mean deviation is rigidly defined and is easy to understand and calculate.

(*ii*) Mean deviation is based on all the observations and is thus definitely a better measure of dispersion than the range and quartile deviation.

(*iii*) The averaging of the absolute deviations from an average irons out the irregularities in the distribution and thus mean deviation provides an accurate and true measure of dispersion.

(*iv*) As compared with standard deviation (discussed in next article § 6·9), it is less affected by extreme observations.

(*v*) Since mean deviation is based on the deviations about an average, it provides a better measure for comparison about the formation of different distributions.

Demerits. (*i*) The strongest objection against mean deviation is that while computing its value we take the *absolute* value of the deviations about an average and ignore the signs of the deviations.

(*ii*) The step of ignoring the signs of the deviations is mathematically unsound and illogical. It creates artificiality and renders mean deviation useless for further mathematical treatment. This drawback necessitates the requirement of another measure of variability which, in addition to being based on all the observations is also amenable to further algebraic manipulations.

(*iii*) It is not a satisfactory measure when taken about mode or while dealing with a fairly skewed distribution. As already pointed out, theoretically mean deviation gives the best result when it is calculated about median. But median is not a satisfactory measure when the distribution has great variations.

(*iv*) It is rarely used in sociological studies.

(*v*) It cannot be computed for distributions with open end classes.

(*vi*) Mean deviation tends to increase with the size of the sample though not proportionately and not so rapidly as range.

6·8·4. Uses. In spite of its mathematical drawbacks, mean deviation has found favour with economists and business statisticians because of its simplicity, accuracy and the fact that standard deviations (discussed in § 6·9) gives greater weightage to the deviations of extreme observations. Mean deviation is frequently useful in computing the distribution of personal wealth in a community or a nation since for this, extremely rich as well as extremely poor people should be taken into consideration. Regarding the practical utility of mean deviation as a measure of variability, it may be worthwhile to quote that in the studies relating to forecasting business cycles, the National Bureau of Economic Research has found that the mean deviation is most practical measure of dispersion to use for this purpose.

6·8·5. Relative Measures of Mean Deviation. The measures of mean deviation as defined in (6·10), (6·11) and (6·12) are absolute measures depending on the units of measurement. The relative measure of dispersion, called the *coefficient of mean deviation* is given by :

$$\text{Coefficient of M.D.} = \frac{\text{Mean Deviation}}{\text{Average about which it is calculated}} \qquad \ldots(6\cdot15)$$

$$\therefore \qquad \text{Coefficient of M.D. about mean} = \frac{\text{M.D.}}{\text{Mean}} \qquad \ldots(6\cdot15a)$$

and

$$\text{Coefficient of M.D. about median} = \frac{\text{M.D.}}{\text{Median}} \qquad \ldots(6\cdot15b)$$

The coefficients of mean deviation defined in (6·15), (6·15*a*) and (6·15*b*) are pure numbers independent of the units of measurement and are useful for comparing the variability of different distributions.

Example 6·5. *Calculate the mean deviation from mean for the following data.*

Class Interval	:	*2—4*	*4—6*	*6—8*	*8—10*
Frequency	:	*3*	*4*	*2*	*1*

Solution.

COMPUTATION OF MEAN AND M.D. FROM MEAN

Class	*Mid-Value* (X)	*Frequency* (f)	$d = X - 5$	fd	$\lvert X - \overline{X} \rvert = \lvert X - 5{\cdot}2 \rvert$	$f \lvert X - \overline{X} \rvert$	$f \lvert d \rvert$*
2—4	3	3	−2	−6	2·2	6·6	6
4—6	5	4	0	0	0·2	0·8	0
6—8	7	2	2	4	1·8	3·6	4
8—10	9	1	4	4	3·8	3·8	4
		$\sum f = 10$		$\sum fd = 2$		$\sum f \lvert X - \overline{X} \rvert = 14{\cdot}8$	$\sum f \lvert d \rvert = 14$

$$\overline{X} = A + \frac{\sum fd}{N} = 5 + \frac{2}{10} = 5{\cdot}2$$

$$\text{M.D. about mean} = \frac{1}{N} \sum f \lvert X - \overline{X} \rvert = \frac{14{\cdot}8}{10} = 1{\cdot}48$$

* Last column $f \lvert d \rvert$ is not required for this method. It is needed for the short-cut method given below.

Aliter. Short-cut Method. We can use the deviations from arbitrary point $a = 5$, directly to compute the M.D. from mean without computing the values $\lvert X - \overline{X} \rvert$. This is particularly useful when $\overline{X}$ is in fractions (decimals) in which case the usual formula is quite laborious. For this we need the last column $f \lvert d \rvert$. [*c.f.* (6·13), § 6·8·2]. Using the formula (6·13), we get

$$\text{M.D. about mean} = \frac{1}{N} \left[\sum f \lvert d \rvert + (\overline{X} - a) \left(\sum f_B - \sum f_A \right) \right]$$

where

$\sum f_B$ = Sum of all the class frequencies before and including the mean class *i.e.*, the class in which mean lies.

Here mean is 5·2 and it lies in the class 4—6.

$\therefore \quad \sum f_B = 4 + 3 = 7$

$\sum f_A$ = Sum of all the class frequencies after the mean class = 2 + 1 = 3

or $\quad \sum f_A = N - \sum f_B = 10 - 7 = 3.$

$$\therefore \quad \text{M.D. about mean} = \frac{1}{10} \left[14 + (5{\cdot}2 - 5) \times (7 - 3) \right] = \frac{14 + 0{\cdot}8}{10} = \frac{14{\cdot}8}{10} = 1{\cdot}48.$$

Remark. The value obtained by the short-cut method coincides with the value obtained by the direct method and rightly so because the arbitrary point $A = 5$ is near the mean value 5·2 (*c.f.* Remark 2, § 6·8·2).

Example 6·6. (*a*) *Find the Mean Deviation from the Mean for the following data* :

Class Interval :	*0—10*	*10—20*	*20—30*	*30—40*	*40—50*	*50—60*	*60—70*
Frequency	*8*	*12*	*10*	*8*	*3*	*2*	*7*

[*C.A.* (*Foundation*), *Nov. 1996*]

(*b*) *Also find the mean deviation about median.*

(*c*) *Compare the results obtained in* (*a*) *and* (*b*).

Solution.

CALCULATIONS FOR M.D. ABOUT MEAN AND MEDIAN

Class Interval	*Mid-value* (X)	*Frequency* (f)	*Less than c.f.*	fX	$\lvert X - \overline{X} \rvert = \lvert X - 29 \rvert$	$f \lvert X - \overline{X} \rvert$	$\lvert X - Md \rvert = \lvert X - 22 \rvert$	$f \lvert X - Md \rvert$
0—10	5	8	8	40	24	192	17	136
10—20	15	12	20	180	14	168	7	84
20—30	25	10	30	250	4	40	3	30
30—40	35	8	38	280	6	48	13	104
40—50	45	3	41	135	16	48	23	69
50—60	55	2	43	110	26	52	33	66
60—70	65	7	50	455	36	252	43	301
Total		$N = 50$		$\sum fX = 1{,}450$		$\sum f \lvert X - \overline{X} \rvert = 800$		$\sum f \lvert X - Md \rvert = 790$

(a). Mean $(\overline{X}) = \frac{1}{N}\Sigma fX = \frac{1,450}{50} = 29.$

Mean Deviation about mean $= \frac{1}{N}\Sigma f\,|X - \overline{X}| = \frac{800}{50} = 16.$

(b) (N/2) = (50/2)= 25. The c.f. just greate than 25 is 30. Hence, the corresponding class 20—30 is the median class. Using the median formula, we get

$$Md = l + \frac{h}{f}\left(\frac{N}{2} - C\right) = 20 + \frac{10}{25}(25 - 20) = 20 + 2 = 22$$

∴ Mean Deviation about median $= \frac{1}{N}\Sigma f\,|X - Md| = \frac{790}{50} = 15{\cdot}8$

(c) From (a) and (b), we observe that :

M.D. about median < M.D. about mean.

In fact, we have the following general result :

"Mean deviation is least when taken about median."

Example 6·7. *Calculate mean deviation from the median for the following data :*

Marks less than :	*80*	*70*	*60*	*50*	*40*	*30*	*20*	*10*
No. of Students :	*100*	*90*	*80*	*60*	*32*	*20*	*13*	*5*

Solution. First of all we shall convert the given cumulative frequency distribution table into ordinary frequency distribution as given in the following table.

COMPUTATION OF M.D. FROM MEDIAN

Marks	*c.f.*	*Frequency (f)*	*Mid-value of class (X)*	$\|X - Md\|$	$f\|X - Md\|$
0—10	5	5	5	41·43	207·15
10—20	13	13 − 5 = 8	15	31·43	251·44
20—30	20	20 − 13 = 7	25	21·43	150·00
30—40	32	32 − 20 = 12	35	11·43	137·16
40—50	60	60 − 32 = 28	45	1·43	40·04
50—60	80	80 − 60 = 20	55	8·57	171·14
60—70	90	90 − 80 = 10	65	18·57	185·70
70—80	100	100 − 90 = 10	75	28·57	285·70
		$N = \Sigma f = 100$			$\Sigma f\|X - Md\| = 1428{\cdot}6$

Here N/2 = 50. Since the *c.f.* just greater than 50 is 60, the corresponding class 40—50 is the median class.

∴ $$Md = l + \frac{h}{f}\left(\frac{N}{2} - C\right) = 40 + \frac{10}{28}(50 - 32) = 40 + 6{\cdot}43 = 46{\cdot}43.$$

∴ $$\text{M.D. about } Md = \frac{1}{N}\Sigma f\,|X - Md| = \frac{1428{\cdot}6}{100} = 14{\cdot}286 \simeq 14{\cdot}29.$$

Aliter. Since median value comes out to be in fractions, we can do the above question conveniently by the short-cut method *i.e.*, by taking the deviations from any arbitrary point a = 45, (say), lying in the median class.

MEAN DEVIATION BY SHORT-CUT METHOD

Marks (X)	*f*	$d = X - 45$	$\|d\|$	$f\|d\|$
5	5	−40	40	200
15	8	−30	30	240
25	7	−20	20	140
35	12	−10	10	120
45	28	0	0	0
55	20	10	10	200
65	10	20	20	200
75	10	30	30	300
	$\Sigma f = 100$			$\Sigma f\|d\| = 1400$

Using formula (6·13*a*), we get

$$\text{M.D. about } Md = \frac{1}{N}\left[\sum f|d| + (Md - a)\,(\sum f_B' - \sum f_A'\right]$$

where

$$\sum f_B' = \text{Sum of the frequencies before and including the median value } viz., \ 46{\cdot}3.$$

$$= 5 + 8 + 7 + 12 + 28 = 60$$

$$\sum f_A' = N - \sum f_B' = 100 - 60 = 40$$

$$\therefore \quad \text{M.D. about } Md = \left[\frac{1400 + (46{\cdot}43 - 45)\,(60 - 40)}{100}\right]\left[\frac{1400 + 1{\cdot}43 \times 20}{100}\right]$$

$$= \left[\frac{1400 + 28{\cdot}6}{100}\right] = \frac{1428{\cdot}6}{100} = 14{\cdot}286 \simeq 14{\cdot}29.$$

Remark. As in the last question, the values of M.D. obtained by the direct method and the short-cut method are same, since the *arbitrary value 'a' is taken in the median class.*

Example. 6.8. *If* $2x_i + 3y_i = 5;\ i = 1, 2, \ldots, n$ *and mean deviation of* $x_1, x_2, \ldots, x_n$ *about their mean is 12, find the mean deviation of* $y_1, y_2, \ldots, y_n$ *about their mean.* [*I.C.W.A.* (*Foundation*), *Dec. 2006*]

Solution. M.D. (X) about mean = 12 (Given). ...(*)

Also $\qquad 2x_i + 3y_i = 5 \;\Rightarrow\; y_i = -\frac{2}{3}x_i - \frac{5}{3};\ i = 1, 2, \ldots, n$ ...(**)

We know that if

$Y = AX + B$, then M.D. of (Y) about mean = $|A| \times$ [M.D. (X) about mean], [From 6.12*a*]

where $|A|$ is the modulus value of A.

$\therefore$ M.D. (Y) about mean = $\left|-\frac{2}{3}\right| \times$ [M.D. (X) about mean] $= \frac{2}{3} \times 12 = 8$ [From (*)]

Example 6·9. *Mean deviation may be calculated from the arithmetic mean or the median or the mode. Which of these three measures is the minimum ?*

Five towns A, B, C, D and E lie in that order along a road. The distances in kilometres of the towns as measured from A are A —0, B—5, C—9, D—16, E—20, A new college is to be established at one of these 5 places, and the number of students who would join the college are A—39, B—911, C—46, D—193, and E—716. The criterion for choosing the location is that the total distance travelled by the students, as measured in student-kilometres should be a minimum. (Thus if the college is located at D, 46 students from C will travel in all 46 × 7 = 322 student-kilometres). Where should the college be located ? Justify your result.

Solution. Mean deviation calculated from the median is the minimum.

Let X denote the distance (in kms.) as measured from the town A. Then the frequency distribution of the distances covered by the students in going to the college is as given in the adjoining table.

Town	*Distance from town A* (X)	*No. of students* (f)	*Less than c.f.*
A	0	39	39
B	5	911	950
C	9	46	996
D	16	193	1189
E	20	716	$N = 1905$

We are given that the criterion for choosing the location of the college is that the total distance travelled by the students, as measured in student-kilometres should be minimum. Since mean deviation is minimum when calculated from median, the total distance travelled by the students, as measured in student-kilometres will be minimum at the point X = *Median*, of the frequency distribution of X.

Here (N/2) = (1905/2) = 952·5. The *c.f.* just greater than 952·5 is 996. Hence, the corresponding value of X = 9, is the median. Since X = 9, corresponds to the town C, the college should be located at the town C.

EXERCISE 6·2

1. What do you mean by 'mean deviation'. Discuss its relative merits over range and quartile deviation as a measure of dispersion. Also point out its limitations.

2. Calculate mean deviation about A.M. from the following :

Value (x)	:	10	11	12	13
Frequency (f)	:	3	12	18	12

Ans. A.M. = 11·87 ; M.D. = 0·71.

3. Calculate the mean deviation about meadian of the series :

x	2·5	3·5	4·5	5·5	6·5	7·5	8·5	9·5	10·5
f	2	3	5	6	6	4	6	4	14

Ans. M.D. (about median) = 2·22.

4. Compute the quartile deviation and mean deviation from median for the following data.

Height in inches	*No. of students*	*Height in inches*	*No. of students*
58	15	63	22
59	20	64	22
60	32	65	10
61	35	66	8
62	33	—	—

Ans. Q.D. = 1·5 ; M.D. (about median) = 1·73.

5. With median as the base, calculate the mean deviation and compare the variability of the two series A and B.

Series A :	3484	4572	4124	3682	5624	4388	3680	4308
Series B :	487	508	620	382	408	266	186	218

Ans. Series A : Md = 4216 ; M.D. = 490·25 ; Coeff. of M.D. = 0·116;
Series B : Md = 395 ; M.D. = 121·38 ; Coeff. of M.D. = 0·307. Series B is more variable.

6. Compare the dispersion of the following series by using the co-efficient of mean deviation.

Age (years)	:	16	17	18	19	20	21	22	23	24	Total
No. of boys	:	4	5	7	12	20	13	5	0	4	70
No. of girls	:	2	0	4	8	15	10	6	3	2	50

Ans. Coeff. of M.D. about median (boys) = 0·0685 ; Coeff. of M.D. about median (girls) = 0·0630.

7. Calculate the mean deviation from the mean for the following data :

Marks	:	0—10	10—20	20—30	30—40	40—50	50—60	60—70
No. of Students	:	6	5	8	15	7	6	3

Ans. Mean = 33·4 ; M.D. about mean = 13·184. [*C.A. (Foundation), May 1999*]

8. (*a*) Mean deviation may be calculated from the arithmetic mean or the median or the mode ? Which of these three measures is the minimum ?

(*b*) Find out mean deviation and its coefficient from median from the following series :

Size of items	:	4	6	8	10	12	14	16
Frequency	:	2	1	3	6	4	3	1

Ans. 2·4 ; 0·24

9. Calculate the mean deviation about the mean for the following data :

x	:	5	15	25	35	45	55	65
f	:	8	12	10	8	3	2	7

[*C.A. (Foundation), May 2001*]

Also find the M.D. about median and comment on the results obtained in (*a*) and (*b*).

Ans. Mean = 29; M.D. about mean = 16. ; Median = 22 ; M.D. about median = 15·8.

10. Calculate mean deviation from median from the following data :

Class interval	*(f)*	*Class interval*	*(f)*
20—25	6	50—55	10
25—30	12	55—60	8
30—40	17	60—70	5
40—45	30	70—80	2
45—50	10		

Also calculate coefficient of mean deviation.

Ans. 8·75 ; 0·206.

11. The following distribution gives the difference in age between husband and wife in a particular community :

Difference in years :	0—5	5—10	10—15	15—20	20—25	25—30	30—35	35—40
Frequency :	449	705	507	281	109	52	16	4

Calculate mean deviation about median from these data. What light does it throw on the social conditions of a community ?

Ans. M.D. about median = 5·24.

12. Find the median and mean deviation of the following data :

Size :	0—10	10—20	20—30	30—40	40—50	50—60	60—70
Frequency :	7	12	18	25	16	14	8

Ans. Median = 35·2 ; M.D. = 13·148. [*Mysore Univ. B.Com., 1998*]

13. Calculate the value of coefficient of mean deviation (from median) of the following data :

Marks	*No. of Students*	*Marks*	*No. of Students*
10—20	2	50—60	25
20—30	6	60—70	20
30—40	12	70—80	10
40—50	18	80—90	7

Ans. Median = 54·8 ; M.D. about median = 12·95; Coefficient of M.D. = 0·2363.

14. Compute the mean deviation from the median and from mean for the following distribution of the scores of 50 college students.

Score :	140—150	150—160	160—170	170—180	180—190	190—200
Frequency :	4	6	10	10	9	3

Ans. 10·24 ; 10·56.

15. Calculate Mean Deviation from Median from the following data :

Wages in Rs. (Mid-value) :	125	175	225	275	325
No. of persons :	3	8	21	6	2

Ans. Median = 221·43 ; M.D. (Median) = 31·607.

6·9. STANDARD DEVIATION

Standard deviation, usually denoted by the letter σ (small sigma) of the Greek alphabet was first suggested by Karl Pearson as a measure of dispersion in 1893. It is defined as the positive square root of the arithmetic mean of the squares of the deviations of the given observations from their arithmetic mean. Thus if $X_1, X_2, \ldots, X_n$ is a set of n observations then its standard deviation is given by :

$$\sigma = \sqrt{\frac{1}{n}\Sigma (X - \overline{X})^2} \qquad \ldots(6\cdot16)$$

where $\overline{X} = \frac{1}{n}\Sigma X$, is the arithmetic mean of the given values. ...(6·16*a*)

Steps for Computation of Standard Deviation

1. Compute the arithmetic mean $\overline{X}$ by the formula (6·16*a*).

2. Compute the deviation $(X - \overline{X})$ of each observation from arithmetic mean *i.e.*, obtain

$$X_1 - \overline{X},\ X_2 - \overline{X}, \ldots, X_n - \overline{X}.$$

3. Square each of the deviations obtained in step 2 *i.e.*, compute $(X_1 - \overline{X})^2, (X_2 - \overline{X})^2, ..., (X_n - \overline{X})^2$.

4. Find the sum of the squared deviations in step 3 given by :

$$\Sigma (X - \overline{X})^2 = (X_1 - \overline{X})^2 + (X_2 - \overline{X})^2 + \ldots + (X_n - \overline{X})^2.$$

5. Divide this sum in step 4 by n to obtain $\frac{1}{n} \Sigma (X - \overline{X})^2$.

6. Take the positive square root of the value obtained in step 5.

7. The resulting value gives the standard deviation of the distribution.

In case of frequency distribution, the standard deviation is given by :

$$\sigma = \sqrt{\frac{1}{N} \Sigma f(X - \overline{X})^2} \qquad \ldots(6·17)$$

where X is the value of the variable or the mid-value of the class (in case of grouped or continuous frequency distributions) ; f is the corresponding frequency of the value X ; $N = \Sigma f$, is the total frequency and

$$\overline{X} = \frac{1}{N} \Sigma fX \qquad \ldots(6·17a)$$

is the arithmetic mean of the distribution.

Steps for Computation of Standard Deviation in case of Frequency Distribution

1. Compute $\overline{X}$ by the formula (6·17*a*) or the usual step deviation formula discussed in Chapter 5.

2. Compute deviations $(X - \overline{X})$ from the mean for each value of the variable X.

3. Obtain the squares of the deviations obtained in step 2 *i.e.*, compute $(X - \overline{X})^2$.

4. Multiply each of the squared deviations obtained in step 3 by the corresponding frequency to get $f(X - \overline{X})^2$.

5. Find the sum of the values obtained in step 4 to get $\Sigma f(X - \overline{X})^2$.

6. Divide the sum obtained in step 5 by $N = \Sigma f$, the total frequency.

7. The positive square root of the value obtained in step 6 gives the standard deviation of the distribution.

Remarks 1. It may be pointed out that although mean deviation could be calculated about any one of the averages (*M, Md* or *Mo*), *standard deviation is always computed about arithmetic mean.*

2. To be more precise, the standard deviation of the variable X will be denoted by σ_x. This notation will be useful when we have to deal with the standard deviation of two or more variables.

3. Standard deviation abbreviated as S.D. or *s.d.* is always taken as the *positive* square root in (6·16) or (6·17).

4. The value of *s.d.* depends on the numerical value of the deviations $(X_1 - \overline{X}), (X_2 - \overline{X}), \ldots, (X_n - \overline{X})$. Thus the value of σ will be greater if the values of X are scattered widely away from the mean. Thus a small value of σ will imply that the distribution is homogeneous and a large value of σ will imply that it is heterogeneous. In particular *s.d.* is zero if each of the deviations is zero *i.e.*, $\sigma = 0$ if and only if,

$$X_1 - \overline{X} = 0,\ X_2 - \overline{X} = 0, \ldots, X_n - \overline{X} = 0 \quad \Rightarrow \quad X_1 = X_2 = X_3 = \ldots = X_n = \overline{X},$$

which is the case if the variable assumes the constant value.

Thus, $\sigma = 0$ if and only if, $\quad X_1 = X_2 = X_3 = \ldots = X_n = k$ (constant) $\qquad \ldots(6·17b)$

In other words, $\sigma = 0$ *if and only if all the observations are equal.*

As an illustration, let us suppose that the variable X takes the same constant values, say, 6, 6, 6, 6, 6. Then

$$\overline{X} = \frac{1}{5} \Sigma X = \frac{6+6+6+6+6}{5} = \frac{30}{5} = 6$$

X	6	6	6	6	6
$X - \overline{X} = X - 6$	0	0	0	0	0

$$\therefore \qquad \text{S.D.}\ (\sigma) = \sqrt{\frac{1}{5} \Sigma (X - \overline{X})^2} = \sqrt{\frac{1}{5}(0)} = 0$$

6·9·1. Mathematical Properties of Standard Deviation. Standard deviation possesses a number of interesting and important mathematical properties which are given below.

1. *Standard deviation is independent of change of origin but not of scale.*

If $d = X - A$, then $\sigma_x = \sigma_d$

But if $d = \dfrac{X-A}{h}$, $h > 0$, then $\sigma_x = h\ \sigma_d$

2. *Standard deviation is the minimum value of the root mean square deviation* (§ 6·9·3)

3. *S.D. ≤ Range* *i.e.*, $\sigma \le X_{max} - X_{min}$

[For Proof, see Remark to § 6·9·2.]

4. *Standard deviation is suitable for further mathematical treatment*. If we know the sizes, means and standard deviations of two or more groups, then we can obtain the standard deviation of the group obtained on combining all the groups. [For details see § 6·10]

5. The standard deviation of the first n natural numbers *viz.*, 1, 2, 3, ..., n is $\sqrt{(n^2-1)/12}$

[For Proof, see Example 6·23(*a*).]

6. The Empirical Rule. For a symmetrical bell shaped distribution, we have *approximately* the following area properties.

(*i*) 68% of the observations lie in the range : Mean ± 1·σ.

(*ii*) 95% of the observations lie in the range : Mean ± 2.σ.

(*iii*) 99% of the observations lie in the range : Mean ± 3.σ..

7. The approximate relationship between quartile deviation (Q.D.), mean deviation (M.D.) and standard deviation (σ) is :

$$\text{Q.D.} \simeq \frac{2}{3}\sigma \quad \text{and} \quad \text{M.D.} \simeq \frac{4}{5}\sigma \quad \Rightarrow \quad \text{Q.D. : M.D. : S.D. :: } 10 : 12 : 15$$

8. For any discrete distribution, standard deviation is not less than mean deviation about mean *i.e.*,

S.D. (σ) ≥ Mean Deviation about mean.

6·9·2. Merits and Demerits of Standard Deviation

Merits. Standard deviation is by far the most important and widely used measure of dispersion. It is rigidly defined and based on all the observations. The squaring of the deviations $(X - \overline{X})$ removes the drawback of ignoring the signs of deviations in computing the mean diviation. This step renders it suitable for further mathematical treatment. The variance of the pooled (combined) series is given by formula (6·30) in § 6·10.

Moreover, of all the measures of dispersion, standard deviation is affected least by fluctuations of sampling.

Thus, we see that standard deviation satisfies almost all the properties laid down for an ideal measure of dispersion except for the general nature of extracting the square root which is not readily comprehensible for a non-mathematical person. It may also be pointed out that standard deviation gives greater weight to extreme values and as such has not found favour with economists or businessmen who are more interested in the results of the modal class. Taking into consideration the pros and cons and also the wide applications of standard deviation in statistical theory, such as in skewness, kurtosis, correlation and regression analysis, sampling theory and tests of significance, we may regard standard deviation as the best and the most powerful measure of dispersion.

Remark. Since $X - \overline{X} \le R$ (Range), for all values of X *viz.*, $X_1, X_2, \ldots, X_n$, we get

$$\sigma^2 = \frac{1}{N}\Sigma f(X-\overline{X})^2$$

$$= \frac{1}{N}\left[f_1(X_1-\overline{X})^2 + f_2(X_2-\overline{X})^2 + \ldots + f_n(X_n-\overline{X})^2\right] \le \frac{1}{N}\left[f_1 R^2 + f_2R^2 + \ldots + f_n R^2\right]$$

$$(\because X_1 - \overline{X} \le R,\ X_2 - \overline{X} \le R, \ldots, X_n - \overline{X} \le R)$$

$$\therefore \quad \sigma^2 \le \frac{1}{N} \cdot R^2 (f_1 + f_2 + \ldots + f_n) = \frac{1}{N} R^2 . N = R^2$$

$$\Rightarrow \quad \sigma^2 \le R^2 \quad \Rightarrow \quad \sigma \le R \quad \Rightarrow \quad s.d. \le \text{Range.}$$

6·9·3. Variance and Mean Square Deviation. *Variance is the square of the standard deviation and is denoted by* σ^2. For a frequency distribution. variance is given by :

$$\sigma^2 = \frac{1}{N} \Sigma f(X - \bar{X})^2 \qquad \ldots(6·18)$$

where the symbols have already been explained in (6·17).

The *mean square deviation*, usually denoted by s^2 is defined as

$$s^2 = \frac{1}{N} \Sigma f(X - A \qquad \ldots(6·19)$$

where A is any arbitrary number.

The square root of the mean square deviation is called *root mean square deviation* and given by :

$$s = \sqrt{\frac{1}{N} \Sigma f (X - A)^2} \qquad \ldots(6·20)$$

Relation between σ^2 and s^2. We have

$$s^2 \ge \sigma^2 \quad \Rightarrow \quad s \ge \sigma \qquad \ldots(6·21)$$

In other words, *mean square deviation is not less than the variance or the root mean square deviation is not less than the standard deviation.*

The sign of equality will hold in (6·21) *i.e.,* $s^2 = \sigma^2$ if and only if $\bar{X} = A$ ...(6·22)

Thus, s^2 will be least when $\bar{X} = A$. Hence, *mean square deviation or equivalently root mean square deviation is least when deviations are taken from the arithmetic mean and variance (standard deviation) is the minimum value of mean square deviation (root mean square deviation).*

Important Remark

The variance σ^2 is in squared units. For example, for the distribution of heights (in inches) of a group of individuals, σ^2 is expressed in (inches)^2, a concept which is difficult to visualise and interpret. To overcome this problem, we try to measure the variation in the sample data in the same units as those of the original measurements by calculating the standard deviation (S.D.), which is defined as the positive square root of variance. Hence, in practice, we use standard deviation, rather than variance as the basic unit of variability.

6·9·4. Different Formulae for Calculating Variance. By definition, the variance of the random variable X denoted by σ^2 or more precisely by σ_x^2, is given by

$$\sigma_x^2 = \frac{1}{N} \Sigma f (X - \bar{X})^2 \qquad \ldots(6·23)$$

where $\Sigma f = N$, is the total frequency.

If X is not a whole number but comes out to be in fractions, the computation of σ_x^2 by the above formula becomes very cumbersome and time-consuming. In order to overcome this difficulty we shall develop different versions of the formula (6·23) which reduce the arithmetical calculations to a great extent and are very useful for numerical computation of standard deviation.

Formula 1. $$\sigma_x^2 = \frac{1}{N} \Sigma f X^2 - \bar{X}^2 = \frac{1}{N} \Sigma f X^2 - \left(\frac{1}{N} \Sigma f X\right)^2 \qquad \ldots(6·24)$$

Formula 2. If $d = X - A$, where A is arbitrary constant, then

$$\sigma_x^2 = \sigma_d^2 = \frac{1}{N} \Sigma f d^2 - \left(\frac{1}{N} \Sigma f d\right)^2 \qquad \ldots(6·25)$$

(6·24) is a much convenient form to use than the formula (6·23). But if the values of X and f are large, the computation of fX, fX^2 is quite time- consuming. In that case we use the step-deviation method in which we take the deviations of the given values of X from any arbitrary point A. Generally, 'A' is taken to be a value lying in the middle part of the distribution, although the formula (6.25) holds for any value of A.

(6·25) leads to the following important conclusion :

"The variance and consequently the standard deviation of a distribution is independent of the change of origin".

Thus, if we add (subtract) a constant to (from) each observation of the series, its variance remains same.

Mathematically this means that :

$$\text{Var}(X+a) = \text{Var}(X-b) = \text{Var } X, \text{ where } a \text{ and } b \text{ are constants.} \quad \ldots(6{\cdot}25a)$$

Formula 3. If we change the origin and scale in X *i.e.*, if we take :

$$d = \frac{X-A}{h};\ h > 0, \text{ then}$$

$$\sigma_x^2 = h^2 \sigma_d^2 = h^2 \left[\frac{1}{N}\Sigma fd^2 - \left(\frac{1}{N}(\Sigma fd)^2\right)\right] \quad \ldots(6{\cdot}26)$$

In case of grouped or continuous frequency distribution, it is convenient to change the scale also. Thus, if h is the magnitude of the class interval (or if h is the common factor in the values of the variable X), then we may take

$$d = \frac{X-A}{h},\ h > 0 \quad \text{and} \quad \text{use } (6{\cdot}26)$$

Remarks 1. Formula (6.26) also leads to the following result.

$$\text{Var}(aX) = a^2\,\text{Var}(X) \quad \Rightarrow \quad \text{S.D.}(aX) = a\,\text{S.D.}(X) \quad \ldots(6{\cdot}26a)$$

where Var (X) denotes the variance of X and a is a constant.

This shows that *variance* (or *s.d.*) *is not independent of change of scale.*

Combining the results obtained in (6·25) and (6·26) we conclude that :

"Variance or standard deviation is independent of the change of origin but not of the scale".

2. For numerical problems, a somewhat more convenient form of (6·26) may be used. Rewriting (6·26), we get

$$\sigma_x^2 = \frac{h^2}{N^2}\left[N\Sigma fd^2 - (\Sigma fd)^2\right] \Rightarrow \sigma_x = \frac{h}{N}\left[N\Sigma fd^2 - (\Sigma fd)^2\right]^{1/2} \Rightarrow \sigma_x = h\,.\,\sigma_d \quad \ldots(6{\cdot}27)$$

3. Different Formulae for Variance for Raw Data

If $x_1, x_2, \ldots, x_n$ are the n observations, then

$$\sigma_x^2 = \frac{1}{n}\Sigma(X-\overline{X})^2 \quad \ldots(6{\cdot}28)$$

$$\Rightarrow \quad \sigma_x^2 = \frac{1}{n}\Sigma X^2 - \overline{X}^{\,2} = \frac{1}{n}\Sigma X^2 - \left(\frac{1}{n}\Sigma X\right)^2 \quad [\text{Taking } f = 1 \text{ and } N = n \text{ in } (6{\cdot}24)] \quad \ldots(6{\cdot}28a)$$

4. If we are given $\overline{X}$ and σ_x^2, then we can obtain the values of ΣX and ΣX^2 as discussed below.

From (6·28*a*), we have

$$\overline{X} = \frac{1}{n}\Sigma X \quad \Rightarrow \quad \Sigma X = n\overline{X} \quad \ldots(6{\cdot}28b)$$

and

$$\sigma_x^2 = \frac{1}{n}\Sigma X^2 - \overline{X}^2 \quad \Rightarrow \quad \Sigma X^2 = n(\sigma_x^2 + \overline{X}^2) \quad \ldots(6{\cdot}28c)$$

Formulae (6·28*b*) and (6·28*c*) are very useful when we are given the values of the mean and standard deviation (or variance) and later on it is found that one or more of the observations are wrong and it is required to compute the mean and variance after replacing the wrong values by correct values or after deleting the wrong values. For illustrations, see Examples 6·24 to 6·26.

Example 6·10. *Calculate the standard deviation of the following observations on a certain variable :*

240·12, 240·13, 240·15, 240·12, 240·17,
240·15, 240·17, 240·16, 240·22, 240·21

Solution.

$$\overline{X} = \frac{\Sigma X}{10} = \frac{2401 \cdot 60}{10} = 240 \cdot 16$$

$$\sigma^2 = \frac{1}{n}\Sigma(X - \overline{X})^2 = \frac{0 \cdot 0106}{10} = 0 \cdot 00106$$

$$\therefore \; s.d. \,(\sigma) = (0 \cdot 00106)^{\frac{1}{2}}$$
$$= \text{Antilog}\left[\tfrac{1}{2}\log(0 \cdot 00106)\right]$$
$$= \text{Antilog}\left[\tfrac{1}{2}(\bar{3} \cdot 0253)\right]$$
$$= \text{Antilog}\left[\tfrac{1}{2}(-3 + 0 \cdot 0253)\right]$$
$$= \text{Antilog}\left[\tfrac{1}{2}(-2 \cdot 9747)\right]$$
$$= \text{Antilog}(-1 \cdot 4173) = \text{Antilog}(\bar{2} \cdot 5127)$$
$$= 0 \cdot 03256$$

COMPUTATION OF STANDARD DEVIATION

X	$X - \overline{X}$	$(X - \overline{X})^2$
240·12	− 0·04	0·0016
240·13	− 0·03	0·0009
240·15	− 0·01	0·0001
240·12	− 0·04	0·0016
240·17	0·01	0·0001
240·15	− 0·01	0·0001
240·17	0·01	0·0001
240·16	0·00	0
240·22	0·06	0·0036
240·21	0·05	0·0025
$\Sigma X = 2401 \cdot 60$	$\Sigma(X - \overline{X}) = 0$	$\Sigma(X - \overline{X})^2 = 0 \cdot 0106$

Example 6·11. *Complete a table showing the frequencies with which words of different numbers of letters occur in the extract reproduced below (omitting punctuation marks) treating as the variable the number of letters in each word, and obtain the mean and standard deviation of the distribution :*

"Her eyes were blue : blue as autumn distance — blue as the blue we see, between the retreating mouldings of hills and woody slopes on a sunny September morning : a misty and shady blue, that had no beginning or surface, and was looked into rather than at."

Solution. Here we take the variable (X) as the number of letters in each word in the extract given above. We find that in the extract given above there are words with number of letters ranging from 1 to 10. Hence, the variable X takes the values from 1 to 10. The frequency distribution is easily obtained by using 'tally marks' as given in the following Table.

No. of letters in a word (X)	*Frequency (f)*	$d = X - A$ $= X - 6$	*fd*	*fd*^{2}
1	2	−5	−10	50
2	8	− 4	−32	128
3	9	−3	−27	81
4	10	−2	−20	40
5	5	−1	−5	5
6	4	0	0	0
7	3	1	3	3
8	1	2	2	4
9	3	3	9	27
10	1	4	4	16
Total	$N = \Sigma f = 46$		$\Sigma fd = -76$	$\Sigma fd^2 = 354$

$$\text{Mean} = A + \frac{\Sigma fd}{N} = 6 + \left(\frac{-76}{46}\right)$$
$$= 6 - 1 \cdot 65 = 4 \cdot 35$$

$$\sigma^2 = \frac{1}{N}\Sigma fd^2 - \left(\frac{1}{N}\Sigma fd\right)^2$$
$$= \frac{354}{46} - (-1 \cdot 65)^2$$
$$= 7 \cdot 6956 - 2 \cdot 7225 = 4 \cdot 9731$$
$$\Rightarrow \quad \sigma = \sqrt{4 \cdot 9731} = 2 \cdot 23.$$

Example 6·12. *Calculate the mean and standard deviation from the following data :*

Value :	*90—99*	*80—89*	*70—79*	*60—69*	*50—59*	*40—49*	*30—39*
Frequency :	2	*12*	22	20	*14*	*4*	*1*

Solution.

CALCULATIONS FOR MEAN AND S.D.

Class	*Mid-value* (x)	*Frequency* (f)	$d = \frac{x - 64 \cdot 5}{10}$	*fd*	*fd*²
90—99	94·5	2	3	6	18
80—89	84·5	12	2	24	48
70—79	74·5	22	1	22	22
60—69	64·5	20	0	0	0
50—59	54·5	14	−1	−14	14
40—49	44·5	4	−2	− 8	16
30—39	34·5	1	−3	−3	9
Total		$N = 75$		$\Sigma fd = 27$	$\Sigma fd^2 = 127$

$$\text{Mean } = A + \frac{h \Sigma fd}{N} = 64 \cdot 5 + \frac{10 \times 27}{75} = 64 \cdot 5 + 3 \cdot 6 = 68 \cdot 1$$

$$\text{S.D. } = h \cdot \sqrt{\frac{\Sigma fd^2}{N} - \left(\frac{\Sigma fd}{N}\right)^2} = 10 \times \sqrt{\frac{127}{75} - \left(\frac{27}{75}\right)^2} = 10 \times \sqrt{1 \cdot 6933 - 0 \cdot 1296}$$

$$= 10 \times \sqrt{1 \cdot 5637} = 10 \times 1 \cdot 2505 = 12 \cdot 505.$$

Example 6·13. *The arithmetic mean and the standard deviation of a set of 9 items are 43 and 5 respectively. If an item of value 63 is added to the set, find the mean and standard deviation of 10 items.*

[*Delhi Univ. B.A.* (*Econ. Hons.*), *2006*]

Solution. We are given : $n = 9,\ \bar{x} = 43$ and $\sigma = 5$.

$$\bar{x} = \frac{\Sigma x}{n} \quad \Rightarrow \quad \Sigma x = n\bar{x} = 9 \times 43 = 387 \qquad \ldots(i)$$

Also $$\sigma^2 = \frac{\Sigma x^2}{n} - (\bar{x})^2 \quad \Rightarrow \quad \Sigma x^2 = n(\sigma^2 + \bar{x}^2)$$

$$\therefore \quad \Sigma x^2 = 9(25 + 43^2) = 9(25 + 1849) = 9 \times 1874 = 16866 \qquad \ldots(ii)$$

If a new item 63 is added, then number of items becomes 10.

$$\text{New } (\Sigma x) = \Sigma x + 63 = 387 + 63 = 450 \qquad \text{[From } (i)]$$

$$\therefore \quad \text{New mean } = \frac{450}{10} = 45$$

$$\text{New } (\Sigma x^2) = \Sigma x^2 + 63^2 = 16866 + 3969 = 20835$$

$$\text{New } s.d. = \sqrt{\frac{\text{New } (\Sigma x^2)}{10} - (\text{New mean})^2} = \sqrt{\frac{20835}{10} - (45)^2}$$

$$= \sqrt{2083 \cdot 5 - 2025} = \sqrt{58 \cdot 5} = 7 \cdot 65.$$

Example 6·14. *Twenty passengers were found ticketless on a bus. The sum of squares and the S.D. of the amount found in their pockets were Rs. 2,000·00 and Rs. 6·00 respectively. If the total fine imposed on these passengers is equal to the total amount recovered from them and fine imposed is uniform, what is the amount each one of them has to pay as fine ? What difficulties do you visualize if such a system of penalty were imposed ?*

[*Delhi Univ. B.A.* (*Econ.*)*Hons.*, *1993*]

Solution. Let x_i, $i = 1, 2, \ldots, 20$ be the amount (in Rs.) found in the pocket of the *i*th passenger. Then we are given :

$$n = 20, \quad \sum_{i=1}^{20} x_i^2 = \text{Rs. } 2{,}000 \quad \text{and} \quad \text{s.d.}(\sigma) = \text{Rs. } 6 \qquad \ldots(i)$$

The total fine imposed on the ticketless passengers is given to be equal to the total amount recovered from them.

$\therefore$ Total fine imposed on the 20 passengers $= \sum_{i=1}^{20} x_i$.

Further, since the fine imposed is uniform among all the 20 passengers,

$\therefore$ Fine to be paid by each passenger $= \frac{1}{20} \sum_{i=1}^{n} x_i = \bar{x}$ ... (*ii*)

We have : $\sigma^2 = \frac{1}{n}\Sigma x_i^2 - \bar{x}^2 \quad \Rightarrow \quad \bar{x}^2 = \frac{1}{20}\Sigma x_i^2 - \sigma^2$

$\therefore \quad \bar{x}^2 = \text{Rs.}^2 \left(\frac{2000}{20} - 6^2\right) = \text{Rs.}^2 (100 - 36) = \text{Rs.}^2\, 64, \Rightarrow \bar{x} = \text{Rs. } 8$ [From (*i*)]

Hence, using (*ii*), the fine paid by each of the passengers is Rs. 8.

If among these ticketless passengers, there are a few rich persons with large sums of money in their pockets, then an obvious shortcoming of this system of imposing penalty is that, it will give undue heavy penalty to the poor passengers (with smaller amounts of money in their pockets).

Example 6.15. *The variance of a series of numbers 2, 3, 11 and x is* $12\frac{1}{4}$. *Find the value of x.*

[*I.C.W.A. (Foundation), June 2006*]

Solution. We are given $n = 4$.

X	2	3	11	x	$\Sigma X = 16 + x$
X^2	4	9	121	x^2	$\Sigma X^2 = x^2 + 134$

$$\sigma_X^2 = \frac{\Sigma X^2}{n} - \left(\frac{\Sigma X}{n}\right)^2 = \frac{x^2 + 134}{4} - \left(\frac{16 + x}{4}\right)^2$$

$$= \frac{1}{16}\left[4(x^2 + 134) - (16 + x)^2\right] = \frac{1}{16}\left[4x^2 + 536 - (256 + x^2 + 32x)\right]$$

$$\Rightarrow \quad \sigma_X^2 = \frac{1}{16}\left[3x^2 - 32x + 280\right] = 12\frac{1}{4} = \frac{49}{4} \text{ (Given).}$$

$$\Rightarrow \quad 3x^2 - 32x + 280 = 49 \times 4 = 196 \quad \Rightarrow \quad 3x^2 - 32x + 84 = 0$$

$$\therefore \quad x = \frac{32 \pm \sqrt{(-32)^2 - 4 \times 3 \times 84}}{2 \times 3} = \frac{32 \pm \sqrt{1024 - 1008}}{6} = \frac{32 \pm 4}{6}$$

$$\Rightarrow \quad x = \left(\frac{32 + 4}{6} \text{ or } \frac{32 - 4}{6}\right) = \left(6 \text{ or } \frac{14}{3}\right).$$

Example 6·16. *The mean of 5 observations is 4·4 and the variance is 8·24. If three of the five observations are 1, 2 and 6, find the values of the other two.* [*Delhi Univ. B.A. (Econ. Hons.), 2004*]

Solution. We are given $n = 5$, $\bar{x} = 4{\cdot}4$ and $\sigma^2 = 8{\cdot}24$

We have : $\Sigma x = n\bar{x} = 5 \times 4{\cdot}4 = 22$

and $\Sigma x^2 = n(\sigma^2 + \bar{x}^2) = 5(8{\cdot}24 + 19{\cdot}36) = 5 \times 27{\cdot}60 = 138$

Three observations are 1, 2 and 6. Let the two unknown observations be x_1 and x_2. Then

$$\Sigma x = 1 + 2 + 6 + x_1 + x_2 = 22 \quad \Rightarrow \quad x_1 + x_2 = 22 - 9 = 13 \qquad \ldots(*)$$

$$\Sigma x^2 = 1^2 + 2^2 + 6^2 + x_1^2 + x_2^2 = 138 \quad \Rightarrow \quad x_1^2 + x_2^2 = 138 - 41 = 97 \qquad \ldots(**)$$

Substituting the value of x_2 from (*) in (**) we get

$$x_1^2 + (13 - x_1)^2 = 97$$

$$\Rightarrow \quad x_1^2 + [13^2 + x_1^2 - 2 \times 13 \times x_1] = 97 \qquad [\because (a - b)^2 = a^2 + b^2 - 2ab]$$

$$\Rightarrow \quad x_1^2 + (169 + x_1^2 - 26x_1) = 97$$

$$\Rightarrow \quad 2x_1^2 - 26x_1 + 72 = 0$$

Solving as a quadratic equation in x_1, we get

$$x_1 = \frac{26 \pm \sqrt{(26)^2 - 4 \times 2 \times 72}}{2 \times 2} = \frac{26 \pm \sqrt{676 - 576}}{4} = \frac{26 \pm 10}{4}$$

$$= \frac{26 + 10}{4} \text{ or } \frac{26 - 10}{4} = 9 \text{ or } 4$$

Substituting in (*), we get $x_1 = 9 \Rightarrow x_2 = 13 - 9 = 4$ or $x_1 = 4 \Rightarrow x_2 = 13 - 4 = 9$

Hence, the other two numbers are 4 and 9.

Example 6.17. (*a*) *For a group of 10 items,*

$$\sum_{i=1}^{10} (X_i - 2) = 40 \quad \text{and} \quad \sum_{i=1}^{10} X_i^2 = 495.$$

Then find the variance of this group. [*I.C.W.A. (Foundation), June 2005*]

(*b*) *For 10 values $X_1, X_2, ..., X_{10}$ of the variable X,*

$$\sum_{i=1}^{10} X_i = 110 \quad \text{and} \quad \sum_{i=1}^{10} (X_i - 5)^2 = 1{,}000.$$

Find variance of X. [*I.C.W.A. (Foundation), June 2006*]

Solution. (*a*) In the usual notations, we are given :

$n = 10$; $\Sigma X^2 = 495$ and

$\Sigma (X - 2) = 40 \quad \Rightarrow \quad \Sigma X - 2n = 40 \quad \Rightarrow \quad \Sigma X = 40 + 2 \times 10 = 60$

$$\therefore \quad \sigma_X^2 = \frac{\Sigma X^2}{n} - \left(\frac{\Sigma X}{n}\right)^2 = \frac{495}{10} - \left(\frac{60}{10}\right)^2 = 49.5 - 36 = 13.5$$

(*b*) We are given : $n = 10$, $\Sigma X = 110$ and $\Sigma (X - 5)^2 = 1{,}000$.

Let $d = X - A = X - 5$, $(A = 5)$. Then, we have

$\Sigma d = \Sigma (X - 5) = \Sigma X - 5 \times n = 110 - 5 \times 10 = 60$ and $\Sigma d^2 = \Sigma (X - 5)^2 = 1{,}000$.

Since variance is independent of change of origin, we get :

$$\sigma_X^2 = \sigma_d^2 = \frac{\Sigma d^2}{n} - \left(\frac{\Sigma d}{n}\right)^2 = \frac{1{,}000}{10} - \left(\frac{60}{10}\right)^2 = 100 - 36 = 64.$$

Example 6.18. *For the numbers 5, 6, 7, 8, 10, 12, if S_1 and S_2 are the respective Root Mean Square Deviations about the mean and about an arbitrary number 9, show that $17S_2^2 = 20 S_1^2$.*

[*I.C.W.A. (Foundation), June 2003*]

Solution. We have

$$n = 6, \quad \overline{X} = \frac{\Sigma X}{n} = \frac{48}{6} = 8$$

S_1^2 = Mean Square Deviation about mean

$$= \frac{1}{n} \Sigma (X - \overline{X})^2 = \frac{34}{6} = \frac{17}{3}$$

S_2^2 = Mean Square Deviation about the point '9'

$$= \frac{1}{n} \Sigma (X - 9)^2 = \frac{40}{6} = \frac{20}{3}$$

CALCULATIONS FOR MEAN SQUARE DEVIATIONS

X	$X - \overline{X}$ $= X - 8$	$(X - \overline{X})^2$	$(X - 9)$	$(X - 9)^2$
5	−3	9	−4	16
6	−2	4	−3	9
7	−1	1	−2	4
8	0	0	−1	1
10	2	4	1	1
12	4	16	3	9
$\Sigma X = 48$		$\Sigma(X - \overline{X})^2 = 34$		$\Sigma(X - 9)^2 = 40$

$$\therefore \quad \frac{S_1^2}{S_2^2} = \frac{17}{3} \times \frac{3}{20} = \frac{17}{20} \quad \Rightarrow \quad 17 S_2^2 = 20 S_1^2$$

Example 6·19. *A charitable organisation decided to give old age pensions to people over sixty years of age. The scale of pensions were fixed as follow :*

Age group	*60—65*	*Rs. 200 per month*
"	*65—70*	*Rs. 250 per month*
"	*70—75*	*Rs. 300 per month*
"	*75—80*	*Rs. 350 per month*
"	*80—85*	*Rs. 400 per month*

The ages of 25 persons who secured the pensions right are as given below :

74, 62, 84, 72, 61, 83, 72, 81, 64, 71, 63, 61, 60,
67, 74, 64, 79, 73, 75, 76, 69, 68, 78, 66, 67

Calculate monthly average pensions payable per person and the standard deviation.

[*Delhi Univ. B.Com. (Hons.) (External), 2005*]

Solution. First of all we shall prepare the frequency distribution of the 25 persons with respect to age in the age-groups 60—65, 65—70,..., 80—85 (as suggested by the above data) by using the method of tally marks. Then we shall compute the arithmetic mean of the pension payable per person and also its standard deviation, as explained in the following table.

COMPUTATION OF MEAN AND STANDARD DEVIATION

Age Group	*Tally makrs*	*Frequency (f)*	*Monthly pension (in Rs.)*	$d = \frac{X-300}{50}$	*fd*	fd^2
60—65	卌 ||	7	200	−2	−14	28
65—70	卌	5	250	−1	−5	5
70—75	卌 |	6	300	0	0	0
75—80	||||	4	350	1	4	4
80—85	|||	3	400	2	6	12
		$N = 25$			$\Sigma fd = -9$	$\Sigma fd^2 = 49$

Average monthly pension is given by :

$$\overline{X} = A + \frac{h\Sigma fd}{N} = 300 + \frac{50 \times (-9)}{25} = (300 - 18) = \text{Rs. } 282$$

Standard deviation of monthly pension is :

$$\sigma = h \cdot \sqrt{\frac{\Sigma fd^2}{N} - \left(\frac{\Sigma fd}{N}\right)^2} = \frac{h}{N}\sqrt{N\,\Sigma fd^2 - (\Sigma fd)^2} = \frac{50}{25}\sqrt{25 \times 49 - (-9)^2}$$

$$= 2\sqrt{1225 - 81} = 2\sqrt{1144} = 2 \text{ Antilog}\left(\tfrac{1}{2}\log 1144\right)$$

$$= 2 \text{ Antilog}\left(\tfrac{1}{2} \times 3{\cdot}0585\right) = 2 \text{ Antilog } (1{\cdot}5292) = 2 \times 33{\cdot}83 = \text{Rs. } 67{\cdot}66.$$

Example 6·20. *You are the incharge of the rationing department of a state affected by food shortage. The following information is received from your local investigators :*

Area	*Mean Calories*	*Standard Deviation of Calories*
X	*2,500*	*500*
Y	*2,200*	*300*

The estimated requirement of an adult is taken at 3,000 calories daily and absolute minimum at 1,250. Comment on the reported figures and determine which area needs more urgent action.

[*Delhi Univ. B.Com. (Hons.), 2002*]

Solution. We shall compute the 3-sigma limits $\overline{x} \pm 3\sigma$ for each area, which will include approximately 99·73% of the population observation [assuming that the distribution is approximately normal].

	3-σ Limits = $\overline{X} \pm 3\sigma$
Area X	$2500 \pm 3 \times 500 = 2500 \pm 1500 = (1000, 4000)$
Area Y	$2200 \pm 3 \times 300 = 2200 \pm 900 = (1300, 3100)$

The absolute daily minimum calories requirement for a person is 1250. From the above figures we observe that almost all the persons in the area Y are getting more than the minimum calories requirement as the lower limit in this area is 1300. However, since in the area X, the lower 3-σ limit is 1000 which is less than 1250, quite a number of people in area X are not getting the minimum requirement of 1250 calories. Hence, as the incharge of the rationing department, it becomes my duty to take urgent action for the people of area X.

Example 6·21. *Find the proportion of items lying within : (i) mean* $\pm \sigma$ *and (ii) mean* $\pm 2\sigma$, *of the following distribution.*

Class	*Frequency*	*Class*	*Frequency*
11—12	*5*	*21—22*	*395*
13—14	*426*	*23—24*	*38*
15—16	*720*	*25—26*	*8*
17—18	*741*	*27—28*	*5*
19—20	*665*	*29—30*	*7*

Solution.

COMPUTATION OF MEAN AND S.D.

Class interval	*Mid-value (X)*	$d = \frac{X - 19\cdot5}{2}$	f	fd	fd^2
11—12	11·5	–4	5	–20	80
13—14	13·5	–3	426	–1278	3834
15—16	15·5	–2	720	–1440	2880
17—18	17·5	–1	741	–741	741
19—20	19·5	0	665	0	0
21—22	21·5	1	395	395	395
23—24	23·5	2	38	76	152
25—26	25·5	3	8	24	72
27—28	27·5	4	5	20	80
29—30	29·5	5	7	35	175
			$\Sigma f = 3010$	$\Sigma fd = -2929$	$\Sigma fd^2 = 8409$

$$\text{Mean} = A + \frac{h \sum fd}{N} = 19\cdot5 + \frac{2 \times (-2929)}{3010} = 19\cdot5 - 1\cdot946 = 17\cdot55$$

$$\sigma = h\sqrt{\frac{\sum fd^2}{N} - \left(\frac{\sum fd}{N}\right)^2} = 2 \times \sqrt{\frac{8409}{3010} - \left(\frac{-2929}{3010}\right)^2}$$

$$= 2 \times \sqrt{2\cdot7937 - (0\cdot9731)^2} = 2 \times \sqrt{2\cdot7937 - 0\cdot9469}$$

$$= 2 \times \sqrt{1\cdot8464} = 2 \times 1\cdot35897 = 2\cdot7179 \approx 2\cdot72$$

$\therefore$ Mean $\pm \sigma = 17\cdot55 \pm 2\cdot72 = 20\cdot27$ and $14\cdot83$

and Mean $\pm 2\sigma = 17\cdot55 \pm 2 \times 2\cdot72 = 17\cdot55 \pm 5\cdot44 = 22\cdot99$ and $12\cdot11$.

The number of items lying within Mean $\pm \sigma$ *i.e.*, within 14·83 and 20·27 is 720 + 741 + 665 = 2126, and the proportion of items lying within Mean $\pm \sigma$ is :

$$\frac{2,126}{3,010} = 0\cdot7063 \qquad i.e., \qquad 70\cdot63\%$$

The number of items lying within Mean ± 2σ *i.e.*, within 12·11 and 22·99 is : 426 + 720 + 741 + 665 + 395 = 2,947. Hence, the proportion of items lying within Mean ± 2σ is :

$$\frac{2,947}{3,010} = 0·9791 \qquad i.e., \qquad 97·91\%$$

Example 6·22. *The mean and standard deviation of the frequency distribution of a continuous random variable X are 40·604 lbs. and 7·92 lbs. respectively. The distribution after change of origin and scale is as follows :*

d :	*–3*	*–2*	*–1*	*0*	*1*	*2*	*3*	*4*	*Total*
f :	*3*	*15*	*45*	*57*	*50*	*36*	*25*	*9*	*240*

where d = (X – A)/h and f is the frequency of X. Determine the actual class intervals.

Solution.

COMPUTATION OF MEAN AND S.D.

d	*f*	*fd*	*fd²*
–3	3	–9	27
–2	15	–30	60
–1	45	–45	45
0	57	0	0
1	50	50	50
2	36	72	144
3	25	75	225
4	9	36	144
	$N = \Sigma f = 240$	$\Sigma fd = 149$	$\Sigma fd^2 = 695$

We are given : $d = (X - A)/h$

$$\overline{X} = 40·604 \quad \text{and} \quad \sigma_x = 7·92$$

$$\overline{X} = A + \frac{h \Sigma fd}{N}$$

$$\Rightarrow \quad 40·604 = A + h\left(\frac{149}{240}\right)$$

$$\Rightarrow \quad 40·604 = A + 0·621h \qquad \ldots(*)$$

$$\sigma_x = h\sqrt{\frac{\Sigma fd^2}{N} - \left(\frac{\Sigma fd}{N}\right)^2}$$

$$\Rightarrow \quad 7·92 = h\sqrt{\frac{695}{240} - \left(\frac{149}{240}\right)^2} = h\sqrt{2·8958 - (0·6208)^2}$$

$$= h\sqrt{2·8958 - 0·3854} = h\sqrt{2·5104} = 1·5844\, h$$

$$\Rightarrow \quad h = \frac{7·92}{1·5844} = 4·9987 \simeq 5$$

Substituting in (*), we get

$$A = 40·604 - 5 \times 0·621$$
$$= 40·604 - 3·105 = 37·499 \simeq 37·5$$

The value

$$d = 0 \quad \Rightarrow \quad X - A = 0 \quad \Rightarrow \quad X = A = 37·5$$

Since the magnitude of the class interval is $h = 5$, the boundaries of the corresponding class are (37·5 – 2·5, 37·5 + 2·5) *i.e.*, (35, 40). Thus the actual frequency distribution is as given in the adjoining table.

d	*X = Mid-value of Class*	*Class Interval*	*Frequency*
–3	22·5	20—25	3
–2	27·5	25—30	15
–1	32·5	30—35	45
0	37·5	35—40	57
1	42·5	40—45	50
2	47·5	45—50	36
3	52·5	50—55	25
4	57·5	55—60	9

Example 6·23. (*a*) *Find the mean and standard deviation of the first n natural numbers.*

(*b*) *Hence deduce the mean and s.d. of the numbers 1, 2, 3, 4, 5, 6, 7, 8, 9, 10.*

Solution. (*a*) If the variable *X* denotes the natural number, then the first *n* natural numbers are 1, 2, 3, …, *n*.

X	1	2	3	…	n
X^2	1^2	2^2	3^2	…	n^2

$$\text{Mean} = \frac{\Sigma X}{n} = \frac{1+2+3+\ldots+n}{n} = \frac{n(n+1)}{2}\cdot\frac{1}{n} = \frac{n+1}{2} \qquad \ldots(*)$$

$$\text{Variance} = \frac{\Sigma X^2}{n} - \overline{X}^2 = \frac{1^2+2^2+3^3+\ldots+n^2}{n} - \left(\frac{n+1}{2}\right)^2$$

$$= \frac{n(n+1)(2n+1)}{6n} - \frac{(n+1)^2}{4} = \frac{(n+1)}{12}\left[2(2n+1) - 3(n+1)\right]$$

$$= \frac{(n+1)}{12}\left[4n+2-3n-3\right] = \frac{(n+1)(n-1)}{12}$$

$$\therefore \quad \sigma^2 = \frac{n^2-1}{12} \quad \Rightarrow \quad s.d.\ (\sigma) = \sqrt{\frac{n^2-1}{12}} \qquad \ldots(**)$$

Note. This is a standard result and should be committed to memory.

(*b*) **Deduction.** We have to find mean and s.d. of the first 10 natural numbers. Taking $n = 10$ in (*) and (**), we get respectively :

$$\text{Mean} = \frac{10+1}{2} = \frac{11}{2} = 5{\cdot}5\ ; \qquad s.d.\ (\sigma) = \sqrt{\frac{10^2-1}{12}} = \sqrt{\frac{100-1}{12}} = \sqrt{8{\cdot}25} = 2{\cdot}87.$$

Example 6·24. *The arithmetic mean and standard deviation of series of 20 items were calculated by a student as 20 cm. and 5 cm. respectively. But while calculating them an item 13 was misread as 30. Find the correct arithmetic mean and standard deviation.*

Solution. We are given $n = 20$, $\overline{X} = 20$ cms, $\sigma = 5$ cms ; Wrong value used = 30 ; Correct value = 13

We have : $\Sigma X = n\overline{X} = 20 \times 20 = 400$ and $\Sigma X^2 = n(\sigma^2 + \overline{X}^2) = 20(25 + 400) = 8500$

If the wrong observation 30 is replaced by the correct value 13, then the number of observations remains same *viz.*, 20 and

Corrected $\Sigma X = 400 - 30 + 13 = 383$; Corrected $\Sigma X^2 = 8500 - (30)^2 + (13)^2 = 7769$

$$\therefore \quad \text{Corrected mean} = \frac{\text{Corrected }(\Sigma X)}{n} = \frac{383}{20} = 19{\cdot}15$$

$$\text{Corrected } \sigma^2 = \frac{\text{Corrected }(\Sigma X)^2}{n} - (\text{Corrected mean})^2$$

$$= \frac{7769}{20} - (19{\cdot}15)^2 = 388{\cdot}45 - 366{\cdot}72 = 21{\cdot}73$$

$$\therefore \quad \text{Corrected } s.d.\ (\sigma) = \sqrt{21{\cdot}73} = 4{\cdot}6615.$$

Example 6·25. *The mean and the variance of ten observations are known to be 17 and 33 respectively. Later it is found that one observation (i.e., 26) is inaccurate and is removed. What is the mean and standard deviation of the remaining ?*

[*Delhi Univ. B.A. (Econ. Hons.), 2009; C.A. (Foundation), May 2002*]

Solution. In the usual notations, we are given : $n = 10$, $\overline{X} = 17$ and $\sigma^2 = 33$

$$\Sigma X = n\overline{X} = 10 \times 17 = 170 \quad \text{and} \quad \Sigma X^2 = n(\sigma^2 + \overline{X}^2) = 10\,(33 + 289) = 3220$$

If the inaccurate observation (26) is removed, then for the remaining $n - 1 = 10 - 1 = 9$ observations, the values of ΣX and ΣX^2 are given by :

$$\text{Corrected } \Sigma X = (\Sigma X) - 26 = 170 - 26 = 144$$

$$\text{Corrected } \Sigma X^2 = (\Sigma X^2) - 26^2 = 3220 - 676 = 2544$$

The mean ($\overline{X}_1$) and variance (σ_1^2) of the remaining 9 observations are given by :

$$\text{New mean } (\overline{X}_1) = \frac{\text{Corrected } \Sigma X}{9} = \frac{144}{9} = 16$$

$$\text{New variance } (\sigma_1^2) = \frac{\text{Corrected } \Sigma X^2}{9} - (\overline{X}_1)^2 = \frac{2544}{9} - 256 = 282{\cdot}67 - 256 = 26{\cdot}67.$$

Example 6·26. *For a frequency distribution of marks in Sociology of 200 candidates (grouped in intervals 0—5, 5—10,...,etc.), the mean and the standard deviation was found to be 45 and 15. Later it was discovered that the score 53 was misread as 63 in obtaining the frequency distribution. Find the correct mean and standard deviation corresponding to the correct frequency distribution.*

Solution. We are given $N = 200, \overline{X} = 45$ and $\sigma = 15$. These values have been obtained on using the wrong value 63 while the correct value is 53. In case of grouped or continuous frequency distribution, the value of X used for computing the mean and the standard deviation, is the mid-value of the class interval. Since the wrong value 63 lies in the interval 60—65 with the mid-value 62·5 and the correct value 53 lies in the interval 50—55 with mid-value 52·5, the question amounts to finding the correct values of $\overline{X}$ and σ if the wrong value 62·5 is replaced by the correct value 52·5.

$\therefore$ We have $N = 200, \quad \overline{X} = 45, \quad \sigma = 15$

Wrong value used = 62·5 ; Correct value = 52·5

$$\Sigma fX = N\overline{X} = 200 \times 45 = 9000$$

$$\Sigma fX^2 = N(\sigma^2 + \overline{X}^2) = 200\ (15^2 + 45^2)$$
$$= 200(225 + 2025) = 200 \times 2250 = 450000$$

$\therefore$ Corrected $\Sigma fX = 9000 - 62{\cdot}5 + 52{\cdot}5 = 8990$

$$\text{Corrected } \Sigma fX^2 = 450000 - (62{\cdot}5)^2 + (52{\cdot}5)^2$$
$$= 450000 - [(62{\cdot}5)^2 - (52{\cdot}5)^2]$$
$$= 450000 - (62{\cdot}5 + 52{\cdot}5)\ (62{\cdot}5 - 52{\cdot}5)$$
$$= 450000 - 115 \times 10 = 450000 - 1150$$
$$= 448850$$

$$\therefore \qquad \text{Corrected mean } = \frac{\text{Corrected } \Sigma fX}{N} = \frac{8990}{200} = 44{\cdot}95$$

$$\text{Corrected } \sigma = \sqrt{\frac{\text{Corrected } \Sigma fX^2}{N} - (\text{Corrected mean})^2}$$

$$= \sqrt{\frac{448850}{200} - (44{\cdot}95)^2} = \sqrt{2244{\cdot}25 - 2020{\cdot}50} = \sqrt{223{\cdot}75} = 14{\cdot}96.$$

EXERCISE 6·3

1. (*a*) Explain with suitable example the term variation. What purposes does a measure of variation serve ? Comment on some of the well-known measures of variation along with their respective merits and demerits. [*Delhi Univ. MBA, 2000*]

(*b*) What is a measure of dispersion ? Discuss four important measures of spread indicating their uses. [*Andhra Pradesh Univ. B.Com., 1998*]

2. What is meant by dispersion ? In your opinion which is the best method of finding out dispersion and why ? [*Delhi Univ. B.Com. (Pass), 1999*]

3. What are the chief requisites of a good measure of dispersion ? In the light of those, comment on some of the well-known measures of dispersion.

4. (*a*) What do you understand by absolute and relative measures of dispersion ? Explain advantages of the relative measures over the absolute measures of dispersion.

(*b*) Define mean deviation and standard deviation. Explain, why economists prefer mean deviation to standard deviation in their analysis.

5. (*a*) Compare mean deviation and standard deviation as measures of variation. Which of the two is a better measure ? Why ? [*Delhi Univ. B.Com. (Hons.), 2001*]

(*b*) Explain the mathematical properties of standard deviation. Why is standard deviation used more than mean deviation ? [*Delhi Univ. B.Com. (Hons.), 2009*]

6. What is standard deviation ? Explain its superiority over other measures of dispersion.

7. Give the various formulae for computing the standard deviation.

8. State giving reasons whether the following statements are true or false :

(*i*) Standard deviation can never be negative.

(*ii*) The sum of squared deviations measured from mean is least.

Ans. (*i*) True, (*ii*) True.

9. For the numbers (X) : 1, 3, 4, 5 and 12, find :

(*i*) the value (v) for which $\Sigma\ (X - v)^2$ is minimized.

(*ii*) the value (v) for which $\Sigma\ | X - v |$ is minimized. [*Delhi Univ. B.A. (Econ. Hons.), 2009*]

Ans. (*i*) $\Sigma (X - v)^2$ is minimum when $v = \overline{X} = \frac{1}{5}(1 + 3 + 4 + 5 + 12) = 5$

(*ii*) $\Sigma | X - v |$ is minimum when v = Median of (1, 3, 4, 5, 12) = 4

10. Calculate standard deviation of the following marks obtained by 5 students in a tutorial group :

Marks Obtained : 8, 12, 13, 15, 22 *[Delhi Univ. B.Com. (Pass), 1997]*

Ans. $\sigma^2 = \frac{\Sigma x^2}{n} - \left(\frac{\Sigma x}{n}\right)^2 = \frac{1086}{5} - \left(\frac{70}{5}\right)^2 = 21{\cdot}2 \quad \Rightarrow \quad \sigma = \sqrt{21{\cdot}2} = 4{\cdot}6.$

11. Why is standard deviation considered to be the best measure of dispersion ? Find the variance if $\Sigma d^2 = 150$ and $N = 6$. Deviations are taken from actual mean. *[Delhi Univ. B.Com. (Pass), 1998]*

Ans. $\sigma^2 = \frac{150}{6} = 25.$

12. (*a*) From the following information, find the standard deviation of x and y variables :

$\Sigma x = 235, \quad \Sigma y = 250, \quad \Sigma x^2 = 6750, \quad \Sigma y^2 = 6840, \quad N = 10.$ *[Delhi Univ. B.Com. (Hons.) 1997]*

Ans. $\sigma_x = 11{\cdot}08;\ \sigma_y = 7{\cdot}68.$

(*b*) You are given the following raw sums in a statistical survey of two variables X and Y :

$\Sigma X = 240, \quad \Sigma Y = 250, \quad \Sigma X^2 = 6400$ and $\Sigma Y^2 = 7060.$

Ten items are included in each survey. Compute Standard Deviation of the X and Y variables.

[Delhi Univ. B.Com. (Pass), 1996]

Ans. $\sigma_x = 8,\ \sigma_y = 9.$

13. (*a*) State a formula for computing standard deviation of n natural numbers 1, 2, ..., n.

[Delhi Univ. B.Com. (Pass), 2000]

Ans. $\sigma = \sqrt{(n^2 - 1)/12}.$

(*b*) Show that the standard deviation of the natural numbers 1, 2, 3, 4 and 5 is $\sqrt{2}$. *[Kerala Univ. B.Com., 1996]*

(*c*) Mean of 10 items is 50 and S.D. is 14. Find the sum of the squares of all the items.

[Mahatma Gandhi Univ. B.Com., April 1998]

Ans. $\Sigma x^2 = 26960$

14. Calculate standard deviation of the following series.

Daily Wages of Workers (in Rs.)	*No. of Workers*	*Daily Wages of Workers (in Rs.)*	*No. of Workers*	*Daily Wages of Workers (in Rs.)*	*No. of Workers*
100—105	200	120—125	350	140—145	280
105—110	210	125—130	520	145—150	210
110—115	230	130—135	410	150—155	160
115—120	320	135—140	320	155—160	90

Ans. *s.d.* = 14.244

15. Find out the mean and standard deviation of the following data.

Age under (years) :	10	20	30	40	50	60	70	80
No. of persons dying :	15	30	53	75	100	110	115	125

Ans. Mean = 35.16 years, S.D. = 19.76 years.

16. In the following data, two class frequencies are missing.

Class Interval	*Frequency*	*Class Interval*	*Frequency*
100—110	4	150—160	—
110—120	7	160—170	16
120—130	15	170—180	10
130—140	—	180—190	6
140—150	40	190—200	3

However, it was possible to ascertain that the total number of frequencies was 150 and that the median has been correctly found out as 146·25. You are required to find with the help of information given :

(*i*) The two missing frequencies.

(*ii*) Having found the missing frequencies, calculate arithmetic mean and standard deviation.

(*iii*) Without using the direct formula, find the value of mode.

Ans. (*i*) 24, 25; (*ii*) A.M. = 147·33, *s.d.* = 19·2; (*iii*) Mode = 144·09.

17. The following table gives the distribution of income of households based on hypothetical data :

Income (Rs.)	*Percentage of households*	*Income (Rs.)*	*Percentage of households*
Under 100	7·2	500—599	14·9
100—199	11·7	600—699	10·4
200—299	12·1	700—999	9·0
300—399	14·8	1000 and above	4·0
400—499	15·9		

(*i*) What are the problems involved in computing standard deviation from the above data ?

(*ii*) Compute a suitable measure of dispersion.

Ans. (*ii*) Compute Quartile Deviation. Q.D. = 169·425 ; Coeff. of Q.D. = 0·404.

18. The standard deviation calculated from a set of 32 observations is 5. If the sum of the observations is 80, what is the sum of the squares of these observations ?

Ans. $\Sigma X^2 = 1000$.

19. The mean of 200 items is 48 and their standard deviation is 3. Find the sum and sum of squares of all items.

Ans. 9,600 ; 4,62,600.

20. Given : No. of observations (N) = 100; Arithmetic average ($\overline{X}$) = 2 ; Standard deviation (s_x) = 4 find ΣX and ΣX^2.

Ans. $\Sigma X = 200$, $\Sigma X^2 = 2000$.

21. The mean of 5 observations is 3 and variance is 2. If three of the five observations are 1, 3, 5, find the other two.

Ans. 2, 4.

22. An association doing charity work decided to give old age pension to people of 60 years and above in age. The scales of pension were fixed as follows :

Age group 60—65 ;	Rs. 400	per month
Age group 65—70 ;	Rs. 500	per month
Age group 70—75 ;	Rs. 600	per month
Age group 75—80 ;	Rs. 700	per month
Age group 80—85 ;	Rs. 800	per month
85 and above ;	Rs. 1000	per month.

The ages of 30 persons who secured the pension right are given below :

62	65	68	72	75	77	82	85	90	78
75	61	60	68	72	76	78	79	80	82
68	75	94	98	73	77	68	65	71	89

Calculate the monthly average pension payable and the standard deviation .

Ans. Average monthly pension = Rs. 676·70; *s.d.* = Rs. 183·80.

23. Treating the number of letters in each word in the following passage as the variable X, prepare the frequency distribution table and obtain its mean, median, mode and standard deviation.

"The reliability of data must always be examined before any attempt is made to base conclusions upon them. This is true of all data, but particularly so of numerical data, which do not carry their quality written large on them. It is a waste of time to apply the refined theoretical methods of Statistics to data which are suspect from the beginning."

Ans. Mean = 4·565, Median = 4, Mode = 3, S.D. = 2·673.

24. A collar manufacturer is considering the production of a new style of collar to attract young men. The following statistics of new circumferences are available based on measurements of a typical group :

Mid-value (in inches)	*No. of students*	*Mid-value (in inches)*	*No. of students*
12·0	4	14·5	18
12·5	8	15·0	10
13·0	13	15·5	7
13·5	20	16·0	5
14·0	25		

Use the criterion $\overline{X} \pm 3\sigma$ to obtain the largest and the smallest size of collar he should make in order to meet the needs of practically all his customers having in mind that collars are worn on an average 3/4 inches larger than neck size.

Hint. Mean = 13·968″; S.D. = 0·964″. ; Limits for collar size are given by : [Mean ± 3 *s.d.*] + 3/4 ;

Largest collar size = 14·718 + 2·892 = 17·61″ ; Smallest collar size = 14·718 – 2·892 = 11·826″

25. The following data represent the percentage impurities in a certain chemical substance.

Percentage of impurities	*Frequency*	*Percentage of impurities*	*Frequency*
Less than 5	0	10—10·9	45
5—5·9	1	11—11·9	30
6—6·9	6	12—12·9	5
7—7·9	29	13—13·9	3
8—8·9	75	14—14·9	1
9—9·9	85		

(*i*) Calculate the mean and standard deviation.

(*ii*) Find the number of frequency lying between (A.M. ± 2 S.D.).

Ans. (*i*) Mean = 9·3857, S.D. = 1·3924; (*ii*) 267.

26. The following distribution was obtained by a change of origin and scale of variable X :

d :	– 4	– 3	– 2	– 1	0	1	2	3	4
f :	4	8	14	18	20	14	10	6	6

Write down the frequency distribution of X if it is given that mean and variance are 59·5 and 413 respectively.

Ans.

C.I.	f	C.I.	f	C.I.	f
15·5—25·5	4	45·5—55·5	18	75·5—85·5	10
25·5—35·5	8	55·5—65·5	20	85·5—95·5	6
35·5—45·5	14	65·5—75·5	14	95·5—105·5	6
				Total	100

27. Mean and standard deviation of the following continuous series are 31 and 15·9 respectively. The distribution after taking step deviation is as follows :

d :	– 3	– 2	– 1	0	1	2	3
f :	10	15	25	25	10	10	5

Determine the actual class intervals. [*G.G.I.P. Univ., B.B.A., May 2004*]

Ans. 0—10, 10—20, 20—30, 30—40, 40—50, 50—60, 60—70.

28. (*a*) The mean and standard deviation of a sample of 100 observations were calculated as 40 and 5·1 respectively by a student who took by mistake 50 instead of 40 for one observation. Calculate the correct mean and standard deviation.

Ans. Corrected mean = 39·9 and *s.d.* = 5.

(*b*) For a number of 51 observations, the arithmetic mean and standard deviation are 58·5 and 11 respectively. It was found after the calculations were made that one of the observations recorded as 15 was incorrect. Find the mean and standard deviation of the 50 observations if this incorrect observation is omitted.

Ans. Mean = 59·37 and S.D. (σ) = 9·21.

29. The mean and the standard deviation of a sample of size 10 were found to be 9·5 and 2·5 respectively. Later on, an additional observation became available. This was 15·0 and was included in the original sample. Find the mean and the standard deviation of the 11 observations.

Ans. Mean = 10, *s.d.* = 2·86.

30. (*a*) The mean and standard deviation of 20 items are found to be 10 and 2 respectively. At the time of checking it was found that one item 8 was incorrect. Calculate the mean and standard deviation if

(*i*) the wrong item is omitted, and

(*ii*) it is replaced by 12.

(*b*) A study of the age of 100 film stars grouped in intervals of 10—12, 12—14,..., etc., revealed the mean age and standard deviation to be 32·02 and 13·18 respectively. While checking it was discovered that the age 57 was misread as 27. Calculate the correct mean age and standard deviation.

Ans. (*a*) (*i*) Mean = 10·1053, *s.d.* = 1·997; (*ii*) Mean = 10·2 *s.d.* = 1·99.

(*b*) Mean = 32·32; *s.d.* =13·402.

31. (*a*) Mean and Standard Deviation of 100 items are found to be 40 and 10. At the time of calculation two items are wrongly taken as 30 and 70 instead of 3 and 27. Find the correct mean and correct standard deviation.

Ans. Mean = 39·3 ; S.D. = 10·24 [*Delhi Univ. B.Com. (Pass), 2001*]

(*b*) Mean and coefficient of standard deviation of 100 items are found by a student as 50 and 0·1. If at the time of calculations two items are wrongly taken as 40 and 50 instead of 60 and 30, find the correct mean and standard deviation. [*Delhi Univ. B.Com. (Hons.), 1996*]

Hint. $n = 100, \quad \bar{x} = 50, \quad \frac{\sigma}{\bar{x}} = 0 \cdot 1 \quad \Rightarrow \quad \sigma = \frac{\bar{x}}{10} = 5 \quad \Rightarrow \quad \sigma^2 = 25.$

Ans. Mean = 50, $\sigma = \sqrt{29} = 5{\cdot}39$.

(*c*) The mean and the standard deviation of a characteristic of 100 items were found to be 60 and 10 respectively. At the time of calculations, two items were wrongly taken as 5 and 45 instead of 30 and 20. Calculate the corrected mean and corrected standard deviation. [*Delhi Univ. B.Com. (Hons.), 2009; C.A. (Foundation), June 1993*]

Ans. Corrected mean = 60, Corrected S.D. = 9·62

32. *Fill in the blanks :*

(*i*) Algebraic sum of deviations is zero from ......

(*ii*) The sum of absolute deviations is minimum from ......

(*iii*) Standard deviation is always ...... than range.

(*iv*) Standard deviation is always ...... than mean deviation.

(*v*) The mean and *s.d.* of 100 observations are 50 and 10 respectively.

The new :

(*a*) Mean = ..., *s.d.* = ..., if 2 is added to each observation.

(*b*) Mean = ..., *s.d.* = ..., if 3 is subtracted from each observation.

(*c*) Mean = ..., *s.d.* = ..., if each observation is multiplied by 5

(*d*) If 2 is subtracted from each observation and then it is divided by 5.

(*vi*) Variance is the ...... value of mean square deviation.

(*vii*) If $Q_1 = 10$, $Q_3 = 40$, the coefficient of quartile deviation is ......

(*viii*) If 25% of the items in a distribution are less than 10 and 25% are more than 40, the quartile deviation is ......

(*ix*) The median and *s.d.* of a distribution are 15 and 5 respectively. If each item is increased by 5, the new median = ... and *s.d.* = ...

(*x*) A computer showed that the *s.d.* of 40 observations ranging from 120 to 150 is 35. The answer is correct/wrong. Tick right one.

Ans. (*i*) Arithmetic mean (*ii*) Median (*iii*) Less (*iv*) Greater (*v*) (*a*) 52, 10 (*b*) 47, 10 (*c*) 250, 50 (*d*) 9·6, 2 (*vi*) Minimum (*vii*) 0·6 (*viii*) 15 (*ix*) 20, 5 (*x*) Wrong, since *s.d.* can't exceed range.

6·10. STANDARD DEVIATION OF THE COMBINED SERIES

As already pointed out, standard deviation is suitable for algebraic manipulations *i.e.,* if we are given the averages, the sizes and the standard deviations of a number of groups, then we can obtain the standard deviation of the resultant group obtained on combining the different groups. Thus if

$\sigma_1, \sigma_2, \ldots, \sigma_k$ are the standard deviations; $\bar{X}_1, \bar{X}_2, \ldots, \bar{X}_k$ are the arithmetic means;

and $n_1, n_2, \ldots, n_k$ are the sizes, of k groups respectively,

then the standard deviation σ of the combined group of size $N = n_1 + n_2 + \ldots + n_k$ is given by the formula

$$N\sigma^2 = n_1(\sigma_1^2 + d_1^2) + n_2(\sigma_2^2 + d_2^2) + \ldots + n_k(\sigma_k^2 + d_k^2) \qquad \ldots (6{\cdot}29)$$

where

$$d_1 = \bar{X}_1 - \bar{X}; \quad d_2 = \bar{X}_2 - \bar{X}, \quad \ldots, \quad d_k = \bar{X}_k - \bar{X} \qquad \ldots (6{\cdot}29a)$$

and

$$\bar{X} = \frac{n_1\bar{X}_1 + n_2\bar{X}_2 + \ldots + n_k\bar{X}_k}{n_1 + n_2 + \ldots + n_k}, \text{ is the mean of the combined group.} \qquad \ldots (6{\cdot}29b)$$

Thus the standard deviation of the combined group is given by :

$$\sigma = \left[\frac{n_1(\sigma_1^2 + d_1^2) + n_2(\sigma_2^2 + d_2^2) + \ldots + n_k(\sigma_k^2 + d_k^2)}{n_1 + n_2 + \ldots + n_k}\right]^{1/2} \qquad \ldots (6{\cdot}30)$$

In particular, for two groups we get from (6·33) :

$$(n_1 + n_2)\,\sigma^2 = n_1(\sigma_1^2 + d_1^2) + n_2(\sigma_2^2 + d_2^2) \qquad \ldots (6{\cdot}31)$$

where $d_1 = \overline{X}_1 - \overline{X} = \overline{X}_1 - \dfrac{n_1\overline{X}_1 + n_2\overline{X}_2}{n_1 + n_2} = \dfrac{n_2(\overline{X}_1 - \overline{X}_2)}{n_1 + n_2}$

and $d_2 = \overline{X}_2 - \overline{X} = \overline{X}_2 - \dfrac{n_1\overline{X}_1 + n_2\overline{X}_2}{n_1 + n_2} = \dfrac{n_1(\overline{X}_2 - \overline{X}_1)}{n_1 + n_2}$

Rewriting (6·35) and substituting the values of d_1 and d_2, we get

$$\begin{aligned}(n_1 + n_2)\,\sigma^2 &= n_1\sigma_1^2 + n_2\sigma_2^2 + n_1 d_1^2 + n_2 d_2^2\\ &= n_1\sigma_1^2 + n_2\sigma_2^2 + \frac{n_1 n_2(\overline{X}_1 - \overline{X}_2)^2}{(n_1 + n_2)^2}(n_1 + n_2)\\ &= n_1\sigma_1^2 + n_2\sigma_2^2 + \frac{n_1 n_2(\overline{X}_1 - \overline{X}_2)^2}{n_1 + n_2}\end{aligned}$$

$$\Rightarrow \qquad \sigma = \left[\frac{n_1^2\sigma_1^2 + n_2\sigma_2^2}{n_1 + n_2} + \frac{n_1 n_2(\overline{X}_1 - \overline{X}_2)^2}{(n_1 + n_2)^2}\right]^{1/2} \qquad \ldots (6{\cdot}31a)$$

Thus, for two groups, the formula (6·35*a*) can be used with convenience, since all the values are already given.

Example 6·27. *The means of two samples of sizes 50 and 100 respectively are 54·1 and 50·3 and the standard deviations are 8 and 7. Obtain the standard deviation of the sample of size 150 obtained by combining the two samples.*

Solution. In the usual notations we are given :

$$n_1 = 50,\quad n_2 = 100,\quad \overline{X}_1 = 54{\cdot}1,\quad \overline{X}_2 = 50{\cdot}3,\quad \sigma_1 = 8,\quad \sigma_2 = 7.$$

The mean $\overline{X}$ of the combined sample of size 150 obtained on pooling the two samples is given by :

$$\overline{X} = \frac{n_1\overline{X}_1 + n_2\overline{X}_2}{n_1 + n_2} = \frac{50 \times 54{\cdot}1 + 100 \times 50{\cdot}3}{50 + 100} = \frac{2705 + 5030}{150} = \frac{7735}{150} = 51{\cdot}57.$$

$$d_1 = \overline{X}_1 - \overline{X} = 54{\cdot}10 - 51{\cdot}57 = 2{\cdot}53; \quad d_2 = \overline{X}_2 - \overline{X} = 50{\cdot}30 - 51{\cdot}57 = -\,1{\cdot}27$$

Hence, the variance σ^2 of the combined sample of size 150 is given by :

$$\begin{aligned}(n_1 + n_2)\,\sigma^2 &= n_1(\sigma_1^2 + d_1^2) + n_2(\sigma_2^2 + d_2^2)\\ \Rightarrow \quad 150\sigma^2 &= 50[8^2 + (2{\cdot}53)^2] + 100[7^2 + (-\,1{\cdot}27)^2]\\ &= 50(64 + 6{\cdot}3504) + 100(49 + 1{\cdot}6129)\end{aligned}$$

$$\therefore \quad \sigma^2 = \frac{3517{\cdot}52 + 5061{\cdot}29}{150} = \frac{8578{\cdot}81}{150} = 57{\cdot}1921 \quad \Rightarrow \quad \sigma = \sqrt{57{\cdot}1921} = 7{\cdot}5625.$$

Example 6·28. *The mean weight of 150 students is 60 kgs. The mean weights of boys and girls are 70 kgs. and 55 kgs respectively, and the standard deviations are 10 kgs. and 15 kgs. respectively. Find the number of boys and the combined standard deviation.*

Solution. In the usual notations, we are given :

$$n = n_1 + n_2 = 150;\ \bar{x} = 60 \text{ kg.};\ \bar{x}_1 = 70 \text{ kg};\ \bar{x}_2 = 55 \text{ kg};\ \sigma_1 = 10 \text{ kg.};\ \sigma_2 = 15 \text{ kg.} \qquad \ldots (*)$$

where the subscripts 1 and 2 refer to boys and girls respectively. We have :

$$\bar{x} = \frac{n_1\bar{x}_1 + n_2\bar{x}_2}{n_1 + n_2} \quad \Rightarrow \quad \frac{70n_1 + 55n_2}{150} = 60 \qquad \text{[From (*)]}$$

$$\therefore \quad 14n_1 + 11(150 - n_1) = 60 \times 30 = 1800 \quad \Rightarrow \quad 3n_1 = 1800 - 1650 = 150 \quad \Rightarrow \quad n_1 = \frac{150}{3} = 50$$

$$\therefore \qquad n_2 = 150 - n_1 = 150 - 50 = 100.$$

Hence, the numbr of boys is $n_1 = 50$ and the number of girls is $n_2 = 100$.

The combined variance (for boys and girls together) is given by :

$$\sigma^2 = \frac{1}{n_1 + n_2}\left[n_1(\sigma_1^2 + d_1^2) + n_2(\sigma_2^2 + d_2^2)\right]$$

where $d_1 = \bar{x}_1 - \bar{x} = (70 - 60)$ kg. = 10kg. ; $d_2 = \bar{x}_2 - \bar{x} = (55 - 60)$ kg. = – 5 kg.

$$\therefore \quad \sigma^2 = \frac{1}{150}\left[50(10^2 + 10^2) + 100(15^2 + (-5)^2)\right] = \frac{10000 + 25000}{150} = \frac{700}{3} = 233{\cdot}33$$

$$\Rightarrow \quad s.d.\ (\sigma) = \sqrt{233{\cdot}33} = 15{\cdot}275.$$

Example 6·29. *For a group containing 100 observations, the arithmetic mean and the standard deviation are 8 and $\sqrt{10{\cdot}5}$ respectively. For 50 observations selected from these 100 observations, the mean and standard deviation are 10 and 2 respectively. Calculate values of the mean and standard deviation for the other half.*

Solution. In the usual notations, we are given :

$$n = 100,\ \bar{x} = 8,\ \sigma = \sqrt{10{\cdot}5} \Rightarrow \sigma^2 = 10{\cdot}5;\ n_1 = 50,\ \bar{x}_1 = 10,\ \sigma_1 = 2;\ n_2 = 100 - 50 = 50$$

We want $\bar{x}_2$ and σ_2.

$$\bar{x} = \frac{n_1\bar{x}_1 + n_2\bar{x}_2}{n_1 + n_2} \Rightarrow 8 = \frac{50 \times 10 + 50 \times \bar{x}_2}{100}$$

$$\therefore \quad 800 = 500 + 50\bar{x}_2 \Rightarrow 50\bar{x}_2 = 800 - 500 = 300 \Rightarrow \bar{x}_2 = \frac{300}{50} = 6$$

$$d_1 = \bar{x}_1 - \bar{x} = 10 - 8 = 2 \Rightarrow d_1^2 = 4;\quad d_2 = \bar{x}_2 - \bar{x} = 6 - 8 = -2 \Rightarrow d_2^2 = 4$$

$$(n_1 + n_2)\sigma^2 = n_1(\sigma_1^2 + d_1^2) + n_2(\sigma_2^2 + d_2^2)$$

$$\Rightarrow \quad 100 \times 10{\cdot}5 = 50(4 + 4) + 50(\sigma_2^2 + 4)$$

$$\Rightarrow \quad 1050 = 400 + 50\sigma_2^2 + 200 \Rightarrow \sigma_2^2 = \frac{1050 - 600}{50} = \frac{450}{50} = 9 \Rightarrow \sigma_2 = 3,$$

since *s.d.* is always positive.

Example 6·30. *Find the missing information from the following :*

	Group I	*Group II*	*Group III*	*Combined*
Number	*50*	*?*	*90*	*200*
Standard Deviation	*6*	*7*	*?*	*7·746*
Mean	*113*	*?*	*115*	*116*

(Himachal Pradesh Univ. B.Com., 1998)

Solution.

	Group 1	*Group 2*	*Group 3*	*Combined Group*
Number	$n_1 = 50$	$n_2 = ?$	$n_3 = 90$	$n_1 + n_2 + n_3 = 200$
s.d.	$\sigma_1 = 6$	$\sigma_2 = 7$	$\sigma_3 = ?$	$\sigma = 7{\cdot}746$
Mean	$\bar{X}_1 = 113$	$\bar{X}_2 = ?$	$\bar{X}_3 = 115$	$\bar{X} = 116$

We have three unknown values *viz.*, n_2, σ_3 and $\bar{X}_2$. To determine these three values we need three equations which are given below :

$$n_1 + n_2 + n_3 = 200 \quad \ldots(i) \quad ; \quad \bar{X} = \frac{n_1\bar{X}_1 + n_2\bar{X}_2 + n_3\bar{X}_3}{n_1 + n_2 + n_3} \quad \ldots(ii)$$

and $(n_1 + n_2 + n_3)\sigma^2 = n_1(\sigma_1^2 + d_1^2) + n_2(\sigma_2^2 + d_2^2) + n_3(\sigma_3^2 + d_3^2)$ ... (*iii*)

From (*i*) we get $n_2 = 200 - (n_1 + n_3) = 200 - (50 + 90) = 60$ ... (*iv*)

Using (*ii*) we get :

$$200 \times 116 = 50 \times 113 + 60\,\overline{X}_2 + 90 \times 115$$

$$\Rightarrow \quad 23200 = 5650 + 60\overline{X}_2 + 10350$$

$$\Rightarrow \quad 60\overline{X}_2 = 23200 - (5650 + 10350)$$

$$= 23200 - 16000 = 7200$$

$$\Rightarrow \quad \overline{X}_2 = \frac{7200}{60} = 120 \qquad \ldots (v)$$

$$\therefore \quad d_1 = \overline{X}_1 - \overline{X} = 113 - 116 = -3$$

$$d_2 = \overline{X}_2 - \overline{X} = 120 - 116 = 4$$

$$d_3 = \overline{X}_3 - \overline{X} = 115 - 116 = -1$$

Substituting these values in (*iii*), we get

$$200 \times (7{\cdot}746)^2 = 50(36 + 9) + 60(49 + 16) + 90(\sigma_3^2 + 1)$$

$$\Rightarrow \quad 200 \times 60{\cdot}000516 = 50 \times 45 + 60 \times 65 + 90 + 90\sigma_3^2$$

$$\Rightarrow \quad 12000 = 2250 + 3900 + 90 + 90\sigma_3^2$$

$$\Rightarrow \quad \sigma_3^2 = \frac{12000 - 6240}{90} = \frac{5760}{90} = 64 \quad \Rightarrow \quad \sigma_3 = 8$$

Hence, the unknown constants are : $n_2 = 60$, $\overline{X}_2 = 120$ and $\sigma_3 = 8$.

6·11. COEFFICIENT OF VARIATION

Standard deviation is only an absolute measure of dispersion, depending upon the units of measurement. The relative measure of dispersion based on standard deviation is called the coefficient of standard deviation and is given by :

$$\text{Coefficient of Standard Deviation} = \frac{\sigma}{\overline{X}} \qquad \ldots (6{\cdot}32)$$

This is a pure number independent of the units of measurement and thus, is suitable for comparing the variability, homogeneity or uniformity of two or more distributions.

We have already discussed the relative measures of dispersion based on range, quartile deviation and mean deviation. Since standard deviation is by far the best measure of dispersion, for comparing the homogeneity or heterogeneity of two or more distributions, we generally compute the coefficient of standard deviation unless asked otherwise.

100 times the coefficient of dispersion based on standard deviation is called the *coefficient of variation*, abbreviated as C.V. Thus,

$$\text{C.V.} = 100 \times \frac{\sigma}{\overline{X}} \qquad \ldots (6{\cdot}33)$$

According to Professor Karl Pearson who suggested this measure, "*coefficient of variation is the percentage variation in mean, standard deviation being considered as the total variation in the mean*".

For comparing the variability of two distributions we compute the coefficient of variation for each distribution. A distribution with smaller C.V. is said to be more homogeneous or uniform or less variable than the other and the series with greater C.V. is said to be more heterogeneous or more variable than the other.

Remark. Some authors define coefficient of variation as the "coefficient of standard deviation expressed as a percentage". For example, if mean = 15 and *s.d.* = 3, then

$$\text{C.V.} = \frac{s.d.}{\text{Mean}} = \frac{3}{15} = 0.20 \quad \Rightarrow \quad \text{C.V.} = 20\% \qquad \ldots (6{\cdot}33a)$$

If we are given the coefficient of variation as a percentage, (like 25% or 10%), then we will use the formula (6·33*a*).

Example 6·31. *Comment on the following :*

For a set of 10 observations : mean = 5, s.d. = 2 and C.V. = 60%.

Solution. We are given : $n = 10, \bar{x} = 5$ and $\sigma = 2$

Using (6.37*a*), we get $\text{C.V.} = \frac{\sigma}{\bar{x}} = \frac{2}{5} = 0{\cdot}40 = 40\%$

But we are given C.V. = 60%. Hence, the given statement is wrong.

Example 6·32. *If $N = 10$, $\bar{X} = 12$, $\Sigma X^2 = 1530$, find the coefficient of variation.*

Solution. We have :

$$\sigma^2 = \frac{1}{n}\Sigma X^2 - (\bar{X})^2 = \frac{1530}{10} - (12)^2 = 153 - 144 = 9 \quad \Rightarrow \quad \sigma = 3$$

[Negative sign is rejected since *s.d.* is always non-negative]

$$\therefore \quad \text{C.V.} = \frac{100 \times \sigma}{\bar{X}} = \frac{100 \times 3}{12} = 25 \qquad \text{[Using (6·37)]}$$

Example 6·33. *The arithmetic mean of runs scored by three batsmen—Vijay, Subhash and Kumar in the same series of 10 innings are 50, 48 and 12 respectively. The standard deviation of their runs are respectively, 15, 12 and 2. Who is the most consistent of the three ? If one of the three is to be selected, who will be selected ?*

Solution. Let $\bar{X}_1, \bar{X}_2, \bar{X}_3$ be the means and $\sigma_1, \sigma_2, \sigma_3$ the standard deviation of the runs scored by Vijay, Subhash and Kumar respectively. Then we are given :

$$\bar{X}_1 = 50, \quad \bar{X} = 48, \quad \bar{X}_3 = 12; \quad \sigma_1 = 15, \quad \sigma_2 = 12, \quad \sigma_3 = 2$$

$$\text{C.V. of runs scored by Vijay} = \frac{100\sigma_1}{\bar{X}_1} = \frac{100 \times 15}{50} = 30$$

$$\text{C.V. of runs scored by Subhash} = \frac{100\sigma_2}{\bar{X}_2} = \frac{100 \times 12}{48} = 25$$

$$\text{C.V. of runs scored by Kumar} = \frac{100\sigma_3}{\bar{X}_3} = \frac{100 \times 2}{12} = 16.67$$

The decision regarding the selection of player may be based on two considerations :

(*i*) If we want a consistent player (which is statistically sound decision), then Kumar is to be selected, since C.V. of the runs is smallest for Kumar.

(*ii*) If we want to select a player whose expected score is the highest, then Vijay will be selected.

Remark. In fact, the best way will be to select a person who is consistent and also has the highest expected score.

Example 6·34. *A batsman Mr. A is more consistent in his last 10 innings as compared to another batsman Mr. B. Therefore, Mr. A is also a higher run getter". Comment.* [*Delhi Univ. B.Com. (Pass), 1999*]

Solution. The consistency of a batsman is judged on the basis of coefficient of variation. The batsman *A* is more consistent than batsman *B* if

$$\text{C.V. }(A) < \text{C.V. }(B) \quad \Rightarrow \quad 100\frac{\sigma_A}{\bar{x}_A} < 100\frac{\sigma_B}{\bar{x}_B} \quad \Rightarrow \quad \frac{\sigma_A}{\bar{x}_A} < \frac{\sigma_B}{\bar{x}_B} \quad \Rightarrow \quad \frac{\bar{x}_A}{\bar{x}_B} > \frac{\sigma_A}{\sigma_B} \qquad \ldots (i)$$

The batsman *A* will be higher run getter than batsman *B* if

$$\bar{x}_A > \bar{x}_B \quad \Rightarrow \quad \frac{\bar{x}_A}{\bar{x}_B} > 1 \qquad \ldots (ii)$$

Since, in general, (*i*) does not necessarily imply (*ii*), the given statement is not true, in general.

In order to conclude that *A* is also a higher run getter, we must be given the values of $\bar{x}_A$ and $\bar{x}_B$ and they should satisfy (*ii*).

Example 6·35. *Coefficien of variation of two series are 75% and 90% and their standard deviations are 15 and 18 respectively. Find their means.*

Solution. We are given : $\sigma_1 = 15$ and $\sigma_2 = 18$

C.V. of I series $= 75\% = \frac{75}{100}$; C.V. of II series $= 90\% = \frac{90}{100}$

Using (6·37*a*), we have : $\text{C.V.} = \frac{\sigma}{\text{Mean}} \Rightarrow \text{Mean} = \frac{\sigma}{\text{C.V.}}$

$\therefore$ Mean of I series $= \frac{\sigma_1}{\text{C.V. (I)}} = \frac{15 \times 100}{75} = 20;$

and Mean of II series $= \frac{\sigma_2}{\text{C.V.(II)}} = \frac{18 \times 100}{90} = 20$

Example 6·36. *"After settlement the average weekly wage in a factory had increased from Rs. 8,000 to Rs. 12,000 and the standard deviation had increased from Rs. 100 to Rs. 150. After settlement the wage has become higher and more uniform." Do you agree ?*

Solution. It is given that after settlement the average weekly wages of workers have gone up from Rs. 8,000 to Rs. 12,000. This implies that the total wages received per week by all the workers together have increased. However, we cannot conclude that the wage of each individual has increased.

Regarding uniformity of the wages, we have to calculate the coefficient of variation of the wages of workers before the settlement and after the settlement.

C.V. of wages before the settlement $= \frac{100 \times 100}{8{,}000} = 1.25$

C.V. of wages after the settlement $= \frac{100 \times 150}{12{,}000} = 1.25$

Since the coefficient of variation of wages before the settlement and after the settlement is same, there is no change in the variability of distribution of wages after the settlement. Hence, it is wrong to say that the wages have become more uniform (less variable) after the settlement.

Example 6·37. *A study of B.A. (Hons.) Economics examination results of 1000 students in 1990 gave the mean grade as 78 and the standard deviation as 8·0. A similar study in 1995 revealed the mean grade of the group as 80 and the standard deviation as 7·6. In which year was there the greater*

(i) absolute dispersion, *(ii) relative dispersion ?*

What can we say about the average performance of the students over time ?

[*Delhi Univ. B.A. (Econ. Hons.), 1999*]

Solution. In the usual notations, we are given :

Year 1990 : $\bar{X}_1 = 78;\ \sigma_1 = 8{\cdot}0;$ *Year 1995* : $\bar{X}_2 = 80,\ \sigma_2 = 7{\cdot}6$

(*i*) We know that the best absolute measure of dispersion is the standard deviation.

Since $\sigma_1 > \sigma_2$, in 1990 there was greater absolute dispersion.

(*ii*) The relative measure of dispersion is given by the coefficient of variation.

$\text{C.V. (1990)} = \frac{100\ \sigma_1}{\bar{X}_1} = \frac{100 \times 8.0}{78} = 10.26$; $\text{C.V. (1995)} = \frac{100\ \sigma_2}{\bar{X}_2} = \frac{100 \times 7{\cdot}6}{80} = 9{\cdot}50$

Since C.V. (1990) > C.V. (1999), the relative dispersion is greater in 1990.

We observe that $\bar{X}_2 > \bar{X}_1$ and C.V. (1995) < C.V. (1990). Hence, it can be said that over the time from 1990 to 1995, the average performance of the students has increased (improved) and they have become more consistent (less variable).

Example 6.38. *Explain the difference between absolute and relative dispersion. If 20 is subtracted from every observation in a data set, then the coefficient of variation of the resulting data set is 20%. If 40 is added to every observation of the same data set, then the coefficient of variation of the resulting set of data is 10%. Find the mean and standard deviation of the original set of data.*

[*Delhi Univ. B.Com. (Hons.), 2004*]

Solution. Let $\overline{X}$ be the mean and $\sigma_X = \sigma$, be the standard deviation of the data observations

Let $U = X - 20 \Rightarrow \overline{U} = \overline{X} - 20$ and $\sigma_U = \sigma_X = \sigma$

and $V = X + 40 \Rightarrow \overline{V} = \overline{X} + 40$ and $\sigma_V = \sigma_X = \sigma$ $\Bigg\}$ [$\because$ *s.d.* is independent of change of origin]

$$C.V.\ (U) = \frac{100\ \sigma_U}{\overline{U}} = \frac{100\ \sigma}{\overline{X} - 20} = 20 \text{ (Given)} \qquad \ldots(i)$$

$$\text{and} \quad C.V.\ (V) = \frac{100\ \sigma_V}{\overline{V}} = \frac{100\ \sigma}{\overline{X} + 40} = 10 \text{ (Given)} \qquad \ldots(ii)$$

Dividing (*i*) by (*ii*) we get $\dfrac{\overline{X} + 40}{\overline{X} - 20} = 2 \quad \Rightarrow \quad \overline{X} = 800$

Substituting in (*i*), we get $\dfrac{100\sigma}{60} = 20 \quad \Rightarrow \quad \sigma = 12$

Example 6·39. *An analysis of the monthly wages paid to workers in two firms A and B, belonging to the same industry, gives the following results :*

	Firm A	*Firm B*
Number of wages earners	*550*	*650*
Average monthly wages (in '00 Rs.)	*50*	*45*
Standard deviation of the distribution of wages (in '00 Rs.)	$\sqrt{90}$	$\sqrt{120}$

Answer the following questions with proper justifications :

(*a*) *Which firm A or B pays larger amount as monthly wages ?*

(*b*) *In which firm A or B, is there greater variability in individual wages ?*

(*c*) *What are the measures of (i) average monthly wages and (ii) standard deviation in the distribution of individual wages of all workers in the two firms taken together ?*

Solution. Let n_1, n_2 denote the sizes $\overline{X}_1$, $\overline{X}_2$ the means and σ_1, σ_2 the standard deviations of the monthly wages (in Rs.) of the workers in the firms *A* and *B* respectively. Then we are given :

$n_1 = 550, \quad \overline{X}_1 = 50, \quad \sigma_1 = \sqrt{90} \quad \Rightarrow \quad \sigma_1^2 = 90$

$n_2 = 650, \quad \overline{X}_2 = 45, \quad \sigma_2 = \sqrt{120} \quad \Rightarrow \quad \sigma_2^2 = 120$

(*a*) We know that

$$\text{Average monthly wages} = \frac{\text{Total monthly wages paid by the firm}}{\text{No. of workers in the firm}}$$

$\Rightarrow$ Total monthly wages paid by the firm = (No. of workers in the firm) × (Average monthly wages)

$\therefore$ Total monthly wages paid by firm $A = n_1\overline{X}_1 = \text{Rs. } 550 \times 50 = \text{Rs. } 27{,}500$ hundred

Total monthly wages paid by firm $B = n_2\overline{X}_2 = \text{Rs. } 650 \times 45 = \text{Rs. } 29{,}250$ hundred

Hence the firm *B* pays out larger amount as monthly wages, the excess of the monthly wages paid over firm *A* being

Rs. (29,250 – 27,500) hundred = Rs. 1,750 hundred

(*b*) In order to find out which firm has more variation in individual wages, we have to compute the coefficient of variation (C.V.) of the distribution of monthly wages for each of the two firms *A* and *B*.

$$\text{C.V. for firm } A = \frac{100\ \sigma_1}{\overline{X}_1} = \frac{100\sqrt{90}}{50} = 2 \times 9{\cdot}487 = 18{\cdot}974$$

$$\text{C.V. for firm } B = \frac{100\ \sigma_2}{\overline{X}_2} = \frac{100\sqrt{120}}{45} = \frac{20 \times 10{\cdot}954}{9} = \frac{219{\cdot}080}{9} = 24{\cdot}34$$

Since C.V. for firm B is greater than the C.V. for firm A, firm B has greater variability in individual wages.

(c) (i) The average monthly wage, say, $\overline{X}$, of all the workers in the two firms A and B taken together is given by :

$$\overline{X} = \frac{n_1\overline{X}_1 + n_2\overline{X}_2}{n_1 + n_2} = \text{Rs. } \frac{500 \times 50 + 650 \times 45}{550 + 650} \text{ hundred}$$

$$= \text{Rs. } \frac{27{,}500 + 29{,}250}{1{,}200} \text{ hundred} = \text{Rs. } \frac{56{,}750}{1{,}200} \text{ hundred} = \text{Rs. } 47{\cdot}29 \text{ hundred} = \text{Rs. } 4{,}729.$$

(ii) The variance σ^2 of the distribution of monthly wages of all the workers in the two firms A and B taken together is given by :

$$(n_1 + n_2)\,\sigma^2 = n_1(\sigma_1^2 + d_1^2) + n_2(\sigma_2^2 + d_2^2) \qquad \ldots (*)$$

$$d_1 = \overline{X}_1 - \overline{X} = 50 - 47{\cdot}29 = 2{\cdot}71 \quad \Rightarrow \quad d_1^2 = 7{\cdot}344$$

and $$d_2 = \overline{X}_2 - \overline{X} = 45 - 47{\cdot}29 = -2{\cdot}29 \quad \Rightarrow \quad d_2^2 = 5{\cdot}244$$

Substituting in (*), we get

$$1200\sigma^2 = 550\,(90 + 7{\cdot}344) + 650\,(120 + 5{\cdot}244) = 550 \times 97{\cdot}344 + 650 \times 125{\cdot}244$$
$$= 53539{\cdot}2 + 81408{\cdot}6 = 134947{\cdot}8$$

$$\Rightarrow \quad \sigma^2 = \frac{134947{\cdot}8}{1200} = 112{\cdot}4565 \text{ Rs.}^2 \Rightarrow \sigma = \text{Rs. } \sqrt{112{\cdot}4565} \text{ hundred} = \text{Rs. } 10{\cdot}60 \text{ hundred} = \text{Rs. } 1060$$

Example 6·40. *From the prices X and Y of shares A and B respectively given below, state which share is more stable in value.*

Price of Share A (X) :	*55*	*54*	*52*	*53*	*56*	*58*	*52*	*50*	*51*	*49*
Price of Share B (Y) :	*108*	*107*	*105*	*105*	*106*	*107*	*104*	*103*	*104*	*101*

Solution.

COMPUTATION OF MEAN AND S.D. OF PRICES OF SHARES A AND B

SHARE A			*SHARE B*		
X	$X - \overline{X} = X - 53$	$(X - \overline{X})^2$	Y	$Y - \overline{Y} = Y - 105$	$(Y - \overline{Y})^2$
55	2	4	108	3	9
54	1	1	107	2	4
52	– 1	1	105	0	0
53	0	0	105	0	0
56	3	9	106	1	1
58	5	25	107	2	4
52	–1	1	104	–1	1
50	–3	9	103	–2	4
51	–2	4	104	–1	1
49	– 4	16	101	– 4	16
$\Sigma X = 530$	$\Sigma(X - \overline{X}) = 0$	$\Sigma(X - \overline{X})^2 = 70$	$\Sigma Y = 1050$	0	$\Sigma(Y - \overline{Y})^2 = 40$

$$\overline{X} = \frac{\Sigma X}{n} = \frac{530}{10} = 53 \quad , \quad \sigma_x^2 = \frac{1}{n}\Sigma(X - \overline{X})^2 = \frac{70}{10} = 7 \quad \Rightarrow \quad \sigma_x = \sqrt{7} = 2{\cdot}646$$

$$\overline{Y} = \frac{\Sigma Y}{n} = \frac{1050}{10} = 105 \quad , \quad \sigma_y^2 = \frac{1}{n}\Sigma(Y - \overline{Y})^2 = \frac{40}{10} = 4 \quad \Rightarrow \quad \sigma_y = \sqrt{4} = 2$$

$$\text{C.V. }(X) = \frac{100 \times \sigma_x}{\overline{X}} = \frac{100 \times 2.646}{53} = 4{\cdot}99 \quad ; \quad \text{C.V. }(Y) = \frac{100 \times \sigma_y}{\overline{Y}} = \frac{100 \times 2}{105} = 1{\cdot}90$$

Since C.V. (Y) is less than C.V. (X), the share B is more stable in value.

Example 6·41. *Goals scored by two teams A and B in a football season were as shown in adjoinging table.*

By calculating the coefficient of variation in each case, find which team may be considered more consistent.

Number of goals scored in a match	*Number of matches*	
	A team	*B team*
0	*27*	*17*
1	*9*	*9*
2	*8*	*6*
3	*5*	*5*
4	*4*	*3*

Solution.

CALCUALTIONS FOR C.V. FOR TEAMS A AND B

No. of goals scored in a match (X)	*TEAM A* No. of matches (f_1)	f_1X	f_1X^2	*TEAM B* No. of matches (f_2)	f_2X	f_2X^2
0	27	0	0	17	0	0
1	9	9	9	9	9	9
2	8	16	32	6	12	24
3	5	15	45	5	15	45
4	4	16	64	3	12	48
Total	$\Sigma f_1 = 53$	$\Sigma f_1 X = 56$	$\Sigma f_1X^2 = 150$	$\Sigma f_2 = 40$	$\Sigma f_2X = 48$	$\Sigma f_2X^2 = 126$

$$\bar{X}_A = \frac{\Sigma f_1 X}{\Sigma f_1} = \frac{56}{53} = 1{\cdot}06$$

$$\sigma_A^2 = \frac{\Sigma f_1 X^2}{\Sigma f_1} - (\bar{X}_A)^2 = \frac{150}{53} - (1{\cdot}06)^2$$

$$= 2{\cdot}83 - 1{\cdot}1236 = 1{\cdot}7064$$

$$\sigma_A = \sqrt{1{\cdot}7064} = 1{\cdot}3063$$

$$\therefore \text{ C.V. for team } A = \frac{100 \times \sigma_A}{\bar{X}_A} = \frac{100 \times 1{\cdot}3063}{1{\cdot}06} = 123{\cdot}24$$

$$\bar{X}_B = \frac{\Sigma f_2 X}{\Sigma f_2} = \frac{48}{40} = 1{\cdot}2$$

$$\sigma_B^2 = \frac{\Sigma f_2 X^2}{\Sigma f_2} - (\bar{X}_B)^2 = \frac{126}{40} - (1{\cdot}2)^2$$

$$= 3{\cdot}15 - 1{\cdot}44 = 1{\cdot}71$$

$$\Rightarrow \quad \sigma_B = \sqrt{1{\cdot}71} = 1{\cdot}308$$

$$\therefore \text{ C.V. for team } B = \frac{100 \times \sigma_B}{\bar{X}_B} = \frac{100 \times 1{\cdot}308}{1{\cdot}2} = 109{\cdot}0$$

Since C.V. for team *B* is less then C.V. for team *A*, team *B* may be considered to be more consistent.

6·12. RELATIONS BETWEEN VARIOUS MEASURES OF DISPERSION

For a Normal distribution (*c.f.* Chapter 14 on theoretical distributions) we have the following relations between the different measures of dispersion :

(*i*) Mean ± Q.D. covers 50% of the observations of the distribution.

(*ii*) Mean ± M.D. covers 57·5% of the observations.

(*iii*) Mean ± σ includes 68·27% of the observations.

(*iv*) Mean ± 2σ includes 95·45% of the observations.

(*v*) Mean ± 3σ includes 99·73% of the observations.

(*vi*) Q.D. = $0{\cdot}6745\sigma \approx \frac{2}{3}\sigma$ (approximately). ... (6·34)

(*vii*) M.D. = $\sqrt{\frac{2}{\pi}}\,.\,\sigma = 0{\cdot}7979 \approx \frac{4}{5}\sigma$ (approximately). ... (6·35)

(*viii*) Q.D. = 0·8459 M.D. [From (*vi*) and (*vii*), on dividing and transposing]

$\Rightarrow$ Q.D. = $\frac{5}{6}$ M.D. (approximately) ... (6·36)

Combining the results (*vi*), (*vii*), and (*viii*) we get approximately :

$$3 \text{ Q.D.} = 2 \text{ S.D.} \quad ; \quad 5 \text{ M.D.} = 4 \text{ S.D.} \quad ; \quad 6 \text{ Q.D.} = 5 \text{ M.D.}$$

$$\Rightarrow \quad 4 \text{ S.D.} = 5 \text{ M.D.} = 6 \text{ Q.D.}$$

Thus we see that standard deviation ensures the highest degree of reliability and Q.D. the lowest.

(*ix*) We have :

$$\text{Q.D.} : \text{M.D.} : \text{S.D.} :: \tfrac{2}{3}\sigma : \tfrac{4}{5}\sigma : \sigma$$

$$\Rightarrow \quad \text{Q.D.} : \text{M.D.} : \text{S.D.} :: 10 : 12 : 15 \qquad \ldots(6\cdot37)$$

(*x*) Range = 6 S.D. = 6σ ...(6·38)

Remarks 1. Rigorously speaking, the above results for various measures of dispersion hold for Normal distribution discussed in Chapter 14 on theoretical distributions. However, these results are approximately true even for symmetrical distributions or moderately asymmetrical (skewed) distributions.

2. In the above results we have expressed various measures of dispersion in terms of standard deviation. We give below the relations expressing standard deviation in terms of other measures of dispersion.

$$\left.\begin{aligned} \text{S.D.} &= 1\cdot2533 \text{ M.D.} \simeq \tfrac{5}{4} \text{M.D.} \\ \text{S.D.} &= 1\cdot4826 \text{ Q.D.} \simeq \tfrac{3}{2} \text{Q.D.} \\ \text{S.D.} &= \tfrac{1}{6} \text{Range} \end{aligned}\right\} \qquad \ldots(6\cdot39)$$

Also we have : M.D. = 1·1830 Q.D. $\simeq \frac{6}{5}$ Q.D. ...(6·40)

EXERCISE 6·4

1. (*a*) What do you understand by absolute and relative measure of dispersion ? Explain advantages of the relative measures over the absolute measures of dispersion.

(*b*) What do you understand by coefficient of variation ? What purpose does it serve ?

2. Prove that the coefficient of variation of the first *n* natural numbers is : $\sqrt{\dfrac{(n-1)}{3(n+1)}}$.

[*Delhi Univ. B.A. Econ. (Hons.), 2006, 2003*]

3. The arithmetic means of runs secured by the three batsmen, *X*, *Y* and *Z* in a series of 10 innings are 50, 48 and 12 respectively. The standard deviations of their runs are 15, 12 and 2 respectively. Who is the most consistent of the three ?

Ans. C.V. (*X*) = 30 ; C.V. (*Y*) = 25 ; C.V. (*Z*) = 16·67. Batsman *Z* is the most consistent.

4. Two samples *A* and *B* have the same standard deviations, but the mean of *A* is greater than that of *B*. The coefficient of variation of *A* is

(*i*) greater than that of *B*. (*ii*) less than that of *B*.
(*iii*) equal to that of *B*. (*iv*) None of these.

Ans. (*i*)

5. (*a*) The coefficient of variation of a distribution is 60% and its standard deviation is 12. Find out its mean.

(*b*) Find the coefficient of variation if variance is 16, number of items is 20 and sum of the items is 160.

[*Bangalore Univ. B.Com., 1998*]

Ans. (*a*)Mean = 20 ; (*b*) C.V. = 50%.

6. (*a*)Coefficients of variation of two series are 60% and 80%. Their standard deviations are 20 and 16 respectively. What are their arithmetic means ?

(*b*) Coefficients of variation of two series are 60% and 80%. Their standard deviations are 24 and 20 respectively. What are their arithmetic means ? [*Delhi Univ. B.Com. (Pass), 1997*]

Ans. (*a*) 33·3, 20; (*b*) 40, 25.

7. Comment on the statement : "After settlement the average weekly wage in a factory had increased from Rs. 800 to Rs. 1200 and the standard deviation had increased from 200 to 250. After settlement, the wages have become higher and more uniform.

Ans. Yes.

8. Weekly average wages of workers in a factory increase from Rs. 800 to Rs. 1200 and standard deviation increases from Rs. 100 to Rs. 500. Have the wages become less uniform now ?

Ans. C.V.(Initial wages) = 12·5 ; C.V. (Revised wages) = 41·67. Yes, the revised wages are more variable.

9. A study of examination results of a batch of students showed the average marks secured as 50 with a standard deviation of 2 in the first year of their studies. The same batch showed an average of 60 marks with an increased standard deviation of 3, after five years of studies. Can you say that the batch as a whole showed improved performance ?

Ans. Improved performance (better average) and more consistent.

10. The means and standard deviations of two brands of light bulbs are given below :

	Brand 1	*Brand 2*
Mean	800 hours	770 hours
S.D.	100 hours	60 hours

Calculate a measure of relative dispersions for the two brands and interpret the results.

[Delhi Univ. B.Com. (Hons.), 2000]

Ans. C.V. (I) = 12·5; C.V. (II) = 7·79 ; Brand II is more uniform.

11. The following is the record number of bricks laid each day for 10 days by two bricklayers *A* and *B*. Calculate the coefficient of variation in each case and discuss the relative consistency of the two bricklayers.

A	700	675	725	625	650	700	650	700	600	650
B	550	600	575	550	650	600	550	525	625	600

If each of the values in respect of worker *A* is decreased by 10 and each of the values for worker *B* is increased by 50, how will it affect the results obtained earlier ?

[Delhi Univ. B.Com. (Hons), 2007]

Ans. $\overline{X}_A = 667.5$ $\sigma_A = 37.165$; $\overline{X}_B = 582.5,$ $\sigma_B = 37.165$

$$C.V.\ (A) = \frac{37.165}{667.5} \times 100 = 5.57 \quad ; \quad C.V.\ (B) = \frac{37.165}{582.5} \times 100 = 6.37$$

$C.V.\ (A) < C.V.\ (B) \quad \Rightarrow$ Brick layer *A* is more consistent.

Since *S.D.* is independent of change of origin, we have :

New Mean : $\overline{X}_A{}' = 667.5 - 10 = 657.5$; $\overline{X}_B{}' = 582.50 + 50 = 632.50$

$\sigma_A{}' = \sigma_A = 37.165$; $\sigma_B{}' = \sigma_B = 37.165$

[New *C.V.* (*A*) − 5.65] < [New *C.V.* (*B*) = 5.88]. Result is not affected.

12. The number of employees, average wages per employee and variance of the wages per employee for two factories are given below :

	Factory A	*Factory B*
Number of Employees	100	200
Average Wage per Employee (Rs.)	120	200
Variance of the Wages per Employee (Rs.)	16	25

In which factory is there greater variation in the distribution of wages per employee ?

[C.A. (Foundation), May 2000]

Ans. C.V.(*A*) = 3·3; C.V. (*B*) = 2·5. There is greater variability in Factory *A*.

13. The number of employees, wages per employee and the variance of the wages per employee for two factories are given below :

	Factory A	*Factory B*
No. of employees	50	100
Average wages per employee per month (in Rs.)	120	85
Variance of the wages per employee per month (in Rs.)	9	16

In which factory is there greater variation in the distribution of wages per employee ?

Ans. In factory *B* ; C.V. (*A*) = 2·5, C.V. (*B*) = 4·7.

14. Two workers on the same job show the following results over a long period of time :

	Worker A	*Worker B*
Mean time of completing the job (minutes)	30	25
Standard deviation (minutes)	6	4

(*i*) Which worker appears to be more consistent in the time he requires to complete the job ?

(*ii*) Which worker appears to be faster in completing the job ? Explain.

Ans. (*i*) *B*, (*ii*) *B* ($\because \overline{X}_B < \overline{X}_A$).

15. The mean and standard deviation of 200 items are found to be 60 and 20 respectively. At the time of calculations, two items were wrongly taken as 3 and 67 instead of 13 and 17. Find the correct mean and standard deviation. What is the correct coefficient of variation ?

Ans. Corrected mean = 59·8, *s.d.* = 20·09; C.V. = 33·60.

16. The mean and standard deviation of a series of 100 items were found to be 60 and 10 respectively. While calculating, two items were wrongly taken as 5 and 45 instead of 30 and 20. Calculate corrected variance and corrected coefficient of variation. *[Delhi Univ. B.Com. (Hons.), 2009]*

Ans. Corrected (σ^2) = 92.50 ; Corrected *C.V.* = 16.03

17. For the following distribution of marks obtained, find the arithmetic mean, the standard deviation and the coefficient of variation.

Marks obtained :	0—5	5—10	10—15	15—20	20—25	25—30	30—35	35—40
No. of students :	2	5	7	13	21	16	8	3

Ans. A.M. = 21·9; σ = 7·9931; C.V. = 36·5.

18. Data on the annual earnings of professors and physicians in a certain town yield the following results :

Professors : $\overline{x}_1$ = Rs.16,000, σ_1 = Rs. 2,000 *Physicians* : $\overline{x}_2$ = Rs.23,000, σ_2 = Rs. 4,000

Are the professors' earnings more or less variable than the physicians' ? *[Delhi Univ. B.A. (Econ. Hons.), 1990]*

Ans. C.V. (Professors) = 12·50, C.V. (Physicians) =17·39; Professors' earnings are less variable.

19. (*a*) Verify the correctness of the following statement : "A batsman scored at an average of 60 runs an inning against Pakistan. The standard deviation of the runs scored by him was 12. A year later against Australia, his average came down to 50 runs an inning and the standard deviation of the runs scored fell down to 9. Therefore, it is correct to say that his performance was worse against Australia and that there was lesser consistency in his batting against Australia". *[Delhi Univ. B.Com. (Hons.), 1986]*

Ans. C.V. (Australia) = 18, C.V. (Pakistan) = 20. Greater consistency against Australia.

$\overline{X}$ (Against Pakistan) > $\overline{X}$ (Against Australia); better performance against Pakistan than against Australia.

(*b*) The following is the record of goals scored by team *A* in the football season :

No. of goals scored by team A in a match :	0	1	2	3	4
Number of matches :	1	9	7	5	3

For team *B* the average number of goals scored per match was 2·5 with a standard deviation of 1·25 goals. Find which team may be considered more consistent.

Ans. C.V. (*A*) = 54·77, C.V. (*B*) = 50; *B* is more consistent.

20. During the 10 weeks of a session, the marks obtained by two candidates, Ramesh and Suresh, taking the Computer Programme course are given below :

Ramesh :	58	59	60	54	65	66	52	75	69	52
Suresh :	87	89	78	71	73	84	65	66	56	46

(*i*) Who is the better scorer — Ramesh or Suresh ?

(*ii*) Who is more consistent ? *[Delhi Univ. B.Com. (Pass), 1998]*

Ans. Ramesh : $\overline{x}_1$ = 61, σ_1 = 7·25, C.V. = 11·89 ; Suresh : $\overline{x}_2$ = 71·5, σ_2 = 13·08, C.V. = 18·29

(*i*) Suresh is better scorer ($\because \overline{x}_2 > \overline{x}_1$). ; (*ii*) Ramesh is more consistent.

21. Complete the table showing the frequencies with which words of different number of letters occur in the extract reproduced below (omitting punctuation marks) treating as the variable the number of letters in each word, and obtain the coefficient of variation of the distribution :

"Her eyes were blue; blue as autumn distance—blue as the blue we see between the retreating mouldings of hills and woody slopes on a sunny September morning : a misty and shady blue, that had no beginning or surface, and was looked into rather than at".

Ans. $\overline{X} = 4·35$; $\sigma = 2·23$; C.V. = 51·04.

22. Compile a table, showing the frequencies with which words of different number of letters occur in the extract reproduced below (omitting punctuation marks) treating as the variable the number of letters in each word, and obtain the mean, median and the coefficient of variation of the distribution :

"Success in the examination confers no absolute right to appointment unless Government is satisfied, after such enquiry as may be considered necessary, that the candidate is suitable in all respects for appointment to the public service".

Ans. Mean = 5·5; Median = 5; *s.d.* = 3·12; C.V. = 56·7.

23.

No of goals scored in a match :		0	1	2	3	4
No. of Matches	Team A :	27	9	8	5	1
	Team B :	1	5	8	9	27

Ans. C.V. (*A*) = 127·84; C.V. (*B*) = 36·06; Team *B* is more consistent.

24. Lives of two models of refrigerators in a recent survey are shown in adjoinging table.

What is the average life of each model of these refrigerators ? Which model has greater uniformity ?

Life (*No. of years*)	*No. of refrigerators* Model A	*Model B*
0—2	5	2
2—4	16	7
4—6	13	12
6—8	7	19
8—10	5	9
10—12	4	1

Ans. $\overline{X}_a = 5·12$ years ; C.V. (*A*) = 54·88; $\overline{X}_b = 6·16$ years. C.V. (*B*) = 36.2; Model *B* has greater uniformity.

25. A purchasing agent obtained samples of incandescent lamps from two suppliers. He had the samples tested in his own labouratory for the length of life with the following results :

Length of life in hours	*Samples from* Company A	*Company B*
700 and under 900	10	3
900 and under 1,100	16	42
1,100 and under 1,300	26	12
1,300 and under 1,500	8	3

Which company's lamps are more uniform ?

Ans. C.V. (*A*) = 16·7, C.V. (*B*) = 11·9. Lamps of company *B* are more uniform.

26. Two brands of tyres are tested with the following results :

(*a*) Which brand of tyres have greater average life ?

(*b*) Compare the variability and state which brand of tyres would you use on your fleet of trucks ?

Life (in '000 miles)	*No. of tyres of brand* X	Y
20—25	1	0
25—30	22	24
30—35	64	76
35—40	10	0
40—45	3	0

[*Bangalore Univ. B.Com., 1997*]

Ans. $\overline{X}$= 32·1 thousand miles, $\sigma_x = 3·137$ thousand miles, C.V. (*X*) = 9·77;

$\overline{Y}$ = 31·3 thousand miles, $\sigma_y = 0·912$ thousand miles, C.V. (*Y*) = 2·914.

(*a*) Brand *X* ; (*b*) Brand *X* tyres are more variable; Brand *Y*.

27. The mean and standard deviation of the marks obtained by two groups of students, consisting of 50 each, are given below. Calculate the mean and standard deviation of the marks obtained by all the 100 students :

Group	*Mean*	*Standard Deviation*
1	60	8
2	55	7

[*C.A. (Foundation), Nov. 1999*]

Ans. $\bar{x}_{12} = 57{\cdot}5, \quad \sigma_{12} = 7{\cdot}92.$

28. For a group of 50 male workers, the mean and standard deviation of their weekly wages are Rs. 63 and Rs. 9 respectively. For a group of 40 female workers these are Rs. 54 and Rs. 6 respectively. Find the standard deviation for the combined group of 90 workers.

Ans. $\sigma = 9.$

29. The first of the two samples has 100 items with mean 15 and standard deviation 3. If the whole group has 250 items with mean 15·6 and standard deviation $\sqrt{13{\cdot}44}$, find mean and the standard deviation of the second group.

Ans. $\overline{X}_2 = 16; \sigma_2 = 4.$

30. For two groups of observations the following results were available :

Group I :	$\Sigma(X-5) = 8;$	$\Sigma(X-5)^2 = 40;$	$N_1 = 20$
Group II :	$\Sigma(X-8) = -10;$	$\Sigma(X-8)^2 = 70;$	$N_2 = 25$

Find the mean and the standard deviation of the 45 observations obtained by combining the two groups.

[*Delhi Univ. B.Com. (Hons.), 2006*]

Hint. Expand $\Sigma(X-5)$, $\Sigma(X-5)^2$, $\Sigma(X-8)$ and $\Sigma(X-8)^2$, and find ΣX and ΣX^2 for each group.

For combined group : $\Sigma X = 108 + 190 = 298,\quad \Sigma X^2 = 620 + 1510 = 2130,\quad N = 45.$

Ans. $\overline{X}_{12} = 6{\cdot}622, \; \sigma_{12} = 1{\cdot}865.$

31. A company has three establishments E_1, E_2, E_3 in three cities. Analysis of the monthly salaries paid to the employees in the three establishments is given bellow :

	E_1	E_2	E_3
Number of employees	20	25	40
Average monthly salary (Rs.)	305	300	340
Standard deviation of monthly salary (Rs.)	50	40	45

Find the average and the standard deviation of the monthly salaries of all the 85 employees in the company.

Ans. Mean = Rs. 320; *s.d.* = Rs. 48·69.

32. Calculate the missing information from the following data.

	Variable A	*Variable B*	*Variable C*	*Combined*
Total Number	175	?	225	500
Mean	220	240	?	235
Standard Deviation	?	6·3	5·9	5·4

Ans. $n_B = 100; \; \overline{X}_C = 244{\cdot}4, \; \sigma_A = 18{\cdot}36.$

33. For a group of 30 male workers, the mean and standard deviation of weekly overtime work (No. of hours) are 10 and 4 respectively; for 20 female workers the mean and standard deviation are 5 and 3 respectively. (*i*) Calculate the mean for the two groups taken together. (*ii*) Is the overtime work more variable for the male group than for the female group ? Explain. [*Delhi Univ. B.A. (Econ.) Hons., 1991*]

Ans. (*i*) 8 hours.

(*ii*) C.V. males (= 40) < C.V. females (= 60) $\Rightarrow$ Overtime work for males is less variable.

34. An analysis of the monthly wages paid to workers in two firms *A* and *B*, belonging to the same industry, gives the following results :

	Firm A	*Firm B*
Number of wage-earners	586	648
Average monthly wage	Rs. 52·5	Rs. 47·5
Variance of the distribution of wage	100	121

(*a*) Which firm, *A* or *B*, pays out the larger amount as monthly wages ?

(*b*) In which firm, *A* or *B*, is there greater variability in individual wages ?

(*c*) What are the measures of (*i*) average monthly wage, and (*ii*) the variability in individual wages, of all the workers in the two firms, *A* and *B*, taken together.

Ans. (*a*) *B*; (*b*) In Firm *B*; (*c*) $\overline{X}$ = Rs. 49·87; σ = Rs. 10·83.

35. For two firms *A* and *B*, the following details are available :

		A	B
Number of employees	:	100	200
Average salary (Rs.)	:	1,600	1,800
Standard deviation of salary (Rs.)	:	16	18

(*i*) Which firm pays large package of salary ?

(*ii*) Which firm shows greater variability in the distribution of salary.

(*iii*) Compute the combined average salary and combined variance of both the firms.

[*Delhi Univ. B.Com. (Pass), 2000*]

Ans. (*i*) *B*; (*ii*) C.V. (*A*) = 1, C.V. (*B*) = 1. Both firms show equal variability.

(*iii*) $\bar{x}_{12}$ = Rs. 1,733·33 and σ^2_{12} = Rs². 9190·22

36. If the mean deviation of a moderately skewed distribution is 7·2 unit, find the standard deviation as well as quartile deviation.

Ans. S.D. $\simeq \frac{5}{4}$ M.D. = 9; Q.D. $\simeq \frac{5}{6}$ M.D. = 6·0.

37. For a series, the value of Mean Deviation is 15. Find the most likely value of its quartile deviation.

[*Delhi Univ. B.Com. (Pass), 2002*]

Ans. Q.D. = $\frac{5}{6}$ M.D. = 12·5.

6·13. LORENZ CURVE

Lorenz curve is a graphic method of studying the dispersion in a distribution. It was first used by Max O. Lorenz, an economic statistician for the measurement of economic inequalities such as in the distribution of income and wealth between different countries or between different periods of time. But today, Lorenz curve is also used in business to study the disparities of the distribution of wages, profits, turnover, production, population, etc.

A very distinctive feature of the Lorenz curve consists in dealing with the cumulative values of the variable and the cumulative frequencies rather than its absolute values and the given frequencies. The technique of drawing the curve is fairly simple and consists of the following steps :

(*i*) The size of the item (variable value) and the frequencies are both cumulated. Taking grand total for each as 100, express these cumulated totals for the variable and the frequencies as percentages of their corresponding grand totals.

(*ii*) Now take coordinate axes, *X*-axis representing the percentages of the cumulated frequencies (x) and *Y*-axis representing the percentages of the cumulated values of the variable (y). Both x and y take the values from 0 to 100 as shown in the Fig. 6·1.

(*iii*) Draw the diagonal line $y = x$ joining the origin O (0, 0) with the point $P(100, 100)$ as shown in the diagram. The line *OP* will make an angle of 45° with the *X*-axis and is called the *line of equal distribution.*

(*iv*) Plot the percentages of the cumulated values of the variable (y) against the percentages of the corresponding cumulated frequencies (x) for the given distribution and join these points with a smooth free-hand curve. Obviously, for any given distribution this curve will never cross the line of equal distribution *OP*. It will always lie below *OP* unless the distribution is uniform (equal) in which case it will coincide with *OP*.

Thus when the distribution of items is not proportionately equal, the variability (dispersion) is indicated and the curve is farther from the line of equal distribution OP. The greater the variability, the greater is the distance of the curve from OP.

Let us consider the Lorenz curve diagram (Fig. 6.1), for the distribution of income, (say).

In the diagram, *OP* is the line of equal distribution of income. If the plotted cumulative percentages lie on this line, there is no variability in the distribution of income of persons. The points lying on the curve OAP indicate a less degree of variability as compared to the points lying on the curve *OBP*. Variability is still greater, when the points lie on the curve *OCP*. Thus a measure of variability of the distribution is provided by the distance of the curve of the cumulated percentages of the given distribution from the line of equal distribution.

LORENZ CURVE

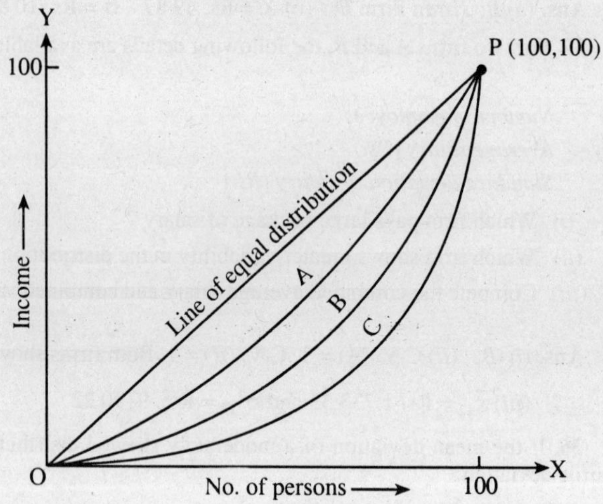

Fig. 6·1.

Remarks 1. An obvious disadvantage of the Lorenz curve is that it gives us only a relative idea of the dispersion as compared with the line of equal distribution. It does not provide us any numerical value of the variability for the given distribution. Accordingly it should be used together with some numerical measure of dispersion. However, this should not undermine the utility of Lorenz curve in studying the variability of the distributions particularly relating to income, wealth, wages, profits, lands, and capitals, etc.

2. From the Lorenz curve we can immediately find out as to what percentage of persons (frequencies) correspond to a given percentage of the item (variable value).

Example 6·42. *From the following table giving data regarding income of workers in a factory, draw a graph (Lorenz curve) to study the inequality of income :*

Income (in Rs.)	*No. of workers in the factory*
Below 500	*6,000*
500—1,000	*4,250*
1,000—2,000	*3,600*
2,000—3,000	*1,500*
3,000—4,000	*650*

Solution.

CALCULATIONS FOR LORENZ CURVE

Income (in Rs.)	*Mid-value*	*Cumulative income*	*Percentage of cumulative income*	*No. of Workers (f)*	*Cumulative frequency*	*Percentage of cumulative frequency*
(1)	(2)	(3)	(4)	(5)	(6)	(7)
0—500	250	250	2·94	6,000	6,000	37·5
500—1000	750	1,000	11.76	4,250	10.250	64.1
1000—2000	1500	2,500	29.41	3,600	13,850	86.6
2000—3000	2500	5,000	58.82	1,500	15,350	95.9
3000—4000	3500	8,500	100.00	650	16,000	100.0
Total	8500			16,000		

The Lorenz curve (Fig. 6·2) prominently exhibits the inequality of the distribution of income among the factory workers.

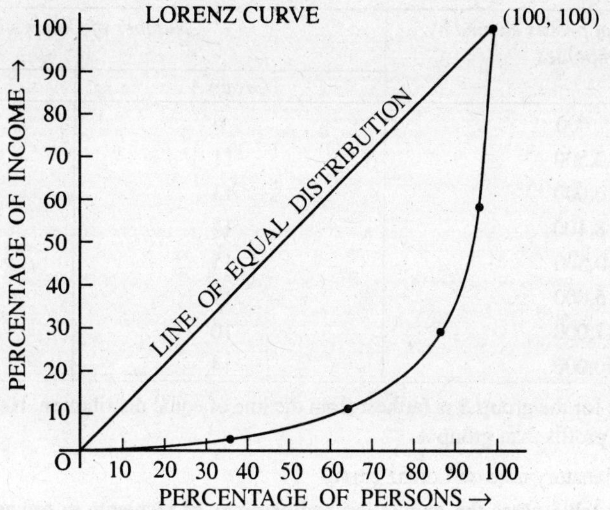

Fig. 6·2.

Remark. From the Lorenz curve we observe that 70% of the persons get only 15% of income and 90% of the persons get only 35% of the income.

EXERCISE 6·5

1. What is Lorenz curve ? How do you construct it ? What is its use?

2. From the following table giving data regarding income of employees in two factories, draw a graph (Lorenz Curve) to show which factory has greater inequalities of income :

Income ('00 Rs.)	:	Below 200	200—500	500—1,000	1,000—2,000	2,000—3,000
Factory A	:	7,000	1,000	1,200	800	500
Factory B	:	800	1,200	1,500	400	200

3. Industrial relations have been deteriorating in the Wessex factory of JK Limited and personnel management has established that a contributory factor is the inequalities of earnings of operators paid on the basis of an incentive scheme.

Operators work an eight-hour day and bonus is paid progressively after measured work equivalent to 360 standard minutes has been produced.

Table *A*, on right side, shows the position for the month of June 1975 in respect of operator production.

Improvements are made in working conditions in the areas where poor performances were recorded and subsequently in October 1975 the results in Table *B*, were measured.

Standard minutes produced per operator per day	*Table A (June 1975) Number of operators*	*Table B (October 1975) Number of operators*
300	10	4
320	32	11
340	20	11
360	18	9
380	2	10
400	5	12
420	5	12
440	5	11
460	3	10
480	—	5
500	—	5

(*a*) Present the data in Tables *A* and *B* in the form of a Lorenz curve.

(*b*) Comment on the results.

Ans. Group *A* represents greater inequality of distribution than group *B*.

4. The frequency distribution of marks obtained in Mathematics (*M*) and English (*E*) are as follows :

Mid-value of marks	:	5	15	25	35	45	55	65	75	85	95
No. of students (*M*)	:	10	12	13	14	22	27	20	12	11	9
No. of students (*E*)	:	1	2	26	50	59	40	10	8	3	1

Analyse the data by drawing the Lorenz curves on the same diagram and describe the main features you observe.

5. Draw Lorenz Curve for the comparison of profits of two groups of companies, *A* and *B*, in business. What is your conclusion ?

Total Amount of profits earned by companies	*Number of Companies in*	
	Group A	*Group B*
600	6	1
2,500	11	19
6,000	13	26
8,400	14	14
10,500	15	14
15,000	17	13
17,000	10	6
40,000	14	7

Ans. Lorenz curve for the group *B* is farthest from the line of equal distribution. Hence, group *B* represents greater inequality of profits than group *A*.

6. (*a*) Write an explanatory note on Lorenz curve.

(*b*) The following table gives the population and earnings of residents in towns *A* and *B*. Represent the data graphically so as to bring out the inequality of the distribution of the earnings of residents.

Town A	*No. of persons :*	50	50	50	50	50	50	50	50	50	50
	Earnings (Rs. daily)	35	50	75	115	160	180	225	300	425	925
Town B	*No. of persons :*	100	140	60	50	200	90	60	40	160	100
	Earnings (Rs. daily)	160	320	120	280	400	400	280	920	240	960

Ans. Inequality of incomes is more prominent in Town *A*.

EXERCISE 6·6
(Objective Type Questions)

I. Match the correct parts to make a valid statement :

(*a*) Algebraic sum of deviations from mean	(*i*) $Q_3 - Q_1$
(*b*) Coefficient of Mean Deviation	(*ii*) $\dfrac{100\,\sigma}{\text{Mean}}$
(*c*) Variance	(*iii*) Zero
(*d*) Quartile Deviation	(*iv*) $\dfrac{1}{N}\Sigma f\,\lvert X - \overline{X}\rvert$
(*e*) Coefficient of Variation	(*v*) $\dfrac{1}{N}\Sigma f\,(X - \overline{X})^2$
(*f*) Sum of absolute deviations from median	(*vi*) $\dfrac{\text{M.D. about Mean}}{\text{Mean}}$
(*g*) Interquartile range	(*vii*) $(Q_3 - Q_1)/2$
(*h*) Mean deviation	(*viii*) Minimum

Ans. (*a*) — (*iii*); (*b*) — (*vi*); (*c*) — (*v*); (*d*) — (*vii*);
(*e*) — (*ii*); (*f*) — (*viii*); (*g*) — (*i*); (*h*) — (*iv*).

II. In the following questions, tick the *correct* answer :

(*i*) Algebraic sum of deviations from mean is :
(*a*) Positive, (*b*) Negative, (*c*) Zero, (*d*) Different for each case.

(*ii*) Sum of squares of deviations is minimum when taken from :
(*a*) Mean, (*b*) Median, (*c*) Mode, (*d*) None of these.

(*iii*) Sum of absolute deviations is minimum when measured from :
(*a*) Mean, (*b*) Median, (*c*) Mode, (*d*) None of these.

(*iv*) For a discrete frequency distribution :

(*a*) S.D. ≤ M.D., (*b*) S.D. ≥ M.D., (*c*) S.D. > M.D., (*d*) S.D. < M.D.

(*e*) None of these, where M.D. = Mean Deviation from mean.

(*v*) The range of a given distribution is

(*a*) greater than *s.d.*, (*b*) Less than *s.d.*, (*c*) Equal to *s.d.*, (*d*) None of these.

(*vi*) The measure of dispersion independent of frequencies of the given distribution is

(*a*) Range, (*b*) *s.d.*, (*c*) M.D., (*d*) Q.D.

(*vii*) In case of open end classes, an appropriate measure of dispersion to be used is

(*a*) Range, (*b*) Q.D., (*c*) M.D., (*d*) *s.d.*

(*viii*) Measure of dispersion which is affected most by extreme observations is.

(*a*) Range, (*b*) Q.D., (*c*) M.D., (*d*) *s.d.*

(*ix*) Mean deviation from median (*Md*) is given by

(*a*) $\frac{\Sigma|X-Md|}{n}$, (*b*) $\frac{\Sigma|X-Md|}{\sqrt{n}}$, (*c*) $\sqrt{\frac{\Sigma|X-Md|^2}{n}}$, (*d*) $\frac{\Sigma|X-Md|^2}{n}$.

(*x*) Quartile deviation is given by :

(*a*) Q_3-Q_1, (*b*) $\frac{Q_3-Q_2}{2}$, (*c*) $\frac{Q_2-Q_1}{2}$, (*d*) $\frac{Q_3-Q_1}{2}$.

(*xi*) Step deviation formula for variance is :

(*a*) $\frac{\Sigma d^2}{n^2}-\left(\frac{\Sigma d}{n}\right)^2$, (*b*) $\frac{\Sigma d^2}{n}-\left(\frac{\Sigma d}{n}\right)^2$, (*c*) $\left(\frac{\Sigma d}{n}\right)^2-\frac{\Sigma d}{n^2}$, (*d*) $\left(\frac{\Sigma d^2}{n}\right)^2-\left(\frac{\Sigma d}{n}\right)^2$.

(*xii*) If the distribution is approximately normal, then

(*a*) M.D. $=\frac{2}{5}\sigma$, (*b*) M.D. $=\frac{3}{5}\sigma$, (*c*) M.D. $=\frac{4}{5}\sigma$, (*d*) None of these.

(*xiii*) For a normal distribution,

(*a*) Q.D. $=\frac{1}{3}\sigma$, (*b*) Q.D $=\frac{2}{3}\sigma$, (*c*) Q.D. $=\sigma$, (*d*) None of these.

(*xiv*) For a normal distribution,

(*a*) Q.D. > M.D., (*b*) Q.D. < M.D., (*c*) Q.D. = M.D.

(*xv*) For a normal distribution, the range mean ± 1.σ covers

(*a*) 65%, (*b*) 68·26%, (*c*) 85%, (*d*) 95% of the items.

Ans. (*i*) — (*c*); (*ii*) — (*a*); (*iii*) — (*b*); (*iv*) — (*b*); (*v*) — (*a*);
(*vi*) — (*a*); (*vii*) — (*b*); (*viii*) — (*a*); (*ix*) — (*a*); (*x*) — (*d*);
(*xi*) — (*b*); (*xii*) — (*c*); (*xiii*) — (*b*); (*xiv*) — (*b*); (*xv*) — (*b*).

III. Fill in the blanks :

(*i*) Algebraic sum of deviations is zero from ......

(*ii*) The sum of absolute deviations is minimum from ......

(*iii*) Standard deviation is always ...... than range.

(*iv*) Standard deviation is always ...... than mean deviation.

(*v*) All relative measures of dispersion are ...... from units of measurement.

(*vi*) Variance is the ......value of mean square deviation.

(*vii*) If $Q_1 = 10$, $Q_3 = 40$, the coefficient of quartile deviation is ......

(*viii*) If 25% of the items in a distribution are less than 10 and 25% are more than 40, quartile deviation is ......

(*ix*) The median and *s.d.* of distribution are 15 and 5 respectively. If each item is increased by 5, the new median = ... and *s.d.* = ...

(*x*) A computer showed that the *s.d.* of 40 observations ranging from 120 to 150 is 35. The answer is correct/wrong. Tick right one.

Ans. (*i*) Arithmetic mean (*ii*) Median (*iii*) Less (*iv*) Greater (*v*) Free
(*vi*) Minimum (*vii*) 0·6 (*viii*) 15 (*ix*) 20, 5 (*x*) Wrong, since s.d. can't exceed range.

IV. Fill in the blanks :

(*i*) The ...... the Lorenz Curve is from the line of equal distribution, the greater is the variability in the series.

(*ii*) Quartile deviation is ...... measure of dispersion.

(*iii*) If $Q_1 = 20$ and $Q_3 = 50$, the coefficient of quartile deviation is ......

(*iv*) If in a series, coefficient of variation is 64 and mean 10, the standard deviation shall be ......

Ans. (*i*) Farther (*ii*) Absolute (*iii*) 0·375 (*iv*) 6·4.

V. State whether the following statements are true or false. In case of false statements, give the correct statement.

(*i*) Algebraic sum of deviations from mean is minimum.

(*ii*) Mean deviation is least when calculated from median.

(*iii*) Variance is always non-negative.

(*iv*) Mean, standard deviation and coefficient of variation have same units.

(*v*) Relative measures of dispersion are independent of units of measurement.

(*vi*) Mean and standard deviation are independent of change of origin.

(*vii*) Variance is square of standard deviation.

(*viii*) Standard deviation is independent of change of origin and scale.

(*ix*) Variance is the minimum value of mean square deviation.

(*x*) Q.D. $= \frac{2}{3} \times$ (*s.d.*), always.

(*xi*) Mean deviation can never be negative.

(*xii*) M.D. $= \frac{2}{3} \times \sigma$, for normal distribution.

(*xiii*) If mean and *s.d.* of a distribution are 20 and 4 respectively, C.V. = 15%.

(*xiv*) If each value in a distribution of 5 observations is 10, then its mean is 10 and variance is 1.

(*xv*) In a discrete distribution s.d. ≥ M.D. (about mean).

Ans. (*i*) False, (*ii*) True, (*iii*) True, (*iv*) False, (*v*) True, (*vi*) False, (*vii*) True, (*viii*) False, (*ix*) True, (*x*) False, (*xi*) True, (*xii*) False, (*xiii*) False, (*xiv*) False, (*xv*) True.

VI. The mean and *s.d.* of 100 observations are 50 and 10 respectively. Find the new mean and standard deviation,

(*i*) if 2 is added to each observation. (*ii*) if 3 is subtracted from each observation.

(*iii*) if each observation is multiplied by 5. (*iv*) if 2 is subtracted from each observation and then it is divided by 5.

Ans. (*i*) 52,10, (*ii*) 47, 10, (*iii*) 250, 50 (*iv*) 9·6, 2

VII. The sum of squares of deviations of 15 observations from their mean 20 is 240. Find (*i*) *s.d.* and (*ii*) C.V.

Ans. $\sigma = 4$, C.V. = 20.

VIII. State, giving reasons, whether the following statements are true or false.

(*i*) Standard deviation can never be negative

(*ii*) Sum of squares of deviations measured from mean is least.

Ans. (*i*) True, (*ii*) True.

IX. Comment briefly on the following statements :

(*i*) The mean of the combined series lies between the means of the two component series.

(*ii*) The standard deviation of the combined series lies between the standard deviations of the two component series.

(*iii*) Mean can never be equal to standard deviation.

(*iv*) Mean can never be equal to variance.

(*v*) A consistent cricket player has greater variability in test scores.

Ans. (*i*) True (*ii*) False (*iii*) False (*iv*) False (*v*) False.

X. Comment briefly on the following statements :

(*i*) The median is the point about which the sum of squared deviations is minimum.

(*ii*) Since $\Sigma(X_i - \overline{X}) = 0, \quad \therefore \Sigma(X_i - \overline{X})^2 = 0.$

(*iii*) A computer obtained the standard deviation of 25 observations whose values ranged from 65 to 85 as 25.

(*iv*) A student obtained the mean and variance of a set of 10 observations as 10, – 5 respectively.

(*v*) The range is the perfect measure of variability as it includes all the measurements.

(*vi*) For the distribution of 5 observations :

$$8,\quad 8,\quad 8,\quad 8,\quad 8,$$

$$\text{mean} = 8 \text{ and variance} = 8$$

(*vii*) If the mean and *s.d.* of distribution *A* are smaller than the mean and *s.d.* of distribution *B* respectively, then the distribution *A* is more uniform (less variable) than the distribution *B*.

Ans. (*i*) False, (*ii*) False, (*iii*) False, (*iv*) False, (*v*) False, (*vi*) False, (*vii*) False.

XI. (*a*) If *s.d.* of a group is 15, find the most likely value of (*i*) Mean deviation and (*ii*) Quartile deviation of that group.

(*b*) If mean deviation of a distribution is 20, find the most likely value of (*i*) *s.d.* and (*ii*) Q.D.

(*c*) If quartile deviation of a distribution is 6, find the most likely value of (*i*) *s.d.* and (*ii*) M.D.

(*d*) If quartile deviation of a distribution is 20 and its mean is 60, obtain the most likely value of (*i*) Coefficient of variation, (*ii*) Mean deviation and (*iii*) Coefficient of mean deviation.

In all the above parts. assume that the distribution is normal.

Ans. (*a*) M.D. = 12, Q.D. = 10, (*b*) *s.d.* = 25, Q.D. = 16·67, (*c*) *s.d.* = 9, M.D. = 7·2, (*d*) C.V. = 50, M.D. = 24, Coefficient of M.D. = 0·4.

7 Skewness, Moments and Kurtosis

7·1. INTRODUCTION

It was pointed out in the last two chapters that we need statistical measures which will reveal clearly the salient features of a frequency distribution. The measures of central tendency tell us about the concentration of the observations about the middle of the distribution and the measures of dispersion give us an idea about the spread or scatter of the observations about some measure of central tendency. We may come across frequency distributions which differ very widely in their nature and composition and yet may have the same central tendency and dispersion. For example, the following two frequency distributions have the same mean $\bar{X} = 15$ and standard deviation $\sigma = 6$, yet they give histograms which differ very widely in shape and size.

Frequency distribution I		*Frequency distribution II*	
Class	*Frequency*	*Class*	*Frequency*
0—5	10	0—5	10
5—10	30	5—10	40
10—15	60	10—15	30
15—20	60	15—20	90
20—25	30	20—25	20
25—30	10	25—30	10

Thus these two measures *viz.*, central tendency and dispersion are inadequate to characterise a distribution completely and they must be supported and supplemented by two more measures *viz.*, *skewness* and *kurtosis* which we shall discuss in the following sections. Skewness helps us to study the shape *i.e.*, symmetry or asymmetry of the distribution while kurtosis refers to the flatness or peakedness of the curve which can be drawn with the help of the given data. These four measures *viz.*, central tendency, dispersion, skewness and kurtosis are sufficient to describe a frequency distribution completely.

7·2. SKEWNESS

Literal meaning of skewness is *'lack of symmetry'*. We study skewness to have an idea about the shape of the curve which we can draw with the help of the given frequency distribution. It helps us to determine the nature and extent of the concentration of the observations towards the higher or lower values of the variable. In a symmetrical frequency distribution which is unimodal, if the frequency curve or histogram is folded about the ordinate at the mean, the two halves so obtained will coincide with each other. In other words, in a symmetrical distribution equal distances on either side of the central value will have same frequencies and consequently both the tails, (left and right), of the curve would also be equal in shape and length (Fig. 7.1). A distribution is said to be skewed if :

• (*i*) The frequency curve of the distribution is not a symmetric bell-shaped curve but it is stretched more to one side than to the other. In other words, it has a longer tail to one side (left or right) than to the other. A frequency distribution for which the curve has a longer tail towards the right is said to be *positively skewed* (Fig. 7.2) and if the longer tail lies towards the left, it is said to be *negatively skewed* (Fig. 7.3).

Figures 7·1 to 7·3 are given on page7·2.

(*ii*) The values of mean (M), median (Md) and mode (Mo) fall at different points *i.e.,* they do not coincide.

(*iii*) Quartiles Q_1 and Q_3 are not equidistant from the median *i.e.,*

$$Q_3 - Md \neq Md - Q_1$$

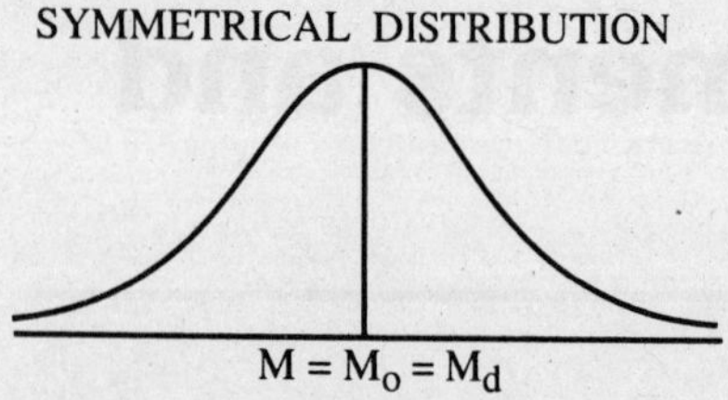

Fig. 7.1.

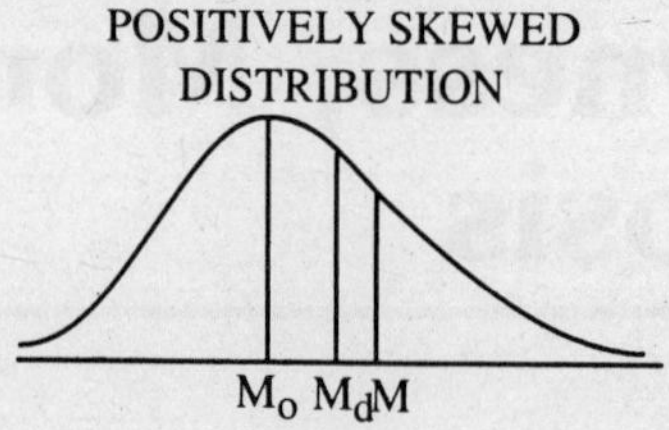

Fig. 7.2.

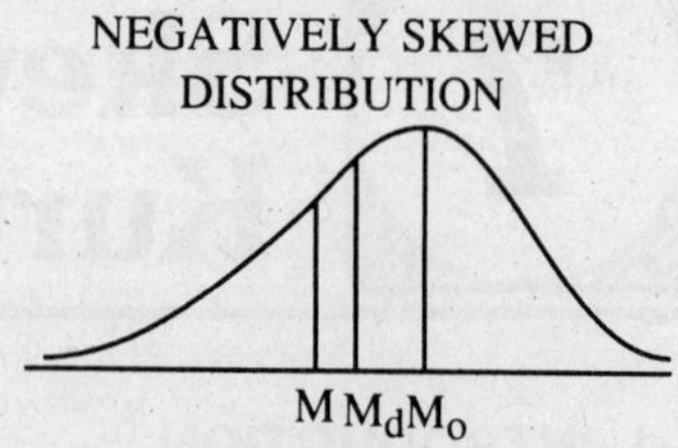

Fig. 7.3.

Remark. Since the extreme values give longer tails, a positively skewed distribution will have greater variation towards the higher values of the variable and a negatively skewed distribution will have greater variation towards the lower values of the variable. For example the distribution of mortality (death) rates *w.r.t.* the age after ignoring the accidental deaths will give a positively skewed distribution. However, most of the phenomena relating to business and economic statistics give rise to negatively skewed distribution. For instance, the distributions of the quantity demanded *w.r.t.* the price; or the number of depositors *w.r.t.* savings in a bank or the number of persons *w.r.t.* their incomes or wages in a city will give negatively skewed curves.

7·2·1. Measures of Skewness. Various measures of skewness (Sk) are :

(1) $Sk = \text{Mean} - \text{Median} = M - Md$ ...(7·1)

or $Sk = \text{Mean} - \text{Mode} = M - Mo$ ...(7·1 *a*)

(2) $Sk = (Q_3 - Md) - (Md - Q_1) = Q_3 + Q_1 - 2\ Md$ ...(7·2)

These are the *absolute measures of skewness* and are not of much practical utility because of the following reasons :

(*i*) Since the absolute measures of skewness involve the units of measurement, they cannot be used for comparative study of the two distributions measured in different units of measurement.

(*ii*) Even if the distributions are having the same units of measurement, the absolute measures are not recommended because we may come across different distributions which have more or less identical skewness (absolute measures) but which vary widely in the measures of central tendency and dispersion.

Thus for comparing two or more distributions for skewness we compute the *relative measures of skewness*, also commonly known as *coefficients of skewness* which are pure numbers independent of the units of measurement. Moreover, in a relative measure of skewness, the disturbing factor of variation or dispersion is eliminated by dividing the absolute measure of skewness by a suitable measure of dispersion. The following are the coefficients of skewness which are commonly used.

7·2·2. Karl Pearson's Coefficient of Skewness. This is given by the formula :

$$Sk = \frac{Mean - Mode}{s.d.} = \frac{M - Mo}{\sigma} \quad ...(7·3)$$

But quite often, mode is ill-defined and is thus quite difficult to locate. In such a situation, we use the following *empirical relationship between the mean, median and mode for a moderately asymmetrical (skewed) distribution* :

$$Mo = 3Md - 2M \quad ...(7·4)$$

Substituting in (7·3), we get

$$Sk = \frac{M - (3Md - 2M)}{\sigma} = \frac{3(M - Md)}{\sigma} \quad ...(7·5)$$

Remarks 1. Theoretically, Karl Pearson's Coefficient of Skewness *lies between the limits* ± 3, *but these limits are rarely attained in practice.*

2. From (7·3) and (7·5), skewness is zero if $M = Mo = Md$. In other words, *for a symmetrical distribution mean, mode and median coincide i.e.,* $M = Md = Mo$.

3. $Sk > 0$, if $M > Md > Mo$ or if $Mo < Md < M$ ...(7·6)

Thus, *for a positively skewed distribution, the value of the mean is the greatest of the three measures and the value of mode is the least of the three measures.*

If the distribution is negatively skewed, the inequality in (7·9) is reversed *i.e.,* the inequalities 'greater than' (*i.e.,* >) and 'less than' (*i.e.,* <) are interchanged. Thus :

$Sk < 0$, if $M < Md < Mo$ or if $Mo > Md > M$ ...(7·7)

In other words, *for a negatively skewed distribution, of the three measures of central tendency viz., mean, median and mode, the mode has the maximum value and the mean has the least value.*

4. While 'dispersion' studies the degree of variation in the given distribution. skewness attempts at studying the *direction of* variation. Extreme variations towards higher values of the variable give a positively skewed distribution while in a negatively skewed distribution, the extreme variations are towards the lower values of the variable.

5. In Pearson's coefficient of skewness, the disturbing factor of variation is eliminated by dividing the absolute measure of skewness $M - Mo$ by the measure of dispersion σ (standard deviation).

6. If the distribution is symmetrical, say, about mean, then

$$\text{Mean} - X_{min} = X_{max} - \text{Mean} \quad \text{...(7·8)}$$

$$\Rightarrow \quad X_{max} + X_{min} = 2\ \text{Mean} \quad \text{...(7.8a)}$$

$$\text{Also} \quad X_{max} - X_{min} = \text{Range} \quad \text{...(7.9)}$$

Adding and subtracting (7.8*a*) and (7.9), we get respectively :

$$2\,X_{max} = 2\ \text{Mean} + \text{Range} \quad \Rightarrow \quad X_{max} = \text{Mean} + \frac{1}{2}\text{Range} \quad \text{...(7.10)}$$

$$2\,X_{min} = 2\ \text{Mean} - \text{Range} \quad \Rightarrow \quad X_{min} = \text{Mean} - \frac{1}{2}\text{Range} \quad \text{...(7.10a)}$$

Example 7·1. *A distribution of wages paid to workers would show that, although a few reach very high levels, most workers are at lower level of wages. If you were an employer, resisting worker's claim for an increase of wages, which average would suit your case? Do you think your argument will be different if you are a trade union leader ? Explain.* [*Delhi Univ. B.A.* (*Econ. Hons.*), *1997*]

Solution. The distribution of wages paid to the workers would show that, although a few reach very high levels, most workers are at lower level of wages. This implies that the distribution of wages of workers in the factory is positively skewed so that

Mean > Median > Mode ⇒ Mode < Median < Mean.

Since mode is the least of the three averages mean, median and mode, the average that will suit the employer most (to resist workers claim for higher wages) will be *mode*.

By similar argument, since mean is the largest of the three averages, it will suit most to the trade union leader.

Example 7.2. *In a symmetrical distribution the mean, standard deviation and range of marks for a group of 20 students are 50, 10 and 30 respectively. Find the mean marks and standard deviation of marks, if the students with the highest and the lowest marks are excluded.* [*Delhi Univ. B.Com.* (*Hons.*), *2004*]

Solution. We are given a *symmetrical* distribution in which,

No. of observations (n) = 20 ; Mean ($\overline{X}$) = 50 ; *s.d.* (σ) = 10 and Range = 30 ...(*)

Since the distribution is symmetrical (about mean) , we have

$$\text{Mean} - X_{min} = X_{max} - \text{Mean}$$

$$\Rightarrow \quad X_{max} + X_{min} = 2\ \text{Mean} = 2 \times 50 = 100 \qquad \text{[From (*)]} \quad \text{...(**)}$$

Also $X_{max} - X_{min} = \text{Range} = 30$ (Given) ...(***)

Adding and subtracting (**) and (***), we get respectively

$$2\,X_{max} = 130 \quad \Rightarrow \quad X_{max} = \frac{130}{2} = 65 \quad \text{and} \quad 2\,X_{min} = 70 \quad \Rightarrow \quad X_{min} = \frac{70}{2} = 35$$

Thus the given problem reduces to :

"Given $n = 20$, $\overline{X} = 50$ and $\sigma_X = 10$, obtain the mean and standard deviation if two observations 65 and 35 are omitted."

$$\overline{X} = \frac{\Sigma X}{n} \quad \Rightarrow \quad \Sigma X = n\overline{X} = 20 \times 50 = 1{,}000$$

$$\sigma^2 = 10^2 = 100 \quad \Rightarrow \quad \Sigma X^2 = n\,(\sigma^2 + \overline{X}^2) = 20\,(100 + 2{,}500) = 52{,}000$$

On omitting the two observations 35 and 65, for the remaining, $N = n - 2 = 20 - 2 = 18$ observations, we have

$$\sum_{i=1}^{18} X_i = \Sigma X - (35 + 65) = 1{,}000 - 100 = 900$$

$$\sum_{i=1}^{18} X_i^2 = \Sigma X^2 - (35^2 + 65^2) = 52{,}000 - (1{,}225 + 4{,}225) = 46{,}550$$

$$\therefore \quad \text{New Mean } (\overline{X}\,') = \frac{1}{18}\sum_{i=1}^{18} X_i = \frac{900}{18} = 50 = \overline{X}$$

$$\text{and} \quad \text{New } s.d. \; (\sigma') = \sqrt{\frac{1}{18}\sum_{i=1}^{18} X_i^2 - (\overline{X}\,')^2} = \sqrt{\frac{46{,}550}{18} - 50^2} = \sqrt{\frac{1{,}550}{18}} = \sqrt{86{\cdot}11} = 9{\cdot}28$$

Aliter : For a symmetrical distribution (about mean) we have, [From (7·10) and (7·10*a*)],

$$X_{max} = \text{Mean} + \frac{1}{2}\text{Range} \quad \text{and} \quad X_{min} = \text{Mean} - \frac{1}{2}\text{Range}$$

Example 7·3. *Calculate Karl Pearson's co-efficient of skewness from the following data :*

Size	:	*1*	*2*	*3*	*4*	*5*	*6*	*7*
Frequency	:	*10*	*18*	*30*	*25*	*12*	*3*	*2*

Solution.

COMPUTATION OF MEAN, MODE AND S.D.

Size (x)	*Frequency (f)*	*f.x*	*f.x²*
1	10	10	10
2	18	36.	72
3	30	90	270
4	25	100	400
5	12	60	300
6	3	18	108
7	2	14	98
Total	$N = 100$	$\Sigma fx = 328$	$\Sigma fx^2 = 1258$

$$\text{Mean } (M) = \frac{\Sigma fx}{N} = \frac{328}{100} = 3{\cdot}28$$

$$\text{S.D. } (\sigma) = \sqrt{\frac{\Sigma fx^2}{N} - \left(\frac{\Sigma fx}{N}\right)^2} = \sqrt{\frac{1258}{100} - \left(\frac{328}{100}\right)^2}$$

$$= \sqrt{12{\cdot}58 - 10{\cdot}7584} = \sqrt{1{\cdot}8216} = 1{\cdot}3497$$

Since the maximum frequency is 30, corresponding value of *x viz.*, 3 is the mode. Thus Mode (*Mo*) = 3.

Karl Pearson's Coefficient of Skewness is given by

$$Sk = \frac{M - Mo}{\sigma} = \frac{3{\cdot}28 - 3{\cdot}00}{1{\cdot}3497} = \frac{0{\cdot}28}{1{\cdot}3497} = 0{\cdot}2075$$

Hence, the distribution is slightly positively skewed.

Example 7·4. *Calculate Karl Pearson's Coefficient of Skewness from the data given below :*

Hourly wages (Rs.)	*No. of workers*	*Hourly wages (Rs.)*	*No. of workers*
40—50	5	90—100	30
50—60	6	100—110	36
60—70	8	110—120	50
70—80	10	120—130	60
80—90	25	130—140	70

Solution

COMPUTATION OF MEAN, MEDIAN AND S.D.

Hourly wages (Rs.)	*Mid-value (X)*	*No. of workers (f)*	$d = \frac{X-85}{10}$	*fd*	fd^2	*'Less than' c.f.*
40—50	45	5	−4	−20	80	5
50—60	55	6	−3	−18	54	11
60—70	65	8	−2	−16	32	19
70—80	75	10	−1	−10	10	29
80—90	85	25	0	0	0	54
90—100	95	30	1	30	30	84
100—110	105	36	2	72	144	120
110—120	115	50	3	150	450	170
120—130	125	60	4	240	960	230
130—140	135	70	5	350	1750	300
		$N = \Sigma f = 300$		$\Sigma fd = 778$	$\Sigma fd^2 = 3510$	

Since the maximum frequency *viz.*, 70 occurs towards the end of the frequency distribution, mode is ill-defined in this case. Hence, we obtain Karl Pearson's coefficient of skewness using median *viz.*, by the formula :

$$Sk = \frac{3\,(\text{Mean} - \text{Median})}{\sigma} \qquad \ldots(*)$$

$$\text{Mean} = A + \frac{h\Sigma fd}{N} = 85 + \frac{10 \times 778}{300} = 85 + 25{\cdot}93 = \text{Rs. } 110{\cdot}93$$

$$\text{s.d. } (\sigma) = h \,.\, \sqrt{\frac{\Sigma fd^2}{N} - \left(\frac{\Sigma fd}{N}\right)^2} = 10 \times \sqrt{\frac{3510}{300} - \left(\frac{778}{300}\right)^2}$$

$$= 10 \times \sqrt{11{\cdot}7 - (2{\cdot}5932)^2} = 10 \times \sqrt{11{\cdot}7 - 6{\cdot}7252}$$

$$= 10 \times \sqrt{4{\cdot}9748} = 10 \times 2{\cdot}23043 = \text{Rs. } 22{\cdot}3043$$

$\frac{N}{2} = \frac{300}{2} = 150$. The *c.f.* just greater than 150 is 170. Hence, the corresponding class 110—120 is the median class. Using the median formula, we get

$$\text{Median} = l + \frac{h}{f}\left(\frac{N}{2} - c\right) = 110 + \frac{10}{50}(150 - 120) = 110 + \frac{30}{5} = 116$$

Substituting these values in (*), we get

$$Sk = \frac{3\,(110{\cdot}93 - 116)}{22{\cdot}3043} = -\frac{3 \times 5{\cdot}07}{22{\cdot}3043} = \frac{-15{\cdot}21}{22{\cdot}3043} = -\,0{\cdot}6819$$

Hence, the given distribution is negatively skewed.

Example 7·5. *Consider the following distributions :*

	Distribution A	*Distribution B*
Mean	*100*	*90*
Median	*90*	*80*
Standard Deviation	*10*	*10*

(i) Distribution A has the same degree of the variation as distribution B.

(ii) Both distributions have the same degree of skewness. True/False ? Comment, giving reasons.

[Delhi Univ. B.Com. (Hons.), 2008]

Solution.

(*i*) C.V. for distribution $A = 100 \times \dfrac{\sigma_A}{\bar{X}_A} = 100 \times \dfrac{10}{100} = 10$

C.V. for distribution $B = 100 \times \dfrac{\sigma_B}{\bar{X}_B} = 100 \times \dfrac{10}{90} = 11{\cdot}11$

Since C.V. (*B*) > C.V. (*A*), the distribution *B* is more variable than the distribution *A*. Hence, the given statement that the distribution *A* has the same degree of variation as distribution *B* is wrong.

(*ii*) Karl Pearson's coefficient of skewness for the distributions *A* and *B* is given by :

$$Sk\,(A) = \frac{3(M - Md)}{\sigma} = \frac{3(100 - 90)}{10} = 3 \;;\; Sk\,(B) = \frac{3(90 - 80)}{10} = 3$$

Since $Sk(A) = Sk(B) = 3$, the statement that both the distributions have the same degree of skewness is true.

Example 7·6. (*a*) *In a moderately asymmetrical distribution, the mode and mean are 32·1 and 35·4 respectively. Calculate the median.*

(*b*) *From a moderately skewed distribution of retail prices for men's shirts, it is found that the mean price is Rs. 200 and the median price is Rs. 170. If the coefficient of variation is 20%, find the Pearsonian coefficient of skewness of the distribution.* [*Delhi Univ. B.Com. (Hons.), 2009; B.A. (Econ. Hons.), 2008*]

Solution (*a*) For a moderately asymmetrical distribution, we have

$$Mo = 3Md - 2M \quad \Rightarrow \quad 3Md = Mo + 2M \quad \Rightarrow \quad Md = \frac{1}{3}(Mo + 2M)$$

$$\therefore \quad Md = \frac{1}{3}(32{\cdot}1 + 2 \times 35{\cdot}4) = \frac{1}{3}(32{\cdot}1 + 70{\cdot}8) = \frac{102{\cdot}9}{3} = 34{\cdot}3$$

(*b*) We are given : Mean (*M*) = Rs. 200, Median (*Md*) = Rs. 170

$$\text{and} \quad C.V. = 20\% \quad \Rightarrow \quad \frac{100\,\sigma}{M} = 20 \quad \Rightarrow \quad \sigma = \frac{20M}{100} = \text{Rs. } \frac{20 \times 200}{100} = \text{Rs. } 40.$$

$$Sk\,(\text{Karl Pearson}) = \frac{3\,(M - Md)}{\sigma} = \frac{3\,(200 - 170)}{40} = \frac{9}{4} = 2{\cdot}25$$

Example 7·7. *Pearson's coefficient of skewness for a distribution is 0·4 and its coefficient of variation is 30%. Its mode is 88, find mean and median.* [*Delhi Univ. B.Com. (Hons.), 1997*]

Solution. We are given Mode = *Mo* = 88, Karl Pearson's coefficient of skewness is :

$$Sk = \frac{M - Mo}{\sigma} = \frac{M - 88}{\sigma} = 0{\cdot}4 \text{ (given)} \qquad \ldots(*)$$

$$\text{C.V.} = \frac{100\,\sigma}{M} = 30 \text{ (given)} \quad \Rightarrow \quad \sigma = \frac{30M}{100} = 0{\cdot}3M \qquad \ldots(**)$$

From (*) and (**), we get

$$M - 88 = 0{\cdot}4\sigma = 0{\cdot}4 \times 0{\cdot}3\,M \quad \Rightarrow \quad M - 0{\cdot}12M = 88 \quad \Rightarrow \quad (1 - 0{\cdot}12)\,M = 88 \Rightarrow M = \frac{88}{0{\cdot}88} = 100$$

Substituting in (**), we get $\sigma = 0{\cdot}3 \times 100 = 30$

Using the empirical relation between mean, median and mode for a moderately asymmetrical distribution *viz.*,

$$Mo = 3Md - 2M \quad \Rightarrow \quad 3Md = Mo + 2M, \quad \text{we get :}$$

$$Md = \tfrac{1}{3}(Mo + 2M) = \tfrac{1}{3}(88 + 2 \times 100) = \frac{288}{3} = 96$$

Hence, Mean = 100 and Median = 96.

Example 7·8. *Pearson's measure of skewness of a distribution is 0·5. Its median and mode are respectively 42 and 36. Find the Coefficient of Variation.*

Solution. We are given : Median = 42, Mode = 36 ...(*)

and Pearson's coefficient of skewness = 0·5 $\Rightarrow$ $Sk = \frac{\text{Mean} - \text{Mode}}{\sigma} = 0{\cdot}5$ ...(**)

To find *s.d.* (σ), we shall first find the value of mean, by using the empirical relationship between mean, median and mode for a moderately asymmetrical distribution *viz.*,

$$\text{Mode} = 3\text{ Median} - 2\text{ Mean} \quad \Rightarrow \quad \text{Mean} = \frac{3\text{ Median} - \text{Mode}}{2} = \frac{3 \times 42 - 36}{2} = \frac{126 - 36}{2} = \frac{90}{2} = 45$$

$$\text{Substituting in (**), we get :} \quad (s.d.)\ \sigma = \frac{\text{Mean} - \text{Mode}}{0{\cdot}5} = \frac{45 - 36}{0{\cdot}5} = \frac{9}{0{\cdot}5} = 18$$

$$\text{Coefficient of Variation (C.V.)} = \frac{100 \times \sigma}{\text{Mean}} = \frac{100 \times 18}{45} = 40$$

Hence, C.V. is 40.

Example 7·9. *The sum of 50 observations is 500 and the sum of their squares is 6,000 and median is 12. Compute the coefficient of variation and the coefficient of skewness.* [*Delhi Univ. B.Com.* (*Pass*), *2000*]

Solution. In the usual notations, we are given :

$$n = 50,\ \Sigma x = 500 \quad \text{and} \quad \Sigma x^2 = 6{,}000\ ;\ \text{Median} = 12$$

$$\therefore \quad \text{Mean } (\bar{x}) = \frac{\Sigma x}{n} = \frac{500}{50} = 10\ ;\ \sigma^2 = \frac{\Sigma x^2}{n} - \bar{x}^2 = \frac{6{,}000}{50} - 100 = 20 \quad \Rightarrow \quad \sigma = \sqrt{20} = 4{\cdot}47$$

$$\text{Coefficient of Variation (C.V.)} = \frac{100\,\sigma}{\bar{x}} = \frac{100 \times 4{\cdot}47}{10} = 44{\cdot}7$$

Karl Pearson's coefficient of skewness is given by :

$$Sk = \frac{3(\text{Mean} - \text{Median})}{\sigma} = \frac{3(10 - 12)}{4{\cdot}47} = \frac{-6}{4{\cdot}47} = -1{\cdot}34.$$

Example 7·10. *The following information was obtained from the records of a factory relating to the wages.*

Arithmetic Mean: Rs. 56·80; Median : Rs. 59·50; S.D. : Rs. 12·40

Give as much information as you can about the distribution of wages.

Solution. We can obtain the following information from the above data :

(*i*) Since Md = Rs. 59·50, we conclude that 50% of the workers in the factory obtain the wages above Rs. 59·50.

(*ii*) $$\text{C.V.} = \frac{100\,\sigma}{M} = \frac{100 \times 12{\cdot}40}{56{\cdot}80} = 21{\cdot}83$$

(*iii*) Karl Pearson's coefficient of skewness is given by :

$$Sk = \frac{3(M - Md)}{\sigma} = \frac{3(56{\cdot}80 - 59{\cdot}50)}{12{\cdot}40} = \frac{3 \times (-2{\cdot}70)}{12{\cdot}40} = \frac{-8{\cdot}1}{12{\cdot}4} = -0{\cdot}65$$

Hence, the distribution of wages is negatively skewed *i.e.*, it has a longer tail towards the left.

(*iv*) Using the empirical relation between M, Md and Mo for a moderately asymmetrical distribution, we get

$$Mo = 3Md - 2M = 3 \times 59{\cdot}50 - 2 \times 56{\cdot}80 = 178{\cdot}50 - 113{\cdot}60 = \text{Rs. } 64{\cdot}90.$$

Example 7·11. *You are given the position in a factory before and after the settlement of an industrial dispute. Comment on the gains or losses from the point of view of workers and that of management.*

	Before	*After*
No. of workers	*3,000*	*2,900*
Mean wage (in Rs.)	*220*	*230*
Median wage (in Rs.)	*250*	*240*
Standard deviation (in Rs.)	*30*	*26*

[*Delhi Univ. B.Com. (Hons.), 2006*]

Solution. On the basis of the above data we are in a position to make the following comments :

(*i*) The number of workers after the dispute has decreased from 3000 to 2900. Obviously this is a definite loss to the persons thrown out or retrenched. It may also be a loss to the management if their retrenchment affects the efficiency of work adversely.

(*ii*) We know that :

$$\text{Average wage} = \frac{\text{Total wages paid}}{\text{Total No. of workers}}$$

$$\Rightarrow \quad \text{Total wages paid} = (\text{Average wage}) \times (\text{Total No. of workers})$$

Hence,

Total wages paid by the management before the dispute $= \text{Rs. } 3000 \times 220 = \text{Rs. } 6{,}60{,}000$

Total wages paid by the management after the dispute $= \text{Rs. } 2900 \times 230 = \text{Rs. } 6{,}67{,}000$

Thus we see that the total wages paid by the management have gone up after the dispute (the additional wage bill being Rs. 7000), although the number of workers has been reduced from 3000 to 2900. This is due to the fact that the average wage per worker has increased after the dispute - which is a distinct advantage to the workers.

It may be pointed out that the increased wages paid by the management (Rs. 7000) should not be viewed as a disadvantage to the management unless we have definite reasons to believe that the efficiency and productivity have not gone up after the dispute. However, the loss to the managements due to higher wage bill, will be more than compensated if after the dispute, there is a definite increase in the efficiency of the workers or/and increase in productivity.

(*iii*) Although the number of workers has decreased from 3000 to 2900 after the dispute, the average wage per worker has gone up from Rs. 220 to 230. This might probably be a consequence of the retrenchment of casual labour or temporary labour working on daily wages or so with relatively lower wages.

(*iv*) The median wage after the dispute has come down from Rs. 250 to Rs. 240. This implies that before the dispute upper 50% of the workers were getting wages above Rs. 250 whereas after the dispute they get wages only above Rs. 240.

(*v*) Using the empirical relation between mean, median and mode (for a moderately asymmetrical distribution) *viz.*,

$$\text{Mode} = 3 \text{ Median} - 2 \text{ Mean}$$

We get

$$\text{Mode (before dispute)} = 3 \times 250 - 2 \times 220 = \text{Rs. } 310$$

$$\text{Mode (after dispute)} = 3 \times 240 - 2 \times 230 = \text{Rs. } 260$$

Thus, we find that the modal wage has come down from Rs. 310 (before dispute) to Rs. 260 (after dispute). Thus after the dispute there is concentration of wages around a much smaller value.

(*vi*)

$$\text{C.V.} = \frac{100 \times (s.d.)}{\text{Mean}}$$

$$\therefore \text{ C.V. (before dispute)} = \frac{100 \times 30}{220} = 13{\cdot}64 \quad \text{and} \quad \text{C.V. (after dispute)} = \frac{100 \times 26}{230} = 11{\cdot}30$$

Since C.V. has decreased from 13·64 to 11·30, the distribution of wages has become less variable *i.e.*, more consistent or uniform after the settlement of the dispute. Thus, after the settlement there are less disparities in wages and from management point it will result in greater satisfaction to the workers.

(*vii*) Since we are given mean and median, we can calculate Karl Pearson's coefficient of skewness for studying the symmetry of the distribution of wages before the dispute and after the dispute *viz.*, $Sk = 3(M - Md))/\sigma$

$$Sk \text{ (before dispute)} = \frac{3(220 - 250)}{30} = -3 \quad \text{and} \quad Sk \text{ (after dispute)} = \frac{3(230 - 240)}{26} = -1{\cdot}15$$

Thus the highly negatively skewed distribution (before the dispute) has become a moderately negatively skewed distribution (after the dispute). This implies that the curve of distribution of wages after the dispute has a less longer tail towards the left. In other words, the number of workers getting lower wages has increased.

EXERCISE 7·1

1. (*a*) Explain the concept of skewness. Draw the sketch of a skewed frequency distribution and show the position of the mean, median and mode when the distribution is asymmetric. (*Delhi Univ. B.Com., 1997*)

(*b*) Explain the concept of positive and negative skewness.

(*c*) Show graphically the positions of mean, median and mode in a positively and negatively skewed series. [*Delhi Univ. B.Com. (Pass), 1998*]

2. Comment on the following :

(*a*) In a symmetrical distribution, we have mean = median ≠ mode. [*Delhi Univ. B.Com. (Hons.) 2002*]

(*b*) "A series representing U-shaped curve is symmetrical." Comment. [*Delhi Univ. B.Com. (Pass), 2001*]

3. (*a*) The values of mean and median are 30 and 40 respectively in a frequency distribution. Is the distribution skewed? If yes, state the direction of skewness. [*Delhi Univ. B.Com. (Pass), 2002*]

Ans. Mean < Median, the distribution is negatively skewed.

(*b*) The mean for a symmetrical distribution is 50·6. Find the values of median and mode. [*C.S. (Foundation), June 2001*]

Ans. Median = Mode = 50·6.

4. (*a*) Define Pearson's measure of skewness. What is the difference between relative measure and the absolute measure of skewness.

(*b*) From the following data find out Karl Pearson's co-efficient of skewness :

Measurement	:	10	11	12	13	14	15
Frequency	:	2	4	10	8	5	1

Ans. 0·3478.

5. Calculate the Pearson's coefficient of skewness from the following :

Wages (Rs.)	:	0—10	10—20	20—30	30—40	40—50
No. of Workers	:	15	20	30	25	10

Ans. 0·1845.

6. Calculate Karl Pearson's coefficient of skewness from the following data and explain its significance :

Wages	:	70—80	80—90	90—100	100—110	110—120	120—130	130—140	140—150
No. of Persons	:	12	18	35	42	50	45	20	8

[*Delhi Univ. B.Com. (Hons.), 2000*]

Ans. M = Rs. 110·43, Mo = Rs. 116·15, σ = Rs. 17·26, Sk = – 0·3316.

7. The mean, standard deviation and range of a symmetrical distribution of weights of a group of 20 boys are 40 kgs., 5 kgs. and 6 kgs. respectively. Find the mean and standard deviation of the group if the lightest and heaviest boys are excluded. [*Delhi Univ. B.A. (Econ. Hons.), 2004*]

Ans. Mean = 40 , *s.d.* (σ) = 5.17

Hint. Proceed as in Example 7.2.

8. Calculate the Pearson's measure of skewness on the basis of Mean, Mode and Standard Deviation.

Mid-value (X)	:	14.5	15.5	16.5	17.5	18.5	19.5	20.5	21.5
f	:	35	40	48	100	125	87	43	22

Hint. The corresponding classes are : 14—15, 15—16, ..., 21—22.

Ans. Mean = 18.07 , Mode = 18.4, σ = 1.775, Skewness (Pearson) = – 0.186

9. From the following data of age of employees, calculate coefficient of skewness and comment on the result :

Age below (yrs.)	:	25	30	35	40	45	50	55
No. of employees	:	8	20	40	65	80	92	100

[*Delhi Univ. MBA, 1997*]

Ans. $\bar{x}$ = 37·25 yrs.; *Mo* = 36·67 yrs.; σ = 16·99 yrs.; *Sk* (Karl Pearson) = 0·07.

10. Calculate Karl Pearson's coefficient of skewness from the following series :

Wt. in kgs.	:	Below 40	40—50	50—60	60—70	70—80
No. of persons	:	10	16	18	25	20
Wt. in kgs.	:	80—90	90—100	100 and above		
No. of persons	:	4	4	3		

Hint. Take the first class as 30—40 and the last class as 100—110.

Ans. Mean = 62·200 kg, Mode = 65·833 kg, σ = 16·857 kg., *Sk* = – 0·2155.

11. Calculate Karl Pearson's coefficient of skewness from the following data :

Marks (above)	:	0	10	20	30	40	50	60	70	80
No. of students	:	150	140	100	80	80	70	30	14	0

Hint. Locate mode by the method of grouping ; two modal classes 10—20 and 50—60; mode ill-defined. Find median.

Ans. $Sk = 3(M - Md)/\sigma = -0{\cdot}6622$.

12. The daily expenditure of 100 families is given below :

Daily Expenditure	:	0—20	20—40	40—60	60—80	80—100
No. of Families	:	13	?	27	?	16

If the mode of the distribution is 44, calculate the Karl Pearson coefficient of skewness.

Ans. Frequency for the class 20—40 is 25 and for the class 60—80 is 19.

$$Sk \text{ (Karl Pearson)} = \frac{50-44}{25{\cdot}3} = 0{\cdot}24.$$

13. The following facts are gathered before and after an industrial dispute :

	Before dispute	*After dispute*
No. of workers employed	515	509
Mean wages	Rs. 49·50	Rs. 52·70
Median wages	Rs. 52·80	Rs. 50·00
Variance of wages	(Rs.)^2 121·00	(Rs.)^2 144·00

Compare the position before and after the dispute in respect of

(*a*) total wages, (*b*) modal wages, (*c*) standard deviation, and (*d*) skewness.

Ans.

	Before dispute	*After dispute*
(*i*) Total wages	Rs. 25,492·50	Rs. 26,849·75
(*ii*) Modal wages	Rs. 59·40	Rs. 44·50
(*iii*) C.V.	22·22	22·74
(*iv*) Skewness	– 0·90	0·69

14. You are given the position in a factory before and after the settlement of an industrial dispute.

	Before Dispute	*After Dispute*
No. of workers	3,000	2,900
Mean wages (Rs.)	220	230
Median wages (Rs.)	250	240
Standard deviation (Rs.)	30	26

Comment on the gains and losses from the point of view of workers and that of management.

[*Delhi Univ. B.Com. (Hons.), 2006*]

Hint. Proceed as in Example **7.13.**

15. You are given below the following details relating to the wages is respect of two factories from which it is concluded that the skewness and variability are same in both the factories.

		Factory A	*Factory B*
Arithmetic Mean	:	50	45
Mode	:	45	50
Variance	:	100	100

Point out the mistake or the wrong inference in the above statement.

Ans. C.V. $(A) = 20$, C.V. $(B) = 22{\cdot}2$; $Sk(A) = +0{\cdot}5$, $Sk(B) = -0{\cdot}5$.

16. The sum of 20 observations is 300 and its sum of squares is 5,000 and median is 15. Find the coefficient of skewness and coefficient of variation. *[Delhi Univ. B.Com. (Hons.), 2007]*

Ans. $Sk = 0$, C.V. $= \frac{5}{15} \times 100 = 33{\cdot}3$.

17. For a group of 10 items $\sum X = 452$, $\sum X^2 = 24{,}270$ and Mode $= 43{\cdot}7$. Find the Pearsonian coefficient of skewness.

Ans. $Sk = 0{\cdot}08$.

18. If the mode and mean of a moderately asymmetrical series are respectively 16 inches and 15·6 inches, would be its most probable median ?

Ans. Median = 15·73 inches.

19. In a slightly skew distribution the arithmetic mean is Rs. 45 and the median is Rs. 48. Find the approximate value of mode.

Ans. Mode = Rs. 54.

20. In a frequency distribution, Karl Pearson's coefficient of skewness revealed that the distribution was skewed to the left to an extent of 0·6. Its mean value was less than its modal value by 4·8. What was the standard deviation ?

Ans. $\sigma = 8$.

21. In a distribution mean = 65, median = 70 and the coefficient of skewness is – 0·6. Find mode and coefficient of variation. (Assume that the distribution is moderately asymmetrical.)

Ans. Mode = 80, *C.V.* = 38·46

22. In a certain distribution the following results were obtained :

Arithmetic Mean $(\bar{X}) = 45$; Median = 48; Coefficient of skewness = – 0·4

The person who gave you this data, failed to give you S.D. (Standard Deviation). You are required to estimate it with the help of the above data. *[Delhi Univ. B.Com. (Hons.), 1997]*

Ans. $\sigma = 22{\cdot}5$.

23. Karl Pearson's measure of skewness of a distribution is 0·5. The median and mode of the distribution are respectively, 42 and 32.

Find : *(i)* Mean, *(ii)* the S.D., *(iii)* the coefficient of variation. *[Delhi Univ. B.A. (Econ. Hons.), 2000]*

Ans. *(i)* 47, *(ii)* 30, *(iii)* 63·83.

24. Karl Pearson's coefficient of skewness of a distribution is 0·32. Its standard deviation is 6·5 and mean is 29·6. Find the mode and median of the distribution.

If the mode of the above is 24·8, what will be the standard deviation ? *[Delhi Univ. B.Com. (Hons.), 1998]*

Ans. Mode = 27·52, Median = 28·91, $\sigma = 15$.

25. Karl Pearson's coefficient of skewness of a distribution is +0·40. Its standard deviation is 8 and mean is 30. Find the mode and median of the distribution.

Ans. Mode = 26·8, Median = 28·93.

26. The median, mode and coefficient of skewness for a certain distribution are respectively 17·4, 15·3 and 0·35. Calculate the coefficient of variation.

Ans. Mean = 18·45; C.V. = 48·78.

27. Karl Pearson's coefficient of skewness of a distribution is 0.5. Its mean is 30 and coefficient of variation is 20%. Find the mode and median of the distribution. *[Delhi Univ. B.A. (Econ. Hons.), 2007]*

Ans. $\sigma = 6$, Median = 29, Mode = 27.

28. *(a)* A frequency distribution is positively skewed. The mean of the distribution is :

Greater than the mode, Less than the mode, Equal to the mode, None of these.

Tick the correct answer.

(*b*) In a moderatly skewed distribution the values of mean and median are 5 and 6 respectively. The value of mode in such a situation is approximately equal to... .

(*i*) 8 (*ii*) 11 (*iii*) 16 (*iv*) None of these.

Ans. (*a*) $M > Mo$, (*b*) : (*i*) 8.

29. State the empirical relationship among mean, median and mode in a symmetrical and moderately asymmetrical frequency distribution. How does it help in estimating mode and measuring skewness ?

Given that mean of a distribution in 50 and mode in 58;

(*i*) Calculate the median;

(*ii*) What can you say about the shape of the distribution ? Explain, Why ? [*Delhi Univ. B.A.. (Econ. Hons.), 2009*]

Ans. (*i*) $Md = 52.67$; (*ii*) $M < Md < M_0 \Rightarrow$ Distribution is negatively skewed.

30. In a moderately asymmetrical distribution :

(*i*) The mode and median are 300 and 240 respectively. Find the value of mean.

(*ii*) Mean = 200 and Mode = 150. Find the value of median. [*C.S.* (*Foundation*), *Dec. 2001*]

Ans. (*i*) Mean = 210, (*ii*) Median = 183·33.

31. Which group is more skewed ?

(*i*) Mean = 22 ; Median = 24 ; s.d. = 10. (*ii*) Mean = 22 ; Median = 25 ; s.d. = 12.

Ans. *Sk* (*i*) = – 0·60 ; *Sk* (*ii*) = – 0·75. Group (*ii*) is more skewed to the left.

32. What is the relationship between mean, mode and median ? What is the condition under which this relationship holds ? Locate graphically the position of the three measures in the case of both negatively as well as positively skewed distribution.

Ans. Mode = 3 Median – 2 Mean, for a moderately asymmetrical distribution.

7·2·3. Bowley's Coefficient of Skewness. Prof. A.L. Bowley's coefficient of skewness is based on the quartiles and is given by :

$$Sk = \frac{(Q_3 - Md) - (Md - Q_1)}{(Q_3 - Md) + (Md - Q_1)} \quad \Rightarrow \quad Sk = \frac{Q_3 + Q_1 - 2Md}{Q_3 - Q_1} \qquad ...(7·11)$$

Remarks 1. Bowley's coefficient of skewness is also known as *Quartile coefficient of skewness* and is especially useful in situations where quartiles and median are used *viz.*, :

(*i*) When the mode is ill-defined and extreme observations are present in the data.

(*ii*) When the distribution has open end classes or unequal class intervals.

In these situations, Pearson's coefficient of skewness cannot be used.

2. From (7·11), we observe that :

$$Sk = 0, \text{ if } Q_3 - Md = Md - Q_1 \qquad ...(7·12)$$

This implies that for a symmetrical distribution (***Sk*** = 0), median is equidistant from the upper and lower quartiles. Moreover, skewness is *positive* if :

$$Q_3 - Md > Md - Q_1 \quad \Rightarrow \quad Q_3 + Q_1 > 2Md \qquad ...(7·13)$$

and skewness is *negative* if :

$$Q_3 - Md < Md - Q_1 \quad \Rightarrow \quad Q_3 + Q_1 < 2Md \qquad ...(7·14)$$

3. Limits for Bowley's Coefficient of Skewness.

$$|Sk \text{ (Bowley)}| \leq 1 \quad \Rightarrow \quad -1 \leq Sk \text{ (Bowley)} \leq 1. \qquad ...(7·15)$$

Thus, Bowley's coefficient of skewness ranges from –1 to 1.

Further, we note from (7·11) that :

$$Sk = +1, \text{ if } Md - Q_1 = 0, \quad i.e., \quad \text{if } Md = Q_1 \qquad ...(7·15a)$$

and

$$Sk = -1, \text{ if } Q_3 - Md = 0, \quad i.e., \quad \text{if } Q_3 = Md \qquad ...(7·15b)$$

4. It should be clearly understood that the values of the coefficient of skewness obtained by Bowley's formula and Pearson's formula are not comparable, although in each case, *Sk* = 0 implies the absence of skewness *i.e.*, the distribution is symmetrical. It may even happen that one of them gives positive skewness while the other gives negative skewness. (See Example 7·17)

5. The only and perhaps quite serious limitations of this coefficient is that it is based only on the central 50% of the data and ignores the remaining 50% of the data towards the extremes.

7·2·4. Kelly's Measure of Skewness. The drawback of Bowley's coefficient of skewness, (*viz.*, that it ignores the 50% of the data towards the extremes), can be partially removed by taking two deciles or percentiles equidistant from the median value. The refinement was suggested by Kelly. *Kelly's percentile (or decile)* measure of skewness is given by :

$$Sk = (P_{90} - P_{50}) - (P_{50} - P_{10}) = P_{90} + P_{10} - 2P_{50} \qquad \ldots(7\cdot16)$$

But $P_{90} = D_9$ and $P_{10} = D_1$. Hence, (7·16) can be re-written as :

$$Sk = (D_9 - D_5) - (D_5 - D_1) = D_9 + D_1 - 2D_5 \qquad \ldots(7\cdot16a)$$

P_i and D_i are the ith percentile and decile respectively of the given distribution.

(7·16) or (7·16*a*) gives an absolute measure of skewness. However, for practical purposes, we generally compute the coefficient of skewness, which is given by :

$$Sk\text{ (Kelly)} = \frac{(P_{90} - P_{50}) - (P_{50} - P_{10})}{(P_{90} - P_{50}) + (P_{50} - P_{10})} = \frac{P_{90} + P_{10} - 2P_{50}}{P_{90} - P_{10}} \qquad \ldots(7\cdot17)$$

$$= \frac{D_9 + D_1 - 2D_5}{D_9 - D_1} \qquad \ldots(7\cdot17a)$$

Remarks 1. We have : $D_5 = P_{50} =$ Median. Hence, from (7·17) and (7·17*a*), we get

$$Sk\text{ (Kelly)} = \frac{P_{90} + P_{10} - 2Md}{P_{90} - P_{10}} = \frac{D_9 + D_1 - 2Md}{D_9 - D_1} \qquad \ldots(7\cdot18)$$

2. This method is primarily of theoretical importance only and is seldom used in practice.

7·2·5. Coefficient of Skewness based on Moments. This coefficient is based on the 2nd and 3rd moments about mean and is discussed in detail in § 7·5.

Example 7·12. *Comment on the following* :

(*i*) *The mode of a distribution cannot be less than arithmetic mean.*

(*ii*) *If Q_1, Q_2, Q_3 be respectively the lower quartile, the median and the upper quartile of a distribution, then $Q_2 - Q_1 = Q_3 - Q_2$.*

Solution. (*i*) The given statement is not true in general. Mode of a distribution cannot be lower than arithmetic mean or in other words, arithmetic mean is greater than mode only for a positively skewed distribution. However, Mean = Mode for a symmetrical distribution, while for a negatively skewed distribution Mean < Mode.

(*ii*) The statement : $Q_3 - Q_2 = Q_2 - Q_1$,

is true only for a symmetrical distribution. However, if the distribution is skewed, then

$$Q_3 - Q_2 \neq Q_2 - Q_1$$

If $Q_3 - Q_2 > Q_2 - Q_1 \Rightarrow Q_1 + Q_3 > 2Q_2$, the distribution is positively skewed.

and if $Q_3 - Q_2 < Q_2 - Q_1 \Rightarrow Q_1 + Q_3 < 2Q_2$, the distribution is negatively skewed.

Example 7·13. *Calculate Bowley's coefficient of skewness of the following data* :

Weight (lbs)	*No. of persons*	*Weight (lbs)*	*No. of persons*	*Weight (lbs)*	*No. of persons*
Under 100	1	*130—139*	145	*170—179*	12
100—109	14	*140—149*	121	*180—189*	5
110—119	66	*150—159*	65	*190—199*	2
120—129	122	*160—169*	31	*200 and over*	2

COMPUTATION OF QUARTILES

Weight (lbs)	No. of persons (f)	'Less than' c.f.	Class boundaries
0—99	1	1	0 — 99·5
100—109	14	15	99·5—109·5
110—119	66	81	109·5—119·5
120—129	122	203	119·5—129·5
130—139	145	348	129·5—139·5
140—149	121	469	139·5—149·5
150—159	65	534	149·5—159·5
160—169	31	565	159·5—169·5
170—179	12	577	169·5—179·5
180—189	5	582	179·5—189·5
190—199	2	584	189·5—199·5
200—209	2	N = 586	199·5—209·5

Solution. Here we are given the frequency distribution with inclusive type classes. Since the formulae for median and quartiles are based on continuous frequency distribution with exclusive type classes without any gaps, we obtain the class boundaries which are given in the last column of the adjoining table.

Here $N = 586, \frac{N}{4} = 146·5, \frac{N}{2} = 293, \frac{3N}{4} = 439·5$

The *c.f.* just greater than *N*/2 *i.e.*, 293 is 348. Hence, the corresponding class 129·5—139·5 is the median class. Using the Median formula, we get

$$Md\ (Q_2) = 129·5 + \frac{10}{145}(293 - 203)$$

$$= 129·5 + \frac{10 \times 90}{145} = 129·50 + 6·21 = 135·71$$

The *c.f.* just greater than *N*/4 *i.e.*, 146·5 is 203. Hence, the corresponding class 119·5—129·5 contains Q_1

$$\therefore \quad Q_1 = 119·5 + \frac{10}{122}(146·5 - 81) = 119·5 + \frac{10 \times 65·5}{122} = 119·50 + 5·37 = 124·87$$

The *c.f.* just greater than 3*N*/4 *i.e.*, 439·5 is 469. Hence, the corresponding class 139·5—149·5 contains Q_3.

$$\therefore \quad Q_3 = 139·5 + \frac{10}{121}(439·5 - 348) = 139·5 + \frac{10 \times 91·5}{121} = 139·50 + 7·56 = 147·06$$

Bowley's coefficient of skewness is given by :

$$Sk\ (\text{Bowley}) = \frac{Q_3 + Q_1 - 2Md}{Q_3 - Q_1} = \frac{147·06 + 124·87 - 2 \times 135·71}{147·06 - 124·87} = \frac{271·93 - 271·42}{22·19} = \frac{0·51}{22·19} = 0·0298.$$

Example 7·14. *Calculate the coefficient of skewness from the following data by using quartiles.*

Marks	*No. of students*	*Marks*	*No. of students*
Above 0	*180*	*Above 60*	*65*
Above 15	*160*	*Above 75*	*20*
Above 30	*130*	*Above 90*	*5*
Above 45	*100*		

COMPUTATION OF QUARTILES

Marks	*Number of students (f)*	*'Less than' c.f.*
0—15	180 – 160 = 20	20
15—30	160 – 130 = 30	50
30—45	130 – 100 = 30	80
45—60	100 – 65 = 35	115
60—75	65 – 20 = 45	160
75—90	20 – 5 = 15	175
above 90	5	180
Total	$N = \Sigma f = 180$	

Solution. We are given 'more than' cumulative frequency distribution. To compute quartiles, we first express it as a continuous frequency distribution without any gaps as given in the adjoining table.

$$\frac{N}{2} = \frac{180}{2} = 90, \ \frac{N}{4} = \frac{180}{4} = 45 \ \text{and} \ \frac{3N}{4} = 135$$

The c.f. just greater than *N*/2 *i.e.*, 90 is 115. Hence the corresponding class 45—60 is the median class.

$$\therefore \quad Md = l + \frac{h}{f}\left(\frac{N}{2} - c\right) = 45 + \frac{15}{35}\left(90 - 80\right) = 45 + \frac{15 \times 10}{35} = 45 + 4·29 = 49·29$$

The *c.f.* just greater than *N*/4 *i.e.*, 45 is 50. Hence, the corresponding class 15—30 contains Q_1.

$$\therefore \quad Q_1 = l + \frac{h}{f}\left(\frac{N}{4} - C\right) = 15 + \frac{15}{30}\left(45 - 20\right) = 15 + \frac{15 \times 25}{30} = 15 + 12·5 = 27·5$$

The *c.f.* just greater than 3*N*/4 *i.e.*, 135 is 160. Hence, the corresponding class 60—75 contains Q_3.

$\therefore \quad Q_3 = l + \frac{h}{f}\left(\frac{3N}{4} - C\right) = 60 + \frac{15}{45}\left(135 - 115\right) = 60 + \frac{20}{3} = 60 + 6{\cdot}67 = 66{\cdot}67$

Hence, Bowley's coefficient of skewness based on quartiles is given by :

$$Sk\text{ (Bowley)} = \frac{Q_3 + Q_1 - 2Md}{Q_3 - Q_1} = \frac{66{\cdot}67 + 27{\cdot}50 - 2 \times 49{\cdot}29}{66{\cdot}67 - 27{\cdot}50} = \frac{94{\cdot}17 - 98{\cdot}58}{39{\cdot}17} = -\frac{4{\cdot}41}{39{\cdot}17} = -0{\cdot}1126$$

Example 7·15. *If the first quartile is 142 and the semi-interquartile range is 18, find the median (assuming the distribution to be symmetrical.* [*Delhi Univ. B.Com. (Hons.), 1997*]

Solution. We are given : $Q_1 = 142$; and $\frac{Q_3 - Q_1}{2} = 18 \Rightarrow Q_3 = Q_1 + 2 \times 18 = 142 + 36 = 178$

If the distribution is symmetrical, then

$$Sk\text{ (Bowley)} = \frac{(Q_3 - Md) - (Md - Q_1)}{(Q_3 - Md) + (Md - Q_1)} = 0 \Rightarrow Q_3 - Md = Md - Q_1$$

$$\therefore \quad Md = \tfrac{1}{2}(Q_1 + Q_3) = \frac{142 + 178}{2} = 160$$

Example 7·16(*a*). *In a frequency distribution the coefficient of skewness based on quartiles is 0·6. If the sum of the upper and lower quartiles is 100 and median is 38, find the value of upper and lower quartiles.*

(*b*) *The mean, mode an Q.D. of a distribution are 42, 36 and 15 respectively. If its Bowley's coefficient of skewness is 1/3, find the values of the two quartiles. Also state the empirical relationship between mean, mode and median.* [*Delhi Univ. B.Com. (Hons.), 2008*]

Solution. (*a*) We are given :

$$Sk = \frac{Q_3 + Q_1 - 2Md}{Q_3 - Q_1} = 0{\cdot}6 \quad \ldots(*) \quad \text{Also} \quad Q_3 + Q_1 = 100 \quad \text{and} \quad \text{Median} = 38 \quad \ldots(**)$$

Substituting from (**) in (*), we get

$$\frac{100 - 2 \times 38}{Q_3 - Q_1} = 0{\cdot}6 \quad \Rightarrow \quad Q_3 - Q_1 = \frac{100 - 76}{0{\cdot}6} = \frac{24}{0{\cdot}6} = 40$$

Thus, we have : $Q_3 + Q_1 = 100$ and $Q_3 - Q_1 = 40$

Adding and subtracting, we get respectively

$$2Q_3 = 140 \Rightarrow Q_3 = \frac{140}{2} = 70; \quad \text{and} \quad 2Q_1 = 60 \Rightarrow Q_1 = \frac{60}{2} = 30$$

Hence, the values of the upper and lower quartiles are 70 and 30 respectively.

(*b*) We are given : Mean = 42, Mode = 36 ...(1)

and $Q.D. = \frac{Q_3 - Q_1}{2} = 15 \quad \Rightarrow \quad Q_3 - Q_1 = 30$ ...(2)

The empirical relation between mean, mode and median is :

Mean – Mode = 3 (Mean – Median) ⇒ Mode = 3 Median – 2 Mean ...(3)

From (1) and (3), we get $36 = 3Md - 2 \times 42 \quad \Rightarrow \quad Md = \frac{1}{3}(36 + 84) = 40$ ...(4)

Bowley's coefficient of skewness is given by :

$$Sk\text{ (Bowley)} = \frac{Q_3 + Q_1 - 2\,Md}{Q_3 - Q_1} = \frac{1}{3} \text{ (Given)}$$

$$\Rightarrow \quad Q_3 + Q_1 = 2\,Md + \frac{1}{3}(Q_3 - Q_1) = 2 \times 40 + \frac{30}{3} = 90 \quad \text{[From (2) and (4)]}$$

$$\therefore \quad Q_3 - Q_1 = 30 \quad \text{and} \quad Q_3 + Q_1 = 90.$$

Adding and subtracting we get respectively.

$$2\,Q_3 = 120 \Rightarrow Q_3 = 60 \quad \text{and} \quad 2Q_1 = 60 \Rightarrow Q_1 = 30.$$

Example 7·17. *From the information given below, calculate Karl Pearson's coefficient of skewness and also quartile coefficient of skewness :*

Measure	*Place A*	*Place B*
Mean	*150*	*140*
Median	*142*	*155*
Standard deviation	*30*	*55*
Third quartile	*195*	*260*
First quartile	*62*	*80*

Solution. *Place A* :

$$Sk \text{ (Karl Pearson)} = \frac{3(M - Md)}{\sigma} = \frac{3(150 - 142)}{30} = \frac{8}{10} = 0·8$$

$$Sk \text{ (Bowley)} = \frac{Q_3 + Q_1 - 2Md}{Q_3 - Q_1} = \frac{195 + 62 - 2 \times 142}{195 - 62} = \frac{257 - 284}{133} = -\frac{27}{133} = -0·203$$

Place B :

$$Sk \text{ (Karl Pearson)} = \frac{3(M - Md)}{\sigma} = \frac{3(140 - 155)}{55} = \frac{3 \times (-15)}{55} = -\frac{9}{11} = -0·82$$

$$Sk \text{ (Bowley)} = \frac{Q_3 + Q_1 - 2Md}{Q_3 - Q_1} = \frac{260 + 80 - 2 \times 155}{260 - 80} = \frac{340 - 310}{180} = \frac{1}{6} = 0·167$$

Note: See Remark 4 to § 7.2.3

EXERCISE 7·2

1. What is 'Skewness' ? What are the tests of skewness ? Draw different sketches to indicate different types of skewness and locate roughly the relative positions of mean, median and mode in cash case.

2. Give any three measures of skewness of a frequency distribution. Explain briefly (not exceeding ten lines) with suitable diagrams the term 'Skewness' as mentioned above.

3. Distinguish between Karl Pearson's and Bowley's measures of skewness. Which one of these would you prefer and why ? *[Delhi Univ. MBA, 2000]*

4. Explain the meaning of skewness using sketches of frequency curves. State the different measures of skewness that are commonly used. How does skewness differ from dispersion ?

5. What are quartiles ? How are they used to measure skewness ?

6. Describe Bowley's measure of skewness. Show that it lies between ±1. Under what conditions these limits are attained ?

7. The weekly wages earned by one hundred workers of a factory are as follows. Find the absolute measures of dispersion and skewness based on quartiles and interpret the results.

Weekly wages ('00 Rs.)	*No. of workers*	*Weekly wages ('00 Rs.)*	*No. of workers*
12·5—17·5	12	37·5—42·5	10
17·5—22·5	16	42·5—47·5	6
22·5—27·5	25	47·5—52·5	3
27·5—32·5	14	52·5—57·5	1
32·5—37·5	13		

Ans. $Q.D. = 7·01$; $Sk = (Q_3 - Md) - (Md - Q_1) = 3·34$.

8. Find out the coefficient of skewness using Bowley's formula from the following figures :

Income (in Rs.) :	100—199	200—299	300—399	400—499	500—599	600—699	700—799	800—899
No. of Persons :	39	25	49	62	38	37	32	18

Ans. $Sk = 0·1146$.

9. The figures in the adjoining table relate to the size of capital of companies :

Find out (*i*) the median size of the capital;

(*ii*) the coefficient of skewness with the help of Bowley's measure of skewness.

What conclusion do you draw from the skewness measured by you ?

Capital in Lakhs of Rs.	*No. of Companies*
1—5	20
6—10	27
11—15	29
16—20	38
21—25	48
26—30	53
31—35	70

Ans. Median = 23·47 ; Sk (Bowley) = – 0·119.

10. For the frequency distribution given below, calculate the coefficient of skewness based on the quartiles :

Class Limits	:	10—19	20—29	30—39	40—49	50—59	60—69	70—79	80—89
Frequency	:	5	9	14	20	25	15	8	4

Ans. – 0·103.

11. Calculate the coefficient of skewness based n quartiles and median from the following data :

Variable	:	0—10	10—20	20—30	30—40	40—50	50—60	60—70	70—80
Frequency	:	12	16	26	38	22	15	7	4

[*Osmania Univ. B.Com., 1998*]

Ans. $Q_1 = 22{\cdot}69$, $Q_3 = 45{\cdot}91$, Median (Q_2) = 34·21, *Sk* (Bowley) = 0·008.

12. By using the quartiles, find a measure of skewness for the following distribution.

Annual Sales (Rs. '000)	*No. of firms*	*Annual Sales (Rs. '000)*	*No. of firms*
Less than 20	30	Less than 70	644
" " 30	225	" " 80	650
" " 40	465	" " 90	665
" " 50	580	" " 100	680
" " 60	634		

[*Bangalore Univ. B.Com., 1998*]

Ans. $Q_1 = 27{\cdot}18$; $Q_3 = 43{\cdot}90$; Median = 34·79 ; *Sk* (Bowley) = 0·0903.

13. Calculate Bowley's coefficient of skewness for the following data :

Income equal to or more than	*No. of Persons*	*Income equal to or more than*	*No. of Persons*
100	1000	600	200
200	950	700	150
300	700	800	100
400	600	900	50
500	500	1000	0

Assume that income is a continuous variable.

Ans. *Sk* = – 0·4506.

14. (*a*) Find out Quartile coefficient of skewness in a series where

$$Q_1 = 18, \quad Q_3 = 25, \quad \text{Mode} = 21 \quad \text{and} \quad \text{Mean} = 18.$$

[*Delhi Univ. B.Com. (Pass) 1999*]

Hint. Mode = $3Md - 2$ Mean $\Rightarrow$ $Md = 19$

Ans. 0·714.

(*b*) Find the coefficient of skewness from the following information :

Difference of two quartiles = 8 ; Mode = 11, Sum of two quartiles = 22 ; Mean = 8.

[*Delhi Univ. B.Com. (Hons.), 1997*]

Hint. $Q_3 - Q_1 = 8$, $Q_3 + Q_1 = 22$ $\Rightarrow$ $Q_1 = 7$, $Q_3 = 15$; $Mo = 3Md - 2M$ $\Rightarrow$ $Md = \frac{11 + 16}{3} = 9$

Ans. S_k (Bowley) = 0·5.

15. (*a*) If the quartile coefficient of skewness is 0·5, quartile deviation is 8 and the first quartile is 16, find the median of the distribution. [*Delhi Univ. B.A. (Econ. Hons.), 2002*]

Ans. Median = 20.

(*b*) The measure of skewness for a certain distribution is – 0·8. If the lower and the upper quartiles are 44·1 and 56·6 respectively, find the median.

Ans. Md = 55·35.

16. (*a*) The coefficient of skewness for a certain distribution based on the quartiles is – 0·8. If the sum of the upper and lower quartiles is 100·7 and median is 55·35, find the values of the upper and lower quartiles.

Ans. $Q_3 = 56{\cdot}6$; $Q_1 = 44{\cdot}1$.

(*b*) In a frequency distribution, coefficient of skewness based on quartiles is 0·6. If the sum of upper and lower quartiles is 100 and median is 38, find the values of lower and upper quartiles. [*Delhi Univ. B.Com. (Hons.), 1993*]

Ans. $Q_1 = 30, Q_3 = 70.$

17. In a distribution, the difference of the two quartiles is 15 and their sum is 35 and the median is 20. Find the coefficient of skewness.

Ans. *Sk* (Bowley) = – 0·33.

18. If the First Quartile is 48 and Quartile Deviation is 6, find the Median (assuming the distribution to be symmetrical). [*Delhi Univ. B.Com. (Pass), 1996*]

Ans. $Md = \frac{1}{2}(Q_3 + Q_1) = \frac{48 + 60}{2} = 54.$

19. Fill in the blank :

"If $Q_1 = 6$, $Q_3 = 10$ and Bowley's coefficient of skewness is 0·5, then the value of median will be equal to…."

Ans. $Md = 7$.

20. Particulars relating to the wage distribution of two manufacturing firms are as follows :

	Firm 'A'	*Firm 'B'*
	Rs.	Rs.
Mean wage	175	180
Median wage	172	170
Modal wage	167	162
Quartiles	162 ; 178	165 ; 185
S.D.	13	19

Compare the two distributions.

Ans. C.V. (Firm *A*) = 7·43, C.V. (Firm *B*) = 10·56; Bowley's coeff. of skewness (Firm *A*) = – 0·25, skewness (Firm *B*) = 0·5; Karl Pearson coeff. of skewness (Firm *A*) = 0·615, skewness (Firm *B*) = 0·947.

21. Find out Bowley's coefficient of skewness from the following data and show which section is more skewed :

Income in '00 Rs.	:	55—58	58—61	61—64	64—67	67—70
Section A	:	12	17	23	18	11
Section B	:	20	22	25	13	4

Ans. Bowley's coefficient of skewness (*A*) = – 0·0061. ; Bowley's coefficient of skewness (*B*) = – 0·06. For the comparison of these negative skewnesses, we compare their absolute values. Section *B* is more skewed.

7·3. MOMENTS

Moment is a term generally used in physics or mechanics and provides us a measure of the turning or the rotating effect of a force about some point. The moment of a force, say, *F* about some point *P* is given by the product of the magnitude of the force (*F*) and the perpendicular distance (*p*) between the point of reference and direction of the force [Fig. 7·4] *i.e.*,

$$\text{Moment} = p \times F$$

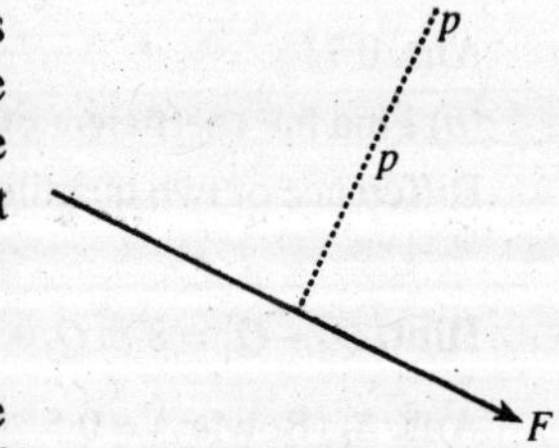

Fig. 7·4.

However, the term moment as used in physics has nothing to do with the moment used in Statistics, the only analogy being that in Statistics we talk of moment of random variable about some point and these moments are used to describe the various characteristics of a frequency distribution *viz*., central tendency, dispersion, skewness and kurtosis.

Let the random variable *X* have a frequency distribution

X	x_1	x_2	x_3 ……	x_n	
f	f_1	f_3	f_3 ……	f_n	$\Sigma f = N$

Let $\bar{x} = \dfrac{\Sigma fx}{\Sigma f} = \dfrac{\Sigma fx}{N}$, be its arithmetic mean.

7·3·1. Moments about Mean. The rth moment of X about the mean $\bar{x}$, usually denoted by μ_r [where μ is the letter Mu of the Greek alphabet] is defined as

$$\mu_r = \frac{1}{N}\sum f(x-\bar{x})^r \; ; r = 0, 1, 2, 3, \ldots \qquad \ldots(7·19)$$

$$= \frac{1}{N}\left[f_1(x_1-\bar{x})^r + f_2(x_2-\bar{x})^r + \ldots + f_n(x_n-\bar{x})^r\right] \qquad \ldots(7·19a)$$

In particular putting $r = 0$ in (7·19), we get

$$\mu_0 = \frac{1}{N}\sum f(x-\bar{x})^0 = \frac{1}{N}\sum f = \frac{1}{N}\cdot N \qquad [\because (x-\bar{x})^0 = 1 \text{ and } \sum f = N]$$

$$\therefore \quad \mu_0 = 1. \qquad \ldots(7·20)$$

Putting $r = 1$ in (7·19), we get $\mu_1 = \frac{1}{N}\sum f(x-\bar{x}) = 0,$ ...(7·21)

because the algebraic sum of deviations of a given set of observations from their mean is zero. Thus, *the first moment about mean is always zero.*

Again taking $r = 2$, we get $\mu_2 = \frac{1}{N}\sum f(x-\bar{x})^2 = \sigma_x^2$ ...(7·22)

Hence, the *second moment about mean gives the variance of the distribution.*

Also $\mu_3 = \frac{1}{N}\sum f(x-\bar{x})^3$ and $\mu_4 = \frac{1}{N}\sum f(x-\bar{x})^4$ ...(7·23)

7·3·2. Moments about Arbitrary Point A. The rth moment of X about any arbitrary point A, usually denoted by μ_r' is defined as :

$$\mu_r' = \frac{1}{N}\sum f(x-A)^r \quad ; \quad r = 0, 1, 2, 3, \ldots \qquad \ldots(7·24)$$

$$= \frac{1}{N}\left[f_1(x_1-A)^r + f_2(x_2-A)^r + \ldots + f_n(x_n-A)^r\right] \qquad \ldots(7·24a)$$

In particular taking $r = 0$ and $r = 1$ in (7·24), we get respectively

$$\mu_0' = \frac{1}{N}\sum f(x-A)^0 = \frac{1}{N}\sum f = 1 \qquad \ldots(7·25)$$

$$\mu_1' = \frac{1}{N}\sum f(x-A) = \frac{1}{N}\left[\sum fx - A\sum f\right] \qquad (\because A \text{ is constant})$$

$$= \frac{1}{N}\left[\sum fx - AN\right] = \frac{1}{N}\sum fx - A$$

$$= \bar{x} - A \qquad \ldots(7·26)$$

$$\Rightarrow \quad \bar{x} = A + \mu'_1 \qquad \ldots(7·27)$$

where μ_1' is the first moment about the point 'A'.

Taking $r = 2, 3, 4$ in (7·24), we get respectively

$$\mu_2' = \text{Second moment about } A = \frac{1}{N}\sum f(x-A)^2 \qquad \ldots(7·28)$$

$$\mu_3' = \text{Third moment about } A = \frac{1}{N}\sum f(x-A)^3 \qquad \ldots(7·28\,a)$$

$$\mu_4' = \text{Fourth moment about } A = \frac{1}{N}\sum f(x-A)^4 \qquad \ldots(7·28\,b)$$

Remarks 1. μ_r, the rth moment about the mean ; $r = 1, 2, 3, \ldots$ are also called the *central moments* and μ'_r, the rth moment about any arbitrary point A are also known as *raw moments*.

2. In particular, if we take $A = 0$ in (7·27), we get

$$\bar{x} = 0 + \mu_1' \text{ (about origin)} \qquad \ldots(7·28\,c)$$

Hence, the *first moment about origin gives mean.*

7·3·3. Relation between Moments about Mean and Moments about Arbitrary Point 'A'.

We have

$$\mu_r = \mu_r' - {}^rC_1\mu'_{r-1}\mu_1' + {}^rC_2\mu'_{r-2}\,\mu'^2_1 - {}^rC_3\mu'_{r-3}\,\mu'^3_1 + \ldots + (-1)^r\,\mu_1'^r \qquad \ldots(7·29)$$

Remarks 1. We summarise below the important results on moments :

$$\left.\begin{aligned} \mu_0 = 1 \quad \text{and} \quad \mu_1 &= 0 \\ \text{Mean } (\bar{x}) &= A + \mu_1' \end{aligned}\right\} \qquad \ldots(7\cdot30)$$

$$\left.\begin{aligned} \text{Variance } &= \sigma_x^2 = \mu_2 = \mu_2' - \mu_1'^2 \\ \mu_3 &= \mu_3' - 3\mu_2'\,\mu_1' + 2\mu_1'^3 \\ \mu_4 &= \mu_4' - 4\mu_3'\,\mu_1' + 6\mu_2'\,\mu_1'^2 - 3\mu_1'^4) \end{aligned}\right\} \qquad \ldots(7\cdot31)$$

The results in (7·30) and (7·31) are of fundamental importance in Statistics and should be committed to memory. Thus, *if we know the first four moments about any arbitrary point A, we can obtain the measures of central tendency* [$\bar{x} = \mu_1'$ *(about origin)*], *dispersion* ($\mu_2 = \sigma^2$), *skewness* (μ_3 *or* β_1) *and kurtosis* (β_2). [The last two measures are discussed in the Sections § 7·5 and § 7·6]. Since, these four measures enable us to have a fairly good idea about the nature and the form of the given frequency distribution, in practice we generally compute only the first four moments and not the higher moments.

2. In case of a symmetrical distribution, if the deviations of the given observations from their arithmetic mean are raised to any odd power, the sum of positive deviations equals the sum of the negative deviations and accordingly the overall sum is zero, *i.e.,* if the distribution is symmetrical then :

$$\Sigma f(x-\bar{x}) = \Sigma f(x-\bar{x})^3 = \Sigma f(x-\bar{x})^5 = \Sigma f(x-\bar{x})^7 = \ldots = 0$$

Dividing by $N = \Sigma f$, we get for a symmetrical distribution :

$$\mu_1 = \mu_3 = \mu_5 = \mu_7 = \ldots = 0$$

$$\Rightarrow \qquad \mu_{2r+1} = 0\,;\ r = 0, 1, 2, 3, \ldots \qquad \ldots(7\cdot32)$$

Hence, for *a symmetrical distribution, all the odd order moments about mean vanish.* Accordingly, odd order moments, specially 3rd moment is used as a measure of skewness.

3. We have $\qquad \mu_2 = \mu_2' - \mu_1'^2$

Since $\mu_1'^2$, being the square of a real quantity is always non-negative, we get

$$\mu_2 = \mu_2' - (\text{some non-negative quantity}) \quad \Rightarrow \quad \mu_2 \le \mu_2'$$

$\therefore$ Variance $\le$ Mean square deviation or S.D. $\le$ Root mean square deviation ...(7·33)

4. For obtaining the moments of a grouped (continuous) frequency distribution, if we change the scale also in X by taking

$$d = \frac{x-A}{h} \quad \Rightarrow \quad x - A = hd \qquad \ldots(7\cdot33a)$$

then

$$\begin{aligned} \mu_r' &= r^{th} \text{ moment of } X \text{ about point } X = A \\ &= \frac{1}{N}\Sigma f(x-A)^r = \frac{1}{N}\Sigma f\,.\,h^r d^r \qquad \text{[From (7·33}a\text{)]} \end{aligned}$$

$$\Rightarrow \qquad \mu_r' = h^r\,.\,\frac{1}{N}\Sigma f d^r \qquad \ldots(7\cdot33b)$$

In particular, we have

$$\mu_1' = h\,.\,\frac{1}{N}\Sigma f d; \quad \mu_2' = h^2\,.\,\frac{1}{N}\Sigma f d^2; \quad \mu_3' = h^3\,.\frac{1}{N}\Sigma f d^3; \quad \mu_4' = h^4\,.\frac{1}{N}\Sigma f d^4 \qquad \ldots(7\cdot33c)$$

Finally, on using the relation (7·31), we obtain the moments about mean.

For numerical computations, if the mean of the distribution comes out to be integral (*i.e., a* whole number), then it is convenient to obtain the moments about mean directly by the formula

$$\mu_r = \frac{1}{N}\Sigma f(x-\bar{x})^r \qquad \ldots(7\cdot33d)$$

However, for grouped (continuous) frequency distribution, the calculations are simplified by changing the scale also in X. If we take

$$z = \frac{x-\bar{x}}{h} \quad \Rightarrow \quad x - \bar{x} = hz \qquad \ldots(7\cdot34)$$

then, we have $\mu_r = \frac{1}{N} \Sigma f . (hz)^r \quad \Rightarrow \quad \mu_r = h^r . \left[\frac{1}{N} \Sigma f z^r\right]$ ...(7·35)

a formula which is more convenient to use.

4. Converse. We can obtain μ_r' in terms of μ_r as given below :

$$\mu'_r = \mu_r + {}^rC_1\, \mu_{r-1}\, \mu_1' + {}^rC_2\, \mu_{r-2}\, \mu_1'^2 + \ldots + \mu_1'^r, \quad \ldots(7\cdot36)$$

In particular, taking $r = 2$, 3 and 4 in (7·36) and simplifying we shall get respectively :

$$\left.\begin{aligned} \mu_2' &= \mu_2 + \mu_1'^2 \\ \mu_3' &= \mu_3 + 3\mu_2\, \mu_1' + \mu_1'^3 \\ \mu_4' &= \mu_4 + 4\mu_3\, \mu_1' + 6\mu_2\, \mu_1'^2 + \mu_1'^4 \end{aligned}\right\} \quad \ldots(7\cdot37)$$

These formulae enable us to compute moments about any arbitrary point, if we are given mean and moments about the mean.

7·3·4. Effect of Change of Origin and Scale on Moments about Mean. Let us change the origin and scale in the variable x to obtain a new variable u as defined below :

$$u = \frac{x - a}{h} \quad \Rightarrow \quad x = a + hu \quad \ldots(7\cdot38)$$

Then, $\mu_r(x) = h^r \mu_r(u)$ ...(7·39)

Hence, rth moment of the variable x about its mean is equal to h^r times the rth moment of the variable u about its mean. The result does not depend on 'a'. Hence, we conclude that the moments about mean (*i.e.*, central moments) are invariant under change of origin but not of scale.

7·3·5. Sheppard's Correction for Moments. In case of grouped or continuous frequency distribution, for the calculation of moments, the value of the variable X is taken as the mid-point of the corresponding class. This is based on the assumption that the frequencies are concentrated at the mid-points of the corresonding classes. This assumption is approximately true for distributions which are symmetrical or moderately skewed and for which the class intervals are not greater than one-twentieth (1/20th) of the range of the distribution. However, in practice, this assumption is not true in general and consequently some error, known as '*grouping error*' is introduced in the calculation of moments. W.F. Sheppard proved that if

(*i*) the frequency distribution is continuous, and

(*ii*) the frequency tapers off to zero in both directions,

the effect due to grouping at the mid-point of the intervals can be corrected by the following formulae, known as Sheppard's corrections :

$$\left.\begin{aligned} \mu_2 \text{ (corrected)} &= \mu_2 - \frac{h^2}{12} \\ \mu_3 \text{ (corrected)} &= \mu_3 \\ \mu_4 \text{ (corrected)} &= \mu_4 - \frac{1}{2} h^2 \mu_2 + \frac{7}{240} h^4 \end{aligned}\right\} \quad \ldots(7\cdot40)$$

where h is the width of the class interval.

Remark. This correction is valid only for symmetrical or slightly asymmetrical continuous distributions and cannot be applied in the case of extremely asymmetrical (skewed) distributions like J-shaped or inverted J-shaped or U-shaped distributions. As a safeguard against sampling errors, this correction should be applied only if the total frequency is fairly large, say, greater than 1000.

7·3·6. Charlier Checks. We have, on using binomial expansion for positive integral index,

$$\left.\begin{aligned} x + 1 &= x + 1 \\ (x + 1)^2 &= x^2 + 2x + 1 \\ (x + 1)^3 &= x^3 + 3x^2 + 3x + 1 \\ (x + 1)^4 &= x^4 + 4x^3 + 6x^2 + 4x + 1 \end{aligned}\right\} \quad \ldots(*)$$

Multiplying both sides of (*) by f and adding over different values of the variable X, we get the following identities,

$$\left.\begin{aligned} \Sigma f(x+1) &= \Sigma fx + N \\ \Sigma f(x+1)^2 &= \Sigma fx^2 + 2\Sigma fx + N \\ \Sigma f(x+1)^3 &= \Sigma fx^3 + 3\Sigma fx^2 + 3\Sigma fx + N \\ \Sigma f(x+1)^4 &= \Sigma fx^4 + 4\Sigma fx^3 + 6\Sigma fx^2 + 4\Sigma fx + N \end{aligned}\right\} \quad \ldots(7·41)$$

These identities are known as Charlier checks and are used in checking the calculations in the computation of the first four moments.

7·4. KARL PEARSON'S BETA (β) AND GAMMA (γ) COEFFICIENTS BASED ON MOMENTS

Prof. Karl Pearson defined the following four coefficients based on the 1st four central moments.

$$\beta_1 = \frac{\mu_3^2}{\mu_2^3} \quad \ldots(7·42)$$

$$\beta_2 = \frac{\mu_4}{\mu_2^2} = \frac{\mu_4}{\sigma^4} \quad \ldots(7·43)$$

$$\gamma_1 = \sqrt{\beta_1} = \frac{\mu_3}{\mu_2^{3/2}} = \frac{\mu_3}{\sigma^3} \qquad (\because \mu_2 = \sigma^2) \quad \ldots(7·44)$$

$$\gamma_2 = \beta_2 - 3 = \frac{\mu_4}{\mu_2^2} - 3 \quad \ldots(7·45)$$

It may be stated here that these coefficients are pure numbers independent of units of measurement and as such can be conveniently used for comparative studies. In practice they are used as measures of skewness and kurtosis as discussed in the following sections.

Remark. Sometimes, another coefficient based on moments *viz.,* Alpha (α) coefficient is used. Alpha coefficients are defined as

$$\alpha_1 = \frac{\mu_1}{\sigma} = 0, \quad \alpha_2 = \frac{\mu_2}{\sigma^2} = 1, \quad \alpha_3 = \frac{\mu_3}{\sigma^3} = \sqrt{\beta_1} = \gamma_1, \quad \alpha_4 = \frac{\mu_4}{\sigma^4} = \beta_2 \quad \ldots(7·46)$$

7·5. COEFFICIENT OF SKEWNESS BASED ON MOMENTS

Based on the first four moments, Karl Pearson's coefficient of skewness becomes

$$Sk = \frac{\sqrt{\beta_1}\,(\beta_2 + 3)}{2(5\beta_2 - 6\beta_1 - 9)} \quad \ldots(7·47)$$

where β_1 and β_2 are Pearson's coefficients defined in (7·42) and (7·43) in terms of the first four central moments. Formula (7·47) will give positive skewness if $M > Mo$ and negative skewness if $M < Mo$. $Sk = 0$, if $\beta_1 = 0$ or $\beta_2 + 3 = 0 \quad \Rightarrow \quad \beta_2 = -3$.

But $\quad \mu_4 = \frac{1}{N}\Sigma f(x - \bar{x})^4 > 0$ and $\mu_2 = \frac{1}{N}\Sigma f(x - \bar{x})^2 > 0$

$$\therefore \quad \beta_2 = \frac{\mu_4}{\mu_2^2} > 0$$

Since β_2 cannot be negative, $Sk = 0$ if $\beta_1 = 0$ or if $\mu_3 = 0$. Hence, *for a symmetrical distribution,* $\beta_1 = 0$. Accordingly, *β_1 may be taken as a relative measure of skewness based on moments.*

Remark. The coefficient β_1 as a measure of skewness has a serious limitation. μ_3 being the sum of the cubes of the deviations from the mean may be positive or negative but μ_3^2 is always positive. Also μ_2 being the variance is always positive. Hence, $\beta_1 = \mu_3^2/\mu_2^3$, is always positive. Thus β_1, as a measure of skewness is not able to tell us about the direction (positive or negative) of skewness. This drawback is removed in Karl Pearson's coefficient [Gamma One, (γ_1)] which is defined as the positive square root of β_1, *i.e.* ;

$$\gamma_1 = +\sqrt{\beta_1} = \frac{\mu_3}{\mu_2^{3/2}} = \frac{\mu_3}{\sigma^3} \qquad \text{...(7·48)}$$

Thus, *the sign of skewness depends upon μ_3. If μ_3 is positive we get positive skewness and if μ_3 is negative, we get negative skewness.*

7·6. KURTOSIS

So far we have studied three measures *viz.*, central tendency, dispersion and skewness to describe the characteristics of a frequency distribution. However, even if we know all these three measures we are not in a position to characterise a distribution completely. The following diagram (Fig. 7.5) will clarify the point.

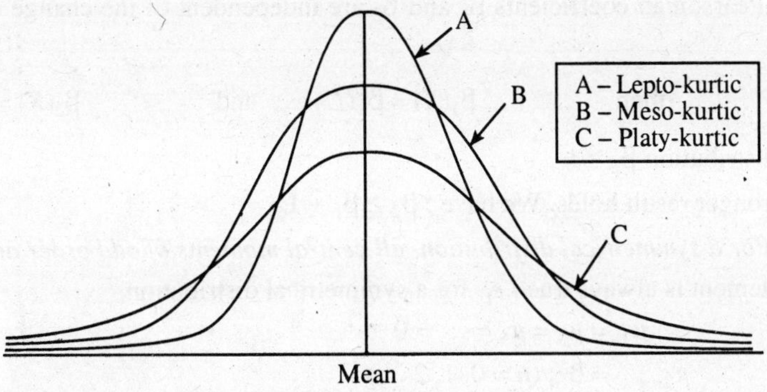

Fig. 7·5.

All the three curves are symmetrical about the mean and have same variation (range). In order to identify a distribution completely we need one more measure which Prof. Karl Pearson called '*convexity of the curve*' or its '*Kurtosis*'. While skewness helps us in identifying the right or left tails of the frequency curve, kurtosis enables us to have an idea about the shape and nature of the hump (middle part) of a frequency distribution. In other words, *kurtosis is concerned with the flatness or peakedness of the frequency curve.*

Curve of type *B* which is neither flat nor peaked is known as *Normal curve* and shape of its hump is accepted as a standard one. Curves with humps of the form of normal curve are said to have *normal kurtosis* and are termed as *meso-kurtic*. The curves of the type *A*., which are more peaked than the normal curve are known as *lepto-kurtic* and are said to *lack kurtosis* or to have *negative kurtosis*. On the other hand, curves of the type *C*, which are flatter than the normal curve are called *platy-kurtic* and they are said to possess *kurtosis in excess* or have *positive kurtosis*.

As a measure of kurtosis, Karl Pearson gave the coefficient Beta two (β_2) or its derivative Gamma two (γ_2) defined as follows :

$$\beta_2 = \frac{\mu_4}{\mu_2^2} = \frac{\mu_4}{\sigma^4} \qquad \text{...(7·49)}$$

$$\gamma_2 = \beta_2 - 3 = \frac{\mu_4}{\sigma^4} - 3 = \frac{\mu_4 - 3\sigma^4}{\sigma^4} \qquad \text{...(7·50)}$$

For a normal or meso-kurtic curve (Type *B*), $\beta_2 = 3$ or $\gamma_2 = 0$. For a lepto-kurtic curve (Type *A*), $\beta_2 > 3$ or $\gamma_2 > 0$ and for a platy-kurtic curve (Type *C*), $\beta_2 < 3$ or $\gamma_2 < 0$.

It is interesting to quote here the words of a British statistician W.S. Gosset (who wrote under the pen name of Student), who very humorously explains the use of the terms platy-kurtic and lepto-kurtic in the following sentence : *"Platykurtic curves like the platypus, are squat with short tails ; lepto-kurtic curves are high with long tails like the kangaroos noted for leaping."*

Gosset's little but humorous sketch is given below :

Fig. 7.6 (*a*).

Fig. 7.6 (*b*).

Remarks 1. The Pearsonian coefficients β_1 and β_2 are independent of the change of origin and scale *i.e.,* if we take :

$$U = \frac{X - A}{h}, h > 0 \quad \text{then} \quad \beta_1(X) = \beta_1(U) \quad \text{and} \quad \beta_2(X) = \beta_2(U)$$

2. For a discrete distribution $\beta_2 \geq 1$.

In fact, a much stronger result holds. We have : $\beta_2 \geq \beta_1 + 1$.

Example 7·18. *"For a symmetrical distribution, all central moments of odd order are zero." Comment.*

Solution. The statement is always true *i.e.,* for a symmetrical distribution,

$$\mu_1 = \mu_3 = \mu_5 = \ldots = 0$$

i.e., $$\mu_{2n+1} = 0 \quad ; (n = 0, 1, 2, \ldots)$$

[For detailed discussion see Remark 2, § 7·3·3]

Example 7·19. *Calculate the first four moments about the mean for the following data and comment on the nature of the distribution :*

x :	1	2	3	4	5	6	7	8	9
f :	1	6	13	25	30	22	9	5	2

[Delhi Univ. B.Com. (Hons.), 1999]

Solution. CALCULATIONS FOR MOMENTS

x	f	$d = x - 5$	fd	fd^2	fd^3	fd^4
1	1	−4	−4	16	−64	256
2	6	−3	−18	54	−162	486
3	13	−2	−26	52	−104	208
4	25	−1	−25	25	−25	25
5	30	0	0	0	0	0
6	22	1	22	22	22	22
7	9	2	18	36	72	144
8	5	3	15	45	135	405
9	2	4	8	32	128	512
	$\sum f = 113$	$\sum d = 0$	$\sum fd = -10$	$\sum fd^2 = 282$	$\sum fd^3 = 2$	$\sum fd^4 = 2058$

Moments About the Point $x = 5$

$$d = x - A = x - 5, (A = 5) \; ; N = \sum f = 113$$

$$\mu_1' = \frac{\sum fd}{N} = \frac{-10}{113} = -0{\cdot}0885 \qquad \mu_3' = \frac{\sum fd^3}{N} = \frac{2}{113} = 0{\cdot}0177$$

$$\mu_2' = \frac{\sum fd^2}{N} = \frac{282}{113} = 2{\cdot}4956 \qquad \mu_4' = \frac{\sum fd^4}{N} = \frac{2058}{113} = 18{\cdot}2124$$

$$\therefore \quad \text{Mean} = A + \mu_1' = 5 + (-0{\cdot}0885) = 4{\cdot}9115$$

Moments About Mean

$\mu_1 = 0$

$\mu_2 = \mu_2' - \mu_1'^2 = 2{\cdot}4956 - (-0{\cdot}0885)^2$
$= 2{\cdot}4956 - 0{\cdot}0078 = 2{\cdot}4878$

$\mu_3 = \mu_3' - 3\mu_2'\mu_1' + 2\mu_1'^3$
$= 0{\cdot}0177 - 3 \times 2{\cdot}4956 \times (-0{\cdot}0885) + 2 \times (-0{\cdot}0885)^3$
$= 0{\cdot}0177 + 0{\cdot}66258 - 0{\cdot}001386$
$= 0{\cdot}6789$

$\mu_4 = \mu_4' - 4\mu_3'\mu_1' + 6\mu_2'\mu_1'^2 - 3\mu_1'^4$
$= 18{\cdot}2124 - 4 \times (0{\cdot}0177) \times (-0{\cdot}0885) + 6 \times 2{\cdot}4956 \times (-0{\cdot}0885)^2 - 3(-0{\cdot}0885)^4$
$= 18{\cdot}2124 + 0{\cdot}00626 + 0{\cdot}11728 - 0{\cdot}000184$
$= 18{\cdot}3357$

Moment Coefficients of Skewness

$$\beta_1 = \frac{\mu_3^2}{\mu_2^3} = \frac{(0{\cdot}6789)^2}{(2{\cdot}4878)^3} = \frac{0{\cdot}4609}{15{\cdot}3974} = 0{\cdot}0299$$

$$\gamma_1 = \frac{\mu_3}{\mu_2^{3/2}} = \frac{\mu_3}{\mu_2\sqrt{\mu_2}} = \frac{0{\cdot}6789}{3{\cdot}9239} = 0{\cdot}173 \text{ or } \gamma_1 = \sqrt{\beta_1} = +\sqrt{0{\cdot}0299} = +0{\cdot}173 \quad (\because \mu_3 \text{ is positive})$$

Kurtosis

$$\beta_2 = \frac{\mu_4}{\mu_2^2} = \frac{18{\cdot}3357}{(2{\cdot}4878)^2} = \frac{18{\cdot}3357}{6{\cdot}1891} = 2{\cdot}9626 \quad \Rightarrow \quad \gamma_2 = \beta_2 - 3 = -0{\cdot}0373.$$

Interpretation

Since $\gamma_1 = 0{\cdot}173$, the given distribution is *very slightly positively skewed.*

Since $\beta_2 = 2{\cdot}9626 \simeq 3$, the given distribution is more or less normal or meso-kurtic. However, since $\beta_2 < 3$ ($\gamma_2 = -0{\cdot}04$), the given frequency curve is *slightly Platy-kurtic* and is *slightly flatter than the normal curve.*

Example 7·20. *From the following data, calculate moments about assumed mean 25 and convert them into central moments :*

X	:	*0—10*	*10—20*	*20—30*	*30—40*
f	:	*1*	*3*	*4*	*2*

[*Delhi Univ. B.Com.* (*Hons.*), *2000*]

Solution. CALCULATIONS FOR MOMENTS ABOUT THE POINT $X = 25$

Class	*Mid-value* (*X*)	*f*	$d = \frac{x-25}{10}$	*fd*	fd^2	fd^3	fd^4
0—10	5	1	−2	−2	4	−8	16
10—20	15	3	−1	−3	3	−3	3
20—30	25	4	0	0	0	0	0
30—40	35	2	1	2	2	2	2
Total		$N = \sum f = 10$		$\sum fd = -3$	$\sum fd^2 = 9$	$\sum fd^3 = -9$	$\sum fd^4 = 21$

Moments about the Point $X = 25$

$$\mu_1' = h \cdot \frac{\sum fd}{N} = \frac{10 \times (-3)}{10} = -3$$

$$\mu_2' = h^2 \cdot \frac{\sum fd^2}{N} = \frac{10^2 \times 9}{10} = 90$$

$$\mu_3' = \frac{h^3 \times \sum fd^3}{N} = \frac{10^3 \times (-9)}{10} = -900$$

$$\mu_4' = \frac{h^4 . \sum fd^4}{N} = \frac{10^4 \times 21}{10} = 21{,}000$$

Central Moments (Moments About Mean)

$\mu_1 = 0$

$\mu_3 = \mu_3' - 3\mu_2'\mu_1' + 2\mu_1'^3$
$= -900 - 3 \times 90 \times (-3) + 2(-3)^3$
$= -900 + 810 - 54 = -144$

$\mu_2 = \mu_2' - \mu_1'^2 = 90 - 9 = 81$

$\mu_4 = \mu_4' - 4\mu_3'\mu_1' + 6\mu_2'\mu_1'^2 - 3\mu_1'^4$
$= 21{,}000 - 4 \times (-900) \times (-3) + 6 \times 90 \times (-3)^2 - 3 \times (-3)^4$
$= 21{,}000 - 10{,}800 + 4{,}860 - 243$
$= 14{,}817$

Example 7·21. *The first three moments of a distribution about the value 67 of the variable are 0·45, 8·73 and 8·91. Calculate the second and third central moments, and the moment coefficient of skewness. Indicate the nature of the distribution.* [*Delhi Univ. B.A.* (*Econ. Hons. I*), *2000*]

Solution. In the usual notations we are given :

$$A = 67,\ \mu_1' = 0{\cdot}45,\ \mu_2' = 8{\cdot}73 \quad \text{and} \quad \mu_3' = 8{\cdot}91$$

The second and third central moments are given by :

$$\mu_2 = \mu_2' - \mu_1'^2 = 8{\cdot}73 - (0{\cdot}45)^2 = 8{\cdot}73 - 0{\cdot}2025 = 8{\cdot}5275$$

$$\mu_3 = \mu_3' - 3\,\mu_2'\,\mu_1' + 2\mu_1'^3 = 8{\cdot}91 - 3 \times 8{\cdot}73 \times 0{\cdot}45 + 2 \times (0{\cdot}45)^3$$

$$= 8{\cdot}91 - 11{\cdot}7855 + 0{\cdot}18225 = -2{\cdot}6933$$

Hence, the variance of the distribution is

$$\sigma^2 = \mu_2 = 8{\cdot}5275 \quad \Rightarrow \quad \sigma(\text{s.d.}) = \sqrt{8{\cdot}5275} = 2{\cdot}9202$$

Since μ_3 is negative, the given distribution is negatively skewed. In other words, the frequency curve has a longer tail towards the left. Karl Pearson's moment coefficient of skewness is given by :

$$\gamma_1 = \frac{\mu_3}{\mu_2^{3/2}} = \frac{\mu_3}{\mu_2\sqrt{\mu_2}} = \frac{-2{\cdot}6933}{8{\cdot}5275 \times 2{\cdot}9202} = \frac{-2{\cdot}6933}{24{\cdot}9020} = -0{\cdot}1082 \Rightarrow \beta_1 = \frac{\mu_3^2}{\mu_2^3} = (-0{\cdot}1082)^2 = 0{\cdot}0117$$

Since γ_1 and β_1 are approximately zero, the given distribution is approximately symmetrical.

Example 7·22. *The first four moments of a distribution about the origin are 1, 4, 10 and 46 respectively. Obtain the various characteristics of the distribution on the basis of the information given. Comment upon the nature of the distribution.*

Solution. We are given the first four moments about origin. In the usual notations we have :

$$A = 0,\ \mu_1' = 1,\ \mu_2' = 4,\ \mu_3' = 10 \quad \text{and} \quad \mu_4' = 46$$

The measure of central tendency is given by :

$$\text{Mean}\ (\bar{x}) = \text{First moment about origin} = \mu_1' = 1$$

The measure of dispersion is given by :

$$\text{Variance}\ (\sigma^2) = \mu_2 = \mu_2' - \mu_1'^2 = 4 - 1 = 3 \quad \Rightarrow \quad \text{s.d.}\ (\sigma) = \sqrt{3} = 1{\cdot}732$$

$$\mu_3 = \mu_3' - 3\mu_2'\,\mu_1' + 2\mu_1'^3 = 10 - 3 \times 4 \times 1 + 2 \times 1 = 10 - 12 + 2 = 0$$

Karl Pearson's moment coefficient of skewness is given by :

$$\gamma_1 = \frac{\mu_3}{\mu_2^{3/2}} = 0 \quad \Rightarrow \quad \beta_1 = \frac{\mu_3^2}{\mu_2^3} = 0$$

Since $\gamma_1 = 0$, the given distribution is symmetrical, *i.e.*, Mean = Median = Mode,

for the given distribution. Moreover, the quartiles are equidistant from the median *i.e.*,

$$Q_3 - \text{Median} = \text{Median} - Q_1$$

$$\mu_4 = \mu_4' - 4\mu_3'\,\mu_1' + 6\mu_2'\,\mu_1'^2 - 3\mu_1'^4$$

$$= 46 - 4 \times 10 \times 1 + 6 \times 4 \times 1 - 3 \times 1 = 46 - 40 + 24 - 3 = 27$$

Hence, Karl Pearson's measure of Kurtosis is given by :

$$\beta_2 = \frac{\mu_4}{\mu_2^2} = \frac{27}{3^2} = 3 \quad \Rightarrow \quad \gamma_2 = \beta_2 - 3 = 0$$

Since $\beta_2 = 3$, the given distribution is Normal (Meso-kurtic).

Since $\beta_1 = 0$ and $\beta_2 = 3$, the given distribution is a normal distribution with

$$\text{Mean } (\bar{x}) = 1 \text{ and s.d. } (\sigma) = \sqrt{3} = 1{\cdot}732.$$

Example. 7.23. *Given that the mean of a distribution is 5, variance is 9 and the moment coefficient of skewness is – 1, find the first three moments about origin.* [Delhi Univ. B.A. (Econ. Hons.), 2009]

Solution. We are given Mean $(\bar{X}) = 5$, Variance $(\sigma^2) = \mu_2 = 9 \Rightarrow \sigma = 3$;

and $\gamma_1 = \dfrac{\mu_3}{\sigma^3} = -1 \Rightarrow \mu_3 = -27.$

We want moments about *the point A* = 0.

$$\text{Mean } (\bar{X}) = A + \mu_1' \Rightarrow 5 = 0 + \mu_1' \Rightarrow \mu_1' = 5$$

$$\mu_2 = \mu_2' - \mu_1'^2 \Rightarrow 9 = \mu_2' - 5^2 \Rightarrow \mu_2' = 34$$

$$\mu_3 = \mu_3' - 3\mu_2'\mu_1' + 2\mu_1'^3 \Rightarrow -27 = \mu_3' - 3 \times 34 \times 5 + 2 \times 5^3 \Rightarrow \mu_3' = -27 + 510 - 250 = 233$$

Example 7·24. *If $\sqrt{\beta_1} = 1$, $\beta_2 = 4$ and variance = 9, find the values of third and fourth central moments and comment upon the nature of the distribution.* [Delhi Univ. B.A. (Econ. Hons.), 2007]

Solution. We are given $\sqrt{\beta_1} = +1$, $\beta_2 = 4$ and Variance $= \mu_2 = 9$ ...(*)

$$\sqrt{\beta_1} = 1 \Rightarrow \sqrt{\frac{\mu_3^2}{\mu_2^3}} = 1 \Rightarrow \mu_3 = \mu_2^{3/2} \,.\, 1 = 9^{3/2} \,.\, 1 = 3^3 = 27 \qquad \left[\text{or } \beta_1 = \frac{\mu_3}{\sigma^3}\right]$$

Also $\beta_2 = 4 \Rightarrow \dfrac{\mu_4}{\mu_2^2} = 4 \Rightarrow \mu_4 = 4 \times 9 \times 9 = 324$

$\therefore \quad \mu_3 = 27$ and $\mu_4 = 324$.

Nature of the Distribution. Since $\gamma_1 = \sqrt{\beta_1} \neq 0$ and $\gamma_1 = 1$, the distribution is moderately positively skewed. ($\because \mu_3 > 0$).

Also $\beta_2 = 4 > 3$. Hence, the given distribution is *lepto-kurtic i.e.,* more peaked than the normal curve.

Example 7·25. *For a meso-kurtic distribution, the first moment about 7 is 23 and the second moment about origin is 1000. Find the coefficient of variation and the fourth moment about the mean.*

[Delhi Univ. B.Com. (Hons.), 2008; Delhi Univ. B.A. (Econ. Hons.), 2002]

Solution. Since the distribution is given to be meso-kurtic, we have :

$$\beta_2 = 3 \Rightarrow \frac{\mu_4}{\mu_2^2} = 3 \Rightarrow \mu_4 = 3\mu_2^2 \qquad ...(i)$$

First moment about '7' is 23 *i.e.,* μ_1' (about 7) = 23 (Given)

$$\therefore \quad \text{Mean} = 7 + \mu_1' = 7 + 23 = 30 \qquad ...(ii)$$

But mean is the first moment about origin.

$\therefore \quad \mu_1'$ (about origin) = 30

Moments About Origin

μ_1' = Mean = 30; μ_2' = 1,000 (Given)

$\therefore \quad \mu_2 = \mu_2' - \mu_1'^2 = 1000 - 30^2 = 100 \Rightarrow$ Variance $(\sigma^2) = 100 \Rightarrow$ s.d. $(\sigma) = 10$

$$\text{Coefficient of Variation (C.V.)} = \frac{100 \times \text{s.d.}}{\text{Mean}} = \frac{100 \times 10}{30} = 33{\cdot}33$$

Substituting the value of $\mu_2 = 100$, in (*i*), the fourth moment about mean is given by :

$$\mu_4 = 3 \times 100^2 = 30{,}000.$$

Example 7·26. (*a*) *You are given the following information :*

Class	*f*	*Class*	*f*	*Class*	*f*
40—41	*1*	*45—46*	*20*	*50—51*	*19*
41—	*2*	*46—*	*38*	*51—*	*14*
42—	*4*	*47—*	*52*	*52—*	*6*
43—	*7*	*48—*	*40*	*53—*	*4*
44—45	*12*	*49—50*	*29*	*54—55*	*2*

Calculate the first four moments about 47·5. Convert these into moments about the mean and calculate β_1 *and* β_2.

(*b*) *Also apply Sheppard's corrections to moments.*

Solution.

CALCULATIONS FOR MOMENTS

Class	*Mid-value (X)*	*f*	$d = X - 47{\cdot}5$	*fd*	fd^2	fd^3	fd^4
40—41	40·5	1	–7	–7	49	–343	2391
41—42	41·5	2	–6	–12	72	– 432	2592
42—43	42·5	4	–5	–20	100	–500	2500
43—44	43·5	7	– 4	–28	112	– 448	1792
44—45	44·5	12	–3	–36	108	–324	972
45—46	45·5	20	–2	– 40	80	–160	320
46—47	46·5	38	–1	–38	38	–38	38
47—48	47·5	52	0	0	0	0	0
48—49	48·5	40	1	40	40	40	40
49—50	49·5	29	2	58	116	232	464
50—51	50·5	19	3	57	171	513	1539
51—52	51·5	14	4	56	224	896	3584
52—53	52·5	6	5	30	150	750	3750
53—54	53·5	4	6	24	144	864	5184
54—55	54·5	2	7	14	98	986	4802
Total		$N = 250$		$\Sigma fd = 98$	$\Sigma fd^2 = 1502$	$\Sigma fd^3 = 1736$	$\Sigma fd^4 = 29968$

First four Moments about A = 47·5. Since $h = 1$, we have :

$$\mu_1' = \frac{1}{N}\Sigma fd = \frac{98}{250} = 0{\cdot}392 \qquad \mu_3' = \frac{1}{N}\Sigma fd^3 = \frac{1736}{250} = 6{\cdot}944$$

$$\mu_2' = \frac{1}{N}\Sigma fd^2 = \frac{1502}{250} = 6{\cdot}008 \qquad \mu_4' = \frac{1}{N}\Sigma fd^4 = \frac{29968}{250} = 119{\cdot}872$$

First four Moments about Mean :

$$\text{Mean} = 47{\cdot}5 + \mu_1' = 47{\cdot}5 + 0{\cdot}392 = 47{\cdot}892$$

$$\mu_1 = 0$$

$$\mu_2 = \mu_2' - \mu_1'^2 = 6{\cdot}008 - (0{\cdot}392)^2 = 6{\cdot}008 - 0{\cdot}1537 = 5{\cdot}854$$

$$\mu_3 = \mu_3' - 3\mu_2'\,\mu_1' + 2\mu_1'^3 = 6{\cdot}944 - 3 \times 6{\cdot}008 \times 0{\cdot}392 + 2 \times (0{\cdot}392)^3$$

$$= 6{\cdot}944 - 18{\cdot}024 \times 0{\cdot}392 + 2 \times 0{\cdot}0602$$

$$\Rightarrow \quad \mu_3 = 6{\cdot}944 - 7{\cdot}0654 + 0{\cdot}1204 = -\,0{\cdot}001 \simeq 0$$

$$\mu_4 = \mu_4' - 4\mu_3'\mu_1' + 6\mu_2'\mu_1'^2 - 3\mu_1'^4$$
$$= 119{\cdot}872 - 4 \times 6{\cdot}944 \times 0{\cdot}392 + 6 \times 6{\cdot}008 \times (0{\cdot}392)^2 - 3 \times (0{\cdot}392)^4$$
$$= 119{\cdot}872 - 10{\cdot}888 + 5{\cdot}539 - 0{\cdot}071 = 114{\cdot}452$$

$$\beta_1 = \frac{\mu_3^2}{\mu_2^3} \simeq 0 \quad ; \quad (\because \mu_3 = 0) \quad \text{and} \quad \beta_2 = \frac{\mu_4}{\mu_2^2} = \frac{114{\cdot}452}{(5{\cdot}854)^2} = \frac{114{\cdot}452}{34{\cdot}269} = 3{\cdot}34$$

(*b*) **Sheppard's Corrections**. Using (7·40), we have :

$$\mu_2 \text{ (Corrected)} = \mu_2 - \frac{h^2}{12} = 5{\cdot}854 - \frac{1}{12} \qquad (\because h = \text{Magnitude of class interval} = 1)$$
$$= 5{\cdot}854 - 3{\cdot}083 = 5{\cdot}771$$

$$\mu_3 \text{ (Corrected)} = \mu_3 \simeq 0$$

$$\mu_4 \text{ (Corrected)} = \mu_4 - \frac{1}{2}h^2\mu_2 + \frac{7}{240}h^4 = 114{\cdot}452 - \frac{1}{2} \times 5{\cdot}854 + \frac{7}{240} \qquad (\because h = 1)$$
$$= 114{\cdot}452 - 2{\cdot}927 + 0{\cdot}029 = 111{\cdot}554.$$

Example 7.27. *For a distribution, it has been found that the first four moments about 27 are 0, 256, – 2871 and 188462 respectively. Obtain the first four moments about zero. Also calculate the value of β_1 and β_2, and comment.* [*Delhi Univ. B.Com. (Hons.) 2007, 2006*]

Solution. We are given :

$$A = 27; \quad \mu_1' = 0, \quad \mu_2' = 256, \quad \mu_3' = -2871; \quad \mu_4' = 188462$$

Mean $= A + \mu_1' = 27 + 0 = 27$

Hence, the moments about '$A = 27$' are same as moments about mean.

$$\Rightarrow \quad \mu_2 = \mu_2' = 256, \quad \mu_3 = \mu_3' = -2871; \quad \mu_4 = \mu_4' = 188462$$

Moments about Origin

$$\mu_1' = \text{Mean} = \mathbf{27}$$
$$\mu_2' = \mu_2 + \mu_1'^2 = 256 + 27^2 = 256 + 729 = \mathbf{985}$$
$$\mu_3' = \mu_3 + 3\mu_2\mu_1' + \mu_1'^3 = -2871 + 3 \times 256 \times 27 + 27^3$$
$$= -2871 + 20736 + 19683 = \mathbf{37548}$$
$$\mu_4' = \mu_4 + 4\mu_3\mu_1' + 6\mu_2\mu_1'^2 + \mu_1'^4$$
$$= 188462 + 4 \times (-2871) \times 27 + 6 \times 256 \times 27^2 + 27^4$$
$$= 188462 - 310068 + 1119744 + 531441 = \mathbf{1529579}$$

$$\beta_1 = \frac{\mu_3^2}{\mu_2^3} = \frac{(-2871)^2}{(256)^3} = \frac{8242641}{16777216} = 0{\cdot}4913 \quad ; \quad \gamma_1 = \frac{\mu_3}{\mu_2^{3/2}} = \frac{-2871}{\sqrt{16777216}} = \frac{-2871}{4096} = -0{\cdot}701$$

$$\beta_2 = \frac{\mu_4}{\mu_2^2} = \frac{188462}{(256)^2} = \frac{188462}{65536} = 2{\cdot}876 \quad \Rightarrow \quad \gamma_2 = \beta_2 - 3 = -0{\cdot}124$$

Since $\beta_1 \neq 0$, the distribution is not symmetrical.

Since $\mu_3 < 0$, $\gamma_1 = -0{\cdot}701 < 0$, the distribution is moderately negatively skewed.

$\beta_2 < 3 \Rightarrow$ Distribution is moderately platy-kurtic.

Example 7·28. *The first four moments of a distribution about the value 4 of the variable are –1·5, 17, –30 and 108. Find the moments about mean, β_1 and β_2.*

Find also the moments about (i) the origin, and (ii) the point $x = 2$.

Solution. In the usual notations, we are given $A = 4$ and $\mu_1' = -1{\cdot}5$, $\mu_2' = 17$, $\mu_3' = -30$ and $\mu_4' = 108$.

Moments about Mean :

$\mu_2 = \mu_2' - \mu_1'^2 = 17 - (-1{\cdot}5)^2 = 17 - 2{\cdot}25$
$= 14{\cdot}75$

$\mu_3 = \mu_3' - 3\mu_2'\mu_1' + 2\mu_1'^3$
$= -30 - 3 \times (17) \times (-1{\cdot}5) + 2(-1{\cdot}5)^3$
$= -30 + 76{\cdot}5 - 6{\cdot}75 = 39{\cdot}75$

$\mu_4 = \mu_4' - 4\mu_3'\mu_1' + 6\mu_2'\mu_1'^2 - 3\mu_1'^4$
$= 108 - 4(-30)(-1{\cdot}5) + 6(17)(-1{\cdot}5)^2 - 3(-1{\cdot}5)^4$
$= 108 - 180 + 229{\cdot}5 - 15{\cdot}1875$
$= 142{\cdot}3125$

Hence, $\beta_1 = \dfrac{\mu_3^2}{\mu_2^3} = \dfrac{(39{\cdot}75)^2}{(14{\cdot}75)^3} = \dfrac{1580{\cdot}06}{3209{\cdot}05} = 0{\cdot}4924$; $\beta_2 = \dfrac{\mu_4}{\mu_2^2} = \dfrac{142{\cdot}3125}{(14{\cdot}75)^2} = \dfrac{142{\cdot}3125}{217{\cdot}5625} = 0{\cdot}6541$

Also Mean $(\bar{x}) = A + \mu_1' = 4 + (-1{\cdot}5) = 2{\cdot}5$

Note. Since for a discrete distribution, $\beta_2 \geq 1$, [See Remark 2 to § 7.6], there seems to be some error in the problem.

Moments about Origin. We have

$$\bar{x} = 2{\cdot}5, \quad \mu_2 = 14{\cdot}75, \quad \mu_3 = 39{\cdot}75 \quad \text{and} \quad \mu_4 = 142{\cdot}31 \ (approx.)$$

We know $\bar{x} = A + \mu_1'$, where μ_1' is the first moment about the point $x = A$. Taking $A = 0$, we get the first moment about origin as $\mu_1' = \text{mean} = 2{\cdot}5$.

Using (7·35), we get

$$\mu_2' = \mu_2 + \mu_1'^2 = 14{\cdot}75 + (2{\cdot}5)^2 = 14{\cdot}75 + 6{\cdot}25 = 21$$

$$\mu_3' = \mu_3 + 3\mu_2\mu_1' + \mu_1'^3 = 39{\cdot}75 + 3(14{\cdot}75)(2{\cdot}5) + (2{\cdot}5)^3$$
$$= 39{\cdot}75 + 110{\cdot}625 + 15{\cdot}625 = 166$$

$$\mu_4' = \mu_4 + 4\mu_3\mu_1' + 6\mu_2\mu_1'^2 + \mu_1'^4$$
$$= 142{\cdot}3125 + 4(39{\cdot}75)(2{\cdot}5) + 6(14{\cdot}75)(2{\cdot}5)^2 + (2{\cdot}5)^4$$
$$= 142{\cdot}3125 + 397{\cdot}5 + 553{\cdot}125 + 39{\cdot}0625 = 1132$$

Moments about the Point $x = 2$. We have $\bar{x} = A + \mu_1'$. Taking $A = 2$, the first moment about the point $x = 2$ is

$$\mu_1' = \bar{x} - 2 = 2{\cdot}5 - 2 = 0{\cdot}5$$

Using (7·35), we get

$$\mu_2' = \mu_2 + \mu_1'^2 = 14{\cdot}75 + 0{\cdot}25 = 15$$

$$\mu_3' = \mu_3 + 3\mu_2\mu_1' + \mu_1^3 = 39{\cdot}75 + 3(14{\cdot}75)(0{\cdot}5) + (0{\cdot}5)^3$$
$$= 39{\cdot}75 + 22{\cdot}125 + 0{\cdot}125 = 62$$

$$\mu_4' = \mu_4 + 4\mu_3\mu_1' + 6\mu_2\mu_1'^2 + \mu_1'^4$$
$$= 142{\cdot}3125 + 4(39{\cdot}75)(0{\cdot}5) + 6(14{\cdot}75)(0{\cdot}5)^2 + (0{\cdot}5)^4$$
$$= 142{\cdot}3125 + 79{\cdot}5 + 22{\cdot}125 + 0{\cdot}0625 = 244$$

Example 7·29. *Examine whether the following results of a piece of computation for obtaining the second central moment are consistent or not ; $N = 120$, $\Sigma fX = -125$, $\Sigma fX^2 = 128$.*

Solution. We have

$$\mu_2 = \frac{\Sigma fX^2}{N} - \left(\frac{\Sigma fX}{N}\right)^2 = \frac{128}{120} - \left(\frac{-125}{120}\right)^2 = 1{\cdot}0670 - 1{\cdot}0816 = -\,0{\cdot}0146,$$

which is impossible, since variance cannot be negative. Hence, the given data are inconsistent.

EXERCISE 7·3.

1. (*a*) Distinguish between "Skewness" and "Kurtosis" and bring out their importance in describing frequency distributions.

(*b*) "Averages, dispension, skewness and kurtosis are complementary to one another in understanding a frequency distribution." Elucidate.

2. (a) Explain the terms Skewness and Kurtosis used in connection with the frequency distribution of a continuous variable. Give the different measures of skewness (any three of the measures to be given) and kurtosis.

(b) Define skewness and describe briefly the various tests of skewness. [*Himachal Pradesh Univ. B.Com., 1998*]

(c) Explain briefly how the measures of skewness and kurtosis can be used in describing a frequency distribution.

(d) What do you mean by 'skewness' ? How is skewness different from kurtosis ?

3. (a) Explain the relation between the central moments and raw moments of a frequency distribution and hence express the first four central moments in terms of the raw moments.

(b) What are the raw and central moments of a distribution ? Show that the central moments are invariant under change of origin but not of scale.

4(a) Define moments. "A frequency distribution can be described almost completely by the first four moments and two measures based on moments." Examine the statement. [*Delhi Univ. B.Com. (Hons.), 1996*]

(b) Define moments. How are moments helpful in the study of the different aspects of the formation of a frequency distribution ? [*Delhi Univ. B.Com. (Hons.) (External), 2006*]

5. Indicate whether two distributions with the same means, standard deviations and coefficients of skewness must have same peakedness. [*Delhi Univ. B.Com. (Hons.), 1999*]

6. Prove that for any frequency distribution :

(i) Kurtosis is greater than unity.

(ii) Quartile coefficient of skewness is less than 1 numerically.

7. Prove any *two* of the following :

(i) The sum of squares of deviations is the least when deviations are taken from the mean.

(ii) The standard deviation is affected by the change of scale but not by the change of origin.

(iii) The moment coefficient of kurtosis is not affected by the change of scale.

[*Delhi Univ. B.A. (Econ. Hons.), 1991*]

8. Prove that the moment coefficient of kurtosis is not affected by the change of scale.

[*Delhi Univ. B.A. (Econ. Hons.),1996*]

9. Define Pearsonian coefficients β_1 and β_2, and discuss their utility in Statistics. Define moment coefficient of skewness. Discuss its utility and limitations, if any.

10. (a) Find the first, second, third and fourth central moments of the set of numbers 2, 4, 6, 8.

Ans. $\mu_1 = 0,\ \mu_2 = 5,\ \mu_3 = 0,\ \mu_4 = 41.$

(b) Given the following data, compute the moment coefficient of skewness and comment on the result.

X :	2	3	7	8	10

[*Delhi Univ. B.A. (Econ. Hons.), 1991*]

Hint. $\overline{X} = 6;\ \mu_2 = \frac{1}{5}\Sigma(x-\bar{x})^2 = \frac{46}{5} = 9{\cdot}2\ ;\ \mu_3 = \frac{1}{5}\Sigma(x-\bar{x})^3 = \frac{-18}{5} = -3{\cdot}6$

$$\beta_1 = 0{\cdot}0166 \Rightarrow \gamma_1 = \sqrt{0{\cdot}0166} = -0{\cdot}12$$ (Negative sign is taken because μ_3 is negative).

Hence, the distribution is *very slightly negatively skewed*, or it is approximately symmetrical ($\because \beta_1 \cong 0$).

11. Calculate β_1 and β_2 (measures of skewness and kurtosis) for the following frequency distribution and hence comment on the type of the frequency distribution :

x :	2	3	4	5	6
f :	1	3	7	2	1

Ans. $\beta_1 = 0{\cdot}0204\ ;\ \beta_2 = 3{\cdot}1080$. Distribution is approximately normal.

12. Find the first four moments about the mean for the following distribution.

Height (in inches) :	60—62	63—65	66—68	69—71	72—74
Frequency :	5	18	42	27	8

Ans. $\mu_1 = 0,\ \mu_2 = 8{\cdot}5275,\ \mu_3 = -2{\cdot}6933,\ \mu_4 = 199{\cdot}3759.$

13. Find the variance, skewness and kurtosis of the following distribution by the method of moments :

Class interval :	0—10	10—20	20–30	30–40
Frequency :	1	4	3	2

Ans. $\sigma^2 = 84,\ \gamma_1 = 0{\cdot}0935,\ \beta_2 = 2{\cdot}102.$

14. Explain Sheppard's corrections for Grouping Errors. What are the conditions to be satisfied for the application of Sheppard's corrections ? *[Delhi Univ. B.Com. (Hons.), (External), 2006]*

15. For the following distribution, calculate the first four central moments and two beta co-efficients :

Class Interval	:	20—30	30—40	40—50	50—60	60—70	70—80	80—90
Frequency	:	5	14	20	25	17	11	8

[Delhi Univ. B.Com. (Hons.), 2001]

Ans. $\mu_1 = 0$, $\mu_2 = 254$, $\mu_3 = 540$, $\mu_4 = 1{,}49{,}000$; $\beta_1 = 0{\cdot}0178$, $\beta_2 = 2{\cdot}3095$.

16. The first two moments of a distribution about the value 5 of the variable are 2 and 20. Find the mean and the variance.

Ans. Mean = 7, Variance = 16.

17. The first three moments of a distribution about the value 2 are 1, 22 and 10. Find its mean, standard deviation and the moment measure of skewness.

Ans. Mean = 3, $\sigma = 4{\cdot}58$, $\gamma_1 = -0{\cdot}5614$.

18. If the first three moments about the origin for a distribution are 10,225 and 0 respectively, calculate the fist three moments about the value 5 for the distribution. *[Delhi Univ. B.A. (Econ. Hons.), 2005]*

Ans. 5, 150, – 2750.

19. For a distribution, the mean is 10, variance is 16, γ_1 is +1 and β_2 is 4. Obtain the first four moments about the origin, *i.e.,* zero. Comment upon the nature of distribution. *[Delhi Univ. B.Com. (Hons.), 2005]*

Ans. Moments about origin : $\mu_1' = 10$, $\mu_2' = 116$, $\mu_3' = 1544$, $\mu_4' = 23184$. The distribution is positively skewed and leptokurtic.

20. The arithmetic mean of a certain distribution is 5. The second and the third moments about the mean are 20 and 140 respectively. Find the third moment of the distribution about 10.

Ans. μ_3' (about 10) = –285.

21. In a certain distribution the first four moments about the point 4 are 1·5, 17, –30 and 108 respectively. Find the kurtosis of the frequency curve and comment on its shape.

Ans. $\beta_2 = 2{\cdot}3088$. Distt. is Platy-kurtic.

22. The first four moments of a distribution about the value 4 are – 1·5, 17, – 30 and 108 respectively. Calculate : (*i*) Moments about mean; (*ii*) Skewness; (*iii*) Show whether the distribution is Leptokurtic or Platykurtic. *[Delhi Univ. B.Com. (Hons.), 2009]*

Ans. (*i*) $\mu_1 = 0$, $\mu_2 = \sigma^2 = 14{\cdot}75$, $\mu_3 = 39{\cdot}75$, $\mu_4 = 142{\cdot}3125$.

(*ii*) Skewness $(\gamma_1) = (\mu_3/\sigma^3) = 0{\cdot}7018$

(*iii*) $\beta_2 = (\mu_4/\mu_2^2) = 0{\cdot}654 < 3 \Rightarrow$ Distribution is platykurtic.

Note . See Example 7·28.

23. The first four central moments are 0, 4, 8 and 144. Examine the skewness and kurtosis.

Ans. $\gamma_1 = 1$, $\beta_2 = 9 \Rightarrow \gamma_2 = 6$.

24. The central moments of a distribution are given by : $\mu_2 = 140$, $\mu_3 = 148$, $\mu_4 = 6030$. Calculate the moment measures of skewness and kurtosis and comment on the shape of the distribution.

Ans. $\gamma_1 = 0{\cdot}0893$; $\beta_2 = 0{\cdot}3076$; Distribution is approximately symmetrical and platy-kurtic.

25. The first four moments of a distribution about value 2 are 1, 2·5, 5·5 and 16 respectively. Calculate the four moments about mean and comment on the nature of the distribution. *[Delhi Univ. B.Com. (Hons.), 2002]*

26. The first four moments of a distribution about the value 3 are 1, 2·5, 5·5 and 16 respectively. Do you think that the distribution is leptokurtic ? *[Delhi Univ. B.A. (Econ. Hons.), 2009]*

Ans. $\mu_2 = 1{\cdot}5$, $\mu_3 = 0$, $\mu_4 = 6$; $\beta_2 = 2{\cdot}67 < 3$. Distribution is platy-kurtic and *not leptokurtic.*

27. The first four moments of a distribution about the value 5 are equal to 2, 20, 40 and 50. Obtain the mean, variance, $\sqrt{\beta_1}$ and β_2 for the distribution and comment. *[Delhi Univ. B.A. (Econ. Hons.), 1993]*

Ans. Mean = 7, Variance = $\mu_2 = 16$; $\mu_3 = -64$, $\mu_4 = 162$.

$$\gamma_1 = \sqrt{\beta_1} = \frac{\mu_3}{\mu_2^{3/2}} = \frac{-64}{64} = -1. \text{ (Negatively skewed) ; } \beta_2 = \frac{\mu_4}{\mu_2^2} = \frac{162}{256} = 0{\cdot}63 \text{ (Platy-kurtic)}$$

28. The following data are given to an economist for the purpose of economic analysis. The data refer to the length of a certain type of batteries.

$N = 100$, $\Sigma fd = 50$, $\Sigma fd^2 = 1970$, $\Sigma fd^3 = 2948$ and $\Sigma fd^4 = 86{,}752$, in which $d = (X - 48)$. Do you think that the distribution is platykurtic ? [*Delhi Univ. B.Com. (Hons.), 1998*]

Ans. $\beta_2 = 2{\cdot}214$; $\beta_2 < 3$, distribution is platy-kurtic.

29. The standard deviation of a symmetrical distribution is 5. What must be the value of the fourth moment about the mean in order that the distribution be (*a*) lepto-kurtic, (*b*) meso-kurtic, and (*c*) platy-kurtic ?

Ans. Distribution is (*a*) lepto-kurtic if $\mu_4 > 1875$; (*b*) meso-kurtic if $\mu_4 = 1875$; (*c*) platy-kurtic if $\mu_4 < 1875$.

30. From the data given below, first calculate the first four moments about an arbitrary value and then after Sheppard's corrections, calculate the first four moments about the mean. Also calculate β_2 and comment on its value.

Average number of hours worked per week by workers in 100 industries in 1998.

Hours worked	:	30—33	33—36	36—39	39–42	42—45	45—48
No. of Industries	:	2	4	26	47	15	6

Ans. Moments after applying Sheppard's correction are :

$$\mu_1 = 0,\quad \mu_2 = 8{\cdot}01,\quad \mu_3 = -20{\cdot}69,\quad \mu_4 = 249{\cdot}393.$$

31. (*a*) The first four moments of a distribution about the value 4 are –1·5, 17, –130, 108. Find whether the data are consistent.

Ans. $\mu_4 = 108 - 780 + 229{\cdot}5 - 15{\cdot}1875 = -457{\cdot}6875$. Since μ_4 is negative, data are inconsistent.

(*b*) The first four moments of a distribution about 3 are 1, 3, 6 and 8. Is the data consistent ? Explain [*Delhi Univ. B.A. (Econ. Hons.), 2009*]

Ans. Inconsistent, because $\mu_4 = -1$ (< 0), which is not possible.

(*c*) For a distribution, the first four moments about zero are 2, 5, 16 and 30. Is the data consistent ? Explain. [*Delhi Univ. B.A. (Econ. Hons.), 2007*]

Ans. Data are inconsistent because $\mu_4 = -26$ (Negative), which is not possible.

32. (*a*) The standard deviation of a symmetrical distribution is given to be 5. What must be the value of the fourth moment about the mean in order that the distribution is meso-kurtic ? [*Delhi Univ. B.A. (Econ. Hons.), 1999*]

(*b*) The standard deviation of symmetrical distribution is 3. What must be the value of the 4th moment about the mean in order that the distribution be mesokurtic ? [*Maharishi Dayanand Univ. M.Com., 1999*]

Ans. (*a*) = 1875, (*b*) 243.

(*c*) Comment on the following :

The standard deviation of a symmetrical distribution is 3 and the value of fourth moment about mean is 243 in order that the distribution is mesokurtic. [*Delhi Univ. B.Com. (Hons.), 2009*]

Ans. True; because for Mesokurtic distribution : $\beta_2 = 3$.

33. Fill in the blanks :

(*a*) (*i*) If $\beta_2 = 3$, the curve is called ......
(*ii*) If $\beta_2 > 3$, the curve is called ......
(*iii*) If $\beta_2 < 3$, the curve is called ......
(*iv*) If $\beta_1 = 0$, the curve is called ......

(*b*) (*i*) β_1 is always ... ($\geq$, $=$, $\leq$).
(*ii*) μ_4 is always ... ($\geq$, $=$, $\leq$).
(*iii*) μ_2 is always ... ($\geq$, $=$, $\leq$).
(*iv*) β_2 is always ... ($\geq$, $=$, $\leq$)

Comment on the result when equality sign holds.

Ans. (*a*) (*i*) Mesokurtic, (*ii*) Leptokurtic, (*iii*) Platykurtic (*iv*) Symmetrical

(*b*) (*i*) $\beta_1 \geq 0$, (*ii*) $\mu_4 \geq 0$, (*iii*) $\mu_2 \geq 0$, (*iv*) $\beta_2 \geq 1$.

34. Fill in the blanks :

(*i*) Literal meaning of skewness is ".......''
(*ii*) Kurtosis is a measure of ...... of the frequency curve.
(*iii*) For a symmetrical distribution, mean, median and mode ......
(*iv*) If Mean < Mode, the distribution is ...... skewed.
(*v*) If Mean > Median, the distribution is ...... skewed.
(*vi*) Bowley's coefficient of skewness lies between ...... and ......
(*vii*) $\beta_1 = 0$ implies that distribution is ......
(*viii*) If $\gamma_1 > 0$, the distribution is ...... skewed.

(*ix*) If $\gamma_1 < 0$, the distribution is ...... skewed.

(*x*) For a normal curve β_2 ......

(*xi*) If $\beta_2 > 3$, the curve is called ......

(*xii*) If $\beta_2 < 3$, the curve is called ......

(*xiii*) An absolute measure of skewness based on moments is ......

(*xiv*) An absolute measure of skewness based on quartiles is ......

(*xv*) Relative measure of skewness based on mean, s.d. and mode is ......

(*xvi*) Relative measure of kurtosis is ......

(*xvii*) Relative measure of skewness in terms of moments is ......

(*xviii*) For a moderately asymmetrical distribution : Mean – Median = ? (Mean – Mode)

(*xix*) If $\mu_3 = -1{\cdot}48$, the curve of the given distribution is stretched more to the ......than to the ......

(*xx*) For a symmetrical distribution, ... are equidistant from ......

(*xxi*) Mean = First moment about ......

(*xxii*) Variance = ... moment about mean.

(*xxiii*) If μ_1' is the first moment about the point 'A', then Mean = ...

(*xxiv*) $\beta_1 = \dfrac{\mu_3^2}{\cdots\cdots}$; $\beta_2 = \dfrac{\cdots}{\mu_2^2}$; $\gamma_1 = \cdots\cdots$; $\gamma_2 = \cdots\cdots$

(*xxv*) In a moderately asymmetrical distribution the distance between ... and ... is ... the distance between ... and ...

Ans.

(*i*) Lack of symmetry, (*ii*) Convexity (flatness or peakedness), (*iii*) Coincide, (*iv*) Negatively,

(*v*) Positively, (*vi*) –1 and 1, (*vii*) Symmetrical, (*viii*) Positively,

(*ix*) Negatively, (*x*) 3, (*xi*) Lepto-kurtic, (*xii*) Platy-kurtic,

(*xii*) μ_3, (*xiv*) $(Q_3 - Md) - (Md - Q_1)$, (*xv*) $(M - Mo)/\sigma$, (*xvi*) β_2 or γ_2,

(*xvii*) β_1 or γ_1, (*xviii*) 1/3, (*xix*) Left, Right, (*xx*) Quartiles, median,

(*xxi*) Origin (*i.e.*, A = 0), (*xxii*) Second, (*xxiii*) $A + \mu_1'$, (*xxiv*) μ_2^3, μ_4, $\sqrt{\beta_1} = \dfrac{\mu_3}{\mu_2^{3/2}}$, $\gamma_2 = \beta_2 - 3$,

(*xxv*) Mean, Mode, Thrice, Mean, Median.

35. State whether the following statements are true (*T*) or false (*F*).

(*i*) Skewness studies the flatness or peakedness of the distribution.

(*ii*) Kurtosis means 'lack of symmetry'.

(*iii*) For a symmetrical distribution $\beta_1 = 0$.

(*iv*) Skewness and kurtosis help us in studying the shape of the frequency curve.

(*v*) Bowley's coefficient of skewness lies between –3 and 3.

(*vi*) Two distributions having the same values of mean, s.d. and skewness must have the same kurtosis.

(*vii*) A positively skewed distribution curve is stretched more to the right than to the left.

(*viii*) If $\beta_2 > 3$, the curve is called platy-kurtic.

(*ix*) If $\beta_2 = 3$, the curve is called normal.

(*x*) β_1 is always non-negative.

(*xi*) β_2 can be negative.

(*xii*) Variance = μ_2 (2nd moment about mean).

(*xiii*) For a symmetrical distribution : $\mu_1 = \mu_3 = \mu_5 = \cdots\cdots = 0$

(*xiv*) For a symmetrical distribution : Mean > Median > Mode.

(*xv*) $\beta_1 = \dfrac{\mu_4}{\mu_3^2}$

Ans.

(*i*) F, (*ii*) F, (*iii*) T, (*iv*) T, (*v*) F

(*vi*) F, (*vii*) T, (*viii*) F, (*ix*) T, (*x*) T,

(*xi*) F, (*xii*) T, (*xiii*) T, (*xiv*) F, (*xv*) F.

8 Correlation Analysis

8·1. INTRODUCTION

So far we have confined our discussion to univariate distributions only *i.e.,* the distributions involving only one variable and also saw how the various measures of central tendency, dispersion, skewness and kurtosis can be used for the purposes of comparison and analysis. We may, however, come across certain series where each item of the series may assume the values of two or more variables. If we measure the heights and weights of *n* individuals, we obtain a series in which each unit (individual) of the series assumes two values—one relating to heights and the other relating to weights. Such distribution, in which each unit of the series assumes two values is called a *bivariate distribution.* Further, if we measure more than two variables on each unit of a distribution, it is called a *multivariate distribution.* In a series, the units on which different measurements are taken may be of almost any nature such as different individuals, times, places, etc. For example we may have :

(*i*) The series of marks of *individuals* in two subjects in an examination.

(*ii*) The series of sales revenue and advertising expenditure of different companies in a *particular year.*

(*iii*) The series of exports of raw cotton in crores of rupees and imports of manufactured goods during *number of years from 1989 to 1994*, say.

(*iv*) The series of ages of husbands and wives in a sample of selected *married couples* and so on.

Thus in a bivariate distribution we are given a set of pairs of observations, one value of each pair being the values of each of the two variables.

In a bivariate distribution, we may be interested to find if there is any relationship between the two variables under study. The *correlation* is a statistical tool which studies the relationship between two variables and *correlation analysis* involves various methods and techniques used for studying and measuring the extent of the relationship between the two variables.

WHAT THEY SAY ABOUT CORRELATION — SOME DEFINITIONS AND USES

"When the relationship is of a quantitative nature, the appropriate statistical tool for discovering and measuring the relationship and expressing it in a brief formula is known as correlation."—**Croxton and Cowden**

"Correlation is an analysis of the covariation between two or more variables." —**A.M. Tuttle**

"Correlation analysis contributes to the understanding of economic behaviour, aids in locating the critically important variables on which others depend, may reveal to the economist the connections by which disturbances spread and suggest to him the paths through which stabilising forces may become effective."—**W.A. Neiswanger**

"The effect of correlation is to reduce the range of uncertainty of our prediction." —**Tippett**

Two variables are said to be correlated if the change in one variable results in a corresponding change in the other variable.

8·1·1. Types of Correlation

(*a*) *POSITIVE AND NEGATIVE CORRELATION*

If the values of the two variables deviate in the same direction *i.e.,* if the increase in the values of one variable results, on an average, in a corresponding increase in the values of the other variable or if a decrease in the values of one variable results, on an average, in a corresponding decrease in the values of the other variable, correlation is said to be *positive or direct.*

Some examples of series of positive correlation are :

(*i*) Heights and weights.
(*ii*) The family income and expenditure on luxury items.
(*iii*) Amount of rainfall and yield of crop (up to a point).
(*iv*) Price and supply of a commodity and so on.

On the other hand, correlation is said to be *negative* or *inverse* if the variables deviate in the opposite direction *i.e.,* if the increase (decrease) in the values of one variable results, on the average, in a corresponding decrease (increase) in the values of the other variable.

Some examples of negative correlation are the series relating to :

(*i*) Price and demand of a commodity.
(*ii*) Volume and pressure of a perfect gas.
(*iii*) Sale of woollen garments and the day temperature, and so on.

(*b*) *LINEAR AND NON-LINEAR CORRELATION*

The correlation between two variables is said to be *linear* if corresponding to a unit change in one variable, there is a constant change in the other variable over the entire range of the values. For example, let us consider the following data :

x	1	2	3	4	5
y	5	7	9	11	13

Thus for a unit change in the value of x, there is a constant change *viz.,* 2 in the corresponding values of y. Mathematically, above data can be expressed by the relation

$$y = 2x + 3$$

In general, two variables x and y are said to be linearly related, if there exists a relationship of the form

$$y = a + bx \qquad \dots (*)$$

between them. But we know that (*) is the equation of a straight line with slope 'b' and which makes an intercept 'a' on the y-axis [*c.f.* $y = mx + c$ form of equation of the line]. Hence, if the values of the two variables are plotted as points in the xy-plane, we shall get a straight line. This can be easily checked for the example given above. Such phenomena occur frequently in physical sciences but in economics and social sciences, we very rarely come across the data which give a straight line graph. The relationship between two variables is said to be *non-linear or curvilinear* if corresponding to a unit change in one variable, the other variable does not change at a constant rate but at fluctuating rate. In such cases if the data are plotted on the xy-plane, we do not get a straight line curve. Mathematically speaking, the correlation is said to be non-linear if the slope of the plotted curve is not constant. Such phenomena are common in the data relating to economics and social sciences.

Since the techniques for the analysis and measurement of non-linear relation are quite complicated and tedious as compared to the methods of studying and measuring linear relationship, we generally assume that the relationship between the two variables under study is linear. In this chapter, we shall confine ourselves to the measurement of linear relationship only. The measurement of non-linear relationship is, however, beyond the scope of this book.

Remark. The study of correlation is easy in physical sciences since on the basis of experimental results, it is easy to establish mathematical relationship between two or more variables under study. But in social and economic sciences, it is very difficult to establish mathematical relationship between the variables under study since in such phenomena, the values of the variables under study are affected simultaneously by multiplicity of factors and it is extremely difficult, sometimes impossible, to study the effects of each factor separately. Hence, in the data relating to social and economic phenomena, the study of correlation cannot be as accurate and precise.

8·1·2. Correlation and Causation. Correlation analysis enables us to have an idea about the degree and direction of the relationship between the two variables under study. However, it fails to reflect upon the cause and effect relationship between the variables. In a bivariate distribution, if the variables have the cause and effect relationship, they are bound to vary in sympathy with each other and, therefore, there is bound to be a high degree of correlation between them. In other words, causation always implies correlation. However, the converse is not true *i.e.,* even a fairly high degree of correlation between the two variables need not imply a cause and effect relationship between them. The high degree of correlation between the variables may be due to the following reasons :

1. *Mutual dependence.* The phenomena under study may inter-influence each other. Such situations are usually observed in data relating to economic and business situations. For instance, it is well-known principle in economics that prices of a commodity are influenced by the forces of supply and demand. For instance, if the price of a commodity increases, its demand generally decreases (other factors remaining constant). Here increased price is the cause and reduction in demand is the effect. However, a decrease in the demand of a commodity due to emigration of the people or due to fashion or some other factors like changes in the tastes and habits of people may result in decrease in its price. Here, the cause is the reduced demand and the effect is the reduced price. Accordingly, the two variables may show a good degree of correlation due to interaction of each on the other, yet it becomes very difficult to isolate the exact cause from the effect.

2. *Both the variables being influenced by the same external factors.* A high degree of correlation between the two variables may be due to the effect or interaction of a third variable or a number of variables on each of these two variables. For example, a fairly high degree of correlation may be observed between the yield per hectare of two crops, say, rice and potato, due to the effect of a number of factors like favourable weather conditions, fertilizers used, irrigation facilities, etc., on each of them. But none of the two is the cause of the other.

3. *Pure chance.* It may happen that a small randomly selected sample from a bivariate distribution may show a fairly high degree of correlation though, actually, the variables may not be correlated in the population. Such correlation may be attributed to chance fluctuations. Moreover, the conscious or unconscious bias on the part of the investigator, in the selection of the sample may also result in high degree of correlation in the sample. In this connection, it may be worthwhile to make a mention of the two phenomena where a fairly high degree of correlation may be observed, though it is not possible to conceive them as being causally related. For example, we may observe a high degree of correlation between the size of shoe and the intelligence of a group of persons. Such correlation is called *spurious* or *non-sense* correlation. [For details see § 8·4·2 (*iii*).]

8·2. METHODS OF STUDYING CORRELATION

We shall confine our discussion to the methods of ascertaining only *linear relationship* between two variables (series). The commonly used methods for studying the correlation between two variables are :

(*i*) Scatter diagram method.
(*ii*) Karl Pearson's coefficient of correlation (Covariance method).
(*iii*) Two-way frequency table (Bivariate correlation method).
(*iv*) Rank method.
(*v*) Concurrent deviations method.

8·3. SCATTER DIAGRAM METHOD

Scatter diagram is one of the simplest ways of diagrammatic representation of a bivariate distribution and provides us one of simplest tools of ascertaining the correlation between two variables. Suppose we are given n pairs of values $(x_1, y_1), (x_2, y_2), \ldots, (x_n, y_n)$ of two variables X and Y. For example, if the variables X and Y denote the height and weight respectively, then the pairs $(x_1, y_1), (x_2, y_2), \ldots, (x_n, y_n)$ may represent the heights and weights (in pairs) of n individuals. These n points may be plotted as dots (.) on the x-axis and y-axis in the xy-plane. (It is customary to take the dependent variable along the y-axis and independent variable along the x-axis.) The diagram of dots so obtained is known as *scatter diagram.* From scatter diagram we can form a fairly good, though rough, idea about the relationship between the two variables. The following points may be borne in mind in interpreting the scatter diagram regarding the correlation between the two variables :

(*i*) If the points are very dense *i.e.*, very close to each other, a fairly good amount of correlation may be expected between the two variables. On the other hand, if the points are widely scattered, a poor correlation may be expected between them.

(*ii*) If the points on the scatter diagram reveal any trend (either upward or downward), the variables are said to be correlated and if no trend is revealed, the variables are uncorrelated.

(*iii*) If there is an upward trend rising from lower left hand corner and going upward to the upper right hand corner, the correlation is positive since this reveals that the values of the two variables move in the same direction. If, on the other hand, the points depict a downward trend from the upper left hand corner to the lower right hand corner, the correlation is negative since in this case the values of the two variables move in the opposite directions.

(*iv*) In particular, if all the points lie on a straight line starting from the left bottom and going up towards the right top, the correlation is perfect and positive, and if all the points lie on a straight line starting from left top and coming down to right bottom, the correlation is perfect and negative.

The following diagrams of the scattered data depict different forms of correlation.

PERFECT POSITIVE CORRELATION

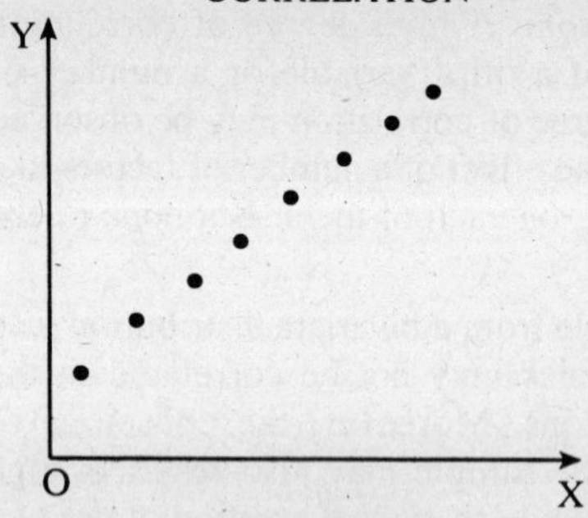

Fig. 8.1.

PERFECT NEGATIVE CORRELATION

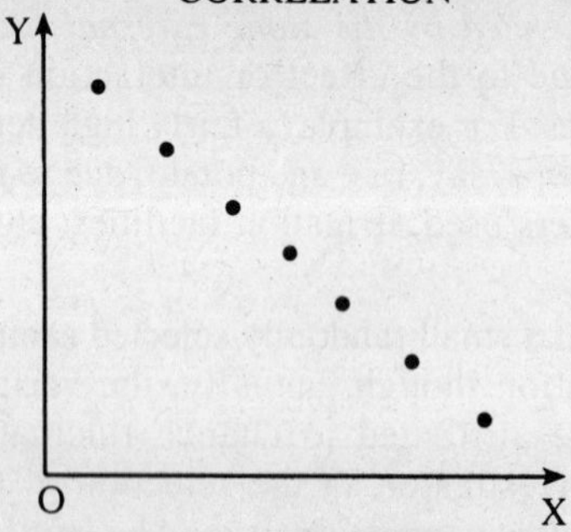

Fig. 8.2.

LOW DEGREE OF POSITIVE CORRELATION

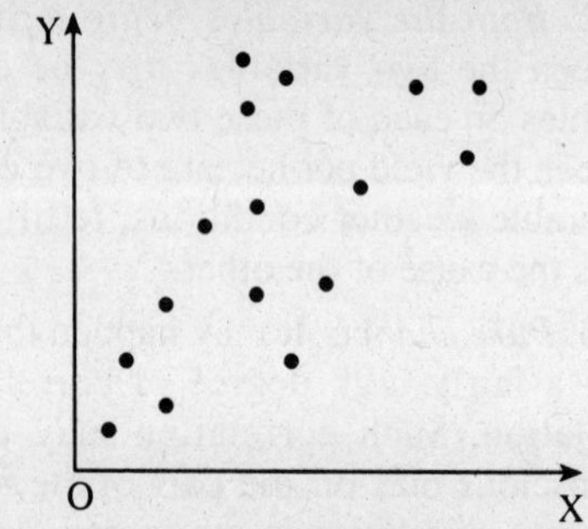

Fig. 8.3.

LOW DEGREE OF NEGATIVE CORRELATION

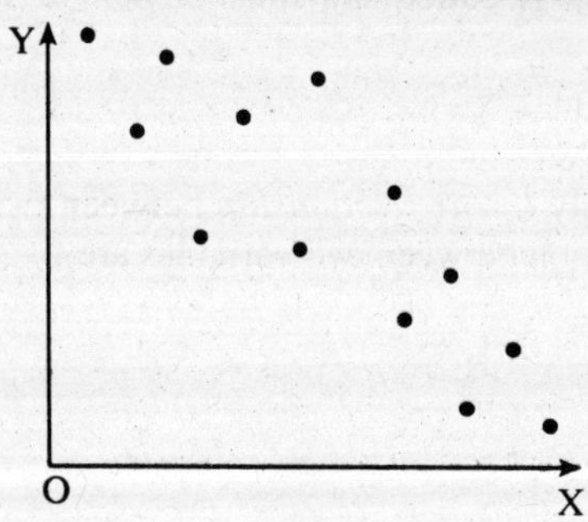

Fig. 8.4.

HIGH DEGREE OF POSITIVE CORRELATION

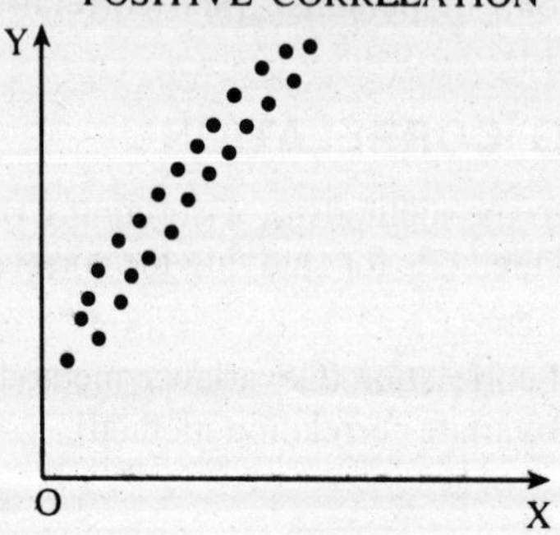

Fig. 8.5.

HIGH DEGREE OF NEGATIVE CORRELATION

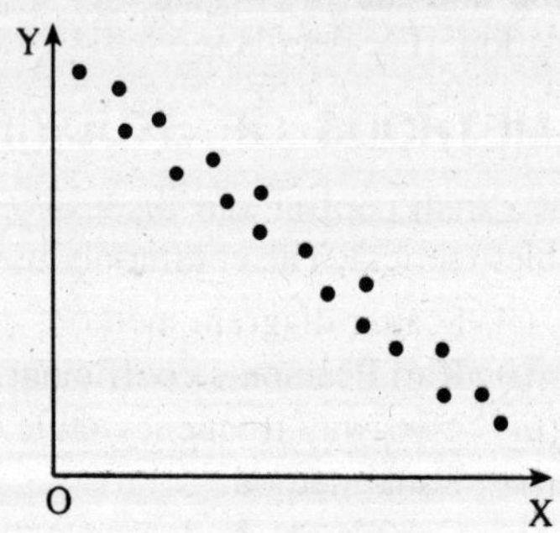

Fig. 8.6.

NO CORRELATION

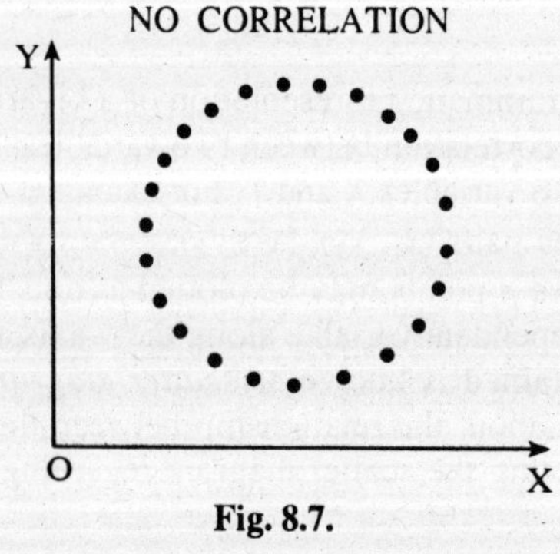

Fig. 8.7.

NO CORRELATION

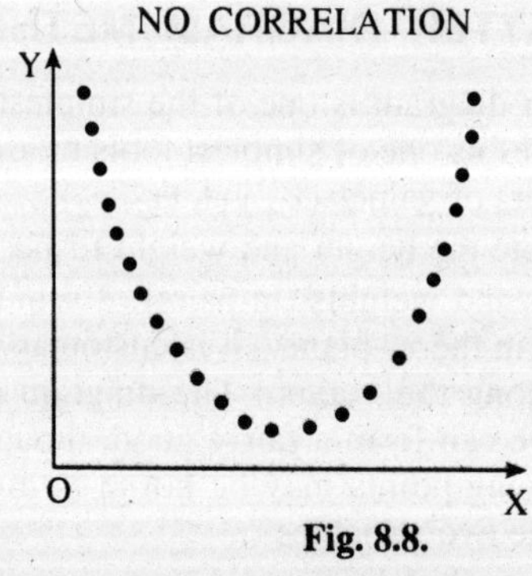

Fig. 8.8.

Remarks 1. The method of scatter diagram is readily comprehensible and enables us to form a rough idea of the nature of the relationship between the two variables merely by inspection of the graph. Moreover, this method is not affected by extreme observations whereas all mathematical formulae of ascertaining correlation between two variables are affected by extreme observations. However, this method is not suitable if the number of observations is fairly large.

2. The method of scatter diagram only tells us about the nature of the relationship whether it is positive or negative and whether it is high or low. It does not provide us an exact measure of the extent of the relationship between the two variables.

3. The scatter diagram enables us to obtain an *approximate estimating line* or *line of best fit by free hand method.* The method generally consists in stretching a piece of thread through the plotted points to locate the best possible line. However, a rigorous method of obtaining the line of best fit is discussed in next chapter (Regression Analysis).

Example 8·1. *Following are the heights and weights of 10 students of a B.Com. class.*

Height (in inches)	*X*	:	*62*	*72*	*68*	*58*	*65*	*70*	*66*	*63*	*60*	*72*
Weight (in kgs.)	*Y*	:	*50*	*65*	*63*	*50*	*54*	*60*	*61*	*55*	*54*	*65*

Draw a scatter diagram and indicate whether the correlation is positive or negative.

Solution. The scatter diagram of the above data is shown below.

SCATTER DIAGRAM

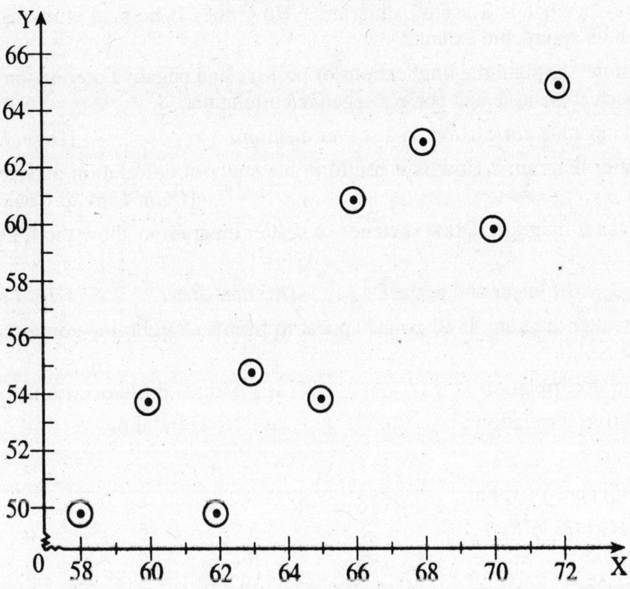

Fig. 8.9.

Since the points are dense *i.e.,* close to each other, we may expect a high degree of correlation between the series of heights and weights. Further, since the points reveal an upward trend starting from left bottom and going up towards the right top, the correlation is positive. Hence, we may expect a fairly high degree of positive correlation between the series of heights and weights in the class of B.Com. students.

EXERCISE 8·1

1. Explain the concept of correlation. Clearly explain with suitable illustrations its role in dealing with business problems.

2. (*a*) Define correlation. Explain various types of correlation with suitable examples.

[*Delhi Univ. B.Com. (Pass), 2000*]

(*b*) State the nature of the following correlations (positive, negative or no correlation) :

(*i*) Sale of woollen garments and the day temperature;

(*ii*) The colour of the saree and the intelligence of the lady who wears it ; and

(*iii*) Amount of rainfall and yield of crop.

3. Define correlation. Discuss its significance. Does correlation always signify causal relationship between two variables ? Explain with illustration.

4. (*a*) Does the high degree of correlation between the two variables signify the existence of cause and effect relationship between the two variables ?

(*b*) Does correlation imply causation between two variables ? *[Delhi Univ. B.Com. (Hons.), 2008]*

5. (*a*) What is '*spurious correlation*' and '*non-sense or chance correlation*' ? Explain with the help of an example. *[Delhi Univ. B.Com. (Pass), 1997]*

(*b*) Comment on the following statement : "A high degree of positive correlation between the 'size of the shoe' and the 'intelligence' of a group of individuals implies that people with bigger shoe size are more intelligent than the people with lower shoe size".

6. How far do you agree with the conclusion drawn in the following case ? Why ?

Two series — quantity of money in circulation and general price index — are found to possess positive correlation of a fairly high order. From this, it is concluded that one is the cause and the other the effect in a direct causal relationship.

7. (*a*) Distinguish clearly between :

(*i*) Positive and Negative correlation ; (*ii*) Linear and non-linear correlation.

(*b*) "If the two or more quantities vary in sympathy so that movements in one tend to be accompanied by corresponding movements in other(s), then they are said to be correlated." Discuss.

8. What is correlation ? What is a scatter diagram ? How does it help in studying correlation between two variables, in respect of both its nature and extent ?

9. (*a*) What is correlation ? Explain the implications of positive and negative correlation. Show by means of scatter diagram, the presence of perfect positive and perfect negative correlation. *[C.A. (Foundation), May 1996]*

(*b*) Illustrate a perfect negative correlation on a scatter diagram. *[Delhi Univ. B.Com. (Pass), 1998]*

10. (*a*) What is a scatter diagram ? How is it useful in the study of correlation between two variables ? Explain with suitable examples. *[Delhi Univ. B.Com. (Hons.), (External), 2006]*

(*b*) Write a note on scatter diagram. Draw sketches of scatter diagram to show the following correlation between two variables *x* and *y* :

(*i*) linear ; (*ii*) linear and perfect; (*iii*) non-linear; (*iv*) *x* and *y* uncorrelated.

(*c*) While drawing a scatter diagram, if all points appear to form a straight line going downward from left to right, then it is inferred that there is :

(*i*) Perfect positive correlation ; (*ii*) Simple positive correlation;
(*iii*) Perfect negative correlation ; (*iv*) No correlation.

Ans. (*iii*)

11. Given the following pairs of values :

Capital employed (Crores of Rs.)	:	2	3	5	6	8	9
Profits (Lakhs of Rs.)	:	6	5	7	8	12	11

(*a*) Make a scatter diagram.

(*b*) Do you think that there is any correlation between profits and capital employed ? Is it positive or negative ? Is it high or low ?

(*c*) By graphic inspection, draw an estimating line.

12. "Even a high degree of correlation does not mean that a relationship of cause and effect exists between the two correlated variables". Discuss.

13. Draw a scatter diagram from the following data :

Height (inches)	:	62	72	70	60	67	70	64	65	60	70
Weight (lbs.)	:	50	65	63	52	56	60	59	58	54	65

Also indicate whether correlation is positive or negative.

Ans. Positive Correlation.

14. Draw a scatter diagram for the data given below and interpret it.

X :	10	20	30	40	50	60	70	80
Y :	32	20	24	36	40	28	38	44

8·4. KARL PEARSON'S COEFFICIENT OF CORRELATION (COVARIANCE METHOD)

A mathematical method for measuring the intensity or the magnitude of *linear relationship* between two variable series was suggested by Karl Pearson (1867-1936), a great British Bio-metrician and Statistician and is by far the most widely used method in practice.

Karl Pearson's measure, known as Pearsonian correlation coefficient between two variables (series) X and Y, usually denoted by $r(X, Y)$ or r_{xy} or simply r, is a numerical measure of linear relationship between them and is defined as the ratio of the covariance between X and Y, written as Cov (x, y), to the product of the standard deviations of X and Y. Symbolically,

$$r = \frac{\text{Cov}(x, y)}{\sigma_x \sigma_y} \qquad \ldots (8\cdot1)$$

If $(x_1, y_1), (x_2, y_2), \ldots, (x_n, y_n)$ are n pairs of observations of the variables X and Y in a bivariate distribution, then

$$\text{Cov}(x, y) = \frac{1}{n}\sum(x-\bar{x})(y-\bar{y}) \;;\; \sigma_x = \sqrt{\frac{1}{n}\sum(x-\bar{x})^2} \;;\; \sigma_y = \sqrt{\frac{1}{n}\sum(y-\bar{y})^2} \qquad \ldots (8\cdot2)$$

summation being taken over n pairs of observations. Substituting in (8·1), we get

$$r = \frac{\frac{1}{n}\sum(x-\bar{x})(y-\bar{y})}{\sqrt{\frac{1}{n}\sum(x-\bar{x})^2 \cdot \frac{1}{n}\sum(y-\bar{y})^2}} = \frac{\sum(x-\bar{x})(y-\bar{y})}{\sqrt{\sum(x-\bar{x})^2 \sum(y-\bar{y})^2}} \qquad \ldots (8\cdot3)$$

The formula (8·3) can also be written as : $$r = \frac{\sum dx\, dy}{\sqrt{\sum dx^2 \cdot \sum dy^2}} \qquad \ldots (8\cdot3a)$$

where dx and dy denote the deviations of x and y values from their arithmetic means $\bar{x}$ and $\bar{y}$ respectively *i.e.*,

$$dx = x - \bar{x}\,,\quad dy = y - \bar{y} \qquad \ldots (8\cdot3b)$$

Simplifying (8·2), we get

$$\text{Cov}(x, y) = \frac{1}{n}\sum xy - \bar{x}\,\bar{y} \qquad \ldots (8\cdot4)$$

$$\Rightarrow \quad \text{Cov}(x, y) = \frac{1}{n}\sum xy - \left(\frac{\sum x}{n}\right)\left(\frac{\sum y}{n}\right) = \frac{1}{n^2}\left[n\sum xy - \left(\sum x\right)\left(\sum y\right)\right] \qquad \ldots (8\cdot4a)$$

$$\sigma_x^2 = \frac{1}{n}\sum(x-\bar{x})^2 = \frac{1}{n}\sum x^2 - \bar{x}^2 \qquad [\textit{c.f.}\ \text{Chapter 6}]$$

$$= \frac{1}{n}\sum x^2 - \left(\frac{\sum x}{n}\right)^2 = \frac{1}{n^2}\left[n\sum x^2 - \left(\sum x\right)^2\right] \qquad \ldots (8\cdot4b)$$

Similarly, we have, $$\sigma_y^2 = \frac{1}{n^2}\left[n\sum y^2 - \left(\sum y\right)^2\right] \qquad \ldots (8\cdot4c)$$

Substituting from (8·4*a*), (8·4*b*) and (8·4*c*) in (8·1), we get

$$r = \frac{\frac{1}{n^2}\left[n\sum xy - \left(\sum x\right)\left(\sum y\right)\right]}{\sqrt{\frac{1}{n^2}\left\{n\sum x^2 - \left(\sum x\right)^2\right\}} \cdot \sqrt{\frac{1}{n^2}\left\{n\sum y^2 - \left(\sum y\right)^2\right\}}}$$

$$= \frac{n\sum xy - \left(\sum x\right)\left(\sum y\right)}{\sqrt{\left[n\sum x^2 - \left(\sum x\right)^2\right]\left[n\sum y^2 - \left(\sum y\right)^2\right]}} \qquad \ldots (8\cdot5)$$

Remarks. Formula (8·3) or (8·3*a*) is quite convenient to apply if the means $\bar{x}$ and $\bar{y}$ come out to be integers (*i.e.*, whole numbers). If $\bar{x}$ or /and $\bar{y}$ is (are) fractional then the formula (8·3) or (8·3*a*) is quite cumbersome to apply, since the computations of $\sum(x-\bar{x})^2$, $\sum(y-\bar{y})^2$ and $\sum(x-\bar{x})(y-\bar{y})$ are quite time consuming and tedious. In such a case formula (8·5) may be used provided the values of x or/and y are small. But if x and y assume large values, the calculation of $\sum x^2$, $\sum y^2$ and $\sum xy$ is again quite time consuming.

Thus if (*i*) $\bar{x}$ and $\bar{y}$ are fractional and (*ii*) x and y assume large values, the formulae (8·3) and (8·5) are not generally used for numerical problems. In such cases, the *step deviation method* where we take the deviations of the variables X and Y from any arbitrary points, is used. We shall discuss this method after the properties of correlation coefficient (*c.f.* § 8·4·1).

2. Karl Pearson's correlation coefficient is also known as the *product moment correlation coefficient.*

Example 8·2. *Calculate Karl Pearson's coefficient of correlation between expenditure on advertising and sales from the data given below.*

Advertising expenses ('000 Rs.)	:	39	65	62	90	82	75	25	98	36	78
Sales (lakh Rs.)	:	47	53	58	86	62	68	60	91	51	84

Solution. Let the advertising expenses (in '000 Rs.) be denoted by the variable x and the sales (in lakh Rs.) be denoted by the variable y.

CALCULATIONS FOR CORRELATION COEFFICIENT

x	y	$dx = x - \bar{x} = x - 65$	$dy = y - \bar{y} = y - 66$	dx^2	dy^2	$dxdy$
39	47	−26	−19	676	361	494
65	53	0	−13	0	169	0
62	58	−3	−8	9	64	24
90	86	25	20	625	400	500
82	62	17	−4	289	16	−68
75	68	10	2	100	4	20
25	60	−40	−6	1600	36	240
98	91	33	25	1089	625	825
36	51	−29	−15	841	225	435
78	84	13	18	169	324	234
$\Sigma x = 650$	$\Sigma y = 660$	$\Sigma dx = 0$	$\Sigma dy = 0$	$\Sigma dx^2 = 5398$	$\Sigma dy^2 = 2224$	$\Sigma dxdy = 2704$

$$\bar{x} = \frac{\Sigma x}{n} = \frac{650}{10} = 65 \; ; \quad \bar{y} = \frac{\Sigma y}{n} = \frac{660}{10} = 66 \; ; \qquad \therefore \quad dx = x - \bar{x} = x - 65 \; ; \quad dy = y - \bar{y} = y - 66$$

$$r = \frac{\Sigma dxdy}{\sqrt{\Sigma dx^2 . \Sigma dy^2}} = \frac{2704}{\sqrt{5398 \times 2224}} = \frac{2704}{\sqrt{12005152}} = \frac{2704}{3464 \cdot 8451} = 0 \cdot 7804$$

Aliter.

$$\Rightarrow \qquad \log r = \log 2704 - \tfrac{1}{2}[\log 5398 + \log 2224]$$

$$= 3 \cdot 4320 - \tfrac{1}{2}(3 \cdot 7325 + 3 \cdot 3472) = 3 \cdot 4320 - 3 \cdot 53985 = -0 \cdot 10785 = \bar{1} \cdot 89215$$

$$\Rightarrow \qquad r = \text{Antilog}(\bar{1} \cdot 89215) = 0 \cdot 7802$$

Hence, there is a fairly high degree of positive correlation between expenditure on advertising and sales. We may, therefore, conclude that in general, sales have increased with an increase in the advertising expenses.

Example 8·3. *From the following table calculate the coefficient of correlation by Karl Pearson's method.*

X	6	2	10	4	8
Y	9	11	?	8	7

Arithmetic means of X and Y series are 6 and 8 respectively.

Solution. First of all we shall find the missing value of Y. Let the missing value in Y-series be a. Then the mean $\bar{y}$ is given by :

$$\bar{y} = \frac{\Sigma Y}{n} = \frac{9 + 11 + a + 8 + 7}{5} = \frac{35 + a}{5} = 8 \text{ (given)}$$

$$\Rightarrow \quad 35 + a = 5 \times 8 = 40 \quad \Rightarrow \quad a = 40 - 35 = 5$$

CALCULATION OF CORRELATION COEFFICIENT

X	Y	$X - \overline{X} = X - 6$	$(Y - \overline{Y}) = Y - 8$	$(X - \overline{X})^2$	$(Y - \overline{Y})^2$	$(X - \overline{X})(Y - \overline{Y})$
6	9	0	1	0	1	0
2	11	– 4	3	16	9	– 12
10	5	4	– 3	16	9	– 12
4	8	– 2	0	4	0	0
8	7	2	– 1	4	1	– 2
$\Sigma X = 30$	$\Sigma Y = 40$	0	0	$\Sigma(X - \overline{X})^2 = 40$	$\Sigma(Y - \overline{Y})^2 = 20$	$\Sigma(X - \overline{X})(Y - \overline{Y}) = -26$

We have $\quad \overline{X} = \frac{\Sigma X}{5} = \frac{30}{5} = 6, \quad \overline{Y} = \frac{\Sigma Y}{5} = \frac{40}{5} = 8$

Karl Pearson's correlation coefficient is given by :

$$r = \frac{\text{Cov}(X, Y)}{\sigma_x \sigma_y} = \frac{\Sigma(X - \overline{X})(Y - \overline{Y})}{\sqrt{\Sigma(X - \overline{X})^2 \, \Sigma(Y - \overline{Y})^2}} = \frac{-26}{\sqrt{40 \times 20}} = \frac{-26}{\sqrt{800}} = \frac{-26}{28 \cdot 2843} = -0 \cdot 9192 \simeq -0 \cdot 92$$

Example 8·4. *Calculate the coefficient of correlation between X and Y series from the following data :*

	Series X	*Series Y*
No. of pairs of observations	*15*	*15*
Arithmetic mean	*25*	*18*
Standard deviation	*3·01*	*3·03*
Sum of squares of deviations from mean	*136*	*138*

Summation of product deviations of X and Y series from their respective arithmetic means = 122.

Solution. In the usual notations, we are given :

$$n = 15, \quad \bar{x} = 25, \quad \bar{y} = 18, \quad \sigma_x = 3 \cdot 01, \quad \sigma_y = 3 \cdot 03$$

$$\Sigma(x - \bar{x})^2 = 136, \quad \Sigma(y - \bar{y})^2 = 138, \quad \text{and} \quad \Sigma (x - \bar{x})(y - \bar{y}) = 122.$$

Karl Pearson's correlation coefficient between X-series and Y-series is given by

$$r = \frac{\Sigma (x - \bar{x})(y - \bar{y})}{n \, \sigma_x \, \sigma_y} = \frac{122}{15 \times 3 \cdot 01 \times 3 \cdot 03} = \frac{122}{136 \cdot 8049} = 0 \cdot 8918$$

Remark. Here some of the given data are superfluous *viz.*, $\bar{x}$, $\bar{y}$, $\Sigma(x - \bar{x})^2$, $\Sigma(y - \bar{y})^2$.

Aliter. We may also compute the correlation coefficient using the formula

$$r = \frac{\Sigma(x - \bar{x})(y - \bar{y})}{\sqrt{\Sigma(x - \bar{x})^2 \, \Sigma(y - \bar{y})^2}} = \frac{122}{\sqrt{136 \times 138}} = \frac{122}{\sqrt{18768}} = \frac{122}{136 \cdot 9964} = 0 \cdot 8905$$

If we use this formula, then the data relating to n, $\bar{x}$, $\bar{y}$, σ_x and σ_y are superfluous.

Example 8·5. *The coefficient of correlation between two variables X and Y is 0·48. The covariance is 36. The variance of X is 16. Find the standard deviation of Y.*

Solution. We are given :

$$r_{xy} = 0 \cdot 48, \; \text{Cov}(X, Y) = 36, \; \sigma_x^2 = 16 \quad \Rightarrow \quad \sigma_x = 4$$

We have : $\quad r_{xy} = \frac{\text{Cov}(X, Y)}{\sigma_x \sigma_y} \quad \Rightarrow \quad \sigma_y = \frac{\text{Cov}(X, Y)}{\sigma_x \, r_{xy}} = \frac{36}{4 \times 0 \cdot 48} = \frac{9}{0 \cdot 48} = 18 \cdot 75.$

Example 8·6. *Given the following information :*
$r_{xy} = 0{\cdot}8$, $\sum xy = 60$, $\sigma_y = 2{\cdot}5$ *and* $\sum x^2 = 90$, *where x and y are the deviations from the respective means, find the number of items (n).* [Delhi Univ. B.Com. (Hons.), 2002]

Solution. We have : $\sigma_x^2 = \frac{1}{n}\sum(X-\overline{X})^2 = \frac{1}{n}\sum x^2 = \frac{90}{n}$ $\quad (\because X - \overline{X} = x)$

$$r = \frac{\sum(X-\overline{X})(Y-\overline{Y})}{n\,\sigma_X\,\sigma_Y} = \frac{\sum xy}{n\sigma_x\sigma_y} \qquad [\because X-\overline{X}=x\ ;\ Y-\overline{Y}=y\ ;\ \sigma_X=\sigma_x, \sigma_Y=\sigma_y]$$

$$\Rightarrow \quad 0{\cdot}8 = \frac{60}{n\sqrt{\frac{90}{n}}\,.\,(2{\cdot}5)} = \frac{60\times 2}{\sqrt{n}\sqrt{90}\times 5} = \frac{24}{\sqrt{n}\sqrt{90}} \Rightarrow n = \frac{24\times 24}{90\times 0{\cdot}8\times 0{\cdot}8} = 10.$$

Example 8.7. *The covariance of two perfectly correlated variables X and Y is 96. Determine σ_X and σ_Y if it is known that variance of X and that of Y is in the ratio of 4 : 9*
[Delhi Univ. B.A. (Econ. Hons.), 2008]

Solution. We are given : Cov $(X, Y) = 96$ ...(1) ; $\frac{\sigma_X^2}{\sigma_Y^2} = \frac{4}{9} \Rightarrow \frac{\sigma_X}{\sigma_Y} = \frac{2}{3} \Rightarrow \sigma_X = \frac{2}{3}\sigma_Y$ ...(2)

The correlation coefficient $r = r(X, Y)$ is given by

$$r = \frac{\text{Cov}(X, Y)}{\sigma_X\sigma_Y} = \frac{96}{\frac{2}{3}\sigma_Y\,.\,\sigma_Y} = \frac{144}{\sigma_Y^2} \qquad \text{[From (1) and (2)]} \quad ...(3)$$

For perfectly correlated variables, we have $r = r(X, Y) = \pm 1$. But since Cov $(X, Y) = 96 > 0$, r is also positive. Hence $r = +1$.

Substituting in (3), we get ; $1 = \frac{144}{\sigma_Y^2} \Rightarrow \sigma_Y^2 = 144 \Rightarrow \sigma_Y = 12$

Substituting in (2), we get : $\sigma_X = \frac{2}{3}\sigma_Y = \frac{2}{3}\times 12 = 8$

$\therefore \quad \sigma_X = 8, \quad \sigma_Y = 12.$

Example 8.8. *Given below is the information relating to marks in Statistics (X) and marks in Accountancy (Y) obtained by the students of a class.*

Covariance between X and Y = 144 ; Second moment of X about 20 = 244;
First moment of X about 20 = 10 ; Arithmetic mean of Y = 45
Correlation coefficient between X and Y = 0·75.

Calculate coefficient of variation of marks of Statistics and that of marks of Accountancy. In which subject the performance of students is more consistent ? [Delhi Univ. B.Com. (Hons.), (External). 2005]

Solution. We are given : Cov $(X, Y) = 144$; $r_{XY} = 0.75$; $\overline{Y} = 45$ ...(*i*)

μ_1' = First moment of X about '20' = 10 $\Rightarrow \overline{X} = A + \mu_1' = 20 + 10 = 30$ ...(*ii*)

μ_2' = Second moment of X about '20' = 244 $\Rightarrow \mu_2 = \mu_2' - \mu_1'^2 = 244 - 100 = 144$ (*iii*)

$\therefore \quad \sigma_X^2 = \mu_2 = 144 \Rightarrow \sigma_X = \sqrt{144} = 12$ ...(*iv*)

$$r_{XY} = \frac{\text{Cov}(X, Y)}{\sigma_X\,\sigma_Y} \Rightarrow 0{\cdot}75 = \frac{144}{12\,\sigma_Y} \Rightarrow \sigma_Y = \frac{12}{(3/4)} = 16 \quad ...(v)$$

The coefficient of variation (*C.V.*) of marks of Statistics and Accountancy are given by :

$$C.V.\text{ (Statistics)} = C.V.(X) = \frac{\sigma_X}{\overline{X}}\times 100 = \frac{12}{30}\times 100 = 40 \qquad \text{[From (iii) and (iv)]}$$

$$C.V.\text{ (Accountancy)} = C.V.(Y) = \frac{\sigma_Y}{\overline{Y}}\times 100 = \frac{16}{45}\times 100 = 35{\cdot}55 \qquad \text{[From (i) and (v)]}$$

Since *C.V.* (*Y*) < *C.V.* (*X*), the performance of the students is more consistent in accountancy.

Example 8·9. *A computer while calculating correlation coefficient between two variables X and Y from 25 pairs of observations obtained the following results :*

$$n = 25,\quad \Sigma X = 125,\quad \Sigma X^2 = 650,\quad \Sigma Y = 100,\quad \Sigma Y^2 = 460,\quad \Sigma XY = 508$$

It was, however, discovered at the time of checking that two pairs of observations were not correctly copied. They were taken as (6, 14) and (8, 6) while the correct values were (8, 12) and (6, 8). Prove that the correct value of the correlation coefficient should be 2 / 3. [*Delhi Univ. B.Com. (Hons.) 2008*]

Solution.

Corrected $\Sigma X = 125 - 6 - 8 + 8 + 6 = 125$; Corrected $\Sigma Y = 100 - 14 - 6 + 12 + 8 = 100$

Corrected $\Sigma X^2 = 650 - 6^2 - 8^2 + 8^2 + 6^2 = 650$; Corrected $\Sigma Y^2 = 460 - 14^2 - 6^2 + 12^2 + 8^2 = 436$

Corrected $\Sigma XY = 508 - 6 \times 14 - 8 \times 6 + 8 \times 12 + 6 \times 8 = 520$

Corrected value of r is given by :

$$r = \frac{n\Sigma XY - (\Sigma X)(\Sigma Y)}{\sqrt{[n\Sigma X^2 - (\Sigma X)^2] \times [n\Sigma Y^2 - (\Sigma Y)^2]}} = \frac{25 \times 520 - 125 \times 100}{\sqrt{[25 \times 650 - (125)^2] \times [25 \times 436 - (100)^2]}}$$

$$= \frac{13000 - 12500}{\sqrt{(16255 - 15625) \times (10900 - 10000)}} = \frac{500}{\sqrt{625 \times 900}} = \frac{500}{25 \times 30} = \frac{2}{3}$$

8·4·1. Properties of Correlation Coefficient

Property I. Limits for Correlation Coefficient

Pearsonian correlation coefficient can not exceed 1 numerically. In other words it lies between –1 and +1. Symbolically,

$$-1 \le r \le 1 \qquad \ldots(8 \cdot 6)$$

Remarks 1. This result provides us a check on our calculations. If in any problem, the obtained value of r lies outside the limits $\pm$ 1, this implies that there is some mistake in our calculations.

2. $r = +1$ implies perfect positive correlation between the variables and $r = -1$ implies perfect negative correlation between the variables.

Property II. *Correlation coefficient is independent of the change of origin and scale.* Mathematically, if X and Y are the given variables and they are transformed to the new variables U and V by the change of origin and scale *viz.*,

$$u = \frac{x - A}{h} \quad \text{and} \quad v = \frac{y - B}{k};\ h > 0,\ k > 0 \qquad \ldots(8 \cdot 7)$$

where A, B, h and k are constants, $h > 0, k > 0$, then the correlation coefficient between x and y is same as the correlation coefficient between u and v *i.e.,*

$$r(x, y) = r(u, v) \quad \Rightarrow \quad r_{xy} = r_{uv} \qquad \ldots(8 \cdot 7a)$$

Remark. This is one of the very important properties of the correlation coefficient and is extremely helpful in numerical computation of r. We had already stated [*c.f.* Remark to § 8·4] that formulae (8·3) and (8·5) become quite tedious to use in numerical problems if $\bar{x}$ and /or $\bar{y}$ are in fractions or if x and y are large. In such cases we can conveniently change the origin and scale (if possible) in X or/and Y to get new variables U and V and compute the correlation between U and V by the formula

$$r_{uv} = \frac{\Sigma(u - \bar{u})(v - \bar{v})}{\sqrt{\Sigma(u - \bar{u})^2 . \Sigma(v - \bar{v})^2}} = \frac{n\Sigma uv - (\Sigma u)(\Sigma v)}{\sqrt{[n\Sigma u^2 - (\Sigma u)^2][n\Sigma v^2 - (\Sigma v)^2]}} \qquad \ldots(8 \cdot 7b)$$

Now using the property II, we finally get : $r_{xy} = r_{uv}$.

Property III. *Two independent variables are uncorrelated but the converse is not true.*

Proof. We have proved in (8·4) that

$$\text{Cov}(x, y) = \frac{1}{n}\Sigma xy - \bar{x} . \bar{y} = E(xy) - E(x)E(y), \qquad \ldots(*)$$

because expected value of a variable is nothing but its arithmetic mean. [See Chapter 13 on Expectation].

If x and y are independent variables then [*c.f.* Chapter 13 on Expectation],

$$E(x \,.\, y) = E(x)E(y)$$

Substituting in (*), we get

$$\text{Cov}(x, y) = E(x)E(y) - E(x)E(y) = 0$$

Hence, if x and y are independent then

$$r_{xy} = \frac{\text{Cov}(x, y)}{\sigma_x \sigma_y} = \frac{0}{\sigma_x \sigma_y} = 0$$

$\Rightarrow$ Independent variables are uncorrelated.

Converse. However, the converse of the theorem is not true *i.e.,* uncorrelated variables need not necessarily be independent. As an illustration consider the following bivariate distribution.

x	-4	-3	-2	-1	1	2	3	4	$\Sigma x = 0$
y	16	9	4	1	1	4	9	16	$\Sigma y = 60$
xy	-64	-27	-8	-1	1	8	27	64	$\Sigma xy = 0$

$$\therefore \quad r_{xy} = \frac{n\Sigma xy - (\Sigma x)(\Sigma y)}{\sqrt{n\Sigma x^2 - (\Sigma x)^2}\,\sqrt{n\Sigma y^2 - (\Sigma y)^2}} = \frac{8 \times 0 - 0 \times 60}{\sqrt{n\Sigma x^2 - (\Sigma x)^2}\sqrt{n\Sigma y^2 - (\Sigma y)^2}} = 0,$$

because zero divided by any finite quantity is zero. Hence, in the above example the variables x and y are uncorrelated. But if we examine the data carefully, we find that x and y are not independent but are connected by the relation $y = x^2$. The above example illustrates that uncorrelated variables need not be independent.

Remarks 1. One should not be confused with the words of uncorrelation and independence. $r_{xy} = 0$ *i.e., uncorrelation between the variables x and y simply implies the absence of any linear (straight line) relationship between them.* They may, however, be related in some other form (other than straight line) *e.g.,* quadratic (as we have seen in the above example), logarithmic or trigonometric form.

2. Some more properties of the correlation coefficient will be discussed in the next chapter on Regression Analysis.

Property IV.

$$r(aX + b, cY + d) = \frac{a \times c}{|a \times c|} \cdot r(X, Y) \qquad \ldots(8.8)$$

where $|a \times c|$ is the modulus value of $a \times c$.

Remarks 1. Since correlation coefficient is independent of change of origin, we get :

$$r(aX + b, cY + d) = r(aX, cY) = \frac{a \times c}{|a \times c|} \cdot r(X, Y).$$

2. Some Results on Covariance. If $U = aX + b$ and $V = CY + d$, then

$$\text{Cov}(U, V) = ac \,.\, \text{Cov}(X, Y)$$

$$\Rightarrow \quad \text{Cov}[aX + b \;,\; CY + d] = ac.\, \text{Cov}(X, Y) \qquad \ldots(i)$$

In particular, taking $b = 0 = d$, in (*i*) we get; $\text{Cov}(aX, cY) = ac.\, \text{Cov}(X, Y)$ ... (*ii*)

Taking $a = c = 1$ in (*i*), we get : $\text{Cov}(X + b, Y + d) = \text{Cov}(X, Y)$ ...(*iii*)

The above results can be restated as follows :

$$\left.\begin{aligned} \text{Cov}(X + A, Y + B) &= \text{Cov}(X, Y) \\ \text{Cov}(AX, BY) &= AB \,.\, \text{Cov}(X, Y) \\ \text{Cov}(AX + C, BY + D) &= AB\, \text{Cov}(X, Y) \end{aligned}\right\} \qquad \ldots(8.9)$$

where A, B, C and D are constants.

Property V. If the variables x and y are connected by the linear equation $ax + by + c = 0$, then the correlation coefficient between x and y is $(+1)$ if the signs of a and b are different and (-1) if the signs of a and b are alike.

Symbolically, if $ax + by + c = 0$, then

$$r = r(x, y) = \begin{cases} +1, & \text{if } a \text{ and } b \text{ are of opposite signs} \\ -1, & \text{if a and } b \text{ are of same sign} \end{cases}$$

Example 8·10. *The total of the multiplication of deviation of X and Y = 3044. No. of pairs of the observations is 10. Total of deviations of X = – 170. Total of deviations of Y = – 20. Total of the squares of deviations of X = 8288. Total of the squares of deviations of Y = 2264.*

Find out the coefficient of correlation when the arbitrary means of X and Y are 82 and 68 respectively.

[*Delhi Univ. B.Com. (Pass), 2001*]

Solution. Let $U = X - 82$ and $V = Y - 68$. Then we are given :

$$n = 10,\ \Sigma UV = 3044,\quad \Sigma U = -170,\quad \Sigma V = -20,\quad \Sigma U^2 = 8288,\quad \Sigma V^2 = 2264.$$

Since the correlation coefficient (r) is independent of change of origin, we have

$$r(X, Y) = r(U, V) = \frac{n\,\Sigma UV - (\Sigma U)(\Sigma V)}{\sqrt{[n\,\Sigma U^2 - (\Sigma U)^2]\,[n\,\Sigma V^2 - (\Sigma V)^2]}}$$

$$= \frac{10 \times 3044 - (-170)(-20)}{\sqrt{[10 \times 8288 - (-170)^2][10 \times 2264 - (-20)^2]}} = \frac{30440 - 3400}{\sqrt{82880 - 28900}\,\sqrt{22640 - 400}}$$

$$= \frac{27040}{\sqrt{53980}\,\sqrt{22240}} = \frac{27040}{232{\cdot}34 \times 149{\cdot}13} = \frac{27040}{34648{\cdot}86} = +\,0{\cdot}78$$

Example 8·11. *Calculate correlation coefficient r(x, y) from the following data :*

$$n = 10,\quad \Sigma x = 140,\quad \Sigma y = 150,\quad \Sigma(x - 10)^2 = 180,\quad \Sigma(y - 15)^2 = 215,\quad \Sigma(x - 10)(y - 15) = 60$$

[*Delhi Univ. B.Com. (Hons.), 2007*]

Solution. Let us take $u = x - 10$ and $v = y - 15$. Then, we have

$$\Sigma u = \Sigma(x - 10) = \Sigma x - 10 \times n = 140 - 100 = 40$$

$$\Sigma v = \Sigma(y - 15) = \Sigma y - 15 \times n = 150 - 150 = 0$$

$$\Sigma u^2 = \Sigma(x - 10)^2 = 180\ ;\quad \Sigma v^2 = \Sigma(y - 15)^2 = 215\ ;\quad \Sigma uv = \Sigma(x - 10)(y - 15) = 60$$

$$\therefore \quad r_{xy} = r_{uv} = \frac{n\,\Sigma uv - (\Sigma u)(\Sigma v)}{\sqrt{[n\,\Sigma u^2 - (\Sigma u)^2]\,[n\,\Sigma v^2 - (\Sigma v)^2]}}$$

$$= \frac{10 \times 60 - 40 \times 0}{\sqrt{[10 \times 180 - (40)^2][10 \times 215 - 0]}} = \frac{600}{\sqrt{200 \times 2150}} = \frac{6}{\sqrt{43}} = \frac{6}{6{\cdot}557} = 0{\cdot}915.$$

Example 8·12. *Calculate the coefficient of correlation for the ages of husbands and wives :*

Age of Husband (years)	*23,*	*27,*	*28*	*29,*	*30,*	*31,*	*33,*	*35,*	*36,*	*39*
Age of Wife (years)	*18,*	*22,*	*23,*	*24,*	*25,*	*26,*	*28,*	*29,*	*30,*	*32*

Solution.

CALCULATIONS FOR CORRELATION COEFFICIENT

x	y	$u = x - 31$	$v = y - 25$	u^2	v^2	uv
23	18	– 8	–7	64	49	56
27	22	– 4	–3	16	9	12
28	23	–3	–2	9	4	6
29	24	–2	–1	4	1	2
30	25	–1	0	1	0	0
31	26	0	1	0	1	0
33	28	2	3	4	9	6
35	29	4	4	16	16	16
36	30	5	5	25	25	25
39	32	8	7	64	49	56
$\Sigma x = 311$	$\Sigma y = 257$	$\Sigma u = 1$	$\Sigma v = 7$	$\Sigma u^2 = 203$	$\Sigma v^2 = 163$	$\Sigma uv = 179$

Karl Pearson's correlation coefficient between U and V is given by

$$r_{uv} = \frac{n\Sigma uv - (\Sigma u)(\Sigma v)}{\sqrt{[n\Sigma u^2 - (\Sigma u)^2][n\Sigma v^2 - (\Sigma v)^2]}} = \frac{10\times179 - 1\times7}{\sqrt{[10\times203-(1)^2][10\times163-(7)^2]}}$$

$$= \frac{1790-7}{\sqrt{(2030-1)(1630-49)}} = \frac{1783}{\sqrt{2029\times1581}} = \frac{1783}{45\cdot04\times39\cdot76} = \frac{1783}{1790\cdot79} = 0\cdot9956.$$

Since Karl Pearson's correlation coefficient (r) is independent of change of origin, we get

$$r_{xy} = r_{uv} = 0\cdot9956.$$

Note. It may be noted that the values of x and y, except for the last three pairs, are connected by the linear relation : $y = x - 5$. Further, as the value of x decreases (increases), the value of y also decreases (increases). Hence, we may expect a very high degree of positive correlation (almost perfect) with the value of r approaching + 1.

Example 8·13. *Find Karl Pearson's coefficient of correlation between sales and expenses of the following ten firms :*

Firm	*1*	*2*	*3*	*4*	*5*	*6*	*7*	*8*	*9*	*10*
Sales ('000 units)	*50*	*50*	*55*	*60*	*65*	*65*	*65*	*60*	*60*	*50*
Expenses ('000 rupees)	*11*	*13*	*14*	*16*	*16*	*15*	*15*	*14*	*13*	*13*

Solution. Let sales (in thousand units) of a firm be denoted by X and expenses (in '000 rupees) be denoted by Y. It may be noted that we can take out factor 5 common in X series. Hence, it will be convenient to change the scale also in X. Taking 65 and 13 as working means for X and Y respectively, let us take :

$$u = (x - 65)/5 \quad ; \quad v = y - 13.$$

CALCULATIONS FOR CORRELATION COEFFICIENT

Firms	x	y	$u = \frac{x-65}{5}$	$v = y - 13$	u^2	v^2	uv
1	50	11	– 3	– 2	9	4	6
2	50	13	– 3	0	9	0	0
3	55	14	– 2	1	4	1	– 2
4	60	16	– 1	3	1	9	– 3
5	65	16	0	3	0	9	0
6	65	15	0	2	0	4	0
7	65	15	0	2	0	4	0
8	60	14	– 1	1	1	1	– 1
9	60	13	– 1	0	1	0	0
10	50	13	– 3	0	9	0	0
	$\Sigma x = 580$	$\Sigma y = 140$	$\Sigma u = -14$	$\Sigma v = 10$	$\Sigma u^2 = 34$	$\Sigma v^2 = 32$	$\Sigma uv = 0$

Karl Pearson's correlation coefficient between u and v is given by

$$r_{uv} = \frac{n\Sigma uv - (\Sigma u)(\Sigma v)}{\sqrt{[n\Sigma u^2 - (\Sigma u)^2][n\Sigma v^2 - (\Sigma v)^2]}} = \frac{10\times0-(-14)\times(10)}{\sqrt{[10\times34-(-14)^2]\times[10\times32-(10)^2]}}$$

$$= \frac{140}{\sqrt{(340-196)\times(320-100)}} = \frac{140}{\sqrt{144\times220}} = \frac{140}{\sqrt{31680}} = \frac{140}{177\cdot99} = 0\cdot7866.$$

Since correlation coefficient is independent of change of origin and scale, we finally have :

$$r_{xy} = r_{uv} = 0\cdot7866.$$

Aliter. We have : $\bar{x} = \frac{\Sigma x}{n} = \frac{580}{10} = 58 \quad ; \quad \bar{y} = \frac{\Sigma y}{n} = \frac{140}{10} = 14.$

Since $\bar{x}$ and $\bar{y}$ are integers, it will be convenient to compute r by taking the deviations from means directly, *i.e.*, by taking :

$$dx = x - \bar{x} = x - 58 \; ; \; dy = y - \bar{y} = y - 14,$$ and use the formula (8·3a). [Try it.]

Example 8·14. *Find Karl Pearson's coefficient of correlation between the age and the playing habit of the people from the following information. Also mention what does your calculated 'r' indicate.*

Age group (years)	*No. of people*	*No. of players*
15 and less than 20	*200*	*150*
20 and less than 25	*270*	*162*
25 and less than 30	*340*	*170*
30 and less than 35	*360*	*180*
35 and less than 40	*400*	*180*
40 and less than 45	*300*	*120*

[*Delhi Univ. B.Com. (Hons.), (External), 2006; Delhi Univ. B.Com. (Pass), 2002*]

Solution. We want to find Karl Pearson's correlation coefficient between the age and the playing habit of the people. To do this, we first express the number of players in each age group on a common base *i.e.,* we find the number of players out of a fixed number of persons (a common base) which may be taken as 100 or 1000 or some other convenient figure. Here we express the number of players as a percentage of the total people in each age group.

Now we compute Karl Pearson's correlation coefficient between age (x) and the percentage of players in each age group (y).

Age group (yrs.) (*1*)	No. of people (2)	No. of players (3)	Percentage of players (y) (4) $= \frac{(3)}{(2)} \times 100$
15—20	200	150	$\frac{150}{200} \times 100 = 75$
20—25	270	162	$\frac{162}{270} \times 100 = 60$
25—30	340	170	$\frac{170}{340} \times 100 = 50$
30—35	360	180	$\frac{180}{360} \times 100 = 50$
35—40	400	180	$\frac{180}{400} \times 100 = 45$
40—45	300	120	$\frac{120}{300} \times 100 = 40$

CALCULATIONS FOR CORRELATION COEFFICIENT

Age-group	*Mid-value* (x)	y	$u = \frac{x - 27{\cdot}5}{5}$	$v = \frac{y - 50}{5}$	u^2	v^2	uv
15—20	17·5	75	– 2	5	4	25	– 10
20—25	22·5	60	– 1	2	1	4	– 2
25—30	27·5	50	0	0	0	0	0
30—35	32·5	50	1	0	1	0	0
35—40	37·5	45	2	– 1	4	1	– 2
40—45	42·5	40	3	– 2	9	4	– 6
Total			$\Sigma u = 3$	$\Sigma v = 4$	$\Sigma u^2 = 19$	$\Sigma v^2 = 34$	$\Sigma uv = -20$

Since correlation coefficient is independent of change of origin and scale we have :

$$r_{xy} = r_{uv} = \frac{n\Sigma uv - (\Sigma u)(\Sigma v)}{\sqrt{[n\Sigma u^2 - (\Sigma u)^2] \cdot [n\Sigma v^2 - (\Sigma v)^2]}} = \frac{6 \times (-20) - (3) \times (4)}{\sqrt{[6 \times 19 - (3)^2] \cdot [6 \times 34 - (4)^2]}}$$

$$= \frac{-120 - 12}{\sqrt{(114 - 9) \times (204 - 16)}} = \frac{-132}{\sqrt{105 \times 118}} = \frac{-132}{\sqrt{19740}} = \frac{-132}{140{\cdot}4991} = -0{\cdot}9395.$$

Thus, we conclude that there is a very high degree of negative correlation, (almost perfect negative correlation) between age (x) and playing habit (y). This implies that with advancement in age, the people's interest in playing goes on decreasing and the scatter diagram of the (x, y) values gives points clustering almost around a straight line starting from left top and going to right bottom.

Example 8·15. (*i*) *Compute the correlation coefficient between the corresponding values of X and Y in the following table :*

X	*2*	*4*	*5*	*6*	*8*	*11*
Y	*18*	*12*	*10*	*8*	*7*	*5*

(ii) Multiply each X value in the table by 2 and add 6. Multiply each value of Y in the table by 3 and subtract 15. Find the correlation coefficient between the two new sets of values. Explain why you do or do not obtain the same result as in (i).

Solution. *(i)*

COMPUTATION OF CORRELATION COEFFICIENT

X	Y	$X-\overline{X}=X-6$	$Y-\overline{Y}=Y-10$	$(X-\overline{X})^2$	$(Y-\overline{Y})^2$	$(X-\overline{X})(Y-\overline{Y})$
2	18	−4	8	16	64	−32
4	12	−2	2	4	4	−4
5	10	−1	0	1	0	0
6	8	0	−2	0	4	0
8	7	2	−3	4	9	−6
11	5	5	−5	25	25	−25
$\Sigma X=36$	$\Sigma Y=60$	$\Sigma(X-\overline{X})=0$	$\Sigma(Y-\overline{Y})=0$	$\Sigma(X-\overline{X})^2=50$	$\Sigma(Y-\overline{Y})^2=106$	$\Sigma(X-\overline{X})(Y-\overline{Y})=-67$

We have : $\overline{X}=\frac{1}{6}\Sigma X=\frac{36}{6}=6,$ and $\overline{Y}=\frac{1}{6}\Sigma Y=\frac{60}{6}=10$

Hence the correlation coefficient between X and Y is given by :

$$r_{xy}=\frac{\Sigma(X-\overline{X})(Y-\overline{Y})}{[\Sigma(X-\overline{X})^2\,\Sigma(Y-\overline{Y})^2]^{1/2}}=\frac{-67}{\sqrt{50\times 106}}=\frac{-67}{\sqrt{5300}}=\frac{-67}{72\cdot 81}=-0\cdot 92$$

Hence, the variables X and Y are highly *negatively* correlated.

(ii) Let us define new variables U and V as : $U=2X+6$ and $V=3Y-15$

We are now required to find the correlation coefficient between the new sets of values of variables U and V as given in the following table.

COMPUTATION OF CORRELATION COEFFICIENT BETWEEN U AND V

X	Y	$U=2X+6$	$V=3Y-15$	U^2	V^2	UV
2	18	10	39	100	1521	390
4	12	14	21	196	441	294
5	10	16	15	256	225	240
6	8	18	9	324	81	162
8	7	22	6	484	36	132
11	5	28	0	784	0	0
Totals		$\Sigma U=108$	$\Sigma V=90$	$\Sigma U^2=2144$	$\Sigma V^2=2304$	$\Sigma UV=1218$

$$\therefore\quad r_{uv}=\frac{n\Sigma UV-(\Sigma U)(\Sigma V)}{\sqrt{n\Sigma U^2-(\Sigma U)^2}\sqrt{n\Sigma V^2-(\Sigma V)^2}}=\frac{6\times 1218-108\times 90}{\sqrt{6\times 2144-(108)^2}\times\sqrt{6\times 2304-(90)^2}}$$

$$=\frac{7308-9720}{\sqrt{(12864-11664)(13824-8100)}}=\frac{-2412}{\sqrt{1200\times 5724}}=\frac{-2412}{\sqrt{6868800}}=\frac{-2412}{2620\cdot 8395}=-0\cdot 92$$

Example 8·16. *If the relation between two random variables x and y is 2x + 3y = 4, then the correlation coefficient between them is :*

(i) – 2/3, (ii) 1, (iii) – 1, (iv) none of these.

[I.C.W.A. (Intermediate), June 2000]

Solution. Since x and y are connected by the linear relation :

$$2x+3y=4 \quad\Rightarrow\quad y=-\frac{2}{3}x+\frac{4}{3}, \qquad \ldots (*)$$

there is perfect correlation between x and y, *i.e.*, $r=\pm 1$. Further from (*), we observe that as x increases, y decreases. Hence, there is perfect negative correlation between x and y.

$\therefore \quad r=-1 \quad\Rightarrow$ *(iii)* is the correct answer.

Aliter. If x and y are connected by the linear relation $ax + by + c = 0$, then

$$r = r(x, y) = \begin{cases} +1, & \text{if } a \text{ and } b \text{ have opposite signs.} \\ -1, & \text{if } a \text{ and } b \text{ have same sign.} \end{cases}$$

We are given $2x + 3y = 4$. Since $a = 2$ and $b = 3$, have the same sign, $r = r(x, y) = -1$.

Example 8·17. *For the bivariate data* $[(x, y)] = [(20, 5), (21, 4), (22, 3)]$, *the correlation coefficient between x and y is :*

(i) 0, (ii) 1, (iii) – 1, (iv) 0·5. *[I.C.W.A. (Intermediate), June 2002]*

Solution. From the given data, we observe that

$$20 + 5 = 25, \quad 21 + 4 = 25 \quad \text{and} \quad 22 + 3 = 25.$$

Thus, x and y are connected by the *linear* relation : $x + y = 25$ ... (*)

$\Rightarrow$ There is *perfect correlation between x and y* $\Rightarrow$ $r = \pm 1$ ... (**)

From (*), we get $y = 25 - x$

$\therefore$ As x increases, y decreases (by the same amount).

$\Rightarrow$ *x and y are negatively correlated* ... (***)

From (**) and (***), we conclude that $r = r(X, Y) = -1$.

Aliter. We can compute the value of $r(X, Y)$ from the given data by using the formula. This is left as an exercise to the reader.

Example 8·18. *(a) The correlation coefficient between two variables X and Y is found to be 0·4. What is the correlation between 2x and (– y) ?* *[Delhi Univ. B.A. (Econ., Hons.), 1997]*

(b) "If the correlation coefficient between two variables x and y is positive, then the coefficient of correlation between – x and – y is also positive" Comment. *[Delhi Univ. B.A. (Econ. Hons.), 1996]*

Solution. (*a*) We are given : $r(x, y) = 0{\cdot}4$ ... (*i*)

We know that : $r(aX, cY) = \dfrac{a \times c}{|a| \times |c|} \cdot r(X, Y)$ ... (*)

Using (*) and (*i*), we get :

$$r(2x, -y) = r(2x, -1\cdot y) = \frac{2 \times (-1)}{|2| \times |-1|}\, r(x, y) = \frac{-2 \times 0{\cdot}4}{2 \times 1} = -0{\cdot}4$$

(*b*) We are given : $r(x, y) > 0$... (*ii*)

Using (*), we get

$$r(-x, -y) = r(-1.x, -1.y) = \frac{(-1) \times (-1)}{|-1| \times |-1|} \cdot r(x, y) = r(x, y)$$

Hence, if $r(x, y)$ is positive, then $r(-x, -y)$ is also positive.

8·4·2. Assumptions Underlying Karl Pearson's Correlation Coefficient. Pearsonian correlation coefficient r is based on the following assumptions :

(*i*) *The variables X and Y under study are linearly related.* In other words, the scatter diagram of the data will given a straight line curve.

(*ii*) *Each of the variables (series) is being affected by a large number of independent contributory causes of such a nature as to produce normal distribution.* For example, the variables (series) relating to ages, heights, weights, supply, price, etc., conform to this assumption. In the words of Karl Pearson :

"The sizes of the complex organs (something measureable) are determined by a great variety of independent contributing causes, for example, climate, nourishment, physical training and innumerable other causes which cannot be individually observed or their effects measured." Karl Pearson further observes, "The variations in intensity of the contributory causes are small as compared with their absolute intensity and these variations follow the normal law of distribution."

(*iii*) *The forces so operating on each of the variable series are not independent of each other but are related in a causal fashion.* In other words, cause and effect relationship exists between different forces operating on the items of the two variable series. These forces must be common to both the series. If the operating forces are entirely independent of each other and not related in any fashion, then there cannot be any correlation between the variables under study.

For example the correlation coefficient between :

(a) the series of heights and income of individuals over a period of time,

(b) the series of marriage rate and the rate of agricultural production in a country over a period of time,

(c) the series relating to the size of the shoe and intelligence of a group of individuals, should be zero, since the forces affecting the two variable series in each of the above cases are entirely independent of each other.

However, if in any of the above cases the value of r for a given set of data is not zero, then such correlation is termed as *chance correlation* or *spurious* or *non-sense correlation.*

[Also see § 8·1·2.]

8·4·3. Interpretation of r. The following general points may be borne in mind while interpreting an observed value of correlation coefficient r :

(i) $r = +1$ implies that there is perfect positive correlation between the variables. In other words, the scatter diagram will be a straight line starting from left bottom and rising upwards to the right top as shown in Fig. 8·1, § 8·3.

(ii) If $r = -1$, there is perfect negative correlation between the variables. In this case scatter diagram will again be a straight line as shown in Fig. 8·1, § 8·3.

(iii) If $r = 0$, the variables are uncorrelated. In other words, there is no linear (straight line) relationship between the variables. However, $r = 0$ does not imply that the variables are independent [*c.f.* Property III, page 8·11].

(iv) For other values of r lying between + 1 and – 1, there are no set guidelines for its interpretation. The maximum we can conclude is that nearer is the value of r to 1, the closer is the relation between the variables and nearer is the value of r to 0, the less close is the relationship between them. One should be very careful in interpreting the value of r as it is often mis-interpreted.

(v) The reliability or the significance of the value of the correlation coefficient depends on a number of factors. One of the ways of testing the significance of r is finding its probable error [*c.f.* § 8·5], which in addition to the value of r takes into account the size of the sample also.

(vi) Another more useful measure for interpreting the value of r is the coefficient of determination [*c.f.* § 8·9]. It is observed there that *the closeness of the relationship between two variables is not proportional to r.*

8·5. PROBABLE ERROR

After computing the value of the correlation coefficient, the next step is to find the extent to which it is dependable. Probable error of correlation coefficient, usually denoted by *P.E.*(r) is an old measure of testing the reliability of an observed value of correlation coefficient in so far as it depends upon the conditions of random sampling.

If r is the observed correlation coefficient in a sample of n pairs of observations then its standard error, usually denoted by *S.E.* (r) is given by :

$$S.E.(r) = \frac{1 - r^2}{\sqrt{n}} \qquad \ldots (8{\cdot}10)$$

Probable error of the correlation coefficient is given by :

$$P.E.\,(r) = 0{\cdot}6745 \times S.E.\,(r) = 0{\cdot}6745\,\frac{(1 - r^2)}{\sqrt{n}} \qquad \ldots (8{\cdot}11)$$

The reason for taking the factor 0·6745 is that in a normal distribution 50% of the observations lie in the range $\mu \pm 0{\cdot}6745\,\sigma$, where μ is the mean and σ is the *s.d.*

According to Secrist, "The probable error of the correlation coefficient is an amount which if added to and subtracted from the mean correlation coefficient, produces amounts within which the chances are even that a coefficient of correlation from a series selected at random will fall."

Uses of Probable Error

1. The probable error of correlation coefficient may be used to determine the limits within which the population correlation coefficient may be expected to lie.

Limits for population correlation coefficient are

$$r \pm P.E.\ (r) \qquad \ldots (8\cdot12)$$

This implies that if we take another random sample of the same size n from the same population from which the first sample was taken, then the observed value of the correlation coefficient, say, r_1 in the second sample can be expected to lie within the limits given in (8·12).

2. *P.E.* (r) may be used to test if an observed value of sample correlation coefficient is significant of any correlation in the population. The following guidelines may be used :

(*i*) If $r < P.E.\ (r)$ *i.e.*, if the observed value of r is less than its *P.E.*, then correlation is not at all significant.

(*ii*) If $r > 6\ P.E.\ (r)$ *i.e.*, if observed value of r is greater than 6 times its *P.E.*, then r is definitely significant.

(*iii*) In other situations, nothing can be concluded with certainty.

Important Remarks 1. Sometimes, *P.E.* may lead to fallacious conclusions particularly when n, the number of pairs of observations, is small. In order to use *P.E.* effectively, n should be fairly large. However, a rigorous test for testing the significance of an observed sample correlation coefficient is provided by Student's t test.

2. *P.E.* can be used only under the following conditions :

(*i*) The data must have been drawn from a normal population.

(*ii*) The conditions of random sampling should prevail in selecting sampled observations.

Example 8·19. (*a*) *Find Karl Pearson's coefficient of correlation from the following series of marks secured by 10 students in a class test in Mathematics and Statistics :*

Marks in Mathematics.	:	45	70	65	30	90	40	50	75	85	60
Marks in Statistics	:	35	90	70	40	95	40	60	80	80	50

Also calculate its probable error. Assume 60 and 65 as working means.

(*b*) *Hence discuss if the value of r is significant or not. Also compute the limits within which the population correlation coefficient may be expected to lie.*

Solution. (*a*) Let the marks in mathematics be denoted by the variable X and the marks in statistics by the variable Y. It may be noted that we can take out the factor 5 common in each of the X and Y series. Hence, it will be convenient to change the scale also. Taking 60 and 65 as working means for X and Y series respectively, let us take :

$$u = \frac{x - 60}{5} \quad \text{and} \quad v = \frac{y - 65}{5}$$

CALCULATIONS FOR CORRELATION COEFFICIENT

x	y	u	v	u^2	v^2	uv
45	35	−3	−6	9	36	18
70	90	2	5	4	25	10
65	70	1	1	1	1	1
30	40	−6	−5	36	25	30
90	95	6	6	36	36	36
40	40	−4	−5	16	25	20
50	60	−2	−1	4	1	2
75	80	3	3	9	9	9
85	80	5	3	25	9	15
60	50	0	−3	0	9	0
Total :		2	−2	140	176	141

We have :

$$r = \frac{n\Sigma uv - (\Sigma u)(\Sigma v)}{\sqrt{[n\Sigma u^2 - (\Sigma u)^2] \times [n\Sigma v^2 - (\Sigma v)^2]}}$$

$$= \frac{10 \times 141 - 2 \times (-2)}{\sqrt{(10 \times 140 - 4)(10 \times 176 - 4)}}$$

$$= \frac{1414}{\sqrt{1396 \times 1756}}$$

$$\Rightarrow \log r = \log 1414 - \tfrac{1}{2}[\log 1396 + \log 1756]$$

$$= 3\cdot1504 - \tfrac{1}{2}[3\cdot1449 + 3\cdot2445]$$

$$= 3\cdot1504 - \tfrac{1}{2} \times 6\cdot3894$$

$$= 3\cdot1504 - 3\cdot1947 = -0\cdot0443 = \bar{1}\cdot9557$$

$\Rightarrow \quad r = \text{Antilog}\ (\bar{1}\cdot 9557) = 0\cdot 9031 = 0\cdot 9$

$\therefore \quad r_{xy} = r_{uv} \simeq 0\cdot 9.$

Probable Error of Correlation Coefficient is given by :

$$P.E.\ (r) = 0\cdot 6745\ \frac{1-r^2}{\sqrt{n}} = \frac{0\cdot 6745 \times 0\cdot 19}{\sqrt{10}} = \frac{0\cdot 128155}{3\cdot 1623} = 0\cdot 0405.$$

(*b*) **Significance of *r*.** We have

$$r = 0\cdot 9 \quad \text{and} \quad 6\ P.E.\ (r) = 6 \times 0\cdot 0405 = 0\cdot 2430.$$

Since r is much greater than 6 $P.E.$ (r), the value of r is highly significant.

Remark. Since the value of r is significant, it implies that ordinarily, higher the marks of a candidate in Mathematics, higher is his score in Statistics also and lower the marks of a candidate in Mathematics, lower is his score in Statistics also. However, it does not mean that all the students who are good in Mathematics are also good in Statistics and all those students who are poor in Mathematics are also poor in Statistics. It should be clearly borne in mind that "*the coefficient of correlation expresses the relationship between two series and not between the individual items of the series*".

Limits for Population Correlation Coefficient are :

$$r \pm P.E.(r) = 0\cdot 9031 \pm 0\cdot 0405 \quad i.e., \quad 0\cdot 8626 \quad \text{and} \quad 0\cdot 9436.$$

This implies that if we take another sample of size 10 from the same population, then its correlation coefficient can be expected to lie between 0·8626 and 0·9436.

Example 8·20. *Test the significance of correlation for the following values based on the number of observations (i) 10, and (ii) 100, r = + 0·4 and + 0·9.*

Solution. We know that an observed value of r is definitely significant if

$$r > 6\ P.E.(r) \quad \Rightarrow \quad \frac{r}{P.E.(r)} > 6$$

In this case, we have :

No. of observations	*r*	*P.E. (r)*	$\frac{r}{P.E.\ (r)}$	*Significance of r.*
10	0·4	$0\cdot 6745\ \frac{1-(0\cdot 4)^2}{\sqrt{10}} = 0\cdot 18$	$\frac{0\cdot 4}{0\cdot 18} = 2\cdot 22 < 6$	Not significant
100	0·4	$0\cdot 6745\ \frac{1-(0\cdot 4)^2}{\sqrt{100}} = 0\cdot 06$	$\frac{0\cdot 4}{0\cdot 06} = 6\cdot 67 > 6$	Significant
10	0·9	$0\cdot 6745\ \frac{1-(0\cdot 9)^2}{\sqrt{10}} = 0\cdot 04$	$\frac{0\cdot 9}{0\cdot 04} = 22\cdot 5 > 6$	Highly significant
100	0·9	$0\cdot 6745\ \frac{1-(0\cdot 9)^2}{\sqrt{100}} = 0\cdot 128$	$\frac{0\cdot 9}{0\cdot 13} = 7 > 6$	Significant

EXERCISE 8·2

1. Explain the meaning and significance of the concept of correlation. How will you calculate it from statistical point of view.

2. (*a*) Define Karl Pearson's coefficient of correlation. What is it intended to measure ?

(*b*) What are the special characteristics of Karl Pearson's coefficient of correlation ? What are the underlying assumptions on which this formula is based ?

(*c*) How do you interpret a calculated value of Karl Pearson's coefficient of correlation ? Discuss in particular the values of $r = 0$, $r = -1$ and $r = +1$.

3. (*a*) Explain what is meant by coefficient of correlation between two variables. What are the different methods of finding correlation ? Distinguish between Positive and Negative correlation. [*Calicut Univ. B.Com., 1997*]

(*b*) Write down an expression for the Karl Pearson's coefficient of linear correlation. Why is it termed as the coefficient of linear correlation ? Explain. [*Delhi Univ. B.A. (Econ., Hons.), 1997*]

4. Define product moment correlation coefficient between two variables x and y. State its limits. Draw the scatter diagram for the extreme cases.

5. (*a*) If *x* and *y* are independent variates then prove that they are uncorrelated. Is the converse true ? Explain your answer with the help of an example.

(*b*) Prove that two independent variables are uncorrelated. By giving an example, show that the converse is not true. Explain the reason ? [*Guru Nanak Dev Univ. MBA, 1994*]

(*c*) Comment on the following statement :

If the coefficient of correlation between two variables is zero, it does not mean that the variables are unrelated. [*Delhi Univ. B.Com. (Hons.), 2002*]

6. Discuss the statistical validity of the following statements :

(*a*) "High positive coefficient of correlation between increase in the sale of a newspaper and increase in the number of crimes, leads to the conclusion that newspaper reading may be responsible for the increase in the number of crimes."

(*b*) "A high positive value of *r* between the increase in cigarette smoking and increase in lung cancer establishes that cigarette smoking is responsible for lung cancer."

(*c*) If the coefficient of correlation between the annual value of exports during the last ten years and the annual number of children born during the same period is + 0·9, what inference, if any, would you draw ? [*Delhi Univ. B.A. (Econ. Hons.), 1996*]

7. Comment on the following :

(*a*) "Positive correlation $r = 0{\cdot}9$, is found between the number of children born and exports over last decade.". [*Delhi Univ. B.Com. (Hons.), 2001*]

(*b*) The correlation coefficient between the railway accidents in a particular year and the babies born in that year was found to be 0·8.

8. (*a*) Define a scatter diagram. Draw the scatter diagram when (*i*) $r = +1$, (*ii*) $r = -1$ and (*iii*) $r = 0$, where *r* is the correlation coefficient. [*I.C.W.A. (Intermediate), Dec. 2001*]

(*b*) What is a scatter diagram ? Give the procedure of drawing a scatter diagram. Draw scatter diagrams when the coefficient of correlation $r = +1$ and $r = -1$. [*C.A. (Foundation), May 2000*]

9. The production manager of a company maintains that the flow time in days (*y*), depends on the number of operations (*x*) to be performed. The following data give the necessary information :

x :	2	2	3	4	4	5	6	6	7	7
y :	8	13	14	11	20	10	22	26	22	25

Plot a scatter diagram. Calculate the value of the Karl Pearson's Product Moment Correlation Coefficient . [*I.C.W.A. (Intermediate), Dec. 1995*]

Ans. $r(x, y) = 0{\cdot}78$.

10. Making use of the data given below, calculate the coefficient of correlation r_{12}

Case :	*A*	*B*	*C*	*D*	*E*	*F*	*G*	*H*
X_1 :	10	6	9	10	12	13	11	9
X_2 :	9	4	6	9	11	13	8	4

Ans. $r_{12} = 0{\cdot}8958$.

11. Calculate Karl Pearson's coefficient of correlation from the following data, using 20 as the working mean for price and 70 as the working mean for demand :

Price :	14	16	17	18	19	20	21	22	23
Demand :	84	78	70	75	66	67	62	58	60

[*Delhi Univ. B.Com. (Pass), 1999*]

Ans. $r = -0{\cdot}954$.

12. Calculate the Karl Pearson's coefficient of correlation from the following data :

		Percentage of Marks				*Percentage of Marks*	
No.	*Subject*	*First Term*	*Second Term*	*No.*	*Subject*	*First Term*	*Second Term*
1.	Hindi	75	62	5.	Commerce	77	69
2.	English	81	68	6.	Mathematics	81	72
3.	Economics	70	65	7.	Statistics	84	76
4.	Accounts	76	60	8.	Costing	75	72

[*Delhi Univ. B.Com. (Pass), 2000*]

Ans. $r = 0{\cdot}623$.

13. Calculate the Karl Pearson's coefficient of correlation for the following ages of husbands and wives at the time of their marriage :

Age of husband (in years) :	23	27	28	28	28	30	30	33	35	38
Age of wife (in years) :	18	20	22	27	21	29	27	29	28	29

Ans. $r = 0{\cdot}8013$.

14. Calculate the Pearson's coefficient of correlation from the following data using 44 and 26 respectively as the origin of X and Y :

X :	43	44	46	40	44	42	45	42	38	40	42	57
Y :	29	31	19	18	19	27	27	29	41	30	26	10

[*Osmania Univ. B.Com., 1998*]

Ans. $r_{xy} = -0{\cdot}7326$.

15. The following table gives the distribution of the total population and those who are totally or partially blind among them. Find out if there is any relation between age and blindness.

Age (Years) :	0—10	10—20	20—30	30—40	40—50	50—60	60—70	70—80
No. of Persons ('000) :	100	60	40	36	24	11	6	3
Blind :	55	40	40	40	36	22	18	15

Hint. Here we shall find the correlation coefficient between age (X) and the number of blinds per lakh (Y) as given in the following table.

X	5	15	25	35	45	55	65	75
Y	55	67	100	111	150	200	300	500

Ans. $r = 0{\cdot}8982$.

16. With the following data in 6 cities, calculate the coefficient of correlation by Pearson's method between the density of population and the death rate.

Cities	*Area in square miles*	*Population (in '000)*	*No. of deaths*
A	150	30	300
B	180	90	1440
C	100	40	560
D	60	42	840
E	120	72	1224
F	80	24	312

[*C.A. (Intermediate). May 1981*]

Hint. Find r between, Density $= \dfrac{\text{Population}}{\text{Area}}$; and Death Rate $= \dfrac{\text{No. of deaths}}{\text{Population}} \times 1000$.

Ans. $r = 0{\cdot}9876$.

17. Calculate the correlation coefficient from the following data :

X :	12	9	8	10	11	13	7
Y :	14	8	6	9	11	12	3

Let now each value of X be multiplied by 2 and then 6 be added to it. Similarly multiply each value of Y by 3 and subtract 2 from it. What will be the correlation coefficient between the new series of X and Y.

[*C.A. (Foundation), May 1997*]

Ans. Let $U = 2X + 6$, $V = 3Y - 2$. Since correlation coefficient is independent of change of origin and scale,

$$r(U, V) = r(X, Y) = 0{\cdot}9485.$$

18. (*a*) Given : $\Sigma X = 125$, $\Sigma Y = 100$, $\Sigma X^2 = 650$, $\Sigma Y^2 = 436$, $\Sigma XY = 520$ and $n = 25$, obtain the value of Karl Pearson's correlation coefficient $r(X, Y)$.

Ans. 0·67.

19. You are given the following information relating to a frequency distribution comprising of 10 observations.

$\overline{X} = 5{\cdot}5$, $\overline{Y} = 4{\cdot}0$, $\Sigma X^2 = 385$, $\Sigma Y^2 = 192$; $\Sigma(X + Y)^2 = 947$,

Find r_{xy}

[*Punjab Univ. B.Com., 1994*]

Hint. Use $\Sigma(X + Y)^2 = \Sigma X^2 + \Sigma Y^2 + 2\,\Sigma XY$ and find $\Sigma XY = 185$.

Ans. $r(X, Y) = -0{\cdot}681$.

20. A computer while calculating the correlation coefficient between the variables X and Y obtained the following results :

$$N = 30,\ \Sigma X = 120,\ \Sigma X^2 = 600,\ \Sigma Y = 90,\ \Sigma Y^2 = 250,\ \Sigma XY = 356$$

It was, however, later discovered at the time of checking that it had copied down two pairs of observations as :

X	Y
8	10
12	7

while the correct values were,

X	Y
8	12
10	8

Obtain the correct value of the correlation coefficient between X and Y. [*I.C.W.A. Dec., 2003*]

Ans. $r = 0{\cdot}0504$

21. Coefficient of correlation between X and Y for 20 items is 0·3; mean of X is 15 and that of Y 20, standard deviations are 4 and 5 respectively. At the time of calculations one pair ($x = 27$, $y = 30$) was wrongly taken as ($x = 17$, $y = 35$). Find the correct coefficient of correlation. [*Delhi Univ. B.Com. (Hons.), (External), 2007*]

Ans. Correct value of correlation coefficient = 0·5153.

22. In order to find the correlation coefficient between two variables X and Y from 12 pairs of observations, the following calculations were made :

$$\Sigma X = 30,\ \Sigma Y = 5,\ \Sigma X^2 = 670,\ \Sigma Y^2 = 285,\ \Sigma XY = 334$$

On subsequent verification it was found that the pair ($X = 11$, $Y = 4$) was copied wrongly, the correct value being ($X = 10$, $Y = 14$). Find the correct value of correlation coefficient.

Ans. 0·78.

23. What do you understand by the probable error of correlation coefficient ? Explain how it can be used to :

(*i*) Interpret the significance of an observed value of sample correlation coefficient.

(*ii*) Determine the limits for the population correlation coefficient.

24. Calculate the coefficient of correlation and find its probable error from the following data :

X :	7	6	5	4	3	2	1
Y :	18	16	14	12	10	6	8

Ans. $r_{xy} = 0{\cdot}9643$; $P.E.\ (r) = 0{\cdot}0179$.

25. Find Karl Pearson's correlation coefficient between age and playing habit of the following students :

Age (years)	:	15	16	17	18	19	20
No. of students	:	250	200	150	120	100	80
Regular players	:	200	150	90	48	30	12

Also calculate the probable error and point out if coefficient of correlation is significant.

[*Himachal Pradesh Univ. M.B.A. 1998; Delhi Univ. B.Com. (Hons.), 1996*]

Hint. Find r between age (X) and percentage of regular players (Y).

Ans. $r_{xy} = -0{\cdot}9912$; $P.E.(r) = 0{\cdot}0048$; r is highly significant.

26. Calculate Karl Pearson's coefficient of correlation for the following series.

Price (in Rs.)	:	110—111	111—112	112—113	113—114	114—115	115—116
Demand (in kg.)	:	600	640	640	680	700	780
Price (in Rs.)	:	116—117	117—118	118—119			
Demand (in kg.)	:	830	900	1,000			

Also calculate the probable error of the correlation coefficient. From your result can you assert that the demand is correlated with price ?

Hint. Find correlation coefficient between x : Mid-value of price (in Rs.) and y demand (in kg.)

Ans. $r = 0{\cdot}9651$; $P.E.\ (r) = 0{\cdot}0154$.

27. (*a*) A student calculates the value of r as 0·7 when the number of items (n) in the sample is 25. Find the limits within which r lies for another sample from the same universe.

Ans. Required limits for r are 0·767 and 0·633.

(*b*) A student calculates the value of r as 0·7 when the value of N is 5 and concludes that r is highly significant. Is he correct ? [*Delhi Univ. B.Com. (Hons.), 1997*]

Ans. $\dfrac{r}{P.E.(r)} = \dfrac{0{\cdot}7\sqrt{5}}{0{\cdot}6745 \times 0{\cdot}51} = 4{\cdot}55 < 6$. Not significant.

28. The correlation coefficient between Physics and Mathematics final marks for a group of 21 students was computed to be 0·80. Find 95% confidence limits for the coefficient.

Ans. Required limits $= r \pm 1{\cdot}96\ P.E.(r) = 0{\cdot}8 \pm 1{\cdot}96 \times 0{\cdot}05299 = 0{\cdot}6961$ and $0{\cdot}9039$.

29. The deviations from the respective means of X and Y series are given below :

x :	−4	−3	−2	−1	0	1	2	3	4
y :	3	−3	−4	0	4	1	2	−2	−1

Calculate Karl Pearson's coefficient of correlation from the above data. *[Delhi Univ. B.Com. (Pass), 1995]*

Hint. $\text{Cov}(X, Y) = \dfrac{1}{n}\Sigma xy = 0.$

Ans. $r(X,Y) = 0.$

30. Calculate the coefficient correlation between X and Y series from the following data :

	X series	*Y series*
No. of observations	15	15
Arithmetic mean	25	18
Standard deviation	5	5

$\Sigma[(X-25)(Y-18)] = 125.$ *[Delhi Univ. B.Com. (Pass), 1995]*

Ans. $r_{XY} = \dfrac{\Sigma(X-\overline{X})(Y-\overline{Y})}{n\,\sigma_X\sigma_Y} = \dfrac{\Sigma(X-25)(Y-18)}{15 \times 5 \times 5} = \dfrac{125}{15 \times 25} = 0{\cdot}33$

31. Given $n = 10$; $\Sigma x = 100$; $\Sigma y = 150$; $\Sigma(x-10)^2 = 180$; $\Sigma(y-15)^2 = 25$; $\Sigma(x-10)(y-15) = 60$;
Obtain Karl Pearson's correlation coefficient. [**Ans.** $(2/\sqrt{5}) = 0{\cdot}8944$]

32. In a correlation study the results were

$\Sigma xy = 40$, $N = 100$, $\Sigma x^2 = 80$, $\Sigma y^2 = 20$, where $x = X - \overline{X}$ and $y = Y - \overline{Y}$

The correlation coefficient is :

(*a*) + 1·0 (*b*) −1·0 (*c*) zero (*d*) None of these.

Ans. (*a*).

33. Given $r = 0{\cdot}8$, $\Sigma xy = 60$, $\sigma_y = 2{\cdot}5$ and $\Sigma x^2 = 90$
Find the number of items. Here x and y are deviations from respective means.

Ans. $n = 10$.

34. (*a*) The following results are obtained between two series. Compute the coefficient of correlation.

	X Series	*Y Series*
Number of items	7	7
Arithmetic mean	4	8
Sum of square of deviations from arithmetic mean	28	76

Summation of products of deviations of X and Y series from their respective means = 46

Ans. $r = 0{\cdot}997$.

(*b*) From the following data calculate the coefficient of correlation between two variables X and Y :

(*i*) Number of items in X-series or Y-series = 12.

(*ii*) Sum of the squares of deviation from mean : 360 for X-series and 250 for Y-series.

(*iii*) Sum of the products of deviations of the two series from their respective means = 225.

Ans. $r_{xy} = 0{\cdot}75$.

35. (*a*) The coefficient of correlation between two variables X and Y is 0·38. Their covariance is 10·2. The variance of X is 16. Find the standard deviation of Y-series.

Ans. $\sigma_y = 6{\cdot}71$.

(*b*) The covariance between the length and weight of five items is 6 and their standard deviations are 2·45 and 2·61 respectively. Find the coefficient of correlation between length and weight. *[Delhi Univ. B.Com. (Hons.), 2000]*

Ans. $r = 0{\cdot}9383$.

36. (*a*) The coefficient of correlation between two variates X and Y is 0·8 and their covariance is 20. If the variance of X series is 16, find the standard deviation of Y series. *[C.A. (Foundation), June 1993]*

Ans. $\sigma_y = 6{\cdot}25$.

(*b*) The coefficient of correlation between two variables X and Y is 0·4 and their co-variance is 10. If variance of X series is 9, find the second moment about mean of Y series. [*Delhi Univ. B.Com. (Hons.), 1996*]

Hint. Second moment about mean of Y series is σ_y^2.

Ans. $\sigma_y^2 = (8·33)^2 = 69·39$.

37. (*a*) For the bivariate data : $\{(x, y) = (10, 4), (11, 3), (12, 2)\ (14, 0), (8, 6)\}$, the coefficient of correlation between x and y is :

(*i*) – 1 (*ii*) 0·5 (*iii*) 1 (*iv*) 0

(*b*) For the bivariate data : $\{(x, y) : (15, 3), (20, 8), (25, 13), (30, 18)\}$ the coefficient of correlation between x and y is :

(*i*) 1 (*ii*) – 1 (*iii*) 0 (*iv*) 0·5

Ans. (*a*) $x + y = 14$; $r = -1$ (*b*) $x - y = 12$; $r = +1$.

38. (*a*) Given that the correlation between x and y is 0·5, what is the correlation between $2x - 4$ and $3 - 2y$?

Ans. $r = -0·5$.

(*b*) Point out the inconsistency in the statement :

"The correlation coefficient of $3x$ and $-2y$ is the same as the correlation coefficient of x and y."

[*I.C.W.A. (Intermediate), Dec. 1998*]

Ans. $r(3x, -2y) = -r(x, y)$. Statement is inconsistent.

39. (*a*) The corresponding values of the variables are given below :

X :	2	3	5	8	9
Y :	4	6	10	16	18

The correlation coefficient between the variables is : – 1, 0, 1 or none of these. Justify your answer.

Ans. $r_{xy} = +1$.

(*b*) Let r be the correlation between x and y. What is the correlation coefficient between :

(*i*) $(3x + 1)$ and $(2y - 3)$, and (*ii*) x and $-y$?

Explain your answers.

Ans. (*i*) r, (*ii*) $-r$.

(*c*) If $U = 2x + 11$ and $V = 3y + 7$, what will be correlation coefficient between U and V ? Justify your statement.

Ans. $r_{uv} = r_{xy}$.

(*d*) Are the following statements valid ? Justify your answer :

(*i*) Positive value of correlation coefficient between x and y implies that if x decreases, y tends to increase.

(*ii*) Correlation coefficient is independent of the origin of reference but is dependent on the units of measurement.

(*iii*) Correlation coefficient between x and y turned out to be 1·25.

Ans. (*i*) False, (*ii*) False, (*iii*) Impossible.

40. Comment on the following, giving reasons for your conclusions :

(*a*) If the correlation coefficient between two variables X and Y is positive, then

(*i*) the correlation coefficient between $-X$ and $-Y$ is positive.

(*ii*) the correlation coefficient between X and $-Y$ or $-X$ and Y is positive.

(*b*) The correlation coefficient between two variables is 1·4.

(*c*) If the variables are independent then they are uncorrelated.

(*d*) Correlation coefficient can be calculated only if the two variables are measured in the same units.

(*e*) If the correlation coefficient between two variables is zero, then the variables are independent.

(*f*) The value of r cannot be negative.

(*g*) r measures every type of relationship between the two variables.

(*h*) "The closeness of relationship between two variables is proportional to r."

(*i*) A student while studying correlation between smoking and drinking found a value of r as high as 1·62.

8·6. CORRELATION IN BIVARIATE FREQUENCY TABLE

If in a bivariate distribution the data are fairly large, they may be summarised in the form of a two-way table. Here for each variable, the values are grouped into various classes (not necessarily the same for both the variables), keeping in view the same considerations as in the case of univariate distribution. For example, if there are m classes for the X-variable series and n classes for the Y-variable series then there will be $m \times n$ cells in the two-way table. By going through the different pairs of the values (x, y) and using tally marks we can find the frequency for each cell and thus obtain the so-called bivariate frequency table as shown below.

BIVARIATE FREQUENCY TABLE

X Series → / *Y Series* ↓	*Classes* / *Mid Points*: x_1 x_2 ... x ... ... x_m	*Total of frequencies of Y*
Classes / *Mid Points*: y_1, y_2, y, ⋮, y_n	$f(x, y)$	f_y
Total of frequencies of X	f_x	Total $\Sigma f_x = \Sigma f_y = N$

Here $f(x, y)$ is the frequency of the pair (x, y).

The formula for computing the correlation coefficient between X and Y for the bivariate frequency table is

$$r = \frac{N \sum x y f(x, y) - (\sum x f_x)(\sum y f_y)}{\sqrt{[N \sum x^2 f_x - (\sum x f_x)^2] \times [N \sum y^2 f_y - (\sum y f_y)^2]}} \qquad \dots (8·13)$$

where N is the total frequency. If there is no confusion we may use the formula :

$$r = r_{xy} = \frac{N \Sigma f x y - (\Sigma f x)(\Sigma f y)}{\sqrt{[N \Sigma f x^2 - (\Sigma f x)^2] \times [N \Sigma f y^2 - (\Sigma f y)^2]}} \qquad \dots (8·13a)$$

where the frequency f used for the product xy is nothing but $f(x, y)$ and the frequency f used in the sums Σfx and Σfy are respectively the frequencies of x and y, *viz.*, f_x & f_y as explained in the above table. If we change the origin and scale in X and Y by transforming them to the new variables U and V by

$$u = \frac{x - A}{h} \quad \text{and} \quad v = \frac{y - B}{k}\ ; \quad h > 0, \ k > 0$$

where h and k are the widths of the x-classes and y-classes respectively and A and B are constants, then by Property II of r, we have :

$$r_{xy} = r_{uv} = \frac{N \Sigma f u v - (\Sigma f u)(\Sigma f v)}{\sqrt{[N \Sigma f u^2 - (\Sigma f u)^2] \times [N \Sigma f v^2 - (\Sigma f v)^2]}} \qquad \dots (8·14)$$

We shall explain the method by means of examples.

Example 8·21. *Family income and its percentage spent on food in the case of hundred families gave the following bivariate frequency distribution. Calculate the coefficient of correlation and interpret its value.*

Food Expenditure	*Family income (Rs.)*				
(in %)	*200—300*	*300—400*	*400—500*	*500—600*	*600—700*
10—15	—	—	—	3	7
15—20	—	4	9	4	3
20—25	7	6	12	5	—
25—30	3	10	19	8	—

[*Delhi Univ. M.B.A., 2000*]

Solution. Let us denote the income (in Rupees) by the variable X and the food expenditure (%) by the variable Y.

Steps 1. Find the mid-points of various classes for X and Y series.

2. Change the origin and scale in X-series and Y-series by transforming them to new variables u and v as defined below :

$$u = \frac{x - A}{h} = \frac{x - 450}{100}, \qquad \text{and} \qquad v = \frac{y - B}{k} = \frac{y - 17{\cdot}5}{5},$$

where x denotes the mid-points of the X-sereis and y denotes the mid-points of the Y-series, and h and k are the magnitudes of the classes of X and Y series respectively.

3. For each class of X, find the total of cell frequencies of all the classes of Y and similarly for each class of Y, find the total of cell frequencies of all the classes of X.

4. Multiply the frequencies of x by the corresponding values of the variable u and find the sum $\sum fu$.

5. Multiply the frequencies of y by the corresponding values of the variable v and find the sum $\sum fv$.

6. Multiply the frequency of each cell by the corresponding values of u and v and write the product $f \times u \times v$ within a square in the right hand top corner for each cell. For example for $u = -1$ and $v = 2$, the cell frequency f is 10. Therefore, the product of f, u and v is $(-1) \times (2) \times 10 = -20$ which is written within a square on the right hand top of cell. Similarly, for $u = 2$ and $v = 1$, the product $fuv = 0 \times 2 \times 1 = 0$, and so on for all the remaining cell frequencies.

7. Add together all the figures in the top corner squares as obtained in step 6 to get the last column fuv for each of the X and Y series. Finally, find the total of the last column to get $\sum fuv$.

8. Multiply the values of fu and fv by the corresponding values of u and v respectively to get the columns for fu^2 and fv^2. Add these values to obtain $\sum fu^2$ and $\sum fv^2$.

The above calculations are shown in the table given on next page 8.28.

$$r_{uv} = \frac{N\sum fuv - (\sum fu)(\sum fv)}{\sqrt{[N\sum fu^2 - (\sum fu)^2] \times [N\sum fv^2 - (\sum fv)^2]}}$$

$$= \frac{100 \times (-48) - 0 \times 100}{\sqrt{(100 \times 120 - 0) \times [100 \times 200 - (100)^2]}} = \frac{-4800}{\sqrt{12000 \times (20000 - 10000)}} \qquad \text{[From page 8·28]}$$

$$= \frac{-4800}{\sqrt{12000 \times 10000}} = \frac{-48}{\sqrt{120 \times 100}} = \frac{-48}{\sqrt{12000}} = \frac{-48}{109{\cdot}54} = -0{\cdot}4382$$

Hence, $\qquad r_{xy} = r_{uv} = -0{\cdot}4381 \qquad$ [By Property II of r]

Example. 8·22. *Calculate Karl Pearson's coefficient of correlation from the data given below :*

Marks	*Age in Years*				
	18	*19*	*20*	*21*	*22*
20—25	3	2	—	—	—
15—20	—	5	4	—	—
10—15	—	—	7	10	—
5—10	—	—	—	3	2
0—5	—	—	—	3	1

Solution. If we denote the age in years by the variable X and the mid-point of the class intervals of marks by the variable Y and take

$$u = X - 20; \quad \text{and} \quad v = \frac{Y - 12{\cdot}5}{5},$$

then the bivariate correlation table is as given on page 8.29.

CALCULATIONS FOR CORRELATION COEFFICIENT

	$X \rightarrow$		200—300	300—400	400—500	500—600	600—700				
		Mid pt. x	250	350	450	550	650				
$Y \downarrow$	Mid pt. y	$U \rightarrow$ $V \downarrow$	-2	-1	0	1	2	f	fv	fv^2	fuv
10—15	12·5	-1	[0]	[0]	[0]	3 [-3]	7 [-14]	10	-10	10	-17
15—20	17·5	0	[0]	4 [0]	9 [0]	4 [0]	3 [0]	20	0	0	0
20—25	22·5	1	7 [-14]	6 [-6]	12 [0]	5 [5]	[0]	30	30	30	-15
25—30	27·5	2	3 [-12]	10 [-20]	19 [0]	8 [16]	[0]	40	80	160	-16
		f	10	20	40	20	10	$N = 100$	$\sum fv = 100$	$\sum fv^2 = 200$	$\sum fuv = -48$
		fu	-20	-20	0	20	20	$\sum fu = 0$			
		fu^2	40	20	0	20	40	$\sum fu^2 = 120$			
		fuv	-26	-26	0	18	-14	$\sum fuv = -48$			

CALCULATIONS FOR CORRELATION COEFFICIENT

Marks Y ↓ / Age in years → X	u → / v ↓	18 (u = −2)	19 (u = −1)	20 (u = 0)	21 (u = 1)	22 (u = 2)	Total f	fv	fv^2	fuv
22·5	2	3 [−12]	2 [−4]	[0]	[0]	[0]	5	10	20	−16
17·5	1	[0]	5 [−5]	4 [0]	[0]	[0]	9	9	9	−5
12·5	0	[0]	[0]	7 [0]	19 [0]	[0]	17	0	0	0
7·5	−1	[0]	[0]	[0]	3 [−3]	2 [−4]	5	−5	5	−7
2·5	−2	[0]	[0]	[0]	3 [−6]	1 [−4]	4	−8	16	−10
	Total f	3	7	11	16	3	$N = 40$	$\Sigma fv = 6$	$\Sigma fv^2 = 50$	$\Sigma fuv = -38$
	fu	−6	−7	0	16	6	$\Sigma fu = 9$			
	fu^2	12	7	0	16	12	$\Sigma fu^2 = 47$			
	fuv	−12	−9	0	−9	−8	$\Sigma fuv = -38$			

$$r_{uv} = \frac{N\Sigma fuv - (\Sigma fu)(\Sigma fv)}{\sqrt{[N\Sigma fu^2 - (\Sigma fu)^2] \times [N\Sigma fv^2 - (\Sigma fv)^2]}} = \frac{40\times(-38)-9\times 6}{\sqrt{[40\times 47-(9)^2]\times[40\times 50-(6)^2]}} \quad \text{[From page 8·29]}$$

$$= \frac{-1520-54}{\sqrt{(1880-81)(2000-36)}} = \frac{-1574}{\sqrt{1799\times 1964}} = \frac{-1574}{\sqrt{3533236}} = \frac{-1574}{1879{\cdot}69} = 0{\cdot}8373$$

But since correlation coefficient is independent of change of origin and scale, [*c.f.* Property II of *r*], we get

$$r_{xy} = r_{uv} = -0{\cdot}8373.$$

EXERCISE 8·3

1. Write a brief note on the correlation table.

The following are the marks obtained by 24 students in a class test of Statistics and Mathematics :

Roll No. of Students	:	1	2	3	4	5	6	7	8	9	10	11	12
Marks in Statistics	:	15	0	1	3	16	2	18	5	4	17	6	19
Marks in Mathematics	:	13	1	2	7	8	9	12	9	17	16	6	18
Roll No. of Students	:	13	14	15	16	17	18	19	20	21	22	23	24
Marks in Statistics	:	14	9	8	13	10	13	11	11	12	18	9	7
Marks in Mathematics	:	11	3	5	4	10	11	14	7	18	15	15	3

Prepare a correlation table taking the magnitude of each class interval as four marks and the first class interval as "equal to 0 and less than 4". Calculate Karl Pearson's coefficient of correlation between the marks in Statistics and marks in Mathematics from the correlation table and comment on it.

Ans. $r = 0{\cdot}5717$.

2. What is a bivariate table ? Write the formula you use for calculating coefficient of correlation from such a table, explaining the symbols used. What does a negative value of the coefficient of correlation indicate ?

3. Calculate the coefficient of correlation between the ages of husbands and wives and its probable error from the following table :

	Ages of husbands (years)					
Ages of wives (years)	20—30	30—40	40—50	50—60	60—70	Total
15—25	5	9	3	—	—	17
25—35	—	10	25	2	—	37
35—45	—	1	12	2	—	15
45—55	—	—	4	16	5	25
55—65	—	—	—	4	2	6
Total	5	20	44	24	7	100

Ans. $r = 0{\cdot}7953$; $P.E.\ (r) = 0{\cdot}0248$.

4. (*a*) Given the data in the adjoining table, calculate the correlation coefficient, *r*, between *X* and *Y*.

X \ Y	30—50	50—70	70—90
0—5	10	6	2
5—10	3	5	4
10—15	4	7	9

[*Delhi Univ. B.A. (Econ. Hons.), 1991*]

Ans. $r = 0{\cdot}375$.

(*b*) Given the following table, obtain r_{xy}.

x \ y	30—50	50—70	70—90	Total
0—5	10	6	2	18
5—10	3	—	4	12
10—15	4	7	—	20
Total	17	—	15	50

[*Delhi Univ. B.A. (Econ. Hons.), 2004*]

Hint. First, obtain the missing values from given totals

Ans. $r = 0{\cdot}375$.

5. Calculate the product moment coefficient of correlation for the adjoining bivariate distribution.

y \ x	5	10	15	20
11	2	4	5	4
17	5	3	6	2
23	3	1	2	3

Ans. $r = -0.0856$.

6. The following table gives the distribution of income and expenditure of 100 families. Find the coefficient of correlation and its probable error. State whether the correlation coefficient is significant or not.

Income (in '00 Rs.)	*Percentage Expenditure on Food (X)*				
Y	10—20	20—30	30—40	40—50	50—60
350—450	—	—	—	—	5
450—550	—	—	1	10	9
550—650	—	4	12	25	3
650—750	4	16	2	2	—
750—850	2	5	—	—	—

Ans. -0.8248.

7. A sample of 100 firms was taken and these were classified according to the sales executed by them and profits earned consequently. The results are shown in the table given below. Determine the correlation coefficient between sales and profits and also its probable error.

Profits	*Sales (in lakhs of Rs.)*						
(in '000 Rs.)	7—8	8—9	9—10	10—11	11—12	12—13	Total
50—70	5	3	—	—	—	—	8
70—90	3	8	5	4	—	—	20
90—110	1	—	7	11	2	2	23
110—130	—	4	5	15	6	—	30
130—150	—	—	2	7	4	6	19
Total	9	15	19	37	12	8	100

Ans. $r = 0.6627$; $P.E.(r) = 0.0378$.

8·7. RANK CORRELATION METHOD

Sometimes we come across statistical series in which the variables under consideration are not capable of quantitative measurement but can be arranged in serial order. This happens when we are dealing with qualitative characteristics (attributes) such as honesty, beauty, character, morality, etc., which cannot be measured quantitatively but can be arranged serially. In such situations Karl Pearson's coefficient of correlation cannot be used as such. Charles Edward Spearman, a British psychologist, developed a formula in 1904 which consists in obtaining the correlation coefficient between the ranks of n individuals in the two attributes under study.

Suppose we want to find if two characteristics A, say, intelligence and B, say, beauty are related or not. Both the characteristics are incapable of quantitative measurements but we can arrange a group of n individuals in order of merit (ranks) *w.r.t.* proficiency in the two characteristics. Let the random variables X and Y denote the ranks of the individuals in the characteristics A and B respectively. If we assume that there is no tie, *i.e.*, if no two individuals get the same rank in a characteristic then, obviously, X and Y assume numerical values ranging from 1 to n.

The Pearsonian correlation coefficient between the ranks X and Y is called the rank correlation coefficient between the characteristics A and B for that group of individuals.

Spearman's rank correlation coefficient, usually denoted by ρ (Rho) is given by the formula

$$\rho = 1 - \frac{6\Sigma d^2}{n(n^2-1)} \qquad \ldots (8·15)$$

where d is the difference between the pair of ranks of the same individual in the two characteristics and n is the number of pairs.

8·7·1. Limits for ρ. Spearman's rank correlation coefficient lies between -1 and $+1$, *i.e.*,

$$-1 \le \rho \le 1 \qquad \ldots (8·16)$$

Remark. Since the square of a real quantity is always non-negative, *i.e.*, ≥ 0, Σd^2 being the sum of non-negative quantities is also non-negative. Further since n is also positive we get from (8·15)

$$\rho = 1 - [\text{some non-negative quantity}]$$

$$\Rightarrow \quad \rho \leq 1, \qquad \ldots(i)$$

the sign of equality holds *i.e.*, $\rho = 1$ if and only if $\Sigma d^2 = 0$. Now, $\Sigma d^2 = 0$ if and only if each $d = 0$, *i.e.*, the ranks of an individual are same in both the characteristics. Following table gives one such possibility.

x	1	2	3	...	n
y	1	2	3	...	n

On the other hand, ρ will be minimum *i.e.*, $\rho = -1$ if Σd^2 is maximum, *i.e.*, if the deviations d are maximum which is so if the ranks of the individuals in the two characteristics are in the reverse (opposite) order as given in the following table.

Individual	1	2	3	...	$n-1$	n
x	1	2	3	...	$n-1$	n
y	n	$n-1$	$n-2$	...	2	1

Note. From the above table, we observe that : $x + y = n + 1$. Also $x - y = d$

8·7·2. Computation of Rank Correlation Coefficient. We shall discuss below the method of computing the Spearman's rank correlation coefficient ρ under the following situations :

(*i*) When actual ranks are given.

(*ii*) When ranks are not given.

CASE (I) — WHEN ACTUAL RANKS ARE GIVEN

In this situation the following steps are involved :

(*i*) Compute d, the difference of ranks.

(*ii*) Compute d^2.

(*iii*) Obtain the sum Σd^2.

(*iv*) Use formula (8·15) to get the value of ρ.

Example 8·23. *The ranks of the same 15 students in two subjects A and B are given below ; the two numbers within the brackets denoting the ranks of the same student in A and B respectively. (1, 10), (2, 7), (3, 2), (4, 6), (5, 4), (6, 8), (7, 3), (8, 1), (9, 11), (10, 15), (11, 9), (12, 5), (13, 14), (14, 12), (15, 13). Use Spearman's formula to find the rank correlation coefficient.* [*Sukhadia Univ. MBA, 1998*]

Solution.

CALCULATION OF SPEARMAN'S CORRELATION COEFFICIENT

Rank in A (x)	*Rank in B* (y)	$d = x - y$	d^2
1	10	−9	81
2	7	−5	25
3	2	1	1
4	6	−2	4
5	4	1	1
6	8	−2	4
7	3	4	16
8	1	7	49
9	11	−2	4
10	15	−5	25
11	9	2	4
12	5	7	49
13	14	−1	1
14	12	2	4
15	13	2	4
		$\Sigma d = 0$	$\Sigma d^2 = 272$

Spearman's rank correlation coefficient ρ is given by :

$$\rho = 1 - \frac{6\Sigma d^2}{n(n^2-1)}$$

$$= 1 - \frac{6 \times 272}{15(225-1)}$$

$$= 1 - \frac{6 \times 272}{15 \times 224}$$

$$= 1 - \frac{17}{35} = \frac{18}{35}$$

$$= 0{\cdot}51$$

Example 8·24. *Ten competitors in a beauty contest are ranked by three judges in the following order :*

1st Judge	:	*1*	*6*	*5*	*10*	*3*	*2*	*4*	*9*	*7*	*8*
2nd Judge	:	*3*	*5*	*8*	*4*	*7*	*10*	*2*	*1*	*6*	*9*
3rd Judge	:	*6*	*4*	*9*	*8*	*1*	*2*	*3*	*10*	*5*	*7*

Use the rank correlation coefficient to determine which pair of judges has the nearest approach to common tastes in beauty.

Solution. Let R_1, R_2 and R_3 denote the ranks given by the first, second and third judges respectively and let ρ_{ij} be the rank correlation coefficient between the ranks given by ith and jth judges, $i \neq j = 1, 2, 3$. Let $d_{ij} = R_i - R_j$, be the difference of ranks of an individual given by the ith and jth judge.

CALCULATION OF RANK CORRELATION COEFFICIENT

R_1	R_2	R_3	$d_{12} = R_1 - R_2$	$d_{13} = R_1 - R_3$	$d_{23} = R_2 - R_3$	d_{12}^2	d_{13}^2	d_{23}^2
1	3	6	−2	−5	−3	4	25	9
6	5	4	1	2	1	1	4	1
5	8	9	−3	−4	−1	9	16	1
10	4	8	6	2	−4	36	4	16
3	7	1	−4	2	6	16	4	36
2	10	2	−8	0	8	64	0	64
4	2	3	2	1	−1	4	1	1
9	1	10	8	−1	−9	64	1	81
7	6	5	1	2	1	1	4	1
8	9	7	−1	1	2	1	1	4
			$\Sigma d_{12} = 0$	$\Sigma d_{13} = 0$	$\Sigma d_{23} = 0$	$\Sigma d_{12}^2 = 200$	$\Sigma d_{13}^2 = 60$	$\Sigma d_{23}^2 = 214$

We have $n = 10$.

Spearman's rank correlation coefficients are given by :

$$\rho_{12} = 1 - \frac{6\Sigma d_{12}^2}{n(n^2-1)} = 1 - \frac{6 \times 200}{10 \times 99} = -\frac{7}{33} = -0{\cdot}2121$$

$$\rho_{13} = 1 - \frac{6\Sigma d_{13}^2}{n(n^2-1)} = 1 - \frac{6 \times 60}{10 \times 99} = \frac{7}{11} = 0{\cdot}6363$$

$$\rho_{23} = 1 - \frac{6\Sigma d_{23}^2}{n(n^2-1)} = 1 - \frac{6 \times 214}{10 \times 99} = -\frac{49}{165} = -0{\cdot}2970$$

Since ρ_{13} is maximum, the pair of first and third judges has the nearest approach to common tastes in beauty.

Remark. Since ρ_{12} and ρ_{23} are negative, the pair of judges (1, 2) and (2, 3) have opposite (divergent) tastes for beauty.

CASE (II)—WHEN RANKS ARE NOT GIVEN

Spearman's rank correlation formula (8·15) can also be used even if we are dealing with variables which are measured quantitatively, *i.e.*, when the actual data but not the ranks relating to two variables are given. In such a case we shall have to convert the data into ranks. The highest (smallest) observation is given the rank 1. The next highest (next lowest) observation is given rank 2 and so on. It is immaterial in which way (descending or ascending) the ranks are assigned. However, the same approach should be followed for all the variables under consideration.

Example 8·25. *Calculate Spearman's rank correlation coefficient between advertisement cost and sales from the following data :*

Advertisement cost ('000 Rs.)	:	*39*	*65*	*62*	*90*	*82*	*75*	*25*	*98*	*36*	*78*
Sales (lakhs Rs.)	:	*47*	*53*	*58*	*86*	*62*	*68*	*60*	*91*	*51*	*84*

Solution. Let X denote the advertisement cost ('000 Rs.) and Y denote the sales (lakhs Rs.).

CALCULATION OF RANK CORRELATION COEFFICIENT

X	Y	*Rank of X (x)*	*Rank of Y (y)*	$d = x - y$	d^2
39	47	8	10	−2	4
65	53	6	8	−2	4
62	58	7	7	0	0
90	86	2	2	0	0
82	62	3	5	−2	4
75	68	5	4	1	1
25	60	10	6	4	16
98	91	1	1	0	0
36	51	9	9	0	0
78	84	4	3	1	1
				$\Sigma d = 0$	$\Sigma d^2 = 30$

Here $n = 10$

$$\therefore \qquad \rho = 1 - \frac{6\Sigma d^2}{n(n^2-1)} = 1 - \frac{6 \times 30}{10 \times 99} = 1 - \frac{2}{11} = \frac{9}{11} = 0{\cdot}82.$$

Example 8·26. *A test in Statistics was taken by 7 students. The teacher ranked his pupils according to their academic achievement. The order of achievement from high to low, together with family income for each pupil, is given as follows :*

Rai (Rs. 8,700), Bhatnagar (Rs. 4,200), Tuli (Rs. 5,700), Desai (Rs. 8,200), Gupta (Rs. 20,000), Chaudhri (Rs. 18,000) and Singh (Rs. 17,500).

Compute the Spearman's rank correlation between academic achievement and family income.

[*Delhi Univ. B.Com.* (*Pass*), *1999*]

Solution. Let us define the following variables.

X : Academic achievement ; Y : Family income (Rupees)

CALCULATIONS FOR RANK CORRELATION COEFFICIENT

Student	*Rank X (x)*	*Income (Rs.) Y*	*Rank Y (y)*	$d = x - y$	d^2
Rai	1	8,700	4	−3	9
Bhatnagar	2	4,200	7	−5	25
Tuli	3	5,700	6	−3	9
Desai	4	8,200	5	−1	1
Gupta	5	20,000	1	4	16
Chaudhri	6	18,000	2	4	16
Singh	7	17,500	3	4	16
				$\Sigma d = 0$	$\Sigma d^2 = 92$

Spearman's rank correlation coefficient between academic achievement (X) and family income (Y) is given by :

$$\rho_{xy} = 1 - \frac{6\,\Sigma d^2}{n(n^2-1)} = 1 - \frac{6 \times 92}{7 \times 48} = 1 - \frac{23}{14} = -\frac{9}{14} = -\,0{\cdot}6429.$$

REPEATED RANKS

In case of attributes if there is a tie *i.e.*, if any two or more individuals are placed together in any classification *w.r.t.* an attribute or if in case of variable data there is more than one item with the same value in either or both the series, then Spearman's formula (8·15) for calculating the rank correlation coefficient breaks down, since in this case the variables X [the ranks of individuals in characteristic A (1st series)] and Y [the ranks of individuals in characteristic B (2nd series)] do not take the values from 1 to n and consequently $\bar{x} \neq \bar{y}$, while in proving (8·15) we had assumed that $\bar{x} = \bar{y}$.

In this case, common ranks are assigned to the repeated items. These common ranks are the arithmetic mean of the ranks which these items would have got if they were different from each other and the next item will get the rank next to the rank used in computing the common rank. For example, suppose an item is repeated at rank 4. Then the common rank to be assigned to each item is (4 + 5)/2, *i.e.*, 4·5 which is the average of 4 and 5, the ranks which these observations would have assumed if they were different. The next item will be assigned the rank 6. If an item is repeated thrice at rank 7, then the common rank to be assigned to each value will be (7 + 8 + 9)/3, *i.e.*, 8 which is the arithmetic mean of 7, 8 and 9, *viz.*, the ranks these observations would have got if they were different from each other. The next rank to be assigned will be 10.

If only a small proportion of the ranks are tied, this technique may be applied together with formula (8·15). If a large proportion of ranks are tied, it is advisable to apply an *adjustment* or *a correction factor* (*C.F.*) to (8·15) as explained below.

"In the formula (8·15) add the factor $m(m^2 - 1)/12$ to Σd^2, *where m is the number of times an item is repeated. This correction factor is to be added for each repeated value in both the series."*

Example 8·27. *A psychologist wanted to compare two methods A and B of teaching. He selected a random sample of 22 students. He grouped them into 11 pairs so that the students in a pair have approximately equal scrores on an intelligence test. In each pair one student was taught by method A and the other by method B and examined after the course. The marks obtained by them are tabulated below :*

Pair	:	*1*	*2*	*3*	*4*	*5*	*6*	*7*	*8*	*9*	*10*	*11*
A	:	*24*	*29*	*19*	*14*	*30*	*19*	*27*	*30*	*20*	*28*	*11*
B	:	*37*	*35*	*16*	*26*	*23*	*27*	*19*	*20*	*16*	*11*	*21*

Find the rank correlation coefficient.

Solution. Let variable X denote the scores of students taught by method A and Y denote the scores of students taught by method B.

CALCULATIONS FOR RANK CORRELATION COEFFICIENT

X	Y	*Rank of X* (x)	*Rank of Y* (y)	$d = x - y$	d^2
24	37	6	1	5	25
29	35	3	2	1	1
19	16	8·5	9·5	−1	1
14	26	10	4	6	36
30	23	1·5	5	−3·5	12·25
19	27	8·5	3	5·5	30·25
27	19	5	8	−3	9·00
30	20	1·5	7	−5·5	30·25
20	16	7	9·5	−2·5	6·25
28	11	4	11	−7	49·00
11	21	11	6	5	25·00
				$\Sigma d = 0$	$\Sigma d^2 = 225·00$

In the X-series, we see that the value 30 occurs twice. The common rank assigned to each of these values is 1·5, the arithmetic mean of 1 and 2, the ranks which these observations would have taken if they were different. The next value 29 gets the next rank, *viz.*, 3. Again, the value 19 occurs twice. The common rank assigned to it is 8·5, the arithmetic mean of 8 and 9 and the next value, *viz.*, 14 gets the rank 10. Similarly, in the y-series the value 16 occurs twice and the common rank assigned to each is 9·5, the arithmetic mean of 9 and 10. The next value *viz.*, 11 gets the rank 11.

Hence, we see that in the X-series the items 19 and 30 are repeated, each occurring twice and in the Y-series the item 16 is repeated. Thus in each of the three cases $m = 2$. Hence on applying the correction factor $\dfrac{m(m^2-1)}{12}$ for each repeated item, we get

$$\rho = 1 - \frac{6\left[\Sigma d^2 + \frac{2(4-1)}{12} + \frac{2(4-1)}{12} + \frac{2(4-1)}{12}\right]}{11(121-1)} \qquad (\because\ n = 11)$$

$$= 1 - \frac{6 \times 226·5}{11 \times 120} = 1 - 1·0225 = -0·0225.$$

Example 8·28. *From the following data calculate the rank correlation coefficient after making adjustment for tied ranks.*

x :	*48*	*33*	*40*	*9*	*16*	*16*	*65*	*24*	*16*	*57*
y :	*13*	*13*	*24*	*6*	*15*	*4*	*20*	*9*	*6*	*19*

[*I.C.W.A. (Intermediate), June 2002*]

Solution. R_x = Rank of *x*-value ; R_y = Rank of *y*-value

Explanation of Ranks

In the *x*-series, we see that the value 16 is repeated three times. The common rank assigned to each of these values is 8, the arithmetic mean of 7, 8 and 9, the ranks which these observations would have taken if they were different. The next value 9 gets the next rank *viz.*, 10

Similarly, in the *y*-series the observation 13 occurs twice. The common rank assigned to each is 5·5, the arithmetic mean of 5 and 6, and the next value 9 gets the next rank 7. Again the value 6 is repeated twice and each is given the common rank (8 + 9)/2 *i.e.*, 8·5 and the next value 4 gets the rank 10.

x	y	R_x	R_y	$d = R_x - R_y$	d^2
48	13	3	5·5	–2·5	6·25
33	13	5	5·5	– 0·5	0·25
40	24	4	1	3	9
9	6	10	8·5	1·5	2·25
16	15	8	4	4	16
16	4	8	10	–2	4
65	20	1	2	–1	1
24	9	6	7	–1	1
16	6	8	8·5	– 0·5	0·25
57	19	2	3	–1	1
Total				$\Sigma d = 0$	$\Sigma d^2 = 41$

Correction Factor (C.F.)

Spearman's rank correlation coefficient for repeated ranks gives :

Repeated value	*No. of times it occurs (m)*	*C.F.* $m(m^2 - 1)/12$
x–series : 16	3	3 (9 – 1)/12 = 2
y–series : 13	2	2(4 – 1)/12 = 0·5
6	2	2(4 – 1)/12 = 0·5
Total		3

$$\rho = 1 - \frac{6}{n(n^2-1)}\left[\Sigma d^2 + \Sigma \frac{m(m^2-1)}{12}\right]$$

$$= 1 - \frac{6}{10(100-1)}\left[41 + 3\right] = 1 - \frac{6 \times 44}{10 \times 99}$$

$$= 1 - \frac{4}{15} = \frac{11}{15} = 0{\cdot}7333.$$

Example 8.29. *Find the Rank correlation Coefficient from the following marks awarded by the examiners in Statistics.*

Roll No.	*By Examiner A*	*By Examiner B*	*By Examiner C*
1	*24*	*37*	*30*
2	*29*	*35*	*28*
3	*19*	*16*	*20*
4	*14*	*26*	*25*
5	*30*	*23*	*25*
6	*19*	*27*	*30*
7	*27*	*19*	*20*
8	*30*	*20*	*24*
9	*20*	*16*	*22*
10	*28*	*11*	*29*
11	*11*	*21*	*15*

[*Delhi Univ. B.Com. (Hons.), 2005*]

Solution· First of all we shall convert the markets awarded by different examiners to the candidates into ranks, as given in the following table.

Rok Nos·	*Marks awarded by Examiner A*	*Rank* (R_A)	*Marks awarded by Examiner B*	*Rank* (R_B)	*Marks awarded by Examiner C*	*Rank* (R_C)	$d_{AB} = R_A - R_B$	$d_{AC} = R_A - R_C$	$d_{BC} = R_B - R_C$	d^2_{AB}	d^2_{AC}	d^2_{BC}
1	24	6	37	1	30	1·5	5	4·5	– 0·5	25	20·25	0·25
2	29	3	35	2	28	4	1	– 1	– 2	1	1	4
3	19	8·5	16	9·5	20	9·5	– 1	– 1	0	1	1	0
4	14	10	26	4	25	5·5	6	4·5	– 1·5	36	20·25	2·25
5	30	1·5	23	5	25	5·5	– 3·5	– 4	– 0·5	12·25	16	0·25
6	19	8·5	27	3	30	1·5	5·5	7	1·5	30·25	49	2·25
7	27	5	19	8	20	9·5	– 3	– 4·5	– 1·5	9	20·25	2·25
8	30	1·5	20	7	24	7	– 5·5	– 5·5	0	30·25	30·25	0
9	20	7	16	9·5	22	8	– 2·5	– 1	1·5	6·25	1	2·25
10	28	4	11	11	29	3	– 7	1	8	49	1	64
11	11	11	21	6	15	11	5	0	– 5	25	0	25
										Σd^2_{AB} = 225	Σd^2_{AC} = 160	Σd^2_{BC} = 102·5

We are given $n = 11$.

$$\rho_{AB} = 1 - \frac{6\left[\Sigma d_{AB}^2 + \frac{m(m^2-1)}{12} \text{ for each repeated rank in } A \text{ and } B \text{ series}\right]}{n(n^2-1)}$$

$$= 1 - \frac{6\left[225 + \frac{2(2^2-1)}{12} + \frac{2(2^2-1)}{12} + \frac{2(2^2-1)}{12}\right]}{11(121-1)}$$

$$= 1 - \frac{6 \times 226{\cdot}5}{11 \times 120} = 1 - \frac{226{\cdot}5}{220} = -\frac{26{\cdot}5}{220} = -0{\cdot}0295$$

Similarly

$$\rho_{AC} = 1 - \frac{6\,[\Sigma d_{AC}^2 + \text{correction for Repeated Ranks}]}{n(n^2-1)}$$

$$= 1 - \frac{6\left[160 + 2\left\{\frac{2(2^2-1)}{12}\right\} + 3\left\{\frac{2(2^2-1)}{12}\right\}\right]}{11 \times (121-1)}$$

$$= 1 - \frac{6(160 + 2{\cdot}5)}{1 \times 220} = 1 - \frac{162{\cdot}5}{220} = \frac{57{\cdot}5}{220} = 0{\cdot}2614$$

$$\rho_{BC} = 1 - \frac{6\left[102{\cdot}5 + \frac{2(2^2-1)}{12} + 3\left\{\frac{2(2^2-1)}{12}\right\}\right]}{11(121-1)}$$

$$= \frac{6 \times 104{\cdot}5}{11 \times 120} = 1 - \frac{104{\cdot}5}{220} = \frac{115{\cdot}5}{220} = 0{\cdot}5250$$

Example 8·30. *The value of Spearman's rank correlation coefficient for certain pairs of number of observations, was found to be 2/3. The sum of squares of the differences between corresponding ranks was 55. Find the number of pairs.*

Solution. We are given $\rho = 2/3$ and $\sum d^2 = 55$. If n is the number of pairs of observations, we have :

$$\rho = 1 - \frac{6\Sigma d^2}{n(n^2-1)} \quad \Rightarrow \quad \frac{2}{3} = 1 - \frac{6 \times 55}{n(n^2-1)}$$

$$\Rightarrow \quad \frac{330}{n(n^2-1)} = 1 - \frac{2}{3} = \frac{1}{3} \quad \Rightarrow \quad n(n^2-1) = 3 \times 330 = 990 \quad \Rightarrow \quad n^3 - n - 990 = 0 \qquad \ldots(*)$$

By hit and trial we find that on putting $n = 10$ in (*),

$$\text{L.H.S.} = 10^3 - 10 - 990 = 1000 - 1000 = 0 = \text{R.H.S.}$$

Hence, by Remainder Theorem, $(n - 10)$ is a factor of $n^3 - n - 990$. On dividing $n^3 - n - 990$ by $(n - 10)$, we obtain the other factor of $n^3 - n - 990$ as $n^2 + 10n + 99$.

$$\therefore \quad (*) \quad \Rightarrow \quad (n-10)(n^2+10n+99) = 0$$

$$\Rightarrow \quad n - 10 = 0 \quad \text{or} \quad n^2 + 10n + 99 = 0$$

$$\Rightarrow \quad n = 10 \quad \text{or} \quad n = \frac{-10 \pm \sqrt{100-396}}{2} \quad \text{(Imaginary values)}$$

Hence, $n = 10$ is the only permissible value. Hence, the number of pairs is 10.

Example 8·31. *The coefficient of rank correlation between Micro-Economics and Statistics marks of 10 students was found to be 0·5. It was later discovered that the difference in ranks in two subjects obtained by one of the students was wrongly taken as 3 instead of 7. Find the correct value of coefficient of rank correlation.* *[Delhi Univ. B.A. (Econ. Hons.), 2006]*

Solution. We are given $n = 10$, $\rho = 0{\cdot}5$. Using (8·15), we get

$$0{\cdot}5 = 1 - \frac{6\Sigma d^2}{n(n^2-1)} = 1 - \frac{6\Sigma d^2}{10 \times 99} \quad \Rightarrow \quad \frac{6\Sigma d^2}{990} = 1 - 0{\cdot}5 = 0{\cdot}5 \quad \Rightarrow \quad \Sigma d^2 = \frac{990}{6 \times 2} = 82{\cdot}5$$

Since one difference was wrongly taken as 3 instead of 7, the correct value of Σd^2 is given by :

$$\text{Corrected } \Sigma d^2 = 82{\cdot}5 - 3^2 + 7^2 = 82{\cdot}5 - 9 + 49 = 122{\cdot}5$$

$$\therefore \quad \text{Corrected } \rho = 1 - \frac{6 \times 122{\cdot}5}{10 \times 99} = 1 - \frac{49}{66} = 1 - 0{\cdot}7424 = 0{\cdot}2576$$

8·7·3. Remarks on Spearman's Rank Correlation Coefficient

1. We always have $\Sigma d = 0$, which provides a check for numerical calculations.

2. Since Spearman's rank correlation coefficient ρ is nothing but Pearsonian correlation coefficient between the ranks, it can be interpreted in the same way as the Karl Pearson's correlation coefficient.

3. Karl Pearson's correlation coefficient assumes that the parent population from which sample observations are drawn is normal. If this assumption is violated then we need a measure which is distribution-free (or non-parametric). A distribution-free measure is one which does not make any assumptions about the parameters of the population. Spearman's ρ is such a measure (*i.e.*, distribution-free), since no strict assumptions are made about the form of the population from which sample observations are drawn.

4. Spearman's formula is easy to understand and apply as compared with Karl Pearson's formula. The values obtained by the two formulae, *viz.*, Pearsonian r and Spearman's ρ are generally different. The difference arises due to the fact that when ranking is used instead of full set of observations, there is always some loss of information. Unless many ties exist, the coefficient of rank correlation should be only slightly lower than the Pearsonian coefficient.

5. Spearman's formula is the only formula to be used for finding correlation coefficient if we are dealing with qualitative characteristics which cannot be measured quantitatively but can be arranged serially. It can also be used where actual data are given. In case of extreme observations, Spearman's formula is preferred to Pearson's formula.

6. Spearman's formula has its limitations also. It is not practicable in the case of bivariate frequency distribution (Correlation Table). For $n > 30$, this formula should not be used unless the ranks are given, since in the contrary case the calculations are quite time consuming.

EXERCISE 8·4

1. (*a*) What is Spearman's rank correlation coefficient ? Discuss its usefulness.

(*b*) Explain the difference between Karl Pearson's (product moment) correlation coefficient and rank correlation coefficient.

2. (*a*) What are the advantages of Spearman's rank correlation coefficient over Karl Pearson's correlation coefficient ? Explain the method of calculating Spearman's correlation coefficient.

(*b*) Define rank correlation coefficient. When is it preferred to Karl Pearson's coefficient of correlation ?

(*c*) Distinguish between Karl Pearson's coefficient of correlation and Spearman's rank correlation coefficient. Explain with the help of an example when Spearman rank correlation coefficient results to + 1, – 1 and between – 1 to + 1. [*Delhi Univ. B.Com. (Hons.), 2009*]

3. Define Rank Correlation. Write down Spearman's formula for rank correlation coefficient ρ. What are the limits of ρ ? Interpret the case when ρ assumes the minimum value.

4. Rankings of 10 trainees at the beginning (x) and at the end (y) of a certain course are given below :

Trainees	*A*	*B*	*C*	*D*	*E*	*F*	*G*	*H*	*I*	*J*
x	1	6	3	9	5	2	7	10	8	4
y	6	8	3	7	2	1	5	9	4	10

Calculate Spearman's rank correlation coefficient. [*I.C.W.A. (Intermediate), June 1995*]

Ans. $\rho = 0{\cdot}394$.

5. The ranks of same 16 students in Mathematics and Physics are as follows. Two numbers within brackets denote the ranks of the students in Mathematics and Physics.

(1, 1) (2, 10) (3, 3) (4, 4) (5, 5) (6, 7) (7, 2) (8, 6) (9, 8) (10, 11) (11, 15) (12, 9) (13, 14) (14, 12) (15, 16) (16, 13).

Calculate the rank correlation coefficient for proficiencies of this group in Mathematics and Physics.

Ans. $\rho = 0{\cdot}8$.

6. Two judges in a beauty competition rank the 12 entries as follows :

X	1	2	3	4	5	6	7	8	9	10	11	12
Y	12	9	6	10	3	5	4	7	8	2	11	1

What degree of agreement is there between the two judges.

Ans. $\rho = -\,0{\cdot}454$

7. Ten competitors in a beauty contest are ranked by three judges in the following order :

1st Judge	1	5	4	8	9	6	10	7	3	2
2nd Judge	4	8	7	6	5	9	10	3	2	1
3rd Judge	6	7	8	1	5	10	9	2	3	4

Use the rank correlation coefficient to discuss which pair of judges has the nearest approach to beauty.

Ans. $\rho_{12} = 0{\cdot}5515$, $\rho_{13} = 0{\cdot}0545$, $\rho_{23} = 0{\cdot}7333$.

The pair of 2nd and 3rd judges has the nearest approach to common tastes in beauty.

8. For the following data, calculate the Coefficient of Rank Correlation.

x	80	91	99	71	61	81	70	59
y	123	135	154	110	105	134	121	106

Ans. $\rho = 0{\cdot}9524$. [*C.A. (Foundation), May 2001*]

9. The following are the marks obtained by a group of students in two papers. Calculate the rank coefficient of correlation.

Economics	78	36	98	25	75	82	92	62	65	39
Statistics	84	51	91	69	68	62	86	58	35	49

Ans. $\rho = 0{\cdot}6121$.

10. Calculate Spearman's coefficient of rank correlation for the following data of scores in psychological tests (x) and arithmetical ability (y) of 10 children.

Child	A	B	C	D	E	F	G	H	I	J
x :	105	104	102	101	100	99	98	96	93	92
y :	101	103	100	98	95	96	104	92	97	94

Ans. $\rho = 0{\cdot}6$.

11. How do you modify Spearman's rank correlation formula for tied ranks ? Compute the Coefficient of Rank Correlation between X and Y from the data given below :

X :	8	10	7	15	3	20	21	5	10	14	8	16	22	19	6
Y :	3	12	8	13	20	9	14	11	4	16	15	10	18	23	25

Ans. $\rho = 1 - \frac{6 \times (539 + 0{\cdot}5 + 0{\cdot}5)}{15 \times 224} = 0{\cdot}0357.$ *[Delhi Univ. B.Com. (Pass), 1998]*

12. Given the following aptitude and I.Q. scores for a group of students. Find the coefficient of rank correlation.

Aptitude Score :	57	58	59	59	60	61	60	64
I.Q. Score :	97	108	95	106	120	126	113	110

[Delhi Univ. B.A. (Eon. Hons.), 2009]

Ans. $\rho = 1 - \frac{6 \times (24 + 0.5 = 0.5)}{8\,(64 - 1)} = 1 - \frac{150}{504} = 0.7024$

13. The following data relate to the marks obtained by 10 students of a class in Statistics and Costing :

Marks in Statistics :	30	38	28	27	28	23	30	33	28	35
Marks in Costing :	29	27	22	29	20	29	18	21	27	22

Obtain the rank correlation coefficient. *[Delhi Univ. B.Com. (Hons.), 2001]*

Ans. $\rho = -\,0{\cdot}3515$.

14. Find the coefficient of rank correlation between the marks obtained in Mathematics (x) and those in Statistics (y) by 10 students of certain class out of a total of 50 marks in each subject.

Student No. :	1	2	3	4	5	6	7	8	9	10
x :	12	18	32	18	25	24	25	40	38	22
y :	16	15	28	16	24	22	28	36	34	19

Ans. $\rho = 0{\cdot}95$.

15. From the following data, calculate the coefficient of rank correlation between x and y.

x :	32	35	49	60	43	37	43	49	10	20
y :	40	30	70	20	30	50	72	60	45	25

Ans. $\rho = -\,0{\cdot}0758$.

16. When is rank correlation coefficient preferred to Karl Pearson's method ? In a bivariate sample, the sum of squares of differences between the ranks of observed values of two variables is 231 and the correlation coefficient between them is – 0·4. Find the number of pairs. *[Delhi Univ. B.Com. (Hons.) (External), 2006]*

Ans. $n = 10$.

Hint. $\rho = 1 - \frac{6\sum d^2}{n\,(n^2 - 1)} \Rightarrow n\,(n^2 - 1) = \frac{6\sum d^2}{1 - \rho} = \frac{6 \times 231}{1{\cdot}4} = 990$

$\Rightarrow \quad n^3 - n - 990 = 0 \quad \Rightarrow \quad n = 10$ [See Example 8.30]

17. If the rank correlation coefficient is 0·6 and the sum of the squares of differences of ranks is 66, then the number of pairs is

(*i*) 8. (*ii*) 9. (*iii*) 10. (*iv*) 11.

Ans. (*iii*). *[I.C.W.A. (Intermediate), June 2001]*

18. Coefficient of correlation between debenture prices and share prices is found to be 0·143. If the sum of the squares of differences in ranks is given to be 48, find the value of n.

Ans. $n = 7$.

19. The coefficient of rank correlation of the marks obtained by 10 students in biology and chemistry was found to be 0·8. It was later discovered that the difference in ranks in the two subjects obtained by one of the students was wrongly taken as 7 instead of 9. Find the correct coefficient of rank correlation.

Ans. Correct value of $\rho = 0{\cdot}6061$.

20. The coefficient of rank correlation of the marks obtained by 10 students in Statistics and Accountancy was found to be 0·2. It was later discovered that the difference in ranks in the two subjects obtained by one of the students was wrongly taken as 9 instead of 7. Find the correct value of coefficient of rank correlation.

[*Delhi Univ. B.Com (Hons.), 1992*]

Ans. Correct $(\rho) = 0{\cdot}3939$.

21. The rank correlation of a physical fitness contest involving 12 participants was calculated as 0·6. However it was later discovered that the difference in ranks of a participant was read as 8 instead of 3. Find the correct value of rank correlation. [*Delhi Univ. B.A. (Econ. Hons.), 2009*]

Ans. 0·7924.

22. Mention the correct answer.

The ranks according to two attributes in a sample are given below :

R_1	:	1	2	3	4	5
R_2	:	5	4	3	2	1

The rank correlation between them is :

0, +1, –1, None of these.

Ans. $\rho = -1$.

8·8. METHOD OF CONCURRENT DEVIATIONS

This is very casual method of determining the correlation between two series when we are not very serious about its precision. This is based on the signs of the deviations (*i.e.*, direction of the change) of the values of the variable from its preceding value and does not take into account the exact magnitude of the values of the variables. Thus we put a plus (+) sign, minus (–) sign or equality (=) sign for the deviation if the value of the variable is greater than, less than or equal to the preceding value respectively. The deviations in the values of two variables are said to be concurrent if they have the same sign, *i.e.*, either both deviations are positive or both are negative or both are equal. The formula used for computing correlation coefficient r by this method is given by

$$r = \pm\sqrt{\pm\left(\frac{2c-n}{n}\right)} \qquad \ldots(8{\cdot}17)$$

where c is the number of pairs of concurrent deviations and n is the number of pairs of deviations. In the formula (8·17) plus/minus sign to be taken inside and outside the square root is of fundamental importance. Since $-1 \leq r \leq 1$, the quantity inside the square root, *viz.*, $\pm\left(\frac{2c-n}{n}\right)$ must be positive, otherwise r will be imaginary which is not possible.

Thus if $(2c - n)$ is positive, we take positive sign in and outside the square root in (8·17) and if $(2c - n)$ is negative, we take negative sign in and outside the square root in (8·17).

Remarks 1. It should be clearly noted that here n is not the number of pairs of observations but it is the number of pairs of deviations and as such it is one less than the number of pairs of observations.

2. r computed by formula (8·17) is also known as *coefficient of concurrent deviations.*

3. Coefficient of concurrent deviations is primarily based on the following principle :

"*If the short time fluctuations of the time series are positively correlated or in other words, if their deviations are concurrent, their curves would move in the same direction and would indicate positive correlation between them.*"

Thus r computed from (8·17) ordinarily indicates the relationship between short time fluctuations only.

Example 8·32. *Calculate the coefficient of concurrent deviations from the data given below :*

Year	:	*1993*	*1994*	*1995*	*1996*	*1997*	*1998*	*1999*	*2000*	*2001*
Supply	:	*160*	*164*	*172*	*182*	*166*	*170*	*178*	*192*	*186*
Price	:	*292*	*280*	*260*	*234*	*266*	*254*	*230*	*190*	*200*

Solution.

CALCULATION OF COEFFICIENT OF CONCURRENT DEVIATIONS

Year	*Supply*	*Sign of deviation from preceding value (x)*	*Price*	*Sign of deviation from preceding value (y)*	*Product of deviations (xy)*
1993	160		292		
1994	164	+	280	–	–
1995	172	+	260	–	–
1996	182	+	234	–	–
1997	166	–	266	+	–
1998	170	+	254	–	–
1999	178	+	230	–	–
2000	192	+	190	–	–
2001	186	–	200	+	–

Here we have : n = Number of pairs of deviations = 9 – 1 = 8

$c = 0$, since there is no pair of deviations having like signs, *i.e.*, since no product deviations xy is positive.

Coefficient of concurrent deviations is given by

$$r = \pm \sqrt{\pm\left(\frac{2c-n}{n}\right)} = \pm \sqrt{\pm\left(\frac{0-8}{8}\right)} = \pm\sqrt{\pm(-1)}$$

Since $2c - n = -8$, *i.e.*, (negative), we take negative sign inside and outside the square root to get,

$$r = \sqrt{-(-1)} = -1$$

Hence, there is perfect negative correlation between the supply and the price.

Example 8·33. *Calculate the coefficient of concurrent deviations for the following data :*

Supply	:	*65*	*40*	*35*	*75*	*63*	*80*	*35*	*20*	*80*	*60*	*50*
Demand	:	*60*	*55*	*50*	*56*	*30*	*70*	*40*	*35*	*80*	*75*	*80*

[C.A. (*Foundation*), *Nov. 1997*]

Solution.

CALCULATIONS FOR COEFFICIENT OF CONCURRENT DEVIATIONS

Supply (*X*)	*Sign of the deviation from preceding value* (*x*)	*Demand* (*Y*)	*Sign of the deviation from preceding value* (*y*)	*Product of deviations* (*xy*)
65		60		
40	–	55	–	+
35	–	50	–	+
75	+	56	+	+
63	–	30	–	+
80	+	70	+	+
35	–	40	–	+
20	–	35	–	+
80	+	80	+	+
60	–	75	–	+
50	–	80	+	–

Here we have : n = Number of pairs of deviations = 11 – 1 = 10

c = Number of pairs of deviations having like signs = 9

The coefficient of concurrent deviations is given by :

$$r = \pm \sqrt{\pm\frac{(2c-n)}{n}} = \pm \sqrt{\pm\frac{2\times 9-10}{10}} = \pm\sqrt{\pm 0{\cdot}8}$$

Since $2c - n = 8$, is positive, we take positive sign inside and outside the square root so that :

$$r = +\sqrt{0{\cdot}8} = 0{\cdot}89.$$

EXERCISE 8·5

1. (*a*) Explain the method of concurrent deviations for computing the correlation between two variable series.

(*b*) Give the points of strength and weakness of finding out the relationship between two variables by the method of concurrent deviations.

2. Obtain the coefficient of correlation between price of rice and rainfall from the data given below by means of concurrent deviations.

Year	*Price of rice (in Rs.) per quintal*	*Annual rainfall in centimetres*	*Year*	*Price of rice (in Rs.) per quintal*	*Annual rainfall in centimetres*
1959	175	315	1965	196	353
1960	160	340	1966	190	333
1961	158	350	1967	191	390
1962	200	350	1968	195	340
1963	198	330	1969	196	380
1964	195	335	1970	204	340

Ans. $r = -0{\cdot}3015$.

3. Calculate the coefficient of correlation by the method of concurrent deviations from the following data :

Year :	1991	1992	1993	1994	1995	1996	1997	1998	1999
Supply :	80	82	86	91	83	85	89	96	93
Price :	146	140	130	117	133	127	115	95	100

Ans. $r = -1$.

4. Calculate the coefficient of correlation, using the method of concurrent deviations between supply and demand of an item for a ten year period as given below :

Year :	1981	1982	1983	1984	1985	1986	1987	1988	1989	1990
Supply :	125	160	164	174	155	170	165	162	172	175
Demand :	115	125	192	190	165	174	124	127	152	169

[*C.A.* (*Foundation*), *Nov. 1995*]

Ans. $r = 0{\cdot}75$.

5. Calculate the coefficient of correlation by the concurrent deviations method.

Supply :	112	125	126	118	118	121	125	125	131	135
Price :	106	102	102	104	98	96	97	97	95	90

Ans. $r = -0{\cdot}7$.

6. Calculate correlation coefficient by concurrent deviations method :

X :	150	135	90	140	100
Y :	60	50	100	80	90

Ans. $r = -0{\cdot}7071$.

7. Calculate coefficient of concurrent deviations from the following data :

x :	100	120	135	135	115	110	110
y :	50	40	60	60	80	55	65

Ans. $r = 0$.

8. Calculate the coefficient of concurrent deviations from the following data :

No. of pairs of observations = 96

No. of pairs of concurrent deviations = 36

Ans. $r = -0{\cdot}492$.

8·9. COEFFICIENT OF DETERMINATION

Coefficient of correlation between two variable series is a measure of linear relationship between them and indicates the amount of variation of one variable which is associated with or is accounted for by another variable. A more useful and readily comprehensible measure for this purpose is the *coefficient of determination* which gives the percentage variation in the dependent variable that is accounted for by the independent variable. In other words, the coefficient of determination gives the ratio of the explained variance to the total variance. The coefficient of determination is given by the square of the correlation coefficient, *i.e.*, r^2. Thus,

$$\text{Coefficient of determination} = r^2 = \frac{\text{Explained Variance}}{\text{Total Variance}} \qquad \ldots(8{\cdot}18)$$

The coefficient of determination is a much useful and better measure for interpreting the value of r. According to Tuttle :

"*The coefficient of correlation has been grossly over-rated and is used entirely too much. Its square, the coefficient of determination is a much more useful measure of the linear covariation of two variables. The reader should develop the habit of squaring every correlation coefficient he finds, cited or stated before coming to any conclusion about the extent of the linear relationship between the two correlated variables.*"

For example, if the value of $r = 0{\cdot}8$, we cannot conclude that 80% of the variation in the relative series (dependent variable) is due to the variation in the subject series (independent variable). But the coefficient of determination in this case is $r^2 = 0{\cdot}64$ which implies that only 64% of the variation in the relative series has been explained by the subject series and the remaining 36% of the variation is due to other factors.

By the same argument while comparing two correlation coefficients, one of which is 0·4 and the other is 0·8 it is misleading to conclude that the correlation in the second case is twice as high as correlation in the first case. The coefficient of determination clearly explains this viewpoint, since in the case $r = 0{\cdot}4$, the coefficient of determination is 0·16 and in the case $r = 0{\cdot}8$, the coefficient of determination is 0·64, from which we conclude that correlation in the second case is four times as high as correlation in the first case.

Remarks 1. The above discussion implies that :

"*The closeness of the relationship between two variables as determined by correlation coefficient r is not proportional.*"

2. The following table gives the values of the coefficient of determination (r^2) for different values of r.

r	0·1	0·2	0·3	0·4	0·5	0·6	0·7	0·8	0·9	1·0
r^2	0·01	0·04	0·09	0·16	0·25	0·36	0·49	0·64	0·81	1·00

It may be seen from the above table that as the value of r decreases, r^2 decreases very rapidly except in two particular cases $r = 0$ and $r = 1$ when we get $r^2 = r$.

3. Coefficient of determination is always non-negative and as such it does not tell us about the direction of the relationship (whether it is positive or negative) between the two series.

4. Coefficient of Non-determination. The ratio of the unexplained variation to the total variation is called the coefficient of *non-determination*. It is usually denoted by K^2 and is given by the formula :

$$K^2 = \frac{\text{Un-explained Variance}}{\text{Total Variance}} = 1 - \frac{\text{Explained Variance}}{\text{Total Variance}} = 1 - r^2 \quad \ldots(8{\cdot}19)$$

5. Coefficient of Alienation. The coefficient of alienation is given by the square root of the coefficient of non-determination, *i.e.*, by K as given below :

$$K = \pm\sqrt{1 - r^2}. \quad \ldots(8{\cdot}19a)$$

EXERCISE 8·6

1. (*a*) If the correlation coefficient is 0·7, then what is the coefficient of determination ? Also interpret its value. [*C.A. (Foundation), Nov. 1997*]

(*b*) What is the coefficient of determination ? How is it useful in interpreting the value of an observed correlation coefficient r ? Explain with the help of an example.

(*c*) "A high value of the coefficient of determination is neither necessary nor sufficient to ensure a causal relationship between X and Y." Explain. [*Delhi Univ. B.A. (Econ. Hons.), 2005*]

2. Explain the terms :

(*i*) Coefficient of non-determination, (*ii*) Coefficient of alienation,

and give their physical interpretation.

3. (*a*) A correlation coefficient of 0·5 does not mean that 50% of the data are explained. Comment. [*Delhi Univ. B.Com. (Hons.), 1998*]

Ans. Statement is true. Only 25% of the variation is explained.

(*b*) Do you agree with the statement : "$r = 0{\cdot}8$ implies that 80% of the data are explained."

Ans. No. Only 64% of the data are explained.

4. The coefficient of correlation between consumption expenditure (c) and disposable income (y) in a study was found to be + 0·6. What percentage of variation in c is explained by variation in y ?

Ans. 36% of the variation in c is explained by variation in y.

5. (*a*) A correlation between two variables has a value $r = 0{\cdot}6$ and a correlation between other two variables is 0·3. Does it mean that the first correlation is twice as strong as the second ?

(*b*) Correlation between two variables has a value of 0·9 and a correlation between other two variables is 0·3. Can we infer that the first correlation is thrice as strong as the second ? Give reasons. [*Osmania Univ. B.Com., 1997*]

Ans. (*a*) No. (*b*) No.

6. Comment on the following :

"The closeness of the relationship between two variables as determined by r, the correlation coefficient between them, is proportional."

Ans. Statement is wrong.

7. If correlation coefficient between random variables x and y is +ve, comment on the following statements :

(*i*) Correlation coefficient between $-x$ and $-y$ is +ve.

(*ii*) We cannot infer about the sign of correlation between x and $-y$.

(*iii*) Interpret the result $r^2 = 0{\cdot}64$, where r^2 is co-efficient of determination.

[*Delhi Univ. B.A. (Econ. Hons.), 2000*]

Ans. (*i*) True. (*ii*) False. $r(x, -y) = -\, r(x, y) < 0$

(*iii*) 64% of variation in Y is explained by the linear regression of Y on X. [*c.f. Chapter 9.*]

8. If the correlation coefficient between X and Y is 0.4 and between U and V is 0.8, does this imply that the extent of association between U and V is twice as that between X and Y ? [*Delhi Univ. B.A. (Econ. Hons.), 1999*]

9. Calculate correlation coefficient and coefficient of determination from the following data.

$$n = 10, \quad \Sigma X = 140, \quad \Sigma Y = 150$$

$$\Sigma (X-10)^2 = 180, \quad \Sigma (Y-15)^2 = 215, \quad \Sigma (X-10)(Y-15) = 60.$$

[*Delhi Univ. B.Com. (Hons.), (External), 2007*]

Ans. $r = 0{\cdot}915$; Coefficient of determination $= r^2 = 0{\cdot}8372$

Hint. $U = X - 10, \quad V = Y - 15, \quad n = 10$

$$\Sigma U = \Sigma X - 10 \times 10 = 140 - 100 = 40\;; \qquad \Sigma V = \Sigma Y - 15 \times 10 = 150 - 150 = 0$$

$$\Sigma U^2 = 180; \quad \Sigma V^2 = 215\;; \quad \Sigma UV = 60$$

$$r_{XY} = r_{UV} = \frac{n\,\Sigma UV - (\Sigma U)(\Sigma V)}{\sqrt{[n\,\Sigma U^2 - (\Sigma U)^2]\,[n\,\Sigma V^2 - (\Sigma V)^2]}} = 0{\cdot}915$$

8.10. LAG AND LEAD CORRELATION

When there exists a cause and effect relationship between two time series, it is usually observed that there is a time lag between the changes in the values of the independent variable (also called the subject series) and the dependent variable (also called the relative series). Such phenomenon is usually observed in most of the economic and business time series. For example, the monthly advertisement expenditure of a firm on its product and the sales of the product have a fairly good degree of positive correlation. However, the effect of the advertisement expenditure will be felt on the increased sales of the product only after a certain period of time, which may be 3 or 4 months or even more. This tendency on the part of the effect (change in the dependent variable or relative) to occur sometimes after the occurrence of the cause (change in independent variable or subject) is known as '*lag*'.

If it is known that 'lag' exists between two time series, it is imperative to make adjustment for it, before computing the correlation coefficient between the two series otherwise fallacious conclusions will be drawn.

In order to make allowance for the 'lag', it is necessary to determine the 'time-lag' *i.e.*, to estimate the time period which lapses before the change in the dependent variable is affected after a change in the independent variable. The 'period of lag' can be estimated by plotting the two series on a graph paper and noting the time distance between the peaks/troughs of two curves. If the peak (trough) in dependent variable (sales) comes after k-months of the peak (trough) in the independent variable (advertisement expenditure), then there is k-month time-lag between the two variables. Here we say that 'advertisement expenditure curve' will lead by k-months and the 'sales curve' would lag by k-months.

Illustration. Let us consider the following hypothetical time series values of monthly advertisement expenditure (in '000 Rs.) and sales (in '000 Rs.) of the product of a firm.

Month	*Advertisement expenditure ('000 Rs.) (x)*	*Sales ('000 Rs.) (y)*	*Month*	*x*	*y*
Jan.	x_1	y_1	July	x_7	y_7
Feb.	x_2	y_2	Aug.	x_8	y_8
March	x_3	y_3	Sept.	x_9	y_9
April	x_4	y_4	Oct.	x_{10}	y_{10}
May	x_5	y_5	Nov.	x_{11}	y_{11}
June	x_6	y_6	Dec.	x_{12}	y_{12}

Suppose that 'advertisement expenditure' is known to have its effect on the 'sales' after 3 months. After making allowance for this 'time-lag' of 3-months, the correct value of correlation coefficient is obtained on computing Karl Pearson's correlation coefficient between the following two-series values.

x	x_1	x_2	x_3	x_4	x_5	x_6	x_7	x_8	x_9
y	y_4	y_5	y_6	y_7	y_8	y_9	y_{10}	y_{11}	y_{12}

Note : The study of 'Lag-correlation' is specially useful in the study of economic and business time series.

9 Linear Regression Analysis

9·1. INTRODUCTION

The literal or dictionary meaning of the word '*Regression*' is '*stepping back* or *returning to the average value*'. The term was first used by British biometrician Sir Francis Galton in the later part of the 19th century in connection with some studies he made on estimating the extent to which the stature of the sons of tall parents reverts or regresses back to the mean stature of the population. He studied the relationship between the heights of about one thousand fathers and sons and published the results in a paper '*Regression towards Mediocrity in Hereditary Stature*'. The interesting features of his study were :

(*i*) The tall fathers have tall sons and short fathers have short sons.

(*ii*) The average height of the sons of group of tall fathers is less than that of the fathers and the average height of the sons of a group of short fathers is more than that of the fathers.

In other words, Galton's studies revealed that the off springs of abnormally tall or short parents tend to revert or step back to the average height of the population, a phenomenon which Galton described as Regression to Mediocrity.

He concluded that if the average height of a certain group of fathers is 'a' cms. above (below) the general average height then average height of their sons will be $(a \times r)$ cms. above (below) the general average height where r is the correlation coefficients between the heights of the given group of fathers and their sons. In this case correlation is positive and since $|r| \leq 1$ we have $a \times r \leq a$. This supports the result in (*ii*) above.

But today the word regression as used in Statistics has a much wider perspective without any reference to biometry. Regression analysis, in the general sense, means the estimation or prediction of the unknown value of one variable from the known value of the other variable. It is one of the very important statistical tools which is extensively used in almost all sciences — natural, social and physical. It is specially used in business and economics to study the relationship between two or more variables that are related causally and for estimation of demand and supply curves, cost functions, production and consumption functions, etc.

Prediction or estimation is one of the major problems in almost all spheres of human activity. The estimation or prediction of future production, consumption, prices, investments, sales, profits, income, etc., are of paramount importance to a businessman or economist. Population estimates and population projections are indispensable for efficient planning of an economy. The pharmaceutical concerns are interested in studying or estimating the effect of new drugs on patients. Regression analysis is one of the very scientific techniques for making such predictions. In the words of M.M. Blair "*Regression analysis is a mathematical measure of the average relationship between two or more variables in terms of the original units of the data*".

We come across a number of inter-related events in our day-to-day life. For instance, the yield of a crop depends on the rainfall, the cost or price of a product depends on the production and advertising expenditure, the demand for a particular product depends on its price, expenditure of a person depends on his income, and so on. The regression analysis confined to the study of only two variables at a time is termed as *simple regression*. But quite often the values of a particular phenomenon may be affected by multiplicity of factors. The regression analysis for studying more than two variables at a time is known as *multiple regression*. However, in this chapter we shall confine ourselves to simple regression only.

In regression analysis there are two types of variables. The variable whose value is influenced or is to be predicted is called *dependent variable* and the variable which influences the values or is used for prediction, is called *independent variable.* In regression analysis independent variable is also known as *regressor or predictor or explanator* while the dependent variable is also known as *regressed* or *explained variable.*

9·2. LINEAR AND NON-LINEAR REGRESSION

If the given bivariate data are plotted on a graph, the points so obtained on the scatter diagram will more or less concentrate round a curve, called the '*curve of regression*'. Often such a curve is not distinct and is quite confusing and sometimes complicated too. The mathematical equation of the regression curve, usually called the *regression equation*, enables us to study the average change in the value of the dependent variable for any given value of the independent variable.

If the regression curve is a straight line, we say that there is *linear regression* between the variables under study. The equation of such a curve is the equation of a straight line, *i.e.*, a first degree equation in the variables x and y. In case of linear regression the values of the dependent variable increase by a constant absolute amount for a unit change in the value of the independent variable. However, if the curve of regression is not a straight line, the regression is termed as *curved or non-linear regression.* The regression equation will be a functional relation between x and y involving terms in x and y of degree higher than one, *i.e.*, involving terms of the type x^2, y^2, xy, etc. However, in this chapter we shall confine our discussion to linear regression between two variables only.

9·3. LINES OF REGRESSION

Line of regression is the line which gives the best estimate of one variable for any given value of the other variable. In case of two variables x and y, we shall have two lines of regression; one of y on x and the other of x on y.

Definition. *Line of regression of y on x is the line which gives the best estimate for the value of y for any specified value of x.*

Similarly, *line of regression of x on y is the line which gives the best estimate for the value of x for any specified value of y.*

The term best fit is interpreted in accordance with the *Principle of Least Squares which consists in minimising the sum of the squares of the residuals or the errors of estimates, i.e., the deviations between the given observed values of the variable and their corresponding estimated values as given by the line of best fit.* We may minimise the sum of the squares of the errors parallel to y-axis or parallel to x-axis, the former (*i.e.*, minimising the sum of squares of errors parallel to y-axis), gives the equation of the line of regression of y on x and the latter, *viz.*, minimising the sum of squares of the errors parallel to x-axis gives the equation of the line of regression of x on y.

We shall explain below the technique of deriving the equation of the line of regression of y on x.

9·3·1. Derivation of Line of Regression of y on x. Let (x_1, y_1), (x_2, y_2), ..., (x_n, y_n), be n pairs of observations on the two variables x and y under study. Let

$$y = a + bx \qquad \dots (9·1)$$

be the line of regression (best fit) of y on x.

For any given point $P_i\ (x_i, y_i)$ in the scatter diagram, the error of estimate or residual as given by the line of best fit (9·1) is $P_i H_i$. Now, the x-coordinate of H_i is same as that of P_i, *viz.*, x_i and since $H_i\ (x_i)$ lies on the line (9·1), the y-coordinate of H_i, *i.e.*, $H_i M$ is given by $(a + bx_i)$. Hence, the error of estimate for P_i is given by

$$P_i H_i = P_i M - H_i M$$

$$= y_i - (a + bx_i) \qquad \dots (9·2)$$

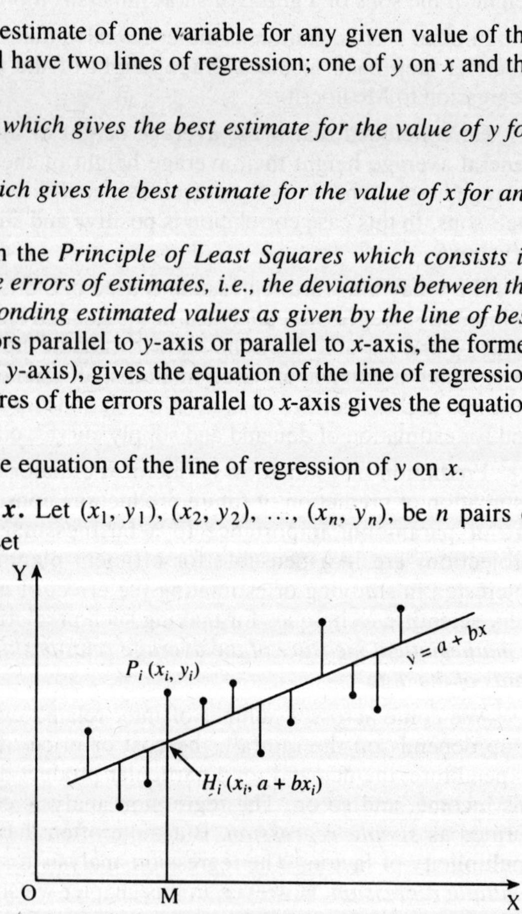

Fig. 9·1.

This is the error (parallel to the y-axis) for the ith point. We will have such errors for all the points on scatter diagram. For the points which lie above the line, the error would be positive and for the points which lie below the line, the error would be negative.

According to the principle of least squares, we have to determine the constants a and b in (9·1) such that the sum of the squares of the errors of estimates is minimum. In other words, we have to minimise

$$E = \sum_{i=1}^{n} P_i H_i^2 = \sum_{i=1}^{n} (y_i - a - bx_i)^2 \qquad \ldots(9·3)$$

subject to variations in a and b.

We may also write E as :

$$E = \Sigma(y - y_e)^2 = \Sigma(y - a - bx)^2, \qquad \ldots(9·3a)$$

where y_e is the estimated value of y as given by (9·1) for given value of x and summation (Σ) is taken over the n pairs of observations.

Using the principle of maxima and minima in differential calculus, E will have an extremum (maximum or minimum) for variations in a and b if its partial derivatives *w.r.t.* a and b vanish separately. Hence from (9·3a), we get

$$\frac{\partial E}{\partial a} = 0 \quad \text{and} \quad \frac{\partial E}{\partial b} = 0 \qquad \ldots(9·4)$$

$$\Rightarrow \qquad \Sigma y = na + b\Sigma x \qquad \ldots(9·5)$$

$$\text{and} \qquad \Sigma xy = a\Sigma x + b\Sigma x^2 \qquad \ldots(9·6)$$

These equations are known as the *normal equations* for estimating a and b. The quantities Σx, Σx^2, Σy, Σxy can be obtained from the given set of n points $(x_1, y_1), (x_2, y_2), \ldots, (x_n, y_n)$ and we can solve the equations (9·5) and (9·6) simultaneously for a and b, to get :

$$a = \frac{(\Sigma x^2)(\Sigma y) - (\Sigma x)(\Sigma xy)}{n\Sigma x^2 - (\Sigma x)^2} \quad \ldots(9·7) \quad \text{and} \quad b = \frac{n\Sigma xy - (\Sigma x)(\Sigma y)}{n\Sigma x^2 - (\Sigma x)^2} \qquad \ldots(9·8)$$

Substituting these values of a and b from (9·7) and (9·8) in (9·1), we get the required equation of the line of regression of y on x.

The equation of the line of regression of y on x can be obtained in a much more systematic and simplified form in terms of $\bar{x}$, $\bar{y}$, σ_x, σ_y and $r = r_{xy}$ as explained below.

Dividing both sides of (9·5) by n, the total number of pairs, we get

$$\frac{1}{n}\Sigma y = a + b \, . \, \frac{1}{n}\Sigma x \quad \Rightarrow \quad \bar{y} = a + b\bar{x} \qquad \ldots(9·9)$$

This implies that *line of best fit, i.e., regression of y on x passes through the point* $(\bar{x}, \bar{y})$. *Or in other words, the point* $(\bar{x}, \bar{y})$ *lies on the line of regression of y on x.*

From (9.8), we get :

$$b = \frac{\text{Cov}(x, y)}{\sigma_x^2} \qquad \ldots(9·10)$$

We find that the equation (9·1) is in the slope-intercept form, *viz.*, $y = mx + c$. Hence *b represents the slope of the line of regression of y on x*. Further, we have proved in (9·9) that this line (*i.e.*, line of regression of y on x) passes through the point $(\bar{x}, \bar{y})$. Hence, using the slope-point form of the equation of a line, the required equation of the line of regression of y on x becomes :

$$y - \bar{y} = b(x - \bar{x}) \qquad \ldots(9·11)$$

$$\text{or} \qquad y - \bar{y} = \frac{\text{Cov}(x, y)}{\sigma_x^2} \cdot (x - \bar{x}) \qquad \ldots(9·12)$$

$$\text{But} \qquad r = r_{xy} = \frac{\text{Cov}(x, y)}{\sigma_x \sigma_y} \quad \Rightarrow \quad \text{Cov}(x, y) = r\,\sigma_x \sigma_y$$

Substituting in (9·12), we may also write the equation of the line of regression of y on x as :

$$y-\bar{y} = \frac{r\sigma_x\sigma_y}{\sigma_x^2}(x-\bar{x}) \quad \Rightarrow \quad y-\bar{y} = \frac{r\,\sigma_y}{\sigma_x}(x-\bar{x}) \qquad \ldots(9·13)$$

Remarks 1. $\frac{\partial E}{\partial a} = 0$ and $\frac{\partial E}{\partial b} = 0$, is only a requirement for extremum (maxima or minima) of E.

The necessary and sufficient conditions for a minima of E for variations in a and b are :

$$(i)\quad \frac{\partial E}{\partial a} = 0, \quad \frac{\partial E}{\partial b} = 0 \qquad \ldots(*)$$

and
$$(ii)\quad \frac{\partial^2 E}{\partial a^2} > 0 \quad \text{and} \quad \Delta = \begin{vmatrix} \frac{\partial^2 E}{\partial a^2} & \frac{\partial^2 E}{\partial a\,\partial b} \\ \frac{\partial^2 E}{\partial b\,\partial a} & \frac{\partial^2 E}{\partial b^2} \end{vmatrix} > 0 \qquad \ldots(**)$$

Theorem. *The solution of the least square equations (9.5) and (9.6), provides a minimum of E defined in (9.3).*

The proof of this theorem is beyond the scope of the book.

2. From (9·4) we have :

$$\Sigma(y-a-bx) = 0 \quad \Rightarrow \quad \Sigma(y-y_e) = 0 \qquad \ldots(9·14)$$

where y_e is the estimated value of y for a given value of x as given by the line of regression of y on x (9·1).

3. The line of regression of y on x passes through the point $(\bar{x}, \bar{y})$.

4. Fitting of linear and non-linear regression (trends) is discussed in detail in Chapter 11 on '*Time Series Analysis*' for determining the trend values.

9·3·2. Line of Regression of x on y. The line of regression of x on y is the line which gives the best estimate of x for any given value of y. It is also obtained by the principle of least squares on minimising the sum of squares of the errors parallel to the x-axis (See Fig. 9·2). By starting with the equation of the form :

$$x = A + By, \qquad \ldots(9·15)$$

and minimising the sum of the squares of errors of estimates of x, *i.e.*, deviations between the given values of x and their estimates given by line of regression of x on y, *viz.*, (9·17), *i.e.*, minimising

$$E = \Sigma(x-A-By)^2, \qquad \ldots(9·16)$$

we shall get the normal equations for estimating A and B as :

$$\Sigma x = nA + B\Sigma y \quad \text{and} \quad \Sigma xy = A\Sigma y + B\Sigma y^2 \qquad \ldots(9·17)$$

Solving (9·17) simultaneously for A and B, we shall get

$$A = \frac{(\Sigma y^2)(\Sigma x) - (\Sigma y)(\Sigma xy)}{n\Sigma y^2 - (\Sigma y)^2} \qquad \ldots(9·18)$$

and
$$B = \frac{n\Sigma xy - (\Sigma x)(\Sigma y)}{n\Sigma y^2 - (\Sigma y)^2} \qquad \ldots(9·19)$$

Substituting these values of A and B in (9·15), we shall get the required equation of line of regression of x on y.

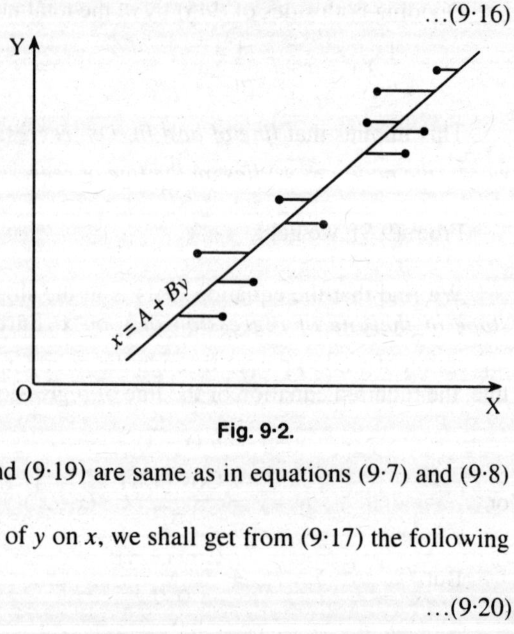

Fig. 9·2.

Remark. The values of A and B obtained in (9·18) and (9·19) are same as in equations (9·7) and (9·8) with x changed to y and y to x.

Proceeding exactly as in the case of line of regression of y on x, we shall get from (9·17) the following results :

$$(i)\qquad \bar{x} = A + B\bar{y} \qquad \ldots(9·20)$$

This implies that the line of regression of x on y passes through the point $(\bar{x}, \bar{y})$.

(*ii*) $$B = \frac{\text{Cov}(x, y)}{\sigma_y^2} = \frac{r\sigma_x}{\sigma_y} \quad \ldots(9\cdot21)$$

(*iii*) The equation of the line of regression of x on y is

$$x - \bar{x} = B(y - \bar{y}) \quad \ldots(9\cdot22)$$

$$\Rightarrow \quad x - \bar{x} = \frac{\text{Cov}(x, y)}{\sigma_y^2}(y - \bar{y}) \quad \ldots(9\cdot23)$$

$$\Rightarrow \quad x - \bar{x} = \frac{r\sigma_x}{\sigma_y}(y - \bar{y}) \quad \ldots(9\cdot24)$$

The derivation of these results is left as an exercise to the reader.

Remarks 1. The regression equation (9·13) implies that the line of regression of y on x passes through the point $(\bar{x}, \bar{y})$. Similarly (9·24) implies that the line of regression of x on y also passes through the point $(\bar{x}, \bar{y})$. Hence *both the lines of regression pass through the point $(\bar{x}, \bar{y})$. In other words, the mean values $(\bar{x}, \bar{y})$ can be obtained as the point of intersection of the two regression lines.*

2. *Why two lines of regression* ? There are always two lines of regression, one of y on x and the other of x on y. The line of regression of y on x (9·12) or (9·13) is used to estimate or predict the value of y for any given value of x, *i.e.*, when y is a dependent variable and x is an independent variable. The estimate so obtained will be best in the sense that it will have the minimum possible error as defined by the principle of least squares. We can also obtain an estimate of x for any given value of y by using equation (9·13) but the estimate so obtained will not be best since (9·13) is obtained on minimising the sum of the squares of errors of estimates in y and not in x. Hence to estimate or predict x for any given value of y, we use the regression equation of x on y (9·24) which is derived on minimising the sum of the squares of errors of estimates in x. Here x is a dependent variable and y is an independent variable. The two regression equations are not reversible or interchangeable because of the simple reason that the basis and assumptions for deriving these equations are quite different. The regression equation of y on x is obtained on minimising the sum of the square of the errors parallel to the y-axis while the regression equation of x on y is obtained on minimising the sum of squares of the errors parallel to the x-axis.

In a particular case of perfect correlation, positive or negative *i.e.*, $r = \pm 1$, the equation of line of regression of y on x becomes :

$$y - \bar{y} = \pm\frac{\sigma_y}{\sigma_x}(x - \bar{x}) \quad \Rightarrow \quad \frac{y - \bar{y}}{\sigma_y} = \pm\left(\frac{x - \bar{x}}{\sigma_x}\right) \quad \ldots(*)$$

Similarly, the equation of the line of regression of x on y becomes :

$$x - \bar{x} = \pm\frac{\sigma_x}{\sigma_y}(y - \bar{y}) \quad \Rightarrow \quad \frac{y - \bar{y}}{\sigma_y} = \pm\left(\frac{x - \bar{x}}{\sigma_x}\right), \quad \ldots(**)$$

which is same as (*).

Hence in case of perfect correlation, ($r = \pm 1$), both the lines of regression coincide. Therefore, *in general, we always have two lines of regression except in the particular case of perfect correlation ($r = \pm 1$) when both the lines coincide and we get only one line.*

9·3·3. Angle Between the Regression Lines.

If θ is the acute angle between the two lines of regression then

$$\theta = \tan^{-1}\left\{\frac{\sigma_x\sigma_y}{\sigma_x^2 + \sigma_y^2}\left(\frac{1 - r^2}{|r|}\right)\right\} \quad \ldots(9\cdot25)$$

In particular, if $r = \pm 1$ then $\quad \theta = \tan^{-1}(0) \quad \Rightarrow \quad \theta = 0$ or π.

i.e., the two lines are either coincident ($\theta = 0$) or they are parallel ($\theta = \pi$). But since both the lines of regression intersect at the point $(\bar{x}, \bar{y})$, they cannot be parallel. Hence *in case of perfect correlation, positive or negative, the two lines of regression coincide.*

If $r = 0$, then from (9·28), $\theta = \tan^{-1}(\infty) = \pi/2$,

i.e., if the variables are uncorrelated, the two lines of regression become perpendicular to each other.

Remarks 1. When $r = 0$ *i.e.*, when x and y are uncorrelated, then the lines of regression of y on x, and x on y are given respectively by [From (9·13) and (9·24)],

$$y - \bar{y} = 0 \quad \Rightarrow \quad y = \bar{y} \quad \text{and} \quad x - \bar{x} = 0 \quad \Rightarrow \quad x = \bar{x}$$

$y = \bar{y}$, represents a line parallel to X-axis at a distance of $\bar{y}$ units from the origin and $x = \bar{x}$, represents a line parallel to Y-axis at a distance of $\bar{x}$ units from the origin.

Hence, *if $r = 0$, the two lines of regression are perpendicular to each other and are parallel to x-axis and y-axis respectively*, as shown in Fig 9·2(a).

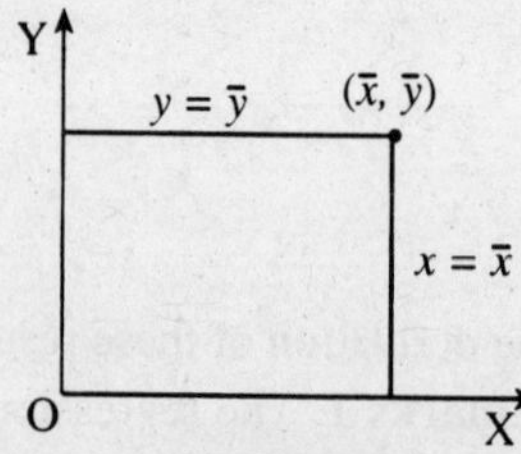

Fig. 9·2(*a*).

2. We have seen above that if $r = 0$ (variables uncorrelated), the two lines of regression are perpendicular to each other and if $r = \pm 1$, $\theta = 0$, *i.e.*, the two lines coincide. This leads us to the conclusion that for higher degree of correlation between the variables, the angle between the lines is smaller, *i.e.*, the two lines of regression are nearer to each other. On the other hand, the angle between the lines increases, *i.e.*, the lines of regression move apart as the value of correlation coefficient decreases. In other words, if the lines of regression make a larger angle, they indicate a poor degree of correlation between the variables and ultimately for $\theta = \pi/2$, *i.e.*, the lines becoming perpendicular if no correlation exists between the variables. Thus by plotting the lines of regression on a graph paper, we can have an approximate idea about the degree of correlation between the two variables under study. Some illustrations are given below in Fig. 9·3(a) to Fig. 9·3(e).

TWO LINES COINCIDE ($r = -1$)

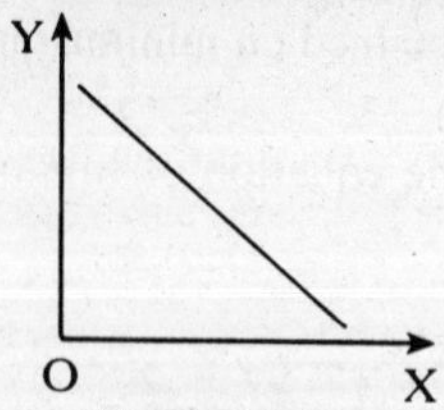

Fig. 9·3(*a*).

TWO LINES COINCIDE ($r = 1$)

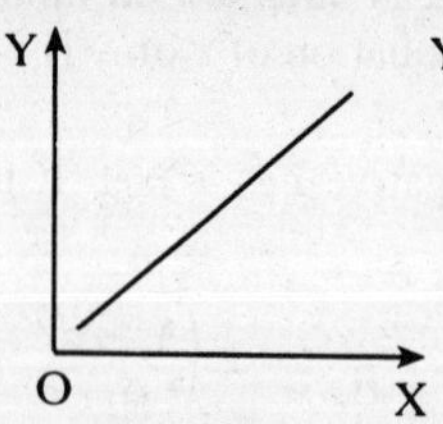

Fig. 9·3(*b*).

TWO LINES PERPENDICULAR ($r = 0$)

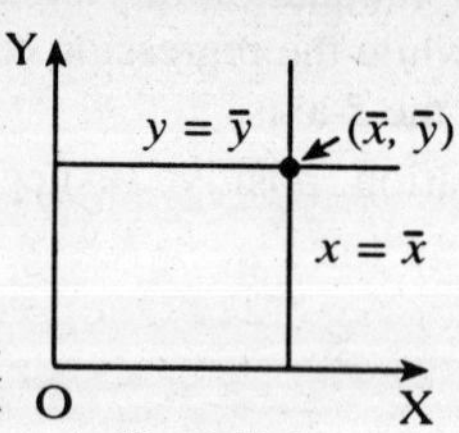

Fig. 9·3(*c*).

TWO LINES APART (LOW DEGREE OF CORRELATION)

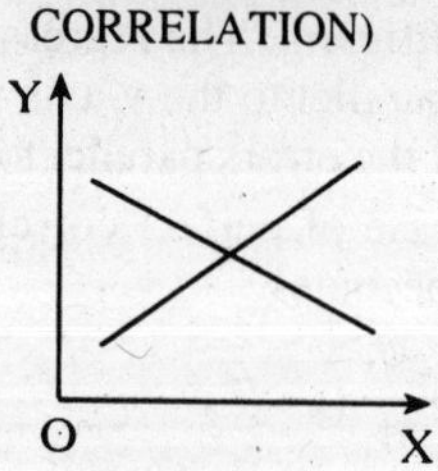

Fig. 9·3 (*d*).

TWO LINES CLOSER (HIGH DEGREE OF CORRELATION)

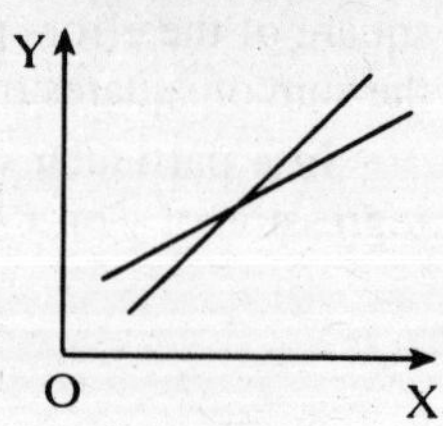

Fig. 9·3(*e*).

9·4. COEFFICIENTS OF REGRESSION

Let us consider the line of regression of y on x, *viz.*,

$$y = a + bx$$

The coefficient 'b' which is the slope of the line of regression of y on x is called the *coefficient of regression* of y on x. *It represents the increment in the value of the dependent variable y for a unit change in the value of the independent variable x.* In other words, it represents the rate of change of y *w.r.t.* x. For notational convenience, the slope b, *i.e.*, coefficient of regression of y on x is written as b_{yx}.

Similarly in the regression equation of x on y, *viz.*,

$$x = A + By,$$

the coefficient B represents the change in the value of dependent variable x for a unit change in the value of independent variable y and is called the *coefficient of regression of x on y*. For notational convenience, it is written as b_{xy}.

Notations

b_{yx} = Coefficient of regression of y on x.

b_{xy} = Coefficient of regression of x on y.

From (9·10), the coefficient of regression of y on x is given by

$$b_{yx} = \frac{\text{Cov}(x, y)}{\sigma_x^2} = \frac{r\,\sigma_y}{\sigma_x} \qquad [\because \text{Cov}(x, y) = r\,\sigma_x\,\sigma_y.] \qquad \ldots(9\cdot26)$$

Similarly from (9·21), the coefficient of regression of x on y is given by :

$$b_{xy} = \frac{\text{Cov}(x, y)}{\sigma_y^2} = \frac{r\,\sigma_x}{\sigma_y} \qquad \ldots(9\cdot27)$$

Accordingly, the equation of the line of regression of y on x becomes

$$y - \bar{y} = b_{yx}(x - \bar{x}), \qquad \ldots(9\cdot28)$$

and the equation of the line of regression of x on y becomes :

$$x - \bar{x} = b_{xy}(y - \bar{y}) \qquad \ldots(9\cdot29)$$

Remarks 1. For numerical computations of the equations of line of regression of y on x, and x on y, the following formulae for the regression coefficients b_{yx} and b_{xy} are very convenient to use.

$$b_{yx} = \frac{\text{Cov}(x, y)}{\sigma_x^2} = \frac{\Sigma(x - \bar{x})(y - \bar{y})}{\Sigma(x - \bar{x})^2} = \frac{n\Sigma xy - (\Sigma x)(\Sigma y)}{n\Sigma x^2 - (\Sigma x)^2} \qquad \ldots(9\cdot30)$$

and $$b_{xy} = \frac{\text{Cov}(x, y)}{\sigma_y^2} = \frac{\Sigma(x - \bar{x})(y - \bar{y})}{\Sigma(y - \bar{y})^2} = \frac{n\Sigma xy - (\Sigma x)(\Sigma y)}{n\Sigma y^2 - (\Sigma y)^2} \qquad \ldots(9\cdot31)$$

Formulae (9·30) and (9·31) are very useful for computing the values of regression coefficients from given set of n points $(x_1, y_1), (x_2, y_2), \ldots, (x_n, y_n)$.

Other convenient formulae to be used for finding the regression coefficients for numerical problems are :

$$b_{yx} = \frac{r\,\sigma_y}{\sigma_x} \quad \text{and} \quad b_{xy} = \frac{r\,\sigma_x}{\sigma_y} \qquad \ldots(9\cdot32)$$

2. Correlation coefficient between two variables x and y is a symmetrical function between x and y, *i.e.*, $r_{xy} = r_{yx}$. However, the regression coefficients are not symmetric functions of x and y, *i.e.*, $b_{yx} \neq b_{xy}$.

3. We have :

$$b_{yx} = \frac{\text{Cov}(x, y)}{\sigma_x^2} \ldots(*), \qquad b_{xy} = \frac{\text{Cov}(x, y)}{\sigma_y^2} \ldots(**), \qquad r_{xy} = \frac{\text{Cov}(x, y)}{\sigma_x\,\sigma_y} \ldots(***)$$

From (*) and (**), we observe that the sign of each regression coefficient b_{yx} and b_{xy} depends on the covariance term, since $\sigma_x > 0$ and $\sigma_y > 0$. *If Cov (x, y) is positive, both the regression coefficients are positive and if Cov (x, y) is negative, both the regression coefficients are negative.*

4. Further, since $\sigma_x > 0$ and $\sigma_y > 0$, the sign of each of r, b_{yx} and b_{xy} depends on the covariance term. If Cov (x, y) is positive, all the three are positive and if Cov (x, y) is negative, all the three are negative. This result can be stated slightly differently as follows :

The sign of correlation coefficient is same as that of the regression coefficients. If regression coefficients are positive, r is positive and if regression coefficients are negative, r is negative.

9·4·1. Theorems on Regression Coefficients

Theorem 9·1. The correlation coefficient is the geometric mean between the regression coefficients *i.e.*,

$$r^2 = b_{yx} \cdot b_{xy} \qquad \ldots(9\cdot33)$$

Proof. We have, $b_{yx} = \dfrac{\text{Cov}(x, y)}{\sigma_x^2} = r \cdot \dfrac{\sigma_y}{\sigma_x}$ ...(9·34) and $b_{xy} = \dfrac{\text{Cov}(x, y)}{\sigma_y^2} = r \cdot \dfrac{\sigma_x}{\sigma_y}$ ...(9·35)

Multiplying (9·34) and (9·35), we get $r^2 = b_{yx} \cdot b_{xy} \Rightarrow r = \pm\sqrt{b_{yx} \cdot b_{xy}}$ ...(9·36)

which establishes the result.

Remark. The sign to be taken before the square root is same as that of regression coefficients. *If the regression coefficients are positive, we take positive sign in (9·36) and if regression coefficients are negative, we take negative sign in (9·36).*

Theorem 9·2. If one of the regression coefficients is greater than unity (one), the other must be less than unity.

Proof. If one of the regression coefficients is greater than 1, then the other must be less than one because otherwise, on using (9·33), we shall get :

$$r^2 = b_{yx} \cdot b_{xy} > 1,$$

which is impossible, since $0 \le r^2 \le 1$.

Theorem 9·3. The arithmetic mean of the modulus value of the regression coefficients is greater than the modulus value of the correlation coefficient

i.e., $$\frac{1}{2}\left[\,|\,b_{yx}\,| + |\,b_{xy}\,|\,\right] > |\,r\,| \quad \ldots(9.37)$$

Theorem 9·4. Regression coefficients are independent of change of origin but not of scale.

Symbolically, if we transform from x and y to new variables u and v by change of origin and scale, *viz.*,

$$u = \frac{x-a}{h},\quad v = \frac{y-b}{k},\quad \text{where } a,\ b,\ h\ (>0) \text{ and } k(>0) \text{ are constants,} \quad \ldots(9·38)$$

Then $$b_{yx} = \frac{k}{h}\, b_{vu} \quad \text{and} \quad b_{xy} = \frac{h}{k} \cdot b_{uv} \quad \ldots(9·39)$$

In particular if we take $h = k = 1$, *i.e.,* we transform the variables x and y to u and v by the relation :

$$u = x - a \quad \text{and} \quad v = y - b \quad \ldots(9·40)$$

i.e., by change of origin only, then from (9·39), we get

$$b_{xy} = b_{uv} = \frac{n\sum uv - (\sum u)(\sum v)}{n\sum v^2 - (\sum v)^2} \quad \ldots(9·40a) \quad \text{and} \quad b_{yx} = b_{vu} = \frac{n\sum uv - (\sum u)(\sum v)}{n\sum u^2 - (\sum u)^2} \quad \ldots(9·40b)$$

These formulae are very useful for obtaining the equations of the lines of regression if the mean values $\bar{x}$ and / or $\bar{y}$ come out to be in fractions or if the values of x and y are large.

Example 9·1. *From the following data, obtain the two regression equations :*

Sales :	*91*	*97*	*108*	*121*	*67*	*124*	*51*	*73*	*111*	*57*
Purchases :	*71*	*75*	*69*	*97*	*70*	*91*	*39*	*61*	*80*	*47*

Solution. Let us denote the sales by the variable X and the purchases by the variable Y.

CALCULATIONS FOR REGRESSION EQUATIONS

x	y	$dx = x - \bar{x}$	$dy = y - \bar{y}$	dx^2	dy^2	$dxdy$
91	71	1	1	1	1	1
97	75	7	5	49	25	35
108	69	18	–1	324	1	–18
121	97	31	27	961	729	837
67	70	– 23	0	529	0	0
124	91	34	21	1156	441	714
51	39	–39	–31	1521	961	1209
73	61	–17	– 9	289	81	153
111	80	21	10	441	100	210
57	47	–33	–23	1089	529	759
$\sum x = 900$	$\sum y = 700$	$\sum dx = 0$	$\sum dy = 0$	$\sum dx^2 = 6360$	$\sum dy^2 = 2868$	$\sum dx\, dy = 3900$

We have $$\bar{x} = \frac{\sum x}{n} = \frac{900}{10} = 90\,; \quad \text{and} \quad \bar{y} = \frac{\sum y}{n} = \frac{700}{10} = 70$$

$$b_{yx} = \frac{\sum(x-\bar{x})(y-\bar{y})}{\sum(x-\bar{x})^2} = \frac{\sum dx\, dy}{\sum dx^2} = \frac{3900}{6360} = 0·6132$$

$$b_{xy} = \frac{\Sigma(x-\bar{x})(y-\bar{y})}{\Sigma(y-\bar{y})^2} = \frac{\Sigma\, dx\, dy}{\Sigma dy^2} = \frac{3900}{2868} = 1{\cdot}361$$

Regression Equations

Equation of line of regression of y on x is	Equation of line of regression of x on y is
$y-\bar{y} = b_{yx}(x-\bar{x})$	$x-\bar{x} = b_{xy}(y-\bar{y})$
$\Rightarrow\ y-70 = 0{\cdot}6132\,(x-90)$	$\Rightarrow\ x-90 = 1{\cdot}361\,(y-70)$
$= 0{\cdot}6132x - 55{\cdot}188$	$= 1{\cdot}361y - 95{\cdot}27$
$\Rightarrow\ y = 0{\cdot}6132x - 55{\cdot}188 + 70{\cdot}000$	$\Rightarrow\ x = 1{\cdot}361y - 95{\cdot}27 + 90{\cdot}00$
$\Rightarrow\ y = 0{\cdot}6132x + 14{\cdot}812$	$\Rightarrow\ x = 1{\cdot}361y - 5{\cdot}27$

Remark. We have

$$r^2 = b_{yx}\, b_{xy} = 0{\cdot}6132 \times 1{\cdot}361 = 0{\cdot}8346 \quad \Rightarrow \quad r = \pm\sqrt{0{\cdot}8346} = \pm\, 0{\cdot}9135$$

But since, both the regression coefficients are positive, r must be positive. Hence, $r = 0{\cdot}9135$.

Example 9·2. *From the data given below find :*

(a) The two regression coefficients. *(b) The two regression equations.*

(c) The coefficient of correlation between the marks in Economics and Statistics.

(d) The most likely marks in Statistics when marks in Economics are 30.

Marks in Economics	:	25	28	35	32	31	36	29	38	34	32
Marks in Statistics	:	43	46	49	41	36	32	31	30	33	39

[*Himachal Pradesh Univ. M.A. (Econ.), 2003*]

Solution. Let us denote the marks in Economics by the variable X and the marks in Statistics by the variable Y.

CALCULATIONS FOR REGRESSION EQUATIONS

x	y	$dx = x-\bar{x} = x-32$	$dy = y-\bar{y} = y-38$	dx^2	dy^2	$dxdy$
25	43	−7	5	49	25	−35
28	46	−4	8	16	64	−32
35	49	3	11	9	121	33
32	41	0	3	0	9	0
31	36	−1	−2	1	4	2
36	32	4	−6	16	36	−24
29	31	−3	−7	9	49	21
38	30	6	−8	36	64	−48
34	33	2	−5	4	25	−10
32	39	0	1	0	1	0
$\Sigma x = 320$	$\Sigma y = 380$	$\Sigma dx = 0$	$\Sigma dy = 0$	$\Sigma dx^2 = 140$	$\Sigma dy^2 = 398$	$\Sigma dxdy = -93$

Here, $\bar{x} = \dfrac{\Sigma x}{n} = \dfrac{320}{10} = 32$; and $\bar{y} = \dfrac{\Sigma y}{n} = \dfrac{380}{10} = 38.$

(*a*) **Regression Coefficients**

Coefficient of regression of y on $x = b_{yx} = \dfrac{\Sigma(x-\bar{x})(y-\bar{y})}{\Sigma(x-\bar{x})^2} = \dfrac{\Sigma\, dxdy}{\Sigma\, dx^2} = \dfrac{-93}{140} = -\,0{\cdot}6643$

Coefficient of regression of x on $y = b_{xy} = \dfrac{\Sigma(x-\bar{x})(y-\bar{y})}{\Sigma(y-\bar{y})^2} = \dfrac{\Sigma\, dx\, dy}{\Sigma\, dy^2} = \dfrac{-93}{398} = -\,0{\cdot}2337$

(*b*) **Regression Equations**

Equation of the line of regression of x on y is :

$$x - \bar{x} = b_{xy}(y - \bar{y})$$
$$\Rightarrow \quad x - 32 = -0{\cdot}2337(y - 38)$$
$$= -0{\cdot}2337y + 0{\cdot}2337 \times 38$$
$$= -0{\cdot}2337y + 8{\cdot}8806$$
$$\Rightarrow \quad x = -0{\cdot}2337y + 32 + 8{\cdot}8806$$
$$\Rightarrow \quad x = -0{\cdot}2337y + 40{\cdot}8806$$

Equation of the line of regression of y on x is :

$$y - \bar{y} = b_{yx}(x - \bar{x})$$
$$\Rightarrow \quad y - 38 = -0{\cdot}6643(x - 32)$$
$$\Rightarrow \quad y = -0{\cdot}6643x + 38 + 0{\cdot}6643 \times 32$$
$$= -0{\cdot}6643x + 38 + 21{\cdot}2576$$
$$\Rightarrow \quad y = -0{\cdot}6643x + 59{\cdot}2576 \quad \ldots(*)$$

(*c*) **Correlation Coefficient.** We have

$$r^2 = b_{yx} \cdot b_{xy} = (-0{\cdot}6643) \times (-0{\cdot}2337) = 0{\cdot}1552 \quad \Rightarrow \quad r = \pm\sqrt{0{\cdot}1552} = \pm 0{\cdot}394$$

Since both the regression coefficients are negative, r must be negative. Hence, we get $r = -0{\cdot}394$.

(*d*) In order to estimate the most likely marks in Statistics (y) when marks in Economics (x) are 30, we shall use the line of regression of y on x *viz.*, the equation (*). Taking $x = 30$ in (*), the required estimate is given by

$$y = -0{\cdot}6643 \times 30 + 59{\cdot}2576 = -19{\cdot}929 + 59{\cdot}2576 = 39{\cdot}3286$$

Hence, the most likely marks in Statistics when marks in Economics are 30, are $39{\cdot}3286 \simeq 39$.

Example 9·3. *A panel of judges A and B graded seven debators and independently awarded the following marks :*

Debator		*1*	*2*	*3*	*4*	*5*	*6*	*7*
Marks by A	:	*40*	*34*	*28*	*30*	*44*	*38*	*31*
Marks by B	:	*32*	*39*	*26*	*30*	*38*	*34*	*28*

An eighth debator was awarded 36 marks by Judge A while Judge B was not present.

If Judge B was also present, how many marks would you expect him to award to eighth debator assuming same degree of relationship exists in judgement ?

[*Delhi Univ. B.Com (Hons.), 1993; Himachal Pradesh Univ. M.A. (Econ.), June 1999, Allahabad Univ. M.Com. 2002*]

Solution. Let the marks awarded by Judge '*A*' be denoted by the variable X and the marks awarded by Judge '*B*' by the variable Y.

CALCULATIONS FOR REGRESSION EQUATIONS

Debator	x	y	$u = x - A = x - 35$	$v = y - B = y - 30$	u^2	v^2	uv
1	40	32	5	2	25	4	10
2	34	39	–1	9	1	81	–9
3	28	26	–7	–4	49	16	28
4	30	30	–5	0	25	0	0
5	44	38	9	8	81	64	72
6	38	34	3	4	9	16	12
7	31	28	–4	–2	16	4	8
Total			$\sum u = 0$	$\sum v = 17$	$\sum u^2 = 206$	$\sum v^2 = 185$	$\sum uv = 121$

The marks awarded by Judge A to the eighth debator are given to be 36, *i.e.*, we are given $x = 36$. We want to find the marks which would have been given to the 8th debator by Judge B, if he were present. In other words, we want to find y when $x = 36$. To do this we need the equation of line of regression of y on x. In the usual notations we have :

$$\bar{x} = A + \frac{\sum u}{n} = 35 + \frac{0}{7} = 35, \qquad \bar{y} = B + \frac{\sum v}{n} = 30 + \frac{17}{7} = 32{\cdot}4286$$

$$b_{yx} = b_{vu} = \frac{n\sum uv - (\sum u)(\sum v)}{n\sum u^2 - (\sum u)^2} = \frac{7 \times 121 - 0 \times 17}{7 \times 206 - 0} = \frac{121}{206} = 0{\cdot}5874$$

The equation of line of regression of y on x is given by

$$y - \bar{y} = b_{yx}(x - \bar{x})$$

$$\Rightarrow \quad y - 32{\cdot}4286 = 0{\cdot}5874\,(x - 35)$$

$$= 0{\cdot}5874x - 0{\cdot}5874 \times 35$$

$$\Rightarrow \quad y = 0{\cdot}5874x - 20{\cdot}5590 + 32{\cdot}4286$$

$$\Rightarrow \quad y = 0{\cdot}5874x + 11{\cdot}8696$$

When $x = 36$, $\quad y = 0{\cdot}5874 \times 36 + 11{\cdot}8696 = 21{\cdot}1464 + 11{\cdot}8696 = 33{\cdot}016$

Hence, if the Judge B were also present, he would have given 33 marks to the eighth debator.

Example 9·4. *A departmental store gives in-service training to its salesmen which is followed by a test. It is considering whether it should terminate the service of any salesman who does not do well in the test. The following data give the test scores and sales made by nine salesmen during a certain period :*

Test scores :	*14*	*19*	*24*	*21*	*26*	*22*	*15*	*20*	*19*
Sales ('000 Rs.) :	*31*	*36*	*48*	*37*	*50*	*45*	*33*	*41*	*39*

Calculate the coefficient of correlation between the test scores and the sales. Does it indicate that the termination of services of low test scores is justified ? If the firm wants a minimum sales volume of Rs. 30,000, what is the minimum test score that will ensure continuation of service ? Also estimate the most probable sales volume of a salesman making a score of 28. [*Delhi Univ. B.Com. (Hons.), 2003*]

Solution. Let x denote the test scores of the salesmen and y denote their corresponding sales (in '000 Rs.)

CALCULATIONS FOR REGRESSION LINES

x	y	$dx = x - \bar{x} = x - 20$	$dy = y - \bar{y} = y - 40$	dx^2	dy^2	$dxdy$
14	31	−6	−9	36	81	54
19	36	−1	−4	1	16	04
24	48	4	8	16	64	32
21	37	1	−3	1	9	−03
26	50	6	10	36	100	60
22	45	2	5	4	25	10
15	33	−5	−7	25	49	35
20	41	0	1	0	1	0
19	39	−1	−1	1	1	01
180	360	$\Sigma\, dx = 0$	$\Sigma\, dy = 0$	$\Sigma\, dx^2 = 120$	$\Sigma\, dy^2 = 346$	$\Sigma\, dxdy = 193$

Then $\quad \bar{x} = \dfrac{\Sigma x}{n} = \dfrac{180}{9} = 20 \; ; \qquad \bar{y} = \dfrac{\Sigma y}{n} = \dfrac{360}{9} = 40$

b_{yx} = Coefficient of regression of y on x

$$= \frac{\Sigma\, dxdy}{\Sigma\, dx^2} = \frac{193}{120} = 1{\cdot}6083$$

b_{xy} = Coefficient of regression of x on y

$$= \frac{\Sigma\, dxdy}{\Sigma\, dy^2} = \frac{193}{346} = 0{\cdot}5578$$

Karl Pearson's correlation coefficient r between x and y is given by :

$$r^2 = b_{yx} \cdot b_{xy} = 1{\cdot}6083 \times 0{\cdot}5578 = 0{\cdot}8971 \quad \Rightarrow \quad r = \pm\sqrt{0{\cdot}8971} = \pm\, 0{\cdot}9471$$

Since, the regression coefficients are positive, r is also positive. $\quad \therefore \quad r = +\,0{\cdot}9471$.

Aliter. $$r_{xy} = \frac{\Sigma\, dxdy}{\sqrt{\Sigma dx^2 \cdot \Sigma dy^2}} = \frac{193}{\sqrt{120 \times 346}} = \frac{193}{\sqrt{41520}} = \frac{193}{203{\cdot}7646} = 0{\cdot}9472$$

Thus, we see that there is a very high degree of positive correlation between the test scores (x) and the sales ('000 Rs.) (y). This justifies the proposal for the termination of service of those with low test scores.

Regression Equations

To obtain the test sclore (x) for given sales (y), we use the equation of the line of regression of x on y.

The equation of line of regression of x on y is :

$$x - \bar{x} = b_{xy}(y - \bar{y})$$

$$\Rightarrow \quad x - 20 = 0{\cdot}5578\,(y - 40) = 0{\cdot}5578y - 22{\cdot}312$$

$$\Rightarrow \quad x = 0{\cdot}5578y - 22{\cdot}312 + 20$$

$$\Rightarrow \quad x = 0{\cdot}5578y - 2{\cdot}312 \qquad \ldots(*)$$

Hence to ensure the continuation of service, the minimum test score (x) corresponding to a minimum sales volume (y) of Rs. 30,000 = 30 ('000 Rs.) is obtained on putting $y = 30$ in (*) and is given by :

$$x = 0{\cdot}5578 \times 30 - 2{\cdot}312 = 16{\cdot}734 - 2{\cdot}312$$

$$= 14{\cdot}422 \simeq 14$$

To estimate the sales volume (y) of a salesman with given test score (x), we use the line of regression of y on x, which is given by :

$$y - \bar{y} = b_{yx}(x - \bar{x})$$

$$\Rightarrow \quad y - 40 = 1{\cdot}6083\,(x - 20)$$

$$= 1{\cdot}6083x - 32{\cdot}1660$$

$$\Rightarrow \quad y = 1{\cdot}6083x - 32{\cdot}1660 + 40$$

$$\Rightarrow \quad y = 1{\cdot}6083x + 7{\cdot}8340$$

Hence the estimated sales volume of a salesman with test score of 28 is (in '000 Rs.)

$$y = 1{\cdot}6083 \times 28 + 7{\cdot}8340$$

$$= 45{\cdot}0324 + 7{\cdot}8340$$

$$= 52{\cdot}8664 \text{ ('000 Rs.)}$$

$$= \text{Rs. } 52{,}866{\cdot}40$$

Example 9·5. *The data about the sales and advertisement expenditure of a firm is given below :*

	Sales (in crores of Rs.)	*Advertisement expenditure (in crores of Rs.)*
Means	*40*	*6*
Standard deviations	*10*	*1·5*

Coefficient of correlation = r = 0·9

(i) Estimate the likely sales for a proposed advertisement expenditure of Rs. 10 crores.

(ii) What should be the advertisement expenditure if the firm proposes a sales target of 60 crores of rupees ?

Solution. Let the variable x denote the sales (in crores of Rs.) and the variable y denote the advertisement expenditure (in crores of Rs.). Then, in usual notations, we are given :

$$\bar{x} = 40, \quad \sigma_x = 10\,; \quad \bar{y} = 6, \quad \sigma_y = 1{\cdot}5, \quad r = r_{xy} = 0{\cdot}9$$

(*i*) To estimate the likely sales (x) for given advertisement expenditure (y), we need the regression equation of x on y which is given by :

$$x - \bar{x} = \frac{r\,\sigma_x}{\sigma_y}(y - \bar{y}) \;\Rightarrow\; x = \frac{r\,\sigma_x}{\sigma_y}(y - \bar{y}) + \bar{x} \;\Rightarrow\; x = \frac{0{\cdot}9 \times 10}{1{\cdot}5}(y - 6) + 40 = 6(y - 6) + 40 \qquad \ldots(*)$$

Hence the estimated sales (x) for a proposed advertisement expenditure (y) of Rs. 10 crores are obtained on putting $y = 10$ in (*) and are given by :

$$x = 6(10 - 6) + 40 = 6 \times 4 + 40 = 64 \text{ crores of Rs.}$$

(*ii*) To estimate the advertisement expenditure (y) for proposed sales (x), we need the equation of line of regression of y on x which is given by :

$$y - \bar{y} = \frac{r\,\sigma_y}{\sigma_x}(x - \bar{x}) \;\Rightarrow\; y = \frac{r\,\sigma_y}{\sigma_x}(x - \bar{x}) + \bar{y} \;\Rightarrow\; y = \frac{0{\cdot}9 \times 1{\cdot}5}{10}(x - 40) + 6 = 0{\cdot}135\,(x - 40) + 6 \ldots(**)$$

Hence the likely advertisement expenditure (y) of the firm for proposed sales target (x) of 60 crores of Rs. is obtained on taking $x = 60$ in (**) and is given by :

$$y = 0{\cdot}135\,(60 - 40) + 6 = 0{\cdot}135 \times 20 + 6 = 2{\cdot}7 + 6 = 8{\cdot}7 \text{ crores of Rs.}$$

Example 9·6. *Point out the inconsistency, if any, in the following statement.*

"The regression equation of y on x is 2y + 3x = 4 and the correlation coefficient between x and y is 0·8". [*I.C.W.A. (Intermediate), Dec. 1998*]

Solution. Line of regression of y on x is :

$$2y + 3x = 4 \quad \Rightarrow \quad y = -\frac{3}{2}x + 2$$

$\therefore$ b_{yx} = Coefficient of regression of y on $x = -\frac{3}{2}$.

Also $r_{xy} = 0{\cdot}8$ (Given).

Since b_{yx} and r_{xy} have different signs, the given statement is wrong (inconsistent).

Remark. The sign of the correlation coefficient (r_{xy}) and the regression coefficients b_{yx} and b_{xy} must be same, each depending on the sign of the covariance term Cov (x, y).

Example 9·7. *The following is an estimated supply regression for sugar :*

$$Y = 0{\cdot}025 + 1{\cdot}5X$$

where Y is supply in kilos and X is price (Rs.) per kilo.

(*i*) *Interpret the coefficient of variable X.*

(*ii*) *Predict the supply when price is Rs. 20 per kilo.*

(*iii*) *Given that r(x, y) = 1 in the above case, interpret the implied relationship between price and quantity supplied.* [*Delhi Univ. B.A.* (*Econ. Hons.*), *1998*]

Solution. The regression equation of Y (supply in kgs.) on X (price in Rupees per kg.) is given to be :

$$Y = 0{\cdot}025 + 1{\cdot}5\,X = a + bX, \text{ (say)} \qquad \ldots(*)$$

(*i*) The coefficient of the variable X *viz.*, $b = 1{\cdot}5$, is the coefficient of regression of Y on X. It reflects the unit change in the value of Y, for a unit change in the corresponding value of X. This means that if the price of sugar goes up by Re. 1 per kg., the estimated supply of sugar goes up by 1·5 kg.

(*ii*) From (*), the estimated supply of sugar when its price is Rs. 20 per kg. is given by :

$$\hat{Y} = 0{\cdot}025 + 1{\cdot}5 \times 20 = 30{\cdot}025 \text{ kg.}$$

(*iii*) $r(X, Y) = 1$, implies that the relationship between X and Y is exactly linear. This means that all the observed values (X, Y) lie on a straight line.

Example 9·8. (*a*) *The coefficient of regression of Y on X is $b_{YX} = 1{\cdot}2$. If*

$$U = \frac{X - 100}{2} \quad \text{and} \quad V = \frac{Y - 200}{3}\text{; find } b_{VU}.$$ [*Delhi Univ. B.A.* (*Econ. Hons.*), *1998*]

(*b*) *The covariance between X and Y is 900 and the standard deviations of X and Y are 15 and 80 respectively.*

If two variables S and T are defined as : $S = \dfrac{20 - X}{5}$ *and* $T = \dfrac{50 + Y}{8}$,

find the slope coefficients of the regressions of : (i) S on T and (ii) T on S.

[*Delhi Univ. B.A.* (*Econ. Hons.*), *2005*]

Solution. (*a*) Using formula (9· 39), we get : $b_{YX} = \frac{k}{h} \cdot b_{VU} = \frac{3}{2}\,b_{VU}$; $(h = 2, k = 3)$

$$\Rightarrow \quad b_{VU} = \frac{2}{3}\,b_{YX} = \frac{2}{3} \times 1{\cdot}2 = 0{\cdot}8$$

(*b*) We are given : $\text{Cov}(X, Y) = 900 \quad ; \quad \sigma_X = 15 \quad ; \quad \sigma_Y = 80 \qquad \ldots(1)$

$$S = \frac{20 - X}{5} \Rightarrow \text{Var}(S) = \text{Var}\left[-\frac{1}{5}(X - 20)\right] = \left(-\frac{1}{5}\right)^2 \text{Var}(X) = \frac{1}{25} \times 15^2 = 9 \quad \text{[From (1)]}$$

and
$$T = \frac{50 + Y}{8} \Rightarrow \text{Var}(T) = \text{Var}\left[\frac{50 + Y}{8}\right] = \left(\frac{1}{8}\right)^2 \text{Var}(Y) = \frac{80^2}{64} = 100 \quad \text{[From (1)]}$$

$$[\because \text{Var}(aX) = a^2\,\text{Var}(X) \quad \text{and} \quad V(X \pm A) = \text{Var}(X)]$$

$$\therefore \text{ Cov}(S, T) = \text{Cov}\left[\frac{20-X}{5}, \frac{50+Y}{8}\right] = \frac{1}{5\times 8}\text{ Cov}[20-X, 50+Y]$$

$$= \frac{1}{40}\text{ Cov}(-X, Y) = -\frac{1}{40}\text{ Cov}(X, Y) = -\frac{900}{40} = -\frac{45}{2} \quad \text{[From (1)]}$$

The slopes coefficients of regression of S on T and T on S are given respectively by

(*i*) $b_{ST} = \dfrac{\text{Cov}(S, T)}{\text{Var}(T)} = \dfrac{-45/2}{100} = -\dfrac{9}{40}$ and (*ii*) $b_{TS} = \dfrac{\text{Cov}(S, T)}{\text{Var}(S)} = \dfrac{-45/2}{9} = -\dfrac{5}{2}$

Example 9·9. *By using the following data, find out the two lines of regression and from them compute the Karl Pearson's coefficient of correlation.*

$\Sigma X = 250$; $\Sigma Y = 300$; $\Sigma XY = 7{,}900$; $\Sigma X^2 = 6{,}500$; $\Sigma Y^2 = 10{,}000$; *and* $N = 10$.

Solution. We have :

$$\overline{X} = \frac{\Sigma X}{N} = \frac{250}{10} = 25 \quad ; \quad \overline{Y} = \frac{\Sigma Y}{N} = \frac{300}{10} = 30$$

$$b_{YX} = \text{Coefficient of regression of } Y \text{ on } X = \frac{N\Sigma XY - (\Sigma X)(\Sigma Y)}{N\Sigma X^2 - (\Sigma X)^2}$$

$$= \frac{10\times 7900 - 250\times 300}{10\times 6500 - (250)^2} = \frac{79000 - 75000}{65000 - 62500} = \frac{4000}{2500} = 1{\cdot}6$$

$$b_{XY} = \text{Coefficient of regression of } X \text{ on } Y = \frac{N\Sigma XY - (\Sigma X)(\Sigma Y)}{N\Sigma Y^2 - (\Sigma Y)^2}$$

$$= \frac{10\times 7900 - 250\times 300}{10\times 10000 - (300)^2} = \frac{79000 - 75000}{100000 - 90000} = \frac{4000}{10000} = 0{\cdot}4$$

Hence correlation coefficient r_{XY} between X and Y is given by :

$$r_{XY}^2 = b_{YX} \cdot b_{XY} = 1{\cdot}6 \times 0{\cdot}4 = 0{\cdot}64 \quad \Rightarrow \quad r_{XY} = \pm\sqrt{0{\cdot}64} = \pm 0{\cdot}8$$

Since the regression coefficients are positive, we take $r = +0{\cdot}8$.

Regression Equations

Regression equation of Y on X	*Regression equation of X on Y*
$Y - \overline{Y} = b_{YX}(X - \overline{X})$	$X - \overline{X} = b_{XY}(Y - \overline{Y})$
$\Rightarrow \quad Y - 30 = 1{\cdot}6(X - 25)$	$\Rightarrow \quad X - 25 = 0{\cdot}4(Y - 30)$
$\Rightarrow \quad Y = 1{\cdot}6X - 40 + 30$	$\Rightarrow \quad X = 0{\cdot}4Y - 12 + 25$
$\Rightarrow \quad Y = 1{\cdot}6X - 10$	$\Rightarrow \quad X = 0{\cdot}4Y + 13$

Example 9·10. *In the estimation of regression equations of two variables X and Y the following results were obtained :*

$\Sigma X = 900$, $\Sigma Y = 700$, $n = 10$; $\Sigma x^2 = 6360$, $\Sigma y^2 = 2860$, $\Sigma xy = 3900$,

where x and y are deviations from respective means. Obtain the two regression equations.

[Delhi Univ. B.Com (Hons.), 2008]

Solution. The coefficients of regression of Y on X, and X on y are given respectively by :

$$b_{YX} = \frac{\text{Cov}(X, Y)}{\sigma_x^2} = \frac{\Sigma(X-\overline{X})(Y-\overline{Y})}{\Sigma(X-\overline{X})^2} = \frac{\Sigma xy}{\Sigma x^2} = \frac{3900}{6360} = 0{\cdot}6132$$

$$b_{XY} = \frac{\text{Cov}(X, Y)}{\sigma_y^2} = \frac{\Sigma(X-\overline{X})(Y-\overline{Y})}{\Sigma(Y-\overline{Y})^2} = \frac{\Sigma xy}{\Sigma y^2} = \frac{3900}{2860} = 1{\cdot}3636$$

$$\overline{X} = \frac{\Sigma X}{n} = \frac{900}{10} = 90 \qquad \overline{Y} = \frac{\Sigma Y}{n} = \frac{700}{10} = 70$$

Regression Equations

Regression equation of Y on X :	Regression equation of X on Y :
$Y - \overline{Y} = b_{YX}(X - \overline{X})$	$X - \overline{X} = b_{XY}(Y - \overline{Y})$
$\Rightarrow \quad Y - 70 = 0{\cdot}6132\,(X - 90)$	$\Rightarrow \quad X - 90 = 1{\cdot}3636\,(Y - 70)$
$\Rightarrow \quad Y = 0{\cdot}6132X - 55{\cdot}188 + 70$	$\Rightarrow \quad X = 1{\cdot}3636Y - 95{\cdot}452 + 70$
$\Rightarrow \quad Y = 0{\cdot}6132X + 14{\cdot}812$	$\Rightarrow \quad X = 1{\cdot}3636Y - 5{\cdot}452$

Example 9·11. *For a set of 10 pairs of values of x and y, the regression line of x on y is $x - 2y + 12 = 0$; mean and standard deviation of y being 8 and 2 respectively. Later it is known that a pair $(x = 3, y = 8)$ was wrongly recorded and the correct pair detected is $(x = 8, y = 3)$. Find the correct regression line of x on y.* *[I.C.W.A. (Intermediate), June 1998]*

Solution. In the usual notations we are given : $n = 10, \quad \bar{y} = 8, \quad \sigma_y = 2$ ... (*)

The equation of the line of regression of x on y is : $x - 2y + 12 = 0$ (Given). Since the lines of regression pass through the point $(\bar{x}, \bar{y})$, we get

$$\bar{x} - 2\bar{y} + 12 = 0 \quad \Rightarrow \quad \bar{x} = 2\bar{y} - 12 = 2 \times 8 - 12 = 4 \qquad \text{[Using (*)]}$$

Also $$x - 2y + 12 = 0 \quad \Rightarrow \quad x = 2y - 12 \qquad b_{xy} = 2$$

$$\therefore \quad \frac{\text{Cov}(x, y)}{\sigma_y^2} = 2 \quad \Rightarrow \quad \text{Cov}(x, y) = 2 \times 2^2 = 8 \qquad \text{[From (*)]}$$

$$\Rightarrow \quad \frac{\sum xy}{n} - \bar{x}\,\bar{y} = 8 \quad \Rightarrow \quad \sum xy = 10\,(8 + 4 \times 8) = 10 \times 40 = 400$$

$$\sigma_y = 2 \quad \Rightarrow \quad \sigma_y^2 = \frac{\sum y^2}{n} - \bar{y}^2 = 4 \quad \Rightarrow \quad \sum y^2 = 10\,(4 + 8^2) = 680$$

$\therefore$ We have $\bar{x} = 4, \quad \bar{y} = 8, \quad \sum y^2 = 680, \quad \sum xy = 400$

Wrong pair = $(x = 3, y = 8)$; Correct pair = $(x = 8, y = 3)$

Corrected Values. [Suffix c stands for corrected values]

$$\bar{x}_c = \frac{n\bar{x} - 3 + 8}{n} = \frac{10 \times 4 + 5}{10} = \frac{9}{2} \quad ; \quad \bar{y}_c = \frac{n\bar{y} - 8 + 3}{n} = \frac{10 \times 8 - 5}{10} = \frac{15}{2}$$

$$(\textstyle\sum y^2)_c = \sum y^2 - 8^2 + 3^2 = 680 - 64 + 9 = 625 \ ; \ (\sum xy)_c = \sum xy - 3 \times 8 + 8 \times 3 = 400 - 24 + 24 = 400$$

$$(\sigma_y^2)_c = \frac{(\sum y^2)_c}{n} - [(\bar{y})_c]^2 = \frac{625}{10} - \frac{225}{4} = \frac{1250 - 1125}{20} = \frac{25}{4}$$

$$[\text{Cov}(xy)]_c = \frac{(\sum xy)_c}{n} - (\bar{x}_c) \times (\bar{y}_c) = \frac{400}{10} - \frac{9}{2} \times \frac{15}{2} = 40 - \frac{135}{4} = \frac{25}{4}$$

$$\therefore \quad (b_{xy})_c = \frac{[\text{Cov}(x, y)]_c}{(\sigma_y^2)_c} = \frac{25/4}{25/4} = 1$$

Corrected line of regression of x on y becomes :

$$x - \bar{x}_c = (b_{xy})_c\,(y - \bar{y}_c) \quad \Rightarrow \quad x - \frac{9}{2} = 1\left(y - \frac{15}{2}\right) \quad \Rightarrow \quad x = y - 3.$$

EXERCISE 9·1

1. (*a*) Explain the concept of regression and point out its usefulness in dealing with business problems.

(*b*) What is a scatter diagram ? Indicate by means of suitable scatter diagrams different types of correlation that may exist between the variables in bivariate data. What are regression lines ? Write down the main points of distinction between correlation analysis and regression analysis.

2. Distinguish between correlation and regression analysis and indicate the utility of regression analysis in economic activities. *[C.A. (Foundation), Nov. 1996]*

3. (*a*) What is regression analysis ? How does it differ from correlation ? Why there are, in general, two regression equations ?

(*b*) Comment on the following :

"Regression equations are irreversible". [*Delhi Univ. B.Com. (Hons.), 2002*]

4. Given a scatter diagram of bivariate data involving variables *X* and *Y*. Find the conditions of minimisation of $\Sigma(Y_i - Y_e)^2$ and hence derive normal equations for the linear regression of *Y* upon *X*. What sum is to be minimised when *X* is regressed upon *Y* and what are the normal equations in this case ?

5. Derive the normal equations for the regression of *Y* on *X* for a data comprising of *n* pairs of values of *X* and *Y*. Show that the mean of the error terms is zero. [*Delhi Univ. B.A. (Econ. Hons.), 2005*]

Hint. $Y = a + bX$ ...... (*i*) (Regression equation of *Y* on *X*)

Normal equations are :

$\Sigma Y = na + b\Sigma X$ ...(*ii*) and $\Sigma XY = a\Sigma X + b\Sigma X^2$ ...(*iii*)

Mean of error terms is given by :

$$\bar{e} = \frac{1}{n}\sum_{i=1}^{n}(Y_i - \hat{Y}_i) = \frac{1}{n}\sum_{i=1}^{n}(Y_i - a - bX_i) \quad \text{[From (i)]}$$

$$= \frac{1}{n}[\Sigma Y_i - na - b\Sigma X_i] = 0. \quad \text{[From (ii)]}$$

6. What is linear regression ? Why are there, in general, two regression lines ? When do they coincide ? Explain the use of regression equations in economic enquiry.

7. (*a*) It is said that regression equations are irreversible meaning thereby that you cannot find out the regression equation of *x* on *y* from that of *y* on *x*. Justify the comment with special reference to the principle of least squares.

(*b*) Explain the term 'Regression'. Why do we take, in general, two regression lines ? When are the regression lines (*i*) perpendicular to each other and (*ii*) coincident ?

8. What are regression lines ? Why is it necessary to consider two lines of regression ? In case the two lines are identical, prove that the correlation coefficient is +1 or –1. If the two variables are independent, show that the two regression lines are perpendicular.

9. What is the angle between the two lines of regression ? Discuss the nature of the lines for the following particular cases :

(*i*) $r = \pm 1$. (*ii*) $r = 0$.

10. What is the difference between correlation and regression coefficients ? Can correlation coefficient be computed out of regression coefficients ? If yes, how ?

11. (*a*) Define regression coefficients. What information do they supply ?

(*b*) Let b_{yx} and b_{xy} stand for the coefficients of regression of *Y* on *X* and *X* on *Y* respectively. Show that :

$r_{xy} = \sqrt{b_{xy} \times b_{yx}}$ [*Delhi Univ. B.A. (Econ. Hons.), 1997*]

12. Given the following values of *x* and *y* :

x :	3	5	6	8	9	11
y :	2	3	4	6	5	8

find the equation of regression of

(*i*) *y* on *x* and (*ii*) *x* on *y*.

Interpret the results.

Ans. $y = 0{\cdot}7143x - 0{\cdot}3334$; $x = 1{\cdot}2857y + 1{\cdot}0001$.

13. Obtain the equations of the two lines of regression for the data given below :

X :	1	2	3	4	5	6	7	8	9
Y :	9	8	10	12	11	13	14	16	15

Ans. $Y = 0{\cdot}95X + 7{\cdot}25$; $X = 0{\cdot}95Y + 7{\cdot}25$.

14. From the following data of the age of husband and the age of wife, form two regression lines and calculate the husband's age when the wife's age is 16.

Husband's age :	36	23	27	28	28	29	30	31	33	35
Wife's age :	29	18	20	22	27	21	29	27	29	28

Ans. Husband's age : *x* ; Wife's age : *y*

$y = 0{\cdot}95x - 3{\cdot}5$; $x = 0{\cdot}8y + 10$; $(x)_{y=16} = 22{\cdot}8$.

15. Find the regression equation of y on x where y and x are the marks obtained by 10 students as given below :

y :	20	60	55	45	75	35	25	90	10	50
x :	20	45	65	40	55	35	15	80	25	50

[*C.A. (Foundation), May 2002*]

Ans. $b_{yx} = 1{\cdot}105$; $y = 1{\cdot}105x - 1{\cdot}015$.

16. The following data give the experience of machine operators and their performance ratings as given by the number of good parts turned out per 100 pieces :

Operator		:	1	2	3	4	5	6	7	8
Experience (in years)	(*X*)	:	16	12	18	4	3	10	5	12
Performance Ratings	(*Y*)	:	87	88	89	68	78	80	75	83

Calculate the regression line of performance ratings on experience and estimate the probable performance if an operator has 7 years experience. [*Himachal Pradesh Univ. B.Com., 1996*]

Ans. $Y = 69{\cdot}67 + 1{\cdot}133\,X$; 77·601.

17. You are given the data relating to purchases and sales. Obtain the two regression equations by the method of least squares and estimate the likely sales when the purchases equal 100.

Purchases	:	62	72	98	76	81	56	76	92	88	49
Sales	:	112	124	131	117	132	96	120	136	97	85

Ans. Purchase : x; Sales : y ; $x = 0{\cdot}6515y + 0{\cdot}0775$

$y = 0{\cdot}7825y + 56{\cdot}3125$; 134·5625.

18. The height of fathers and sons is given in the following table. Find the two lines of regression and estimate the expected average height of the son when the height of the father is 67·5 inches.

Height of father (in inches)	:	65	66	67	67	68	69	71	73
Height of son (in inches)	:	67	68	64	68	72	70	69	70

Ans. $y = 0{\cdot}4242x + 39{\cdot}5484$; $x = 0{\cdot}525y + 32{\cdot}2875$; 68·18 inches.

19. The following table gives the ages and blood pressure of 10 women.

Age (X)	:	56	42	36	47	49	42	60	72	63	55
Blood Pressure (Y)	:	147	125	118	128	145	140	155	160	149	150

(*i*) Find the correlation coefficient between *X* and *Y*.

(*ii*) Determine the least square regression equation of *Y* on *X*.

(*iii*) Estimate the blood pressure of a woman whose age is 45 years.

Ans. (*i*) $r = 0{\cdot}89$, (*ii*) $Y = 83{\cdot}758 + 1{\cdot}11X$, (*iii*) When $X = 45$, $Y = 134$.

20. A panel of two judges *P* and *Q* graded seven dramatic performances by independently awarding marks as follows :

Performance	:	1	2	3	4	5	6	7
Marks by P	:	46	42	44	40	43	41	45
Marks by Q	:	40	38	36	35	39	37	41

The eighth performance, which Judge *Q* could not attend, was awarded 37 marks by Judge *P*. If Judge *Q* had also been present, how many marks would be expected to have been awarded by him to the eighth performance ?

Ans. $33{\cdot}5 \simeq 34$.

21. The following table gives the normal weight of a baby during the first six months of life :

Age in months	:	0	2	3	5	6
Weight in lbs.	:	5	7	8	10	12

Estimate the weight of a baby at the age of 4 months.

Ans. 9·2982 lbs.

22. You are given the following data :

	x	y
Arithmetic Mean	36	85
Standard Deviation	11	8

Correlation coefficient between x and $y = 0{\cdot}66$

(*i*) Find two regression equations. (*ii*) Estimate value of x when $y = 75$.

Ans. (*i*) $y = 0{\cdot}48x + 67{\cdot}72$; $x = 0{\cdot}9075y - 41{\cdot}1375$, (*ii*) 26·925.

23. Given the information : Sum of $X = 5$; Sum of $Y = 4$
Sum of squares of deviations from the mean of $X = 40$; Sum of squares of deviations from the mean of $Y = 50$
Sum of the products of deviations from the means of X and $Y = 32$; Number of pairs of observations = 10
Calculate :

(*i*) regression coefficient of Y on X ; (*ii*) regression coefficient of X on Y ;
(*iii*) Karl Pearson's coefficient of correlation. [*Delhi Univ. B.A. (Econ. Hons.), 1999*]

Ans. $b_{YX} = 0{\cdot}80$; $b_{XY} = 0{\cdot}64$; $r(X, Y) = 0{\cdot}7156$.

24. For some bi-variate data, the following results were obtained :

Mean value of variable $X = 53{\cdot}2$ and of $Y = 39{\cdot}5$.
Regression Coefficient of Y and $X = -1{\cdot}5$ and of X on $Y = -0{\cdot}38$.
What should be the most likely value of X when $Y = 50$?

Also find the coefficient of correlation between two variables. [*Delhi Univ. B.Com. (Hons.), 2005*]

Ans. $\hat{X} = 53{\cdot}2 + (-1{\cdot}5)(50 - 39{\cdot}5) = 49{\cdot}21$; $r = -\sqrt{(-1{\cdot}5)(-0{\cdot}38)} = -\sqrt{\cdot 57} = -0{\cdot}7549$

25. For a particular product, the sales (y) and the advertisement expenditure (x) for 10 years, provide the results

$$\Sigma x = 15,\ \Sigma y = 110,\ \Sigma xy = 400,\ \Sigma x^2 = 250,\ \Sigma y^2 = 3200.$$

Find the regression line of y on x and the estimated value of y for $x = 10$. [*I.C.W.A (Intermediate), Dec. 2001*]

Ans. $y = 1{\cdot}033x + 9{\cdot}4505$; $(\hat{y})_{x=10} = 19{\cdot}781$.

26. Calculate the correlation coefficient from the following results :

$N = 10$, $\Sigma X = 350$, $\Sigma Y = 310$, $\Sigma(X - 35)^2 = 162$, $\Sigma(Y - 31)^2 = 222$, $\Sigma(X - 35)(Y - 31) = 92$.

Also find the regression line of Y on X. [*Delhi Univ. B.A. (Econ. Hons.), 2007*]

Hint. $\overline{X} = 35$, $\overline{Y} = 31$ $\Rightarrow$ $\Sigma(x - 35)^2 = \Sigma(x - \overline{x})^2 = 162$ and so on.

Ans. $r(X, Y) = 0{\cdot}485$; $Y = 0{\cdot}568X + 11{\cdot}12$.

27. For bivariate data, you are given the following :

$\Sigma(X - 58) = 46$; $\Sigma(Y - 58) = 9$, $\Sigma(X - 58)^2 = 3086$, $\Sigma(Y - 58)^2 = 483$; $\Sigma(X - 58)(Y - 58) = 1095$.

Number of pairs of observations is 7. You are required to determine the two regression equations and the coefficient of correlation between X and Y. [*Delhi Univ. B.Com. (Hons.), 2000*]

Hint. Let $U = X - 58$, $V = Y - 58$. ; Then we are given ΣU, ΣV, ΣU^2, ΣV^2 and ΣUV.

$\overline{X} = 58 + \overline{U}$; $\overline{Y} = 58 + \overline{V}$; $b_{YX} = b_{VU}$ and $b_{XY} = b_{UV}$

Ans. Regression Equations

Y on X : $Y = 0{\cdot}372X + 35{\cdot}266$; X on Y : $X = 2{\cdot}197Y - 65{\cdot}680$; $r(X, Y) = 0{\cdot}904$.

28. If the two regression lines corresponding to two variables X and Y meet at a point (2, 3), $V(X) = 4$, $V(Y) = 1$ and correlation coefficient between X and Y is $\frac{1}{2}$, the estimated value of Y for $X = 6$ is :

(*i*) 2, (*ii*) 4, (*iii*) 7, (*iv*) None of these.

[*I.C.W.A. (Intermediate), Dec. 1999*]

Hint. Lines of regression intersect at the point $(\overline{x}, \overline{y}) = (2, 3)$.

Ans. (*ii*).

29. Let the two variables X and Y have the covariance and correlation coefficient between them as 2 and 0·5 respectively and $V(X) = 2V(Y)$, then the regression coefficient of X on Y is

(*i*) 1, (*ii*) $\frac{1}{2}$, (*iii*) $\frac{1}{4}$, (*iv*) None of these.

[*I.C.W.A. (Intermediate), June 2001*]

Ans. (*iv*) $b_{xy} = 1/\sqrt{2}$

30. For a bivariate data the mean value of X is 20 and the mean value of Y is 45. The regression coefficient of Y on X is 4 and that of X on Y is 1/9. Find

(*i*) The coefficient of correlation.
(*ii*) The standard deviation of X if the standard deviation of Y is 12.
(*iii*) Also write down the equations of regression lines.

Ans. (*i*) 0·67, (*ii*) $\sigma_x = 2$, (*iii*) Regression = *ns* of y on x and x on y are respectively : $y = 4x - 35$, $9x = y + 135$.

31. From the following results, obtain the two regression equations and estimate the yield of crops when the rainfall is 22 cms. and the rainfall when the yield is 600 kgs.

	Yield in kgs. (X)	*Rainfall in cms.* (Y)
Mean	508·4	26·7
S.D.	36·8	4·6

Coefficient of correlation between yield and rainfall is 0·52. [*C.A. (Foundation), Nov. 2001*]

Ans. $y = 4{\cdot}16x + 397{\cdot}328$; $x = 0{\cdot}065y - 6{\cdot}346$; 488·85 kgs. ; 32·654 cms.

32. The following table shows the mean and standard deviation of the prices of two shares in a stock exchange.

Share	*Mean (in Rs.)*	*Standard deviation (in Rs.)*
A Ltd.	39·5	10·8
B Ltd.	47·5	16·0

If the coefficient of correlation between the prices of two shares is 0·42, find the most likely price of share. *A* corresponding to a price of Rs. 55 observed in the case of share *B*. [*Delhi Univ. (FMS), M.B.A. Oct. 2002*]

Ans. $X = 0.27Y + 26.675$; Rs. 41.52.

33. Given the following information :

		X	Y
Mean	:	6	8
Standard Deviation	:	5	13

Coefficient of Determination = 0·64

Find : (*i*) b_{YX} and b_{XY} and (*ii*) Value of Y when $X = 100$. [*Delhi Univ. B.A. (Econ. Hon.) 2009*]

Ans. (*i*) $r^2 = 0{\cdot}64 \Rightarrow r = \pm 0{\cdot}8$;

$$r = 0{\cdot}8 \Rightarrow b_{YX} = r\frac{\sigma_Y}{\sigma_X} = 2{\cdot}08 \ ; \quad b_{XY} = r\frac{\sigma_X}{\sigma_Y} = 0{\cdot}31$$

$$r = -0{\cdot}8 \Rightarrow b_{YX} = -2{\cdot}08 \ ; \quad b_{XY} = -0{\cdot}31$$

(*ii*) $(\hat{Y})_{X=100} = \overline{Y} + b_{YX}(100 - \overline{X}) = 8 + 2{\cdot}08\,(100 - 6) = 203{\cdot}52$; [Assume : $b_{YX} > 0$].

34. A survey was conducted to study the relationship between expenditure on accommodation (X) and expenditure on food and entertainment (Y) and the following results were obtained :

	Mean	*S.D.*
Expenditure on accommodation	Rs. 173	63·15
Expenditure on food and entertainment	Rs. 47·8	22·98

Coefficient of correlation = + 0·57

Write down the equation of regression of X on Y and estimate the expenditure on food and entertainment, if the expenditure on accommodation is Rs. 200. [*Bangalore Univ. B.Com., 1998*]

Ans. $Y = 0{\cdot}207X + 11{\cdot}99$, $(Y)_{X=200}$ = Rs. 53·29

35. Find out the regression coefficients of Y on X, and X on Y on the basis of the following data :

$\Sigma X = 50$, $\overline{X} = 5$, $\Sigma Y = 60$, $\overline{Y} = 6$, $\Sigma XY = 350$, Variance of $X = 4$, Variance of $Y = 9$.

Ans. $b_{yx} = 1{\cdot}25$, $b_{xy} = 0{\cdot}56$.

36. In order to find the correlation coefficient between two variables X and Y from 12 pairs of observations, the following calculations were made :

$\Sigma X = 30$; $\Sigma X^2 = 670$; $\Sigma Y = 5$; $\Sigma Y^2 = 285$; $\Sigma XY = 344$

On subsequent verification it was discovered that the pair ($X = 11$, $Y = 4$) was copied wrongly, the correct values being ($X = 10$, $Y = 14$). After making necessary correction, find :

(*a*) the two regression coefficients ; (*b*) the two regression equations ; (*c*) the correlation coefficient.

[*Delhi Univ. B.Com. (Hons.), 1990*]

Ans. (*a*) $b_{yx} = 0{\cdot}694$; $b_{xy} = 0{\cdot}898$ (*b*) : Y on X : $y = 0{\cdot}694x - 0{\cdot}427$; X on Y : $x = 0{\cdot}898y + 1{\cdot}294$

(*c*) $r(x, y) = 0{\cdot}7894 \simeq 0{\cdot}79$.

9·5. TO FIND THE MEAN VALUES $(\overline{x}, \overline{Y})$ FROM THE TWO LINES OF REGRESSION

Let us suppose that the two lines of regression are :

$$a_1 x + b_1 y + c_1 = 0 \qquad \ldots(9·41)$$

and

$$a_2 x + b_2 y + c_2 = 0 \qquad \ldots(9·42)$$

We have already discussed that *both the lines of regression pass through the point* $(\overline{x}, \overline{y})$. *In other words,* $(\overline{x}, \overline{y})$ *is the point of intersection of the two lines of regression.* Hence, solving (9·41) and (9·42) simultaneously, we get

$$\frac{\overline{x}}{b_1c_2 - b_2c_1} = \frac{\overline{y}}{c_1a_2 - c_2a_1} = \frac{1}{a_1b_2 - a_2b_1} \quad \Rightarrow \quad \overline{x} = \frac{b_1c_2 - b_2c_1}{a_1b_2 - a_2b_1}, \quad \overline{y} = \frac{c_1a_2 - c_2a_1}{a_1b_2 - a_2b_1} \qquad \ldots(9·43)$$

9·6. TO FIND THE REGRESSION COEFFICIENTS AND THE CORRELATION COEFFICIENT FROM THE TWO LINES OF REGRESSION

Let (9·41) and (9·42) be the given lines of regression and let us suppose that (9·41) is the line of regression of y on x and (9·42) is the line of regression of x on y. To obtain b_{yx}, the coefficient of regression of y on x, write the regression equation of y on x in the form $y = a + bx$. Then b, the coefficient of x gives the value of b_{yx}. Similarly to obtain b_{xy}, write the equation of regression of x on y in the form $x = A + By$. Then B, the coefficient of y gives b_{xy}. Therefore, re-writing (9·41), we get the regression equation of y on x :

$$y = -\frac{a_1}{b_1}x - \frac{c_1}{b_1} \quad \Rightarrow \quad b_{yx} = -\frac{a_1}{b_1} \qquad \ldots(9·44)$$

Similarly re-writing (9·42), we get regression equation of x on y as :

$$x = -\frac{b_2}{a_2}y - \frac{c_2}{a_2} \quad \Rightarrow \quad b_{xy} = -\frac{b_2}{a_2} \qquad \ldots(9·45)$$

The correlation coefficient r between x and y can now be obtained by using the formula

$$r^2 = b_{yx} \cdot b_{xy} = \left(-\frac{a_1}{b_1}\right) \times \left(-\frac{b_2}{a_2}\right) = \frac{a_1b_2}{a_2b_1} \quad \Rightarrow \quad r = \pm\sqrt{\frac{a_1b_2}{a_2b_1}}, \qquad \ldots(9·46)$$

the sign to be taken before the square root is same as that of the regression coefficients. If regression coefficients are positive, we take positive sign and if they are negative, we take negative sign in (9·46).

Remark. *Given the two lines of regression (9·41) and (9·42) how to determine which is the line of regression of y on x and which is the line of regression of x on y ?* Incidentally, the above discussion enables us to answer this question. By supposing (9·41) and (9·42) to be equations of the lines of regression of y on x and x on y respectively, we can obtain b_{yx} and b_{xy} and hence r^2. If $r^2 < 1$, our supposition, *i.e.*, (9·41) is equation of regression of y on x and (9·42) is equation of regression of x on y is true. However, if r^2 comes out to be greater than 1, then our supposition is wrong because r^2 must lie between 0 and 1. In this case we shall conclude that (9·41) is the equation of regression of x on y and (9·42) is the equation of regression of y on x.

Example 9·12. *The lines of regression of a bivariate population are :*

$$8x - 10y + 66 = 0 \quad \ldots(*) \qquad 40x - 18y = 214 \quad \ldots(**)$$

The variance of x is 9. Find

(i) The mean values of x and y; (ii) Correlation coefficient between x and y; (iii) Standard deviation of y.

Solution. (*i*) Since both the lines of regression pass through the mean values, the point $(\overline{x}, \overline{y})$ must satisfy (*) and (**). Hence, we get

$$8\overline{x} - 10\overline{y} + 66 = 0 \quad \ldots(1) \qquad \text{and} \qquad 40\overline{x} - 18\overline{y} - 214 = 0 \quad \ldots(2)$$

Multiplying (1) by 5, we get $40\bar{x} - 50\,\bar{y} + 330 = 0$

Subtracting (3) from (2), we get $32\,\bar{y} = 544 \quad \Rightarrow \quad \bar{y} = \frac{544}{32} = 17$ ... (3)

Substituting in (1), we get

$$8\bar{x} - 10 \times 17 + 66 = 0 \quad \Rightarrow \quad 8\,\bar{x} = 170 - 66 = 104 \quad \Rightarrow \quad \bar{x} = \frac{104}{8} = 13$$

Hence, the mean values are given by : $\bar{x} = 13, \bar{y} = 17$.

(*ii*) Let us suppose that (*) is the equation of line of regression of y on x and (**) is the equation of line of regression of x on y.

Re-writing (*), we get $10y = 8x + 66 \quad \Rightarrow \quad y = \frac{8}{10}x + \frac{66}{100}$

$\therefore \quad b_{yx}$ = Coefficient of regression of y on $x = \frac{8}{10} = \frac{4}{5}$

Re-writing (**), we get $40x = 18y + 214 \quad \Rightarrow \quad x = \frac{18}{40}y + \frac{214}{40}$

$\therefore \quad b_{xy}$ = Coefficient of regression x on $y = \frac{18}{40}$

Hence, $\quad r^2 = b_{yx} \cdot b_{xy} = \frac{8}{10} \times \frac{18}{40} = \frac{9}{25} \quad \Rightarrow \quad r = \pm\sqrt{\frac{9}{25}} = \pm\frac{3}{5} = \pm 0{\cdot}6$

Since both the regression coefficients are positive, r must be positive. Hence, we take $r = 0{\cdot}6$.

(*iii*) We are given : $\quad \sigma_x^2 = 9 \quad \Rightarrow \quad \sigma_x = \pm 3$.

But since standard deviation is always non-negative, we take $\sigma_x = 3$.

We have : $\quad b_{yx} = \frac{r\,\sigma_y}{\sigma_x} \quad \Rightarrow \quad \frac{4}{5} = \frac{3}{5} \cdot \frac{\sigma_y}{3} \quad \Rightarrow \quad \sigma_y = 4$

Remarks 1. It can be verified that the values of $\bar{x} = 13$ and $\bar{y} = 17$ as obtained in part (*i*) satisfy both the equations (*) and (**). In numerical problems of this type, this check should invariably be applied to ascertain the correctness of the answer.

2. If we had assumed that (*) is the equation of the line of regression of x on y and (**) is the equation of line of regression of y on x, then re-writing (*) and (**) we get respectively :

$$8x = 10y - 66 \quad \Rightarrow \quad x = \frac{10}{8}y - \frac{66}{8} \quad \Rightarrow \quad b_{xy} = \frac{10}{8}$$

$$18y = 40x - 214 \quad \Rightarrow \quad y = \frac{40}{18}x - \frac{214}{18} \quad \Rightarrow \quad b_{yx} = \frac{40}{18}$$

$$\therefore \quad r^2 = b_{xy} \cdot b_{yx} = \frac{10}{8} \times \frac{40}{18} = \frac{25}{9} = 2{\cdot}78.$$

But since r^2 always lies between 0 and 1, *i.e.*, since r^2 cannot exceed 1, our supposition that (*) is line of regression of x on y and (**) is the line of regression of y on x is wrong.

Example 9·13. (*a*) *For two variables x and y with the same mean, the regression equations are*

$$y = 2x + b \text{ and } x = 3y + \beta. \text{ Then } \frac{b}{\beta} \text{ is :}$$

(*i*) $\frac{1}{2}$, (*ii*) $\frac{3}{2}$, (*iii*) $\frac{1}{4}$, (*iv*) $\frac{2}{3}$. [*I.C.W.A. (Intermediate), Dec. 2001*]

(*b*) *Given below is the information relating to a bivariate distribution :*

Regression equation of Y on X : Y = 20 + 0·4 X

Mean of X = 30 ; Correlation coefficient between X and Y = 0·8.

Find the regression equation of X on Y [*Delhi Univ. B.Com (Hons.) External 2005*]

Solution. Regression equations are :

$$y = 2x + b \quad \text{and} \quad x = 3y + \beta \qquad ...(*)$$

Since the two variables x and y have the same mean, let : $\bar{x} = \bar{y} = \mu$, (say). ...(**)

Since the lines of regression pass through the point ($\bar{x}, \bar{y}$), we get from (*) :

$\bar{y} = 2\bar{x} + b$ and $\bar{x} = 3\bar{y} + \beta$ $\Rightarrow$ $\mu = 2\mu + b$ [From(**)] and $\mu = 3\mu + \beta$ [From (**)]

$\Rightarrow$ $\mu = -b$ and $\mu = -\beta/2$

$\therefore$ $\mu = -b = -\dfrac{\beta}{2}$ $\Rightarrow$ $\dfrac{b}{\beta} = \dfrac{1}{2}$ $\Rightarrow$ (*i*) is the correct answer.

(*b*) In the usual notations we are given $\bar{X} = 30$ and $r = r_{XY} = 0{\cdot}8$ ...(*)

and Regression equation of Y on X : $Y = 20 + 0{\cdot}4X$ ...(**)

$\Rightarrow$ b_{YX} = Coefficient of Regression of Y on $X = 0{\cdot}4$ ...(***)

Since the two lines of regression pass through the means ($\bar{X}, \bar{Y}$), we get from (**),

$$\bar{Y} = 20 + 0{\cdot}4\,\bar{X} = 20 + 0{\cdot}4 \times 30 = 32 \qquad \text{[From (*)]}$$

Also $r^2 = b_{YX} \, . \, b_{XY}$ $\Rightarrow$ $b_{XY} = \dfrac{r^2}{b_{YX}} = \dfrac{(0{\cdot}8)^2}{0{\cdot}4} = 1{\cdot}6$ [From (*) and (***)]

Hence, the equation of regression of X on Y is given by

$$X - \bar{X} = b_{XY}(Y - \bar{Y}) \Rightarrow X - 30 = 1{\cdot}6\,(Y - 32) = 1{\cdot}6Y - 51{\cdot}2 \Rightarrow X = 1{\cdot}6Y - 21{\cdot}2$$

Example 9·14. *For 100 students of a class, the regression equation of marks in Statistics (X) on the marks in Commerce (Y) is 3Y – 5X + 180 = 0. The mean marks in Commerce is 50 and variance of marks in Statistics is 4/9th of the variance of marks in Commerce. Find the mean marks in Statistics and the coefficient of correlation between marks in the two subjects.*

[Delhi Univ. B.Com. (Hons.), 2005, C.A. (Foundation), May 2000]

Solution. Let X denote marks in Statistics and Y denote marks in Commerce. In the usual notations we are given :

$n = 100$, $\bar{Y} = 50$, $\sigma_x^2 = \frac{4}{9}\sigma_y^2$ $\Rightarrow$ $\dfrac{\sigma_y}{\sigma_x} = \sqrt{\dfrac{9}{4}} = \dfrac{3}{2}$ ...(*)

The line of regression of X on Y is given to be :

$3Y - 5X + 180 = 0$ $\Rightarrow$ $5X = 3Y + 180$ $\Rightarrow$ $X = \frac{3}{5}Y + 36$ ...(**)

Since the lines of regression pass through the point ($\bar{X}, \bar{Y}$), we get from (**)

$$\bar{X} = \tfrac{3}{5}\bar{Y} + 36 = \tfrac{3}{5}(50) + 36 = 66 \qquad \text{[From (*)]}$$

Hence, the mean marks in Statistics are 66.

From (**), the coefficient of regression of X on Y is given by :

$b_{xy} = r\dfrac{\sigma_x}{\sigma_y} = \dfrac{3}{5}$ $\Rightarrow$ $r = \dfrac{3}{5}\dfrac{\sigma_y}{\sigma_x} = \dfrac{3}{5} \times \dfrac{3}{2} = 0{\cdot}9$ [From (*)]

Hence, the correlation coefficient between the marks in Statistics and Commerce is $r = 0{\cdot}9$.

Example 9·15. *If the two lines of regression are :*

4x – 5y + 30 = 0 and 20x – 9y – 107 = 0,

which of these is the line of regression of x on y, and y on x. Find r_{xy} and σ_y when $\sigma_x = 3$.

Solution. We are given the regression lines as :

$4x - 5y + 30 = 0$ ...(*i*) and $20x - 9y - 107 = 0$ ...(*ii*)

Let (*i*) be the equation of the line of regression of x on y and (*ii*) be the equation of the line of regression of y on x.

From (*i*), we get $x = \frac{5}{4}y - \frac{30}{4}$ $\Rightarrow$ $b_{xy} = \frac{5}{4}$

From (*ii*), we get $y = \frac{20}{9}x - \frac{107}{9}$ $\Rightarrow$ $b_{yx} = \frac{20}{9}$

$\therefore$ $r^2 = b_{yx} \cdot b_{xy} = \frac{20}{9} \times \frac{5}{4} = 2{\cdot}7778.$

Since $r^2 > 1$, our supposition is wrong. [$\because$ We always have $0 \le r^2 \le 1$]

Hence, (*i*) is the line of regression of *y* on *x* and (*ii*) is the line of regression of *x* on *y*.

Re-writing (*i*), we get : $5y = 4x + 30$ $\Rightarrow$ $y = \frac{4}{5}x + 6$ $\Rightarrow$ $b_{yx} = \frac{4}{5}$

Re-writing (*ii*), we get : $20x = 9y + 107$ $\Rightarrow$ $x = \frac{9}{20}y + \frac{107}{20}$ $\Rightarrow$ $b_{xy} = \frac{9}{20}$

$\therefore$ $r^2 = b_{yx} \cdot b_{xy} = \frac{4}{5} \times \frac{9}{20} = 0{\cdot}36$ $\Rightarrow$ $r = \pm\sqrt{0{\cdot}36} = \pm 0{\cdot}6$

Since both the regression coefficients are positive, *r* must be positive. Hence, we take $r = r_{xy} = 0{\cdot}6$.

We are given, $\sigma_x = 3$

We have $b_{yx} = r\frac{\sigma_y}{\sigma_x}$ $\Rightarrow$ $\sigma_y = \frac{b_{yx} \cdot \sigma_x}{r} = \frac{4}{5} \times \frac{3}{0{\cdot}6} = 4$

Example 9·16. *Comment on the following results obtained from given data :*

For a bivariate distribution :

(*i*) *Coefficient of regression of Y on X is 4·2* and *Coefficient of regression of X on Y is 0·50.*

(*ii*) $b_{yx} = 2{\cdot}4$ *and* $b_{xy} = -0{\cdot}4$.

Solution. (*i*) We are given that : $b_{yx} = 4{\cdot}2$ and $b_{xy} = 0{\cdot}5$ $\Rightarrow$ $r^2 = b_{yx} \cdot b_{xy} = 4{\cdot}2 \times 0{\cdot}5 = 2{\cdot}10 > 1$

But we know that *r* cannot exceed unity numerically, *i.e.*, $-1 \le r \le 1$ $\Rightarrow$ $r^2 \le 1$

Hence, the given statement is wrong.

(*ii*) $b_{yx} = 2{\cdot}4$ and $b_{xy} = -0{\cdot}4$, is not possible, since both the regression coefficients must have the same sign.

9·7. STANDARD ERROR OF AN ESTIMATE

The regression equations enable us to estimate (predict) the value of the dependent variable for any given value of the independent variable. The estimates so obtained are, however, not perfect. A measure of the precision of the estimates so obtained from the regression equations is provided by the *Standard Error* (S.E.) of the estimate. Standard error is a word analogous to standard deviation (which is a measure of dispersion of the observations about the mean of the distribution) and gives us a measure of the scatter of the observations about the line of regression. Thus

$$S_{yx} = \text{S.E. of estimate of } y \text{ for given } x = \sqrt{\frac{1}{N}\Sigma(y - y_e)^2} = \sqrt{\frac{(\text{Unexplained Variation in } y)}{N}} \quad \ldots(9{\cdot}47)$$

where y_e is the estimated value of *y* for given value of *x* obtained from the line of regression of *y* on *x* and *N* is the number of the given pairs of observations. [Explained and Unexplained Variations are discussed below].

Similarly,

$$S_{xy} = \text{S.E. of estimate of } x \text{ for given } y = \sqrt{\frac{1}{N}\Sigma(x - x_e)^2} = \sqrt{\frac{(\text{Unexplained Variation in } x)}{N}} \quad \ldots(9{\cdot}48)$$

The computation of standard error of estimates by above formulae is quite tedious as it requires the computations of the error of estimates $y - y_e$ for each *x* and $x - x_e$ for each *y*. However, a much more convenient formula for numerical computations is given below.

$$S_{yx} = \sigma_y(1 - r^2)^{1/2} \Rightarrow S_{yx}^2 = \sigma_y^2(1 - r^2) \quad \ldots(9{\cdot}49)$$

$$S_{xy} = \sigma_x(1 - r^2)^{1/2} \Rightarrow S_{xy}^2 = \sigma_x^2(1 - r^2) \quad \ldots(9{\cdot}50)$$

where $r = r_{xy}$ is the correlation coefficient between the two variables *x* and *y*.

Remark. Limits For *r*. Since $S_{yx}^2 \geq 0$ and $S_{xy}^2 \geq 0$, and $\sigma_y^2 > 0$ and $\sigma_x^2 > 0$, we have :

$$1 - r^2 \geq 0 \quad \Rightarrow \quad r^2 \leq 1 \quad \Rightarrow \quad |r| \leq 1 \quad \Rightarrow \quad -1 \leq r \leq 1;$$

Hence, the correlation coefficient lies between the limits – 1 and 1.

9·7·1. Explained and Unexplained Variation. The total variation in y-values can be split into two parts :

(*i*) The *Explained Variation, i.e.,* the variation in y which is explained by the variable x.

(*ii*) The *Unexplained Variation, i.e.,* the variation in y which is unexplained by the variable x. This part of variation is due to some other factors (variables) affecting the total variation in y-values.

Mathematically, we can write :

$$\Sigma(y - \bar{y})^2 = \Sigma\left[(y - y_e) + (y_e - \bar{y})\right]^2$$

$$= \Sigma(y - y_e)^2 + \Sigma(y_e - \bar{y})^2, \qquad ...(9·51)$$

the product term vanishes since $\Sigma(y - y_e) = 0$. [*c.f.* (9·14)]

The first term on the R.H.S. in (9·51), *viz.*, $\Sigma(y - y_e)^2$ is called the *Unexplained Variation* in y and the second term, *viz.*, $\Sigma(y_e - \bar{y})^2$ is called the *Explained Variation.*

The ratio of explained variation to the total variation is known as the coefficient of determination (r^2), *i.e.,*

$$r^2 = \frac{\text{Explained Variation}}{\text{Total Variation}} \quad \Rightarrow \quad r^2 = \frac{\Sigma(y_e - \bar{y})^2}{\sigma_y^2} = \frac{S_{ye}^2}{\sigma_y^2} \qquad ...(9·52)$$

Example 9·17. *The weights of a calf taken at weekly intervals are given below.*

Age (in weeks) :	*1*	*2*	*3*	*4*	*5*	*6*	*7*	*8*	*9*	*10*
Weight (in lbs.) :	*52·5*	*58·7*	*65·0*	*70·2*	*75·4*	*81·1*	*87·2*	*95·5*	*102·2*	*108·4*

(*i*) *Fit a linear regression equation to this data by the principle of least squares.*

(*ii*) *Calculate the average rate of growth per week.*

(*iii*) *Obtain an estimate of the weight of the calf at the age of 13 weeks.*

(*iv*) *Estimate the weights of the calf at ages 1, 2, ..., 10 weeks respectively using the regression equation obtained in* (*i*).

(*v*) *Find the error* (*e*) *in each case for the estimated values obtained in* (*iv*) *and verify that* $\Sigma e = 0$.

(*vi*) *Also obtain the standard error of the estimate.*

Solution. Let the random variable X denote age (in weeks) and Y denote the weight (in lbs.) of the calf. We are given $n = 10$.

CALCULATIONS FOR REGRESSION EQUATION AND S.E. OF ESTIMATE

(x) (1)	y (2)	x^2 (3)	xy (4)	$y_e = 45·73 + 6·16\,x$ (5)	$e = y - y_e$ (6)	$(y - y_e)^2$ (7)
1	52·5	1	52·5	51·89	0·61	0·3721
2	58·7	4	117·4	58·05	0·65	0·4225
3	65·0	9	195·0	64·21	0·79	0·6241
4	70·2	16	280·8	70·37	–0·17	0·0289
5	75·4	25	377·0	76·53	–1·13	1·2769
6	81·1	36	486·6	82·69	–1·59	2·5281
7	87·2	49	610·4	88·85	–1·65	2·7225
8	95·5	64	764·0	95·01	0·49	0·2401
9	102·2	81	919·8	101·17	1·03	1·0609
10	108·4	100	1084·0	107·33	1·07	1·1449
$\Sigma x = 55$	$\Sigma y = 796·2$	$\Sigma x^2 = 385$	$\Sigma xy = 4887·5$		$\Sigma(y - y_e) = 0·1$	$\Sigma(y - y_e)^2 = 10·421$

(*i*) Let us consider the regression equation of y on x, *viz.*,

$$y = a + bx \qquad \ldots(*)$$

Constants 'a' and 'b' are given by : [*c.f.* (9·7) and (9·8)]

$$a = \frac{(\sum x^2)(\sum y) - (\sum x)(\sum xy)}{n\sum x^2 - (\sum x)^2} = \frac{385 \times 796{\cdot}2 - 55 \times 4887{\cdot}5}{10 \times 385(55)^2}$$

$$= \frac{306537 - 268812{\cdot}5}{3850 - 3025} = \frac{37724{\cdot}5}{825} = 45{\cdot}73$$

$$b = \frac{n\sum xy - (\sum x)(\sum y)}{n\sum x^2 - (\sum x)^2} = \frac{10 \times 4887{\cdot}5 - 55 \times 796{\cdot}2}{10 \times 385 - (55)^2}$$

$$= \frac{48875 - 43791}{3850 - 3025} = \frac{5084}{825} = 6{\cdot}16$$

Substituting these values of a and b in (*), the equation of the line of regression of y on x becomes :

$$y = 45{\cdot}73 + 6{\cdot}16\,x \qquad \ldots(**)$$

(*ii*) The weights of the calf after 1, 2, 3, ... weeks as given by the regression equation (*) are : $a + b$, $a + 2b$, $a + 3b$, ... Hence, the average rate of growth per week is b lbs. *i.e.*, 6·16 lbs.

(*iii*) The estimated weight of the calf at the age 13 weeks is obtained on putting $x = 13$ in (**) and is given by :

$$(\hat{Y})_{x=13} = 45{\cdot}73 + 6{\cdot}16 \times 13 = 45{\cdot}73 + 80{\cdot}08 = 125{\cdot}81 \text{ lbs.}$$

(*iv*) From regression equation we, have :

When $x = 1$, $y_e = 45{\cdot}73 + 6{\cdot}16 = 51{\cdot}89$; when $x = 2$, $y_e = 45{\cdot}73 + 6{\cdot}16 \times 2 = 58{\cdot}05$

and so on. These estimated values (y_e) for different values of x from 1 to 10 are given in the column 5 of the calculation table.

(*v*) Errors of estimates or residuals are given by :

$e = y - y_e$ = [Values in column (2) – Values in column (5) of the calculation table]

and are given in column (6) of the calculation table. From the table, we find that :

$$\sum e = \sum (y - y_e) = 4{\cdot}64 - 4{\cdot}54 = 0{\cdot}1.$$

Note. We should have got $\sum e = 0$. However, in this case it is not zero. The difference is due to the rounding of the constants a and b up to two decimals.

(*vi*) **Standard Error of the Estimate of** Y (for any given X), *i.e.*, S_{yx} is given by

$$S_{yx} = \sqrt{\frac{1}{n}\sum (y - y_e)^2} = \sqrt{\frac{10{\cdot}421}{10}} = \sqrt{1{\cdot}0421} = 1{\cdot}02.$$

Example 9·18. *In fitting of a regression of Y on X to a bivariate distribution consisting of 9 observations, the explained and unexplained variations were computed as 24 and 36 respectively. Find (i) the coefficient of determination and (ii) standard error of the estimate of Y on X.*

[*Delhi Univ. B.A. (Econ. Hons.), 1997*]

Solution. (*i*) In the usual notations, we are given

$n = 9$, Explained Variation = 24 ; Unexplained Variation = 36

Total Variation = Explained Variation + Unexplained Variation = 24 + 36 = 60

$$\therefore \quad \sum (y - \bar{y})^2 = 60 \quad \Rightarrow \quad \sigma_y^2 = \frac{1}{n}\sum (y - \bar{y})^2 = \frac{60}{9} = \frac{20}{3}$$

$$\text{Coefficient of determination } (r^2) = \frac{\text{Explained Variation}}{\text{Total Variation}} = \frac{24}{60} = 0{\cdot}4$$

(*ii*) The standard error (S.E.) of the estimate of Y on X, denoted by S_{yx} is given by :

$$S_{yx} = \sigma_y \sqrt{(1-r^2)} = \sqrt{\sigma_y^2 (1-r^2)} = \sqrt{\frac{20}{3}(1-0\cdot4)} = \sqrt{\frac{20}{3}\times 0\cdot6} = \sqrt{4} = 2.$$

Example 9·19. *In a partially destroyed record, for the estimation of the two lines of regression from a bivariate data (X, Y), the following results were available :*

Coefficient of regression of Y on X = –1·6 ; Coefficient of regression of X on Y = – 0·4

Standard error of the estimate of Y on X = 3

Find :

(*i*) *Coefficient of correlation between X and Y.* (*ii*) *Standard deviations σ_X and σ_Y*

(*iii*) *Standard error of the estimate of X on Y.* [*Delhi Univ. B.A.* (*Econ. Hons.*), *1998*]

Solution. In the usual notations, we are given :

$$b_{yx} = -1\cdot6 \;;\quad b_{xy} = -0\cdot4 \;;\quad S_{yx} = 3 \qquad \ldots(1)$$

(*i*) Coefficient of correlation $r = r(X, Y)$ is given by :

$$r^2 = b_{yx}\,.\,b_{xy} = (-1\cdot6)\times(-0\cdot4) = 0\cdot64 \quad\Rightarrow\quad r = \pm\sqrt{0\cdot64} = \pm\,0\cdot8$$

Since the regression coefficients are negative, r is also negative.

$$\therefore \qquad r = -\,0\cdot8 \qquad \ldots(2)$$

(*ii*) The standard error of estimate of Y on X is given by

$$S_{yx} = \sigma_y\,(1-r^2)^{1/2} \quad\Rightarrow\quad \sigma_y = \frac{S_{yx}}{(1-r^2)^{1/2}}$$

$$\therefore \qquad \sigma_y = \frac{3}{\sqrt{1-0\cdot64}} = \frac{3}{\sqrt{0\cdot36}} = \frac{3}{0\cdot6} = 5 \qquad \text{[From (1) and (2)]} \qquad \ldots(3)$$

$$\text{Also} \qquad b_{yx} = \frac{r\,\sigma_y}{\sigma_x} \quad\Rightarrow\quad \sigma_x = \frac{r\,\sigma_y}{b_{yx}} = \frac{(-0\cdot8)\times5}{-1\cdot6} = 2\cdot5. \qquad \text{[From (1), (2) and (3)]}$$

(*iii*) Standard error of estimate of X on Y is given by :

$$S_{xy} = \sigma_x\,(1-r^2)^{1/2} = 2\cdot5\,(1-0\cdot64)^{1/2} = 2\cdot5\times0\cdot6 = 1\cdot5.$$

9·8. REGRESSION EQUATIONS FOR A BIVARIATE FREQUENCY TABLE

The computation of correlation coefficient r for a bivariate frequency table, commonly known as correlation table, has been discussed in Chapter 8. The calculation of r involves the computation of $\bar{x}$, $\bar{y}$, σ_x, σ_y. Since the equations of the two lines of regression, *viz.*, line of regression of y on x, and x on y are respectively :

$$y - \bar{y} = b_{yx}\,(x-\bar{x}) = \frac{r\,\sigma_y}{\sigma_x}\,(x-\bar{x}) \qquad \text{and} \qquad x-\bar{x} = b_{xy}\,(y-\bar{y}) = \frac{r\,\sigma_x}{\sigma_y}\,(y-\bar{y}),$$

the calculations for obtaining these equations will be more or less same. However, it may be remarked here that the regression coefficients b_{yx} and b_{xy} are independent of change of origin but not of scale, *i.e.*, if we take

$$u = \frac{x-a}{h} \quad\text{and}\quad v = \frac{y-b}{k}\;;\quad\text{then}\quad b_{yx} = \frac{k}{h}\,b_{vu} \quad\text{and}\quad b_{xy} = \frac{h}{k}\,b_{uv}$$

This point has to be borne in mind in computing the regression coefficients. We will explain the technique by means of an example.

Example 9·20. *Following table gives the ages (in years) of husbands and wives for 50 newly married couples. Find the two regression lines. Also estimate*

(a) the age of husband when wife is 20 and (b) the age of wife when husband is 30.

Age of wife	*Age of husband*			
	20—25	*25—30*	*30—35*	*Total*
16—20	*9*	*14*	—	*23*
20—24	*6*	*11*	*3*	*20*
24—28	—	—	*7*	*7*
Total	*15*	*25*	*10*	*50*

Also find the standard error of the estimates. [*Delhi Univ. B.Com. (Hons.), 1997*]

Solution. Let us denote the age (in years) of husband by the variable X and age of wife by the variable Y. Let x and y denote the mid-points of the corresponding classes of X and Y series respectively. If we take

$$u = \frac{x-A}{h} = \frac{x-27\cdot5}{5} \quad ; \quad v = \frac{y-B}{k} = \frac{y-22}{4},$$

the table for computing the two lines of regression is given below.

$$\bar{u} = \frac{\sum fu}{N} = \frac{-5}{50} = -0\cdot1 \qquad \bar{x} = A + h\bar{u} = 27\cdot5 + 5 \times (-0\cdot1) = 27\cdot5 - 0\cdot5 = 27$$

$$\bar{v} = \frac{\sum fv}{N} = \frac{-16}{50} = -0\cdot32 \qquad \bar{y} = B + k\bar{v} = 22 + 4 \times (-0\cdot32) = 22 - 1\cdot28 = 20\cdot72$$

CALCULATIONS FOR REGRESSION EQUATIONS

(Figures in brackets are the fuv values shown in the small boxes of the cells.)

		Age of Husband →	20—25	25—30	30—35				
		Mid. pt. (x)	22·5	27·5	32·5				
Age of Wife ↓	Mid. pt (y)	u → v ↓	−1	0	1	f	fv	fv^2	fuv
16—20	18	−1	9 [9]	14 [0]	[0]	23	−23	23	9
20—24	22	0	6 [0]	11 [0]	3 [0]	20	0	0	0
24—28	26	1	[0]	[0]	7 [7]	7	7	7	7
		f	15	25	10	$N = 50$	$\sum fv = -16$	$\sum fv^2 = 30$	$\sum fuv = 16$
		fu	−15	0	10	$\sum fu = -5$			
		fu^2	15	0	10	$\sum fu^2 = 25$			
		fuv	9	0	7	$\sum fuv = 16$			

$$b_{yx} = \frac{k}{h}\left[\frac{N\sum fuv - (\sum fu)(\sum fv)}{N\sum fu^2 - (\sum fu)^2}\right]$$

$$= \frac{4}{5}\left[\frac{50 \times 16 - (-5) \times (-16)}{50 \times 25 - (-5)^2}\right] = \frac{4}{5}\left[\frac{800-80}{1250-25}\right]$$

$$= \frac{4}{5} \times \frac{720}{1225} = 0\cdot4702$$

$$b_{xy} = \frac{h}{k}\left[\frac{N\sum fuv - (\sum fu)(\sum fv)}{N\sum fv^2 - (\sum fv)^2}\right]$$

$$= \frac{5}{4}\left[\frac{800-80}{50 \times 30 - (-16)^2}\right]$$

$$= \frac{5}{4} \times \frac{720}{1244} = 0\cdot7235$$

Regression Equation of y on x

$$y - \bar{y} = b_{yx}(x - \bar{x})$$

$$\Rightarrow \quad y - 20{\cdot}72 = 0{\cdot}4702(x - 27)$$

$$= 0{\cdot}4702x - 12{\cdot}6954$$

$$y = 0{\cdot}4702x + 20{\cdot}72 - 12{\cdot}6954$$

$$= 0{\cdot}4702x + 8{\cdot}0246$$

Hence, the most likely age of wife (y) when the age of husband (x) is 30 years is given by

$$y = 0{\cdot}4702 \times 30 + 8{\cdot}0246$$

$$= 14{\cdot}1060 + 8{\cdot}0246$$

$$= 22{\cdot}1306$$

$$= 22 \text{ years (approximately)}$$

Regression Equation of x on y

$$x - \bar{x} = b_{xy}(y - \bar{y})$$

$$\Rightarrow \quad x - 27 = 0{\cdot}7235(y - 20{\cdot}72)$$

$$= 0{\cdot}7235y - 14{\cdot}991$$

$$\Rightarrow \quad x = 0{\cdot}7235y + 27{\cdot}000 - 14{\cdot}991$$

$$\Rightarrow \quad x = 0{\cdot}7235y + 12{\cdot}009$$

Hence, the most likely age of husband (x) when the age of wife (y) is 20 years is given by :

$$x = 0{\cdot}7235 \times 20 + 12{\cdot}009$$

$$= 14{\cdot}470 + 12{\cdot}009$$

$$= 26{\cdot}479$$

$$= 26{\cdot}5 \text{ years (approximately)}$$

Computation of Standard Errors of Estimate

$$\sigma_x = \frac{h}{N}\sqrt{N\sum fu^2 - (\sum fu)^2} = \frac{5}{50}\sqrt{50 \times 25 - (-5)^2} = \frac{\sqrt{1225}}{10} = \frac{35}{10} = 3{\cdot}5$$

$$\sigma_y = \frac{k}{N}\sqrt{N\sum fv^2 - (\sum fv)^2} = \frac{4}{50}\sqrt{50 \times 30 - (-16)^2} = \frac{4}{50} \times \sqrt{1244} = \frac{4}{50} \times 35{\cdot}27 = 2{\cdot}82$$

$$r^2 = b_{yx} \cdot b_{xy} = 0{\cdot}4702 \times 0{\cdot}7235 = 0{\cdot}34$$

S.E. of estimate of y (for given x) :

$$S_{yx} = \sigma_y(1 - r^2)^{1/2} = 2{\cdot}82(1 - 0{\cdot}34)^{1/2}$$

$$= 2{\cdot}82 \times 8{\cdot}124 = 22{\cdot}91$$

S.E. of estimate of x (for given y) :

$$S_{xy} = \sigma_x(1 - r^2)^{1/2} = 3{\cdot}5(1 - 0{\cdot}34)^{1/2}$$

$$= 3{\cdot}5 \times 8{\cdot}124 = 28{\cdot}434$$

9·9. CORRELATION ANALYSIS Vs. REGRESSION ANALYSIS

1. Correlation literally means the relationship between two or more variables which vary in sympathy so that the movements in one tend to be accompanied by the corresponding movements in the other(s). On the other hand, regression means stepping back or returning to the average value and is a mathematical measure expressing the average relationship between the two variables.

2. Correlation coefficient 'r_{xy}' between two variables x and y is a measure of the direction and degree of the *linear* relationship between two variables which is mutual. It is symmetric, *i.e.*, $r_{yx} = r_{xy}$ and it is immaterial which of x and y is dependent variable and which is independent variable.

Regression analysis aims at establishing the functional relationship between the two variables under study and then using this relationship to predict or estimate the value of the dependent variable for any given value of the independent variable. It also reflects upon the nature of the variable, *i.e.*, which is dependent variable and which is independent variable. Regression coefficients are not symmetric in x and y, *i.e.*, $b_{yx} \neq b_{xy}$.

3. Correlation need not imply cause and effect relationship between the variables under study. [For details see § 8·1·2, page 8·2. However, regression analysis clearly indicates the cause and effect relationship between the variables. The variable corresponding to cause is taken as independent variable and the variable corresponding to effect is taken as dependent variable.

4. Correlation coefficient r_{xy} is a relative measure of the linear relationship between x and y and is independent of the units of measurement. It is a pure number lying between ± 1.

On the other hand, the regression coefficients, b_{yx} and b_{xy} are absolute measures representing the change in the value of the variable $y(x)$, for a unit change in the value of the variable $x(y)$. Once the functional form of regression curve is known, by substituting the value of the dependent variable we can obtain the value of the independent variable and this value will be in the units of measurement of the variable.

5. There may be *non-sense correlation* between two variables which is due to pure chance and has no practical relevance, *e.g.*, the correlation between the size of shoe and the intelligence of a group of individuals. There is no such thing like non-sense regression.

6. Correlation analysis is confined *only* to the study of linear relationship between the variables and, therefore, has limited applications. Regression analysis has much wider applications as it studies linear as well as non-linear relationship between the variables

EXERCISE 9·2

1. Given two lines of regression, explain how you will find :

(*i*) the mean values ($\bar{x}, \bar{y}$) ; (*ii*) the regression coefficients b_{yx} and b_{xy},

(*iii*) the correlation coefficient r_{xy} ; (*iv*) the ratio of the s.d.'s σ_x / σ_y.

2. The equations of two lines of regression obtained in a correlation analysis are given below :

$$2X = 8 - 3Y \quad \text{and} \quad 2Y = 5 - X.$$

Obtain the value of the correlation coefficient.

Ans. $r = -0{\cdot}866$.

3. You are supplied with the following data :

$$4x - 5y + 33 = 0 \qquad 20x - 9y - 107 = 0 \qquad \text{Variance } x = 9$$

Calculate :

(*i*) the mean values of *x* and *y* ; (*ii*) standard deviation of *y* ; (*iii*) coefficient of correlation between *x* and *y*.

Ans. (*i*) $\bar{x} = 13, \bar{y} = 17$, (*ii*) $\sigma_y = 4$, (*iii*) $r_{xy} = 0{\cdot}6$

4. The equations of two lines of regression obtained in a correlation analysis are the following :

$$2x + 3y - 8 = 0 \quad \text{and} \quad x + 2y - 5 = 0$$

Obtain the value of the correlation coefficient and the variance of *y*, given that the variance of *x* is 12.

Ans. $r = -0{\cdot}87$, $\sigma_y^2 = 4$.

5. The lines of regression of a bi-variate distribution are as follows :

$$5X - 145 = -10Y \quad ; \quad 14Y - 208 = -8X.$$

It is given that the variance of $X = 4$. You are required to find out the mean values of *X* and *Y*, and the standard deviation of *Y*. Also find out coefficient of correlation between *X* and *Y*. [*Delhi Univ. B.Com. (Hons.), 2001*]

Ans. $\bar{X} = 5$, $\bar{Y} = 12$, $\sigma_y = 1{\cdot}07$, $r(X, Y) = -0{\cdot}935$.

6. Regression equations of two variables *X* and *Y* are as follows :

$$3X + 2Y = 26 \quad \ldots(*) \quad \text{and} \quad 6X + Y = 31 \quad \ldots(**)$$

Find :

(*i*) the means of *X* and *Y*, (*ii*) the regression coefficients of *X* on *Y* and *Y* on *X*,

(*iii*) the coefficient of correlation between *X* and *Y*, (*iv*) the most probable value of *Y* when $X = 5$,

(*v*) the ratio of variances of the variables. [*I.C.W.A. (Intermediate), Dec. 1998*]

Ans. $\bar{x} = 4$, $\bar{y} = 7$, (*ii*) $b_{xy} = -1/6$, $b_{yx} = -3/2$, (*iii*) $r_{xy} = -0{\cdot}5$, (*iv*) 5·5, (*v*) $\sigma_y^2 : \sigma_x^2 = 9 : 1$.

7. Consider the two regression lines :

$$3X + 2Y = 26 \quad \ldots(*) \quad \text{and} \quad 6X + Y = 31 \quad \ldots(**)$$

(*i*) Find their point of intersection and interpret it.

(*ii*) Find correlation coefficient between *X* and *Y*.

(*iii*) Show that the regression estimate of *Y* for $X = 0$ is 13 whereas regression estimate of *X* for $Y = 13$ is 3. Explain the cause of difference. [*Delhi Univ. B.Com. (Hons), (External) 2005*]

Hint. (*i*) Solving; $\bar{X} = 4, \bar{Y} = 7$ (*ii*) $r^2 = \left(-\frac{3}{2}\right) \times \left(-\frac{1}{6}\right) = \frac{1}{4} \Rightarrow r = -\frac{1}{2}$

(*iii*) (*) is the regression equation of *Y* on *X* and (**) is the regression equation of *X* on *Y*.

$$\text{When } X = 0,\ \hat{Y} = \frac{26}{2} = 13 \text{ [From (*)]}; \quad \text{When } Y = 13,\ \hat{X} = \frac{31 - 13}{6} = 3$$

8. Given the regression lines as : $3x + 2y = 26$ and $6x + y = 31$, find their point of intersection and interpret it. Also find the correlation coefficient between *x* and *y*. [*C.A. (Foundation), May 2001*]

Ans. Point of intersection of the lines of regression gives the mean values : ($\bar{x} = 4$ and $\bar{y} = 7$) ; $r_{xy} = -0{\cdot}25$

9. (*a*) If the two regression lines are $3y + 9x = 46$ and $3x + 12y = 19$, determine which one of these is the regression line of y on x and which one is that of x on y. Also find the means, correlation coefficient and ratio of the variances of x and y. [*Delhi Univ. B.Com. (Hons.), (External), 2006*]

Ans. (*i*) $3y + 9x = 46$ ... (*) $\quad 3x + 12y = 19$ ...(**)

(*) is Regression Equation of x on y and (**) is Regression Equation of y on x.

(*ii*) $\bar{x} = 5, \ \bar{y} = \frac{1}{3}$ $\quad$ (*iii*) $r_{xy} = -\sqrt{\left(-\frac{1}{3}\right)\left(-\frac{1}{4}\right)} = -\sqrt{\frac{1}{12}} = -0{\cdot}289$ $\quad$ (*iv*) $\sigma_x^2 : \sigma_y^2 = 4 : 3$.

(*b*) The equations of two regression lines between two variables are expressed as

$$2x - 3y = 0 \quad \text{and} \quad 4y - 5x - 8 = 0.$$

(*i*) Identify which of the two can be called regression of y on x, and of x on y.

(*ii*) Find $\bar{x}$ and $\bar{y}$ and (*iii*) correlation coefficient (r) from the equations.

[*Delhi Univ. B.A. (Econ. Hons.), 2008; C.A. (Foundation), May 1999*]

Ans. (*i*) Regression of y on x : $2x - 3y = 0$: x on y : $4y - 5x - 8 = 0$;

(*ii*) $\bar{x} = -(24/7) - 3{\cdot}43$, $\bar{y} = -(16/7) - 2{\cdot}29$; (*iii*) $r = 0{\cdot}73$.

10. For random variables X and Y with the same mean, the two regression equations are

$Y = aX + b$ and $X = \alpha Y + \beta$. Show that $\frac{b}{\beta} = \frac{1-a}{1-\alpha}$. [*Delhi Univ. B.A. (Econ. Hons.), 2003*]

Hint. Proceed as in Example 9.13(*a*).

11. For 50 students of a class, the regression equation of marks in Statistics (x) on marks in Accountancy (y) is $3y - 5x + 180 = 0$. The mean marks in Accountancy is 44 and variance of marks in Statistics is 9/16th of the variance of marks in Accountancy. Find the mean marks in Statistics and coefficient of correlation between marks in two subjects.

[*Delhi Univ. B.Com. (Hons.), 1994*]

Ans. $\bar{x} = 62{\cdot}4$; $r_{xy} = 0{\cdot}8$.

12. For fifty students of a class, the regression equation of marks in Statistics (y) on the marks in Accountancy (x) is $4y - 5x - 8 = 0$. Average marks in Accountancy are 40. The ratio of the standard deviations $\sigma_y : \sigma_x$ is 5 : 2. Find the average marks in Statistics and the coefficient of correlation between the marks in two subjects.

Ans. $\bar{y} = 52$, $r_{xy} = 0{\cdot}5$.

13. Given $x = 4y + 5$ and $y = kx + 4$, are the lines of regression of x on y, and y on x respectively. If k is positive, prove that it cannot exceed 1/4. If $k = 1/16$, find the means of the two variables and coefficient of correlation between them. [*Delhi Univ. B.com. (Hons.), 2006; Poona Univ. M.B.A. 2003*]

Hint. $r^2 = b_{yx} \cdot b_{xy} = 4 \cdot k \leq 1 \quad \Rightarrow \quad k \leq \frac{1}{4}$.

Ans. $\bar{x} = 28$, $\bar{y} = 5{\cdot}75$, $r = 0{\cdot}5$.

14. If $a_1 x + b_1 y + c_1 = 0$ and $a_2 x + b_2 y + c_2 = 0$

are the equations of the lines of regression of y on x and x on y respectively, then prove that $a_1 b_2 \leq a_2 b_1$.

Hint. $r^2 = b_{yx} \cdot b_{xy} = \left(-\frac{a_1}{b_1}\right) \times \left(-\frac{b_2}{a_2}\right) \leq 1$.

15. What do you mean by Standard Error (S.E.) of an estimate ? Give expressions for the S.E. of estimate of y for given x and S.E. of estimate of x for given y, assuming linear regression between x and y.

16. (*a*) What is 'explained variation' and 'unexplained variation' ? How is it related to S.E. of an estimate ?

In a regression analysis, the sum of squares of the deviations about the mean for the predicted scores is 80 and the sum of squares of the error is 40, what is r^2 ? Explain. [*Delhi Univ. B.A. (Econ. Hons.), 2009*]

Ans. $r^2 = \dfrac{\Sigma(\hat{Y}_i - \bar{Y})^2}{\Sigma(Y_i - \bar{Y})^2} = \dfrac{\Sigma(\hat{Y}_i - \bar{Y})^2}{\Sigma(Y_i - \hat{Y}_i)^2 + \Sigma(\hat{Y}_i - \bar{Y})^2} = \dfrac{80}{40 + 80} = \dfrac{2}{3} = 0{\cdot}67$

(*b*) Given : Unexplained variation = 19·22, Explained variation = 19·70, determine the coefficient of correlation.

Ans. $r^2 = \dfrac{\text{Explained variation}}{\text{Total variation}} = \dfrac{19{\cdot}70}{19{\cdot}70 + 19{\cdot}22} = \dfrac{19{\cdot}70}{38{\cdot}92} = 0{\cdot}5062 \quad \Rightarrow \quad r = \pm 0{\cdot}7115$.

17. Explain the concept of standard error of estimate. What is the significance of standard error of estimate ? How will you find standard error of estimate for the equations of Y on X, and X on Y. [*Delhi Univ. B.Com. (Hons.), 2006*]

18. (*a*) Explain the concept of standard error of estimate of the linear regression of Y on X. Can you express it in terms of correlation coefficient ? What is the standard error of estimating Y from X if $r = 1$?

[*Delhi Univ. B.A. (Econ. Hons.), 1995*]

Ans. $S_{yx} = \sigma_y (1 - r^2)^{1/2}$; $S_{yx} = 0$ if $r = 1$.

(*b*) Find out the standard error in estimating y from x from the following regression equations :

$3y - 2x - 10 = 0$ and $2y - x - 50 = 0$

It is known that the variance of y is 9. [*Delhi Univ. B.A. (Econ. Hons.), 2003*]

Ans. $r^2 = b_{yx} \cdot b_{xy} = \frac{1}{2} \times \frac{3}{2} = \frac{3}{4}$; $\sigma_y = 3$, $S_{yx} = 1{\cdot}5$.

19. You are given the following information about advertising expenditure (X) and sales (Y) :

	Advertising Expenditure (X) (Rs. Crores)	Sales (Y) (Rs. Crores)
Mean	10	90
Standard Deviation	3	12

Correlation coefficient $r_{XY} = 0{\cdot}8$.

(*i*) Estimate the two linear regression equations of Y on X, and X on Y.

(*ii*) What should be the advertising budget if the company wants to attain sales target of Rs. 120 crores ?

(*iii*) What is the standard error of the estimate in the regression of Y on X. [*Delhi Univ. B.A. (Econ. Hons.), 2006*]

Ans. (*i*) $Y = 3{\cdot}2\,X + 58$ and $X = 0{\cdot}2\,Y - 8$; (*ii*) $(\hat{X})_{Y=120} = 0{\cdot}2 \times 120 - 8 = 16$ crores. (*iii*) $S_{yx} = 7{\cdot}2$

20. The regression equations of X on Y and Y on X (not necessarily in that order) are

$10X + 3Y = 25$ and $6X + 5Y = 31$. The variance of X is 4.

Find :

(*i*) The means of X and Y.

(*ii*) The predicted value of X when Y is 1 and the predicted value of Y when $X = 2$.

(*iii*) The correlation coefficient between X and Y.

(*iv*) The standard error of estimate in the regression of Y on X. [*Delhi Univ. B.A. (Econ. Hons.), 2002*]

Hint. (*iv*) $S_{yx} = \sigma_y (1 - r^2)^{1/2}$; $b_{yx} = \dfrac{r\sigma_y}{\sigma_x} = -\frac{6}{5} \Rightarrow \sigma_y = 4$.

Ans. (*i*) $\bar{X} = 1$, $\bar{Y} = 5$ (*ii*) $(\hat{X})_{Y=1} = 2{\cdot}2$; $(\hat{Y})_{X=2} = 3{\cdot}8$ (*iii*) $r(X, Y) = -0{\cdot}6$ (*iv*) $S_{yx} = 3{\cdot}2$.

21. (*a*) The equations of the two lines of regression obtained in a correlation analysis between two variables x and y are :

$2x = 8 - 3y$ and $2y = 5 - x$; and Var $(x) = 4$.

Find : (*i*) Mean values of x and y. ; (*ii*) Identify the lines of regression.

(*iii*) Two regression coefficients. ; (*iv*) Correlation coefficient $r(x, y)$.

(*v*) Coefficient of determination. ; (*vi*) Variance of y

(*vii*) Standard error of estimate of y on x and x on y. [*Delhi Univ. B.A. (Econ. Hons.), 1996*]

[*Delhi Univ. B.Com. (Hons.), 2004*]

Ans. (*i*) $\bar{x} = 1$, $\bar{y} = 2$

(*ii*) $2x = 8 - 3y$ is the line of regression of x on y and $2y = 5 - x$ is the line of regression of y on x.

(*iii*) $b_{yx} = -\frac{1}{2}$, $b_{xy} = -\frac{3}{2}$; (*iv*) $r(x, y) = -\frac{\sqrt{3}}{2} = -0{\cdot}866$

(*v*) $r^2 = 0{\cdot}75$ (*vi*) $\sigma_y^2 = 4/3$ (*vii*) $S_{yx} = 0{\cdot}578$, $S_{xy} = 1$

22. Find :

(*i*) the regression coefficients b_{YX} and b_{XY} ; (*ii*) correlation coefficient r_{XY}, and

(*iii*) the standard error of the estimate of Y on X from the following data :

$\Sigma XY = 350$; $\bar{X} = 5$; $\bar{Y} = 6$; $\Sigma X = 50$; $\Sigma Y = 60$; Var $(X) = 4$; Var $(Y) = 9$.

[*Delhi Univ. B.A. (Econ. Hons.), 2007*]

Hint. $\bar{X} = \frac{\Sigma X}{n} \Rightarrow n = \frac{\Sigma X}{\bar{X}} = \frac{50}{5} = 10$ or $n = \frac{\Sigma Y}{\bar{Y}} = \frac{60}{6} = 10.$

$$\text{Cov}(X, Y) = \frac{\Sigma XY}{n} - \bar{X}\,\bar{Y} = \frac{350}{10} - 5 \times 6 = 5; \quad \sigma_X^2 = 4; \quad \sigma_Y^2 = 9$$

$$\therefore \quad r = \frac{\text{Cov}(X, Y)}{\sigma_X \sigma_Y} = \frac{5}{6}; \quad b_{YX} = \frac{\text{Cov}(X, Y)}{\sigma_X^2} = \frac{5}{4}; \quad b_{XY} = \frac{\text{Cov}(X, Y)}{\sigma_Y^2} = \frac{5}{9}$$

$$S_{YX} = \sigma_Y (1 - r^2)^{1/2} = 3 . \frac{\sqrt{11}}{6} = \frac{\sqrt{11}}{2}$$

23. Given the standard deviations σ_x and σ_y for two correlated variates x and y in a large sample :

(*a*) What is the standard error in estimating y from x if $r = 0$?

(*b*) By how much is the error reduced if r is increased to 0·5 ?

(*c*) What is the standard error in estimating y from x if $r = 1$?

Ans. (*a*) $S_{yx} = \sigma_y$, (*b*) 0·14 σ_y, (*c*) $S_{yx} = 0$.

24. Calculate the coefficient of correlation and two lines of regression from the following data :

Sales Revenue (Lakh Rs.)	*Advertising Expenditure* 5—15	15—25	25—35	35—45
75—125	3	4	4	8
125—175	8	6	5	7
175—225	2	2	3	4
225—275	3	3	2	2

[*Delhi Univ. M.B.A., 1996*]

Ans. $X = 172{\cdot}655 - 0{\cdot}5165Y$; $Y = 30{\cdot}4 - 0{\cdot}0273X$; $r = 0{\cdot}119$.

25. Given the following data compute the two coefficients of regression and Karl Pearson's coefficient of correlation.

X \ Y	0—20	20—40	40—60
10—25	10	5	3
25—40	4	40	8
40—55	6	9	15

[*Delhi Univ.. B.Com. (Hons.) 1995 ; B.A. (Econ. Hons.), 1992*]

Ans. $b_{YX} = 0{\cdot}4375$; $b_{xy} = 0{\cdot}2511$; $r(x, y) = 0{\cdot}3314$.

EXERCISE 9·3
(OBJECTIVE TYPE QUESTIONS)

1. If two regression coefficients are 0·8 and 1·2, what would be the value of the coefficient of correlation ?

Ans. 0·9798.

2. Given $b_{yx} = -1{\cdot}4$ and $b_{xy} = -0{\cdot}5$, calculate r_{xy}.

Ans. $r_{xy} = -0{\cdot}84$.

3. (*a*) Comment on the following :

For a bivariate distribution, the coefficient of regression of y on x is 4·2 and coefficient of regression of x on y is 0·5.

(*b*) If two regression coefficients are 0·8 and 0·6, what would be the value of the coefficient of correlation ?

(*c*) A student while studying correlation between smoking and drinking found a value of $r = 2{\cdot}46$. Discuss.

(*d*) For a bivariate distribution : $b_{yx} = 2{\cdot}8$; $b_{xy} = -0{\cdot}3$. Comment.

Ans. (*a*) $r^2 = 4{\cdot}2 \times 0{\cdot}5 = 2{\cdot}1 > 1$. Statement is wrong. (*b*) 0·69. (*c*) Wrong, since $-1 \le r \le 1$. (*d*) Wrong, since both the regression coefficients must have the same sign.

4. With $b_{xy} = 0{\cdot}5$, $r = 0{\cdot}8$ and variance of $Y = 16$, the standard deviation of X equals to...

(a) 2·5 (b) 6·4 (c) 10·0 (d) 25·6

Ans. $\sigma_x = 2{\cdot}5$.

5. Given regression coefficients of x on y and y on x as 0·85 and 0·89, find the value of coefficient of correlation.

Ans. $r = 0{\cdot}8698$.

6. From the following regression equations, find $\bar{x}$ and $\bar{y}$.

$$Y \text{ on } X \ : \ 2Y - X - 50 = 0 \quad ; \quad X \text{ on } Y \ : \ 3Y - 2X - 10 = 0$$

Ans. $\bar{x} = 130$, $\bar{y} = 90$.

7. A student obtained the two regression lines as :

$$2x - 5y - 7 = 0 \qquad \text{and} \qquad 3x + 2y - 8 = 0$$

Do you agree with him ?

Ans. No. $b_{yx} = 2/5$, $b_{xy} = -2/3$. Impossible, because both the regression coefficients must have the same sign.

8. Comment on the following statements :

(i) The correlation coefficient (r_{xy}) between X and Y is 0·90 and the regression coefficient β_{xy} is – 1.

(ii) If the two coefficients of regression are negative then their correlation coefficient is positive.

(iii) $r_{xy} = 0{\cdot}9$, $\beta_{xy} = 2{\cdot}04$, $\beta_{yx} = -3{\cdot}2$.

Ans. (i) Wrong, (ii) Wrong, (iii) Wrong [r_{xy}, β_{xy} and β_{yx} must have the same sign].

9. Discuss briefly the importance of regression analysis. Interpret the following values :

(i) Product-moment coefficient of correlation is 0.

(ii) Regression coefficient of Y on X is $-1{\cdot}75$.

(iii) Coefficient of rank correlation = 1.

10. (i) "The regression equations of Y on X and X on Y are irreversible." Explain.

(ii) "A correlation coefficient $r = 0{\cdot}8$ indicates a relationship twice as close as $r = 0{\cdot}4$." Comment.

(iii) "Even a high degree of correlation does not mean that a relationship of cause and effect exists between the two correlated variables." Why ?

11. Indicate whether the following statements are True or False. Give reasons :

1. If the coefficient of correlation between two variables X and Y is 0·8, then coefficient of correlation between $-X$ and $-Y$ is $-0{\cdot}8$.

2. If the coefficient of correlation between X and Y is perfect, the two lines of regression of X on Y, and Y on X are reversible. *[Delhi Univ. B.Com (Hons.) 2004]*

Ans. 1. $r(-X, -Y) = (-1)(-1)\, r(X, Y) = 0{\cdot}8$; *False*

2. If $r = \pm 1$, the two lines of regression coincide. $\Rightarrow$ Two regression lines are reversible; *True*.

10 Index Numbers

10·1. INTRODUCTION

Index numbers are indicators which reflect the relative changes in the level of a certain phenomenon in any given period (or over a specified period of time) called the *current period* with respect to its values in some fixed period, called the *base period* selected for comparison. The phenomenon or variable under consideration may be :

(*i*) The price of a particular commodity like steel, gold, leather, etc., or a group of commodities like consumer goods, cereals, milk and milk products, cosmetics, etc.

(*ii*) Volume of trade, factory production, industrial or agricultural production, imports or exports, stocks and shares, sales and profits of a business house and so on.

(*iii*) The national income of a country, wage structure of workers in various sectors, bank deposits, foreign exchange reserves, cost of living of persons of a particular community, class or profession and so on.

Definition. "*Index numbers are statistical devices designed to measure the relative change in the level of a phenomenon (variable or a group of variables) with respect to time, geographical location or other characteristics such as income, profession, etc.*" In other words, index numbers are specialised type of rates, ratios, percentages which give the general level of magnitude of a group of distinct but related variables in two or more situations.

For example, suppose we are interested in studying the general change in the price level of consumer goods, *i.e.,* goods or commodities consumed by the people belonging to a particular section of society, say, low income group or middle income group or labour class and so on. Obviously these changes are not directly measurable as the price quotations of the various commodities are available in different units, *e.g.,* cereals (wheat, rice, pulses, etc.), are quoted in Rs. per quintal or kg.; water in Rs. per gallon; milk, petrol, kerosene, etc., in Rs. per litre; cloth in Rs. per metre and so on.

Further, the prices of some of the commodities may be increasing while those of others may be decreasing during the *two* periods and the rates of increase or decrease may be different for different commodities. *Index number* is a statistical device which enables us to arrive at a single representative figure which gives the general level of the price of the phenomenon (commodities) in an extensive group. According to Wheldon :

"*Index number is a statistical device for indicating the relative movements of the data where measurement of actual movements is difficult or incapable of being made.*"

F.Y. Edgeworth gave the classical definition of index numbers as follows :

"*Index number shows by its variations the changes in a magnitude which is not susceptible either of accurate measurement in itself or of direct valuation in practice.*"

10·2. USES OF INDEX NUMBERS

The first index number was constructed by an Italian, Mr. Carli, in 1764 to compare the changes in price for the year 1750 (current year) with the price level in 1500 (base year) in order to study the effect of discovery of America on the price level in Italy. Though originally designed to study the general level of prices or accordingly purchasing power of money, today index numbers are extensively used for a variety of purposes in economics, business, management, etc., and for quantitative data relating to production, consumption, profits, personnel and financial matters, etc., for comparing changes in the level of phenomenon for two periods, places, etc. In fact, there is hardly any field of quantitative measurements where index numbers are not constructed. They are used in almost all sciences — natural, social and physical. The main uses of index numbers can be summarised as follows :

1. *Index Numbers as Economic Barometers.* Index numbers are indispensable tools for the management personnel of any government organisation or individual business concern and in business planning and formulation of executive decisions. The indices of prices (wholesale and retail), output (volume of trade, import and export, industrial and agricultural production) and bank deposits, foreign exchange and reserves, etc., throw light on the nature of, and variation in, the general economic and business activity of the country. A careful study of these indices gives us a fairly good appraisal of the general trade, economic development and business activity of the country. In the words of G. Simpson and F. Kafka :

"*Index numbers are today one of the most widely used statistical devices...They are used to take the pulse of the economy and they have come to be used as indicators of inflationary or deflationary tendencies.*"

Like barometers which are used in Physics and Chemistry to measure atmospheric pressure, index numbers are rightly termed as '*economic barometers*' or '*barometers of economic activity*' which measure the pressure of economic and business behaviour.

2. *Index Numbers Help in Studying Trends and Tendencies.* Since the index numbers study the relative changes in the level of a phenomenon at different periods of time, they are specially useful for the study of the general trend for a group phenomena in a time series data. The indices of output (industrial and agricultural production), volume of trade, import and export, etc., are extremely useful for studying the changes in the level of phenomenon due to the various components of a time series, *viz.*, secular trend, seasonal and cyclical variations and irregular components and reflect upon the general trend of production and business activity. As a measure of average change in extensive group, the index numbers can be used to forecast future events. For instance, if a businessman is interested in establishing a new industry, the study of the trend of changes in the prices, wages and incomes in different industries is extremely helpful to him to frame a general idea of the comparative courses which the future holds for different undertakings.

3. *Index Numbers Help in Formulating Decisions and Policies.* Index numbers of the data relating to prices, production, profits, imports and exports, personnel and financial matters are indispensable for any organisation in efficient planning and formulation of executive decisions. For example, the cost of living index numbers are used by the government and the industrial and business concerns for the regulation of dearness allowance (D.A.) or grant of bonus to the workers so as to enable them to meet the increased cost of living from time to time. The excise duty on the production or sales of a commodity is regulated according to the index numbers of the consumption of the commodity from time to time. Similarly, the indices of consumption of various commodities help in the planning of their future production. Although index numbers are now widely used to study the general economic and business conditions of the society, they are also applied with advantage by sociologists (population indices), psychologists (I.Q.'s), health and educational authorities, etc., for formulating and revising their policies from time to time.

4. *Price Indices Measure the Purchasing Power of Money.* The cost of living index numbers determine whether the real wages are rising or falling, money wages remaining unchanged. In other words, they help us in computing the real wages which are obtained on dividing the money wages by the corresponding price index and multiplying by 100. Real wages help us in determining the purchasing power of money. For example, suppose that the cost of living index for any year, say, 1979 for a particular class of people with 1970 as base year is 150. If a person belonging to that class gets Rs. 300 in 1970, then in order to maintain the same standard of living as in 1970 (other factors remaining constant) his salary in 1979 should be $\frac{150}{100} \times 300$ = Rs. 450. In other words, if a person gets Rs. 450 in 1979, then his real wages are $\frac{450}{150} \times 100$ = Rs. 300 *i.e.*, the purchasing power of money has reduced to 2/3.

5. *Index Numbers are Used for Deflation.* Consumer price indices or cost of living index numbers are used for deflation of net national product, income value series in national accounts. The technique of obtaining real wages from the given nominal wages (as explained in use 4 above) can be used to find real

income from inflated money income, real sales from nominal sales and so on by taking into account appropriate index numbers.

For detailed discussion on (4) and (5) See § 10·8·3.

10·3. TYPES OF INDEX NUMBERS

Index numbers may be broadly classified into various categories depending upon the type of the phenomenon or variable in which the relative changes are to be studied. Although index numbers can be constructed for measuring relative changes in any field of quantitative measurement, we shall primarily confine the discussion to the data relating to economics and business *i.e.*, data relating to prices, production (output) and consumption. In this context index numbers may be broadly classified into the following three categories :

1. Price Index Numbers. The price index numbers measure the general changes in the prices. They are further sub-divided into the following classes :

(*a*) **Wholesale Price Index Numbers.** The wholesale price index numbers reflect the changes in the general price level of a country. The official general purpose index number of wholesale prices in India was first compiled by the Economic Adviser, Ministry of Commerce and Industry (now the Ministry of Commerce) in 1947 (with year ending August 1939 as base year) and revised series was started in April 1956 (with 1952-53 and base year). The new series of index number of wholesale price (1961-62 base year) was started on the recommendations of "Wholesale Price Index Revision Committee". It covered 139 commodities, 225 markets and 774 quotations. The revised series of index numbers of whole-sale prices with 1970-1971 as base year was introduced since the first week of January, 1977.

(*b*) **Retail Price Index Numbers.** These indices reflect the general changes in the retail prices of various commodities such as consumption goods, stocks and shares, bank deposits, government bonds, etc. In India, these indices are constructed by Labour Ministry in the form of Labour Bureau Index Number of Retail Prices—Urban Centres and Rural Centres.

Consumer Price Index, commonly known as the Cost of Living Index is a specialised kind of retail price index and enables us to study the effect of changes in the prices of a basket of goods or commodities on the purchasing power or cost of living of a particular class or section of the people like labour class, industrial or agricultural worker, low income or middle income class, etc. In India, cost of living index numbers are available for (*i*) Central Government employees, (*ii*) middle class people, and (*iii*) working class.

2. Quantity Index Numbers. Quantity index numbers study the changes in the volume of goods produced (manufactured), consumed or distributed, like the indices of agricultural production, industrial production, imports and exports, etc. They are extremely helpful in studying the level of physical output in an economy.

3. Value Index Numbers. These are intended to study the change in the total value (price multiplied by quantity) of production such as indices of retail sales or profits or inventories. However, these indices are not as common as price and quantity indices.

10·4. PROBLEMS IN THE CONSTRUCTION OF INDEX NUMBERS

As already pointed out, index numbers are very powerful statistical tools for measuring the changes in the level of any phenomenon over two different periods of time. It is, therefore, imperative that utmost care is exercised in the computation and construction of these indices. Index numbers which are not properly compiled will, not only lead to wrong and fallacious conclusions but might also prove to be dangerous. The construction of the index numbers requires a careful study of the following points which may be termed as *preliminaries* to the construction of index numbers.

1. The Purpose of Index Numbers. The first and the foremost problem in the construction of index numbers is to define in clear and concrete terms the objective or the purpose for which the index number is required. The purpose of the index would help in deciding about the nature of the statistics (data) to be collected, the statistical techniques (formulae) to be used and also has a determining effect on some other related problems like the selection of commodities, selection of base period, the average to be used and so on. For example, if we want to study the changes in the cost of living (*i.e.*, consumer price index) the class of people for which the index is designed, *viz.*, agricultural or industrial workers, low income group, middle income group, etc., should be clearly specified because the consumption pattern of the commodities by the people of different classes varies considerably. Similarly, if the objective is to study the general changes in the price level in a country then the price quotations are to be obtained from "the wholesale market and relatively a large number of commodities or items are to be included in its construction as compared with the number of items in the construction of cost of living index for a specified class of people. In the absence of the purpose of the index being clearly specified, we are liable to collect some irrelevant information which may never be used and also omit some important data or items which might ultimately lead to fallacious conclusions and wastage of resources.

2. Selection of Commodities or Items. Once the purpose of the index is explicitly specified, the next problem is the selection of the commodities or items to be used for its construction. In the selection of commodities the following points may be borne in mind :

(*i*) The commodities selected should be relevant to the purpose of the index. For example, if we want to study the effect of change in prices on the cost of living of low income group (poor families), then we should select only those commodities or items which are generally consumed or utilised by the people belonging to the group and proper care should be taken not to include items which are consumed by middle income and high income groups. In this connection, the selection of high quality cosmetics, and the luxury items like scooter, television, refrigerator, etc., will have no relevance. The commodities should thus be representative of the habits, tastes, customs and consumption pattern of the class of people for whom the index is intended.

As already pointed out, index number gives the general level of a phenomenon in an extensive group. It is practically impossible to take into account all the items in the group. For example, in the construction of price index, from technical point of view we should study the price changes in all the items or commodities. However, from practical point of view, it is neither possible nor desirable to take into account all the items. We resort to sampling and only a few representative items are selected from the whole lot. The ideal solution lies in :

(*a*) Classifying the whole relevant group of items or commodities into relatively homogeneous sub-groups like : (*i*) Food (cereals — rice, wheat, pulses, grams, etc., milk and milk products; fruits; vegetables; meat, poultry, and fish; bakery products and so on), (*ii*) Clothing, (*iii*) Fuel and Lighting (including electrical appliances), (*iv*) House Rent, (*v*) Miscellaneous (including items like education, entertainment, medical expenses, washerman, newspaper, etc.

(*b*) Selecting an adequate number of representative items from each group (so that the final sample is a stratified sample and not a random sample). Further, within each group, the more important items of consumption by the particular group of people are selected first and from among the remaining items as many more items are selected as our resources (in terms of time, money and administration) permit. Thus, even within each stratum (sub-group) the sample drawn is not random.

(*ii*) The total number of commodities selected for the index should neither be too small nor too large, because if it is too small, then the index number will not be representative and if it is too large, then the computational work may be uneconomical in terms of time and money and may even be tedious. The number of commodities selected should be fairly enough consistent with the ease of handling and computation.

(*iii*) In order to arrive at meaningful and valid comparisons it is essential that the commodities selected for the construction of the index number are of the same quality or grade in different periods, or in other words they remain more or less stable in quality for reasonably long periods. Hence, in order to avoid any confusion about the quality of commodities due to time lag, graded or standardised items or commodities should be selected as far as possible.

3. Data for Index Numbers. The raw data for the construction of index numbers are the prices of the selected commodities together with their quantities consumed for different periods. These data must be obtained from reliable sources like standard trade journals (publications of Chambers of Commerce); reputed periodicals and newspapers like *Eastern Economist, Economic Times, The Financial Express, Indian Journal of Economics*, etc.; periodical special reports from producers, exporters, etc., or in the absence of all these through reliable and unbiased field agency. The basic principles of data collection *viz.*, accuracy, suitability or comparability, and adequacy should be kept in mind in using secondary data. [For details see § 2·6]. Above all, the data collected must be relevant to the purpose of the index. For example, if we want to study the changes in the general price level in a country, then the price quotations for the selected commodities must be obtained from the wholesale market and not from the retail shops. Since it is neither possible nor desirable to collect the price quotations of a commodity from all the markets in the country, an adequate number of representative markets which are well known for trading in that particular commodity is selected at random. After the places or markets from which price quotations are to be obtained have been selected, the next job is to appoint an authority, who will supply the price quotations from time to time on regular basis, since price indices are often computed yearly, monthly and even weekly. This may be achieved either by appointing additional staff in the selected places or asking a private institution or local field agency to do the job. Care must be exercised to see that the agency is unbiased. Moreover, to apply cross-checks on the price quotations supplied by the agency, the price quotations may also be obtained from other independent agency in that place, from time to time.

4. Selection of Base Period. As already pointed out the base period is the period selected for comparisons of the relative changes in the level of a phenomenon from time to time. The index for base period is always taken as 100. The following points in conformity with the objectives of the index should serve as guidelines for selecting a base period :

(*i*) *Base period should be a period of normal and stable economic conditions, i.e.*, it should be free from all sorts of abnormalities and random or irregular fluctuations like earthquakes, wars, floods, famines, labour strikes, lockouts, economic boom and depression. For instance, if the base period is taken as a period of economic boom so that prices of various goods and commodities are very low, then the index will be over-stated while if the base period is a period of depression or economic instability, so that the prices of consumption goods are abnormally high, then the index will be under-stated. However, the selection of a strictly normal period is not an easy job. A period which is normal in one respect may be abnormal in some other respect. Accordingly, sometimes an average of two or more years is taken as base period and the average prices and quantities of the commodities consumed in these years are taken as base year prices and quantities.

(*ii*) *The base period should not be too distant from the given period.* Due to rapid and dynamic pace of events these days, it is desirable that the base period should not be very far off from the current period because the comparisons are valid and meaningful if they are made between two periods with relatively familiar set of circumstances. If the time lag is too much between the current and the base periods then it is very likely that there may be an appreciable change in the tastes, customs, habits, and fashions of the people, thereby, affecting the consumption pattern of the various commodities to a marked extent. It is also possible that during this long period some of the goods or commodities consumed in the base year have become obsolete or outdated and have been replaced by new commodities of better quality. In such situations, comparison will be very difficult to make. Keeping this point in view the base period in the Economic Adviser's Index Number of Wholesale Prices in India has been recently shifted from *1960-61 to 1970-71.* Similarly, for the grant of dearness allowance (D.A.) or increment to the workers, the prices should be compared with the period when last D.A. was granted or announced.

(*iii*) *Fixed-base or Chain-base.* If the period of comparison is kept fixed for all current years, it is called fixed-base period. However, because of the points raised in (*ii*) above, sometimes chain-base method is used, in which the changes in the prices for any given year are compared with the prices in the preceding year. [For details see Chain-base Index Numbers discussed in § 10·7.]

5. Type of Average to be Used. The changes in the prices of various commodities have to be combined to arrive at a single index which will reflect the average change in the price level of the commodities in the composite group. This is done by averaging them. Since index numbers are specialised averages, a judicious selection of the average to be used for their construction is of great importance. The commonly used averages are :

(*i*) Arithmetic Mean (A.M.).

(*ii*) Geometric Mean (G.M.).

(*iii*) Median.

Median is the easiest of all the three to calculate but since it completely ignores the extreme observations and is more affected by a few middle items, it is seldom used. Arithmetic mean is also not recommended theoretically as it is very much affected by extreme observations. However, from the theoretical considerations, geometric mean is the most appropriate average in this case because :

(*i*) In index number we deal with ratios and relative changes and geometric mean gives equal weights to equal ratios of change. [G.M. of ratios = Ratio of G.M.'s]. For example, if the price of a commodity is doubled and that of the other is halved then the geometric mean is not affected while the arithmetic mean will show an increase of 25%.

(*ii*) It gives more importance to small items and less importance to large items and is, therefore, not unduly affected by extreme and violent fluctuations in the observations.

(*iii*) Index numbers based on geometric mean are reversible [See Time Reversal Test § 10·6·2].

Hence from theoretic considerations, for the sake of greater accuracy and precision, geometric mean should be preferred. However, in practice, because of its computational difficulties, geometric mean is not used as much as arithmetic mean. Basically, the effective choice of an appropriate average for the construction of an index number is between the arithmetic mean and geometric mean, each of which is commonly used in practice but gives different figures for the index.

6. System of Weighting. The commodities included for the construction of index numbers like food, clothing, housing, light and fuel, etc., are not of equal importance. In order that the index is representative of the average changes in the level of phenomenon for the composite group, proper weights should be assigned to different commodities according to their relative importance in the group. Thus, in practice, we may have two types of index numbers.

(*i*) *Unweighted Index Numbers.* The index numbers constructed without assigning any weights to different items are called unweighted index numbers.

(*ii*) *Weighted Index Numbers.* These are obtained after assigning weights to different items according to their relative importance in the group. In fact, unweighted index numbers may also be looked upon as weighted index numbers where the weight of each commodity is unity.

The system of weighting and the question of allocation of appropriate weights to various items is of fundamental importance and constitutes an important aspect of the construction of index numbers. The weights may be assigned to the various commodities in any manner deemed appropriate to bring out their economic importance. For example, the production figures, consumption figures or distribution figures may be taken as weights. The most commonly adopted systems of weighting are :

(*i*) *Quantity weights* in which the various commodities are attached importance according to the amount of their quantity used, purchased or consumed.

(*ii*) *The value weights* in which the importance to the various items is assigned according to the expenditure involved on them.

The choice of different systems of weighting *w.r.t.* the quantities consumed or the total values in the base year or the current year or sometimes their arithmetic or geometric crosses gives rise to a number of formulae for the construction of index numbers, discussed in § 10·5 and very much depends on the purpose of the index and availability of the data.

Regarding the system of weighting to be adopted for constructing index numbers, it is worthwhile to quote the words of A.L. Bowley :

"The discussion of proper weights to be used has occupied a space in statistical literature out of all proportions to its significance, for it may be said at once that no great importance need be attached to the special choice of weights ; one of the most convenient facts of statistical theory is that, given certain conditions, the same result is obtained with sufficient closeness whatever logical system of weights is applied."

However, he is not totally against the weighting and suggested the arithmetic cross of Laspeyre's and Paasche's formulae discussed in § 10·5·2.

7. Choice of Formula. The choice of the formula to be used depends on the availability of the data regarding the prices and the quantities of the selected commodities in the base and/or current year. Before discussing various formulae, we give below notations and terminology.

Notations and Terminology

Base Year. The year selected for comparison, *i.e.,* the year *w.r.t.* which comparisons are made. It is denoted by the suffix zero '0'.

Current Year. The year for which comparisons are sought or required. It is denoted by the suffix 1.

p_0 : Price of a commodity in the base year.

p_1 : Price of a commodity in the current year.

q_0 : Quantity of a commodity consumed or purchased during the base year.

q_1 : Quantity of a commodity consumed or purchased in the current year.

w : Weight assigned to a commodity according to its relative importance in the group.

I : Simple Index Number or Price Relative obtained on expressing current year price as a percentage of the base year price and is given by

$$I = \text{Price Relative} = \frac{p_1}{p_0} \times 100 \qquad \ldots (10\cdot1)$$

P_{01} : Price Index Number for the current year *w.r.t.* the base year.

P_{10} : Price Index Number for the base year *w.r.t.* the current year.

Q_{01} : Quantity Index Number for the current year *w.r.t.* the base year.

Q_{10} : Quantity Index Number for the base year *w.r.t.* the current year.

V_{01} : Value Index for the current year *w.r.t.* the base year.

Remark. To be more precise and specific we have :

p_{0j} : Price of the *j*th commodity in the base year, $j = 1, 2, \ldots, n$, (say).

p_{1j} : Price of the *j*th commodity in the current year.

Similarly, q_{0j} and q_{1j} are the quantities of the *j*th commodity in the base year and the current year respectively.

$\sum\limits_{j=1}^{n} p_{0j}$ is total price of all the n commodities in the base year and $\sum\limits_{j=1}^{n} q_{0j}$ is the total quantity of all the commodities consumed in the base year. Similarly

$$\sum_{j=1}^{n} p_{0j} \cdot q_{0j} = \sum_{j=1}^{n} v_{0j},$$

is the total value of all the commodities consumed in the base year. However, for the sake of notational convenience we shall write :

$$\sum_{j=1}^{n} p_{0j} = \Sigma p_0 \qquad \sum_{j=1}^{n} q_{0j} = \Sigma q_0,$$

$$\sum_{j=1}^{n} p_{0j}\, q_{0j} = \Sigma p_0 q_0\,; \qquad \sum_{j=1}^{n} p_{1j}\, q_{1j} = \Sigma p_1 q_1$$

and so on, the summation being taken over the n selected commodities.

10·5. METHODS OF CONSTRUCTING INDEX NUMBERS

We shall now discuss the various techniques or methods used for the construction of index numbers.

Since price indices are most important of all the indices, we shall describe their construction in detail in the following section. The quantity indices can be obtained from price indices by interchanging the price (p) and quantity (q) in the final formula.

10·5·1. Simple (Unweighted) Aggregate Method. This is the simplest of all the methods of constructing index numbers and consists in expressing the total price, *i.e.,* aggregate of prices (of all the selected commodities) in the current year as a percentage of the aggregate of prices in the base year. Thus, the price index for the current year *w.r.t.* the base year is given by :

$$P_{01} = \frac{\sum p_1}{\sum p_0} \times 100 \qquad \ldots (10·2)$$

where $\sum p_1$ is the aggregate of prices (of all the selected commodities) in the current year and $\sum p_0$ is the aggregate of prices in the base year.

This method, though simple, is not reliable and has the following limitations :

(*i*) The prices of various commodities may be quoted in different units, *e.g.*, cereals may be quoted in Rs. per quintal or kg.; liquids like milk, petrol, kerosene may be quoted in Rs. per litre; cloth may be quoted in Rs. per metre and so on. Thus, the index is influenced very much by the units in which commodities are quoted and accordingly some of the commodities may get more importance because they are quoted in a particular unit. For example, if wheat price is quoted in Rs. per kg. the index would be entirely different than if it is quoted in Rs. per quintal, the latter representation will very much emphasise its importance. This index is liable to be misused since unscrupulous and selfish persons might manipulate its value to suit one's requirements by changing the units of measurement of some of the items from 100 gms. to kg. ; from kg. to quintal and so on.

(*ii*) In this method the various commodities are weighted according to the magnitudes of their prices and accordingly commodities which are highly priced exert a greater influence on the value of the index than the commodities which are low-priced. Hence, this index is dominated by commodities with large figure quotations.

(*iii*) The relative importance of the various commodities is not taken into consideration.

Remark. Based on this method, the quantity index is given by the formula :

$$Q_{01} = \frac{\sum q_1}{\sum q_0} \times 100 \qquad \ldots (10·3)$$

where $\sum q_0$ and $\sum q_1$ are the quantities of all the selected commodities consumed in the base year and the current year respectively.

Example 10·1. *From the following data calculate Index Number by Simple Aggregate Method.*

Commodity	:	*A*	*B*	*C*	*D*
Price in 1980 (*Rs.*)	:	*162*	*256*	*257*	*132*
Price in 1981 (*Rs.*)	:	*171*	*164*	*189*	*145*

Solution.

TABLE 10·1

COMPUTATION OF PRICE INDEX NUMBER

Commodity	*Price* (*in Rupees*)	
	1980 (p_0)	*1981* (p_1)
A	162	171
B	256	164
C	257	189
D	132	145
Total	$\sum p_0 = 807$	$\sum p_1 = 669$

The price index number using Simple Aggregate Method is given by :

$$P_{01} = \frac{\sum p_1}{\sum p_0} \times 100 = \frac{669}{807} \times 100 = 82·90$$

10·5·2. Weighted Aggregate Method. In this method, appropriate weights are assigned to various commodities to reflect their relative importance in the group. The weights can be production figures, consumption figures or distribution figures. For the construction of the price index numbers, quantity weights are used, *i.e.*, the amount of the quantity consumed, purchased or marketed. If w is the weight attached to a commodity, then the price index is given by

$$P_{01} = \frac{\sum w p_1}{\sum w p_0} \times 100 \qquad \ldots (10·4)$$

By using different systems of weighting we get a number of formulae. Some of the important formulae are given on page 10·9.

Laspeyre's Price Index or Base Year Method. Taking base year quantities as weights, *i.e.*, $w = q_0$ in (10·4), we get *Laspeyre's Price Index* given by :

$$P_{01}^{La} = \frac{\Sigma p_1 q_0}{\Sigma p_0 q_0} \times 100 \qquad \ldots (10\cdot5)$$

This formula was devised by French Economist Laspeyre in 1817.

Paasche's Price Index. If we take current year quantities as weights in (10·4) we obtain *Paasche's Price Index* which is given by :

$$P_{01}^{Pa} = \frac{\Sigma p_1 q_1}{\Sigma p_0 q_1} \times 100 \qquad \ldots (10\cdot6)$$

This formula was given by German Statistician Paasche in 1874.

Dorbish-Bowley Price Index. This index is given by the arithmetic mean of Laspeyre's and Paasche's price index numbers and we have :

$$P_{01}^{DB} = \frac{1}{2}\left[\frac{\Sigma p_1 q_0}{\Sigma p_0 q_0} + \frac{\Sigma p_1 q_1}{\Sigma p_0 q_1}\right] \times 100 \qquad \ldots (10\cdot7)$$

This is also sometimes known as *L-P* formula.

Fisher's Price Index. Irving Fisher advocated the geometric cross of Laspeyre's and Paasche's price index numbers and is given by :

$$P_{01}^{F} = [P_{01}^{La} \times P_{01}^{Pa}]^{1/2} = \left[\frac{\Sigma p_1 q_0}{\Sigma p_0 q_0} \times \frac{\Sigma p_1 q_1}{\Sigma p_0 q_1}\right]^{1/2} \times 100 \qquad \ldots (10\cdot8)$$

Fisher's index is termed as an *Ideal* index since it satisfies time reversal and factor reversal tests for the consistency of index numbers. [For details, see § 10·6.]

Marshall-Edgeworth Price Index. Taking the arithmetic cross of the quantities in the base year and the current year as weights *i.e.*, $w = (q_0 + q_1)/2$, we obtain the Marshall-Edgeworth (M.E.) formula given by

$$P_{01}^{ME} = \frac{\Sigma p_1 (q_0 + q_1)/2}{\Sigma p_0 (q_0 + q_1)/2} \times 10 = \frac{\Sigma p_1 (q_0 + q_1)}{\Sigma p_0 (q_0 + q_1)} \times 100 \qquad \ldots (10\cdot9)$$

$$= \left[\frac{\Sigma p_1 q_0 + \Sigma p_1 q_1}{\Sigma p_0 q_0 + \Sigma p_0 q_1}\right] \times 100 \qquad \ldots (10\cdot9a)$$

Walsch Price Index. Instead of taking the arithmetic mean of base year and current year quantities as weights, if we take their geometric mean, *i.e.*, $w = \sqrt{q_0 q_1}$, then we obtain Walsch Index given by the formula :

$$P_{01}^{Wa} = \frac{\Sigma p_1 \sqrt{q_0 q_1}}{\Sigma p_0 \sqrt{q_0 q_1}} \times 100 \qquad \ldots (10\cdot10)$$

Kelly's Price Index or Fixed Weights Index. This formula, named after Truman L. Kelly, requires the weights to be fixed for all periods and is also sometimes known as *aggregative index with fixed weights* and is given by the formula :

$$P_{01}^{K} = \frac{\Sigma p_1 q}{\Sigma p_0 q} \times 100 \qquad \ldots (10\cdot11)$$

where the weights are the quantities (q) which may refer to some period (not necessarily the base year or the current year) and are kept constant for all periods. The average (A.M. or G.M.) of the quantities consumed of two, three or more years may be used as weights.

Kelly's fixed base index has a distinct advantage over Laspeyre's index because unlike Laspeyre's index the change in the base year does not necessitate a corresponding change in the weights which can be kept constant until new data become available to revise the index. As such, currently this index is finding great favour and becoming quite popular. The Labour Bureau wholesale price index in U.S.A. is based on this method.

Remarks 1. In all the above formulae, the summation is taken over the various commodities selected for the construction of the index number.

2. Laspeyre's Index vs. Paasche's Index. Laspeyre's price index is based on the assumption that the quantities consumed in the base year and the current year are same, an assumption which is not true in general. If the consumption of some of the commodities or items decreases in the current year due to rise in their prices or due to changes in the habits, tastes and customs of the people, then Laspeyre's index which is based on base year quantities as weights gives relatively more weightage for such commodities (whose prices rise sharply) and consequently the numerator in (10·5) is relatively larger. Hence, Laspeyre's index is expected to have an *'upward bias'* as it over-estimates the true value. Similarly, if the consumption of certain commodities increases in the current year due to decrease in their prices (or changes in the tastes, habits and customs of the people), then Paasche's index which uses current year quantities as weights gives more weightage to such commodities (whose prices decline much). Accordingly, Paasche's index has a *'downward bias'* and is expected to under-estimate the true value. However, it should not be inferred that Laspeyre's index must be larger than Paasche's index always. The conditions under which Laspeyre's index is greater than, equal to or less than Paasche's index have been obtained in Example 10·11. In this context it may be worthwhile to quote the following words of Karmal.

"If the prices of all the goods change in the same ratio then Laspeyre's and Paasche's price index numbers will be equal, for then the weighting system is irrelevant; or if the quantities of all the goods change in the same ratio, they will be equal for then the two weighting systems are the same relatively."

In general, the true value of the price index lies somewhere between the two.

Since the weights change for every year, Paasche's price index numbers require much more computational work as compared with Laspeyre's price index numbers.

3. Marshall-Edgeworth and Fisher's Index Numbers. These formulae are a sort of compromise between Laspeyre's price index (which has an upward bias) and Paasche's price index (which has a downward bias) and have no bias in any known direction. They provide a better estimate of the true price index. However, since both these formulae require the base year and current year prices and quantities for their computation, they have practical limitations because it is very difficult and rather expensive also to obtain correct information regarding these weights. Further, these formulae require much more computational work than Laspeyre's or Paasche's price index numbers. Moreover, although Fisher's index is termed as *ideal* index since it satisfies *Time Reversal* and *Factor Reversal* tests for the consistency of index numbers (discussed later), it is rarely used in practice because of its computational difficulties and statisticians prefer to rely on simple, though less exact, Laspeyre's and Paasche's index numbers. It may be remarked that both Fisher's index and Marshall-Edgeworth index lie between Laspeyre's and Paasche's indices.

4. Quantity Indices. As already discussed, quantity index numbers reflect the relative changes in the quantity or volume of goods produced, consumed, marketed or distributed in any given year *w.r.t.* to some base year. The formulae for quantity indices are obtained from the formulae (10·4) to (10·11) on interchanging prices (p) and quantities (q). Thus, for example,

$$Q_{01}^{La} = \frac{\Sigma\, q_1 p_0}{\Sigma\, q_0 p_0} \times 100 = \frac{\Sigma\, p_0 q_1}{\Sigma\, p_0 q_0} \times 100 \qquad \ldots(10\cdot12)$$

$$Q_{01}^{Pa} = \frac{\Sigma\, q_1 p_1}{\Sigma\, q_0 p_1} \times 100 = \frac{\Sigma\, p_1 q_1}{\Sigma\, p_1 q_0} \times 100 \qquad \ldots(10\cdot13)$$

$$Q_{01}^{F} = [Q_{01}^{La} \times Q_{01}^{Pa}]^{1/2} = \sqrt{\frac{\Sigma\, p_0 q_1}{\Sigma\, p_0 q_0} \times \frac{\Sigma\, p_1 q_1}{\Sigma\, p_1 q_0}} \times 100 \qquad \ldots(10\cdot14)$$

$$Q_{01}^{ME} = \frac{\Sigma\, q_1 (p_0 + p_1)}{\Sigma\, q_0 (p_0 + p_1)} \times 100 = \frac{\Sigma\, q_1 p_0 + \Sigma\, q_1 p_1}{\Sigma\, q_0 p_0 + \Sigma\, q_0 p_1} \times 100 \qquad \ldots(10\cdot15)$$

and so on.

5. Value Indices. Value index numbers are obtained on expressing the total value (or expenditure) in any given year as a percentage of the same in the base year. Symbolically, we write

$$V_{01} = \frac{\text{Total value in current year}}{\text{Total value in base year}} \times 100 \quad \Rightarrow \quad V_{01} = \frac{\Sigma p_1 q_1}{\Sigma p_0 q_0} \times 100 \qquad \ldots(10 \cdot 16)$$

We shall now discuss some numerical illustrations based on the above formulae.

Example 10·2. *The table below gives details of price and consumption of 5 commodities for 1995 and 1997. Using an appropriate formula arrive at an index number for 1997 prices with 1995 as base.*

Commodities	*Price per unit 1995 (Rs.)*	*Price per unit 1997 (Rs.)*	*Consumption value 1995 (Rs.)*
Rice	*40*	*48*	*800*
Wheat	*25*	*27*	*400*
Oil	*95*	*105*	*760*
Fish	*110*	*120*	*1100*
Milk	*80*	*100*	*480*

[*I.C.W.A. (Intermediate), Dec. 1998*]

Solution. Since we are given the base year (1995) consumption values (p_0q_0) and current year quantities (q_1) are not given, the appropriate formula for index number is Laspeyre's price index.

TABLE 10·2. **CALCULATIONS FOR LASPEYRE'S PRICE INDEX**

Commodity	*Base Year 1995*		*Current Year 1997*		
	Price per unit (p_0) *(Rs.)*	*Consumption Value (Rs.)* p_0q_0	*Price per unit* (p_1) *(Rs.)*	$q_0 = \frac{(3)}{(2)}$	p_1q_0
(1)	(2)	(3)	(4)		
Rice	40	800	48	20	960
Wheat	25	400	27	16	432
Oil	95	760	105	8	840
Fish	110	1100	120	10	1,200
Milk	80	480	100	6	600
		$\Sigma p_0 q_0 = 3{,}540$			$\Sigma p_1 q_0 = 4{,}032$

Laspeyre's price index for 1997 *w.r.t.* base 1995 is given by :

$$P_{01}^{La} = \frac{\Sigma p_1 q_0}{\Sigma p_0 q_0} \times 100 = \frac{4{,}032}{3{,}540} \times 100 = 113 \cdot 8983 \simeq 113 \cdot 9.$$

Example 10·3. *(a) From the following data calculate price index numbers for 1980 with 1970 as base by (i) Laspeyre's method, (ii) Paasche's method, (iii) Marshall-Edgeworth method, and (iv) Fisher's ideal method.*

Commodities	*1970*		*1980*	
	Price	*Quantity*	*Price*	*Quantity*
A	*20*	*8*	*40*	*6*
B	*50*	*10*	*60*	*5*
C	*40*	*15*	*50*	*15*
D	*20*	*20*	*20*	*25*

(b) It is stated that Marshall-Edgeworth index number is a good approximation to Fisher's ideal index number. Verify this for the data in Part (a).

Solution.

TABLE 10·3. **CALCULATIONS FOR PRICE INDICES BY DIFFERENT FORMULAE**

Commodities	*1970*		*1980*					
	p_0	q_0	p_1	q_1	$p_0 q_0$	$p_0 q_1$	$p_1 q_0$	$p_1 q_1$
A	20	8	40	6	160	120	320	240
B	50	10	60	5	500	250	600	300
C	40	15	50	15	600	600	750	750
D	20	20	20	25	400	500	400	500
					$\Sigma p_0 q_0 = 1660$	$\Sigma p_0 q_1 = 1470$	$\Sigma p_1 q_0 = 2070$	$\Sigma p_1 q_1 = 1790$

(*i*) **Laspeyre's Price Index :** $P_{01}^{La} = \frac{\sum p_1 q_0}{\sum p_0 q_0} \times 100 = \frac{2070}{1660} \times 100 = 1{\cdot}24699 \times 100 = 124{\cdot}699$

(*ii*) **Paasche's Price Index :** $P_{01}^{Pa} = \frac{\sum p_1 q_1}{\sum p_0 q_1} \times 100 = \frac{1790}{1470} \times 100 = 1{\cdot}2177 \times 100 = 121{\cdot}77$

(*iii*) **Marshall-Edgeworth Price Index :**

$$P_{01}^{ME} = \left(\frac{\sum p_1 q_0 + \sum p_1 q_1}{\sum p_0 q_0 + \sum p_0 q_1}\right) \times 100 = \left(\frac{2070 + 1790}{1660 + 1470}\right) \times 100 = \frac{3860}{3130} \times 100 = 123{\cdot}32$$

(*iv*) **Fisher's Price Index**

$$P_{01}^{F} = \sqrt{\frac{\sum p_1 q_0}{\sum p_0 q_0} \times \frac{\sum p_1 q_1}{\sum p_0 q_1}} \times 100 = \sqrt{\frac{2070}{1660} \times \frac{1790}{1470}} \times 100$$

$$= \sqrt{1{\cdot}24699 \times 1{\cdot}2177} \times 100 = \sqrt{1{\cdot}51846} \times 100 = 1{\cdot}23226 \times 100 = 123{\cdot}23.$$

Aliter :

$$P_{01}^{F} = \sqrt{P_{01}^{La} \times P_{01}^{Pa}} = \sqrt{124{\cdot}699 \times 121{\cdot}77} = \sqrt{15184{\cdot}597} = 123{\cdot}23$$

(*b*) Since $P_{01}^{ME} = 123{\cdot}32$ and $P_{01}^{F} = 123{\cdot}23$, are approximately equal, Marshall-Edgeworth index number is a good approximation to Fisher's ideal index number.

Example 10·4. *From the data given below construct index number of the group of four commodities by using Fisher's Ideal Formula* :

Commodities	*Base Year*		*Current Year*	
	Price per unit (Rs.)	*Expenditure (Rs.)*	*Price per unit (Rs.)*	*Expenditure (Rs.)*
A	2	40	5	75
B	4	16	8	40
C	1	10	2	24
D	5	25	10	60

Solution. In this problem we are given the expenditure (*e*) and the prices (*p*) per unit for different commodities. We have

$$\text{Expenditure} = \text{Price} \times \text{Quantity} \quad \Rightarrow \quad \text{Quantity} = \frac{\text{Expenditure}}{\text{Price}} \quad \Rightarrow \quad q = \frac{e}{p} \qquad \ldots(*)$$

Using (*) we shall first obtain the quantities consumed for the base year and the current year as given in the following table.

TABLE 10·4. COMPUTATION OF FISHER'S IDEAL INDEX NUMBER

Commodities	p_0	p_0q_0	q_0	p_1	p_1q_1	q_1	p_1q_0	p_0q_1
A	2	40	20	5	75	15	100	30
B	4	16	4	8	40	5	32	20
C	1	10	10	2	24	12	20	12
D	5	25	5	10	60	6	50	30
		$\sum p_0 q_0 = 91$			$\sum p_1 q_1 = 199$		$\sum p_1 q_0 = 202$	$\sum p_0 q_1 = 92$

Hence, Fisher's Ideal Price Index is given by

$$P_{01}^{F} = \sqrt{\frac{\sum p_1 q_0}{\sum p_0 q_0} \times \frac{\sum p_1 q_1}{\sum p_0 q_1}} \times 100 = \sqrt{\frac{202 \times 199}{91 \times 92}} \times 100$$

$$= \sqrt{\frac{40198}{8372}} \times 100 = \sqrt{4{\cdot}8015} \times 100 = 2{\cdot}1912 \times 100 = 219{\cdot}12.$$

Example 10·5. (*a*) *Compute price index and quantity index numbers for the year 2000 with 1995 as base year, using*
(*i*) *Laspeyre's Method,*
(*ii*) *Paasche's Method.*

Commodity	*Quantity (units)*		*Value (Rs.)*	
	1995	*2000*	*1995*	*2000*
A	*100*	*150*	*500*	*900*
B	*80*	*100*	*320*	*500*
C	*60*	*72*	*150*	*360*
D	*30*	*33*	*360*	*297*

(b) *Also compute Fisher's price and quantity index numbers.* [*I.C.W.A. (Intermediate), June 2002*]

Solution. We are given the quantities and the values of the commodities in the base year and the current year. We know that :

$$\text{Value} = \text{Price} \times \text{Quantity} \quad \Rightarrow \quad \text{Price} = \frac{\text{Value}}{\text{Quantity}} \quad ...(*)$$

Using (*), we can obtain the quantities consumed in the base year and the current year.

TABLE 10·5. CALCULATIONS FOR LASPEYRE'S, PAASCHE'S AND FISHER'S INDEX NUMBERS

q_0 (1)	q_1 (2)	p_0q_0 (3)	p_0 (4) = (3) ÷ (1)	p_1q_1 (5)	p_1 (6) = (5) ÷ (2)	p_1q_0	p_0q_1
100	150	500	5	900	6	600	750
80	100	320	4	500	5	400	400
60	72	150	2·5	360	5	300	180
30	33	360	12	297	9	270	396
		$\Sigma p_0 q_0 = 1330$		$\Sigma p_1 q_1 = 2057$		$\Sigma p_1 q_0 = 1570$	$\Sigma p_0 q_1 = 1726$

(i) *Laspeyre's Price and Quantity Indices.*

$$P_{01}^{La} = \frac{\Sigma p_1 q_0}{\Sigma p_0 q_0} \times 100 = \frac{1570}{1330} \times 100 = 118{\cdot}045$$

$$Q_{01}^{La} = \frac{\Sigma q_1 p_0}{\Sigma q_0 p_0} \times 100 = \frac{1726}{1330} \times 100 = 129{\cdot}744$$

(ii) *Paasche's Prince and Quantity Indices*

$$P_{01}^{Pa} = \frac{\Sigma p_1 q_1}{\Sigma p_0 q_1} \times 100 = \frac{2057}{1726} \times 100 = 119{\cdot}177$$

$$Q_{01}^{Pa} = \frac{\Sigma q_1 p_1}{\Sigma q_0 p_1} \times 100 = \frac{2057}{1570} \times 100 = 131{\cdot}019$$

(b) **Fisher's Price and Quantity Indices**

$$P_{01}^{F} = \sqrt{P_{01}^{La} \times P_{01}^{Pa}} = \sqrt{118{\cdot}045 \times 119{\cdot}177} = \sqrt{14068{\cdot}248} = 118{\cdot}610$$

$$Q_{01}^{F} = \sqrt{Q_{01}^{La} \times Q_{01}^{Pa}} = \sqrt{129{\cdot}774 \times 131{\cdot}019} = \sqrt{17002{\cdot}859} = 130{\cdot}395.$$

Example 10·6. *Compute by Fisher's formula the Quantity Index Number from the data given below :*

Articles	*1994* Price (Rs.)	*1994* Total Value (Rs.)	*1996* Price (Rs.)	*1996* Total Value (Rs.)
A	5	50	4	48
B	8	48	7	49
C	6	18	5	20

Solution. Here we are given the total values (v) for the current and base years which are given by :

$$\text{Total Value} = \text{Price} \times \text{Quantity} \quad \Rightarrow \quad v = p \times q \quad \rightarrow \quad q = v/p \quad ...(*)$$

Hence, the quantity consumed for base and current years is obtained on dividing the total value by the corresponding price.

TABLE 10·6. COMPUTATION OF FISHER'S QUANTITY INDEX NUMBER

Article	p_0	$v_0 = p_0q_0$	q_0	p_1	$v_1 = p_1q_1$	q_1	p_0q_1	p_1q_0
A	5	50	10	4	48	12	60	40
B	8	48	6	7	49	7	56	42
C	6	18	3	5	20	4	24	15
		$\Sigma p_0 q_0 = 116$			$\Sigma p_1 q_1 = 117$		$\Sigma p_0 q_1 = 140$	$\Sigma p_1 q_0 = 97$

Fisher's quantity index number for 1996 with base year 1994 is given by the formula

$$Q_{01}^{F} = \sqrt{\frac{\Sigma q_1 p_0}{\Sigma q_0 p_0} \times \frac{\Sigma q_1 p_1}{\Sigma q_0 p_1}} \times 100 = \sqrt{\frac{\Sigma p_0 q_1 \times \Sigma p_1 q_1}{\Sigma p_0 q_0 \times \Sigma p_1 q_0}} \times 100$$

$$= \sqrt{\frac{140 \times 117}{116 \times 97}} \times 100 = \sqrt{\frac{16380}{11252}} \times 100 = \sqrt{1{\cdot}4557} \times 100 = 1{\cdot}2065 \times 100 = 120{\cdot}65.$$

Example 10·7. *Given the data in the adjoining Table, where p and q respectively stand for price and quantity and subscripts stand for time period, find x, if the ratio between Laspeyre's (L) and Paasche's (P) index numbers is*

$$L : P :: 28 : 27$$

	Commodities	
	A	B
p_0	1	1
q_0	10	5
p_1	2	x
q_1	5	2

Solution.

TABLE 10·7. **CALCULATIONS FOR LASPEYRE'S AND PAASCHE'S INDICES**

Commodities	p_0	q_0	p_1	q_1	$p_0 q_0$	$p_0 q_1$	$p_1 q_0$	$p_1 q_1$
A	1	10	2	5	10	5	20	10
B	1	5	x	2	5	2	$5x$	$2x$
					$\Sigma p_0 q_0 = 15$	$\Sigma p_0 q_1 = 7$	$\Sigma p_1 q_0 = 20 + 5x$	$\Sigma p_1 q_1 = 10 + 2x$

We are given : $\dfrac{P_{01}^{La}}{P_{01}^{Pa}} = \dfrac{28}{27}$ ...(*)

$$P_{01}^{La} = \frac{\Sigma p_1 q_0}{\Sigma p_0 q_0} \times 100 = \left(\frac{20 + 5x}{15}\right) \times 100 = \left(\frac{4 + x}{3}\right) \times 100 \quad ; \quad P_{01}^{Pa} = \frac{\Sigma p_1 q_1}{\Sigma p_0 q_1} \times 100 = \left(\frac{10 + 2x}{7}\right) \times 100$$

Substituting in (*) we get :

$$\frac{\left(\dfrac{4 + x}{3}\right)}{\left(\dfrac{10 + 2x}{7}\right)} = \frac{28}{27} \quad \Rightarrow \quad \frac{7(4 + x)}{3(10 + 2x)} = \frac{28}{27} \quad \Rightarrow \quad \frac{4 + x}{10 + 2x} = \frac{4}{9}$$

$$\Rightarrow \quad 9(4 + x) = 4(10 + 2x) \quad \Rightarrow \quad 36 + 9x = 40 + 8x \quad \Rightarrow \quad x = 4$$

Example 10·8. *Calculate the weighted price index from the following data ;*

Materials required	*Unit*	*Quantity required*	*Price (Rs.)*	
			1963	*1973*
Cement	*100 lb.*	*500 lb.*	*5·0*	*8·0*
Timber	*c.ft.*	*2,000 c.ft.*	*9·5*	*14·2*
Steel sheets	*cwt.*	*50 cwt.*	*34·0*	*42·20*
Bricks	*per '000*	*20,000*	*12·0*	*24·0*

Solution. Since the quantities (weights) required of different materials are fixed for both the base and current years, we will use Kelly's formula for finding out price index.

Further, for cement unit is 100 lbs. and the quantity required is 500 lbs. Hence, the quantity consumed per unit for cement is 500/100 = 5. Similarly, the quantity consumed per unit for bricks is 20,000/1,000 = 20.

TABLE 10·8. **COMPUTATION OF KELLY'S INDEX NUMBER**

Materials required	*Unit*	*Quantity required*	*q*	*Price (Rs.)* 1963	*Price (Rs.)* 1973		
				p_0	p_1	$q\,p_0$	$q\,p_1$
Cement	100 lb	500 lb.	5	5·0	8·0	25	40
Timber	c.ft.	2,000 c.ft.	2000	9·5	14·2	19,000	28,400
Steel sheets	cwt.	50 cwt.	50	34·0	42·0	1,700	2,100
Bricks	per '000	20,000	20	12·0	24·0	240	480
						$\Sigma q\,p_0 = 20{,}965$	$\Sigma q\,p_1 = 31{,}020$

Kelly's Price Index is given by : $P_{01}{}^K = \dfrac{\Sigma\, q\, p_1}{\Sigma\, q\, p_0} \times 100 = \dfrac{31020}{20965} \times 100 = 147{\cdot}96$

10·5·3. Simple Average of Price Relatives. In this method, first of all we obtain the *price relatives* for each commodity. The price relatives are obtained by expressing the price of the commodity in the current year as a percentage of its price in the base year, *i.e.*,

$$P = \text{Price Relative for a commodity} = \frac{p_1}{p_0} \times 100 \qquad \ldots(10{\cdot}17)$$

Price-relatives are the simplest form of the index numbers for each commodity. The price index for the composite group is obtained on averaging these price-relatives by using some suitable measure of central tendency, usually arithmetic mean (A.M.) or geometric mean (G.M.). Price index using simple arithmetic mean of the relatives is given by :

$$P_0\ (A.M.) = \frac{1}{n}\Sigma\left(\frac{p_1}{p_0} \times 100\right) = \frac{1}{n}\Sigma P \qquad \ldots(10{\cdot}18)$$

where n is the number of commodities in the group.

Using simple geometric mean of the price relatives, the price index is given by :

$$P_{01}\ (G.M.) = \left[\Pi\left(\frac{p_1}{p_0} \times 100\right)\right]^{1/n} = \left[\Pi\, P\right]^{1/n} \qquad \ldots(10{\cdot}19)$$

where Π denotes the product of the price-relatives for the n commodities. To evaluate (10·19), we use logarithms. Taking logarithm of both sides in (10·19), we get

$$\log P_{01}\ (G.M.) = \frac{1}{n}\Sigma \log\left(\frac{p_1}{p_0} \times 100\right) = \frac{1}{n}\Sigma \log P \;\Rightarrow\; P_{01}\ (G.M.) = \text{Antilog}\left[\frac{1}{n}\Sigma \log P\right] \ldots(10{\cdot}19a)$$

Merits and Demerits. The index number based on the simple average of the price-relatives overcomes some of the drawbacks of the 'simple aggregate method', *viz.*,

(*i*) Price-relatives are pure numbers independent of the units of measurement and hence the index number based on their average is not affected by the units in which the prices are quoted.

(*ii*) The extreme observations (large and small price quotations) do not influence the index unduly. It gives equal importance to all observations.

The drawback of this method is that it gives equal weights to all the commodities and thus neglects their relative importance in the group. This drawback is removed by taking the weighted average of the price-relatives as discussed in § 10·5·4.

Another limitation of this method is the choice of the average to be used. As already discussed, G.M., though difficult to compute, is theoretically a better average than A.M. However, because of the computational ease, A.M. is used in practice. Some economists, notably F.Y. Edgeworth advocated the use of harmonic mean for averaging the price-relatives but it did not find favour with others and is seldom used.

Remark. The distribution of the price-relatives is found to be positively skewed and the skewness increases as the base is shifted more and more away from the given year.

Example 10·9. *Construct Index Number for each year from the following average annual wholesale prices of cotton with 1993 as base* :

Year	*Wholesale Prices (Rs.)*	*Year*	*Wholesale Prices (Rs.)*
1993	*75*	*1998*	*70*
1994	*50*	*1999*	*69*
1995	*65*	*2000*	*75*
1996	*60*	*2001*	*84*
1997	*72*	*2002*	*80*

Solution. The index numbers for each year are obtained by expressing the prices in the current year as a percentage of the price in the base year 1993.

TABLE 10·9. **COMPUTATION OF PRICE INDEX NUMBERS**

Year	*Wholesale Prices (Rs.)*	*Index Number (Base : 1993 = 100)*	*Year*	*Wholesale Prices (Rs.)*	*Index Number (Base : 1993 = 100)*
1993	75	100	1998	70	$\frac{70}{75} \times 100 =$ 93·33
1994	50	$\frac{50}{75} \times 100 =$ 66·67	1999	69	$\frac{69}{75} \times 100 =$ 92·00
1995	65	$\frac{65}{75} \times 100 =$ 86·67	2000	75	$\frac{75}{75} \times 100 =$ 100·00
1996	60	$\frac{60}{75} \times 100 =$ 80·00	2001	84	$\frac{84}{75} \times 100 =$ 112·00
1997	72	$\frac{72}{75} \times 100 =$ 96·00	2002	80	$\frac{80}{75} \times 100 =$ 106·67

Example 10·10. *The following are the prices (in Rs.) of commodities in 1995 and 2000. Calculate a price index based on price-relatives using the arithmetic mean as well as geometric mean.*

Year	*Commodity*					
	A	*B*	*C*	*D*	*E*	*F*
1995	*45*	*60*	*20*	*50*	*85*	*120*
2000	*55*	*70*	*30*	*75*	*90*	*130*

Solution.

TABLE 10·10. **CALCULATIONS FOR PRICE INDEX BASED ON A.M. AND G.M.**

Commodity	*Price*		*Price Relative*	
	In 1995 (p_0)	*In 2000* (p_1)	$P = \frac{p_1}{p_0} \times 100$	*log P*
A	45	55	122·22	2·0871
B	60	70	116·67	2·0667
C	20	30	150·00	2·1761
D	50	75	150·00	2·1761
E	85	90	105·88	2·0246
F	120	130	108·33	2·0347
			$\Sigma P = 753{\cdot}1$	$\Sigma \log P = 12{\cdot}5653$

Index Number based on Arithmetic Mean is :

$$P_{01} \text{ (A.M.)} = \frac{1}{n}\Sigma\left(\frac{p_1}{p_0}\right) \times 100 = \frac{1}{n}\Sigma P = \frac{753{\cdot}1}{6} = 125{\cdot}517$$

Index Number based on Geometric Mean is given by :

$$\log P_{01} \text{ (G.M.)} = \frac{1}{n}\Sigma \log P = \frac{1}{6} \times 12{\cdot}5653 = 2{\cdot}0942 \;\Rightarrow\; P_{01} \text{ (G.M.)} = \text{Antilog } (2{\cdot}0942) = 124{\cdot}3.$$

Example 10·11. *Calculate Price Index for 1995 and 1996 using 1990 as base year from the following data* :

Commodity	*Prices (Rs. per unit)*		
	1990	*1995*	*1996*
A	*5*	*6*	*4*
B	*7*	*10*	*7*
C	*8*	*12*	*6*
D	*20*	*17*	*16*
E	*500*	*550*	*540*

Solution.

TABLE 10·11. **CALCULATIONS FOR PRICE INDICES**

Commodity	*Prices*			*Price Relatives*	
	1990 p_0	*1995* p_1	*1996* p_2	*For 1995* $(p_1/p_0)\times 100$	*For 1996* $(p_2/p_0)\times 100$
A	5	6	4	120·00	80·00
B	7	10	7	142·86	100·00
C	8	12	6	150·00	75·00
D	20	17	16	85·00	80·00
E	500	550	540	110·00	108·00
Total				607·86	443·00

$$\text{Price index for 1995} = \frac{1}{5}\sum\left(\frac{p_1}{p_0}\times 100\right) = \frac{607{\cdot}86}{5} = 121{\cdot}57$$

$$\text{Price index for 1996} = \frac{1}{5}\sum\left(\frac{p_2}{p_0}\times 100\right) = \frac{443{\cdot}00}{5} = 88{\cdot}6$$

10·5·4. Weighted Average of Price Relatives. The shortcoming of Simple Average of Relatives Method which assumes that all the relatives are equally important is overcome in this method which consists in assigning appropriate weights to the relatives according to the relative importance of the different commodities in the group. Thus, the index for the whole group is obtained on taking the *weighted* average, usually A.M. or G.M. of the price-relatives. Thus, based on weighted A.M., the price index is given by :

$$P_{01}\,(\text{A.M.}) = \frac{\sum\left[W\left(\frac{p_1}{p_0}\times 100\right)\right]}{\sum W} = \frac{\sum WP}{\sum W} \qquad \ldots(10{\cdot}20)$$

where W is the weight attached to the price-relative P.

STEPS FOR COMPUTING P_{01} (A.M.) IN (10·20)

1. Find the price-relatives (P) for each commodity, *i.e.*, compute $P = \dfrac{p_1}{p_0}\times 100$

2. Multiply the price-relatives in Step 1 by the corresponding weights (W) assigned to get the product WP.

3. Obtain the sum of products obtained in Step 2 for all the commodities to get $\sum WP$.

4. Divide the sum in Step 3 by $\sum W$, the total of the weights assigned.

The resulting figure gives the price index based on the weighted average of price-relatives.

The price index based on the weighted geometric mean of price-relatives is given by

$$P_{01}\,(\text{weighted G.M.}) = \left[\prod\left\{\left(\frac{p_1}{p_0}\times 100\right)^W\right\}\right]^{1/\sum W} = \left[\prod (P^W)\right]^{1/\sum W} \qquad \ldots(10{\cdot}21)$$

Taking logarithm of both sides, we get

$$\log\left[P_{01}\,(\text{weighted G.M.})\right] = \frac{\sum W\log P}{\sum W} \;\Rightarrow\; P_{01}\,(\text{weighted G.M.}) = \text{Antilog}\left[\frac{\sum W\log P}{\sum W}\right] \qquad \ldots(10{\cdot}22)$$

For computational purposes, formula (10·22) is used and requires the following steps.

STEPS FOR COMPUTING P_{01} (G.M.) IN (10·22)

1. Compute the price-relatives $P = (P_1/P_0) \times 100$, for each commodity.
2. Find the logarithms of all the price-relatives. This gives us log P values.
3. Multiply log P values for each commodity by the corresponding weights (W) assigned. This will give (W. log P) values.
4. Find the sum of the values (W. log P) in Step 3 over all the commodities to get $\Sigma W \log P$.
5. Divide the sum obtained in Step 4 by ΣW, the sum of weights.
6. Antilog of the value obtained in Step 5 gives required price index.

Remarks 1. Since price-relatives are the simplest form of the index numbers, we may also use the notation I for P, *i.e.*, we may write

$$I = \frac{p_1}{p_0} \times 100 \qquad \ldots(10 \cdot 23)$$

2. In the usual notations, we have :

$$P_{01}{}^{La} = \frac{\Sigma p_1 q_0}{\Sigma p_0 q_0} \times 100 = \frac{\Sigma\left[\left(\frac{p_1}{p_0} \times 100\right) p_0\, q_0\right]}{\Sigma p_0 q_0} = \frac{\Sigma PW}{\Sigma W} \qquad \ldots(*)$$

where $\qquad P = \frac{p_1}{p_0} \times 100$, is the price-relative of the commodity

and $\qquad W = p_0\, q_0$, is the value of the commodity in the base year,

the summation being taken over different commodities.

From (*), we conclude that *Laspeyre's price index is the weighted mean of the price-relatives, the corresponding weights being the values of the commodities in the base year.*

Similarly, Paasche's price index number is given by :

$$P_{01}{}^{Pa} = \frac{\Sigma p_1 q_1}{\Sigma p_0 q_1} \times 100 = \frac{\Sigma\left[\left(\frac{p_1}{p_0} \times 100\right) p_0\, q_1\right]}{\Sigma p_0\, q_1} = \frac{\Sigma WP}{\Sigma W} \qquad \ldots(**)$$

where $\qquad P = \frac{p_1}{p_0} \times 100 \qquad$ and $\qquad W = p_0\, q_1$.

Hence, *Paasche's price index can be expressed as the weighted mean of the price-relatives, the corresponding weights being* $w = p_0 q_1$ *i.e., the values obtained on taking the current year quantities at the base year prices.*

Example 10·12. *The following table gives the prices of some food items in the base year and current year and the quantities sold in the base year. Calculate the weighted index number by using the weighted average of price-relatives.*

Items	*Base Year Quantities (Units)*	*Base Year Price (in Rs.)*	*Current Year Price (in Rs.)*
A	7	18·00	21·60
B	6	3·00	4·65
C	16	7·50	9·00
D	21	2·50	2·25

[*C.A.* (*Foundation*), *May 1999*]

Solution.

TABLE 10·12. **CALCULATIONS FOR PRICE I. NO. USING PRICE RELATIVES**

Item	*Base Year Quantities Weights (W)*	*Prices in Rupees*		*Price Relatives*	
		Base Year (p_0)	*Current Year* (p_1)	$P = \frac{p_1}{p_0} \times 100$	*WP*
A	7	18·00	21·60	120	840
B	6	3·00	4·65	155	930
C	16	7·50	9·00	120	1920
D	21	2·50	2·25	90	1890
	$\Sigma W = 50$				$\Sigma WP = 5580$

Price index number for the current year (Base Year = 100), using weighted average of price-relatives is given by :

$$P_{01} \text{ (Weighted A.M.)} = \frac{\Sigma WP}{\Sigma W} = \frac{5580}{50} = 111{\cdot}6.$$

Example 10·13. *Calculate index number of prices for 1995 on the basis of 1990 from the data given below :*

Commodity	*Weight*	*Price per unit 1990 (Rs.)*	*Price per unit 1995 (Rs.)*
A	40	16	20
B	25	40	50
C	20	12	15
D	15	2	3

If the weights of commodities A, B, C, D are increased in the ratio 1 : 2 : 3 : 4, what will be increase in index number ? [*I.C.W.A. (Intermediate), June 1998*]

Solution.

TABLE 10·13. **CALCULATIONS FOR INDEX NUMBERS**

Commodity	*Weight (W)*	*Price per unit in Rupees*		*Price Relative*	*WP*	*Increased Weight* $(W_1)^*$	W_1P
		1990 (p_0)	*1995* (p_1)	$P = \frac{p_1}{p_0} \times 100$			
A	40	16	20	125	5000	$40 + \frac{40}{10} = 44$	5500
B	25	40	50	125	3125	$25 + \frac{2 \times 25}{10} = 30$	3750
C	20	12	15	125	2500	$20 + \frac{3 \times 20}{10} = 26$	3250
D	15	2	3	150	2250	$15 + \frac{4 \times 15}{10} = 21$	3150
	$\Sigma W = 100$				$\Sigma WP = 12875$	$\Sigma W_1 = 121$	$\Sigma W_1P = 15650$

* Since the weights of the commodities are increased in the ratio 1 : 2 : 3 : 4, (Total = 10), the increase in weights are :

$(A) : \frac{1}{10} \times 40 = 4,\quad (B) : \frac{2}{10} \times 25 = 5,\quad (C) : \frac{3}{10} \times 20 = 6,\quad (D) : \frac{4}{10} \times 15 = 6$

$$\text{Original Index Number } (I) = \frac{\Sigma WP}{\Sigma W} = \frac{12875}{100} = 128{\cdot}75$$

$$\text{New Index Number } (I_1) = \frac{\Sigma W_1P}{\Sigma W_1} = \frac{15650}{121} = 129{\cdot}34$$

$\therefore$ Increase in the Index Number $= I_1 - I = 0{\cdot}59.$

Example 10·14. *An enquiry into the budgets of middle class families in a family gave the following information :*

Expenses on →	*Food*	*Rent*	*Clothing*	*Fuel*	*Others*
	30%	*15%*	*20%*	*10%*	*25%*
Prices (in Rs.) in 1997	*100*	*20*	*70*	*20*	*40*
Prices (in Rs.) in 1998	*90*	*20*	*60*	*15*	*55*

Compute the price index number using :

(i) Weighted A.M. of price-relatives. *(ii) Weighted G.M. of price-relatives.*

Solution.

TABLE 10·14. **COMPUTATION OF PRICE INDEX USING A.M. & G.M.**

Groups	*Weights (W)*	*Price* 1997 (p_0)	1998 (p_1)	*Price Relatives* $P = \frac{p_1}{p_0} \times 100$	*WP*	*log P*	*W log P*
Food	30	100	90	90·0	2700	1·9542	58·626
Rent	15	20	20	100·0	1500	2·0000	30·000
Clothing	20	70	60	85·7	1714	1·9330	38·660
Fuel	10	20	15	75·0	750	1·8751	18·751
Others	25	40	55	137·5	3437·5	2·1383	53·457
					$\Sigma WP = 10101·5$		$\Sigma W \log P = 199·494$

(*i*) Index Number for 1998 *w.r.t* base year 1997, based on the weighted arithmetic mean of price-relatives is given by

$$P_{01} \text{ (A.M.)} = \frac{\Sigma WP}{\Sigma W} = \frac{10101·5}{100} = 101·015$$

(*ii*) Index Number for 1998 *w.r.t* base year 1997, based on the weighted geometric mean of price-relatives is given by

$$\log P_{01} \text{ (G.M.)} = \frac{\Sigma W \log P}{\Sigma W} = \frac{199·494}{100} = 1·9949 \Rightarrow P_{01} \text{ (G.M.)} = \text{Antilog } (1·9949) = 98·83.$$

EXERCISE 10·1

1. (*a*) What is an index number ? Explain the various problems involved in the construction of index numbers ?

(*b*) Discuss the problems faced while constructing an index number. [*Delhi Univ. B.Com. (Pass), 2000*]

(*c*) What are the important points which have to be considered in the construction of index numbers ? [*C.A. (Foundation), May 1997*]

2. "For constructing index numbers the best method on theoretical ground is not the best method from practical point of view." Discuss. [*Delhi Univ. B.Com. (Hons.), 1999*]

3. It has been stated that the technique of index number construction involves four major factors :

(*a*) choice of items ; (*b*) base period ; (*c*) form of average ; (*d*) weighting system.

Do you agree with this view ? If so, explain these four factors and discuss the problems to which they give rise. If you do not agree, give your main views on the main problems involved in index number construction.

4. "An index number is a special type of average". Discuss.

5. "In the construction of index numbers, the advantages of geometric mean are greater than those of arithmetic mean". Discuss. [*Delhi Univ. B.com. (Hons.), 2007*]

6. What are index numbers ? Why are they called economic barometers ? [*Delhi Univ. B.Com. (Pass), 2002*]

7. (*a*) What is implied by "weighting" in the process of index number construction ? Why is it necessary ? What are the commonly proposed weighting schemes ?

(*b*) What is the importance of weighting in the construction of index numbers ? Which of the three—mean, median and geometric mean—will you prefer in calculating index numbers and why ?

8. (*a*) What are Index Numbers ? How are they constructed ? Explain the role of weights in the construction of general Price Index Numbers.

(*b*) Distinguish between unweighted and weighted index numbers. Enumerate some of the important methods of weighting a price index and discuss their relative merits and demerits.

9. (*a*) Explain that the Laspeyre's Method has an upward bias while the Paasche's Method has a downward bias. Point out, under what conditions

(*i*) they give equal results, (*ii*) Laspeyre's method gives a result lesser than Paasche's method.

(*b*) Distinguish between the methods of assigning weights in Laspeyre's and Paasche's price index numbers. Show that Laspeyre's price index is greater than Paasche's price index in case of rising prices.

[*Delhi Univ. B.A.* (*Econ. Hons.*), *2000*]

10. On the basis of figures of production of generators given below, construct :

(*i*) Quantity index; and ; (*ii*) Price index (using 1990 as base) :

Year	:	1990	1991	1992	1993	1994
Units Produced (in thousands)	:	24	30	32	38	44
Value of Output (in Rs. Million)	:	192	255	272	361	451

[*Delhi Univ. B.A.* (*Econ. Hons.*), *2005*]

Ans.

Year	:	1990	1991	1992	1993	1994
Price Index	:	100	106.25	106.25	118.75	128.12
Quantity Index	:	100	125	133.33	158.33	183.33

Hint. Price $= \dfrac{\text{Value of output}}{\text{Units produced }(q)}$; $P.I = \dfrac{p_i}{p_0} \times 100$; $Q.\,I. = \dfrac{q_i}{q_0} \times 100$; Base '0' = 1990.

11. What is the difference between Laspeyre's and Paasche's systems of weights in compiling a price index ? Calculate both Laspeyre's and Paasche's aggregative price indices for the year 2000 from the following data :

Commodities	*Quantity*		*Price Per Unit (Rs.)*	
	1999	*2000*	*1999*	*2000*
A	3	5	20	25
B	4	6	25	30
C	2	3	30	25
D	1	2	10	7·50

Ans. 109·78 ; 109·72.

12. From the data given below compute Laspeyre's and Paasche's index numbers.

Commodities	*Price*		*Quantity*	
	1995	*2001*	*1995*	*2001*
A	4	10	50	40
B	3	9	10	2
C	2	4	5	2

(Price and Quantity figures are in appropriate units).

Ans. 254·16 ; 250·58.

13. The geometric mean of index numbers of Laspeyre and Paasche is 229·5648 while the sum of Laspeyre's and Paasche's index number is 480. Find out Laspeyre's and Paasche's indices. [*C.A. PEE-1, May 2005*]

Ans. and **Hint.** Let $P_{01}^{La} = a$ and $P_{01}^{Pa} = b$. Then, we are given :

$$\sqrt{ab} = 229{\cdot}5648 \quad \Rightarrow \quad ab = 52699{\cdot}99 \simeq 52700 \quad \text{and} \quad a + b = 480 \qquad \ldots(i)$$

$$(a-b)^2 = (a+b)^2 - 4\,ab = 230400 - 210800 = 19600 \quad \Rightarrow \quad a - b = \sqrt{19600} = 140 \quad \ldots(ii)$$

Adding and substracting (*i*) and (*ii*), we get : $a = 310$, $b = 170$.

14. (*a*) Using Paasche's formula, compute the quantity index and the price index numbers for 2000 with 1996 as base year :

Commodity	Quantity Units		Value in (Rs.)	
	1996	2000	1996	2000
A	100	150	500	900
B	80	100	320	500
C	60	72	150	360
D	30	33	360	297

(*b*) For the above problem also compute price index by

(*i*) Marshall-Edgeworth formula ; (*ii*) Fisher's formula ; (*iii*) Dorbish-Bowley formula ; (*iv*) Walsch formula.

Ans. (*a*) $P_{01}^{Pa} = 119{\cdot}2$; $Q_{01}^{Pa} = 131{\cdot}09$; (*b*) (*i*) 118·68, (*ii*) 118·62, (*iii*) 118·6225, (*iv*) 118·64.

15. "Marshall-Edgeworth index number is a good approximation to the Fisher's Ideal Index Number."—Verify the truth of this statement from the following data :

Year	Rice		Wheat		Jowar	
	Price	Quantity	Price	Quantity	Price	Quantity
1970	9·3	100	6·4	11	5·1	5
1977	4·5	90	3·7	10	2·7	3

Ans. $P_{01}^{ME} = 49{\cdot}135$; $P_{01}^{F} = 49{\cdot}134$.

16. A company spent Rs. 50, Rs. 48, Rs. 18 and Rs. 42 during 1998. The company increased the expenditure to Rs. 100, Rs. 98, Rs. 60 and Rs. 102 during 1999 respectively on four commodities. If the units of four commodities purchased during 1998 and 1999 are identical *i.e.*, 5, 2, 6 and 17, compute the price index for 1999 by the most suitable method.

[*Delhi Univ. B.Com. (Pass), 2000*]

Ans. $I = \dfrac{\Sigma p_1 q}{\Sigma p_0 q} = \left(\dfrac{100+98+60+102}{50+48+18+42}\right) \times 100 = 227{\cdot}85.$

17. From the data given below construct an index number of the group of four commodities by using

(*i*) Simple Aggregate Method and (*ii*) Fisher's Ideal Formula.

Commodities	Base Year (1996)		Current Year (1997)	
	Price per unit	Expenditure (Rs.)	Price per unit	Expenditure (Rs.)
1	2	40	5	75
2	4	16	8	40
3	1	10	2	24
4	5	25	10	60

Ans. (*i*) 208·33 ; (*ii*) 219·13.

18. Using Fisher's Ideal Formula, compute price and quantity index numbers for 1984 with 1982 as base year, given the following information :

Year	Commodity A		Commodity B		Commodity C	
	Price (Rs.)	Quantity (kg.)	Price (Rs.)	Quantity (kg.)	Price (Rs.)	Quantity (kg.)
1982	5	10	8	6	6	3
1984	4	12	7	7	5	4

Ans. $P_{01}^{F} = 83{\cdot}59$, $Q_{01}^{F} = 120{\cdot}6$.

19. What are Index Numbers ? Why are they called economic barometers ?

On the basis of the following information, calculate the Fisher's Ideal Price Index Number :

Commodities	Base Year Price	Base Year Quantity	Current Year Price	Current Year Quantity
A	2	40	6	50
B	4	50	8	40
C	6	20	9	30
D	8	10	6	20
E	10	10	5	20

Ans. $P_{01}^{F} = 149{\cdot}15$.

20. (*a*) What is an Index Number ? Briefly describe the uses of Index Numbers.

(*b*) Calculate Fisher's Ideal Index from the following data :

Items	Base Year		Current Year	
	Quantity	Price	Quantity	Price
A	15	4	10	6
B	20	3	25	4
C	10	6	20	5
D	30	5	25	5

[*Delhi Univ. B.Com. (Pass), 1996*]

Ans. $P_{01}^{F} = 109{\cdot}5$.

21. Find Laspeyre's, Paasche's and Fisher's price and quantity index numbers from the following data :

Commodity	Base Year		Current Year	
	Price (Rs.)	Quantity (kg.)	Price (Rs.)	Quantity (kg.)
A	5	25	6	30
B	10	5	15	4
C	3	40	2	50
D	6	30	8	35

[*C.A. (Foundation), May 2007*]

Ans. $P_{01}^{La} = 114{\cdot}74$, $P_{01}^{Pa} = 112{\cdot}73$, $P_{01}^{F} = 113{\cdot}73$; $Q_{01}^{La} = 115{\cdot}79$, $Q_{01}^{Pa} = 113{\cdot}76$, $Q_{01}^{F} = 114{\cdot}77$.

22. Given that $\Sigma p_1 q_1 = 250$, $\Sigma p_0 q_0 = 150$, Paasche's Index Number = 150 and Dorbish-Bowley's Index Number = 145, find out (*i*) Fisher's Ideal Index Number ; and (*ii*) Marshall-Edgeworth's Index Number.

[*Delhi Univ. B.Com. (Hons.), 2007*]

Hint. Paasche's I.No. $= \dfrac{\Sigma p_1 q_1}{\Sigma p_0 q_1} \times 100 = 150 \quad \Rightarrow \quad \Sigma p_0 q_1 = \dfrac{250 \times 100}{150} = \dfrac{500}{3}$

Dorbish-Bowley's I.No. $= \frac{1}{2}\left[\dfrac{\Sigma p_1 q_0}{\Sigma p_0 q_0} + \dfrac{\Sigma p_1 q_1}{\Sigma p_0 q_1}\right] = 145 \quad \Rightarrow \quad \Sigma p_1 q_0 \simeq 210$ (*approx.*)

Ans. $P_{01}^{F} = 100\sqrt{2.1} = 144{\cdot}9$; $P_{01}^{ME} = 145.26$

23. From the following data, construct a price index number of the group of four commodities by using Fisher's Ideal Formula.

Commodity	Base Year Price per unit	Base Year Expenditure Rs.	Current Year Price per unit	Current Year Expenditure Rs.
A	2	40	5	75
B	4	16	8	40
C	1	10	2	24
D	5	25	10	60

[*Himachal Pradesh Univ. B.Com., 1996*]

Ans. $P_{01}^{F} = 219{\cdot}1$.

24. From the information given below find the price index for the Year II with Year I as base by using Fisher's ideal index number formula.

Commodities	Price (Rs.)/unit		Total value (Rs.)	
	Year I	Year II	Year I	Year II
A	35	36	700	756
B	31	40	465	480
C	30	32	240	320
D	20	22	40	44

[*I.C.W.A. (Intermediate), June 2001*]

Ans. $P_{01}^{F} = \sqrt{112 \cdot 11 \times 110 \cdot 57} = 111 \cdot 34$.

25. From the following data, construct Quantity Index Number by

(*i*) Fisher's Method; and (*ii*) Marshall-Edgeworth's Method.

Commodity	Base Year		Current Year	
	Price (Rs.)	Quantity (kgs.)	Expenditure (Rs.)	Quantity (kgs.)
A	25	40	2,000	50
B	22	18	1,200	30
C	54	16	1,320	44
D	20	40	1,350	45
E	18	30	630	15

[*Delhi Univ. B.Com. (Hons.), 1997*]

Ans. (*i*) 136·85, (*ii*) 134·94.

26. From the data given below, calculate quantity index numbers for the year 2000 by using :

(*i*) Laspeyre's , (*ii*) Paasche's and (*iii*) Fisher's, formulae.

Commodity	Year 1999		Year 2000	
	Price	Value	Price	Value
A	10	70	11	115·50
B	5	45	10	45
C	6	30	5	45

[*C.S. (Foundation), Dec. 2000*]

Ans. (*i*) $Q_{01}^{La} = 125 \cdot 17$, (*ii*) $Q_{01}^{Pa} = 107 \cdot 03$, (*iii*) $Q_{01}^{F} = 115 \cdot 75$.

27. (*a*) What is an Index Number ? Explain the terms — Price Relative ; Quantity Relative ; and Value Relative— with reference to a single commodity.

(*b*) What do you understand by price-relatives ? Discuss the method of constructing index numbers based on them.

28. (*a*) Show that Laspeyre's price index can be written as the weighted average of price-relatives. What are the weights. [*Delhi Univ. B.A. (Econ. Hons.), 1998*]

(*b*) Can Paasche's price index be expressed as the weighted average of price-relatives ? If yes, identify the weights.

29. Calculate the index number by using geometric mean.

Commodity	Base Year Price	Current Year Price
A	2	7
B	4	5

Ans. 209·17.

30. The following are the prices of commodities in 1998 and 1999. Calculate a price index based on price-relatives, using the *geometric mean*.

Year	Commodity					
	A	B	C	D	E	F
1998	45	60	20	50	85	120
1999	60	70	30	75	90	130

Ans. 126.

31. The price quotations of four different commodities for 1990 and 1995 are given below. Calculate the index number for 1995 with 1990 as base by using (*i*) simple average of price-relatives, (*ii*) weighted average of price relatives.

Commodity	*Weight*	*Price in Rupees*	
		1995	*1990*
A	5	4·50	2·00
B	7	3·20	2·50
C	6	4·50	3·00
D	2	1·80	1·00

Ans. (*i*) 170·75, (*ii*) 164·05.

32. Calculate price index of the following data by taking Base 1995 = 100, by weighted average of relatives method :

Commodities	*1995* *Price (Rs.)*	*Quantity*	*1996* *Price (Rs.)*
A	20	2	25
B	10	3	12
C	12	5	18
D	16	4	16
E	5	7	4

Ans. 110·48.

33. Calculate the index number for 1998 with 1990 as base using the Weighted Average of Price Relatives Method for the following data :

Commodity	*Weight*	*Price (in Rs.)*	
		1990	*1998*
A	2	12	24
B	8	8	12
C	4	15	27
D	5	6	18
E	1	10	12

[*Delhi Univ. B.Com. (Pass), 1999*]

Ans. I. No. $= \frac{\Sigma WP}{\Sigma W} = \frac{3{,}940}{20} = 197.$

34. Compute the Weighted Index Numbers for 1997 and 1999 (Based on 1996) by relative method from the following data. Also interpret the computed index numbers.

Years		*Commodities*			
		A	*B*	*C*	*D*
1996	Price	6	8	9	12
	Weight	5	3	1	1
1997	Price	9	10	6	10
1998	Price	12	12	9	15
1999	Price	15	14	12	20

[*Delhi Univ. B.Com. (Pass), 2001*]

Ans. Base 1996 = 100 ; Price I. No. for 1997 = 127·50 ; Price I. No. for 1999 = 207·50.

35. The price relatives and weights of a set of commodities are given in the following table :

Commodity	*A*	*B*	*C*	*D*
Price Relatives	125	120	127	119
Weights	W_1	$2W_1$	W_2	$W_2 + 3$

If the sum of the weights is 40 and the index for the set is 122, find the values of W_1 and W_2

[*Delhi Univ. B.Com. (Hons.), (External), 2007; Himachal Pradesh Univ. M.A. (Econ.), 2005*]

Ans. $W_1 = 7$, $W_2 = 8$

Hint. P = Price Relative; W : weights, I = Index Number

$$I = \frac{\Sigma WP}{\Sigma W} \Rightarrow 365W_1 + 246\,W_2 + 357 = 40 \times 122 = 4880 \Rightarrow 365\,W_1 + 246\,W_2 - 4523 = 0 \quad \ldots(i)$$

Also $\Sigma W = 3W_1 + 2W_2 + 3 = 40$ (given) $\Rightarrow 3W_1 + 2W_2 - 37 = 0$. ...(ii)

Solving (i) and (ii), we get $W_1 = 7$, $W_2 = 8$.

36. Given below are the prices and weights of given commodities for the years 1990, 1991 and 1992 :

Commodity	*Weight*	*Prices in Rupees*		
		1990	*1991*	*1992*
A	20	12·00	18·00	24·00
B	15	3·00	6·00	15·00
C	10	12·50	18·75	25·00
D	40	10·00	30·00	50·00
E	15	4·50	9·00	13·50

Using either aggregative method or relative method, calculate the weighted price index numbers for 1991 and 1992, taking 1990 as the base year.

Ans. Price indices based on Price Relatives are : For 1991 : 225 ; For 1992 : 380.

10·6. TESTS OF CONSISTENCY OF INDEX NUMBER FORMULAE

In § 10·5 we have discussed various formulae for the construction of index numbers. None of the formulae measures the price changes or quantity changes with exactitude or perfection and has some bias. The problem is to choose the most appropriate formula in a given situation. As a measure of the formula error a number of mathematical tests, known as the *tests of consistency* of index number formulae have been suggested. In this section we shall discuss these tests, which are also sometimes termed as the *criteria for a good index number.*

10·6·1. Unit Test. This test requires that the index number formula should be independent of the units in which the prices or quantities of various commodities are quoted. All the formulae discussed in § 10·5 except the index number based on Simple Aggregate of Prices (Quantities) satisfy this test.

10·6·2. Time Reversal Test. The time reversal test, proposed by Prof. Irving Fisher requires the index number formula to possess time consistency by working both forward and backward *w.r.t.* time. In his (Fisher's) words :

"The formula for calculating an index number should be such that it gives the same ratio between one point of comparison and the other, no matter which of the two is taken as the base or putting it another way, the index number reckoned forward should be reciprocal of the one reckoned backward."

In other words, if the index numbers are computed for the same data relating to two periods by the same formula but with the bases reversed, then the two index numbers so obtained should be the reciprocals of each other. Mathematically, we should have (omitting the factor 100),

$$P_{01} \times P_{10} = 1 \quad \ldots(10{\cdot}17)$$

or more generally

$$P_{ab} \times P_{ba} = 1 \quad \ldots(10{\cdot}18)$$

where P_{ab} is the price index (without factor 100) for year '*b*' with year '*a*' as base and P_{ba} is the price index (without factor 100) for year '*a*' with year '*b*' as base.

Time reversal test is satisfied by the following index number formulae :

(*i*) Simple aggregate index [*c.f.* Example 10·17 (*i*)]

(*ii*) Marshall-Edgeworth formula [*c.f.* Example 10·17 (*iii*)]

(*iii*) Walsch formula [*c.f.* Example 10·17 (*iv*)]

(*iv*) Fisher's ideal formula [*c.f.* Example 10·17 (*v*)]

(*v*) Kelly's fixed weight formula (Proved below)

(*vi*) Simple Geometric Mean of Price Relatives formula (Proved below)

(*vii*) Weighted Geometric Mean of Price Relatives formula with fixed weights.

Laspeyre's and Paasche's index numbers do not satisfy this test [*c.f.* Example 10·17 (*ii*) and 10·17 (*vi*)].

Let us verify this test for Kelly's fixed weight formula. We have (without factor 100)

$$P_{01}{}^{K} = \frac{\Sigma W p_1}{\Sigma W p_0} \quad \text{and} \quad P_{10}{}^{K} = \frac{\Sigma W p_0}{\Sigma W p_1}$$

$$\therefore \quad P_{01}{}^{K} \times P_{10}{}^{K} = \frac{\Sigma W p_1}{\Sigma W p_0} \times \frac{\Sigma W p_0}{\Sigma W p_1} = 1$$

Hence, Kelly 's fixed weight formula satisfies time reversal test.

For the index number based on simple G.M. of price-relatives, we have :

$$P_{01}\,(\text{G.M.}) = \left[\left(\Pi \frac{p_1}{p_0} \right) \right]^{1/n} \quad \text{and} \quad P_{10}\,(\text{G.M.}) = \left[\left(\Pi \frac{p_0}{p_1} \right) \right]^{1/n}$$

$$P_{01}\,(\text{G.M.}) \times P_{10}\,(\text{G.M.}) = \left[\Pi \left(\frac{p_1}{p_0} \right) \right]^{1/n} \times \left[\Pi \left(\frac{p_0}{p_1} \right) \right]^{1/n} = \left[\Pi \left(\frac{p_1}{p_0} \right) \times \Pi \left(\frac{p_0}{p_1} \right) \right]^{1/n} = 1$$

Hence, the simple geometric mean of price-relatives formula satisfies time reversal test. Similarly, the test can be verified for the weighted geometric mean of price-relatives index with fixed weights.

Remarks 1. P_{10} can be obtained from the formula for P_{01} by interchanging the subscripts 0 and 1, *i.e.*, replacing 0 by 1 and 1 by 0.

2. If Laspeyre's price index number is equal to Paasche's price index number, then in the usual notations, we have :

$$P_{01}{}^{La} = P_{01}{}^{Pa} \quad \Rightarrow \quad \frac{\Sigma p_1 q_0}{\Sigma p_0 q_0} \times 100 = \frac{\Sigma p_1 q_1}{\Sigma p_0 q_1} \times 100$$

$$\Rightarrow \quad (\Sigma p_1 q_0)\,(\Sigma p_0 q_1) = (\Sigma p_1 q_1)\,(\Sigma p_0 q_0), \quad \ldots(*)$$

the summation being taken over different commodities.

Without factor 100, we have :

$$P_{01}{}^{La}\, P_{10}{}^{La} = \frac{\Sigma p_1 q_0}{\Sigma p_0 q_0} \times \frac{\Sigma p_0 q_1}{\Sigma p_1 q_1} = 1 \quad \text{[From (*)]}$$

Therefore, Laspeyre's price index satisfies the time reversal test.

Without factor 100, we have :

$$P_{01}{}^{Pa}\, P_{10}{}^{Pa} = \frac{\Sigma p_1 q_1}{\Sigma p_0 q_1} \times \frac{\Sigma p_0 q_0}{\Sigma p_1 q_0} = 1 \quad \text{[From (*)]}$$

Therefore, Paasche's price index satisfies the time reversal test.

Hence, *if Laspeyre's price index is equal to Paasche's price index, then both of these index numbers satisfy the time reversal test.*

10·6·3. Factor Reversal Test. This is the second of the two important tests of consistency proposed by Prof. Irving Fisher. According to him :

"*Just as our formula should permit the interchange of two times without giving inconsistent results, so it ought to permit interchanging the prices and quantities without giving inconsistent results—i.e., the two results multiplied together should give the true value ratio, except for a constant of proportionality.*"

This implies that if the price and quantity indices are obtained for the same data, same base and current periods and using the same formula, then their product (without the factor 100) should give the true value ratio, since price multiplied by quantity gives total value. Symbolically, we should have (without factor 100),

$$P_{01} \times Q_{01} = \frac{\Sigma p_1 q_1}{\Sigma p_0 q_0} = V_{01} \quad \ldots(10\cdot19)$$

where $\Sigma\, p_1 q_1$ and $\Sigma\, p_0 q_0$ denote the total value in the current and base year respectively.

Fisher's formula satisfies the factor reversal test. [*c.f.* Example 10·17 (*v*)]. In fact, Fisher's index is the only index satisfying this test as none of the formulae discussed in § 10·5 satisfies this test. Proofs for some of them, *viz*., Laspeyre's, Paasche's, Marshall-Edgeworth, Simple Aggregate and Walsch index numbers do not satisfy the factor reversal test are given in Example 10·17.

Remarks 1. Since Fisher's index is the only index which satisfies both the time reversal and factor reversal tests, it is sometimes termed as Fisher's *Ideal Index*.

2. If Laspeyre's price index is equal to Paasche's price index, then in the usual notations, we have :

$$P_{01}^{La} = P_{01}^{Pa} \Rightarrow \frac{\sum p_1 q_0}{\sum p_0 q_0} \times 100 = \frac{\sum p_1 q_1}{\sum p_0 q_1} \times 100 \Rightarrow (\sum p_1 q_0)(\sum p_0 q_1) = (\sum p_0 q_0)(\sum p_1 q_1), \quad \ldots(**)$$

the summation being taken over different commodities.

$$P_{01}^{La} = \frac{\sum p_1 q_0}{\sum p_0 q_0} \text{ (Without factor 100)}$$

$$Q_{01}^{La} = \frac{\sum p_0 q_1}{\sum p_0 q_0} = \frac{\sum p_1 q_1}{\sum p_1 q_0} \quad \text{[From (**)]}$$

$$\therefore P_{01}^{La} \cdot Q_{01}^{La} = \frac{\sum p_1 q_0}{\sum p_0 q_0} \times \frac{\sum p_1 q_1}{\sum p_1 q_0} = \frac{\sum p_1 q_1}{\sum p_0 q_0} = V_{01}$$

$\Rightarrow$ Laspeyre's price index satisfies the factor reversal test.

$$P_{01}^{Pa} = \frac{\sum p_1 q_1}{\sum p_0 q_1} \text{ (Without factor 100)}$$

$$Q_{01}^{Pa} = \frac{\sum p_1 q_1}{\sum p_1 q_0} = \frac{\sum p_0 q_1}{\sum p_0 q_0} \quad \text{[From (**)]}$$

$$\therefore P_{01}^{Pa} \cdot Q_{01}^{Pa} = \frac{\sum p_1 q_1}{\sum p_0 q_1} \times \frac{\sum p_0 q_1}{\sum p_0 q_0} = \frac{\sum p_1 q_1}{\sum p_0 q_0} = V_{01}$$

$\Rightarrow$ Paasche's price index satisfies the factor reversal test.

Hence, *if Laspeyre's price index is equal to Paasche's price index, then both of these index numbers satisfy the factor reversal test.*

10·6·4. Circular Test. Circular test, first suggested by Westergaard, is an extension of time reversal test for more than two periods and is based on the shiftability of the base period. This requires the index to work in a circular manner and this property enables us to find the index numbers from period to period without referring back to the original base each time. For three periods *a, b, c,* the test requires :

$$P_{ab} \times P_{bc} \times P_{ca} = 1, \; a \neq b \neq c \qquad \ldots(10·20)$$

where P_{ij} is the price index (without factor 100) for period '*j*' with period '*i*' as base. In the usual notations, (10·20) can be stated as :

$$P_{01} \times P_{12} \times P_{20} = 1 \qquad \ldots(10·21)$$

For instance, $$P_{01}^{La} \times P_{12}^{La} \times P_{20}^{La} = \frac{\sum p_1 q_0}{\sum p_0 q_0} \times \frac{\sum p_2 q_1}{\sum p_1 q_1} \times \frac{\sum p_0 q_2}{\sum p_2 q_2} \neq 1.$$

Hence, Laspeyre's index does not satisfy the circular test. Similarly, it can be verified that none of Paasche's, M.E.'s, Walsch's, and Fisher's indices satisfies this test. In fact, circular test is not satisfied by any of the weighted aggregative formulae with changing weights, *i.e.*, if the weights used in the construction of index numbers P_{01}, P_{12} and P_{20} change. This test is satisfied *only* by the index number formulae based on :

(*i*) Simple geometric mean of the price-relatives, and

(*ii*) Kelly's fixed base method.

For example, for the index numbers based on simple geometric mean of price-relatives, we have :

$$P_{01} \times P_{12} \times P_{20} = \left[\Pi\left(\frac{p_1}{p_0}\right)\right]^{1/n} \times \left[\Pi\left(\frac{p_2}{p_1}\right)\right]^{1/n} \times \left[\Pi\left(\frac{p_0}{p_2}\right)\right]^{1/n}$$

$$= \left[\Pi\left(\frac{p_1}{p_0}\right) \times \Pi\left(\frac{p_2}{p_1}\right) \times \Pi\left(\frac{p_0}{p_2}\right)\right]^{1/n} = 1.$$

Hence circular test holds in this case.

Similarly, the index number based on Kelly's fixed weight formula gives (without factor 100)

$$P_{01} \times P_{12} \times P_{20} = \frac{\Sigma Wp_1}{\Sigma Wp_0} \times \frac{\Sigma Wp_2}{\Sigma Wp_1} \times \frac{\Sigma Wp_0}{\Sigma Wp_2} = 1.$$

Remark. *Generalisation of (10·21).* The circular test can be generalised to the case of more than three periods to give :

$$P_{01} \times P_{12} \times P_{23} \times \ldots \times P_{n-1,\, n} \times P_{n,\,0} = 1 \qquad \ldots(10·22)$$

where the indices are considered without the factor 100.

Example 10·15. *For the following data prove that the Fisher's Ideal Index satisfies both the Time Reversal Test and the Factor Reversal Test and calculate its value.*

	Base Year		*Current Year*	
Commodity	*Price*	*Quantity*	*Price*	*Quantity*
A	6	50	10	56
B	2	100	2	120
C	4	60	6	60
D	10	30	12	24

Solution.

TABLE 10·15. **COMPUTATION OF FISHER'S INDEX**

Commodity	p_0	q_0	p_1	q_1	p_0q_0	p_0q_1	p_1q_0	p_1q_1
A	6	50	10	56	300	336	500	560
B	2	100	2	120	200	240	200	240
C	4	60	6	60	240	240	360	360
D	10	30	12	24	300	240	360	288
					$\Sigma p_0q_0 =$ 1040	$\Sigma p_0q_1 =$ 1056	$\Sigma p_1q_0 =$ 1420	$\Sigma p_1q_1 =$ 1448

Fisher's price index : $(P_{01}{}^F) = 100 \times \sqrt{\dfrac{\Sigma p_1q_0 \times \Sigma p_1q_1}{\Sigma p_0q_0 \times \Sigma p_0q_1}} = 100 \times \sqrt{\dfrac{1420 \times 1448}{1040 \times 1056}}$

$$= 100 \times \sqrt{\frac{2056160}{1098240}} = 100 \times \sqrt{1·8722} = 100 \times 1·3683 = 136·83$$

Time Reversal Test : We have $P_{01}{}^F = 1·3683$ (without factor 100)

and $$P_{10}{}^F = \frac{\Sigma p_0q_1 \times \Sigma p_0q_0}{\Sigma p_1q_1 \times \Sigma p_1q_0} \quad \text{(without factor 100)}$$

$$= \sqrt{\frac{1056 \times 1040}{1448 \times 1420}} = \sqrt{\frac{1098240}{2056160}} = \sqrt{0·5341} = 0·7308$$

$\therefore \quad P_{01}{}^F \times P_{10}{}^F = 1·3683 \times 0·7308 = 0·9999 \simeq 1.$

Hence, Fisher's index satisfies time reversal test.

Factor Reversal Test. We have (without factor 100)

$$Q_{01}{}^F = \left[\frac{\Sigma q_1p_0 \times \Sigma q_1p_1}{\Sigma q_0p_0 \times \Sigma q_0p_1}\right]^{\frac{1}{2}} = \left[\frac{\Sigma p_0q_1 \times \Sigma p_1q_1}{\Sigma p_0q_0 \times \Sigma p_1q_0}\right]^{\frac{1}{2}}$$

$$= \left[\frac{1056 \times 1448}{1040 \times 1420}\right]^{\frac{1}{2}} = \sqrt{\frac{1529088}{1476800}} = \sqrt{1·035406} = 1·0175$$

$\therefore \quad P_{01}{}^F \times Q_{01}{}^F = 1·3683 \times 1·0175 = 1·3922$ and $\dfrac{\Sigma V_1}{\Sigma V_0} = \dfrac{\Sigma p_1q_1}{\Sigma p_0q_0} = \dfrac{1448}{1040} = 1·3923$

$\therefore \quad P_{01}{}^F \times Q_{01}{}^F = \dfrac{\Sigma V_1}{\Sigma V_0} \quad \Rightarrow$ Fisher's index satisfies Factor Reversal Test also.

Aliter : We have (without factor 100)

$$P_{01}{}^F = \sqrt{\frac{\Sigma p_1 q_0 \times \Sigma p_1 q_1}{\Sigma p_0 q_0 \times \Sigma p_0 q_1}} = \sqrt{\frac{1420 \times 1448}{1040 \times 1056}} \quad ; \quad P_{10}{}^F = \sqrt{\frac{\Sigma p_0 q_1 \times \Sigma p_0 q_0}{\Sigma p_1 q_1 \times \Sigma p_1 q_0}} = \sqrt{\frac{1056 \times 1040}{1448 \times 1420}}$$

$$\therefore \quad P_{01}{}^F \times P_{10}{}^F = \sqrt{\left[\frac{1420 \times 1448 \times 1056 \times 1040}{1040 \times 1056 \times 1448 \times 1420}\right]} = \sqrt{1} = 1.$$

Hence, Fisher's Index satisfies Time Reversal Test.

$$Q_{01}{}^F = \sqrt{\frac{\Sigma p_0 q_1 \times \Sigma p_1 q_1}{\Sigma p_0 q_0 \times \Sigma p_1 q_0}} = \sqrt{\frac{1056 \times 1448}{1040 \times 1420}}$$

$$\therefore \quad P_{01}{}^F \times Q_{01}{}^F = \sqrt{\left(\frac{1420 \times 1448}{1040 \times 1056}\right) \times \left(\frac{1056 \times 1448}{1040 \times 1420}\right)} = \sqrt{\left(\frac{1448}{1040}\right)^2} = \frac{1448}{1040} = \frac{\Sigma p_1 q_1}{\Sigma p_0 q_0}$$

Hence, Fisher's index satisfies Factor Reversal Test.

Remark. If we are not asked to compute Fisher's index but simply to test if it satisfies Time Reversal or/and Factor Reversal Tests, then the alternative method given above is very convenient for numerical computations.

Example 10·16. *Calculate Laspeyre's, Paasche's and Fisher's indices for the following data. Also examine which of the above indices satisfy (i) Time reversal test, (ii) Factor reversal test.*

Commodity	*Base Year*		*Current Year*	
	Price	*Quantity*	*Price*	*Quantity*
A	6·5	500	10·8	560
B	2·8	124	2·9	148
C	4·7	69	8·2	78
D	10·9	38	13·4	24
E	8·6	49	10·8	27

Solution.

TABLE 10·16. **COMPUTATIONS FOR LASPEYRE'S, PAASCHE'S AND FISHER'S INDICES**

Commodity	p_0	q_0	p_1	q_1	p_0q_0	p_1q_0	p_0q_1	p_1q_1
A	6·5	500	10·8	560	3250·0	5400·0	3640·0	6048·0
B	2·8	124	2·9	148	347·2	359·6	414·4	429·2
C	4·7	69	8·2	78	324·3	565·8	366·6	639·6
D	10·9	38	13·4	24	414·2	509·2	261·6	321·6
E	8·6	49	10·8	27	421·4	529·2	232·2	291·6
					4757·1	7363·8	4914·8	7730·0

(i) $$P_{01}{}^{La} = \frac{\Sigma p_1 q_0}{\Sigma p_0 q_0} \times 100 = \frac{7363·8}{4757·1} \times 100 = 1·5480 \times 100 = 154·80$$

(ii) $$P_{01}{}^{Pa} = \frac{\Sigma p_1 q_1}{\Sigma p_0 q_1} \times 100 = \frac{7730·0}{4914·8} \times 100 = 1·5728 \times 100 = 157·28$$

(iii) $$P_{01}{}^F = (P_{01}{}^{Pa} \times P_{01}{}^{La})^{1/2} = (154·80 \times 157·28)^{1/2} = 156·03$$

(iv) $$Q_{01}{}^{La} = \frac{\Sigma q_1 p_0}{\Sigma q_0 p_0} \times 100 = \frac{4914·8}{4757·1} \times 100 = 1·0121 \times 100 = 101·21$$

(v) $$Q_{01}{}^{Pa} = \frac{\Sigma q_1 p_1}{\Sigma q_0 p_1} \times 100 = \frac{7730·0}{7363·8} \times 100 = 1·0497 \times 100 = 104·97$$

(vi) $$Q_{01}{}^F = \sqrt{(Q_{01}{}^{La} \times Q_{01}{}^{Pa})} = \sqrt{(101·21 \times 104·97)} = 10·06 \times 10·24 = 103·01$$

Time Reversal Test : We should have (without factor 100) : $P_{01} \times P_{10} = 1$

(vii) $$P_{10}^{La} = \frac{\Sigma p_0 q_1}{\Sigma p_1 q_1} \times 100 = \frac{4914 \cdot 8}{7730 \cdot 0} \times 100 = 0 \cdot 6358 \times 100 = 63 \cdot 58$$

(viii) $$P_{10}^{Pa} = \frac{\Sigma p_0 q_0}{\Sigma p_1 q_0} \times 100 = \frac{4757 \cdot 1}{7363 \cdot 8} \times 100 = 0 \cdot 6460 \times 100 = 64 \cdot 60$$

(ix) $$P_{10}^{F} = (P_{10}^{La} \times P_{10}^{Pa})^{1/2} = \sqrt{(63 \cdot 58 \times 64 \cdot 60)} = 7 \cdot 97 \times 8 \cdot 04 = 64 \cdot 08$$

Hence,

$$P_{01}^{La} \times P_{10}^{La} = 1 \cdot 5480 \times 0 \cdot 6358 = 0 \cdot 9842 \neq 1 \quad \text{and} \quad P_{01}^{Pa} \times P_{10}^{Pa} = 1 \cdot 5728 \times 0 \cdot 6460 = 1 \cdot 0161 \neq 1$$

$$P_{01}^{F} \times P_{10}^{F} = 1 \cdot 5602 \times 0 \cdot 6408 = 0 \cdot 9998 \simeq 1$$

Hence, Fisher's formula satisfies the time reversal test. Laspeyre's and Paasche's formulae do not satisfy this test.

Factor Reversal Test. We should have : $P_{01} \times Q_{01} = \dfrac{\Sigma p_1 q_1}{\Sigma p_0 q_0}$

(x) $P_{01}^{La} \times Q_{01}^{La} = 1 \cdot 5480 \times 1 \cdot 0121 = 1 \cdot 5667$; (xi) $P_{01}^{Pa} \times Q_{01}^{Pa} = 1 \cdot 5728 \times 1 \cdot 0497 = 1 \cdot 6510$

(xii) $P_{01}^{F} \times Q_{01}^{F} = 1 \cdot 5603 \times 1 \cdot 0301 = 1 \cdot 6073$; (xiii) $\dfrac{\Sigma V_1}{\Sigma V_0} = \dfrac{\Sigma p_1 q_1}{\Sigma p_0 q_0} = \dfrac{7730}{4757 \cdot 1} = 1 \cdot 6249$

$$\therefore \quad P_{01}^{F} \times Q_{01}^{F} \simeq \frac{\Sigma p_1 q_1}{\Sigma p_0 q_0}$$

Fisher's formula satisfies factor reversal test also. Laspeyre's and Paasche's formulae do not satisfy this test.

Example 10·17. *Explain fully the concept and use of an index number. Discuss the role of weighting in the construction of index numbers. Describe the reversal tests for index numbers and examine the following formula in the light of these tests :*

(i) $\dfrac{\Sigma p_1}{\Sigma p_0} \times 100$ (ii) $\dfrac{\Sigma q_0 p_1}{\Sigma q_0 p_0} \times 100$ (iii) $\dfrac{\Sigma (q_0 + q_1) p_1}{\Sigma (q_0 + q_1) p_0} \times 100$

(iv) $\dfrac{\Sigma \sqrt{q_0 q_1}\, p_1}{\Sigma \sqrt{q_0 q_1}\, p_0} \times 100$ (v) $\sqrt{\dfrac{\Sigma p_1 q_0}{\Sigma p_0 q_0} \times \dfrac{\Sigma p_1 q_1}{\Sigma p_0 q_1}} \times 100$ (vi) $\dfrac{\Sigma q_1 p_1}{\Sigma q_1 p_0} \times 100$

Solution. We have (without the factor 100)

(i) $$P_{01} = \frac{\Sigma p_1}{\Sigma p_0}, \quad P_{10} = \frac{\Sigma p_0}{\Sigma p_1}, \quad Q_{01} = \frac{\Sigma q_1}{\Sigma q_0}$$

This is the Simple Aggregative Type of Index Number.

$$P_{01} \times P_{10} = \frac{\Sigma p_1}{\Sigma p_0} \times \frac{\Sigma p_0}{\Sigma p_1} = 1.$$

Hence, the given index (Simple Aggregative Price Index) satisfies Time Reversal Test.

Also $$P_{01} \times Q_{01} = \frac{\Sigma p_1}{\Sigma p_0} \times \frac{\Sigma q_1}{\Sigma q_0} \neq \frac{\Sigma p_1 q_1}{\Sigma p_0 q_0}$$

Hence the given index does not satisfy Factor Reversal Test.

(ii) $$P_{01} = \frac{\Sigma p_1 q_0}{\Sigma p_0 q_0}, \quad P_{10} = \frac{\Sigma p_0 q_1}{\Sigma p_1 q_1}, \quad Q_{01} = \frac{\Sigma p_0 q_1}{\Sigma p_0 q_0}$$

The given index is nothing but Laspeyre's Price Index.

$$\therefore \quad P_{01}^{La} \times P_{10}^{La} = \frac{\Sigma p_1 q_0}{\Sigma p_0 q_0} \times \frac{\Sigma p_0 q_1}{\Sigma p_1 q_1} \neq 1$$

Hence, the given index (Laspeyre's Index) does not satisfy Time Reversal Test.

$$P_{01}^{La} \times Q_{01}^{La} = \frac{\Sigma p_1 q_0}{\Sigma p_0 q_0} \times \frac{\Sigma p_0 q_1}{\Sigma p_0 q_0} \neq \frac{\Sigma p_1 q_1}{\Sigma p_0 q_0}$$

Hence, Laspeyre's Index does not satisfy Factor Reversal Test.

(*iii*) $$P_{01} = \frac{\Sigma p_1 (q_0 + q_1)}{\Sigma p_0 (q_0 + q_1)}; \quad P_{10} = \frac{\Sigma p_0 (q_1 + q_0)}{\Sigma p_1 (q_1 + q_0)}; \quad Q_{01} = \frac{\Sigma q_1 (p_0 + p_1)}{\Sigma q_0 (p_0 + p_1)}$$

The given index is nothing but Marshall-Edgeworth Price Index Number.

$$P_{01}^{ME} \times P_{10}^{ME} = \frac{\Sigma p_1 (q_0 + q_1)}{\Sigma p_0 (q_0 + q_1)} \times \frac{\Sigma p_0 (q_1 + q_0)}{\Sigma p_1 (q_1 + q_0)} = 1.$$

Hence, Marshall-Edgeworth Index Number satisfies Time Reversal Test.

$$P_{01}^{ME} \times Q_{01}^{ME} = \frac{\Sigma p_1 (q_0 + q_1)}{\Sigma p_0 (q_0 + q_1)} \times \frac{\Sigma q_1 (p_0 + p_1)}{\Sigma q_0 (p_0 + p_1)} \neq \frac{\Sigma p_1 q_1}{\Sigma p_0 q_0}$$

Thus, Marshall-Edgeworth Index number does not satisfy Factor Reversal Test.

(*iv*) $$P_{01} = \frac{\Sigma p_1 \sqrt{q_0 q_1}}{\Sigma p_0 \sqrt{q_0 q_1}}; \quad P_{10} = \frac{\Sigma p_0 \sqrt{q_1 q_0}}{\Sigma p_1 \sqrt{q_1 q_0}}; \quad Q_{01} = \frac{\Sigma q_1 \sqrt{p_0 p_1}}{\Sigma q_0 \sqrt{p_0 p_1}}$$

The given index number is the Walsch Price Index Number.

$$P_{01}^{Wa} \times P_{10}^{Wa} = \frac{\Sigma p_1 \sqrt{q_0 q_1}}{\Sigma p_0 \sqrt{q_0 q_1}} \times \frac{\Sigma p_0 \sqrt{q_1 q_0}}{\Sigma p_1 \sqrt{q_1 q_0}} = 1$$

Hence, Walsch Price Index satisfies Time Reversal Test.

$$\therefore \quad P_{01}^{Wa}\, Q_{01}^{Wa} = \frac{\Sigma p_1 \sqrt{q_0 q_1}}{\Sigma p_0 \sqrt{q_0 q_1}} \times \frac{\Sigma q_1 \sqrt{p_0 p_1}}{\Sigma q_0 \sqrt{p_0 p_1}} \neq \frac{\Sigma p_1 q_1}{\Sigma p_0 q_0}$$

Hence, Walsch Price Index does not satisfy Factor Reversal Test.

(*v*) $$P_{01} = \sqrt{\frac{\Sigma p_1 q_0}{\Sigma p_0 q_0} \times \frac{\Sigma p_1 q_1}{\Sigma p_0 q_1}}; \qquad P_{10} = \sqrt{\frac{\Sigma p_0 q_1}{\Sigma p_1 q_1} \times \frac{\Sigma p_0 q_0}{\Sigma p_1 q_0}}$$

The given index number is Fisher's Price Index Number.

$$\therefore \quad P_{01}^{F} \times P_{10}^{F} = \sqrt{\frac{\Sigma p_1 q_0}{\Sigma p_0 q_0} \times \frac{\Sigma p_1 q_1}{\Sigma p_0 q_1}} \times \sqrt{\frac{\Sigma p_0 q_1}{\Sigma p_1 q_1} \times \frac{\Sigma p_0 q_0}{\Sigma p_1 q_0}}$$

$$= \sqrt{\left[\frac{\Sigma p_1 q_0 \times \Sigma p_1 q_1 \times \Sigma p_0 q_1 \times \Sigma p_0 q_0}{\Sigma p_0 q_0 \times \Sigma p_0 q_1 \times \Sigma p_1 q_1 \times \Sigma p_1 q_0}\right]} = \sqrt{1} = 1.$$

Hence, Fisher's Index satisfies Time Reversal Test.

$$Q_{01}^{F} = \sqrt{\frac{\Sigma q_1 p_0}{\Sigma q_0 p_0} \times \frac{\Sigma q_1 p_1}{\Sigma q_0 p_1}} = \sqrt{\frac{\Sigma p_0 q_1}{\Sigma p_0 q_0} \times \frac{\Sigma p_1 q_1}{\Sigma p_1 q_0}}$$

$$\therefore \quad P_{01}^{F} \times Q_{01}^{F} = \sqrt{\frac{\Sigma p_1 q_0}{\Sigma p_0 q_0} \times \frac{\Sigma p_1 q_1}{\Sigma p_0 q_1}} \times \sqrt{\frac{\Sigma p_0 q_1}{\Sigma p_0 q_0} \times \frac{\Sigma p_1 q_1}{\Sigma p_1 q_0}}$$

$$= \sqrt{\left[\frac{\Sigma p_1 q_0 \times \Sigma p_1 q_1 \times \Sigma p_0 q_1 \times \Sigma p_1 q_1}{\Sigma p_0 q_0 \times \Sigma p_0 q_1 \times \Sigma p_0 q_0 \times \Sigma p_1 q_0}\right]} = \sqrt{\frac{(\Sigma p_1 q_1)^2}{(\Sigma p_0 q_0)^2}} = \frac{\Sigma p_1 q_1}{\Sigma p_0 q_0}$$

Hence, Fisher's Price Index satisfies Factor Reversal Test.

(*vi*) $$P_{01} = \frac{\Sigma p_1 q_1}{\Sigma p_0 q_1}; \quad P_{10} = \frac{\Sigma p_0 q_0}{\Sigma p_1 q_0}; \quad Q_{01} = \frac{\Sigma q_1 p_1}{\Sigma q_0 p_1}$$

This Index is Paasche's Price Index.

$$P_{01}{}^{Pa} \times P_{10}{}^{Pa} = \frac{\Sigma p_1 q_1}{\Sigma p_0 q_1} \times \frac{\Sigma p_0 q_0}{\Sigma p_1 q_0} \neq 1$$

Hence, Paasche's Price Index does not satisfy Time Reversal Test.

$$\therefore \quad P_{01}{}^{Pa} \times Q_{01}{}^{Pa} = \frac{\Sigma p_1 q_1}{\Sigma p_0 q_1} \times \frac{\Sigma p_1 q_1}{\Sigma p_1 q_0} \neq \frac{\Sigma p_1 q_1}{\Sigma p_0 q_0}$$

Hence, Paasche's Price Index does not satisfy Factor Reversal Test.

EXERCISE 10·2

1. (*a*) What do you mean by tests of consistency for an index number ?

(*b*) What are the various tests of adequacy of index numbers ? [*C.A.* (*Foundation*), *Nov. 1997*]

2. Explain the time reversal and factor reversal tests. Examine whether Laspeyre's and Paasche's index numbers satisfy these tests.

3. Discuss Laspeyre's, Paasche's and Fisher's index numbers. Which of the three would you prefer and why ?

4. What do you understand by :

(*i*) Factor Reversal Test ; and (*ii*) Time Reversal Test.

Prove that Fisher's index number satisfies both these tests.

5. (*a*) Briefly discuss the superiority of Fisher's Index Number formula over those of Laspeyre's and Paasche's Index Numbers. [*Delhi Univ. B.Com.* (*Pass*), *1998*]

(*b*) What is meant by reversibility of an index number ? Describe the time and factor reversal tests in the theory of index numbers. Give a formula which satisfies both these tests. [*C.A.* (*Foundation*), *Nov. 1995*]

6. (*a*) What is Fisher's Ideal Index ? Why is it called ideal ? Show that it satisfies both the time reversal test as well as the factor reversal test.

(*b*) Is Fisher's index really an ideal index ? Give reasons in support of your answer.

7. Distinguish between Laspeyre's and Paassche's index numbers. When will they be equal ? Why is it that Fisher's index number is called Ideal Index Number ?

8. (*a*) Explain the time reversal and factor reversal tests. Examine whether Fisher's price index satisfies time reversal test. [*Delhi Univ. B.A.* (*Econ. Hons.*), *2000*]

(*b*) Explain the concepts of time reversal test and factor reversal test and show that Fisher's ideal index satisfies both these tests. [*Delhi Univ. B.Com.* (*Hons.*), *2000*]

9. (*a*) Define Laspeyre's price index number and Paasche's price index number. Explain time-reversal test and check if this test is satisfied by Paasche's price index number. [*C.A.* (*Foundation*), *May 1997*]

(*b*) What do you mean by time reversal test for Index Numbers ? Show that Laspeyre's and Paasche's index numbers do not satisfy it and that Fisher's Ideal Index does. [*Delhi Univ. B.Com.* (*Pass*), *1999*]

(*c*) If Laspeyre's price index is equal to Paasche's price index, show that Paasche's index number will satisfy the time reversal test. [*Delhi Univ. B.A.* (*Econ. Hons.*), *2009*]

(*d*) Show under what conditions, the time reversal test will be satisfied by Paasche's price index.

[*Delhi Univ. B.A.* (*Econ. Hons.*), *2007*]

10. (*a*) State the tests for adequacy of index numbers. Under what conditions does the Laspeyre's index satisfy the factor reversal test ? [*Delhi Univ. B.A.* (*Econ. Hons.*), *2005, 2002*]

(*b*) Prove that Laspeyre's and Paasche's price index numbers satisfy :

(*i*) the Time Reversal Test ; (*ii*) the Factor Reversal Test,

if and only if both are equal. [*Delhi Univ. B.A.* (*Econ. Hons.*), *2008, 2002*]

11. What is Fisher's "ideal" index number ? Show that it satisfies "time reversal test" but not "circular test". Show that if prices are rising, the Paasche's price index normally understates the price rise and the Laspeyre's price index overstates it.

12. What are time reversal and factor reversal tests ? State their uses.

Test whether the index number due to Walsch given by : $I = \dfrac{\Sigma p_1 \sqrt{q_0 q_1}}{\Sigma p_0 \sqrt{q_0 q_1}} \times 100$, satisfies time reversal test.

13. With the usual notations the Marshall-Edgeworth index number is defined as : $\dfrac{\Sigma p_1 (q_0 + q_1)}{\Sigma p_0 (q_0 + q_1)} \times 100$

and Fisher's ideal index number is defined as : $\sqrt{\dfrac{\Sigma p_1 q_0}{\Sigma p_0 q_0} \times \dfrac{\Sigma p_1 q_1}{\Sigma p_0 q_1}} \times 100$

Show which tests are satisfied by these formulae.

14. What are factor and time-reversal tests in index number theory ? Do you consider these properties as essential requisites of an index number ?

Examine the following index numbers for presence or absence of the above two properties.

(*i*) $100 \times \dfrac{\Sigma q_1 p_1}{\Sigma q_1 p_0}$, (*ii*) $100 \times \sqrt{\left(\dfrac{\Sigma q_0 p_1 \cdot \Sigma q_1 p_1}{\Sigma q_0 p_0 \cdot \Sigma q_1 p_0}\right)}$

where p and q denote, as usual, prices and quantities respectively.

15. State giving reasons, whether the following statement is true or false :

Factor reversal test of Index Numbers is : $P_{01} \times Q_{01} = \dfrac{\Sigma p_1 q_1}{\Sigma p_1 q_0}$

Ans. False.

16. From the adjoining data find the index numbers for the current year and the base year based on each other and show that the Geometric Mean makes it reversible but the Arithmetic Mean does not.

Commodity	*Prices*	
	Base Year	*Current Year*
A	25	55
B	30	45

Ans. P_{01} (*A.M.*) = 185 ; P_{01} (*G.M.*) = 181·66 ; P_{10} (*A.M.*) = 56·06 ; P_{10} (G.M.) = 55·05.
P_{01} (*A.M.*) $\times P_{10}$ (*A.M.*) $\neq 1$; P_{01} (*G.M.*) $\times P_{10}$ (*G.M.*) = 1, (without the factor 100).

17. Compute Fisher's index number on the basis of the following data :

Commodity	*Base Year*		*Current Year*	
	Price (in '00 Rs.)	*Expenditure (in '00 Rs.)*	*Price (in '00 Rs.)*	*Expenditure (in '00 Rs.)*
A	5	25	10	60
B	1	10	2	24
C	4	16	8	40
D	2	40	5	75

Also apply Factor Reversal Test to the above index number.

Ans. $P_{01}{}^F = 219{\cdot}12$.

18. Using the following data, show whether the time reversal test is satisfied by Fisher's price index.

Commodity	p_0	q_0	p_1	q_1
A	12	30	14	20
B	10	20	15	16

[*Delhi Univ. B.A. (Econ. Hons.), 2009*]

Ans. Yes.

19. Using the following data show that the Fisher ideal index satisfies both the time reversal and factor reversal tests.

Commodity	*Base Year*		*Current Year*	
	Price	*Quantity*	*Price*	*Quantity*
A	6	50	10	60
B	2	100	2	120
C	4	60	6	60

Ans. $P_{01}{}^F = 143{\cdot}05$. [*Delhi Univ. B.A. (Econ.Hons.), 1999*]

20. Following are the values :

$\Sigma p_0 q_0 = 425$ $\Sigma p_1 q_0 = 505$ $\Sigma p_1 q_1 = 530$ $\Sigma p_0 q_1 = 470$

Show that Fisher's method, Paasche's and Marshall method either satisfy time reversal test and factor reversal test or do not satisfy both or one of them.

[*Delhi Univ. B.Com. (Hons.), 1996*]

Hint. Fisher's index satisfies both the tests; Marshall-Edgeworth index satisfies Time Reversal Test only and Paasche's index satisfies none of these tests.

21. (*a*) What do you mean by Time Reversal Test, Factor Reversal Test and Circular Test. Give the list of the formulae which satisfy the above tests respectively.

(*b*) Prove that the Fisher's index number does not satisfy the circular test.

10·7. CHAIN INDICES OR CHAIN BASE INDEX NUMBERS

The various formulae discussed for the construction of index numbers are based on the fixed base method and they reflect the relative changes in the level of a phenomenon in any period called *current period* with its changes in some particular fixed year called the *base year*. Fixed base indices, though simple to construct have their limitations, some of which are outlined below :

(*i*) Due to the dynamic pace of events these days, there may be a considerable change in the tastes, customs, fashions, etc., of the society and consequently in the consumption pattern of the people. Hence, if the base year is quite distant from the current year, the comparisons on the basis of fixed base indices may be unrealistic, unreliable and may even be misleading.

(*ii*) The changes in the fashions and habits of the people, during the two periods (current year and fixed base year) might lead to new innovations and new products might have come in the market. Moreover, some of the commodities or items which were largely consumed in the base year might have become outdated and may have to be discarded. This is not possible under the fixed base method as it requires the same set of commodities or items to be used in both the periods.

(*iii*) Because of the inherent changes in the consumption patterns of the people due to time lag, the relative importance of the various commodities in the two periods may change considerably, thus, necessitating a revision in the original weights.

Keeping these limitations in mind, it was felt that the data for the two periods being compared should be as homogeneous as possible and this is best attained by taking two adjacent periods. Accordingly, instead of fixed base method, we use the chain base method in which the relative changes in the level of phenomenon for any period are compared with that of the immediately preceding period.

The chain base method thus consists in computing a series of index numbers (by a suitable method) for each year with the preceding year as the base year. If P_{ab} denotes the price index for current period '*b*' with respect to the base period '*a*', then we compute series of indices $P_{01}, P_{12}, P_{23}, \ldots, P_{r-1,\, r}$ if we are given the data for $(r + 1)$ periods. These indices are called *Link Index Numbers or Link Relatives*. The basic chain indices (C.I.) are obtained from these link relatives by successive multiplication as given below :

$$\left.\begin{aligned} P_{01} &= \text{First Link} \\ P_{02} &= P_{01} \times P_{12} \\ P_{03} &= (P_{01} \times P_{12}) \times P_{23} = P_{02} \times P_{23} \\ &\;\;\vdots \quad \vdots \quad \vdots \\ P_{0r} &= P_{0,\, r-1} \times P_{r-1,\, r} \end{aligned}\right\} \qquad \ldots(10\cdot23)$$

Thus, the steps in the construction of the chain base index numbers may be summarised as follows :

1. For each commodity, express the price in any year as a percentage of its price in the preceding year. This gives the link relatives (L.R.). Thus

$$\text{L.R. for period } i = \frac{p_i}{p_{i-1}} \times 100, \ (i = 1, 2, \ldots, r) \qquad \ldots(10\cdot24)$$

2. Chain base indices (C.B.I.) are obtained on multiplying the link relatives successively as explained in (10·24). Thus

$$\text{C.B.I for any year} = \frac{\text{Current Year L.R.} \times \text{Preceding Year C.B.I.}}{100} \qquad \ldots(10\cdot25)$$

Remarks 1. Obviously, the techniques of computing the index number by the 'fixed base' and the 'chain base' methods are different, the former (F.B.I.) using the original (raw) data while the latter (C.B.I.) using the Link Relatives.

If there is only one series of observations, *i.e.,* if we are given the prices (quantities) of only one commodity (item) for different years, then the fixed base indices and the chain base indices will always be same [See Example 10·18]. Hence, in such a case we should always use the fixed base method since it requires much less calculations as compared with chain base method.

However, if there are more than two series, then the chain base indices and fixed base indices would usually be different except for the first two years, for which they will always be equal [See Example 10·20].

2. *Conversion of Chain Base Index Numbers to Fixed Base Index Numbers.* Fixed base index (F.B.I.) numbers can be obtained from the chain base index (C.B.I.) numbers by using the following formula :

$$\text{Current Year F.B.I.} = \frac{\text{Current year C.B.I.} \times \text{Previous Year F.B.I.}}{100}, \quad \ldots(10{\cdot}26)$$

the F.B.I. for the first period being same as the C.B.I. for the first period.

10·7·1. Uses of Chain Base Index Numbers. (1) In the chain base method the comparisons are made with the immediate past (preceding year) and accordingly the data (for the two periods being compared) are relatively homogeneous. The comparisons are, therefore, more valid and meaningful and the resulting index is more representative of the current trends in the tastes, habits, customs and fashions of the society. Hence, the chain base indices are specially useful to a businessman who is basically interested in comparison between the values of a phenomenon at two consecutive periods rather than the values of the phenomenon at any period with its value in some distant fixed base period.

According to Mudgett, the chain base method gives better account of the dynamics of the transition from base year to given year than other methods.

2. In the chain base method, new commodities or items may be included and the old and obsolete items may be deleted without impairing comparability and without requiring the recalculation of the entire series of index numbers, which is necessary in case of fixed base method. Moreover, the weights of the various commodities can be adjusted frequently. This flexibility greatly increases the utility of the chain indices over the fixed base index numbers. According to Marshall and Edgeworth, chain base indices are the best means of making short-term comparisons.

10·7·2. Limitations of Chain Base Index Numbers. The chain indices are relatively tedious and time consuming to calculate as compared with fixed base indices. They are suitable only for short range comparisons and the long range comparisons of the chain indices are not really valid. It is very difficult to understand the significance of these indices, and give physical interpretations to them.

Example 10·18. *Convert the following fixed base index numbers into chain base index numbers :*

Year :	*1990*	*1991*	*1992*	*1993*	*1994*	*1995*
F.B.I. :	*376*	*392*	*408*	*380*	*392*	*400*

Solution.

TABLE 10·17. **CONVERSION OF F.B.I. TO C.B.I.**

Year	*F.B.I.*	*Link Relatives*	*Chain Index*
1990	376	...	376
1991	392	$\frac{392}{376} \times 100 = 104{\cdot}26$	$\frac{376 \times 104{\cdot}26}{100} = 392$
1992	408	$\frac{408}{392} \times 100 = 104{\cdot}08$	$\frac{392 \times 104{\cdot}08}{100} = 408$
1993	380	$\frac{380}{408} \times 100 = 93{\cdot}14$	$\frac{408 \times 93{\cdot}14}{100} = 380$
1994	392	$\frac{392}{380} \times 100 = 103{\cdot}16$	$\frac{380 \times 103{\cdot}16}{100} = 392$
1995	400	$\frac{400}{392} \times 100 = 102{\cdot}04$	$\frac{392 \times 102{\cdot}04}{100} = 400$

Remark. *It may be noted that the chain base indices are same as the fixed base indices. In fact this will always be true for a single fixed series of index numbers.*

Example 10·19. *From the chain base index numbers given below, find fixed base index numbers :*

Year	:	*1995*	*1996*	*1997*	*1998*	*1999*
Chain base index	:	*80*	*110*	*120*	*90*	*140*

Solution. Using formula (10·27), *viz.*,

$$\text{Current year F.B.I.} = \frac{\text{Current year C.B.I.} \times \text{Previous year F.B.I.}}{100},$$

the first year F.B.I. being same as first year C.B.I.; we obtain the F.B.I. numbers as given in Table 10·18.

TABLE 10·18. **CONVERSION OF C.B.I. NUMBERS TO F.B.I. NUMBERS**

Year	*Chain Index Number*	*Fixed Base Index Number*
1995	80	80
1996	110	$\frac{80 \times 110}{100} = 88$
1997	120	$\frac{88 \times 120}{100} = 105{\cdot}60$
1998	90	$\frac{105{\cdot}6 \times 90}{100} = 95{\cdot}04$
1999	140	$\frac{95{\cdot}04 \times 140}{100} = 133{\cdot}06$

Example 10·20. (*a*) *From the following prices of three groups of commodities for the years 1995 to 1999, find the chain base index numbers chained to 1995.*

Groups	*1995*	*1996*	*1997*	*1998*	*1999*
I	*4*	*6*	*8*	*10*	*12*
II	*16*	*20*	*24*	*30*	*36*
III	*8*	*10*	*16*	*20*	*24*

(b) Also find fixed base index numbers with 1995 as base year.

Solution.

(*a*) TABLE 10·19. **COMPUTATION OF CHAIN BASE INDEX NUMBERS**

Group	Relatives based on preceding year				
	1995	*1996*	*1997*	*1998*	*1999*
I	100	$\frac{6}{4} \times 100 = 150$	$\frac{8}{6} \times 100 = 133{\cdot}33$	$\frac{10}{8} \times 100 = 125$	$\frac{12}{10} \times 100 = 120$
II	100	$\frac{20}{16} \times 100 = 125$	$\frac{24}{20} \times 100 = 120{\cdot}00$	$\frac{30}{24} \times 100 = 125$	$\frac{36}{30} \times 100 = 120$
III	100	$\frac{10}{8} \times 100 = 125$	$\frac{16}{10} \times 100 = 160{\cdot}00$	$\frac{20}{16} \times 100 = 125$	$\frac{24}{20} \times 100 = 120$
Total of L.R.	300	400	413·33	375	360
Average L.R. (A.M.)	100	133·33	137·78	125	120
Chain Indices	100	$\frac{100 \times 133{\cdot}33}{100} = 133{\cdot}33$	$\frac{137{\cdot}78 \times 133{\cdot}33}{100} = 183{\cdot}70$	$\frac{125 \times 183{\cdot}70}{100} = 229{\cdot}63$	$\frac{120 \times 229{\cdot}63}{100} = 275{\cdot}56$

(b) TABLE 10·20. COMPUTATION OF FIXED BASE INDEX NUMBERS

Group	Price Relatives (1995 = 100)				
	1995	*1996*	*1997*	*1998*	*1999*
I	100	$\frac{6}{4} \times 100 = 150$	$\frac{8}{4} \times 100 = 200$	$\frac{10}{4} \times 100 = 250$	$\frac{12}{4} \times 100 = 300$
II	100	$\frac{20}{16} \times 100 = 125$	$\frac{24}{16} \times 100 = 150$	$\frac{30}{16} \times 100 = 187{\cdot}5$	$\frac{36}{16} \times 100 = 225$
III	100	$\frac{10}{8} \times 100 = 125$	$\frac{16}{8} \times 100 = 200$	$\frac{20}{8} \times 100 = 250$	$\frac{24}{8} \times 100 = 300$
Total of Relatives	300	400	550	687·5	825
Index No. (Average of Relatives)	100	133·33	183·33	229·17	275

Remark. It may be observed that the index numbers obtained by both the methods are same for the first two years and they are different for the remaining years. This is due to the averaging (combining) of the values for different groups.

EXERCISE 10·3

1. (*a*) What are the Chain Base Index Numbers ? How are they constructed ? What are their uses ?

(*b*) Discuss the advantages of chain indices over fixed base indices. Also state their limitations.

(*c*) Explain the difference between fixed base index and chain base index. Write the formula to convert the chain base index to fixed base index. *[Delhi Univ. B.Com. (Pass), 2000]*

2. (*a*) Distinguish between 'Fixed' and 'Chain' base indices. Give a suitable illustration to show the difference.

(*b*) Distinguish between fixed base and chain base index numbers. What are their relative merits and demerits ?

(*c*) Explain briefly the fixed base method and the chain base method of constructing index numbers. Point out the advantages and disadvantages of the two methods.

3. From the fixed base index numbers given below, find out chain base index numbers :

Year :	1996	1997	1998	1999	2000	2001
Index No. :	200	220	240	250	280	300

Ans. 200, 220, 240, 250, 280, 300.

4. Convert the following series of index numbers to chain base indices :

Year :	1990	1991	1992	1993	1994	1995	1996	1997
Index No. (Base 1990) :	100	110	125	133	149	139	150	165

Ans. 100, 110, 125, 133, 149, 139, 150, 165.

5. Convert the following link relatives into price relatives, taking 1995 as the base :

Year :	1995	1996	1997	1998	1999	2000
Link Relatives :	120	150	180	225	270	324

Ans.

Fixed Base Index Numbers :	120,	180,	324,	729,	1968,	6376
Fixed Base Index Nos. (Base 1995 = 100) :	100,	149·99,	269·99,	607·48,	1639·93,	5313·12

6. From the fixed base index numbers given below obtain chain base index numbers.

Year :	1993	1994	1995	1996	1997	1998
Index No. :	150	180	120	120	80	96

Ans. 150, 180, 120, 120, 80, 96.

7. From the chain base index numbers given below, prepare fixed base index numbers.

Year :	1994	1995	1996	1997	1998
Index No. :	90	110	115	120	130

Ans. 90, 99, 113·85, 136·62, 177·61.

8. From the chain base index numbers given below, prepare fixed base index numbers.

Year :	1991	1992	1993	1994	1995
Index No. :	110	160	140	100	150

Ans. 110, 176, 246·4, 492·8, 739·2.

9. Prepare fixed base index numbers from the chain base index numbers given below :

Year	:	1991	1992	1993	1994	1995	1996
Index No.	:	92	102	104	98	103	101

Ans. 92, 93·84, 97·59, 95·64, 98·51, 99·50.

10. From the following annual average prices of three commodities given in rupees per unit, find chain index numbers based on 1997 :

Commodities	*1997*	*1998*	*1999*	*2000*	*2001*
X	8	10	12	15	12
Y	10	12	15	18	20
Z	6	9	12	15	18

Ans. 100, 131·67, 166·05, 204·79, 212·36.

11. Assuming that all the goods can be assigned equal weights, calculate the chain base index numbers for the years 1996 to 2000 on the basis of the following price-relatives :

$$\left[\text{Price Relative} = \frac{\text{Current year's price}}{\text{Last year's price}} \times 100\right]$$

	Goods A	*Goods B*	*Goods C*	*Goods D*	*Goods E*
1996	100	100	100	100	100
1997	90	125	134	118	133
1998	89	61	60	115	125
1999	112	200	80	93	140
2000	122	66	150	86	86

Ans. 100, 120, 108, 135, 137·7.

12. The price index of crude oil was 120 in 1997 with 1995 as base year and 130 in 1998 with 1997 as base. The price of crude further increased by 20% in 1999 over 1998 and decreased by 10% in 2000 over 1999. It further decreased by 10% in 2001 over 2000. Obtain the chain base index of crude prices for the year 2001 over 1995.

[Delhi Univ. B.A. (Econ. Hons.), 2006]

Hint. Chain Indices—Chained to Base 1995 :

Year	1995	1997	1998	1999	2000	2001
Chain Index. Chained to Base 1995 = 100	100	120	$\frac{130}{100} \times 120 = 156$	$\frac{(100+20)}{20} \times 156$ = 187.20	$\frac{(100-10)}{100} \times 187.20$ = 168.48	$\frac{(100-10)}{100} \times 168.48$ = 151.63

13. Calculate the Chain Base Index Numbers from the following data :

Commodity	*Prices in Rupees*				
	1991	*1992*	*1993*	*1994*	*1995*
A	2	3	4	2	7
B	3	6	9	4	3
C	4	12	20	8	16
D	5	7	18	11	22

[Delhi Univ. B.Com. (Hons.), 1998]

Ans. 100, 197·50, 349·16, 170·70, 352·07.

14. Calculate the chain base index numbers from the data given below :

Year	*Price of Commodities (in Rs.)*				
	A	B	C	D	E
1996	10	20	12	40	100
1997	12	22	14	45	110
1998	11	25	18	49	106
1999	14	28	10	43	102
2000	15	23	9	42	101

Ans. 100, 113.83, 122.74, 117.54, 111.88.

10·8. BASE SHIFTING, SPLICING AND DEFLATING OF INDEX NUMBERS

10·8·1. Base Shifting. Base shifting means the changing of the *given* base period (year) of a series of index numbers and recasting them into a new series based on some recent *new* base period. This step is quite often necessary under the following situations :

(*i*) When the base year is too old or too distant from the current period to make meaningful and valid comparisons. As already pointed out [Selection of Base Period § 10·4], the base year should be normal year of economic stability not too far distant from the given year.

(*ii*) If we want to compare series of index numbers with different base periods, to make quick and valid comparisons both the series must be expressed with a common base period.

Base shifting requires the recomputation of the entire series of the index numbers with the new base. However, this is a very difficult and time consuming job. A relatively much simple, though approximate method consists in taking the index number of the new base year as 100 and then *expressing the given series of index numbers as a percentage of the index number of the time period selected as the new base year*. Thus, the series of index numbers, recast with a new base is obtained by the formula :

$$\text{Recast I. No. of any year} = \frac{\text{Old I. No. of the year}}{\text{I. No. of new base year}} \times 100 \qquad \ldots(10\cdot27)$$

$$= \left(\frac{100}{\text{I. No. of new base year}}\right) \times (\text{Old I. No. of the year}) \qquad \ldots(10\cdot27a)$$

In other words, the new series of index numbers is obtained on multiplying the old index numbers with a common factor :

$$\frac{100}{\text{I. No. of New Base Year}} \qquad \ldots(10\cdot28)$$

The technique is explained below by numerical illustrations.

Remark. Rigorously speaking the above method is applicable only if the given index numbers satisfy the circular test (*i.e.*, Index Number based on Kelly's fixed base method or simple geometric mean of price-relatives). However, most of the index numbers based on other methods also yield results, which are practically, quite close to the theoretically correct values.

Example 10·21. *Reconstruct the following indices using 2000 as the base.*

Year :	*1996*	*1997*	*1998*	*1999*	*2000*	*2001*	*2002*
Index Nos. :	*110*	*130*	*150*	*175*	*180*	*200*	*220*

Solution.

TABLE 10·21. **INDEX NUMBERS (BASE 2000 = 100)**

Year	*Index No.*	*Index Number (Base 2000 = 100)*
1996	110	$\frac{100}{180} \times 110 = 61\cdot11$
1997	130	$\frac{100}{180} \times 130 = 72\cdot22$
1998	150	$\frac{100}{180} \times 150 = 83\cdot33$
1999	175	$\frac{100}{180} \times 175 = 97\cdot22$
2000	180	100·00
2001	200	$\frac{100}{180} \times 200 = 111\cdot11$
2002	220	$\frac{100}{180} \times 220 = 122\cdot22$

Example 10·22. *An index is at 100 in 1981. It rises 4% in 1982, falls 6% in 1983, falls 4% in 1984 and rises 3% in 1985. Calculate the index numbers for the five years with 1983 as base.*

Solution.

TABLE 10·22. **INDEX NUMBERS (BASE 1983 = 100)**

Year	*Index Number (Base 1981 = 100)*	*Index Number (Base 1983 = 100)*
1981	100	$\frac{100}{97 \cdot 76} \times 100 = 102 \cdot 32$
1982	$100 + 4 = 104$	$\frac{100}{97 \cdot 76} \times 104 = 106 \cdot 40$
1983	$\frac{94}{100} \times 104 = 97 \cdot 76$	100·00
1984	$\frac{96}{100} \times 97 \cdot 76 = 93 \cdot 85$	$\frac{100}{97 \cdot 76} \times 93 \cdot 85 = 96 \cdot 00$
1985	$\frac{103}{100} \times 93 \cdot 85 = 96 \cdot 66$	$\frac{100}{97 \cdot 76} \times 96 \cdot 66 = 98 \cdot 88$

10·8·2. Splicing. An application of the principle of base shifting is in the technique of splicing which consists in combining two or more overlapping series of index numbers to obtain a single continuous series. This continuity of the series of index number is required to facilitate comparisons. Let us suppose that we have a series of index numbers with some base period, say, 'a' and it is discontinued in the period 'b' and with the terminating period of the first series as base, *i.e.*, period 'b' as base, a second series of index numbers (with the same items) is constructed by the same method (formula). In order to secure continuity in comparisons the two series are *put together* or *spliced* together to get a continuous series. The method is explained in Table 10·23.

TABLE 10·23. **SPLICING OF TWO INDEX NUMBER SERIES**

Year	*Series I Base 'a'*	*Series II Base 'b'*	*Series II Spliced to Series I (Base 'a')*	*Series I Spliced to Series II (Base 'b')*
a	100		100	$\frac{100}{a_r} \times 100$
$a + 1$	a_1		a_1	$\frac{100}{a_r} \times a_1$
$a + 2$	a_2		a_2	$\frac{100}{a_r} \times a_2$
⋮	⋮	⋮	⋮	⋮
$b - 1$	a_{r-1}		a_{r-1}	$\frac{100}{a_r} \times a_{r-1}$
b	a_r	100	a_r	100
$b + 1$		b_1	$\frac{a_r}{100} \times b_1$	b_1
$b + 2$		b_2	$\frac{a_r}{100} \times b_2$	b_2
$b + 3$		b_3	$\frac{a_r}{100} \times b_3$	b_3
⋮	⋮	⋮	⋮	⋮

Explanation. When series II is spliced to series I to get a continuous series with base 'a', 100 of II series becomes a_r.

$\Rightarrow$ b_1 of II series becomes $\frac{a_r}{100} \times b_1$,

and b_2 of II series becomes $\frac{a_r}{100} \times b_2$,

and so on. Thus, multiplying each index of the series II with constant factor $\frac{a_r}{100}$, we get the new series of index numbers spliced to series I (Base 'a'). In this case series I is also said to be *spliced forward.*

If we splice series I to series II to get a new continuous series with base '*b*', then

$$\Rightarrow \quad \begin{cases} a_r \text{ of 1st series becomes } 100, \\ a_{r-1} \text{ of Ist series becomes } \dfrac{100}{a_r} \times a_{r-1}, \\ \vdots \qquad \vdots \qquad \vdots \\ a_2 \text{ of Ist series becomes } \dfrac{100}{a_r} \times a_2, \end{cases}$$

and so on. Thus, the new series of index numbers with series I spliced to series II (Base '*b*') is obtained on multiplying each index of series I by new constant factor $\left(\dfrac{100}{a_r}\right)$. In this case we also say that series II is *spliced backward.* We give below some numerical illustrations to explain the technique.

Remark. It may be pointed out that like base shifting, the technique of splicing will give accurate results only for the index numbers which satisfy circular test, *i.e.*, the index numbers based on Kelly's fixed weight method or simple geometric mean of relatives.

Example 10·23. *Given the following values :*

	A	*B*
1964	$\sum p_0 q_0 =$ *Rs. 10*	
1965	$\sum p_1 q_0 =$ *Rs. 12*	
1966	$\sum p_2 q_0 =$ *Rs. 15*	
1967	$\sum p_3 q_0 =$ *Rs. 20*	$\sum p_3 q_3 =$ *Rs. 25*
1968		$\sum p_4 q_3 =$ *Rs. 30*
1969		$\sum p_5 q_3 =$ *Rs. 40*
1970		$\sum p_6 q_3 =$ *Rs. 45*

(*i*) *Calculate two price indices : A with q_0 as weights and B with q_3 as weights.*

(*ii*) *Splice the two series so as to make 'A' a continuous series.* [*Delhi Univ. B.A.*, (*Econ. Hons.*), *1994*]

Solution.

TABLE 10·24. **INDEX NUMBER SERIES B SPLICED TO SERIES A**

Year (1)	*INDEX NUMBER SERIES* *A* (*q_0 as weights*) (*Base 1964*) (2)	*INDEX NUMBER SERIES* *B* (*q_3 as weights*) (*Base 1967*) (3)	*Index No. Series 'B' Spliced to Series 'A'* (*Base 1964*) (4) $= \frac{200}{100} \times (3)$
1964	100		100
1965	$\frac{12}{10} \times 100 = 120$		120
1966	$\frac{15}{10} \times 100 = 150$		150
1967	$\frac{20}{10} \times 100 = 200$	100	200
1968		$\frac{30}{25} \times 100 = 120$	$\frac{200}{100} \times 120 = 240$
1969		$\frac{40}{25} \times 100 = 160$	$\frac{200}{100} \times 160 = 320$
1970		$\frac{45}{25} \times 100 = 180$	$\frac{200}{100} \times 180 = 360$

(*i*) Index numbers for series *A* with q_0 as weights (Base 1964 = 100) are given in column (2) of the above table and the index numbers for series *B* with q_3 as weights (Base 1967 = 100) are given in column (3) of the above table.

(*ii*) To splice the two series so as to make '*A*', a continuous series (with Base 1964 = 100), we have to splice series '*B*' to series '*A*', as done in the last column of the Table 10·24.

Example 10·24. *Given below are two price index series. Splice them on the base 1994 = 100. By what per cent did the price of steel rise between 1990 and 1995 ?*

Year	*Old price index for Steel : (Base 1985 = 100)*	*New price index for Steel : (Base 1994 = 100)*
1990	*141·5*	
1991	*163·7*	
1992	*158·2*	
1993	*156·8*	*99·8*
1994	*157·1*	*100·0*
1995		*102·3*

Solution.

TABLE 10·25. **SPLICING OF OLD PRICE INDEX TO NEW PRICE INDEX**

Year	*Old price index for Steel : (Base 1985 = 100)*	*New price index for Steel : (Base 1994 = 100)*
1990	141·5	$\frac{100}{157 \cdot 1} \times 141 \cdot 5 = 90 \cdot 07$
1991	163·7	$\frac{100}{157 \cdot 1} \times 163 \cdot 7 = 104 \cdot 20$
1992	158·2	$\frac{100}{157 \cdot 1} \times 158 \cdot 2 = 100 \cdot 70$
1993	156·8	$\frac{100}{157 \cdot 1} \times 156 \cdot 8 = 99 \cdot 81$
1994	157·1	100·0
1995		102·3

Hence, the percentage increase in the price of steel between 1990 and 1995 is

$$\frac{102 \cdot 30 - 90 \cdot 07}{90 \cdot 07} \times 100 = 0 \cdot 1358 \times 100 = 13 \cdot 58$$

Hence required increase is 13·58%.

Remark. When the old index is spliced to the new index (Base 1994), the index number for 1994, *viz.*, 157·1 becomes 100.

Hence, the multiplying factor for splicing is $\frac{100}{157 \cdot 1} = 0 \cdot 6365$.

Example 10.25. *Two sets of indices, one with 1976 as base and the other with 1984 as base, are given below.*

Year :	*1976*	*1977*	*1978*	*1979*	*1980*	*1981*	*1982*	*1983*	*1984*
Index A	*100*	*110*	*120*	*190*	*300*	*330*	*360*	*390*	*400*
Year	*1984*	*1985*	*1986*	*1987*	*1988*	*1989*	*1990*		
Index B	*100*	*105*	*90*	*95*	*102*	*110*	*96*		

You are required to splice the Index B to Index A. Then also shift the base to 1986

[*Delhi Univ. B.Com. (Hons.), 2009*]

Solution.

TABLE 10·26 : **INDEX 'B' SPLICED TO INDEX 'A', THEN BASE SHIFTED TO 1986**

Year	*Index A (Base 1976)*	*Index B (Base 1984)*	*Index B Spliced to Index A (Base 1976)*	*New Index (Base 1986)*
(1)	(2)	(3)	$(4) = \frac{400}{100} \times (3) = 4 \times (3)$	$(5) = \frac{100}{360} \times (4)$
1976	100		100	$\frac{100}{3 \cdot 6} = 27 \cdot 78$
1977	110		110	$\frac{110}{3 \cdot 6} = 30 \cdot 56$
1978	120		120	$\frac{120}{3 \cdot 6} = 33 \cdot 33$

1979	190		190	$\frac{190}{3\cdot6} = 52\cdot78$
1980	300		300	$\frac{300}{3\cdot6} = 83\cdot33$
1981	330		330	$\frac{330}{3\cdot6} = 91\cdot67$
1982	360		360	$\frac{360}{3\cdot6} = 100$
1983	390		390	$\frac{390}{3\cdot6} = 108\cdot33$
1984	400	100	$4 \times 100 = 400$	$\frac{400}{3\cdot6} = 111\cdot11$
1985		105	$4 \times 105 = 420$	$\frac{420}{3\cdot6} = 116\cdot67$
1986		90	$4 \times 90 = 360$	$\frac{360}{3\cdot6} = 100$
1987		95	$4 \times 95 = 380$	$\frac{380}{3\cdot6} = 105\cdot56$
1988		102	$4 \times 102 = 408$	$\frac{408}{3\cdot6} = 113\cdot33$
1989		110	$4 \times 110 = 440$	$\frac{440}{3\cdot6} = 122\cdot22$
1990		96	$4 \times 96 = 384$	$\frac{384}{3\cdot6} = 106\cdot67$

Example 10·26. *In 1920, a Statistical Bureau started an index of production based on 1914 with the following results :*

Year	*1914 (Base)*	*1920*	*1929*
Index	*100*	*120*	*200*

In 1936, the Bureau reconstructed the index on a plan with base 1929.

Year	*1929 (Base)*	*1935*
Index	*100*	*150*

In 1936, the Bureau again reconstructed the index on yet another plan with the base year 1935.

Year	*1935 (Base)*	*1939*	*1943*
Index	*100*	*120*	*150*

Obtain a continuous series with the base 1935, by splicing the three series.

Solution. First of all we shall splice the first series (Base 1914) to the second series (Base 1929). In doing so the old index number for 1929, *viz*., 200 becomes 100. Hence, the multiplying factor for splicing is $\frac{100}{200} = 0\cdot5$.

Then we splice with new continuous series (Base 1929) to the third series (Base 1935). Here the old index number of 1935, *viz*., 150 becomes 100. Hence, the multiplying factor for splicing is $\frac{100}{150} = 0\cdot6667$.

TABLE 10·27. **SPLICING OF INDEX NUMBERS**

Year	*First series (Base 1914)*	*First series spliced to second (Base 1929)*	*1st two series spliced to third series (Base 1935)*
1914	100	$\frac{100}{200} \times 100 = 50$	$\frac{100}{150} \times 50 = 33\cdot33$
1920	120	$\frac{100}{200} \times 120 = 60$	$\frac{100}{150} \times 60 = 40\cdot00$
1929	200	100	$\frac{100}{150} \times 100 = 66\cdot67$
1935		150	100
1939			120
1943			150

Example 10.27. *Prepare a special series of index numbers with 1995 = 100, from the following three series of index numbers :*

Year	*1990*	*1991*	*1992*	*1993*	*1994*	*1995*	*1996*
Index A	*100*	*120*	*135*				
Index B			*100*	*115*	*125*	*145*	
Index C						*100*	*110*

[*Delhi Univ. B.A. (Econ. Hons.), 2006*]

Solution.

TABLE 10. 28. **INDEX NUMBER SERIES A AND B SPLICED TO SERIES C**

Year	*Index A*	*Index B*	*Index A spliced to Index B (Base 1992)*	*Index C*	*Indices A and B Spliced to Index C (Base 1995)*
1990	100		$\frac{100}{135} \times 100 = 74{\cdot}07$		$\frac{100}{145} \times 74{\cdot}07 = 51{\cdot}08$
1991	120		$\frac{100}{135} \times 120 = 88{\cdot}89$		$\frac{100}{145} \times 88{\cdot}89 = 61{\cdot}30$
1992	135	100	100		$\frac{100}{145} \times 100 = 68{\cdot}97$
1993		115	115		$\frac{100}{145} \times 115 = 79{\cdot}31$
1994		125	125		$\frac{100}{145} \times 125 = 86{\cdot}21$
1995		145	145	100	100
1996				110	110

10·8·3. Deflating of Index Numbers. Deflating means adjusting, correcting or reducing a value which is inflated. Hence, by deflating of the price index numbers we mean adjusting them after making allowance for the effect of changing price levels. This is particularly desirable in the case of an economy which has inflationary trends because in such an economy, the increase in the prices of commodities or items over a period of years means a fall in their *real incomes* (which is defined as the purchasing power of money), and accordingly a rise in their *money income* or *nominal income* may not amount to a rise in their real income. Thus, it becomes necessary to adjust or correct nominal wages in accordance with the rise in the corresponding price index to arrive at the real income. The purchasing power is given by the reciprocal of the index number and consequently the real income (or wages) is obtained on dividing the money or nominal income by the corresponding appropriate price index and multiplying the result by 100. Symbolically,

$$\text{Real Wages} = \frac{\text{Money or Nominal Wages}}{\text{Price Index}} \times 100 \quad \text{...(10·29)}$$

The real income is also known as *deflated income*.

This technique is extensively used to deflate value series or value indices, rupee sales, inventories, incomes, wages and so on.

Example 10·28. *During a certain period, the consumer price index increased from 110 to 200, and the salary of a worker also increased from 3,500 to 5,000. What is the real gain, if any, to the worker.*

[*Delhi Univ. B.A. (Econ. Hons.), 2009*]

Solution. Real wages in the first period = Rs. $\frac{3{,}500}{110} \times 100$ = Rs. 3,181·82

Real wages in the record (current) period = Rs. $\frac{5{,}000}{200} \times 100$ = Rs. 2,500

Since the real wages have come down from Rs. 3,181·82 in the first period to Rs. 2,500 in the second (current) period, the worker has a real loss of Rs. (3,181·82 – 2,500) = Rs. 681·82.

Example 10·29. *The consumer price index for a group of workers was 250 in 1994 with 1980 as the base.*

(i) Compute the purchasing power of a rupee in 1994 compared to 1980.

(ii) At what value of consumer price index would the purchasing power of a rupee be 25 paise ?

[*Delhi Univ. B.A. (Econ. Hons.), 1998*]

Solution. (*i*) Purchasing power (P.P) of a rupee in 1994 with respect to the base period 1980 is given by :

$$\text{P.P. of a rupee} = \frac{100}{\text{Consumer Price Index for 1994 } w.r.t. \text{ base 1980}} = \text{Rs. } \frac{100}{250} = \text{Re. } 0{\cdot}40. \qquad \ldots(*)$$

This implies that if a person was spending Re. 0·40 (*i.e.*, 40 paise) to buy a certain basket of goods in 1980, in 1994 he has to spend Re. 1 to buy the same basket of goods.

(*ii*) If we want the purchasing power of a rupee to be Re. 0·25 in 1994, then from (*), we get

$$\text{Consumer price index for 1994 with respect to base 1980} = \frac{100}{\text{P.P. of a rupee}} = \frac{100}{0{\cdot}25} = 400.$$

Example 10·30. *The table given below shows the average wages in rupees per week of a group of industrial workers during the years 1980-87. The consumer price indices for these years with 1980 as base are also shown :*

Year	:	*1980*	*1981*	*1982*	*1983*	*1984*	*1985*	*1986*	*1987*
Average Wage of Workers (Rs.)	:	*119*	*133*	*144*	*157*	*175*	*184*	*189*	*194*
Consumer Price Index	:	*100*	*107·6*	*106·6*	*107·6*	*116·2*	*118·9*	*119·8*	*120·2*

(i) Determine the Real Wage of workers during the years 1980-87 as compared with their wages in 1980.

(ii) Determine the purchasing power of Rupee for the year 1987 as compared to the year 1980. What is the significance of this result ? [*Delhi Univ. B.Com. (Hons.),1996*]

Solution. Real wages are obtained on dividing the average wages by the corresponding index number and multiplying by 100, and are given in Table 10·29.

TABLE 10·29. COMPUTATION OF REAL WAGES

Year	*Average wages of workers* (1)	*Consumer price index (Base : 1980 = 100)* (2)	*Real wages of workers* $(3) = \frac{(1)}{(2)} \times 100$
1980	119	100	$\frac{119}{100} \times 100 = 119{\cdot}00$
1981	133	107·6	$\frac{133}{107{\cdot}6} \times 100 = 123{\cdot}61$
1982	144	106·6	$\frac{144}{106{\cdot}6} \times 100 = 135{\cdot}08$
1983	157	107·6	$\frac{157}{107{\cdot}6} \times 100 = 145{\cdot}91$
1984	175	116·2	$\frac{175}{116{\cdot}2} \times 100 = 150{\cdot}60$
1985	184	118·9	$\frac{184}{118{\cdot}9} \times 100 = 154{\cdot}75$
1986	189	119·8	$\frac{189}{119{\cdot}8} \times 100 = 157{\cdot}76$
1987	194	120·2	$\frac{194}{120{\cdot}2} \times 100 = 161{\cdot}39$

The purchasing power of the rupee in any year as compared to the year 1980 is given by the reciprocal of the corresponding consumer price index.

Hence, the purchasing power of rupee in 1987 as compared to the year 1980 = $\frac{100}{120 \cdot 2} = 0 \cdot 83$.

This implies that in 1987 we have to spend Re. 1 for buying a commodity which cost 83 paise in 1980. This means that although the average wage of the worker in 1987 is much more than his wages in 1980, in fact he is not better off than in 1980, since the purchasing power of the rupee has in reality, sloped to Re. 0·83 *i.e.*, eighty-three paise only.

Example 10·31. *The ajoining table gives the annual income of a person and the general price index number for the period 1988 to 1996. Prepare index number to show the changes in the real income of the person.*

[*Delhi Univ. B.Com. (Hons.), 2000*]

Year	*Annual Income in Rs.*	*Price Index Number*
1988	*36,000*	*100*
1989	*42,000*	*120*
1990	*50,000*	*145*
1991	*55,000*	*160*
1992	*60,000*	*250*
1993	*64,000*	*320*
1994	*68,000*	*450*
1995	*72,000*	*530*
1996	*75,000*	*600*

Solution.

TABLE 10·30. **COMPUTATION OF INDICES OF REAL INCOME**

Year (*1*)	*Annual Income* (*in Rs.*) (*2*)	*Price Index Number* (*3*)	*Real Income* $(4) = \frac{(2)}{(3)} \times 100$	*Real Income Indices* (*1988 = 100*) $(5) = \frac{100}{36,000} \times (4)$
1988	36,000	100	$\frac{36,000}{100} \times 100 = 36,000$	100
1989	42,000	120	$\frac{42,000}{120} \times 100 = 35,000$	$\frac{35,000}{36,000} \times 100 = 97 \cdot 22$
1990	50,000	145	$\frac{50,000}{145} \times 100 = 34,482 \cdot 75$	$\frac{34,482 \cdot 75}{36,000} \times 100 = 95 \cdot 78$
1991	55,000	160	$\frac{55,000}{160} \times 100 = 34,375$	$\frac{34,375}{36,000} \times 100 = 95 \cdot 48$
1992	60,000	250	$\frac{60,000}{250} \times 100 = 24,000$	$\frac{24,000}{36,000} \times 100 = 66 \cdot 66$
1993	64,000	320	$\frac{64,000}{320} \times 100 = 20,000$	$\frac{20,000}{36,000} \times 100 = 55 \cdot 55$
1994	68,000	450	$\frac{68,000}{450} \times 100 = 15,111 \cdot 11$	$\frac{15,111 \cdot 11}{36,000} \times 100 = 41 \cdot 97$
1995	72,000	530	$\frac{72,000}{530} \times 100 = 13,589 \cdot 90$	$\frac{13,589 \cdot 90}{36,000} \times 100 = 37 \cdot 75$
1996	75,000	600	$\frac{75,000}{600} \times 100 = 12,500$	$\frac{12,500}{36,000} \times 100 = 34 \cdot 72$

Example 10.32. *The adjoining Table gives data on national income (Rs. '000 crores) and wholesale price index numbers (1981 = 100) :*

Calculate :

(i) the national income at 1981 prices,

(ii) index of real income for each year (base year 1993).

Year	*National Income (Rs. '000 cr.)*	*WPI (1981 = 100)*
1993	*781*	*248*
1994	*914*	*275*
1995	*1067*	*296*
1996	*1237*	*315*
1997	*1384*	*330*
1998	*1612*	*353*

[*Delhi Univ. B.A. (Econ. Hons.), 2007*]

Solution.

TABLE 10·31 : CALCULATIONS FOR INDICES OF REAL INCOME

Years (1)	*N.I (Rs. '000 Cr.)* (2)	*WPI (1981 = 100)* (3)	*N.I (Rs. '000 Cr.) at 1981 Prices* $(4) = \frac{100 \times (2)}{(3)}$	*Index of Real Income (Base 1993 = 100)* $(5) = \frac{100}{315} \times (4) = 0{\cdot}3175 \times (4)$
1993	781	248	$\frac{781}{248} \times 100 \simeq 315$	100
1994	914	275	$\frac{914}{275} \times 100 \simeq 332$	105
1995	1067	296	$\frac{1067}{296} \times 100 \simeq 360$	114
1996	1237	315	$\frac{1237}{315} \times 100 \simeq 393$	125
1997	1384	330	$\frac{1384}{330} \times 100 \simeq 419$	133
1998	1612	353	$\frac{1612}{353} \times 100 \simeq 457$	145

EXERCISE 10·4

1. What is 'base shifting' ? Why does it become necessary to shift the base of index numbers ? Give an example of the shifting of base of index numbers.

2. Explain, with examples, the shifting and splicing techniques in index numbers. [*C.A.* (*Foundation*), *May 1996*]

3. The following are price index numbers (Base 1985 = 100)

Year :	1985	1986	1987	1988	1989	1990	1991	1992	1993	1994	1995
Index No. :	100	120	122	116	120	120	137	136	149	156	137

Shift the base to 1990 and recast the index numbers.

Ans. 83·33, 100, 101·67, 96·67, 100, 100, 114·17, 113·33, 124·17, 130·00, 114·17.

4. The following are the index numbers of wholesale prices of a certain commodity based on 1992 :

Year :	1992	1993	1994	1995	1996
Index No. :	100	108	120	150	210

Shift the base to 1994 and obtain new index numbers.

Ans. 83·33, 90, 100, 125, 175.

5. In the following series of index numbers shift the base from 1990 to 1993.

Year :	1990	1991	1992	1993	1994	1995	1996	1997
Index No. :	100	105	110	125	135	180	195	205

Ans. 80, 84, 88, 100, 108, 144, 156, 164.

6. The following are the index numbers of prices based on 1997 prices. Shift the base from 1997 to 2001 :

Year :	1997	1998	1999	2000	2001	2002	2003	2004	2005
Index Number :	100	140	260	340	400	450	500	260	240

[*Delhi Univ. B.A.* (*Econ. Hons.*), *2008*]

Ans. (Base 2001 = 100) : 25, 35, 65, 85, 100, 112·50, 125, 65, 60.

7. Given below are two sets of indices one with 1985 as base and the other with 1992 as base :

(*a*) *Year*	*Index No.*	(*b*) *Year*	*Index No.*
1985	100	1992	100
1986	115	1993	105
1987	122	1994	118
1988	150	1995	98
1989	200	1996	102
1990	220	1997	105
1991	240	1998	120
1992	250	1999	125

The index number (*a*) with 1985 base was discontinued in 1992. It is desired to splice the second index number (*b*) with 1992 base to the first index number for the sake of continuity. How will it be done so that the combined series has a common base of 1985 ?

Ans.	1985	1986	...	1992	1993	1994	1995	1996	1997	1998	1999
	100	115	...	250	262·5	295	245	255	262·5	300	312·5

8. Given below are two sets of indices. For the purpose of continuity of records, you are required to construct a combined series with the year 1983 as the base :

Year	*I set — Price Relatives*	*II set — Link Relatives*
1980	100	
1981	120	
1982	125	
1983	150	
1984		110
1985		120
1986		95
1987		105

[*Delhi Univ. B.Com. (Hons.), 1999*]

Ans. I. No.'s from 1980 to 1987 (Base 1983 = 100) are : 66·7, 80, 83·3, 100, 110, 120, 95, 105.

9. Combine the two series of index numbers given below to obtain a new series with (*i*) 1963 = 100, (*ii*) 1960 = 100.

WHOLESALE PRICE INDEX

Year	*Old Series 1958 = 100*	*Revised Series 1963 = 100*
1960	111	—
1961	113	—
1962	115	—
1963	119	100
1964	134	112
1965	—	122

State the assumptions underlying your calculations. [*Delhi Univ. B.A. (Econ. Hons.), 1990*]

Ans. (*i*) 93·27, 94·95, 96·63, 100, 112, 122;

(*ii*) 100, 101·80, 103·60, 107·21, 120·72, 131·50* $\left[(*) : \frac{134 \times 122}{112} \times \frac{100}{111} = 131\cdot50 \right]$.

10. Given below are two index number series. Splice them on the base 1974 = 100.

Year		*1970*	*1971*	*1972*	*1973*	*1974*	*1975*
Old Price Index for Steel (Base 1965 = 100)	:	141·5	163·7	158·2	156·8	157·1	
New Price Index (Base 1974 = 100) :					99·8	100·0	102·3

[*Delhi Univ. B.A. (Econ. Hons.), 2000*]

Ans.	*Year* :	1970	1971	1972	1973	1974	1975
	I. No. :	90·06	104·20	100·69	99·80	100	102·3

11. (*a*) A firm in a certain industry has an index of material prices based on movements in the prices of selected materials weighted by the quantities consumed in the base year. The price index series based on 1980 = 100, for the years 1990 - 1995 was as follows :

1990	1991	1992	1993	1994	1995
120·3	122·1	126·4	125·2	127·0	131·6

In 1995, the index was completely revised to take into account a change in the type of materials used. The new index, based on 1995 = 100, showed the following values :

1995	1996	1997
100	106·3	109·4

(*i*) Splice the new index to the old, *i.e.*, splice 'forward'; (*ii*) Splice the old index to the new, *i.e.*, splice 'backward'.

Ans. (*i*)	1996	1997	(*ii*)	1990	1991	1992	1993	1994
	139·9	144		91·4	92·8	96·0	95·1	96·5

(b) What are the uses of 'base shifting' of an Index Number series ? Prepare a spliced series of index numbers with 2003 as base from the following series :

Years	1998	1999	2000	2001	2002	2003	2004
Index A	100	120	135				
Index B			100	115	125	145	
Index C						100	110

[Delhi Univ. B.Com. (Hons.), (External), 2005]

Ans.

Year	1996	1999	2000	2001	2002	2003	2004
Splicing indices A and B to C (Base 2003)	51·08	61·30	68·97	79·31	86·21	100	110

12. (a) What is meant by (i) base shifting, (ii) splicing and deflating of index numbers ? Explain and illustrate.

(b) What do you understand by deflating of index numbers ? What is the need for deflating the index numbers ? Illustrate your answer with the help of an example.

13. (a) Explain how index number is used to measure the purchasing power of money.

(b) What do you understand by deflating of index numbers ? Illustrate your answer with the help of an example.

14. Given the following data :

Year	:	1995	1996	1997	1998	1999	2000	2001
Monthly Pay (Rs.)	:	10,500	11,000	11,500	12,500	13,500	14,000	14,500
Price Index	:	115	120	130	138	144	150	160

(i) Calculate the real monthly pay for each year.

(ii) In which year did the emploree have the highest purchasing power ?

(iii) Whar percentage increase in the monthly pay for the year 2001 is required (if any) to compensate him with the purchasing power in the year of this highest real pay ? [Delhi Univ. B.Com. (Hons.), 2007]

Ans. (i)

Year :	1995	1996	1997	1998	1999	2000	2001
Real Monthly pay (Rs.)	9130·43	9166·67	8846·15	9057·97	9375·00	9333·33	9062·50

(ii) Highest purchasing power corresponds to the year 1999, which is the year of highest real wages (Rs. 9375·00)

(iii) Required monthly increase in pay in 2001 = $\left(\dfrac{9375{\cdot}00 - 9062{\cdot}50}{9062{\cdot}50}\right) \times 100\% = 3{\cdot}448\%$

15. Mean monthly wages (x) and cost of living index numbers (y) for the years 1990 to 1995 are given below :

Year :	1990	1991	1992	1993	1994	1995
Rs. x :	360	400	480	520	550	590
y :	100	104	115	160	210	260

In which year the real income was (i) the highest, (ii) the lowest ?

Ans. (i) 1992, (ii) 1995.

16. The table below shows the average wages in rupees per day of a group of industrial workers during the years 1960-1971. The consumer price indices for these years with Base (1960 = 100) are also shown.

(a) Determine the Real Wages of the workers during the years 1960-1971 as compared with their wages in 1960.

Year :	1960	1961	1962	1963	1964	1965	1966	1967	1968	1969	1970	1971
Average wage of workers :	1·19	1·33	1·44	1·57	1·75	1·84	1·89	1·94	1·97	2·13	2·28	2·45
Consumer price index :	100	107·6	106·6	107·6	116·2	118·8	119·8	120·2	119·9	121·7	125·9	129·3

(b) Determine the purchasing power of the Rupee for the year 1971 as compared to the year 1960. What is the significance of this result ?

Ans. (a) Real wages (in Rs.) for 1960 to 1971 :

1·19, 1·24, 1·35, 1·46, 1·51, 1·55, 1·58, 1·61, 1·64, 1·75, 1·81, 1·89.

(b) Re. 0·77.

16. The following data relate to the average weekly income of workers and the price index :

Years	1995	1996	1997	1998	1999	2000
Weekly Income (Rs.)	800	819	825	876	920	924
Price Index (1995 = 100)	100	105	110	120	125	135

Calculate real income of workers during the years 1995 to 2000. *[Delhi Univ. B.A. (Econ. Hons.), 2007]*

Ans. Real Income (Rs.) : 800, 780, 750, 730, 736, 684.

17. The following data relate to the income of the people and General Index Number of Prices of a certain region. Calculate —

(*i*) Real income, and (*ii*) Index Numbers of Real Income with 1983 as base.

Year	:	1983	1984	1985	1986	1987	1988	1989
Income (in '00 Rs.)	:	800	819	825	876	920	938	924
General Price Index Number	:	100	105	110	120	125	140	140
Ans. Real Wages	:	800,	780,	750,	730,	736,	670,	660
I. No. of Real Wages	:	100,	97·5,	93·75,	91·25,	92,	83·75,	82·5

18. Given the following data :

Year	:	2000	2001	2002	2003
Monthly Pay (Rs.)	:	22,500	23,500	24,000	24,500
Price Index	:	142	148	155	162

(*i*) Calculate the real monthly income for each year.

(*ii*) Calculate the index of real wages for each year with 2,000 as base year.

[Delhi Univ. B.A. (Econ. Hons.), 2009]

Ans. (*i*) Real Wages (in Rs.)	:	15845	15878	15484	15123
(*ii*) Indices of Real Wages (2000 = 100)	:	1009	100·21	97·72	95·44

19. The employees of an American Company have presented the following data in support of their contention that they are entitled to a wage adjustment. Dollar amounts shown represent the average weekly take-home pay of the group.

Year	:	1983	1984	1985	1986
Pay	:	240	250	260	280
Index	:	120	150	160	200

(*i*) Compute the real wages.

(*ii*) Compute the amount of pay needed in 1986 to provide buying power equal to that enjoyed in 1983.

[Delhi Univ. B.A. (Econ. Hons.), 1995]

Ans. (*i*) Year :	1983	1984	1985	1986
Real Wages (Dollars) :	200	166·67	162·50	140

(*ii*) $\frac{240}{120} \times 200$ Dollars = 400 Dollars.

20. The following data gives the average monthly income of a teacher and general index of price during 1990-97. Prepare the index number to show that change in the real income of the teacher and comment on price increase.

Year	:	1990	1991	1992	1993	1994	1995	1996	1997
Income	:	4,000	4,400	4,800	5,200	5,600	6,000	6,400	6,800
Index	:	100	130	160	220	270	330	400	490

[Himachal Pradesh Univ. B.Com., 1997]

Ans. Real Income Indices (Base 1990 = 100) :

100·00, 84·62, 75·00, 59·09, 51·85, 45·45, 40·00, 34·69.

10·9. COST OF LIVING INDEX NUMBER

The wholesale price index numbers measure the changes in the general level of prices and they fail to reflect the effect of the increase or decrease of prices on the cost of living of different classes or groups of people in a society. Cost of living index numbers, also termed as *'Consumer Price Index Numbers*, or

'*Retail Price Index Numbers*' are designed to measure the effects of changes in the prices of a basket of goods and services on the purchasing power of a particular section or class of the society during any given (*current*) period *w.r.t.* some fixed (*base*) period. They reflect upon the average increase in the cost of the commodities consumed by a class of people so that they can maintain the same standard of living in the current year as in the base year. Due to the wide variations in the tastes, customs and fashions of different sections or classes of people, their consumption patterns of various commodities also differ widely from class to class or group to group (like poor, lower income group, high income group, labour class, industrial workers, agricultural workers) and even within the same class or group from region to region (rural, urban, plane, hills, etc.). Accordingly, the price movements affect these people (belonging to different class or group or region) differently. Hence, to study the effect of rise or fall in the prices of various commodities consumed by a particular group or class of people on their cost of living, the '*cost of living*' Index Numbers are constructed separately for different classes of people or groups or sections of the society and also for different geographical areas like town, city, rural area, urban area, hilly area and so on.

Remark. It should be clearly understood that the cost of living index numbers measure the changes in the cost of living or purchasing power of a particular class of people due to the movements (rise or fall) in the retail prices only. They do not measure the changes in the cost of living as a consequence of changes in the living standards. The cost of living index numbers should not be interpreted as a measure of '*Standard of Living*'. Cost of living index numbers are based on (retail) prices and price is a factor which affects the purchasing power of the class of the people. But price of the commodities or consumer goods is only one of the various factors on which the standard of living of people depends, some other factors being family size, its age and sex-wise composition, its income and occupation, place, region, etc., none of which is taken into account while computing the cost of living index number. Accordingly, the Sixth International Conference of Labour Statisticians held under the auspices of the International Labour Organisation (I.L.O.) in 1949 recommended the replacement of term '*Cost of Living*' index by a more appropriate term "*Consumer Price Index*' or '*Retail Price Index*'.

10·9·1. Main Steps in the Construction of Cost of Living Index Numbers

(*a*) **Scope and Coverage.** As in the case of any index number, the first step in the construction of cost of living index numbers is to specify clearly the class of people (low income, high income, labour class, industrial worker, agricultural worker, etc.), for whom the index is desired. In addition to the class of people, the geographical area such as rural area, urban area, city or town, or a locality of a town, etc., should also be clearly defined. The class should form, as far as possible, a homogeneous group *w.r.t.* income.

Remark. As already pointed out, the cost of living index is intended to study the variations in the cost of living (due to the price movements) of a particular class of people living in a particular region. For example, we can't construct a single cost of living index number for, say, low income class for the whole country because there is wide variation in the retail prices of commodities and the consumption pattern of this class of people in different regions (states) of the country. Thus, the relative importance of different commodities will be different in different regions. For example, in Bengal rice and fish are relatively more important as compared with wheat and meat. Accordingly the '*class of people*' together with their region or place of stay should be clearly specified.

(*b*) **Family Budget Enquiry.** After step (*a*), the next step is to conduct a sample *family budget enquiry*. This is done by selecting a sample of adequate number of representative families from the class of people for whom the index is designed. The enquiry should be conducted in a normal period of economic stability. The objective of the enquiry is to find out the expenses which an average family (of the given class) incurs on different items of consumption. The enquiry furnishes the information on the following points :

1. *The nature, quality and quantity of the commodities consumed by given class of people.*

The commodities are broadly classified into the following five major groups.

(*i*) Food. (*ii*) Clothing. (*iii*) Fuel and Lighting. (*iv*) House Rent. and (*v*) Miscellaneous.

Each of these major groups is further sub-divided into smaller groups termed as *sub-groups*. For instance, the group 'Food' may be sub-divided into cereals (wheat, rice, pulses, etc.) ; meat, fish and poultry ; milk and milk products ; fats and oils ; fruits and vegetables ; condiments and spices ; sugar ; nonalcoholic beverages ; pan, supari and tobacco, etc. Similarly, 'Clothing' may cover clothing, bedding, foot-wear, etc. The last item 'Miscellaneous' includes items like medical care, education and reading, amusement and recreation, gifts and charities, transport and communication, household requisites, personal care and effects and so on. It, however, does not include non-consumption money transactions such as payments towards provident fund, insurance premiums, purchase of savings certificates and bonds, etc.

The procedure of selection of commodities for the construction of the index has been discussed in detail in § 10·4. Care should be taken to include only those items or commodities which are primarily consumed by the given class of people for whom the index is to be constructed.

2. *The retail prices of different commodities selected for the index.* The price quotations for the selected commodities should be obtained from 'local markets' where the class of people reside or from super bazar, fair-price shops or cooperative stores or departmental stores from where they usually do their shopping. [For details see § 10·4.]

3. From the prices of the commodities and their quantities consumed, we can obtain :

(*i*) The expenditure on each item (in a group) expressed as a ratio of the expenditure on the whole group, and

(*ii*) The expenditure on each group expressed as a proportion of the expenditure on all the groups.

10·9·2. Construction of Cost of Living Index Numbers. As already pointed out, the relative importance of different items of consumption is different for different classes or groups of people and even within the same class from region to region. Accordingly, the cost of living indices are obtained as weighted indices, by taking into consideration the relative importance of the commodities which is decided on the basis of the amount spent on various items. The cost of living index numbers are constructed by the following methods :

Method 1. *Aggregate Expenditure Method or Weighted Aggregate Method.* In this method, the quantities consumed in the base year are used as weights. Thus in the usual notations :

$$\text{Cost of Living Index} = \frac{\Sigma p_1 q_0}{\Sigma p_0 q_0} \times 100 \qquad \ldots(10\cdot30)$$

$$= \frac{\text{Total expenditure in current year}}{\text{Total expenditure in base year}} \times 100,$$

total expenditure in current year is obtained with base year quantities as weights.

Formula (10·30) is nothing but *Laspeyre's price index.*

Method 2. *Family Budget Method or Method of Weighted Relatives.* In this method the cost of living index is obtained on taking the weighted average of price-relatives, the weights being the values of the quantities consumed in the base year. Thus, if we write

$$I = \text{Price Relative} = \frac{p_1}{p_0} \times 100 \quad \text{and} \quad W = p_0 q_0, \text{ then}$$

$$\text{Cost of Living Index} = \frac{\Sigma WI}{\Sigma W} \qquad \ldots(10\cdot31)$$

Substituting the values of W and I, we get

$$\text{Cost of Living Index} = \frac{\Sigma p_0 q_0 \left(\frac{p_1}{p_0} \times 100\right)}{\Sigma p_0 q_0} = \frac{\Sigma p_1 q_0}{\Sigma p_0 q_0} \times 100$$

which is same as (10·30).

Remark. Thus we see that the cost of living index numbers obtained by both the methods are same.

10·9·3. Uses of Cost of Living Index Numbers.

1. Cost of living index numbers are used to determine the purchasing power of money and for computing the real wages (income) from the nominal or money wages (income). We have :

$$\text{Purchasing Power of Money} = \frac{1}{\text{Cost of Living Index Number}} \quad \ldots (10{\cdot}31a)$$

$$\text{Real Wages} = \frac{\text{Money Wages}}{\text{Cost of Living Index}} \times 100 \quad \ldots (10{\cdot}31b)$$

Thus, cost of living index number enables us to find if the real wages are rising or falling, the money wages remaining unchanged.

2. The Government (Central and / or State) and many big industrial and business units use the cost of living index numbers to regulate the dearness allowance (D.A.) or grant of bonus to the employees in order to compensate them for increased cost of living due to price rise. They are used by the government for the formulation of price policy, wage policy and general economic policies.

3. Cost of living indices are used for deflating income and value series in national accounts. [For details see § 10·8·3—Deflation of Index Numbers.]

4. Cost of living index numbers are used widely in wage negotiations and wage contracts. For example, they are used for automatic adjustment of wages under *'Escalator Clauses'* in collective bargaining agreements. Escalator clause provides for certain point automatic increase in the wages corresponding to a unit increase in the consumer price index.

Example 10·33. *In the construction of a certain Cost of Living Index Number, the following group index numbers were found. Calculate the Cost of Living Index Number by using :*

(i) the weighted arithmetic mean, and (ii) the weighted geometric mean.

Group	*Food*	*Fuel and Lighting*	*Clothing*	*House Rent*	*Miscellaneous*
Index Numbers	*350*	*200*	*240*	*160*	*250*
Weights	*5*	*1*	*1*	*1*	*2*

Solution.

TABLE 10·32. **COMPUTATION OF CONSUMER PRICE INDEX USING A.M. AND G.M.**

Group	*Index Number (I)*	*Weights (W)*	*WI*	*log I*	*W log I*
Food	350	5	1750	2·5441	12·7205
Fuel and Lighting	200	1	200	2·3010	2·3010
Clothing	240	1	240	2·3802	2·3802
House Rent	160	1	160	2·2041	2·2041
Miscellaneous	250	2	500	2·3979	4·7958
		$\Sigma W = 10$	$\Sigma WI = 2850$		$\Sigma W \log I = 24{\cdot}4016$

The consumer price index using Arithmetic Mean = $P_{01}\text{ (A.M.)} = \dfrac{\Sigma WI}{\Sigma W} = \dfrac{2850}{10} = 285$

Using Geometric Mean, the consumer price index is given by :

$$\log P_{01}\text{ (G.M.)} = \frac{\Sigma W \log I}{\Sigma W} = \frac{24{\cdot}4016}{10} = 2{\cdot}4401 \quad \Rightarrow \quad P_{01}\text{ (G.M.)} = \text{Antilog } (2{\cdot}4401) = 275{\cdot}4$$

Example 10·34. *Calculate the Cost of Living Index Number from the following data :*

Items	*Price*		*Weights*
	Base Year	*Current Year*	
Food	*30*	*47*	*4*
Fuel	*8*	*12*	*1*
Clothing	*14*	*18*	*3*
House Rent	*22*	*15*	*2*
Miscellaneous	*25*	*30*	*1*

Solution.

TABLE 10·33. **CALCULATIONS FOR COST OF LIVING INDEX NUMBER**

Items	*Weights (W)*	*Prices*		*Price Relatives*	
		Base Year (p_0)	*Current Year* (p_1)	$P = \frac{p_1}{p_0} \times 100$	*WP*
Food	4	30	47	156·67	626·67
Fuel	1	8	12	150·00	150·00
Clothing	3	14	18	128·57	385·71
House Rent	2	22	15	68·18	136·36
Miscellaneous	1	25	30	120·00	120·00
	$\Sigma W = 11$				$\Sigma WP = 1418{\cdot}74$

$$\text{Cost of Living Index Number} = \frac{\Sigma WP}{\Sigma W} = \frac{1418{\cdot}74}{11} = 128{\cdot}98.$$

Example 10·35. *In 1981 for working class people wheat was selling at an average price of Rs. 16 per 10 kg., cloth at Rs. 4 per metre, house rent at Rs. 50 per house and miscellaneous items at Rs. 20 per unit. By 1991 cost of wheat rose by Rs. 8 per 10 kg., house rent by Rs. 30 per house and miscellaneous items doubled the price. The weights of the groups in order were in the ratio 1 : 2 : 4 : 1. The working class cost of living index number for the year 1991 with 1981 as base was 175%. By how much cloth price rose during the period 1981-91 ?* [*I.C.W.A. (Intermediate), June 2001*]

Solution. Let us suppose that the cloth price in 1991 was Rs. x per metre and let the weights for the four groups : Wheat, Cloth, House Rent and Miscellaneous be k, $2k$, $4k$ and k respectively, so that they are in the ratio 1 : 2 : 4 : 1.

TABLE 10·34. **CALCULATIONS FOR COST OF LIVING INDEX NO.**

Group	*Unit*	*Price*		*Weight*	$P = \frac{p_1}{p_0} \times 100$	*W P*
		1981 (p_0)	*1991* (p_1)	(*W*)		
Wheat	10 kg.	16	16 + 8 = 24	k	150	150 k
Cloth	1 metre	4	x	2 k	25x	50 xk
House Rent	1 house	50	50 + 30 = 80	4 k	160	640 k
Miscellaneous	1 unit	20	2 × 20 = 40	k	200	200 k
Total				$\Sigma W = 8k$		$\Sigma\ WP = (990\,k + 50\,x\,k)$

Cost of living index number for 1991 with 1981 as base is given by

$$\frac{\Sigma WP}{\Sigma W} = 175 \quad \text{(Given)} \quad \Rightarrow \quad \frac{(990 + 50x)\,k}{8\,k} = 175$$

$$\therefore \quad 990 + 50x = 175 \times 8 \quad \Rightarrow \quad x = \frac{1400 - 990}{50} = \frac{410}{50} = 8{\cdot}20$$

Hence, during the period 1981-91, the price of the cloth rose by :

$$\text{Rs. } (x - 4) = \text{Rs. } (8{\cdot}20 - 4) = \text{Rs. } 4{\cdot}20 \text{ per metre.}$$

Example 10·36. *In calculating a certain cost of living index no. the following weights were used : Food 15, Clothing 3, Rent 4, Fuel and Light 2, Miscellaneous 1. Calculate the index for a date when the average percentage increases in prices of items in the various groups over the base period were 32, 54, 47, 78 and 58 respectively.*

Suppose a business executive was earning Rs. 2,050 in the base period. What should be his salary in the current period if his standard of living is to remain the same ? [*Delhi Univ. B.Com. (Pass), 1998*]

Solution. The current index number for each item is obtained on adding 100 to the percentage increase in price.

TABLE 10·35. **CALCULATIONS FOR COST OF LIVING INDEX**

Group (1)	*Average % increase in price* (2)	*Group Index (I)* (3) = 100 + (2)	*Weight* (W)	*WI*
Food	32	132	15	1,980
Clothing	54	154	3	462
Rent	47	147	4	588
Fuel and Light	78	178	2	356
Miscellaneous	58	158	1	158
			$\Sigma W = 25$	$\Sigma WI = 3{,}544$

$$\text{Cost of Living Index} = \frac{\Sigma WI}{\Sigma W} = \frac{3{,}544}{25} = 141{\cdot}76.$$

This implies that if a person was getting Rs. 100 in the base year, then in order to fully compensate the business executive for rise in prices, his salary in the current period should be Rs. 141·76. Hence, if a business executive was earning Rs. 2,050 in the base period, his salary in the current period should be :

$$\text{Rs. } \frac{141{\cdot}76}{100} \times 2{,}050 = \text{Rs. } 2{,}906{\cdot}08$$

in order to enable him to maintain the same standard of living *w.r.t.* price rise, other factors remaining constant.

Example 10·37. *A textile worker in the city of Mumbai earns Rs. 3500 per month. The cost of living index for a particular month is given as 136. Using the following data, find out the amounts he spent on house rent and clothing.*

Group	*Expenditure*	*Group Index*
Food	*1400*	*180*
Clothing	*?*	*150*
House Rent	*?*	*100*
Fuel and Lighting	*560*	*110*
Miscellaneous	*630*	*80*

[*Delhi Univ. B.Com. (Hons.), 1997*]

Solution. Let the expenditure on house rent, and fuel and lighting be Rs. x and Rs. y respectively.

TABLE 10·36. **COMPUTATION OF COST OF LIVING INDEX**

Group	*Expenditure* (W)	*Group Index (I)*	*WI*
Food	1400	180	252000
Clothing	x	150	$150x$
House Rent	y	100	$100y$
Fuel and Lighting	560	110	61600
Miscellaneous	630	80	50400
		$\Sigma W = 3500 = x + y + 2590$	$\Sigma WI = 364000 + 150x + 100y$

$$\text{Cost of living index} = \frac{\Sigma WI}{\Sigma W} = \frac{364000 + 150x + 100y}{3500} = 136 \quad \text{(Given)}$$

$\Rightarrow$ $364000 + 150x + 100y = 136 \times 3500 = 476000$

$\Rightarrow$ $150x + 100y = 476000 - 364000 = 112000$ ...(*)

Also $\Sigma W = x + y + 2590 = 3500$ (Given) $\Rightarrow$ $x + y = 3500 - 2590 = 910$ ...(**)

Multiplying (**) by 100, we get $100x + 100y = 91000$ ...(***)

Subtracting (***) from (*), we have : $50x = 112000 - 91000 = 21000 \Rightarrow x = \frac{21000}{50} = 420$

Substituting in (**), we get $y = 910 - x = 910 - 420 = 490$

Hence, the worker spent Rs. 420 on clothing and Rs. 490 on house rent.

Example 10·38. (*a*)*The data below show the percentage increase in price of a few selected food items and the weights attached to each of them. Calculate the index number for the food group.*

Food items	:	*Rice*	*Wheat*	*Dal*	*Ghee*	*Oil*	*Spices*	*Milk*	*Fish*	*Veget-ables*	*Refres-hments*
Weight	:	*33*	*11*	*8*	*5*	*5*	*3*	*7*	*9*	*9*	*10*
Percentage increase in price	:	*180*	*202*	*115*	*212*	*175*	*517*	*260*	*426*	*332*	*279*

(*b*) *Using the above food index and the information given below, calculate the cost of living index number.*

Group	:	*Food*	*Clothing*	*Fuel & Light*	*Rent & Rates*	*Miscellaneous*
Index	:	—	*310*	*220*	*150*	*300*
Weight	:	*60*	*5*	*8*	*9*	*18*

[*Delhi Univ. B.Com. (Hons.), 2006*]

Solution. The current index number for each item is obtained on adding 100 to the percentage increase in price.

TABLE 10·37 (*a*)
CALCULATIONS FOR FOOD INDEX

Food items	*Weight (W)*	*Percentage increase*	*Current Index (I)*	*WI*
Rice	33	180	280	9,240
Wheat	11	202	302	3,322
Dal	8	115	215	1,720
Ghee	5	212	312	1,560
Oil	5	175	275	1,375
Spices	3	517	617	1,851
Milk	7	260	360	2,520
Fish	9	426	526	4,734
Vegetables	9	332	432	3,888
Refreshments	10	279	379	3,790
Total	$\Sigma W = 100$	—	—	$\Sigma WI =$ 34,000

TABLE 10·37 (*b*). **CALCULATIONS FOR COST OF LIVING INDEX**

Group	*Index* (I_1)	*Weight* (W_1)	W_1I_1
Food	340	60	20,400
Clothing	310	5	1,550
Fuel and Light	220	8	1,760
Rent and Rates	150	9	1,350
Miscellaneous	300	18	5,400
Total		$\Sigma W_1 = 100$	$\Sigma W_1I_1 =$ 30,460

(*a*) Index number for the food group $= \dfrac{\Sigma WI}{\Sigma W} = \dfrac{34000}{100} = 340$;

(*b*) Cost of Living Index $= \dfrac{\Sigma W_1I_1}{\Sigma W_1} = \dfrac{30460}{100} = 304{\cdot}6$

Example 10·39. *From the following data relating to working class consumer price index of a city, calculate index numbers for 1998 and 1999.*

Group	:	*Food*	*Clothing*	*Fuel and Lighting*	*House Rent*	*Miscellaneous*
Weights	:	*48*	*18*	*7*	*13*	*14*
Group Indices 1998	:	*110*	*120*	*110*	*100*	*110*
Group Indices 1999	:	*130*	*125*	*120*	*100*	*135*

The wages were increased by 8% in 1999. Is this increase sufficient ?

Solution.

TABLE 10·38. **COMPUTATION OF INDEX NUMBERS FOR 1998 AND 1999**

Group	*Weights (W)*	*Group Indices 1998 (I_1)*	*Group Indices 1999 (I_2)*	WI_1	WI_2
Food	48	110	130	5280	6240
Clothing	18	120	125	2160	2250
Fuel and Lighting	7	110	120	770	840
House Rent	13	100	100	1300	1300
Miscellaneous	14	110	135	1540	1890
	$\Sigma W = 100$			$\Sigma WI_1 = 11050$	$\Sigma WI_2 = 12520$

Index number for 1998 = $\frac{\Sigma WI_1}{\Sigma W} = \frac{11050}{100} = 110{\cdot}5$; Index number for 1999 = $\frac{\Sigma WI_2}{\Sigma W} = \frac{12520}{100} = 125{\cdot}20$

Hence, increase in the consumer price number from 1998 to 1999 is 125·2 – 110·5 = 14·7

Hence, the percentage increase in the price index for 1999 is $\frac{14{\cdot}7}{110{\cdot}5} \times 100 = 13{\cdot}3$.

Therefore, an increase of 8% in the wages in 1999 is insufficient to maintain the same standard of living as in 1998.

Example 10·40. *An enquiry into the budgets of the middle class families of a certain city revealed that on an average the percentage expenses on the different groups were :*

Food 45, Rent 15, Clothing 12, Fuel and Light 8, Miscellaneous 20.

The group index numbers for the current year as compared with a fixed base period were respectively 410, 150, 343, 248 and 285. Calculate the Cost of Living Index Number for the current year.

Mr. X was getting Rs. 2,400 in the base period and Rs. 4,300 in the current year. State how much he ought to have received as extra allowance to maintain his former standard of living.

Solution. The percentage expenses on different groups may be regarded as the weights attached to them.

Cost of living index is given by :

$$\frac{\Sigma WI}{\Sigma W} = \frac{45 \times 410 + 15 \times 150 + 12 \times 343 + 8 \times 248 + 20 \times 285}{45 + 15 + 12 + 8 + 20} = \frac{32{,}500}{100} = 325$$

This implies that if a person was getting Rs. 100 in the base year then, in order that he is fully compensated for rise in prices, his salary in the current year should be Rs. 325. Hence, if Mr. X was getting Rs. 2,400 in the base year, his salary in the current period should be

$$\text{Rs. } \frac{325}{100} \times 2{,}400 = \text{Rs. } 7{,}800 \text{ p.m.}$$

in order to enable him to maintain the same standard of living *w.r.t.* rise in prices, other factors remaining constant. But current salary of Mr. X is given to be Rs. 4,300. Hence, he ought to receive an extra allowance of Rs. 7,800 – 4,300 = Rs. 3,500 to maintain the same standard of living as in the base year.

Example 10·41. *The following table gives the cost of living index number for 1998 with 1986 as base for different commodity groups :*

Food, Clothings, Fuel and Light, Rent and Miscellaneous as 440, 500, 350, 400 and 250 respectively with their weights in order in the ratio 15 : 1 : 2 : 3 : 4.

Obtain the overall cost of living index number. Suppose a person was earning Rs. 4,000 in 1986. What should be his salary in 1998 to maintain the same standard of living as in 1986 ?

[*I.C.W.A. (Intermediate), June 2000*]

Solution. Since the weights for the commodity groups : Food, Clothings, Fuel and Light, Rent, and Miscellaneous are given to be in the ratio 15 : 1 : 2 : 3 : 4 respectively, let the corresponding weights be $15x$, x, $2x$, $3x$ and $4x$ respectively.

TABLE 10·39.

COMPUTATION OF OVERALL C.O.L. INDEX NUMBER

Commodity Group	*C.O.L. index for 1998 w.r.t. base 1986 (I)*	*Weights (W)*	$W \times I$
Food	440	$15x$	$6600x$
Clothings	500	x	$500x$
Fuel and Light	350	$2x$	$700x$
Rent	400	$3x$	$1200x$
Miscellaneous	250	$4x$	$1000x$
		$\Sigma W = 25x$	$\Sigma WI = 10{,}000x$

Overall Cost of Living Index Number for 1998 with respect to base year 1986 is given by :

$$\frac{\Sigma WI}{\Sigma W} = \frac{10{,}000x}{25x} = 400.$$

This implies that if a person was getting Rs. 100 in the base year (1986), in order that he is fully compensated for rise in prices, his salary in the current period (1998) should be Rs. 400. Hence, if a person was earning Rs. 4,000 in 1986, then his salary in 1998 should be :

$$\text{Rs. } \frac{400}{100} \times 4{,}000 = \text{Rs. } 16{,}000$$

in order to enable him to maintain the same standard of living *w.r.t.* rise in prices, other factors remaining constant.

Example 10·42. *In a working class consumer price index number of a particular town, the weights corresponding to different groups of items were as follows :*

Food — 55, Fuel — 15, Clothing — 10, Rent — 12 and Miscellaneous — 8.

In Oct. 1999, the D.A. was fixed by a mill of that town at 182 per cent for the workers which fully compensated for the rise in prices of food and rent but did not compensate for anything else. Another mill of the same town paid D.A. of 46·5 per cent which compensated for the rise in fuel and miscellaneous groups. It is known that rise in food is double than that of fuel and the rise in miscellaneous group is double that of rent.

Find the rise in food, fuel, rent and miscellaneous groups. [*Delhi Univ. B.Com. (Hons.), 2002*]

Solution. Let us suppose that the percentage rise in fuel is x and in rent is y. Then we are given that the percentage increase in food is $2x$ and in the miscellaneous group is $2y$. Since nothing is mentioned about rise in clothing group we presume that it is unaffected *i.e.*, the current index for clothing remains same as in base year *viz*., 100.

First Mill. Since the first mill announced D.A. of 182%, the current index obtained is 100 + 182 = 282. Further, since the mill fully compensated the workers for rise in prices of food and rent only and not the other groups, the group index used for food was $(100 + 2x)$ and for rent was $(100 + y)$. Hence, taking the indices of other groups as 100 each, the consumer price index is given by

$$\frac{\Sigma WI}{\Sigma W} = \frac{55(100+2x) + 15 \times 100 + 10 \times 100 + 12(100+y) + 8 \times 100}{100} = 282$$

$$\Rightarrow \quad 110x + 12y + 100 \times 100 = 282 \times 100 \quad \Rightarrow \quad 110x + 12y = 18{,}200 \quad \ldots(*)$$

Second Mill. Since the second mill announced a D.A. of 46·5% to its workers fully compensating the rise in prices in fuel and miscellaneous groups and not other groups, using the same argument as above, we shall get :

$$\frac{1}{100}\left[55 \times 100 + 15(100 + x) + 10 \times 100 + 12 \times 100 + 8(100 + 2y)\right] = 100 + 46{\cdot}5$$

$$\Rightarrow \quad 15x + 16y + 100 \times 100 = 146{\cdot}5 \times 100 \quad \Rightarrow \quad 15x + 16y = 4{,}650 \ldots(**)$$

Multiplying (*) by 4 and (**) by 3, and subtracting, we get

$$(440 - 45)x = 72{,}800 - 13{,}950 \quad \rightarrow \quad x = \frac{58{,}850}{395} = 148{\cdot}99$$

Substituting this value in (**), we get

$$16y = 4{,}650 - 15 \times 148{\cdot}99 = 4{,}650 - 2{,}234{\cdot}85 = 2415{\cdot}15 \quad \Rightarrow \quad y = \frac{2415{\cdot}15}{16} = 150{\cdot}95$$

Hence, the percentage increase in different groups is as follows :

Group	*Food*	*Fuel*	*Rent*	*Miscellaneous*
Percentage increase	$2x = 297{\cdot}98$	$x = 148{\cdot}99$	$y = 150{\cdot}95$	$2y = 301{\cdot}90$

10·10. LIMITATIONS OF INDEX NUMBERS

Although index numbers are very important tools for studying the economic and business activity of a country, they have their limitations and as such should be used and interpreted with caution. The following are some of their limitations :

(1) Since index numbers are based on the sample data, they are only approximate indicators and may not exactly represent the changes in the relative level of a phenomenon.

(2) There is likelihood of error being introduced at each stage of the construction of the index numbers, *viz.*,

(*i*) Selection of commodities.

(*ii*) Selection of the base period.

(*iii*) Collection of the data relating to prices and quantities of the commodities.

(*iv*) Choice of the formula — the system of weighting to be used.

(*v*) The average to be used for obtaining the index for the composite group of commodities.

As already pointed out, the selection of various commodities to be included for construction of the index and the selection of various markets or stores from where to collect the data relating to prices and quantities of the commodities is not on the basis of a random sample because randomness will be at the cost of representativeness but is done on the basis of a stratified-cum-deliberate or purposive sample. The commodities are usually classified into relatively homogeneous groups (or strata) and from within each group (or stratum) more important commodities are selected first and from the remaining as many more commodities are selected at random consistent with resources at our disposal in terms of time and money. The deliberate or purposive sampling makes the sample subjective in nature and consequently some sort of personal bias is likely to creep in and attempts should be made to minimise this error.

(3) Due to dynamic pace of events and scientific advancements these days, there is a rapid change in the tastes, customs, fashions and consequently in the consumption patterns of the various commodities among the people in a society. Accordingly, index numbers (which require that the items and their qualities should remain same over period of time) may not be able to keep pace with the changes in the nature and quality of the commodities and hence may not be really representative one.

(4) There is no formula which measures the price change or quantity change of a given body of data with exactitude or perfection. Accordingly, there is inherent in each index an error termed as '*formula error*'. For example, Laspeyre's index has an upward bias while Paasche's index has a downward bias. A measure of formula error is provided by the difference between these two indices. Moreover, index numbers are special type of averages and the type of average used for their construction has its own field of utility and limitations. Thus, the index numbers may not really be representative.

(5) By suitable choice of the base year, commodities, price and quantity quotations, index numbers are liable to be manipulated by unscrupulous and selfish persons to obtain the desired results.

In spite of all the above limitations, index numbers, if properly constructed and not deliberately distorted are extremely useful 'economic' barometers.

EXERCISE 10·5

1. (*a*) What is a cost of living index number ? What does it measure ? Discuss briefly its uses and limitations.

(*b*) What do you understand by cost of living index numbers ? Describe briefly the various steps involved in their construction.

(*c*) "Cost of living index number is essentially a consumer price index." Discuss. State the important steps involved in its construction. What are its uses ?

2. What are the points that are taken into consideration in choosing the base period and determining the weights in the preparation of cost of living index numbers ?

3. Give a detailed account of the method of construction of a Consumer Price Index. Interpret the formula you will use in this connection.

4. What is an *Index Number* ? Describe the general lines on which you would proceed to construct a cost of living index for factory workers in an industrial area.

5. How does the method of construction of a consumer price index differ from that of the construction of a wholesale price index ? Explain by taking an illustration.

6. (*a*) How are index numbers constructed ? Discuss the importance of the choices of base year and selection of weighting in the construction of a cost of living index number.

(*b*) What are the difficulties to be faced in the construction of cost of living index ? How are they overcome in the actual construction of the index ?

7. (*a*) Explain the uses and limitations of index numbers.

(*b*) What is an 'index number' ? Explain the significance of index numbers. [*C.S.* (*Foundation*), *June 2001*]

(*c*) Mention the areas in which index numbers are useful in spite of their limitations.

[*C.A.* (*Foundation*), *June 1993*]

8. Find the cost of living index for the following data :

Group	Food	Clothing	Rent	Fuel and Lighting	Miscellaneous
Group Index	180	150	100	110	80
Weight	140	42	49	56	63

Ans. 136.

9. In the construction of a certain Cost of Living Index Number, the following group index numbers were found. Calculate the Cost of Living Index Number by using :

(*i*) The weighted arithmetic mean ; and (*ii*) The weighted geometric mean.

Group	Food	Fuel and Lighting	Clothing	House Rent	Miscellaneous
Index Number	352	200	230	160	190
Weights	48	10	8	12	15

Ans. (*i*) 274·26, (*ii*) 261·1.

10. "The average salary of employees of a certain organisation has tripled over last ten years. Therefore, their standard of living has increased three times over this period." Do you agree ? Explain.

[*Delhi Univ. B.Com.* (*Hons.*), *2001*]

11. A worker earned Rs. 900 per month in 1990. The cost of living index increased by 70% between 1990 and 1993. How much extra income should the worker have earned in 1993 so that he could buy the same quantities as in 1990 ? [*Delhi Univ. B.Com.* (*Hons.*), *1994*]

Ans. Rs. $12 \times \left[\left(\frac{170}{100} \times 900 \right) - 900 \right]$ = Rs. 7,560.

12. During a certain period the cost of living index number goes up from 110 to 200 and the salary of the worker is also increased from Rs. 325 to Rs. 550. Does the worker really gain, and if so, by how much in real terms ?

[*Delhi Univ. B.Com.* (*Hons.*), *1993*]

Ans. Loss of Rs. 90·90.

13. Following information relating to workers in an industrial town is given.

Items of consumption	*Consumer Price Index in 2000* (*1990 = 100*)	*Proportion of expenditure on the items*
(*i*) Food, drinks and tobacco	225	52%
(*ii*) Clothing	175	8%
(*iii*) Fuel and Lighting	155	10%
(*iv*) Housing	250	14%
(*v*) Miscellaneous	150	16%

Average wage per month in 1990 was Rs. 2000. What should be the average wage per worker per month in 2000 in that town so that the standard of living of the workers does not fall below the 1990 level ?

Ans. Rs. 4110.

14. The adjoining table gives the cost of living index numbers for different groups with their respective weights for the year 1992 (Base Year : 1982). Calculate the overall Cost of Living Index Number.

Mr. Bose got a salary of Rs. 550 in 1982. Determine how much he should have to receive as salary in 1992 to maintain his same standard of living as in 1982.

Group	*Cost of living index*	*Weight*
Food	525	40
Clothing	325	16
Light & Fuel	240	15
Rent	180	20
Others	200	9

[*I.C.W.A.* (*Intermediate*), *Dec. 1996* ; *Madras Univ. B.Com., 1996*]

Ans. 352 ; Rs. 1936.

15. The adjoining information relating to workers in an industrial town is given.

Average wage per month in 2,000 is Rs. 2,000. What should be dearness allowance expressed as % of wages ? What should be the average wage per worker per month in 2005 in that town so that the standard of living of worker does not fall below the 2000 level ?

Item of Consumption	*Consumer price Index 2005 (2000 = 100)*	*Proportion of Expenditure on Item*
Food	132	60%
Clothing	154	12%
Fuel and Lighting	147	16%
Housing	178	8%
Miscellaneous	158	4%

[Delhi Univ. B.Com. (Hons.), 2008]

Ans. CPI in 2005 = $(\Sigma WI/\Sigma W) = (14176/100) = 141{\cdot}76$

The pay of worker in 2005 should be Rs. $\left(\frac{2000 \times 141{\cdot}76}{100}\right)$ = Rs. 2835·20

D.A. expressed as % of wages = $\frac{\text{Rs. }(2835{\cdot}20 - 2000)}{\text{Rs. }2000} \times 100 = 41{\cdot}76\%$

16. Incomplete information obtained from a partially destroyed records on cost of living analysis is given below:

Group	*Group Index*	*Percent (%) of Total Expenditure*
Food	268	60
Clothing	280	Not available
Housing	210	50
Fuel and Electricity	240	5
Miscellaneous	260	Not available

The cost of living index with percent of total expenditure as weight was found to be 255·8 Estimate the missing weights. *[Delhi Univ. B.Com. (Hons.), 2005; I.C.W.A. (Stage 2), Dec. 2003]*

Ans. Clothing : 10 ; Miscellaneous : 5.

17. The monthly income of a person is Rs. 10,500. It is given that the cost of living index for a particular month is 136. Find out the amount spent by that person :

(*i*) On food; and (*ii*) On clothing.

Item	Food	Rent	Clothing	Fuel and Power	Miscellaneous
Expenditure (Rs.)	?	1470	?	1680	1890
Index	180	100	150	110	80

[Delhi Univ. B.Com. (Hons.), 2001]

Hint. $\Sigma W = 10{,}500$.

Ans. Food : 4,200 ; Clothing : 1,260.

18. A textile worker in the city of Ahmedabad earns Rs. 750 p.m. The cost of living index for January, 1986, is given as 160. Using the following data, find out the amounts he spends on (*i*) Food and (*ii*) Rent.

Group	*Expenditure (Rs.)*	*Group Index*
(*i*) Food	?	190
(*ii*) Clothing	125	181
(*iii*) Rent	?	140
(*iv*) Fuel and Lighting	100	118
(*v*) Miscellaneous	75	101

[Delhi Univ. B.Com. (Hons.), 1993]

Ans. (*i*) Rs. 300, (*ii*) Rs. 150.

19. In calculating cost of living index the following weights were used : Food $8\frac{1}{2}$, Rent 2, Clothing $2\frac{1}{2}$, Fuel and Light 1, Miscellaneous 11. Calculate the index number for a data when the percentage increase in prices of the various items over prices of July, 1998 = 100 were 31, 57, 90, 75 and 88 respectively.

Ans. 152·2.

20. In calculating a certain cost of living index number, the following weights were used. Food 15, Clothing 3, Rent 4, Fuel and Light 2, Miscellaneous 1. Calculate the index for a data when the average percentage increases in prices of items in the various groups over the base period were 32, 54, 47, 78 and 58 respectively.

Suppose a business executive was earning Rs. 2,050 in the base period. What should be his salary in the current period if his standard of living is to remain the same ? [*Bangalore Univ. B.Com., 1999*]

Ans. 141·76 ; Rs. 2,906·08.

21. (*a*) The cost of living index uses the following weighs :

Food 40, Rent 15, Clothing 10, Fuel 10, Miscellaneous 15. During the period 2000 – 05, the cost of living index raised from 100 to 205·83. Over the same period the percentage rises in prices were :

Rent 60, Clothing 180, Fuel 75 and Miscellaneous 165. What is the percentage change in the price of food ?

[*Delhi Univ. B.Com. (Hons.), 2006*]

Hint. Let percentage rise in price of food be *x*.

$$\text{Then,} \qquad \text{Index} = \frac{\Sigma WI}{\Sigma W} = \frac{[40 \times (100 + x) + 15 \times 160 + 10 \times 280 + 10 \times 175 + 15 \times 265]}{40 + 15 + 10 + 10 + 15}$$

$$\Rightarrow \qquad 205{\cdot}83 = \frac{14925 + 40x}{90} \qquad \Rightarrow \qquad x = \frac{18524{\cdot}7 - 14925}{40} = 89{\cdot}99 \simeq 90.$$

Ans. 90

(*b*) The relative importance of the following eight groups of family expenditure was found to be-food 348, rent 88, clothing 97, fuel and light 65, household durable goods 71, miscellaneous goods 35, services 79, drink and tobacco 217. The corresponding % age increase in price for Oct. 1975 gave the following values — 25, 1, 22, 18, 14, 13, ? and 4. Calculate the percentage increase in group — services, if the percentage increase for whole group is 15·278.

Ans. 11.

22. From some given data, the retail price index based on five items, *viz.*, Food, Rent and Rates, Fuel and Light, Clothing and Miscellaneous was calculated as 205. Percentage increases in prices over the base period are given below :

Rent and Rates 60, Clothing 210, Fuel and Light 120, Miscellaneous 130.

Calculate the percentage increase in the Food Group, given that the weights of different items are as follows :

Food 60, Rent and Rates 16, Fuel and Light 8, Clothing 12, Miscellaneous 4, All items 100.

Ans. 92·3% increase in food group.

23. Calculate the cost of living index number from the following data :

Group/Commodities	*Weights* W	*Group/Commodity Index Number* I
Food	71	370
Clothing	3	423
Fuel, etc.	9	469
House Rent	7	110
Miscellaneous	10	279

[*C.A. (Foundation), Nov. 2001*]

Ans. 353·20.

24. "Index numbers are the barometers of economic activity." Explain.

The subgroup indices of the consumer price index number of workers of an industrial town for the year 2003 (with base 1998) were :

Food	Cloth	Fuel and Light	House Rent	Miscellaneous
180	140	125	200	150 .

The weights of the various subgroups are 50, 9, 6, 15 and 20 respectively. It is proposed to fix industrial dearness allowance such that the employees are compensated fully for the rise in prices of food and house rent but only to the extent of fifty percent of increase in prices of rest of the sub-groups. What should be the dearness allowance expressed as a percentage of wages ? [*Delhi Univ. B.Com. (Hons.), 2004*]

Hint. Since the employees are compensated fully for the rise in prices of food and house rent but only to the extent of 50% of increase in the prices of the rest of the sub-groups, for calculating the C.O.L. Index (for giving compensation) we will take the indices of cloth, fuel and light, and miscellaneous items as :

$$100 + \frac{40}{2} = 120, \quad 100 + \frac{25}{2} = 112{\cdot}5 \quad \text{and} \quad 100 + \frac{50}{2} = 125, \text{ respectively.}$$

$$\therefore \quad \text{C.O.L. Index (for 2003)} = \frac{[180 \times 50 + 120 \times 9 + 112{\cdot}5 \times 6 + 200 \times 15 + 125 \times 20]}{50 + 9 + 6 + 15 + 20} = 162{\cdot}55$$

Hence, the dearness allowance to be given to employees should be 62·55% of their wages in 1998.

25. The group indices and the corresponding weights for the working class cost of living index numbers in an industrial city for the years 1996 and 2000 are given below :

Group	*Weight*	*Group Index* 1996	*Group Index* 2000
Food	71	370	380
Clothing	3	423	504
Fuel, etc.	9	469	336
House Rent	7	110	116
Miscellaneous	10	279	283

(*a*) Compute the cost of living indices for the two years 1996 and 2000.

(*b*) If a worker was getting Rs. 3,000 per month in 1996, do you think that he should be given some extra allowance so that he can maintain his 1996 standard of living ? If so, what should be the minimum amount of this extra allowance ?

Ans. (*a*) 353·20 ; 351·58. (*b*) No extra allowance should be given.

26. Labour and capital are used in two different proportions in products *A* and *B*, but the price of each input is equal for both products. On the basis of the information given in the attached table, prepare, for the year 2000 separate price indices for labour and capital.

	Product A	*Product B*
Weight for labour	60	70
Weight for capital	40	30
Cost of Production Index for 2000 (Base Year 1990 = 100)	340	330

Ans. P_{01} (Labour) = 300 ; P_{01} (Capital) = 400.

27. An enquiry into the budgets of the middle class families in a certain city in India gave the following information :

Expenses on	*Food*	*Fuel*	*Clothing*	*Rent*	*Misc.*
	35%	10%	20%	15%	20%
Price 1995 (Rs.)	150	25	75	30	40
Price 1996 (Rs.)	145	23	65	30	45

What is the cost of living index number of 1996 as compared with that of 1995 ?

Ans. 102·86.

28. Use the formula $I_x = \dfrac{\Sigma\, q_0 p_x}{\Sigma\, q_0 p_0} \times 100$, and find the consumer price index for 2000 with 1989 as base with the help of the following data. Interpret the Index Number so obtained.

Item No.	*Quantity consumed in 1989* (q_0)	*Price per unit in 1989* (p_0)	*Price per unit in 2000* (p_x)
1	75	3·4	9·6
2	16	2·5	8·5
3	15	7·6	12·6
4	22	4·5	7·5
5	13	7·0	11·0
6	3	2·0	4·0

Ans. 225·61.

29. Construct the consumer price index numbers for 1999 and 2000 from the indices given below :

Year	*Food*	*Rent*	*Clothing*	*Fuel*	*Music*
1998	100	100	100	100	100
1999	102	100	103	100	97
2000	106	102	105	101	98

Assume the following weights for the different groups :

Food	*Rent*	*Clothing*	*Fuel*	*Music*
60	16	12	8	4

Ans. For 1999 : 101·44 ; For 2000 : 104·52.

30. Index of Industrial Production covers three groups of industries. This index increased from 106·4 to 150·2 from one point of time to another. The index numbers of individual three groups of industries, over the same period, changed as follows : Mining and Quarrying from 102·0 to 144·1 ; Manufacturing from 106·5 to 146·6 ; Electricity from 110·4 to 189·9.

Determine the weights for the individual groups of industries.

Ans. (9·9, 81·2, 8·9) ≃ (10, 81, 9).

31. If the Consumer Price Index (for the same class of people and with same base year) is higher for Delhi than that for Mumbai, does it necessarily mean that Delhi is more expensive (for this class of people) than Mumbai. Give reasons in support of your answer.

32. Owing to change in prices, the consumer price index of the working class in a certain area rose in a month by one quarter of what it was before, to 225. The index of food became 252 from 198, that of clothing from 185 to 205, that of fuel and lighting from 175 to 195, and that of miscellaneous from 138 to 212. The index of rent, however, remained unchanged at 150. It was known that weight of clothing, rent, and fuel and lighting were the same. Find out the exact weights of all the groups. *[Delhi Univ. B.Com (Hons.), (External), 2007]*

Hint. Let I_1 and I_2 be the index numbers in the beginning of the month and the end of the month respectively. Then we are given :

$$I_2 = 225 \quad \text{and} \quad I_2 = \left(1 + \frac{1}{4}\right) I_1 = \frac{5}{4} I_1 \quad \Rightarrow \quad I_1 = \frac{4}{5} I_2 = \frac{4}{5} \times 225 = 180$$

Let the weights of food, clothing, fuel and lighting, rent, and miscellaneous items be x, z, z, z, y respectively. Then, by the given data, we shall get :

$$I_1 = \frac{\Sigma WI}{\Sigma W} = \frac{198x + 138y + 510z}{x + y + 3z} = 180 \quad \Rightarrow \quad 3x - 7y - 5z = 0 \qquad \ldots(i)$$

and
$$I_2 = \frac{\Sigma WI}{\Sigma W} = \frac{252x + 212y + 550z}{x + y + 3z} = 225 \quad \Rightarrow \quad 27x - 13y - 125z = 0 \qquad \ldots(ii)$$

Also $\Sigma W = x + y + 3z = 100$ ...(*iii*)

Solving (*i*), (*ii*) and (*iii*) simultaneously, we shall get $x = 54, \quad y = 16, \quad z = 10.$

Ans. Food : 54, Clothing : 10, Fuel and Lighting : 10, Rent : 10, Miscellaneous : 16.

33. In a working class consumer price index number of a particular town the weights corresponding to different groups of items were as follows :

Food — 55, Fuel — 15, Clothing — 10, Rent — 8 and Miscellaneous — 12.

In Oct. 2000, the D.A. was fixed by a mill of that town at 182 per cent for the workers which fully compensated for the rise in prices of food and rent but did not compensate for anything else. Another mill of the same town paid D.A. of 46·5 per cent which compensated for the rise in fuel and miscellaneous groups. It is known that rise in food is double than that of fuel and the rise in miscellaneous group is double than that of rent.

Find the rise in food, fuel, rent and miscellaneous groups.

Ans. Percentage increase is :

Food : 317·14 ; Fuel : 158·57 ; Rent : 94·64 ; Miscellaneous : 189·28.

34. The estimated per capita income for India in 1931-32 was Rs. 65. The estimate for 1972-73 was Rs. 650. In 1972-73, every Indian was, therefore, 10 times more prosperous than in 1931-32". Comment.

35. (*a*) What is an index number ? Describe the limitations of index numbers.

(*b*) "Index numbers are used to measure the changes in some quantity which we cannot observe directly".

Explain the above statement and point out the uses and limitations of index numbers.

11 Time Series Analysis

11·1. INTRODUCTION

A time series is an arrangement of statistical data in a chronological order, *i.e.,* in accordance with its time of occurrence. It reflects the dynamic pace of movements of a phenomenon over a period of time. Most of the series relating to Economics, Business and Commerce, *e.g.,* the series relating to prices, production and consumption of various commodities; agricultural and industrial production, national income and foreign exchange reserves ; investment, sales and profits of business houses ; bank deposits and bank clearings, prices and dividends of shares in a stock exchange market, etc., are all time series spread over a long period of time. Accordingly, time series have an important and significant place in Business and Economics, and basically most of the statistical techniques for the analysis of time series data have been developed by economists. However, these techniques can also be applied for the study of behaviour of any phenomenon collected chronologically over a period of time in any discipline relating to natural and social sciences, though not directly related to economics or business. According to Ya-lun Chou :

"A time series may be defined as a collection of readings belonging to different time periods, of some economic variable or composite of variables".

Mathematically, a time series is defined by the functional relationship

$$y = f(t) \qquad \ldots(11\cdot1)$$

where y is the value of the phenomenon (or variable) under consideration at time t. For example,

(*i*) the population (y) of a country or a place in different years (t),

(*ii*) the number of births and deaths (y) in different months (t) of the year,

(*iii*) the sale (y) of a departmental store in different months (t) of the year,

(*iv*) the temperature (y) of a place on different days (t) of the week,

and so on constitute time series. Thus, if the values of a phenomenon or variable at times $t_1, t_2, \ldots, t_n$ are $y_1, y_2, \ldots, y_n$ respectively, then the series

t :	t_1	t_2	t_3	...	t_n
y :	y_1	y_2	y_3	...	y_n

constitutes a time series. Thus, a time series invariably gives a bivariate distribution, one of the two variables being time (t) and the other being the value (y) of the phenomenon at different points of time. The values of t may be given yearly, monthly, weekly, daily or even hourly, usually but not always at equal intervals of time. As already discussed in Chapter 4, the graph of a time series, known as *Historigram,* is obtained on plotting the data on a graph paper taking the independent variable t along the x-axis and the dependent variable y along the y-axis.

11·2. COMPONENTS OF A TIME SERIES

If the values of a phenomenon are observed at different periods of time, the values so obtained will show appreciable variations or changes. These fluctuations are due to the fact that the value of the phenomenon is affected not by a single factor but due to the cumulative effect of a multiplicity of factors pulling it up and down. However, if the various forces were in a state of equilibrium, then the time series will remain constant. For example, the sales (y) of a product are influenced by (*i*) advertisement expenditure, (*ii*) the price of the product, (*iii*) the income of the people, (*iv*) other competitive products in the market, (*v*) tastes, fashions, habits and customs of the people and so on. Similarly, the price of a particular product depends on its demand, various competitive products in the market, raw materials, transportation expenses, investment, and so on. The various forces affecting the values of a phenomenon in a time series may be broadly classified into the following four categories, commonly known as the *components of a time series*, some or all of which are present (in a given time series) in varying degrees.

(*a*) Secular Trend or Long-term Movement (*T*).

(*b*) Periodic Movements or Short-term Fluctuations :

(*i*) Seasonal Variations (*S*), (*ii*) Cyclical Variations (*C*).

(*c*) Random or Irregular Variations (*R* or *I*).

The value (y) of a phenomenon observed at any time (t) is the net effect of the interaction of above components. We shall explain these components briefly in the following sections.

11·2·1. Secular Trend. The general tendency of the time series data to increase or decrease or stagnate during a *long* period of time is called the *secular trend* or *simple trend*. This phenomenon is usually observed in most of the series relating to Economics and Business, *e.g.*, an upward tendency is usually observed in time series relating to population, production and sales of products, prices, incomes, money in circulation, etc., while a downward tendency is noticed in the time series relating to deaths, epidemics, etc., due to advancement in medical technology, improved medical facilities, better sanitation, diet, etc. According to Simpson and Kafka :

"*Trend, also called secular or long-term trend, is the basic tendency of a series...to grow or decline over a period of time. The concept of trend does not include short-range oscillations, but rather the steady movement over a long time.*"

Remarks 1. It should be clearly understood that trend is the *general, smooth, long-term average tendency*. It is not necessary that the increase or decline should be in the same direction throughout the given period. It may be possible that different tendencies of increase, decrease or stability are observed in different sections of time. However, the overall tendency may be upward, downward or stable. Such tendencies are the result of the forces which are more or less constant for a long time or which change very gradually and continuously over a long period of time such as the change in the population, tastes, habits and customs of the people in a society, and so on. They operate in an evolutionary manner and do not reflect sudden changes. For example, the effect of population increase over a long period of time on the expansion of various sectors like agriculture, industry, education, textiles, etc., is a continuous but gradual process. Similarly, the growth or decline in a number of economic time series is the interaction of forces like advances in production technology, large-scale production, improved marketing management and business organisation, the invention and discovery of new natural resources and the exhaustion of the existing resources and so on – all of which are gradual processes.

2. The term '*long period of time*' is a relative term and cannot be defined exactly. It would very much depend on the nature of the data. In certain phenomenon, a period as small as few hours may be sufficiently long, while in others even a period as long as 3- 4 years may not be sufficient. For example, to have an idea about the production of a particular product (agricultural or industrial production), an increase over the past 20 or 30 months will not reflect a secular change for which we must have data for 7-8 years. In such a phenomenon, the values for short period (2-3 years) are unduly affected by cyclic variation (discussed later) and will into reveal the true trend. In order to have true picture of the trend, the time series values must be examined over a period covering at least two or three complete cycles.

On the other hand, if we count the number of bacterial population (living organisms) of a culture subjected to strong germicide every 20 seconds for 1 hour, then the set of 180 readings showing a general pattern would be termed as secular movement.

3. *Linear and Non-Linear (Curvi-Linear) Trend.* If the time series values plotted on graph cluster more or less round a straight line, the trend exhibited by the time series is termed as *Linear* otherwise *Non-Linear* (*Curvi-Linear*)—See Figures 11·1 and 11·2. In a straight line trend, the time series values increase or decrease more or less by a constant absolute amount, *i.e.*, the rate of growth (or decline) is constant. Although, in practice, linear trend is commonly used, it is rarely observed in economic and business data. In an economic and business phenomenon, the rate of growth or decline is not of constant nature throughout but varies considerably in different sectors of time. Usually, in the beginning, the growth is slow, then rapid which is further accelerated for quite some time, after which it becomes stationary or stable for some period and finally retards slowly.

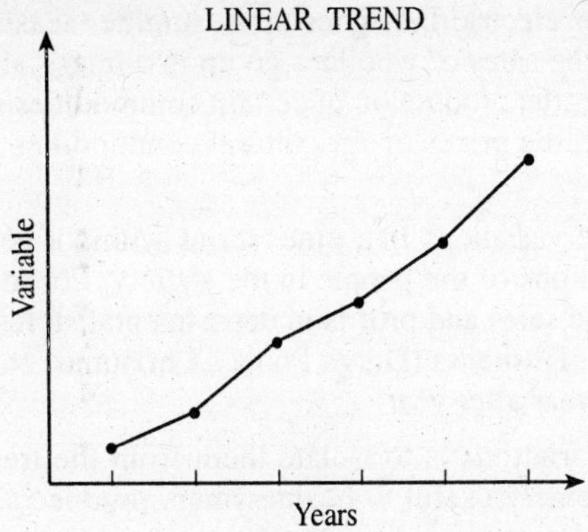

Fig. 11·1.

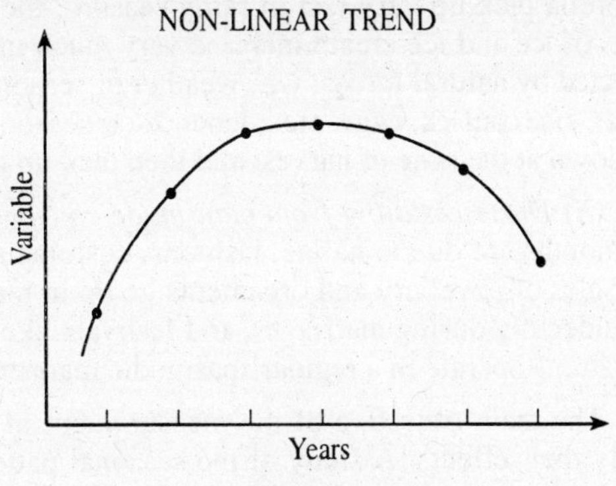

Fig. 11·2.

4. It is not necessary that all the series must exhibit a rising or declining trend. Certain phenomena may give rise to time series whose values fluctuate round a constant reading which does not change with time, *e.g.,* the series relating to temperature or barometric readings (pressure) of a particular place.

5. Uses of Trend. (*i*) The study of the data over a long period of time enables us to have a general idea about the pattern of the behaviour of the phenomenon under consideration. This helps in business forecasting and planning future operations. For example, if the time series data for a particular phenomenon exhibits a trend in a particular direction, then under the assumption that the same pattern will continue in the near future, an assumption which is quite reasonable unless there are some fundamental and drastic changes in the forces affecting the phenomenon—we can forecast the values of the phenomenon for future also. The accuracy of the trend curve or trend equation or the estimates obtained from them will depend on the reliability of the type of trend fitted to the given data. (For details, see Measurement of Trend - Least Square Method.) The trend values are of paramount importance to a businessman in providing him the rough estimates of the values of the phenomenon in the near future. For instance, an idea about the approximate sales or demand for a product is extremely useful to a businessman in planning future operations and formulating policies regarding inventory, production, etc.

(*ii*) By isolating trend values from the given time series, (By dividing the given time series values by the trend values or subtracting trend values from the given time series values - See [Models (11·1) and (11·2) discussed later], we can study the short-term and irregular movements.

(*iii*) Trend analysis enables us to compare two or more time series over different periods of time and draw important conclusions about them.

11·2·2. Short-Term Variations. In addition to the long-term movements there are inherent in most of the time series, a number of forces which repeat themselves periodically or almost periodically over a period of time and thus prevent the smooth flow of the values of the series in a particular direction. Such forces give rise to the so-called *short-term variations* which may be classified into the following two categories :

(*i*) Sesonal Variations (S), and (*ii*) Cyclical Variations (C).

Seasonal Variations (S). These variations in a time series are due to the rhythmic forces which operate in a regular and periodic manner over a span of less than a year, *i.e.,* during a period of 12 months and have the same or almost same pattern year after year. Thus, seasonal variations in a time series will be there if the data are recorded quarterly (every three months), monthly, weekly, daily, hourly, and so on. Although in each of the above cases, the amplitudes of the seasonal variations are different, all of them have the same period, *viz.,* 1 year. Thus *in a time series data where only annual figures are given, there are no seasonal variations.* Most of economic time series are influenced by seasonal swings, *e.g.,* prices, production and consumption of commodities ; sales and profits in a departmental store ; bank clearings and bank deposits, etc., are all affected by seasonal variations. The seasonal variations may be attributed to the following two causes :

(*i*) *Those resulting from natural forces.* As the name suggests, the various seasons or weather conditions and climatic changes play an important role in seasonal movements. For instance, the sales of umbrella pick up very fast in rainy season ; the demand for electric fans goes up in summer season ; the sales of ice and ice-cream increase very much in summer ; the sales of woollens go up in winter - all being affected by natural forces, *viz.*, weather or seasons. Likewise, the production of certain commodities such as sugar, rice, pulses, eggs, etc., depends on seasons. Similarly, the prices of agricultural commodities always go down at the time of harvest and then pick up gradually.

(*ii*) *Those resulting from man-made conventions.* These variations in a time series within a period of 12 months are due to habits, fashions, customs and conventions of the people in the society. For instance, the sales of jewellery and ornaments go up in marriages ; the sales and profits in departmental stores go up considerably during marriages, and festivals like Deepawali, Dushehra (Durga Pooja), Christmas, etc. Such variations operate in a regular spasmodic manner and recur year after year.

The main objective of the measurement of seasonal variations is to isolate them from the trend and study their effects. A study of the seasonal patterns is extremely useful to businessmen, producers, sales-managers, etc., in planning future operations and in formulation of policy decisions regarding purchase, production, inventory control, personnel requirements, selling and advertising programmes. In the absence of any knowledge of seasonal variations, a seasonal upswing may be mistaken as indicator of better business conditions while a seasonal slump may be mis-interpreted as deteriorating business conditions. Thus, to understand the behaviour of the phenomenon in a time series properly, the time series data must be adjusted for seasonal variations. [This is done by isolating them from trend and other components on dividing the given time series values (y) by the seasonal variations (S). [See Model (11·1).] This technique is called *de-seasonalisation* of data and is discussed in detail later (*c.f.* § 11·6·5).

Cyclical Variations (C). The oscillatory movements in a time series with period of oscillation greater than one year are termed as *cyclical variations*. These variations in a time series are due to ups and downs recurring after a period greater than one year. The cyclical fluctuations, though more or less regular, are not necessarily uniformly periodic, *i.e.,* they may or may not follow exactly similar patterns after equal intervals of time. One complete period which normally lasts from 7 to 9 years is termed as a '*cycle*'. These oscillatory movements in any business activity are the outcome of the so-called '*Business Cycles*' *which are the four-phased cycles comprising prosperity (boom), recession, depression and recovery from time to time.* These booms and depressions in any business activity follow each other with steady regularity and the complete cycle from the peak of one boom to the peak of next boom usually lasts from 7 to 9 years. Most of the economic and business series, *e.g.,* series relating to production, prices, wages, investments, etc., are affected by cyclical upswings and downswings.

The study of cyclical variations is of great importance to business executives in the formulation of policies aimed at stabilising the level of business activity. A knowledge of the cyclic component enables a businessman to have an idea about the periodicity of the booms and depressions and accordingly he can take timely steps for maintaining stable market for his product.

11·2·3. Random or Irregular Variations. Mixed up with cyclical and seasonal variations, there is inherent in every time series another factor called *random or irregular variations*. These fluctuations are purely random and are the result of such unforeseen and unpredictable forces which operate in absolutely erratic and irregular manner. Such variations do not exhibit any definite pattern and there is no regular period or time of their occurrence, hence they are named irregular variations. These powerful variations are usually caused by numerous non-recurring factors like floods, famines, wars, earthquakes, strikes and lockouts, epidemics, revolution, etc., which behave in a very erratic and unpredictable manner. Normally, they are short-term variations but sometimes their effect is so intense that they may give rise to new cyclical or other movements. Irregular variations are also known as *episodic* fluctuations and include all types of variations in a time series data which are not accounted for by trend, seasonal and cyclical variations.

Because of their absolutely random character, it is not possible to isolate such variations and study them exclusively nor we can forecast or estimate them precisely. The best that can be done about such variations is to obtain their rough estimates (from past experience) and accordingly make provisions for such abnormalities during normal times in business.

11·3. ANALYSIS OF TIME SERIES

The time series analysis consists of :

(*i*) Identifying or determining the various forces or influences whose interaction produces the variations in the time series.

(*ii*) Isolating, studying, analysing and measuring them independently, *i.e.*, by holding other things constant.

The time series analysis is of great importance not only to businessman or an economist but also to people working in various disciplines in natural, social and physical sciences. Some of its uses are enumerated below :

(*i*) It enables us to *study the past behaviour of the phenomenon under consideration, i.e.,* to determine the type and nature of the variations in the data.

(*ii*) The segregation and study of the various components is of paramount importance to a businessman in the planning of future operations and in the formulation of executive and policy decisions.

(*iii*) It helps to compare the actual current performance or accomplishments with the expected ones (on the basis of the past performances) and analyse the causes of such variations, if any.

(*iv*) It enables us to predict or estimate or forecast the behaviour of the phenomenon in future which is very essential for business planning.

(*v*) It helps us to compare the changes in the values of different phenomena at different times or places, etc.

11·4. MATHEMATICAL MODELS FOR TIME SERIES

The following are the two models commonly used for the decomposition of a time series into its components.

(*i*) **Additive Model or Decomposition by Additive Hypothesis.** According to the additive model, the time series can be expressed as :

$$Y = T + S + C + I \qquad \ldots(11\cdot1)$$

or more precisely

$$Y_t = T_t + S_t + C_t + I_t \qquad \ldots(11\cdot1a)$$

where $Y\,(Y_t)$ is the time series value at time t, and T_t , S_t , C_t and I_t represent the trend, seasonal, cyclical and random variations at time t. In this model $S = S_t$, $C = C_t$ and $I = I_t$ are absolute quantities which can take positive and negative values so that :

$$\Sigma S = \Sigma S_t = 0, \text{ for any year,}$$

$$\Sigma C = \Sigma C_t = 0, \text{ for any cycle,}$$

and

$$\Sigma I = \Sigma I_t = 0, \text{ in the long-term period.}$$

The additive model assumes that all the four components of the time series operate independently of each other so that none of these components has any effect on the remaining three. This implies that the trend, however, fast or slow, it may be, has no effect on the seasonal and cyclical components ; nor do seasonal swings have any impact on cyclical variations and conversely. However, this assumption is not true in most of the economic and business time series where the four components of the time series are not independent of each other. For instance, the seasonal or cyclical variations may virtually be wiped off by very sharp rising or declining trend. Similarly, strong and powerful seasonal swings may intensify or even precipitate a change in the cyclical fluctuations.

(*ii*) **Multiplicative Model or Decomposition by Multiplicative Hypothesis.** Keeping the above points, in view, most of the economic and business time series are characterised by the following classical multiplicative model :

$$Y = T \times S \times C \times I \qquad \ldots(11\cdot2)$$

or more precisely

$$Y_t = T_t \times S_t \times C_t \times I_t \qquad \ldots(11\cdot2a)$$

This model assumes that the four components of the time series are due to different causes but they are not necessarily independent and they can affect each other. In this model S, C and I are not viewed as absolute amounts but rather as relative variations. Except for the trend component T, the other components S, C and I are expressed as rates or indices fluctuating above or below 1 such that the geometric means of all the $S = S_t$ values in a year, $C = C_t$ values in a cycle or $I = I_t$ values in a long-term period are unity.

Taking logarithm of both sides in (11·2), we get

$$\log Y = \log T + \log S + \log C + \log I \qquad \text{...(11·3)}$$

which is nothing but the additive model fitted to the logarithms of the given time series values.

Remarks 1. Most of the time series relating to economic and business phenomena conform to the multiplicative model (11·2). In practice, additive model (11·1) is rarely used.

2. Mixed Models. In addition to the additive and multiplicative models discussed above, the components in a time series may be combined in a large number of other ways. The different models, defined under different assumptions, will yield different results. Some of the *mixed models* resulting from different combinations of additive and multiplicative models are given below :

$$Y = TCS + I \qquad \text{...(11·4)}$$

$$Y = TC + SI \qquad \text{...(11·5)}$$

$$Y = T + SCI \qquad \text{...(11·6)}$$

$$Y = T + S + CI \qquad \text{...(11·7)}$$

3. The model (11·1) or (11·2) can be used to obtain a measure of one or more of the components by elimination, *viz.*, subtraction or division. For example, if trend component (T) is known, then using multiplicative model, it can be isolated from the given time series to give :

$$S \times C \times I = \frac{Y}{T} = \frac{\text{Original Values}}{\text{Trend Values}} \qquad \text{...(11·8)}$$

Thus, for the *annual data,* for which the seasonal component S is not there, we have

$$Y = T \times C \times I \quad \Rightarrow \quad C \times I = \frac{Y}{T} \qquad \text{...(11·8a)}$$

In the following sections we shall discuss various techniques for the measurement of different components of a time series.

11·5. MEASUREMENT OF TREND

The following are the four methods which are generally used for the study and measurement of the trend component in a time series.

(i) *Graphic* (or *Free-hand* Curve Fitting) Method.

(ii) Method of *Semi-Averages.*

(iii) Method of *Curve Fitting* by the *Principle of Least Squares.*

(iv) Method of *Moving Averages.*

11·5·1. Graphic or Free Hand Curve Fitting Method. This is the simplest and the most flexible method of estimating the secular trend and consists in first obtaining a historigram by plotting the time series values on a graph paper and then drawing a free-hand smooth curve through these points so that it accurately reflects the long-term tendency of the data. The smoothing of the curve eliminates the other components, *viz.*, seasonal, cyclical and random variations. In order to obtain proper trend line or curve, the following points may be borne in mind :

(i) It should be smooth.

(ii) The number of points above the trend curve/line should be more or less equal to the number of points below it.

(iii) The sum of the vertical deviations of the given points above the trend line should be approximately equal to the sum of vertical deviations of the points below the trend line so that the total positive deviations are more or less balanced against total negative deviations.

(iv) The sum of the squares of the vertical deviations of the given points from the trend line/curve is minimum possible.

[The points (*iii*) and (*iv*) conform to the principle of average (Arithmetic Mean) because the algebraic sum of the deviations of the given observations from their arithmetic mean is zero and the sum of the squared deviations is minimum when taken about mean.]

(v) If the cycles are present in the data then the trend line should be so drawn that :

(a) It has equal number of cycles above and below it.

(b) It bisects the cycles so that the areas of the cycles above and below the trend line are approximately same.

(vi) The minor short-term fluctuations or abrupt and sudden variations may be ignored.

Merits. (*i*) It is very simple and time-saving method and does not require any mathematical calculations.

(*ii*) It is a very flexible method in the sense that it can be used to describe all types of trend – linear as well as non-linear.

Demerits. (*i*) The strongest objection to this method is that it is highly subjective in nature. The trend curve so obtained will very much depend on the personal bias and judgement of the investigator handling the data and consequently different persons will obtain different trend curves for the same set of data. Thus, a proper and judicious use of this method requires great skill and expertise on the part of the investigator and this very much restricts the popularity and utility of this method. This method, though simple and flexible, is seldom used in practice because of the inherent bias of the investigator.

(*ii*) It does not help to measure trend.

(*iii*) Because of the subjective nature of the free-hand trend curve, it will be dangerous to use it for forecasting or making predictions.

11·5·2. Method of Semi-Averages. As compared with graphic method, this method has more objective approach. In this method, the whole time series data is classified into two equal parts *w.r.t.* time. For example, if we are given the time series values for 10 years from 1985 to 1994 then the two equal parts will be the data corresponding to periods 1985 to 1989 and 1990 to 1994. However, in case of odd number of years, the two equal parts are obtained on omitting the value for the middle period. Thus, for example, for the data for 9 years from 1990 to 1998, the two parts will be the data for years 1990 to 1993 and 1995 to 1998, the value for the middle year, *viz.*, 1994 being omitted. Having divided the given series into two equal parts, we next compute the arithmetic mean of time-series values for each half separately. These means are called ***semi-averages***. Then these semi-averages are plotted as points against the middle point of the respective time periods covered by each part. The line joining these points gives the straight line trend fitting the given data.

As an illustration, for the time series data for 1985 to 1994, we have :

	Part I	*Part II*
Period :	1985 to 1989	1990 to 1994
Semi-Average :	$\bar{x}_1 = \dfrac{y_1 + y_2 + y_3 + y_4 + y_5}{5}$	$\bar{x}_2 = \dfrac{y_6 + y_7 + \ldots + y_{10}}{5}$
Middle of time period :	1987	1992

$\bar{x}_1$ is plotted against 1987 and $\bar{x}_2$ is plotted against 1992. The trend line is obtained on joining the points so obtained, *viz.*, the points (1987, $\bar{x}_1$) and (1992, $\bar{x}_2$) by a straight line. In the above case, the two parts consisted of an odd number of years, *viz.*, 5 and hence the middle time period is computed easily. However, if the two halves consist of even numbers of years as in the next case given above; *viz.*, the years 1990 to 1993 and 1995 to 1998, the centring of average time period is slightly difficult. In this case $\bar{x}_1$ (the mean of the values for the years 1990 to 1993) will be plotted against the mean of the two middle years of the period 1990 to 1993, *viz.*, the mean of the years 1991 and 1992. Similarly, $\bar{x}_2$ will be plotted against the mean of the years 1996 and 1997.

Merits. (*i*) An obvious advantage of this method is its objectivity in the sense that it does not depend on personal judgement and everyone who uses this method gets the same trend line and hence the same trend values.

(*ii*) It is easy to understand and apply as compared with the moving average or the least square methods of measuring trend.

(*iii*) The line can be extended both ways to obtain future or past estimates.

Limitations. (*i*) This method assumes the presence of linear trend (in the time series values) which may not exist.

(*ii*) The use of arithmetic mean (for obtaining semi-averages) may also be questioned because of its limitations.

Accordingly, the trend values obtained by this method and the predicted values for future are not precise and reliable.

Example 11·1. *Apply the method of semi-averages for determining trend of the following data and estimate the value for 2000 :*

Years	:	*1993*	*1994*	*1995*	*1996*	*1997*	*1998*
Sales (thousand units)	:	*20*	*24*	*22*	*30*	*28*	*32*

If the actual figure of sales for 2000 is 35,000 units, how do you account for the difference between the figures you obtain and the actual figures given to you ?

Solution. Here $n = 6$ (even), and hence the two parts will be 1993 to 1995 and 1996 to 1998.

TABLE 11·1. **CALCULATIONS FOR TREND BY SEMI-AVERAGES**

Year	*Sales (thousand units)*	*3-Yearly Semi-Totals*	*Semi-Average (A.M.)*
1993	20		
1994	24 →	66	$\frac{66}{3} = 22$
1995	22		
1996	30		
1997	28 →	90	$\frac{90}{3} = 30$
1998	32		

Here the semi-average 22 is to be plotted against the mid-year of first part, *i.e.*, 1994 and the semi-average 30 is to be plotted against the mid-year of second part, *viz.*, 1997. The trend line is shown in the Fig. 11·3.

Remark. The trend values for different years can be read from the trend line graph. Alternately, the average increment in value of sales (thousand units) for 3 years from 1994 to 1997 is 30 – 22 = 8 ('000 units). Hence, the yearly increment in sales is (8/3) = 2·667 ('000 units).

Now the trend value of sales for 1994 is the average of first part, *viz.*, 22 ('000 units) and for 1997 is 30 ('000 units). Hence using the fact that the yearly increment in sales is 2·667 ('000 units), the trend values for sales of various years can be obtained as shown in Table 11·1A.

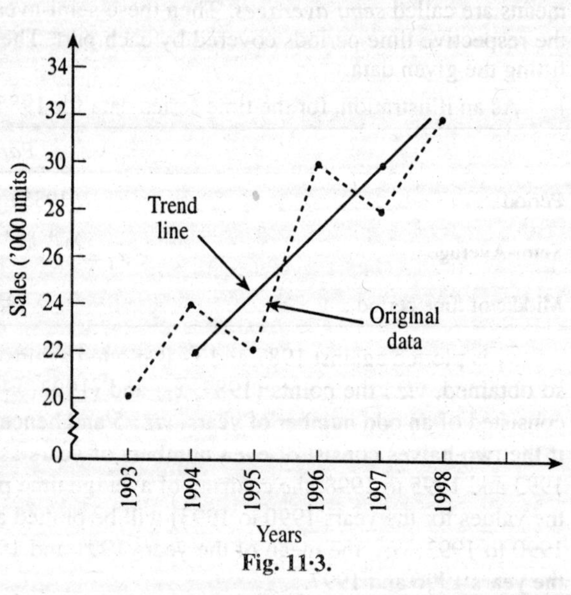

Fig. 11·3.

TABLE 11·1A. COMPUTATION OF TREND VALUES

Year	*Trend Values ('000 units)*	*Year*	*Trend Values ('000 units)*
1993	22 – 2·667 = 19·333	1997	30
1994	22	1998	30 + 2·667 = 32·667
1995	22 + 2·667 = 24·667	1999	32·667 + 2·667 = 35·334
1996	24·667 + 2·667 = 27·334	2000	35·334 + 2·667 = 38·001

Thus the estimated (trend) value for sales in 2000 is 38,001 units. This trend value differs from the given value of 35,000 units because it has been obtained under the assumption that there is a linear relationship between the given time series values which in this case (as is obvious from the graph of the original data) is not true. Moreover, in computing the trend value, the effects of seasonal, cyclical and irregular variations have been completely ignored while the observed values are affected by these factors.

Example 11·2. *From the following series of annual data, find the trend line by the method of semi-averages. Also estimate the value for 1999.*

Year :	*1990*	*1991*	*1992*	*1993*	*1994*	*1995*	*1996*	*1997*	*1998*
Actual Value :	*170*	*231*	*261*	*267*	*278*	*302*	*299*	*298*	*340*

Solution. Here the number of years is 9, *i.e.,* odd. The two middle parts will be 1990 to 1993 and 1995 to 1998, the value for middle year, *viz.,* 1994 being ignored.

TABLE 11·2. CALCULATIONS FOR TREND BY SEMI-AVERAGES

Year	*Actual Value*	*4 Yearly Semi-Totals*	*Semi-Average*
1990	170		
1991	231		
1992	261	→ 929	$\frac{929}{4} = 232{\cdot}25 \simeq 232$
1993	267		
1994	278		
1995	302		
1996	299		
1997	298	→ 1239	$\frac{1239}{4} = 309{\cdot}75 \simeq 310$
1998	340		

The value 232 is plotted against the middle of the years 1991 and 1992 and the value 310 is plotted against the middle of the years 1996 and 1997. The trend line graph is shown in Fig. 11·4.

From the graph we see that the estimated (trend) value for 1999 is 348.

Aliter. *Trend Value for 1999* : From the calculations in the above table we observe that the increment in the actual value from middle of 1991-92 to the middle of 1996-97, *i.e.,* for 5 years is 310 – 232 = 78. Hence the yearly increment is 78/5. We also find that the average trend value for middle of 1996-97 is 310. Hence the trend value for 1999 is given by

$$310 + \frac{5}{2} \times \frac{78}{5} = 310 + 39 = 349.$$

This value differs from the graph value of 348 obtained from the trend line because of the reason given in Example 11·1 and also because we have obtained the calculations by rounding the decimals.

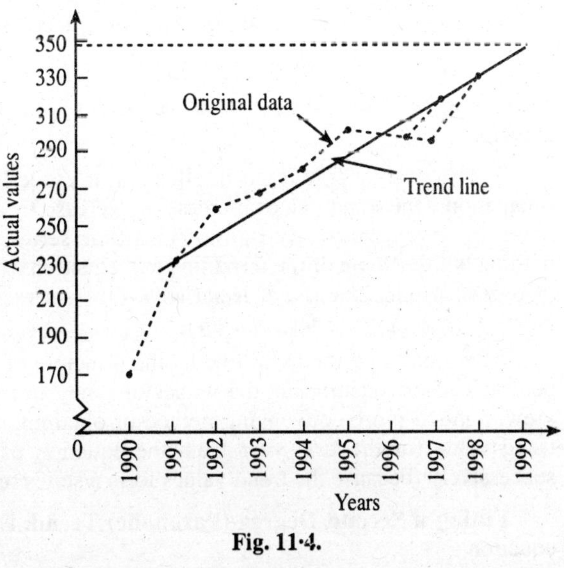

Fig. 11·4.

11·5·3. Method of Curve Fitting by the Principle of Least Squares. The principle of least squares provides us an analytical or mathematical device to obtain an objective fit to the trend of the given time series. Most of the data relating to economic and business time series conform to definite laws of growth or decay and accordingly in such a situation analytical trend fitting will be more reliable for forecasting and predictions. This technique can be used to fit linear as well as non-linear trends.

Fitting of Linear Trend. Let the straight line trend between the given time-series values (y) and time (t) be given by the equation :

$$y = a + bt \qquad \text{...(11·9)}$$

Then for any given time 't', the estimated value y_e of y as given by this equation is :

$$y_e = a + bt \qquad \text{...(11·10)}$$

As discussed in details in Chapter 9 – Linear Regression Analysis, the principle of least squares consists in estimating the values of a and b in (11·9) so that the sum of the squares of errors of estimate

$$E = \Sigma(y - y_e)^2 = \Sigma(y - a - bt)^2, \qquad \text{...(11·11)}$$

is minimum, the summation being taken over given values of the time series. This will be so if :

$$\frac{\partial E}{\partial a} = 0 = -2\Sigma\,(y - a - bt) \quad \text{and} \quad \frac{\partial E}{\partial b} = 0 = -2\,\Sigma\; t\,(y - a - bt) \qquad \text{... (*)}$$

which, on simplification, gives the *normal equations* or *least square equations* for estimating a and b as

$$\Sigma y = na + b\Sigma t \quad \text{...(11·12)} \qquad \text{and} \qquad \Sigma\, t\, y = a\Sigma t + b\Sigma t^2, \qquad \text{...(11·13)}$$

where n is the number of time series pairs (t, y). It may be seen that equation (11·12) is obtained on taking sum of both sides in equation (11·9). Equation (11·13) is obtained on multiplying equation (11·9) by t and then summing both sides over the given values of the series.

Solving (11·12) and (11·13) for a and b and substituting these values in (11·9), we finally get the equation of the straight line trend.

Remarks 1. The values of a and b obtained on solving the equations (11·12) and (11·13) provide a minimum of E defined in (11·11).

Further the first equation of (*) implies

$$\Sigma(y - a - bt) = 0 \quad \Rightarrow \quad \Sigma(y - y_e) = 0.$$

Hence the least square trend line is obtained so that :

$$(i)\ \Sigma(y - y_e) = 0 \quad \Rightarrow \quad \Sigma y = \Sigma y_e,$$

i.e., the sum of the given values and the sum of trend values are equal ,

and $(ii)\ \Sigma\,(y - y_e)^2$ is minimum.

where y is the observed time series value and y_e is the corresponding trend value given by the trend line (11·9).

2. The straight line trend implies that irrespective of the seasonal and cyclical swings and irregular fluctuations, the trend values increase or decrease by a constant absolute amount 'b' per unit of time. Thus, if we are given the yearly figures for a time series, then the coefficient 'b' in the line (11·9), which is nothing but the *slope* of the trend line [*c.f.* equation of a line in the form : $y = mx + c$], gives the *annual rate of growth.* Hence, the *linear trend values form a series in arithmetic progression, the common difference being 'b', the slope of the trend line.*

After obtaining the trend line by the principle of least squares, the trend values for different years can be obtained on substituting the values of time t in the trend equation. However, from practical point of view, a much more convenient method of obtaining the trend values of different years is to compute the trend value for the first year from the equation of the trend line and then add the value of 'b' to it successively (because the trend values form a series in A.P. with common difference 'b').

Fitting a Second Degree (Parabolic) Trend. Let the second degree parabolic trend be given by the equation :

$$y = a + bt + ct^2 \qquad \text{...(11·14)}$$

Then for any given value of t, the trend value is given by :

$$y_e = a + bt + ct^2$$

Thus, if y_e is the trend value corresponding to an observed value y, then according to the principle of least squares we have to obtain the values of a, b and c in (11·14) so that

$$E = \Sigma\,(y - y_e)^2 = \Sigma(y - a - bt - ct^2)^2$$

is minimum for variations in a, b and c. Thus, the normal or least square equations for estimating a, b and c are given by :

$$\left.\begin{aligned} \frac{\partial E}{\partial a} &= 0 = -2\Sigma\,(y - a - bt - ct^2) \\ \frac{\partial E}{\partial b} &= 0 = -2\Sigma\, t\,(y - a - bt - ct^2) \\ \frac{\partial E}{\partial c} &= 0 = -2\Sigma\, t^2\,(y - a - bt - ct^2) \end{aligned}\right\} \Rightarrow \left.\begin{aligned} \Sigma y &= na + b\Sigma\, t + c\Sigma\, t^2 \\ \Sigma\, t\,y &= a\Sigma\, t + b\Sigma\, t^2 + c\Sigma\, t^3 \\ \Sigma\, t^2 y &= a\Sigma\, t^2 + b\Sigma\, t^3 + c\Sigma\, t^4 \end{aligned}\right\} \quad ...(11\cdot15)$$

the summation being taken over the values of the time series.

The first equation in (11·15) is obtained on summing both sides of (11·14). The second equation is obtained on multiplying (11·14) with t, [the coefficient of second constant b in (11·14)] and then summing both sides. The third equation is obtained on multiplying both sides of (11·14) with t^2 [the coefficient of c, the third constant in (11·14)] and then summing over values of the series.

For given time series, the values Σy, $\Sigma\, t\, y$, $\Sigma\, t^2 y$, $\Sigma\, t$, $\Sigma\, t^2$, $\Sigma\, t^3$ and $\Sigma\, t^4$ can be calculated and equations (11·15) can be solved for a, b and c. With these values of a, b, c, the parabolic curve (11·14) is the trend curve of best fit.

Remark. Change of Origin. Usually, the values of t are for different years, say, 1990, 1991,..., 1999 and thus computation of $\Sigma\, t$, $\Sigma\, t^2$, $\Sigma\, t^3$, $\Sigma\, t^4$, etc., and hence the solution of equations (11·12) and (11·13) for linear trend or equations (11·15) for parabolic trend is quite tedious and time consuming. However, it may be remarked that the time variable t in the time series has no magnitudinal value but it has only positional or locational importance. Hence, we can shift the origin in the time variable according to our convenience and assign it the consecutive values 0, 1, 2,..., etc.. The time period allotted to the value 0 is known as the *period of origin*. This might slightly facilitate the solution of the normal equations. However, the algebraic computations can be simplified to a great extent by shifting the origin in time variable t to a new variable x in such a way that we always get $\Sigma\, x = \Sigma\, x^3 = 0$. The *technique* is explained below and *can be applied only if the values of t are given to be equidistant,* say, at an interval h.

If *n, the number of time series values is odd, then* the transformation is :

$$x = \frac{t - \text{middle value}}{\text{Interval }(h)} \quad ...(11\cdot16)$$

Thus, if we are given yearly figures for, say, 1990, 1991, 1992, ..., 1996, *i.e.*, $n = 7$, then

$$x = \frac{t - \text{middle year}}{1} = t - 1993 \quad ...(*)$$

Putting t = 1990, 1991, 1992, ..., 1996 in (*), we get $x = -3, -2, -1, 0, 1, 2$ and 3 respectively so that $\Sigma\, x = \Sigma\, x^3 = 0$.

If n is even then, the transformation is :

$$x = \frac{t - (\text{Arithmetic mean of two middle values})}{\frac{1}{2}\,(\text{Interval})} \quad ...(11\cdot17)$$

Thus, if we are given the yearly values for, say, 1995, 1996, 1997,..., 2002, then

$$x = \frac{t - \frac{1}{2}(1998 + 1999)}{\frac{1}{2}} = 2\,(t - 1998\cdot5) = 2t - 3997 \quad ...(**)$$

Putting $t = 1995, 1996, \ldots, 2002$ in (**), we get respectively :

$$x = -7, -5, -3, -1, 1, 3, 5, 7 \qquad \text{so that} \qquad \sum x = \sum x^3 = 0$$

The transformations (*) or (**) will always give $\sum x = 0 = \sum x^3$, and this reduces the algebraic calculations for the solution of normal equations to a great extent. For example, for the linear trend

$$y = a + bx, \qquad \ldots(11\cdot18)$$

where x is defined either by (11·16) or (11·17) according as n is odd or even, the normal equations for estimating a and b become :

$$\sum y = na + b\sum x \qquad \text{and} \qquad \sum xy = a\sum x + b\sum x^2$$

but $\sum x = 0$. Hence these equations give :

$$\sum y = na \quad \text{and} \quad \sum xy = b\sum x^2 \quad \Rightarrow \quad a = \frac{\sum y}{n} \quad \text{and} \quad b = \frac{\sum xy}{\sum x^2} \qquad \ldots(11\cdot19)$$

With these values of a and b, (11·18) gives the equation of the trend line.

Similarly, for the parabolic trend : $y = a + bx + cx^2, \qquad \ldots(11\cdot20)$

the normal equations for estimating a, b and c are

$$\left.\begin{aligned} \sum y &= na + b\sum x + c\sum x^2 \\ \sum xy &= a\sum x + b\sum x^2 + c\sum x^3 \\ \sum x^2 y &= a\sum x^2 + b\sum x^3 + c\sum x^4 \end{aligned}\right\} \text{which reduce to} \left.\begin{aligned} \sum y &= na + c\sum x^2 \quad &\ldots(i) \\ \sum xy &= b\sum x^2 \quad &\ldots(ii) \\ \sum x^2 y &= a\sum x^2 + c\sum x^4 \quad &\ldots(iii) \end{aligned}\right\} \quad [\because \sum x = \sum x^3 = 0]$$

Equation (*ii*) gives the value of $b = \dfrac{\sum xy}{\sum x^2}$ and equations (*i*) and (*iii*) can be solved simultaneously for a and c. With these values of a, b and c the curve (11·20) becomes the parabolic trend curve of best fit.

Fitting of Exponential Trend. The exponential curve is given by the equation :

$$y = ab^t \qquad \ldots(11\cdot21)$$

Taking logarithm of both sides, we get

$$\log y = \log a + t \log b \quad \Rightarrow \quad Y = A + Bt \qquad \ldots(11\cdot22)$$

where $\quad Y = \log y \; ; \; A = \log a \quad \text{and} \quad B = \log b \qquad \ldots(11\cdot23)$

(11·22) is a straight line trend between Y and t. Hence, the normal equations for estimating A and B are [*c.f.* equations (11·12) and (11·13)] :

$$\sum Y = nA + B\sum t \qquad \text{and} \qquad \sum tY = A\sum t + B\sum t^2$$

These equations can be solved for A and B and we finally get on using (11·23) :

$$a = \text{Antilog } (A) \qquad \text{and} \qquad b = \text{Antilog } (B) \qquad \ldots(11\cdot24)$$

With these values of a and b, the curve (11·21) becomes best exponential trend curve.

Remark. As already explained in the fitting of linear and parabolic trend, we can change the origin in t to new variable x such that $\sum x = 0$ and then considering the trend curve $y = ab^x$, the calculations can be reduced to a great extent.

Merits and Limitations of Trend Fitting by Principle of Least Squares

Merits. The method of least squares is the most popular and widely used method of fitting mathematical functions to a given set of observations. It has the following advantages :

(*i*) Because of its analytical or mathematical character, this method completely eliminates the element of subjective judgement or personal bias on the part of the investigator.

(*ii*) Unlike the method of moving averages (discussed in § 11·5·6), this method enables us to compute the trend values for all the given time periods in the series.

(*iii*) The trend equation can be used to estimate or predict the values of the variable for any period t in future or even in the intermediate periods of the given series and the forecasted values are also quite reliable.

(*iv*) The curve fitting by the principle of least squares is the *only* technique which enables us to obtain the rate of growth per annum, for yearly data, if linear trend is fitted. If we fit the linear trend $y = a + bx$, where x is obtained from t by change of origin such that $\sum x = 0$, then for the yearly data, the annual rate of growth is b or $2b$ according as the number of years is odd or even respectively.

Demerits. (*i*) The most serious limitation of the method is the determination of the type of the trend curve to be fitted, *viz.*, whether we should fit a linear or a parabolic trend or some other more complicated trend curve. [This is discussed in detail in § 11·5·5.] Assumptions about the type of trend to be fitted might introduce some bias.

(*ii*) The addition of even a single new observation necessitates all the calculations to be done afresh which is not so in the case of moving average method.

(*iii*) This method requires more calculations and is quite tedious and time consuming as compared with other methods. It is rather difficult for a non-mathematical person (layman) to understand and use.

(*iv*) Future predictions or forecasts based on this method are based only on the long-term variations, *i.e.*, trend and completely ignore the cyclical, seasonal and irregular fluctuations.

(*v*) It cannot be used to fit growth curves (Modified exponential curve, Gompertz curve and Logistic curve) to which most of the economic and business time series conform. The discussion, however, is beyond the scope of the book

We shall now discuss some numerical examples to illustrate the technique of curve fitting by the principle of least squares.

Example 11·3. *Fit a linear trend to the following data by the least squares method. Verify that* $\Sigma(y - y_e) = 0$, *where* y_e *is the corresponding trend value of* y.

Year	:	*1990*	*1992*	*1994*	*1996*	*1998*
Production (in '000 units)	:	*18*	*21*	*23*	*27*	*16*

Also estimate the production for the year 1999. [*Delhi Univ. B.Com. (Pass), 1999*]

Solution. Here $n = 5$ *i.e.*, odd. Hence, we shift the origin to the middle of the time period *viz.*, the year 1994.

Let $\quad x = t - 1994 \qquad \ldots(i)$

Let the trend line of y (production) on x be :

$$y = a + bx \text{ (Origin 1994)} \qquad \ldots(ii)$$

TABLE 11·3. **COMPUTATION OF STRAIGHT LINE TREND**

Year (*t*)	*Production ('000 units)* (*y*)	$x = t - 1994$	x^2	xy	*Trend Values ('000 units)* $(y_e) = 21 + 0{\cdot}1x$	$y - y_e$ *('000 units)*
1990	18	−4	16	−72	21 − 0·4 = 20·6	−2·6
1992	21	−2	4	−42	21 − 0·2 = 20·8	0·2
1994	23	0	0	0	21·0	2·0
1996	27	2	4	54	21 + 0·2 = 21·2	5·8
1998	16	4	16	64	20 + 0·4 = 21·4	−5·4
	$\sum y = 105$	$\sum x = 0$	$\sum x^2 = 40$	$\sum xy = 4$		$\Sigma(y - y_e) = 0$

The normal equations for estimating a and b in (*ii*) are :

$$\Sigma y = na + b\Sigma x \quad \text{and} \quad \Sigma xy = a\Sigma x + b\Sigma x^2$$

$$\Rightarrow \quad 105 = 5a + b \times 0 \quad \Rightarrow \quad 4 = a \times 0 + b \times 40$$

$$\Rightarrow \quad a = \frac{105}{5} = 21 \quad \Rightarrow \quad b = \frac{4}{40} = \frac{1}{10} = 0{\cdot}1$$

Substituting in (*ii*), the straight line trend equation is given by :

$$y = 21 + 0{\cdot}1x, \quad \text{(Origin : 1994)} \qquad \ldots(iii)$$

[x units = 1 year and y = Production (in '000 units).]

Putting $x = -4, -2, 0, 2$ and 4 in (*iii*), we obtain the trend values (y_e) for the years 1990, 1992,..., 1998 respectively, as given in the last but one column of the Table 11·3.

The difference $(y - y_e)$ is calculated in the last column of the table. We have :

$$\Sigma(y - y_e) = -2{\cdot}6 + 0{\cdot}2 + 2{\cdot}0 + 5{\cdot}8 - 5{\cdot}4 = 8 - 8 = 0, \text{ as required.}$$

Estimated Production for 1999. Taking $t = 1999$ in (*i*), we get $x = 1999 - 1994 = 5$. Substituting $x = 5$ in (*iii*), the estimated production for 1999 is given by :

$$(y_e)_{1999} = 21 + 0{\cdot}1 \times 5 = 21 + 0{\cdot}5 = 21{\cdot}5 \text{ thousand units.}$$

Example 11·4. *Below are given the figures of production (in thousand tons) of a sugar factory :*

Year	:	*1999*	*2000*	*2001*	*2002*	*2003*	*2004*	*2005*
Production	:	*77*	*88*	*94*	*85*	*91*	*98*	*90*

(*i*) *Fit a straight line by the method of 'least squares' and show the trend values.*

(*ii*) *What is the monthly increase in production ?*

(*iii*) *Eliminate the trend by using both additive and multiplicative models.*

[Delhi Univ. B.Com. (Hons.), (External), 2007]

Solution.

TABLE 11·4. COMPUTATION OF STRAIGHT LINE TREND

Year	*Production (in '000 tons)*	$x = t - 2002$	xy	x^2	*Trend Values (in '000 tons)* $y_e = 89 + 2x$
1999	77	–3	–231	9	83
2000	88	–2	–176	4	85
2001	94	–1	– 94	1	87
2002	85	0	0	0	89
2003	91	1	91	1	91
2004	98	2	196	4	93
2005	90	3	270	9	95
Total	$\Sigma y = 623$	$\Sigma x = 0$	$\Sigma xy = 56$	$\Sigma x^2 = 28$	$\Sigma y_e = 623$

(*i*) Let the straight line trend of y on x be given by :

$$y = a + bx \qquad \text{...(*)}$$

where the origin is July 2002 and x unit = 1 year. The normal equations for estimating a and b in (*) are :

$$\Sigma y = na + b\Sigma x \quad \text{and} \quad \Sigma xy = a\Sigma x + b\Sigma x^2$$

$$\Rightarrow \quad a = \frac{\Sigma y}{n} = \frac{623}{7} = 89 \quad \text{and} \quad b = \frac{\Sigma xy}{\Sigma x^2} = \frac{56}{28} = 2 \qquad [\because \ \Sigma x = 0]$$

Hence, the straight line trend is given by the equation :

$$y = 89 + 2x \quad \text{(Origin : 2002)} \qquad \text{...(**)}$$

[x units = 1 year and y = Annual production of sugar (in '000 tons)]

Putting $x = -3, -2, -1, 0, 1, 2, 3$ in (**), we get the trend values for the years 1999 to 2005 respectively and are shown in the last column of the Table 11·4. It may be checked that $\Sigma y = \Sigma y_e$, as required by the principle of least squares.

(*ii*) From (*) it is obvious that the trend values increase by a constant amount 'b' units every year. Thus, the yearly increase in production is 'b' units, *i.e.*, $2 \times 1000 = 2000$ tons.

Hence, the monthly increase in production $= \frac{2000}{12} = 166{\cdot}67$ tons.

(*iii*) Assuming multiplicative model, the trend values are eliminated on dividing the given values (y) by the trend values (y_e). However, if we assume the additive model, the trend eliminated values are given by $(y - y_e)$ [See Table 11·5]. The resulting values contain short-term (cyclic) variations and irregular variations. Since the data are annual, the seasonal variations are absent.

TABLE 11·5. **ELIMINATION OF TREND**

Year	Trend eliminated values (in '000 tons) based on	
	Additive Model $(y - y_e)$	Multiplicative Model (y / y_e)
1999	$77 - 83 = -6$	$77 \div 83 = 0{\cdot}93$
2000	$88 - 85 = 3$	$88 \div 85 = 1{\cdot}04$
2001	$94 - 87 = 7$	$94 \div 87 = 1{\cdot}08$
2002	$85 - 89 = -4$	$85 \div 89 = 0{\cdot}96$
2003	$91 - 91 = 0$	$91 \div 91 = 1{\cdot}00$
2004	$98 - 93 = 5$	$98 \div 93 = 1{\cdot}05$
2005	$90 - 95 = -5$	$90 \div 95 = 0{\cdot}95$

Example 11·5. *The sales of a company in million of rupees for the years 1994 — 2001 are given below:*

Year :	*1994*	*1995*	*1996*	*1997*	*1998*	*1999*	*2000*	*2001*
Sales :	*550*	*560*	*555*	*585*	*540*	*525*	*545*	*585*

(i) Find the linear trend equation.

(ii) Estimate the sales for the year 1993.

(iii) Find the slope of the straight line trend

(iv) Do the figures show a rising trend or a falling trend ?

Solution. (*i*) In this case, since *n*, the number of pairs is even, *viz.*, 8, we shift the origin to the time which is the arithmetic mean of the two middle times, *viz.*, 1997 and 1998 and we take :

$$x = \frac{t - \left(\dfrac{1997 + 1998}{2}\right)}{\frac{1}{2}\cdot\text{(Interval)}} = 2(t - 1997{\cdot}5) = 2t - 3995 \qquad \ldots(i)$$

Thus taking :

$t = 1997$, we get $x = 3994 - 3995 = -1$; $t = 1996$, we get $x = 3992 - 3995 = -3$

and so on. Let the linear trend equation between *y* and *x* be given by :

$$y = a + bx\ ,\ x = 2(t - 1997{\cdot}5) \qquad \ldots(ii)$$

where *x* units = $\frac{1}{2}$ year and *y* = Annual sales in million of Rs.

TABLE 11·6. **COMPUTATIONS FOR LINEAR TREND**

Year (t)	Sales (y)	$x = 2(t - 1997{\cdot}5)$	xy	x^2	Trend values (in Million Rs.) $y_e = 555{\cdot}63 + 0{\cdot}21x$
1994	550	–7	–3850	49	$555{\cdot}63 - 7 \times 0{\cdot}21 = 554{\cdot}16$
1995	560	–5	–2800	25	$555{\cdot}63 - 5 \times 0{\cdot}21 = 554{\cdot}58$
1996	555	–3	–1665	9	$555{\cdot}63 - 3 \times 0{\cdot}21 = 555{\cdot}00$
1997	585	–1	– 585	1	$555{\cdot}63 - 1 \times 0{\cdot}21 = 555{\cdot}42$
1998	540	1	540	1	$555{\cdot}63 + 1 \times 0{\cdot}21 = 555{\cdot}84$
1999	525	3	1575	9	$555{\cdot}63 + 3 \times 0{\cdot}21 = 556{\cdot}26$
2000	545	5	2725	25	$555{\cdot}63 + 5 \times 0{\cdot}21 = 556{\cdot}68$
2001	585	7	4095	49	$555{\cdot}63 + 7 \times 0{\cdot}21 = 557{\cdot}10$
Total	$\Sigma y = 4445$	$\Sigma x = 0$	$\Sigma xy = 35$	$\Sigma x^2 = 168$	

The normal equations for estimating *a* and *b* in (*ii*) are :

$$\Sigma y = na + b\Sigma x \qquad\qquad \Sigma xy = a\Sigma x + b\Sigma x^2$$

$$\Rightarrow\ 4445 = 8a + 0 \qquad\qquad \Rightarrow\ 35 = a \times 0 + 168b$$

$$\Rightarrow\ a = \frac{4445}{8} = 555{\cdot}63 \qquad\qquad \Rightarrow\ b = \frac{35}{168} = 0{\cdot}21$$

Substituting in (*ii*), the straight line trend is given by the equation :

$$y = 555{\cdot}63 + 0{\cdot}21x \quad \ldots(iii)$$

Putting $x = -7, -5, -3, -1, 1, 3, 5$ and 7 in (*iii*), we get the trend values of sales for the years 1994 to 2001 respectively. The trend values are shown in the last column of the Table 11·6.

(*ii*) The estimated sales for 1993 are obtained on putting $t = 1993$ in :

$$x = 2(t - 1997{\cdot}5) = 2(1993 - 1997{\cdot}5) = -9$$

Substituting in (*iii*), the estimated sales for 1993 are :

$$(y_e)_{1993} = 555{\cdot}63 + 0{\cdot}21 \times (-9) = 555{\cdot}63 - 1{\cdot}89 = 553{\cdot}74 \text{ million Rs.}$$

(*iii*) The slope of straight line trend (*iii*) is given by $b = 0{\cdot}21$.

[*c.f.* the slope-intercept form of the equation of a straight line : $y = mx + c$, where m is the slope of the line and c is the intercept made by it on the line.]

(*iv*) The slope of the trend line represents the rate of growth (sales) per unit time *i.e.*, annually. Since the slope $b = 0{\cdot}21$ is positive, the given data exhibits a rising trend.

Remarks 1. If the slope of the trend line comes out to be negative, then the given time series will exhibit a declining (decreasing) trend.

2. $b = 0{\cdot}21$, implies that there is an annual increase of Rs. 0·21 million *i.e.*, Rs. 2,10,000 in the sales of the company.

Example 11·6. *Calculate the quarterly trend values by the method of least square for the following quarterly data for the last five years given below.*

Year	*I Quarter*	*II Quarter*	*III Quarter*	*IV Quarter*
1994	*60*	*80*	*72*	*68*
1995	*68*	*104*	*100*	*88*
1996	*80*	*116*	*108*	*96*
1997	*108*	*152*	*136*	*124*
1998	*160*	*184*	*172*	*164*

[*Delhi Univ. B.Com. (Hons.), 1999*]

Solution. Here we will fit linear trend equation between the average quarterly values (*Y*) and the time variable *X* (year).

TABLE 11·7. **CALCULATIONS FOR LINEAR TREND**

Year (*X*)	*Total of quarterly values*	*Average of quarterly values* (*Y*)	$U = X - 1996$	U^2	*UY*	*Trend Values* ($Y_e = 112 + 24U$)
1994	280	70	–2	4	–140	112 + 24 (–2) = 64
1995	360	90	–1	1	–90	112 + 24 (–1) = 88
1996	400	100	0	0	0	112 + 24 (0) = 112
1997	520	130	1	1	130	112 + 24 (1) = 136
1998	680	170	2	4	340	112 + 24 (2) = 160
Total		$\Sigma Y = 560$	$\Sigma U = 0$	$\Sigma U^2 = 10$	$\Sigma UY = 240$	

The normal equations for fitting the linear trend equation :

$$Y = a + bU, \; (U = X - 1996) \quad \ldots(i)$$

are

$$\left.\begin{aligned} \Sigma Y &= na + b\Sigma U \\ \Sigma UY &= a\Sigma U + b\Sigma U^2 \end{aligned}\right\} \Rightarrow \begin{aligned} a &= \frac{\Sigma Y}{n} = \frac{560}{5} = 112 \\ b &= \frac{\Sigma UY}{\Sigma U^2} = \frac{240}{10} = 24 \end{aligned}$$

∴ The linear trend equation is :

$$Y = 112 + 24U, \; (U = X - 1996) \quad \ldots(ii)$$

Putting $U = -2, -1, 0, 1$ and 2 in (*ii*), we get the trend values (for average quarterly values) for the years 1994 to 1998 respectively, as given in the last column of the Table 11·7.

From (*i*) or (*ii*), yearly increment in trend value = $b = 24$

$\therefore$ Quarterly increment = $\frac{24}{4} = 6.$

We can now obtain the quarterly trend values for different years as explained below.

From the Table 11·7, the trend value for the middle quarter (*i.e.*, half of the second quarter and half of the third quarter) of 1994 is 64. Since the quarterly increment is 6, the trend values for the second and third quarter of 1994 are $64 - \frac{1}{2} \times 6 = 61$ and $64 + \frac{1}{2} \times 6 = 67$, respectively. Consequently, the trend value for the first quarter of 1994 is $61 - 6 = 55$ and for the fourth quarter of 1994 is $67 + 6 = 73$. Similarly, we can obtain the trend values for different quarters of the remaining years by adding 6 to the preceding value, as given in the Table 11·8.

TABLE 11·8. **QUARTERLY TREND VALUES**

Year	*1st Quarter*	*2nd Quarter*	*3rd Quarter*	*4th Quarter*
1994	55	61	67	73
1995	79	85	91	97
1996	103	109	115	121
1997	127	133	139	145
1998	151	157	163	169

Example 11·7. *The linear trend of sales of a company is Rs. 6,50,000 in 1995 and it rises by Rs. 16,500 per year.*

(*i*) *Write down the trend equation.*

(*ii*) *If the company knows that its sales in 1998 will be 10% below the forecasted trend sales, find its expected sales in 1998.* [*Delhi Univ. B.A. (Econ. Hons.), 1998*]

Solution. (*i*) The sales of the company are Rs. 6,50,000 in 1995 and they exhibit a linear trend with a constant rise of Rs. 16,500 per year. Hence, the annual trend equation of the sales of the company is :

$$Y_t = 6{,}50{,}000 + 16{,}500\, t \quad \ldots(*)$$

(Y_t : Annual sales in Rupees ; t units = 1 year ; Origin : 1995).

(*ii*) Using the trend equation (*), the estimated sales of the company in 1998 *i.e.*, when $t = 3$, are given by :

$$(\hat{Y}_t)_{1998} = \text{Rs. } (6{,}50{,}000 + 16{,}500 \times 3) = \text{Rs. } (6{,}50{,}000 + 49{,}500) = \text{Rs. } 6{,}99{,}500.$$

$$\therefore \quad \text{Actual Sales in 1998} = \text{Rs.}\left[6{,}99{,}500 - \frac{10}{100} \times 6{,}99{,}500\right] = \text{Rs. } (6{,}99{,}500 - 69{,}950) = \text{Rs. } 6{,}29{,}550$$

Example 11·8. *Fit a second degree parabola to the following data.*

X	:	*1*	*2*	*3*	*4*	*5*
Y	:	*1090*	*1220*	*1390*	*1625*	*1915*

[*Delhi Univ. B.Com. (Hons.) 2008 ; C.A. (Foundation), May 2001*]

Solution.

TABLE 11·9. **CALCULATIONS FOR PARABOLIC TREND**

X	Y	$U = X - 3$	$V = \frac{Y - 1450}{5}$	U^2	U^3	U^4	UV	U^2V
1	1090	–2	–72	4	– 8	16	144	–288
2	1220	–1	– 46	1	–1	1	46	–46
3	1390	0	–12	0	0	0	0	0
4	1625	1	35	1	1	1	35	35
5	1915	2	93	4	8	16	186	372
Total		$\Sigma U = 0$	$\Sigma V = -2$	$\Sigma U^2 = 10$	$\Sigma U^3 = 0$	$\Sigma U^4 = 34$	$\Sigma UV = 411$	$\Sigma U^2V = 73$

Let the parabola of best fit of V on U be :

$$V = a + bU + cU^2 \quad \ldots(i)$$

where $U = X - 3$ and $V = \frac{Y - 1450}{5}$ ...(ii)

Then the normal equations for estimating a, b and c are :

$$\left.\begin{aligned} \Sigma V &= na + b\Sigma U + c\Sigma U^2 \\ \Sigma UV &= a\Sigma U + b\Sigma U^2 + c\Sigma U^3 \\ \Sigma U^2V &= a\Sigma U^2 + b\Sigma U^3 + c\Sigma U^4 \end{aligned}\right\} \Rightarrow \begin{aligned} -2 &= 5a + 10c & \ldots(iii) \\ 411 &= 10b & \ldots(iv) \\ 73 &= 10a + 34c & \ldots(v) \end{aligned}$$

$(iv) \Rightarrow b = \frac{411}{10} = 41{\cdot}1$ ...(vi)

$(v) - 2 \times (iii)$ gives : $73 + 4 = 34c - 20c = 14c \Rightarrow c = \frac{77}{14} = 5{\cdot}5$ ...(vii)

Substituting the value of c in (iii), we get

$$5a = -2 - 10\,(5{\cdot}5) = -57 \Rightarrow a = \frac{-57}{5} = -11{\cdot}4 \quad \ldots(viii)$$

Substituting the values of a, b, c from (vi), (vii) and (viii) in (i), the parabola of best fit of V on U becomes :

$$V = -11{\cdot}4 + 41{\cdot}1\,U + 5{\cdot}5\,U^2 \quad \ldots(ix)$$

where U and V are given by (ii).

Substituting the values of U and V from (ii) in (ix), the second degree parabola of best fit of Y on X becomes :

$$\begin{aligned} \frac{Y - 1450}{5} &= -11{\cdot}4 + 41{\cdot}1\,(X - 3) + 5{\cdot}5\,(X - 3)^2 \\ &= -11{\cdot}4 + 41{\cdot}1\,X - 123{\cdot}3 + 5{\cdot}5\,(X^2 - 6X + 9) \\ &= 5{\cdot}5X^2 + (41{\cdot}1 - 33)\,X + (-11{\cdot}4 - 123{\cdot}3 + 49{\cdot}5) \\ &= 5{\cdot}5X^2 + 8{\cdot}1X - 85{\cdot}2 \end{aligned}$$

$$\Rightarrow \quad Y - 1450 = 27{\cdot}5X^2 + 40{\cdot}5X - 426 \quad \Rightarrow \quad Y = 27{\cdot}5X^2 + 40{\cdot}5X + 1024$$

Example 11·9. *The prices of a commodity during 2001—2006 are given below. Fit a parabola $Y = a + bX + cX^2$ to these data. Estimate the price for the year 2007 :*

Year (X) :	*2001*	*2002*	*2003*	*2004*	*2005*	*2006*
Price (Rs.) (Y) :	100	107	128	140	181	192

[*Delhi Univ. B.Com. (Hons.), 2006*]

Solution. Here, the number of pairs of observations $n = 6$ *i.e.,* even. Hence, shifting the origin to the arithmetic mean of two middle years, let us take :

$$t = \frac{X - \frac{1}{2}(2003 + 2004)}{\frac{1}{2}\,\text{(Interval)}} = \frac{X - 2003{\cdot}5}{\frac{1}{2} \times 1} = 2(X - 2003{\cdot}5), \quad \ldots(*)$$

where X : Years ; Y : Price of commodity (in Rs.).

The values of t for $X = 2001$ to 2006 [From (*)] are respectively –5, –3, –1, 1, 3, 5.

Let the parabolic trend equation of Y on t be :

$$Y = a + bt + ct^2 \; ; \quad t = X - 2003{\cdot}5 \quad \ldots(**)$$

where t unit $= \frac{1}{2}$ year and Y is price of the commodity in Rs.

TABLE 11·10. CALCULATIONS FOR PARABOLIC TREND

Year (X)	Price (in (Rs.) Y	t	t^2	t^3	t^4	ty	t^2y
2001	100	–5	25	–125	625	–500	2500
2002	107	–3	9	–27	81	–321	963
2003	128	–1	1	–1	1	–128	128
2004	140	1	1	1	1	140	140
2005	181	3	9	27	81	543	1629
2006	192	5	25	125	625	960	4800
$n = 6$	$\Sigma Y = 848$	$\Sigma t = 0$	$\Sigma t^2 = 70$	$\Sigma t^3 = 0$	$\Sigma t^4 = 1414$	$\Sigma tY = 694$	$\Sigma t^2Y = 10160$

The normal equations for estimating a, b & c in (**) are :

$$\Sigma Y = na + b\Sigma t + c\Sigma t^2 \qquad 848 = 6a + 70c \qquad ...(i)$$

$$\Sigma tY = a\Sigma t + b\Sigma t^2 + c\Sigma t^3 \quad \Rightarrow \quad 694 = 70b \qquad ...(ii)$$

$$\Sigma t^2Y = a\Sigma t^2 + b\Sigma t^3 + c\Sigma t^4 \qquad 10160 = 70a + 1414c \qquad ...(iii)$$

$$(ii) \quad \Rightarrow \quad b = \frac{694}{70} = 9{\cdot}914 \qquad ...(iv)$$

Multiplying (i) by 35 and (iii) by 3 and then subtracting, we get

$$29680 - 30480 = (210a + 2450c) - (210a + 4242c)$$

$$\Rightarrow \quad -800 = -1792c \quad \Rightarrow \quad c = \frac{800}{1792} = 0{\cdot}446 \qquad ...(v)$$

Substituting the value of c in (i), we get

$$848 = 6a + 31{\cdot}22 \quad \Rightarrow \quad a = \frac{848 - 31{\cdot}22}{6} = \frac{816{\cdot}78}{6} = 136{\cdot}130 \qquad ...(vi)$$

Substituting the values of a, b and c from (iv), (v) and (vi) in (**), we get the parabolic trend equation as :

$$Y = 136{\cdot}130 + 9{\cdot}914t + 0{\cdot}446t^2 \quad ; \quad t = 2\,(X - 2003{\cdot}5) \qquad ...(vii)$$

Estimation of price for 2007

When $X = 2007$, $t = 2\,(2007 - 2003{\cdot}5) = 2 \times 3{\cdot}5 = 7$.

Putting $t = 7$ in (vii), the estimated price of the commodity for the year 2007 is

$$\hat{Y}_{x=2007} = \hat{Y}_{t=7} = \text{Rs. } (136{\cdot}130 + 9{\cdot}914 \times 7 + 0{\cdot}446 \times 7^2)$$

$$= \text{Rs. } (136{\cdot}130 + 69{\cdot}396 + 21{\cdot}854) = \text{Rs. } 227{\cdot}38$$

Example 11·10. *Fit a trend function $y = A \,.\, B^x$ to the following data.*

x :	1	2	3	4	5
y :	1·6	4·5	13·8	40·2	125·0

Solution. Here we have to fit the exponential curve

$$y = A \,.\, B^x \qquad ...(i)$$

Taking logarithm of both sides, we get

$$\log y = \log A + x \log B$$

$$\Rightarrow \quad Y = a + bx \qquad ...(ii)$$

where $\quad Y = \log y \,;\quad a = \log A \quad$ and $\quad b = \log B \qquad ...(iii)$

Equation (ii) is straight line between the variables Y and x and hence the normal equations for estimating a and b are :

$$\Sigma Y = na + b\Sigma x \qquad \text{and} \qquad \Sigma xY = a\Sigma x + b\Sigma x^2 \qquad ...(iv)$$

TABLE 11·11. COMPUTATION OF EXPONENTIAL TREND

x	y	$Y = \log y$	xY	x^2	Trend Values (y_e)
1	1·6	0·2041	0·2041	1	1·5573 ≃ 1·6
2	4·5	0·6532	1·3064	4	4·6361 ≃ 4·6
3	13·8	1·1399	3·4197	9	13·8017 ≃ 13·8
4	40·2	1·6042	6·4168	16	41·0877 ≃ 41·1
5	125·0	2·0969	10·4845	25	122·3180 ≃ 122·3
$\Sigma x = 15$		$\Sigma Y = 5·6983$	$\Sigma xY = 21·8315$	$\Sigma x^2 = 55$	

Substituting in (*iv*), the normal equations for estimating a and b become :

$$5·6983 = 5a + 15b \quad \ldots(v) \qquad \text{and} \qquad 21·8315 = 15a + 55b \quad \ldots(vi)$$

(*vi*) $-3 \times$ (*v*) gives :

$$21·8315 - 3 \times 5·6983 = 55b - 45b \Rightarrow 10b = 4·7366 \Rightarrow b = \frac{4·7366}{10} = 0·4737$$

Substituting the value of b in (*v*), we get

$$a = \frac{1}{5}(5·6983 - 15 \times 0·4737) = \frac{1}{5}(5·6983 - 7·1055) = -\frac{1}{5} \times 1·4072 = -0·2814$$

Hence using (*iii*), we get $\qquad B = \text{Antilog}(b) = \text{Antilog}(0·4737) = 2·977$

$$A = \text{Antilog}(a) = \text{Antilog}(-0·2814) = \text{Antilog}(\bar{1}·7186) = 0·5231$$

Substituting the values of A and B in (*i*), the required trend function is given by :

$$y = 0·5231 \times (2·977)^x \quad \ldots(vii)$$

Putting x = 1, 2, 3, 4 and 5 in (*vii*), we get the trend values which are shown in the last column of the Table 11·11. For example,

$(y_e)_1 = 0·5231 \times 2·977 = 1·5573$; $\quad (y_e)_2 = 0·5231 \times (2·977)^2 = 1·5573 \times 2·977 = 4·6361$

$(y_e)_3 = 4·6361 \times 2·977 = 13·8017$; and so on.

Remark. In fact, we observe that the trend values given by (*vii*) form a series in Geometric Progression (G.P.) with common ratio $r = 2·977$. Hence, if we compute the trend value for $x = 1$, then trend values for x = 2, 3, 4, etc., can be obtained on multiplying this value by the common ratio r = 2·977 successively.

Example 11·11. *You are given the population figures of India as follows :*

Census Year (x) :	*1911*	*1921*	*1931*	*1941*	*1951*	*1961*	*1971*
Population (in crores) (y) :	*25·0*	*25·1*	*27·9*	*31·9*	*36·1*	*43·9*	*54·7*

Fit an exponential trend $y = ab^x$ to the above data by the method of least squares and find the trend values. Estimate the population in 1981.

Solution. Here n = 7, is odd. Further, since the population figures are given at equal intervals of 10 years, we define :

$$u = \frac{x - \text{middle value}}{\text{Interval}} = \frac{x - 1941}{10} \quad \ldots(i)$$

and consider the trend curve ; $\qquad y = a \, . \, b^u \quad \ldots(ii)$

Taking logarithm of both sides :

$$\log y = \log a + u \log b \Rightarrow Y = A + Bu \quad \ldots(iii)$$

where $\quad Y = \log y, \quad A = \log a, \quad B = \log b$

The normal equations for estimating A and B in (*iii*) are given by (since $\Sigma u = 0$) :

$$\Sigma Y = nA \quad \text{and} \quad \Sigma uY = B \Sigma u^2 \Rightarrow A = \frac{\Sigma Y}{n} \quad \text{and} \quad B = \frac{\Sigma uY}{\Sigma u^2} \quad \ldots(iv)$$

TABLE 11·12. COMPUTATION OF EXPONENTIAL TREND

Year (x)	Population (in crores) (y)	$u = \frac{x-1941}{10}$	$Y = \log y$	u^2	uY	Trend Value (in crores) $y_e = 33{\cdot}6 \times (1{\cdot}142)^u$
1911	25·0	−3	1·3979	9	−4·1937	25·76 ÷ 1·142 = 2·56
1921	25·1	−2	1·3997	4	−2·7994	29·42 ÷ 1·142 = 25·76
1931	27·9	−1	1·4456	1	−1·4456	33·60 ÷ 1·142 = 29·42
1941	31·9	0	1·5038	0	0	33·60
1951	36·1	1	1·5575	1	1·5575	33·6 × 1·142 = 38·37
1961	43·9	2	1·6425	4	3·2850	38·37 × 1·142 = 43·82
1971	54·7	3	1·7380	9	5·2140	43·82 × 1·142 = 50·04
Total	$\Sigma y = 244{\cdot}6$	0	$\Sigma Y = 10{\cdot}6850$	$\Sigma u^2 = 28$	$\Sigma uY = 1{\cdot}6178$	$\Sigma y_e = 243{\cdot}57$

Using (*iv*), we get

$$A = \frac{10{\cdot}6850}{7} = 1{\cdot}5264 \quad \Rightarrow \quad a = \text{Antilog}(A) = \text{Antilog}(1{\cdot}5264) = 33{\cdot}60$$

$$B = \frac{1{\cdot}6178}{28} = 0{\cdot}0578 \quad \Rightarrow \quad b = \text{Antilog}(B) = \text{Antilog}(0{\cdot}0578) = 1{\cdot}142$$

Substituting the values of a and b in (*ii*), we get the exponential trend equation as :

$$y = 33{\cdot}60 \times (1{\cdot}142)^u, \quad \text{where} \quad u = \frac{(x-1941)}{10} \qquad \ldots(v)$$

The trend values for the years 1911 to 1971 can be obtained from (*v*) on putting $u = -3, -2, \ldots, 2, 3$ respectively. For instance,

$$(y_e)_{x=1941} = (y_e)_{u=0} = 33{\cdot}60$$

Since the trend values given by (*v*) are in G.P. with common ratio $r = b = 1{\cdot}142$, the trend values for years 1951, 1961 and 1971 are obtained on multiplying 33·60 by 1·142 successively and similarly the trend values for 1931, 1921 and 1911 are obtained on dividing 33·60 by 1·142 successively. The trend values are given in the last column of Table 11·12.

Estimate of Population in 1981. For $x = 1981$, we get $u = \frac{x-1941}{10} = \frac{1981-1941}{10} = 4.$

Hence putting $u = 4$ in (*v*), we get the estimated population of 1981 as :

$$(y_e)_{1981} = 33{\cdot}6 \times (1{\cdot}142)^4 = (33{\cdot}6) \times (1{\cdot}142)^3 \times 1{\cdot}142$$

$$= (y_e)_{1971} \times 1{\cdot}142 = 50{\cdot}04 \times 1{\cdot}142 = 57{\cdot}15 \text{ (crores)}.$$

Or

$$(y_e)_{1981} = 33{\cdot}6 \times (1{\cdot}30416)^2 = 33{\cdot}6 \times 1{\cdot}700844 = 57{\cdot}15 \text{ (crores)}.$$

Remark. We should get $\Sigma y = \Sigma y_e$. However, in the Table 11·13, $\Sigma y \neq \Sigma y_e$. The difference is due to the rounding of the constants a and b in (*ii*), to two decimal places.

Example 11·12. *The annual trend equations for consumption of butter (in '000 kgs.) for three districts I, II and III respectively are given below. Comment on the pattern of change of consumption over time for each district.*

$$(i)\ Y_t = 200 - 0{\cdot}012\,t \quad ; \quad (ii)\ Y_t = 225\,(1{\cdot}015)^t \quad ; \quad (iii)\ Y_t = 250\,(0{\cdot}978)^t$$

[*Delhi Univ. B.A. (Econ Hons.), 1998*]

Solution. (*i*) In district I, the annual trend model is

$$Y_t = 200 - 0{\cdot}012\,t \qquad \ldots(1)$$

which is linear of the form $Y_t = a + bt$ ...(1*a*)

The constant '*b*' in 1(*a*) reflect the constant annual growth (increase if $b > 0$ and decrease if $b < 0$) in the consumption of butter.

Hence, in district 1, the initial consumption ($t = 0$) of butter is a = 200,000 kg. and it decreases by $0{\cdot}012 \times 1000$ kg. = 12kg., every subsequent year.

(ii) and (iii). The trend models in districts II and III are the growth models of the form :

$$Y_t = P_0\,(1 + r)^t, \qquad \ldots(*)$$

where P_0 is the initial value of Y_t (at $t = 0$) and r is the rate of growth per annum (Compound Interest Formula).

District II. The trend model is :

$$Y_t = 225\,(1{\cdot}015)^t = 225\,(1 + 0{\cdot}015)^t \qquad \ldots(2)$$

Hence, in district II, the initial consumption of butter (Y_0) is 225,000 kg and it increases at the compound rate of $r = 0{\cdot}015 = 1{\cdot}5\%$ per annum.

District III. The trend model is :

$$Y_t = 250\,(0{\cdot}978)^t = 250\,(1 - 0{\cdot}022)^t \qquad \ldots(3)$$

Hence, in district III, the initial consumption of butter is 250,000 kg. and it decreases at the compound rate of $r = 0{\cdot}022 = 2{\cdot}2\%$ per annum.

11·5·4. Conversion of Trend Equation. Any trend equation

$$y_e = f(t) \qquad \ldots(*)$$

depends on three factors, *viz.*,

(*i*) The origin of time reference.

(*ii*) The units of time, *viz.*, yearly, monthly, weekly, etc.

(*iii*) The units of the given values, *i.e.*, the time series values relate to annual figures, monthly figures or monthly averages.

The trend equation (*) may be recomputed after redefining these factors to suit our convenience. We shall discuss below two points :

(1) Shifting of origin and

(2) Conversion of annual trend equation to monthly trend equation when :

(*a*) The y-values are in annual totals and

(*b*) The y-values are given as monthly averages.

Shifting of Origin. Quite often, to facilitate comparisons among trend values, it becomes desirable to shift the origin (the time period of reference) in a time series to some convenient point. We shall explain the technique by an example.

Let the straight line *annual* trend equation be given by :

$$y_e = a + bx \qquad \ldots(11{\cdot}25)$$

where Origin : 1990 (1st July) ; x units : one year; y units : Annual Totals.

The constant 'a' in the trend equation (11·31) is the trend value at the year of origin, *viz.*, 1990, *i.e.*,

$$(y_e)_{1990} = a$$

Now, if we want to change the time series to have its origin in, say, 1995, *i.e.*, we want to shift the new trend origin 5 years hence, then the new trend equation is obtained on changing the value of x to $x + 5$ in (11·25). Thus, the new trend equation becomes :

$$y_e = a + b\,(x + 5), \qquad \ldots(11{\cdot}26)$$

Origin : 1995 (1st July), *i.e.*, $x = 0$ when $t = 1995$.

Similarly, if we want to shift the origin to 1987, *i.e.*, 3 years back, the new trend equation becomes :

$$y_e = a + b\,(x - 3), \qquad \ldots(11{\cdot}27)$$

Origin : 1987 (1st July), *i.e.*, $x = 0$ when $t = 1987$.

Thus, shifting of origin only affects the value of the constant 'a' in the equation (11·25), while slope 'b' of the equation remains the same.

Conversion of Annual Trend Equation to Monthly Trend Equation. Let us again consider the annual trend equation (11·25). The slope 'b' in the equation represents the annual increment in the y-values.

Since the average monthly figure is obtained on dividing the total annual figure by 12, the trend equation (11·25) converted to *average monthly values* becomes :

$$y_e = \frac{a}{12} + \frac{b}{12}x \qquad \text{...(11·28)}$$

where Origin : 1990 (1st July) ; x units : One year y units : Monthly figures.

For example, we may say that average monthly production of sugar, say, for four years 1990, 1991, 1992 and 1993 are y_1, y_2, y_3, y_4 respectively. Thus, the x unit is years, though we are given average monthly values.

In equation (11·28) the coefficient of x, *viz.*, $b/12$ represents the increment in y-values on a monthly basis but from one month in a year to the corresponding month in the following (next) year. In order to obtain a monthly trend equation in which the x values are also in units of one month, and as the coefficient of x represents an increment in trend values from month to month, the coefficient $b/12$ in equation (11·28) has to be further divided by 12. Thus, the monthly trend equation becomes :

$$y = \frac{a}{12} + \frac{b}{144}x \qquad \text{...(11·29)}$$

where Origin : 1990 (1st July) ; x units : One month ; y units : Average monthly values.

Thus, if we want to shift the origin in (11·29) from 1st July to middle of November, *i.e.*, four and half months hence, then equation (11·29) reduces to :

$$y_e = \frac{a}{12} + \frac{b}{144}(x + 4·5) \qquad \text{...(11·30)}$$

where Origin : 15th November, 1990 ; x units : One month, y units : Average monthly values.

Similarly, if the origin in monthly trend equation (11·29) is shifted to middle March, *i.e.*, $3\frac{1}{2}$ months back, it reduces to :

$$y_e = \frac{a}{12} + \frac{b}{144}(x - 3·5) \qquad \text{...(11·31)}$$

Remark. The annual trend equation (11·25) can also be reduced to quarterly trend equation which will be given by :

$$y_e = \frac{a}{4} + \frac{b}{4 \times 12} \cdot x \quad \Rightarrow \quad y_e = \frac{a}{4} + \frac{b}{48}x \qquad \text{...(11·32)}$$

where Origin : 1990 (1st July) ; x units : One quarter ; y units : Quarterly values.

Example 11·13. *The equation for yearly sales in ('000 Rs.) for a commodity with 1st July, 2001, as origin is* $Y = 81·6 + 28·8X$.

(*i*) *Determine the trend equation to give monthly trend values with 15th Jan., 2002 as origin, and*

(*ii*) *Calculate the trend values for March 2002 to August 2002.*

Solution. (*i*) The given annual trend equation reduced to monthly values becomes :

$$y_e = \frac{81·6}{12} + \frac{28·8}{144}x \quad \Rightarrow \quad y_e = 6·8 + 0·2x \qquad \text{...(*)}$$

[Origin : (1st July 2001 ; x unit = 1 month ; y unit = average monthly sales (in '000 Rs.)]

We want to shift the origin to January 2002, *viz.*, middle of January, *i.e.*, 15th Jan., 2002. In other words, we have to shift the origin $6\frac{1}{2}$ months forward and the required equation is obtained on changing x to $x + 6·5$ in (*). Hence, the new trend equation is given by :

$$\begin{aligned} y_e &= 6·8 + 0·2(x + 6·5) \\ &= 6·8 + 0·2x + 1·3 \\ &= 8·1 + 0·2x \end{aligned} \qquad \text{...(**)}$$

[Origin : 15th Jan., 2002 ; x unit = 1 month ; y unit = average monthly sales (in '000 Rs.)]

(ii) Finally, the trend values for middle of March 2002 to middle of August 2002 are obtained on taking $x = 2, 3, 4, 5, 6, 7$ respectively in (**) and are given in Table 11·13.

TABLE 11·13. COMPUTATION OF TREND VALUES

Month	x	Trend Values (Rs. '000) $y_e = 8{\cdot}1 + 0{\cdot}2\,x$	y_e (Rs.)
March	2	$8{\cdot}1 + 0{\cdot}2 \times 2 = 8{\cdot}5$	8500
April	3	$8{\cdot}1 + 0{\cdot}2 \times 3 = 8{\cdot}7$	8700
May	4	$8{\cdot}1 + 0{\cdot}2 \times 4 = 8{\cdot}9$	8900
June	5	$8{\cdot}1 + 0{\cdot}2 \times 5 = 9{\cdot}1$	9100
July	6	$8{\cdot}1 + 0{\cdot}2 \times 6 = 9{\cdot}3$	9300
August	7	$8{\cdot}1 + 0{\cdot}2 \times 7 = 9{\cdot}5$	9500

Example 11·14. *The trend equation for the yearly sales of a commodity with 1st July, 1991 as origin is*

$$Y_e = 96 + 28{\cdot}8X + 4X^2 \text{ (where X-unit = 1 year)} :$$

(i) *Determine monthly trend equation with January 1992 as origin.*

(ii) *Compute trend values for August 1991 and March 1992.* [Delhi Univ. B.Com. (Hons.), 2002]

Solution. (i) The given *annual* trend equation reduced to monthly values becomes :

$$Y_e = \frac{96}{12} + \frac{28{\cdot}8}{12 \times 12}X + \frac{4}{12 \times 12 \times 12}X^2$$

$$\Rightarrow \quad Y_e = 8 + 0{\cdot}2\,X + 0{\cdot}0023X^2 \quad \ldots(*)$$

[Origin : 1st July 1991 ; X unit = 1 month ; Y unit = Average monthly sales]

We want to shift the origin to January 1992 *viz.*, middle of January *i.e.*, 15th Jan. 1992. In other words, we want to shift the origin 6 months forward and the required equation is obtained on changing X to $X + 6{\cdot}5$ in (*). Hence, the required trend equation becomes :

$$\begin{aligned} Y_e &= 8 + 0{\cdot}2\,(X + 6{\cdot}5) + 0{\cdot}0023\,(X + 6{\cdot}5)^2 \\ &= 8 + 0{\cdot}2\,X + 1{\cdot}3 + 0{\cdot}0023\,(X^2 + 13X + 42{\cdot}25) \\ &= 9{\cdot}3 + 0{\cdot}2\,X + 0{\cdot}0023\,X^2 + 0{\cdot}0299\,X + 0{\cdot}0972 \\ &= 9{\cdot}3972 + 0{\cdot}2299\,X + 0{\cdot}0023X^2 \end{aligned} \quad \ldots(**)$$

[Origin : 15th January, 1992 ; X unit = 1 month ; Y unit = Average monthly sales]

(ii) The trend value for August 1991 *i.e.*, 15th Aug., 1991 is obtained on taking $X = 1{\cdot}5$ in (*)

$$(\hat{Y})_{\text{Aug. 1991}} = 8 + 0{\cdot}2 \times 1{\cdot}5 + 0.0023 \times (1{\cdot}5)^2 = 8 + 0{\cdot}3 + 0{\cdot}005 = 8{\cdot}305$$

The trend value for March 1992 *i.e.*, (15th March, 1992) in obtained on taking $X = 2$ in (**)

$$\begin{aligned} \therefore \quad (\hat{Y})_{\text{March 1992}} &= 9{\cdot}3972 + 0{\cdot}2299 \times 2 + 0{\cdot}0023 \times 2^2 \\ &= 9{\cdot}3972 + 0{\cdot}4598 + 0{\cdot}0092 = 9{\cdot}8662 \end{aligned}$$

OR We can also obtain the trend value for March 1992 (15th March, 1992) on taking $X = 8{\cdot}5$ in (*).

Example 11·15. *The following is a monthly trend equation :*

$$Y_e = 20 + 2X \quad \ldots(*)$$

[Origin : Jan., 1992 ; X unit = One month ; Y unit = Monthly sales (in '000 Rupees)]

Convert it into an annual trend equation. [Delhi Univ. B.Com. (Hons.), 1998]

Solution. To convert the monthly trend equation (*) to annual trend equation, we should first of all shift the origin from mid-January 1992 to the middle of the year 1992 *i.e.*, to 1st July, 1992. In other words, we should advance the value of X by 5·5. Thus, the given equation (*) gives :

$$\begin{aligned} y_e &= 20 + 2\,(X + 5{\cdot}5) \\ &= 31 + 2X = a + bX, \text{ (say)}, \quad \text{(Origin : 1st July, 1992)} \end{aligned} \quad \ldots(i)$$

where y_e is the monthly sales and X unit = 1 month.

To obtain the annual trend equation, we shall multiply 'a' by 12 and 'b' by 144 in (ii), thus giving :

$$y_e = 12 \times 31 + 144 \times 2X \quad \Rightarrow \quad y_e = 372 + 288X \,;$$

where Origin : 1st July, 1992 ; X unit = 1 Year ; Y unit = Annual sales (in '000 Rs.).

11·5·5. Selection of the Type of Trend. As already pointed out, the greatest limitation of the trend fitting by the principle of least squares is the choice of the mathematical curve to be fitted to the given data. A number of mathematical curves for describing the given data have been discussed in the last section and the choice of a particular type requires great skill, intelligence and expertise. The historigram (graph) of the given time series enables us to have a fairly good idea about the type of the trend. The graph will clearly reveal if the trend is linear (straight line) or curvilinear (non-linear). If the graph exhibits a curvilinear trend then further approximation to the type of the trend curve can be obtained on plotting the data on a semi-logarithmic scale. [For details see Chapter 4, § 4·4·5]. A careful study of the graph obtained on plotting the data on an arithmetic or semi-logarithmic scale often provides adequate basis for selecting the type of trend. In this connection, the following points may be helpful.

(i) If the time series values increase or decrease by a constant absolute amount, *i.e.*, they form a series in arithmetic progression, then the straight line trend, [$y = a + bt$], is used, the slope 'b' of the line representing the constant rate of change per unit of time. In this case the historigram will give a straight line graph.

(ii) If the trend is non-linear, then the data are plotted on a semi-logarithmic scale. If the graph so obtained gives a straight line, it implies that the values increase or decrease by a constant percentage (rather than a constant absolute amount) *i.e.*, they form a series in geometric progression and the appropriate trend curve to be used is the exponential curve ($y = a\,b^t$).

Alternatively, the calculus of finite differences [*c.f.* Chapter on Interpolation and Extrapolation] can be used to decide about the type of the trend curve. The difference operator Δ is defined as :

$$\Delta y_t = y_{t+h} - y_t$$

where y_t represents the time series value at time t and 'h' is *equal* interval at which the values are given. If we are given annual data, *i.e.*, data are given at an equal interval of $h = 1$, then

$$\Delta\, y_1 = y_2 - y_1 \,; \qquad \Delta\, y_2 = y_3 - y_2 \,; \qquad \Delta\, y_3 = y_4 - y_3 \,; \quad \text{and so on.}$$

We state below the important theorem on which the conclusions are based :

"*If $y = y_t = f(t)$ is a polynomial of nth degree in t, then n^{th} differences $\Delta^n\, y = \Delta^n f(t)$, are constant, and $(n+1)^{th}$ and higher differences are zero*".

The following points, based on the calculus of finite differences may serve as guidelines for selecting the type of trend :

(i) If the first differences are approximately constant *i.e.*,

$$\Delta y_t = \text{constant, for all values of } t \text{ (approximately)},$$

i.e., if $\quad y_2 - y_1 = y_3 - y_2 = y_4 - y_3 = \ldots$, (approximately),

use the straight line trend ($y = a + bt$).

(ii) If 2nd differences are constant *i.e.*, if $\Delta^2\, y = \Delta^2\, y_t$ = constant (approximately) for all t, then use a second degree parabolic trend :

$$y = a + b\,t + c\,t^2.$$

(iii) If $\Delta \log y = \Delta \log y_t$ = constant (approximately), the appropriate trend is exponential *i.e.*, $y = a\,b^t$.

EXERCISE 11·1

1. (a) What is a time series ? What are its main components ? Give illustrations for each of them.

(b) Discuss briefly the various components of a time series. [*Delhi Univ. B.Com. (Hon.), 2008*]

2. (a) What is meant by Time Series Analysis ? Discuss its importance in business. [*Delhi Univ. B.Com. (Hons.), 1997*]

(b) Discuss briefly the importance of time series analysis in business and economics. What are the components of a time series ? Give an example of each component.

3. (*a*) Explain briefly the additive and multiplicative models of time series. [*Delhi Univ. B.A.* (*Econ. Hons.*), *1999*]

(*b*) How do the multiplicative and additive models of time series differ from each other ? [*Delhi Univ. B.A.* (*Econ. Hons.*), *2000*]

(*c*) What are the commonly used models in a time series analysis ? Discuss the underlying assumptions of each model. [*Delhi Univ. B.A..* (*Econ. Hons.*),*1997*]

(*d*) How do the additive and multiplicative models of time series differ from each other ? Why is the multiplicative model the most commonly used assumption in time series analysis ?

4. (*a*) Define trend. Enumerate the different methods of measuring secular trend in a given time series.

(*b*) Write about the various methods of isolating trend from the raw data. Explain them by giving statistical examples.

(*c*) Explain the different components of a time series. State the reasons for choosing the least square method out of the available measures for obtaining trend values.

5. (*a*) What is 'Secular Trend' ? Discuss any one method of isolating trend values in a time series. [*Delhi Univ. B.Com.* (*Hons.*), *2000*]

(*b*) What are the objectives of time series analysis ? Why do we need to separate out the trend movements from the periodic fluctuations ? Explain. [*Delhi Univ. B.A.* (*Econ. Hons.*), *1998*]

6. (*a*) Distinguish between secular trend, seasonal variations and cyclical fluctuations. How would you measure secular trend in any given data ?

(*b*) What are secular trend and cyclical, seasonal and irregular fluctuations ? Describe the methods of isolation of trend.

7. (*a*) Discuss the relative merits and demerits of 'free-hand curve' method for studying trend. What points will you keep in mind in drawing such a trend curve ?

With the help of graph paper, obtain the trend curve :

Year :	1982	1983	1984	1985	1986	1987	1988
Value :	64	82	97	71	78	112	115
Year :	1989	1990	1991	1992	1993	1994	
Value :	131	88	100	146	150	120	

(*b*) What are different methods of measuring trend ? Explain the methods of eliminating trend in a time series. Which one do you consider better ? [*Delhi Univ. B.Com.* (*Hons.*), *2009*]

8. Explain trend fitting by the method of semi-averages. Discuss its relative merits and demerits.

Compute the trend values by the method of semi-averages from the data given below :

Year :	1992	1993	1994	1995	1996	1997	1998	1999
No. of sheep (*in lakhs*) :	56	55	51	47	42	38	35	32

Ans. Trend values (in lakhs) for the years 1992 to 1999 are : 59, 56, 50·5, 46·5, 41·5, 37, 32·5, 28.

9. (*a*) The sale of a commodity in tonnes varied from January 1999 to December 1999 in the following manner :

280	300	280	280	270	240
230	230	220	200	210	200

Find a trend by the method of semi-average. [*Delhi Univ. B.Com.* (*Pass*), *2001*]

(*b*) Fit a trend line from the following data by using semi-average method :

Year :	1993	1994	1995	1996	1997	1998
Profits (*in '000 Rs.*) :	100	120	140	150	130	200

Ans. Joining the points (1994, 120) and (1997, 160), we get the trend line.

10. Explain the principle of least squares. How is it used in trend fitting ? What are the relative merits and demerits of trend fitting by the principle of least squares ?

11. What are the components of a time series ? How would you isolate trend by the method of least squares ? Illustrate your answer by an example.

12. Fit a straight line trend to the following data using the method of least squares and calculate the production for the year 2001 :

Year :	1996	1997	1998	1999	2000
Production (*'000 tons*) :	83	92	74	90	166

[*C.S.* (*Foundation*), *June 2002*]

Ans. $Y = 101 + 16{\cdot}4X$; (X-Origin = 1998) ; Estimated production for 2001 is 150·2 ('000 tons).

13. Fit a straight line trend to the following data by Least Squares Method :

Year	:	1991	1993	1995	1997	1999
Production	:	18	21	23	27	16

Specify the year of origin. Estimate production for the years 1998 and 2000. [*Delhi Univ. B.Com.* (*Pass*), *2002*]

Ans. $Y = 21 + 0{\cdot}1\ X$, [Origin X : 1995] ; $(\hat{Y})_{1998} = 21{\cdot}3$; $(\hat{Y})_{2000} = 21{\cdot}5$.

14. Fit a straight line trend to the following data and estimate the the value of output for the yera 2007.

Year	:	1997	1998	1999	2000	2001	2002	2003
Production of steel (in million tons)	:	60	72	75	65	80	85	95

[*Delhi Univ. B.A.* (*Econ. Hons.*), *2006*]

Ans. $y_e = 76 + 4{\cdot}86\ x$ (Origin : 2000) ; y : (million tons) ; $(y_e)_{2007} = 110{\cdot}02$ (million tons)

15. Below are given the figures of production (in thousand quintals) of a sugar factory :

Year	:	1993	1994	1995	1996	1997	1998	1999
Production (in '000 quintals)	:	80	90	92	83	94	99	92

(*i*) Fit a straight line trend to these figures by the method of least squares.
(*ii*) Show the given data and the trend line on the graph paper. ; (*iii*) Estimate the production in 2002.
(*iv*) Find the slope of the straight line trend. ; (*v*) Do the figures show a rising trend or a falling trend ?
(*vi*) What does the difference between the given figures and trend values indicate ?

Ans. (*i*) $y_e = 90 + 2x$; Origin : 1996 (1st July).
Trend Values ('000 quintals) : 84, 86, 88, 90, 92, 94, 96.
(*iii*) $(y_e)_{2002} = 102$ ('000 quintals) ; (*iv*) Slope = 2 ('000 quintals). (*v*) Rising trend ; since slope is positive.

16. Fit a straight line trend to the time series data given below by 'least squares method' and predict the sales for the year 2000 :

Year (t)	:	1993	1994	1995	1996	1997	1998	1999
Sales (in lakh Rs.) (Y)	:	25	30	38	50	62	80	95

[*C.S.* (*Foundation*), *June 2000*]

Ans. Straight line trend : $Y = 54{\cdot}29 + 11{\cdot}93\ X$; ($X = t - 1996$).
Estimated sales for 2000 are : $\hat{Y} = [54{\cdot}29 + 11{\cdot}93\ (2000 - 1996)]$ = Rs. 102·01 lakhs.

17. Fit a straight line trend to the following data by least squares method taking 1999 as the year of origin and estimate exports for the year 2005.

Year	:	1996	1997	1998	1999	2000	2001	2002
Exports (in tonnes)	:	47	50	53	65	62	64	72

[*Delhi Univ. B.A.* (*Econ. Hons.*), *2008*]

Ans. Straight line trend : $Y = 59 + 4X$; ($X = t - 1999$).
Estimated exports for 2005 : $\hat{Y} = 59 + 4 \times 6 = 83$ tonnes.

18. Using the method of least squares, fit a straight line to the following data and find the trend values and short term fluctuations.

Year	:	1990	1991	1992	1993	1994	1995	1996	1997	1998
Values	:	232	226	220	180	190	168	162	152	144

[*I.C.W.A.* (*Intermediate*), *June 2002*]

Ans. Trend Values (y_e) : 234, 222, 210, 198, 186, 174, 162, 150, 138.
Short-term fluctuations : $(y - y_e)$: − 2, 4, 6, −18, 4, − 6, 0, 2, 6 (Assuming additive model).

19. You are given the exports of electronic goods from 1990 to 1999. Fit a linear trend to the exports data and estimate the expected exports for the year 2005.

Year	:	1990	1992	1994	1996	1998	1999
Exports (crores Rs.)	:	11	16	13	18	22	20

[*Delhi Univ. B.Com.* (*Pass*), *2000*]

Ans. $y = 11{\cdot}529 + 1{\cdot}063x$; (Origin 1990) ; $(\hat{y})_{2005} = 27{\cdot}474$ (crores Rs.).

20. (*a*) The following table shows the consumption of butter in a district in different years. Obtain the trend values by the method of least squares.

Year	:	1989	1990	1991	1992	1993	1994
Consumption ('000 kgs)	:	60	80	90	120	145	170

(*b*) Also obtain the monthly increase in consumption of butter.

Ans. (*a*) $y_e = 110{\cdot}83 + 11{\cdot}07x$; $x = 2\,(t - 1991{\cdot}5)$.

Trend Values in ('000 kgs.) : 55·48, 77·62, 99·76, 121·90, 144·04, 166·18.

(*b*) Monthly increase in consumption of butter = 1·8450 ('000 kgs.). = 1845 kgs.

21. Fit a straight line trend equation by the method of least squares and estimate the value for 1999.

Year	:	1990	1991	1992	1993	1994	1995	1996	1997
Value	:	380	400	650	720	690	600	870	930

Ans. $y_e = 655 + 35{\cdot}83x$; $x = 2(t - 1993{\cdot}5)$.

Trend Values : 404·19, 475·85, 547·51, 619·17, 690·83, 762·49, 834·15, 905·81. ; $(y_e)_{1999} = 1049{\cdot}13$.

22. The following data relate to the number of passenger cars (in millions) produced from 1963 to 1970 :

Year	:	1963	1964	1965	1966	1967	1968	1969	1970
Number	:	6·7	5·3	4·3	6·1	5·6	7·9	5·8	6·1

Fit a straight line trend by the method of least squares to the above time series data. Use your result to estimate the production in 1970 and compare it with actual production.

Ans. $y = 5{\cdot}975 + 0{\cdot}0512x$; $x = 2(t - 1966{\cdot}5)$; $(y_e)_{1970} = 6{\cdot}3337$ millions.

23. In a study of its sales, a motor company obtained the following least square trend equation :

$y = 1{,}600 + 200x$ (origin 1980 , x units = 1 year , y = total number of units sold annually).

The company has physical facilities to produce only 3,600 units a year and it believes that it is reasonable to assume that at least for the next decade the trend will continue as before.

(*a*) What is the average annual increase in the number of units sold ?

(*b*) By what year will the company's expected sales have equalled its present physical capacity ?

(*c*) Estimate the annual sales for 1995.

How much in excess of company's present physical capacity is this estimated value ?

Ans. (*a*) 200 units, (*b*) In 1990, (*c*) 4,600 units. ; Excess = 4600 – 3600 = 1000 units.

24. Convert the following annual trend equation for total sales of a company to a monthly trend equation :

$$Y = 162 + 15{\cdot}8\,X$$

(Origin : 1975 ; Scale : 1 unit of X = 1 year).

Forecast the sales for June, 1978 by the two equations. Compare your results.

Ans. $y = 13{\cdot}5 + 0{\cdot}1097x$; [Origin : 1975, x unit = 1 month ; y unit = Monthly Sales]

25. The trend of the annual sales of Bharat Aluminium Company is described by the following equation :

$y_e = 12 + 0{\cdot}7x$; [Origin : 1990 ; x unit = 1 year and y unit = Annual production]

Step the equation down to a month to month basis and shift the origin to 1st January 1990.

Ans. $y_e = 1 + \frac{0{\cdot}7}{144}x$; [Origin : 1st July 1990 ; x unit = 1 month] ; $y_e = 0{\cdot}9712 + 0{\cdot}0048\,x$; [Origin : 1st Jan., 1990].

26. The trend equation for certain production is given by $y = 3{,}600 + 288t$, where

y : Annual production in thousand tons ; t : Time with origin, the year 1990 and unit = 1 year.

Estimate the trend value of the production for September 1994. [*I.C.W.A. (Intermediate), June 2000*]

Hint. Monthly trend equation is given by :

$$y = \frac{3{,}600}{12} + \frac{288}{144}t = 300 + 2t \quad ; \quad \text{Origin : 1st July, 1990} \quad ; \quad t : \text{Unit 1 month} \quad ; \quad y : \text{Monthly production.} \quad (*)$$

For September 1994 *i.e.,* 15th September, 1994 ; $t = 4 \times 12 + 2{\cdot}5 = 50{\cdot}5$ in (*).

∴ Estimated production for 1994 = 300 + 2 × 50·5 = 401 thousand tons.

27. You are given the following trend equation by the method of least squares of a company selling readymade garments :

$$Y = 480 + 36X$$

Origin : 1988 ; X = Unit of one year ; Y = Number of units sold per year.

(*i*) Convert the above trend equation into a monthly trend equation; and

(*ii*) Estimate the sale for the month of Oct. 1994. [*Delhi Univ. B.Com. (Hons.), 1994*]

Ans. (*i*) Monthly trend equation :

$Y = 40 + 0{\cdot}25X$; Origin 1st July, 1988 ; X unit : 1 month ; Y: No. of units sold per month

(*ii*) Estimated sales for month of October (mid-October) 1994 : $\hat{Y} = 40 + 0{\cdot}25\,(12 \times 6 + 3{\cdot}5) = 58{\cdot}87$.

28. For each of the following, derive the monthly trend equation (shift origin also to a month);

(*i*)	$Y_t = 960 + 72X$;	Origin : 1998,	X unit : 1 year,	Y unit : Annual Sales of coffee in Rs.
(*ii*)	$Y_t = 169{\cdot}58 + 78X$;	Origin : 1995,	X unit : 1 year,	Y unit : Average monthly production
(*iii*)	$Y_t = 2760 + 212X$;	Origin : 1997,	X unit : 1/2 year,	Y unit : Annual earnings in Rs.
(*iv*)	$Y_t = 72 + 12X$;	Origin : 1995,	X unit : 1/2 year,	Y unit : Average monthly production.

[*Delhi Univ. B.Com. (Hons.), 2006*]

Hint and Ans.

(*i*) $Y_t = \dfrac{960}{12} + \dfrac{72}{12 \times 12}(X + 0{\cdot}5) = 80{\cdot}25 + 0{\cdot}5\,X$;

Origin = 15 July 1998, X unit = One month, Y unit = Average monthly sales of coffee in Rs.

(*ii*) $Y_t = 169{\cdot}58 + \dfrac{78}{12}(X + 0{\cdot}5) = 172{\cdot}83 + 6{\cdot}5\,X$;

Origin = 15th July 1995, X unit = One month, Y unit = Average monthly production.

(*iii*) $Y_t = \dfrac{2760}{12} + \dfrac{212}{12 \times 6}(X + 0{\cdot}5) = 231{\cdot}47 + 2{\cdot}94\,X$;

Origin = 15th July 1997, X unit = One month, Y unit = Average monthly earning in Rs.

(*iv*) $Y_t = 72 + \dfrac{12}{6}(X + 0{\cdot}5) = 73 + 2X$;

Origin = 15th July 1995, X unit = One month, Y unit = Average monthly production.

29. Trend equation for yearly sales (in '000 Rs.) for a commodity with year 1999 as origin is $Y = 81{\cdot}6 + 28{\cdot}8X$. Determine the trend equation to give the monthly trend values with January 2000 as origin and calculate the trend value for March, 2000.

Ans. $y_e = 8{\cdot}1 + 0{\cdot}2x$; Origin : Middle of January 2000 ; x unit = 1 month; y unit = Average monthly sales ('000 Rs.).

30. (*a*) Explain the methods of fitting of the quadratic and exponential curves. How would you use the fitted curves for forecasting ?

(*b*) Distinguish between Trend and Exponential Trend. [*Delhi Univ. B.Com (Hons.), 1998*]

31. Fit a parabolic curve of second degree to the data given below and estimate the value for 1999 and comment on it :

Years	:	1993	1994	1995	1996	1997
Sales (in '000 Rs.)	:	10	12	13	10	8

Ans. $y_e = 12{\cdot}314 - 0{\cdot}6x - 0{\cdot}857x^2$

Trend Values : 10·086, 12·057, 12·314, 10·857, 7·686

$(y_e)_{1999} = -3{\cdot}798$ (thousand Rs.). Since the sales cannot be negative, the given second degree parabolic curve is not a good fit to the given data.

32. Find a non-linear trend equation from the following three normal equations obtained from the origin 1994 and estimate the value for 1997 :

$10 = 5a + 10b + 30c,$ $26 = 10a + 30b + 100c,$ $86 = 30a + 100b + 354c.$

[*Delhi Univ. B.Com. (Hons.), 1996*]

Hint. Solving these equations for a, b and c, we shall get : $a = \frac{38}{35}$, $b = \frac{1}{35}$, $c = \frac{1}{7}$.

Ans. Trend equation is :

$$Y = \frac{38}{35} + \frac{1}{35}x + \frac{1}{7}x^2 \;;\quad \text{Origin : 1994,} \quad (x = X - 1994).$$

33. Calculate trend values for the following data using a second degree equation :

Year (t)	:	1984	1985	1986	1987	1988	1989	1990
Output (thousand tons) (Y)	:	100	107	128	140	181	192	200

[*Delhi Univ. B.Com. (Hons.), 1992*]

Ans. $Y = 149{\cdot}10 + 18{\cdot}68X + 0{\cdot}16X^2$; [Origin : 1987 *i.e.*, $X = t - 1987$]

$(\hat{Y})_{1993} = 266{\cdot}94$ (thousand tons).

34. Fit an equation of the form $Y = a + bX + cX^2$, to the data given below :

X	:	1	2	3	4	5
Y	:	25	28	33	39	46

Also obtain the trend values. Is the parabolic trend a good fit ?

Ans. $Y = 32{\cdot}92 + 5{\cdot}3t + 0{\cdot}64t^2$; where $t = X - 3$. ...(*)

$\Rightarrow$ $Y = 22{\cdot}78 + 1{\cdot}46X + 0{\cdot}64X^2$

Trend Values : $X = (1, 2, 3, 4, 5)$; $Y_e = (24{\cdot}88,\ 28{\cdot}26,\ 32{\cdot}92,\ 38{\cdot}86,\ 46{\cdot}08)$

Since the original values (Y) and the corresponding trend values (Y_e) are very close, we may conclude that the parabolic trend (*) is a very good fit to the given data.

35. Fit a parabolic trend $y = a + bx + cx^2$ to the following data, where Y denotes the output (in thousand units) :

Year (X)	:	1981	1982	1983	1984	1985	1986	1987	1988	1989
Y	:	2	6	7	8	10	11	11	10	9

Also compute the trend values. Estimate the value of 1990. [*Delhi. Univ. B.Com. (Hons.), 2000*]

Ans. $y = 10{\cdot}02 + 0{\cdot}85x - 0{\cdot}27x^2$; (x : origin 1985)

Trend values for years 1981 to 1989 are respectively (in '000 units) :

2·30, 5·04, 7·24, 8·90, 10·02, 10·60, 10·64, 10·14, 9·10.

$(\hat{y})_{1990} = 7{\cdot}52$ thousand units.

36. The sales of a company (in thousands of Rupees) for the years 2000 to 2006 are given in the following table.

Year (x)	2000	2001	2002	2003	2004	2005	2006
Sales ('000 Rs.) (y)	32	47	65	92	132	190	275

Fit the exponential trend equation $y = a\,b^x$, to the given data and estimate the sales for 2007.

[*Delhi Univ. B.Com. (Hons.), 2007*]

Ans. $y = a\,b^t$; $t = x - 2003$ $\Rightarrow$ $y = 93{\cdot}49 \times (1{\cdot}427)^{x-2003}$; $(\hat{y})_{x=2007}$ = Rs. 380,000.

37. The sales of a company in lakhs of rupees for the years 1995 to 1999 are given below :

Year (x)	:	1995	1996	1997	1998	1999
Sales (y)	:	65	92	132	190	275

Estimate the sales for the year 2000 using an equation of the form $y = a\,b^x$.

Ans. $y = 132{\cdot}7\ (1{\cdot}435)^x$; (Origin : 1997) ; $(y_e)_{2000} = 392{\cdot}127$ (lakh Rs.).

38. Given the following population figures for India, estimate, the population for 1991, using an equation of the form $y = AB^x$.

Census year (X)	:	1921	1931	1941	1951	1961	1971	1981
Population (Y) (in crores)	:	25·1	27·9	31·9	36·1	43·9	54·8	68·5

Ans. $y = 38{\cdot}83 \times (1{\cdot}182)^u$; $u = (X - 1951)/10$; $(y_e)_{1991} = 75{\cdot}7946$ (crores).

39. Fit a trend function $Y = AB^X$, to the following data :

X	1	2	3	4	5
Y	2·08	6·74	23·10	45·27	138

[*Delhi Univ. B.Com. (Hons.), 2005*]

Ans. $Y = 18{\cdot}25 \times (2{\cdot}8)^x$, $x = X - 3$.

11·5·6. Method of Moving Averages. Method of moving averages is a very simple and flexible method of measuring trend. It consists in obtaining a series of moving averages, (arithmetic means), of successive overlapping groups or sections of the time series. The averaging process smoothens out fluctuations and the ups and downs in the given data. The moving average is characterised by a constant known as the *period* or *extent* of the moving average. Thus, the moving average of period 'm' is a series of successive averages (A.M.'s) of m overlapping values at a time, starting with 1st, 2nd, 3rd value and so on. Thus, for the time series values $y_1, y_2, y_3, y_4, y_5, \ldots$ for different time periods, the moving average (M.A.) values of period 'm' are given by :

$$\text{1st M.A.} \frac{y_1 + y_2 + \ldots + y_m}{m}, \text{ 2nd M.A.} = \frac{y_2 + y_3 + \ldots + y_{m+1}}{m}, \text{ 3rd M.A.} = \frac{y_3 + y_4 + \ldots + y_{m+2}}{m}, \text{ and so on.}$$

We shall discuss two cases.

Case (*i*) **When *Period is Odd.*** If the period 'm' of the moving average is odd. then the successive values of the moving averages are placed against the middle values of the corresponding time intervals. For example, if m =5, the first moving average value is placed against the middle period. *i.e.,* 3rd, the second M.A. value is placed against the time period 4 and so on.

Case (*ii*). **When Period is Even.** If the period 'm' of the M.A. is even, then there are two middle periods and the M.A. values are placed in between the two middle periods of the time intervals it covers. Obviously, in this case, the M.A. values will not coincide with a period of the given time series and an attempt is made to synchronise them with the original data by taking a two-period average of the moving averages and placing them in between the corresponding time periods. This technique is called *centering* and the corresponding moving average values are called *centred moving averages.* In particular, if the period m = 4, the first moving average value is placed against the middle of 2nd and 3rd time intervals; the second moving average value is placed in between 3rd and 4th time periods and so on. These values are given by :

$$\bar{y}_1 = \tfrac{1}{4}\left(y_1 + y_2 + y_3 + y_4\right), \quad \bar{y}_2 = \tfrac{1}{4}\left(y_2 + y_3 + y_4 + y_5\right), \quad \bar{y}_3 = \tfrac{1}{4}\left(y_3 + y_4 + y_5 + y_6\right) \qquad \ldots (11\cdot33)$$

and so on. The centred moving averages are obtained on taking 2-period M.A. of $\bar{y}_1, \bar{y}_2, \bar{y}_3$, and so on. Thus,

$$\begin{aligned}
\text{First Centred M.A.} &= \tfrac{1}{2}(\bar{y}_1 + \bar{y}_2) \\
&= \tfrac{1}{2}\left[\tfrac{1}{4}(y_1 + y_2 + y_3 + y_4) + \tfrac{1}{4}(y_2 + y_3 + y_4 + y_5)\right] \\
&= \tfrac{1}{8}\left[(y_1 + y_2 + y_3 + y_4) + (y_2 + y_3 + y_4 + y_5)\right] \\
&= \tfrac{1}{8}\left[y_1 + 2y_2 + 2y_3 + 2y_4 + y_5\right] \qquad \ldots (11\cdot34)
\end{aligned}$$

$$\text{Similarly, Second M.A.} = \tfrac{1}{8}(y_2 + 2y_3 + 2y_4 + 2y_5 + y_6), \qquad \ldots (11\cdot34a)$$

and so on. These centred moving averages are placed against the time periods 3, 4, 5, ... and so on. Equation (11·34) may be regarded as a weighed average of y_1, y_2, y_3, y_4 and y_5, the corresponding weights being 1, 2, 2, 2, 1, *i.e.,*

$$\bar{Y} = \frac{w_1y_1 + w_2y_2 + w_3y_3 + w_4y_4 + w_5y_5}{w_1 + w_2 + w_3 + w_4 + w_5} = \frac{\Sigma wy}{\Sigma w}, \text{ where } w_1 = w_5 = 1 \text{ and } w_2 = w_3 = w_4 = 2.$$

Similar interpretation can be given to (11·34a)

From (11·34) and (11·34a) we see that *a centred moving average of period 4 is equivalent to a weighted moving average of period 5, the corresponding weights being 1, 2, 2, 2, 1.* [For verification of this result, see Example 11·20]

The moving average values plotted against time give the trend curve. The basic problem in M.A. method is the determination of period 'm' and this is discussed in Remark 3 below.

Remarks. 1. Moving Average and Linear Trend. *If the time series data does not contain any movements except the trend which when plotted on a graph gives a straight line curve, then the moving average will reproduce the series.* The following example will clarify the point.

Year (t)	Values (y)	3-Yearly M.A.	5-Yearly M.A.	7-Yearly. M.A.
1	10	—	—	—
2	14	14	—	—
3	18	18	18	—
4	22	22	22.	22
5	26	26	26	26
6	30	30	30	30
7	34	34	34	34
8	38	38	38	38
9	42	42	42	—
10	46	46	—	—
11	50	—	—	—

Thus the trend values by the moving average of extent 3, 5, 7 and so on coincide with the original series.

Note that in this case, the given values exhibit a linear trend $y = 6 + 4t$.

2. Moving Average and Curvilinear Trend. *If the data does not contain any oscillatory or irregular movements and has only general trend and the historigram (graph) of the time series gives a curve which is convex (concave) to the base, then the trend values computed by moving average method will give another curve parallel to the given curve but above (below) it.* In other words, if there are no variations in the data except the trend which is curvilinear, then the moving average values, when plotted, will exhibit the same curvilinear pattern but slightly away from the given historigram. Further, *greater the period of the moving average, the farther will be trend curve from the original historigram.* In other words, the difference between the trend values and the original values becomes larger as the period of the moving average increases.

3. Period of Moving Average. The moving average will completely eliminate the oscillatory movements if :

(*i*) The period of the moving average is equal to or a multiple of the period of oscillatory movements provided they are regular in period or amplitude, and

(*ii*) The trend is linear or approximately so.

Hence, to compute correct trend values by the method of moving averages, the *period or extent of the moving average should be same as the period of the cyclic movements in the series.* However, if the period of moving average is less or more than the period of the cyclic movement then it (M.A.) will only reduce their effect.

Quite often, we come across time series data which do not exhibit regular cyclic movements and might reflect different cycles with varying periods which may be determined on drawing the historigram of the given time series and observing the time distances between various peaks. In such a situation, the period of the moving average is taken as the average period of the various cycles present in the data.

4. Moving Average and Polynomial Trend. In most of the economic and business time series the trend is rarely linear and accordingly, if the trend is curvilinear, the moving average values will give a distorted picture of the trend. In such a case the correct trend values are obtained by taking a weighted moving average of the given values. The weights to be used will depend on the period of the M.A. and the degree of the polynomial trend to be fitted. For example, the weights for a moving average [5, 2], *i.e.,* a moving average of extent 5 for a parabolic trend are given by :

$$\left(-\frac{3}{35},\ \frac{12}{35},\ \frac{17}{35},\ \frac{12}{35},\ -\frac{3}{35}\right) \qquad \dots (*)$$

Thus, the first moving average value for series $y_1, y_2, y_3, \dots$ is given by :

$$\frac{1}{35}\left(-3y_1 + 12y_2 + 17y_3 + 12y_4 - 3y_5\right).$$

The weights for the moving average [7, 2], *i.e.*, a M.A. of period 7 for parabolic trend are :

$$\left(\frac{-2}{21}, \frac{3}{21}, \frac{6}{21}, \frac{7}{21}, \frac{6}{21}, \frac{3}{21}, \frac{-2}{21}\right) \qquad \ldots (**)$$

and the first trend value is given by :

$$\frac{1}{21}\left[-2y_1 + 3y_2 + 6y_3 + 7y_4 + 6y_5 + 3y_6 - 2y_7\right]$$

It may be observed that :

(*i*) the weights for the M.A. are symmetric about the middle value, and

(*ii*) the sum of weights is unity.

5. Effect of Moving Average on Irregular Fluctuations. The moving average smoothens the ups and downs present in the original data and, therefore, reduces the intensity of irregular fluctuations to some extent. It can't eliminate them completely. However, greater the period of the moving average (up to a certain limit), the greater is the amount of reduction in their intensity. Thus, from point of view of reducing irregular variations, long-period moving average is recommended. However, we have pointed out in Remark 2, that greater the period of moving average, farther are the trend values from the original values. In other worlds, longer period of moving average is likely to give a distorted picture of the trend values. Accordingly, as a compromise, the period of moving average should neither be too large nor too small. *The optimum period of the moving average is the one that coincides with or is a multiple of the period of the cycle in the time series as it would completely eliminate cyclical variations, reduce the irregular variations and, therefore, give the best possible values of the trend.*

We shall now discuss numerical problems to explain the technique of obtaining trend values by moving average method.

Example 11·16. *Calculate (i) three yearly (ii) five yearly, moving averages for the following data and comment on the results.*

Year :	*1990*	*1991*	*1992*	*1993*	*1994*	*1995*	*1996*	*1997*	*1998*	*1999*	*2000*
y :	*242*	*250*	*252*	*249*	*253*	*255*	*251*	*257*	*260*	*265*	*262*

Solution. The 3 yearly and 5 yearly moving average values are given in Table 11·14.

TABLE 11·14. COMPUTATION OF 3 AND 5-YEARLY M.A. VALUES

Year (1)	*y* (2)	*3-yearly moving totals* (3)	*3-yearly moving averages (Trend values)* (4) = (3) ÷ 3	*5-yearly moving totals* (5)	*5-yearly M.A. (Trend values)* (6) = (5) ÷ 5
1990	242	—	—	—	—
1991	250	744	248·0	—	—
1992	252	751	250·3	1246	249·2
1993	249	754	251·3	1259	251·8
1994	253	757	252·3	1260	252·0
1995	255	759	253·0	1265	253·0
1996	251	763	254·3	1276	255·2
1997	257	768	256·0	1288	257·6
1998	260	782	260·7	1295	259·0
1999	265	787	262·3	—	—
2000	262	—	—	—	—

Comments. As the period of the M.A. increases, the trend values move away from the original values.

Example 11·17. *Calculate the trend values by the method of moving average, assuming a four-yearly cycle, from the following data relating to sugar production in India :*

Year	*Sugar Production (lakh tonnes)*	*Year*	*Sugar Production (lakh tonnes)*
1971	*37·4*	*1977*	*48·4*
1972	*31·1*	*1978*	*64·6*
1973	*38·7*	*1979*	*58·4*
1974	*39·5*	*1980*	*38·6*
1975	*47·9*	*1981*	*51·4*
1976	*42·6*	*1982*	*84·4*

Solution. Since we are given that the data follows a four yearly cycle, we shall compute the trend values by using moving average of period 4, as shown in Table 11·15

TABLE 11·15. COMPUTATION OF 4 - YEARLY MOVING AVERAGES

Year	*Sugar production (lakh tonnes)*	*4-yearly moving totals*	*4-yearly moving average*	*2-period moving total of col. (4)*	*Centred moving average [Trend values]*
(1)	*(2)*	*(3)*	*(4) = (3) ÷ 4*	*(5)*	*(6) = (5) ÷ 2*
1971	37·4				
1972	31·1				
		← 146·7	36·675		
1973	38·7			← 75·975	37·99
		← 157·2	39·300		
1974	39·5			← 81·475	40·74
		← 168·7	42·175		
1975	47·9			← 66·755	43·39
		← 178·4	44·600		
1976	42·6			← 95·475	47·74
		← 203·5	50·875		
1977	48·4			← 104·375	52·19
		← 214·0	53·500		
1978	64·6			← 106·000	53·00
		← 210·0	52·500		
1979	58·4			← 105·750	52·88
		← 213·0	53·250		
1980	38·6			← 111·450	55·73
		← 232·8	58·200		
1981	51·4				
1982	84·4				

Example 11·18. *Determine the period of the moving average for the following data and calculate moving averages for that period :*

Year :	*1*	*2*	*3*	*4*	*5*	*6*	*7*	*8*	*9*	*10*	*11*	*12*	*13*	*14*	*15*
Value :	*130*	*127*	*124*	*135*	*140*	*132*	*129*	*127*	*145*	*158*	*153*	*146*	*145*	*164*	*170*

Solution. Since the peaks of the given data occur at the years 1, 5, 10 and 15, the data clearly exhibits a regular cyclic movement with period 5. Hence, the period of the moving average for determining the trend values is also 5, *viz.*, the period of the cyclic variations.

TABLE 11·16. **COMPUTATION OF FIVE-YEARLY MOVING AVERAGE**

Year (1)	*Value* (2)	*5-yearly Moving totals* (3)	*5-yearly M.A. (Trend Values)* (4) = (3) ÷ 5
1	130	—	—
2	127	—	—
3	124	656	131·2
4	135	658	131·6
5	140	660	132·0
6	132	663	132·6
7	129	673	134·6
8	127	691	138·2
9	145	712	142·4
10	158	729	145·8
11	153	747	149·4
12	146	766	153·2
13	145	778	155·6
14	164	—	—
15	170	—	—

Example 11·19. *What is moving average ? What are its uses in analysis of time series ?*

Given the numbers 2, 6, 1, 5, 3, 7, 2; write down the weighted moving average of period 3, the weights being 1, 4, 1.

Solution. The weighted moving average is obtained on dividing the weighted moving totals by the sum of the weights, *viz.*, 1 + 4 + 1 = 6. Thus,

$$\text{Weighted M.A.} = \frac{\Sigma WX}{\Sigma W} = \frac{\Sigma WX}{6} \qquad \ldots (*)$$

The weighted moving average values are obtained in the last column of Table 11·17.

TABLE 11·17

COMPUTATION OF WEIGHTED M.A. OF PERIOD 3

Values (X) (1)	*Weighted moving totals of period 3* (2)	*Weighted M.A. of period 3* (3) = (2) ÷ 6
2		
6	$1\times2+4\times6+1\times1=27$	$27\div6=4{\cdot}5$
1	$1\times6+4\times1+1\times5=15$	$15\div6=2{\cdot}5$
5	$1\times1+4\times5+1\times3=24$	$24\div6=4{\cdot}0$
3	$1\times5+4\times3+1\times7=24$	$24\div6=4{\cdot}0$
7	$1\times3+4\times7+1\times2=33$	$33\div6=5{\cdot}5$
2		

Example 11·20. *For the following series of observations, verify that the 4-year centred moving average is equivalent to a 5-year weighted moving average with weights 1, 2, 2, 2, 1 respectively :*

Year :	*1989*	*1990*	*1991*	*1992*	*1993*	*1994*	*1995*	*1996*	*1997*	*1998*	*1999*
Annual Sales (Rs. '000)	*2*	*6*	*1*	*5*	*3*	*7*	*2*	*6*	*4*	*8*	*3*

Solution.

TABLE 11·18. COMPUTATION OF 4-YEARLY MOVING AVERAGES

Year	*Annual sales ('000 Rs.)*	*4-yearly moving totals*	*4-yearly M.A.*	*2-point moving total of col. (4)*	*4-yearly moving average (centred)*
(1)	*(2)*	*(3)*	*(4) = (3) ÷ 4*	*(5)*	*(6) = (5) ÷ 2*
1989	2				
1990	6				
		← 14	3·50		
1991	1			← 7·25	3·63
		← 15	3·75		
1992	5			← 7·75	3·88
		← 16	4·00		
1993	3			← 8·25	4·13
		← 17	4·25		
1994	7			← 8·75	4·38
		← 18	4·50		
1995	2			← 9·25	4·63
		← 19	4·75		
1996	6			← 9·75	4·88
		← 20	5·00		
1997	4			← 10·25	5·13
		← 21	5·25		
1998	8				
1999	3				

As in the earlier example, the weighted average is obtained on dividing the weighted totals by the sum of the weights, *i.e.*, by using the formula :

$$\text{Weighted M.A.} = \frac{\Sigma wy}{\Sigma w}, \quad \text{where} \quad \Sigma w = 1 + 2 + 2 + 2 + 1 = 8.$$

TABLE 11·19. COMPUTATION OF 5-YEARLY WEIGHTED M.A. VALUES

Year	*Sales('000 Rs.) (y)*	*5-yearly weighted moving totals*	*5-yearly weighted moving average*
(1)	*(2)*	*(3)*	*(4) = (3) ÷ 8*
1989	2		
1990	6		
1991	1	$1 \times 2 + 2\,(6 + 1 + 5) + 1 \times 3 = 29$	3.63
1992	5	$1 \times 6 + 2\,(1 + 5 + 3) + 1 \times 7 = 31$	3·88
1993	3	$1 \times 1 + 2\,(5 + 3 + 7) + 1 \times 2 = 33$	4·13
1994	7	$1 \times 5 + 2(3 + 7 + 2) + 1 \times 6 = 35$	4·38
1995	2	$1 \times 3 + 2\,(7 + 2 + 6) + 1 \times 4 = 37$	4·63
1996	6	$1 \times 7 + 2\,(2 + 6 + 4) + 1 \times 8 = 39$	4·88
1997	4	$1 \times 2 + 2\,(6 + 4 + 8) + 1 \times 3 = 41$	5.13
1998	8		
1999	3		

From Tables 11·18 and 11.19 we see that the 4-yearly centred moving average is equivalent to 5-yearly weighted moving average with weights 1, 2, 2, 2, 1 respectively.

Remark. This result is true, in general, for any time series. Here we have just verified the result for the given time series.

Merits and Demerits of Moving Average Method

Merits 1. This method does not require any mathematical complexities and is quite simple to understand and use as compared with the principle of least squares method.

2. Unlike the 'free hand curve' method, this method does not involve any element of subjectivity since the choice of the period of moving average is determined by the oscillatory movements in the data and not by the personal judgement of the investigator.

3. Unlike the method of trend fitting by principle of least squares, the moving average method is quite flexible in the sense that a few more observations may be added to the given data without affecting the trend values already obtained. The addition of some new observations will simply result in some more trend values at the end.

4. The oscillatory movements can be completely eliminated by choosing the period of the M.A. equal to or multiple of the period of cyclic movement in the given series. [See Remark 3, § 11·5·6.] A proper choice of the period also reduces the irregular fluctuations to some extent. [See Remark 5, § 11·5·6]

5. In addition to the measurement of trend, the method of moving averages is also used for measurement of seasonal, cyclical and irregular fluctuations.

Limitations. 1. An obvious limitation of the moving average method is that we cannot obtain the trend values for all the given observations. We have to forego the trend values for some observations at both the extremes (*i.e.*, in the beginning and at the end) depending on the period of the moving average. For example, for a moving average of period 5, 7 and 9, we lose the trend values for the first and last 2, 3 and 4 values respectively.

2. Since the trend values obtained by moving average method cannot be expressed by any functional relationship, this method cannot be used for forecasting or predicting future values which is the main objective of trend analysis.

3. The selection of the period of moving average is very important and is not easy to determine particularly when the time series does not exhibit cycles which are regular in period and amplitude. In such a case the moving average will not completely eliminate the oscillatory movements and consequently the moving average values will not represent a true picture of the general trend. [See Remark 3, § 11·5·6 for determining the period of M.A.]

4. In case of non-linear trend, which is generally the case in most of economic and business time series, the trend values given by the moving average method are biased and they lie either above or below the true sweep of the data. According to Waugh :

"If the trend line is concave downwards (like the side of a bowl), the value of the moving average will always be too high, if the trend is concave upward (like the side of a derby pot), the value of the moving average will always be tool low."

As already pointed out, [see Remark 4, § 11·5·6], in case of polynomial trend, appropriate trend values are obtained by using a weighted moving average with suitable weights.

Keeping in view the limitations, the moving average method is recommended under the following situations :

(*i*) If trend is linear or approximately so.

(*ii*) The oscillatory movements describing the given time series are regular both in period and amplitude.

(*iii*) If forecasting is not required.

EXERCISE 11·2

1. (*a*) Explain the method of moving average. How is it used in measuring trend in the analysis of a time series ?

(*b*) Explain how tend is obtained by the method of moving averages in the analysis of a time series. What are the merits and demerits of the method ?

(*c*) State the conditions under which a moving average can be recommended for trend analysis. How will you determine the period of the moving average ?

(*d*) Why does economic time series data exhibit seasonal and random fluctuations ? List the steps you would take to construct a seasonal index by the ratio to moving average method. Mention the assumptions taken to permit this construction. [*Delhi Univ. BA. (Econ. Hons.), 2005*]

2. (*a*) What is Time Series ? Mention its chief components. What is a moving average ? What are its uses in Time Series analysis ?

(*b*) Explain how trend is eliminated from a time series by the moving average method. Use a suitable illustration.

3. (*a*) How are the moving Average (M.A.) values affected if the period of M.A. is increased ?

What is the effect of increase of the period of M.A. on the irregular fluctuations ?

(*b*) What are the limitations and advantages of the moving average method of trend fitting ?

(*c*) Why are moving averages calculated in analysing a time series ? How is the period of the moving average determined ?

(*d*) Explain the importance and different components of a time series. Discuss the relative merits and demerits of moving average method and least squares method for obtaining trend values.

4. Explain briefly the various methods of determining trend in a time series.

Using three-year moving averages, determine the trend and short-term fluctuations. Plot the original and trend values on the same graph paper.

Year	1988	1989	1990	1991	1992	1993	1994	1995	1996	1997
Production (in '000 tonnes)	21	22	23	25	24	22	25	26	27	26

Ans. Trend (3 yearly M.A). 22, 23·3, 24, 23·7, 23·7, 24·3, 26, 26·3.

Using additive model, short-term fluctuations are : 0, – 0·3, 1·0, 0·3, – 1·7, 0·7, 0, 0·7

5. Assuming an additive model, apply 3 year moving averages to obtain the trend-free series for years 2 to 6.

Year :	1	2	3	4	5	6	7
Exports (Rs. lakhs) :	126	130	137	141	145	155	159

[*Delhi Univ. B.A. (Econ. Hons.), 1992*]

Ans. Year	1	2	3	4	5	6	7
M.A. Values	—	131	136	141	147	153	—
Trend free Values	—	– 1	1	0	– 2	2	—

6. From the following data, calculate the trend values using four-yearly moving average :

Year :	1989	1990	1991	1992	1993	1994	1995	1996	1997
Values :	506	620	1036	673	588	696	1116	738	663

[*C.A. (Foundation), Nov. 2001*]

Ans. M.A. Values for 1991 to 1995 respectively are : 719, 738·75, 758·25, 776·375, 793·875

7. Assume a four-year cycle, calculate the trend by the method of moving average from the following data relating to production of tea in a certain tea estate :

Year	1961	1962	1963	1964	1965	1966	1967	1968	1969	1970
Production (Kg.)	464	515	518	467	502	540	557	571	586	612

Ans. 4-yearly M.A.'s for 1963 to 1968 respectively are : [*I.C.W.A. (Intermediate), Dec. 1999*]

495·70, 503·60, 511·60, 529·50, 553·00, 572·50

8. From the given data, compute 'trend' and 'short-term variations' by the Moving Average Method, assuming a four-yearly cycle and multiplicative model.

Year :	1990	1991	1992	1993	1994	1995	1996	1997	1998	1999	2000
Sales :	75	60	55	60	65	70	70	75	85	100	70

Ans. M.A. Values. : 61 25, 61·25, 64·37, 68·12, 72·50, 78·75, 82·50.

Trend eliminated values : 89·80, 97·96, 100·98, 102·76, 96·55, 95·24, 103·03

9. Eliminate trend by moving average method and comment.

Year	*1st Quarter*	*2nd Quarter*	*3rd Quarter*	*4th Quarter*
1995	40	35	38	40
1996	42	37	39	38
1997	41	35	38	42

[*Delhi Univ. B.Com. (Hons.), 1998*]

Ans. M.A. Values (M.A.V) and the Trend Eliminated Values (T.E.V) (Assuming multiplicative model) from 3rd Quarter 1995 to 2nd Quarter 1997. respectively are :

M. A. V.	38.5,	39.0,	39.375,	39.25,	38.875,	38.5,	38.125,	38.5;
T. E. V.	98.70,	102.56,	106.67,	94.27,	100.32	98.70,	107.54,	90.91

10. What is trend in a time series ? The following table gives the annual sales (in Rs. 1,000) of a commodity :

Year :	1980	1981	1982	1983	1984	1985	1986	1987	1988	1989	1990
Sales :	710	705	680	687	757	629	644	783	781	805	872

Determine the trend by calculating the 5 yearly moving averages. [*I.C.W.A,. (Intermediate), June 1995*]

Ans. 5 year M.A. (Trend) values for 1982 to 1988 are respectively : (Rs. 1,000) :

707.80, 691.60, 679.40, 700.00, 718.80, 728.4, 777.0.

11. Find the trend for the following series using a three-year weighted moving average with weights 1, 2, 1.

Year :	1	2	3	4	5	6	7
Value :	2	4	5	7	8	10	13

Ans. 3·75, 5·25, 6·75, 8·25, 10·25

12. For the following series of observations, verify that the 2-year centred moving average is equivalent to a 3-year weighted moving average with weights 1, 2, 1 respectively.

Year :	1994	1995	1996	1997	1998	1999	2000
Values :	2	4	5	7	8	10	13

[*I.C.W.A. (Intermediate), June 2002*]

Ans. M.A. Values for 1995 to 1999 are respectively : 3·75, 5·25, 6·75, 8·25, 10·25.

13. For the following data, verify that the 5-yearly weighted moving average trend values with weights 1, 2, 2, 2, 1 respectively are equivalent to 4-yearly centred moving average trend values.

Year :	1995	1996	1997	1998	1999	2000	2001	2002	2003	2004	2005
Sales (Rs. in lakhs) :	5	3	7	6	4	8	9	10	8	9	9

[*Delhi Univ. B.Com. (Hons.), 2009*]

Ans. M.A's for 1997 to 2003 are : 5.125, 5.625, 6.500, 7.250, 8.250, 8.875, 9.000

11·6. MEASUREMENT OF SEASONAL VARIATIONS

As already pointed out, by seasonal variabtions in a time series we mean the variations due to such forces which operate in a regular periodic manner with period less than one year. The study of such variations, which are predominantly exhibited by most of the economic and business time series, is of paramount importance to a businessman or sales manager for planning future production and in scheduling purchases, inventory control, personnel requirements, and selling and advertising programmes. The objectives for studying seasonal patterns in a time series may be classified as follows :

(*i*) To isolate the seasonal variations, *i.e.*, to determine the effect of seasonal swings on the value of a given phenomenon, and

(*ii*) To eliminate them, *i.e.*, to determine the value of the phenomenon if there were no seasonal ups and downs in the series. This is called *de-seasonalising the given data and is* necessary for the study of cyclic variations.

Obviously, for the study of seasonal variations, the time series data must be given for 'parts' of a year *viz.*, monthly quarterly, weekly, daily or hourly. The study of seasonal variations assumes that the seasonal pattern is superimposed on the values of a given series independently in the sense that a particular month (for monthly data), or quarter (for quarterly data) will always exert a particular effect on the values of the series. Seasonal variations are measured as relative effect in terms of ratios or percentages, assuming multiplicative model and occasionally as absolute changes assuming additive model of time series. The following are different methods of measuring seasonal variations :

(i) *Method of 'Simple Averages'*. (ii) *'Ratio to Trend' method.*

(iii) *'Ratio to Moving Average' method.* (iv) *'Link Relative' method.*

11·6·1. Method of Simple Averages. This is the simplest method of measuring seasonal variations in a time series and involves the following steps. (We shall explain the steps for monthly data. They can be modified accordingly for quarterly, weekly or daily data).

(i) Arrange the data by years and months.

(ii) Compute the average (Arithmetic Mean) $\bar{x}_i$ for ith month ; $i = 1, 2, \ldots, 12$. Thus, $\bar{x}_1, \bar{x}_2, \ldots, \bar{x}_{12}$ are the average values for January, February, ..., December respectively, the average being taken over different years, say, k in number.

(iii) Obtain the overall average $\bar{x}$ of these averages obtained in step (ii). This is given by :

$$\bar{x} = \frac{\bar{x}_1 + \bar{x}_2 + \ldots + \bar{x}_{12}}{12} \qquad \ldots (11·35)$$

(iv) Seasonal indices (*S.I.*) for different months are obtained on expressing each monthly average as a percentage of the overall average, $\bar{x}$ *i.e.,*

$$\text{Seasonal Index for any month} = \frac{\text{Monthly Average}}{\bar{x}} \times 100 \qquad \ldots (11·36)$$

Thus, $\text{Seasonal Index for January} = \frac{\bar{x}_1}{\bar{x}} \times 100$; $\text{Seasonal Index for February} = \frac{\bar{x}_2}{\bar{x}} \times 100$

⋮

$$\text{Seasonal Index for December} = \frac{\bar{x}_{12}}{\bar{x}} \times 100$$

Remarks. 1. If we are given quarterly data for different years then we compute average value $\bar{x}_i$, (i = 1, 2, 3, 4), for each quarter over different years and then

$$\bar{x} = \frac{1}{4}\left(\bar{x}_1 + \bar{x}_2 + \bar{x}_3 + \bar{x}_4\right) \qquad \ldots (11·37)$$

Finally, seasonal index numbers for different quarters are given by the formula :

$$\text{Seasonal Index for } i\text{th quarter} = \frac{\bar{x}_i}{\bar{x}} \times 100 \; ; \; i = 1, 2, 3, 4 \qquad \ldots (11·38)$$

2. The sum of the seasonal indices must be 1200 for monthly data and 400 for quarterly data.

3. From computational point of view, a somewhat convenient formula for computing the seasonal index (*S.I.*) is obtained on substituting the value of $\bar{x}$ in (11·36). Thus we get :

$$\text{S.I. for any month} = \frac{\text{Monthly Average}}{(\bar{x}_1 + \bar{x}_2 + \ldots + \bar{x}_{12})/12} \times 100 = \frac{\text{Monthly Average} \times 1200}{\text{Sum of monthly averages}} \qquad \ldots (11·39)$$

Similarly we shall have :

$$\text{S.I. for any quarter} = \frac{\text{Quarterly Average} \times 400}{\text{Sum of quarterly averages}} \qquad \ldots (11·40)$$

A more simplified formula is as follows :

If T_i is the total for ith season, [i = 1, 2, ... , 12 for monthly data], over the given k different years then :

$$\bar{x}_i = \frac{T_i}{k}, \; (i = 1, 2, \ldots, 12) \quad \text{and} \quad \bar{x} = \frac{1}{12}\sum_i \bar{x}_i = \frac{1}{12}\sum_i \left(\frac{T_i}{k}\right) = \frac{1}{12k}\sum_i T_i = \frac{1}{k}\bar{T}$$

$$\text{Seasonal Index for } i\text{th Season} = \frac{\bar{x}_i}{\bar{x}} \times 100 = \frac{T_i / k}{T / k} \times 100 = \frac{T_i}{T} \times 100. \quad \dots (11\cdot40a)$$

So, *instead of seasonal means we may use seasonal totals.*

Limitations. The method of simple averages, though very simple to apply gives only approximate estimates of the pattern of seasonal variations in the series. It assumes that the data do not contain any trend and cyclical fluctuations at all or their effect on the time series values is not quite significant. This is a very serious limitation since most of the economic and business time series exhibit definite trends and are affected to a great extent by cycles. Accordingly, the indices obtained by this method do not truly represent the seasonal swings in the data because they include the influence of trend and cyclic variations also. This method tries to eliminate the random or irregular component by averaging the monthly (or quarterly) values over different years. In order to arrive at any meaningful seasonal indices, first of all trend effects should be eliminated from the given values. This is done in the next two methods, *viz.*, 'ratio to trend' method and 'ratio to moving average' method.

Example 11·21. *Use the method of monthly averages to determine the monthly indices for the following data of production of a commodity for the years 2004, 2005, 2006.*

Month	*PRODUCTION IN LAKHS OF TONNES*			*Month*	*PRODUCTION IN LAKHS OF TONNES*		
	2004	*2005*	*2006*		*2004*	*2005*	*2006*
January	*12*	*15*	*16*	*July*	*16*	*17*	*16*
February	*11*	*14*	*15*	*August*	*13*	*12*	*13*
March	*10*	*13*	*14*	*September*	*11*	*13*	*10*
April	*14*	*16*	*16*	*October*	*10*	*12*	*10*
May	*15*	*16*	*15*	*November*	*12*	*13*	*11*
June	*15*	*15*	*17*	*December*	*15*	*14*	*15*

Solution

TABLE 11·20. **COMPUTATION OF SEASONAL INDICES**

Month	*Production in lakhs of tonnes*				*Seasonal Indices*
	2004	*2005*	*2006*	*Total*	
(1)	*(2)*	*(3)*	*(4)*	*(5)*	$(6) = \frac{(5)}{41} \times 100$
January	12	15	16	43	104·88
February	11	14	15	40	97·56
March	10	13	14	37	90·24
April	14	16	16	46	112·20
May	15	16	15	46	112·20
June	15	15	17	47	114·63
July	16	17	16	49	119·51
August	13	12	13	38	92·68
September	11	13	10	34	82·93
October	10	12	10	32	78·05
November	12	13	11	36	87·80
December	15	14	15	44	107·32
Total				492	1200
Average				$\frac{492}{12} = 41$	$\frac{1200}{12} = 100$

Aliter. Instead of using the totals (over different years) for different months, we could use the average values for different months. For example, the average production for *i*th month is given by :

$$\bar{x}_i = \frac{T_i}{3}, (i = 1, 2, \ldots, 12) \quad ; \quad \text{where } T_i \text{ is the total production for } i\text{th month.}$$

For example : $\bar{x}_1 = \frac{T_1}{3} = \frac{43}{3} = 14·33$; $\bar{x}_2 = \frac{T_2}{3} = \frac{40}{3} = 13·33$ and so on.

Now proceed as in Example 11·22.

Example 11·22. *Compute the seasonal index for the following data assuming that there is no need to adjust the data for the trend.*

Quarter :	*2000*	*2001*	*2002*	*2003*	*2004*	*2005*
I	*3·5*	*3·5*	*3·5*	*4·0*	*4·1*	*4·2*
II	*3·9*	*4·1*	*3·9*	*4·6*	*4·4*	*4·6*
III	*3·4*	*3·7*	*3·7*	*3·8*	*4·2*	*4·3*
IV	*3·6*	*4·8*	*4·0*	*4·5*	*4·5*	*4·7*

Solution. Since we are given that there is no need to adjust the data for trend, the appropriate method for computing the seasonal indices is '*simple average*' method.

TABLE 11·21. **COMPUTATION OF SEASONAL INDICES**

Year	*I Qrt*	*II Qrt*	*III Qrt*	*IV Qrt*
2000	3·5	3·9	3·4	3·6
2001	3·5	4·1	3·7	4·8
2002	3·5	3·9	3·7	4·0
2003	4·0	4·6	3·8	4·5
2004	4·1	4·4	4·2	4·5
2005	4·2	4·6	4·3	4·7
Total	22·8	25·5	23·1	26·1
Average (A.M.)	3·80	4·25	3·85	4·35
Seasonal Indices	$\frac{3·8}{4·06} \times 100 = 93·60$	$\frac{4·25}{4·06} \times 100 = 104·68$	$\frac{3·85}{4·06} \times 100 = 94·83$	$\frac{4·35}{4·06} \times 100 = 107·14$

The average of the averages is :

$$\bar{x} = \frac{3·80 + 4·25 + 3·85 + 4·35}{4} = \frac{16·25}{4} = 4·06.$$

11·6·2. Ratio to Trend Method. This method is an improvement over the 'simple average' method of measuring seasonality and is based on the assumption that the seasonal fluctuations for any season (month, for monthly data and quarter, for quarterly data) are a constant factor of the trend. The following are the steps for measuring seasonal indices by this method.

(*i*) Compute the trend values (monthly or quarterly as the case may be), by the principle of least squares by fitting an appropriate mathematical curve (straight line, second degree parabolic curve or exponential curve, etc.).

(*ii*) Assuming multiplicative model of time series, the trend is eliminated by dividing the given time series values for each season (month or quarter) by the corresponding trend values and multiplying by 100. Thus

$$\text{Trend eliminated values } = \frac{Y}{T} \times 100 = \frac{TSCI}{T} \times 100 \quad \ldots (11·41)$$

$$= SCI \times 100 \quad \ldots (11·41a)$$

These percentages will, therefore, include seasonal, cyclical and irregular fluctuations. Further steps are more or less same as in the 'simple average' method.

(*iii*) Arrange these trend eliminated values according to years and months or quarters. An attempt is made to eliminate the cyclical and irregular variations by averaging the percentages for different months or quarters, over the given years. Arithmetic mean or median may be used for averaging. These averages give the preliminary indices of seasonal variations for different seasons (months or quarters).

(*iv*) Lastly, these seasonal indices are adjusted to a total of 1200 for monthly data or 400 for quarterly data by multiplying each of them with a constant factor k given by

$$k = \frac{1200}{\text{Sum of monthly indices}} \quad or \quad k = \frac{400}{\text{Sum of quarterly indices}}$$

for monthly or quarterly data respectively. This step amounts to expressing the preliminary seasonal indices as a percentage of their arithmetic mean.

Merits and Demerits. Since this method determines the indices of seasonal variations after eliminating the trend component, it definitely gives more representative values of seasonal swings as compared with the 'simple average' method. However, the averaging process over different years will not completely eliminate the cyclical effects particularly, if the cyclical swings are obvious and pronounced in the given series. Accordingly, the indices of seasonal variations obtained by this method are mingled with cyclical effects also and are, therefore, biased and not truly representative. Hence, this method is recommended if the cyclical movements are either absent or if present, their effect is not so significant. If the data exhibits pronounced cyclical swings, then the seasonal indices based on '*Ratio to Moving Average*' method, discussed in § 11·6·3 will reflect the seasonal variations better than this method. However, as compared with moving average method, a distinct advantage of this method is that trend values can be obtained for each month (quarter) for which data are available, whereas there is loss of information of certain trend values (in the beginning and at the end) in the ratio to moving average method.

Remark. If we are given the monthly (or quarterly) figures for different years, then the fitting of trend equation to monthly (quarterly) data which involves a fairly large number of observations, by the principle of least squares is quite tedious and time consuming. In such a situation, the calculations are simplified to a great extent by first fitting the trend equation to annual totals or *average* monthly or quarterly values and then adjusting or modifying it to monthly or quarterly values as explained in equations (11·29) and (11·32), § 11·5·4. This technique is explained in the Example 11·23.

Example 11·23. *Using 'Ratio to Trend' method, determine the quarterly seasonal indices for the following data.*

Production of Coal (in Million of Tons)

Year	*I Qrt.*	*II Qrt.*	*III Qrt.*	*IV Qrt.*
1	68	60	61	63
2	70	58	56	60
3	68	63	68	67
4	65	56	56	62
5	60	55	55	58

Solution.

TABLE 11·22. **COMPUTATION OF LINEAR TREND**

Year (*t*)	*Total of quarterly values*	*Average of quarterly values* (*y*)	$x = t - 3$	x^2	xy	*Trend Values (Million tons)* $y_e = 61{\cdot}4 - 1{\cdot}45x$
1	252	63·0	−2	4	−126	64·30
2	244	61·0	−1	1	−61	62·85
3	266	66·5	0	0	0	61·40
4	242	60·5	1	1	60·5	59·95
5	224	56·0	2	4	112	58·50
		$\Sigma y = 307$	$\Sigma x = 0$	$\Sigma x^2 = 10$	$\Sigma xy = -14{\cdot}5$	

Let the straight line trend equation be :

$$y = a + bx \qquad \dots (*)$$

Origin : 3rd year ; x units : 1 year, and y units : Average quarterly production (in Million tons).

The normal (least-requare) equations for estimating a and b in (*) are :

$$\Sigma y = na + b\Sigma x \quad \text{and} \quad \Sigma xy = a\Sigma x + b\Sigma x^2$$

Since $\Sigma x = 0$, these give : $a = \frac{\Sigma y}{n} = \frac{307}{5} = 61{\cdot}4$; $b = \frac{\Sigma xy}{\Sigma x^2} = \frac{-14{\cdot}5}{10} = -1{\cdot}45$

Hence, the straight line trend is given by the equation :

$$y_e = 61{\cdot}4 - 1{\cdot}45\,x, \qquad \dots (**)$$

Origin : 3rd year ; x unit = 1 year ; y unit : Average *quarterly* production. (Million tons)

Putting $x = -2, -1, 0, 1, 2$ we obtain the average quarterly trend values for the years 1 to 5 respectively, which are given in the last column of the above table.

From the trend equation (**), we observe that :

Yearly increment in the trend values = $b = -1{\cdot}45$ $\Rightarrow$ Quarterly increment = $\frac{-1{\cdot}45}{4} = -0{\cdot}36$

The negative value of b implies that we have a declining trend. Now we have to determine the quarterly trend values for each year.

The average quarterly trend value for the 1st year is 64·30. This is, in fact the trend value for the middle quarter, *i.e.,* half of the 2nd quarter and half of 3rd quarter, for the first year. Since the quarterly increment is – 0·36, we obtain the trend values for the 2nd and 3rd quarters of first year as :

$64{\cdot}30 - \frac{1}{2}(-0{\cdot}36)$ and $64{\cdot}30 + \frac{1}{2}(-0{\cdot}36)$ *i.e.,* $64{\cdot}30 + 0{\cdot}18$ and $64{\cdot}30 - 0{\cdot}18$ *i.e.,* 64·48 and 64·12

respectively. The trend value for 1st quarter, now becomes 64·48 + 0·36 = 64·84. Since the quarterly increment is – 0·36, the trend values for the 4th quarter of 1st year and remaining quarters of other years are obtained on subtracting 0·36 from the value of 3rd quarter, *viz.,* 64·12 successively. Trend values are given in the Table 11·23.

TABLE 11·23. COMPUTATION OF SEASONAL INDICES

	Trend Values				*Trend Eliminated Values (Given values as % of Trend values)*				
Year	*I Qrt*	*II Qrt*	*III Qrt*	*IV Qrt*	*I Qrt*	*II Qrt*	*III Qrt*	*IV Qrt*	
1	64·84	64·48	64·12	63·76	104·87	93·05	95·13	98·81	
2	63·39	63·03	62·67	62·61	110·43	92·02	89·36	96·29	
3	61·94	61·58	61·22	60·86	109·78	102·31	111·07	110·09	
4	60·50	60·14	59·78	59·42	107·44	98·10	93·68	104·34	
5	59·06	58·70	58·34	57·98	101·59	93·70	87·42	100·03	
				Total	534·11	479·18	476·66	509·56	Total
				Average (A.M.) (Seasonal Indices)	106·82	95·84	95·33	101·91	399.9
				Adjusted Seasonal Indices	106·85	95·86	95·35	101·94	

Sum of seasonal indices = 106·82 + 95·84 + 95·33 + 101·91 = 399·90

Since this is not exactly 400, the seasonal indices obtained as arithmetic mean are adjusted to a total 400 by multiplying each of them with a constant factor k, called *correction factor* given by :

$$k = \frac{400}{399{\cdot}9} = 1{\cdot}00025$$

Remarks. 1. Since the sum of seasonal indices is 399·9 which is approximately 400, we may not apply any adjustment in this case.

2. Rounding to whole numbers, the quarterly seasonal indices are 107, 96, 95, 102 respectively.

3. In obtaining the trend values, we fitted a linear trend equation to average quarterly production. However, we could have fitted a straight line trend to annual (total) values and then, finally adjusted the trend equation to quarterly values [*c.f.* (11·32)].

11·6·3. 'Ratio to Moving Average' Method. This is an improvement over the 'Ratio to Trend' method as it tries to eliminate the cyclical variations which are mixed up with seasonal indices in the 'Ratio to Trend' method. 'Ratio to Moving Average' is the most widely used method of measuring seasonal fluctuations and involves the following steps :

(*i*) Obtain centred 12-month (4-quarter) moving average values for the given series. Since the variations recur after a span of 12 months for monthly data (4-quarters for quarterly data), a 12-month (4-quarter) moving average will completely eliminate the seasonal variations provided they are of constant pattern and intensity. Accordingly, the 12-month (4-quarter) moving average values may be regarded to contain trend and cyclic components, *viz.*, $T \times C$, as averaging process tries to eliminate the irregular component.

(*ii*) Express the original values as a percentage of centred moving average values for all months (quarters) except for the first 6 months (2 quarters) and 6 months (2 quarters) at the end. Using multiplicative model of time series, these percentages give :

$$\frac{\text{Original value}}{\text{M.A. value}} \times 100 = \frac{TSCI}{TC} \times 100 = SI \times 100 \qquad \ldots (11·42)$$

Hence the 'ratio to moving average' represents the seasonal and irregular components.

(*iii*) As in the 'simple averages' and 'ratio to trend' methods, arrange these percentages according to years and months (quarters). Preliminary seasonal indices are obtained on eliminating the irregular component by averaging these percentages for each month (quarter), the average being taken over different years. Arithmetic mean or median may be used for averaging.

(*iv*) The sum of these indices should be 1200 (or 400) for monthly (or quarterly) data. If it is not so, then these seasonal indices obtained in step (*iii*) are adjusted to a total of 1200 (or 400) by multiplying each of them with a constant factor

$$k = \frac{1200}{\text{Sum of monthly indices}}, \quad \text{or} \quad k = \frac{400}{\text{Sum of quarterly indices}},$$

for monthly and quarterly data respectively. This last step amounts to expressing each of the preliminary indices as a percentage of their arithmetic mean.

Merits and Demerits. 'Ratio to moving average' is the most satisfactory and widely used method for estimating the seasonal fluctuations in a time series because it irons out both trend and cyclical components from the indices of seasonal variations. However, it should be kept in mind that it will give true seasonal indices provided the cyclical fluctuations are regular in periodicity as well as amplitude. An obvious drawback of this method is that there is loss of some trend values in the beginning and at the end and accordingly seasonal indices for first six months (or 2 quarters) of the first year and last six months (or 2 quarters) of the last year cannot be determined.

Remarks. 1. Specific Seasonal Index and Typical Seasonal Index. The seasonal indices for each month (quarter) of different years are also known as *specific seasonals* and the average of specific seasonals for each month (quarter) for a number of years are termed as *typical seasonals.*

2. Additive Model. If we use additive model of the time series, then the method of moving averages for computing seasonal indices involves the following steps. [We shall state the steps for monthly data and these can be modified accordingly for quarterly and other data.]

(*i*) Obtain 12-month moving average values. These will contain trend and cyclic components, *i.e.*, they will represent $(T + C)$.

(*ii*) Trend eliminated values are obtained on subtracting these moving average values from the given time series values to give :

$$y - \text{M.A. values } = (T + S + C + I) - (T + C) = S + I \qquad \ldots (11·43)$$

(*iii*) Irregular Component is eliminated on averaging these $(S + I)$ values for each month over different years and we get the preliminary indices for each month.

(*iv*) Sum of these indices should be zero. In case it is not so, the preliminary indices obtained in step (*iii*) are adjusted to a total of zero by *subtracting* from each of them a constant factor,

$$k = \frac{1}{12}\left[\text{Sum of the monthly seasonal indices}\right]$$

'Ratio to Moving Average' method, using the multiplicative model is illustrated in Examples 11·24 and 11·25.

Example 11·24. *Calculate seasonal indices by the 'ratio to moving average method' from the following data of the sales (y) of a Firm in lakhs of Rupees.*

Year	*I Quarter*	*II Quarter*	*III Quarter*	*IV Quarter*
2001	*68*	*62*	*61*	*63*
2002	*65*	*58*	*66*	*61*
2003	*68*	*63*	*63*	*67*

Solution.

TABLE 11·24. **COMPUTATION OF MOVING AVERAGES**

Year (1)	*Sales (y) (Rs. lakhs)* (2)	*4-Quarterly Moving Totals.* (3)	*4-Qrt. M.A.* (4)	*2-Pd M.T. of col. (4)* (5)	*4-Qrt. M.A. Centred* (6)	*Ratio to M.A. Values* $(7) = \frac{(2)}{(6)} \times 100$
2001 I Qrt.	68					
II Qrt.	62					
		← 254	63.50			
III Qrt.	61			126·25	63·125	96·63
		← 251	62·75			
IV Qrt.	63			124·50	62·250	101·20
		← 247	61·75			
2002 I Qrt.	65			124·75	62·375	104·21
		← 252	63·00			
II Qrt.	58			125·50	62·750	92·43
		← 250	62·50			
III Qrt.	66			125·75	62·875	104·97
		← 253	63·25			
IV Qrt.	61			127·75	63·875	95·50
		← 258	64·50			
2003 I Qrt.	68			128·25	64·125	106·04
		← 255	63·75			
II Qrt.	63			129·00	64·500	97·67
		← 261	65·25			
III Qrt.	63					
IV Qrt.	67					

TABLE 11·24A. **COMPUTATION OF SEASONAL INDICES**

Year	*Trend Eliminated Values* *I Qrt.*	*II Qrt.*	*III Qrt.*	*IV Qrt.*	
2001	—	—	96·63	101·20	
2002	104·21	92·43	104·97	95·50	
2003	106·04	97·67	—		
Total	210·25	190·10	201·60	196·70	Total
Average (A.M.) (S.I.)	105·13	95·05	100·80	98·35	399·33
Adjusted Seasonal Indices	105·31	95·21	100·97	98·52	400·01

Sum of seasonal indices = 105·13 + 95·05 + 100·80 + 98·35 = 399·33

which is less than 400. These indicese are, therefore, adjusted to a total of 400 by multiplying each of them by a constant factor :

$$k = \frac{400}{399 \cdot 33} = 1 \cdot 0017$$

The adjusted seasonal indices are given in the last row of Table 11·24A.

Example 11·25. *Calculate the seasonal indices by the 'ratio to moving average' method from the following data.*

Year	*Quarter*	*Y*	*4-Quarterly Moving Average*
2005	*I*	*75*	
	II	*60*	
	III	*54*	*63·375*
	IV	*59*	*65·375*

2006	*I*	*86*	*67·125*
	II	*65*	*70·875*
	III	*63*	*74·000*
	IV	*80*	*75·375*
2007	*I*	*90*	*76·625*
	II	*72*	*77·625*
	III	*66*	*79·500*
	IV	*85*	*81·500*
2008	*I*	*100*	*83·000*
	II	*78*	*84·750*
	III	*72*	
	IV	*93*	

Solution.

TABLE 11·25. **CALCULATION OF SEASONAL INDICES**

Year	*Trend Eliminated Values* $\left(\textit{Given values as a percentage of M.A. Values, i.e., } \frac{y}{M.A.} \times 100\right)$ *I Qrt.*	*II Qrt.*	*III Qrt.*	*IV Qrt.*	
2005	—	—	85·2071	90·2485	
2006	128·1192	91·7108	85·1351	106·1360	
2007	117·4551	92·7536	89·0189	104·2945	
2008	120·4819	92·0354	—	—	
Total	366·0562	276·4998	253·3611	300·6790	
Average (A.M.) (S.I.)	122·0187	92·1666	84·4537	100·2263	Total 398·8653
Adjusted Seasonal Indices	122·3604	92·4247	84·6902	100·5069	399·9822 ≈ 400

The seasonal indices obtained as averages (A.M.) above are adjusted to a total of 400, by multiplying each of them by a constant factor,

$$k = \frac{400}{\text{Sum of Seasonal Indices}} = \frac{400}{398 \cdot 8653} = 1 \cdot 0028$$

The adjusted seasonal indices are given in the last row of the above table.

11·6·4. Method of Link Relatives. We have already discussed the concept of '*Link Relatives*' in the last chapter while discussing chain index numbers. Link relative (L.R.) is the value of the given phenomenon in any season (month, for monthly data ; quarter, for quarterly data ; day, for weekly data and so on), expressed as a percentage of its value in the preceding season. We shall explain the method for monthly data and it can be modified accordingly for quarterly or weekly data. Thus,

$$\text{Link Relative for any month} = \frac{\text{Current month's value}}{\text{Previous month's value}} \times 100 \qquad \ldots(11 \cdot 44)$$

For example,

$$\text{L.R. for March} = \frac{\text{Value (figure) for March}}{\text{Value (figure) for February}} \times 100 \qquad \ldots(11 \cdot 44a)$$

The construction of indices of seasonal variations by the Link Relatives method, also known as Pearson's method, involves the following steps.

(*i*) Convert the original data into link relatives by formula (11·44*a*), *i.e.*, express each value as a percentage of the preceding value.

(*ii*) As in the case of 'Ratio to Trend' or 'Ratio to M.A.' method, average these link relatives for each month, the average being taken over the given number of years. Arithmetic mean or median may be used for averaging. Median is preferred to A.M. as the latter gives undue importance to extreme observations which are not basically due to seasonal swings.

(*iii*) Convert these link relatives (L.R.) into chain relatives (C.R.) on the basis of 1st season by the formula :

$$\text{C.R. for any month} = \frac{\text{L.R. of that month} \times \text{C.R. of preceding month}}{100} \qquad \ldots(11\cdot45)$$

the chain relative for January being taken as 100. For example :

$$\text{C.R. for February} = \frac{\text{L.R. of Feb.} \times \text{C.R. of January}}{100}$$

$$= \text{L.R. of February} \qquad (\because \text{ C.R. of Jan.} = 100)$$

$$\text{C.R. for March} = \frac{\text{L.R. of March} \times \text{C.R. of Feb.}}{100}$$

$$\vdots \qquad \vdots \qquad \vdots$$

$$\text{C.R. for December} = \frac{\text{L.R. of Dec.} \times \text{C.R. of Nov.}}{100}$$

(*iv*) Obtain the C.R. for first month *viz.*, January on the basis of the December chain relative, which is given by :

$$\text{New C.R. for January} = \frac{\text{L.R. of January} \times \text{C.R. of Dec.}}{100} \qquad \ldots(11\cdot46)$$

Usually, this will not be 100 due to the effect of long-term secular trend and accordingly the chain indices are to be adjusted or corrected for the effect of trend.

(*v*) This adjustment is done by subtracting a '*correction factor*' from each of the chain relatives.

$$\text{Let us write : } d = \tfrac{1}{12}\,[\text{New C.R. for January} - 100] \qquad \ldots(11\cdot47)$$

If we assume a straight line trend, then the correction factor for February, March,..., December is d, $2d$,..., $11d$ respectively.

(*vi*) The indices of seasonal variation are obtained on adjusting these corrected chain relatives to a total of 1200, by expressing each of them as a percentage of their arithmetic mean. This amounts to multiplying each of them by a constant factor,

$$k = \frac{1200}{\text{Sum of the corrected monthly chain relatives}}$$

Remark. For quarterly data, we write

$$d = \tfrac{1}{4}\,[\text{New C.R. for 1st Quarter} - 100]$$

and the corrected C.R.'s for 2nd, 3rd and 4th quarter are obtained on subtracting d, $2d$ and $3d$ from the C.R.'s obtained in step (*iii*).

Finally, adjust these corrected C.R.'s to a total of 400, by multiplying each of them by a constant factor,

$$k = \frac{400}{\text{Sum of the corrected quarterly C.R.'s}}$$

to get the indices of seasonal variation.

Merits and Demerits : (*i*) The averaged link relatives include both the cyclic and trend components. Though trend is subsequently eliminated by applying correction, the indices obtained will be truly representative only if the data really exhibits a straight line trend. However, this is not so in most of the economic and business time series.

(*ii*) Though not so easy to understand as the moving average method, the actual calculations involved in this method are much less extentisve than the 'Ratio to M.A.' or 'Ratio to Trend' method.

(*iii*) There is loss of only one link relative *i.e.*, for the first season while in case of moving average method we lose some of the values (trend and seasonal) in the beginning and at the end. Thus, 'Link Relatives' method utilises the data more completely.

Example 11·26. *Compute the seasonal indices by the 'Link Relatives' method for the following data :*

Wheat Prices (in Rupees per 10 kg.)

Quarter	*Year →*	*2002*	*2003*	*2004*	*2005*
1st (Jan.-March		*75*	*86*	*90*	*100*
2nd (April-June)		*60*	*65*	*72*	*78*
3rd (July-Sept.)		*54*	*63*	*66*	*72*
4th (Oct.-Dec.)		*59*	*80*	*85*	*93*

Solution.

TABLE 11·26 : **COMPUTATION OF SEASONAL INDICES BY LINK RELATIVES METHOD**

	LINK RELATIVES				
Year	*I Qrt.*	*II Qrt.*	*III Qrt.*	*IV Qrt.*	
2002	—	80·00	90·00	109·26	
2003	145·76	75·58	96·92	126·98	
2004	112·50	80·00	91·67	128·79	
2005	117·65	78·00	92·31	129·17	
Total of L.R.'s	375·91	313·58	370·90	494·20	
Average L.R. (A.M.)	125·303	78·395	92·725	123·550	
Chain Relatives	100·000	$\frac{78·395 \times 100}{100} = 78·395$	$\frac{78·395 \times 92·725}{100} = 72·690$	$\frac{123·55 \times 72·69}{100} = 89·810$	Total
Adjusted C.R's	100	$78·395 - 3·135 = 75·26$	$72·690 - 6·270 = 66·42$	$89·810 - 9·405 = 80·41$	322·09
Seasonal Indices	124·20	93·47	82·49	99·87	400·03

The New (Second) C.R. for 1st quarter is :

$$\frac{\text{L.R. of 1st Qrt.} \times \text{C.R. of last (4th) Qrt.}}{100} = \frac{125·303 \times 89·81}{100} = 112·54.$$

We have :
$$d = \tfrac{1}{4}\,[\text{New C.R. of 1st Qrt.} - 100] = \tfrac{1}{4}(112·54 - 100) = 3·135$$

Adjusted C.R.'s for 2nd, 3rd and 4th quarters are obtained on subtracting d, $2d$ and $3d$ from the corresponding C.R.'s.

$$\text{Sum of adjusted C.R.'s} = 100 + 75·26 + 66·42 + 80·41 = 322·09.$$

Indices of seasonal variations are obtained on adjusting these adjusted C.R.'s to a total of 400 by multiplying each one of them with a constant factor,

$$k = \frac{400}{\text{Sum of adjusted C.R.'s}} = \frac{400}{322·09} = 1·242,$$

and are given in the last row of the Table 11·26.

Remark. The values of seasonal indices for the same data obtained by the 'Ratio to M.A. Method' in Example 11·25 compare reasonably well with the values of S.I.'s by 'Link Relative Method' as obtained *above*.

11·6·5. Deseasonalisation of Data. As already pointed out, the objective of studying seasonal variations is : (*i*) to measure them and (*ii*) to eliminate them from the given series. Elimination of the seasonal effects from the given values is termed as *deseasonalisation of the data.* It helps us to adjust the given time series for seasonal variations, thus leaving us with trend component, cyclical and irregular movements. Assuming multiplicative model of the time series, the deseasonalised (seasonality eliminated) values are obtained on dividing the given values by the corresponding indices of seasonal variations.

$$\text{Deseasonalised Datx} = \frac{y}{S} = \frac{TCSI}{S} = TCI \qquad ...(11·48)$$

Deseasonalisation is specially needed for the study of cyclic component. It also helps businessmen and management executives for planning future production programmes, for forecasting and for managerial control. It also helps in proper interpretation of the data. For example, if the values are not adjusted for seasonality, then seasonal upswings (or downswings) may be misinterpreted as periods of boom and prosperity (or depression) in business.

Remark. In case of absolute seasonal variations (additive model of time series), the deseasonalised values are obtained on subtracting the seasonal variations from the given values. Thus,

$$\text{Deseasonalised Data } = y - S = (T + S + C + I) - S = T + C + I \qquad \ldots(11.49)$$

Example 11·27. *The quarterly seasonal indices of freight movements on a railway line are given below.*

Quarter	*I*	*II*	*III*	*IV*
Seasonal Index	*70*	*110*	*100*	*120*

If the total freight for the first quarter of 1991 is 350,000 tonnes, compute the traffic to be expected in the remaining quarters. (You may assume that there is no trend.) *[Delhi Univ. B.A. (Econ. Hons.), 1999]*

Solution. We are given that the total freight movements on the given railway line are 3,50,000 tonnes. Under the assumption that there is no trend, the estimated freight for different quarters can be computed as given in the following table.

Quarter	*I*	*II*	*III*	*IV*
Seasonal Index	70	110	100	120
Expected freight (in tonnes)	3,50,000 (Given)	$\frac{3,50,000}{70} \times 110 = 5,50,000$	$\frac{3,50,000}{70} \times 100 = 5,00,000$	$\frac{3,50,000}{70} \times 120 = 6,00,000$

Example 11·28. *Deseasonalise the following data with the help of the seasonal data given below.*

Month	*Cash Balance ('000) Rs.*	*Seasonal Index*
January	*360*	*120*
February	*400*	*80*
March	*550*	*110*
April	*360*	*90*
May	*350*	*70*
June	*550*	*100*

Solution. Deseasonalised values are obtained on dividing the given time series values (Y) by the seasonal effect — assuming that the given series data follows multiplicative model of decomposition. We have :

$$\text{Seasonal effect} = \frac{\text{Seasonal Index}}{100} = \frac{\text{S.I.}}{100}$$

Hence, using multiplicative model : $Y = T \times S \times C \times I$;

$$\text{Deseasonalised value} = \frac{Y}{\text{Seasonal effect}} = \frac{Y}{\text{S.I.}} \times 100$$

TABLE 11·27. **COMPUTATION OF DESEASONALISED VALUES**

Month	*Cash Balance ('000 Rs.) (Y)*	*Seasonal Index (S.I.)*	*Deseasonalised Value* $= \frac{Y}{S.I.} \times 100$
January	360	120	$\frac{360}{120} \times 100 = 300$
February	400	80	$\frac{400}{80} \times 100 = 500$
March	550	110	$\frac{550}{110} \times 100 = 500$
April	360	90	$\frac{360}{90} \times 100 = 400$
May	350	70	$\frac{350}{70} \times 100 = 500$
June	550	100	$\frac{550}{100} \times 100 = 550$

Remark. If we assume the additive model of decomposition, then the deseasonalised values are given by (Y – S.I.).

Example 11·29. *The seasonal indices of the sales of garments of a particular type in a certain shop are given below :*

Quarter	*Jan.-March*	*Apr.-June*	*July-Sept.*	*Oct.-Dec.*
Seasonal index	*97*	*85*	*83*	*135*

If the total sales in the first quarter of a year be worth Rs. 15,000 and sales are expected to rise by 4% in each quarter, determine how much worth of garments of this type be kept in stock by the shop-owner to meet the demand for each of three quarters of the year.

Solution. Since the sales are expected to rise by 4% in each quarter, we have :

Expected sales in any quarter = 104% of the value of previous quarter. ...(*)

Taking into account the seasonal index (S.I.) for each quarter we have :

Stock in any quarter = (Expected Sales × S.I.) of that quarter. ...(**)

Using the formulae in (*) and (**), we can find the stock which the shop-owner should keep in the shop to meet the demand for each of the three other quarters of the year as explained below :

Quarter (1)	*Seasonal index* (2)	*Seasonal effect* (3)	*Expected sales (in Rs.)* (4)	*Stock worth (Rs.)* (5) = (3) × (4)
Jan.-March	97	0·97	15,000	14,550
Apr.-June	85	0·85	$\frac{104}{100} \times 15{,}000 = 15{,}600$	13,260
July-Sept.	83	0·83	$\frac{104}{100} \times 15{,}600 = 16{,}224$	13,466
Oct.-Dec.	135	1·35	$\frac{104}{100} \times 16{,}224 = 16{,}873$	22,779

Example 11·30. *The sale of a company rose from Rs. 60,000 in the month of August to Rs. 69,000 in the month of September. The seasonal indices for these two months are 105 and 140 respectively. The owner of the company was not at all satisfied with the rise of sales in the month of September by Rs. 9,000. He expected much more because of the seasonal index for that month. What was his estimate of sales for the month of September ?*

Solution. The owner of the company was justifiably not satisfied with the rise of sales of Rs. (69,000 – 60,000) = Rs. 9,000 from August to September because on the basis of the seasonal index of September, the estimated sales for September should have been :

$$\text{Rs. } \frac{60{,}000}{105} \times 140 = \text{Rs. } 80{,}000$$

Thus the actual sales of Rs. 69,000 for September is much below the expected sales and hence the dissatisfaction of the owner is justified.

Aliter. Actual sales for August are Rs. 60,000 and seasonal index for August is 105. Hence the seasonal effect for August is 1·05 and accordingly the expected monthly sales are :

$$\text{Rs. } 60{,}000 \div 1{\cdot}05 = \text{Rs. } \frac{60{,}000}{1{\cdot}05}$$

Seasonal effect for September is 140 ÷ 100 = 1·40 and, therefore, the estimated sales for September are :

$$\text{Rs. } \frac{60{,}000}{1{\cdot}05} \times 1{\cdot}40 = \text{Rs. } 80{,}000$$

Example 11·31. *On the basis of quarterly sales (in Rs. lakhs) of a certain commodity for the years 2001-2005 the following calculations were made :*

Trend :

y = 25·0 + 0·6t, with origin at 1st quarter of 2001,

where t = time units (one quarter), and y = quarterly sales (Rs. lakhs).

Seasonal variations :

Quarter	*1st*	*2nd*	*3rd*	*4th*
Seasonal index	*90*	*95*	*110*	*105*

Estimate the quarterly sales for the year 2002 (use multiplicative model).

Solution. Since, in the trend equation :

$$y = 25{\cdot}0 + 0{\cdot}6t, \qquad \ldots(*)$$

1st quarter of 2001 is origin, we have $t = 0$ for 1st quarter. Further, since time unit is one quarter we have t =1, 2, and 3 for 2nd, 3rd and 4th quarters respectively of the year 2001.

Hence, the values of t for 1st, 2nd, 3rd and 4th quarters of 2002 are 4, 5, 6 and 7 respectively. Using multiplicative model of time series *i.e.,*

$$y = T \times S \times C \times I,$$

the estimated quarterly sales for the year 2002 are obtained in the Table 11.28.

TABLE 11·28. **ESTIMATED QUARTERLY SALES FOR 2002**

Quarter of 2002	*t*	*Trend Values (Rs. lakhs)* $y_e = 25 + 0{\cdot}6t$	*Seasonal Effect* $S = \frac{\text{Seasonal Index}}{100}$	*Estimated Sales (Rs. lakhs)* $y_e \times S$
1	4	$25 + 0{\cdot}6 \times 4 = 27{\cdot}4$	0·90	24·66
2	5	$25 + 0{\cdot}6 \times 5 = 28{\cdot}0$	0·95	26·60
3	6	$25 + 0{\cdot}6 \times 6 = 28{\cdot}6$	1·10	31·46
4	7	$25 + 0{\cdot}6 \times 7 = 29{\cdot}2$	1·05	30·66

11·7. MEASUREMENT OF CYCLICAL VARIATIONS

An approximate or crude method of measuring cyclical variations is the '*Residual Method*' which consists in first estimating trend (T) and seasonal (S) components and then eliminating their effect from the given time series. Assuming multiplicative model of the time series, these components (T and S) are eliminated on dividing the given time series values by $T \times S$ *viz.,*

$$\frac{Y}{T \times S} = \frac{TSCI}{TS} = CI, \qquad \ldots(11{\cdot}50)$$

thus leaving us with cyclical and irregular movements.

If we ignore the random or irregular variations or assume that their effect is not very significant, then the values obtained in (11·50) may be taken to reflect cyclical variations.

To arrive at better estimates of cyclical fluctuations, the irregular component (I) should be eliminated from the CI values obtained in (11·50). But irregular movements, by their nature, cannot be determined as they are the residuals after adjusting the given data for trend, seasonal and cyclical variations. An attempt is then made to iron out or smoothen the irregular component by taking a moving average of these CI values.

Steps in the computation of cyclical variations by the 'residual method' may be summarised as follows :

(*i*) Compute trend values (T) and the seasonal indices (S) preferably by the moving average method. S should be in fraction form and not in percentage form.

(*ii*) Divide given values by $T \times S$. This step may be divided into two steps *viz.*

(*a*) Divide Y by T to get SCI.

(*b*) Divide SCI by S to get CI.

(*iii*) Take M.A. of the CI values obtained in Step (*ii*) above. For monthly data, often 3-month or 5-month moving average may be used.

Remarks 1. The 'residual method' will give effective results only if the trend component and seasonal fluctuations are correctly measured. This is, by far, the most commonly used method of measuring cyclical variations.

2. The problem of taking M.A. of the CI values involves two questions :

(*i*) Period of M.A.

(*ii*) Weighting system to be used.

For a detailed study of these, the reader is referred to Applied General Statistics by Croxton and Cowden.

3. The other methods for studying the cyclical variations are :

(*i*) Reference Cycle Analysis Method.
(*ii*) Direct Percentage Variation Method.
(*iii*) Fitting of Sine Functions Method or Harmonic Analysis.

For a detailed study of these methods the reader, is referred to Applied General Statistics by Croxton and Cowden.

Example 11·32. *Obtain the estimates of the cyclical variations for the data of Example 11·25.*

Solution.

TABLE 11·29. **COMPUTATION OF INDICES OF CYCLICAL VARIATIONS**

Year	*Quarter*	*Original Values (Y)*	*Seasonal Index (S)**	$\frac{Y}{S}\times 100 = TCI$	*Trend (M.A.) (T)*	$\frac{\text{Col. (5)}}{\text{Col. (6)}}\times 100 = 100\ CI$	*3-Quarterly M.A. of Col. (7)*
(1)	*(2)*	*(3)*	*(4)*	*(5)*	*(6)*	*(7)*	*(8)*
2005	1	75	122·36	61·29	—		
	2	60	92·42	64·92	—		
	3	54	84·69	63·76	63·375	100·61	—
2006	4	59	100·51	58·70	65·375	89·79	98·37
	1	86	122·36	70·28	67·125	104·70	97·91
	2	65	92·42	70·33	70·875	99·23	101·49
	3	63	84·69	74·39	74·000	100·53	101·78
2007	4	80	100·51	79·59	75·375	105·59	100·70
	1	90	122·36	73·55	76·625	95·99	100·65
	2	72	92·42	77·91	77·625	100·37	98·13
	3	66	84·69	77·93	79·500	98·03	100·72
	4	85	100·51	84·57	81·500	103·77	100·09
2008	1	100	122·36	81·73	83·000	98·47	100·61
	2	78	92·42	84·40	84·750	99·59	—
	3	72	84·69	85·02	—		
	4	93	100·51	92·53	—		

* The values of seasonal indices for different quarters and the M.A. values are taken as obtained in Example 11·25.

Last coloum (8) of Table 11·29 gives indices of cyclical variations.

11·8. MEASUREMENT OF IRREGULAR VARIATIONS

By the nature of movements, no formula, however approximate, can be suggested to obtain an estimate of the irregular component in a time series. In practice, the three components of a time series *viz.*, Trend (*T*), Seasonal (*S*) and Cyclical (*C*) are obtained and the irregular component is obtained as a residual which is unaccounted for by these components after eliminating them from the given series. Using the multiplicative model of time series, the random or irregular component is given by :

$$\frac{Y}{TSC} = \frac{TSCI}{TSC} = I, \qquad ...(11·51)$$

where *S* and *C* are in fractional form and not in percentage form.

However, in practice, the cycle behaves in an erratic manner because successive cycles vary widely in period, amplitude and pattern and accordingly it is very difficult to measure the cyclical variations accurately. Moreover, they are so much inter-mixed with irregular variations that, quite often, it becomes practically impossible to separate them. Accordingly, in analysis of time series, trend and seasonal components are measured separately and after eliminating their effect the cyclical and irregular fluctuations $(C \times I)$ are left together.

Remark. Although the random or irregular component cannot be estimated accurately, we can obtain an estimate of the variance of the random component by the "*Variate Difference*" method. The discussion is, however, beyond the scope of the book.

11·9. TIME SERIES ANALYSIS IN FORECASTING

In this chapter we described the various components of a time series and the methods for isolating and measuring them independently. In forecasting, we project the past trend and seasonal variations into the future. These forecasts will be reliable,

(*i*) If the time series data used for the forecasts is reliable.

(*ii*) If the past trends were regular and going to last for quite sometime in future.

(*iii*) If an appropriate and accurate trend curve is fitted to the given data [See § 11·5·5]

However, due to changes in the sociological, economical and political scenario, the business environment in future may undergo significant changes as compared to the environment that existed when the time series data were collected. In such situations, the current forecasts will not be reliable.

EXERCISE 11·3

1. What do you understand by 'seasonal variations' in time series data ? Explain with few examples, the utility of such a study.

2. (*a*) Explain the meaning of time series. What are its main components ? How would you study seasonal variations in a time series ?

(*b*) What are different components of an economic time series ? Name the methods of determining seasonal index.

(*c*) What do you understand by seasonal indices ? What methods are used to determine them ?

3. (*a*) What are seasonal variations ? Explain any method of determining these.

[*Delhi Univ. B.A.* (*Econ. Hons.*), *1999*]

(*b*) "All periodic variations are not necessarily seasonal." Discuss this statement with suitable examples.

[*Delhi Univ. B.A.* (*Econ. Hons.*), *1997*]

(*c*) Explain the different components of an economic time series. How would you statistically eliminate the influence of seasonal and cyclical factors on the long period movement of any series ?

4. Explain what is meant by seasonal fluctuations of a time series. Discuss the different methods for determining seasonal fluctuations of a given time series. Discuss the relative merits and demerits of each of these methods. Also state the conditions of applicability for each of the methods.

5. What do you mean by seasonal fluctuations in time series. Give examples.

Explain the method of 'Simple Averages' for obtaining indices of seasonal variations. Discuss its relative merits and demerits.

6. Compute the seasonal averages, and seasonal indices for the following time-series.

Month	1994	1995	1996	Month	1994	1995	1996
Jan.	15	23	25	July.	20	22	30
Feb.	16	22	25	Aug.	28	28	34
March	18	28	35	Sept.	29	32	38
April	18	27	36	Oct.	33	37	47
May	23	31	36	Nov.	33	34	41
June	23	28	30	Dec.	38	44	53

[**Hint.** Use Method of Simple Averages.]

Ans. 70, 70, 90, 90, 100, 90, 80, 100, 110, 130, 120, 150.

7. Assuming no trend in the series, calculate seasonal indices for the following data :

	Quarter			(in units)
Year	*I*	*II*	*III*	*IV*
1994	78	66	84	80
1995	76	74	82	78
1996	72	68	80	70
1997	74	70	84	74
1998	76	74	86	82

[*C.A. (Foundation), May 1999*]

[**Hint.** Use the method of simple averages.]

Ans. Seasonal Indices for the four quarters are : 98·43 ; 92·15 ; 108·90 ; 100·52.

8. Explain 'ratio to trend' method of measuring seasonal variations and discuss its relative merits and demerits. Find seasonal variations by the ratio-to-trend method from the data given below :

Year	*1st Quarter*	*2nd Quarter*	*3rd Quarter*	*4th Quarter*
1993	30	40	36	34
1994	34	52	50	44
1995	40	58	54	48
1996	54	76	68	62
1997	80	92	86	82

Ans. Straight line trend is given by : $y = 56 + 12x$,

Origin : 1995 (1st July) : x units = 1 year ; y units : Average quarterly values.

Seasonal Indices : 92·0, 117·4, 102·1, 88·5

9. Find the seasonal variations by the ratio to trend method from the data given below :

	Quarter			
Year	*I*	*II*	*III*	*IV*
2001	60	80	72	68
2002	68	104	100	88
2003	80	116	108	96
2004	108	152	136	124
2005	160	184	172	164

[*Delhi Univ. B.Com. (Hons.), (External), 2006*]

Ans.

Quarter	Q_1	Q_2	Q_3	Q_4
S.I. (Adjusted)	92·05	117·36	102·13	88·46

10. (*a*) Describe the 'ratio to moving average' and the 'ratio to trend' methods of estimating seasonal indices. Compare the two methods.

(*b*) Explain why 'ratio to moving average' method is considered to be the best measure of seasonal fluctuations.

(*c*) Explain, step by step, the 'ratio to moving average' method of determining seasonal index.

[*Delhi Univ. B.A. (Econ. Hons.), 2000*]

11. From the given ratios of observed values to trend values (%), calculate seasonal indices. If sales for 2001 are expected to be Rs. 2,000 lakhs, what are the likely sales for individual quarters ?

Out of additive and multiplicative models in time series analysis, which is better and why ? [*Delhi Univ. B.Com. (Hons.), 2008*]

Years	*Quarters*			
	I	*II*	*III*	*IV*
1997	80	95	80	110
1998	101	104	90	110
1999	100	95	90	100
2000	115	110	100	120

Ans. S.I. : 99, 101, 90, 110

12. Calculate seasonal indices from the following data :

Year	*Ratio to Moving Averages (%)* Quarters *I*	*II*	*III*	*IV*
1987	—	—	85·21	90·25
1988	128·12	91·71	96·10	103·90
1989	112·33	100·35	78·13	97·88
1990	105·26	103·50	—	—

[*Delhi Univ. B.Com.* (*Hons.*), *1991*]

Ans. 115·93, 99·12, 87·01, 97·93.

13. Calculate the seasonal indices from the following ratio-to-moving average values expressed in percentage :

Season → / *Year*	*Summer*	*Rain*	*Winter*
1999	—	101·75	107·14
2000	96·18	92·30	114·00
2001	92·45	95·20	118·18

Ans. S.I. (Summer) 93·127 ; (Rain) 95·202 ; (Winter) 111·682. [*C.A.* (*Foundation*), *May 2002*]

14. The following are the figures of quarterly production, for which some four quarterly centered moving averages have been calculated :

Year	*Quarter*	*Production*	*Moving average*
1992	1	216	—
	2	281	—
	3	209	227·00
	4	200	226·13
1993	1	220	229·88
	2	270	237·50
	3	250	243·75
	4	220	252·50
1994	1	250	
	2	310	
	3	280	
	4	246	

Calculate the remaining values of moving averages. Treating the moving averages as trend values, compute the seasonal indices.

Ans. M.A. values for I and II Quarter of 1994 are : 261·25 , 268·25.

Assuming multiplicative model of time series, Seasonal Indices are : 96·65, 115·77, 98·29, 88·67.

15. Given the following quarterly sales figures in thousands of rupees for the years 1996-1999, find the specific seasonals by the method of moving averages.

	I	*II*	*III*	*IV*
1996	290	280	285	310
1997	320	305	310	330
1998	340	321	320	340
1999	270	360	362	380

Ans. 104·25, 97·94, 96·52, 101·29.

16. (*a*) Enumerate the various steps you would take in determining seasonal indices by Link Relative Method.

(*b*) What do you mean by Link Relative ? Explain the 'link relative method' of computing indices of seasonal variations. Discuss its merits and demerits.

17. Obtain the seasonal indices by the link relative method, for the following data :

AVERAGE QUARTERLY PRICE OF A COMMODITY

Quarter	*Years* *1996*	*1997*	*1998*	*1999*	*2000*
I	30	35	31	31	34
II	26	28	29	31	36
III	22	22	28	25	26
IV	31	36	32	35	33

Ans. 108·02, 99·75, 81·23, 111·00. [*C.A.* (*Foundation*), *May 2000*]

18. Calculate seasonal index by link relative method :

LINK RELATIVES

Quarter	*1991*	*1992*	*1993*	*1994*	*1995*
I	—	80	88	80	83
II	120	117	129	125	117
III	133	113	111	115	120
IV	83	89	93	96	79

[*Delhi Univ. B.Com. (Hons.), 1996*]

Ans. 82·47, 99·29, 116·74, 101·49.

19. (*a*) Explain the meaning of deseasonalising data. What purpose does it serve ?

(*b*) A large company estimates its average monthly sales in a particular year to be Rs. 2,00,000. The seasonal indices of the sales data are as follows :

Month	*Seasonal index*	*Month*	*Seasonal index*	*Month*	*Seasonal index*
January	76	May	137	September	100
February	77	June	122	October	102
March	98	July	101	November	82
April	128	August	104	December	73

Using this information, draw up a monthly sales budget for the company (assume that there is no trend).

Ans. Estimated Sales (in '000 Rs.) for January to December are :

152, 154, 196, 256, 274, 244, 202, 208, 200, 204, 164, 146.

20. (*a*) What do you understand by deseasonalisation of data ? Explain its uses.

(*b*) The seasonal indices of sales of a firm are as under :

January	106	May	98	September	92
February	105	June	96	October	102
March	101	July	93	November	106
April	104	August	89	December	108

If the firm is expecting total sales of Rs. 42,00,000 during 2006, estimate the sales for the individual months of 2006.

Hint. Average monthly sales for 2006 is Rs. (42,00,000 ÷ 12) = Rs. 3,50,000.

Ans. Estimated sales (in '000 Rs.) for January to December of 2006 are :

371, 367·5, 353·5, 364, 343, 336, 325·5, 311·5, 322, 357, 371, 378.

21. The quarterly seasonal indices of the sales of a popular brand of colour television of a company, in Delhi, are given below :

Quarter	:	*I*	*II*	*III*	*IV*
Seasonal Index	:	130	90	75	105

It the total sales for the first quarter of 1997 is Rs. 6,50,000, estimate the worth of televisions to be kept in store to meet the demand in other quarters. Assume that there is no trend.

[*Delhi Univ. BA. (Econ. Hons.) 1997*]

Hint. The estimated worth of televisions to be kept in store to meet the demand for the *i*th quarter is :

$$\frac{\text{Sales of 1st quarter}}{\text{S.I. of 1st quarter}} \times (\text{S.I. of } i\text{th quarter}) \; ; \; i = 2, 3, 4$$

Ans. *Quarter*	:	II	III	IV
Inventory to be kept (in Rs.)	:	4,50,000	3,75,000	5,25,000

22. The seasonal indices of the sale of garments of a particular type in a store are given below :

Quarter	:	*I*	*II*	*III*	*IV*
Seasonal Index	:	98	89	83	130

If the total sales in the first quarter of a year be worth Rs. 10,000, find how much worth of garments of this type should be kept in stock to meet the demand in each of the remaining quarters. [*I.C.W.A. (Intermediate), 1995*]

Ans. Garments to be kept (in Rs.) : II Qtr : 9081·63 ; III Qtr : 8469·39 ; IV Qtr : 13265·30.

23. The sales of particualr product of a company rose from Rs. 40,000 in March to Rs. 48,000 in April 1997. The company's seasonal indices for these two months are 105 and 140 respectively. The owner of the company expressed dissatisfaction with the April sales, but the Sales Manager said that he was quite pleased with the Rs. 8,000 increase. What argument should the owner of the company have used to reply to the Sales Manager ?

The Sales Manager also predicted on the basis of the April sales that the total 1997 sales were going to be Rs. 5,76,000. Criticise the Sales Manager's estimate and explain how the estimate of Rs. 4,11,000 may be arrived at.

Ans. Owner's estimate of sales for April 1997 = $\frac{40,000}{105} \times 140$ = Rs. 53333·33

Sales manager ignored the S.I. for April 1997.

Owner's estimate of Annual Sales for 1997 = $\frac{48,000}{1·4} \times 12$ = Rs. 4,11,000 (nearest thousand)

24. The sale of a reputed organisation rose from Rs. 1,26,000 in the month of August 1993 to Rs. 1,38,000 in the month of September 1993. The seasonal indices for the two months were 105 and 140. The General Manager was not at all satisfied with rise of the sales in the month of September 1993 by Rs. 12,000. He expected much more because of seasonal index for the month. What was his expectations of sales for the month of September 1993 ?

[*Delhi Univ. B.Com. (Hons.), 1994*]

Hint. G.M's estimate of sales for Sept. 1993 = Rs. $\frac{1,26,000}{105} \times 140$ = Rs. 1,68,000.

25. The sales of readymade garments of a particular brand, of a departmental store rose from Rs. 25,000 in January to Rs. 30,000 in February, the seasonal indices for these months being 105 and 135 respectively. While the sales manager of the store was satisfied with Rs. 5,000 increase, the owner of the store expressed his dissatisfaction. Who is right ? Justify your answer.

Ans. Expected sales in February should be Rs. $\left(\frac{25,000}{105} \times 135\right)$ = Rs. 32142·86. The owner of the store is right.

26. The trend equation for quarterly sales of a firm is estimated to be as follows : $Y = 20 + 2X$,

where Y is sales per quarter in millions of rupees, the unit of X is one quarter and the origin is the middle of the first quarter (Jan.-March) of 1999. The seasonal indices of sales for the four quarters are as follows :

Quarter	:	I	II	III	IV
Seasonal Indices	:	120	105	85	90

Estimate the actual sales for each quarter of 2004. [*Delhi Univ. B.Com. (Hons.) 2004*]

Ans.

Quarter	:	I	II	III	IV
Estimated Sales (in Million (Rs.)	:	72	65·1	54·4	59·4

Hint : $Y = 20 + 2X$; [Origin : Middle of 1st quarter of 1999]

$X = 0$, for middle of 1st quarter of 1999,

$\Rightarrow$ $X = 4, 8, 12, 16, 20$ for middle of first quarter of 2000, 2001, 2002, 2003, 2004 respectively.

$\therefore$ For 2004, $X = 20, 21, 22$ and 23 for Q_1, Q_2, Q_3 and Q_4 respectively.

[Now proceed as in Example 11·31]

27. On the basis of quarterly sales in (Rs. lakhs) of a certain commodity for the years 1994-95, the following calculations were made :

$Y = 20 + 0·5\, X$ with origin : 1st quarter of 1994

X unit = one quarter ; Y = Quarterly sales (Rs. lakhs)

SEASONAL VARIATIONS

Quarter	I	II	III	IV
Seasonal Index	80	90	120	110

Estimate the quarterly sales for each of the four quarters of 1995, using the multiplicative model.

[*Delhi Univ. B.A. (Econ. Hons.), 2000*]

Ans. Estimated quarterly sales for the four quarters of 1995 (in Rs. lakh) are

17·60, 20·25, 27·60, 25·85 respectively.

28. Calculate the seasonal index numbers from the following data of sales of goods X :

RATIO OF OBSERVED VALUES TO TREND VALUES (%)

Year	*Q I*	*Q II*	*Q III*	*Q IV*
2001	108	130	107	93
2002	86	120	110	91
2003	92	118	104	88
2004	78	100	94	78
2005	82	110	98	86
2006	106	118	105	98

If the sales of goods X by a firm in the first quarter of 2007 are worth Rs. 20,000, determine how much worth of the goods should be kept in stock by the firm to meet the demand in each of the remaining three quarters of 2007 by using the seasonal index numbers calculated above. *[Delhi Univ. B.Com. (Hons.), 2007]*

Ans.	*I Quarter*	*II Quarter*	*III Quarter*	*IV Quarter*
S.I.	92	116	103	89
Estimated sales for 2007 (Rs.)		$\frac{20,000}{92} \times 116 = 25217{\cdot}39$	$\frac{20,000}{92} \times 103 = 22391{\cdot}30$	$\frac{20,000}{92} \times 89 = 19347{\cdot}83$

29. What are the different components of a time series ? Explain how you will measure short period fluctuations in a time series.

30. How is the analysis of time series useful in business and industry ? Describe briefly, the phases of a business cycle.

31. (*a*) Explain the term "cyclical component of a time series". Describe a method for obtaining this component from a given series of monthly data. Explain any procedure known to you for detecting the presence of a cyclical component.

(*b*) Explain 'seasonal variations' and 'cyclical variations'. How are they different from each other ? Explain any method of deseasonalizing of data. *[Delhi Univ. B.A. (Econ. Hons.), 1999]*

32. Explain the nature of cyclical variations in a time series. How do seasonal variations differ from them ? Give an outline of the moving average method of measuring seasonal variations.

33. What do you understand by irregular fluctuations in a time series ? How can they be measured ?

EXERCISE 11·4

Short and Objective Type Questions

1. Explain time series.

2. Explain the various components of a time series.

3. Outline briefly the use of Time Series Analysis.

4. Enumerate the various components of a time series.

5. What do you mean by Secular Trend ? Give examples.

6. Explain the meaning of seasonal variations, with illustrations.

7. (*a*) What are cyclic variations ? How are they caused ?

(*b*) Give the four phases of Business Cycle.

8. How do cyclical variations differ from seasonal variations ?

9. What are irregular variations ? How are they caused ?

10. What do you understand by 'Additive Model' in time series analysis ? State clearly the assumptions.

11. What do you understand by 'Multiplicative Model' in time series analysis ? State clearly its assumptions.

12. Of the Additive and Multiplicative Models in time series analysis, which is better and why ?

13. Enumerate the different methods of estimating :

(*i*) Trend, (*ii*) Seasonal variations,

in time series analysis.

14. Suppose you have fitted a straight line trend

$y = 85{\cdot}6 + 2{\cdot}4x$; Origin 2000 ; x unit = 1 year , y = Annual production of sugar (in '000 quintals)

(*i*) What is the slope of the trend line ? (*ii*) What is the monthly increase in production ?

(*iii*) Does the trend line exhibit an increasing trend or decreasing trend ?

(*iv*) Shift the trend equation to 1995. (*v*) Convert the equation to monthly trend.

15. What do you understand by 'Deseasonalisation of Data' ? Explain by means of an illustration.

16. Fill in the blanks :

(*i*) ...... is the overall tendency of the time series data to ...... or ...... over a ...... period of time.

(*ii*) Short term variations are classified as :

(*a*) = ..., (*b*) ......

(*iii*) The period of the moving average should be equal to ......

(*iv*) If the trend is absent in the data, then the seasonal indices are computed by ......

(v) Cyclical variations are caused by ......

(vi) The time series data exhibits ...... trend if the rate of growth is constant.

(vii) The least square linear trend equation $y = a + bx$ exhibits ...... trend if $b > 0$ and ...... trend if $b < 0$.

(viii) The four phase of a business cycle (in order) are ......

(ix) Using Multiplicative Model of Time Series, the time series values (y) are given by : $y =$ ...... where......

(x) The annual trend equation : $y = a + bx$, [x unit = 1 year; y : annual sales] reduced to monthly trend equation is : $y =$ ......

(xi) For the annual data, ... component is absent.

(xii) Seasonal variations are the short-term variations with period......

(xiii) The most widely used method of measuring seasonal variations is..........

(xiv) For the additive model in time series analysis, for annual data the difference $Y - T$ represents......

(xv) The most important factors causing seasonal variations are........

Ans. (i) Trend, increase, decrease, long.
(ii) (a) Seasonal, (b) Cyclical.
(iii) Period of oscillatory movements.
(iv) Method of Simple Averages.
(v) Trade or Business Cycles.
(vi) Linear.
(vii) Rising, declining
(viii) Economic boom (prosperity), recession, depression and recovery (improvement).
(ix) $Y = T \times S \times C \times I$, (x) $y = \frac{a}{12} + \frac{b}{144}x$
(xi) Seasonal. (xii) Less than one year.
(xiii) Ratio to M.A. Method.
(xiv) Cyclical and Irregular components.
(xv) Weather (seasons) and social customs.

17. With which components of a time series would you mainly associate each of the following ? Why ?

(a) (i) A fire in a factory delaying production for three weeks.
(ii) An era of prosperity.
(iii) Sales of a textile firm during Deepawali
(iv) A need for increased wheat production due to constant increase in population,
(v) Recession.
(vi) The increase in day temperature from winter to summer. [*Delhi Univ. B.Com. (Pass), 2001*]

Ans. (i) Irregular (ii) Cyclical (iii) Seasonal (iv) Long-term trend (v) Cyclical (vi) Seasonal.

(b) (i) A strike in a factory delaying production for 10 days.
(ii) A decline in ice-cream sales during November to March.
(iii) The increase in day temperature from winter to summer.
(iv) Diwali sales in a departmental store.
(v) Fall in death rate due to advances in science.
(vi) Rainfall in Delhi in July 2002.
(vii) Increase in money in circulation for the last 10 years.
(viii) Rainfall in Delhi that occurred for a week in December 2001.
(ix) Inflation.
(x) An increase in employment during harvest time.

Ans. (i) Irregular (ii) Seasonal (iii) Cyclical (iv) Seasonal (v) Long-term trend
(vi) Seasonal (vii) Trend (viii) Irregular (ix) Cyclical (x) Seasonal.

18. Write down the four characteristic movements of a time series. With which characteristic movement of a time series would you associate : (i) a recession, (ii) decline in death due to advances in medical science ?

Ans. (i) Cyclical, (ii) Secular Trend.

19. Cyclical fluctuations are caused by :

(i) Strikes and lockouts (ii) Floods (iii) Wars (iv) None of these.

Ans. (iv)

20. Write the normal equations to determine the constants a, b, c in fitting the trend equations :

(i) $y = a + bx$; (ii) $y = a + bx + cx^2$,

given the n observations on each of the variables x and y.

21. What is the physical interpretation of the constants a and b in the linear trend equation $y = a + bx$?

22. How are the values of the constants b and c affected if we shift the origin in the trend equation $y = a + bx + cx^2$?

12 Theory of Probability

12·1. INTRODUCTION

If an experiment is performed repeatedly under essentially homogeneous and similar conditions, the result or what is commonly termed as *outcome* may be classified as follows :

(*a*) It is unique or certain

(*b*) It is not definite but may be one of the various possibilities depending on the experiment.

The phenomenon under category (*a*) where the result can be predicted with certainty is known as *deterministic* or *predictable* phenomenon. In a deterministic phenomenon, the conditions under which an experiment is performed, uniquely determine the outcome of the experiment. For instance :

(*i*) In case of a perfect gas we have *Boyle's* law which states,

$$\text{Pressure} \times \text{Volume} = \text{Constant} \qquad i.e., \qquad P\,V = \text{Constant} \qquad \Rightarrow \qquad V \propto \frac{1}{P},$$

provided the temperature remains constant.

(*ii*) The distance (s) covered by a particle after time (t) is given by

$$s = ut + \frac{1}{2}at^2$$

where u is the initial velocity and a is the acceleration.

(*iii*) If dilute sulphuric acid is added to zinc, we get hydrogen.

Thus, most of the phenomena in physical and chemical sciences are of a deterministic nature. However, there exist a number of phenomena as generated by category (*b*) where the results cannot be predicted with certainty and are known as *unpredictable* or *probabilistic* phenomena. Such phenomena are frequently observed in economics, business and social sciences or even in our day-to-day life. For example,

(*i*) The sex of a baby to be born cannot be predicted with certainty.

(*ii*) A sales (or production) manager cannot say with certainty if he will achieve the sales (or production) target in the season.

(*iii*) If an electric bulb or tube has lasted for 3 months, nothing can be said about its future life.

(*iv*) In toss of a uniform coin, we are not sure if we shall get head or tail.

(*v*) A producer can not ascertain the future demand of his product with certainty.

Even in out day-to-day life we say or hear phrases like "It may rain today" ; "Probably I will get a first class in the examination"; "India might draw or win the cricket series against Australia"; and so on. In all the above cases there is involved an element of uncertainty or chance. A numerical measure of uncertainty is provided by a very important branch of Statistics called the "*Theory of Probability*". In the words of Prof. Ya-Lin-Chou : "*Statistics is the science of decision making with calculated risks in the face of uncertainty*".

12·2. SHORT HISTORY

The theory of probability has its origin in the games of chance related to gambling, for instance, throwing of dice or coin, drawing cards from a pack of cards and so on. Jerome Cardan (1501-1576) an Italian mathematician was the first man to write a book on the subject entitled "Book on Games of

Chance", (*Liber de Ludo Aleae*) which was published after his death in 1663. It is a valuable treatise on the hazards of the game of chance and contains a number of rules by which the risks of gambling could be minimised and one could protect oneself against cheating. However, a systematic and scientific foundation of the mathematical theory of probability was laid in mid-seventeenth century by the French mathematicians Blaise Pascal (1623-62) and Pierre de Fermat (1601-65) while solving a problem for sharing the stake in an incomplete gambling match posed by a notable French gambler and nobleman Chevalier-de-Mere. The lengthy correspondence between these two mathematicians, who ultimately solved the problem, resulted in the scientific development of the subject of probability. The next stalwart in this field was the Swiss mathematician James Bernoulli (1654-1705) who made extensive study of the subject for twenty years. His 'Treatise on Probability' (*Arts Conjectandi*), which was published posthumously by his nephew in 1713, is a major contribution to the theory of Probability and Combinatorics. A. De-Moivre (1667-1754) also contributed a lot to this subject and published his work in his famous book '*The Doctrines of Chances*' in 1718. Thomas Bayes (1702-61) introduced the concept of *Inverse probability*. The French mathematician Pierre-Simon de Laplace (1749-1827) after an extensive research over a number of years published his monumental work '*Theorie Analytique des probabilities.* (Theory of Analytical Probability), in 1812. This resulted in what is called the *classical theory of probability*. R.A. Fisher, Von-Mises introduced the empirical approach to the theory of probability through the notion of sample space.

Russian mathematicians have made very great contributions to the modern theory of probability. Main contributors, to mention only a few, are Chebychev (1821-94) who founded the Russian School of Statisticians ; A. Markov (1856-1922), Khinchine (Law of Large Numbers), Liapounoff (Central Limit Theorem), Gnedenko and A.N. Kolmogorov. Kolmogorov axiomised the theory of probability and his small book '*Foundations of Probability*' published in 1933 introduced probability as a set function and is considered as a classic.

Today the subject has been developed to a great extent and there is not even a single discipline in social, physical or natural sciences where probability theory is not used. It is extensively used in the quantitative analysis of business and economic problems. It is an essential tool in statistical inference and forms the basis of the '*Decision Theory*', *viz.,* decision making in the face of uncertainty with calculated risks.

12·3. TERMINOLOGY

As already discussed above there are three approaches to probability :

(*i*) Classical approach,
(*ii*) Empirical approach,
(*iii*) Axiomatic approach.

In this section we shall explain the various terms which are used in the definition of probability under different approaches. Concepts will be explained with reference to simple experiments relating to tossing of coins, throwing of a die* or drawing cards from a pack of cards. Unless otherwise stated, we shall assume that coin or die is *uniform* or *unbiased* or *regular* and pack of cards is well shuffled.

Random Experiment. An experiment is called a *random experiment* if when conducted repeatedly under essentially homogeneous conditions, the result is not unique but may be any one of the various possible outcomes.

Trial and Event. Performing of a random experiment is called a *trial* and outcome or combination of outcomes are termed as *events*. For example :

(*i*) If a coin is tossed repeatedly, the result is not unique. We may get any of the two faces, head or tail. Thus tossing of a coin is a random experiment or trial and getting of a head or tail is an event.

(*ii*) Similarly, throwing of a die is a trial and getting any one of the faces 1, 2, ..., 6 is an event, or getting of an odd number or an even number is an event ; or getting a number greater than 4 or less than 3 are events.

(*iii*) Drawing of two balls from an urn containing '*a*' red balls and '*b*' white balls is a trial and getting of both red balls, or both white balls, or one red and one white ball are events.

---

* A die is a homogeneous cube with six faces marked with numbers from 1 to 6. Plural of the word die is dice.

Event is called *simple* if it corresponds to a single possible outcome of the experiment or trial otherwise it is known as a *compound* or *composite* event. Thus, in tossing of a single die, the event of getting '5' is a simple event but the event 'getting an even number', is a composite event.

Exhaustive Cases. The total number of possible outcomes of a random experiment is called the *exhaustive cases* for the experiment. Thus, in toss of a single coin, we can get head (*H*) or tail (*T*). Hence exhaustive number of cases is 2, *viz.*, (*H, T*). If two coins are tossed, the various possibilities are *HH, HT, TH, TT* where *HT* means head on the first coin and tail on second coin, and *TH* means tail on the first coin and head on the second coin and so on. Thus, in case of toss of two coins, exhaustive number of cases is 4, *i.e.*, 2^2. Similarly, in a toss of three coins the possible number of outcomes is :

$$
\begin{aligned}
&(H, T) \times (H, T) \times (H, T) \\
&= (HH, HT, TH, TT) \times (H, T) \\
&= HHH, HTH, THH, TTH, HHT, HTT, THT, TTT
\end{aligned}
$$

Therefore, in case of toss of 3 coins the exhaustive number or cases is $8 = 2^3$. In general, in a throw of n coins, the exhaustive number of cases is 2^n.

In a throw of a die, exhaustive number of cases is 6, since we can get any one of the six faces marked 1, 2, 3, 4, 5 or 6. If two dice are thrown, the possible outcomes are :

(1, 1)	(1, 2)	(1, 3)	(1, 4)	(1, 5)	(1, 6)
(2, 1)	(2, 2)	(2, 3)	(2, 4)	(2, 5)	(2, 6)
(3, 1)	(3, 2)	(3, 3)	(3, 4)	(3, 5)	(3, 6)
(4, 1)	(4, 2)	(4, 3)	(4, 4)	(4, 5)	(4, 6)
(5, 1)	(5, 2)	(5, 3)	(5, 4)	(5, 5)	(5, 6)
(6, 1)	(6, 2)	(6, 3)	(6, 4)	(6, 5)	(6, 6)

i.e., 36 ordered pairs where pair (i, j) means number i on the first die and j on the second die, i and j both taking the values from 1 to 6. Hence, in the case of a throw of two dice exhaustive number of cases is $36 = 6^2$. Thus, for a throw of 3 dice, exhaustive number of cases will be $216 = 6^3$, and for n dice they will be 6^n.

If r cards are drawn from a pack of cards, the exhaustive number of cases is ${}^nC_r = \binom{n}{r}$, since r cards can be drawn out of n cards in $\binom{n}{r}$ ways.

Favourable Cases or Events. The number of outcomes of a random experiment which entail (or result in) the happening of an event are termed as the cases favourable to the event. For example :

(*i*) In a toss of two coins, the number of cases favourable to the event '*exactly one head*' is 2, *viz.*, *HT*, *TH* and for getting '*two heads*' is one *viz.*, *HH*.

(*ii*) In drawing a card from a pack of cards, the cases favourable to 'getting a diamond' are 13 and to 'getting an ace of spade' is only 1.

Mutually Exclusive Events or Cases. Two or more events are said to be mutually exclusive if the happening of any one of them excludes the happening of all others in the same experiment. For example, in toss of a coin, the events 'head' and 'tail' are mutually exclusive because if head comes, we can't get tail and if tail comes we can't get head. Similarly, in the throw of a die, the six faces numbered 1, 2, 3, 4, 5 and 6 are mutually exclusive. Thus, events are said to be mutually exclusive if no two or more of them can happen simultaneously.

Equally Likely Cases. The outcomes are said to be *equally likely* or *equally probable* if none of them is expected to occur in preference to other. Thus, in tossing of a coin (dice), all the outcomes, *viz.*, *H, T* (the faces 1, 2, 3, 4, 5, 6) are equally likely if the coin (die) is unbiased.

Independent Events. Events are said to be independent of each other if happening of any one of them is not affected by and does not affect the happening of any one of others. For example :

(*i*) In tossing of a die repeatedly, the event of getting '5' in 1st throw is independent of getting '5' in second, third or subsequent throws.

(*ii*) In drawing cards from a pack of cards, the result of the second draw will depend upon the card drawn in the first draw. However, if the card drawn in the first draw is replaced before drawing the second card, then the result of second draw will be independent of the 1st draw.

Similarly, drawing of balls from an urn gives independent events if the draws are made with replacement. If the balls drawn in the earlier draws are not replaced, the resulting draws will not be independent.

12·4. MATHEMATICAL PRELIMINARIES

12·4·1. Set Theory. *A set is a well defined collection or aggregate of objects having given properties and specified according to a well defined rule.* For example, letters in the English alphabet ; vowels (or consonants) in the English alphabet ; Prime Ministers of India ; Colleges in Delhi, etc., are all sets. The objects comprising the set are known as its *elements.* Sets are usually represented by the capital letters of the English alphabet, *viz.*, *A, B, C,* etc. We shall use the following symbols :

$\in$: Belongs to ; $\notin$: Does not belong to ; $\subset$: Contained in ; $\supset$: Contains

If x is an element of the set A we write $x \in A$ and if x is not an element of set A we write $x \notin A$. A set is written by enclosing its elements within curly brackets. For example :

A = Set of first 10 natural numbers	B = Set of odd positive integers
$= \{ 1, 2, 3, 4, 5, 6, 7, 8, 9, 10 \}$	$= \{ 1, 3, 5, 7, \ldots \}$
$= \{ x : x \in N ; x \leq 10 \}$	$= \{ x : x = 2n + 1, n \in I^+ \}$

Null Set. A set having no element at all is called a *null* or an *empty* set. It is denoted by the symbol ϕ (Phi). For example, if two dice are thrown and A is a set of points on the two dice so that their sum is greater than 12, then A is a null set. Also

$$B = \{ x : x^2 + 1 = 0, x \text{ real} \} = \phi,$$

since the solution of the equation $x^2 + 1 = 0$, is always imaginary.

Sub-set. A set A is said to be a proper subset of B if every element of A is also an element of B and there is at least one element of B which is not an element of A and we write $A \subset B$.

If latter restriction is removed, then A is said to be a subset of B and we write $A \subseteq B$.

Equality of Two Sets. Two sets A and B are said to be equal, if every element of A is an element of B and if every element of B is an element of A. Mathematically,

$$A = B \text{ if } x \in A \Rightarrow x \in B \quad \text{and} \quad x \in B \Rightarrow x \in A$$

Remarks. 1. Every set is a subset of itself, *i.e.*, $A \subset A$.

2. The null set ϕ is a subset of every set, *i.e.*, $\phi \subset A$.

Universal Set. In any problem, the overall limiting set, of which all the sets under consideration are subsets, is called an universal set. We shall denote it by S. The universal set will vary from situation to situation.

ALGEBRA OF SETS

The *union* of two sets A and B, denoted by $A \cup B$, is defined as a set of elements which belong to either A or B or both. Symbolically, we write

$$A \cup B = \{ x : x \in A \text{ or } x \in B \}$$

For example if $A = \{ 1, 2, 3, 4 \}$, $B = \{3, 4, 5, 6 \}$ then $A \cup B = \{ 1, 2, 3, 4, 5, 6 \}$

The *intersection* of two sets A and B, denoted by $A \cap B$, is defined as a set whose elements belong to both A and B. Symbolically we write :

$$A \cap B = \{ x : x \in A \text{ and } x \in B \}$$

Thus, in the above case $A \cap B = \{ 3, 4 \}$

Two sets A and B are said to be *disjoint* or *mutually exclusive* if they do not have any common point. Mathematically, A and B are said to be disjoint if their intersection is a null set

i.e., if $A \cap B = \phi$

The *complement* of a set A, usually denoted by $\bar{A}$ or A' or A^c is the set of elements which do not belong to the set A but which belong to the universal set S. Symbolically,

$$\bar{A} \text{ or } A^c = \{ x : x \notin A \text{ and } x \in S \}$$

Remark. Obviously A and A^c are disjoint *i.e.*, $A \cap A^c = \phi$.

The *difference* of two sets A and B, denoted by $A - B$ is the set of elements which belong to A but not to B. Symbolically,

$$A - B = \{ x : x \in A \text{ and } x \notin B \}$$

This can also be written as :

$$A - B = \{ x : x \in (A \cap \bar{B}) \}$$

Thus $A - B$ is equivalent to $A \cap \bar{B}$.

Laws of Set Theory. If A, B and C are subsets of the universal set S, then the following laws hold :

Commutative Laws :

$$A \cup B = B \cup A \qquad \text{(For Union)}$$
$$A \cap B = B \cap A \qquad \text{(For intersection)}$$

Associative Laws :

$$A \cup (B \cup C) = (A \cup B) \cup C \qquad \text{(For Union)}$$
$$A \cap (B \cap C) = (A \cap B) \cap C \qquad \text{(For intersection)}$$

Distributive Laws :

$$A \cap (B \cup C) = (A \cap B) \cup (A \cap C)$$
$$A \cup (B \cap C) = (A \cup B) \cap (A \cup C)$$

Hence intersection is distributive w.r.t. union and union is distributive w.r.t. intersection.

Difference Laws :

$$A - B = A \cap \bar{B}$$
$$A - B = A - (A \cap B) = (A \cup B) - B$$

Complementary Laws :

$$A \cup A^c = S \quad ; \quad A \cap A^c = \phi$$
$$A \cup S = S \quad ; \quad (\because A \subset S) \quad ; \quad A \cap S = A$$
$$A \cup \phi = A \quad ; \quad A \cap \phi = \phi$$

De-Morgan's Laws of Complementation :

$$(A \cup B)^c = A^c \cap B^c$$

i.e., the complement of the union is equal to the intersection of the complements and

$$(A \cap B)^c = A^c \cup B^c$$

i.e., the complement of intersection is equal to the union of complements.

The various operations on sets, *viz*., union, intersection, difference and complementation can be expressed diagrammatically through Venn diagrams given below :

UNION OF TWO SETS

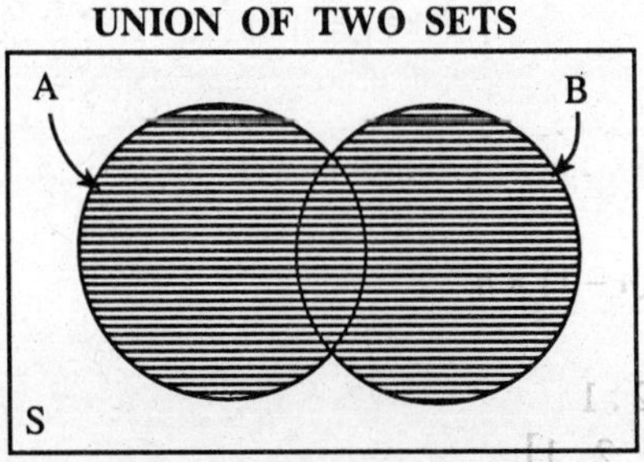

$A \cup B = B \cup A$ = Shaded region

Fig. 12·1

INTERSECTION OF TWO SETS

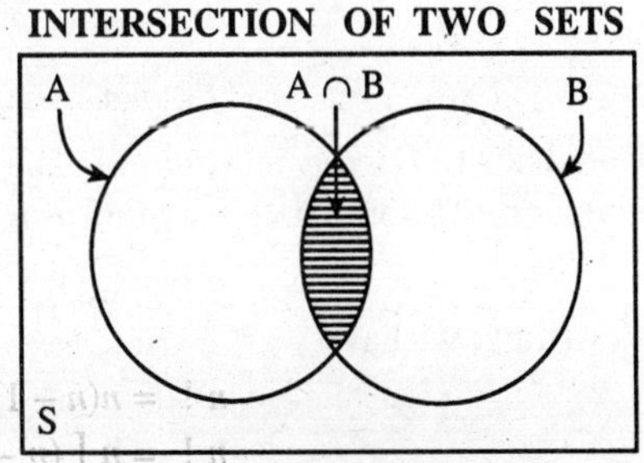

$A \cap B = B \cap A$ = Shaded region

Fig. 12·2

DISJOINT SETS

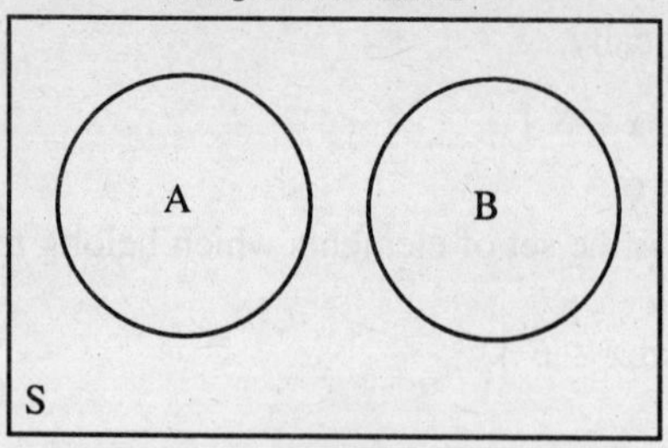

$A \cap B = \phi$

Fig. 12·3.

COMPLEMENT OF A SET

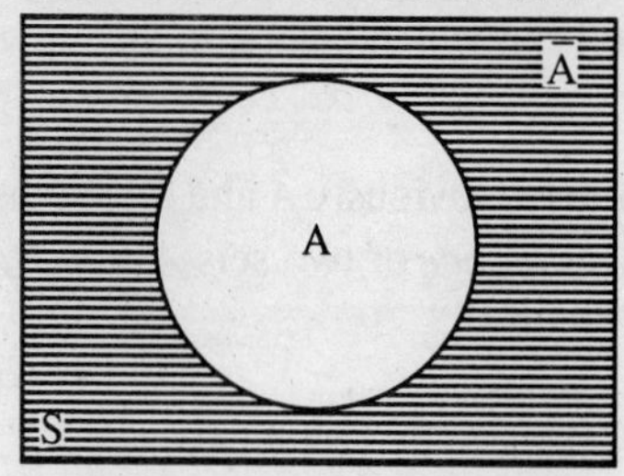

$\bar{A} = S - A =$ Shaded region

Fig. 12·4.

The laws of complementation can be generalised to n sets. If $A_i \subset S$; $i = 1, 2, \ldots, n$ then

$$\left(\bigcup_{i=1}^{n} A_i\right)^c = \bigcap_{i=1}^{n} (A_i{}^c) \quad \text{and} \quad \left(\bigcap_{i=1}^{n} A_i\right)^c = \bigcup_{i=1}^{n} (A_i^c)$$

Idempotency Law :

$$A \cup A = A \quad \text{and} \quad A \cap A = A$$

12·4·2. Permutation and Combination. The word *permutation* in simple language means 'arrangement' and the word *combination* means 'group' or 'selection'. Let us consider three letters *A*, *B* and *C*. The permutations of these three letters taken two at a time will be *AB, BC, CA, BA, CB* and *AC*, *i.e.*, 6 in all whereas the combinations of three letters taken two at a time will be *AB, BC* and *CA*, *i.e.*, 3 in all. It should be noted that in combinations, the order of the elements (letters in this case) is immaterial, *i.e.*, *AB* and *BA* form the same combination but these are different arrangements. Similarly, in case of 4 letters *A, B C, D*, the total number of combinations taking three at a time is : *ABC, ABD, ACD, BCD*, *i.e.*, 4 in all. However, each of these combinations gives six different arrangements. For example, different arrangements of the combination *ABC* are *ABC, ACB, BAC, BCA, CAB, CBA*.

Hence, the total number of permutations (arrangements) of 4 letters taking 3 at a time is $4 \times 6 = 24$.

Permutation (Definition). *A permutation of n different objects taken r at a time, denoted by* ${}^nP_r$, *is an ordered arrangement of only r objects of the n objects.*

We shall now state, without proof, some important results on permutation in the forms of theorems.

Theorem 12·1. *The number of different permutations of n different objects taken r at a time without repetition is*

$${}^nP_r = n(n-1)(n-2) \ldots (n-r+1) \qquad \ldots(12·1)$$

i.e., it is a continued product of r factors starting with n and differing by unity. For example :

$${}^3P_2 = 3 \times 2 = 6 \quad ; \quad {}^4P_3 = 4 \times 3 \times 2 = 24 \quad ; \quad \text{and so on.}$$

In particular, the total number of permutations of n distinct objects, taken all at a time is given by :

$${}^nP_n = n(n-1)\, n-2) \ldots 1 \qquad [\text{ Take } r = n \text{ in } (12·1)]$$

$$\Rightarrow \quad {}^nP_n = n\,! \qquad \ldots(12·2)$$

Remarks 1. *Factorial Notation.* The product of first n natural numbers, *viz.*, 1, 2, 3, ..., n is called factorial n or n-factorial and is written as $n\,!$ or $\underline{|n}$. Thus,

$$n\,! = \underline{|n} = 1 \times 2 \times 3 \times \ldots \times (n-1) \times n \qquad \ldots(12·3)$$

Rewriting, we have

$$n\,! = n(n-1)(n-2) \ldots 3 \,.\, 2 \,.\, 1$$

$$\Rightarrow \quad n\,! = n\,[\,(n-1)(n-2) \ldots 3 \,.\, 2 \,.\, 1]$$

$$\Rightarrow \quad n\,! = n(n-1)\,! \qquad \ldots(12·4)$$

Repeated application of (12·4) gives :

$$n\,! = n(n-1)\,(n-2)\,!$$
$$= n(n-1)\,(n-2)\,(n-3)\,!$$

and so on. For example, we have :

$$5\,! = 5 \times 4 \times 3 \times 2 \times 1 = 120$$
$$= 5 \times 4\,!$$
$$= 5 \times 4 \times 3\,!$$

and so on.

By convention, we take $0\,! = 1$, *i.e.*, 0 factorial is defined as 1.

2. We have

$$^nP_r = n(n-1)\,(n-2)\,\ldots\,(n-r+1)$$
$$= \frac{n\,(n-1)\,(n-2)\,\ldots\,(n-r+1)\,(n-r)\,(n-r-1)\,\ldots\,3\,.\,2\,.\,1}{(n-r)\,(n-r-1)\,\ldots\,3\,.\,2\,.\,1}$$

$$^nP_r = \frac{n\,!}{(n-r)\,!}, \qquad \ldots(12\cdot5)$$

a form which is much more convenient to remember and use for computational purposes.

Theorem 12·2. *The number of different permutations of n different (distinct) objects, taken r at a time with repetition is :*

$$^nP_r = n^r \qquad \ldots(12\cdot6)$$

In particular, $^nP_n = n^n$

Theorem 12·3. *The number of permutations of n different objects all at a time round a circle is* $(n-1)\,!$

Theorem 12·4 (Permutation of objects not all distinct). *The number of permutations of n objects taken all at time, when n_1 objects are alike of one kind, n_2 objects are alike of second kind, ..., n_k objects are alike of kth kind is given by*

$$\frac{n\,!}{n_1\,!\,n_2\,!\,\ldots\,n_k\,!} \qquad \ldots(12\cdot7)$$

For example, total number of arrangements of the letters of the word ALLAHABAD taken all at a time is given by :

$$\frac{9\,!}{4\,!\,2\,!} = \frac{9 \times 8 \times 7 \times 6 \times 5}{2} = 7560,$$

because in this word, there are 9 letters out of which 4 are of one kind, *i.e.*, *A* ; 2 are of 2nd kind, *i.e.*, *L* and rest are all different occurring once and $1\,! = 1$.

Theorem 12·5 (Fundamental Rule of Counting). *If one operation can be performed in p different ways and another operation can be performed in q different ways. then the two operations when associated together can be performed in* $p \times q$ *ways.*

The result can be generalised to more than two operations.

For example, if there are five routes of journey from place *A* to place *B*, then the total number of ways of making a return journey (*i.e.*, going from *A* to *B* and then coming back from *B* to *A*) are $5 \times 5 = 25$, since one can go from *A* to *B* in 5 ways and come back from *B* to *A* in 5 ways and anyone of the ways of going can be associated with any one of the ways of coming.

Combination (Definition). *A combination of n different objects taken r at a time, denoted by* ^nC_r *or* $\binom{n}{r}$ *is a selection of only r objects out of the n objects, without any regard to the order of arrangement.*

Theorem 12·6. *The number of different combinations of n different objects taken r at a time, without repetition, is*

$$^nC_r = \binom{n}{r} = \frac{n!}{r!(n-r)!} \quad ; \quad r \le n \qquad \text{...(12·8)}$$

$$= \frac{^nP_r}{r!} \qquad \text{[Using (12·5)]} \qquad \text{...(12·8 a)}$$

and with repetition is $\binom{n+r-1}{r}$ or $^{n+r-1}C_r$.

Remark. $^nC_0, {}^nC_1, \ldots, {}^nC_n$ are known as *Binomial Coefficients.* We have $^nC_0 = 1 = {}^nC_n$.

Theorem 12·7. $^nC_r = {}^nC_{n-r}$; $r = 0, 1, 2, \ldots, n$ ...(12·9)

Theorem 12·8. $^nC_r + {}^nC_{r-1} = {}^{n+1}C_r$ ...(12·10)

Theorem 12·9. (Sum of Binomial Coefficients)

$$^nC_0 + {}^nC_1 + {}^nC_2 + \ldots + {}^nC_n = 2^n \qquad \text{...(12·11)}$$

12·5. MATHEMATICAL OR CLASSICAL OR 'A PRIORI' PROBABILITY

Definition. *If a random experiment results in N exhaustive, mutually exclusive and equally likely outcomes (cases) out of which m are favourable to the happening of an event A, then the probability of occurrence of A, usually denoted by P(A) is given by :*

$$P(A) = \frac{\text{Favourable number of cases to } A}{\text{Exhaustive number of cases}} = \frac{m}{N} \qquad \text{...(12·12)}$$

This definition was given by James Bernoulli who was the first man to obtain a quantitative measure of uncertainty.

Remarks. 1. Obviously, the number of cases favourable to the complementry event $\bar{A}$ *i.e.,* non-happening of event A are $(N - m)$ and hence by definition, the probability of non-occurrence of A is given by :

$$P(\bar{A}) = \frac{\text{Favourable No. of cases to } \bar{A}}{\text{Exhaustive number of cases}} = \frac{N-m}{N} = 1 - \frac{m}{N}$$

$$\Rightarrow \quad P(\bar{A}) = 1 - P(A) \qquad \text{...(12·13)} \qquad \Rightarrow \quad P(A) + P(\bar{A}) = 1 \qquad \text{...(12·14)}$$

2. Since m and N are non-negative integers, $P(A) \ge 0$. Further, since the favourable number of cases to A are always less than or equal to the total number of cases N, *i.e.,* $m \le N$, we have $P(A) \le 1$. Hence probability of any event is a number lying between 0 and 1, *i.e.,*

$$0 \le P(A) \le 1, \qquad \text{...(12·15)}$$

for any event A. If $P(A) = 0$, then A is called an *impossible or null* event. If $P(A) = 1$, then A is called a *certain* event.

3. The probability of happening of the event A, *i.e.,* $P(A)$ is also known as the probability of success and is usually written as p and the probability of the non-happening of A, *i.e.,* $P(\bar{A})$ is known as the probability of failure, which is usually denoted by q. Thus, from (12·13) and (12·14), we get

$$q = 1 - p \quad \Rightarrow \quad p + q = 1 \qquad \text{...(12·16)}$$

4. According to the above definition, the probability of getting a head in a toss of an unbiased coin is $\frac{1}{2}$, since the two exhaustive cases H and T (assuming the coin does not stand on its edge), are mutually exclusive and equally likely and one is favourable to getting a head. Similarly, in drawing a card from a well shuffled pack of cards, the probability of getting an ace is 4/52 = 1/13. Thus, the classical definition of probability does not require the actual experimentation, *i.e.,* no experimental data are needed for its computation, nor it is based on previous experience. It enables us to obtain probability by logical reasoning prior to making any actual trials and hence it is also known as '*a priori*' or *theoretical* or *mathematical probability.*

5. Limitations. The classical probability has its short-comings and fails in the following situations :

(*i*) If N, the exhaustive number of outcomes of the random experiment is infinite.

(*ii*) If the various outcomes of the random experiment are not equally likely. For example, if a person jumps from the top of Qutab Minar, then the probability of his survival will not be 50%, since in this case the two mutually exclusive and exhaustive outcomes, *viz.*, survival and death are not equally likely.

(*iii*) If the actual value of N is not known. Suppose an urn contains some balls of two colours, say red and white, their number being unknown. If we actually draw the balls from the urn, then we may form some idea about the ratio of red to the white balls in the urn. In the absence of any such experimentation (which is the case in classical probability), we cannot draw any conclusion in such a situation regarding the probability of drawing a white or a red ball from the urn. This drawback is overcome, in the statistical or empirical probability which we discuss below.

12·6. STATISTICAL OR EMPIRICAL PROBABILITY

Definition. (Von Mises). *If an experiment is performed repeatedly under essentially homogeneous and identical conditions, then the limiting value of the ratio of the number of times the event occurs to the number of trials, as the number of trials becomes indefinitely large, is called the probability of happening of the event, it being assumed that the limit is finite and unique.*

Suppose that an event A occurs m times in N repetitions of a random experiment. Then the ratio m/N gives the *relative frequency* of the event A and it will not vary appreciably from one trial to another. In the limiting case when N becomes sufficiently large, it more or less settles to a number which is called the probability of A. Symbolically,

$$P(A) = \lim_{N \to \infty} \frac{m}{N} \qquad \ldots(12\cdot17)$$

Remarks 1. Since in the relative frequency approach, the probability is obtained objectively by repetitive empirical observations, it is also known as *Empirical Probability.*

2. The empirical probability provides validity to the classical theory of probability. If an unbiased coin is tossed at random, then the classical probability gives the probability of a head as $\frac{1}{2}$. Thus, if we toss an unbiased coin 20 times, then classical probability suggests we should have 10 heads. However, in practice, this will not generally be true. In fact in 20 throws of a coin, we may get no head at all or 1 or 2 heads. However, the empirical probability suggests that if a coin is tossed a large number of times, say 500 times, we should on the average expect 50% heads and 50% tails. Thus, the empirical probability approaches the classical probability as the number of trials becomes indefinitely large.

3. Limitations. It may be remarked that the empirical probability $P(A)$ defined in (12·17) can never be obtained in practice and we can only attempt at a close estimate of $P(A)$ by making N sufficiently large. The following are the limitations of the experiment.

(*i*) The experimental conditions may not remain essentially homogeneous and identical in a large number of repititions of the experiment.

(*ii*) The relative frequency m/N, may not attain a unique value, no matter however large N may be.

Example 12·1. *A uniform die is thrown at random. Find the probability that the number on it is :*

(*i*) *5,* (*ii*) *greater than 4,* (*iii*) *even.*

Solution. Since the dice can fall with any one of the faces 1, 2, 3, 4, 5, and 6, the exhaustive number of cases is 6.

(*i*) The number of cases favourable to the event of getting '5' is only 1.

$\therefore$ Required probability = 1/6.

(*ii*) The number of cases favourable to the event of getting a number greater than 4 is 2, *viz.*, 5 and 6.

$\therefore$ Required probability $= \frac{2}{6} = \frac{1}{3}$

(*iii*) Favourable cases for getting an even number are 2, 4 and 6, *i.e.*, 3 in all.

$\therefore$ Required probability $= \frac{3}{6} = \frac{1}{2}$

Example 12·2. *In a single throw with two uniform dice find the probability of throwing*

(i) *Five,* (ii) *Eight.*

Solution. Exhaustive number of cases in a single throw with two dice is $6^2 = 36$.

(i) Sum of '5' can be obtained on the two dice in the following mutually exclusive ways :

(1, 4,), (4, 1), (2, 3), (3, 2) *i.e.,* 4 cases in all where the first and second number in the bracket ( ) refer to the numbers on the 1st and 2nd dice respectively.

$$\therefore \quad \text{Required probability} = \frac{4}{36} = \frac{1}{9}$$

(ii) The cases favourable to the event of getting sum of 8 on two dice are :

(2, 6), (6, 2), (3, 5), (5, 3), (4, 4) *i.e.,* 5 *distinct* cases in all.

$$\therefore \quad \text{Required probability} = \frac{5}{36}\,.$$

Example 12·3. *Four cards are drawn at random from a pack of 52 cards. Find the probability that*

(i) *They are a king, a queen, a jack and an ace.*

(ii) *Two are kings and two are aces.*

(iii) *All are diamonds.*

(iv) *Two are red and two are black.*

(v) *There is one card of each suit.*

(vi) *There are two cards of clubs and two cards of diamonds.*

Solution. Four cards can be drawn from a well shuffled pack of 52 cards in ${}^{52}C_4$ ways, which gives the exhaustive number of cases.

(i) 1 king can be drawn out of the 4 kings is ${}^4C_1 = 4$ ways. Similarly, 1 queen, 1 jack and an ace can each be drawn in ${}^4C_1 = 4$ ways. Since any one of the ways of drawing a king can be associated with any one of the ways of drawing a queen, a jack and an ace, the favourable number of cases are ${}^4C_1 \times {}^4C_1 \times {}^4C_1 \times {}^4C_1$.

$$\text{Hence, required probability} = \frac{{}^4C_1 \times {}^4C_1 \times {}^4C_1 \times {}^4C_1}{{}^{52}C_4} = \frac{256}{{}^{52}C_4}$$

(ii) $$\text{Required probability} = \frac{{}^4C_2 \times {}^4C_2}{{}^{52}C_4}$$

(iii) Since 4 cards can be drawn out of 13 cards (since there are 13 cards of diamond in a pack of cards) in ${}^{13}C_4$ ways,

$$\text{Required probability} = \frac{{}^{13}C_4}{{}^{52}C_4}\,.$$

(iv) Since there are 26 red cards (of diamonds and hearts) and 26 black cards (of spades and clubs) in a pack of cards,

$$\text{Required probability} = \frac{{}^{26}C_2 \times {}^{26}C_2}{{}^{52}C_4}$$

(v) Since, in a pack of cards there are 13 cards of each suit,

$$\text{Required probability} = \frac{{}^{13}C_1 \times {}^{13}C_1 \times {}^{13}C_1 \times {}^{13}C_1}{{}^{52}C_4}$$

(vi) $$\text{Required probability} = \frac{{}^{13}C_2 \times {}^{13}C_2}{{}^{52}C_4}$$

Example 12·4. *What is the chance that a non-leap year should have fifty-three sundays ?*

Solution. A non-leap year consists of 365 days *i.e.,* 52 full weeks and one over-day. A non-leap year will consist of 53 sundays if this over-day is sunday. This over-day can be anyone of the possible outcomes :

(*i*) Sunday (*ii*) Monday (*iii*) Tuesday (*iv*) Wednesday (*v*) Thursday (*vi*) Friday (*vii*) Saturday *i.e.*, 7 outcomes in all. Of these, the number of ways favourable to the required event *viz.*, the over-day being Sunday is 1.

$\therefore$ Required probability $= \frac{1}{7}\cdot$

Example 12·5. *If six dice are rolled, then the probability that all show different faces is*

(*i*) $\frac{1}{6^6}$ (*ii*) $\frac{6}{6^6}$ (*iii*) $\frac{6!}{6^6}$ (*iv*) *None of the above.*

[*I.C.W.A. (Intermediate), June 2002*]

Solution. In a random roll of six dice, the exhaustive number of cases is $n(S) = 6^6$. ...(*)

Define the event E : All the six dice show different faces.

We can get any one of the six faces 1, 2, 3, 4, 5, 6, on the first dice. For the happening of E, the second die must show any one of the remaining 5 faces, the third die must show any one of the remaining 4 faces, and so on, the 6th die must show the remaining last face.

Hence, by the principle of counting, the number of cases favourable to the happening of E are

$$n(E) = 6 \times 5 \times 4 \times 3 \times 2 \times 1 = 6\,!.$$

$$\therefore \quad P(E) = \frac{n(E)}{n(S)} = \frac{6\,!}{6^6}$$

$\Rightarrow$ (*iii*) is the correct answer.

Example 12·6. *A bag contains 20 tickets marked with numbers 1 to 20. One ticket is drawn at random. Find the probability that it will be a multiple of* (*i*) *2 or 5,* (*ii*) *3 or 5.*

Solution. One ticket can be drawn out of 20 tickets in $^{20}C_1 = 20$ ways, which determine the exhaustive number of cases.

(*i*) The number of cases favourable to getting the ticket number which is :

(*a*) a multiple of 2 are 2, 4, 6, 8, 10, 12, 14, 16, 18, 20 *i.e.*, 10 cases.

(*b*) a multiple of 5 are 5, 10, 15, 20 *i.e.*, 4 cases.

Of these, two cases *viz.*, 10 and 20 are duplicated. Hence the number of *distinct* cases favourable to getting a number which is a multiple of 2 or 5 are $10 + 4 - 2 = 12$.

$\therefore$ Required probability $= \frac{12}{20} = \frac{3}{5} = 0{\cdot}6$.

(*ii*) The cases favourable to getting a multiple of 3 are 3, 6, 9, 12, 15, 18 *i.e.*, 6 cases in all and getting a multiple of 5 are 5, 10, 15, 20 *i.e.*, 4 cases in all. Of these, one case *viz.*, 15 is duplicated.

Hence, the number of *distinct* cases favourable to getting a multiple of 3 or 5 is $6 + 4 - 1 = 9$.

$\therefore$ Required probability $= \frac{9}{20} = 0{\cdot}45$

Example 12·7. *An urn contains 8 white and 3 red balls. If two balls are drawn at random, find the probability that*

(*i*) *both are white,* (*ii*) *both are red,* (*iii*) *one is of each colour.*

Solution. Total number of balls in the urn is 8 + 3 = 11. Since 2 balls can be drawn out of 11 balls in $^{11}C_2$ ways,

$$\text{Exhaustive number of cases} = {}^{11}C_2 = \frac{11 \times 10}{2} = 55$$

(*i*) If both the drawn balls are white, they must be selected out of the 8 white balls and this can be done in $^{8}C_2 = \frac{8 \times 7}{2} = 28$ ways.

$\therefore$ Probability that both the balls are white $= \frac{28}{55}$

(*ii*) If both the drawn balls are red, they must be drawn out of the 3 red balls and this can be done in $^{3}C_2 = 3$ ways. Hence, the probability that both the drawn balls are red $= \frac{3}{55}\cdot$

(*iii*) The number of favourable cases for drawing one white ball and one red ball is

$$^8C_1 \times {}^3C_1 = 8 \times 3 = 24$$

∴ Probability that one ball is white and other is red $= \frac{24}{55}$.

Example 12·8. *The letters of the word 'article' are arranged at random. Find the probability that the vowels may occupy the even places.*

Solution. The word 'article' contains 7 distinct letters which can be arranged among themselves in 7 ! ways. Hence exhaustive number of cases is 7 !.

In the word 'article' there are 3 vowels, *viz.*, *a, i* and *e* and these are to be placed in, three even places, *viz.*, 2nd, 4th and 6th place. This can be done in 3 !, ways. For each arrangement, the remaining 4 consonants can be arranged in 4 ! ways. Hence, associating these two operations, the number of favourable cases for the vowels to occupy even places is 3 ! × 4 !.

∴ Required probability $= \frac{3\,!\,4\,!}{7\,!} = \frac{3\,!}{7 \times 6 \times 5} = \frac{1}{35}$.

Example 12·9. *The letters of the word 'failure' are arranged at random. Find the probability that the consonants may occupy only odd positions.*

Solution. There are 7 distinct letters in the word 'failure' and they can be arranged among themselves in 7 ! ways, which gives the exhaustive number of cases.

In the word '*failure*' there are 4 vowels *viz.*, *a i, u* and *e*, and 3 consonants *viz., f, l. r.* These 3 consonants are to be placed in the 4 odd places *viz.*, 1st, 3rd, 5th and 7th and this can be done in $^4C_3$ ways. Further these 3 consonants can be arranged among themselves in 3 ! ways and the remaining 4 vowels can be arranged among themselves in 4 ! ways. Associating all these operations, total number of favourable cases for the consonants to occupy *only* odd positions is $^4C_3 \times 3\,! \times 4\,!$.

∴ Required probability $= \frac{^4C_3 \times 3\,! \times 4\,!}{7\,!} = \frac{4 \times 3\,!}{7 \times 6 \times 5} = \frac{4}{35}$.

Example 12·10. *Twenty books are placed at random in a shelf. Find the probability that a particular pair of books shall be :*

(*i*) *Always together* (*ii*) *Never together.*

Solution. Since 20 books can be arranged among themselves in 20 ! ways, the exhaustive number of cases is 20 !.

(*i*) Let us now regard that the two particular books are tagged together so that we shall regard them as a single book. Thus, now we have (20 – 1) = 19 books which can he arranged among themselves in 19 ! ways. But the two books which are fastened together can be arranged among themselves in 2 ! ways. Hence, associating these two operations, the number of favourable cases for getting a particular pair of books always together is 19 ! × 2 !.

∴ Required probability $= \frac{19\,! \times 2\,!}{20\,!} = \frac{2}{20} = \frac{1}{10}$.

(*ii*) Total number of arrangement of 20 books among themselves is 20 ! and the total number of arrangements that a particular pair of books will always be together is 19 ! × 2, [See part (*i*)]. Hence, the number of arrangements in which a particular pair of books is never together is :

$$20\,! - 2 \times 19\,! = (20-2) \times 19\,! = 18 \times 19\,!$$

∴ Required probability $= \frac{18 \times 19\,!}{20\,!} = \frac{18}{20} = \frac{9}{10}$

Aliter :

P [A particular pair of books shall never be together]

$= 1 - P$ [A particular pair of books is always together]

$= 1 - \frac{1}{10} = \frac{9}{.0}$.

Example 12·11. *n persons are seated on n chairs at a round table. Find the probability that two specified persons are sitting next to each other.*

Solution. The n persons can be seated in n chairs at a round table in $(n-1)!$ ways, which gives the exhaustive number of cases.

If two specified persons, say, A and B sit together, then regarding A and B fixed together, we get $(n-1)$ persons in all, who can be seated at a round table in $(n-2)!$ ways. Further, since A and B can interchange their positions in $2!$ ways, total number of favourable cases of getting A and B together is $(n-2)! \times 2!$. Hence the required probability is

$$\frac{(n-2)! \times 2!}{(n-1)!} = \frac{2}{n-1}.$$

Aliter. Let us suppose that of the n persons, two persons, say, A and B are to be seated together at a round table. After one of these two persons, say A occupies the chair, the other person B can occupy any one of the remaining $(n-1)$ chairs. Out of these $(n-1)$ seats, the number of seats favourable to making B sit next to A is 2 (since B can sit on either side of A). Hence the required probability is $2/(n-1)$.

Example 12·12. *In a village of 21 inhabitants, a person tells a rumour to a second person, who in turn repeats it to a third person, etc. At each step the recipient of the rumour is chosen at random from the 20 people available. Find the probability that the rumour will be told 10 times without :*

(*i*) *returning to the originator* ; (*ii*) *being repeated to any person*

[*Delhi Univ. B.A.* (*Econ. Hons.*), *2002*]

Solution. Since any person can tell the rumour to any one of the remaining $21-1=20$ people in 20 ways, the exhaustive number of cases that the rumour will be told 10 times is 20^{10}.

(*i*) Let us define the event :

E_1 : The rumour will be told 10 times without returning to the originator.

The originator can tell the rumour to any one of the remaining 20 persons in 20 ways, and each of the $10-1=9$ recipients of the rumour can tell it to any of the remaining $20-1=19$ persons (without returning it to the originator) in 19 ways. Hence the favourable number of cases for E_1 are 20×19^9. The required probability is given by :

$$P(E_1) = \frac{20 \times 19^9}{20^{10}} = \left(\frac{19}{20}\right)^9$$

(*ii*) Let us define the event :

E_2 : The rumour is told 10 times without being repeated to any person.

In this case the first person (narrator) can tell the rumour to any one of the available $21-1=20$ persons; the second person can tell the rumour to any one of the remaining $20-1=19$ persons ; the third person can tell the rumour to anyone of the remaining $20-2=18$ persons ; ... ; the 10th person can tell the rumour to any one of the remaining $20-9=11$ persons.

Hence, the favourable number of cases for E_2 are $20 \times 19 \times 18 \times \ldots \times 11$.

$$\therefore \quad \text{Required Probability} = P(E_2) = \frac{20 \times 19 \times 18 \times \ldots \times 11}{20^{10}}.$$

Example 12·13. *If 10 men, among whom are A and B, stand in a row, what is the probability that there will be exactly 3 men between A and B ?* [*Delhi Univ. B.A.* (*Econ. Hons.*), *2002*]

Solution. If 10 men stand in a row, then A can occupy any one of the 10 positions and B can occupy any one of the remaining 9 positions. Hence, the exhaustive number of cases for the positions of two men A and B are $10 \times 9 = 90$.

The cases favourable to the event that there are exactly 3 men between A and B are given below :

(*i*) A is in the 1st position and B is in the 5th position.
(*ii*) A is in the 2nd position and B is in the 6th position.
⋮
(*vi*) A is in the 6th position and B is in the 10th position.

Further, since A and B can interchange their positions,

The total number of favourable cases $= 2 \times 6 = 12$.

$\therefore$ Required probability $= \frac{12}{90} = \frac{2}{15} = 0{\cdot}1333$.

Example 12·14. *In a random arrangement of the letters of the word 'MATHEMATICS', find the probability that all the vowels come together.*

Solution. The total number of permutations of the letters of the word '*MATHEMATICS*' are

$$\frac{11!}{2!\,2!\,2!},$$

because it contains 11 letters, of which 2 are A's, 2M's, 2T's, and remaining are all different.

The word *MATHEMATICS* contains 4 vowels *viz., AEAI,* (2 A's being identical). To obtain the total number of arrangements in which these 4 vowels come together, we regard them as tied together, forming only one letter so that, the total number of letters in *MATHEMATICS* may be taken as $11 - 3 = 8$, out of which 2 are M's, 2 are T's and rest distinct and therefore, their number of arrangements is given by

$$\frac{8!}{2!\,2!}$$

Further, the four vowels *AEAI*, two of which are identical and rest distinct can be arranged among themselves in $\frac{4!}{2!}$ ways. Hence, the total number of arrangements favourable to getting all vowels together is :

$$\frac{8!}{2!\,2!} \times \frac{4!}{2!}$$

$$\therefore \quad \text{Required probability} = \frac{8!\,4!}{2!\,2!\,2!} \div \frac{11!}{2!\,2!\,2!}$$

$$= \frac{8!\,4!}{11!} = \frac{4!}{11 \times 10 \times 9} = \frac{4}{165}.$$

Example 12·15. *There are four hotels in a certain town. If 3 men check into hotels in a day, what is the probability that each checks into a different hotel ?*

Solution. Since each man can check into any one of the four hotels in ${}^4C_1 = 4$ ways, the 3 men can check into 4 hotels in $4 \times 4 \times 4 = 64$ ways, which gives the exhaustive number of cases.

If three men are to check into different hotels, then first man can check into any one of the 4 hotels in ${}^4C_1 = 4$ ways ; the second man can check into any one of the remaining 3 hotels in ${}^3C_1 = 3$ ways ; and the third man can check into any one of the remaining two hotels in ${}^2C_1 = 2$ ways. Hence, favourable number of cases for each man checking into a different hotel is :

$${}^4C_1 \times {}^3C_1 \times {}^2C_1 = 4 \times 3 \times 2 = 24$$

$\therefore$ Required probability $= \frac{24}{64} = \frac{3}{8} = 0{\cdot}375$.

EXERCISE 12·1

1. Explain the concept of probability following :

(*i*) Mathematical or 'a Priori' approach,

(*ii*) Relative frequency or empirical approach.

2. (*a*) Define random experiment, trial and event.

(*b*) What do you understand by (*i*) equally likely, (*ii*) mutually exclusive and (*iii*) independent events.

(*c*) Define independent and mutually exclusive events. Can two events be mutually exclusive and independent simultaneously ? Support your answer with an example.

3. (*a*) Explain the different approaches to probability. [*Delhi Univ. B.Com. (Hons.), 2002*]

(*b*) List the reasons for classical definition of probability not being very satisfactory. Give the modern definition of probability. [*C.A. (Foundation), Nov. 1997*]

(*c*) Describe briefly the various schools of thought on probability. Discuss their limitations, if any.

4. (*a*) What is the probability that a leap year selected at random will contain 53 Sundays ?

[*Delhi Uiv. B.A. (Econ. Hons.), 2008*]

(*b*) A leap year selected at random will contain either 53 Sundays or 53 Mondays is

(*i*) $\frac{1}{7}$, (*ii*) $\frac{2}{7}$, (*iii*) $\frac{3}{7}$, (*iv*) $\frac{4}{7}$.

[*I.C.W.A. (Intermediate), Dec. 2001*]

Ans. (*a*) $\frac{2}{7}$ (*b*) $\frac{3}{7}$ (*i.e., iii*).

5. In a single throw of two dice, what is the probability of getting

(*i*) a total of 8 ; and (*ii*) Total different from 8 :

Ans. (*i*) 5/36, (*ii*) 31/36.

6. Prove that in a single throw with a pair of dice, the probability of getting the sum of 7 is equal to 1/6 and the probability of getting the sum of 10 is equal to 1/12.

7. In a single throw of two dice, find

(*i*) *P* (odd number on first dice and 6 on the second), (*ii*) *P* (a number > 4 on each die),

(*iii*) *P* (a total of 11), (*iv*) *P* (a total of 9 or 11), (*v*) *P* (a total greater than 8).

Ans. (*i*) $\frac{1}{12}$, (*ii*) $\frac{1}{9}$, (*iii*) $\frac{1}{18}$, (*iv*) $\frac{1}{6}$, (*v*) $\frac{5}{18}$.

8. In the play of two dice, the thrower loses if his first throw is 2, 4 or 12. He wins if his first throw is a 5 or 11. Find the ratio between his probability of losing and probability of winning in the first throw.

[*C.A. (Foundation), Dec. 1993 ; Delhi Univ. B.Com.* (*Hons.*) *1998*]

Hint. Number of favourable cases for getting

(*i*) 2, 4 or 12 is 1 + 3 + 1 = 5 ; (*ii*) 5 or 11 is 4 + 2 = 6

Ans. Required Probability = $\frac{5/36}{6/36} = \frac{5}{6}$.

9. If a pair of dice is thrown, find the probability that the sum of the digits on them is neither 7 nor 11.

[*C.A.* (*Foundation*), *Nov. 1995*]

Ans. (7/9) = 0·78.

10. Tickets are numbered from 1 to 100. They are well shuffled and a ticket is drawn at random. What is the probability that the drawn ticket has :

(*a*) an even number ? (*b*) a number 5 or a multiple of 5 ?

(*c*) a number which is greater than 75 ? (*d*) a number which is a square ?

Ans. (*a*) 0·5, (*b*) 0·2, (*c*) 0·25, (*d*) 0·10.

11. There are 17 balls, numbered from 1 to 17 in a bag. If a person selects one ball at random, what is the probability that the number printed on the ball will be an even number greater than 9 ?

Ans. 4 / 17.

12. An integer is chosen at random from the first 200 positive integers. What is the probability that integer chosen is divisible by 6 or 8 ?

Ans. 1/4.

13. One ticket is drawn at random from a bag containing 30 tickets numbered from 1 to 30. Find the probability that

(*i*) It is multiple of 5 or 7 ; (*ii*) It is multiple of 3 or 5.

Ans. (*i*) 1/3, (*ii*) 7/15.

14. A number is chosen from each of the two sets :

1, 2, 3, 4, 5, 6, 7, 8, 9, ; 1, 2, 3, 4, 5, 6, 7, 8, 9.

If p_1 is the probability that the sum of the two numbers be 10 and p_2 the probability that their sum be 8, find $p_1 + p_2$.

Ans. 16 / 81.

15. A bag contains 7 white and 9 black balls. Two balls are drawn in succession at random. What is the probability that one of them is white and the other is black ?

Ans. 21/40.

16. A bag contains eight balls, five being red and three white. If a man selects two balls at random from the bag, what is the probability that he will get one ball of each colour ? *[Delhi Univ. B.Com. (Hons.), 1997]*

Ans. $\frac{^5C_1 \times {}^3C_1}{^8C_2} = \frac{15}{28}$.

17. A bag contains 5 white and 3 black balls. Two balls are drawn at random one after the other without replacement. Find the probability that balls drawn are black.

Ans. $\frac{3}{28}$.

18. A bag contains 4 white, 5 red and 6 green balls. Three balls are drawn at random. What is the probability that a white, a red and a green ball are drawn ?

Ans. 24 / 91.

19. A bag contains 8 black, 3 red and 9 white balls. If 3 balls are drawn at random, find the probability that

(*a*) all are black, (*b*) 2 are black and 1 is white, (*c*) 1 is of each colour,
(*d*) the balls are drawn in the order black, red and white, (*e*) None is red.

Ans. (*a*) $\frac{14}{285}$, (*b*) $\frac{21}{95}$, (*c*) $\frac{18}{95}$, (*d*) $\frac{3}{95}$, (*e*) $\frac{34}{57}$.

20. The Federal Match Company has forty female employees and sixty male employees. If two employees are selected at random, what is the probability that

(*i*) both will be males, (*ii*) both will be females, (*iii*) there will be one of each sex ?

Since the three events are collectively exhaustive and mutually exclusive, what is the sum of the three probabilities ?

Ans. (*i*) 0·357, (*ii*) 0·157, (*iii*) 0·4848. ; 1.

21. Among the 90 pieces of mail delivered to an office, 50 are addressed to the accounting department and 40 are addressed to the marketing department. If two of these pieces of mail are delivered to the manager's office by mistake, and the selection is random, what are the probabilities that :

(*i*) Both of them should have been delivered to the accounting department;
(*ii*) Both of them should have been delivered to the marketing department;
(*iii*) One should have been delivered to the accounting department and the other to be marketing department ?

[Delhi Univ. M.Com. 2002]

Ans. (*i*) $\frac{^{50}C_2}{^{90}C_2} = 0{\cdot}3059$; $\frac{^{40}C_2}{^{90}C_2} = 0{\cdot}1948$; $\frac{^{50}C_1 \times {}^{40}C_1}{^{90}C_2} = 0{\cdot}4994$

22. If a single draw is made from a pack of 52 cards, what is the probability of securing either an ace of spades or a jack of clubs.

Ans. 1 / 26.

23. (*a*) Four cards are drawn from a full pack of cards. Find the probability that two are spades and two are hearts ?

(*b*) From a pack of 52 cards, 4 are accidentally dropped. Find the chance that

(*i*) they will consist of a knave, a queen, a king and ace. (*ii*) they are the 4 honours of the same suit,
(*iii*) they be one from each suit, (*iv*) two of them are red and two are black.

Ans. (*a*) $\frac{^{13}C_2 \times {}^{13}C_2}{^{52}C_4} = \frac{468}{20825}$. (*b*) (*i*) $\frac{256}{^{52}C_4}$, (*ii*) $\frac{4}{^{52}C_4}$, (*iii*) $\frac{(^{13}C_1)^4}{^{52}C_4}$, (*iv*) $\frac{^{26}C_2 \times {}^{26}C_2}{^{52}C_4}$.

24. What is the probability of getting 9 cards of the same suit in one hand at a game of bridge ?

Ans. $4 \times {}^{13}C_9 \times {}^{39}C_4 / {}^{52}C_4$.

25. The letters of the word *Triangle* are arranged at random. Find the probability that the word so formed

(*i*) starts with *T*, (*ii*) ends with *E*, (*iii*) starts with *T* and ends with *E*.

Ans. (*i*) $\frac{1}{8}$, (*ii*) $\frac{1}{8}$, (*iii*) $\frac{1}{56}$.

26. In a random arrangement of the letters of the word *VIOLENT*, find the chance that the vowels *I, O, E* occupy odd positions only.

Ans. $\frac{^4C_3 \times 3\,!\,4\,!}{7\,!} = \frac{4}{35}$.

27. In a random arrangement of the letters of the word Allahabad, find the chance that the vowels occupy the even places.

Ans. $\frac{1 \times 5!}{2!} \div \frac{9!}{4!\,2!} = \frac{1}{126}$.

28. The letters of the word *ARRANGE* are arranged at random. Find the chance that :

(*i*) The two *R*'s come together. (*ii*) The two *R*'s do not come together.

(*iii*) The two *R*'s and the two *A*'s come together.

Ans. (*i*) $\frac{6!}{2!} \div \frac{7!}{2!\,2!} = 360 \div 1260 = \frac{2}{7}$; (*ii*) $(1260 - 360) \div 1260 = \frac{5}{7}$; (*iii*) $\frac{5!}{1260} = \frac{2}{21}$.

29. *A* and *B* stand in a ring with 10 other persons. If the arrangement of the persons is at random, find the chance that (*i*) there are exactly three persons between *A* and *B*, (*ii*) *A* and *B* stand together.

Ans. (*i*) 2 / 11, (*ii*) 2 / 11.

30. The first twelve letters of the English alphabet are written down at random. What is the probability that

(*a*) There are 4 letters between *A* and *B* ? ; (*b*) *A* and *B* are written down side by side ?

Ans. (*a*) 7 / 66 , (*b*) 1 / 6.

31. Seven persons sit in a row at random. Find the chance that :

(*i*) Three persons *A, B, C* sit together in a particular order. ; (*ii*) *A, B, C* sit together in any order.

(*iii*) *B* and *C* occupy the end seats. ; (*iv*) *C* always occupies the middle seat.

Ans. (*i*) $\frac{5!}{7!} = \frac{1}{42}$, (*ii*) $\frac{5!\,3!}{7!} = \frac{1}{7}$, (*iii*) $\frac{5! \times 2}{7!} = \frac{1}{21}$, (*iv*) $\frac{6!}{7!} = \frac{1}{7}$.

32. Five digited numbers are formed from the digits 1, 2, 3, 4, 5. Find the chance that the number formed is greater than 23000.

Ans. $\frac{3! + 3 \times 4!}{5!} = \frac{78}{5!} = \frac{13}{20}$.

33. Twelve balls are distributed at random among three boxes. What is the probability that the first box will contain 3 balls ?

Ans. $\frac{{}^{12}C_3 \times 2^9}{3^{12}}$.

34. If n biscuits are distributed at random among N beggars, find the chance that a particular beggar receives r $(< n)$ biscuits.

Ans. $\frac{{}^{n}C_r \times (N-1)^{n-r}}{N^r}$.

12·7. AXIOMATIC PROBABILITY

The modern theory of probability is based on the axiomatic approach introduced by the Russian mathematician A.N. Kolmogorov in 1930's. Kolmogorov axiomised the theory of probability and his small book '*Foundations of Probability*', published in 1933, introduces probability as a set function and is considered as a classic. In axiomatic approach, to start with, some concepts are laid down and certain *properties* or *postulates*, commonly known as *axioms*, are defined and from these axioms alone the entire theory is developed by logic of deduction. The axiomatic definition of probability includes both the classical and empirical definitions of probability and at the same time is free from their drawbacks. Before giving axiomatic definition of probability, we shall explain certain concepts, used therein.

Sample Space. *The set of all possible outcomes of a random experiment is known as the sample space and is denoted by S.* In other words, sample space is the set of all exhaustive cases of the random experiment. The outcomes of the experiment are also known as *sample points*. Mathematically, if $e_1, e_2, \ldots, e_n$ are the mutually exclusive possible outcomes of a random experiment, then the set $S = \{e_1, e_2, \ldots, e_n\}$ is said to be sample space of the experiment. The elements of S possess the following properties :

(*i*) Each of the e_i's $(i = 1, 2, \ldots, n)$ is outcome of the experiment.

(*ii*) Any repetition of the experiment results in an outcome corresponding to one and only one of the e_i's.

Remark. We shall write $n(S)$ to denote the number of elements *i.e.*, sample points in S.

Illustrations. 1. If a coin is tossed at random, the sample space is $S = (H, T)$ and $n(S) = 2$.

If two coins are tossed then the sample space is given by :

$$S = \{ (H, T) \times (H, T) \} = \{ HH, HT, TH, TT \}$$

and $$n(S) = 4 = 2^2$$

In a toss of three coins,

$$S = \{ (H, T) \times (H, T) \times (H, T) \} = \{ (HH, HT, TH, TT) \times (H, T) \}$$
$$= \{ HHH, \ HTH, \ THH, \ TTH, \ HHT, HTT, THT, TTT \}$$

and $$n(S) = 8 = 2^3$$

In general, in a random toss of N coins, $n(S) = 2^N$.

2. If two dice are thrown, then the sample space consists of 36 points as given below.

$$S = \left\{ \begin{matrix} (1, 1), & (1, 2), & (1, 3), & (1, 4), & (1, 5), & (1, 6) \\ (2, 1), & (2, 2), & (2, 3), & (2, 4), & (2, 5), & (2, 6) \\ \vdots & \vdots & \vdots & \vdots & \vdots & \vdots \\ (6, 1), & (6, 2), & (6, 3), & (6, 4), & (6, 5), & (6, 6) \end{matrix} \right\} \quad ; \quad n(S) = 36 = 6^2$$

In general, in a random toss of N dice, $n(S) = 6^N$

Event. *Of all the possible outcomes in the sample space of a random experiment, some outcomes satisfy a specified description, which we call an event.* For example, as already discussed, in a toss of 3 coins the sample space is given by :

$$S = \{ HHH, \ HTH, THH, \ TTH, \ HHT, \ HTT, \ THT, \ TTT \}$$
$$= \{ w_1, w_2, w_3, w_4, w_5, w_6, w_7, w_8 \}, \text{ say,} \qquad \ldots(12{\cdot}18)$$

where $w_1 = HHH, \quad w_2 = HTH, \quad w_3 = THH, \quad \ldots, \quad w_8 = TTT.$

For this sample space we can define a number of events, some of which are given below ;

E_1 : Event of getting all heads $= \{ HHH \} = \{ w_1 \}$

E_2 : Event of getting exactly two heads $= \{ HTH, THH, HHT \} = \{ w_2, w_3, w_5 \}$

E_3 : Event of getting at least two heads

$$= \{ w_1, \ w_2, \ w_3, \ w_5 \} = \{ w_1 \} \cup \{ w_2, \ w_3, \ w_5 \} = E_1 \cup E_2,$$

where E_1 and E_2 are disjoint. ...(*)

E_4 : Event of getting exactly one head $= \{ w_4, \ w_6, \ w_7 \}$

E_5 : Event of getting at least one head

$$= \{ w_1, w_2, w_3, w_4, w_5, w_6, w_7 \} = \{ w_1, w_2, w_3, w_5 \} \cup \{ w_4, w_6, w_7 \}$$
$$= E_3 \cup E_4 = E_1 \cup E_2 \cup E_4, \text{ where } E_1, E_2 \text{ and } E_4 \text{ are disjoint.} \qquad \text{[From (*)]}$$

E_6 : Event of getting all tails $= \{ TTT \} = \{ w_8 \}$.

Thus, rigorously speaking *an event may be defined as a non-empty sub-set of the sample space.* Every event may be expressed as a disjoint union of the single element subsets of S or a disjoint union of some subsets of S. Since events are nothing but sets, the algebra of sets may be used to deal with them.

The two events A and B are said to be *disjoint* or *mutually exclusive* if they cannot happen simultaneously *i.e.*, if their intersection is a null set. Thus if A and B are disjoint events, then

$$A \cap B = \phi \quad \Rightarrow \quad P(A \cap B) = P(\phi) = 0 \qquad \ldots(12{\cdot}19)$$

Thus $P(A \cap B) = 0$, provides us with a criterion for finding if A and B are mutually exclusive.

Axiomatic Probability (Definition). Given a sample space of a random experiment, the probability of the occurrence of any event A is defined as a set function $P(A)$ satisfying the following axioms.

Axiom 1. $P(A)$ is defined, is real and non-negative *i.e.*,

$$P(A) \geq 0 \ \textit{(Axiom of non-negativity)} \qquad \ldots(12.19a)$$

Axiom 2. $P(S) = 1$ (*Axiom of certainty*) ...(12·20)

Axiom 3. If $A_1, A_2, \ldots, A_n$ is any finite or infinite sequence of disjoint events of S, then

$$P\left(\bigcup_{i=1}^{n} A_i\right) = \sum_{i=1}^{n} P(A_i) \quad \text{or} \quad P\left(\bigcup_{i=1}^{\infty} A_i\right) = \sum_{i=1}^{\infty} P(A_i) \text{ (Axiom of additivity)} \quad \ldots(12\cdot21)$$

Events as Sets - Glossary of Probability Terms

If A and B are two events then :

$A \cup B$: An event which represents the happening of *at least one* of the events A and B, (*i.e.*, either A occurs or B occurs or both A and B occur).

$A \cap B$: An event which represents the simultaneous happening of both the events A and B.

$\bar{A}$: A does not happen.

$\bar{A} \cap \bar{B}$: Neither A nor B happens *i.e.*, none of A and B happens.

$\bar{A} \cap B$: A does not happen but B happens.

$(A \cap \bar{B}) \cup (\bar{A} \cap B)$: Exactly one of the two events A and B happens.

The above notations can be generalised for n events, say, $A_1, A_2, \ldots, A_n$. Thus :

$A_1 \cap A_2 \cap \ldots \cap A_n$: *A compound* event which represents the simultaneous happening of all the events $A_1, A_2 \ldots, A_n$.

$A_1 \cup A_2 \cup \ldots \cup A_n$: An event which represents the happening of *at least one* of the events $A_1, A_2, \ldots, A_n$. This involves the events of the type $A_1, A_2, \ldots, A_n$ (one at a time) ;

$A_i \cap A_j$, $(i \neq j = 1, 2, \ldots, n)$ *i.e.*, simultaneous happening of two at a time ;

$A_i \cap A_j \cap A_k$, $(i \neq j \neq k = 1, 2, \ldots, n)$, *i.e.*, simultaneous happening of three at a time, ..., and $A_1 \cap A_2 \cap \ldots \cap A_n$ *i.e.*, all the n at a time.

However, if $A_1, A_2, \ldots, A_n$ are *mutually disjoint*, they can not happen simultaneously, *i.e.*, $A_i \cap A_j$, $A_i \cap A_j \cap A_k$, ..., $A_1 \cap A_2 \cap \ldots \cap A_n$, are all null events and in that case $A_1 \cup A_2 \cup \ldots \cup A_n$ will represent the happening of *any one* of the events $A_1, A_2, \ldots, A_n$.

Probability - Mathematical Notion. Let us suppose that S is the sample space of a *random experiment* with a large number of trials with sample points (number of all possible outcomes) N, *i.e.*, $n(S) = N$. Let the number of occurrences (sample points) favourable to the event A be denoted by $n(A)$. Then the frequency interpretation of the probability gives :

$$P(A) = \frac{n(A)}{n(S)} = \frac{n(A)}{N} \quad \ldots(12\cdot21a)$$

But in practical problems, writing down the elements of S and counting the number of cases favourable to a given event often proves quite tedious. For example, if a die is thrown three times, then total number of sample points would be $6^3 = 216$ and if 3 cards are drawn from a pack of cards without replacement there would be $52 \times 51 \times 50 = 132{,}600$ sample points. To write them is a very difficult task and is quite often unnecessary. However, in such situations the computation of probabilities can be facilitated to a great extent by the two fundamental theorems of probability - the addition theorem and the multiplication theorem discussed below.

12·8. ADDITION THEOREM OF PROBABILITY

Theorem 12·9. *The probability of occurrence of at least one of the two events A and B is given by :*

$$P(A \cup B) = P(A) + P(B) - P(A \cap B) \quad \ldots(12\cdot22)$$

Proof. Let us suppose that a random experiment results in a sample space S with N sample points (exhaustive number of cases). Then by definition :

$$P(A \cup B) = \frac{n(A \cup B)}{n(S)} = \frac{n(A \cup B)}{N} \qquad \ldots(12{\cdot}23)$$

where $n(A \cup B)$ is the number of occurrences (sample points) favourable to the event $(A \cup B)$.

From the Fig. 12·5, we get :

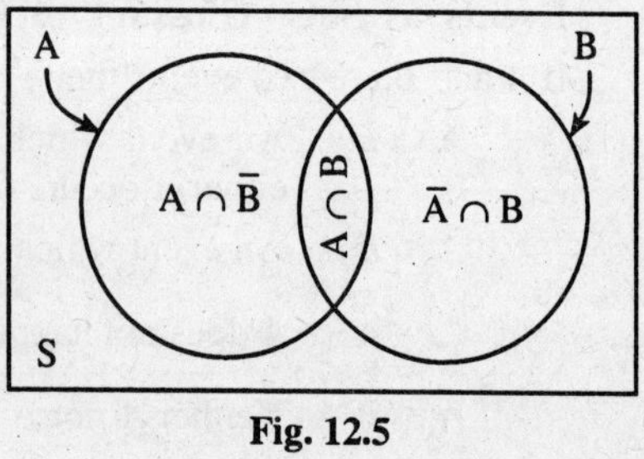

Fig. 12.5

$$\begin{aligned} P(A \cup B) &= \frac{[n(A) - n(A \cap B)] + n(A \cap B) + [n(B) - n(A \cap B)]}{N} \\ &= \frac{n(A) + n(B) - n(A \cap B)}{N} \\ &= \frac{n(A)}{N} + \frac{n(B)}{N} - \frac{n(A \cap B)}{N} \\ &= P(A) + P(B) - P(A \cap B) \end{aligned}$$

Remark. Since $P(A \cap B) \geq 0$, we get from (12·22) :

$$P(A \cup B) \leq P(A) + P(B) \qquad \ldots(12{\cdot}23a)$$

In particular, for two events A_1 and A_2, we have

$$P(A_1 \cup A_2) \leq P(A_1) + P(A_2) \qquad \ldots(12{\cdot}23b)$$

For three events A_1, A_2 and A_3, we have

$$\begin{aligned} P[A_1 \cup A_2 \cup A_3] &= P[(A_1 \cup A_2) \cup A_3] \\ &\leq P(A_1 \cup A_2) + P(A_3) \qquad [\text{From (12·23}a\text{) with } A = A_1 \cup A_2 \text{ and } B = A_3] \end{aligned}$$

$$\Rightarrow \quad P(A_1 \cup A_2 \cup A_3) \leq P(A_1) + P(A_2) + P(A_3) \qquad [\text{From (12·23}b\text{)}] \qquad \ldots(12{\cdot}23c)$$

Proceeding similarly, we have in general,

$$P(A_1 \cup A_2 \cup A_3 \cup \ldots \cup A_n) \leq P(A_1) + P(A_2) + P(A_3) + \ldots + P(A_n)$$

12·8·1. Addition Theorem of Probability for Mutually Exclusive Events. If the events A and B are mutually disjoint, *i.e.*, if $A \cap B = \phi$ then

$$P(A \cap B) = \frac{n(A \cap B)}{N} = \frac{n(\phi)}{N} = 0, \qquad \ldots(*)$$

because $n(\phi) = 0$, as a null set does not contain any sample point. In case of disjoint events, $A \cup B$ represents the happening of *anyone* of the events A and B. Hence, substituting from (*) in (12·22) we get the addition theorem as follows :

Theorem 12·10. *The probability of happening of any one of the two mutually disjoint events is equal to the sum of their individual probabilities. Symbolically, for disjoint events A and B,*

$$P(A \cup B) = P(A) + P(B) \qquad \ldots(12{\cdot}24)$$

12·8·2. Generalisation of (12·22). For three events A, B and C, the probability of the occurrence of at least one of them is given by

$$\begin{aligned} P(A \cup B \cup C) &= \frac{n(A \cup B \cup C)}{N} \\ &= \frac{1}{N}\left[n(A) + n(B) + n(C) - n(A \cap B) - n(B \cap C) - n(A \cap C) + n(A \cap B \cap C)\right] \\ &= \frac{n(A)}{N} + \frac{n(B)}{N} + \frac{n(C)}{N} - \frac{n(A \cap B)}{N} - \frac{n(B \cap C)}{N} - \frac{n(A \cap C)}{N} + \frac{n(A \cap B \cap C)}{N} \\ &= P(A) + P(B) + P(C) - P(A \cap B) - P(B \cap C) - P(A \cap C) + P(A \cap B \cap C) \qquad \ldots(12{\cdot}25) \end{aligned}$$

In particular, if *A, B* and *C* are mutually exclusive (disjoint), then

$$A \cap B = A \cap C = B \cap C = \phi \qquad \text{and} \qquad A \cap B \cap C = \phi$$

$$\Rightarrow \qquad n(A \cap B) = n(A \cap C) = n(B \cap C) = n(A \cap B \cap C) = 0$$

Hence, substituting in (12·25), *the probability of occurrence of any one of the mutually exclusive events A, B and C is equal to the sum of their individual probabilities given by* :

$$P(A \cup B \cup C) = P(A) + P(B) + P(C) \qquad \ldots(12\cdot26)$$

In general, if $A_1, A_2, \ldots, A_n$ are *mutually exclusive* then

$$P(A_1 \cup A_2 \cup \ldots \cup A_n) = P(A_1) + P(A_2) + \ldots + P(A_n) \qquad \ldots(12\cdot27)$$

i.e., the probability of occurrence of any of the n mutually disjoint events $A_1, A_2, \ldots, A_n$ *is equal to the sum of their individual probabilities.*

Important Remark. *How to use Addition Theorem (12·27) in Numerical Problems* ? Suppose we want to find the probability of occurrence of an event *A*. Then from practical point of view, we try to work out the several mutually exclusive ways (events) in which the event *A* can materialise. Let these possible mutually exclusive forms of *A* be $A_1, A_2, \ldots, A_n$. Then we can write

$$A = A_1 \cup A_2 \cup A_3 \cup \ldots \cup A_n$$

where $A_1, A_2, \ldots, A_n$ are mutually exclusive. Hence using (12·27), we get

$$P(A) = P(A_1 \cup A_2 \cup \ldots \cup A_n)$$
$$= P(A_1) + P(A_2) + \ldots + P(A_n)$$

Hence the working rule for numerical problems may be summarised as follows :

"The probability of occurrence of any event A is the sum of the probabilities of happening of its all possible mutually exclusive forms $A_1, A_2, \ldots, A_n$*".*

12·9. THEOREM OF COMPOUND PROBABILITY OR MULTIPLICATION THEOREM OF PROBABILITY

Theorem 12·11. *The probability of simultaneous happening of two events A and B is given by* :

$$\left.\begin{aligned} P(A \cap B) &= P(A) \,.\, P(B \mid A) \,;\; P(A) \neq 0 \\ \text{or} \quad P(B \cap A) &= P(B) \,.\, P(A \mid B) \,;\; P(B) \neq 0 \end{aligned}\right\} \qquad \ldots(12\cdot28)$$

where P (B | A) is the conditional probability of happening of B under the condition that A has happened and P (A | B) is the conditional probability of happening of A under the condition that B has happened.

In other words, the probability of the simultaneous happening of the two events *A* and *B* is the product of two probabilities, namely: the probability of the first event times the conditional probability of the second event, given that the first event has already occurred. We may take any one of the events *A* or *B* as the first event.

Proof. Let *A* and *B* be the events associated with the sample space *S* of a random experiment with exhaustive number of outcomes (sample points) *N, i.e., n*(*S*) = *N*. Then by definition :

$$P(A \cap B) = \frac{n(A \cap B)}{n(S)} \qquad \ldots(12\cdot29)$$

For the conditional event *A* | *B* (*i.e.,* the happening of *A* under the condition that *B* has happened), the favourable outcomes (sample points) must be out of the sample points of *B*. In other words, for the event *A* | *B*, the sample space is *B* and hence

$$P(A \mid B) = \frac{n(A \cap B)}{n(B)} \qquad \ldots(12\cdot30)$$

Similarly, we have

$$P(B \mid A) = \frac{n(B \cap A)}{n(A)} \qquad \ldots(12\cdot31)$$

Rewriting (12·29), we get

$$P(A \cap B) = \frac{n(A)}{n(S)} \times \frac{n(A \cap B)}{n(A)} = P(A) \cdot P(B \mid A) \qquad \text{[From (12·31)]}$$

Also
$$P(A \cap B) = \frac{n(B)}{n(S)} \times \frac{n(A \cap B)}{n(B)} = P(B) \cdot P(A \mid B) \qquad \text{[From (12·30)]}$$

Generalisation of Multiplication Theorem of Probability. The multiplication theorem of probability can be extended to more than two events. Thus, for three events A_1, A_2 and A_3, we have

$$P(A_1 \cap A_2 \cap A_3) = P(A_1) \cdot P(A_2 \mid A_1) \cdot P(A_3 \mid A_1 \cap A_2) \qquad \ldots(12·32)$$

In general, for n events $A_1, A_2, \ldots, A_n$, we have

$$P(A_1 \cap A_2 \cap \ldots \cap A_n) = P(A_1) \cdot P(A_2 \mid A_1) \cdot P(A_3 \mid A_1 \cap A_2) \times \ldots \times P(A_n \mid A_1 \cap A_2 \cap \ldots \cap A_{n-1})$$

...(12·32*a*)

12·9·1. Independent Events. Events are said to be independent of each other if happening of any one of them is not affected by and does not affect the happening of any one of the others.

If A and B are independent events so that the probability of occurrence or non-occurrence of A is not affected by occurrence or non-occurrence of B, then we have

$$P(A \mid B) = P(A) \quad \text{and} \quad P(B \mid A) = P(B) \qquad \ldots(12·33)$$

12·9·2. Multiplication Theorem for Independent Events. *Two events A and B are independent if and only if*

$$P(A \cap B) = P(A) \cdot P(B) \qquad \ldots(12·34)$$

i.e., if the probability of the simultaneous happening of two events is equal to the product of their individual probabilities.

Proof. For two events A and B, we have

$$P(A \cap B) = P(A) \cdot P(B \mid A) = P(B) \cdot P(A \mid B) \qquad \ldots(*)$$

If Part. If A and B are independent, then

$$P(A \mid B) = P(A) \quad \text{and} \quad P(B \mid A) = P(B) \qquad \ldots(**)$$

Substituting in (*), we get

$$P(A \cap B) = P(A) \cdot P(B)$$

Only if Part. If (12·34) holds, then using (*), we get

$$P(B \mid A) = P(B) \quad \text{and} \quad P(A \mid B) = P(A)$$

$\Rightarrow$ A and B are independent.

Hence, $$P(A \cap B) = P(A) \cdot P(B), \qquad \ldots(12·34a)$$

provides a necessary and sufficient condition for the independence of two events A and B.

By this we mean that if A and B are independent events, then (12·34) holds and conversely, if (12·34) holds, then A and B are independent events.

Generalisation. The result in (12·34) can be generalised to more than two events.

The n events $A_1, A_2, A_3, \ldots, A_n$ *are independent if and only if*

$$P(A_1 \cap A_2 \cap A_3 \cap \ldots \cap A_n) = P(A_1) \cdot P(A_2) \cdot P(A_3) \ldots P(A_n) \qquad \ldots(12·35)$$

i.e., the probability of the simultaneous happening of n events is equal to the product of the probabilities of their individual happenings.

We shall now give below some results in the form of theorems, which will be frequently used in the solution of numerical problems

Theorem 12·12. $P(\bar{A}) = 1 - P(A) \Rightarrow P(A) + P(\bar{A}) = 1$ ...(12·36)

Theorem 12·13. (*i*) $P(\bar{A} \cap B) = P(B) - P(A \cap B)$ ...(12·37)

(*ii*) $P(A \cap \bar{B}) = P(A) - P(A \cap B)$ ...(12·38)

Remark. We know that for every event E, $P(E) \geq 0$. Hence from (12·37), we get

$$P(B) - P(A \cap B) = P(\bar{A} \cap B) \geq 0 \quad \Rightarrow \quad P(B) \geq P(A \cap B) \quad \Rightarrow \quad P(A \cap B) \leq P(B) \quad \ldots(12\cdot39)$$

Similarly from (12·38), we get

$$P(A) - P(A \cap B) = P(A \cap \bar{B}) \geq 0 \quad \Rightarrow \quad P(A) \geq P(A \cap B) \quad \Rightarrow \quad P(A \cap B) \leq P(A) \quad \ldots(12\cdot40)$$

Theorem 12·14. If $A \subset B$, then $P(A) \leq P(B)$ ...(12·41)

Remark. The results in (12·39) and (12·40) can be immediately deduced from (12·41), since

$$A \cap B \subset A \quad \text{and} \quad A \cap B \subset B.$$

Theorem 12·15. *If events A and B are independent then the events*

(*i*) A and $\bar{B}$ are independent; (*ii*) $\bar{A}$ and B are independent ; (*iii*) $\bar{A}$ and $\bar{B}$ are independent.

Proof. Since the events A and B are independent, we have

$$P(A \cap B) = P(A)\, P(B) \quad \ldots(*)$$

(*i*)
$$\begin{aligned} P(A \cap \bar{B}) &= P(A) - P(A \cap B) \\ &= P(A) - P(A)\, P(B) \quad \text{[From (*)]} \\ &= P(A)\left[1 - P(B)\right] \\ &= P(A)\, P(\bar{B}) \end{aligned}$$

$\Rightarrow$ A and $\bar{B}$ are independent.

(*ii*)
$$\begin{aligned} P(\bar{A} \cap B) &= P(B) - P(A \cap B) \\ &= P(B) - P(A)\, P(B) \quad \text{[From (*)]} \\ &= P(B)\left[1 - P(A)\right] \\ &= P(B)\,.\, P(\bar{A}) \end{aligned}$$

$\Rightarrow$ $\bar{A}$ and B are independent.

(*iii*)
$$\begin{aligned} P(\bar{A} \cap \bar{B}) &= 1 - P(A \cup B) \\ &= 1 - \left[P(A) + P(B) - P(A \cap B)\right] \\ &= 1 - P(A) - P(B) + P(A)\, P(B) \quad \text{[Using (*)]} \\ &= \left[1 - P(A)\right] - P(B)\left[1 - P(A)\right] \\ &= \left[1 - P(A)\right]\left[1 - P(B)\right] \\ &= P(\bar{A})\,.\, P(\bar{B}) \end{aligned}$$

$\Rightarrow$ $\bar{A}$ and $\bar{B}$ are independent events.

Theorem. 12·16. *If* $A_1, \ldots, A_2, \ldots, A_n$ *are independent events with respective probabilities of occurrence* $p_1, p_2, \ldots, p_n$ *then the probability of occurrence of at least one of them is given by* :

$$P(A_1 \cup A_2 \cup \ldots \cup A_n) = 1 - (1 - p_1)(1 - p_2) \ldots (1 - p_n) \quad \ldots(12\cdot42)$$

Proof. We are given :

$$P(A_i) = p_i \quad \Rightarrow \quad P(\bar{A}_i) = 1 - p_i \quad \ldots(i)$$

We know that for any event E, $\quad P(E) + P(\bar{E}) = 1 \quad \ldots(ii)$

Taking $E = A_1 \cup A_2 \cup \ldots \cup A_n$ in (*ii*), we get

$$P(A_1 \cup A_2 \cup \ldots \cup A_n) + P(A_1 \cup A_2 \cup \ldots \cup A_n)^c = 1$$

$$\Rightarrow \quad P(A_1 \cup A_2 \cup \ldots \cup A_n) + P(\bar{A}_1 \cap \bar{A}_2 \cap \ldots \cap \bar{A}_n) = 1 \quad \ldots(12\cdot43)$$

[By De-Morgan's law of complementation, *i.e.*, the complement of the *union* of sets is equal to the *intersection of their complements*].

$$\begin{aligned} \Rightarrow \quad P(A_1 \cup A_2 \cup \ldots \cup A_n) &= 1 - P(\bar{A}_1 \cap \bar{A}_2 \cap \ldots \cap \bar{A}_n) \quad \ldots(12\cdot44) \\ &= 1 - P(\bar{A}_1)\, P(\bar{A}_2) \ldots P(\bar{A}_n), \end{aligned}$$

by compound probability theorem, since, $A_1, A_2, \ldots, A_n$ and consequently $\bar{A}_1, \bar{A}_2, \ldots, \bar{A}_n$ are independent [c.f. Theorem 12·15]. Hence substituting from (*i*), we get

$$P(A_1 \cup A_2 \cup \ldots \cup A_n) = 1 - (1-p_1)(1-p_2)\ldots(1-p_n)$$

Remark. The results in (12·43) and (12·44) are very important and are used quite often in numerical problems. Result (12·43) stated in words gives :

$$P\{\text{Happening of at least one of the events } A_1, A_2, \ldots, A_n\}$$
$$= 1 - P\{\text{None of the events } A_1, A_2, \ldots, A_n \text{ happens}\} \quad \ldots(12\cdot45)$$

or Equivalently,

$$P\{\text{None of the given events happens}\}$$
$$= 1 - P\{\text{At least one of them happens}\} \quad \ldots(12\cdot45a)$$

We shall now discuss numerical problems, explaining the use of addition and multiplication theorems of probability.

Example 12·16. *Let E denote the experiment of tossing a coin three times in succession. Construct the sample space S. Write down the elements of the two events E_1 and E_2, where E_1 is the event that the number of heads exceeds the number of tails and E_2 is the event of getting head in the first trial. Find the probabilities $P(E_1)$ and $P(E_2)$, assuming that all the elements of S are equally likely to occur.*

Solution. The sample space S in a random experiment of "tossing a coin three times in succession", is given by : (H = Head ; T = Tail).

$$S = \{H, T\} \times \{H, T\} \times \{H, T\}$$
$$= \{H, T\} \times \{HH, HT, TH, TT\}$$
$$= \{HHH, HHT, HTH, HTT, THH, THT, TTH, TTT\}$$

The number of elements in the sample space, *i.e.*, the exhaustive number of cases is given by $n(S) = 8$.

The event E_1 : "Number of heads exceeds the number of tails" in a random toss of 3 coins means we should get at least two heads, *i.e.*, two heads and one tail; or all three heads. Thus the sample points of E_1 are :

$$E_1 = \{HHH, \quad HHT, \quad HTH, \quad THH\} \quad \text{and} \quad n(E_1) = 4$$

Similarly, the event E_2 : "Getting head in the first trial" is given by :

$$E_2 = \{HHH, \quad HHT, \quad HTH, \quad HTT\} \quad \text{and} \quad n(E_2) = 4$$

If we assume that all the elements of S are equally likely to occur then

$$P(E_1) = \frac{n(E_1)}{n(S)} = \frac{4}{8} = \frac{1}{2} \quad \text{and} \quad P(E_2) = \frac{n(E_2)}{n(S)} = \frac{4}{8} = \frac{1}{2}.$$

Example 12·17. *A committee of 4 persons is to be appointed from 3 officers of the production department, 4 officers of the purchase department, two officers of the sales department and 1 chartered accountant. Find the probability of forming the committee in the following manner :*

(*i*) *There must be one from each category*

(*ii*) *It should have at least one from the purchase department*

(*iii*) *The chartered accountant must be in the committee.*

Solution. There are in all 3 + 4 + 2 + 1 = 10 people. A committee of 4 can be formed out of these 10 people in $^{10}C_4$ ways. Hence the exhaustive number of cases is :

$$^{10}C_4 = \frac{10 \times 9 \times 8 \times 7}{4\,!} = 210$$

(*i*) The number of favourable cases for the committee to consist of one member from each category (Production, Purchase, Sales & C.A.) is :

$$^3C_1 \times {}^4C_1 \times {}^2C_1 \times {}^1C_1 = 3 \times 4 \times 2 \times 1 = 24$$

$$\therefore \quad \text{Required probability} = \frac{24}{210} = \frac{4}{35} = 0{\cdot}1143$$

(*ii*) The probability 'p' that the committee of 4 has at least one member from the purchase department is given by :

$$p = P[1 \text{ from purchase department and 3 others}] + P[2 \text{ from purchase department and 2 others}]$$
$$+ P[3 \text{ from purchase department and 1 other}] + P[4 \text{ from purchase department}]$$
$$= \frac{^4C_1 \times {^6C_3}}{^{10}C_4} + \frac{^4C_2 \times {^6C_2}}{^{10}C_4} + \frac{^4C_3 \times {^6C_1}}{^{10}C_4} + \frac{^4C_4}{^{10}C_4}$$
$$= \frac{1}{210}\left[4 \times \frac{6 \times 5 \times 4}{3\,!} + \frac{4 \times 3}{2\,!} \times \frac{6 \times 5}{2\,!} + 4 \times 6 + 1\right]$$
$$= \frac{1}{210}\left(80 + 90 + 24 + 1\right) = \frac{195}{210} = 0{\cdot}9286$$

(*ii*) **Aliter.**

$$p = 1 - P\,[\text{There is no person from purchase department}] = 1 - \frac{^6C_4}{^{10}C_4}$$

[Because all the four persons must be selected from production and sales deptts. and C.A.]

$$= 1 - \frac{6 \times 5 \times 4 \times 3}{10 \times 9 \times 8 \times 7} = 1 - \frac{1}{14} = \frac{13}{14} = 0{\cdot}9286.$$

(*iii*) The probability p_1 that the chartered accountant must be in the committee of 4 is given by :

$$p_1 = P\,[\text{Chartered Accountant and 3 others}] = \frac{^1C_1 \times {^9C_3}}{^{10}C_4}$$
$$= \frac{9 \times 8 \times 7}{3\,!} \times \frac{4\,!}{10 \times 9 \times 8 \times 7} = \frac{4}{10} = 0{\cdot}4.$$

Example 12·18. *A committee of four has to be formed from among 3 economists, 4 engineers, 2 statisticians and 1 doctor.*

(*i*) *What is the probability that each of the four professions is represented on the committee ?*

(*ii*) *What is the probability that the committee consists of the doctor and at least one economist ?*

Solution. There are $3 + 4 + 2 + 1 = 10$ members in all and a committee of 4 out of them can be formed in $^{10}C_4$ ways. Hence exhaustive number of cases is :

$$^{10}C_4 = \frac{10 \times 9 \times 8 \times 7}{4\,!} = 210$$

(*i*) Favourable number of cases for the committee to consist of members, one of each profession is :

$$^3C_1 \times {^4C_1} \times {^2C_1} \times 1 = 3 \times 4 \times 2 = 24$$

$\therefore$ Required probability $= \frac{24}{210} = \frac{4}{35} = 0{\cdot}1143$

(*ii*) The probability 'p' that the committee consists of the doctor and at least one economist is given by

$$p = P\,[\text{One doctor, one economist, 2 others}] + P[\text{One doctor, two economists, 1 other}]$$
$$+ P\,[\text{One doctor, 3 economists}]$$
$$= \frac{^1C_1 \times {^3C_1} \times {^6C_2}}{^{10}C_4} + \frac{^1C_1 \times {^3C_2} \times {^6C_1}}{^{10}C_4} + \frac{^1C_1 \times {^3C_3}}{^{10}C_4} = \frac{1}{210}\left[1 \times 3 \times \frac{6 \times 5}{2} + 1 \times 3 \times 6 + 1 \times 1\right]$$
$$= \frac{1}{210}\left(45 + 18 + 1\right) = \frac{64}{210} = \frac{32}{105} = 0{\cdot}3048$$

Example 12·19. *A card is drawn from a well shuffled pack of playing cards. Find the probability that it is either a diamond or a king.*

Solution. Let A denote the event of drawing a diamond and B denote the event of drawing a king from a pack of cards. Then we have

$$P(A) = \frac{13}{52} = \frac{1}{4} \quad \text{and} \quad P(B) = \frac{4}{52} = \frac{1}{13} \quad \text{and we want } P(A \cup B).$$

$$P(A \cup B) = P(A) + P(B) - P(A \cap B) = \frac{1}{4} + \frac{1}{13} - P(A \cap B) \qquad \ldots(*)$$

There is only one case favourable to the event $A \cap B$ *viz.*, king of diamond. Hence, $P(A \cap B) = \frac{1}{52}$

Substituting in (*), we get

$$P(A \cup B) = \tfrac{1}{4} + \tfrac{1}{13} - \tfrac{1}{52} = \frac{13+4-1}{52} = \frac{16}{52} = \frac{4}{13}$$

Example 12·20. *If $P(A) = 0{\cdot}4$, $P(B) = 0.7$ and P (at least one of A and B) = 0.8, find P(only one of A and B).* [*I.C.W.A. (Intermediate), Dec. 1998*]

Solution. We are given : $P(A) = 0.4,\ P(B) = 0.7$ and $P(A \cup B) = 0.8.$ ...(*)

The event "only one of A and B", can materialise in the following mutually disjoint ways :

(*i*) A and not B *i.e.*, $A \cap \bar{B}$ (*ii*) Not A and B *i.e.*, $\bar{A} \cap B$.

Hence the required probability is given by :

$$\begin{aligned} p &= P\ [\text{Only one of } A \text{ and } B] \\ &= P\ (i) + P\ (ii) = P(\bar{A} \cap B) + P\ (A \cap \bar{B}) \\ &= P(B) - P\ (A \cap B) + P(A) - P(A \cap B) \\ &= 0.7 + 0.4 - 2\ P(A \cap B) \end{aligned} \quad ...(**)$$

We have $P(A \cup B) = P(A) + P(B) - P(A \cap B)$

$\Rightarrow \quad P(A \cap B) = P(A) + P(B) - P(A \cup B) = 0.4 + 0.7 - 0.8 = 0.3$ [From (*)] ...(***)

Substituting in (**), we get : $p = 0.7 + 0.4 - 2 \times 0.3 = 0.5$

Aliter.

$$\begin{aligned} p &= P\ [\text{Only one of } A \text{ and } B] = P[\text{At least one of } A \text{ and } B] - P[\text{Both } A \text{ and } B] \\ &= P(A \cup B) - P(A \cap B) = 0.8 - 0.3 = 0.5 \end{aligned}$$

Example 12·21. (*a*) *Choose the correct alternative :*

"For two equally likely, exhaustive and independent events A and B, P(AB) is :
(i) 0, (ii) 0.25, (iii) 0.50, (iv) 1. [*I.C.W.A. (Intermediate), June 1999*]

(*b*) *Comment on the following :*

A and B are two events such that

$$P(A) = \frac{1}{4},\quad P(B) = \frac{1}{3},\quad P\ (A \cup B) = \frac{1}{2}\cdot \textit{Hence}\ \ P(B|A) = \frac{1}{5}\cdot$$ [*Delhi Univ. B.Com. (Hons.), 2009*]

Solution. (*a*) Since A and B are equally likely, $P\ (A) = P(B) = p$, (say). ...(*i*)

Further, since A and B are given to be exhaustive, $P(A) + P(B) = 1 \Rightarrow p + p = 1 \Rightarrow p = \frac{1}{2}$

$$\therefore \quad P\ (A) = P(B) = \tfrac{1}{2}$$

Since A and B are independent also, $P\ (A \cap B) = P\ (A)\ P(B) = \frac{1}{2} \times \frac{1}{2} = \frac{1}{4} = 0{\cdot}25$

$\therefore$ (*ii*) is the correct alternative.

(*b*) $P(A \cup B) = P(A) + P(B) - P(A \cap B) \Rightarrow P(A \cap B) = P(A) + P(B) - P(A \cup B) = \frac{1}{4} + \frac{1}{3} - \frac{1}{2} = \frac{3+4-6}{12} = \frac{1}{12}$

$$\therefore \quad P(B \mid A) = \frac{P(A \cap B)}{P(A)} = \frac{1/(12)}{1/4} = \frac{1}{3}$$

Hence, the given data are inconsistent.

Example 12·22. *Let A and B be the two possible outcomes of an experiment and suppose*

$$P(A) = 0{\cdot}4, \qquad P\ (A \cup B) = 0{\cdot}7 \qquad \textit{and} \qquad P(B) = p$$

(i) For what choice of p are A and B mutually exclusive?

(ii) For what choice of p are A and B independent ?

Solution. (*i*) We have $P(A \cup B) = P(A) + P(B) - P(A \cap B)$

$\therefore \quad P(A \cap B) = P(A) + P(B) - P(A \cup B) = 0{\cdot}4 + p - 0{\cdot}7 = p - 0{\cdot}3$

If A and B are mutually exclusive, then

$$P(A \cap B) = 0 \quad \Rightarrow \quad p - 0{\cdot}3 = 0 \quad \Rightarrow \quad p = 0{\cdot}3$$

(*ii*) A and B are independent if and only if $P(A \cap B) = P(A) \,.\, P(B)$

$$\Rightarrow \quad p - 0{\cdot}3 = (0{\cdot}4) \times p \quad \Rightarrow \quad (1 - 0{\cdot}4)p = 0{\cdot}3 \quad \Rightarrow \quad 0{\cdot}6p = 0{\cdot}3 \quad \Rightarrow \quad p = \frac{0{\cdot}3}{0{\cdot}6} = 0{\cdot}5.$$

Example 12·23. *Prove the following :*

(*i*) *If* $P(A \mid B) \geq P(A)$ *then* $P(B \mid A) \geq P(B)$.

(*ii*) *If* $P(B \mid \bar{A}) = P(B \mid A)$, *then A and B are independent events.*

[*Delhi Univ. B.A. (Econ. Hons.), 2005*]

Solution. (*i*) $P(A \mid B) \geq P(A)$ (Given) $\Rightarrow \dfrac{P(A \cap B)}{P(B)} \geq P(A) \Rightarrow P(A \cap B) \geq P(A) \cdot P(B)$ ...(*)

$$\therefore \quad P(B \mid A) = \frac{P(A \cap B)}{P(A)} \geq \frac{P(A)\,P(B)}{P(A)} \text{ [From (*)]} \quad \Rightarrow \quad P(B \mid A) \geq P(B).$$

(*ii*) $P(B \mid \bar{A}) = P(B \mid A)$ [Given] $\Rightarrow \dfrac{P(\bar{A} \cap B)}{P(\bar{A})} = \dfrac{P(A \cap B)}{P(A)} \Rightarrow \dfrac{P(B) - P(A \cap B)}{1 - P(A)} = \dfrac{P(A \cap B)}{P(A)}$

Cross multiplying and transposing, we get

$$P(A) \cdot P(B) - P(A) \cdot P(A \cap B) = P(A \cap B) - P(A) \cdot P(A \cap B)$$

$$\Rightarrow \quad P(A) \cdot P(B) = P(A \cap B) \Rightarrow A \text{ and } B \text{ are independent.}$$

Example 12·24. *A Chartered Accountant applies for a job in two firms X and Y. He estimates that the probability of his being selected in firm X is 0·7, and being rejected at Y is 0·5 and the probability of at least one of his applications being rejected is 0·6. What is the probability that he will be selected in one of the two firms ?* [*C.A. PEE-1, Nov. 2003*]

Solution. Let A and B denote the events that the chartered accountant is selected in firms X and Y respectively. Then in the usual notations, we are given

$$P(A) = 0{\cdot}7 \Rightarrow P(\bar{A}) = 1 - 0{\cdot}7 = 0{\cdot}3 \quad ; \quad P(\bar{B}) = 0{\cdot}5 \Rightarrow P(B) = 1 - 0{\cdot}5 = 0{\cdot}5 \qquad ...(*)$$

and $\quad P(\bar{A} \cup \bar{B}) = 0{\cdot}6$ ...(**)

We know (By De-Morgan's law)

$$\overline{A \cap B} = \bar{A} \cup \bar{B}$$

$$\therefore \quad P(A \cap B) = 1 - P(\overline{A \cap B}) = 1 - P(\bar{A} \cup \bar{B}) = 1 - 0{\cdot}6 = 0{\cdot}4 \quad \text{[From (**)]} \quad ...(***)$$

The probability that the chartered accountant will be selected in one of the two firms X or Y is given by :

$$P(A \cup B) = P(A) + P(B) - P(A \cap B) = 0{\cdot}7 + 0{\cdot}5 - 0{\cdot}4 = 0{\cdot}8 \quad \text{[From (*) and (***)]}$$

Example 12·25. *Probability that a man will be alive 25 years hence is 0·3 and the probability that his wife will be alive 25 years hence is 0·4. Find the probability that 25 years hence*

(*i*) *both will be alive,* (*ii*) *only the man will be alive,* (*iii*) *only the woman will be alive,*
(*iv*) *none will be alive.* (*v*) *at least one of them will be alive.*

Solution. Let us define the following events :

A : The man will be alive 25 years hence ; B : His wife will be alive 25 years hence.

We are given $P(A) = 0{\cdot}3$ and $P(B) = 0{\cdot}4$.

(*i*) The probability that 25 years hence, both man and his wife will be alive is

$$P(A \cap B) = P(A) \,.\, P(B) = 0{\cdot}3 \times 0{\cdot}4 = 0{\cdot}12 \qquad [\because A \text{ and } B \text{ are independent}]$$

(*ii*) The probability that 25 years hence, only the man will be alive is

$$P(A \cap \bar{B}) = P(A) - P(A \cap B) = 0{\cdot}30 - 0{\cdot}12 = 0{\cdot}18 \qquad [\text{From Part } (i)]$$

(*iii*) The probability that only the woman will be alive 25 years hence is

$$P(\bar{A} \cap B) = P(B) - P(A \cap B) = 0{\cdot}40 - 0{\cdot}12 = 0{\cdot}28 \qquad [\text{From Part } (i)]$$

(*iv*) $P[\text{None will be alive}] = P(\bar{A} \cap \bar{B})$

$$= P(\bar{A})\, P(\bar{B}) = (1 - 0{\cdot}3)\,(1 - 0{\cdot}4) = 0{\cdot}42 \qquad [\because A \text{ and } B \text{ are independent}]$$

(*v*) The probability 'p' that 25 years hence, at least one of them will be alive is

$$p = 1 - P(\text{None will be alive}) = 1 - 0{\cdot}42 = 0{\cdot}58 \qquad [\text{From Part } (iv)]$$

Aliter. Required probability is :

$$P(A \cup B) = P(A) + P(B) - P(A \cap B) = P(A) + P(B) - P(A)\,.\,P(B)$$
$$= 0{\cdot}3 + 0{\cdot}4 - 0{\cdot}3 \times 0{\cdot}4 = 0{\cdot}70 - 0{\cdot}12 = 0{\cdot}58$$

Example 12·26. *The probability that a contractor will get a plumbing contract is 2 / 3, and the probability that he will not get an electric contract is 5 / 9. If the probability of getting at least one contract is 4/5, what is the probability that he will get both the contracts ?*

Solution. Let A and B denote the events that the contractor will get a 'plumbing' contract and 'electric' contract respectively. Then we are given :

$$P(A) = \tfrac{2}{3} \;;\quad P(\bar{B}) = \tfrac{5}{9} \quad \Rightarrow \quad P(B) = 1 - P(\bar{B}) = \tfrac{4}{9}$$

and $\quad P(A \cup B) = \text{Probability that contractor gets at least one contract} = 4/5$

$$\Rightarrow \quad P(A) + P(B) - P(A \cap B) = \tfrac{4}{5} \qquad [\text{By addition theorem of probability}]$$

$$\therefore \quad \tfrac{2}{3} + \tfrac{4}{9} - P(A \cap B) = \tfrac{4}{5} \quad \Rightarrow \quad P(A \cap B) = \tfrac{2}{3} + \tfrac{4}{9} - \tfrac{4}{5} = \frac{30 + 20 - 36}{45} = \frac{14}{45}$$

Hence, the probability that the contractor will get both the contracts is 14 / 45.

Example 12·27. *A problem in statistics is given to two students A and B. The odds in favour of A solving the problem are 6 to 9 and against B solving the problem are 12 to 10. If both A and B attempt, find the probability of the problem being solved.* [*Delhi Univ. B.Com., (Hons.), 2000*]

Solution. Let us define the events :

E_1 : A solves the problem ; E_2 : B solves the problem.

Then we are given :

$$P(E_1) = \frac{6}{6+9} = \frac{6}{15} = \frac{2}{5} \quad \text{and} \quad P(E_2) = \frac{10}{10+12} = \frac{5}{11} \qquad \ldots(i)$$

Assuming that A and B try to solve the problem independently, E_1 and E_2 are independent.

$$\therefore \quad P(E_1 \cap E_2) = P(E_1)\,P(E_2) = \tfrac{2}{5} \times \tfrac{5}{11} = \tfrac{2}{11} \qquad \ldots(ii)$$

The problem will be solved if at least one of the students A and B solves the problem. Hence, the probability of the problem being solved is given by :

$$P(E_1 \cup E_2) = P(E_1) + P(E_2) - P(E_1 \cap E_2)$$
$$= \tfrac{2}{5} + \tfrac{5}{11} - \tfrac{2}{11} = \frac{22 + 25 - 10}{55} = \frac{37}{55} = 0{\cdot}673 \qquad [\text{From } (i) \text{ and } (ii)]$$

OR $\quad P(E_1 \cup E_2) = 1 - P(\bar{E}_1 \cap \bar{E}_2) = 1 - P(\bar{E}_1) \cdot P\bar{E}_2) \qquad [\because E_1 \text{ and } E_2 \text{ are independent}]$

$$= 1 - \left(1 - \tfrac{2}{5}\right)\left(1 - \tfrac{5}{11}\right) = 1 - \tfrac{3}{5} \times \tfrac{6}{11} = \tfrac{37}{55}\cdot$$

Example 12·28. *A problem in Statistics is given to three students A, B and C whose chances of solving it are $\frac{1}{3}$, $\frac{1}{4}$ and $\frac{1}{5}$ respectively. Find the probability that the problem will be solved if they all try independently.*

Solution. Let E_1, E_2 and E_3 denote the events that the problem is solved by A, B and C respectively. Then we have

$$P(E_1)=\frac{1}{3} \quad ; \quad P(E_2)=\frac{1}{4} \quad ; \quad P(E_3)=\frac{1}{5}$$

$$P(\bar{E}_1)=1-P(E_1)=\frac{2}{3} \quad ; \quad P(\bar{E}_2)=1-P(E_2)=\frac{3}{4} \quad ; \quad P(\bar{E}_3)=1-P(E_3)=\frac{4}{5}$$

Problem will be solved if at least one of the three is able to solve it. Hence, the required probability that the poblem will be solved is given by :

$$P(E_1 \cup E_2 \cup E_3 = 1 - P(\bar{E}_1 \cap \bar{E}_2 \cap \bar{E}_3) = 1 - P(\bar{E}_1) \,.\, P(\bar{E}_2) \,.\, P(\bar{E}_3)$$

[By compound probability theorem since E_1, E_2 and E_3 are independent].

$$= 1 - \frac{2}{3} \times \frac{3}{4} \times \frac{4}{5} = 1 - \frac{2}{5} = \frac{3}{5}.$$

Example 12·29. *Find the probability of throwing 6 at least once in six throws with a single die.*

Solution. Let E_i $(i = 1, 2, \ldots, 6)$ denote the event of getting a 6 in the ith throw of a single die. Then

$$P(E_i)=\frac{1}{6} \quad \Rightarrow \quad P(\bar{E}_i)=\frac{5}{6} \quad ; (i = 1, 2, \ldots, 6)$$

The probability that in six throws of a single die, we get 6 at least once is given by :

$$P(E_1 \cup E_2 \cup E_3 \cup E_4 \cup E_5 \cup E_6) = 1 - P(\bar{E}_1 \cap \bar{E}_2 \cap \bar{E}_3 \cap \bar{E}_4 \cap \bar{E}_5 \cap \bar{E}_6)$$

$$= 1 - P(\bar{E}_1) \,.\, P(\bar{E}_2) \,.\, P(\bar{E}_3) \,.\, P(\bar{E}_4) \,.\, P(\bar{E}_5) \,.\, P(\bar{E}_6)$$

[$\because$ $E_1, E_2, \ldots, E_6$ and consequently $\bar{E}_1, \bar{E}_2, \ldots, \bar{E}_6$ are independent, since the throws of the die are independent].

$$= 1 - \left(\frac{5}{6}\right)^6.$$

Example 12·30. *The odds that A speaks the truth are 3 : 2 and the odds that B speaks the truth are 5 : 3. In what percentage of cases are they likely to contradict each other on an identical point ?*

Solution. Let us define the events : E_1 : A speaks the truth ; E_2 : B speaks the truth.

Then $\bar{E}_1$ and $\bar{E}_2$ represent the complementary events that A and B tell a lie respectively. We are given :

$$P(E_1)=\frac{3}{3+2}=\frac{3}{5} \quad \Rightarrow \quad P(\bar{E}_1)=1-\frac{3}{5}=\frac{2}{5} \quad ; \quad P(E_2)=\frac{5}{5+3}=\frac{5}{8} \quad \Rightarrow \quad P(\bar{E}_2)=1-\frac{5}{8}=\frac{3}{8}$$

The event E that A and B contradict each other on an identical point can happen in the following mutually exclusive ways :

(*i*) A speaks the truth and B tells a lie *i.e.*, the event $E_1 \cap \bar{E}_2$ happens.

(*ii*) A tells a lie and B speaks the truth *i.e.*, the event $\bar{E}_1 \cap E_2$ happens.

Hence by addition theorem of probability :

$$P(E) = P(i) + P(ii) = P(E_1 \cap \bar{E}_2) + P(\bar{E}_1 \cap E_2)$$

$$= P(E_1) \,.\, P(\bar{E}_2) + P(\bar{E}_1) \,.\, P(E_2),$$

[By compound probability theorem, since E_1 and E_2 are independent]

$$\therefore \quad P(E) = \frac{3}{5} \times \frac{3}{8} + \frac{2}{5} \times \frac{5}{8} = \frac{9+10}{40} = \frac{19}{40} = 0{\cdot}475$$

Hence, A and B contradict each other on an identical point in 47·5% of the cases.

Example 12·31. *Three groups of children contain respectively 3 girls and 1 boy; 2 girls and 2 boys; 1 girl and 3 boys. One child is selected at random from each group. Show that the chance that the three selected consist of 1 girl and 2 boys is 13 / 32.*

Solution. Let B_1, B_2 and B_3 be the events of drawing a boy from the 1st, 2nd and 3rd group respectively and G_1, G_2 and G_3 be the events of drawing a girl from the 1st, 2nd, and 3rd group respectively, then

$$P(B_1)=\frac{1}{4}, \quad P(B_2)=\frac{2}{4}, \quad P(B_3)=\frac{3}{4} \quad ; \quad \text{and} \quad P(G_1)=\frac{3}{4}, \quad P(G_2)=\frac{2}{4}, \quad P(G_3)=\frac{1}{4}.$$

The required event of getting 1 girl and 2 boys in a random selection of 3 children can materialise in the following mutually exclusive cases :

(*i*) Girl from the first group and boys from the 2nd and 3rd groups *i.e.*, the event $G_1 \cap B_2 \cap B_3$ happens.

(*ii*) Girl from the 2nd group and boys from the 1st and 3rd groups *i.e.*, the event $B_1 \cap G_2 \cap B_3$ happens.

(*iii*) Girl from the 3rd group and boys from the 1st and 2nd groups *i.e.*, the event $B_1 \cap B_2 \cap G_3$ happens.

Hence, by the addition theorem of probability, required probability p is given by :

$$p = P(i) + P(ii) + P(iii)$$
$$= P(G_1 \cap B_2 \cap B_3) + P(B_1 \cap G_2 \cap B_3) + P(B_1 \cap B_2 \cap G_3)$$
$$= P(G_1)\,P(B_2)\,P(B_3) + P(B_1)\,P(G_2)\,P(B_3) + P(B_1)\,P(B_2)\,P(G_3)$$

(Since, the selections from the three groups are independent.)

$$= \frac{3}{4}\times\frac{2}{4}\times\frac{3}{4} + \frac{1}{4}\times\frac{2}{4}\times\frac{3}{4} + \frac{1}{4}\times\frac{2}{4}\times\frac{1}{4} = \frac{18+6+2}{64} = \frac{26}{64} = \frac{13}{32}$$

Example 12·32. *The probability that a management trainee will remain with a company is 0·60. The probability that an employee earns more than Rs. 10,000 per month is 0·50. The probability that an employee is a management trainee who remained with the company or who earns more than Rs. 10,000 per month is 0·70. What is the probability that an employee earns more than Rs. 10,000 per month, given that he is a management trainee who stayed with the company ?*

Solution. Let us define the events :

A : A management trainee will remain with the company

B : An employee earns more than Rs. 10,000 per month.

Then we are given : $\quad P(A) = 0{\cdot}60 \quad$ and $\quad P(B) = 0{\cdot}50$

Further, we are given :

P [A management trainee remains with the company *or* earns more than Rs. 10,000 per month] = 0·70.

$$\Rightarrow \quad P(A \cup B) = 0{\cdot}7$$
$$\Rightarrow \quad P(A) + P(B) - P(A \cap B) = 0{\cdot}7$$
$$\Rightarrow \quad P(A \cap B) = P(A) + P(B) - 0{\cdot}7 = 0{\cdot}6 + 0{\cdot}5 - 0{\cdot}7 = 0{\cdot}4$$

$$\text{Required probability } = P(B \mid A) = \frac{P(A \cap B)}{P(A)} = \frac{0{\cdot}4}{0{\cdot}6} = \frac{2}{3}.$$

Example 12·33. *Two factories manufacture the same machine parts. Each part is classified as having either 0, 1, 2 or 3 manufacturing defects. The joint probability for this is given in the adjoining Table.*

Manufacturer	Number of Defects			
	0	*1*	*2*	*3*
X	*0·1250*	*0·0625*	*0·1875*	*0·1250*
Y	*0·0625*	*0·0625*	*0·1250*	*0·2500*

(i) A part is observed to have no defect. What is the probability that it was produced by X manufacturer ?

(ii) A part is known to have been produced by manufacturer X. What is the probability that the part has no defects ?

(iii) A part is known to have two or more defects. What is the probability that it was manufactured by X ?

(iv) A part is known to have one or more defects. What is the probability that it was manufactured by Y ? [Delhi Univ. B.Com. (Hons.), 2008]

Solution. Let D denote the number of defects observed in the manufactured part.

Joint Probability Distribution

Manufacturer	*Number of Defects (D)* 0	1	2	3	*Total*
X	0·1250	0·0625	0·1875	0·1250	$p_1(X) = 0·5$
Y	0·0625	0·0625	0·1250	0·2500	$p_2(Y) = 0·5$
Total p (D)	0·1875	0·1250	0·3125	0·3750	1·0

(i) P [Part produced by X | No defect] $= \dfrac{P(X \cap D = 0)}{P(D = 0)} = \dfrac{0·1250}{0·1875} = 0·6667$

(ii) $P[D = 0 \mid X] = \dfrac{P(D = 0 \cap X)}{p_1(X)} = \dfrac{0·1250}{0·5} = 0·25$

(iii) $P[X \mid D \geq 2] = \dfrac{P[X \cap D \geq 2]}{P(D \geq 2)} = \dfrac{0·1875 + 0·1250}{0·3125 + 0·3750} = \dfrac{0·3125}{0·6875} = 0·4545$

(iv) $P[Y \mid D \geq 1] = \dfrac{P[Y \cap D \geq 1]}{P(D \geq 1)} = \dfrac{0·0625 + 0·1250 + 0·2500}{0·1250 + 0·3125 + 0·3750} = \dfrac{0·4375}{0·8125} = 0·5385$

Example 12·34. *We have data from 100 economists in academics, private sector, and government, concerning their opinions whether the economy would be stable, expand or contract in the near future. However, a part of the information was lost. Based on remaining data, you are required to create a probability table.*

Economists	*Economy* *Stable (S)*	*Expanding (E)*	*Contracting (C)*	*Total*
Academics (A)	25		20	
Private Sector (R)		7		22
Government (G)	5	8		13
	40			

From the given table find :

(i) P(A) ; (ii) P(E) ; (iii) P(A ∩ E) ; (iv) P(G ∩ C) ; (v) P (E | G) ; (vi) P (G | E).

[Delhi Univ. B.A. (Econ. Hons.), 2006]

Solution. The completed probability table is given below :

PROBABILITY TABLE

Economists	*Economy* *Stable (S)*	*Expanding (E)*	*Contracting (C)*	*Total*
Academics (A)	**25**	65 – 25 – 20 = 20	**20**	100 – 22 – 13 = 65
Private Sector (R)	40 – 25 – 5 = 10	**7**	22 – 10 – 7 = 5	**22**
Government (G)	**5**	**8**	13 – 5 – 8 = 0	**13**
	40	20 + 7 + 8 = 35	100 – 40 – 35 = 25	**100**

Note. Figures in bold are the given figures.

From the probability table, we get

(i) $P(A) = \dfrac{65}{100} = 0·65$ (ii) $P(E) = \dfrac{35}{100} = 0·35$

(iii) $P(A \cap E) = P(A) \cdot P(E \mid A) = 0·65 \times \dfrac{20}{65} = 0·20$ [From Table]

(iv) $P(G \cap C) = P(G) \cdot P(C \mid G) = \dfrac{13}{100} \times 0 = 0$ [From Table]

(v) $P(E \mid G) = \dfrac{P(E \cap G)}{P(G)} = \dfrac{8/100}{13/100} = \dfrac{8}{13} = 0·6154$ [From Table]

(vi) $P(G \mid E) = \dfrac{P(G \cap E)}{P(E)} = \dfrac{8/100}{35/100} = \dfrac{8}{35} = 0·2286$ [From Table]

Example 12·35. *A market research firm is interested in surveying certain attitudes in a small community. There are 125 households broken down according to income, ownership of a telephone or ownership of a T.V.*

	Household with monthly income of Rs. 8,000 or less		*Household with monthly income above Rs. 8,000*	
	Telephone Subscriber	*No Telephone*	*Telephone Subscriber*	*No. Telephone*
Own T.V. set	*27*	*20*	*18*	*10*
No. T.V. set	*18*	*10*	*12*	*10*

(*i*) *What is the probability of obtaining of a T.V. owner in drawing at random ?*

(*ii*) *If a household has monthly income over Rs. 8,000 and is a telephone subscriber, what is the probability that it has a T.V. ?*

(*iii*) *What is the conditional probability of drawing a household that owns a T.V., given that the household is a telephone subscriber ?*

(*iv*) *Are the events 'ownership of a T.V.' and 'telephone subscriber' statistically independent ? Comment.* [*Himachal Pradesh Univ. M.B.A., 1998*]

Solution. Let us define the following events :

A : The house hold owns a TV.

B : The household is a telephone subscriber.

C : The household has monthly income over Rs. 8,000.

Then from the given data we have :

$$P(A) = \frac{27+20+18+10}{125} = \frac{75}{125} = \frac{3}{5}\ ;\ P(B) = \frac{27+18+18+12}{125} = \frac{75}{125} = \frac{3}{5}\ ;\ P(C) = \frac{18+12+10+10}{125} = \frac{50}{125} = \frac{2}{5}$$

$$P(A \cap B) = P\left[\text{The household owns a TV and is a telephone subscriber}\right] = \frac{27+18}{125} = \frac{45}{125} = \frac{9}{25}$$

$$P(B \cap C) = P\left[\text{A household is a telephone subscriber and has monthly income over Rs. 8,000}\right] = \frac{18+12}{125} = \frac{30}{125} = \frac{6}{25}$$

$$P(A \cap B \cap C) = P\left[\begin{array}{c}\text{A household owns a TV, is a telephone subscriber}\\ \text{and has monthly income over Rs. 8,000}\end{array}\right] = \frac{18}{125}$$

(*i*) Required probability $= P(A) = \frac{3}{5} = 0{\cdot}6$

(*ii*) Required probability $= P(A \mid B \cap C) = \dfrac{P(A \cap B \cap C)}{P(B \cap C)} = \dfrac{18/125}{30/125} = \frac{3}{5} = 0{\cdot}6$

(*iii*) Required probability $= P(A \mid B) = \dfrac{P(A \cap B)}{P(B)} = \dfrac{45/125}{75/125} = \frac{3}{5} = 0{\cdot}6$

(*iv*) We have $P(A \cap B) = \frac{9}{25}$ and $P(A) \times P(B) = \frac{3}{5} \times \frac{3}{5} = \frac{9}{25}$.

Since $P(A \cap B) = P(A).P(B)$, A and B are statistically independent.

Example 12·36. *A box of 100 gaskets contains 10 gaskets with type A defects, 5 gaskets with type B defects and 2 gaskets with both types of defects. Find the probabilities that*

(*i*) *a gasket to be drawn has a type B defect under the condition that it has a type A defect, and*

(*ii*) *a gasket to be drawn has no type B defect under the condition that it has no typed A defect.*

[*Delhi Univ. B.Com. (Hons.), (External), 2005; I.C.W.A. (Intermediate), June 1998*]

Solution. Let us define the following events :

E_1 : The gasket has type A defect ; E_2 : The gasket has type B defect

Then : $P(E_1) = \frac{10}{100} = 0{\cdot}10$, $P(E_2) = \frac{5}{100} = 0{\cdot}05$, $P(E_1 \cap E_2) = \frac{2}{100} = 0{\cdot}02$

(*i*) Required probability $= P(E_2 \mid E_1) = \dfrac{P(E_1 \cap E_2)}{P(E_1)} = \dfrac{0{\cdot}02}{0{\cdot}10} = \dfrac{2}{10} = 0{\cdot}2$

(*ii*) Required probability is given by :

$$P(\bar{E}_2 \mid \bar{E}_1) = \frac{P(\bar{E}_1 \cap \bar{E}_2)}{P(\bar{E}_1)} = \frac{1 - P(E_1 \cup E_2)}{P(\bar{E}_1)} = \frac{1 - [P(E_1) + P(E_2) - P(E_1 \cap E_2)]}{1 - P(E_1)}$$

$$= \frac{1 - (0{\cdot}10 + 0{\cdot}05 - 0{\cdot}02)}{1 - 0{\cdot}10} = \frac{0{\cdot}87}{0{\cdot}90} = 0{\cdot}97$$

Example 12·37. *There are 12 balls in a bag, 8 red and 4 green. Three balls are drawn successively without replacement. What is the probability that they are alternately of the same colour ?*

Solution. The required event can materialise in the following mutually exclusive ways :

(*i*) The balls are red, green and red in the first, second and third draw respectively.

(*ii*) The balls are green, red and green in the first, second and third draw respectively.

Hence, by addition theorem of probability, the required probability p is given by : $p = P(i) + P(ii)$ ...(*)

Computation of P(i). Let *A*, *B* and *C* denote the events of drawing a red, green and red ball in the 1st, 2nd and 3rd draw respectively. Since the balls drawn are not replaced before the next draw, the constitution of the bag in the three draws is respectively :

1st draw		2nd draw		3rd draw	
8R	4G	7R	4G	7R	3G

$\therefore \quad P(i) = P(A \cap B \cap C) = P(A) \,.\, P(B \mid A) \,.\, P(C \mid A \cap B)$ [By compound probability theorem]

$$= \frac{8}{12} \times \frac{4}{11} \times \frac{7}{10} = \frac{224}{1320}$$

Computation of P(ii). If the drawn balls are green, red and green in the 1st, 2nd and 3rd draw respectively, then the constitution of the bag for the three draws respectively is :

1st draw		2nd draw		3rd draw	
8R	4G	8R	3G	7R	3G

Hence, by compound probability theorem, $P(ii) = \dfrac{4}{12} \times \dfrac{8}{11} \times \dfrac{3}{10} = \dfrac{96}{1320}$

Substituting in (*), we get : $p = \dfrac{224}{1320} + \dfrac{96}{1320} = \dfrac{224 + 96}{1320} = \dfrac{320}{1320} = \dfrac{8}{33} = 0{\cdot}2424.$

Example 12·38. *A box of nine golf gloves contains two left-handed and seven right-handed gloves :*

(i) If two golves are randomly selected from the box without replacement, what is the probability that (a) both gloves are right handed and (b) one is left-handed and one right-handed glove ?

(ii) If three gloves are selected without replacement, what is the probability that all of them are left-handed ?

(iii) If two golves are randomly selected with replacement, what is the probability that they would both be right-handed ? [*Delhi Univ. B.Com.* (*Hons.*), *2001*]

Solution. The box contains : Left handed gloves = 2 ; Right handed gloves = 7 ; Total = 9

(*i*) *Gloves drawn without replacement* :

Two balls can be drawn out of 9 balls in ${}^9C_2$ ways, which gives the exhaustive number of cases.

(*a*) The number of cases favourable to the event : "both gloves are right handed", is ${}^7C_2$.

$\therefore$ Required probability $= \dfrac{^7C_2}{^9C_2} = \dfrac{7 \times 6}{2} \times \dfrac{2}{9 \times 8} = \dfrac{7}{12} = 0·5833.$

(*b*) The number of cases favourable to the event :

"one left handed and one right handed glove," is $^2C_1 \times {^7C_1} = 2 \times 7$.

$\therefore$ Required probability $= \dfrac{2 \times 7}{^9C_2} = \dfrac{2 \times 7 \times 2}{9 \times 8} = \dfrac{7}{18} = 0·3889.$

(*ii*) If three gloves are selected without replacement then the event : "all the three are left handed", is an impossible event, since the box contains only two left handed gloves.

$\therefore$ Required probability $= 0$.

(*iii*) If two gloves are selected at random with replacement, then the two draws are independent.

$\therefore$ P[Both are right handed gloves]

$= P$[Right handed glove in the first draw] $\times$ P[Right handed glove in the second draw]

$= \dfrac{7}{9} \times \dfrac{7}{9} = \dfrac{49}{81} = 0·6049.$

Example 12·39. *A bag contains 5 white and 3 black balls; another bag contains 4 white and 5 black balls. From any one of these bags a single draw of two balls is made. Find the probability that one of them would be white and the other black ball.*

Solution. Let us define the following events :

A_1 = First bag is selected. ; A_2 : Second bag is selected.

B : In a draw of 2 balls, one is white and the other is black.

The required event of drawing one white ball and one black ball in a draw of two balls can materialise in the following mutually exclusive ways :

(*i*) $A_1 \cap B$ happens, (*ii*) $A_2 \cap B$ happens.

Hence, by addition theorem of probability, the required probability p is given by :

$$p = P(i) + P(ii) = P(A_1 \cap B) + P(A_2 \cap B)$$

$$= P(A_1) \,.\, P(B \mid A_1) + P(A_2).\, P(B \mid A_2) \qquad ...(*)$$

Since there are two bags, the selection of each being equally likely, we have : $P(A_1) = P(A_2) = \frac{1}{2}$

$P(B \mid A_1)$ = Probability of drawing one white and one black ball in a draw of 2 balls from the *first* bag.

$$= \frac{^5C_1 \times {^3C_1}}{^8C_2} = \frac{5 \times 3 \times 2\,!}{8 \times 7} = \frac{15}{28} = 0·5357.$$

$P(B \mid A_2)$ = Probability of drawing one white and one black ball in a draw of 2 balls from the *2nd* bag.

$$= \frac{^4C_1 \times {^5C_1}}{^9C_2} = \frac{4 \times 5 \times 2}{9 \times 8} = \frac{5}{9} = 0·5556.$$

Substituting in (*) we get : $p = \dfrac{1}{2} \times \dfrac{15}{28} + \dfrac{1}{2} \times \dfrac{5}{9} = \dfrac{15}{56} + \dfrac{5}{18} = \dfrac{135 + 140}{504} = \dfrac{275}{504} = 0·5456.$

Example 12·40. *A lady declares that by taking a cup of tea, she can discriminate whether the milk or tea infusion was first added to the cup. It is proposed to test this assertion by means of an experiment with 12 cups of tea, 6 made in one way and 6 in the other, and presenting them to the lady for judgement in a random order.*

(i) Calculate the probability that on the null hypothesis that the lady has no discrimination power, she would judge correctly all the 12 cups, it being known to her that 6 are of each kind.

(ii) Suppose that the 12 cups were presented to the lady in six pairs, each pair to consist cups of each kind in a random order. How would the probability of correctly judging with every cup on the same null hypothesis be altered in this case ?

Which of the two designs would you prefer and why ?

Solution. (*i*) The total number of ways in which 12 cups of tea, 6 made in one way and 6 in the other, can be presented to the lady at random is

$$\frac{12\,!}{6\,!\,6\,!} = 924$$

Of these there is only one way in which the lady can judge all the cups correctly.

$\therefore$ Required probability $= \frac{1}{924} = 0{\cdot}0011.$

(*ii*) If the 12 cups are presented to the lady in pairs, each pair consisting of cups of either kind of tea preparation, the probability that she will correctly judge each pair is $\frac{1}{2}$ and since the 6 presentations of the cups (in pairs) are independent of each other, the probability that the lady will correctly judge all the 6 pairs is given by the compound probability theorem as :

$$\left(\frac{1}{2}\right)^6 = \frac{1}{64} = 0{\cdot}0156.$$

The first method of testing is preferable to the second because the probability of correctly judging all the cups is much less in the first case as compared with the corresponding probability in the second case.

EXERCISE 12·2

1. State and prove the addition theorem of probability for any two events A and B. Rewrite the theorem when A and B are mutually exclusive.

2. (*a*) State and prove the Multiplication Theorem of Probability.

(*b*) State and prove the multiplication theorem of probability. How is the result modified if the events are not independent ?

3. State the axioms of probability. [*Delhi Univ. B.A. (Econ. Hons.), 2008*]

4. (*a*) Explain with examples the rules of Addition and Multiplication in Theory of Probability.

(*b*) State the addition and multiplication rules of probability giving one example of each rule.

[*Delhi Univ. B.Com., (Hons.), 1998*]

5. (*a*) What do you understand by conditional probability ? If

Prob. $(A + B) =$ Prob. $A +$ Prob. B,

are the two events A and B statistically independent ?

(*b*) Explain the meaning of conditional probability of an event. State the addition and multiplication rules of probability.

(*c*) Examine the validity of the following statement :

If $P(A \mid B) = P(A)$, then A and B are independent ? [*C.A. (Foundation), May 2002*]

6. Prove that for two events A and B,

$$P(A \cup B) = P(A) + P(B) - P(A \cap B)$$

What happens if A and B are mutually exclusive ?

7. (*a*) Define independent events.

(*b*) Obtain the necessary and sufficient condition for the independence of two events A and B.

Generalise the result to n events $A_1, A_2, \ldots, A_n$.

8. (*a*) For two events A and B, prove that

$$P(A \cup B) \le P(A) + P(B)$$

(*b*) Prove that :

$$P(A_1 \cup A_2 \cup \ldots\ldots \cup A_n) \le P(A_1) + P(A_2) + \ldots\ldots + P(A_n), \text{ for any events } A_1, A_2, \ldots, A_n.$$

[*Delhi Univ. B.A. (Econ. Hons.), 2002*]

9. (*a*) It is given that the two events A and B are both independent and mutually exclusive. Show that at least one of them must have zero probability. [*Delhi Univ. B.A., (Econ. Hons.), 1998*]

Hint. $P(A \cap B) = P(A) . P(B)$ [$\because$ A and B are independent]

Also $P(A \cap B) = 0$ [$\because$ A and B are mutually exclusive]

$\therefore$ $P(A) P(B) = 0$ $\Rightarrow$ $P(A) = 0$ or $P(B) = 0$

(*b*) Prove that two mutually exclusive events with positive probabilities cannot be independent.

[*Delhi Univ. B.A. (Econ. Hons.), 2008*]

(*c*) Distinguish between independent and mutually exclusive events. When will the events A and B be both independent and mutually exclusive ? [*Delhi Univ. B.A. (Econ. Hons.), 2007*]

10. A statistical experiment consists of asking 3 housewives at random if they wash their dishes with brand X detergent. List the elements of the sample space S using the letter Y for 'yes' and N for 'no'. List the elements of the event : "The second woman interviewed uses brand X". Find the probability of this event if it is assumed that all the elements of S are equally likely to occur.

Ans. 1/2

11. Explain what is meant by sample space.

An unbiased coin is tossed three times. Construct the sample space S. If E_1 denotes the event of 'getting exactly 2 heads' ; E_2 the event of 'getting at least two tails' and E_3 the event of 'getting tail in the first toss' ; write down the elements of these events and find the probabilities of their occurrence, assuming that all the elements of S are equally likely to occur.

Ans. 3/8, 1/2, 1/2.

12. Define the concepts of conditional probability and independent events.

A researcher has to consult a recently published book. The probability of its being available is 0·5 for library A and 0·7 for library B. Assuming the two events to be statistically independent, find out the probability of the book being available in library A and not available in library B ?

Ans. 0·15.

13. If two dice are thrown, what is the probability that the sum of the numbers on the dice is

(*i*) greater than 8 and (*ii*) neither 7 nor 11 ? [*C.A. (Foundation), May 1999*]

Ans. (*i*) 5/18 (*ii*) 7/9.

14. Consider a random experiment in which two dice are tossed. Construct the Sample Space S. Define the following events :

E_1 : Sum of the points on the two dice is 6 ; E_2 : Sum of the points on the two dice is even

E_3 : Sum of the points on the two dice is odd ; E_4 : Sum of the points on the two dice is greater than 12

E_5 : Sum of the points on the two dice is divisible by 3

E_6 : Sum of the points is greater than or equal to 2 and less than or equal to 12.

Write the elements of these events and find the probabilities of their occurrence, assuming that all the elements of S are equally likely.

Ans. 5/36, 1/2, 1/2, 0, 1/3, 1.

15. A card is drawn at random from a well shuffled pack of cards. What is the probability that it is a heart or a queen ?

Ans. 4/13.

16. A piece of electronic equipment has two essential parts A and B. In the past, part A failed 30% of the times, part B failed 20% of the times and both parts failed simultaneously 5% of the times.

Assuming that both parts must operate to enable the equipment to function, what is the probability that the equipment will function ? [*Delhi Univ. B.A. (Econ. Hons.), 1998*]

Ans. $1 - (0·30 + 0·20 - 0·05) = 0·55$.

17. In a certain college, the students engage in various sports in the following proportions :

Football (F) : 60% of all students; Basketball (B) : 50% of all students ;

Both football and basketball : 30% of all students.

If a student is selected at random, what is the probability that he will :

(*i*) play football or basketball ? (*ii*) play neither sports ?

Ans. (*i*) 0·80, (*ii*) 0·20.

18. There are three Engineers and three IAS officers. A committee of 3 is to be formed at random. Find the probability that at least one engineer and at least one IAS officer is in the committee.

[*I.C.W.A. (Intermediate), June 2001*]

Hint. Required probability = P[1 engineer and 2 I.A.S. officers] + P[2 engineers and 1 I.A.S. officer]

Ans. 9/10.

19. Out of the numbers 1 to 120, one is selected at random. What is the probability that it is divisible by 8 or 10 ?

[*C.A. (Foundation), May 1996*]

Ans. 0.2.

20. If $P(A) = \frac{1}{4}$, $P(B) = \frac{2}{5}$ and $P(A \cup B) = \frac{1}{2}$, find

(*i*) $P(A \cap B^c)$ (*ii*) $P(A^c \cup B^c)$, where A and B are two non-mutually exclusive events connected with a random experiment E and A^c is the complementary event of A. [*I.C.W.A. (Intermediate), June 1997*]

Ans. (*i*) 0·1 (*ii*) $P(A^c \cup B^c) = P(A \cap B)^c = 1 - P(A \cap B) = 0{\cdot}85$.

21. The result of an examination given to a class on three papers A, B and C are :

40% Failed in Paper ; 30% Failed in B ; 25% Failed in Paper C
15% Failed in Paper A and B both ; 12% Failed in B and C both ; 10% Failed in A and C both; and
3% Failed in all the three A, B and C.

What is the probability of a randomly selected candidates passing in all the three papers ?

(*Punjab Univ. B.Com., 2000*)

Ans. 0·39.

22. The odds are 9 to 5 against a person who is 50 years living till he is 70 and 8 to 6 against a person who is 60 living till he is 80. Find the probability that at least one of them will be alive after 20 years.

[*Delhi Univ. B.A. (Econ. Hons.), 1996*]

Ans. 31/49.

23. A candidate is selected for interview for three posts. For the first post there are 3 candidates, for the second 4 and for the third 2. What is the probability that the candidate is selected for at least one post ?

[*C.A. (Foundation), Nov., 2001*]

Ans. Required probability $= 1 - \left(1 - \frac{1}{3}\right)\left(1 - \frac{1}{4}\right)\left(1 - \frac{1}{2}\right) = \frac{3}{4}$.

24. A salesman has a 60 per cent chance of making a sale to each customer. The behaviour of successive customers is independent. If two customers A and B enter the shop, what is the probability that the salesman will make a sale to A or B ? [*Delhi Univ. B.A. (Econ. Hons.), 2000*]

Ans. 0·84.

25. Suppose it is 11 to 5 against a person who is now 38 years of age living till he is 73 and 5 to 3 against B, now 43 living till he is 78. Find the chance that at least one of these persons will be alive 35 years hence.

Ans. 0·57.

26. A problem in statistics is given to three students A, B and C whose chances of solving it are 1/3, 1/4 and 1/2 respectively. What is the probability that the problem will be solved ?

Ans. 3/4.

27. Two persons X and Y appear in an interview for two vacancies in the same post. The probability of X's selection is $\frac{1}{5}$ and that of Y's selection is $\frac{1}{3}$. The probability that none of them will be selected is :

(*i*) $\frac{7}{15}$, (*ii*) $\frac{8}{15}$, (*iii*) $\frac{9}{15}$, (*iv*) $\frac{10}{15}$. [*I.C.W.A. (Intermediate), Dec. 2001*]

Ans. (*ii*)

28. The chances of an accident in a factory in a year in the cities A, B, and C are 10 in 50, 10 in 120, and 10 in 60 respectively. The chance that an accident may happen in at least one of them is :

(*i*) $\frac{5}{18}$, (*ii*) $\frac{6}{18}$, (*iii*) $\frac{7}{18}$, (*iv*) $\frac{8}{18}$. [*I.C.W.A. (Intermediate), June 2002*]

Ans. (*iii*).

29. The probability that India wins a cricket test match against England is given to be $\frac{1}{3}$. If India and England play three test matches, what is the probability that :

(*i*) India will lose all the three test matches ? ; (*ii*) India will win at least one test match ?

Ans. (*i*) 8 / 27 (*ii*) 19 / 27.

30. There are 3 economists, 4 engineers, 2 statisticians and 1 doctor. A committee of 4 from among them is to be formed. Find the probability that the committee :

(*i*) Consists of one of each kind ; (*ii*) Has at least one economist ;

(*iii*) Has the doctor as a member and three others.

Ans. (*i*) 4 / 35, (*ii*) 5/6, (*iii*) 2/5.

31. A committee of 4 persons is to be appointed from 7 men and 3 women. What is the probability that the committee contains :

(*i*) Exactly two women; (*ii*) At least one woman. *[C.A. PEE-1, May 2004]*

Ans. (*i*) $\frac{{}^7C_2 \times {}^3C_2}{{}^{10}C_4} = \frac{3}{10} = 0{\cdot}10$ (*ii*) $1 - \frac{{}^7C_4}{{}^{10}C_4} = 1 - \frac{35}{210} = \frac{5}{6} = 0{\cdot}8333.$

32. A committee of 4 persons is to be appointed from 3 officers of the production department, 3 officers of the sales department and 2 officers of the purchase department and 1 cost accountant. Find the probability of forming a committee in the following manner : *[I.C.W.A. (Intermediate), December 1998]*

(*i*) There must be one from each category; (*ii*) It should have at least one from the purchase department.

[I.C.W.A. (Intrmediate), December 1998]

Ans. $\frac{{}^3C_1 \times {}^3C_1 \times {}^2C_1 \times 1}{{}^9C_4} = \frac{1}{7}$; (*ii*) $[({}^2C_1 \times {}^7C_3) + ({}^2C_2 \times {}^7C_2)] \div {}^9C_4 = \frac{13}{18}.$

33. Two men M_1 and M_2 and three women W_1, W_2 and W_3 in a big industrial firm are trying for further promotion for only one post which falls vacant. Those of the same sex have equal probabilities of getting promotion but each man is twice as likely to get promotion as any woman.

(*i*) Find the probability that a woman gets a promotion.

(*ii*) If M_2 and W_2 are husband and wife, find the probability that one of them gets the promotion.

Ans. (*i*) 3/7, (*ii*) 3/7.

34. The odds against student *X* solving a business statistics problem are 8 : 6 and odds in favour of student *Y* solving the same problem are 14 : 16.

(*i*) What is the chance that the problem will be solved if they both try, independently of each other ?

(*ii*) What is the probability that neither solves the problem ?

Ans. (*i*) $\frac{73}{105}$, (*ii*) $\frac{32}{105}$.

35. The odds against *A* solving a problem are 10 to 7 and the odds in favour of *B* solving the problem are 15 to 12. What is the probability that if both of them try, the problem will be solved ? *[Delhi Univ. B.Com. (Hons.), 2006]*

Ans. $1 - \left(\frac{10}{10+7}\right)\left(\frac{12}{15+12}\right) = \frac{113}{153} = 0{\cdot}7386.$

36. *A* speaks truth in 60 per cent cases and *B* speaks truth in 75 per cent cases. In what percentage of cases are they likely to contradict each other in stating the same fact. *[C.A. PEE-1, Nov. 2002]*

Ans. 45%.

37. Given $P(A) = 1/4$, $P(B \mid A) = 1/2$ and $P(A \mid B) = 1/4$, find if

(*i*) *A* and *B* are mutually exclusive, (*ii*) *A* and *B* are independent.

Ans. (*i*) *A* and *B* are not mutually exclusive. (*ii*) *A* and *B* are independent.

38. Given : $P(A) = 0{\cdot}5$ $P(A \cup B) = 0{\cdot}7$, find $P(B)$ if ;

(*i*) *A* and *B* are independent events; (*ii*) *A* and *B* are mutually exclusive events; (*iii*) $P(A \mid B) = 0{\cdot}5$

[Delhi Univ. B.A. (Econ. Hons.), 2005]

Ans. (*i*) 0·4, (*ii*) 0·2, (*iii*) 0·4.

39. It is given that $P(A \cup B) = \frac{5}{6}$, $P(A \cap B) = \frac{1}{3}$ and $P(\bar{B}) = \frac{1}{2}$,

where $P(\bar{B})$ stands for the probability that *B* does not happen. Determine *P* (*A*) and *P* (*B*). Are *A* and *B* independent ?

Ans. $P(A) = 2/3$, $P(B) = 1/2$. *A* and *B* are independent.

40. If $P(A) = \frac{3}{4}$, $P(B) = \frac{1}{2}$, $P(A - B) = \frac{3}{8}$, find the probabilities that

(*i*) exactly one of *A* and *B* occurs, (*ii*) none of them occurs.

Also examine whether the events A and B are independent or not. [*I.C.W.A. (Intermediate), Dec. 1997*]

Ans. (*i*) $\frac{1}{2}$, (*ii*) $\frac{1}{8}$, (*iii*) A and B are independent.

41. Choose the correct alternative :

If $P(A) = 0.4$, $P(A \cup B) = 0.7$, then for two independent events A and B, $P(B)$ is

(*i*) 0.5 (*ii*) 0.75 (*iii*) 0.3 (*iv*) none of these. [*I.C.W.A. (Intermediate), June 2000*]

(*b*) One of the two events A and B must occur. If the chance of A is $\frac{2}{3}$ of that of B, then odds in favour of B are

(*i*) 1 : 3, (*ii*) 3 : 2 (*iii*) 2 : 3 (*iv*) none of these.

[*I.C.W.A. (Intermediate), June 2000*]

Ans. (*a*) : (*i*) ; (*b*) : (*ii*).

42. A university has to select one examiner from a list of 50 persons — 20 of them women and 30 men; 10 of them knowing Hindi and 40 not; 15 of them being teachers and the remaining 35 not. What is the probability of the university selecting a Hindi-knowing woman teacher ?

Ans. $\frac{20}{50} \times \frac{10}{50} \times \frac{15}{50} = \frac{3}{125}$.

43. A man wants to marry a girl having qualities : white complexion - the probability of getting such a girl is one in twenty ; handsome dowry - the probability of getting this is one in fifty ; westernised manners and etiquettes - the probability here is one in hundred. Find the probability of his getting married to such a girl when the possession of these three attributes is independent. (*Punjab Univ. B.Com. 1997*)

Ans. 0·00001.

44. An electronic device is made up of three components A, B, and C. The probability of failure of the component A is 0·01, that of B is 0·1 and that of C is 0·02 in some fixed period of time. Find the probability that the device will work satisfactorily during that period of time assuming that the three components work independently of one another.

Ans. $0{\cdot}99 \times 0{\cdot}9 \times 0{\cdot}98 = 0{\cdot}8732$.

45. Three ships A, B and C sail from England to India. Odds in favour of their arriving safety are 2 : 5, 3 : 7 and 6 : 11 respectively.

Find the probability that they all arrive safely. [*Delhi Univ. B.A. (Econ. Hons.), 2000*]

Ans. $\frac{2}{7} \times \frac{3}{10} \times \frac{6}{17} = 0{\cdot}03$.

46. Lloyd, the captain of the West Indies cricket team, is reported to have observed the rule of calling 'heads' every time the toss was made during the five matches of the last Test series with the Indian team. What is the probability of his winning the toss in all the five matches ?

How will the probability be affected if he had made a rule of tossing a coin privately to decide whether to call 'heads' or 'tails' on each occasion.

Ans. 1/32 ; unaffected.

47. The probability that a man will be alive in 25 years is 3/5, and the probability that his wife will be alive in 25 years is 2/3. Find the probability that (*a*) both will be alive, (*b*) only the man will be alive, (*c*) only the wife will be alive, (*d*) at least one will be alive, (*e*) none will be alive, 25 years hence. [*C.A. PEE-1, May 2003*]

Ans. (*a*) 2 / 5, (*b*) 1/5, (*c*) 4 / 15, (*d*) 13 / 15, (*e*) 2 / 15.

48. The results of conducting an examination in two papers A and B for 20 candidates were recorded as under :

8 passed in paper A ; 7 passed in paper B ; 8 failed in both papers A and B.

If out of these candidates, one is selected at random, find the probability that the candidate

(*i*) passed in both papers A and B, (*ii*) failed only in A, and ; (*iii*) failed in A or B.

Ans. (*i*) 3/20, (*ii*) 1/5, (*iii*) 17/20.

49. A bag contains 8 white and 7 black balls. 4 balls are drawn one by one without replacement. What is the probability that white and black balls appear alternately ?

Ans. 14 / 195.

50. A bag contains 5 white and 3 black balls, and 4 are successively drawn and not replaced. What is the probability that they are alternately of different colours ?

Ans. 1 / 7.

51. A and B toss an ordinary die alternately in succession. The winner is one who throws an ace first. If A is the first to throw, calculate their probabilities of winning the game.

Ans. 6 / 11, 5 / 11.

52. A, B and C, in that order, toss a coin. The first one to throw a head wins. What are their respective chances of winning ? Assume that the game may continue indefinitely. *(Punjab Univ. B.Com., April 1995)*

Ans. $P(A) = 4/7, \quad P(B) = 2/7, \quad P(C) = 1/7.$

53. A and B alternately cut a pack of cards, and the pack is shuffled after each cut. If A starts and the game is continued until one cuts a diamond, what are the respective chances of A and B first cutting a diamond ?

Ans. $4/7, 3/7.$

54. (*a*) A person is known to hit a target in 5 out of 8 shots, whereas another person is known to hit it in 3 out of 5 shots. Find the probability that the target is hit at all when they both try. *[C.A. PEE-I, Nov. 2004]*

Ans. $1 - \left(1 - \frac{5}{13}\right) \times \left(1 - \frac{3}{8}\right) = \frac{8}{13}.$

55. A can hit a target 4 times in 5 shots, B three times in 4 shots and C two times in 3 shots. They fire a volley, what is the probability that the target is damaged if at least two hits are required to damage it. *[Delhi Univ. B.A. (Econ. Hons.), 2006]*

Ans. 5/6.

Hint. The target is damaged if at least two persons hit the target.

$$\text{Required probability} = \frac{4}{5} \times \frac{3}{4} \times \left(1 - \frac{2}{3}\right) + \frac{4}{5}\left(1 - \frac{3}{4}\right) \times \frac{2}{3} + \left(1 - \frac{4}{5}\right) \times \frac{3}{4} \times \frac{2}{3} + \frac{4}{5} \times \frac{3}{4} \times \frac{2}{3} = \frac{50}{60} = \frac{5}{6}.$$

56. Three groups of workers contain 3 men and 1 woman, 2 men and 2 women, and 1 man and 3 women, respectively. One worker is selected at random from each group. What is the probability that the group selected consists of 1 man and 2 women ?

Ans. 13/32.

57. Among the examinees in an examination 30%, 35% and 45% failed in Statistics, in Mathematics and in at least one of the subjects respectively. An examinee is selected at random. Find the probabilities that

(*i*) he failed in Mathematics only, (*ii*) he passed in Statistics if it is known that he failed in Mathematics. *[C.A. (Foundation), May 2002]*

Ans. (*i*) 0.20 ; (*ii*) 0·429.

58. The probability that a person stopping at a petrol pump will get his car's tyres checked is 0·12; the probability that he will get his car's oil checked is 0·29, and the probability that he will get both checked is 0·07.

(*i*) What is the probability that a person stopping at this pump will have neither his car's tyres nor car's oil checked ?

(*ii*) Find the probability that a person who has his car's oil checked will also have his car's tyres checked. *[Delhi Univ. B.Com. (Hons.), 2007]*

Ans. (*i*) 0·66 ; (*ii*) 0·24.

59. The probability that a trainee will remain with a company is 0·8. The probability that an employee earns more than Rs. 20,000 per year is 0·4. The probability that an employee who was a trainee and remained with the company or who earns more than Rs. 20,000 per year is 0·9.

What is the probability that an employee earns more than Rs. 20,000 per year given that he is a trainee who stayed with the company ? *[C.A. (Foundation), Nov. 2000]*

Ans. 3/8.

60. Choose the correct alternative, stating proper reason.

For two events A and B, $P(A) = \frac{1}{3} = 1 - P(B)$, $\quad P(B \mid A) = \frac{1}{4}$, then $P(A \mid B)$ is

(*i*) $\frac{1}{3}$, (*ii*) $\frac{1}{2}$, (*iii*) $\frac{1}{8}$, (*iv*) none of these. *[I.C.W.A. (Intermediate), June 2001]*

Ans. (*iii*).

61. Let A and B be the two events such that $P(A) = \frac{1}{2}$, $P(B) = \frac{1}{3}$ and $P(A \cap B) = \frac{1}{4}$.

Obtain the probabilities (*i*) $P(A \mid B)$, (*ii*) $P(A \cup B)$ and (*iii*) $P(\bar{A} \cap \bar{B})$.

[Delhi Univ. B.A. (Econ. Hons.) 2008; C.A. (Foundation), May 2001]

Ans. (*i*) $\frac{3}{4}$, (*ii*) $\frac{7}{12}$, (*iii*) $\frac{5}{12}$.

62. A and B are two events such that $P(A) = 1/4$, $P(B) = 1/3$, and $P(A \cup B) = 1/2$. Find $P(B \mid A)$.

[Delhi Univ. B.A. (Econ. Hons.), 2008]

Ans. 1/3.

63. A bag contains 10 gold and 8 silver coins. Two successive drawings of 3 coins are made such that :

(*i*) the coins are replaced before the second drawing

(*ii*) the coins are not replaced before the second drawing.

In each case find the probability that the first drawing will give 3 gold coins and the second, 3 silver coins.

[*C.A. (Foundation), May 2000*]

Ans. (*i*) $\frac{35}{3468}$, (*ii*) $\frac{4}{221}$.

64. An urn contains 10 white and 6 black balls. Find the probability that a blind-folded person in one draw shall obtain a white ball, and in the second draw (without replacing the first one) a black ball.

Ans. $\frac{10}{16} \times \frac{6}{15} = \frac{1}{4}$.

65. A group of 200 persons was classified according to age and sex as given below :

Age in years	*Male*	*Female*	*Total*
Below 30	60	50	110
30 and above	80	10	90
Total	140	60	200

(*i*) What is the probability that a randomly chosen person from this group is a male below 30 years of age ?

(*ii*) What is the probability that a person is below 30 years of age, given that he is a male ?

[*I.C.W.A Intermediate), June1995*]

Ans. (*i*) 0·30, (*ii*) = 0·43.

66. The personnel department of a company has records which show the following analysis of its 200 engineers.

Age (in years)	*Bachelor's degree only*	*Master's degree*	*Total*
Under 30	90	10	100
30 to 40	20	30	50
Over 40	40	10	50
Total	150	50	200

If one engineer is selected at random from the company, find :

(*a*) The probability he has only a bachelor's degree.

(*b*) The probability he has a master's degree, given that he is over 40.

(*c*) The probability he is under 30, given that he has only a bachelor's degree.

Ans. (*a*) $\frac{150}{200} = 0{\cdot}75$, (*b*) $\frac{10}{50} = 0{\cdot}2$, (*c*) $\frac{90}{150} = 0{\cdot}6$.

67. Suppose A and B are any two events and that $P(A) = p_1$, $P(B) = p_2$ and $P(A \cap B) = p_3$. Show that the formula of each of the following probabilities in terms of p_1, p_2 and p_3 can be expressed as follows :

(*i*) $P(\bar{A} \cup \bar{B}) = 1 - p_3$ (*ii*) $P(\bar{A} \cap \bar{B}) = 1 - p_1 - p_2 + p_3$ (*iii*) $P(A \cap \bar{B}) = p_1 - p_3$

(*iv*) $P(\bar{A} \cap B) = p_2 - p_3$ (*v*) $P(A \mid B) = \frac{p_3}{p_2}$ and $P(B \mid A) = \frac{p_3}{p_1}$, and

(*vi*) $P(\bar{A} \mid \bar{B}) = \frac{1 - p_1 - p_2 + p_3}{1 - p_2}$ and $P(\bar{B} \mid \bar{A})$ $\frac{1 - p_1 - p_2 + p_3}{1 - p_1}$

OBJECTIVE TYPE QUESTIONS

68. Pick out the correct answer with reasoning :

(*i*) Two dice are thrown and the sums of the numbers on the faces up are obtained. The probability of this sum being 2 is :

(*a*) $\frac{1}{6}$, (*b*) $\frac{1}{36}$, (*c*) $\frac{1}{18}$, (*d*) None of these.

(*ii*) A die is thrown two times and the sum of numbers on the faces up is noted. The probability of this sum being 11 is

$\frac{1}{6}$, $\frac{1}{36}$, $\frac{1}{18}$, None of these.

Ans. (*i*) 1/36, (*ii*) 1/18.

69. Two events A and B are mutually exclusive :

$P(A) = 1/5$ and $P(B) = 1/3$. Find the probability that :

(*i*) Either A or B will occur, (*ii*) Both A and B will occur (*iii*) Neither A nor B will occur.

Ans. (*i*) 8/15, (*ii*) 0, (*iii*) 7/15.

70. Point out the error in the following statement :

The probability that a student will commit exactly one mistake during his laboratory experiments is 0·08 and the probability that he will commit at least one mistake is 0·05.

Ans. Wrong ; The latter probability must be greater than the former.

71. Criticise the following statement :

"The probability of Atul passing an examination is 1/3 and the probability of Vijay passing the same examination is 2/3. Therefore, the probability of either one of them passing in the examination is 1."

Ans. Wrong, because two events are not mutually exclusive.

72. Explain what is wrong with the following statement :

"Four persons are asked the same question by an interviewer. If each has, independently, probability 1/6 of answering correctly, the probability that at least one answers correctly is $4 \times 1/6 = 2/3$."

Ans. Correct answer is $\left[1 - \left(\frac{5}{6}\right)^4\right]$.

73. Discuss and criticise the following :

$P(A) = 2/3$, $P(B) = 1/4$, $P(C) = 1/6$,

for the probabilities of three mutually exclusive events A, B and C.

Ans. Wrong, since sum of probabilities in this case is greater than 1.

74. Explain why there must be a mistake in the following statement :

"A quality control engineer claims that the probabilities that a large consignment of glass bricks contains 0, 1, 2, 3, 4 or 5 defectives are 0·11, 0·23, 0·37, 0·16, 0·09 and 0·05 respectively.

Ans. Sum of probabilities = 1·01 which is impossible. This sum must be 1.

75. If $P(AB)$ is equal to 0·24 and $P(A)$ is equal to 0·60, then $P(B \mid A)$ is......

(*a*) 0·16 (*b*) 0·36 (*c*) 0·84 (*d*) none of these.

Ans. (*d*)

76. Choose the correct alternative, stating proper reasons :

(*a*) One of the two events A and B must occur. If the chance of A is (2/3) of that of B, then odds in favour of B are :

(*i*) 1 : 3, (*ii*) 3 : 2 (*iii*) 2 : 3 (*iv*) none of these.

[*I.C.W.A. (Intermediate), June 2000*]

(*b*) Let A and B be two events such that $P(A) = 0{\cdot}4$, $P(A \cup B) = 0{\cdot}7$ and $P(B) = p$. For what choice of p are A and B independent ?

(*i*) $\frac{1}{2}$, (*ii*) $\frac{1}{3}$, (*iii*) $\frac{3}{4}$, (*iv*) none of these.

[*I.C.W.A. (Intermediate), Dec. 2001*]

77. For two independent events A and B for which $P(A) = \frac{1}{2}$ and $P(B) = \frac{1}{3}$, the probability that at most one of them occurs is

(*i*) $\frac{5}{6}$, (*ii*) $\frac{2}{3}$, (*iii*) $\frac{1}{2}$, (*iv*) none of these.

Ans. (*i*).

78. The chance of drawing a white ball in the first draw and again a white ball in the second draw without replacement of the ball in the first draw from a bag containing 6 white and 4 red balls is

(*a*) 2 / 10 (*b*) 6 / 10 (*c*) 36 / 100 (*d*) 1 / 3.

Ans. (*d*).

79. Explain why there must be a mistake in each of the following statements :

(*i*) If the probability that an ore contains uranium is 0·28, the probability that it does not contain uranium is 0·62.

(*ii*) The probability that a student will get an A-grade in an Economics course is 0·32 and the probability that he will get either an A or a B grade in the same course is 0·27.

(*iii*) A company is working on the construction of two shopping centres. The probability that the larger of the two shopping centres will be completed on time is 0·35 and the probability that both shopping centres will be completed on time is 0·42.

Ans. (*i*) 0·28 + 0·62 = 0·9 ≠ 1. (*ii*) $P(A \text{ or } B)$ must be greater than $P(A)$.
(*iii*) P (both) must be less than P (single).

80. Given that A, B, C are mutually exclusive events, explain why each of the following is not a permissible assignment of probabilities.

(*i*) $P(A) = 0{\cdot}24$, $P(B) = 0{\cdot}4$ and $P(A \cup C) = 0{\cdot}2$

(*ii*) $P(A) = 0{\cdot}7$, $P(B) = 0{\cdot}1$ and $P(B \cap C) = 0{\cdot}3$

(*iii*) $P(A) = 0{\cdot}6$, $P(A \cap \bar{B}) = 0{\cdot}5$.

Ans. (*i*) Since A, B, C are mutually exclusive, we must have

$P(A \cup B \cup C) = P(A) + P(B) + P(C) = P(B) + P(A \cup C) = 1$, which is not so in this case.

(*ii*) $P(B \cap C)$ must be zero $(\because C \cap B) = \phi)$

(*iii*) $P(A \cap B) = P(A) - P(A \cap \bar{B}) = 0{\cdot}1$, which is not possible since A and B are mutually exclusive and hence $P(A \cap B)$ must be 0.

12·11. INVERSE PROBABILITY

One of the important applications of the conditional probability is in the computation of unknown probabilities, on the basis of the information supplied by the experiment or past records. For example, suppose an event has occurred through one of the various mutually disjoint events or reasons. Then the conditional probability that it has occurred due to a particular event or reason is called its *inverse* or *posteriori* probability. These probabilities are computed by *Bayes's Rule*, named so after the British mathematician Thomas Bayes who propounded it in 1763. The revision of old (given) probabilities in the light of the additional information supplied by the experiment or past records is of extreme help to business and management executives in arriving at valid decisions in the face of uncertainties.

Bayes's Theorem (Rule for the Inverse Probability)

Theorem 12·17. *If an event A can only occur in conjunction with one of the n mutually exclusive and exhaustive events* $E_1, E_2, \ldots, E_n$ *and if A actually happens, then the probability that it was preceded by the particular event* E_i $(i = 1, 2, \ldots, n)$ *is given by* :

$$P(E_i \mid A) = \frac{P(A \cap E_i)}{\sum_{i=1}^{n} P(E_i) \, . \, P(A \mid E_i)} = \frac{P(E_i) \, . \, P(A \mid E_i)}{\sum_{i=1}^{n} P(E_i) \, . \, P(A \mid E_i)} \qquad \ldots(12{\cdot}46)$$

Proof. Since the event A can occur in combination with any of the mutually exclusive and exhaustive events $E_1, E_2, \ldots, E_n$, we have

$$A = (A \cap E_1) \cup (A \cap E_2) \cup \ldots \cup (A \cap E_n)$$

where $A \cap E_1, A \cap E_2, \ldots, A \cap E_n$, being the subsets of mutually exclusive events $E_1, E_2, \ldots, E_n$ are all disjoint (mutually exclusive) events. Hence, by the addition theorem of probability, we have

$$\begin{aligned} P(A) &= P(A \cap E_1) + P(A \cap E_2) + \ldots + P(A \cap E_n) \\ &= P(E_1)\, P(A \mid E_1) + P(E_2)\, P(A \mid E_2) + \ldots + P(E_n)\, P(A \mid E_n) \\ &= \sum_{i=1}^{n} P(E_i)\, P(A \mid E_i) \end{aligned} \qquad \ldots(12{\cdot}47)$$

For any particular event E_i, the conditional probability, $P(E_i \mid A)$ is given by :

$$P(E_i \cap A) = P(A)\, P(E_i \mid A)$$

$$\Rightarrow \qquad P(E_i \mid A) = \frac{P(E_i \cap A)}{P(A)} = \frac{P(E_i)\, P(A \mid E_i)}{\sum_{i=1}^{n} P(E_i) \, . \, P(A \mid E_i)} \qquad \text{[From (12·47)]}$$

which is the Bayes's rule for obtaining the conditional probabilities.

Remark. The probabilities $P(E_1)$, $P(E_2)$, ... , $P(E_n)$ which are already given or known before conducting an experiment are termed as *a priori* or *priori* probabilities. The conditional probabilities $P(E_1 | A), P(E_2 | A), ..., P(E_n | A)$, which are computed after conducting the experiment, *viz.*, occurrence of A are termed as *posteriori* probabilities.

Example 12·41. *A restaurant serves two special dishes, A and B to its customers consisting of 60% men and 40% women. 80% of men order dish A and the rest B. 70% of women order B and the rest A. In what ratio of A to B should the restaurant prepare the two dishes ?*

Solution. Let us define the following events :

A : The customer orders for dish 'A' ; B : The customer orders for dish 'B'
M : The customer is a man ; W : The customer is a woman.

∴ We are given :

$P(M) = 0{\cdot}6, \quad P(W) = 0{\cdot}4 \quad ; \quad P(A | M) = 0{\cdot}8, \quad P(B | M) = 0{\cdot}2 \quad ; \quad P(A | W) = 0{\cdot}3, \quad P(B | W) = 0{\cdot}7$

Since the dish 'A' is ordered by men or women, we can write 'A' as disjoint union :

$$A = (A \cap M) \cup (A \cap W)$$

Hence, the probability that the customer orders the dish A is given by :

$$P(A) = P[(A \cap M) \cup (A \cap W)] = P(A \cap M) + P(A \cap W)$$
$$= P(M) \,.\, P(A | M) + P(W) P(A | W) = 0{\cdot}6 \times 0{\cdot}8 + 0{\cdot}4 \times 0{\cdot}3 = 0{\cdot}48 + 0{\cdot}12 = 0{\cdot}6$$

Similarly, the probability that the customer orders for dish B is given by :

$$P(B) = P(M) \,.\, P(B | M) + P(W) \,.\, P(B | W) = 0{\cdot}6 \times 0{\cdot}2 + 0{\cdot}4 \times 0{\cdot}7 = 0{\cdot}12 + 0{\cdot}28 = 0{\cdot}4$$

Hence, the restaurant should prepare the two dishes A and B in the ratio 0·6 : 0·4 *i.e.*, 3 : 2.

Example 12·42. *Two sets of candidates are competing for the positions on the Board of Directors of a company. The probabilities that the first and second sets will win are 0·6 and 0·4 respectively. If the first set wins, the probability of introducing a new product is 0·8, and the corresponding probability if the second set wins is 0·3. What is the probability that the product will be introduced ?*

Solution. Let E_1, E_2 denote the events that the 1st and 2nd sets of candidates respectively win and let E be the event of introducing a new product.

Then we are given :

$P(E_1) = 0{\cdot}6 \quad ; \quad P(E_2) = 0{\cdot}4 \quad ; \quad P(E | E_1) = 0{\cdot}8 \quad ; \quad P(E | E_2) = 0{\cdot}3$

The event E can materials in the following mutually exclusive ways :

(*i*) 1st set wins and the new product is introduced, *i.e.*, $E_1 \cap E$ happens.

(*ii*) Second set wins and the new product is introduced, *i.e.*, $E_2 \cap E$ happens. Thus

$$E = (E_1 \cap E) \cup (E_2 \cap E),$$

where $E_1 \cap E$ and $E_2 \cap E$ are disjoint.

Hence, by addition theorem of probability

$$P(E) = P(E_1 \cap E) + P(E_2 \cap E) = P(E_1) P(E | E_1) + P(E_2) P(E | E_2)$$
$$= 0{\cdot}6 \times 0{\cdot}8 + 0{\cdot}4 \times 0{\cdot}3 = 0{\cdot}48 + 0{\cdot}12 = 0{\cdot}6$$

Example 12·43. *In a bolt factory, machines A, B, C manufacture respectively 25%, 35% and 40% of the total. Of their output 5, 4, 2 per cent are known to be defective bolts. A bolt is drawn at random from the product and is found to be defective. What are the probabilities that it was manufactured by*

(*i*) *Machine A,* (*ii*) *Machine B or C.* [*Delhi Univ. B.Com. (Hons.), 2000*]

Solution. Let E_1, E_2 and E_3 denote respectively the events that the bolt selected at random is manufactured by the machines A, B and C respectively and let E denote the event that it is defective. Then we have :

E_i	E_1	E_2	E_3	Total
$P(E_i)$	0·25	0·35	0·40	1
$P(E \mid E_i)$	0·05	0·04	0·02	
$P(E \cap E_i) = P(E_i) \times P(E \mid E_i)$	0·0125	0·0140	0·0080	$P(E) = 0{\cdot}0345$

(*i*) Hence, the probability that a defective bolt chosen at random is manufactured by factory A is given by Bayes's rule as :

$$P(E_1 \mid E) = \frac{P(E_1)\, P(E \mid E_1)}{\Sigma P(E_i)\, P(E \mid E_i)} = \frac{0{\cdot}0125}{0{\cdot}0345} = \frac{25}{69} = 0{\cdot}36$$

(*ii*) Similarly we get :

$$P(E_2 \mid E) = \frac{0{\cdot}0140}{0{\cdot}0345} = \frac{28}{69} = 0{\cdot}41 \quad ; \quad P(E_3 \mid E) = \frac{0{\cdot}0080}{0{\cdot}0345} = \frac{16}{69} = 0{\cdot}23$$

Hence, the probability that a defective bolt chosen at random is manufactured by machine B or C is :

$$P(E_2 \mid E) + P(E_3 \mid E) = 0{\cdot}41 + 0{\cdot}23 = 0{\cdot}64.$$

OR Required probability $= 1 - P(E_1 \mid E) = 1 - 0{\cdot}36 = 0{\cdot}64.$

TREE DIAGRAM

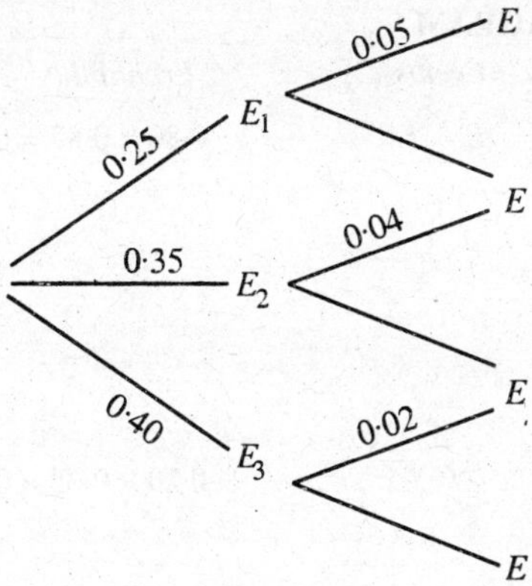

	Events	*Probability*
	$E_1 \cap E$	$0{\cdot}25 \times 0{\cdot}05 = 0{\cdot}0125$
	$E_2 \cap E$	$0{\cdot}35 \times 0{\cdot}04 = 0{\cdot}0140$
	$E_3 \cap E$	$0{\cdot}40 \times 0{\cdot}02 = 0{\cdot}0080$
Total		0·0345

Fig. 12·6

From the above diagram the probability that a defective bolt is manufactured by factory A is

$$P(E_1 \mid E) = \frac{0{\cdot}0125}{0{\cdot}0345} = 0{\cdot}36$$

Similarly, $P(E_2 \mid E) = \dfrac{0{\cdot}0140}{0{\cdot}0345} = 0{\cdot}41$ and $P(E_3 \mid E) = \dfrac{0{\cdot}0080}{0{\cdot}0345} = 0{\cdot}23$

Important Remark. Since $P(E_3)$ is greatest, on the basis of '*a priori*' probabilities alone, we are likely to conclude that a defective bolt drawn at random from the product is manufactured by machine C. After using the additional information we obtain the *posterior* probabilities which give $P(E_2 \mid E)$ as maximum. Thus, we shall now say that it is probable that the defective bolt has been manufactured by machine B, a result which is different from the earlier conclusion. However, latter conclusion is a much valid conclusion as it is based on the entire information at our disposal. Thus, Bayes's rule provides a very powerful tool in improving the quality of probability and this helps the management executives in arriving at valid decisions in the face of uncertainty. Thus, the additional information reduces the importance of the prior probabilities. The only requirement for the use of *Bayesian Rule* is that all the hypotheses under consideration must be valid and that none is assigned 'a prior' probability 0 or 1.

Example 12·44. *A company has two plants to manufacture scooters. Plant I manufactures 80 per cent of the scooters and plant II manufactures 20 per cent. At plant I, 85 out of 100 scooters are rated standard quality or better. At plant II, only 65 out of 100 scooters are rated standard quality or better.*

(*i*) *What is the probability that scooter selected at random came from plant, I if it is known that the scooter is of standard quality ?*

(*ii*) *What is the probability that the scooter came from plant II, if it is known that the scooter is of standard quality ?*

Solution. Let us define the following events :

E_1 : Scooter is manufactured by plant I ; E_2 : Scooter is manufactured by plant II

E : Scooter is rated as standard quality.

Then we are given :

$$P(E_1) = 0·80, \quad P(E_2) = 0·20 \quad ; \quad P(E \mid E_1) = 0·85 \quad P(E \mid E_2) = 0·65$$

(*i*) Required probability is : (By Bayes's Rule)

$$P(E_1 \mid E) = \frac{P(E_1)\, P(E \mid E_1)}{P(E_1)\, P(E \mid E_1) + P(E_2)\, P(E \mid E_2)}$$

$$= \frac{0·80 \times 0·85}{0·80 \times 0·85 + 0·20 \times 0·65} = \frac{0·68}{0·68 + 0·13} = \frac{0·68}{0·81} = 0·84$$

(*ii*) Required probability is given by :

$$P(E_2 \mid E) = \frac{P(E_2)\, P(E \mid E_2)}{P(E_1)\, P(E \mid E_1) + P(E_2)\, P(E \mid E_2)} = \frac{0·20 \times 0·65}{0·80 \times 0·85 + 0·20 \times 0·65} = \frac{0·13}{0·81} = 0·16$$

Aliter

TREE DIAGRAM

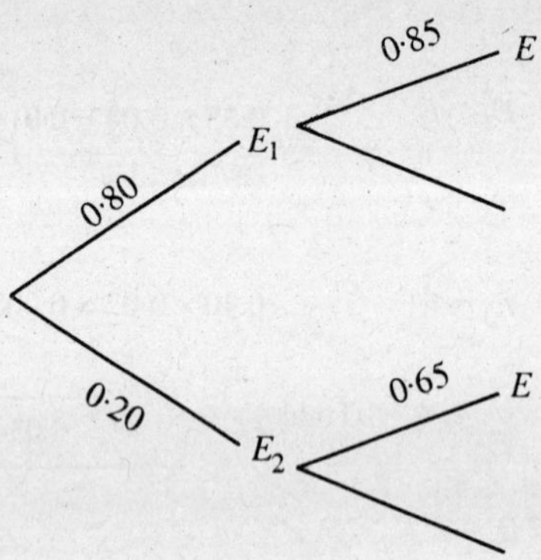

Events	*Probability*
$E \cap E_1$	$0·80 \times 0·85 = 0·68$
$E \cap E_2$	$0·20 \times 0·65 = 0·13$
Total	0·81

Fig. 12·7

(*i*) $P(E_1 \mid E) = \frac{0·68}{0·81} = 0·84$; (*ii*) $P(E_2 \mid E) = \frac{0·13}{0·81} = 0·16$

Example 12·45. *A company launches an advertising campaign of its new product on TV, radio and in print media in an area where 30% watch TV, 50% listen to the radio and the rest rely on newspapers for all information. It is estimated that a person who sees the advertisement on TV will buy the product with probability 0·6. A person who has heard it on radio is expected to buy the product with probability 0·3 and seeing the advertisement in print will convince a person to buy the product with probability 0·1. A consumer, chosen at random, is found to have purchased the product. What is the probability she heard about the product on radio ?* [*Delhi Univ. B.A. (Econ. Hons.), 2007*]

Solution. Define the following events :

E_1 : The person watches T.V.

E_2 : The person listens to radio.

E_3 : The person relies on newspapers, for information.

E : The person buys the new product of the company.

Then, we are given :

$P(E_1) = 0·30$	$P(E \mid E_1) = 0·6$	$P(E_1)) \cdot P(E \mid E_1) = 0·18$
$P(E_2) = 0·50$	$P(E \mid E_2) = 0·3$	$P(E_2) \cdot P(E \mid E_2) = 0·15$
$P(E_3) = 1 - 0·30 - 0·50 = 0·20$	$P(E \mid E_3) = 0·1$	$P(E_3) \cdot P(E \mid E_3) = 0·02$
		Total $P(E) = 0·35$

$$P(E) = \sum_{i=1}^{3} P(E_i)\; P(E \mid E_i) = 0·35$$

The required probability that the consumer who purchased the product, heard about it on the radio is given by (By Bayes Rule) :

$$P(E_2 | E) = \frac{P(E_2) \cdot P(E | E_2)}{\sum_{i=1}^{3} P(E_i) \cdot P(E | E_i)} = \frac{P(E_2)\, P(E | E_2)}{P(E)} = \frac{0\cdot15}{0\cdot35} = \frac{3}{7}$$

Example 12·46. *The results of an investigation by an expert on a fire accident in a skyscraper are summarised below :*

(i) Prob. (there could have been short circuit) = 0·8

(ii) Prob. (LPG cylinder explosion) = 0·2

(iii) Chance of fire accident is 30% given a short circuit and 95% given an LPG explosion.

Based on these, what do you think is the most probable cause of fire ? Statistically justify your answer.

[*Delhi Univ. B.Com. (Hons.), (External), 2007; I.C.W.A. (Intermediate), Dec. 1998*]

Solution. Let us define the following events :

E_1 : Short circuit ; E_2 : LPG explosion ; E : Fire accident.

Then, we are given :

$P(E_1) = 0\cdot8$; $P(E_2) = 0\cdot2$; $P(E | E_1) = 0\cdot30$; $P(E | E_2) = 0\cdot95$

By Bayes' Rule :

$$P(E_1 | E) = \frac{P(E_1) \,.\, P(E | E_1)}{P(E_1)\, P(E | E_1) + P(E_2)\, P(E | E_2)} = \frac{0\cdot8 \times 0\cdot30}{0\cdot8 \times 0\cdot30 + 0\cdot2 \times 0\cdot95} = \frac{0\cdot240}{0\cdot240 + 0\cdot190} = \frac{24}{43}$$

$$P(E_2 | E) = \frac{P(E_2)\, P(E | E_2)}{P(E_1)\, P(E | E_1) + P(E_2)\, P(E | E_2)} = \frac{0\cdot190}{0\cdot430} = \frac{19}{43}$$

OR $\quad P(E_2 | E) = 1 - P(E_1 | E) = 1 - \frac{24}{43} = \frac{19}{43}$

Since $P(E_1 | E) > P(E_2 | E)$, short circuit is the most probable cause of fire.

Example 12·47. *A man has five coins, one of which has two heads. He randomly takes out a coin and tosses it three times.*

(i) What is the probability that it will fall head upward all the times ?

(ii) If it always falls head upward, what is the probability that it is the coin with two heads ?

[*Delhi Univ. B.Com. (Hons.), 2004*]

Solution. Define the following events.

E_1 : Selecting a normal coin ; E_2 : Selecting a coin with two heads,

E : In a random toss of coin three times, the coin falls head upward all the times.

Since, out of the five coins with the man, one coin has two heads, we have :

$$P(E_1) = \frac{4}{5}, \quad P(E_2) = \frac{1}{5}\,; \quad P(E | E_1) = \left(\frac{1}{2}\right)^3 = \frac{1}{8}, \quad P(E | E_2) = 1^3 = \mathbf{1}.$$

(*i*) Required probability is given by :

$$P(E) = P[(E \cap E_1) \cup (E \cap E_2)] = P(E \cap E_1) + PE \cap E_2)$$

$$= P(E_1)\, P(E | E_1) + P(E_2)\, P(E | E_2) = \frac{4}{5} \times \frac{1}{8} + \frac{1}{5} \times 1 = \frac{3}{10} = 0\cdot3$$

(*ii*) Required probability $= P(E_2 | E) = \frac{P(E_2)\, P(E | E_2)}{P(E)} = \frac{(1/5) \times 1}{(3/10)} = \frac{2}{3} = 0\cdot67$ (By Bayes' Rule)

Example 12·48. *Each of the three identical jewellery boxes has 2 drawers. In each drawer of the first box, there is a gold watch. In each drawer of the second box there is a silver watch. In one drawer of the third box, there is a gold watch while in the other drawer there is a silver watch. If we select a box at random, open one of the drawers and find it to contain a silver watch, what is the probability that the other drawer has the gold watch ?*

Solution. Let us define the following events :

E_i : The event that ith box is selected ; $(i = 1, 2, 3)$.

E : The event that the opened drawer of the selected box contains a silver watch.

Then we have :

$$P(E_1) = P(E_2) = P(E_3) = \tfrac{1}{3} \;;\quad P(E \mid E_1) = 0 \;;\quad P(E \mid E_2) = 1 \quad \text{and} \quad P(E \mid E_3) = \tfrac{1}{2} \qquad \ldots(*)$$

We are given that one of the drawers of the selected box contains a silver watch and we want that the second drawer of the box contains a gold watch. This can happen only if the third box is selected because it is only the third box which contains silver and gold watches in its drawers. Hence, we are required to find the probability $P(E_3 \mid E)$.

By Bayes' theorem, the required probability is given by :

$$P(E_3 \mid E) = \frac{P(E_3) \,.\, P(E \mid E_3)}{P(E_1)\, P(E \mid E_1) + P(E_2)\, P(E \mid E_2) + P(E_3)\, P(E \mid E_3)}$$

$$= \frac{\frac{1}{3} \times \frac{1}{2}}{\frac{1}{3} \times 0 + \frac{1}{3} \times 1 + \frac{1}{3} \times \frac{1}{2}} = \frac{\frac{1}{6}}{\frac{1}{3} + \frac{1}{6}} = \frac{1}{3} \qquad \text{[From (*)]}$$

Example 12·49. *An urn contains four balls. Two balls are drawn at random and are found to be white. What is the probability that all the balls are white ?* [*I.C.W.A. (Intermediate), June 2000*]

Solution. Since two balls are drawn and they are found to be white, the urn must contain at least two white balls. Let us define the following events :

E_i $(i = 2, 3, 4)$: The event that the urn contains i white balls.

E : The event that two white balls are drawn.

Since the events E_2, E_3 and E_4 are equally likely, we have : $P(E_2) = P(E_3) = P(E_4) = \frac{1}{3}$ ...(*i*)

$P(E \mid E_2)$ = Probability of drawing two white balls, given that the urn contains 2 white balls.

$$= \frac{{}^2C_2}{{}^4C_2} = \frac{1}{6} \qquad \ldots(ii)$$

Similarly, we have : $P(E \mid E_3) = \dfrac{{}^3C_2}{{}^4C_2} = \dfrac{3}{6} = \dfrac{1}{2}$ and $P(E \mid E_4) = \dfrac{{}^4C_2}{{}^4C_2} = 1$ ...(*iii*)

We want the conditional probability $P(E_4 \mid E)$.

$$P(E_4 \mid E) = \frac{P(E_4)\, P(E \mid E_4)}{P(E_2)\, P(E \mid E_2) + P(E_3)\, P(E \mid E_3) + P(E_4)\, P(E \mid E_4)} \qquad \text{[By Bayes' Rule]}$$

$$= \frac{\frac{1}{3} \times 1}{\frac{1}{3} \times \frac{1}{6} + \frac{1}{3} \times \frac{1}{2} + \frac{1}{3} \times 1} = \frac{\frac{1}{3}}{\frac{1}{18} + \frac{1}{6} + \frac{1}{3}} = \frac{\frac{1}{3}}{\frac{10}{18}} = \frac{3}{5} = 0{\cdot}6. \qquad \text{[From (i), (ii) and (iii)]}$$

Example 12·50. *The contents of urns I, II and III are as follows :*

1 white, 2 black and 3 red balls ; 2 white, 1 black and 1 red balls, and ; 4 white, 5 black and 3 red balls.

One urn is chosen at random and two balls drawn. They happen to be white and red. What is the probability that they came from urns I, II, III ?

Solution. Let E_1, E_2 and E_3 denote the events of choosing 1st, 2nd and 3rd urn respectively and let E be the event that the two balls drawn from the selected urn are white and red. Then we have :

	E_1	E_2	E_3
$P(E_i)$	1/3	1/3	1/3
$P(E \mid E_i)$	$\frac{1 \times 3}{^6C_2} = \frac{1}{5}$	$\frac{2 \times 1}{^4C_2} = \frac{1}{3}$	$\frac{4 \times 3}{^{12}C_2} = \frac{2}{11}$
$P(E \cap E_i) = P(E_i) \times P(E \mid E_i)$	$\frac{1}{3} \times \frac{1}{5} = \frac{1}{15}$	$\frac{1}{3} \times \frac{1}{3} = \frac{1}{9}$	$\frac{1}{3} \times \frac{2}{11} = \frac{2}{33}$

We have : $$\Sigma P(E_i)\, P(E \mid E_i) = \frac{1}{15} + \frac{1}{9} + \frac{2}{33} = \frac{33 + 55 + 30}{495} = \frac{118}{495}$$

Hence by Bayes's rule, the probability that the two white and red balls drawn are from 1st urn is :

$$P(E_1 \mid E) = \frac{P(E_1)\, P(E \mid E_1)}{\Sigma P(E_i)\, P(E \mid E_i)} = \frac{1/15}{118/495} = \frac{33}{118}$$

Similarly, we have $$P(E_2 \mid E) = \frac{P(E_2)\, P(E \mid E_2)}{\Sigma P(E_i)\, P(E \mid E_i)} = \frac{1/9}{118/495} = \frac{55}{118}$$

and $$P(E_3 \mid E) = \frac{2/33}{118/495} = \frac{30}{118} \quad Or \quad P(E_3 \mid E) = 1 - \frac{33}{118} - \frac{55}{118} = \frac{30}{118}.$$

Example 12·51. *A speaks the truth 2 out of 3 times and B 4 out of 5 times ; they agree in the assertion that from a bag containing 6 balls of different colours, a black ball has been drawn. Find the probability that the statement is true.* [*Delhi Univ. B.Com., (Hons.) 2005*]

Solution. The probability of drawing a black ball $= \frac{1}{6}$

The probability of drawing a non-black ball $= \frac{5}{6}$

P {A says black ball to black ball} $= \frac{2}{3}$; P(B says black ball to black ball} $= \frac{4}{5}$

If a black ball has been drawn, the probability that both A and B agree in aserting that it is black is given by compound probability theorem as :

$$\frac{1}{6} \times \frac{2}{3} \times \frac{4}{5} = \frac{4}{45}$$

The probability that A asserts falsely that a certain ball is black $= \left(1 - \frac{2}{3}\right) \times \frac{1}{5} = \frac{1}{15}$, because there are 5 balls of different colours, other than black.

Similarly, the probability that B asserts falsely that a certain ball is black $= \left(1 - \frac{4}{5}\right) \times \frac{1}{5} = \frac{1}{25}$

Hence, if a non-black ball is drawn, the probability that both A and B agree in asserting that it is black is

$$\frac{5}{6} \times \frac{1}{15} \times \frac{1}{25} = \frac{1}{450}$$

After a ball is drawn the probability that both agree in saying truth to the probability that both say false is

$$\frac{4}{45} : \frac{1}{450} = \frac{40}{450} : \frac{1}{450} = 40 : 1$$

$\therefore$ Required probability that the statement is true $= \frac{40}{40 + 1} = \frac{40}{41}$

EXERCISE 12·3

1. Next year there will be three candidates for the position of principal, in the college, Dr. Singhal, Mr. Mehra and Dr. Chatterji, whose chances of getting appointment are in the proportion 4 : 2 : 3 respectively. The probability that Dr. Singhal if selected, will abolish co-education in the college is 0·3. The probability of Mr. Mehra and Dr. Chatterji doing the same are respectively 0·5 and 0·8. What is the probability that co-education will be abolished from the college next year ?

Ans. (23 / 45) = 0·5111

2. Suppose that one of three men, a politician, a businessman, and an educationist, will be appointed as the vice-chancellor of a university. The respective probabilities of their appointments are 0·50, 0·30, 0·20. The probabilities that research activities will be promoted by these people if they are appointed are 0·30, 0·70 and 0·80 respectively. What is the probability that research will be promoted by the new vice-chancellor ?

Ans. 0·52.

3. Assume that a factory has two machines. Past records show that machine 1 produces 30% of the items of output and machine 2 were produces 70% of the items. Further, 5% of the items produced by machine 1 were defective and only 1% produced by machine 2 defective. If a defective item is drawn at random, what is the probability that it was produced by (*i*) machine 1, (*ii*) meahine 2 ?

Ans. (*i*) 0·682, (*ii*) 0·318.

4. In a bolt factory machines *A*, *B* and *C* manufacture respectively 20%, 30% and 50% of the total of its output. Of them 5, 4 and 2 per cent respectively are defective bolts. A bolt is drawn at random from the product and is found to be defective. What is the probability that it was manufactured by machine *B* ? *[I.C.W.A. (Intermediate), Dec. 1998]*

Ans. (3/8) = 0·375.

5. (*a*) Distinguish between a-priori probability and posteriori probability. *[Delhi Univ. B.Com. (Hons.) 1997]*

(*b*) State and prove Bayes Theorem and write a note on its importance in Statistics.

6. A factory produces a certain type of outputs by three types of machines. The respective daily production figures are :

Machine I : 3,000 Units ; *Machine II* : 2,500 Units ; *Machine III* : 4,500 Units.

Past experience shows that 1 per cent of the output produced by Machine I is defective. The corresponding fraction of defectives for the other two machines are 1·2 per cent and 2 per cent respectively. An item is drawn at random from the day's production run and is found to be defective. What is probability that it comes from the output of

(*a*) Machine I, (*b*) Machine II, and (*c*) Machine III ?

Ans. (*a*) 1/5, (*b*) 1/5, (*c*) 3/5.

7. Suppose that a product is produced in three factories *A*, *B and C*. It is known that factory *A* produces twice as many items as factory *B*, and that factories *B and C* produce the same number of products. Assume that it is known that 2 per cent of the items produced by each of the factories *A* and *B* are defective while 4 per cent of those manufactured by factory *C* are defective. All the items produced in three factories are stocked, and an item of product is selected at random. What is the probability that this item is defective ?

Ans. 0·025.

8. A company has three plants to manufacture 8,000 scooters in a month. Out of 8,000 scooters, Plant I manufactures 4,000 scooters, Plant II manufactures 3,000 scooters and Plant III manufactures 1,000 scooters. At Plant I, 85 out of 100 scooters are rated of standard quality or better; at Plant II only 65 out of 100 scooters are rated of standard quality or better, and at Plant III, 60 out of 100 scooters are rated of standard quality or better. What is the probability that the scooter selected at random came from (*i*) Plant I, (*ii*) Plant II and (*iii*) Plant III, if it is known that the scooter is of a standard quality ? *[Delhi Univ. B. Com. (Hons.), 1995]*

Ans. (*i*) 0·571, (*ii*) 0·328, (*iii*) 0·101

9. Due to turnover and absenteeism at an assembly plant, 20% of the items are assembled by inexperienced employees. Management has determined that customers return 12% of the items assembled by inexperienced employees, whereas only 3% of the items assembled by experienced employees are returned. What is the probability that an item was assembled by an inexperienced employee, given that the item was returned ? *[I.C.W.A. (Intermediate), June 1995]*

Ans. 0·5.

10. Suppose there is a chance for a newly constructed building to collapse, whether the design is faulty or not. The chance that the design is faulty is 10%. The chance that the building collapses is 95% if the design is faulty and otherwise it is 45%. It is seen that the building collapsed. What is the probability that it is due to faulty design. *[I.C.W.A. (Intermediate), Dec. 1996]*

Ans. 0·19.

11. (*a*) In a population of workers, suppose 40% are grade school graduates, 50% are high school graduates, and 10% are college graduates. Among the grade school graduates, 10% are unemployed ; among the high school graduates, 5% are unemployed, and among the college graduates 2% are unemployed.

If a worker is chosen at random and found to be unemployed, what is the probability that he is a college graduate ?

Ans. 0·03.

(*b*) Market studies have shown that 30% of chartered accountants leave their jobs to start their own consultancy. Among those who leave their jobs, 60% have a degree in law while 20% of those who do not leave, have a law degree. If a chartered accountant has a law degree, what is the probability he will leave his current job to set up his own consultancy firm ? [*Delhi Univ. B.A. (Econ. Hons.), 2007*]

Hint. E_1 : C.A. leave the jobs ; E_2 : C.A. does not leave the jobs ; E : C.A. has law degree.

Then, we are given : $P(E_1) = 0{\cdot}30 \Rightarrow P(E_2) = 0{\cdot}70$; $P(E \mid E_1) = 0{\cdot}60$ and $P(E \mid E_2) = 0{\cdot}20$

$$\text{Required probability} = P(E_1 \mid E) = \frac{P(E_1)\,P(E \mid E_1)}{\sum\limits_i P(E_i)\,P(E \mid E_i)} = \frac{0{\cdot}0180}{0{\cdot}0320} = \frac{9}{16} = 0{\cdot}5625$$

12. A manufacturing firm produces pipes in two plants I and II, the daily production being 1,500 and 2,000 pipes respectively. The fraction defective of pipes produced by the plants I and II are 0·006 and 0·008 respectively. If a pipe selected at random, from the day's production is found to be defective, what is the probability that it has come from plant I ? [*I.C.W.A. (Intermediate), June 2002*]

Ans. 0·36.

13. You note that your officer is happy in 60% cases of your calls. You have also noticed that if he is happy, he accedes to your requests with a probability of 0·4, whereas if he is not happy, he accedes to your requests with a probability of 0·1. You call on him one day and he accedes to your request. What is the probability of his being happy ? [*Delhi Univ. B.Com. (Hons.), (External), 2006; Himachal Pradesh Univ. M.B.A. 1996*]

Ans. (6/7) = 0·857.

14. The odds against A speaking the truth are 4 : 6, while the odds in favour of B speaking the truth are 7 : 3.

(*i*) What is the probability that A and B contradict each other in stating the same fact ?

(*ii*) A and B agree on a statement, what is the probability that the statement is true ?

Ans. (*i*) 0·46, (*ii*) (21/27) = 0·78

15. In a certain recruitment test there are multiple choice questions. There are four possible answers to each question and of these one is correct. An intelligent student knows 90% of the answers while a weak student knows only 20% answers.

(*i*) If an intelligent student gets the correct answers, what is the probability that he was guessing ?

(*ii*) If a weak student gets the correct answer, what is the probability that he was guessing ?

[*Gujarat Univ. M.B.A., 1995*]

Hint. Define the events : E_1 : The student knows the answer ; E_2 : The student guesses the answer.
E : The student gets the correct answer.

Do the question separately for intelligent students and weak students.

Ans. (*i*) $\dfrac{P(E_2)\,P(E \mid E_2)}{P(E_1)\,P(E \mid E_1) + P(E_2)\,P(E \mid E_2)} = \dfrac{0{\cdot}10 \times 0{\cdot}25}{0{\cdot}90 \times 1 + 0{\cdot}10 \times 0{\cdot}25} = \dfrac{0{\cdot}025}{0{\cdot}925} = \dfrac{1}{37}$ (*ii*) $\dfrac{0{\cdot}80 \times 0{\cdot}25}{0{\cdot}20 \times 1 + 0{\cdot}80 \times 0{\cdot}25} = \dfrac{0{\cdot}2}{0{\cdot}4} = \dfrac{1}{2} = 0{\cdot}5$

16. In a competitive examination, an examine either guesses or copies or knows the answer to a multiple choice question with four choices. The probability that he makes a guess is 0·35 and the probability that he copies the answer is 0·20. The probability that the answer is correct, given that he copied it is 0·15. Find the probability that he :

(*a*) guesses, (*b*) copies, (*c*) knows ,

the answer to the question, given that he correctly answered it.

Ans. (*a*) $\frac{35}{227}$, (*b*) $= \frac{12}{227}$, (*c*) $\frac{180}{227}$.

17. An insurance company insured 2000 scooter drivers, 4000 car drivers and 6000 truck drivers. The probability of an accident involving a scooter, a car and a truck is 1/100, 3/100 and 3/20 respectively. One of the insured persons meets with an accident. What is the probability that he is a :

(*i*) scooter driver, (*ii*) car driver, (*iiii*) truck driver ?

Ans. (*i*) $\frac{1}{52}$, (*ii*) $\frac{3}{26}$, (*iii*) $\frac{45}{52}$.

18. Explain the concept of conditional probability.

An insurance company insured 2,000 scooter drivers, 4,000 car drivers and 6,000 truck drivers. The probability of their accident is 0·1, 0·3 and 0·2 respectively. One of the insured persons meets with an accident. What is the probability that he is a scooter driver ? *[Delhi Univ. B.Com. (Hons.), (External), 2005]*

Ans. $\dfrac{\frac{2}{12}\times 0\cdot 1}{\frac{2}{12}\times 0\cdot 1+\frac{4}{12}\times 0\cdot 3+\frac{6}{12}\times 0\cdot 2}=\dfrac{0\cdot 2}{0\cdot 2+1\cdot 2+1\cdot 2}=\dfrac{2}{26}=\dfrac{1}{13}=0\cdot 0769.$

19. A doctor is to visit a patient. From the past experience, it is known that the probabilities that he will come by car, taxi, scooter or by other means of transport are 0·3, 0·2, 0·1 and 0·4 respectively. The probabilities that he will be late are 1/4, 1/3 and 1/12, if he comes by car, taxi and scooter respectively. But, if he comes by other means of transport, then he will not be late. When he arrives, he is late. What is the probability that he comes by car ?

Ans. $\frac{1}{2}$.

20. The chance that a doctor will diagnose a disease correctly is 60%. The chance that a patient will die by his treatment after correct diagnosis is 40% and the chance of death by wrong diagnosis is 70%. A patient of the doctor who had the disease died. What is the chance that the disease was diagnosed correctly ?

[Delhi Univ. B.A. (Econ. Hons.), 2004]

Ans.

Hint. E_1 : Doctor diagnoses the disease correctly ; E_2 : Doctor diagnoses the disease wrongly

E : The patient dies.

$P(E_1)=0\cdot 60$; $P(E_2)=1-0\cdot 6=0\cdot 40$; $P(E\mid E_1)=0\cdot 40$; $P(E\mid E_2)=0\cdot 70$

$$P(E_1\mid E)=\frac{P(E_1)\,P(E\mid E_1)}{P(E_1)\,P(E\mid E_1)+P(E_2)\,P(E\mid E_2)}=\frac{0\cdot 6\times 0\cdot 4}{0\cdot 6\times 0\cdot 4+0\cdot 4\times 0\cdot 7}=\frac{6}{13}=0\cdot 4615$$

21. There are three identical boxes containing respectively 1 white and 3 red balls, 2 white and 1 red balls ; 4 white and 3 red balls. One box is chosen at random and two balls are drawn : (*i*) find the probability that the balls are white and red, (*ii*) if the balls are white and red, what is the probability that they are from the second box ?

Ans. (*i*) (73 / 126) = 0·5794. (*ii*) (28 / 73) = 0·3836.

22. There are two identical boxes containing respectively 4 white and 3 red balls, 3 white and 7 red balls. A box is chosen at random and a ball is drawn from it. Find the probability that the ball is white. If the ball is white, that is the probability that it is from first box ? *[Delhi Univ. B.A.(Econ. Hons.), 1995]*

Ans. $\frac{61}{140}=0\cdot 4357.$ (*ii*) $\frac{40}{61}=0\cdot 6557.$

23. *A* and *B* are two very weak students of Statistics and their chances of solving a problem correctly are 1/8 and 1/12 respectively. If the probability of their making a common mistake is 1/1001 and they obtain same answer, find the chance that their answer is correct.

Ans. 13/14.

24. *A* speaks the truth 3 times out of 4, and *B* 7 times out of 10 ; they both assert that a white ball has been drawn from a bag containing 6 balls of different colours : find the probability of the truth of the assertion.

Ans. 35/36.

13 Random Variable, Probability Distributions and Mathematical Expectation

13·1. RANDOM VARIABLE

Intuitively, by a random variable (*r.v.*) we mean a real number X associated with the outcomes of a random experiment. It can take any one of the various possible values each with a definite probability. For example, in a throw of a die, if X denotes the number obtained, then X is a random variable which can take any one of the values 1, 2, 3, 4, 5 or 6, each with equal probability 1/6. Similarly, in toss of a coin if X denotes the number of heads, then X is a random variable which can take any one of the two values : 0 (No head, *i.e.,* tail) or 1 (*i.e.,* head), each with equal probability $\frac{1}{2}$.

Let us now consider a random experiment of three tosses of a coin (or three coins tossed simultaneously). Then the sample space S consists of $2^3 = 8$ points as given below :

$$\begin{aligned} S &= \{ (H, T) \times (H, T) \times (H, T) \} \\ &= \{ (HH, HT, TH, TT) \times (H, T) \} \\ &= \{ HHH, HTH, THH, TTH, HHT, HTT, THT, TTT \} \end{aligned}$$

Let us consider the variable X, which is the number of heads obtained. Then, X is a random variable which can take any one of the values 0, 1 or 2.

Outcome	:	*HHH*	*HTH*	*THH*	*TTH*	*HHT*	*HTT*	*THT*	*TTT*
Values of X	:	*3*	2	2	*1*	2	*1*	*1*	*0*

If the sample points in the above order be denoted by $w_1, w_2, w_3, \ldots, w_8$ then to each outcome w of the random experiment, we can assign a real number $X = X(w)$. For example,

$$X(w_1) = 3, \qquad X(w_2) = 2, \qquad X(w_3) = 2, \qquad \ldots, \qquad X(w_8) = 0.$$

Thus, rigorously speaking, random variable may be defined as *a real valued function on the sample space, taking values on the real line* $R(-\infty, \infty)$. In other words, random variable is a function which takes real values which are determined by the outcomes of the random experiment.

Remarks 1. A random variable is denoted by the capital letters $X, Y, Z,\ldots$etc., of the English alphabet and particular values which the random variable takes are denoted by the corresponding small letters of the English alphabet.

2. It should be clearly understood that the actual values which the event assumes is not a random variable. For example, in three tosses of a coin, the number of heads obtained is a random variable which can take any one of the three values 0, 1, 2 or 3 as long as the coin is not tossed. But, after it is tossed and we get two heads, then 2 is not a random variable.

3. Discrete and Continuous Random Variables. If the random variable X assumes only a finite or countably infinite set of values it is known as *discrete* random variable. For example, marks obtained by students in a test, the number of students in a college, the number of defective mangoes in a basket of mangoes, number of accidents taking place on a busy road, etc., are all discrete random variables.

On the other hand, if the *r.v.* X can assume infinite and uncountable set of values, it is said to be a *continuous r.v.*, *e.g.*, the age, height or weight of students in a class are all continuous random variables. In case of a continuous random variable we usually talk of the value in a particular interval and not at a point. Generally discrete *r.v.*'s, represent counted data while continuous *r.v.*'s represent measured data.

13·2. PROBABILITY DISTRIBUTION OF A DISCRETE RANDOM VARIABLE

Let us consider a discrete *r.v.* X which can take the possible values $x_1, x_2, x_3,..., x_n$. With each value of the variable X, we associate a number,

$$p_i = P(X = X_i) \ ; \ i = 1, 2,..., n$$

which is known as the probability of X_i and satisfies the following conditions :

$$(i) \qquad p_i = P(X = X_i) \geq 0, (i = 1, 2,..., n) \qquad ...(13·1)$$

i.e., p_i's are all non-negative and

$$(ii) \quad \sum p_i = p_1 + p_2 + ... + p_n = 1, \qquad ...(13·2)$$

i.e., the total probability is one.

More specifically, let X be a discrete random variable and define :

$$p(x) = P(X = x)$$

such that $p(x) \geq 0$ and $\sum p(x) = 1$, summation being taken over various values of the variable.

The function $p_i = P(X = X_i)$ or $p(x)$ is called the *probability function or more precisely probability mass function (p.m.f)* of the random variable X and the set of all possible ordered pairs $\{x, p(x)\}$, is called the *probability distribution* of the random variable X.

Remark. The concept of probability distribution is analogous to that of frequency distribution. Just as frequency distribution tells us how the total frequency is distributed among different values (or classes) of the variable, similarly a probability distribution tells us how total probability of 1 is distributed among the various values which the random variable can take. It is usually represented in a tabular form given below :

TABLE 13·1 **PROBABILITY DISTRIBUTION OF *r.v.* X**

x	x_1	x_2	x_3	......	x_n
$p(x)$	p_1	p_2	p_3	......	p_n

13·3. PROBABILITY DISTRIBUTION OF A CONTINUOUS RANDOM VARIABLE

Unlike a discrete probability distribution, a continuous probability distribution can not be presented in a tabular form. It has either a formula form or a graphical form. To understand these forms, let us go back to Chapter 4 where we learned how to draw a *histogram* and *frequency polygon* of a grouped frequency distribution for a continuous variable.

A frequency polygon gets smoother and smoother as the sample size gets larger, and the class intervals become more numerous and narrower. Ultimately the density polygon becomes a smooth curve called the *density curve.* The function that defines the curve is called the *probability density function.*

13·3·1. Probability Density Function (p.d.f.) of Continuous random Variable

Let X be a continuous random variable taking values on the interval $[a, b]$.

A function $p(x)$ is said to be the *probability density function* of the continuous random variable X if it satisfies the following properties :

(*i*) $p(x) \geq 0$ for all x in the interval $[a, b]$.

(*ii*) For two distinct numbers c and d in the interval $[a, b]$

$P(c \leq X \leq d)$ = [Area under the probability curve between the ordinates (vertical lines) at $x = c$ and $x = d$] (Fig. 13·1) ... (13·3)

(*iii*) Total area under the probability curve is 1,

i.e., $P(a \leq X \leq b) = 1$ ... (13·3*a*)

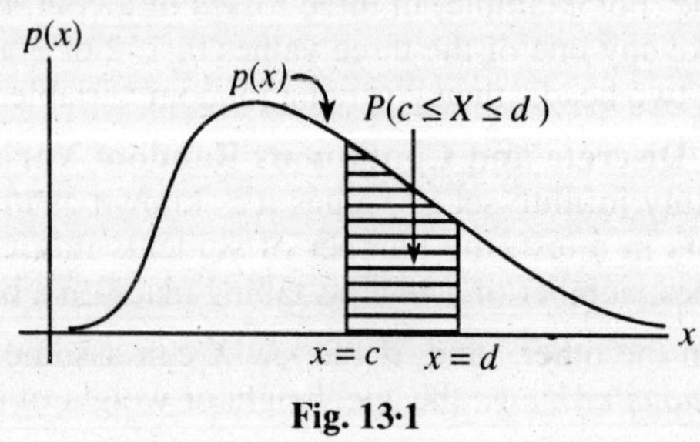

Fig. 13·1

Remarks 1. *For a continuous random variable, the probability at a point is always zero*

i.e., $P(X = c) = 0$, *for all single point values of c.* ... (13·4)

Hence, in case of continuous random variable, we always talk of probabilities in an interval and not at a point (which is always zero).

2. Since in the case of continuous random variable, the probability at a point is always zero, we have

$$P(X = c) = 0 \quad \text{and} \quad P(x = d) = 0 \qquad \text{... (*)}$$

Writing

$$c \le X \le d = (c < X \le d) \cup (X = c)$$
$$c \le X \le d = (c \le X < d) \cup (X = d)$$
$$c \le X \le d = (c < X < d) \cup (X = c) \cup (X = d),$$

all the events on the right hand being mutually exclusive (disjoint), and using (*), and the addition theorem of probability [Axion of Additivity], we get :

$$P(c \le X \le d) = P(c < X \le d) = P(c \le X < d) = P(c < X < d) \qquad \text{... (13·4a)}$$

Hence, *in case of continuous random variable, it does not matter if one or both the end points of the interval (c, d) are included or not.*

However, this result is not true, in general, for discrete random variables.

Illustration. If X is a continuous random variable, then

$$P(X \le 5) = P(X < 5)$$

However, if X is a discrete random variable taking positive integer values, then

$$P(X \le 5) = p(0) + p(1) + p(2) + p(3) + p(4) + p(5)$$

and

$$P(X < 5) = P(X \le 4)$$
$$= p(0) + p(1) + p(2) + p(3) + p(4)$$

Therefore $P(X \le 5) \ne P(X < 5)$, in general.

3. Probability Density Function (Continuous r.v.). In case of a continuous random variable, we do not talk of probability at a particular point (which is always zero) but we always talk of probability in an interval. If $p(x)\,dx$ is the probability that the random variable X takes the value in a small interval of magnitude dx, *e.g.,* $(x, x + dx)$ or $\left(x - \frac{dx}{2}, x + \frac{dx}{2}\right)$, then $p(x)$ is called the *probability density function* (*p.d.f.*) of the *r.v. X.*

13·4. DISTRIBUTION FUNCTION OR CUMULATIVE PROBABILITY FUNCTION

If X is a discrete *r.v.* with probability function $p(x)$ then, the distribution function, usually denoted by $F(x)$ is defined as :

$$F(x) = P(X \le x) \qquad \text{...(13·5)}$$

If X takes integral values, *viz.*, 1, 2, 3, ...then

$$F(x) = P(X = 1) + P(X = 2) + \ldots + P(X = x)$$

$$\Rightarrow \quad F(x) = p(1) + p(2) + p(3) + \ldots + p(x) \qquad \text{...(13·5a)}$$

Remarks. 1. In the above case,

$$F(x - 1) = p(1) + p(2) + \ldots + p(x - 1)$$

$$\therefore \quad F(x) - F(x - 1) = p(x) \quad \Rightarrow \quad p(x) = F(x) - F(x - 1) \qquad \text{...(13·5b)}$$

Hence, if X is a random variable which can take only positive integral values, then probability function can be obtained from distribution function by using (13·5*b*).

2. If X is a continuous *r.v.* with probability density function $p(x)$, then the distribution function is given by the integral

$$F(x) = P(X \le x) = \int_{-\infty}^{x} p(x)\, dx \qquad \text{...(13·5}c\text{)}$$

13·5. MOMENTS

If X is a discrete *r.v.* with probability function $p(x)$ then :

$$\mu'_r = r\text{th moment about any arbitrary point '}A\text{'} = \Sigma\, (x - A)^r . \, p(x) \qquad \text{...(13·6)}$$

$$\mu_r = r\text{th moment about mean } (\bar{x}) = \Sigma (x - \bar{x})^r . \, p(x) \qquad \text{...(13·7)}$$

In particular,

$$\text{Mean } (\bar{x}) = \text{First moment about origin} = \Sigma\, x\, p(x). \qquad \text{...(13·8)}$$

[Taking $A = 0$ and $r = 1$ in (13·6)].

$$\text{Variance } (x) = \mu_2 = \Sigma (x - \bar{x})^2 . \, p(x) \qquad \text{...(13·9)}$$

In the expressions from (13·6) to (13·9), the summation is taken over the various values of the *r.v.* X.

In the case of continuous *r.v.* with *p.d.f.* $p(x)$, the above formulae hold with the only difference that summation is replaced by integration $\left(\int\right)$ over the values of the variable.

Example 13·1. *A die is tossed twice. Getting 'an odd number' is termed as a success. Find the probability distribution of the number of successes.*

Solution. Since the cases favourable to getting an odd number in a throw of a die are (1, 3, 5), *i.e.*, 3 in all,

$$\text{Probability of success}(S) = \frac{3}{6} = \frac{1}{2} \quad ; \quad \text{Probability of failure } (F) = 1 - \frac{1}{2} = \frac{1}{2} \cdot$$

If X denotes the number of successes in two throws of a die, then X is a random variable which takes the values 0, 1, 2.

$$P(X = 0) = P[F \text{ in 1st throw and } F \text{ in 2nd throw}] = P(FF) = P(F) \times P(F) = \frac{1}{2} \times \frac{1}{2} = \frac{1}{4}$$

$$P(X = 1) = P(S \text{ and } F) + P(F \text{ and } S) = P(S)\, P(F) + P(F)\, P(S) = \frac{1}{2} \times \frac{1}{2} + \frac{1}{2} \times \frac{1}{2} = \frac{1}{2}$$

$$P(X = 2) = P(S \text{ and } S) = P(S)\, P(S) = \frac{1}{2} \times \frac{1}{2} = \frac{1}{4}$$

Hence the probability distribution of X is given by :

x	0	1	2
$p(x)$	$\frac{1}{4}$	$\frac{1}{2}$	$\frac{1}{4}$

Example 13·2. *Two cards are drawn*

(a) successively with replacement

(b) simultaneously (successively without replacement),

from a well shuffled deck of 52 cards. Find the probability distribution of the number of aces.

Solution. Let X denote the number of aces obtained in a draw of two cards. Obviously, X is a random variable which can take the values 0, 1 or 2.

(*a*) Probability of drawing an ace $= \frac{4}{52} = \frac{1}{13} \quad \Rightarrow \quad$ Probability of drawing a non-ace $= 1 - \frac{1}{13} = \frac{12}{13}$

Since the cards are drawn with replacement, all the draws are independent.

$$P(X = 2) = P(\text{Ace and Ace}) = P(\text{Ace}) \times P(\text{Ace}) = \frac{1}{13} \times \frac{1}{13} = \frac{1}{169} \cdot$$

$$P(X=1) = P(\text{Ace and Non-ace}) + P(\text{Non-ace and Ace})$$
$$= P(\text{Ace}) \times P(\text{Non-ace}) + P(\text{Non-ace}) \times P(\text{Ace})$$
$$= \frac{1}{13} \times \frac{12}{13} + \frac{12}{13} \times \frac{1}{13} = \frac{24}{169}$$

$$P(X=0) = P(\text{Non-ace and Non-ace}) = P(\text{Non-ace}) \times P(\text{Non-ace}) = \frac{12}{13} \times \frac{12}{13} = \frac{144}{169}$$

Hence, the probability distribution of X is :

x :	0	1	2
$p(x)$:	$\frac{144}{169}$	$\frac{24}{169}$	$\frac{1}{169}$

(*b*) If cards are drawn without replacement, then exhaustive number of cases of drawing 2 cards out of 52 cards is ${}^{52}C_2$.

$$\therefore \quad P(X=0) = P(\text{No ace}) = P(\text{Both cards are non-aces}) = \frac{{}^{48}C_2}{{}^{52}C_2} = \frac{48 \times 47}{52 \times 51} = \frac{188}{221}$$

$$P(X=1) = P(\text{one ace}) = P(\text{one ace and one non-ace}) = \frac{{}^4C_1 \times {}^{48}C_1}{{}^{52}C_2} = \frac{4 \times 48 \times 2}{52 \times 51} = \frac{32}{221}$$

$$P(X=2) = P(\text{both aces}) = \frac{{}^4C_2}{{}^{52}C_2} = \frac{4 \times 3}{52 \times 51} = \frac{1}{221}$$

Hence, the probability distribution of X becomes :

x :	0	1	2
$p(x)$:	$\frac{188}{221}$	$\frac{32}{221}$	$\frac{1}{221}$

Example 13·3. *Obtain the probability distribution of X, the number of heads in three tosses of a coin (or a simultaneous toss of three coins).*

Solution. Obviously, X is a random variable which can take the values 0, 1, 2 or 3. The sample space S consists of $2^3 = 8$ sample points, as given below :

$$S = \{(H, T) \times (H, T) \times (H, T)\}$$
$$= \{(HH, HT, TH, TT) \times (H, T)\}$$
$$= \{HHH, HTH, THH, TTH, HHT, HTT, THT, TTT\}$$

The probability distribution of X is given in Table 13·2.

TABLE 13·2 : **PROBABILITY DISTRIBUTION OF NUMBER OF HEADS IN 3 TOSSES OF A COIN**

No. of heads (x)	*Favourable events*	*No. of favourable cases*	*Probability* $p(x)$
0	$\{TTT\}$	1	$\frac{1}{8}$
1	$\{TTH, HTT, THT\}$	3	$\frac{3}{8}$
2	$\{HTH, THH, HHT\}$	3	$\frac{3}{8}$
3	$\{HHH\}$	1	$\frac{1}{8}$

Example 13·4. *Two dice are rolled at random. Obtain the probability distribution of the sum of the numbers on them.*

Solution. When two dice are rolled, the sample space S consists of $6^2 = 36$, sample points as shown.

Let X denote the sum of the numbers on the two dice. Then X is a random variable which can take the values 2, 3, 4, ..., 12 with the probability distribution given in Table 13·3.

$$S = \left\{ \begin{array}{llll} (1,1), & (1,2), & \ldots, & (1,6) \\ (2,1), & (2,2), & \ldots, & (2,6) \\ \vdots & & & \vdots \\ (6,1), & (6,2), & \ldots, & (6,6) \end{array} \right\}$$

TABLE 13·3. **PROBABILITY DISTRIBUTION OF SUM OF POINTS IN TOSS OF TWO DICE**

Sum of numbers (x)	*Favourable sample points*	*No. of favourable cases*	*Probability* $p(x)$
2	(1, 1)	1	$\frac{1}{36}$
3	(1, 2), (2, 1)	2	$\frac{2}{36}$
4	(1, 3), (3, 1), (2, 2)	3	$\frac{3}{36}$
5	(1, 4), (4, 1), (2, 3), (3, 2)	4	$\frac{4}{36}$
6	(1, 5), (5, 1), (2, 4), (4, 2), (3, 3)	5	$\frac{5}{36}$
7	(1, 6), (6, 1), (2, 5), (5, 2), (3, 4), (4, 3)	6	$\frac{6}{36}$
8	(2, 6), (6, 2), (3, 5), (5, 3), (4, 4)	5	$\frac{5}{36}$
9	(3, 6), (6, 3), (4, 5), (5, 4)	4	$\frac{4}{36}$
10	(4, 6), (6, 4), (5, 5)	3	$\frac{3}{36}$
11	(5, 6), (6, 5)	2	$\frac{2}{36}$
12	(6, 6)	1	$\frac{1}{36}$

Example 13·5. *Four bad apples are mixed accidentally with 20 good apples. Obtain the probability distribution of the number of bad apples in a draw of 2 apples at random.*

Solution. Let X denote the number of bad apples drawn. Then X is a random variable which can take the values 0, 1 or 2.

There are 4 + 20 = 24 apples, in all and the exhaustive number of cases of drawing two apples is ${}^{24}C_2$.

$$\therefore \quad P(X=0) = \frac{{}^{20}C_2}{{}^{24}C_2} = \frac{20 \times 19}{24 \times 23} = \frac{95}{138} \quad ; \quad P(X=1) = \frac{{}^{4}C_1 \times {}^{20}C_1}{{}^{24}C_2} = \frac{2 \times 4 \times 20}{24 \times 23} = \frac{40}{138}$$

$$P(X=2) = \frac{{}^{4}C_2}{{}^{24}C_2} = \frac{4 \times 3}{24 \times 23} = \frac{3}{138}$$

Hence, the probability distribution of X is :

x :	0	1	2
$p(x)$:	$\frac{95}{138}$	$\frac{40}{138}$	$\frac{3}{138}$

EXERCISE 13·1

1. Define a random variable and its probability distribution. Explain by means of two examples.

2. State, with reasons, if the following probability distributions are admissible or not.

(*i*)

x :	0	1	2
$p(x)$:	0·3	0·2	0·5

(*ii*)

x :	–1	0	1
$p(x)$:	0·4	0·4	0·3

(*iii*)

x :	0	1	2	3
$p(x)$:	0·2	0·3	0·3	0·1

(*iv*)

x :	–2	–1	0	1	2
$p(x)$:	0·3	0·4	– 0·2	0·2	0·3

Ans. (*i*) Yes, (*ii*) No, since $\Sigma\, p(x) > 1$, (*iii*) No, since $\Sigma\, p(x) < 1$, (*iv*) No, since $p(0) = -0·2$ which is not possible.

3. Two dice are thrown simultaneously and 'getting a number less than 3' on a die is termed as a success. Obtain the probability distribution of the number of successes.

Ans.

x :	0	1	2
$p(x)$:	4/9	4/9	1/9

4. Obtain the probability distribution of the number of sixes in two tosses of a die.

Ans.

x :	0	1	2
$p(x)$:	$\frac{25}{36}$	$\frac{10}{36}$	$\frac{1}{36}$

5. Obtain the probability distribution of number of heads in two tosses of a coin.

Ans.

x :	0	1	2
$p(x)$:	1/4	2/4	1/4

6. Three cards are drawn at random successively, with replacement, from a well shuffled pack of cards. Getting 'a card of diamonds' is termed as a success. Obtain the probability distribution of the number of successes.

Ans.

x :	0	1	2	3
$p(x)$:	$\frac{27}{64}$	$\frac{27}{64}$	$\frac{9}{64}$	$\frac{1}{64}$

7. Two cards are drawn without replacement, from a well shuffled pack of cards. Obtain the probability distribution of the number of face cards (Jack, Queen, King and Ace).

Ans.

x :	0	1	2
$p(x)$:	$\frac{^{36}C_2}{^{52}C_2}=\frac{105}{221}$	$\frac{^{36}C_1 \times {^{16}C_1}}{^{52}C_2}=\frac{96}{221}$	$\frac{^{16}C_2}{^{52}C_2}=\frac{20}{221}$

8. Five defective mangoes are accidentally mixed with twenty good ones and by looking at them it is not possible to differentiate between them. Four mangoes are drawn at random from the lot. Find the probability distribution of X, the number of defective mangoes.

Ans.

x :	0	1	2	3	4
$p(x)$:	$\frac{^{20}C_4}{^{25}C_4}=\frac{969}{2530}$	$\frac{^5C_1 \times {^{20}C_3}}{^{25}C_4}=\frac{1140}{2530}$	$\frac{^5C_2 \times {^{20}C_2}}{^{25}C_4}=\frac{380}{2530}$	$\frac{^5C_3 \times {^{20}C_1}}{^{25}C_4}=\frac{40}{2530}$	$\frac{^5C_4}{^{25}C_4}=\frac{1}{2530}$

9. Two bad eggs are mixed accidentally with 10 good ones and three are drawn at random from the lot. Obtain the probability distribution of the number of bad eggs drawn.

Ans.

x :	0	1	2	3
$p(x)$:	$\frac{^{10}C_3}{^{12}C_3}=\frac{12}{22}$	$\frac{^2C_1 \times {^{10}C_2}}{^{12}C_3}=\frac{9}{22}$	$\frac{^2C_2 \times {^{10}C_1}}{^{12}C_3}=\frac{1}{22}$	0

10. An urn contains 6 red and 4 white balls. Three balls are drawn at random. Obtain the probability distribution of the number of white balls drawn.

Ans.

x :	0	1	2	3
$p(x)$:	$\frac{5}{30}$	$\frac{15}{30}$	$\frac{9}{30}$	$\frac{1}{30}$

13·6. MATHEMATICAL EXPECTATION

If X is a random variable which can assume any one of the values $x_1, x_2 \ldots, x_n$ with respective probabilities $p_1, p_2, \ldots, p_n$ then the *mathematical expectation* of X, usually called the *expected value* of X and denoted by $E(X)$, is defined as :

$$E(X) = p_1x_1 + p_2x_2 + \ldots + p_nx_n = \Sigma\, p \times x \quad \ldots(13·10)$$

where

$$\Sigma\, p_i = p_1 + p_2 + \ldots + p_n = 1 \quad \ldots(13·11)$$

More precisely, if X is a random variable with probability distribution $\{x, p(x)\}$, then

$$E(X) = \Sigma\, x \times p(x), \quad \ldots(13·12)$$

summation being taken over different values of X.

Physical Interpretation of $E(X)$. Let us consider the following frequency distribution of the random variable X :

X	x_1	x_2	x_3	$\ldots$	x_i	$\ldots$	x_n
f	f_1	f_2	f_3	$\ldots$	f_i	$\ldots$	f_n

Then the mean of the distribution is given by :

$$\bar{x} = \frac{f_1x_1 + f_2x_2 + \ldots + f_n x_n}{N} = \frac{f_1}{N} x_1 + \frac{f_2}{N} x_2 + \ldots + \frac{f_n}{N} x_n \qquad \ldots(*)$$

We observe that, out of total of N cases, f_i cases are favourable to x_i.

$$\therefore \quad P(X = x_i) = \frac{f_i}{N} = p_i, \text{ (say)}, (i = 1, 2, \ldots, n), \quad \Rightarrow \quad \frac{f_1}{N} = p_1, \ \frac{f_2}{N} = p_2, \ \ldots, \ \frac{f_n}{N} = p_n.$$

Substituting in (*) we get :

$$\bar{x} = p_1x_1 + p_2 x_2 + \ldots + p_n x_n \quad \Rightarrow \quad \bar{x} = E(X) \quad \text{[By def. of } E(X)] \qquad \ldots(13·13)$$

Hence, *mathematical expectation of a random variable is nothing but its arithmetic mean.*

Remarks 1. The term 'expected value' is unfortunate in that, it is not in any sense a value which one expects to occur in a particular experiment. But if an experiment is conducted repeatedly a large number of times under essentially homogeneous conditions, then the average of the actual outcomes is the expected value. Sometimes, expected value may give results which are impossible or absurd. For example, the expected value of the number obtained in a random throw of a die is 3·5 [*c.f.* Example 13·6]; the expected value of the number of heads in three tosses of a coin is 1·5 [*c.f.* Example 13·7] ; the expected number of white balls drawn in a draw of 2 balls from an urn containing 7 white and 3 red balls is 1·4 [*c.f.* Example 13·11] ; the results which are unrealistic and absurd.

2. In a game of chance, suppose that a player gains a sum 'a' if he wins and loses a sum 'b' if he does not win, *i.e.*, if he fails. If p and q are probabilities of his success and failure respectively in a single trial, then regarding loss as negative gain, the mathematical expectation of his gain is

$$a \times p + (-b) \times q = ap - bq$$

If the mathematical expectation of the gain of the player is zero, the game is said to be 'fair'. If the mathematical expectation of the gain is greater than 1, then the game is said to be *biased to the player* and if the expectation is negative, the game is said to be *biased against the player.*

We shall now state some theorems without proof. The proofs are beyond the scope of the book.

13·7. THEOREMS ON EXPECTATION

Theorem 13·1. *$E(c) = c$, where c is a constant.* ...(13·14)

Theorem 13·2. *$E(cX) = c\,E(X)$, where c is a constant.* ...(13·15)

Theorem 13·3. *$E(aX + b) = a\,E(X) + b$, where a and b are constants.* ...(13·16)

Theorem 13·4. (Addition Theorem of Expectation). *If X and Y are random variables then*

$$E(X + Y) = E(X) + E(Y), \qquad \ldots(13·17)$$

i.e., Expected value of the sum of two random variables is equal to the sum of their expected values.

The result can be generalised to n variables. *If $X_1, X_2, \ldots, X_n$ are n random variables, then*

$$E(X_1 + X_2 + \ldots + X_n) = E(X_1) + E(X_2) + \ldots + E(X_n) \qquad \ldots(13·18)$$

i.e.,

$$E\left(\sum_{i=1}^{n} X_i\right) = \sum_{i=1}^{n} E(X_i) \quad \text{or} \quad \text{simply} \quad E(\Sigma X) = \Sigma\, E(X) \qquad \ldots(13·19)$$

Corollary. $E(aX + bY) = a\,E(X) + bE(Y)$, where a and b are constants. ...(13·20)

The result follows immediately on using (13·17) and then (13·15).

Theorem 13·5. (Multiplication Theorem of Expectation). *If X and Y are independent random variables, then*

$$E(XY) = E(X)\,.\,E(Y) \qquad \ldots(13·21)$$

i.e., the expected value of the product of two independent random variables is equal to the product of their expected values.

In general, if $X_1, X_2, \ldots, X_n$ *are n independent random variables, then*

$$E(X_1\, X_2\, X_3 \ldots X_n) = E(X_1)\,.\,E(X_2) \ldots E(X_n) \qquad \ldots(13·22)$$

Remark. It should be borne in mind that *the multiplication theorem of expectation holds only for independent events while no such condition on the variables is required for the addition theorem of expectation.*

13·8. VARIANCE OF X IN TERMS OF EXPECTATION

We have

$$\sigma_x^2 = E[X - E(X)]^2 \quad \text{...(13·23)}$$

Also, we have a simplified expression for σ_x^2 given by

$$\Rightarrow \quad \sigma_x^2 = E(X^2) - [E(X)]^2 \quad \text{...(13·24)}$$

For the probability distribution $\{x, p(x)\}$, we have :

$$\text{Mean} = E(X) = \Sigma\, x \times p(x) \quad \text{...(13·25)}$$

and

$$\sigma_x^2 = E(X^2) - [E(X)]^2 = \Sigma\, x^2\, p(x) - [\Sigma\, x\, p(x)]^2 \quad \text{...(13·26)}$$

Theorem 13·6. Var $(X \pm c)$ = Var X, where c is a constant. ...(13·27)

This theorem states *that variance is independent of change of origin.*

Theorem 13·7. Var $(aX) = a^2$. Var (X), where a is a constant. ...(13·28)

This theorem states that *variance is not independent of change of scale.*

Corollary. Combining the results of the above two theorems, we get :

$$\text{Var}\,(aX \pm b) = \text{Var}\,(aX) = a^2\ \text{Var}\,(X) \quad \text{...(13·28}a\text{)}$$

Theorem 13·8. Var $(c) = 0$, where c is constant. ...(13·29)

13·9. COVARIANCE IN TERMS OF EXPECTATION

Let (x_i, y_i), $i = 1, 2, \ldots, n$ be n paired observations on two variables X and Y. Then,

$$E(X) = \frac{1}{n}\sum_{i=1}^{n} x_i = \bar{x}\ ;\quad E(Y) = \frac{1}{n}\sum_{i=1}^{n} y_i = \bar{y}\ ;\quad E(XY) = \frac{1}{n}\sum_{i=1}^{n} x_i y_i \quad \text{...(*)}$$

In Chapter 8, [= ns (8·2) and (8·4)], we defined Cov $(X,. Y) = \frac{1}{n}\Sigma\,(x - \bar{x})\,(y - \bar{y}) = \frac{1}{n}\Sigma xy - \bar{x}\,\bar{y}$

Hence, using (*), in terms of expectation, we have

$$\text{Cov}\,(X, Y) = E\,[(X - \bar{x})\,(Y - \bar{y})] = E\,(XY) - E(X)\,(E(Y)$$

$$\Rightarrow \quad \text{Cov}\,(X, Y) = E\big[\{X - E(X)\}\,\{Y - E(Y)\}\big] = E(XY) - E(X).E(Y) \quad \text{...(13·30)}$$

Theorem 13·9. *If the variables X and Y are independent, then*

$$(a)\ \text{Cov}\,(X, Y) = 0 \qquad \text{and} \qquad (b)\ r\,(X, Y) = 0, \quad \text{...(13·30}a\text{)}$$

where r(X, Y), is the correlation coefficient between X and Y.

Proof. (*a*) If X and Y are independent then $E(XY) = E(X)\cdot E(Y)$ ...(**)

Substituting in (13·30), Cov $(X, Y) = E(X)\,E(Y) - E(X)\,E(Y) = 0$

Hence, *for independent variables X and Y, Cov (X, Y) = 0.*

(*b*) By definition,

$$r(X, Y) = \frac{\text{Cov}\,(X, Y)}{\sigma_X \cdot \sigma_Y} = 0. \qquad \text{[From Part } (a)\text{]}$$

Hence, *two independent variables are uncorrelated.*

Example 13·6. *A die is thrown at random. What is the expectation of the number on it ?*

Solution. Let X denote the number obtained on the die. Then X is a random variable which can take any one of the values 1, 2, 3, ..., 6 each with equal probability 1/6 as given in the adjoining Table.

x	1	2	3	4	5	6
p	1/6	1/6	1/6	1/6	1/6	1/6

$$\therefore \quad E(X) = \sum x \,.\, p(x) = 1 \times \tfrac{1}{6} + 2 \times \tfrac{1}{6} + 3 \times \tfrac{1}{6} + 4 \times \tfrac{1}{6} + 5 \times \tfrac{1}{6} + 6 \times \tfrac{1}{6}$$
$$= \tfrac{1}{6}(1 + 2 + 3 + 4 + 5 + 6) = \tfrac{21}{6} = \tfrac{7}{2} = 3{\cdot}5.$$

Example 13·7. *What is the expected number of heads appearing when a fair coin is tossed three times ?* [*Delhi Univ. B.Com. (Hons.), 1996*]

Solution. Let X denote the number of heads obtained in a random toss of 3 coins. Then the probability distribution of X is [*c.f.* Example 13·3]

x	0	1	2	3
$p(x)$	1/8	3/8	3/8	1/8

$$\therefore \quad E(X) = \sum x\, p(x) = \tfrac{1}{8}\left(0 + 1 \times 3 + 2 \times 3 + 3 \times 1\right) = \tfrac{12}{8} = 1{\cdot}5$$

Example 13·8. *A random variable X is defined as the sum of faces when a pair of dice is thrown. Find the expected value of X.*

Solution. Let the random variable X denote the sum of points obtained on a pair of dice when thrown. Then, the probability distribution of X is (*c.f.* Example 13·4) :

x	2	3	4	5	6	7	8	9	10	11	12
$p(x)$	$\frac{1}{36}$	$\frac{2}{36}$	$\frac{3}{36}$	$\frac{4}{36}$	$\frac{5}{36}$	$\frac{6}{36}$	$\frac{5}{36}$	$\frac{4}{36}$	$\frac{3}{36}$	$\frac{2}{36}$	$\frac{1}{36}$

$$\therefore \quad E(X) = \sum x \,.\, p(x)$$
$$= 2 \times \tfrac{1}{36} + 3 \times \tfrac{2}{36} + 4 \times \tfrac{3}{36} + 5 \times \tfrac{4}{36} + 6 \times \tfrac{5}{36} + 7 \times \tfrac{6}{36} + 8 \times \tfrac{5}{36} + 9 \times \tfrac{4}{36} + 10 \times \tfrac{3}{36} + 11 \times \tfrac{2}{36} + 12 \times \tfrac{1}{36}$$
$$= \tfrac{1}{36}\left[2 + 6 + 12 + 20 + 30 + 42 + 40 + 36 + 30 + 22 + 12\right] = \tfrac{252}{36} = 7$$

Example 13·9. *A contractor spends Rs. 3,000 to prepare for a bid on a construction project which, after deducting manufacturing expenses and the cost of bidding, will yield a profit of Rs. 25,000 if the bid is won. If the chance of winning the bid is ten per cent, compute his expected profit and state the likely decision on whether to bid or not to bid.* [*Delhi Univ. B.A. (Econ. Hons.), 1998*]

Solution. Expenses incurred on preparing the bid = Rs. 3,000.

This will be his loss if the bid is not won by the contractor. Profit if bid is won = Rs. 25,000.

P(Winning the bid) = 10% = 0·10 (Given) ; P(Losing the bid) = 1 – 0·10 = 0·90

∴ Contractor's expected profit

$$= \text{Rs.}\left[25{,}000 \times 0{\cdot}10 + (-3{,}000) \times 0{\cdot}90\right] = \text{Rs.}\ (2{,}500 - 2{,}700) = (-)\ \text{Rs.}\ 200$$

Since the contractor's expected profit is negative, he should not bid.

Example 13·10. *A survey conducted over the last 25 years indicated that in 10 years the winter was mild, in 8 years it was cold and in the remaining 7 years it was very cold.*

A company sells 1000 woollen coats in a mild year, 1300 in a cold year and 2000 in a very cold year.

You are required to find the yearly expected profit of the company if a woollen coat costs Rs. 1730 and it is sold to stores for Rs. 2480.

Solution. From the given data, we obtain the following probability distribution of the number of woollen coats sold in any winter (year).

Winter	*Probability (p)*	*No. of woollen coats sold (x)*	*p.x*
Mild	$\frac{10}{25}$	1000	$\frac{10}{25} \times 1000 = 400$
Cold	$\frac{8}{25}$	1300	$\frac{8}{25} \times 1300 = 416$
Very cold	$\frac{7}{25}$	2000	$\frac{7}{25} \times 2000 = 560$

Hence, the expected number of woollen coats sold in any year is given by :

$$E(x) = \sum p \,.\, x = 400 + 416 + 560 = 1376$$

Since the cost of a woolen coat is Rs. 1730 and it is sold to the stores for Rs. 2480, the company makes a profit of Rs. (2480 – 1730) = Rs. 750 per coat.

Hence, the yearly expected profit of the company is Rs. 1376 × 750 = Rs. 10,32,000.

Example 13·11. *An urn contains 7 white and 3 red balls. Two balls are drawn together, at random, from this urn. Compute the probability that neither of them is white. Find also the probability of getting one white and one red ball. Hence compute the expected number of white balls drawn.*

Solution. From an urn containing 7 white and 3 red balls, two balls can be drawn in ${}^{10}C_2$ ways. Let X denote the number of white balls drawn. The probability distribution of X is obtained as follows :

$$p(0) = \text{Probability that neither of two balls is white}$$

$$= \text{Probability that both balls drawn are red} = \frac{{}^3C_2}{{}^{10}C_2} = \frac{3 \times 2}{10 \times 9} = \frac{1}{15},$$

since 2 balls can be drawn out of 3 red balls in ${}^3C_2$ ways.

$$p(1) = \text{Probability of getting 1 white and 1 red ball} = \frac{{}^7C_1 \times {}^3C_1}{{}^{10}C_2} = \frac{7 \times 3 \times 2}{10 \times 9} = \frac{21}{45},$$

since 1 white ball can be drawn out of 7 white balls in ${}^7C_1$ ways and 1 red ball can be drawn out of 3 red balls in ${}^3C_1$ ways and all these ways can be associated with each other.

$$p(2) = \text{Probability of getting two white balls} = \frac{{}^7C_2}{{}^{10}C_2} = \frac{7 \times 6}{2} \times \frac{2}{10 \times 9} = \frac{21}{45}$$

Hence expected number of white balls drawn is :

$$E(X) = \Sigma\, x.p\,(x) = 0 \times \frac{1}{15} + 1 \times \frac{21}{45} + 2 \times \frac{21}{45} = \frac{21 + 42}{45} = \frac{63}{45} = 1{\cdot}4$$

Example 13·12. *From a bag containing 4 white and 6 red balls, three balls are drawn at random .*

(*i*) *Find the expected number of white balls down.*

(*ii*) *If each white ball drawn carries a reward of Rs. 4 and each red ball Rs. 6, find the expected reward of the draw.* [*Delhi Univ. B.Com (Hons.), 2002*]

Solution. There are 4 white and 6 red balls *i.e.,* 10 balls in the bag.

Three balls can be drawn out of 10 balls in ${}^{10}C_3$ ways, which gives the exhaustive number of cases.

In a random draw of 3 balls from the bag, the number of favourable cases for getting x white balls and consequently $(3 - x)$ red balls, is given by the principle of counting by :

$${}^4C_x \times {}^6C_{3-x} \quad ; \quad x = 0, 1, 2, 3$$

$$\therefore \quad p(x) = \text{Probability of drawing } x \text{ white balls} = \frac{{}^4C_x \times {}^6C_{3-x}}{{}^{10}C_3} \quad ; \quad x = 0, 1, 2, 3$$

$$\Rightarrow \quad p(0) = \frac{{}^4C_0 \times {}^6C_3}{{}^{10}C_3} = \frac{1 \times 6 \times 5 \times 4 \times 3\,!}{3\,! \times 10 \times 9 \times 8} = \frac{1}{6} = \frac{5}{30} \quad ; \quad p(1) = \frac{{}^4C_1 \times {}^6C_2}{{}^{10}C_3} = \frac{4 \times 15}{120} = \frac{15}{30} \,;$$

$$p(2) = \frac{{}^4C_2 \times {}^6C_1}{{}^{10}C_3} = \frac{6 \times 6}{120} = \frac{9}{30} \quad ; \quad p(3) = \frac{{}^4C_3 \times {}^6C_0}{{}^{10}C_3} = \frac{4 \times 1}{120} = \frac{1}{30}$$

The probability distribution of the number of white balls drawn (X) is given in the following table.

The expected number of the white balls drawn is given by :

x	$p(x)$
0	5/30
1	15/30
2	9/30
3	1/30

$$E(X) = \Sigma\, x\, p(x)$$

$$= 0 \times \frac{5}{30} + 1 \times \frac{15}{30} + 2 \times \frac{9}{30} + 3 \times \frac{1}{30}$$

$$= \frac{1}{30}\left(15 + 18 + 3\right) = \frac{36}{30} = \frac{6}{5} = 1{\cdot}2$$

(*ii*) Since each white ball drawn carries a reward of Rs. 4 and each red ball Rs. 6, the reward $R(x)$ for drawing x white balls and consequently $(3 - x)$ red balls in a random draw of 3 balls is given by :

$$\text{Rs. } [4 \times x + 6\,(3 - x)]$$

x	$p(x)$	Reward $R(x)$ in Rs.
0	5/30	$4 \times 0 + 6 \times 3 = 18$
1	15/30	$4 \times 1 + 6 \times 2 = 16$
2	9/30	$4 \times 2 + 6 \times 1 = 14$
3	1/30	$4 \times 3 + 6 \times 0 = 12$

$\therefore$ Expected reward of the draw is :

$$E[R(x)] = \sum R(x).\, p(x)$$
$$= \text{Rs. } \left[\tfrac{5}{30} \times 18 + \tfrac{15}{30} \times 16 + \tfrac{9}{30} \times 14 + \tfrac{1}{30} \times 12\right]$$
$$= \text{Rs. } (3 + 8 + 4{\cdot}20 + 0{\cdot}40)$$
$$= \text{Rs. } 15{\cdot}60$$

Example 13·13. *A bag contains 2 white balls and 3 black balls. Four persons A, B, C and D, in the order named, each draw one ball and do not replace it. The first to draw a white ball receives Rs. 20. Determine their expectations.* [*Delhi Univ. B.A. (Econ. Hons.), 1995*]

Solution. The box contains 2 white and 3 black balls.

Since *A, B, C* and *D* draw the ball successively without replacement and the person who first draws the white ball wins, their respective chances of winning are as follows :

$P(A\text{'s winning}) = P(A \text{ draws a white ball in the first draw}) = \frac{2}{5} = 0{\cdot}4$

$P(B\text{'s winning}) = P(A$ does not get a white ball and in the next draw B gets a white ball$)$

$$= \left(1 - \frac{2}{5}\right) \times \frac{2}{4} = \frac{3}{5} \times \frac{2}{4} = 0{\cdot}3$$

$P(C\text{'s winning}) = P\,[A$ and B do not get a white ball in the first two draws and C gets the white ball in the 3rd draw$]$

$$= \left(1 - \frac{2}{5}\right) \times \left(1 - \frac{2}{4}\right) \times \frac{2}{3} = \frac{3}{5} \times \frac{2}{4} \times \frac{2}{3} = 0{\cdot}2$$

Similarly,

$$P(D\text{'s winning}) = \left(1 - \frac{2}{5}\right)\left(1 - \frac{2}{4}\right)\left(1 - \frac{2}{3}\right) \times \frac{2}{2} = \frac{3}{5} \times \frac{2}{4} \times \frac{1}{3} = 0{\cdot}1$$

or $P(D\text{'s winning}) = 1 - 0{\cdot}4 - 0{\cdot}3 - 0{\cdot}2 = 0{\cdot}1.$

Hence, their respective expectations for a prize of Rs. 20 are :

A's expectation = Rs. $20 \times 0{\cdot}4$ = Rs. 8 ; B's expectation = Rs. $20 \times 0{\cdot}3$ = Rs. 6

C's expectation = Rs. $20 \times 0{\cdot}2$ = Rs. 4 ; D's expectation = Rs. $20 \times 0{\cdot}1$ = Rs. 2

Example 13·14. *A die is tossed twice. Getting 'a number greater than 4' is considered a success. Find the mean and variance of the probability distribution of the number of successes.*

Solution. Since the favourable cases for 'getting a number greater than 4' in a throw of a die are 5 and 6, *i.e.*, 2 in all, we have :

Probability of success $(S) = \frac{2}{6} = \frac{1}{3}$ $\Rightarrow$ Probability of failure $(F) = 1 - \frac{1}{3} = \frac{2}{3}$

Let X denote the number of successes. Then, X is a random variable taking the values 0, 1 and 2.

$$P(X = 0) = P(F \text{ and } F) = P(F) \times P(F) = \frac{2}{3} \times \frac{2}{3} = \frac{4}{9}$$
$$P(X = 1) = P(F \text{ and } S) + P(S \text{ and } F) = P(F).\, P(S) + P(S).\, P(F) = \frac{2}{3} \times \frac{1}{3} + \frac{1}{3} \times \frac{2}{3} = \frac{4}{9}$$
$$P(X = 2) = P(S \text{ and } S) = P(S)\, P(S) = \frac{1}{3} \times \frac{1}{3} = \frac{1}{9}$$

COMPUTATION OF VARIANCE

x	$p(x)$	$x \,.\, p(x)$	$x^2 \,.\, p(x)$
0	4/9	0	0
1	4/9	4/9	4/9
2	1/9	2/9	4/9
Total		$\sum x\, p(x) = \frac{6}{9}$	$\sum x^2\, p(x) = \frac{8}{9}$

$\therefore$ Mean $(\mu) = \sum x \,.\, p(x) = \frac{6}{9} = \frac{2}{3}$

Variance $(\sigma^2) = \sum x^2\, p(x) - [\sum xp(x)]^2$

$$= \frac{8}{9} - \left(\frac{2}{3}\right)^2 = \frac{4}{9}$$

Example 13·15. *A random variable X has the following probability distribution :*

x	:	4	5	6	8
p	:	0·1	0·3	0·4	0·2

Find $E[X - E(X)]^2$. [*C.A. (Foundation), Nov. 2000*)

Solution. $E[X - E(X)]^2 = \text{Var}(X) = E(X^2) - [E(X)]^2$
$= \Sigma px^2 - (\Sigma px)^2$

x	p	px	px^2
4	0·1	0·4	1·6
5	0·3	1·5	7·5
6	0·4	2·4	14·4
8	0·2	1·6	12·8
Total	1	$\Sigma px = 5{\cdot}9$	$\Sigma px^2 = 36{\cdot}3$

$\therefore \quad E[X - E(X)]^2 = \Sigma px^2 - (\Sigma px)^2$
$= 36{\cdot}3 - (5{\cdot}9)^2$
$= 36{\cdot}30 - 34{\cdot}81$
$= 1{\cdot}49$

Example 13·16. *If a random variable X assumes the values 0 and 1 with* $P(X = 0) = 3\,P(X = 1)$, *then* $V(X)$ is :

(*i*) $\frac{1}{16}$ (*ii*) $\frac{2}{16}$ (*iii*) $\frac{3}{16}$ (*iv*) $\frac{4}{16}$

[*I.C.W.A. (Intermediate), June 2002*]

Solution. Let $P(X = 1) = p$ ...(*i*) Then $P(X = 0) = 3P(X = 1) = 3p$ ...(*ii*)

Since the *r.v.* X takes only two values 0 and 1, we have :

$P(X = 0) + P(X = 1) = 1 \Rightarrow 3p + p = 1 \Rightarrow 4p = 1 \Rightarrow p = \frac{1}{4}$

$\therefore \quad P(X = 0) = 3p = \frac{3}{4}$ and $P(X = 1) = p = \frac{1}{4}$

x	$p(x)$	$x\,p(x)$	$x^2p(x)$
0	$\frac{3}{4}$	0	0
1	$\frac{1}{4}$	$\frac{1}{4}$	$\frac{1}{4}$
Total		$\frac{1}{4}$	$\frac{1}{4}$

$\text{Var}(X) = \Sigma x^2 p(x) - [\Sigma x\,p(x)]^2$
$= \frac{1}{4} - \left(\frac{1}{4}\right)^2 = \frac{1}{4} - \frac{1}{16} = \frac{4-1}{16} = \frac{3}{16}$

$\therefore$ (*iii*) is the correct answer.

Example 13·17. *A player tosses two fair coins. He wins Rs. 5 if 2 heads occur, Rs. 2 if 1 head occurs and Re. 1 if no head occurs.*

(*i*) *Find his expected gain.*

(*ii*) *How much should he pay to play the game if it is to be fair ?*

Solution. In a random toss of two fair coins, $n(S) = 2^2 = 4$, and the probability distribution of the number of heads (x) is as obtained below :

No. of heads (x)	Favaourable events	No. of favourable cases	Probability (p)	Gain in Rs. (y)	$p.y$
0	*TT*	1	$\frac{1}{4} = 0{\cdot}25$	1	0·25
1	*HT, TH*	2	$\frac{2}{4} = 0{\cdot}50$	2	1·00
2	*HH*	1	$\frac{1}{4} = 0{\cdot}25$	5	1·25

(*i*) The expected gain of the player is given by :

$$E(y) = \Sigma\, p.y = 0{\cdot}25 + 1 + 1{\cdot}25 = \text{Rs. } 2{\cdot}50$$

(*ii*) The game is said to be fair if the mathematical expectation of the gain of the player is zero. Hence, the player should pay Rs. 2·50 to play the game, if this is to be fair.

13·10. VARIANCE OF LINEAR COMBINATION

Let x and y be the given variables and let us consider a linear combination of these variables given by :

$$u = ax + by \qquad ...(13·31)$$

where a and b are constants.

Then $\text{Var}(u) = \text{Var}(ax + by) = a^2 \text{Var}(x) + b^2 \text{Var}(y) + 2ab \text{Cov}(x, y)$ ...(13·32)

Remark. Similarly, have :

$$\text{Var}(ax - by) = a^2 \text{Var}(x) + b^2 \text{Var}(y) - 2ab \text{Cov}(x, y) \qquad ...(13·32a)$$

If x and y are independent, then Cov $(x, y) = 0$.

Hence, if x and y are independent, then

$$\text{Var}(ax \pm by) = a^2 \text{Var}(x) + b^2 \text{Var}(y) \qquad ...(13·32b)$$

Example 13·18. *If $V(X) = V(Y) = \frac{1}{4}$ and $V(X - Y) = \frac{1}{3}$, the correlation coefficient between random variables X and Y is*

(i) $\frac{1}{3}$; (ii) $-\frac{1}{3}$; (iii) $\frac{2}{3}$; (iv) *none of these.*

[*I.C.W.A. (Intermediate), Dec. 1999*]

Solution. We are given : $\sigma_x^2 = \sigma_y^2 = \frac{1}{4} \Rightarrow \sigma_x = \sigma_y = \frac{1}{2}$. ...(*)

and $\text{Var}(X - Y) = \frac{1}{3}$

$\Rightarrow \text{Var}(X) + \text{Var}(Y) - 2\,\text{Cov}(X, Y) = \frac{1}{3}$ [From (13·32a)]

$\Rightarrow \sigma_x^2 + \sigma_y^2 - 2r\,\sigma_x \sigma_y = \frac{1}{3}$ $\left(\because \dfrac{\text{Cov}(x, y)}{\sigma_x \sigma_y} = r\right)$

$\Rightarrow \frac{1}{4} + \frac{1}{4} - 2r\frac{1}{2}\cdot\frac{1}{2} = \frac{1}{3} \Rightarrow \frac{r}{2} = \frac{1}{2} - \frac{1}{3} = \frac{3-2}{6} = \frac{1}{6} \Rightarrow r = \frac{1}{3}$

$\therefore$ (*i*) is the correct answer.

13·11. JOINT AND MARGINAL PROBABILITY DISTRIBUTIONS

In Chapter 3, § 3·6, we had discussed bivariate frequency distribution and the marginal frequency distributions. Analogously, we have joint and marginal probability distributions.

Let X and Y be two discrete random variables. Let us suppose that X can assume m values $x_1, x_2, \ldots, x_m$ and Y can assume n values $y_1, y_2, \ldots, y_n$. Let us consider the probability of the ordered pair

$$(x_i, y_j),\ i = 1, 2, \ldots, m\ ;\ j = 1, 2, \ldots, n$$

defined by :

$$p_{ij} = P(X = x_i \text{ and } Y = y_j) = p(x_i, y_j) \qquad ...(13·33)$$

The function $p(x, y)$ defined in (13·33) for any ordered pair (x, y) is called the joint probability function of X and Y and is represented in a tabular form as follows :

TABLE 13·4 **JOINT PROBABILITY FUNCTION**

$X \rightarrow$ / $Y \downarrow$	x_1	x_2	x_3	...	x_i	...	...	x_m	*Total*
y_1	p_{11}	p_{21}	p_{31}	...	p_{i1}	...	...	p_{m1}	p_1'
y_2	p_{12}	p_{22}	p_{32}	...	p_{i2}	...	...	p_{m2}	p_2'
y_3	p_{13}	p_{23}	p_{33}	...	p_{i3}	...	...	p_{m3}	p_3'
⋮	⋮	⋮	⋮		⋮			⋮	⋮
y_j	p_{1j}	p_{2j}	p_{3j}	...	p_{ij}	...	...	p_{mj}	p_j'
⋮	⋮	⋮	⋮		⋮			⋮	⋮
y_n	p_{1n}	p_{2n}	p_{3n}	...	p_{in}	...	...	p_{mn}	p_n'
Total	p_1	p_2	p_3	...	p_i	...	...	p_m	1

From the joint probability distribution of X and Y, the *marginal probability function* of X is given by :

$$p_i = P(X = x_i) = p_{i_1} + p_{i_2} + p_{i_3} + \dots p_{in} \quad ; \quad (i = 1, 3 \dots, m)$$

$$= \sum_{j=1}^{n} p_{ij} \qquad \dots(13·34)$$

The set of values $\{x_i, p_i\}$; $i = 1, 2, 3, \dots, m$ gives the *marginal probability distribution* of X. Similarly,

$$p_j' = P(Y = y_j) = p_{1j} + p_{2j} + p_{3j} + \dots + p_{mj}, \ (j = 1, 2, \dots, n)$$

$$= \sum_{i=1}^{m} p_{ij} \qquad \dots(13·35)$$

gives the *marginal probability function of* Y and the set of values $\{y_j, p_j'\}$; $j = 1, 2, 3, \dots, n$ gives the *marginal probability distribution* of Y. It may be noted that :

$$\left.\begin{aligned} &\sum_i \sum_j p_{i_j} = 1 \\ &\sum_i p_i = \sum_i \left(\sum_j p_{ij}\right) = \sum_i \sum_j p_{ij} = 1 \\ &\sum_j p_j' = \sum_j \left(\sum_i p_{ij}\right) = \sum_i \sum_j p_{ij} = 1 \end{aligned}\right\} \qquad \dots(13·36)$$

Remark. Two random variables X and Y are said to be independent if and only if their joint probability function is equal to the product of their marginal probability functions, *i.e.*, if and only if.

$$P(X = x_i \cap Y = y_j) = P(X = x_i) \,.\, P(Y = y_j) \quad i.e., \quad p_{ij} = p_i \times p_j' \qquad \dots(13·37)$$

Example 13·19. *Let X and Y be two random variables each taking three values –1, 0 and 1, and having the joint probability distribution as given in Table 13·5.*

Obtain the marginal probability distributions of X and Y and hence their expected values.

TABLE 13·5

Y \ X	–1	0	1
–1	0	·1	·1
0	·2	·2	·2
1	0	·1	·1

Solution.

TABLE 13·6. COMPUTATION OF MARGINAL PROBABILITY DISTRIBUTIONS

Y↓ \ X→	–1	0	1	Total $g(y)$
–1	0	·1	·1	·1 + ·1 = 0·2
0	·2	·2	·2	·2 + ·2 + ·2 = 0·6
1	0	·1	·1	0 + ·1 + ·1 = 0·2
Total $p(x)$	0 + ·2 + 0 = 0·2	·1 + ·2 + ·1 = 0·4	·1 + ·2 + ·1 = 0·4	$\sum p(x) = \sum g(y) = 1$

The marginal probability distributions of X and Y are as given in Tables 13·7 and 13·8 respectively.

TABLE 13·7. MARGINAL PROBABILITY DISTRIBUTION OF X

x	–1	0	1	Total
$p(x)$	0·2	0·4	0·4	1·0

TABLE 13·8. MARGINAL PROBABILITY DISTRIBUTION OF Y

y	–1	0	1	Total
$g(y)$	0·2	0·6	0·2	1·0

$$\begin{aligned} E(X) &= \sum x\, p(x) \\ &= -1 \times 0·2 + 0 \times 0·4 + 1 \times 0·4 \\ &= -0·2 + 0·4 = 0·2 \end{aligned}$$

$$\begin{aligned} E(Y) &= \sum y g(y) \\ &= -1 \times 0·2 + 0 \times 0·6 + 1 \times 0·2 \\ &= -0·2 + 0·2 = 0 \end{aligned}$$

Example 13·20. *If* $p(x) = \begin{cases} 0{\cdot}1x, & x = 1,2,3,4 \\ 0, & \text{otherwise,} \end{cases}$

Find : (*i*) $P\{x = 1 \text{ or } 2\}$ (*ii*) $P\left\{\frac{1}{2} < x < \frac{5}{2} \;\middle|\; x > 1\right\}$ [*I.C.W.A. (Intermediate), June 2002*]

Solution (*i*) $P(X = 1 \text{ or } 2) = P(X = 1) + P(X = 2) = p(1) + p(2)$

$$= 0{\cdot}1 \times 1 + 0{\cdot}1 \times 2 = 0{\cdot}1 + 0{\cdot}2 = 0{\cdot}3$$

(*ii*) $$P\left\{\frac{1}{2} < X < \frac{5}{2} \;\middle|\; X > 1\right\} = \frac{P\left[\left(\frac{1}{2} < X < \frac{5}{2}\right) \cap X > 1\right]}{P(X > 1)} = \frac{P(X = 2)}{1 - P(X \le 1)}$$

$$= \frac{0{\cdot}1 \times 2}{1 - [p(0) + p(1)]} = \frac{0{\cdot}2}{1 - [0{\cdot}1 \times 0 + 0{\cdot}1 \times 1]} = \frac{0{\cdot}2}{0{\cdot}9} = \frac{2}{9}.$$

EXERCISE 13·2

1. (*a*) Define a random variable and its mathematical expectation.

(*b*) What is mathematical expectation ? How is it useful to a businessman ?

(*c*) Explain the concept of mathematical expectation. [*Delhi Univ. B.Com (Hons.), 2002*]

2. A random variable *X* has the following probability distribution :

X :	–1	0	1	2
Probability :	1/3	1/6	1/6	1/3

Compute the expectation of *X*.

Ans. 1/2.

3. A random variable *X* has the following probability function :

x :	0	1	2	3	4	5	6	7
$p(x)$:	0	k	$2k$	$2k$	$3k$	k^2	$2k^2$	$7k^2 + k$

(*i*) Find *k*, (*ii*) Evaluate $P(X \ge 6)$, $P(X < 6)$, and $P(O < X < 5)$

Hint. (*i*) $\Sigma\, p(x) = 1 \quad \Rightarrow \quad 10k^2 + 9k - 1 = 0 \quad \Rightarrow \quad k = \frac{1}{10}$

(*ii*) $9k^2 + k = \frac{19}{100}$; $\frac{81}{100}$; $\frac{4}{5}$.

4. A random variable *X* has the following probability function.

Values of X, x :	–2	–1	0	1	2	3
$p(x)$:	0·1	k	0·2	$2k$	0·3	k

Find the value of *k*, and calculate mean and variance of *X*.

Ans. 0·1 ; 0·8 and 2·16.

5. A bakery has the following schedule of daily demand for cakes. Find the expected number of cakes demanded per day.

No. of cakes demanded in hundreds	0	1	2	3	4	5	6	7	8	9
Probability	·02	·07	·09	·12	·20	·20	·18	·10	·01	·01

Ans. 508.

6. In a business venture a man can make a profit of Rs. 2,000 with probability of 0·4 or have a loss of Rs. 1,000 with a probability of 0·6. What is his expected profit ?

Ans. Rs. 200.

7. If the probability that the value of a certain stock will remain the same is 0·46, the probability that its value will increase by Re. 0·50 or Re. 1·00 per share are respectively 0·17 and 0·23 and the probability that its value will decrease by Re. 0·25 per share is 0·14, what is the expected gain per share ?

Ans. Re. 0·28.

8. A box contains 12 items of which 3 are defective. A sample of 3 items is selected at random from this box. If X represents the number of defective items in the 3 selected items, describe the random variable X completely and obtain its expectation.

Ans.

x	0	1	2	3
$p(x)$	27/64	27/64	9/64	1/64

; $E(X) = 0{\cdot}75$.

9. A and B throw with one die for a prize of Rs. 99 which is to be won by the player who first throws 6. If A has the first throw, what are their respective expectations ?

Ans. Rs. 54, Rs. 45.

10. A box contains 4 right handed and 6 left handed screws. Two screws are drawn at random without replacement. Let X be the number of left handed screws drawn. Find

(*i*) the probability distribution of X, and (*ii*) expectation of X. [*I.C.W.A. (Intermediate), June 1998*]

Ans. (*i*)

x	0	1	2
$p(x)$	2/15	8/15	5/15

; (*ii*) $E(X) = 1{\cdot}2$.

11. Define expected value of a discrete random variable.

Three items are drawn at random from a box containing 2 defective and 6 non-defective items. Find the expected number of non-defective items drawn. [*C.A. (Foundation), May 1997*]

Ans.

x	0	1	2	3
$p(x)$	0	$\frac{3}{28}$	$\frac{15}{28}$	$\frac{10}{28}$

; $E(X) = 2{\cdot}25$.

12. A box contains 6 tickets. Two of the tickets carry a prize of Rs. 5 each, the other four prizes are of Re. 1 each. If one ticket is drawn, what is the expected value of the prize ? [*C.A. (Foundation), Nov. 1997*]

Hint.

Prize in Rs. (x)	5	1
$p(x)$	$\frac{2}{6}=\frac{1}{3}$	$\frac{4}{6}=\frac{2}{3}$

; $E(X) = 2{\cdot}33$.

13. The probability known is 0·99 that a 30-year old man will survive one year more. An insurance company offers to sell such a man a Rs. 10,000 one-year term life insurance policy at a premium of Rs. 110. What is the insurance company's expected gain ? [*Delhi Univ. B.Com. (Hons.), (Extend.) 2005; I.C.W.A (Intermediate), June 1996*]

Ans. Rs. $[110 \times 0{\cdot}99 - (10{,}000 - 110) \times 0{\cdot}01]$ = Rs. 10.

14. A number is chosen at random from the set 10, 11, 12, ..., 109 ; and another number is chosen at random from the set 12, 13, 14, ..., 61. What are the expected values of their (*i*) sum and (*ii*) product ? [*I.C.W.A. (Intermediate), June 2000*]

Ans. (*i*) $(59{\cdot}5 + 36{\cdot}5) = 96$, (*ii*) $59{\cdot}5 \times 36{\cdot}5 = 2171{\cdot}75$.

15. A random variable has the following probability distribution :

Value of X	:	0	1	2	3
Probability	:	0·1	0·3	0·4	0·2

Find : (*i*) $E(X)$ and, (*ii*) Var (X). [*Delhi Univ. B.A. (Econ. Hons.), 2009*]

Ans. $E(X) = 1{\cdot}7$, Var $(X) = 0{\cdot}81$

16. The probability distribution of a random variable X is given in the adjoining table.

Find (*i*) $E(2X + 5)$ and (*ii*) $E(X^2)$.

x	−2	3	1
$p(x)$	$\frac{1}{3}$	$\frac{1}{2}$	$\frac{1}{6}$

[*C.A. (Foundation), May 2000*]

Ans. $E(X) = 1$; $E(2X + 5) = 7$; $E(X^2) = 6$.

17. Let the random variable X assume the values x_1, x_2 and x_3. Then the function f denoted by $f(x_i) = P(X = x_i)$ is given by :

Values of X, (x)	:	−3	6	9
$P(X = x)$	:	1/6	1/2	1/3

Find $E(X)$, $E(X^2)$ and $E(2X + 1)^2$. [*C.A. PEE-1, Nov. 2003*]

Ans. $E(X) = 5{\cdot}5$; $E(X^2) = 46{\cdot}5$; $E(2X + 1)^2 = 4E(X^2) + 4E(X) + 1 = 209$

18. A fair coin is tossed three times. Let X be the number of tails appearing. Find the probability distribution of X. Calculate the expected value of X. Find also its variance. [*I.C.W.A. (Intermediate), June 2002*]

Ans.

x	0	1	2	3
$p(x)$	1/8	3/8	3/8	1/8

; $E(X) = 3/2$; Var $(X) = 3/4$.

19. A random variable X has the following probability distribution :

Value of X, (x)	:	0	1	2	3
$P(X = x)$	:	1/3	1/2	0	1/6

Find : (*i*) Var (X), (*ii*) Var(Y) where $Y = 2X - 1$. [*Delhi Univ. B.A. (Econ. Hons.), 2008*]

Ans. Var$(X) = 1$; Var$(Y) = $ Var$(2X - 1) = $ Var$(2X) = 2^2$ Var$(X) = 4 \times 1 = 4$.

20. Choose the correct alternative, stating proper reason.

If the random variable X assumes only two values 0 and 1, with $P(X = 0) = 3\,P(X = 1)$, then variance of X is :

(*i*) 0 ; (*ii*) 0·5 ; (*iii*) 0·75 ; (*iv*) none of these.

[*I.C.W.A. (Intermediate), Dec. 1999*]

Ans. Var $(X) = 0{\cdot}1875$; (*iv*) is the correct answer.

21. Five variate values with their probability of occurrence are as follows :

Values of X, x	:	2·0	3·5	4·5	5·0	6·0
$P(X = x) = p(x)$	:	0·1	0·2	0·4	0·2	0·1

Find the variance of X. [*C.A., PEE-1, May 2005*]

Ans. Var$(X) = 19{\cdot}55 - (4{\cdot}30)^2 = 1{\cdot}06$.

22. A die is tossed twice. 'Getting a number less than 3' is termed as success. Obtain the probability distribution and hence the mean and variance of the number of successes.

Ans. Mean = 2/3, Variance = 4/9.

23. Company ABC estimates the net profit on a new product it is launching to be Rs. 3,000,000 if it is successful ; Rs. 1,000,000 if it is 'moderately successful' and a loss of Rs. 1,000,000 if it is 'unsuccessful'. The firm assigns the following probabilities to the different possibilities :

Successful 0·15, 'moderately successful' 0·25 and unsuccessful 0·60.

Find the expected value and variance of the net profit. [*Delhi Univ. B.A. (Econ. Hons.), 1990*]

Ans. $E(X) = $ Rs. 1 lakh ; Var$(X) = 2{\cdot}19$ million (Rs.)^2

24. Let (X, Y) be a pair of discrete random variables each taking three values 1, 2 and 3 with the joint distribution in the adjoining Table.

Y \ X	*1*	2	3
1	5/27	4/27	2/27
2	1/27	3/27	3/27
3	3/27	4/27	2/27

Obtain the marginal probability distributions of X and Y and hence find $E(X)$, $E(Y)$ and $E(X + Y)$. Also find Var (X) and Var (Y).

Ans. $E(X) = E(Y) = \frac{52}{27} = 1{\cdot}93$; $E(X + Y) = 3{\cdot}86$; Var. $(X) = 0{\cdot}58$; Var $(Y) = 0{\cdot}72$

25. A and B play for a prize. A is to throw a die first and win if he throws a 6. If he fails, B is to throw and win if he throws 6 or 5. If B fails, A is to throw again and win if he gets 6, 5 or 4. The game continues in this manner till it is won. The winner is to get a cash prize of Rs. 3,240. What are their respective expected winning ?

[*Delhi Univ. B.A. (Econ. Hons.), 2006*]

Hint. If A throws the die first,

$$P(A\text{'s winning}) = \frac{1}{6} + \left(1 - \frac{1}{6}\right) \cdot \left(1 - \frac{2}{6}\right) \cdot \frac{3}{6} + \left(1 - \frac{1}{6}\right)\left(1 - \frac{2}{6}\right)\left(1 - \frac{3}{6}\right)\left(1 - \frac{4}{6}\right) \cdot \frac{5}{6}$$

$$= \frac{1}{6} + \frac{5}{6} \times \frac{4}{6} \times \frac{3}{6} + \frac{5}{6} \times \frac{4}{6} \times \frac{3}{6} \times \frac{2}{6} \times \frac{5}{6} = \frac{1}{6} + \frac{10}{36} + \frac{25}{324} = 0{\cdot}52$$

$\therefore$ $P(B\text{'s winning}) = 1 - P(A\text{'s winning}) = 1 - 0{\cdot}52 = 0{\cdot}48$

$\therefore$ A's Expected gain = Rs. 3,240 × 0·52 = Rs. 1684·80

B's Expected gain = Rs. 3,240 × 048 = Rs. 1555·20

26. A box contains 8 tickets, 3 of them carry a prize of Rs. 5 each and the remaining 5 a prize of Rs. 2 each.

(1) If one ticket is drawn at random, what is the expected value of the prize ?

(2) If two tickets are drawn at random, what is the expected value of the prize ?

[Delhi Univ. B.Com. (Hons.), (External), 2005]

Hint. X : Prize in (Rs.). Then :

$$(i)\quad E(X) = \text{Rs.}\left[5 \times \frac{3}{8} + 2 \times \frac{5}{8}\right] = \text{Rs. } 3{\cdot}125$$

$$(ii)\quad E(X) = \text{Rs.}\left[(2+2) \times \frac{{}^5C_2}{{}^8C_2} + (2+5) \times \frac{{}^5C_1 \times {}^3C_1}{{}^8C_2} + (5+5) \times \frac{{}^3C_2}{{}^8C_2}\right] = \text{Rs. } \frac{175}{28} = \text{Rs. } 6{\cdot}25$$

14 Theoretical Distributions

14·1. INTRODUCTION

In Chapter 3, we studied the empirical or observed or experimental frequency distributions in which the actual data were collected, classified and tabulated in the form of a frequency distribution. Such data are usually based on sample studies. The statistical measures like the averages, dispersion, skewness, kurtosis, correlation, etc., for the sample frequency distributions, not only give us the nature and form of the sample data but also help us in formulating certain ideas about the characteristics of the population. However, a more scientific way of drawing inferences about the population characteristics is through the study of theoretical distributions which we shall discuss in this chapter. In the population, the values of the variable may be distributed according to some definite probability law which can be expressed mathematically and the corresponding probability distribution is known as theoretical probability distribution. Such probability laws may be based on 'a priori' considerations or 'a posteriori' inferences. These distributions are based on expectations on the basis of previous experience. Theoretical distributions also enable us to fit a mathematical model or a function of the form $y = p(x)$ to the given data.

In Chapter 13, we have already defined the random variable, mathematical expectation, probability function and distribution function, moments, mean and variance in terms of probability function. These provide us the necessary tools for the study of theoretical distributions. In this chapter we shall study the following *univariate* probability distributions :

(*i*) Binomial Distribution
(*ii*) Poisson Distribution
(*iii*) Normal Distribution

The first two distributions are *discrete* probability distributions and the third is a *continuous* probability distribution.

14·2. BINOMIAL DISTRIBUTION

Binomial distribution is also known as the '*Bernoulli distribution*' after the Swiss mathematician James Bernoulli (1654-1705) who discovered it in 1700 and was first published in 1713, eight years after his death. This distribution can be used under the following conditions :

(*i*) The random experiment is performed repeatedly a finite and fixed number of times. In other words n, the number of trials, is finite and fixed.

(*ii*) The outcome of the random experiment (trial) results in the dichotomous classification of events. In other words, the outcome of each trial may be classified into two mutually disjoint categories, called success (the occurrence of the event) and failure (the non-occurrence of the event).

(*iii*) All the trials are independent, *i.e.*, the result of any trial, is not affected in any way, by the preceding trials and doesn't affect the result of succeeding trials.

(*iv*) The probability of success (happening of an event) in any trial is p and is constant for each trial. $q = 1 - p$, is then termed as the probability of failure (non-occurrence of the event) and is constant for each trial.

For example, if we toss a fair coin n times (which is fixed and finite), then the outcome of any trial is one of the mutually exclusive events, *viz.*, head (success) and tail (failure). Further, all the trials are independent, since the result of any throw of a coin does not affect and is not affected by the result of other throws. Moreover, the probability of success (head) in any trial is $\frac{1}{2}$, which is constant for each trial. Hence the coin tossing problems will give rise to Bionomial distribution.

Similarly dice throwing problems will also conform to Binomial distribution.

More precisely, we expect a Binomial distribution under the following conditions :

(*i*) n, the number of trials is finite.

(*ii*) Each trial results in two mutually exclusive and exhaustive outcomes, termed as success and failure.

(*iii*) Trials are independent.

(*iv*) p, the probability of success is constant for each trial. Then $q = 1 - p$, is the probability of failure in any trial.

Remark. The trials satisfying the above four conditions are also known as *Bernoulli trials.*

14·2·1. Probability Function of Binomial Distribution. If X denotes the number of successes in n trials satisfying the above conditions, then X is a random variable which can take the values 0, 1, 2, ..., n ; since in n trials we may get no success (all failures), one success, two successes, ..., or all the n successes.

We are interested in finding the corresponding probabilities of 0, 1, 2, ..., n successes. The general expression for the probability of r successes is given by :

$$p(r) = P(X = r) = {}^nC_r \, p^r . q^{n-r} ; r = 0, 1, 2, \ldots, n \qquad \ldots(14{\cdot}1)$$

Proof. Let S_i denote the success and F_i denote the failure at the ith trial ; $i = 1, 2, \ldots, n$. Then, we have

$$P(S_i) = p \quad \text{and} \quad P(F_i) = q \quad ; \quad i = 1, 2, \ldots, n \qquad \ldots(*)$$

The probability of r successes and consequently $(n - r)$ failures in a sequence of n-trials in *any fixed specified order*, say, $S_1 F_2 S_3 S_4 F_5 F_6 \ldots \ldots S_{n-1} F_n$ where S occurs r times and F occurs $(n - r)$ times is given by :

$$P[S_1 \cap F_2 \cap S_3 \cap S_4 \cap F_5 \cap F_6 \cap \ldots \cap S_{n-1} \cap F_n]$$
$$= P(S_1). P(F_2). P(S_3). P(S_4). P(F_5). P(F_6) \ldots \ldots P(S_{n-1}). P(F_n)$$

[By compound probability theorem, since the trials are independent].

$$= p . q . p . p . q . q . \ldots \ldots p . q \qquad \text{[From (*)]}$$
$$= [p \times p \times p \times \ldots \ldots r \text{ times}] \times [q \times q \times q \times \ldots \ldots (n-r) \text{ times}]$$
$$= p^r . q^{n-r} \qquad \ldots(**)$$

But in n trials, the total number of possible ways of obtaining r successes and $(n - r)$ failures is

$$\frac{n\,!}{r\,!\,(n-r)\,!} = {}^nC_r,$$

all of which are mutually disjoint. The probability for each of these ${}^nC_r$ mutually exclusive ways is same as given in (**), *viz.*, $p^r q^{n-r}$. Hence by the addition theorem of probability, the required probability of getting r successes and consequently $(n - r)$ failures in n trials, in *any order what-so-ever* is given by :

$$P(X = r) = p^r q^{n-r} + p^r q^{n-r} + \ldots + p^r q^{n-r} \; ({}^nC_r \text{ terms})$$
$$= {}^nC_r \, p^r q^{n-r} ; r = 0, 1, 2, \ldots, n$$

Remark. 1. Putting $r = 0, 1, 2, \ldots, n$ in (14·1), we get the probabilities of 0, 1, 2, ..., n successes respectively in n trials and these are tabulated in Table 14·1.

Since these probabilities are the successive terms in the binomial expansion $(q + p)^n$, it is called the Binomial distribution.

2. Total probability is unity, *i.e.*, 1 ;

TABLE 14·1 : BINOMIAL PROBABILITIES

r	$p(r) = P(X = r)$
0	${}^nC_0 p^0 q^n = q^n$
1	${}^nC_1 p^1 q^{n-1}$
2	${}^nC_2 p^2 q^{n-2}$
⋮	⋮
n	${}^nC_n p^n q^0 = p^n$

$$\sum_{r=0}^{n} p(r) = p(0) + p(1) + \ldots + p(n)$$
$$= q^n + {}^nC_1\, q^{n-1} p + {}^nC_2\, q^{n-2} p^2 + \ldots + p^n$$
$$= (q+p)^n = 1 \qquad (\because\ p + q = 1)$$

3. The expression for $P(X = r)$ in (14·1) is known as *the probability (mass) function* of the Binomial distribution with *parameters n and p*. The random variable X following the probability law (14·1) is called a *Binomial Variate* with parameters n and p.

The Binomial distribution is completely determined, *i.e.*, all the probabilities can be obtained, if n and p are known. Obviously, q is known when p is given because $q = 1 - p$.

4. Since the random variable X takes only integral values, Binomial distribution is a *discrete* probability distribution.

5. For n trials, the binomial probability distribution consists of $(n + 1)$ terms, the successive binomial coefficients being,

$${}^nC_0,\ {}^nC_1,\ {}^nC_2, \ldots, {}^nC_{n-1},\ {}^nC_n$$

Since ${}^nC_0 = {}^nC_n = 1$, the first and last coefficient will always be 1. Further, since

$${}^nC_r = {}^nC_{n-r},$$

the binomial coefficients will be symmetric. Moreover, we have for all values of x :

$$(1+x)^n = {}^nC_0 + {}^nC_1 x + {}^nC_2\, x^2 + \ldots + {}^nC_n\, x^n$$

Putting $x = 1$ we get :

$$(1+1)^n = {}^nC_0 + {}^nC_1 + {}^nC_2 + \ldots + {}^nC_n \quad \Rightarrow \quad {}^nC_0 + {}^nC_1 + {}^nC_2 + \ldots + {}^nC_n = 2^n$$

i.e., the sum of binomial coefficients is 2^n.

The values of the Binomial coefficients for different values of n can be obtained conveniently from the Pascal's triangle, named after the French mathematician Blaise Pascal (1623-62) and is given below :

PASCAL'S TRIANGLE
[SHOWING COEFFICIENTS OF TERMS IN $(a + b)^n$]

Value of n	*Binomial coefficients*	*Sum* (2^n)
1	1 1	2
2	1 2 1	4
3	1 3 3 1	8
4	1 4 6 4 1	16
5	1 5 10 10 5 1	32
6	1 6 15 20 15 6 1	64
7	1 7 21 35 35 21 7 1	128
8	1 8 28 56 70 56 28 8 1	256
9	1 9 36 84 126 126 84 36 9 1	512
10	1 10 45 120 210 252 210 120 45 10 1	1,024

It can be easily seen that, taking the first and last terms as 1, each term in the above table can be obtained by adding the two terms on either side of it in the preceding line (*i.e.*, the line above it). As pointed out earlier, it can be easily verified that the bionomial coefficients are symmetric and the sum of the coefficients is 2^n.

14·2·2 Constants of Bionomial Distribution

r	$P(X = r) = p(r)$	$r.\, p(r)$	$r^2 \cdot p(r)$
0	q^n	0	0
1	${}^nC_1\, q^{n-1} p$	$1 \cdot {}^nC_1\, q^{n-1} p$	$1^2 . {}^nC_1\, q^{n-1} p$
2	${}^nC_2\, q^{n-2} p^2$	$2 \cdot {}^nC_2\, q^{n-2} p^2$	$2^2 . {}^nC_2\, q^{n-2} p^2$
3	${}^nC_3\, q^{n-3} p^3$	$3 \cdot {}^nC_3\, q^{n-3} p^3$	$3^3 . {}^nC_3\, q^{n-3} p^3$
⋮	⋮	⋮	⋮
n	p^n	$n p^n$	$n^2 p^n$

$$\text{Mean} = \Sigma r\, p(r) = {}^nC_1\, q^{n-1} p + 2\, {}^nC_2\, q^{n-2} . p^2 + 3\, {}^nC_3\, q^{n-3} p^3 + \ldots + np^n$$

$$= n\, q^{n-1} p + 2 \cdot \frac{n\,(n-1)}{2\,!} q^{n-2} p^2 + \frac{3n\,(n-1)\,(n-2)}{3\,!} q^{n-3} p^3 + \ldots + np^n$$

$$= np \left[q^{n-1} + (n-1)\, q^{n-2} p + \frac{(n-1)\,(n-2)}{2\,!} q^{n-3} p^2 + \ldots + p^{n-1} \right]$$

$$= np \left[q^{n-1} + {}^{n-1}C_1\, q^{n-2} p + {}^{n-1}C_2\, q^{n-3} p^2 + \ldots + p^{n-1} \right]$$

$$= np\,(q+p)^{n-1} \qquad \text{(By Binomial expansion for positive integer index)}$$

$$= np \qquad [\because p + q = 1]$$

$$\text{Variance} = \Sigma r^2\, p(r) - [\Sigma r p(r)]^2 = \Sigma r^2\, p(r) - (\text{mean})^2 \qquad \ldots(*)$$

$$\Sigma r^2\, p(r) = 1^2 \times {}^nC_1\, q^{n-1} p + 2^2\, {}^nC_2\, q^{n-2} p^2 + 3^2\, {}^nC_3\, q^{n-3} p^3 + \ldots + n^2 p^n$$

$$= n\, q^{n-1} p + \frac{4n(n-1)}{2} q^{n-2} p^2 + \frac{9n(n-1)\,(n-2)}{3\,!} q^{n-3} p^3 + \ldots + n^2 p^n$$

$$= np \left[q^{n-1} + 2(n-1)\, q^{n-2} p + \tfrac{3}{2} (n-1)\,(n-2)\, q^{n-3} p^2 + \ldots + np^{n-1} \right]$$

$$= np \left[\left\{ q^{n-1} + (n-1)\, q^{n-2} p + \frac{(n-1)\,(n-2)}{2} q^{n-3} p^2 + \ldots + 1 p^{n-1} \right\} \right.$$

$$\left. + \left\{ (n-1)\, q^{n-2} p + (n-1)\,(n-2)\, q^{n-3} p^2 + \ldots + (n-1)\, p^{n-1} \right\} \right]$$

$$= np \left[\{ (q+p)^{n-1} \} + (n-1)\, p\, \{ q^{n-2} + (n-2)\, q^{n-3} p + \ldots + p^{n-2} \} \right]$$

$$= np \left[(q+p)^{n-1} + (n-1)\, p\, (q+p)^{n-2} \right]$$

$$= np \left[1 + (n-1)\, p \right] \qquad (\because p = q = 1)$$

Substituting in (*) we get

$$\text{Variance} = np[1 + np - p] - (np)^2 = np[1 + np - p - np] = np[1 - p] = npq$$

Hence for the binomial distribution,

$$\text{Mean} = np \quad \ldots(14{\cdot}2) \qquad \text{and} \qquad \text{Variance} = \mu_2 = \sigma^2 = npq \quad \ldots(14{\cdot}3)$$

Similarly we can obtain the other constants given below :

$$\mu_3 = npq\,(q-p) \quad \ldots(14{\cdot}4) \qquad \text{and} \qquad \mu_4 = npq\,[1 + 3pq(n-2)] \quad \ldots(14{\cdot}5)$$

Hence, the moment coefficient of skewness is :

$$\beta_1 = \frac{\mu_3{}^2}{\mu_2{}^3} = \frac{[npq\,(q-p)]^2}{(npq)^3} = \frac{(q-p)^2}{npq} \qquad \ldots(14{\cdot}6)$$

and

$$\gamma_1 = +\sqrt{\beta_1} = \frac{\mu_3}{\mu_2{}^{3/2}} = \frac{q-p}{\sqrt{npq}} \qquad \ldots(14{\cdot}6a)$$

Coefficient of kurtosis is given by :

$$\beta_2 = \frac{\mu_4}{\mu_2{}^2} = \frac{npq[1 + 3pq(n-2)]}{(npq)^2} = \frac{1 + 3pq\,(n-2)}{npq}$$

$$\therefore \quad \beta_2 = 3 + \frac{1 - 6pq}{npq} \quad \ldots(14{\cdot}7) \qquad \text{and} \qquad \gamma_2 = \beta_2 - 3 = \frac{1 - 6pq}{npq} \quad \ldots(14{\cdot}7a)$$

Remarks. 1. Since q is the probability (of failure), we always have $0 < q < 1$.

$$\therefore \qquad \text{Variance} = np \times q < np = \text{Mean} \qquad (\because 0 < q < 1)$$

$$\Rightarrow \qquad \text{Variance} < \text{mean} \qquad \ldots(14{\cdot}7b)$$

Hence for the Binomial distribution variance is less than mean.

2. $\quad \text{Var}(X) = npq = np\,(1-p)$

$$\text{Var}(X) \text{ is maximum when } p = \tfrac{1}{2} \quad \Rightarrow \quad q = 1 - p = 1 - \tfrac{1}{2} = \tfrac{1}{2}.$$

$$\therefore \quad \text{Maximum Variance} = (npq)_{p = q = 1/2} = n \times \tfrac{1}{2} \times \tfrac{1}{2} = \frac{n}{4}$$

Hence, $\quad$ if $X \sim B(n, p)$, $\text{Var}(X) \le \dfrac{n}{4}$ ...(14·7c)

i.e., for the binomial distribution with parameters n and p, variance cannot exceed n/4.

3. As $n \to \infty$, from equations (14·6) and (14·7), we get

$$\beta_1 \to 0, \qquad \gamma_1 \to 0, \qquad \beta_2 \to 3, \qquad \text{and} \qquad \gamma_2 \to 0.$$

4. "*Binomial distribution is symmetrical if $p = q = 0{\cdot}5$. It is positively skewed if $p < 0{\cdot}5$ and negatively skewed if $p > 0{\cdot}5$.*"

14·2·3. Mode of Binomial Distribution. Mode is the value of X which maximises the probability function. Thus if $X = r$ gives mode then we should have

$$p(r) > p(r-1) \quad \text{and} \quad p(r) > p(r+1) \qquad ...(14{\cdot}8)$$

Working Rule to Find Mode of Binomial Distribution. Let X be a Binomial variate with parameters n and p.

Case (I). When $(n+1)p$ is an integer

Let $(n+1)p = k$ (an integer).

In this case the distribution is bi-modal, the two modal values being $X = k$ and $X = k - 1$.

Thus if $n = 9$ and $p = 0{\cdot}4$, then $(n+1)p = 10 \times 0{\cdot}4 = 4$, which is an integer. Hence, in this case the distribution is bi-modal, the two modal values being 4 and $4 - 1 = 3$.

Case (II). When $(n+1)p$ is not an integer

Let $(n+1)p = k_1 + f$, where k_1 is the integral part and f is the fractional part of $(n+1)p$. In this case the distribution has a *unique* mode at $X = k_1$, the integral part of $(n+1)p$.

For example, if $n = 7$ and $p = 0{\cdot}6$, then $(n+1)p = 8 \times 0{\cdot}6 = 4{\cdot}8$. Hence Mode = 4, the integral part of 4·8.

Remark. *If np is a whole number (i.e., integer), then the distribution is unimodal and the mean and mode are equal, each being np.*

Example 14·1. *Ten unbiased coins are tossed simultaneously. Find the probability of obtaining,*

(*i*) *Exactly 6 heads* $\quad$ (*ii*) *At least 8 heads* $\quad$ (*iii*) *No head*
(*iv*) *At least one head* $\quad$ (*v*) *Not more than three heads* $\quad$ (*vi*) *At least 4 heads*

Solution. If p denotes the probability of a head, the $p = q = \frac{1}{2}$. Here $n = 10$. If the random variable X denotes the number of heads, then by the Binomial probability law, the probability of r heads is given by,

$$p(r) = P(X = r) = {}^nC_r \, p^r . q^{n-r}$$

$$= {}^{10}C_r \left(\tfrac{1}{2}\right)^r . \left(\tfrac{1}{2}\right)^{10-r} = {}^{10}C_r . \left(\tfrac{1}{2}\right)^{10} = \frac{1}{1024}\,{}^{10}C_r \qquad ...(*)$$

(*i*) Required probability $= p(6) = \dfrac{1}{1024}\,{}^{10}C_6 = \dfrac{210}{1024} = \dfrac{105}{512}$ [From (*)]

(*ii*) Required probability $= P(X \ge 8) = p(8) + p(9) + p(10)$

$= \dfrac{1}{1024}\left[{}^{10}C_8 + {}^{10}C_9 + {}^{10}C_{10}\right]$ [From (*)]

$= \dfrac{45 + 10 + 1}{1024} = \dfrac{56}{1024} = \dfrac{7}{128}$

(*iii*) Required probability $= P(X = 0) = p(0) = \dfrac{1}{1024}\,{}^{10}C_0 = \dfrac{1}{1024}$ [From (*)]

(*iv*) Required probability $= P$[At least one head]

$= 1 - P$ [No head] $= 1 - p(0)$

$= 1 - \dfrac{1}{1024} = \dfrac{1023}{1024}$ [From Part (*iii*)] (*v*) Required probability $= P(X \le 3) = p(0) + p(1) + p(2) + p(3)$

$$= \frac{1}{1024}\left[{}^{10}C_0 + {}^{10}C_1 + {}^{10}C_2 + {}^{10}C_3\right] = \frac{1+10+45+120}{1024} = \frac{176}{1024} = \frac{11}{64}$$

(*vi*) Required probability $= (X \ge 4) = p(4) + p(5) + \ldots + p(10)$

$$= \frac{1}{1024}\left[{}^{10}C_4 + {}^{10}C_5 + \ldots + {}^{10}C_{10}\right]$$

Last part can be conveniently done as follows :

Required probability $= P(X \ge 4) = 1 - P(X \le 3)$

$$= 1 - \left[p(0) + p(1) + p(2) + p(3)\right] = 1 - \frac{11}{64} = \frac{53}{64} \qquad \text{[From Part } (v)]$$

Example 14·2. *Define Binomial Distribution. What is the probability of guessing correctly at least six of the ten answers in a TRUE-FALSE objective test ?*

Solution. Definition of Binomial Distribution—See Text. In a True-False Objective Test, the probability of guessing an answer correctly is given by :

$$p = \frac{1}{2} \qquad \Rightarrow \qquad q = 1 - p = \frac{1}{2}$$

By Binomial probability law, the probability of guessing correctly x answers in a 10-question test is given by :

$$p(x) = {}^{10}C_x\, p^x q^{10-x} = {}^{10}C_x \left(\frac{1}{2}\right)^x \left(\frac{1}{2}\right)^{10-x}$$

$$= {}^{10}C_x \left(\frac{1}{2}\right)^{10} \;;\quad x = 0, 1, \ldots\ldots, 10. \qquad \ldots(*)$$

Hence the required probability P of guessing correctly at least 6 of the 10 answers is given by :

$$P = p(6) + p(7) + p(8) + p(9) + p(10)$$

$$= \left(\frac{1}{2}\right)^{10}\left[{}^{10}C_6 + {}^{10}C_7 + {}^{10}C_8 + {}^{10}C_9 + {}^{10}C_{10}\right] \qquad \text{[From (*)]}$$

$$= \frac{1}{1024}\left[{}^{10}C_4 + {}^{10}C_3 + {}^{10}C_2 + {}^{10}C_1 + 1\right] \qquad (\because {}^nC_r = {}^nC_{n-r})$$

$$= \frac{1}{1024}\left[\frac{10\times9\times8\times7}{4\,!} + \frac{10\times9\times8}{3\,!} + \frac{10\times9}{2\,!} + 10 + 1\right]$$

$$= \frac{1}{1024}\left[210 + 120 + 45 + 10 + 1\right] = \frac{386}{1024} = \frac{193}{512}.$$

Example 14·3. *A student is to match three historical events (Gandhi's birth, India's freedom and first world war) with three years 1947, 1914 and 1869. If he guesses, with no knowledge of the correct answers, obtain the probability distribution of the number of answers he gets correctly.*

[*Delhi Univ. B.A. (Econ. Hons.), 2006*]

Solution. Since the student guesses the answers to the three questions with no knowledge of correct answers, we have :

p = Probability of answering any question correctly $= \frac{1}{3}$, (which is constant for each question).

Let the *r.v.* X denote the number of correct answers obtained by the student. Then,

$$X \sim B(n, p) \text{ with } n = 3 \text{ and } p = \frac{1}{3} \quad \Rightarrow \quad q = 1 - p = \frac{2}{3}.$$

$p(x)$ = Probability of guessing x correct answers

$$= {}^nC_x\, p^x q^{n-x} = {}^3C_x \left(\frac{1}{3}\right)^x \left(\frac{2}{3}\right)^{3-x} \qquad \text{(By Binomial probability law)}$$

$$= \left(\frac{1}{3}\right)^3 \cdot {}^3C_x\, 2^{3-x} = \frac{1}{27}\cdot {}^3C_x\, 2^{3-x}\;;\quad x = 0, 1, 2, 3.$$

$$\therefore \quad p(0) = \frac{1}{27}\cdot {}^3C_0 . 2^3 = \frac{8}{27} \;;\qquad p(1) = \frac{1}{27}\cdot {}^3C_1 . 2^2 = \frac{3\times4}{27} = \frac{12}{27}$$

$$p(2) = \frac{1}{27}\cdot {}^3C_2 . 2^1 = \frac{3\times2}{27} = \frac{6}{27} \;;\qquad p(3) = \frac{1}{27}\cdot {}^3C_3 . 2^0 = \frac{1}{27}$$

The probability distribution of the number of correct answers (X) is given in the adjoining Table.

TABLE 14·1 : PROBABILITY DISTRIBUTION OF CORRECT ANSWERS

x	0	1	2	3
$p(x)$	8/27	12/27	6/27	1/27

Example 14·4. *Suppose that a Central University has to form a committee of 5 members from a list of 20 candidates out of whom 12 are teachers and 8 are students. If the members of the committee are selected at random, what is the probability that the majority of the committee members are students ?*

[Delhi Univ. B.A. (Econ. Hons.), 2009]

Solution. In the usual notations we have : $n = 5$;

$$p = \text{Probability of selecting a student member} = \frac{8}{20} = \frac{2}{5}$$

$$\Rightarrow \qquad q = \text{Probability of selecting a teacher member} = \frac{12}{20} = \frac{3}{5}$$

Let X denote the number of students selected in the committee. Then $X \sim B(n = 5, p = 2/5)$. Hence, by binomial probability distribution,

$$P(X = r) = p(r) = \binom{5}{r}\left(\frac{2}{5}\right)^r\left(\frac{3}{5}\right)^{5-r} \quad ; \quad r = 0, 1, 2, 3, 4, 5 \qquad \ldots(1)$$

The required probability is given by :

$$P(X \geq 3) = p(3) + p(4) + p(5) = \binom{5}{3}\left(\frac{2}{5}\right)^3 \cdot \left(\frac{3}{5}\right)^2 + \binom{5}{4}\left(\frac{2}{5}\right)^4 \cdot \left(\frac{3}{5}\right) + \binom{5}{5}\left(\frac{2}{5}\right)^5$$

$$= \frac{1}{5^5}\left[10 \times 8 \times 9 + 5 \times 16 \times 3 + 1 \times 32\right] = \frac{720 + 240 + 32}{3125} = \frac{992}{3125} = 0.3174$$

Example 14·5. *The number of tosses of a coin that are needed so that the probability of getting at least one head being 0·875 is*

(*i*) 2, (*ii*) 3, (*iii*) 4, (*iv*) 5. *[I.C.W.A. (Intermediate), Dec. 2001]*

Solution. Let the required number of tosses of the coin be n. Then

$$P[\text{At least one head in } n \text{ tosses of a coin}] = 1 - P[\text{ No head in } n \text{ tosses of a coin}] = 1 - \left(\frac{1}{2}\right)^n$$

We want n so that this probability is 0·875.

$$\therefore \quad 1 - \left(\frac{1}{2}\right)^n = 0{\cdot}875 \quad \Rightarrow \quad \left(\frac{1}{2}\right)^n = 1 - 0{\cdot}875 = 0{\cdot}125 = (0{\cdot}5)^3 = \left(\frac{1}{2}\right)^3 \quad \Rightarrow n = 3$$

$\therefore$ (*ii*) is the correct answer.

Example 14·6. *(a) Find the probability of getting the sum 7 on at least 1 of 3 tosses of a pair of fair dice.*

(b) How many tosses are needed in order that the probability in (a) is greater than 0.95.

[Delhi Univ., B.A. (Econ. Hons.), 2009]

Solution. (*a*) Let p be the probability of getting the sum of 7 in toss of a pair of fair dice. Then

$$p = \frac{6}{36} = \frac{1}{6} \quad \Rightarrow \quad q = 1 - p = \frac{5}{6}$$

[Exhaustive cases = $6^2 = 36$; Favourable cases {(1, 6), (6, 1) (2, 5) (5, 2), (3, 4), (4, 3)} *i.e.* **six.**]

Let the *r.v.* X denote the number of times 7 is obtained in 3 tosses of a pair of dice Then

$$X \sim B\left(n = 3, \ p = \frac{1}{6}\right); \text{ so that}$$

$$P(X = r) = \binom{3}{r} \cdot \left(\frac{1}{6}\right)^r \cdot \left(\frac{5}{6}\right)^{3-r} \quad ; \ r = 0, 1, 2, 3 \qquad \ldots(i)$$

The probability of getting the sum 7 on at least one of the 3 tosses is given by :

$$P(X \geq 1) = 1 - P(X = 0) = 1 - \left(\frac{5}{6}\right)^3 = 1 - \frac{125}{216} = \frac{91}{216} = 0.42 \qquad \text{[From } (i)]$$

(*b*) We want to find *n* so that,

$$1 - P(X = 0) > 0.95 \quad \Rightarrow \quad 1 - \left(\frac{5}{6}\right)^n > 0.95 \quad \Rightarrow \quad \left(\frac{5}{6}\right)^n < 0{\cdot}05 = \frac{1}{20}$$

$$i.e., \quad \left(\frac{6}{5}\right)^n > 20 \quad \Rightarrow \quad (1{\cdot}2)^n > 20 \quad \Rightarrow \quad n \log (1{\cdot}2) > \log 20$$

$$\therefore \quad n > \frac{\log 20}{\log 1{\cdot}2} = \frac{1{\cdot}3010}{0{\cdot}0792} = 16{\cdot}42 \quad \Rightarrow \quad n \geq 17.$$

Example 14·7. *How many dice must be thrown so that there is a better than even chance of obtaining at least one six ?*

Solution. Let us suppose that the dice is thrown *n* times. The probability *P* of obtaining a six at least once in *n* throws of a dice is given by :

$$P = \text{Probability of at least one six in } n \text{ tosses of a dice}$$

$$= 1 - \text{Probability of 'no' six in } n \text{ tosses of a dice} = 1 - \left(\frac{5}{6}\right)^n$$

We want *P* to be greater than 1/2.

$$i.e., \quad 1 - \left(\frac{5}{6}\right)^n > \frac{1}{2} \quad \Rightarrow \quad \frac{1}{2} > \left(\frac{5}{6}\right)^n \quad i.e., \quad 0{\cdot}5 > (0{\cdot}83)^n \qquad \ldots(*)$$

n	1	2	3	4	5	6	...
$(0{\cdot}83)^n$	0·83	0·6889	0·5718	0·4746	0·3939	0·3269	...

By trial, we find that the inequality (*) is satisfied when $n \geq 4$. Hence the dice must be thrown at least 4 times.

Aliter. Proceed as in above Example 14.6.

Example 14·8. *Assume that half the population is vegetarian so that the chance of an individual being a vegetarian is $\frac{1}{2}$· Assuming that 100 investigators each take sample of 10 individuals to see whether they are vegetarians, how many investigators would you expect to report that three people or less were vegetarian ?*

Solution. In the usual notations we have : $n = 10$,

$$p = \text{Probability that an individual is a vegetarian} = \frac{1}{2} \quad ; \quad q = 1 - p = \frac{1}{2}$$

Then by Binomial probability law, the probability that there are *r* vegetarians in a sample of 10 is given by

$$p(r) = {}^{10}C_r\, p^r\, q^{10-r} = {}^{10}C_r \left(\frac{1}{2}\right)^r \left(\frac{1}{2}\right)^{10-r} = {}^{10}C_r \left(\frac{1}{2}\right)^{10} = \frac{1}{1024}\, {}^{10}C_r \qquad \ldots(*)$$

Thus, the probability that in a sample of 10, three or less people are vegetarian is :

$$p(0) + p(1) + p(2) + p(3) = \frac{1}{1024}\left[{}^{10}C_0 + {}^{10}C_1 + {}^{10}C_2 + {}^{10}C_3\right] \qquad \text{[From (*)]}$$

$$= \frac{1}{1024}\left[1 + 10 + 45 + 120\right] = \frac{176}{1024} = \frac{11}{64}$$

Hence, out of 100 investigators, the number of investigators who will report 3 or less vegetarians in a sample of 10 is :

$$100 \times \frac{11}{64} = \frac{275}{16} = 17{\cdot}2 \simeq 17,$$

since the number of investigators cannot be in fraction.

Example 14·9. *In a binomial distribution with 6 independent trials, the probability of 3 and 4 successes is found to be 0·2457 and 0·0819 respectively. Find the parameters p and q of the binomial distribution.* [*Delhi Univ. B.Com. (Hons.), 2002; 1998*]

Solution. Let $X \sim B(n = 6, p)$ where X denotes the number of successes. Then, by binomial probability law, the probability of r successes is given by :

$$p(r) = P(X = r) = {}^6C_r\, p^r q^{6-r}\ ; \quad r = 0, 1, 2, \ldots, 6; \quad (q = 1 - p). \qquad \ldots(*)$$

Putting $r = 3$ and 4 in (*), we get respectively :

$$p(3) = {}^6C_3\, p^3 q^3 = 20\, p^3 q^3 = 0{\cdot}2457 \text{ (Given)} \qquad \ldots(**)$$

$$p(4) = {}^6C_4\, p^4 q^2 = 15\, p^4 q^2 = 0{\cdot}0819 \text{ (Given)} \qquad \ldots(***)$$

$$\left[\because\ {}^6C_3 = \frac{6 \times 5 \times 4}{3\,!} = 20\ ;\quad {}^6C_4 = {}^6C_2 = \frac{6 \times 5}{2} = 15\right]$$

Dividing (***) by (**), we get :

$$\frac{p(4)}{p(3)} = \frac{15p^4 q^2}{20\, p^3 q^3} = \frac{0{\cdot}0819}{0{\cdot}2457} = \frac{1}{3} \quad \Rightarrow \quad \frac{3}{4} \cdot \frac{p}{q} = \frac{1}{3}$$

$$\therefore \quad 9p = 4q = 4(1 - p) \quad \Rightarrow \quad 13p = 4 \quad \Rightarrow \quad p = \frac{4}{13}$$

$$\Rightarrow \quad q = 1 - p = 1 - \frac{4}{13} = \frac{9}{13}$$

Example 14·10. (*a*) *Comment on the following* :

For a binomial distribution, mean = 7 and variance = 11.

[*Delhi Univ. B.Com. (Hons.), 2009*]

(*b*) *A binomial variable on 100 trials has 6 as its standard deviation. This statement is* :

(*i*) *valid,* (*ii*) *invalid* (*iii*) *cannot say.* *Choose the correct alternative.*

[*I.C.W.A. (Intermediate), June 1999*]

Solution. (*a*) For a binomial distribution with parameters n and p.

$$\text{Mean} = np = 7 \quad \ldots(i) \quad ; \quad \text{Variance} = npq = 11 \quad \ldots(ii)$$

Dividing (*ii*) by (*i*), we get : $q = \frac{11}{7} = 1{\cdot}6$,

which is impossible, since q being the probability, must lie between 0 and 1. Hence, the given statement is wrong.

(*b*) We are given : $X \sim B(n, p)$, where $n = 100$

and s.d. $(\sigma) = 6 \quad \Rightarrow \quad$ Variance $(\sigma^2) = 36$.

We know that if $X \sim B(n, p)$, then the maximum value of variance (X) is $n/4$. *i.e.,*

$$\text{Var}(X) \le \frac{n}{4} = \frac{100}{4} = 25. \qquad \text{But, we are given Var}(X) = 36.$$

Hence, the given statement is invalid *i.e.,* (*ii*) is the correct answer.

Example 14·11. *If the probability of a defective bolt is 1/10, find (i) the mean ; (ii) variance ; (iii) moment coefficient of skewness; (iv) kurtosis, for the distribution of defective bolts in a total of 400.*

[*Delhi Univ. B.Com. (Hon.), 2005*]

Solution. In the usual notations, we have : $n = 400, \quad p = \frac{1}{10} = 0{\cdot}1, \quad q = 1 - p = 0{\cdot}9$

According to Binomial probability law :

(*i*) Mean $= np = 400 \times 0{\cdot}1 = 40$; (*ii*) Variance $= npq = 400 \times 0{\cdot}1 \times 0{\cdot}9 = 36$.

(*iii*) The moment coefficient of skewness

$$\beta_1 = \frac{(q-p)^2}{npq} = \frac{(0{\cdot}8)^2}{36} = \frac{0{\cdot}64}{36} = 0{\cdot}01777 \simeq 0{\cdot}018 \quad \Rightarrow \quad \gamma_1 = +\sqrt{\beta_1} = \frac{q-p}{\sqrt{npq}} = \sqrt{0{\cdot}018} = 0{\cdot}134$$

(*iv*) Coefficient of kurtosis is given by :

$$\beta_2 = 3 + \frac{1 - 6pq}{npq} = 3 + \frac{1 - 6 \times 0{\cdot}1 \times 0{\cdot}9}{36} = 3 + \frac{0{\cdot}46}{36} = 3 + 0{\cdot}013 = 3{\cdot}013 \quad \Rightarrow \quad \gamma_2 = \beta_2 - 3 = 0{\cdot}013.$$

Remark. Since $\beta_1 \neq 0$, the distribution is not symmetrical. But since it is nearly zero, it is moderately symmetrical. $\beta_2 > 3$ implies that the distribution is platykurtic.

14·2·4. Fitting of Binomial Distribution. Suppose a random experiment consists of n trials, satisfying the conditions of Binomial distribution and suppose this experiment is repeated N-times. Then the frequency of r successes is given by the formula.

$$N \times p(r) = N \times {}^nC_r\, p^r q^{n-r} \quad ; \quad r = 0, 1, 2, \ldots, n. \qquad \ldots(14·9)$$

Putting $r = 0, 1, 2, \ldots, n$ we get the expected or theoretical frequencies of the Binomial distribution, which are given in the Table 14·2.

TABLE 14·2

No. of Successes (r)	*Expected or Theoretical Frequencies N. p(r)*
0	$N \cdot q^n$
1	$N \cdot {}^nC_1 \cdot q^{n-1} p$
2	$N \cdot {}^nC_2\, q^{n-2} p^2$
⋮	⋮
n	$N \cdot p^n$

If p, the probability of success which is constant for each trial is known, then the expected frequencies can be obtained easily as given in the Table 14·2. However, if p is not known and if we want to graduate or fit a binomial distribution to a given frequency distribution, we first find the mean of the given frequency distribution by the formula $\bar{x} = \Sigma fx / \Sigma f$ and equate it to np, which is the mean of the binomial probability distribution. Hence, p can be estimated by the relation

$$np = \bar{x} \qquad \Rightarrow \qquad p = \frac{\bar{x}}{n} \qquad \ldots(14·10)$$

Then $q = 1 - p$. With these values of p and q, the expected or theoretical Binomial frequencies can be obtained by using the formulae given in the Table 14·2.

Example 14·12. (*a*) *8 coins are tossed at a time, 256 times. Find the expected frequencies of successes (getting a head) and tabulate the results obtained.*

(*b*) *Also obtain the values of the mean and standard deviation of the theoretical (fitted) distribution.*

Solution. In the usual notations, we are given : $n = 8,\ N = 256.$

$$p = \text{Probability of success (head) in a single throw of a coin} = \tfrac{1}{2} \quad \Rightarrow \quad q = 1 - p = \tfrac{1}{2}$$

Hence, by the Binomial probability law, the probability of r successes in a toss of 8 coins is given by :

$$p(r) = {}^nC_r\, p^r q^{n-r} = {}^8C_r \left(\tfrac{1}{2}\right)^r \left(\tfrac{1}{2}\right)^{8-r}$$

$$= {}^8C_r \left(\tfrac{1}{2}\right)^8 = \frac{1}{256}\, {}^8C_r \qquad \ldots(*)$$

Hence, in $N = 256$ throws of 8 coins, the frequency of r successes is :

$$f(r) = N.\, p(r) = 256 \times \frac{1}{256}\, {}^8C_r = {}^8C_r \quad ; r = 0, 1, \ldots, 8.$$

Thus, the expected (theoretical) frequencies are as obtained in Table 14·3.

TABLE 14·3 : EXPECTED BINOMIAL FREQUENCIES

No. of heads	*Expected Frequencies*
0	${}^8C_0 = 1$
1	${}^8C_1 = 8$
2	${}^8C_2 = 28$
3	${}^8C_3 = 56$
4	${}^8C_4 = 70$
5	${}^8C_5 = 56$
6	${}^8C_6 = 28$
7	${}^8C_7 = 8$
8	${}^8C_8 = 1$

(*b*) For the theoretical distribution (Binomial distribution),

$$\text{Mean} = np = 8 \times \tfrac{1}{2} = 4 \quad ; \quad s.d. = \sqrt{npq} = \sqrt{8 \times \tfrac{1}{2} \times \tfrac{1}{2}} = \sqrt{2} = 1·4142$$

Example 14·13. *Fit a binomial distribution to the following data :*

x :	0	1	2	3	4
f :	28	62	46	10	4

Solution. In the usual notations we have : $n = 4 \;\; ; N = \Sigma f = 150$

If p is the parameter of the binomial distribution, then

$$np = \text{Mean of the distribution} = \bar{x} \qquad \ldots(*)$$

$$\bar{x} = \frac{\sum fx}{\sum f} = \frac{0+62+92+30+16}{150} = \frac{200}{150} = \frac{4}{3}$$

Substituting in (*) we get $4 \times p = \frac{4}{3} \Rightarrow p = \frac{1}{3}$ and $q = 1 - p = \frac{2}{3}$

The expected binomial probabilities are given by :

$$p(x) = {}^nC_x\, p^x q^{n-x} = {}^4C_x \left(\frac{1}{3}\right)^x \left(\frac{2}{3}\right)^{4-x} \qquad ...(**)$$

Putting $x = 0$, 1, 2, 3, and 4 in (**), we get the expected binomial probabilities as given in the Table 14·4.

TABLE 14·4 : FITTING OF BINOMIAL DISTRIBUTION

x	$p(x)$	*Expected Binomial Frequency* $f(x) = N.\ p(x) = 150\ p(x)$
0	${}^4C_0 \left(\frac{1}{3}\right)^0 \left(\frac{2}{3}\right)^4 = \frac{16}{81} = 0{\cdot}1975$	$29{\cdot}63 \simeq 30$
1	${}^4C_1 \left(\frac{1}{3}\right) \cdot \left(\frac{2}{3}\right)^3 = \frac{4 \times 8}{81} = 0{\cdot}3951$	$59{\cdot}26 \simeq 59$
2	${}^4C_2 \left(\frac{1}{3}\right)^2 \cdot \left(\frac{2}{3}\right)^2 = \frac{4 \times 3}{2\,!} \times \frac{4}{81} = 0{\cdot}2963$	$44{\cdot}44 \simeq 44$
3	${}^4C_3 \left(\frac{1}{3}\right)^3 \cdot \left(\frac{2}{3}\right) = 4 \times \frac{2}{81} = 0{\cdot}0988$	$14{\cdot}81 \simeq 15$
4	${}^4C_4 \left(\frac{1}{3}\right)^4 = \frac{1}{81} = 0{\cdot}0123$	$1{\cdot}85 \simeq 2$

Hence the fitted binomial distribution is :

x :	0	1	2	3	4	Total
f :	30	59	44	15	2	150

Example 14·14. *Six dice are thrown 729 times. How many times do you expect at least three dice to show a five or six ?*

Solution. Here we are given $n = 6$ and $N = 729$.

Let the event of getting 5 or 6 in the throw of a single die be called a success. Then

$$p = \text{Probability of success} = \frac{1}{6} + \frac{1}{6} = \frac{1}{3} \quad ; \quad q = 1 - p = \frac{2}{3}$$

In a signle throw of 6 dice, the probability of getting r successes (*i.e.*, getting 5 or 6 on r dice) is given by the binomial law :

$$p(r) = {}^nC_r\, p^r q^{n-r} = {}^6C_r \left(\frac{1}{3}\right)^r \left(\frac{2}{3}\right)^{6-r} = \frac{1}{3^6} \cdot {}^6C_r\, 2^{6-r} = \frac{1}{729}\, {}^6C_r \cdot 2^{6-r}$$

Thus, the probability that at least three dice show a 5 or 6 is $p(3) + p(4) + p(5) + p(6)$. Hence, in 729 throws of 6 dice each, the required frequency of getting at least 3 successes is

$$N \times [\, p(3) + p(4) + p(5) + p(6)]$$

$$= 729 \times \frac{1}{729}\left[{}^6C_3 \times 2^3 + {}^6C_4 \times 2^2 + {}^6C_5 \times 2 + {}^6C_6 \times 1\right]$$

$$= [8 \times 20 + 15 \times 4 + 6 \times 2 + 1] = 160 + 60 + 12 + 1 = 233.$$

EXERCISE 14·1

1. What do you understand by theoretical distributions ? Discuss their utility in Statistics.

2. What are the conditions under which a Binomial distribution can be used as an approximation to an observed frequency distribution ? Discuss the conditions carefully.

3. (*a*) What do you understand by 'binomial' distribution ? What are its main features ?

(*b*) Explain the salient features of binomial distribution. State the conditions under which the binomial distribution is used. [*Delhi Univ. B.Com. (Hons.), 2006*]

(*c*) Explain the characteristics of binomial distribution. [*Delhi Univ. B.Com.* (*Hons.*), *2001*]

4. (*a*) Define a binomial variate with parameters n and p and obtain its probability function.

(*b*) Obtain an expression for the mean of the binomial distribution in terms of the number of trials and the probability of success.

(*c*) Obtain the first four moments about mean for the binomial probability distribution, and hence find β_1 and β_2. Prove that as $n \to \infty$, $\beta_1 \to 0$ and $\beta_2 \to 3$.

5. (*a*) Obtain the expression for the mean and variance of a binomial distribution with parameters n and p. Hence show that for the binomial distribution, variance is less than mean.

(*b*) Obtain the variance of a binomial distribution $B(n, p)$. What is its upper bound ?

6. (*a*) What is binomial distribution ? State its important properties.

(*b*) Enumerate some real life situations where binomial distribution is applicable.

7. "A binomial distribution need not necessarily be a symmetrical distribution." Do you agree with the statement ? Give reasons.

8. 12% of the items produced by a machine are defective. What is the probability that out of a random sample of 20 items produced by the machine, 5 are defective ? (Simplification is not necessary).

Ans. $^{20}C_5 \cdot (0{\cdot}12)^5 \cdot (0{\cdot}88)^{15}$.

9. The average number of defective pieces, in the manufacturing of an article, is 1 in 10. Find the probability of getting exactly 3 defective articles in a packet of 10 articles selected at random. [*Delhi Univ. B.A.* (*Econ. Hons.*), *2000*]

Ans. $^{10}C_3\ (0{\cdot}1)^3\ (0{\cdot}9)^7$.

10. The probability that a student will graduate is 0·4. Determine the probability that out of 5 students :

(*i*) none; (*ii*) 1; (*iii*) at least 1 ; and (*iv*) all,

will graduate. [*Delhi Univ. B.Com* (*Hons.*), *1997*]

Ans. (*i*) 0·07776 (*ii*) 0·2592 (*iii*) 0·92224 (*iv*) 0·01024

11. Suppose that the probability is $\frac{1}{2}$ that a car stolen in Delhi will be recovered. Find the probability that at least one out of 20 cars stolen in the city on a particular day will be recovered. [*Delhi Univ. B.A.* (*Econ. Hons.*), *2002*]

Ans. $1 - \left(\frac{1}{2}\right)^{20}$.

12. It is observed that 80% of television viewers watch "Aap Ki Adalat" programme. What is probability that at least 80% of the viewers in a random sample of five, watch this programme ? [*I.C.W.A.* (*Intermediate*), *Dec. 1996*]

Ans and Hint. Required Probability = $P(X \geq 80\ \%$ of 5$) = P(X \geq 4) = 0{\cdot}7373$; $X \sim B\ (n = 5, p = 0{\cdot}8)$

13. If the probability of male birth is 0·5, then the probability that in a family of 4 children there will be at least 1 boy, is

(*i*) $\frac{4}{16}$, (*ii*) $\frac{4}{16}$, (*iii*) $\frac{11}{16}$, (*iv*) $\frac{15}{16}$.

[*I.C.W.A.* (*Intermediate*), *June 1999*]

Ans. (*iv*).

14. The merchant's file of 20 accounts contains 6 delinquent and 14 non-delinquent accounts. An auditor randomly selects 5 of these accounts for examination.

(*i*) What is the probability that the auditor finds exactly 2 delinquent cases ?

(*ii*) Find the expected number of delinquent accounts in the sample selected.

Ans. (*i*) $^5C_2\ (0{\cdot}3)^2 (0{\cdot}7)^3 = 0{\cdot}3087$ (*iii*) $np = 5 \times 0{\cdot}3 = 1{\cdot}5$

15. An oil exploration firm finds that 5% of the test wells it drills, yield a deposit of natural gas. If the firm drills 6 wells, what is the probability that

(*i*) exactly 2 wells, (*ii*) at least one well ; yield gas ? [*I.C.W.A.* (*Intermediate*), *June 1995*]

Ans. (*i*) 0·0305 (*ii*) $1 - (0{\cdot}95)^6 = 0{\cdot}2649$.

16. 20% of the bolts produced by a machine are defective. Obtain the probability distribution of the number of defectives in a sample of 5 bolts chosen at random.

Ans. $p(x) = {}^5C_x \cdot (1/5)^x\ (4/5)^{5-x}$; $x = 0, 1, 2, 3, 4, 5$.

17. Four coins are tossed simultaneously. What is the probability of getting

(*i*) 2 heads and 2 tails, (*ii*) at least two heads, and (*iii*) at least one head.

Ans. (*i*) $\frac{3}{8}$, (*ii*) $\frac{11}{16}$, (*iii*) $\frac{15}{16}$.

18. What do you understand by Binomial distribution ? What are its features ?

Three perfect coins are tossed together. What is the probability of getting at least one head ?

Ans. 7/8.

19. An accountant is to audit 24 accounts of a firm. Sixteen of these are of highly-valued customers. If the accountant selects 4 of the accounts at random, what is the probability that he chooses at least one highly-valued account ?

Ans. 80 / 81.

20. (*a*) Eight coins are thrown simultaneously. Show that the probability of obtaining at least 6 heads is 37 / 256.

(*b*) The average percentage of failures in a certain examination is 40. What is the probability that out of a group of 6 candidates, at least 4 passed in the examination ? [*C.A. (Foundation), Nov. 1997*]

Ans. 0·54432.

21. On an average 2% of the population in an area suffers from T.B. What is the probability that out of 5 persons chosen at random from this area, at least two suffer from T.B. (Simplification is not necessary.)

Ans. $1-(0\cdot98)^4 \times 1\cdot08$.

22. Assuming that it is true that 2 in 10 industrial accidents are due to fatigue, find the probability that—

(*i*) *exactly* 2 of 8 industrial accidents will be due to fatigue.

(*ii*) *at least* 2 of 8 industrial accidents will be due to fatigue.

Ans. (*i*) ${}^8C_2\,(0\cdot2)^2\,(0\cdot8)^6$, (*ii*) $1-(0\cdot8)^7 \times 2\cdot4$.

23. From past weather records, it has been found that, on an average, rain falls on 12 days in June. Find the probability that in a given week of June :

(*i*) the first 4 days will be dry and the remaining three days wet ;

(*ii*) there will be rain on alternate days ; (*iii*) exactly 3 days will be wet.

Ans. (*i*) $\left(\frac{3}{5}\right)^4 \cdot \left(\frac{2}{5}\right)^3$; (*ii*) $\left(\frac{2}{5}\right)^3 \cdot \left(\frac{3}{5}\right)^3$; (*ii*) ${}^7C_3\left(\frac{2}{5}\right)^3\left(\frac{3}{5}\right)^4$.

24. The incidence of occupational disease, in an industry is such that the workmen have a 20% chance of suffering from it. What is the probability that out of six workmen, 4 or more will contract the disease ?

Ans. $\frac{53}{3125} = 0\cdot0169$.

25. An insurance salesman sells policies to five men, all of identical age and good health. According to the actuarial tables, the probability that a man of this particular age will be alive 30 years hence is $\frac{2}{3}$. Find the probability that in 30 years (*i*) all five men, (*ii*) at least one man, (*iii*) at least 3 men, (*iv*) at most three men, will be alive.

[*Delhi Univ. B.Com. (Hons.), 2005*]

Ans. (*i*) $\left(\frac{2}{3}\right)^5 = \frac{32}{243}$; (*ii*) $1-\frac{1}{3^5} = \frac{242}{243}$, (*iii*) $\frac{192}{243}$ (*iv*) $1-\left[{}^5C_4\left(\frac{2}{3}\right)^4\left(\frac{1}{3}\right)+{}^5C_5\left(\frac{2}{3}\right)^5\right]$.

26. The probability of a bomb hitting a target is 1/5. Two bombs are enough to destroy a bridge. If six bombs are aimed at the bridge, find the probability that the bridge is destroyed.

Hint. $n = 6$, $p = 1/5$.

The bridge is destroyed if at least two of the bombs hit it. Hence the required probability that bridge is destroyed is given by

$$p(2)+p(3)+p(4)+p(5)+p(6) = 1-[\,p(0)+p(1)] = 1-\frac{2048}{3125} = 0\cdot345.$$

27. A multiple choice test consists of 8 questions with three answers to each question (of which only one is correct). A student answers each question by rolling a balanced die and checking the first answer if he gets 1 or 2, the second answer if he gets 3 or 4, and the third answer if he gets 5 or 6. To get a distinction, a student must secure at least 75% correct answers. If there is no negative marking, what is the probability that the student secures a distinction ?

Hint. Let X : Number of correct answers. Then $X \sim B\left(n = 8, p = \frac{1}{3}\right)$.

Ans. Required probability = $P(X \geq 75\%$ of $8) = P(X \geq 6) = 0\cdot0197$.

28. Explain the concept of posterior probability. A buyer will accept a certain lot of T.V. tuners if a sample of three picked at random contains at the most one defective. What is the probability that he will accept the lot of twenty tuners if it contains four defectives. [*Delhi Univ. B.Com. (Hons.), 2004*]

Hint. X : Number of defective tuners in the sample. $X \sim B\,(n = 3,\; p = (4/20) = 0{\cdot}2)$

$$\text{Required probability} = P\,(X \le 1) = \sum_{x=0}^{1} {}^3C_x\, p^x (1-p)^{3-x} = (0{\cdot}8)^3 + 3 \times (0{\cdot}2) \times (0{\cdot}8)^2 = 0{\cdot}896.$$

29. A machine produces an average of 20% defective bolts. A batch is accepted if a sample of 5 bolts taken from that batch contains no defective and rejected if the sample contains 3 or more defectives. In other cases, a second sample is taken. What is the probability that the second sample is required ? [*Delhi Uni. B.A. (Econ. Hons.)*, 1994]

Ans. $\left(\frac{1}{5}\right)^5 \left[{}^5C_1 \times 4^4 + {}^5C_2 \times 4^3\right] = 0{\cdot}6144.$

30. The probability of a man hitting the target is $\frac{1}{4}$.

(*a*) If he fires 7 times, what is the probability that he hits the target : (*i*) at least once (*ii*) at least twice ?

(*b*) How many times must he fire so that the probability of his hitting the target is greater than 2 / 3 ?

[*Delhi Univ. B.A. (Econ. Hons.)*, 2004]

Ans. (*a*) (*i*) $1 - (3/4)^7 = 0{\cdot}8666$; (*ii*) $1 - (3/4)^7 - 7.(1/4).(3/4)^6 = 0{\cdot}5553$; (*b*) $n = 4$.

31. In a large group of students, 80% have a recommended Statistic book. 3 students are selected at random.

(*i*) Find the probability distribution of the number of students having the book.

(*ii*) Calculate the mean and variance of the distribution. [*Delhi Univ. B.A. (Econ. Hons.)*, 1991]

Ans. (*i*)

x	0	1	2	3
$p(x)$	0·008	0·096	0·384	0·512

(*ii*) Mean = 2·4, Variance = 0·48.

32. A box contains 10 screws of which 5 are defective. Obtain the probability distribution of the number of defective screws (X) in a sample of 4 screws chosen at random and find $V(X)$. [*I.C.W.A (Intermediate)*, *Dec.* 1999]

Ans. $X \sim B\left(n = 4, p = \frac{1}{2}\right)$;

x	0	1	2	3	4
$p(x)$	$\frac{1}{16}$	$\frac{4}{16}$	$\frac{6}{16}$	$\frac{4}{16}$	$\frac{1}{16}$

; $\sigma_x^2 = 1$.

33. Assuming that half of population is vegetarian and each of 128 investigators takes a sample of 10 individuals to see whether they are vegetarian, how many investigators would you expect to report 2 or less vegetarians ?

[*Delhi Univ. B.A. (Econ. Hons.)*, 2004]

Ans. 7. **Hint.** Proceed as in Example 14.8.

34. In 100 sets of ten tosses of an unbiased coin, in how many cases should we expect :

(*i*) seven heads and three tails, (*ii*) at least seven heads ?

Ans. (*i*) 12, (*ii*) 17.

35. Out of 1,000 families of 3 children each, how many families would you expect to have two boys and one girl, assuming that boys and girls are equally likely ?

Ans. 375.

36. The following statement cannot be true, why ?

"The mean of a binomial distribution is 4 and its standard deviation is 3".

Ans. $q = 2{\cdot}25$, which is impossible.

37. If the probability of a defective bolt is 0·2, find : (*i*) the mean; and (*ii*) the standard deviation, of defective bolts in a total of 900 bolts. [*Delhi Univ. B.Com (Hons.)*, 1994]

Hint. Mean $= np = 900 \times 0{\cdot}2 = 180$; s.d. $= \sqrt{npq} = \sqrt{900 \times 0{\cdot}2 \times 0{\cdot}8} = 12.$

38. What is the mean and variance of the binomial distribution $(0{\cdot}3 + 0{\cdot}7)^{10}$, $q = 0{\cdot}3$?

[*C.A. (Foundation)*, *Nov.* 2000]

Ans. Mean = 7, Variance = 2·1.

39. Find the parameters (n and p), of a binomial distribution which has mean equal to 6 and standard deviation equal to 2. [*Delhi Univ. B.Com. (Hons.)*, 2007]

Ans. $p = 1/3$; $n = 18$.

40. State the conditions under which a binomial distribution is used. Find the binomial distribution if the mean is 12 and the standard deviation is 2. [*C.A. (Foundation)*, *May* 1997]

Ans. $X \sim B\,(n = 18, p = 2/3)$.

41. If the mean and variance of a binomial distribution with parameters (n, p) are 40 and 30 respectively, then parameters are :

(*i*) (40, 0·75) ; (*ii*) (30, 0·25) ; (*iii*) (160, 0·25) ; (*iv*) (120, 0·5).

[*I.C.W.A. (Intermediate), June 1999*]

Ans. (*iii*).

42. The mean of a binomial distribution is 4 and its standard deviation is $\sqrt{3}$. What are the values of n, p and q with usual notations ?

Ans. $n = 16, \quad p = 1/4, \quad q = 3/4.$

43. The mean and variance of a binomial distribution are 3 and 2 respectively. Find the probability that the variate takes the values :

(*i*) Less than or equal to 2, (*ii*) greater than or equal to 7.

Ans. $n = 9, p = 1/3, q = 2/3.$

(*i*) $P(X \le 2) = \frac{58}{9} \times \left(\frac{2}{3}\right)^7 = 0{\cdot}3767$; (*ii*) $P(X \ge 7) = \left(\frac{1}{3}\right)^7 \left(16 + 2 + \frac{1}{9}\right) = 0{\cdot}0083.$

44. A discrete random variable X has mean equal to 6 and variance equal to 2. If it is assumed that the underlying distribution of X is binomial, what is the probability that $5 \le X \le 7$?

Ans. $p = 2/3$ and $n = 9$; Required probability $= 4672 / 3^9$.

45. A binomial distribution on 50 trials has 4 as its standard deviation. The statement is :

(*i*) valid (*ii*) invalid (*iii*) cannot say.

Choose the correct answer.

Ans. (*ii*) Invalid. [**Hint.** For binomial distribution, Variance $\le \frac{n}{4}$.]

46. If a random variate X follows binomial distribution with the values of the parameters as 9 and p, then maximum value of the variance of X is

(*i*) 2, (*ii*) 2·25, (*iii*) 4·5 (*iv*) none of these. [*I.C.W.A (Intermediate), Dec 2001*]

Ans. (*ii*).

47. In a Binomial distribution with 6 independent trials, the probabilities of 3 and 4 successes are found to be 0·2457 and 0·0819 respectively. Find the parameter 'p' of the Binomial distribution.

[*Delhi Univ. B.Com. (Hons.), 2002 ; C.A. (Foundation), June 1993*]

Ans. $p = \frac{4}{13}$.

48. Find the probability of success p for a binomial distribution, if $n = 6$ and $4\,P(X = 4) = P(X = 2)$.

[*C.A. (Foundation), Nov. 1999*]

Ans. $p = \frac{1}{3}$.

Hint. $3p^2 + 2p - 1 = 0 \quad \Rightarrow \quad p = 1/3$ or -1 (Rejected).

49. Obtain the mean and standard deviation of a binomial distribution for which

$P(X = 3) = 16.\, P(X = 7)$ and $n = 10$ [*Delhi Univ. B.Com. (Hons.), (External), 2005*]

Ans. $p = 1/3, \; n = 10$; Mean $= np = 10/3$; $s.d. = \sqrt{npq} = \sqrt{20}/3$.

50. (*a*) What is the most probable number of times an ace will appear if a die is tossed (*i*) 50 times (*ii*) 53 times.

Ans. (*i*) 8, (*ii*) Bimodal ; Modes are 8 and 9.

(*b*) The mode of the bionomial distribution $B\left(7, \frac{1}{3}\right)$ is :

(*i*) 3 (*ii*) 2 (*iii*) $\frac{7}{3}$ (*iv*) $\frac{8}{3}$. [*I.C.W.A. (Intermediate), June 2002*]

Ans. (*ii*).

51. If the probability of defective bolt is 0·1 find

(*a*) the mean and standard deviation for the distribution of defective bolts in a total of 500, and

(*b*) the moment coefficients of skewness and kurtosis of the distribution.

Ans. Mean = 50, s.d. = 6·7, $\gamma_1 = 0{\cdot}119$, $\beta_2 = 3{\cdot}01$, $\gamma_2 = 0{\cdot}01$.

52. Find the standard deviation of a binomial distribution whose mean is 5 and $\mu_3 = 0{\cdot}5$.

Hint. $np = 5,\ \mu_3 = npq\,(q-p) = 0{\cdot}5 \quad \Rightarrow \quad q\,(q-p) = \frac{0{\cdot}5}{5} = 0{\cdot}1$

$\Rightarrow \quad q\,(2q-1) = 0{\cdot}1 \quad \Rightarrow \quad 20\,q^2 - 10\,q - 1 = 0 \quad \Rightarrow \quad q = 0{\cdot}585$

Ans. $\sigma = \sqrt{n\,p\,q} = \sqrt{5 \times 0{\cdot}585} = 1{\cdot}71$.

69. Five fair coins were tossed 100 times. From the following outcomes, calculate the expected frequencies.

No. of heads up :	0	1	2	3	4	5
Observed frequency :	2	10	24	38	18	8

Ans. [3, 16, 31, 31, 16, 3]

53. The screws produced by a certain machine were checked by examining samples of 12. The following table shows the distribution of 128 samples according to the number of defectives they contained.

No. of defectives :	0	1	2	3	4	5	6	7	Total
No. of samples :	7	6	19	35	30	23	7	1	128

Fit a binomial distribution and find the expected frequencies if the chance of a screw being defective is 1/2. Find the mean and variance of the fitted distribution. *[Delhi Univ., (FMS), M.B.A., March 2004]*

Ans. $f(x = N.p(x) = 128 \times {}^7C_x\,(1/2)^x.(1/2)^{7-x} = {}^7C_x \ ;\ x = 0, 1, 2, \ldots, 7$

Expected binomial frequencies are : [1, 7, 21, 35, 35, 21, 7, 1].

For fitted distribution, Mean $= 7 \times \frac{1}{2} = 3.5$; Variance $= 7 \times \frac{1}{2} \times \frac{1}{2} = 1{\cdot}75$

54. The adjoining data due to Wheldon shows the results of throwing 12 dice 4096 times ; a throw of 4, 5 or 6 being called a success .

Success	*Frequency*	*Success*	*Frequency*
0	—	7	847
1	7	8	536
2	60	9	257
3	198	10	71
4	430	11	11
5	731	12	—
6	948		

Find the expected frequencies and compare the actual mean with that of the expected distribution. Calculate the standard deviation of the fitted distribution.

Ans. Expected frequencies are :

1, 12, 66, 220, 495, 792, 924, 792, 495, 220, 66, 12, 1.

Expected mean = 6, Actual mean = 6·139 ; s.d. of fitted distribution $= \sqrt{n\,p\,q} = 1{\cdot}732$.

14·3. POISSON DISTRIBUTION (AS A LIMITING CASE OF BINOMIAL DISTRIBUTION)

Poisson distribution was derived in 1837 by a French mathematician Simeon D. Poisson (1781—1840). Poisson distribution may be obtained as a limiting case of Binomial probability distribution under the following conditions :

(*i*) n, the number of trials is indefinitely large *i.e.*, $n \to \infty$.

(*ii*) p, the constant probability of success for each trial is indefinitely small *i.e.*, $p \to 0$.

(*iii*) $np = m$, (say), is finite.

Under the above three conditions the Binomial probability function (14·1) tends to the probability function of the Poisson distribution given below :

$$p(r) = P(X = r) = \frac{e^{-m}.\,m^r}{r\,!},\ r = 0, 1, 2, 3, \ldots \qquad \ldots(14{\cdot}10)$$

where X is the number of successes (occurrences of the event), $m = np$ and

$e = 2{\cdot}71828$ [The base of the system of Natural logarithms]

and $\quad r\,! = r\,(r-1)\,(r-2) \ldots \times 3 \times 2 \times 1.$

Derivation of (14·10). We shall obtain the limiting form of the binomial probability function (14·1) under the conditions ;

$$n \to \infty \quad \text{and} \quad np = m \quad \Rightarrow \quad p = \frac{m}{n} \quad \text{and} \quad q = 1 - \frac{m}{n}$$

Probability function of Binomial distribution is

$$^{n}C_{r}\, p^{r} q^{n-r} = \frac{n!}{r!\,(n-r)!}\, p^{r} q^{n-r}$$

$$= \frac{n(n-1)(n-2)\ldots[n-(r-1)]}{r!}\left(\frac{m}{n}\right)^{r}\left(1-\frac{m}{n}\right)^{n-r}$$

$$= \frac{m^{r}}{r!}\cdot\frac{n}{n}\cdot\frac{n-1}{n}\cdot\frac{n-2}{n}\cdots\cdots\frac{n-(r-1)}{n}\cdot\left(1-\frac{m}{n}\right)^{n-r}$$

$$= \frac{m^{r}}{r!}\left(1-\frac{1}{n}\right)\left(1-\frac{2}{n}\right)\cdots\cdots\left(1-\frac{r-1}{n}\right)\times\left(1-\frac{m}{n}\right)^{n}\times\left(1-\frac{m}{n}\right)^{-r}$$

Taking the limit as $n \to \infty$, the limiting form of Binomial probability function becomes

$$\frac{m^{r}}{r!}\cdot\lim_{n\to\infty}\left(1-\frac{1}{n}\right)\times\lim_{n\to\infty}\left(1-\frac{2}{n}\right)\times\ldots\times\lim_{n\to\infty}\left(1-\frac{r-1}{n}\right)\times\lim_{n\to\infty}\left(1-\frac{m}{n}\right)^{n}\times\lim_{n\to\infty}\left(1-\frac{m}{n}\right)^{-r}$$

$$= \frac{m^{r}}{r!}\times(1-0)\times(1-0)\times\ldots\times(1-0)\times\lim_{n\to\infty}\left(1-\frac{m}{n}\right)^{n}\times\lim_{n\to\infty}\left(1-\frac{m}{n}\right)^{-r} \qquad \ldots(*)$$

But we know that :

$$\lim_{n\to\infty}\left(1+\frac{a}{n}\right)^{n} = e^{a} \quad \text{and} \quad \lim_{n\to\infty}\left(1+\frac{a}{n}\right)^{A} = 1 \qquad \ldots(14{\cdot}11)$$

if A is constant independent of n. Substituting these values in (*), we get the limiting form of Binomial probability function as

$$\frac{m^{r}}{r!}\times 1\times e^{-m}\times 1 = \frac{e^{-m}\, m^{r}}{r!}$$

Hence the probability function of the Poisson distribution is

$$p(r) = P(X=r) = \frac{e^{-m}\, m^{r}}{r!}\,;\quad r = 0, 1, 2, 3, \ldots$$

as stated in (14·10).

Remarks. 1. Poisson distribution is a discrete probability distribution, since the variable X can take only integral values 0, 1, 2, ... ∞.

TABLE 14·5 : **POISSON PROBABILITIES**

No. of Successes (r)	*Probability* $p(r)$
0	$\frac{e^{-m}\,.\,m^{0}}{0!} = e^{m}$
1	$\frac{e^{-m}\,.\,m}{1!}$
2	$\frac{e^{-m}\,.\,m^{2}}{2!}$
3	$\frac{e^{-m}\,.\,m^{3}}{3!}$
⋮	⋮

2. Putting r = 0, 1, 2, 3 ..., in (14·10), we obtain the probabilities of 0, 1, 2, 3, ..., successes respectively, which are given in the Table 14·5.

The values of e^{-m} for some selected values of m are given in Table V in the Appendix at the end of the book.

3. Total probability is 1.

$$\sum_{r=0}^{\infty} p(r) = e^{-m} + me^{-m} + \frac{m^{2}}{2!}e^{-m} + \frac{m^{3}}{3!}e^{-m} + \ldots$$

$$= e^{-m}\left[1 + m + \frac{m^{2}}{2!} + \frac{m^{3}}{3!} + \ldots\right]$$

$$= e^{-m}\times e^{m} = e^{-m+m} = e^{0} = 1 \qquad \text{[By law of indices]}$$

$$\left[\because\ e^{x} = 1 + x + \frac{x^{2}}{2!} + \frac{x^{3}}{3!} + \ldots\right] \qquad \ldots(14{\cdot}12)$$

4. If we know m, all the probabilities of the Poisson distribution can be obtained. m is, therefore, called the *parameter* of the Poisson distribution.

14·3·1. Utility or Importance of Poisson Distribution. The conditions under which Poisson distribution is obtained as a limiting case of the Binomial distribution and also the conditions for the general model underlying Poisson distribution [*c.f.* remark 5] suggest that Poisson distribution can be used to explain the behaviour of the discrete random variables where the probability of occurrence of the event is very small and the total number of possible cases is sufficiently large. As such Poisson distribution has found application in a variety of fields such as Queuing Theory (waiting time problems), Insurance, Physics, Biology, Business, Economics and Industry. Most of the *Temporal Distributions* (dealing with events which are supposed to occur in equal intervals of time) and the *Spatial Distributions* (dealing with events which are supposed to occur in intervals of equal length along a straight line) follow the Poisson Probability Law. We give below some practical situations where Poisson distribution can be used :

(*i*) The number of telephone calls arriving at a telephone switch board in unit time (say, per minute).

(*ii*) The number of customers arriving at the super market ; say per hour.

(*iii*) The number of defects per unit of manufactured product [This is done for the construction of control chart for number of defects (*c*) in Industrial Quality Control].

(*iv*) To count the number of radio-active disintegrations of a radio-active element per unit of time (Physics).

(*v*) To count the number of bacteria per unit (Biology).

(*vi*) The number of defective material say, pins, blades etc. in a packing manufactured by a good concern.

(*vii*) The number of suicides reported in a particular day or the number of causalities (persons dying) due to a rare disease such as heart attack or cancer or snake bite in a year.

(*viii*) The number of accidents taking place per day on a busy road.

(*ix*) The number of typographical errors per page in a typed material or the number of printing mistakes per page in a book.

14·3·2. Constants of Poisson Distribution

r	$p(r)$	$rp(r)$	$r^2 p(r)$
0	e^{-m}	0	0
1	me^{-m}	$1.\ me^{-m}$	me^{-m}
2	$\frac{m^2 e^{-m}}{2\,!}$	$2.\frac{m^2 e^{-m}}{2\,!}$	$2^2.\frac{m^2 e^{-m}}{2\,!}$
3	$\frac{m^3 e^{-m}}{3\,!}$	$3.\frac{m^3 e^{-m}}{3\,!}$	$3^2.\frac{m^3 e^{-m}}{3\,!}$
4	$\frac{m^4 e^{-m}}{4\,!}$	$4.\frac{m^4 e^{-m}}{4\,!}$	$4^2.\frac{m^4 e^{-m}}{4\,!}$
⋮	⋮	⋮	⋮

$$\text{Mean} = \sum_{r=0}^{\infty} r\ p(r)$$

$$= me^{-m} + 2\frac{m^2 e^{-m}}{2\,!} + 3\,.\frac{m^3 e^{-m}}{3\,!} + 4\,.\frac{m^4 e^{-m}}{4\,!} + \dots$$

$$= me^{-m}\left[1 + m + \frac{m^2}{2\,!} + \frac{m^3}{3\,!} + \dots\right]$$

$$= me^{-m} \times e^m \qquad \text{[Using (14·12)]}$$

$$= me^{-m+m} = m\,e^0$$

$$= m \qquad (\because e^0 = 1) \qquad \dots(14·13)$$

$$\text{Variance} = \Sigma r^2 p(r) - [\Sigma rp(r)]^2$$

$$= \Sigma r^2 p(r) - (\text{mean})^2$$

$$= \Sigma r^2 p(r) - m^2 \qquad \dots(*)$$

$$\Sigma r^2 p(r) = m\,e^{-m} + 2^2\cdot\frac{m^2 e^{-m}}{2\,!} + 3^2\cdot\frac{m^3 e^{-m}}{3\,!} + 4^2\cdot\frac{m^4 e^{-m}}{4\,!} + \dots$$

$$= m\,e^{-m}\left[1 + 2m + \frac{3}{2\,!}m^2 + \frac{4}{3\,!}m^3 + \dots\right]$$

$$= m\,e^{-m}\left[\left\{1 + m + \frac{m^2}{2\,!} + \frac{m^3}{3\,!} + \dots\right\} + \left\{m + \frac{2m^2}{2\,!} + \frac{3m^3}{3\,!} + \dots\right\}\right]$$

$$= m\,e^{-m}\left[\left\{1 + m + \frac{m^2}{2\,!} + \frac{m^3}{3\,!} + \dots\right\} + m\left\{1 + m + \frac{m^2}{2\,!} + \frac{m^3}{3\,!} + \dots\right\}\right]$$

$$= m\,e^{-m}\left[e^m + m\,e^m\right] = m\,e^{-m}\,.\,e^m\,(1 + m) = m(1 + m)\,e^0 \qquad \text{[Using (14·12)]}$$

$$= m(1 + m)$$

Substituting in (*) we get

$$\text{Variance} = m(1+m) - m^2 = m + m^2 - m^2 = m \qquad ...(14\cdot14)$$

Hence *for the Poisson distribution with parameter m, we have Mean = Variance = m* ...(14·15)

i.e., mean and variance are equal, each being equal to the parameter m.

Other Constants : The moments (about mean) of the Poisson distribution are :

$$\mu_1 = 0 \quad ; \quad \mu_2 = \text{Variance} = m \quad ; \quad \mu_3 = m \quad ; \quad \mu_4 = m + 3m^2$$

Hence, $$\beta_1 = \frac{\mu_3^2}{\mu_2^3} = \frac{m^2}{m^3} = \frac{1}{m} \quad \text{and} \quad \gamma_1 = \sqrt{\beta_1} = \frac{1}{\sqrt{m}} \qquad ...(14\cdot16)$$

$$\beta_2 = \frac{\mu_4}{\mu_2^2} = \frac{m+3m^2}{m^2} = 3 + \frac{1}{m} \quad \Rightarrow \quad \gamma_2 = \beta_2 - 3 = \frac{1}{m} \qquad ...(14\cdot17)$$

Remarks 1. As $m \to \infty$, $\beta_1 \to 0$, $\gamma_1 \to 0$, $\beta_2 \to 3$ and $\gamma_2 \to 0$.

2. Since $\mu_3 = m > 0$, from (14·16) we observe that $\gamma_1 > 0$. This means that *Poisson distribution is a positively skewed distribution.* As the value of the parameter m increases, γ_1 decreases and thus skewness is reduced for increasing values of m. In particular as $m \to \infty$ (large values of m), $\gamma_1 \to 0$ and consequently the distribution tends to be symmetrical for large m.

14·3·3. Mode of Poisson Distribution : The Poisson distribution has mode at $X = r$,

$$\text{if } p(r) > p(r-1) \quad \text{and} \quad p(r) > p(r+1).$$

Case (i). When *m* is an integer. If m is an integer, equal to k, (say), then the Poisson distribution is bi-modal, the two modes being at the points $X = k$ and $X = k - 1$.

Case (ii). When *m* is not an integer. If m is not an integer, then the distribution is unimodal, the unique modal value being the integral part of m. For example, if $m = 5\cdot6$, then mode is 5, the integral part of 5·6.

Example 14·15. *Comment on the following :*

For a Poisson distribution, Mean = 8 and Variance = 7.

Solution. The given statement is wrong, since for a Poisson distribution mean and variance are equal.

Example 14·16. *If the standard deviation of a Poisson variable X is $\sqrt{2}$, then the probability that X is strictly positive is*

(*i*) e^2 (*ii*) e^{-2} (*iii*) $1 - e^{-\sqrt{2}}$, (*iv*) none of these.

[*I.C.W.A. (Intermediate) June 2000*]

Solution. Let $X \sim P(\lambda)$. We know that for Poisson distribution with parameter λ,

$$\text{Variance} = \lambda = \left(\sqrt{2}\right)^2 = 2 \qquad \left[\because \text{ s.d.} = \sqrt{2} \text{ (Given)}\right]$$

$$\therefore \quad P(X=r) = \frac{e^{-\lambda} \cdot \lambda^r}{r\,!} = \frac{e^{-2} \cdot 2^r}{r\,!} \quad ; \quad r = 0, 1, 2, \ldots \qquad ...(*)$$

The Probability that X is strictly positive is given by :

$$P(X > 0) = 1 - P(X = 0) = 1 - e^{-2} \qquad \text{[From (*)]}$$

Hence, (*iv*) is the correct answer.

Example 14·17. *Between the hours 2 P.M. and 4 P.M. the average number of phone calls per minute coming into the switch board of a company is 2·35. Find the probability that during one particular minute, there will be at most 2 phone calls. [Given $e^{-2\cdot35} = 0\cdot095374$]*

Solution. If the random variable X denotes the number of telephone calls per minute, then X will follow Poisson distribution with parameter $m = 2\cdot35$ and probability function :

$$P(X=r) = \frac{e^{-m} \cdot m^r}{r\,!} = \frac{e^{-2\cdot35} \times (2\cdot35)^r}{r\,!} \quad ; \quad r = 0, 1, 2 \ldots \qquad ...(*)$$

The probability that during one particular minute there will be at most 2 phone calls is given by :

$$P(X \le 2) = P(X = 0) + P(X = 1) + P(X = 2) = e^{-2\cdot35}\left(1 + 2\cdot35 + \frac{(2\cdot35)^2}{2\,!}\right) \qquad \text{[From (*)]}$$

$$= 0\cdot095374 \times (1 + 2\cdot35 + 2\cdot76125) = 0\cdot095374 \times 6\cdot11125 = 0\cdot5828543.$$

Example 14·18. *It is known from past experience that in a certain plant there are on the average 4 industrial accidents per month. Find the probability that in a given year there will be less than 4 accidents. Assume Poisson distribution.* ($e^{-4} = 0\cdot0183$)

Solution. In the usual notations we are given $m = 4$. If the random variable X denotes the number of accidents in the plant per month, then by Poisson probability law,

$$P(X = r) = \frac{e^{-m}.\, m^r}{r\,!} = \frac{e^{-4}.\, 4^r}{r\,!} \qquad \ldots(*)$$

The required probability that there will be less than 4 accidents is given by

$$P(X < 4) = P(X = 0) + P(X = 1) + P(X = 2) + P(X = 3)$$

$$= e^{-4}\left[1 + 4 + \frac{4^2}{2\,!} + \frac{4^3}{3\,!}\right] = e^{-4}\,[1 + 4 + 8 + 10\cdot67] \qquad \text{[From (*)]}$$

$$= e^{-4} \times 23\cdot67 = 0\cdot0183 \times 23\cdot67 = 0\cdot4332.$$

Example 14·19. *If 5% of the electric bulbs manufactured by a company are defective, use Poisson distribution to find the probability that in a sample of 100 bulbs*

(i) none is defective,

(ii) 5 bulbs will be defective. (*Given* : $e^{-5} = 0\cdot007$).

Solution. Here we are given : $n = 100$,

p = Probability of a defective bulb = 5% = 0·05

Since p is small and n is large, we may approximate the given distribution by Poisson distribution. Hence, the parameter m of the Poisson distribution is :

$$m = np = 100 \times 0\cdot05 = 5$$

Let the random variable X denote the number of defective bulbs in a sample of 100. Then (by Poisson probability law),

$$P(X = r) = \frac{e^{-m}\, m^r}{r\,!} = \frac{e^{-5}\, 5^r}{r\,!};\ r = 0, 1, 2, \ldots \qquad (*)$$

(*i*) The probability that none of the bulbs is defective is given by :

$$P(X = 0) = e^{-5} = 0\cdot007 \qquad \text{[From (*)]}$$

(*ii*) The probability of 5 defective bulbs is given by :

$$P(X = 5) = \frac{e^{-5} \times 5^5}{5\,!} = \frac{0\cdot007 \times 625}{24} = \frac{4\cdot375}{24} = 0\cdot1823.$$

Example 14·20. *A manufacturer of blades knows that 5% of his product is defective. If he sells blades in boxes of 100, and guarantees that not more than 10 blades will be defective, what is the probability (approximately) that a box will fail to meet the guaranteed quality ?*

Solution. p = Probability of a defective blade = 5% = 0·05.

Since the probability of a defective blade is small, we may use Poisson distribution. In the usual notations we are given $n = 100$.

Hence $\quad m = np = 100 \times 0\cdot05 = 5$

If the random variable X denotes the number of defective blades in a box of 100, then (by Poisson probability law),

$$P(X = r) = \frac{e^{-m}.\, m^r}{r\,!} = \frac{e^{-5}\,.\, 5^r}{r\,!}\ ;\ r = 0, 1, 2, \ldots$$

A box will fail to meet the guaranteed quality if the number of defectives in it is more than 10. Hence the required probability is :

$$P(X > 10) = 1 - P(X \le 10) = 1 - \sum_{r=0}^{10} p(r)$$

$$= 1 - \sum_{r=0}^{10} \frac{e^{-5} . 5^r}{r!} = 1 - e^{-5} \sum_{r=0}^{10} \frac{5^r}{r!}$$

Example 14·21. *In a certain factory turning out optical lenses, there is a small chance 1/500 for any one lens to be defective. The lenses are supplied, in packets of 10. Use Poisson distribution to calculate the approximate number of packets containing no defective, one defective, two defective, three defective lenses respectively in a consignment of 20,000 packets. You are given that* $e^{-0·02} = 0·9802$.

Solution. In the usual notations we are given : $N = 20{,}000$; $n = 10$ and

$$p = \text{Probability of a defective optical lense} = \frac{1}{500}$$

$$m = np = 10 \times \frac{1}{500} = \frac{1}{50} = 0·02$$

Let the random variable X denote the number of defective optical lenses in a packet of 10. Then, by Poisson probability law, the probability of r defective lenses in a packet is given by :

$$P(X = r) = \frac{e^{-0·02} (0·02)^r}{r!} = \frac{0·9802 \times (0·02)^r}{r!}$$

Hence in a consignment of 20,000 packets the frequency (number) of packets containing r defective lenses is

$$N.P(X = r) = \frac{20000 \times 0·9802 \times (0·02)^r}{r!} \qquad ...(*)$$

Putting $r = 0, 1, 2$ and 3 in (*), we get respectively

No. of packets containing no defective lens $= 20000 \times 0·9802 = 19604$

No. of packets containing 1 defective lens is

$$= \frac{20000 \times 0·9802 \times (0·02)}{1} = 19604 \times 0·02 = 392·08 \simeq 392$$

No. of packets containing 2 defective lenses is

$$= \frac{20000 \times 0·9802 \times (0·02)^2}{2!} = \frac{392·08 \times 0·02}{2} = 3·9208 \simeq 4$$

No. of packets containing 3 defective lenses is

$$= \frac{20000 \times 0·9802 \times (0·02)^3}{3!} = \frac{3·9208 \times 0·02}{3} = 0·026138 \simeq 0,$$

since the number of packets cannot be in fraction.

Hence, the number of packets containing 0, 1, 2, and 3 defective lenses is respectively 19604, 392, 4, 0.

Example 14·22. *A car hire firm has two cars which it hires out day by day. The number of demands for a car on each day is distributed as a Poisson variate with mean 1·5. Calculate the proportion of days on which* (*i*) *Neither car is used* (*ii*) *Some demand is refused.*

Solution. Let the random variable X denote the number of demands for a car on any day. Then, X follows Poisson distribution with parameter $m = 1·5$.

$$\therefore \quad P(X = r) = \text{Probability of } r \text{ demands for a car on any day.}$$

$$= \frac{e^{-1·5} (1·5)^r}{r!} \qquad ...(*)$$

(*i*) Neither car will be used, if there is no demand for any car. Hence the required proportion of days on which no car is used is given by :

$$P(X = 0) = e^{-1·5} = \text{Antilog } [-1·5 \log_{10} e] \qquad \text{[From (*)]}$$

$$= \text{Antilog } [-1·5 \log_{10} 2·718] = \text{Antilog } [-1·5 \times 0·4343]$$

$$= \text{Antilog } [-0·65145] = \text{Antilog } \left[\bar{1} \cdot 34855\right] = 0·2231$$

(*ii*) Since the firm has only two cars, some demand will be refused if the number of demands per day is greater than 2. Hence, the required proportion is given by :

$$P(X > 2) = 1 - P(X \le 2) = 1 - \left[P(X = 0) + P(X = 1) + P(X = 2) \right]$$

$$= 1 - \left[e^{-1\cdot5} + 1\cdot5 e^{-1\cdot5} + \frac{(1\cdot5)^2}{2\,!} e^{-1\cdot5} \right] = 1 - e^{-1\cdot5} \left[1 + 1\cdot5 + \frac{2\cdot25}{2} \right] \quad \text{[From (*)]}$$

$$= 1 - 0\cdot2231\,(1 + 1\cdot5 + 1\cdot125) = 1 - 0\cdot2231 \times 3\cdot625$$

$$= 1 - 0\cdot80874 = 0\cdot19126.$$

Example 14·23. *The management of a photograph record company has discovered that the number of defects on records appears to follow a Poisson distribution with a mean equal to 0·4.*

(*i*) *What is the probability that a record selected at random will have three defects ?*

(*ii*) *If management sets a policy that all photograph records sold to customers must not have any defects, what per cent of its records production will not be made available for sales because of defects ?*

$e^{-4} = 0\cdot1832$, $e^{-0\cdot4} = 0\cdot6703$. [*Delhi Univ. B.Com. (Hons.), (External), 2007*]

Solution. Let the *r.v.* X denote the number of defects in a record. Then, using Poisson probability model with mean $m = 0\cdot4$, we have :

$$p(r) = P(X = r) = e^{-0\cdot4}\,(0\cdot4)^r / r\,!\;;\; r = 0, 1, 2, \ldots \qquad \ldots(*)$$

(*i*) Required probability $= p(3) = \dfrac{e^{-0\cdot4}\,(0\cdot4)^3}{3\,!} = \dfrac{0\cdot6703 \times 0\cdot064}{6} = 0\cdot00715$

(*ii*) The photographic records will not be made available for sales to the customers even if it contains at least one defect and the required probability is given by :

$$P(X \ge 1) = 1 - P(X = 0) = 1 - p(0) = 1 - e^{-0\cdot4} = 1 - 0\cdot6703 = 0\cdot3297.$$

Hence 32·97% ≃ 33% of its photographic record production will not be made available for sales because of defects.

Example 14·24. *If a random variable X follows Poisson distribution such that P(X = 1) = P(X = 2), find*

(*a*) *The mean and variance of the distribution.* (*b*) *P(X = 0).*

[*Delhi Univ. B.Com (Hons.), 1993 ; C.A. (Foundation), Nov. 1995*]

Solution. Let X be a random variable following Poisson distribution with parameter m. Then, the probability function is given by :

$$P(X = r) = \frac{e^{-m}\,m^r}{r\,!},\; r = 0, 1, 2, \ldots \qquad \ldots(i)$$

Putting $r = 1$ and 2 in (*i*) we get respectively :

$$P(X = 1) = m.e^{-m} \quad \text{and} \quad P(X = 2) = \frac{m^2.\,e^{-m}}{2\,!}.$$

We are given that :

$$P(X = 1) = P(X = 2) \Rightarrow m e^{-m} = \frac{m^2\,e^{-m}}{2\,!} \Rightarrow 2 = m \qquad \text{[Cancelling } m\,e^{-m} \text{ on both sides]}$$

(*a*) Since the mean and variance of a Poisson distribution with parameter are equal, each being equal to *m*, we get

$$\text{Mean} = \text{Variance} = m = 2.$$

(*b*) Putting $r = 0$ in (*i*) we get,

$$P(X = 0) = \frac{e^{-m}\,.\,m^0}{0\,!} = e^{-m} = e^{-2}$$

$$= \text{Antilog}\left[-2\log_{10} e\right] = \text{Antilog}\left[-2\log_{10} 2{\cdot}718\right]$$

$$= \text{Antilog}\,[-2 \times 0{\cdot}4343] = \text{Antilog}\,[-\,0{\cdot}8686] = \text{Antilog}\left[\bar{1}{\cdot}1314\right]$$

$$= 0{\cdot}1353$$

Example 14·25. *If X is a Poisson variable such that*

$P(X = 2) = 9P(X = 4) + 90\,P(X = 6)$, find the mean and variance of X.

[Deli Univ. B.Com. (Hons.), 2008; C.A. PEE-1, May 2003]

Solution. Let X be a Poisson variable with parameter m. Then

$$P(X = r) = \frac{e^{-m} \cdot m^r}{r\,!} \;;\quad r = 0, 1, 2, \ldots \qquad \ldots(*)$$

We are given :

$$P(X = 2) = 9\,P(X = 4) + 90\,P(X = 6)$$

$$\Rightarrow \quad \frac{e^{-m} \cdot m^2}{2\,!} = 9 \times \frac{e^{-m} \cdot m^4}{4\,!} + 90 \times \frac{e^{-m} \cdot m^6}{6\,!} \qquad \text{[From (*)]}$$

$$\Rightarrow \quad \frac{1}{2} = \frac{9\,m^2}{4 \times 3 \times 2 \times 1} + \frac{90\,m^4}{6 \times 5 \times 4 \times 3 \times 2 \times 1} \qquad \text{[Dividing both sides by } e^{-m}\,m^2]$$

$$\Rightarrow \quad 1 = \frac{3}{4} m^2 + \frac{m^4}{4} \quad \Rightarrow \quad 4 = 3m^2 + m^4 \quad \Rightarrow \quad m^4 + 3m^2 - 4 = 0 \qquad \ldots(**)$$

(**) is a quadratic equation in m^2.

$$\therefore \quad m^2 = \frac{-3 \pm \sqrt{9 - 4 \times 1 \times (-4)}}{2 \times 1} = \frac{-3 \pm 5}{2} = (-\,4,\, 1)$$

But m^2 cannot be negative. Therefore, $m^2 = 1 \quad \Rightarrow \quad m = 1 \qquad (\because\ m > 0)$

For the Poisson distribution, mean and variance are equal.

$\therefore$ Mean $= E(X) = m = 1$ and Var $(X) = m = 1$.

14·3·4. Fitting of Poisson Distribution. If we want to fit a Poisson distribution to a given frequency distribution, we compute the mean $\overline{X}$ of the given distribution and take it equal to the mean of the fitted (Poisson) distribution, *i.e.*, we take $m = \overline{X}$. Once m is known, the various probabilities of the Poisson distribution can be obtained, the general formula being

$$p(r) = P(X = r) = \frac{e^{-m} \times m^r}{r\,!} \;;\quad r = 0, 1, 2, 3, \ldots \qquad \ldots(14{\cdot}18)$$

If N is the total observed frequency, then the expected or theoretical frequencies of the Poisson distribution are given by $N \times p\,(r)$.

Expected frequencies can be very conveniently computed as explained in the Table 14·6 :

TABLE 14·6 : **EXPECTED POISSON FREQUENCIES**

Value of Variable (*r*)	*Probability* *p*(*r*)	*Expected or Theoretical Poisson Frequencies f*(*r*) = *NP*(*r*)
0	$p(0) = e^{-m}$	$f(0) = N\,p(0) = Ne^{-m}$
1	$p(1) = me^{-m} = mp(0)$	$f(1) = m\,Np(0) = m\,f(0)$
2	$p(2) = \frac{m^2 e^{-m}}{2\,!} = \frac{m}{2} me^{-m} = \frac{m}{2}\,p(1)$	$f(2) = \frac{m}{2} \cdot N\,p(1) = \frac{m}{2}\,f(1)$
3	$p(3) = \frac{m^3 e^{-m}}{3\,!} = \frac{m}{3}\,\frac{m^2 e^{-m}}{2\,!} = \frac{m}{3}\,p(2)$	$f(3) = \frac{m}{3}\,N\,p(2) = \frac{m}{3}\,f(2)$
4	$p(4) = \frac{m^4 e^{-m}}{4\,!} = \frac{m}{4}\,\frac{m^3 e^{-m}}{3\,!} = \frac{m}{4}\,p(3)$	$f(4) = \frac{m}{4}\,N\,p\,(3) = \frac{m}{4}\,f(3)$
⋮	⋮	⋮

Example 14·26. *Fit a Poisson distribution to the following data and calculate the theoretical frequencies.*

x	:	0	1	2	3	4
f	:	123	59	14	3	1

Solution.

x	0	1	2	3	4	
f	123	59	14	3	1	$\Sigma f = 200$
fx	0	59	28	9	4	$\Sigma fx = 100$

$$\therefore \quad \bar{x} = \frac{\Sigma fx}{\Sigma f} = \frac{100}{200} = 0{\cdot}5.$$

Thus, the mean (m) of the theoretical (Poisson) distribution is $m = \bar{x} = 0{\cdot}5$. By Poisson probability law, the theoretical frequencies are given by :

$$f(r) = Np(r) = 200.\frac{e^{-m}\, m^r}{r\,!} \quad ; \quad r = 0, 1, 2, 3, \ldots$$

$$\therefore \quad f(0) = N\,p(0) = 200 \times e^{-m} = 200 \times e^{-0\cdot 5} = 200 \times 0{\cdot}6065 = 121{\cdot}3.$$

TABLE 14·7 : **COMPUTATION OF EXPECTED FREQUENCIES**

x	*Expected Poisson Frequencies N.p(x)*			
0	$N\,p(0) = 121{\cdot}3$			$\simeq 121$
1	$N\,p(1) = N\,p(0) \times m$	$= 121{\cdot}3 \times 0{\cdot}5$	$= 60{\cdot}65$	$\simeq 61$
2	$N\,p(2) = N\,p(1) \times \frac{m}{2}$	$= \frac{60{\cdot}65 \times 0{\cdot}5}{2}$	$= 15{\cdot}3125$	$\simeq 15$
3	$N\,p(3) = N\,p(2) \times \frac{m}{3}$	$= \frac{15{\cdot}3125 \times 0{\cdot}5}{3}$	$= 2{\cdot}552$	$\simeq 3$
4	$N\,p(4) = N\,p(3) \times \frac{m}{4}$	$= \frac{2{\cdot}552 \times 0{\cdot}5}{4}$	$= 0{\cdot}32$	$\simeq 0$
Total				200

Example 14·27. *A systematic sample of 100 pages was taken from the Concise Oxford Dictionary and the observed frequency distribution of foreign words per page was found to be as follows :*

No. of foreign words per page (X) :	0	1	2	3	4	5	6
Frequency (f) :	48	27	12	7	4	1	1

Calculate the expected frequencies using Poisson distribution. Also compute the mean and variance of fitted distribution.

Solution.

$$\overline{X} = \frac{\Sigma fx}{\Sigma f} = \frac{99}{100} = 0{\cdot}99$$

If the above distribution is approximated by a Poisson distribution, then the parameter (m) of Poisson distribution is given by $m = \bar{x} = 0{\cdot}99$ and by Poisson probability law, the frequency (number) of pages containing r foreign words is given by :

TABLE 14·8 : **FITTING OF POISSON DISTRIBUTION**

x	f	fx
0	48	0
1	27	27
2	12	24
3	7	21
4	4	16
5	1	5
6	1	6
	$\Sigma f = 100$	$\Sigma fx = 99$

$$f(r) = Np(r) = N.P(X = r) = 100 \times \frac{e^{-0\cdot 99}\,(0{\cdot}99)^r}{r\,!}$$

Putting $r = 0, 1, 2, \ldots, 6$, we get the expected frequencies of Poisson distribution.

$$f(0) = N.p(0) = 100 \times e^{-0.99} = 100 \times \text{Antilog}\,[-0.99 \log_{10} e]$$
$$= 100 \times \text{Antilog}\,[-0.99 \times \log_{10} 2.718] = 100 \times \text{Antilog}\,[-0.99 \times 0.4343]$$
$$= 100 \times \text{Antilog}\,[-0.429957] = 100 \times \text{Antilog}\,[\bar{1}.570043]$$
$$= 100 \times 0.3716 = 37.16$$

$$f(1) = \frac{m}{1} f(0) = 37.16 \times 0.99 = 36.7884 \quad ; \quad f(2) = \frac{m}{2} f(1) = 36.7884 \times 0.495 = 18.21$$

$$f(3) = \frac{m}{3} f(2) = 18.21 \times 0.33 = 6.0093 \quad ; \quad f(4) = \frac{m}{4} f(3) = 6.0093 \times 0.2475 = 1.4873$$

$$f(5) = \frac{m}{5} f(4) = 1.4873 \times 0.198 = 0.2945 \quad ; \quad f(6) = \frac{m}{6} f(5) = 0.2945 \times 0.165 = 0.0486$$

Hence the theoretical (expected) frequencies of the Poisson distribution are :

X	:	0	1	2	3	4	5	6
Expected frequencies	:	37·16	36·79	18·21	6·01	1·49	0·29	0·05
(Rounded)	:	37	37	18	6	2	0	0

Since, for Poisson distribution, mean and variance are equal, the mean and variance of theoretical (fitted) distribution are given by :

$$\text{Mean} = \text{Variance} = m = \bar{x} = 0.99.$$

EXERCISE 14·2

1. (*a*) What is Poisson distribution ? Under what conditions is it applicable ?

(*b*) Define Poisson distribution and state the conditions under which this distribution is used.

[*Delhi Univ. B.Com (Hons.), 1996*]

(*c*) Name the six situations where Poison distribution can have applications. [*Delhi Univ. B.Com (Hons.), 1995*]

2. (*a*) Obtain Poisson distribution as a limiting case of the Binomial distribution.

(*b*) Prove that for the Poisson distribution, mean and variance are equal.

3. What are the chief characteristics of Poisson distribution ? Mention three business situations where Poisson model is applicable.

4. Write down the probability function of a Possion distribution whose mean is 2. What is its variance ? Give four examples of Poisson variable.

Ans. Variance = 2.

5. The standard deviation of a Poisson distribution is 2. Find the probability that $X = 3$. (Given $e^{-4} = 0.0183$).

Ans. 0·1952.

6. Define a Poisson distribution.

If X be a Poisson variate with parameter 1, find $P(3 < X < 5)$. [Given $e^{-1} = 0.36783$].

Ans. 0·0153.

7. Between the hours of 2 and 4 P.M., the average number of phone calls per minute coming into the switch-board of a company is 2·5. Find the probability that during one particular minute there will be :

(*i*) no phone call at all, (*ii*) exactly 3 calls, (*iii*) at least 2 calls.

(Given $e^{-2} = 0.13534$ and $e^{-0.5} = 0.60650$)

[*Delhi Univ. B.Com. (HOns.), 2006*]

Ans. (*i*) 0·0821. (*ii*) 0·2138 (*iii*) $1 - e^{-2.5} \sum_{r=0}^{1} \frac{(2.5)^r}{r!} = 0.7127$

8. Write the probability function of Poisson distribution. Give two examples of Poisson variate. Accidents occur on a particular stretch of highway at an average rate of 3 per week. What is the probability that there will be exactly two accidents in a given week ? (Given $e^3 = 20.08$).

Ans. $\frac{9}{2e^3} = 0.2241$.

9. Suppose that the number of claims for missing bagage average 6 per day. Find the probability that on a given day, there will be :

(*i*) No claim; (*ii*) Exactly 6 claims; (*iii*) At least 2 claims. $(e^{-6} = 0{\cdot}00248)$

[*Delhi Univ. B.Com (Hons.), 2001*]

Hint. X : No. of claims for missing baggage per day. Then $X \sim P(\lambda = 6)$.

Ans. (*i*) 0·00248 (*ii*) 0·1607 (*iii*) 0·98264.

10. The average number of customers, who appear at a counter of a certain bank per minute is two. Find the probability that during a given minute :

(*i*) No customer appears (*ii*) Three or more customers appear. $(e^{-2} = 0{\cdot}1353]$

[*C.A. (Foundation), May 1998*]

Ans. (*i*) 0·1353 (*ii*) 0·3235.

11. A guest house has two rooms which it hires out by the day. The number of demand for a room on any day follows Poisson distribution with mean 1·5. Calculate the probability that

(*i*) all rooms are vacant on a particular day, and

(*ii*) some demand is refused on that day. (Given $e^{-1\cdot5} = 0{\cdot}223$) [*I.C.W.A. (Intermediate), June 1999*]

Ans. (*i*) 0·223 (*ii*) 0·1916.

12. Which probability distribution is appropriate to describe the situation where 100 misprints are distributed randomly throughout the 100 pages of a book ? For this distribution, find the probability that a page selected at random will contain at least three misprints. [*C.A. (Foundation), May 2000*]

Ans. $X \sim P\left(\lambda = np = 100 \times \frac{1}{100} = 1\right)$; Required probability = 0·08.

13. Find the probability that at most 5 defective bolts will be found in a box of 200 bolts if it is known that 2 per cent of such bolts are expected to be defective. (You may take the distribution to be Poisson). Take $e^{-4} = 0{\cdot}0183$.

Ans. $e^{-4}\left(1 + 4 + 8 + \frac{32}{3} + \frac{32}{3} + \frac{128}{15}\right) = 0{\cdot}7845$.

14. If 2 per cent of electric bulbs manufactured by a certain company are defective, find the probability that in a sample of 200 bulbs,

(*i*) less than 2 bulbs, (*ii*) more than 3 bulbs, are defective. [Given $e^{-4} = 0{\cdot}0183$]

Ans. (*i*) 0·0915, (*ii*) 0·5669.

15. A manufacturer, who produces medicine bottles, finds that 0·1% of the bottles are defective. Bottles are packed in boxes containing 500 bottles. A drug manufacturer buys 100 boxes from the producer of bottles. Using Poison distribution, find how many boxes will contain :

(*i*) no defective, (*ii*) at least 2 defectives. $[e^{-0\cdot5} = 0{\cdot}6065]$ [*Delhi Univ. (FMS) M.B.A., April 2004*]

Ans. (*i*) 61, (*ii*) 10

Hint. $\lambda = np = 500 \times 0{\cdot}001 = 0{\cdot}5$; $N = 100$

(*i*) $Np(0) = 100 \times 0{\cdot}6065 \simeq 61$ (*ii*) $N.P\,(X \geq 2) = 100\,[1 - P\,(X \leq 1)] \simeq 10$

16. In a town 10 accidents took place in 50 days. Assuming that number of accidents per day follows Poisson distribution, find the probability that there will be at least three accidents per day (given $e^{-0\cdot2} = 0{\cdot}8187$)

(*Punjab Univ. B.Com., 2000*)

Hint. λ = Average number of accidents per day $= \frac{10}{50} = 0{\cdot}2$

Ans. $1 - e^{-0\cdot2}\,(1 + 0{\cdot}2 + 0{\cdot}02) = 0{\cdot}0012$.

17. If the probability that an individual suffers a bad reaction from an injection of a given serum is 0·001, determine the probability that out of 2000 individuals:

(*i*) exactly 3; and ; (*ii*) more than two individuals, will suffer a bad reaction.

[*Delhi Univ. B.Com. (Hons.), 1997*]

Hint. $\lambda = np = 2000 \times 0{\cdot}001 = 2$

Ans. (*i*) $\frac{4}{3}e^{-2} = 0{\cdot}1801$ (*ii*) $1 - 5e^{-2} = 0{\cdot}3245$.

18. One fifth per cent of the blades produced by a blade manufacturing factory turn out to be defective. The blades are supplied in packets of 10. Use Poisson distribution to calculate the approximate number of packets containing no defective, one defective and two defective blades respectively in a consignment of 1,00,000 packets.

(Given $e^{-0\cdot02} = 0{\cdot}9802$). [*Delhi Univ. (FMS), M.B.A. Nov. 2003 ; Delhi Univ. B.Com. (Hons.), 2000*]

Hint. $p = \frac{1}{500}$, $n = 10$, $\lambda = np = 0{\cdot}02$.

Ans. 98020, 1960, 20.

19. A manufacturer of cotter pins knows that 2% of his product is defective. If he sells cotter pins in boxes of 200 and guarantees that not more than 5 pins will be defective, what is the probability that a box will fail to meet the guaranteed quality ? [Given $e^{-4} = 0{\cdot}0183$] [*I.C.W.A. (Intermediate), June 1998*]

Ans. $P(X > 5) = 1 - P(X \le 5) = 0{\cdot}2155$.

20. A manufacturer of pins knows that on an average 5% of his product is defective. He sells pins in boxes of 100, and guarantees that not more than 4 pins will be defective. What is the probability that (*i*) a box will meet the guaranteed quality, (*ii*) A box will fail to meet the guaranteed quality ? ($e^{-5} = {\cdot}0067$). [*Kanpur Univ. M.Com. 2005*]

Ans. (*i*) $e^{-5}\left[1 + 5 + \frac{25}{2!} + \frac{125}{3!} + \frac{625}{4!}\right] = 0{\cdot}0067 \times 65{\cdot}37 = 0{\cdot}438$. (*ii*) $1 - 0{\cdot}438 = 0{\cdot}562$.

21. A distributor of bean seeds determines from extensive tests that 5% of large batch of seeds will not germinate. He sells the seeds in packets of 200 and guarantees 90% germination. Determine the probability that a particular packet will violate the guarantee.

Ans. $1 - \sum_{r=0}^{10} (e^{-10}\, 10^r / r!)$

22. A manufacturer finds that the average demand per day for the mechanics to repair his new products is 1·5, over a period of one year and the demand per day is distributed as Poisson variate. He employs two mechanics. On how many days in one year

(*a*) both the mechanics would be free, (b) some demand is refused.

Ans. (*a*) $365 \times e^{-1\cdot5} = 365 \times 0{\cdot}2231 = 81{\cdot}4$ days

(*b*) $365\left[1 - \left(e^{-1\cdot5} + 1{\cdot}5\, e^{-1\cdot5} + \frac{(1{\cdot}5)^2}{2} e^{-1\cdot5}\right)\right] = 365 \times 0{\cdot}1912 = 69{\cdot}8$ days.

23. If X is a Poisson variate and $P(X = 0) = P(X = 1) = k$, show that $k = \frac{1}{e}$.

24. If a random variable X follows Poisson distribution such that $P(X = 1) = P(X = 2)$, find

(*i*) the mean of the distribution (*ii*) $P(X = 0)$ (*iii*) $P(X > 2)$.

[*Delhi Univ. B.Com.(Hons.), 1999*]

Ans. (*i*) 2, (*ii*) 0·13534 (*iii*) 0·3233.

25. If X be a Poisson random variable such that $P(X = 0) = P(X = 1)$, then $E(X)$ is

(*i*) e; (*ii*) 1; (*iii*) $\frac{1}{e}$; (*iv*) none of these. [*I.C.W.A. (Intermediate), Dec. 1999*]

Ans. (*ii*).

26. State the conditions under which Poisson distribution is used. If a random variable X follows Poisson distribution such that $P(X = 1) = P(X = 2)$, find the mean and variance of the distribution.

[*C.A. (Foundation), Nov. 1995*]

Ans. Mean = Variance = 2.

27. If X is a Poisson variate with mean λ, then $p(x + 1)$ is :

(*i*) $\frac{\lambda}{x+1}\, p(x)$, (*ii*) $\frac{\lambda}{x}\, p(x)$, (*iii*) $\frac{x+1}{\lambda}\, p(x)$, (*iv*) $\frac{x}{\lambda}\, p(x)$.

[*I.C.W.A. (Intermediate), Dec. 2001*]

Ans. (*i*).

28. If a Poisson distribution has a double mode at $X = 1$ *and at* $X = 2$, find $P(X = 1)$.

[*I.C.W.A. (Intermediate), Dec. 2001*]

Ans. $2\, e^{-2}$.

29. The distribution of typing mistakes committed by a typist is given below. Assuming a Poisson model, find the expected frequencies.

Mistakes per page :	0	1	2	3	4	5
No. of pages :	142	156	69	27	5	1

[*I.C.W.A. (Intermediate), June 2002*]

Ans. $m = \frac{\Sigma fx}{\Sigma f} = 1$; [147, 147, 74, 25, 6, 1]

30. A systematic sample of 200 pages was taken from the manuscript typed by a typist and the observed frequency distribution of the typing mistakes per page was found to be as under :

No. of typing mistakes (x)	:	0	1	2	3	4
No. of pages (f)	:	122	60	15	2	1

Fit a Poisson distribution to the above information.

Ans. [121, 61, 15, 3, 0]

31. Fit a Poisson distribution to the following data :

x	:	0	1	2	3	4	5	6
f	:	143	90	42	12	9	3	1

Given that $e^{-0·89} = 0 \cdot 410656$. [*I.C.W.A. (Intermediate), June 2001*]

Ans. 123, 110, 49, 14, 3, 1, 0.

32. 100 car radios are inspected as they come off the production line and the number of defects per set are recorded in the adjoining Table.

Fit a Poisson Distribution to the above data and calculate theoretical frequencies of 0, 1, 2, 3 and 4 defects.

[*Delhi Univ. B.Com. (Hons.), 2009*]

No. of Defects	*No. of Sets*
0	79
1	18
2	2
3	1
4	0

Ans. $\hat{\lambda}$ = Mean = 0·25 ; $e^{-0·25} = 0·7788$. Theoretical Poisson frequencies are : 78, 19·47 $\simeq$ 20*, 2·43 $\simeq$ 2, 0, 0.

* : 19·47 is rounded to 20 to make total frequency = 100.

33. Explain what is wrong with the following statement :

"Since accident statistics show that the probability that a person will be involved in a road accident in a given year is 0·02, the probability that he will be involved in 2 accidents in that year is 0·0004."

Hint. Let $X \sim P(\lambda)$. $P(X \geq 1) = 0·02$ (Given) $\Rightarrow$ $1 - p(0) = 0·02$

$\therefore$ $p(0) = e^{-\lambda} = 0·98$ $\Rightarrow$ $\lambda = 0·02$

Ans. Statement is wrong. The required probability $= P(X = 2) = \dfrac{e^{-\lambda} . \lambda^2}{2!} = 0·000196$.

14·4. NORMAL DISTRIBUTION

The distributions discussed so far, *viz.*, Binomial distribution and Poisson distribution, are discrete probability distributions, since the variables under study were discrete random variables. Now we confine the discussion to continuous probability distributions which arise when the underlying variable is a continuous one.

Normal probability distribution or commonly called the *normal distribution* is one of the most important continuous theoretical distributions in Statistics. Most of the data relating to economic and business statistics or even in social and physical sciences conform to this distribution.

The normal distribution was first discovered by English Mathematician De-Moivre (1667-1754) in 1733 who obtained the mathematical equation for this distribution while dealing with problems arising in the game of chance. Normal distribution is also known as Gaussian distribution (Gaussian Law of Errors) after Karl Friedrich Gauss (1777-1855) who used this distribution to describe the theory of accidental errors of measurements involved in the calculation of orbits of heavenly bodies. Today, normal probability model is one of the most important probability models in statistical analysis.

14·4·1. Equation of Normal Probability Curve. If X is a continuous random variable following normal probability distribution with mean μ and standard deviation σ, then its probability density function (p.d.f.) is given by

$$p(x) = \frac{1}{\sqrt{2\pi} . \sigma} \cdot e^{-\frac{1}{2}\left(\frac{x-\mu}{\sigma}\right)^2}, -\infty < x < \infty \qquad ...(14·19)$$

or

$$p(x) = \frac{1}{\sqrt{2\pi} . \sigma} \cdot e^{-\frac{(x-\mu)^2}{2\sigma^2}}, -\infty < x < \infty \qquad ...(14·19a)$$

where π and e are the constants given by :

$$\pi = \frac{22}{7}, \quad \sqrt{2\pi} = 2{\cdot}5066, \quad \text{and} \quad e = 2{\cdot}71828 \text{ [The base of the system of Natural logarithms.]}$$

Remark *The mean μ and standard deviation σ are called the parameters of the Normal distribution.*

14·4·2. Standard Normal Distribution. If X is a random variable following normal distribution with mean μ and standard deviation σ, then the random variable Z defined as follows :

$$Z = \frac{X - E(X)}{\sigma_x} = \frac{X - \mu}{\sigma}, \qquad \ldots(14{\cdot}20)$$

is called the *standard normal variate* (S.N.V.). We have :

$$E(Z) = 0 \quad \text{and} \quad \text{Var}(Z) = 1 \Rightarrow \sigma_Z = 1.$$

Therefore, *the standard normal variate (S.N.V.) Z has mean 0 and standard deviation 1.*

Hence the probability density function (*p.d.f.*) of *S.N.V. Z* is given by :

$$\phi(z) = \frac{1}{\sqrt{2\pi}} e^{-\frac{z^2}{2}}, -\infty < z < \infty \qquad \ldots(14{\cdot}21)$$

[Taking $x = z$, $\mu = 0$ and $\sigma = 1$ in (14·19)]

This gives the height (ordinate) of standard normal curve at the point z.

Remarks 1. A standard normal variable Z is denoted by $Z \sim N(0, 1)$.

2. From (14·21), we observe that the values of $\phi(z)$ are the same for positive as well as negative values of z *i.e.*, $\phi(-z) = \phi(z)$. *Hence, the standard normal probability curve is symmetric about the line $z = 0$.*

3. Why do we need Standard Normal distribution ?

A normal distribution is characterized by two parameters (constants);

(*i*) the mean (μ) whose position can be located anywhere on the x-axis and

(*ii*) the standard deviation (σ) which determines the spread of its bell shape curve along the x-axis.

If we want to construct tables to compute the areas, say, $P(a \le X \le b)$ under any normal probability curve $N(\mu, \sigma^2)$, we need to construct an infinite number of tables for different combinations of the values of μ and σ, which is practically impossible. In practice we standardize the variable X to obtain the z-scores $Z = (X - \mu)/\sigma$ and then construct the table for the areas under the standard normal probability curve. Hence, by rescaling the normal distribution axis, any normal distribution can be converted into standard normal distribution with mean 0 and *SD* 1. Consequently we need only one table of areas under standard normal curve. Thus, for any normal distribution with mean μ and *SD* σ, this table can be used for obtaining the areas under standard normal curve for almost any interval along the z-axis. Table VI at the end of the book gives the areas under standard normal curve.

14·4·3. Relation between Binomial and Normal Distributions. Normal distribution is a limiting case of the binomial probability distribution under the following conditions :

(*i*) n, the number of trials is indefinitely large, *i.e.*, $n \to \infty$.

(*ii*) Neither p nor q is very small.

We know that for a binomial variate X with parameters n and p, $E(X) = np$ and $\text{Var}(X) = npq$

De-Moivre proved that under the above two conditions, the distribution of standard Binomial variate

$$Z = \frac{X - E(X)}{\sigma_x} = \frac{X - np}{\sqrt{npq}},$$

tends to the distribution of standard Normal variate as given in (14·21).

If p and q are nearly equal (*i.e.*, p is nearly 1/2), then the normal approximation is surprisingly good even for small values of n. However, when p and q are not equal, *i.e.*, when p or q is small, even then the Binomial distribution tends to normal distribution but in this case the convergence is slow. By this we mean that if p and q are not equal then for Binomial distribution to tend to Normal distribution we need relatively larger value of n as compared to the value of n required in the case when p and q are nearly equal. Thus, the normal approximation to the Binomial distribution is better for increasing values of n and is exact in the limiting case as $n \to \infty$.

14·4·4. Relation between Poisson and Normal Distributions. If X is a random variable following Poisson distribution with parameter m, then

$$E(X) = \text{Mean} = m \quad \text{and} \quad \text{Var}(X) = \sigma^2 = m$$

Thus standard Poisson variate becomes : $\dfrac{X - E(X)}{\sigma_x} = \dfrac{X - m}{\sqrt{m}}$

It has been proved that this variate tends to be a Standard Normal Variate if $m \to \infty$. Thus, *Normal distribution may also be regarded as a limiting case of Poisson distribution as the parameter $m \to \infty$.*

14·4·5. Properties of Normal Distribution. The normal probability curve with mean μ and standard deviation σ is given by

$$p(x) = \frac{1}{\sqrt{2\pi}\,.\,\sigma}\,.\; e^{-(x-\mu)^2/2\sigma^2}\ , \quad -\infty < x < \infty \qquad \ldots (*)$$

The standard normal probability curve is given by the equation :

$$\phi(z) = \frac{1}{\sqrt{2\pi}}\, e^{-z^2/2}\ , \quad -\infty < z < \infty \qquad \ldots (**)$$

It has the following properties :

1. The graph of $p(x)$ is the famous bell shaped curve as shown in the Fig. 14·1. The top of the bell is directly above the mean (μ).

NORMAL PROBABILITY CURVE

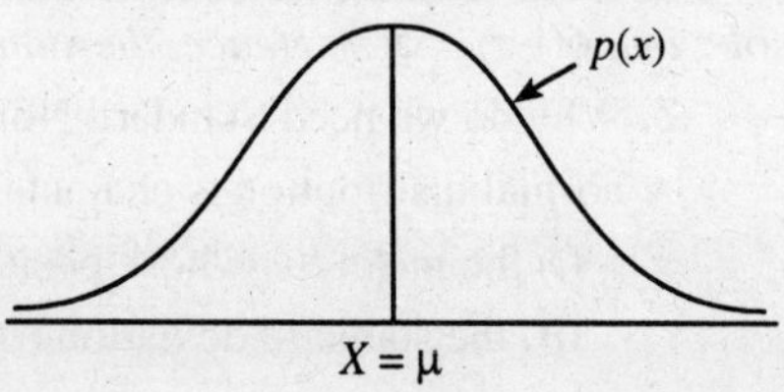

Fig. 14·1

2. The curve is symmetrical about the line $X = \mu$, $(Z = 0)$, *i.e.*, it has the same shape on either side of the line $X = \mu$ (or $Z = 0$).

This is because the equation of the curve $\phi(z)$ remains unchanged if we change z to $-z$.

3. Since the distribution is symmetrical, mean, median and mode coincide. Thus,

$$\text{Mean} = \text{Median} = \text{Mode} = \mu$$

4. Since Mean = Median = μ, the ordinate at $X = \mu$, $(Z = 0)$ divides the whole area into two equal parts. Further, since total area under normal probability curve is 1, the area to the right of the ordinate as well as to the left of the ordinate at $X = \mu$ (or $Z = 0$) is 0·5.

5. Also, by virtue of symmetry, the quartiles are equidistant from median (μ), *i.e.*,

$$Q_3 - Md = Md - Q_1 \quad \Rightarrow \quad Q_1 + Q_3 = 2Md = 2\mu \qquad \ldots (14\cdot22)$$

6. Since the distribution is symmetrical, the moment coefficient of skewness is given by :

$$\beta_1 = 0 \quad \Rightarrow \quad \gamma_1 = 0 \qquad \ldots (14\cdot23)$$

7. The coefficient of kurtosis is given by :

$$\beta_2 = 3 \quad \Rightarrow \quad \gamma_2 = 0 \qquad \ldots (14\cdot24)$$

8. No portion of the curve lies below the x-axis, since $p(x)$ being the probability can never be negative.

9. Theoretically, the range of the distribution is from $-\infty$ to ∞. But practically, Range = 6σ.

10. As x increases numerically [*i.e.*, on either side of $X = \mu$], the value of $p(x)$ decreases rapidly, the maximum probability occurring at $x = \mu$ and is given by [Put $x = \mu$ in (*)]

$$\left[p(x)\right]_{max} = \frac{1}{\sqrt{2\pi}\,.\,\sigma} \qquad \ldots (14\cdot25)$$

Thus, maximum value of $p(x)$ is inversely proportional to the standard deviation. For large values of σ, $p(x)$ decreases, *i.e.*, the curve tends to flatten out and for small values of σ, $p(x)$ increases, *i.e.*, the curve has a sharp peak.

11. Distribution is unimodal, the only mode occurring at $X = \mu$.

12. Since the distribution is symmetrical, all moments of odd order about the mean are zero. Thus

$$\mu_{2n+1} = 0 \; ; \; (n = 0, 1, 2, \ldots) \qquad \ldots (14\cdot26)$$

i.e.,

$$\mu_1 = \mu_3 = \mu_5 = \ldots = 0 \qquad \ldots (14\cdot26a)$$

13. The moments (about mean) of even order are given by :

$$\mu_{2n} = 1.\,3.\,5.\,\ldots\,(2n-1)\,\sigma^{2n}\,, \quad (n = 1, 2, 3\ldots) \qquad \ldots (14\cdot27)$$

Putting $n = 1$ and 2, we get

$$\mu_2 = \sigma^2 \quad \text{and} \quad \mu_4 = 1\cdot3\sigma^4 = 3\sigma^4 \qquad \ldots (14\cdot28)$$

$$\therefore \quad \beta_1 = \frac{\mu_3^2}{\mu_2^3} = 0 \quad \text{and} \quad \beta_2 = \frac{\mu_4}{\mu_2^2} = \frac{3\sigma^4}{\sigma^4} = 3 \qquad \ldots (14\cdot28a)$$

14. X-axis is an asymptote to the curve, *i.e.,* for numerically large value of X (on either side of the line $(X = \mu)$, the curve becomes parallel to the X-axis and is supposed to meet it at infinity.

15. A linear combination of independent normal variates is also a normal variate. If $X_1, X_2, \ldots, X_n$ are independent normal variates with means $\mu_1, \mu_2, \ldots, \mu_n$ and standard deviations $\sigma_1, \sigma_2, \ldots, \sigma_n$ respectively, then their linear combination

$$a_1X_1 + a_2X_2 + \ldots + a_nX_n \qquad \ldots (14\cdot29)$$

where $a_1, a_2, \ldots, a_n$ are constants, is also a normal variate with

$$\left.\begin{aligned} \text{Mean} &= a_1\,\mu_1 + a_2\,\mu_2 \ldots + a_n\,\mu_n \\ \text{and} \quad \text{Variance} &= a_1^2\,\sigma_1^2 + a_2^2\sigma_2^2 + \ldots + a_n^2\sigma_n^2 \end{aligned}\right\} \qquad \ldots (14\cdot29a)$$

In particular, if we take $a_1 = a_2 = \ldots = a_n = 1$ in (14·29) then we get :

"*$X_1 + X_2 + \ldots + X_n$ is a normal variate with mean $\mu_1 + \mu_2 + \ldots + \mu_n$ and variance $\sigma_1^2 + \sigma_2^2 + \ldots + \sigma_n^2$.*" ...(14·29*b*)

Thus, *the sum of independent normal variates is also a normal variate.* This is known as the '*Reproductive or Additive Property*' of the Normal distribution.

If we take $a_1 = a_2 = 1$ and $a_3 = a_4 = \ldots = a_n = 0$, then we have from (14·29) and (14·29*a*) :

$X_1 + X_2$ is a normal variate with mean $\mu_1 + \mu_2$ and variance $\sigma_1^2 + \sigma_2^2$. ...(14·29*c*)

Further if we take $a_1 = 1$ and $a_2 = -1$ and $a_3 = a_4 = \ldots = a_n = 0$, in (14·29) and (14·29*a*) we get :

$X_1 - X_2$ is a normal variate with mean $\mu_1 - \mu_2$ and variance $\sigma_1^2 + \sigma_2^2$. ...(14·29*d*)

Hence, *the sum as well as the difference of independent normal variates is a normal variate.*

Further, if we take $a_1 = a_2 = \ldots = a_n = (1/n)$, then we have from (14·29) and (14·29*a*) :

$$\overline{X} = \frac{1}{n}(X_1 + X_2 + \ldots + X_n) \sim N\left(\frac{1}{n}\sum_{i=1}^{n}\mu_i,\; \frac{1}{n^2}\sum_{i=1}^{n}\sigma_i^2\right) \qquad \ldots (14\cdot29e)$$

Moreover, if $X_1, X_2, \ldots, X_n$ are identically and independently distributed (*i.i.d.*) normal variates, each with mean μ and variance σ^2, *i.e.,* if $X_i \sim N(\mu, \sigma^2)$; $i = 1, 2, \ldots, n$, then from (14·29*e*) we get :

$$\overline{X} = \frac{1}{n}\sum_{i=1}^{n} X_i \sim N\left(\frac{1}{n}\cdot n\mu\,,\; \frac{1}{n^2}\cdot n\sigma^2\right) \quad \Rightarrow \quad \overline{X} \sim N\left(\mu\,,\; \frac{\sigma^2}{n}\right) \qquad \ldots (14\cdot29f)$$

Hence, if $X_1, X_2, \ldots, X_n$ are i.i.d. $N(\mu\,,\, \sigma^2)$, then $\overline{X} \sim N(\mu\,,\, \sigma^2/n)$,

***i.e.* the mean $(\overline{X})$ of n i.i.d. normal variates $N(\mu, \sigma^2)$, is also normally distributed with the same mean (μ) but with variance (σ^2/n).**

16. Mean Deviation (*M.D.*) about mean or median or mode, $[\because M = Md = Mo]$ is given by :

$$M.D. = \sqrt{\frac{2}{\pi}}\,.\,\sigma = 0.7979\,\sigma \cong \frac{4}{5}\,\sigma \qquad \text{... (14·30)}$$

17. Quartiles are given (in terms of μ and σ) by :

$$Q_1 = \mu - 0{\cdot}6745\,\sigma \quad \text{and} \quad Q_3 = \mu + 0{\cdot}6745\,\sigma \qquad \text{... (14·31)}$$

18. Quartile deviation (*Q.D.*) is given by

$$Q.D. = \frac{Q_3 - Q_1}{2} = 0{\cdot}6745\sigma \cong \frac{2}{3}\sigma \qquad \text{[From (14·31)]} \qquad \text{... [(14·32)]}$$

Also $\quad Q.D. = \frac{2}{3}\sigma = \frac{4}{6}\sigma = \frac{5}{6}\times\frac{4}{5}\sigma = \frac{5}{6}M.D. \qquad$ [From (14·30)]

$$\therefore \quad Q.D. = \frac{5}{6}M.D. \qquad \text{... (14·33)}$$

19. We have (approximately) :

$$Q.D. : M.D. : S.D. \quad :: \quad \frac{2}{3}\sigma : \frac{4}{5}\sigma : \sigma \quad :: \quad \frac{2}{3} : \frac{4}{5} : 1$$

$$\Rightarrow \quad Q.D. : M.D. : S.D. \quad :: \quad 10 : 12 : 15 \qquad \text{... (14·34)}$$

20. From (14·30) and (14·33) we also have

$$4S.D. = 5M.D. = 6Q.D. \qquad \text{... (14·35)}$$

21. Points of inflexion of the normal curve are at $X = \mu \pm \sigma$ *i.e.,* they are equidistant from mean at a distance of σ and are given by :

$$\left[x = \mu \pm \sigma, \quad p(x) = \frac{1}{\sigma\,.\,\sqrt{2\pi}}\,e^{-1/2}\right]$$

22. *Area Property.* One of the most fundamental properties of the normal probability curve is the area property. The area under the normal probability curve between the ordinates at $X = \mu - \sigma$ and $x = \mu + \sigma$ is 0·6826. In other words, the range $\mu \pm \sigma$ covers 68·26% of the observations.

The area under the normal probability curve between the ordinates at $X = \mu - 2\sigma$ and $X = \mu + 2\sigma$ is 0·9544 *i.e.,* the range $\mu \pm 2\sigma$ covers more than 95% of the observations.

The area under the normal probability curve between the ordinates at $X = \mu - 3\sigma$ and $X = \mu + 3\sigma$ is 0·9973 *i.e.,* the range $\mu \pm 3\sigma$ covers 99·73% of the observations. Hence, for practical purposes, the range $\mu \pm 3\sigma$ covers the entire area, which is 1 [or all the observations].

The standard normal variate corresponding to X is $Z = \dfrac{X - \mu}{\sigma}$

When $X = \mu + \sigma$, $\quad Z = \dfrac{\mu + \sigma - \mu}{\sigma} = 1$; $\qquad$ When $X = \mu - \sigma$, $\quad Z = \dfrac{\mu - \sigma - \mu}{\sigma} = -1$

When $X = \mu + 2\sigma$, $\quad Z = \dfrac{\mu + 2\sigma - \mu}{\sigma} = 2$; $\qquad$ When $X = \mu - 2\sigma$, $\quad Z = \dfrac{\mu - 2\sigma - \mu}{\sigma} = -2$

When $X = \mu + 3\sigma$, $\quad Z = \dfrac{\mu + 3\sigma - \mu}{\sigma} = 3$; $\qquad$ When $X = \mu - 3\sigma$, $\quad Z = \dfrac{\mu - 3\sigma - \mu}{\sigma} = -3$

Hence the area under the *standard normal probability curve*

(*i*) Between the ordinates at $Z = \pm\, 1$ is 0·6826.

(*ii*) Between the ordinates at $Z = \pm\, 2$ is 0·9544.

(*iii*) Between the ordinates at $Z = \pm\, 3$ is 0·9973.

These areas are exhibited in the Fig. 14·2.

AREAS UNDER NORMAL PROBABILITY CURVE

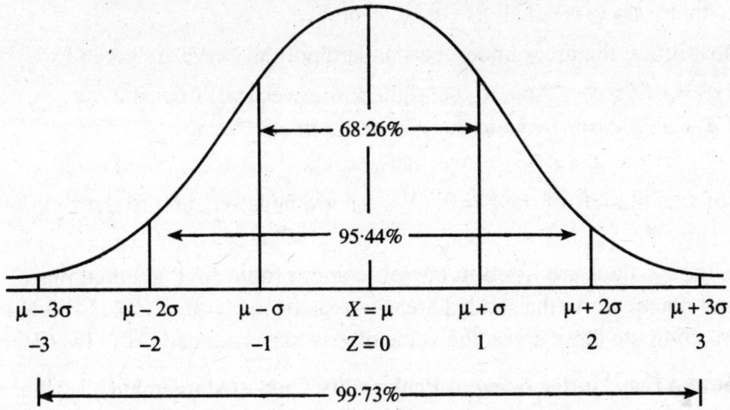

Fig. 14·2

The Table 14·9 gives the areas under the standard normal probability curve for some important values of Z:

TABLE 14·9 : **AREAS UNDER STANDARD NORMAL CURVE**

Distance from the mean ordinates in terms of ± σ	*Area under the curve*
Z = ± 0·6745	50% = 0·50
Z = ± 1·00	68·26% = 0·6826
Z = ± 1·96	95% = 0·95
Z = ± 2·0	95·44% = 0·9544
Z = ± 2·58	99% = 0·99
Z = ± 3·0	99·73% = 0·9973

Remark These values of Z [Table 14·9] and the corresponding areas under the normal probability curve are of great practical utility in Statistics and should be committed to memory.

14·4·6. Areas Under Standard Normal Probability Curve

For $z_1 > 0$,

$$P(0 < Z < z_1) = \text{Area under standard normal curve between } z = 0 \text{ and } z = z_1.$$

$$= \int_0^{z_1} \phi(z)\, dz = \frac{1}{\sqrt{2\pi}} \int_0^{z_1} e^{-\frac{1}{2}z^2}\, dz \qquad \ldots (14·36)$$

The value of this definite integral can be obtained to any degree of accuracy by the numerical approximation procedures and have been tabulated for different values of z_1, at an interval of 0·01. These areas (probabilities) are given in Table VI at the end of the book.

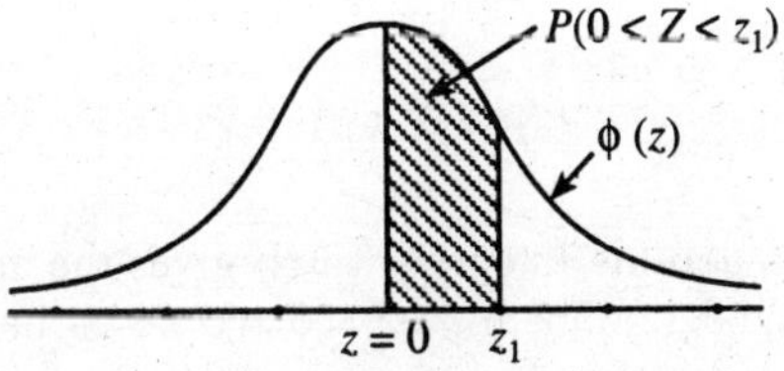

Fig. 14·3

Suppose the area that we are interested in is not between 0 and z. We can still use Tale VI. We discuss below the various possibilities and the technique of reducing the desired area to form 0 to z, after some manipulations.

Remarks. 1. Since standard normal variable Z is a continuous random variable, $P(Z = a) = 0$, where a is a fixed constant. Hence in the problems relating to areas under normal probability curve, it is immaterial whether we take the inequality < or ≤, in computing probabilities.

2. To compute the areas under standard normal probability curve, it is more convenient to express the desired areas in terms of the probabilities and use the symmetric property of the normal distribution.

In the examples that follow, we shall use this technique.

In terms of probabilities, the areas under the standard normal curve are given by :

$P(Z \geq a) = P(Z > a)$ = Area to the right of the (vertical) line at $z = a$.

$P(Z \leq a) = P(Z < a)$ = Area to the left of the line at $z = a$.

$P(a \leq Z \leq b) = P(a < Z < b)$ = Area between the lines at $z = a$ and $z = b$.

3. The values of z to the left of the $z = 0$, $(X = \mu)$, are negative and to the right of $z = 0$ $(X = \mu)$, are positive.

4. In Table VI, the z-values are listed in the left column (upto first decimal place) and across the top row (second decimal place) while the shaded areas (Areas from $Z = 0$ to $Z = z$) [Fig 14·3] are given in the body of the table. To compute these areas, the value of Z is to be rounded off to two decimal places.

How to Compute Areas Under Normal Probability Curve. Mathematically, the area bounded by the curve $p(x)$, X-axis and the ordinates at $X = a$ and $X = b$ is given by the definite integral :

$$\int_a^b p(x)\,dx$$

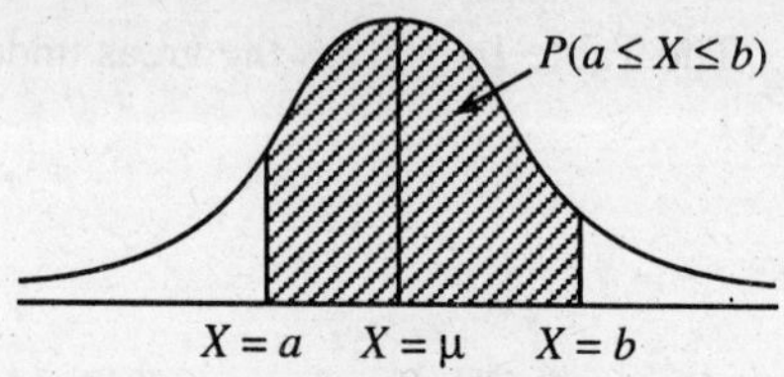

Fig. 14·4(a)

But since $p(x)$ is probability density function, it is represented by

$$P(a \leq X \leq b) = \int_a^b p(x)\,dx, \qquad \ldots (14 \cdot 36a)$$

and is shown in the Fig. 14·4(*a*).

Let us now try to compute the areas under the normal probability curve.

$$P(\mu < X < a) = \int_\mu^a p(x)\,dx$$

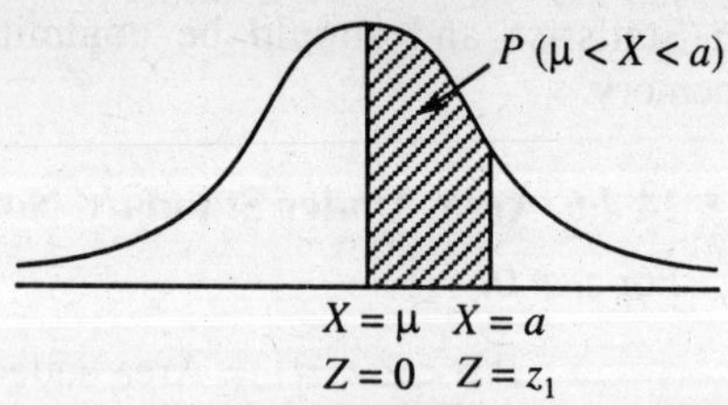

Fig. 14·4(b)

is the area under the normal curve (14·19) enclosed by x-axis and the ordinates at $X = \mu$ and $X = a$ as shown in Fig. 14·4(*b*).

When $X = \mu$, $Z = \dfrac{X-\mu}{\sigma} = \dfrac{\mu-\mu}{\sigma} = 0$; When $X = a$, $Z = \dfrac{a-\mu}{\sigma} = z_1$, (say).

$$\therefore \qquad P(\mu < X < a) = P(0 < Z < z_1) = \int_0^{z_1} \phi(z)\,dz = \frac{1}{\sqrt{2\pi}} \int_0^{z_1} e^{-z^2/2} dz \qquad \ldots (14 \cdot 37)$$

This definite Integral, which gives the area under the standard normal probability curve bounded by z-axis and the ordinates at $Z = 0$ and $Z = z_1$ has been evaluated and tabulated for different values of z_1 at the intervals of 0·01 and are given in Table VI in the Appendix at the end of the book.

In particular we have :

$P(\mu - \sigma < X < \mu + \sigma)$

$= P(-1 < Z < 1)$

$= 2P(0 < Z < 1)$ [By symmetry]

$= 2 \times 0 \cdot 3413$ [From Normal Probability Table VI]

$= 0 \cdot 6826$

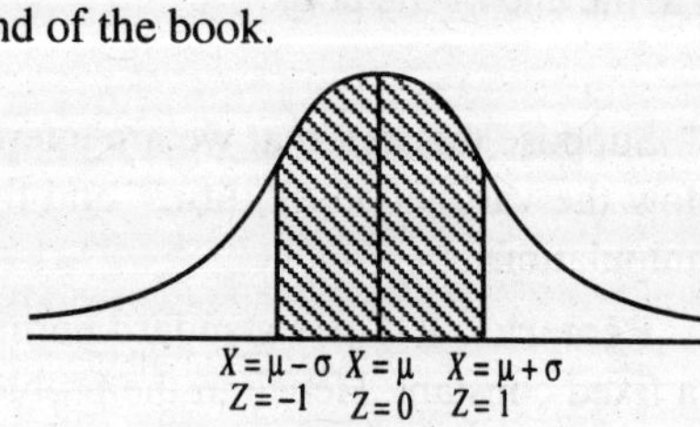

Fig. 14·5

Similarly,

$$P(\mu - 1{\cdot}96\sigma < X < \mu + 1{\cdot}96\sigma) = P(-1{\cdot}96 < Z < 1{\cdot}96) = 2P\,(0 < Z < 1{\cdot}96) = 2 \times 0{\cdot}4750 = 0{\cdot}95$$

$$P(\mu - 2\sigma < X < \mu + 2\sigma) = P(-2 < Z < 2) = 2P\,(0 < Z < 2) = 2 \times 0{\cdot}4772 = 0{\cdot}9544$$

$$P(\mu - 2{\cdot}58\sigma < X < \mu + 2{\cdot}58\sigma) = P(-2{\cdot}58 < Z < 2{\cdot}58) = 2P(0 < Z < 2{\cdot}58) = 2 \times 0{\cdot}495 = 0{\cdot}99$$

$$P(\mu - 3\sigma < X < \mu + 3\sigma) = P\,(-3 < Z < 3) = 2P\,(0 < Z < 3) = 2 \times 0{\cdot}49865 = 0{\cdot}9973.$$

Remarks 1. Since total probability is always 1, we have

$$\int_{-\infty}^{\infty} p(x)dx = \int_{-\infty}^{\infty} \phi(z)dz = 1$$

i.e., the total area under the normal probability curve is 1.

2. Since the areas under the normal probability curve have been tabulated in terms of the standard normal variable Z in the form of definite integral

$$\int_{0}^{z_1} \phi(z)\,dz = P(0 < Z < z_1),$$

for practical problems, we do not deal with the variable X but first convert it to *S.N.V. Z.* Next, we try to convert the required area in the form $P(0 < Z < z_1)$ by using the following results : [See Fig. 14·6].

$$P(X > \mu) = P(Z > 0) = 0{\cdot}5$$

$$P(X < \mu) = P(Z < 0) = 0{\cdot}5$$

and making use of the symmetry property of the distribution.

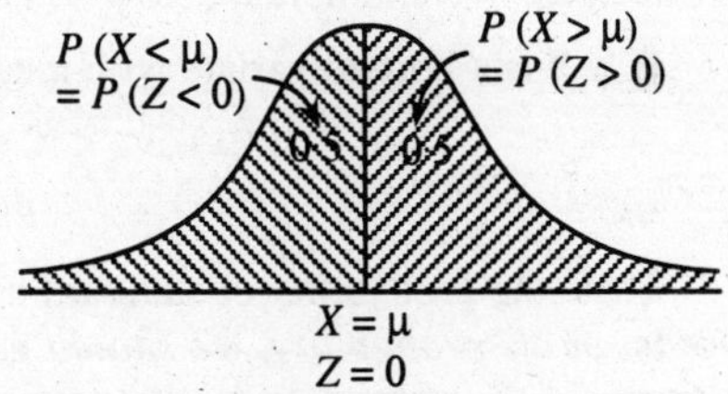

Fig. 14·6

Computation of Area to the Right of the Ordinate at $X = a$, *i.e.,* to find $P(X > a)$.

Case (i). $a > \mu$; i.e., a is to the right of the mean ordinate. [See Fig. 14·7]

Since $a > \mu$, the corresponding value of Z will be positive.

When $X = a$, $Z = \dfrac{a - \mu}{\sigma} = z_1$, (say). [Fig. 14·7]

$$P(X > a) = P(Z > z_1)$$

$$= 0{\cdot}5 - P(0 < Z < z_1)$$

and the probability $P(0 < Z < z_1)$ can be read from the Table VI in the appendix.

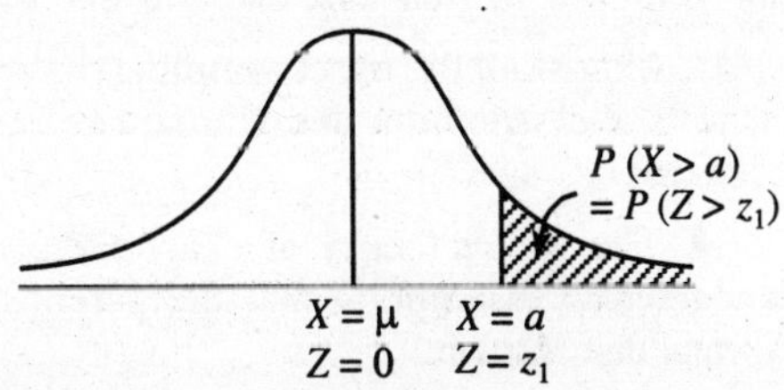

Fig. 14·7

Case (ii). $a < \mu$, i.e., a is to the left of the mean ordinate. [Fig. 14·8]

Since $a < \mu$, the value of Z corresponding to X = a will be negative.

When $X = a$, $Z = \dfrac{a - \mu}{\sigma} = -z_1$, (say). [Fig 14·8]

$\therefore \quad P(X > a) = P(Z > -z_1)$

$= P(-z_1 < Z < 0) + 0{\cdot}5$ [From Fig. 14·8]

$= 0{\cdot}5 + P(0 < Z < z_1)$ [By symmetry]

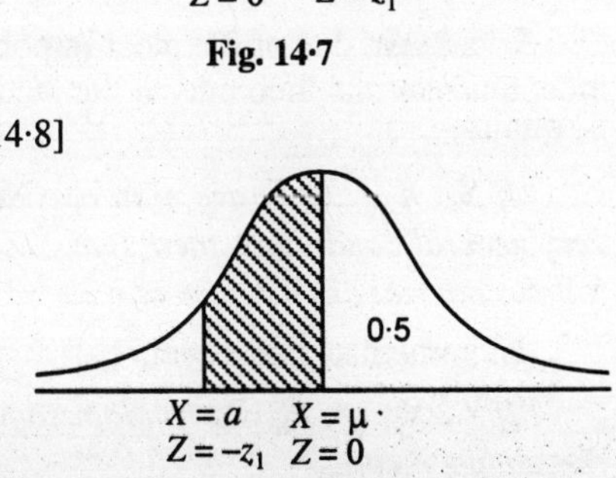

Fig. 14·8

and $P(0 < Z < z_1)$ can be read from the Normal Probability Table VI.

Computation of the Area to the Left of the Ordinate at X = b i.e., to find P(X < b).

Case (i). $b > \mu$ i.e., b is to the right of the ordinate at $X = \mu$. [Fig. 14·9]

Fig. 14·9

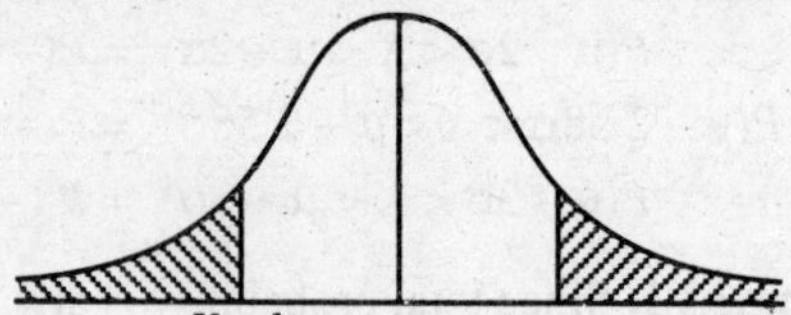

Fig. 14·10

When $X = b$, $$Z = \frac{b-\mu}{\sigma} = z_1, \text{ (say). [See Fig. 14·9]}$$

$\therefore$ $$P(X < b) = P(Z < z_1) = 0{\cdot}5 + P(0 < Z < z_1) \quad \text{[Obvious from Fig. 14·9]}$$

Case (ii). $b < \mu$, i.e., b is to the left of the ordinate at $X = \mu$ [See Fig. 14·10]

$\therefore$ $$P(X < b) = P(Z < -z_1) = P(Z > z_1) \quad \text{[By symmetry]}$$
$$= 0{\cdot}5 - P(0 < Z < z_1)$$

14·4·7. Importance of Normal Distribution. Normal distribution has occupied a very important role in Statistics. We enumerate below some of its important applications.

1. If X is a normal variate with mean μ and variance σ^2, then we have proved that

$$P(\mu - 3\sigma < X < \mu + 3\sigma) = P(-3 < Z < 3) = 0{\cdot}9973$$

$$\Rightarrow \quad P[|Z| > 3] = 1 - 0{\cdot}9973 = 0{\cdot}0027$$

Thus, the probability of standard normal variate going outside the limits ± 3 is practically zero. In other words, *in all probability, we should expect a standard normal variate to lie between the limits* ± 3. This property of the normal distribution forms the basis of entire *large sample theory.* [This discussion is beyond the scope of this book.]

2. Most of the discrete probability distributions (*e.g.*, Binomial distribution, Poisson distribution) tend to normal distribution as *n*, the number of trials increases. For large values of *n*, computation of probability for discrete distributions becomes quite tedious and time consuming. In such cases, normal approximation can be used with great ease and convenience.

3. Almost all the exact sampling distributions, *e.g.*, Student's *t*-distribution, Snedecor's *F*-distribution, Fisher's Z-distribution and Chi square distribution conform to normal distribution for large degrees of freedom (*i.e.*, as $n \to \infty$).

4. The whole theory of exact sample (small sample) tests, *viz.*, *t*, *F*, χ^2 tests, etc., is based on the fundamental assumption that the parent population from which the samples have been drawn follows Normal distribution.

5. Perhaps, one of the most important applications of the Normal distribution is inherent in one of the most fundamental theorems in the theory of Statistics, *viz.*, the *Central Limit Theorem* which may be stated as follows:

"*If $X_1, X_2, ..., X_n$ are n independent random variables following any distribution, then under certain very general conditions, their sum $\sum X = X_1 + X_2 + ... + X_n$ is asymptotically normally distributed, i.e., $\sum X$ follows normal distribution as $n \to \infty$*".

An immediate consequence of this theorem is the following result.

"*If $X_1, X_2, ..., X_n$ is a random sample of size n from any population with mean μ and variance σ^2, then the sample mean*

$$\overline{X} = \frac{1}{n}(X_1 + X_2 + \ldots + X_n) = \frac{1}{n}\sum X,$$

is asymptotically normal (as $n \to \infty$) with mean μ and variance σ^2/n"

6. Normal distribution is used in Statistical Quality Control in Industry for the setting of control limits for the construction of control charts.

[Discussion on topics in Remarks 3 to 6 is beyond the scope of the book.]

7. W.J. Youden of the National Bureau of Standards describes the importance of the Normal distribution artistically in the following words :

THE NORMAL
LAW OF ERROR
STANDS OUT IN THE
EXPERIENCE OF MANKIND
AS ONE OF THE BROADEST
GENERALISATIONS OF NATURAL
PHILOSOPHY. IT SERVES AS THE
GUIDING INSTRUMENT IN RESEARCHES,
IN THE PHYSICAL AND SOCIAL SCIENCES
AND IN MEDICINE, AGRICULTURE AND
ENGINEERING. IT IS AN INDISPENSABLE TOOL FOR
THE ANALYSIS AND THE INTERPRETATION OF THE
BASIC DATA OBTAINED BY OBSERVATION AND EXPERIMENT.

The above presentation, strikingly enough gives the shape of the normal probability curve.

8. Lipman reveals the popularity and importance of normal distribution in the following quotation :

"Every body believes in the law of errors (the normal curve), the experimenters because they think it is a mathematical theorem, the mathematicians because they think it is an experimental fact."

Example 14·28. *Suppose the waist measurements W of 800 girls are normally distributed with mean 66 cms, and standard deviation 5 cms. Find the number N of girls with waists—*

(i) between 65 cms and 70 cms ; (ii) greater than or equal to 72 cms.

Solution. W : Waist measurements (in cms.) of girls.

We are given $W \sim N(\mu, \sigma^2)$, where $\mu = 66$ cms and, $\sigma = 5$ cms.

W (in cms)	65	70	72
$Z = \frac{W-\mu}{\sigma} = \frac{W-66}{5}$ (Standard Normal Variate)	$\frac{65-66}{5} = -0{\cdot}2$	$\frac{70-66}{5} = 0{\cdot}8$	$\frac{72-66}{5} = 1{\cdot}2$

(*i*) The probability that a girl has waist between 65 cms and 70 cms is given by :

$$\begin{aligned} P(65 \le W \le 70) &= P(-0{\cdot}2 \le Z \le 0{\cdot}8) = P(-0{\cdot}2) \le Z \le 0) + P(0 \le Z \le 0{\cdot}8) \\ &= P(0 \le Z \le 0{\cdot}2) + P(0 \le Z \le 0{\cdot}8) \qquad \text{(By symmetry)} \\ &= 0{\cdot}0793 + 0{\cdot}2881 = 0{\cdot}3674 \qquad \text{(From Normal Tables)} \end{aligned}$$

Hence, in a group of 800 girls, the expected number of girls with waists between 65 cms and 70 cms is

$$800 \times 0{\cdot}3674 = 293{\cdot}92 \simeq 294$$

(*ii*) The probability that a girl has waist greater than or equal to 72 cms is given by

$$P(W \ge 72) = P(Z \ge 1{\cdot}2) = 0{\cdot}5 - P(0 \le Z \le 1{\cdot}2) = 0{\cdot}5 - 0{\cdot}3849 = 0{\cdot}1151$$

Hence, in a group of 800 girls, the expected number of girls with waist greater than or equal to 72 cms is :

$$800 \times 0{\cdot}1151 = 92{\cdot}08 \simeq 92.$$

Example 14·29. *Assume the mean height of soldiers to be 68·22 inches with a variance of 10·8 inches².* *How many soldiers in a regiment of 1,000 would you expect to be*

(i) over six feet tall, and (ii) below 5·5 feet ? Assume heights to be normally distributed.

Solution. Let the variable X denote the height (in inches) of the soldiers. Then we are given :

$$\text{Mean} = \mu = 68{\cdot}22 \quad \text{and} \quad \text{Variance} = \sigma^2 = 10{\cdot}8$$

A soldier will be over 6 feet tall if X is greater than $12 \times 6 = 72$ (because X is height in inches).

When $X = 72$, $Z = \dfrac{X-\mu}{\sigma} = \dfrac{72-68{\cdot}22}{\sqrt{10{\cdot}8}} = \dfrac{3{\cdot}78}{3{\cdot}286} = 1{\cdot}15$

The probability that a soldier is over 6 feet = 72″ tall is given by :

$$P(X > 72) = (Z > 1{\cdot}15) = 0{\cdot}5 - P(0 \le Z \le 1{\cdot}15)$$

$$= 0{\cdot}5 - 0{\cdot}3749 = 0{\cdot}1251 \qquad \text{[From Normal Probability Table VI]}$$

Hence, in a regiment of 1,000 soldiers, the number of soldiers over 6 feet tall is :

$$1000 \times 0{\cdot}1251 = 125{\cdot}1 \cong 125$$

(*ii*) The probability that a soldier is below 5·5′ = 66″ is given by :

$$P(X < 66) = P\left(Z < \frac{66-68{\cdot}22}{\sqrt{10{\cdot}8}}\right) = P\left(Z < \frac{-2{\cdot}22}{3{\cdot}286}\right)$$

$$= P(Z < -0{\cdot}6756) = P(Z > 0{\cdot}6756) \qquad \text{(By symmetry)}$$

$$= 0{\cdot}5 - P(0 < Z < 0{\cdot}6756) = 0{\cdot}5 - 0{\cdot}2501 \qquad \text{[From Normal Probability Tables]}$$

$$= 0{\cdot}2499 \text{ (approx.)}$$

Hence, the number of soldiers over 5·5 feet in a regiment of 1,000 soldiers is

$$1000 \times 0{\cdot}2499 = 249{\cdot}9 \simeq 250.$$

Example 14·30. *The average test marks in a particular class is 79. The standard deviation is 5. If the marks are distributed normally, how many students in a class of 200 did not receive marks between 75 and 82 ? Given :*

$$Pr\,\{0 \le Z \le {\cdot}7\} = {\cdot}2580, \qquad Pr\,\{0 \le Z \le {\cdot}8\} = {\cdot}2881$$

$$Pr\,\{0 \le Z \le {\cdot}6\} = {\cdot}2257, \qquad \text{where } Z \text{ is a standard normal variable.}$$

[Delhi Univ. B,.Com. (Hons.), 2005]

Solution. If the random variable X denotes the marks obtained by the students in the given test, then we are given :

$$X \sim N(\mu, \sigma^2) \quad \text{where} \quad \mu = 79 \quad \text{and} \quad \sigma = 5.$$

The probability that a student gets marks between 75 and 82 is given by :

$$P(75 < X < 82) = P\left(\frac{75-79}{5} < Z < \frac{82-79}{5}\right) \qquad \left(\because Z = \frac{X-\mu}{\sigma} = \frac{X-79}{5}\right)$$

$$= P(-0{\cdot}8 < Z < 0{\cdot}6)$$

$$= P(-0{\cdot}8 < Z < 0) + P(0 < Z < 0{\cdot}6)$$

$$= P(0 < Z < 0{\cdot}8) + P(0 < Z < 0{\cdot}6) \qquad \text{(By symmetry)}$$

$$= 0{\cdot}2881 + 0{\cdot}2257 = 0{\cdot}5138$$

The probability p that a student does not get marks between 75 and 82 is given by :

$$p = 1 - P(\text{Student gets marks between 75 and 82})$$

$$= 1 - P(75 < X < 82) = 1 - 0{\cdot}5138 = 0{\cdot}4862$$

Hence, in a class of 200 students, the number of students who did not receive marks between 75 and 82 is given by :

$$200 \times p = 200 \times 0{\cdot}4862 = 97{\cdot}24 \simeq 97.$$

Example 14·31. *The hourly wages of 1,000 workmen are normally distributed around a mean of Rs. 70 and with a standard deviation of Rs. 5. Estimate the number of workers whose houly wages will be :*

(*i*) *between Rs. 69 and Rs. 72* (*ii*) *more than Rs. 75 ;* (*iii*) *less than Rs. 63.*

(*iv*) *Also estimate the lowest hourly wages of the 100 highest paid workers.*

Solution. Let the random variable X denote the hourly wages in Rupees. Then X is a normal variable with mean $\mu = 70$ and $\sigma = 5$. The standard normal variable corresponding to X is

$$Z = \frac{X-\mu}{\sigma} = \frac{X-70}{5}$$

X	63	69	72	75
$Z = \frac{X-70}{5}$	$\frac{63-70}{5} = -1{\cdot}4$	$-0{\cdot}2$	$0{\cdot}4$	1

... (*)

(*i*) $P(69 < X < 72) = P(-0{\cdot}2 < Z < 0{\cdot}4)$ [From (*)]

$= P(-0{\cdot}2 < Z < 0) + P(0 < Z < 0{\cdot}4)$

$= P(0 < Z < 0{\cdot}2) + P(0 < Z < 0{\cdot}4)$ (By symmetry)

$= 0{\cdot}0793 + 0{\cdot}1554 = 0{\cdot}2347$

Hence, the required number of workers is : $1000 \times 0{\cdot}2347 = 234{\cdot}7 \simeq 235$.

(*ii*) We want $P(X > 75)$.

$\therefore$ $P(X > 75) = P(Z > 1)$ [From (*)]

$= 0{\cdot}5 - P(0 < Z < 1)$ [From Fig. 14·11]

$= 0{\cdot}5 - 0{\cdot}3413 = 0{\cdot}1587$

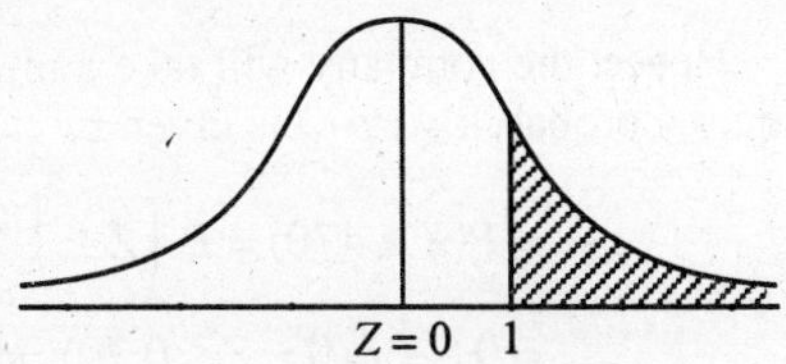

Fig. 14·11

Thus, the number of workers with hourly wages more than Rs. 75 is :

$1000 \times 0{\cdot}1587 = 158{\cdot}7 \simeq 159$

(*iii*) $P(X < 63) = P(Z < -1{\cdot}4)$ [From (*)]

$= P(Z > 1{\cdot}4)$ [By symmetry, Fig. 14·12]

$= 0{\cdot}5 - P(0 < Z < 1{\cdot}4)$

$= 0{\cdot}5 - 0{\cdot}4192 = 0{\cdot}0808.$

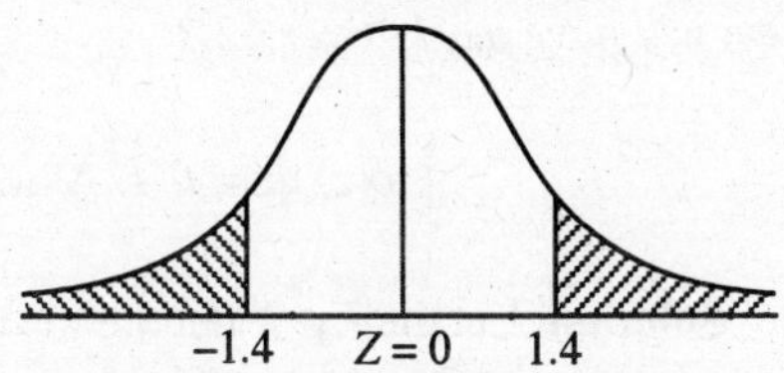

Fig. 14·12

Hence, the number of workers with hourly wages less than Rs. 63 is : $1000 \times 0{\cdot}0808 = 80{\cdot}8 \simeq 81.$

(*iv*) Proportion of the 100 highest paid workers is : $\frac{100}{1000} = \frac{1}{10} = 0{\cdot}10$

We want to determine $X = x_1$, say, such that $P(X > x_1) = 0{\cdot}10$

$$\text{When } X = x_1,\ Z = \frac{x_1 - 70}{5} = z_1, \text{ (say)}. \qquad \ldots (**)$$

Then $P(Z > z_1) = 0{\cdot}10 \Rightarrow P(0 < Z < z_1) = 0{\cdot}5 - 0{\cdot}1 = 0{\cdot}40$

From the Normal Probability Table VI and (**), we get

$$z_1 = \frac{x_1 - 70}{5} = 1{\cdot}28 \text{ (approx.)} \Rightarrow x_1 = 70 + 5 \times 1{\cdot}28 = 70 + 6{\cdot}40 = 76{\cdot}40$$

Hence, the lowest hourly wages of the 100 highest paid workers are Rs. 76·40.

Example 14·32. *Time taken by the crew, of a company, to construct a small bridge is a normal variate with mean 400 labour hours and standard deviation of 100 labour hours.*

(i) What is the probability that the bridge gets constructed between 350 to 450 labour hours ?

(ii) If the company promises to construct the bridge in 450 labour hours or less and agrees to pay a penalty of Rs. 100 for each labour hour spent in excess of 450, what is the probability that the company pays a penalty of at least Rs. 2000 ? [*Delhi Univ. B.A.* (*Econ. Hons.*), *1998*]

Solution. Let X denote the time (in labour hours) to construct the bridge. Then, in the usual notations, we are given : $X \sim N(\mu, \sigma^2)$ where $\mu = 400$ hrs, $\sigma = 100$ hrs.

(*i*) The probability (p_1) that the bridge gets constructed between 350 to 450 labour hours is given by :

$$p_1 = P\,(350 < X < 450)$$

X	$Z = \left(\dfrac{X-\mu}{\sigma}\right) = \dfrac{X-400}{100}$
350	$\dfrac{350-400}{100} = -0{\cdot}5$
450	$\dfrac{450-400}{100} = 0{\cdot}5$

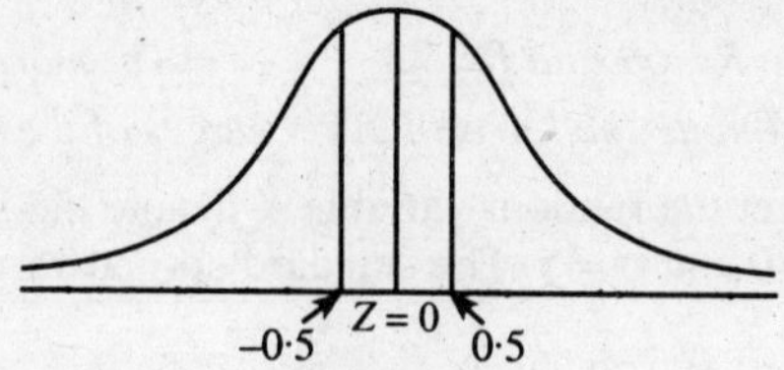

Fig. 14·13

$\therefore$ $p_1 = P\,(-0{\cdot}5 < Z < 0{\cdot}5)$, where $Z \sim N(0, 1)$ [Fig. 14·13]

$= 2\,P\,(0 < Z < 0{\cdot}5)$ (By symmetry)

$= 2 \times 0{\cdot}1915 = 0{\cdot}3830$ (From Normal Probability Tables)

(*ii*) The penalty for each labour hour delay (excess over 450 hours) is Rs. 100, (given).

If the minimum penalty paid by the company is Rs. 2000, then the delay in completing the bridge is

$$\geq \frac{2000}{100} = 20 \text{ hours.}$$

Hence, the company will take a minimum of (450 + 20) = 470 hours, to complete the bridge. Thus, the required probability (p_2) is given by :

$$p_2 = P(X \geq 470) = P\left(Z \geq \frac{470-400}{100}\right) = P\,(Z \geq 0{\cdot}70)$$

$$= 0{\cdot}5 - P(0 \leq Z \leq 0{\cdot}70) = 0{\cdot}5 - 0{\cdot}2580 = 0{\cdot}2420 \qquad \text{[From Normal Probability Tables]}$$

Example 14·33. *Marks obtained by a number of students are assumed to be normally distributed with mean 50 and variance 36. If 4 students are taken at random, what is the probability that exactly two of them will have marks over 62 ?*

$$\int_0^2 \phi(z)\,dz = 0{\cdot}4772 \text{ where } Z \text{ is } N\,(0, 1).$$

[*I.C.W.A.* (*Intermediate*), *June 2002*]

Solution. Let the *r.v.* X denote the marks obtained by the students. Then we are given that :

$$X \sim N(\mu, \sigma^2) \text{ where } \mu = 50 \text{ and } \sigma^2 = 36 \quad \Rightarrow \quad \sigma = 6.$$

The probability 'p' that a student scores marks over 62 in given by :

$$p = P(X > 62) = P(Z > 2) \qquad \left[Z = \frac{X-\mu}{\sigma} = \frac{62-50}{6} = 2\right]$$

$$= 0{\cdot}5 - P(0 \leq Z \leq 2) = 0{\cdot}5 - 0{\cdot}4772 = 0{\cdot}0228$$

$$\left[\text{Given : } \int_0^2 \phi(z)\,dz = 0{\cdot}4772 \quad \Rightarrow \quad P(0 \leq Z \leq 2) = 0{\cdot}4772\right]$$

Let Y denote the *r.v.* that the score of a student is more than 62. If 4 students are selected at random, then Y has a binomial distribution with parameters $n = 4$ and $p = 0{\cdot}0228$ *i.e.*, $Y \sim B(n = 4, p = 0{\cdot}0228)$.

The required probability that exactly 2 of the 4 selected students will have marks over 62 is :

$${}^4C_2\,p^2 q^{4-2} = {}^4C_2\,(0{\cdot}0228)^2\,(0{\cdot}9772)^2 = 6(0{\cdot}00052)\,(0{\cdot}95492) = 0{\cdot}00298 \text{ (approx.)}$$

Example 14·34. *The I.Q.'s of army volunteers in a given year are normally distributed with mean (μ) = 110 and standard deviation (σ) = 10. The army wants to give advanced training to 20% of those recruits with the highest scores. What is the lowest I.Q. score acceptable for the advanced training ?*

[*Delhi Univ. B.A.* (*Econ. Hons.*), *1994*]

Solution. Let the *r.v.* X denote the *I.Q.* of the army volunteers. Then we are given $X \sim N(\mu, \sigma^2)$, where $\mu = 110$, $\sigma = 10$. We want to find x_1 so that

$$P(X > x_1) = 20\% = 0{\cdot}20 \qquad \ldots (i)$$

The standard normal variate $Z = \dfrac{X-\mu}{\sigma} = \dfrac{X-110}{10}$

When $X = x_1$, $\quad Z = \dfrac{x_1 - 110}{10} = z_1$, (say). $\Rightarrow \quad x_1 = 110 + 10z_1$ ... (*ii*)

(*i*) $\Rightarrow \quad P(Z > z_1) = 0{\cdot}20$

$\Rightarrow \quad P(0 < Z < z_1) = 0{\cdot}30$

$\Rightarrow \quad z_1 = 0{\cdot}84$

(From Normal Probability Tables)

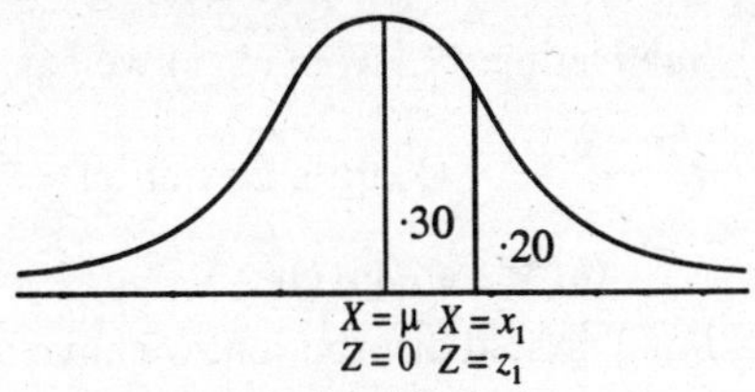

Fig. 14·14

Substituting in (*ii*), we get : $\quad x_1 = 110 + 10 \times 0{\cdot}84 = 118{\cdot}4$.

Hence, the lowest *I.Q.* score acceptable for advanced training is $118{\cdot}4 \simeq 118$.

Example 14·35. *A set of examination marks is approximately normally distributed with a mean of 75 and standard deviation of 5. If the top 5% of students get grade A and the bottom 25% get grade F, what mark is the lowest A and what mark is the highest F ?* [*Delhi Univ. B.Com. (Hons.), (External), 2007*]

Solution. Let X denote the marks in the examination. Then, X is normally distributed with mean $\mu = 75$ and *s.d.* $\sigma = 5$. Let x_1 be the lowest marks for grade A and x_2 be the highest marks for grade F. Then we are given :

$$P(X > x_1) = 0{\cdot}05 \quad \text{and} \quad P(X < x_2) = 0{\cdot}25$$

Then the standard normal variables corresponding to x_1 and x_2 are given by [See Fig. 14·15] :

$$\left.\begin{aligned} Z &= \frac{x_1-\mu}{\sigma} = \frac{x_1 - 75}{5} = z_1, \text{ (say)} \\ Z &= \frac{x_2-\mu}{\sigma} = \frac{x_2 - 75}{5} = -z_2, \text{ (say)} \end{aligned}\right\} \quad \ldots(*)$$

[Note the negative sign for z_2].

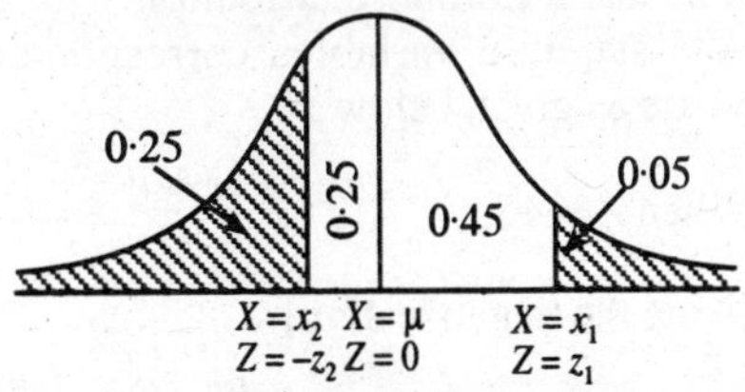

Fig. 14·15

From the figure we obviously get :

$P(0 < Z < z_1) = 0{\cdot}45 \quad \Rightarrow \quad z_1 = 1{\cdot}645$ (approx.) [From Table VI]

$P(-z_2 < Z < 0) = 0{\cdot}25 \quad \Rightarrow \quad P(0 < Z < z_2) = 0{\cdot}25$ (By symmetry)

$\Rightarrow \quad z_2 = 0{\cdot}675$ (approx.) [From Table VI]

Substituting for z_1 and z_2 in (*) we get :

$$x_1 = 75 + 5z_1 = 75 + 5 \times 1{\cdot}645 = 83{\cdot}225 \simeq 83$$

$$x_2 = 75 - 5z_2 = 75 - 5 \times 0{\cdot}675 = 71{\cdot}625 \simeq 72$$

Hence, the lowest mark for grade A is 83 and the highest mark for grade F is 72.

Example 14·36. (*a*) *For a normal distribution with mean μ and standard deviation σ, obtain the first and third quartiles and also the quartile deviation.*

(*b*) *For a normal distribution with mean 50 and s.d. 15, find Q_1 and Q_3.*

Solution. (*a*) By definition of Q_1 and Q_3 we have :

$P(X < Q_1) = 0{\cdot}25$

and $\quad P(X > Q_3) = 0{\cdot}25$

$$\left.\begin{aligned} \text{When } X = Q_1,\ Z &= \frac{Q_1-\mu}{\sigma} = -z_1, \text{ (say)} \\ \text{When } X = Q_3,\ Z &= \frac{Q_3-\mu}{\sigma} = z_1 \end{aligned}\right\} \quad \ldots(*)$$

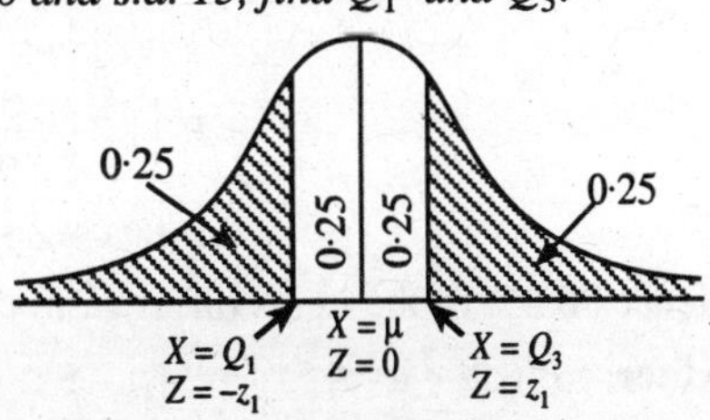

Fig. 14·16

(Obvious from the Fig. 14·16 because of symmetry).

Thus, we get (obvious from the figure) :

$P(0 < Z < z_1) = 0·25 \quad \Rightarrow \quad z_1 = 0·6745$ (approx.) [From Normal Tables]

Substituting in (*) we get :

$Q_1 = \mu - \sigma z_1 = \mu - 0·6745\,\sigma$ ...(**) and $Q_3 = \mu + \sigma z_1 = \mu + 0·6745\,\sigma$ ...(***)

Subtracting (**) from (***) we have : $Q_3 - Q_1 = 2 \times 0·6745\,\sigma$

$$\therefore \quad \text{Quartile Deviation} = \frac{Q_3 - Q_1}{2} = 0·6745\,\sigma \simeq \frac{2}{3}\sigma$$

(*b*) We are given : $\mu = 50, \quad \sigma = 15$

For a normal distribution, we have :

$$Q_1 = \text{Mean} - 0·6745\sigma = 50 - 0·6745 \times 15 = 50 - 10·1175 = 39·8825$$

$$Q_3 = \text{Mean} + 0·6745\sigma = 50 + 0·6745 \times 15 = 50 + 10·1175 = 60·1175$$

Example 14·37. (*i*) *In a normal distribution, 31% of the items are under 45 and 8% are over 64. Find the mean and standard deviation of the distribution.*

(*ii*) *What % of the items differ fromt he mean by a number not more than 5 ?*

[*Delhi Univ. B.A. (Econ. Hons.), 2004*]

Solution. (*i*) Let X denote the variable under consideration. Then we are given :

$P(X < 45) = 0·31$ and $P(X > 64) = 0·08$

If X has a normal distribution with mean μ and *s.d.* σ, then the standard variables corresponding to $X = 45$ and $X = 64$ are as given below :

When $X = 45$, $\quad Z = \dfrac{45 - \mu}{\sigma} = -z_1$, (say). ...(*)

[Note the negative sign]

When $X = 64$, $\quad Z = \dfrac{64 - \mu}{\sigma} = z_2$, (say). ...(**)

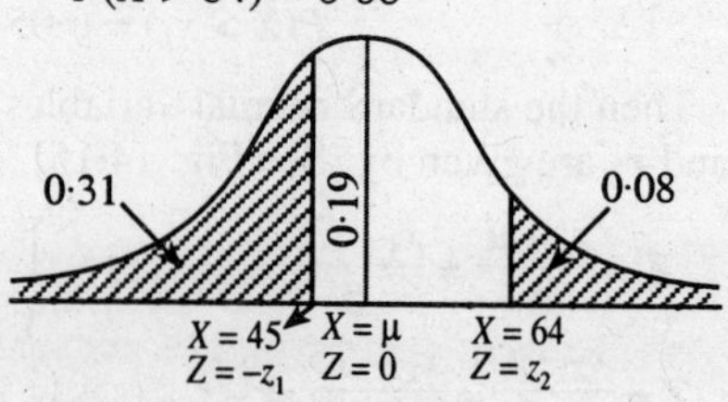

Fig. 14·17

From the Fig. 14·17, it is obvious that

$P(0 < Z < z_2) = 0·42 \quad \Rightarrow \quad z_2 = 1·405$ (From Normal Tables)

Also $\quad P(-z_1 < Z < 0) = 0·19$

$\Rightarrow \quad P(0 < Z < z_1) = 0·19$ [By symmetry]

$\Rightarrow \quad z_1 = 0·496$ [From Normal Tables]

Substituting the values of z_1 and z_2 in (*) and (**) we get :

$45 - \mu = -0·496\sigma$ ...(*i*) and $64 - \mu = 1·405\,\sigma$ ...(*ii*)

Subtracting (*i*) from (*ii*), we have : $19 = 1·901\sigma \quad \Rightarrow \quad \sigma = 10$ (approx.)

Substituting in (*i*), we get : $\mu = 45 + 0·496 \times 10 = 45 + 4·96 = 49·96 \simeq 50$ (approx.)

Hence, mean is 50 and s.d. is 10.

(*ii*) $\quad P[|X - \mu| \not> 5] = P[|X - \mu| \le 5] = P[\sigma|Z| \le 5] \qquad \left[\because Z = \dfrac{X - \mu}{\sigma} \sim N(0, 1)\right]$

$$= P\left(|Z| \le \frac{5}{\sigma}\right) = P(|Z| \le 0·5) = P(-0·5 \le Z \le 0·5) \qquad [\because \sigma = 10]$$

$$= 2\,P(0 \le Z \le 0·5) = 2 \times 0·1915 = 0·3830 \qquad \text{(By Symmetry)}$$

Hence 38·3% of the items differ from the mean by a number not more than 5.

Aliter. $P(|X - \mu| \le 5) = P(\mu - 5 \le X \le \mu + 5) = P(45 \le X \le 55) \qquad (\because \mu = 50)$

$$= P(-0·5 \le Z \le 0·5) = 2\,P(0 \le Z \le 0·5) \qquad \left(\because Z = \frac{X - \mu}{\sigma} = \frac{X - 50}{10}\right)$$

Example 14·38. *In an examination a student passes if he secured 30% or more marks. He is placed in the first, second or third divisions accordingly as he secures 60% or more marks, between 45% and 60% marks and between 30% and 45% respectively. He gets a distinction in case he secures 80% or more marks. It is noticed from the results that 10% of the students failed whereas 5% of them obtained distinction. Calculate the percentage of students placed in the second division. (Assume marks to be normally distributed).* [*Delhi Univ. B.A. (Econ. Hons.), 2006*]

Solution. Let X denote marks in the test. Then $X \sim N(\mu, \sigma^2) \Rightarrow Z = \dfrac{X-\mu}{\sigma} \sim N(0, 1)$.

We are given : $P(X < 30) = 10\% = 0{\cdot}10$ and $P(X > 80) = 5\% = 0{\cdot}05$

The standard normal variates corresponding to $X = 30$ and $X = 80$ are :

$$\frac{30-\mu}{\sigma} = -z_1 \text{ (say), (Note the negative sign) and } \frac{80-\mu}{\sigma} = z_2, \text{ (say), so that}$$

$$\left.\begin{aligned}&\Rightarrow\quad P(Z < -z_1) = 0{\cdot}10 \Rightarrow P(0 \le Z < z_1) = 0{\cdot}40 \Rightarrow z_1 = 1{\cdot}28\\ &\text{and}\quad P(Z > z_2) = 0{\cdot}05 \Rightarrow P(0 \le Z \le z_2) = 0{\cdot}45 \Rightarrow z_2 = 1{\cdot}65\end{aligned}\right\} \text{(From Normal Probability Table)}$$

$$\therefore \quad \frac{30-\mu}{\sigma} = -1{\cdot}28 \quad \text{and} \quad \frac{80-\mu}{\sigma} = 1{\cdot}65$$

Substracting, we get $\dfrac{50}{\sigma} = 2{\cdot}93 \Rightarrow \sigma = \dfrac{50}{2{\cdot}93} = 17{\cdot}06 \simeq 17$

Dividing, we get $\dfrac{80-\mu}{30-\mu} = -1{\cdot}289 \Rightarrow \mu = \dfrac{118{\cdot}67}{2{\cdot}289} = 51{\cdot}84 \simeq 52$

Required probability $= P(45 < X < 60) = P(-0{\cdot}40 < Z < 0{\cdot}48)$

$= P(0 < Z < 0{\cdot}40) + P(0 < Z < 0{\cdot}48) = 0{\cdot}1844 + 0{\cdot}1554 = 0{\cdot}3398$

$\Rightarrow$ $33{\cdot}98\% \simeq 34\%$ of students are placed in second division.

Example 14·39. *The marks of the students in a certain examination are normally distributed with mean marks as 40% and standard deviation, marks as 20%. On this basis, 60% students failed. The result was moderated and 70% students passed. Find the pass marks before and after the moderation.*

[*Delhi Univ. B.Com. (Hons.), 2002*]

Solution. Let the percentage pass marks before the moderation be x_1 and after the moderation be x_2.

If X denotes the percentage of marks obtained in the examination, then we are given :

$$X \sim N(\mu, \sigma^2), \text{ where } \mu = 40 \quad \text{and} \quad \sigma = 20.$$

Before Moderation. Pass marks $= x_1\%$.

60% students failed $\Rightarrow$ 40% students passed

$\therefore$ $P(X \ge x_1) = 0{\cdot}40$

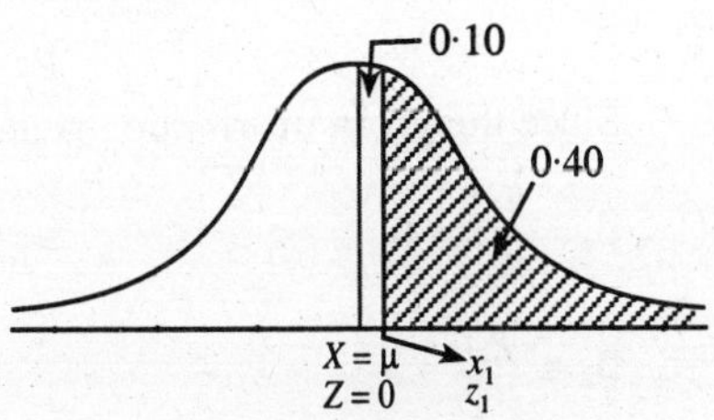

Fig. 14·18

Obviously, x_1 is located to the right of $x = \mu$ [See Fig. 14·18] and consequently the corresponding value of Z is positive.

When $X = x_1$, $Z = \dfrac{x_1 - \mu}{\sigma} = \dfrac{x_1 - 40}{20} = z_1$ (say) ...(*)

$\therefore$ $P(Z \ge z_1) = 0{\cdot}40 \Rightarrow P(0 \le Z \le z_1) = 0{\cdot}10 \Rightarrow z_1 = 0{\cdot}25$ [From Normal Tables]

Substituting in (*), we get : $x_1 = 40 + 20\, z_1 = 40 + 20 \times 0{\cdot}25 = 45$

Hence, the pass marks before the moderation are 45%.

After Moderation. 70% of the students passed. (Given)

Pass marks $= x_2\%$, (say).

$\therefore \qquad P(X \geq x_2) = 0{\cdot}70$

Obviously, x_2 is located to the left of $X = \mu$, [Fig. 14·19] and consequently, the corresponding value of Z will be negative.

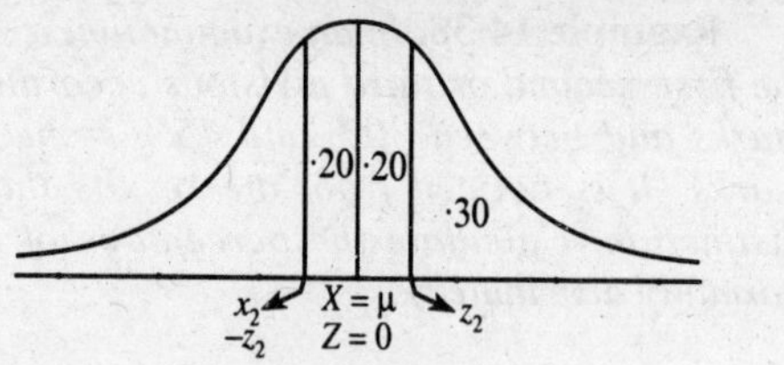

Fig. 14·19

When $X = x_2$, $Z = \dfrac{x_2 - \mu}{\sigma} = \dfrac{x_2 - 40}{20} = -z_2 \qquad \ldots(**)$

[Note the negative sign]

$\therefore \quad P(Z \geq -z_2) = 0{\cdot}70 \quad \Rightarrow \quad p(-z_2 \leq Z \leq 0) + 0{\cdot}50 = 0{\cdot}70$ [From Fig. 14·19]

$\Rightarrow \quad P(0 \leq Z \leq z_2) = 0{\cdot}20$ (By symmetry) $\Rightarrow \quad z_2 = 0{\cdot}525$ (From Normal Tables)

Substituting in (**), we get : $x_2 = 40 + 20 \times (-0{\cdot}525) = 40 - 10{\cdot}5 = 29{\cdot}5$

Hence, the pass marks after moderation are 29·5%.

Example 14·40. *If* $f(x) = \dfrac{2}{\sqrt{\pi}} e^{-4x^2}, \; -\infty < x < \infty,$

is the p.d.f. of a normal distribution, then the variance is :

(i) $\dfrac{1}{\sqrt{2}}$ *(ii)* $\dfrac{1}{2}$ *(iii)* $\dfrac{1}{4}$ *(iv)* $\dfrac{1}{8}$.

[*I.C.W.A. (Intermediate), June 2002*]

Solution. The p.d.f. of normal distribution with mean μ and variance σ^2 is given by :

$$f(x) = \frac{1}{\sqrt{2\pi}\,.\,\sigma} e^{-(x-\mu)^2/2\sigma^2}; \; -\infty < x < \infty \qquad \ldots(*)$$

We are given : $\quad f(x) = \dfrac{2}{\sqrt{\pi}} e^{-4x^2}, \; -\infty < x < \infty \qquad \ldots(**)$

Comparing (*) and (**), we get :

$$\frac{1}{\sqrt{2\pi}\,.\,\sigma} = \frac{2}{\sqrt{\pi}} \quad \Rightarrow \quad \sigma = \frac{1}{2\sqrt{2}} \quad \Rightarrow \quad \sigma^2 = \frac{1}{4 \times 2} = \frac{1}{8}$$

$\therefore$ *(iv)* is the correct answer.

Example 14·41. *For a normal distribution, the first moment about origin is 35 and the second moment about 35 is 10. Find the first four central moments.* [*Delhi Univ. B.A. (Econ. Hons.), 1998*]

Solution. Mean = First moment about origin = 35 (Given), $\ldots(i)$

Second moment about 35 = 10 (Given)

$\Rightarrow$ Second moment about mean = 10 [$\because$ Mean = 35 (From *(i)*)]

$\Rightarrow \qquad \mu_2 = 10 \qquad \ldots(ii)$

Since the given distribution is normal, $\beta_1 = 0$ and $\beta_2 = 3$.

$\beta_1 = \dfrac{\mu_3^2}{\mu_2^3} = 0 \quad \Rightarrow \quad \mu_3 = 0$

$\beta_2 = \dfrac{\mu_4}{\mu_2^2} = 3 \quad \Rightarrow \quad \mu_4 = 3\mu_2^2 = 3 \times 10^2 = 300$ [From *(ii)*]

$\therefore \quad \mu_1 = 0$ (always) ; $\mu_2 = 10$; $\mu_3 = 0$; $\mu_4 = 300$.

Example 14·42. *Write down the probability density function of the normal distribution.*

A factory turns out an article by mass production methods. From past experience it appears that 20 articles on an average are rejected out of every batch of 100. Find the variance of the number of rejects in a batch. What is the probability that the number of rejects in a batch exceeds 30 ?

(Given area under a normal curve between z = 0 and z = 2·5 is 0·4938).

Solution. In the usual notations we have : $n = 100$,

$$p = \text{Probability that an article is rejected} = \frac{20}{100} = \frac{1}{5} \quad \Rightarrow \quad q = 1 - p = 1 - \frac{1}{5} = \frac{4}{5}$$

If the random variable X denotes the number of rejects in a sample of n, then by Binomial probability law we have :

$$E(X) = \mu = \text{Mean number of rejects} = np = = 100 \times \frac{1}{5} = 20$$

$$\text{Var}(X) = \sigma^2 = npq = 100 \times \frac{1}{5} \times \frac{4}{5} = 16$$

If we assume that X is normally distributed, then the probability that the number of rejects in a batch of 100 exceeds 30 is given by :

$$P(X > 30) = P(Z > 2{\cdot}5) \qquad \left(\because\ Z = \frac{X-\mu}{\sigma} = \frac{30-20}{\sqrt{16}} = 2{\cdot}5\right)$$

$$= 0{\cdot}5 - P(0 \le Z \le 2{\cdot}5) = 0{\cdot}5 - 0{\cdot}4938 = 0{\cdot}0062$$

EXERCISE 14·3

1. (*a*) What are the main features of Normal probability distribution ? Can a normal probability distribution be fully determined if we know its mean and standard deviation ?

(*b*) What is normal distribution ? Draw a rough sketch of its probability density function and describe its four important properties.

2. Write down the binomial, the Poisson and the normal probability functions explaining the constants. State the range of the variables in each case. Give one example each of binomial, Poisson and normal variables.

3. What are the chief properties of normal distribution. Discuss briefly the importance of normal distribution in statistical analysis. [*Delhi Univ. B.Com. (Hons.), 2007*]

4. (*a*) Explain the role of normal distribution in statistical analysis and also point out its constraints. (*Himachal Pradesh Univ. M.B.A., 1998*)

(*b*) Give the salient features of a normal distribution. Write its probability function. [*C.A. (Foundation), May 2000, 1997*]

5. State the conditions under which a binomial distribution tends to (*i*) Poisson distribution and (*ii*) normal distribution. Write down the probability function of binomial and Poisson distributions. [*C.A. (Foundation), Nov. 1996*]

6. (*a*) Why does the Normal distribution occupy the most honourable position in statistical analysis.

(*b*) List the chief properties of the Normal distribution. Why is this distribution given a central place in Statistics ?

7. (*a*) Explain the distinctive features of Binomial, Normal and Poisson probability distributions. When does a Binomial distribution tend to become (*i*) a Normal and (*ii*) a Poisson distribution ? Explain clearly.

(*b*) State the conditions under which a random variable possesses a binomial distribution. State the binomial probability function. In what ways is the calculation of probability using a binomial probability function different from the way probability is calculated from the relevant function of the normal distribution. [*Delhi Univ. B.A. (Econ. Hons.), 2005*]

Hint. Normal distribution is a continuous distribution while binomial distribution is a discrete probability distribution. In normal distribution, probabilities are computed as areas under the normal probability curve.

8. (*a*) If X is random variable following normal distribution with mean μ and s.d. σ, write its probability density function (p.d.f.). Also obtain the p.d.f. of standard normal variate $Z = (X - \mu)/\sigma$.

(*b*) What are the properties of a normal distribution ? If the random variable X is normally distributed with mean μ and variance σ^2, show that the mean of the variable $Z = (X - \mu)/\sigma$ is always zero. [*Delhi Univ. B.A. (Econ. Hons.), 2007*]

Hint. $X \sim N(\mu, \sigma^2)$; $Z = \dfrac{X-\mu}{\sigma}$; $E(X) = \mu$.

$$\text{Mean of } Z = E(Z) = E\left(\frac{X-\mu}{\sigma}\right) = \frac{1}{\sigma} E(X-\mu) = \frac{1}{\sigma}[E(X) - \mu] = 0.$$

(*c*) If the random variable X is normally distributed with mean μ and variance σ^2, derive the mean and variance of the variable $Z = (X - \mu)/\sigma$. [*Delhi Univ. B.A. (Econ. Hons.), 2009*]

Ans. $E(Z) = 0$ and $\text{Var}(Z) = 1$.

(*d*) How will you obtain the area (probability) under a normal probability curve ? In particular, if $X \sim N(\mu, \sigma^2)$, obtain

(*i*) $P(X > \mu)$ (*ii*) $P(X < \mu)$ (*iii*) $P(\mu - \sigma < X < \mu + \sigma)$

(*iv*) $P(\mu - 2\sigma < X < \mu + 2\sigma)$ (*v*) $P(\mu - 3\sigma < X < \mu + 3\sigma)$. (*vi*) $P(\mu - 1{\cdot}96\sigma < X < \mu + 1{\cdot}96\sigma)$

Ans. (*i*) 0·5, (*ii*) 0·5, (*iii*) 0·6826, (*iv*) 0·9544, (*v*) 0·9973, (*vi*) 0·95.

9. For a normally distributed variable *X*, what proportion of the observations would be found between $(\mu - \sigma)$ and $(\mu - 3\sigma)$? [*Delhi Univ. B.A. (Econ. Hons.), 2007*]

Hint. $X \sim N(\mu, \sigma^2)$; $Z = \dfrac{X-\mu}{\sigma} \sim N(0, 1)$

$$P(\mu - 3\sigma < X < \mu - \sigma) = P(-3 < Z < -1) = P(1 < Z < 3) \quad \text{[By symmetry]}$$
$$= P(0 < Z < 3) - P(0 < Z < 1) = 0{\cdot}4987 - 0{\cdot}3413 = 0{\cdot}1574$$

10. Let $X \sim N(0, 1)$. Find out which one is greater :

$P(-0{\cdot}5 \le X \le 0{\cdot}1)$ or $P(1 \le X \le 2)$

[*C.A. (Foundation), May 1998*]

Ans. $P(-0{\cdot}5 \le X \le 0{\cdot}1) = 0{\cdot}2313$; $P(1 \le X \le 2) = 0{\cdot}1359$; $\therefore$ $P(-0{\cdot}5 \le X \le 0{\cdot}1)$ is greater.

11. In a sample of 1,000 items, the mean weight and standard deviation are 50 and 10 kilograms respectively. Assuming the distribution to be normal, find the number of items weighing between 40 and 70 kilograms.

[*C.A. PEE-1, Nov. 2004*]

Ans. $1{,}000 \times P(40 \le X \le 70) = 1{,}000 \times P(-1 \le Z \le 2) = 1{,}000 \times 0{\cdot}8185 \simeq 819$.

12. If *x* follows normal distribution *N*(0, 1) and $P(x < 1) = 0{\cdot}84$, then $P(|x| < 1)$ is

(*i*) 0·68, (*ii*) 0·32, (*iii*) 0·16, (*iv*) none of these.

[*I.C.W.A. (Intermediate), June 2001*]

Ans. (*i*).

13. The average daily sale of 500 branch offices was Rs. 150 thousand and the standard deviation Rs. 15 thousand. Assuming the distribution to be normal indicate how many branches have sales between :

(*i*) Rs. 120 thousand and Rs. 145 thousand ? (*ii*) Rs. 140 thousand and Rs. 165 thousand ?

Ans. (*i*) 174, (*ii*) 295.

14. The average monthly sales of 2000 firms are normally distributed with mean Rs. 26,000 and standard deviation Rs. 6,000 Find :

(*i*) the number of firms for which sales exceed Rs. 32,000,

(*ii*) the number of firms with sales between Rs. 28,000 and Rs. 32,000. [*Delhi Univ. B.A. (Econ. Hons.), 2007*]

Ans. (*i*) 317, (*ii*) 424.

15. As a result of tests on 2,000 electric bulbs manufactured by a company, it was found that the lifetime of the bulb was normally distributed with an average life of 2,040 hours and standard deviation of 60 hours. On the basis of the information, estimate the number of the bulbs that is expected to burn for

(*a*) more than 2,150 hours, and (*b*) less than 1,960 hours.

Ans. (*a*) 67, (*b*) 184.

16. (*a*) State the probability distribution function of the Standard Normal Variate ; represent it graphically and mark off the 1σ, 2σ and 3σ limits indicating the areas under the curve enclosed by these limits.

(*b*) The mean weight of 500 male students at a certain college is 151 lbs and the standard deviation is 15 lbs. Assuming that the weights are normally distributed, find how many students weigh :

(*i*) between 120 lbs and 155 lbs ; (*ii*) more than 185 lbs.

Ans. (*a*) 0·3413, 0·4772, 0·49865 ; (*b*) (*i*) 294, (*ii*) 6.

17. A project yields an average cash flow of Rs. 500 lakhs with a standard deviation of Rs. 80 lakhs. Calculate the following probabilities assuming the normal distribution :

(*i*) Cash flow will be more than Rs. 550 lakhs

(*ii*) Cash flow will be less than Rs. 440 lakhs

(*iii*) Cash flow will be between Rs. 450 lakhs and Rs. 530 lakhs. [*Delhi Univ. B.A. (Econ. Hons.), 2008*]

Ans. (*i*) 0·2660, (*ii*) 0·2266, (*iii*) 0·3801.

18. The incomes of a group of 10,000 persons were found to be normally distributed with mean Rs. 750 p.m. and S.D. = Rs. 50. Show that out of this group 95% had income exceeding Rs. 668 and only 5% had income exceeding Rs. 832. [*Delhi Univ. B.A. (Econ. Hons.), 2002*]

19. The average marks obtained in the annual examination is 65 with the s.d. of 10. The top 5% of the students are to receive a scholarship. What is the minimum marks a student must score to be eligible for the scholarship. Assume Normal Distribution. [*Delhi Univ. B.A. (Econ. Hons.), 2009*]

Ans. $X \sim N(\mu = 65, \sigma^2 = 10^2)$. We want $X = x_1$, (say) so that $P(X > x_1) = 0{\cdot}05$.

$$z_1 = [(x_1 - 65) / 10] = 1{\cdot}645 \quad \Rightarrow \quad x_1 = 81{\cdot}45 \simeq 82.$$

20. The weekly wages of tradesmen are normally distributed about a mean of Rs. 150 with a standard deviation of Rs. 12. If all tradesmen were awarded a wage increase of 12 per cent, what would be the mean and standard deviation of the new distribution of tradesmen wages ? [*Delhi Univ. B.A. (Econ. Hons.), 2008*]

Hint. X : Original wages (in Rs.) of tradesman; $E(X)$ = Rs. 150 and σ_X = Rs. 12.

$$U = \text{New Wages} = X + 12\% \, (X) = X + 0{\cdot}12X = 1{\cdot}12X.$$

$$E(U) = 1{\cdot}12 \, E(X) = \text{Rs. } 168 \quad ; \quad \sigma_U = 1{\cdot}12 \, \sigma_X = \text{Rs. } 13{\cdot}44.$$

21. (*a*) Time taken by the crew of a company to construct a small bridge is a normal variate with mean 400 labour hours and standard deviation 200 labour hours.

(*i*) What is the probability that the bridge gets constructed between 350 to 450 labour hours ?

(*ii*) If the company promises to construct the bridge in 450 labour hours or less and agrees to pay a penalty of Rs. 100 for each labour hour spent in excess of 450, what is the probability that the company pays a penalty of at least Rs. 2000 ?

(Area under the normal curve for Z = 0 and Z = 0·25 is 0·0987 , Z = 0·35 is 0·1368).

[*Delhi Univ. B.Com. (Hons.), (External), 2006*]

Ans. (*i*) 0·1974, (*ii*) 0·3632.

Hint. X : Time taken (in labour hours) by the company to build the bridge.

$$X \sim N(\mu = 400, \; \sigma^2 = 200^2) \quad ; \quad Z = [(X - \mu)/\sigma] \sim N(0, 1).$$

Now proceed as in Example 14·32.

(*b*) Time taken by a construction company to construct a flyover is a normal variate with mean 400 labour days and standard deviation of 100 labour days. If the company promises to construct the flyover in 450 days or less and agrees to pay a penalty of Rs. 10,000 for each labour day spent in excess of 450, what is the probability that :

(*i*) the company pays a penalty of at least Rs. 2,00,000 ?

(*ii*) the company takes at most 500 days to complete the flyover ? [*Delhi Univ. B.Com. (Hons.), 2004*]

Ans. (*i*) 0·2420, (*ii*) 0·8413.

Hint. Proceed as in Example 14·32.

$$(i) \; p = P\left(X > 450 + \frac{2{,}00{,}000}{10{,}000}\right) = P(X > 470) \; ; \quad (ii) \; P(X \le 500)$$

22. The weekly wages for workers in a factory are distributed normally with mean Rs. 1,800 and standard deviation Rs. 144. Within what range of wages will 95 per cent of workers' wages lie ?

[*Delhi Univ. B.A. (Econ. Hons.), 2009*]

Ans. (Rs. 1517·76, Rs. 2082·24)

Hint. If $X \sim N(\mu, \sigma^2)$, $P[\mu - 1{\cdot}96\sigma \le X \le \mu + 1{\cdot}96\sigma] = 0{\cdot}95$

$\therefore$ Required range of wages = $\mu \pm 1{\cdot}96\sigma$ = Rs. $[1800 \pm 1{\cdot}96 \times 144]$

23. (*a*) Explain, what do you mean by a standard normal variate .

(*b*) Given a normal distribution with $\mu = 50$ and $\sigma = 10$, find the value of X that has (*i*) 13% of the area to its left and (*ii*) 04% of the area to its right.

Ans. (*b*) (*i*) 38·7, (*ii*) 67·5

24. Two thousand electric bulbs with an average life of 1000 hours and a standard deviation of 200 hours are installed in a town. Assuming the lives of the bulbs to be normally distributed, answer the following :

(*i*) What number of bulbs might be expected to fail in the first 700 burning hours?

(*ii*) What is the minimum burning life of the top one quarter of bulbs ? [*Delhi Univ. B.Com (Hons.), 2001*]

Ans. (*i*) 134 (*ii*) 1134 hours.

Hint. (*ii*) Find x_1 so that $P(X > x_1) = 0{\cdot}25$.

25. In a normal distribution 2·28% of items are under 33 and 84·13% are under 63. What are the mean and standard deviation of the distribution ? Given that $\int_0^z \frac{e^{-\frac{t^2}{2}}}{\sqrt{2\pi}}\, dt = 0{\cdot}3413$ and 0·4772 according as $z = 1$ and 2.

[*I.C.W.A. (Intermediate), Dec. 2001*]

Ans. $\mu = 53$, $\sigma = 10$

26. Suppose that a doorway being constructed is to be used by a class of people whose heights are normally distributed with mean 70 and standard deviation 3″. How much high the doorway should be, without causing more than 25% of the people to bump their heads ? If the height of the door may be fixed at 76″, how many persons out of 5,000 are expected to bump their heads ?

Ans. 72·025″ and 114.

27. Incomes of a group of 10,000 persons were found to be normally distributed with mean Rs. 520 and standard deviation Rs. 60.

Find :

(*i*) the number of persons having income between Rs. 400 and Rs. 550,

(*ii*) the lowest income of the richest 500.

For a standard normal variate t, the area under the curve between $t = 0$ and $t = 0{\cdot}5$ is 0·19146, the area between $t = 0$ and $t = 1{\cdot}645$ is 0·45000 and the area between $t = 0$ and $t = 2$ is 0·47725.

Ans. (*i*) 6687 (*ii*) Rs. 618·70.

28. The distribution of distance between residence and place of work for 1,00,000 people in Delhi is normally distributed with a mean of 10 kilometres and a variance of 25 km². How many people travel more than 18 kms to their place of work ? If 10% of the people who travel the longest distance are to be provided a special allowance, what is the minimum distance from place of work to be eligible for the allowance ? [*Delhi Univ. B.A. (Econ. Hons.), 2005*]

Ans. $1{,}00{,}000 \times P(X > 18) = 1{,}00{,}000 \times 0{\cdot}0548 = 5480$; 16·400 km.

Hint. Find $X = x_1$ (km), say, so that $P(X > x_1) = 0{\cdot}10$.

29. The local authorities in a certain city install 10,000 electric lamps in the streets of the city. If these lamps have an average life of 1,000 burning hours with standard deviation of 200 hours, assuming normality, what number of lamps might be expected to fail (*i*) in the first 800 burning hours ? (*ii*) between 800 and 1,200 burning hours ? After what period of burning hours would you expect that

(*a*) 10% of the lamps would fail ? (*b*) 10% of the lamps would be still burning ?

Ans. (*i*) 1587 (*ii*) 6826. (*a*) 744 hours (*b*) 1256 hours.

Hint. (*a*) Find x_1 *s.t.* $P(X < x_1) = 0{\cdot}10$, $x_1 = 744$; (*b*) Find x_2 *s.t.* $P(X > x_2) = 0{\cdot}10$, $x_2 = 1256$

30. (*a*) In a certain examination the percentage of passes and distinctions were 46 and 9 respectively. Estimate the average marks obtained by the candidates, the minimum pass and distinction marks being 40 and 75 respectively. (Assume the distribution of marks to be normal.)

(*b*) Also determine what would have been the minimum qualifying marks for admission to a re-examination of the failed candidates, had it been desired that the best 25% of them should be given another opportunity of being examined.

Ans. (*a*) $\sigma = 28{\cdot}22$, $\mu = 37{\cdot}178 \simeq 37{\cdot}2$; (*b*) $30{\cdot}43 \simeq 30$

Hint. (*b*) Pass percentage = 46 ; ∴ Percentage of student who failed = 54

Let x_1 be the minimum qualifying marks for re-examination of the failed students. We want x_1 *s.t.*

$$P(x_1 < X < 40) = 25\% \text{ of } (54\%) = 13{\cdot}5\% = 0{\cdot}135$$

31. In a certain examination, mean of marks scored by 400 students is 45 with a standard deviation of 15. Assuming the distribution to be normal, find (*i*) the number of students securing marks between 30 and 60 ; (*ii*) the limits between which marks of the middle 50% of the students lie.

(Area under standard normal curve between $Z = 0$ and $Z = 1$ is 0·3413.)

Ans. (*i*) 273, (*ii*) $Q_1 = 34{\cdot}38$, $Q_3 = 55{\cdot}12$.

32. The mean *I.Q.* (intelligence quotient) of a large number of children of age 14 was 100 and the standard deviation 16. Assuming that the distribution was normal, find

(*i*) What % of the children had *I.Q.* under 80 ?
(*ii*) Between what limits the *I.Q.*s of the middle 40% of the children lay ?
(*iii*) What % of the children had *I.Q.*s within the range $\mu \pm 1{\cdot}96\sigma$?

Ans. (*i*) 10·56% (*ii*) 91·6 , 108·4 (*iii*) 0·95.

33. (*a*) The mean and standard deviation of a normal distribution are 60 and 5′ respectively. Find the inter-quartile range and the mean deviation of the distribution.

Ans. $\dfrac{Q_3 - Q_1}{2} = 0{\cdot}6745 \times \sigma \quad \Rightarrow \quad Q_3 - Q_1 = 6{\cdot}745$; M.D. (about mean) = 4 approx.

(*b*) The median and Q_1 of a normal distribution are 89·0 and 75·5 respectively. Calculate the standard deviation. What is the relationship between Binomial, Normal and Poisson distributions ?

[*Delhi Univ. B.Com. (Hons.), 2008*]

Ans. $\sigma = 20$

Hint. Mean $(\mu) = Md = 89{\cdot}0$ (Given) and $Q_1 = \mu - 0{\cdot}6745\ \sigma = 75{\cdot}5$ (given).

34. What proportion of area of a normal curve is included between (*i*) σ, (*ii*) 2σ, and (*iii*) 3σ distance from the mean ?

For a normal distribution of 100 items, the lower quartile Q_1 is 73 and σ is 15. Find

(*i*) median, (*ii*) limits for central 50% of the distribution, and (*iii*) mean deviation.

Ans. (*i*) Median = 83·12, (*ii*) $Q_1 = 73$, $Q_3 = 93{\cdot}235$, (*iii*) 11·9685.

35. In a distribution exactly normal, 7% of the items are under 35 and 89% are under 63. What are the mean and standard deviation of the distribution ?

[*Delhi Univ. B.Com. (Hons.), 2009*]

Ans. $\mu = 50{\cdot}27$, $\sigma = 10{\cdot}35$.

Hint. $X \sim N(\mu, \sigma^2)$; $P(X < 35) = 0{\cdot}07$ and $P(X < 63) = 0{\cdot}89$

$$\therefore \quad P(Z < -z_1) = 0{\cdot}07 \quad \Rightarrow \quad P(0 < Z < z_1) = 0{\cdot}43 \quad \Rightarrow \quad \frac{35 - \mu}{\sigma} = -z_1 = -1{\cdot}475 \qquad \ldots(1)$$

$$\text{and} \quad P(Z < z_2) = 0{\cdot}89 \quad \Rightarrow \quad P(0 < Z < z_2) = 0{\cdot}39 \quad \Rightarrow \quad \frac{63 - \mu}{\sigma} = z_2 = 1{\cdot}23 \qquad \ldots(2)$$

36. At a certain examination, 10% of the students who appeared for the paper in Statistics got less than 30 marks and 97% of the students got less than 62 marks. Assuming the distribution to be normal, find the mean and the standard deviation of the distribution.

Ans. $\mu = 43{\cdot}04$, $\sigma = 10{\cdot}03$.

37. The following table gives frequencies of occurrence of a variable *X* between certain limits :

Variatble (X)	*Frequency (f)*
Less than 40	30
40 or more but less than 50	33
50 and more	37
	100

The distribution is exactly normal. Find the average and standard deviation of X.

Ans. $\mu = 46·14$, $\sigma = 11·696$.

38. (*a*) If the cauliflowers on a truck are classified as A, B and C according to a size-weight index as : under 75, between 75 and 80, and above 80; find approximately (assuming a normal distribution) the mean and standard deviation of a lot in which A are 58%, B are 38% and C are 4%. [*Delhi Univ. B.A. (Econ. Hons.), 2006*]

Ans. and Hint. X : Size-weight index of cauliflower ; $X \sim N(\mu, \sigma^2)$, (say). (Given).

Class A : $X < 75$; **Class B** : $75 < X < 80$; **Class C** : $X > 80$

Given $P(X < 75) = 58\% = 0·58$ and $P(X > 80) = 4\% = 0·04$

$\Rightarrow \quad P(Z < z_1) = 0·58 \quad \Rightarrow \quad P(0 < Z < z_1) = 0·08 \quad \Rightarrow \quad z_1 = \dfrac{75-\mu}{\sigma} = 0·20$

and $\quad P(Z > z_2) = 0·04 \quad \Rightarrow \quad P(0 < Z < z_2) = 0·46 \quad \Rightarrow \quad z_2 = \dfrac{80-\mu}{\sigma} = 1·75$

Solving, we get : $\mu = 74·35$ and $\sigma = 3·25$.

(*b*) A collection of human skulls is divided into three classes according to the value of a 'length-breadth index' x. Skulls with $x < 75$ are classified as 'long', those with $75 \le x \le 80$ as 'medium', and those with $x > 80$ as 'short'. The percentages of skulls in the three classes in this collection are respectively 58, 38 and 4. Find approximately the mean and standard deviation of x, on the assumption that x is normally distributed.

Ans. $\mu = 74·4$ (approx.), $\sigma = 3·2$ (approx.)

39. In a certain examination 15% of the candidates passed with distinction while 25% of them failed. It is known that a candidate fails if he obtains less than 40 marks (out of 100) while he must obtain at lest 75 marks in order to pass with distinction. Determine mean and standard deviation of the distribution of marks assuming this to be normal.

[*Delhi Univ. B.Com. (Hons.), 2006*]

Ans. $\mu = 53·715$; $\sigma = 20·47$ (approx.).

Hint. $P(Z \le -z_1) = ·25$ and $P(Z \ge z_2) = 0·15$

where $\quad -z_1 = \dfrac{40-\mu}{\sigma} = -0·67$ (approx.) $\quad$ ...(*) $\quad$ and $\quad z_2 = \dfrac{75-\mu}{\sigma} = 1·04$ (approx..) $\quad$ ...(**)

$\Rightarrow \quad 40 - \mu = -0·67\sigma \quad$ and $\quad 75 - \mu = 1·04\,\sigma$

Subtracting we get : $\quad 35 = 1·71\sigma \quad \Rightarrow \quad \sigma = \dfrac{35}{1·71} = 20·47$

Substituting in (*) : $\quad \mu = 40 + 0·67 \times 20·47 = 53·715$.

40. (*a*) A factory turns out an article by mass production methods. From past experience it appears that 10 articles on the average are rejected out of every batch of 100. Find the standard deviation of the number of rejects in a batch, and write down the equation to the normal curve which may be taken to represent the distribution of the number of rejects in a large series of batches of 100.

Ans. $\sigma = 3$; $\quad p(x) = \dfrac{1}{3\sqrt{2\pi}}\, e^{-(x-10)^2/18} \; ; -\infty < x < \infty$

(*b*) Five per cent of the electric bulbs manufactured by a company are defective. Using normal approximation, find the probability that in a sample of 400 bulbs, 30 or more will be defective.

Hint. Mean $(\mu) = np = 400 \times 0·05 = 20$; $\sigma^2 = npq = 400 \times 0·05 \times 0·95 = 19$; $P(X \ge 30) = P(Z \ge 2·29)$

Ans. 0·011.

41. There are 600 business students in the graduate department of an university, and the probability for any student to need a copy of a particular textbook from the university library on any day is 0·05. How many copies of the book should be kept in the university library so that the probability may be greater than 0·90 that none of the students needing a copy from the library has to come back disappointed ? (Use normal approximation to the binomial probability distribution).

Hint. We are given : $n = 600$, $p = 0·05$, $\mu = np = 600 \times 0·05 = 30$,

$\sigma^2 = npq = 600 \times 0·05 \times 0·95 = 28·5 \quad \Rightarrow \quad \sigma = \sqrt{28·5} = 5·3$ (approx.) We want x_1 such that $P(X \le x_1) > 0·90$.

Ans. More than 37 books.

42. If $X \sim N(\mu, \sigma^2)$, what is the value of

(*i*) Median (*ii*) Mode (*iii*) Quartile deviation (*iv*) Mean deviation about mean ?

Ans. (*i*) μ, (*ii*) μ, (*iii*) $0{\cdot}67\,\sigma \simeq \frac{2}{3}\sigma$, (*iv*) $\sqrt{\frac{2}{\pi}}\sigma \simeq \frac{4}{5}\sigma$

43. The distribution of a variable X is given by the *p.d.f* :

$$f(x) = \text{constant} \times \exp\left[-\frac{1}{2}\left(\frac{x-100}{5}\right)^2\right] \quad ; \quad -\infty < x < \infty$$

Write down the values of

(*i*) the constant, (*ii*) the mean, (*iii*) the median (*iv*) the mode (*v*) the standard deviation (*vi*) the mean deviation and (*vii*) the quartile deviation, of the distribution.

Ans. (*i*) $\frac{1}{\sqrt{2\pi}\times 5}$, (*ii*) 100, (*iii*) 100, (*iv*) 100, (*v*) 5, (*vi*) $\sqrt{\frac{2}{\pi}}\times 5 \simeq 4$, (*vii*) $\frac{2}{3}\times 5 = 3{\cdot}33$ (approx.)

44. For a random variable, the probability density function is expressed as :

$$p(x) = \sqrt{\left(\frac{2}{\pi}\right)}\, e^{-2(x-3)^2}, \; -\infty < x < \infty$$

(*i*) Identify the distribution.

(*ii*) Give the values of mean and standard deviation of the distribution.

(*iii*) Write down two important properties of the distribution.

Ans. (*i*) Normal distribution ; (*ii*) Mean $(\mu) = 3$, *s.d.* $(\sigma) = \frac{1}{2}$

(*iii*) Mean = Median = Mode ; $\beta_1 = 0$, $\beta_2 = 3$. Symmetry about mean.

45. (*a*) For a certain normal distribution, the first moment about 8 is 22 and the fourth moment about 30 is 243. Find the coefficient of variation of the distribution. [*Delhi Univ. B.Com. (Hons.), 2004*]

Ans. C.V. = 10

[**Hint.** Let $X \sim N(\mu, \sigma^2)$. Then we have : Mean $(\mu) = A + \mu_1' = 8 + 22 = 30$.

Fourth moment about 30 = Fourth moment about mean = $\mu_4 = 243$ ($\because$ Mean = 30)

$\Rightarrow \quad \mu_4 = 3\sigma^4$ (For Normal Distribution) $\Rightarrow \quad \sigma^4 = \frac{243}{3} = 81 \quad \Rightarrow \quad \sigma = 3$

$$\text{C.V.} = 100\frac{\sigma}{\mu} = \frac{100\times 3}{30} = 10$$

(*b*) For a certain normal distribution, the first moment about 10 is 40 and the fourth moment about 50 is 48. What is the arithmetic mean and standard deviation of the distribution ?

Ans. $\mu = 50, \quad \sigma = 2.$

46. (*a*) If X is a normal variable with mean 10 and variance (1/4), find the mode and show that the modal ordinate is $\sqrt{(2/\pi)}$. [*I.C.W.A (Intermediate), June 1999*]

47. If X be a normal variate with mean 50 and variance $\frac{1}{4}$, then the modal oridinate is

(*i*) $\frac{1}{50\sqrt{2\pi}}$; (*ii*) $\frac{1}{4\sqrt{2\pi}}$; (*iii*) $\frac{1}{2\sqrt{2\pi}}$; (*iv*) $\frac{1}{\sqrt{2\pi}}$.

[*I.C.W.A. (Intermediate), Dec. 1999*]

Ans. (*a*) Mode = 10 ; (*b*) (*iii*).

48. The p.d.f. of a normal distribution is :

$$f(x) = k.\exp\left[-\frac{(x-5)^2}{18}\right] \quad ; \quad -\infty < x < \infty$$

Find the values of k, mean and S.D.

Ans. Mean = 5 , S.D. $(\sigma) = 3$, $k = \frac{1}{3\cdot\sqrt{2\pi}}$

49. .(*a*) Criticise the following statements :

(*i*) The mean of a symmetrical binomial distribution is 5 and the number of trials is 12.

(*ii*) The mean of a Poisson distribution is 5 and the standard deviation is 3.

(*iii*) The mean of a normal distribution is 5 and the third order central moment (μ_3) is 2.

Ans. (*i*) Wrong. Data gives $p = 5/12$, but for symmetrical binomial distribution $p = \frac{1}{2}$.

(*ii*) Wrong, because for P.D., mean = variance.

(*iii*) Wrong, because for normal distribution $\mu_3 = 0$.

(*b*) A student obtained the following results. Comment on the accuracy of his results.

(*i*) For a binomial distribution mean = 4, variance = 3,

(*ii*) For a Poisson distribution, mean = 10, *s.d.* = 5

(*iii*) For a normal distribution, mean = 50, median = 52.

Ans. (*i*) Correct, (*ii*) Wrong, (*iii*) Wrong.

50. (*i*) What is the area under the normal curve within the range Mean ± 2·58 s.d. ?

[*C.A.* (*Foundation*), *May 2001*]

Ans. 99%.

(*ii*) The area under the normal probability curve within the range :

(*a*) Mean ± 1·96 S.D. = ..., (*b*) Mean ± 2 S.D. = ... , (*c*) Mean ± 3 S.D. = ..., (*d*) Mean ± 1·96 S.D.

Ans. (*a*) 95% (*b*) 0·9554 (*c*) 0·9973 (*d*) 0·95

15 Sampling Theory and Design of Sample Surveys

15·1. INTRODUCTION

The science of Statistics may be broadly studied under the following two headings :

(*a*) Descriptive,

(*b*) Inductive.

So far, (Chapter 1 to 11), we have confined the discussion to *Descriptive Statistics* which consists in describing some characteristics of the numerical data. The *Inductive Statistics*, also known as *Statistical Inference*, may be termed as the logic of drawing statistically valid conclusions about the totality of cases or items termed as *population*, in any statistical investigation on the basis of examining a part of the population, termed as *sample*, and which is drawn from the population in scientific manner. In modern '*decision making process*' in different fields of human activity, including the ordinary actions of our daily life, most of our decisions and attitudes depend very much upon the inspection or examination of only a few objects or items out of the total lot. This process of studying only the sample data and then generalising the results to the population (*i.e.,* drawing inferences about the population on the basis of sample study) involves an element of risk, the risk of making wrong decisions. Evaluation of this risk in terms of probability is discussed in Chapter 16. In this chapter will shall discuss the various techniques of drawing samples from the population.

15·2. UNIVERSE OR POPULATION

In any statistical investigation the interest usually lies in studying the various characteristics relating to items or individuals belonging to a particular group. This group of individuals under study is known as the *population* or *universe*. For example, if an enquiry is intended to determine the average per capita income of the people in a particular city, the population will comprise all the earning people in that city. On the other hand if we want to study the expenditure habits of the families in that city, then the population will consist of all the house-holds in that city. Further, if we want to study the quality of the manufactured product in an industrial concern during the day, then the population will consist of the day's total production. Thus, "*In Statistics, population is the aggregate of objects, animate or inanimate, under study in any statistical investigation*". In sampling theory, the population means the larger group from which the samples are drawn.

A population containing a finite number of objects or items is known as *finite population, e.g.,* the students in a college, the day's production in an industrial concern, the population of a city or a town, etc. On the other hand, a population having an infinite number of objects or with the number of objects so large as to appear practically infinite, is termed as an *infinite population, e.g.,* the population of temperatures at various points of thermosphere; the population of the heights, weights or ages of the people in the country (each of these variables can take *any* numerical value in a particular interval), the population of stars in the sky, etc. As will be seen later (Chapter 16), infinite populations are better for sampling studies. The population may further be classified as *existent* or *hypothetical*. A population consisting of concrete objects is known as *existent* population, *e.g.,* the population of (*i*) the books in a library, (*ii*) the aeroplanes in the Indian Air Force, (*iii*) the scooters in Delhi, etc. On the other hand, if the population does not consist of concrete objects, *i.e.,* it consists of imaginary objects then it is called *hypothetical* population. For instance, the populations of the throws of a die or a coin, thrown infinite number of times are hypothetical populations.

15·3. SAMPLING

A finite subset of the population, selected from it with the objective of investigating its properties is called a *sample* and the number of units in the sample is known as the *sample size.* Sampling is a tool which enables us to draw conclusions about the characteristics of the population after studying only those objects or items that are included in the sample.

The main objectives of the sampling theory are :

(*i*) To obtain the optimum results, *i.e.,* the maximum information about the characteristics of the population with the available sources at our disposal in terms of time, money and manpower by studying the sample values only.

(*ii*) To obtain the best possible estimates of the population parameters. [See § 15·4].

Although the scientific development of the theory of sampling has taken place only during the last few decades, the idea of sampling is very old. From times immemorial, people have been using it without knowing that some scientific procedure has been used in arriving at the conclusions. On inspecting the sample of a particular stuff, we arrive at a conclusion about accepting or rejecting it. For example, the consumer examines only a handful of the rice, pulses or any commodity in a shop to assess its quality and then decides to buy it or not. The housewife, usually tastes a spoonful of the cooked products to ascertain if it is properly cooked and also to see if it contains proper quantity of salt or sugar. The consumer ascertains the quality of the grapes by testing one or two from the seller's basket. The intelligence of the individuals in a subject is estimated by the university by giving them a 3-hour test. A businessman orders for the products after examining only a sample from it. In fact, the entire business is done on the basis of display of a few specimen samples only. The error involved in approximations about the population characteristics on the basis of the sample is known as *sampling error* and is inherent and unavoidable in any sampling scheme.

15·4. PARAMETER AND STATISTIC

The statistical constant of the population like mean (μ), variance (σ^2), skewness (β_1), kurtosis (β_2), moments (μ_r), correlation coefficient (ρ), etc., are known as *parameters*. We can compute similar statistical constants for the sample drawn from the given population. Prof. R.A. Fisher termed the statistical constants of the sample like mean ($\bar{x}$), variance (s^2), skewness (b_1), kurtosis (b_2), moments (m_r), correlation coefficient (r), etc., as *statistics*. Obviously, parameters are function of the population values while statistics are functions of the sample observations.

Let us consider a finite population of N units and let $y_1, y_2, \ldots, y_N$ be the observations on the N units in the population. Suppose we draw a sample of size n from this population. Let $x_1, x_2, \ldots, x_n$ be the observations on the sample units. Then we have, by definition :

$$\mu = \frac{1}{N}\left(y_1 + y_2 + \ldots + y_N\right) = \frac{1}{N}\sum_{i=1}^{N} y_i \qquad \ldots(15·1)$$

$$\sigma^2 = \frac{1}{N}\left[(y_1-\mu)^2 + (y_2-\mu)^2 + \ldots + (y_N-\mu)^2\right] = \frac{1}{N}\sum_{i=1}^{N}(y_i-\mu)^2 \qquad \ldots(15·2)$$

The sample mean ($\bar{x}$) and variance (s^2) are given by :

$$\bar{x} = \frac{1}{n}\left(x_1 + x_2 + \ldots + x_n\right) = \frac{1}{n}\sum_{i=1}^{n} x_i \qquad \ldots(15·3)$$

$$s^2 = \frac{1}{n}\left[(x_1-\bar{x})^2 + (x_2-\bar{x})^2 + \ldots + (x_n-\bar{x})^2\right] = \frac{1}{n}\sum_{i=1}^{n}(x_i-\bar{x})^2 \qquad \ldots(15·4)$$

Generally, the population parameters are unknown and their estimates provided by the appropriate sample statistics are used. Obviously, the sample statistics are functions of the sample observations and vary from sample to sample. Thus, if t is any general statistic, then we may write t as a function of the sample observations $x_1, x_2, \ldots, x_n$ as given below :

$$t = t\,(x_1, x_2, \ldots, x_n) \qquad \ldots(15\cdot5)$$

Remark. A statistic $t = t(x_1, x_2, \ldots, x_n)$ is said to be an *unbiased estimate of* the population parameter θ if $E(t) = \theta$. In other words, if

$$E(Statistic) = Parameter, \qquad \ldots(15\cdot5a)$$

then the statistic is said to be an unbiased estimate of the parameter.

15·4·1. Sampling Distribution. If we draw a sample of size n from a given finite population of size N, then the total number of possible samples is:

$$^{N}C_n = \frac{N\,!}{n\,!\,(N-n)\,!} = k, \text{ (say)}.$$

For each of these k sample we can compute some statistic $t = t\,(x_1, x_2, \ldots, x_n)$, in particular the mean $\bar{x}$, the variance s^2, etc., as given in Table 15·1.

TABLE 15·1

Sample Number	Statistic		
	t	$\bar{x}$	s^2
1	t_1	$\bar{x}_1$	s_1^2
2	t_2	$\bar{x}_2$	s_2^2
3	t_3	$\bar{x}_3$	s_3^2
⋮	⋮	⋮	⋮
k	t_k	$\bar{x}_k$	s_k^2

The set of the values of the statistic so obtained, one for each sample, constitutes what is called the *sampling distribution of the statistic*. For example, the values $t_1, t_2, t_3, \ldots, t_k$ determine the sampling distribution of the statistic t. In other words, statistic t may be regarded as a random variable which can take the values $t_1, t_2, t_3, \ldots, t_k$ and we can compute the various statistical constants like mean, variance, skewness kurtosis, etc., for its distribution. For example, the mean and variance of the sampling distribution of the statistic t are given by :

$$\bar{t} = \frac{1}{k}\left(t_1 + t_2 + \ldots + t_k\right) = \frac{1}{k}\sum_{i=1}^{k} t_i \qquad \ldots(15\cdot6)$$

$$\text{Var}\,(t) = \frac{1}{k}\left[(t_1 - \bar{t}\,)^2 + (t_2 - \bar{t}\,)^2 + \ldots + (t_k - \bar{t}\,)^2\right] = \frac{1}{k}\sum_{i=1}^{k}(t_i - \bar{t}\,)^2 \qquad \ldots(15\cdot7)$$

15·4·2. Standard Error. The standard deviation of the sampling distribution of a statistic is known as its *Standard Error* (*S.E.*). Thus, the Standard Error of the statistic t is given by :

$$S.E.\ (t) = \sqrt{\text{Var}\,(t)} = \sqrt{\left[\frac{1}{k}\sum_{i=1}^{k}(t_i - \bar{t}\,)^2\right]} \qquad \ldots(15\cdot8)$$

In particular the S.E. of the sampling distribution of the mean $\bar{x}$ is given by the standard deviation of the values $\bar{x}_1, \bar{x}_2, \ldots, \bar{x}_k$.

The derivation of the standard errors of the sampling distributions of various statistics is quite difficult and beyond the scope of the book. The standard errors of the sampling distributions of some of the well-known statistics, where n is the sample size, σ is the population standard deviation, P is the population proportion and $Q = 1 - P$, n_1 and n_2 represent the sizes of two samples respectively, is given in the Table 15·2.

TABLE 15·2. STANDARD ERROR OF IMPORTANT STATISTICS

S. No.	Statistic	Standard Error
1.	Sample mean ($\bar{x}$)	$\sigma / \sqrt{n}$
2.	Sample proportion 'p'	$\sqrt{PQ/n}$
3.	Sample standard deviation (s)	$\sqrt{\sigma^2 / 2n}$

4.	Sample variance (s^2)	$\sigma^2 \sqrt{2/n}$
5.	Sample median	$1.25331\sigma / \sqrt{n}$
6.	'r' = sample correlation coefficient	$(1-\rho^2)/\sqrt{n}$, ρ being the population correlation coefficient
7.	Difference of two independent sample means: $(\bar{x}_1 - \bar{x}_2)$	$\sqrt{\frac{\sigma_1^2}{n_1} + \frac{\sigma_2^2}{n_2}}$
8.	Difference of two independent sample s.d.'s : $(s_1 - s_2)$	$\sqrt{\frac{\sigma_1^2}{2n_1} + \frac{\sigma_2^2}{2n_2}}$
9.	Difference of two independent sample proportions : $(p_1 - p_2)$	$\sqrt{\frac{P_1Q_1}{n_1} + \frac{P_2Q_2}{n_2}}$

The above formulae for the standard errors are obtained in random sampling from an *infinite* population or from a very large population so that the sample size n is relatively very small as compared with the population size N and consequently n/N is neglected.

Remark. The reciprocal of the *S.E.* of a statistic gives a measure of the precision or reliability of the estimate of the parameter.

15·5. PRINCIPLES OF SAMPLING

The fact that the characteristics of the sample (sample statistics) provide a fairly good idea about the population characteristics (population parameters) is borne out by the theory of probability. We discuss below some important laws which form the basis of the sampling theory.

15·5·1. Law of Statistical Regularity. This law has its origin in the mathematical theory of probability. In the words of L.R. Conner, "*The law of statistical regularity lays down that a group of objects chosen at random from a larger group tends to possess the characteristics of that large group (universe)*". According to King "*the law of statistical regularity lays down that the moderately large number of items chosen at random from a large group are almost sure on the average to possess the characteristics of the large group.*

The principle of statistical regularity impresses upon the following two points :

(*i*) *large sample size.* Logically, it seems that as the sample size increases, the sample is more likely to reveal the true characteristics of the population and thus provide better estimates of the parameters. It is known that the reliability of the sample statistic as an estimate of the population parameter is proportional to the square root of the sample size n. But due to certain limitations in terms of time, money and manpower, it is not always possible to take very large samples. Moreover, the effort and cost of drawing large samples might outlive the utility of the sample study as against the complete enumeration (census).

(*ii*) *Random selection.* The sample should be selected at random from the population. By random selection we mean a selection in which each and every unit in the population has an equal chance of being selected in the sample.

If a sample is selected such that the above two conditions are statisfied, then it will depict the true characteristics of the population fairly accurately and can be used for drawing valid inferences about the population. For example, if we are interested in studying the average height of the students in Delhi University, then it is not desirable to resort to 100% enumeration of the students in the university. A fairly adequate sample of the students from each college may be selected at random and the average height of the students selected in the samples may be computed. Since the sample is random, it would be representative of the population and the average so obtained will not differ much from the true value (*i.e.,* the average computed by the complete enumeration). This difference is attributed to fluctuations of sampling. [For detailed discussion of drawing random samples, see Simple Random Sampling, § 15·11 and Stratified Random Sampling, § 15·12].

15·5·2. Principle of Inertia of Large Numbers. An immediate deduction from the Principle of Statistical Regularity is the *Principle of Inertia of Large Numbers* which states, "*Other things being equal, as the sample size increases, the results tend to be more reliable and accurate*". This is based on the fact that the behaviour of a phenomenon *on mass, i.e.,* on a large scale is generally stable. By this we mean that if individual events are observed, their behaviour may be erratic and unpredictable but when a large number of events are considered, they tend to behave in a stable pattern. This is because a number of forces operate on the given phenomenon and if the units are large, then the typical odd variations in one part of the universe in one direction will get neutralised by the variations in equally bigger part of the universe in the other direction. According to A.L. Bowley, "*Great numbers and averages resulting from them, such as we always obtain in measuring social phenomena, have a great inertia.*" Thus, in dealing with large number, the variation in the component parts tend to balance each other and consequently the variation in the aggregate result is likely to be insignificant. However, it should not be inferred that in case of large numbers, there is no variation at all. Large numbers are relatively more stable in their characteristics than the small numbers. They (large numbers) also exhibit variations but they are of very small magnitude and intensity and are not violent in nature. For example, if a coin is tossed, say, 20 times then nothing can be said with certainty about the proportion of heads. We may get 0, 1, 2, ..., or even all the 20 heads. But if it is thrown at random a very large number of times, say, 5,000 times, then we may expect on the average 50% heads and 50% tails. As another illustration, let us consider the production of a particular commodity, say, rice in two districts in a State for a number of years. The figures will show great variations due to favourable or unfavourable conditions in that particular region. However, the figures for the production of rice for the whole State over number of years will show relatively lesser variations because lower production in some of districts will be compensated by the excessive production in some other districts of the State. Arguing similarly, we find that the production figures for the whole of India will show still lesser variation and for the entire world it would be more or less stable.

15·5·3. Principle of Persistence of Small Numbers. If some of the items in a population possess markedly distinct characteristics from the remaining items, then this tendency would be revealed in the sample values also. Rather this tendency of persistence will be there even if the population size is increased or even in the case of large samples. For example, if the day's production of any manufacturing unit is made 4 times, the proportion of defectives in the lot remains more or less same. This means that the number of defectives in the lot will also increase more or less in the same proportion. Similarly, if a random sample of size n from the lot gives a fraction defective,

$$p = \frac{1}{n} \times (\text{Number of defectives in the sample}),$$

and if the sample size is doubled or trebled, the fraction defective will more or less remain same.

15·5·4. Principle of Validity. A sampling design is termed as valid if it enables us to obtain valid tests and estimates about the population parameters. This principle is satisfied by the samples drawn by the technique of probability sampling discussed in 15·10·2.

15·5·5. Principle of Optimisation. This principle stresses the need of obtaining optimum results in terms of *efficiency* and *cost* of the sampling design with the sources available at our disposal. As has been pointed out earlier, a measure of efficiency or reliability of an estimate of the population parameter is provided by the reciprocal of the standard error of the estimate and the cost of the design is determined by the total expenses incurred in terms of money and manpower. This principle aims at :

(*i*) obtaining a desired level of efficiency at minimum cost and

(*ii*) obtaining maximum possible efficiency with given level of cost.

15·6. CENSUS VERSUS SAMPLE ENUMERATION

For any statistical enquiry in any field of humans activity, whether it is in business, economics or social sciences, the basic problem is to obtain adequate and reliable data relating to the particular phenomenon under study. There are two methods of collecting the data :

(*i*) The Census Method or Complete Enumeration.

(*ii*) The Sample Method or Partial Enumeration.

Census Method. In the census method we resort to 100% inspection of the population and enumerate each and every unit of the population. In the sample method we inspect only a selected representative and adequate fraction (finite subset) of the population and after analysing the results of the sample data we draw coclusions about the characteristics of the population.

The census method seems to provide more accurate and exact information as compared to sample enumeration as the information is collected from each and every unit of the population. Moreover, it affords more extensive and detailed study. For instance, the population census conducted by the Government of India every 10 years collects information not only about the population but also obtains data relating to age, marital status, occupation, religion, education, employment, income, property, etc. The census method has its obvious limitations and drawbacks given below :

(*i*) The complete enumeration of the population requires lot of time, money, manpower and administrative personnel. As such this method can be adopted only by the government and big organisations who have vast resources at their disposal.

(*ii*) Since the entire population is to be enumerated, the census method is usually very time consuming. If the population is sufficiently large, then it is possible that the processing and the analysis of the data might take so much time that when the results are available they are not of much use because of changed conditions.

Remark. *When to use Census Method* ? Census method is recommended in the following situations :

(*a*) If the information is required about each and every unit of the population, there is no way but to resort to 100% enumeration.

(*b*) In any manufacturing process in industry, 100% enumeration should be taken recourse to under the following conditions :

(*i*) The occurrence of a defect may cause loss of life or serious casualty to personnel.

(*ii*) A defect may cause serious malfunction of the equipment.

It may also be desirable to carry out complete census if,

(*i*) N, the lot size is small and

(*ii*) the incoming lot quality is poor or unknown.

Sample Method. The sample method has a number of distinct advantages over the complete enumeration method. Prof. R.A. Fisher sums up the advantages of sampling techniques over complete census in just four words : *Speed, Economy, Adaptability and Scientific Approach.* A properly designed and carefully executed sampling plan yields fairly good results, often better than those obtained by the census method. We now summarise the merits of the sample method over the census method.

1. *Speed, i.e., less time.* Since only a part of the population is to be inspected and examined, the sample method results in considerable amount of saving in time and labour. There is saving in time not only in conducting the sampling enquiry but also in the processing, editing and analysing the data. This is a very sensitive and important point for the statistical investigations where the results are urgently and quickly needed.

2. *Economy, i.e., Reduced Cost of the Enquiry.* The sample method is much more economical than a complete census. In a sample enquiry, there is reduction in the cost of collection of the information, administration, transport, training and man hours. Although, the labour and the expenses of obtaining information per unit are generally large in a sample enquiry than in the census method, the overall expenses of a sample survey are relatively much less, since only a fraction of the population is to be enumerated. This is particularly significant in conducting socio-economic surveys in developing countries with budding economies who cannot afford a complete census because of lack of finances.

3. *Administrative Convenience.* A complete census requires a very huge administrative set up involving lot of personnel, trained investigators and above all the co-ordination between the various operating agencies. On the other hand, the organisation and administration of a sample survey is relatively much convenient as it requires less personnel staff and the field of enquiry is also limited.

4. *Reliability.* In the census, the sampling errors are completely absent. If the non-sampling errors are also absent the results would be 100% accurate. (For sampling and non-sampling errors see § 15·9.] On the other hand, a sample enquiry contains both sampling and non-sampling errors. In spite of this weakness, a carefully designed and scientifically executed sample survey gives results which are more reliable than those obtained from a complete census. This is because of the following reasons :

(*a*) It is always possible to ascertain the extent of sampling error and degree of reliability of the results. Even the desired degree of accuracy can be achieved through sampling using different devices.

(*b*) The non-sampling errors such as due to measuring and recording observations, inaccuracy or incompleteness of informations, location of units, non-response or incomplete response, training of investigators, interpretation of questions, bias of the investigators, etc., are of a more serious nature in a complete census. In a sample survey these errors can be effectively controlled and minimised by

(*i*) employing highly qualified, skilled and trained personnel,

(*ii*) imparting adequate training to the investigators for conducting the enquiry,

(*iii*) better supervision,

(*iv*) using more sophisticated equipment and statistical techniques for the processing and analysis of the relatively limited data.

Lastly, follow-up work in case of non-response or incomplete response can be effectively undertaken in a sample survey than in a census. The effective reduction of the non-sampling errors in a sample survey more than compensates the errors in the estimates due to sampling procedure and thus provides relatively more accurate and reliable results. The efficiency of the sampling procedure lies in the fact that quite often the accuracy of the results of a complete census is ascertained by using some type of sampling check procedure.

5. *Greater Scope.* It appears that there is possibility of obtaining detailed information only in a complete census where each and every unit in the population is enumerated. But in practice because of our limitations in any statistical enquiry in terms of time, money and man hours and because of the fact that sampling procedure results in considerable savings in time, money and labour, it is possible to obtain more detailed and exhaustive information from the limited few units selected in the sample. Obviously, it is relatively easy to collect information on, say, 25 questions from each of 100 units selected in the sample than to obtain the information on, say, 10 questions from each of 1,000 units in the population. Moreover, complete enumeration is impracticable, rather inconceivable if the enquiry requires highly trained personnel and more sophisticated equipment for the collection, processing and analysis of the data. The sampling procedure is more readily adaptable than census for statistical investigations.

6. *Infinite or / and Hypothetical Population.* If the population is inifinite or too large, then sampling procedure is the only way of estimating the parameters of a population. For instance, the number of fish in the sea or the number of wild elephants in a dense forest can be estimated only by sampling method.

Similarly, in case of hypothetical population, as for example in the problem of throwing a die or tossing a coin, where the process may continue large number of times or indefinitely, the sampling procedure is the only scientific technique of estimating the parameters of the population.

7. *Destructive Testing.* If the testing of units is destructive *i.e.*, if in the course of inspection the units are destroyed or affected adversely, then we are left with no other way but to resort to sampling. For example :

(*i*) to estimate the average life of the bulbs or tubes in a given consignment,

(*ii*) to determine the composition of a chemical salt,

(*iii*) to test the breaking strength of chalks manufactured in a factory or to estimate the tensile strength of the steel rods.

(*iv*) to test the quality of explosives, crackers, shells, etc.,

we have to inspect a representative sample, since complete census will destroy all the items.

15·7. LIMITATIONS OF SAMPLING

The merits of sample surveys over complete enumeration can be realised only if :

(*i*) the sample is drawn in a scientific manner,

(*ii*) the appropriate sampling design is used, and

(*iii*) the sample size is adequate.

In spite of the above merits of the sample survey over census, the sampling procedure has its limitations and problems which are enumerated below :

(*i*) If a sample survey is not properly planned (or designed) and executed carefully, the results obtained will not be reliable and quite often might even be misleading. In this context, it may be worthwhile to quote the words of Frederick F. Stephen :

"*Samples are like medicines. They can be harmful when they are taken carelessly or without knowledge of their effects.... Every good sample should have a proper lable with instructions about its use*".

Sampling design must be perfect otherwise it might lead to serious complications in the final results. The omission of a few units in a complete census may be immaterial but non-response or incomplete response from even one or two units in a small sample might have a significant effect on the final result.

(*ii*) An efficient sampling scheme requires the services of qualified, skilled and experienced personnel, better supervision and more sophisticated equipment and statistical techniques for the planning and execution of the survey and for the collection, processing and analysis of the sample data. In the absence of these, the results of the survey may not be reliable.

(*iii*) Sometimes the sample survey might require more time, money and labour than a complete census. This will be so if the sample size is a large proportion of the population size and if complicated weighted system is used.

(*iv*) Sampling procedure cannot be used if we want to obtain information about each and every unit of the population. Further, if the population is too heterogeneous, it may be impossible to use a sampling procedure.

(*v*) Each sampling procedure, discussed in § 15·11 to § 15·16 has its own limitations.

15·8. PRINCIPAL STEPS IN A SAMPLE SURVEY

The following are the principal steps in the planning and execution of the sample surveys :

1. Objectives and Scope of the Survey. As in any statistical investigation, the first step in organising a sampling survey is to define in clear and concrete terms the objectives and scope of the survey. This is of immense help in deciding about the type of data to be collected and also the statistical techniques to be used for the processing and analysis of the data. In the absence of the purpose of the enquiry being explicitly specified, we are bound to collect some irrelevant information which is never used subsequently and also omit some important information which will ultimately lead to fallacious conclusions and wastage of resources. It should be kept in mind that these objects of the survey are commensurate with the sources available at our disposal in terms of cost (money), labour and time limit within which the results of the survey are desired.

2. Defining the Population to be Sampled. The population from which units are to be sampled should be defined clearly without any ambiguity. For example, in field experimentation, the field should be clearly defined in terms of the shape, size, etc., keeping in mind the border line cases so that nothing is left at the discretion of the investigator.

Due to certain practical limitations and problems in dealing with certain units of the population, they are usually eliminated from the scope of the survey. Accordingly, the population from which samples are drawn, usually termed as *sampled population* is usually different, rather much more restricted than the population for which results are desired, usually called the *target population*.

3. The Frame and Sampling Units. The population must be capable of division into what are called *sampling units*. In a sample survey, the sampling units are the units into which the population to be sampled is divided. These units are units of enumeration, *i.e.,* the units on which the observations are to be made. It may be an individual person, a household, a family, a farm, a shop, a firm, a livestock or a block in a locality. A sampling unit should be unambiguous, specific, stable and appropriate to the enquiry. [For details see Chapter 2, § 2·1·2.]

In order to draw a samples of villages in a State, we must have a map of the districts and villages of that state; for selecting house-holds, we must have a list of blocks in the locality; for selecting a group of students in a college, the list of students enrolled in the college is needed. This map, list or other acceptable material which serves as a guide for the population to be covere d is known as the *frame*. The frame may not contain a detailed information about the sampling units. What is desired is that it should have at least enough information so as to enable us to identify and locate the sampling units properly for statistical investigation. An up-to-date and good frame is very important to obtain efficient results in a sample survey because the structure of the sample survey is determined by the *frame*. A frame which is routinely prepared for some purpose should be used only after careful scrutiny and examination as it is usually found to be incomplete or it contains an unknown amount of duplication. Before using such a frame it should be ascertained that it is up-to-date, and free from these defects of incompleteness and duplication. if it is not up-to-date, it should be made so before using it.

4. Data to be Collected. The decision about the type of the data to be collected should be taken keeping in view the nature, objectives and the scope of the survey, the time and finances at our disposal and the degree of accuracy aimed at in the final results. Attempt should be made to eliminate the collection of irrelevant and unnecessary data which are never used subsequently and to ensure that no important or essential information is omitted. An outlying of the tables needed for the results of the survey is quite helpful in this regard.

5. The Questionnaire or Schedule. After deciding about the nature of statistics to be collected, the next step is the preparation of the questionnaire (to be filled by the respondents) or schedule of enquiry (to be completed by the investigators after interviewing people) for collecting the requisite information. The drafting of the questionnaire is a highly specialised job and requires great skill, wisdom, care, efficiency and experience. The questionnaire or the schedule should be designed and drafted with utmost care and caution, keeping in view the knowledge, understanding and the general educational level of respondents. [For detailed discussion on Drafting or Framing the Questionnaire see Chapter 2, § 2·4.]

6. Method of Collecting Information. There are two methods commonly used for obtaining numerical data for human population :

(*i*) Direct Personal Investigation or Interview Method. [For details see Chapter 2, § 2·3·1.]

(*ii*) Mailed Questionnaire Method. [For details see Chapter 2, § 2·3·4.]

A choice between the two methods depends on the objectives of the enquiry, the expenses involved and the accuracy of the results aimed at.

7. Non-Respondents. Due to certain practical problems, it may not be possible to obtain information from each of the sampled units. For instance, if the data are collected by the interview method, the respondent may not be available at his place in spite of repeated visits by the investigator. Similarly, if mailed questionaire method is used, a number of respondents may not return the questionaire at all, while others may supply haphazard, vague, in-complete and un-intelligible information which may not be of much use. This incompleteness of information, known as *non-response*, is very likely to change the results of the survey. In case of large proportion of non-response, the results based on the information supplied by a very small proportion of the selected individuals cannot be regarded as reliable. Attempts should be made to minimise non-response and the reasons for non-response should be recorded by the investigator.

8. Selection of Proper Sampling Design. A judicious decision about the sampling plan to be adopted is of paramount importance in the planning and execution of a sample survey. From among the several available Sampling Designs like Simple Random Sampling, Stratified Random Sampling, Systematic Sampling, etc.[discussed in § 15·11 to 15·16], an appropriate sampling design should be selected, keeping in view the objective of the survey, the nature of the population to be sampled, expenses involved, the time required for the availability of the results and the degree of the precision aimed at. A proper choice of the sampling scheme is of paramount importance in a sample survey. As has been pointed out earlier, a properly and scientifically designed and carefully executed sampling plan might yield results which are even more reliable than those obtained in a complete census. On the other hand, an ill-planned and vaguely executed sampling plan will give results which will not be reliable and quite often may be misleading.

9. Organisation of Field Work. To obtain reliable results in a sample survey, the sampling errors should be minimised. For this it is essential that the field work is properly organised and the personnel engaged in the conducting and execution of the survey should be properly trained to handle the problems of the survey like locating the sample units, use of the equipment and recording of the observations, the methods of collecting the desired information, dealing with non-response, etc. It is also desirable to provide for adequate and frequent supervisory check on the field work.

10. Pilot survey or Pre-Test. From practical point of view it is found useful to conduct a *pre-test* or a guiding survey known as *Pilot Survey*, on a small scale before starting the main survey. This is done to try out the questionnaire and the field methods for obtaining the general information about the population to be sampled. The information supplied by the pilot survey helps in :

(*i*) Estimating the cost of the main sample survey and also the time needed for the availability of the results.

(*ii*) Improving the organisation of the field work by removing the defects or faults observed in the pilot survey.

(*iii*) Formulating effective methods of asking questions and also in the improvement of the questionnaire.

(*iv*) Training of field staff.

(*v*) Disclosing certain problems or troubles that may otherwise be of a serious nature in a large scale main survey.

11. Summary and Analysis of the Data. After the planning and execution of the sample survey, the last step is the analysis of the collected data. It basically involves the following steps :

(*i*) Scrutiny and Editing of the data.

(*ii*) Tabulation of data.

(*iii*) Statistical analysis.

(*iv*) Reports, summary and conclusions.

Appropriate statistical techniques and formulae should be used for obtaining the estimates of desired information. Efforts should be made to minimise the error at each stage. The report should contain a statement of the details of the different stages of the survey, the types of the estimates obtained along with their precisions and so on.

15·9. ERRORS IN STATISTICS

In Statistics, the word 'error' is used to denote the difference between the true value and the estimated or approximated value. In other words 'error' refers to the difference between the true value of a population parameter and its estimate provided by an appropriate sample statistic computed by some statistical device. Thus, in Statistics, the term error is used in a different and much restricted sense. It should be distinguished from mistake or inaccuracies which may be committed in the course of making observations, counting, calculations, etc. These errors in Statistics arise due to a number of factors such as :

(*i*) *Approximations in measurements, e.g.,* the heights of individuals may be approximated to 10th of a centimetre, age may be measured correct to nearest month, weight may be measured correct to 10th of a kilogram, distance may be measured correct to the nearest metre and so on. Thus, in all such measurements, there is bound to be a difference between the observed value and the true value.

(*ii*) *Approximations in rounding* of the figures to the nearest hundreds, thousands, millions, etc., or in the *rounding of decimals.*

(*ii*) The *biases*, due to faulty collection and analysis of the data and biases in the presentation and interpretation of the results.

(*iv*) Personal *biases* of the investigators, and so on.

In any statistical investigation, these errors *i.e.,* the discrepancies between the estimated and the actual values are the net effect of a multiplicity of factors and can be broadly classified into two groups discussed below.

15·9·1. Sampling and Non-Sampling Errors. The inaccuracies or errors in any statistical investigation, *i.e.,* in the collection, processing, analysis and interpretation of the data may be broadly classified as follows :

(*i*) *Sampling Errors* and (*ii*) *Non-Sampling Errors.*

Sampling Errors. In a sample survey, since only a small portion of the population is studied, its results are bound to differ from the census results and thus have a certain amount of error. This error would always be there, no matter that the sample is drawn at random and that it is highly representative. This error is attributed to fluctuations of sampling and is called *sampling error*. Sampling error is due to the fact that only a subset of the population (*i.e.,* sample) has been used to estimate the population parameters and draw inferences about the population. Thus, sampling error is present only in a sample survey and is completely absent in census method.

Sampling errors are primarily due to the following reasons :

1. *Faulty selection of the sample.* Some of the bias is introduced by the use of defective sampling technique for the selection of a sample, *e.g.,* purposive or judgment sampling in which the investigator deliberately selects a representative sample to obtain certain results. This bias can be overcome by strictly adhering to a simple random sample or by selecting a sample at random subject to restrictions which while improving the accuracy are of such nature that they do not introduce bias in the results.

2. *Substitution.* If difficulties arise in enumerating a particular sampling unit included in the random sample, the investigators usually substitute a convenient member of the population. This obviously leads to some bias since the characteristics possessed by the substituted unit will usually be different from those possessed by the unit originally included in the sample.

3. *Faulty demarcation of sampling units.* Bias due to defective demarcation of sampling units is particularly significant in area surveys such as agricultural experiments in the field or crop cutting surveys, etc. In such surveys, while dealing with border-line cases, it depends more or less on the discretion of the investigator whether to include them in the sample or not.

4. *Error due to bias in the estimation method.* Sampling method consists in estimating the parameters of the population by appropriate statistics computed from the sample. Improper choice of the estimation techniques might introduce the error. For example, in simple random sampling, if $x_1, x_2, \ldots, x_n$ are observations on the n sampled units, then the sample variance

$$s^2 = \frac{1}{n} \sum_{i=1}^{n} (x_i - \bar{x})^2$$

is a biased estimate of the population variance σ^2, while an unbiased estimate of σ^2 is given by

$$S^2 = \frac{1}{n-1} \sum_{i=1}^{n} (x_i - \bar{x})^2$$

5. *Variability of the population.* Sampling error also depends on the variability or heterogeneity of the population to be sampled.

Remarks 1. An important feature of the sampling errors is that they follow random or chance variations and tend to cancel out each other on averaging. The statistic computed from the sample differs from the true value of the parameter due to fluctuations of sampling . If a number of independent samples of the same size are drawn form the given population then the same statistic computed for each of the samples will also vary from sample to sample. But the average of the sampling distribution of the statistic *i.e.,* the expected value of the statistic can be expected to equal the true parameter value.

2. A measure of the sampling error is provided by the standard error of the estimate. The knowledge and estimation of the sampling error reduces the element of uncertainty. The reliability or efficiency of a sampling plan is determined by the reciprocal of the standard error of the estimate and is called the *precision* of the estimate. In a sample survey, attempt is made to minimise this sampling error, which is same as increasing the precision of the estimate. In most of the situations it has been observed that standard error of the estimate is inversely proportional to the square root of the sample size. [See Table 15·2. § 15·4·2].

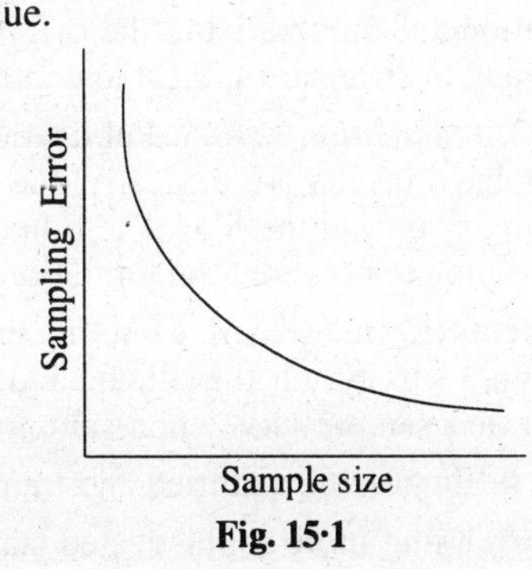

Fig. 15·1

In other words, the reliability or efficiency of the sampling design, which is thus directly proportional to the square root of the sample size, can be increased by taking large samples as shown in Fig. 15·1. However, the sample size can be increased only up to certain limits, keeping in view the time and money factors at our disposal, otherwise the very purpose of the sample survey will be defeated.

Non-Sampling Errors. Non-sampling errors are not attributed to chance and are a consequence of certain factors which are within human control. In other words, they are due to certain causes which can be traced and may arise at any stage of the enquiry, *viz.*, planning and execution of the survey and collection, processing and analysis of the data. Non-sampling errors are thus present both in census surveys as well as sample surveys. Obviously, non-sampling errors will be of large magnitude in a census survey than in a sample survey because they increase with the increase in the number of units to be examined and enumerated. It is very difficult to prepare an exhaustive list of all the sources of non-sampling errors. We enumerate below some of the important factors responsible for non-sampling errors in any survey (census or sample).

1. Faulty planning, including vague and faulty definitions of the population or the statistical units to be used, incomplete list of population-members (*i.e.*, incomplete frame in case of sample survey).

2. Vague and imperfect questionnaire which might result in incomplete or wrong information.

3. Defective methods of interviewing and asking questions.

4. Vagueness about the type of the data to be collected.

5. Exaggerated or wrong answers to the questions which appeal to the pride or prestige or self-interest of the respondents. For example, a person may over-state his education or income or understate his age or he may give wrong statements to safeguard his self-interest.

6. Personal bias of the investigator.

7. Lack of trained and qualified investigators and lack of supervisory staff.

8. Failure of respondents' memory to recall the events or happenings in the past.

9. *Non-response and Inadequate or Incomplete Response.* Bias due to non-response results if in a house-to-house survey the respondent is not available in spite of repeated visits by the investigator or if the respondent refuses to furnish the information. Incomplete response error is introduced if the respondent is unable to furnish information on certain questions or if he is unwilling or even refuses to answer certain questions.

10. *Improper coverage.* If the objects of the survey are not precisely stated in clear cut terms, this may result in

(*i*) the inclusion in the survey of certain units which are to be excluded, or

(*ii*) the exclusion of certain units which were to be included in the survey under the objectives.

For example, in a census to determine the number of individuals in the age group, say, 15 years to 55 years, more or less serious errors may occur in deciding whom to enumerate unless particular community or area is not specified and also the time at which the age is to be specified.

11. *Compiling Errors, i.e.,* wrong calculations or entries made during the processing and analysis of the data. Various operations of data processing such as editing and coding of the responses, punching of cards, tabulation and summarising the original observations made in the survey are a potential source of error. Compilation errors are subject to control *through verification, consistency checks, etc.*

12. *Publication Errors.* Publication errors, *i.e.,* the errors committed during presentation and printing of tabulated results are basically due to two sources. The first refers to the mechanics of publication-the proofing error and the like. The other, which is of a more serious nature, lies in the failure of the survey organisation to point out the limitations of the statistics.

Remark. In a census, sampling error is completely absent so that the total error is non-sampling error. A sample survey, on the other hand, contains both sampling and non-sampling errors. As pointed out earlier, in a sample survey non-sampling errors can be effectively controlled by :

(*i*) Employing qualified and trained personnel for the planning and execution of the survey ;

(*ii*) Using more sophisticated statistical techniques and equipment for the processing and analysis of the data.

(*iii*) Providing adequate supervisory checks on the field work.

(*iv*) Pre-testing or conducting a pilot survey.

(*v*) Through editing and scrutiny of the results.

(*vi*) Effective checking of all the steps in the processing and analysis of the data.

(*vii*) More effective follow up of non-response cases.

(*viii*) Imparting thorough training to the investigators for efficient conduct of the enquiry.

Moreover, the sampling error in a sample survey can be minimised by taking an adequately large sample selected by an appropriate sampling plan. The selection of the sample by 'Probability Samplings' such as Simple Random Sampling, Stratified Random Sampling, Systematic Sampling, etc., [See § 15·10·2; § 15·11; § 15·12, § 15·13], usually gives quite reliable results. In practice, the use of simple random sampling with suitable adaption of stratification of the universe if it is heterogeneous, or the technique of multistage random sampling if there are clearly demarcated stages, gives fairly good results, often better than those given by a complete census.

15·9·2. Biased and Unbiased Errors. In any statistical investigation, whether a complete census or a sample survey, the statistical errors can also be classified as :

(*a*) *Biased Errors* and (*b*) *Unbiased Errors.*

Biased Errors. Biased errors creep in because of :

(*i*) Bias on the part of the enumerator or investigator whose personal beliefs and prejudices are likely to affect the results of the enquiry.

(*ii*) Bias in the measuring instrument or the equipment used for recording the observations.

(*iii*) Bias due to faulty collection of the data, and in the statistical techniques and the formulae used for the analysis of the data.

(*iv*) *Respondents' bias.* An appeal to the pride or prestige of an individual introduces a bias called *prestige* bias by virtue of which he may upgrade his education, occupation, income, etc., or understate his age, thus resulting in wrong answers. Moreover, respondents may furnish wrong information to safeguard their personal interests. For example, for income-tax purposes a person may give an under-statement of his salary or income or assets.

(*v*) *Bias due to Non-response.* [See item 9, Non-sampling Errors.]

(*vi*) *Bias in the Technique of Approximations.* If, while rounding off, each individual value is either approximated to next highest or lowest number so that all the errors move in the same direction, there is bias for overstatement or understatement respectively, For example, if the figures are to be rounded off to the next highest or lowest hundred then each of the values 305 and 396 will be recorded as 400 and 300 respectively.

Owing to their nature, the biased errors have a tendency to grow in magnitude with an increase in the number of the observations and hence are also known as *Cumulative Errors.* Thus, the *magnitude of the biased errors is directly proportional to the number of observations.*

Unbiased Errors. The errors are termed as *unbiased errors* if the estimated or approximated values are likely to err on either side, *i.e.,* if the chances of making an over-estimate is almost same as the chance of making an under-estimate. Since these errors move in both the directions, the errors in one direction are more or less neutralised by the errors in the opposite direction and consequently the ultimate result is not much affected. For example, if the individual values, say, 385, 415, 355, 445 are rounded to the *nearest complete unit, i.e.,* hundred, each one of them would be recorded as 400. In this case the values 385 and 355 give *over-estimating errors* of magnitudes 15 and 45 respectively wile the values 415 and 445 give *under-estimating* errors of magnitudes 15 and 45 respectively and in the ultimate result (approximation) they get neutralised. Thus, if the number of observations is quite large, these unbiased errors will not affect the final result much. Since the errors in one direction compensate for the errors in the other direction, unbiased errors are also termed as *Compensatory Errors.* Thus we observe that the unbiased errors do not grow with the increase in the number of observations but they have a tendency to get neutralised and are minimum in the ultimate analysis and *the magnitude of the unbiased errors is inversely proportional to the number of items.*

15·9·3. Measures of Statistical Errors (Absolute and Relative Errors). A measure of the statistical errors is provided by absolute and relative errors.

Absolute Error. An absolute error (*A.E.*) is the difference between the true value of any particular observed item or variable and its estimated or approximated value. Symbolically, we may write :

$$AE = |a - e|, \qquad \ldots(15\cdot9)$$

where a is the actual value and e is the estimated value and $|a - e|$ represents the modulus value of $(a - e)$ after ignoring the negative sign. For example, if a value 54,87350 is approximated to the nearest lakh, it can be taken as 55 lakhs. Thus

$$AE = |a - e| = |54{,}87{,}350 - 55{,}00{,}000| = |-12{,}650| = 12{,}650$$

The magnitude of the absolute error is quite independent of the magnitude of the actual value. For example, in the above case AE remains same for all those values which have the digit in the 10 thousand place greater than 5. Consequently, absolute errors cannot be compared meaningfully. For example, the above error of 12,650 in a value of 54,87,350 may be quite insignificant or immaterial as compared with an absolute error of 10 in a value of 500. Moreover, these errors are in the units of measurement and as such *AE*s in different units can't be compared meaningfully. In order to facilitate comparison of the errors, they are reduced to pure numbers which are independent of the units of measurement. This is done by calculating the *Relative Error* (*R.E.*) which is defined as the ratio of the absolute error to the actual value. Symbolically,

$$RE = \frac{AE}{\text{Actual value}} = \frac{|a - e|}{a} \qquad \ldots(15\cdot10)$$

Thus in the above example, *RE* which relates the magnitude of the error to the magnitude of the true value, is given by

$$RE = \frac{12{,}650}{54{,}87{,}350} = 0\cdot0023$$

The relative error may also be expressed as percentage.

$$\text{Percentage } RE = \frac{12{,}650}{54{,}87{,}3500} \times 100 = 0\cdot23$$

In statistical analysis, relative error is a much more useful measure than the absolute error as it provides a useful coefficient, (a pure number independent of units of measurement), for comparing the degree of the error of different sets of data.

15·10. TYPES OF SAMPLING

The choice of an appropriate sampling design is of paramount importance in the execution of a sample survey and is generally made keeping in view the objectives and scope of the enquiry and the type of the universe to be sampled. The sampling techniques may be broadly classified as follows :

(*i*) *Purposive or Subjective or Judgment Sampling.*

(*ii*) *Probability Sampling.*

(*iii*) *Mixed Sampling.*

15·10·1. Purposive or Subjective or Judgment Sampling. In this method, a desired number of sample units is selected deliberately or purposely depending upon the object of the enquiry so that only the important items representing the true characteristics of the population are included in the sample.

An obvious and serious drawback of this sampling scheme is that it is highly subjective in nature, since the selection of the sample depends entirely on the personal convenience, beliefs, biases and prejudices of the investigator. For example, if in a socio-economic survey it is desired to study the standard of living of the people in New Delhi and if the investigator wants to show that the standard has gone down, then he may include individuals in the samples only from the low income stratum of the society and exclude the people from the posh colonies like South Extension, Greater Kailash, Jor Bagh, Chanakyapuri and so on. This method cannot be worked out for large samples and is expected to give good results in small samples only provided the selection of the sample is representative. This can be achieved if the investigator is thoroughly skilled and experienced in the field of enquiry and knows the limitations of such a selection. Further, since this scheme does not involve the principle of probability, estimation of the sampling error depends upon the hypothesis which are rarely met in practice.

15·10·2. Probability Sampling. Probability sampling provides a scientific technique of drawing samples from the population according to some laws of chance in which each unit in the universe has some definite pre-assigned probability of being selected in the sample. Different types of sampling are in which :

(*i*) Each sample unit has an equal chance of being selected.
(*ii*) Sampling units have varying probability of being selected.
(*iii*) Probability of selection of a unit is proportional to the sample size.

15·10·3. Mixed Sampling. Sampling design in which the sample units are selected partly according to some probability laws, [given in § 15·10·2 (*i*), (*ii*), (*iii*)] and partly according to a fixed sampling rule (no use of chance), is known as *Mixed Sampling*.

Some of the important types of sampling schemes covered by § 15·10·2 and 15·10·3 are given below :

(*i*) Simple Random Sampling
(*ii*) Stratified Random Sampling
(*iii*) Systematic Sampling
(*iv*) Multistage Sampling
(*v*) Quasi Random Sampling
(*vi*) Area Sampling
(*vii*) Simple Cluster Sampling
(*viii*) Multistage Cluster Sampling
(*ix*) Quota Sampling

We shall discuss below some plans briefly.

Remark. The selection of the sample based on the theory of probability is also known as *random selection* and sometimes the probability sampling is also called *Random Sampling*. It should be borne in mind that in ordinary language randomness means haphazardness or without any purpose or definite law but in Statistics randomness is a well defined concept. According to Simpson and Kafka, "*Random samples are characterised by the way in which they are selected. Randomness is not used in the sense of haphazard or hit or miss*".

15·11. SIMPLE RANDOM SAMPLING

Simple random sampling (S.R.S.) is the technique in which *sample is so drawn that each and every unit in the population has an equal and independent chance of being included in the sample.*

If the unit selected in any draw is not replaced in the population before making the next draw, then it is known as *simple random sampling without replacement* (*srswor*) and if it is replaced back before making the next draw, then the sampling plan is called *simple random sampling with replacement* (*srswr*). Thus, simple random sampling with replacement always amounts to sampling from an infinite population, even though the population is finite.

Remark. Alternative Definition of srswor. If a sample of size n is drawn without replacement from a population of size N then there are ${}^NC_n$ possible samples. Simple Random Sampling is the technique of selecting the sample so that each of these ${}^NC_n$ samples has an equal chance or probability

$$p = \frac{1}{{}^NC_n}, \quad \ldots(15·11)$$

of being selected in the sample.

If sampling is done with replacement, then there are N^n possible samples of size n. In this case, simple random sampling (srswr) gives equal chance

$$p = \frac{1}{N^n}, \quad \ldots(15·12)$$

for each of the N^n samples to be selected.

15·11·1. Selection of a Simple Random Sample. Proper care must be exercised to ensure that the sample drawn is random and therefore, representative of the population. A random sample may be selected by :

(i) *Lottery Method.*

(ii) *Use of Table of Random Numbers.*

Lottery Method. The simplest method of drawing a random sample is the lottery system. This consists in identifying each and every member or unit of the population with a distinct number which is recorded on a slip or a card. These slips should be as homogeneous as possible in shape, size, colour, etc., to avoid the human bias. The lot of these slips or cards is a kind of miniature of the population for sampling purposes. If the population is small, then these slips are put in a bag and thoroughly shuffled and then as many slips as units needed in the sample are drawn one by one, the slips being thoroughly shuffled after each draw. The sampling units corresponding to the numbers on the selected slips will constitute a random sample. For example, let us suppose that we want to draw a random sample of 10 individuals from a population of 100 individuals. We assign the numbers 1 to 100, one number to each individual of the population and prepare 100 identical slips bearing the numbers from 1 to 100. These slips are then placed in a bag or container and shuffled thoroughly. Finally, a sample of 10 slips is drawn out one by one. The individuals bearing the numbers on these selected slips will constitute the desired sample.

If the population to be sampled is fairly large, then we may adopt the lottery method in which all the slips or cards are placed in a metal cylinder which is thrown into a large rotating drum working under a mechanical system. The rotation of the drum results in through mixing or randomisation of the cards. Then a sample of desired size n is drawn out of the container mechanically and the corresponding n sample units constitute the desired random sample.

The lottery method gives a sample which is quite independent of the properties of the population. It is one of the best and most commonly used methods of selecting random samples. It is quite frequently used in the random draw of prizes, in the Tambola games and so on.

Remark. In sampling with replacement (srswr) each card drawn is replaced back in the container before making the next draw.

But in sampling without replacement (srswor) cards once drawn are not returned back. Since cards are drawn one by one, a thorough mixing is required before the next draw.

Use of Table of Random Numbers. The lottery method described above is quite time consuming and cumbersome to use if the population to be sampled is sufficiently large. Moreover, in this method, it is not humanly possible to make all the slips or cards exactly alike and as such some bias is likely to be introduced. Statisticians have avoided this difficulty by considering the random sampling number series. Most of these series are the results of actual sampling operations recorded for future use. The most practical and inexpensive method of selecting a random sample consists in the use of '*Random Number Tables*', which have been so constructed that each of the digits 0, 1, 2, ..., 9 appears with approximately the same frequency and independently of each other. If we have to select a sample from a population of size $N(\leq 99)$, then the numbers can be combined two by two to give pairs from 00 to 99. Similarly if $N \leq 999$ or $N \leq 9999$ and so on, then combining the digits three by three (or four by four and so on), we get numbers from 000 to 999 or 0000 to 9999 and so on. Since each of the digits 0, 1, 2, ..., 9 occurs with approximately the same frequency and independently of each other, so does each of the pairs 00 to 99, triplets 000 to 999 or *quadruplets* 0000 to 9999 and so on.

The method of drawing a random sample comprises the following steps :

(i) Identify N units in the population with the numbers 1 to N.

(ii) Select at random, any page of the '*random number table*' and pick up the numbers in any row, column or diagonal at random.

(iii) The population units corresponding to the numbers selected in step (ii) constitute the random sample.

We give below different sets of random numbers commonly used in practice. The numbers in these tables have been subjected to various statistical tests for randomness of a series and their randomness has been well established for all practical purposes.

1. *Tippet's (1927) Random Number Tables.* (Tracts for computers No. 15, Cambridge University Press).

Tippet random number tables consist of 10,400 four-digited numbers, giving in all 10,400 × 4, *i.e.*, 41,600 digits selected at random from the British census reports.

2. *Fisher and Yates (1938) Tables (in Statistical Tables for Biological, Agricultural and Medical Research)* comprise 15,000 digits arranged in two's. Fisher and Yates obtained these tables by drawing numbers at random from the 10th to 19th digits of A.S. Thomson's 20-figures logarithmic tables.

3. *Kendall and Babington Smiths (1939)* random tables consist of 100,000 digits grouped into 25,000 sets of 4-digited random numbers (Tracts for computers, No. 24, Cambridge University Press).

4. *Rand Corporation (1955), (Free Press, Illinois)* random number tables consist of one million random digits consisting of 200,000 random numbers of 5 digits each.

5. *Table of Random Numbers (The ISI series, Calcutta)* by C.R. Rao, Mitra and Mathai.

The first forty sets from Tippet's Table have been reproduced in Table 15·3, for illustrating their use in the selection of random samples.

TABLE 15·3. EXTRACT FROM TIPPET'S TABLE OF RANDOM NUMBERS

2952	6641	3992	9792	7979	5911	3170	5624
4167	9524	1545	1396	7203	5356	1300	2693
2370	7483	3408	2762	3563	1089	6913	7691
0560	5246	1112	6107	6008	8126	4233	8776
2754	9143	1405	9025	7002	6111	8816	6446

Example 15·1. *Draw a random sample (without replacement) of 15 students from a class of 450 students.*

Solution. First of all we identify the 450 students of the college with numbers from 1 to 450. Starting with the first number in the above extract from Tippett's random number tables and moving row-wise, we pick out, one by one, the three-digited numbers less than or equal to 450, till 15 numbers ≤ 450 are obtained. In this process the numbers over 450 are discarded and the repeated numbers, if any, are taken only once.

The above numbers (Table 15·3), grouped in three's are :

295, 266, 413, 992, 979, 279, 795, 911, 317, 056, 244, 167, 952,
415, 451, 396, 720, 353, 561, 300, 269, 323, 707, 483, 340 ...

Thus the students corresponding to the numbers

295, 266, 413, 279, 317, 56, 244, 167,
415 396, 353, 300, 269, 323, and 340,

constitute the desired random sample of size 15.

Example 15·2. *Use Table 15·3, to draw a random sample (without replacement) of size 5 from a population of 24 units.*

Solution. First of all we identify the 24 units in the population with numbers from 1 to 24. Then in Table 15·3, starting with the first number and moving row-wise, we pick out the numbers in pairs, one by one, discarding those numbers which are greater than 24 and counting the repeated numbers only once, till a selection of 5 numbers below 25 is made. These numbers are : 11, 24, 15, 13, 03. Thus, the units in the population corresponding to these five numbers, constitute the required random sample of size 5.

Remark. In this method a large number of digits are rejected [as in Example 15·2 all digits above 24 are rejected], and thus we need large tables even to draw small samples. It may even happen that extract given from the table of random numbers is so small that we are not able to draw a random sample of the desired size. This difficulty can be overcome by assigning more than one number to each of the sampling units. For instance, in Example 15·2, the first unit may be assigned the numbers :

$$1, 1+24, \quad 1+2\times 24, \quad 1+3\times 24, \quad \text{and so on}$$

i.e., 1, 25, 49, 73, 97, 121, ... and so on.

Similarly the second unit may be assigned the numbers :

2, 26, 50, 74, 98, 122, ... and so on.

Finally, the last unit may be assigned the numbers :

0, 24, 48, 72, 96, 120, ... ,

Following this procedure, the desired sample of size 5 will be given by the units corresponding to the numbers 4, 5, 15, 17, 18 as explained the Table 15·4.

TABLE 15·4

Number from Table 15·3	*Number of the Sampled Unit*
$29 = 5 + 24$	5
$52 = 4 + 2 \times 24$	4
$66 = 18 + 2 \times 24$	18
$41 = 17 + 24$	17
$39 = 15 + 24$	15

We give below another illustration.

Example 15·3. *The adjoining table of ten random numbers of two digits each is provided to the field investigator.*

34	96	61	85	49
78	50	02	27	13

...(*)

How should he use this table to make a random selection of 5 plots out of 40 ?

Solution. In this case we shall first identify the 40 plots with the numbers 1 to 40. In the table in (*) there are only 3 numbers, *viz.*, 34, 02 and 13 which are less than 40 and accordingly we are not able to draw the desired sample of size 5 from this table as such. In this case, we shall assign more than one number to each of the sampling units, *i.e.*, plots. For example, the first plot will be assigned the numbers

$01,\ 01 + 40,\ 01 + 2 \times 40,\ 01 + 3 \times 40,\ \ldots$ and so on,

i.e., 1, 41, 81, 121, 161, 201, ... and so on.

Similarly the second plot will be assigned the numbers

$02,\ 02 + 40,\ 02 + 2 \times 40,\ 02 + 3 \times 40,\ \ldots$

i.e., 02, 42, 82, 122, 162, 202, ... , and so on.

Finally, the last plot, *i.e.,* 40th plot can be assigned the numbers 0, 40, 80, 120, 160, ... and so on.

TABLE 15·5

Number from Table (*)	*Number of the Sampled Plot*
34	34
$96 = 16 + 2 \times 40$	16
$61 = 21 + 40$	21
$85 = 5 + 2 \times 40$	5
$49 = 9 + 40$	9

If we select the first number in (*) and move row-wise we get the adjoining Table 15·5.

Thus, the plot Nos. 5, 9, 16, 21 and 34 constitute the desired sample.

If we select the first number in (*) and move columnwise, the desired sample consists of plot numbers :

34, 38, 16, 10 and 21;

because, $78 = 40 + 38$, $96 = 2 \times 40 + 16$, $50 = 40 + 10$ and $61 = 40 + 21$.

15·11·2. Sampling Distribution of Mean. If $X_1, X_2, \ldots, X_n$, is a random sample of size n from a population with mean μ and variance σ^2, then

$$E(\overline{X}) = \mu \qquad \ldots(15\cdot13)$$

$$\text{and} \quad \text{Var}(\overline{X}) = \frac{\sigma^2}{n} \quad \Rightarrow \quad S.E.(\overline{X}) = \frac{\sigma}{\sqrt{n}}, \qquad \ldots(15.14)$$

if the sample is drawn with replacement.

$$\text{and} \quad \text{Var}(\overline{X}) = \frac{N-n}{N-1} \cdot \frac{\sigma^2}{n} \quad \Rightarrow \quad S.E.(\overline{X}) = \sqrt{\left(\frac{N-n}{N-1}\right) \cdot \frac{\sigma^2}{n}}, \qquad \ldots(15\cdot15)$$

if the sample is drawn without replacement.

Remarks 1. $\text{Var}(\overline{X}) = \dfrac{\sigma^2}{n} \quad \Rightarrow \quad S.E.(\overline{X}) = \dfrac{\sigma}{\sqrt{n}}$

i.e., *S.E.* $(\overline{X})$ is inversely proportional to the square root of the sample size. Hence, larger the sample size, lesser the S.E. $(\overline{X})$ and consequently $\overline{X}$ is a better or more efficient estimator of μ for large values of n.

2. Srswor Vs Srswr. We have

$$\text{Var}\,(\overline{X})_{\text{srswor}} = \frac{\sigma^2}{n}\cdot\left(\frac{N-n}{N-1}\right) < \frac{\sigma^2}{n} = \text{Var}\,(\overline{X})_{\text{srswr}},$$

because $\quad n > 1 \quad \Rightarrow \quad N - n < N - 1 \quad \Rightarrow \quad \dfrac{N-n}{N-1} < 1$

$$\therefore \quad \text{Var}\,(\overline{X})_{\text{srswor}} < \text{Var}\,(\overline{X})_{\text{srswr}} \qquad \text{...(15·16)}$$

i.e., the variance of the sample mean (as an estimate of μ) *is less in srswor as compared with its variance in the case of srswr.* This implies that srswor provides a better (more efficient) estimate of the population mean μ relative to srswr.

15·11·4. Merits and Limitations of Simple Random Sampling

Merits 1. Since it is a probability sampling, it eliminates the bias due to the personal judgment or discretion of the investigator. Accordingly, the sample selected is more representative of the population than in the case of judgment sampling.

2. Because of its random character, it is possible to ascertain the efficiency of the estimates by considering the standard errors of their sampling distributions. As pointed out earlier [See Remark 1 above], $\bar{x}$ as an estimate μ can be made more efficient by taking large samples. Moreover, large sample will be more representative of the population according to the Principle of Statistical Regularity and the Principle of Inertia of Large Numbers and thus provide better results.

3. The theory of random sampling is highly developed so that it enables us to obtain the most reliable and maximum information at the least cost, and results in savings in time, money and labour.

Demerits 1. Simple random sampling requires an up-to-date frame, *i.e.*, a complete and up-to-date list of the population units to be sampled. In practice, since this is not readily available in many inquiries, it restricts the use of this sampling design.

2. In field surveys if the area of coverage is fairly large, then the units selected in the random sample are expected to be scattered widely geographically and thus it may be quite time consuming and costly to collect the requisite information or data.

3. If the sample is not sufficiently large, then it may not be representive of the population and thus may not reflect the true characteristics of the population

4. The numbering of the population units and the preparation of the slips is quite time consuming and uneconomical particularly if the population is large. Accordingly, this method can't be used effectively to collect most of the data in social sciences.

5. For given degree of accuracy, simple random sampling usually requires larger sample as compared to stratified random sampling discussed below. [*See* § 15·12]

6. Sometimes, simple random sample gives results which are highly improbabilistic in nature, *i.e.*, whose probability is very small. For example, a random selection of 13 cards from a pack of 52 cards might give all thirteen cards of spades, say. The probability of the happening of such an event in practice is very very small.

15·12. STRATIFIED RANDOM SAMPLING

In simple random sampling without replacement (*srswor*).

$$\text{Var}\,(\overline{X}) = \frac{\sigma^2}{n}\left(\frac{N-n}{N-1}\right) \qquad \text{...(*)}$$

From (*), we see that Var $(\bar{x})$ can be reduced by

(*i*) Increasing the sample size n, and

(*ii*) Minimising the population variance σ^2.

Thus, apart from increasing the sample size, the only other way of increasing the precision of sample estimate of the population mean is to devise a sampling plan which will effectively reduce the variability in the population. This objective is achieved by *stratified sampling*.

When the population is heterogeneous with respect to the variable or characteristic under study, then the technique of stratified random sampling is used to obtain more efficient results. Stratification means division into layers or groups. Stratified random sampling involves the following steps :

1. Stratify the given population into a number of sub-groups or sub-populations known as *strata* such that :

(*a*) The units within each stratum (sub-group) are as homogeneous as possible.

(*b*) The differences between various strata are as marked as possible, *i.e.*, the stratum means differ as widely as possible.

(*c*) Various strata are non-overlapping. This means each and every unit in the population belongs to one and only one stratum.

The criterion used for the stratification of the universe into various strata is known as ***stratifying factor***. In general, geographical, sociological or economic characteristics form the basis of stratification of the given population. Some of the commonly used stratifying factors are age, sex, income, occupation, education level, geographic area, economic status, etc. Stratification will be effective only if it possesses the three characteristics (*a*), (*b*), (*c*) enumerated above. In many fields of highly skewed distributions, stratification is a very effective and valuable tool.

Thus, in stratified sampling the given population of size N is divided into, say, k relatively homogeneous strata of sizes $N_1, N_2, \ldots, N_k$ respectively such that $N = \sum_{i=1}^{k} N_i$.

2. Draw simple random samples (without replacement) from each of the k strata. Let srswor of size n_i be drawn from the ith strata, ($i = 1, 2, \ldots, k$) such that $\sum_{i=1}^{k} n_i = n$, where n is the total sample size from a population of size N.

The sample of $n = \sum_{i=1}^{k} n_i$, units is known as *Stratified Random Sample* (without replacement) and the technique of drawing such a sample is known as *Stratified Random Sampling.*

Remark. The basic problems in stratified random sampling are :

(*i*) The stratification of the universe into different starta or sub-groups.

(*ii*) The determination of the sizes of the samples to be drawn from different starta.

Both these points are equally important. A faulty stratification cannot be compensated even by taking large samples.

15·12·1. Allocation of Sample Size in Stratified Sampling. To obtain efficient results, the allocation of sample size n_i, ($i = 1, 2, \ldots, k$) *i.e.*, the number of units to be selected from the ith stratum, the total sample size $n = n_1 + n_2 + \ldots + n_k$ being given, is done in the following ways :

(*i*) *Proportional Allocation*

(*ii*) *Neyman's Optimum Allocation*

(*iii*) *Disproportionate Allocation.*

Proportional Allocation. In this, the items are selected from each stratum in the same proportion as they exist in the population. The allocation of sample sizes is termed as proportional if the *sample fraction, i,e,* the ratio of the sample size to the population size, remains the same in all the strata, Mathematically, the principle of proportional allocation gives :

$$\frac{n_1}{N_1} = \frac{n_2}{N_2} = \ldots = \frac{n_k}{N_k} = \frac{n_1 + n_2 + \ldots + n_k}{N_1 + N_2 + \ldots + N_k} = \frac{n}{N} = c, \text{ (Constant)} \qquad \ldots(15{\cdot}17)$$

since the total sample size n, and the population size N are fixed. Hence,

$$n_1 = N_1\left(\frac{n}{N}\right), \quad n_2 = N_2\left(\frac{n}{N}\right), \ldots, \quad n_k = N_k\left(\frac{n}{N}\right)$$

$$\Rightarrow \qquad n_i = N_i\left(\frac{n}{N}\right), (i = 1, 2, \ldots, k) \qquad \ldots(15{\cdot}18)$$

$$\Rightarrow \qquad n_i \propto N_i, \qquad \ldots(15{\cdot}18a)$$

where $c = n/N$, is taken as the constant of proportionality.

Neyman's Optimum Allocation. In this case the size of the samples to be drawn from the various strata is determined so that the variance of the estimate of the population mean is minimum for a fixed total size of the sample. This gives :

$$n_i \propto N_i\,\sigma_i \qquad \ldots(15{\cdot}19)$$

This is known as *Neyman's formula for optimum allocation*. This suggets that greater the value of the product $N_i\,\sigma_i$, *i.e.*, product of size and the variability of the stratum, the larger is the number of units to be sampled from it. Thus, if there are two strata of the same size then a larger sample is to be drawn from the stratum having greater variability, *i.e.*, standard deviation.

Disproportionate Allocation. In this case an equal number of items is taken from every stratum regardless of how the stratum is represented in the population. Sometimes, the proportion may vary from stratum to stratum also. *In short, a stratified sample in which the number of items selected from each stratum is independent of its size is called disproportionate stratified sample.*

Remark. $$\text{Var}(\overline{X})_R \geq \text{Var}(\overline{X}_{st})_P \geq \text{Var}(\overline{X}_{st})_N \qquad \ldots(15{\cdot}20)$$

where $(\overline{X})_R$ is estimate of μ based on simple random sampling and Var $(\overline{X}_{st})_P$ and Var $(\overline{X}_{st})_N$ are the variances of the estimates of μ obtained in stratified random sampling using proportional and Neyman's allocation of the samples. Hence, Neyman's optimum allocation gives the most efficient estimate.

15·12·2. Merits and Demerits of Stratified Random Sampling

Merits 1. More Representative Sample. A properly constructed and executed stratified random sampling plan overcomes the drawbacks of purposive sampling and random sampling and still enjoys the virtues of both these methods by dividing the given universe into a number of homogeneous subgroups with respect to purposive characteristic and then using the technique of random sampling in drawing samples from each stratum. A stratified random sample gives adequate representation to each strata or important section of the population and eliminates the possibility of any important group of the population being completely ignored. The stratified random sampling provides a more representative sample of the population and accordingly results in less variability as compared with other sampling designs.

2. Greater Precision. As a consequence of the reduction in the variability within each stratum, stratified random sampling provides more efficient estimates as compared with simple random sampling. For instance, the sample estimate of the population mean is more efficient in both proportional and Neyman's allocation of the samples to different strata in stratified random sampling as compared with the corresponding estimate obtained in simple random sampling.

3. Administrative Convenience. The division of the population into relatively homogeneous subgroups brings administrative convenience. Unlike random samples, the stratified samples are expected to be localised geographically. This ultimately results in reduction in cost and saving in time in terms of collection of the data, interviewing the respondents and supervision of the field work.

4. Sometimes it is desired to achieve different degrees of accuracy for different segments of the population. Stratified random sampling is the only sampling plan which enables us to obtain the results of known precision for each of the stratum.

5. Quite often, the sampling problems differ quite significantly in different segments of the population. In such a situation, the problem can be tackled effectively through stratified sampling by regarding each segment of the population as a different strata and approaching upon them independently during sampling.

Demerits 1. As already pointed out the success of stratified random sampling depends on :

(*i*) Effective stratification of the universe into homogeneous strata and

(*ii*) Appropriate size of the samples to be drawn from each of the stratum.

If stratification is faulty, the results will be biased. The error due to wrong stratification cannot be compensated even by taking large samples.

The allocation of the sample sizes to different strata requires an accurate knowledge of the population size in each stratum N_i, $i = 1, 2, \ldots, k$. [*c.f.*, Proportional Allocation $n_i \propto N_i$]. Further Neyman's principle of optimum allocation, *viz.*, $n_i \propto N_i\ \sigma_i$, requires an additional knowledge of the variability or standard deviation of each strata. N_i and σ_i, $(i = 1, 2, \ldots, k)$ are usually unknown and are a serious limitation to the effective use of stratified random sampling.

2. Disproportional stratified sampling requires the assignment of weights to different strata and if the weights assigned are faulty, the resulting sample will not be representative and might give biased results.

15·13. SYSTEMATIC SAMPLING

Systematic sampling is slight variation of the simple random sampling in which only the first sample unit is selected at random and the remaining units are automatically selected in a definite sequence at equal spacing from one another. This technique of drawing samples is usually recommended if the complete and up-to-date list of the sampling units, *i.e.*, the frame is available and the units are arranged in some systematic order such as alphabetical, chronological, geographical order, etc. This requires the sampling units in the population to be ordered in such a way that each item in the population is uniquely identified by its order, for example the names of persons in a telephone directory, the list of voters, etc.

Let us suppose that N sampling units in the population are arranged in some systematic order and serially numbered from I to N and we want to draw a sample of size n from it such that

$$N = nk \quad \Rightarrow \quad k = \frac{N}{n} \qquad \ldots(15{\cdot}21)$$

where k is usually called the *sample interval.*

Systematic sampling consists in selecting any unit at random from the first k units numbered from 1 to k and then selecting every kth unit in succession subsequently. Thus, if the first unit selected at random is ith unit, then the systematic sample of size n will consist of the units numbered.

$$i, \quad i + k, \quad i + 2k, \quad \ldots, \quad i + (n - 1)k.$$

The random number 'i' is called the *random start* and its value, in fact, determines the whole sample. As an example, let us suppose that we want to select 50 voters from a list of voters containing 1,000 names arranged systematically. Here

$$n = 50 \quad \text{and} \quad N = 1{,}000 \quad \Rightarrow \quad k = \frac{N}{n} = \frac{1{,}000}{50} = 20$$

We select any number from 1 to 20 at random and the corresponding voter in the list is selected. Suppose the selected number is 6. Then, the systematic sample will consist of 50 voters in the list at serial numbers : 6, 26, 46, 66, ..., 966, 986.

Obviously we can select k possible systematic samples starting with the 1st unit, 2nd unit, ..., kth unit which are enumerated below :

TABLE 15·6

Random Start	*Sample Composition (Units in the Sample)*					
1	1	$1 + k$	....,	$1 + jk$	...	$1 + (n - 1)k$
2	2	$2 + k$	....,	$2 + jk$	...	$2 + (n - 1)k$
⋮	⋮	⋮			⋮	
i	i	$i + k$	....,	$i + jk$	...	$i + (n - 1)k$
⋮	⋮	⋮			⋮	
k	k	$2k$	....,	$(1 + j)k$	...	nk

Thus, k rows of the Table 15·6. give the k-systematic samples. The columns of the above table are also sometimes referred to as *n strata*.

Remark. Systematic random sample appears like a stratified random sample with one unit per stratum.

15·13·1. Merits and Demerits

Merits 1. Systematic sampling is very easy to operate and checking can also be done quickly. Accordingly, it results in considerable saving in time and labour relative to simple random sampling or stratified random sampling.

2. Systematic sampling may be more efficient than simple random sampling provided the frame is complete and up-to-date and the units are arranged serially in a random order like the names in a telephone directory where the units are arranged in alphabetical order. However, even in alphabetical arrangement, certain amount of non-random character may persist.

Demerits 1. Systematic sampling works well only if the complete and up-to-date frame is available and if the units are randomly arranged. However, these requirements are not generally fulfilled.

2. Systematic sampling gives biased results if there are periodic features in the frame and the sampling interval (k) is equal to or a multiple of the period.

The relative efficiency of the systematic sampling over stratified random sampling or simple random sampling without replacement (srswor) largely depends on the properties of the population under study. Without a knowledge of the structure of the population, no hard and fast rules can be laid down and no situations can be pinpointed where the use of systematic sampling is to be recommended.

15·14. CLUSTER SAMPLING

In this case the total population is divided, depending on problem under study, into some recognisable sub-divisions which are termed as *clusters* and a simple random sample of these clusters is drawn. We then observe, measure and interview each and every unit in the selected clusters.

For example, if we are interested in obtaining the income or opinion data in a city, the whole city may be divided into N different blocks or localities (which determine the clusters) and a simple random sample of n blocks is drawn. The individuals in the selected blocks determine the cluster sample.

In using cluster sampling the following points should be borne in mind :

(*i*) Clusters should be as small as possible consistent with the cost and limitations of the survey, and

(*ii*) The number of sampling units in each cluster should be approximately same.

Thus, cluster sampling is not to be recommended if we are sampling areas in the city where there are private residential houses, business and industrial complexes, apartment buildings, etc., with widely varying number of persons or households.

15·15. MULTISTAGE SAMPLING

Instead of enumerating all the sampling units in the selected clusters, one can obtain better and more efficient estimates by resorting to sub-sampling within the clusters. The technique is called *two-stage sampling*, clusters being termed as *primary units* and the units within the clusters as *secondary units.*

The above technique may be generalised to what is called *multistage sampling*. As the name suggests, multistage sampling refers to a sampling technique which is carried out in various stages. Here, the population is regarded as made of a number of primary units, each of which is further composed of a number of secondary stage units and so on, till we ultimately reach the desired sampling unit in which we are interested. For example, if we are interested in obtaining a sample of, say, n households from a particular State, the first stage units may be districts, the second stage units may be villages in the districts and third stage units will be households in the villages. Each stage thus results in a reduction of the sample size.

Multistage sampling consists in sampling first stage units by some suitable method of sampling. From among the selected first stage units, a sub-sample of secondary stage units is drawn by some suitable method of sampling which may be same as or different from the method used in selecting first stage units. Further stages may be added to arrive at a sample of the desired sampling units.

Merits. Multistage sampling is more flexible as compared to other methods of sampling. It is simple to carry out and results in administrative convenience by permitting the field work to be concentrated and yet covering large area.

Most practical advantage of multistage sampling is that we need the second stage frame only for those units which are selected in the first stage sample and this leads to great saving in operational cost. Consequently this technique is of great utility, particularly in surveys of under developed area or pockets where no up-to-date and accurate frame is generally available for sub-division of the material into reasonably small sampling units.

Demerits. Errors are likely to be larger in this method than in any other method. The variability of the estimates under this method may be greater than that of estimates based on simple random sampling. This variability depends on the composition of the primary units. In general, a multistage sampling is usually less efficient than a suitable single stage sampling of the same size.

15·16. QUOTA SAMPLING

Quota sampling may be looked as a special form of stratified sampling. In this method, the investigator is told in advance the number of the sample units he is to examine or enumerate from the stratum assigned to him. In the language of stratified sampling, the quota of the units to be examined by the investigator from the stratum assigned to him is fixed for each investigator. The sampling quotas may be fixed according to some specified characteristic such as income group, sex, occupation, political or religious affiliations, etc. The choice of the particular units or individuals for investigation is left to the investigators themselves. They are merely given the quotas with the specific instruction to inspect (interview) a specified number of units (informants) from each stratum. Quite often the investigator does not make a random selection of the sample units. He usually applies his judgment and discretion in the choice of the sample and tries to get the desired information as quickly as possible. Moreover, in case of non-response from some of the selected sample units (due to certain reasons like non-availability of the respondent even after repeated calls by the investigator, or the inability or refusal of the informant to furnish the requisite information), the investigator selects some fresh units himself to complete his quota. In doing so, he is likely to include some purposive units to get the desired information.

Merits 1. Quota sampling is a stratified-cum-purposive or judgment sampling and thus enjoys the benefits of both. It aims at making the best use of stratification without incurring high costs involved in following any probabilistic method of sampling. There is considerable saving in time and money as the sampled units may be so selected that they are close together.

2. If carefully executed by skilled and experienced investigators who are aware of the limitations of judgment sampling and if proper controls or checks are imposed on the investigators, quota sampling is likely to give quite reliable results.

Demerits. Since quota sampling is a restricted type of judgment sampling, it suffers from all the limitations of judgment or purposive sampling, *viz.*,

(*i*) It may be biased because of the personal beliefs and prejudices of the investigator in the selection of the units or/and inspecting them.

(*ii*) It may involve the bias due to the substitution of the sampled units from where there is no response.

(*iii*) Since it is not based on random sampling, the sampling error cannot be estimated.

In spite of all these shortcomings, the technique of quota sampling is generally adopted in market surveys, political surveys, or surveys of opinion poll where it is very difficult, rather impossible, to identify the strata in advance.

EXERCISE 15·1.

1. Distinguish between a population and a sample. Discuss the relative merits of census and sample methods of collecting data.

2. Point out the importance of sampling in solving business problems. What are the basic principles on which sampling theory rests ?

3. (*a*) Explain the difference between Statistic and Parameter as used in Sampling Theory.

What is Sampling Distribution of a statistic ? Explain it by taking a particular statistic.

(*b*) Explain what do you understand by the sampling distribution of a statistic and its standard error. Discuss the utility of standard error in Statistics.

4. (*a*) Distinguish between a census and a sample enquiry and discuss their comparative advantages.

[*Delhi Univ. B.Com (Pass) 1995*]

(*b*) Distinguish between the 'census' and 'sampling' methods of collection of data, and compare their merits and demerits. Why is sampling method unavoidable in certain situations ?

(*Punjab Univ., M.A. Econ. 1995; Delhi Univ., B.Com., 1998*)

5. Explain briefly (your answer should not exceed about 300 words) why a sample survey is usually preferred to a census survey. Give one example of a situations where a census survey is imperative.

6. (*a*) Describe briefly the Law of Statistical Regularity and state its applications in the economic and social spheres.

(*b*) State and Explain :

(*i*) Law of Statistical Regularity

(*ii*) Law of Inertia of Large Numbers. (*Punjab Univ. M.Com. 1996*)

7. (*a*) What are the different sources of errors in a sample survey ?

(*b*) Describe briefly how these can be controlled.

8. (*a*) Distinguish clearly between sampling and non-sampling errors. Is it true to say that non-sampling errors do not arise in a sample survey ? How will you control these errors ?

(*b*) Distinguish between sampling and non-sampling errors. What are their sources ? How these errors can be controlled ? (*Punjab Univ. M.Com., 1996*)

9. (*a*) What is a statistical error ? Explain the difference between a statistical error and a 'mistake'. Describe the various measures of statistical errors.

(*b*) Explain the concept of biased and unbiased errors. [*Delhi Univ. B.Com. (Pass) 1998, 1999*]

10. Define :

(*i*) Statistical Errors.

(*ii*) Biased and Unbiased Errors.

(*iii*) Sampling and Non-sampling Errors.

(*iv*) Absolute and Relative Errors.

11. What is sampling ? What are the essentials of a good sample ? Name the various methods of sampling and explain them in brief. (*Kurukshetra Univ. B.Com., 1996*)

12. (*a*) Discuss the technique of Judgment or Purposive Sampling.

(*b*) What is Simple Random Sampling ? Discuss its relative merits and demerits.

(*c*) Describe the various methods of drawing a random sample from a finite population.

(*d*) Discuss stratified and systematic sampling (*Punjab Univ. B.Com., April 2000*)

13. (*a*) Distinguish between simple random sampling and purposive sampling.

Describe a procedure for drawing a random sample of size 5 from a population of size 17 (with replacement method).

(*b*) What is simple random sampling ? How would you estimate the total labour force in the State by random sampling ?

14. What are random sampling numbers ? Outline the different random number series and explain how these are used to select a simple random sample.

15. A carefully designed "Sample Survey" is said to be better than a poorly planned and executed "Census". Bring out the merits of sample method of enquiry and at least three of the methods to obtain representative data in a sample.

16. Distinguish between simple random sampling and stratified random sampling.

Describe a procedure of drawing a random sample of size 3 from a population of size 11 by 'without replacement' method.

17. Bring out the important features of

(*i*) Systematic Sampling. (*ii*) Stratified Sampling.

18. "Mere size, of course, does not assure representativeness in a sample. A small random or stratified sample is apt to be much superior to a large but badly selected sample."

Discuss this statement pointing out the advantages, disadvantages and limitations of the sample method.

19. (*a*) Distinguish between random sampling and stratified sampling. Suppose it is desired to survey petrol buying habits of car owners in a particular city. How would you proceed about it ? Draw a brief questionnaire for the purpose.

(*b*) Distinguish between simple random sampling and stratified random sampling. When will you use the latter ? [*Delhi Univ. B.A. (Econ. Hons.), 1999*]

(*c*) Illustrate the difference between proportionate and disproportionate stratified sampling.

[*Delhi Univ. B.Com. (Pass), 1998*]

20. (*a*) Discuss the merits and demerits of stratified sampling method. (*Delhi Univ. M.A. Social work, 1999*)

(*b*) Write a critical note on the merits and limitations of judgement sampling. (*C.A. May, 1993*)

21. While collecting data, under what circumstances would you prefer (*a*) random sampling to deliberate sampling, (*b*) stratified sampling to simple random sampling ? Is quota sampling same as stratified sampling ?

22. Discuss the various techniques which may be used for carrying out a sample survey. Explain how you will minimize sampling errors and biases while using these techniques.

23. What do you mean by sampling ? Briefly explain various methods of sampling ?

(*Osmania Univ. B.Com., 1993*)

24. Three sampling plans to determine the quality of the manufactured product are given below :

(*i*) Inspect every 10th item.

(*ii*) Inspect one item every 10 minutes.

(*iii*) Inspect a random sample of 6 during each hour's production.

State the sampling design in each case. Which one is the most appropriate ? Give reasons.

Ans. (*i*) and (*ii*), Systematic random sampling; (*iii*) Simple random sampling.

25. Would you prefer sampling or complete enumeration in the following cases ? State with reasons.

(*i*) Small number of respondents scattered in the whole country.

(*ii*) A large number of respondents in small cluster. (*iii*) A study in depth.

(*iv*) Tensile strength in a metal (*v*) Corrosion test in the sheets.

Ans. (*i*) Complete enumeration; (*ii*) Either; (*iii*) to (*v*) Sample method.

26. Describe the following sampling plans, and given their relative merits and demerits.

(*i*) Judgment or Purposive Sampling. (*ii*) Simple Random Sampling

(*iii*) Stratified Random Sampling (*iv*) Cluster Sampling

(*v*) Multistage Sampling (*vi*) Quota Sampling

(*vii*) Systematic Sampling.

16 Interpolation and Extrapolation

16·1. INTRODUCTION

Let us suppose that we are given two variables x and y, x being the independent variable and y the dependent variable. We say that y is a function of x and we write it as :

$$y = f(x) = y_x, \text{ (say)}. \qquad \ldots(16{\cdot}1)$$

Suppose we are given the values $x_0, x_1, x_2, \ldots, x_n$ of x and let the corresponding values of y be $y_0, y_1, y_2, \ldots, y_n$ respectively. If we want to estimate the value of y_x for any value of x *between the limits,* x_0 and x_n, this can be done by applying the technique of *Interpolation.* For example, suppose we are given the population census figures (y_x) for the years (x) 1931, 1941, 1951, 1961 and 1971 and we want to estimate the population for any year between 1931 and 1971, say, 1958, 1965, etc. This is done by the method of *interpolation.* However, if we have to estimate the population for the period outside the range 1931—1971, say, for 1926 or 1975, the technique is known as *extrapolation.* Interpolation is defined as the *technique of estimating the value of* y_x *for any intermediate value of the variable* x.

Theile defines interpolation as "*the art of reading between the lines of a table.*"

Interpolation or extrapolation is the technique of obtaining the most likely estimate of a certain quantity (dependent variable) from the given relevant facts, under certain assumptions.

Remarks 1. It should be clearly understood that there is no difference between interpolation and extrapolation as far as estimation methods and underlying assumptions are concerned. The only difference between the two is that *interpolation relates to estimation of a value within the given range of the series while extrapolation deals with obtaining the forecasts or projections (in the past or future) beyond the given range of the series.*

2. The values of the independent variable x are known as *arguments* and the corresponding values of the dependent variable y are known as *entries.*

16·1·1. Assumptions. The techniques of interpolation and extrapolation are based on the following assumptions :

(*i*) *There are no sudden jumps or falls in the values of the dependent variable (entries) for the periods under consideration.* In other words, the values should relate to periods of normal and stable economic conditions, *i.e.,* the given data should be free from all sorts of abnormalities and all sorts of random and irregular fluctuations like earthquakes, wars, floods, epidemics, labour strikes, lock outs, economic boom and depression, and political disturbances, etc., which may result in violent ups and downs in the values of y_x. This means that the data can be represented by a smooth and continuous curve. Mathematically, it means that *the given data can be represented by a polynomial of certain degree* which is determined by the following fundamental theorem in algebra :

"*One and only one polynomial curve of degree less than or equal to n passes through a given set of* $(n + 1)$ *distinct points.*"

Thus, if we are given a set of 4 entries (values of y) then y_x can be represented as a polynomial of 3rd degree, *viz.*, $y_x = a_0 + a_1 x + a_2 x^2 + a_3 x^3$. Similarly if we are given only 3 entries, then y_x can be expressed as a second degree polynomial in x, *viz.*, $y_x = b_0 + b_1 x + b_2 x^2$ and so on.

All the formulae of interpolation are based on the fundamental assumption that the given data can be expressed as a polynomial function (of certain degree) with fair degree of accuracy.

(*ii*) In the absence of the evidence to the contrary, there is regularity in the fluctuations so that the rate of change in the given data has been uniform. Thus, in the example of census population given above, it is assumed that the rate of growth has been consistent (uniform) from the years 1931 to 1971.

Remarks 1. In order to arrive at valid estimates, a fairly good number of arguments and entries should be given.

2. If a number of consecutive missing values are to be estimated from the given data, then the estimates are unlikely to be reliable.

16·1·2. Uses of Interpolation. 1. The need for interpolating missing observations or making forecasts or projections arises in a number of disciplines like economics, business, social sciences, actuarial work, population studies, etc. Some of the examples are ascertaining the most likely prices, business changes, mid-term intercensal population figures, mid-term figures of industrial production from their totals and so on.

2. The interpolation technique has been used to derive the formulae for the computation of median and mode in case of continuous frequency distribution. [See formulae in Chapter 5].

3. Interpolation techniques are used to fill in the gaps in the statistical data for the sake of continuity of information. These gaps in the data may be due to the following reasons :

(*i*) Due to certain financial and organisational difficulties, data may not be collected on census basis and sampling techniques may be used to obtain the relevant information. The intermediate gaps are then filled by interpolation methods.

(*ii*) Data for some periods may not be collected due to certain unavoidable circumstances.

(*iii*) Figures of some of the periods may be erased, destroyed or lost due to certain reasons like improper handling or random and natural causes like fire, floods, etc.

Interpolation techniques help us to obtain the best (most likely) substitutes for the original missing values under certain assumptions discussed in § 16·1·1 and these methods are entirely different from those by which actual data are obtained.

Remark. *Accuracy of Estimates.* Since the interpolation techniques are based on certain assumptions which may not hold good in practice, the estimates so obtained, may not always be accurate or reliable. It is not possible to ascertain the error of estimate. The accuracy of the interpolated values depends on :

(*i*) A knowledge of possible fluctuations in the values of the phenomenon under study, which is provided by the available data at our disposal.

(*ii*) A knowledge about the course of events which affect the value of the phenomenon under investigation. If we know that the estimated value of the given phenomenon at a particular period is affected by random factors like political riots, floods, etc., then the interpolated value should be modified in the light of this information and a better estimate may be obtained.

16·2. METHODS OF INTERPOLATION

The methods of interpolation or extrapolation may be broadly classified as follows :

(*i*) Graphic Method.

(*ii*) Algebraic Method.

We shall discuss these methods in details in the following sections.

16·3. GRAPHIC METHOD

This method consists in representing the given data geometrically by means of a graph. The independent variable is plotted along the *X*-axis and the dependent variable is plotted along the *Y*-axis. The various points so obtained are joined together by a smooth free hand curve. From this curve, which will represent the general trend of the relationship between the two variables, we can read the value of one variable corresponding to any given value of the other variable within the given range of the series. [For Graphs of time series — See Chapter 4, § 4·4·4].

If the value of y (or x) lies outside the given range, *i.e.*, if it is a case of extrapolation, then the smoothed curve is extended to the required point and then the estimated value is read from the graph.

For example, if we want to find the value of y for $x = a$, then at $x = a$, draw a perpendicular to x-axis, meeting the smoothed curve at P. From point P draw a line PQ parallel to X-axis meeting the Y-axis at Q. Then the estimated value of y_x at $x = a$ is OQ.

Graphic method is specially useful in the following situations :

(*i*) Series is correlated (either positively or negatively).

(*ii*) In case of historical or temporal series which exhibit periodical or cyclical fluctuations.

Merits and Demerits. Obviously, graphic method is a very simple and quick method of studying the relationship between two variables. It is also very flexible as it can be used to study all types of trends—linear as well as non-linear.

The strongest drawback of this method is its subjective nature due to the inherent bias of the investigator. Different persons will get different smooth curves for the same set of data, depending on the personal judgment and experience of the investigator. Hence, in spite of its simplicity and flexibility, it is not commonly used in practice. Moreover, because of the subjective nature of the free hand smooth curve, it may be dangerous to use it for forecasting or projections.

Example 16·1. *The following table gives the profits of a firm for the period 1991 to 1996. The figure for 1995 is missing. Interpolate the same by graphic method :*

Year	:	*1991*	*1992*	*1993*	*1994*	*1995*	*1996*
Profits (Rs. in lakhs)	:	*110*	*120*	*115*	*125*	*?*	*130*

Solution. We have to interpolate the missing figure (profits in lakhs of rupees) for the year 1995 by graphic method. We plot the given data on the graph, taking the independent variable years (x) along X-axis and the dependent variable profits (in lakhs of Rs.) along Y-axis [Fig. 16·1]. At $x = 1995$, draw a perpendicular to X-axis meeting the curve in point P. From P draw PM parallel to X-axis meeting Y-axis in M. Then estimated profits (in lakhs of Rs.) for 1995 are $OM = 127{\cdot}5$.

Remark. The answer does not seem to be accurate in this case as the data exhibits rise and fall trend alternate years. The estimated value is overstated in this case whereas actually it should have been less than Rs. 125 lakhs.

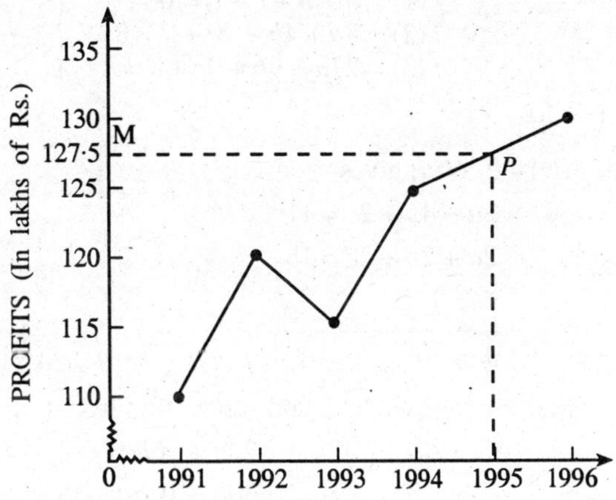

Fig. 16·1

16·4. ALGEBRAIC METHOD

A number of algebraic methods, based on the fundamental assumptions discussed in § 16·1·1, have been developed for interpolation or extrapolation of figures. Some of the commonly used methods are enumerated below and will be discussed in the following sections :

(*i*) Method of Parabolic Fitting.

(*ii*) Methods of Finite Differences. (Newton's forward difference and Newton's backward difference formulae.)

(*iii*) The Binomial Expansion Method.

(*iv*) 'Divided Differences Method' and 'Lagranges Method' for unequal interval of arguments.

16·5. METHOD OF PARABOLIC CURVE FITTING

The form of function $y = f(x)$ or its estimate for any given value of x can be obtained by fitting a polynomial curve to the given set of observations provided the values of x (arguments) are at equal intervals. The method is based on the fundamental theorem of algebra, *viz.*, *one and only one polynomial curve of degree less than or equal to n passes through a given set of* $(n+1)$ *distinct points*". Thus, if we are given $(n+1)$ equidistant arguments and entries, then we can represent the function $y = f(x)$ by a polynomial of nth degree, *viz.*,

$$y = f(x) = a_0 x^n + a_1 x^{n-1} + a_2 x^{n-2} + \ldots + a_{n-1} x + a_n \qquad \ldots(16{\cdot}2)$$

where $a_0, a_1, \ldots, a_n$ are $(n+1)$ constants whose values are to be determined from the $(n+1)$ equations obtained on substituting the given values of x and $y = f(x)$ in (16·2). Solving the $(n+1)$ equations so obtained and substituting the values of $a_0, a_1, \ldots, a_n$ in (16·2), we get the required form of function $y = f(x)$, which can then be used to estimate y for any given value of x. We shall explain the technique by means of an example.

Remark. The method of parabolic curve fitting is quite time consuming and tedious, particularly when the number of entries given is large. For example, if we are given 5 entries, then $y = f(x)$ can be represented by a polynomial of 4th degree which involves 5 unknown constants. To determine these 5 constants we have to solve simultaneous equations in these 5 unknowns which is quite difficult job.

Example 16·2. *Find f(x), given that f(0) = –3, f(1) = 6, f(2) = 8, f(3) = 12. State your assumptions, if any. Hence find f(6).*

Solution. Since we are given 4 entries, we can regard $f(x)$ to be a polynomial of 3rd degree, say,

$$f(x) = ax^3 + bx^2 + cx + d \qquad \ldots(i)$$

This involves 4 unknown constants a, b, c and d.

Putting $x = 0, 1, 2$, and 3 in (*i*) we get respectively :

$$\left.\begin{aligned} f(0) &= d = -3 \\ f(1) &= a + b + c + d = 6 \\ f(2) &= 8a + 4b + 2c + d = 8 \\ f(3) &= 27a + 9b + 3c + d = 12 \end{aligned}\right\} \Rightarrow \left.\begin{aligned} d &= -3 \\ a + b + c &= 6 - d = 9 \\ 8a + 4b + 2c &= 8 - d = 11 \\ 27a + 9b + 3c &= 12 - d = 15 \end{aligned}\right\} \begin{aligned} &\ldots(ii) \\ &\ldots(iii) \\ &\ldots(iv) \\ &\ldots(v) \end{aligned}$$

(*iv*) – 2 × (*iii*) gives

$$\begin{aligned} 8a + 4b + 2c &= 11 \\ 2a + 2b + 2c &= 18 \\ - \quad - \quad - \quad & \quad - \\ \hline 6a + 2b \qquad &= -7 \qquad \ldots(vi) \end{aligned}$$

2 × (*v*) –3 (*iv*) gives :

$$\begin{aligned} 54a + 18b + 6c &= 30 \\ 24a + 12b + 6c &= 33 \\ - \quad - \quad - \quad & \quad - \\ \hline 30a + 6b \qquad &= -3 \qquad \ldots(vii) \end{aligned}$$

Multiplying (*vi*) by 5 and subtracting from (*vii*), we get

$$\begin{aligned} 30a + 6b &= -3 \\ 30a + 10b &= -35 \\ - \quad - \quad & \quad + \\ \hline -4b &= 32 \end{aligned} \quad \Rightarrow \quad b = \frac{-32}{4} = -8$$

Substituting in (*vi*), we get

$$6a - 16 = -7 \quad \Rightarrow \quad 6a = 9 \quad \Rightarrow \quad a = \frac{9}{6} = \frac{3}{2}$$

Substituting the values of a and b in (*iii*), we have

$$c = 9 - a - b = 9 - \frac{3}{2} + 8 = \frac{31}{2}$$

Finally, substituting the values of a, b, c and d in (*i*), we get the form of function $f(x)$ as :

$$f(x) = \frac{3}{2}x^3 - 8x^2 + \frac{31}{2}x - 3 \qquad \ldots(viii)$$

Putting $x = 6$ in (*viii*), we get

$$f(6) = \frac{3}{2} \times 6^3 - 8 \times 6^2 + \frac{31}{2} \times 6 - 3 = 324 - 288 + 93 - 3 = 126$$

16·6. METHOD OF FINITE DIFFERENCES

The calculus of finite differences is a very convenient tool of interpolating figures when the arguments are at equal intervals. Before we develop the different techniques we shall first define the operators Δ and *E*, used extensively in the theory of finite differences.

Let us suppose that the equidistant values of the independent variable x are :

$$a, \quad a+h, \quad a+2h, \quad \ldots, \quad a+nh\ ;$$

where a is known as the *initial argument* (*or origin*), h is known as the common *interval of differencing*. Let the corresponding values of the independent variable $y = f(x)$, be

$$f(a), \quad f(a+h), \quad f(a+2h), \quad \ldots, \quad f(a+nh)\ ;$$

which are known as the *entries*. For example $f(a+h)$ is the entry corresponding to the argument $a+h$, and so on.

Operator Δ. The difference operator Δ (Capital Delta of Greek alphabet) is defined as :

$$\Delta f(x) = f(x+h) - f(x)\ ;\ x = a, a+h, a+2h, \ldots \qquad \ldots(16\cdot3)$$

In particular, taking $x = a, a+h, a+2h, \ldots$in (16·3), we get

$$\begin{aligned} \Delta f(a) &= f(a+h) - f(a) \\ \Delta f(a+h) &= f(a+h+h) - f(a+h) = f(a+2h) - f(a+h) \\ \Delta f(a+2h) &= f(a+3h) - f(a+2h), \end{aligned} \qquad \ldots(16\cdot4)$$

and so on.

The differences defined in (16·4) are known as *first order differences*. By performing the operator Δ on the first order differences in (16·4) we get the *second order differences*, which are denoted by Δ^2. In particular

$$\begin{aligned} \Delta^2 f(a) &= \Delta\left[\,\Delta f(a)\,\right] = \Delta\left[\,f(a+h) - f(a)\,\right] \\ &= \Delta f(a+h) - \Delta f(a) \qquad \ldots(16\cdot5) \\ &= \left[\,f(a+2h) - f(a+h)\,\right] - \left[\,f(a+h) - f(a)\,\right] \\ &= f(a+2h) - 2f(a+h) + f(a), \qquad \ldots(16\cdot5a) \end{aligned}$$

and so on.

Similarly proceeding we can obtain third and higher order differences denoted by $\Delta^3, \Delta^4, \ldots$, and so on. These differences of various orders can be conveniently expressed in the form of a table known as *Finite (Forward) Difference Table*. The following table gives the arguments, entries and the first two differences. The higher order differences can be similarly obtained.

TABLE 16·1 FORWARD DIFFERENCE TABLE

Argument x	*Entry* $y = f(x)$	*First differences* $\Delta f(x)$	*Second differences* $\Delta^2 f(x)$
a	$f(a)$		
		$f(a+h) - f(a) = \Delta f(a)$	
$a+h$	$f(a+h)$		$\Delta f(a+h) - \Delta f(a) = \Delta^2 f(a)$
		$f(a+2h) - f(a+h) = \Delta f(a+h)$	
$a+2h$	$f(a+2h)$		$\Delta f(a+2h) - \Delta f(a+h) = \Delta^2 f(a+h)$
		$f(a+3h) - f(a+2h) = \Delta f(a+2h)$	
$a+3h$	$f(a+3h)$		$\Delta f(a+3h) - \Delta f(a+2h) = \Delta^2 f(a+2h)$
		$f(a+4h) - f(a+3h) = \Delta f(a+3h)$	
$a+4h$	$f(a+4h)$		

$f(a)$ is known as the first entry in the difference table and $\Delta f(a), \Delta^2 f(a)), \Delta^3 f(a), \ldots$, are known as the *leading differences*. This table is also sometimes known as the *diagonal (forward) differences table* since the differences are shown in diagonal pattern.

Operator ∇. The *backward difference* operator denoted by ∇ (Nebula of Green alphabet) is defined as :

$$\nabla f(x+h) = f(x+h) - f(x) = \Delta f(x) \qquad \text{...(16·6)}$$

In other words, the backward difference of $f(x+h)$ is same as forward difference of $f(x)$. The following table gives the arguments, entries and the backward differences up to 2nd order.

TABLE 16·2 **BACKWARD DIFFERENCE TABLE**

Argument x	*Entry* $y = f(x)$	*First differences* $\nabla f(x)$	*Second differences* $\nabla^2 f(x)$
a	$f(a)$		
		$f(a+h) - f(a) = \nabla f(a+h)$	
$a+h$	$f(a+h)$		$\nabla f(a+2h) - \nabla f(a+h) = \nabla^2 f(a+2h)$
		$f(a+2h) - f(a+h) = \nabla f(a+2h)$	
$a+2h$	$f(a+2h)$		$\nabla f(a+3h) - \nabla f(a+2h) = \nabla^2 f(a+3h)$
		$f(a+3h) - f(a+2h) = \nabla f(a+3h)$	
$a+3h$	$f(a+3h)$		$\nabla f(a+4h) - \nabla f(a+3h) = \nabla^2 f(a+4h)$
		$f(a+4h) - f(a+3h) = \nabla f(z+4h)$	
$a+4h$	$f(a+4h)$		

Like the Table 16·1, this table is also known as the *diagonal backward difference table* since the differences are shown in the diagonal pattern.

Remark. Unless stated otherwise, interval of differencing will always be taken as unity (one).

Operator E. In case of the arguments at equal intervals 'h', the operator E is defined as :

$$E f(x) = f(x+h) \qquad \text{...(16·7)}$$

i.e., the operator E is equivalent to increasing the argument by the interval of differencing.

Like second and higher order differences, the operator E^2 means the operator E is performed twice. Thus

$$E^2 f(x) = E[E f(x)] = E[f(x+h)] = f(x+2h) \qquad \text{...(16·8)}$$

In general,

$$E^r f(x) = f(x+rh) \qquad \text{...(16·9)}$$

where h is the interval of differencing. Taking $h = 1$ in (16·9), we get

$$E^r f(x) = f(x+r) \qquad \text{...(16·9}a)$$

In particular

$$E[f(0)] = E^1 f(0) = f(0+1) = f(1) \; ; \; E^2 f(0) = f(0+2) = f(2) \; ; \; E^3 f(0) = f(0+3) = f(3) \; ; \text{..(16·9}b)$$

and so on provided interval of differencing is unity.

Similarly

$$E f(1) = E^1 f(1) = f(1+1) = f(2) \quad ; \quad E^2 f(1) = f(1+2) = f(3) \qquad \text{...(16·9}c)$$

These results are of much practical utility and should be committed to memory.

Relation Between Operators E and Δ. We have, by definition :

$$\Delta f(x) = f(x+h) - f(x) = E f(x) - f(x) \quad \Rightarrow \quad \Delta f(x) = (E-1) f(x)$$

Since $f(x)$ is arbitrary, we get the relation between the operators Δ and E as :

$$\Delta = E - 1 \quad \Rightarrow \quad 1 + \Delta = E \qquad \text{...(16·10)}$$

Remark. Strictly speaking, we should say that the operators E *and* $(1+\Delta)$ are equivalent operators and we use the notation (≡) for equivalence. Thus, we should write $1 + \Delta \equiv E$. However, in practice, we use the equality sign rather than the equivalance sign.

Fundamental Theorem of Finite Differences. If $f(x)$ is a polynomial of nth degree in x, *i.e.*, if

$$f(x) = a_0 x^n + a_1 x^{n-1} + a_2 x^{n-2} + \dots + a_{n-1} x + a_n$$

then $\Delta^n f(x) = a_0 (n!) = \text{constant}$

and $\Delta^r f(x) = 0, \text{ if } r > n$ ...(16·11)

In other words, *the* n^{th} *order difference of a polynomial of* n^{th} *degree is constant and higher order differences are all zero.*

With this background, we are now set to discuss the Newton's forward and backward difference formulae and also to discuss the binomial expansion method of estimating the missing values for arguments at equal intervals.

Remark. It should be understood that the operators E, Δ and ∇ are defined only when the arguments are given to be at equal intervals.

16·7. NEWTON'S FORWARD DIFFERENCE FORMULA

This formula enables us to determine the polynomial form of the function $f(x)$ and hence estimate its value for any given value of x. It is given by the formula :

$$f(x) = f(a) + u\,\Delta f(a) + \frac{u(u-1)}{2!}\Delta^2 f(a) + \frac{u(u-1)(u-2)}{3!}\Delta^3 f(a) + \dots \quad ...(16·12)$$

where x is the period of interpolation, *i.e.*, it is the value corresponding to which entry is required ; a is first argument in the difference table and

$$u = \frac{\text{Period of interpolation} - \text{Period of origin}}{\text{Interval of differencing}} \Rightarrow u = \frac{x-a}{h} \quad ...(16·13)$$

Proof. The proof of (16·12) is very simple and depends on the definition of operator E and the binomial expansion. We have from (16·13),

$$u = \frac{x-a}{h} \Rightarrow x = a + hu$$

$$\begin{aligned}
\therefore \quad f(x) &= f(a + hu) = E^u f(a) && [c.f.\ (16·9)]\\
&= (1+\Delta)^u f(a) && [\text{From } (16·10)]\\
&= (1 + {}^uC_1\,\Delta + {}^uC_2\,\Delta^2 + {}^uC_3\,\Delta^3 + \dots) f(a)\\
&= f(a) + {}^uC_1\,\Delta f(a) + {}^uC_2\,\Delta^2 f(a) + {}^uC_3\,\Delta^3 f(a) + \dots\\
&= f(a) + u\,\Delta f(a) + \frac{u(u-1)}{2!}\Delta^2 f(a) + \frac{u(u-1)(u-2)}{3!}\Delta^3 f(a) + \dots
\end{aligned}$$

as desired.

Remarks 1. Formula (16·12) is also commonly known as *Newton-Gregory formula for forward interpolation.* This is so called because it contains the values of the function $f(x)$ from $f(a)$ onwards to the right and none to the left of $f(a)$. *It is recommended for estimating the value of* $y = f(x)$ *near the beginning* $(x > a)$ *of a set of given values*, because this formula is based on the leading differences which always occur in the beginning of the difference table.

2. It should be noted that the expression in (16·12) is not an infinite series but is a terminating series. The last term depends on the number of given points $(x, y = f(x))$. If we are given $(n + 1)$ entries (points), then $f(x)$ can be approximated by a polynomial of nth degree, so that

$$\Delta^n f(x) = \text{Constant} \Rightarrow \Delta^{n+1} f(x) = 0, \text{ for all values of } x.$$

Hence, in this case, the expression in (16·12) will terminate at $\Delta^n f(x)$ and we shall get $f(x)$, on simplification [of (16·12)] as a polynomial of nth degree in x.

Example 16·3. *If* $y = 2x^3 - x^2 + 3x + 1$, *calculate the values of* y *corresponding to* $x = 0, 1, 2, 3, 4, 5$ *and form the table of differences.*

Solution. Here we have $y_x = 2x^3 - x^2 + 3x + 1$ ...(*)

Putting $x = 0, 1, 2, 3, 4$ and 5 in (*), we get respectively

$$y_0 = 1$$
$$y_1 = 2 \times 1 - 1 + 3 + 1 = 5$$
$$y_2 = 2 \times 8 - 4 + 3 \times 2 + 1 = 19$$
$$y_3 = 2 \times 27 - 9 + 3 \times 3 + 1 = 54 - 9 + 9 + 1 = 55$$
$$y_4 = 2 \times 4^3 - 4^2 + 3 \times 4 + 1 = 2 \times 64 - 16 + 12 + 1 = 125$$
$$y_5 = 2 \times 5^3 - 5^2 + 3 \times 5 + 1 = 250 - 25 + 15 + 1 = 241$$

The difference table is given in Table 16·3

TABLE 16·3 **TABLE OF DIFFERENCES**

x	y_x	Δy_x	$\Delta^2 y_x$	$\Delta^3 y_x$	$\Delta^4 y_x$
0	1				
		4			
1	5		10		
		14		12	
2	19		22		0
		36		12	
3	55		34		0
		70		12	
4	125		46		
		116			
5	241				

Remark. Let us consider the value of y_x and its successive differences as given in the various columns of the difference Table 16·3. We find the following interesting result.

The difference between the two extreme values (the last value and the first value) of any column is equal to the sum of all the values in the next (succeeding) column.

For example, in the Table 16·3,

Difference between the extreme values of Δy_x column = 116 − 4 = 112

Sum of all values of $\Delta^2 y_x$ column = 10 + 22 + 34 + 46 = 112

The reader may verify this result for other columns of Table 16·3.

This result is true not only in Table 16·3 but in all the forward difference tables.

Example 16·4. *Estimate the expectation of life at the age of 16 years by using the following data.*

Age (in years) :	*10*	*15*	*20*	*25*	*30*	*35*
Expectation of life (years) :	*35·4*	*32·3*	*29·2*	*26·0*	*23·2*	*16·4*

Solution. Since the year of interpolation is in the beginning of the table we use Newton's forward difference formula as given below :

$$y_x = y_a + u\,\Delta y_a + \frac{u(u-1)}{2\,!}\Delta^2 y_a + \frac{u(u-1)(u-2)}{3\,!}\Delta^3 y_a + \ldots \qquad \ldots(*)$$

where $u = (x - a)/h$; and x is the year of interpolation, a is the year of origin and h is common interval of differencing.

$$\therefore \qquad u = \frac{16-10}{5} = \frac{6}{5} = 1{\cdot}2 \qquad \ldots(**)$$

The difference table is given in Table 16·4.

TABLE 16·4 **TABLE OF DIFFERENCES**

x	y_x	Δy_x	$\Delta^2 y_x$	$\Delta^3 y_x$	$\Delta^4 y_x$	$\Delta^5 y_x$
10	35·4					
		−3·1				
15	32·3		0			
		−3·1		−0·1		
20	29·2		−0·1		0·6	
		−3·2		0·5		−1·5
25	26·0		0·4		−0·9	
		−2·8		−0·4		
30	23·2		0			
		−2·8				
35	20·4					

Hence, from (*) and (**), we get

$$y_{16} = 35{\cdot}4 + 1{\cdot}2\,(-3{\cdot}1) + \frac{(1{\cdot}2)(1{\cdot}2-1)}{2}\times 0 + \frac{(1{\cdot}2)(1{\cdot}2-1)(1{\cdot}2-2)}{6}\times(-0{\cdot}1)$$
$$+\frac{(1{\cdot}2)(1{\cdot}2-1)(1{\cdot}2-2)(1{\cdot}2-3)}{24}\times(0{\cdot}6) + \frac{(1{\cdot}2)(1{\cdot}2-1)(1{\cdot}2-2)(1{\cdot}2-3)(1{\cdot}2-4)}{120}\times(-1{\cdot}5)$$

$$\Rightarrow \quad y_{16} = 35{\cdot}4 - 3{\cdot}72 + 0 + 0{\cdot}0032 + 0{\cdot}00864 + 0{\cdot}012096 = 31{\cdot}7 \text{ years.}$$

Hence the estimated expectation of life at the age of 16 years by using the given data is 31·7 years.

Example 16·5. *The following results are given :*

$$\sqrt[3]{27} = 3{\cdot}0000 \quad ; \quad \sqrt[3]{28} = 3{\cdot}0369 \quad ; \quad \sqrt[3]{29} = 3{\cdot}0727 \quad ; \quad \sqrt[3]{30} = 3{\cdot}1074$$

Using them, find $\sqrt[3]{26}$.

Solution. Let $y_x = \sqrt[3]{x}$. Then we are given the values of y_{27}, y_{28}, y_{29} and y_{30} and we want y_{26}. Since the values are given at equal intervals, we can apply Newton's forward interpolation formula.

Newton's formula gives :

$$y_x = y_a + u\,\Delta y_a + \frac{u(u-1)}{2!}\Delta^2 y_a + \frac{u(u-1)(u-2)}{3!}\Delta^3 y_a + \ldots \qquad \ldots(*)$$

where $u = (x-a)/h$; x is the value of the argument for which y_x is required, a is the 1st argument in the difference table and h is the common interval of differencing.

TABLE 16·5 **TABLE OF DIFFERENCES**

x	y_x	Δy_x	$\Delta^2 y_x$	$\Delta^3 y_x$
27	3·0000			
		0·0369		
28	3·0369		– 0·0011	
		0·0358		0
29	3·0727		– 0·0011	
		0·0347		
30	3·1074			

$$\therefore \qquad u = \frac{26-27}{1} = -1.$$

Substituting in (*) and using the difference Table 16·5, we get

$$y_{26} = 3{\cdot}0000 - 1\times 0{\cdot}0369 + \frac{(-1)(-2)}{2}\times(-0{\cdot}0011) = 3{\cdot}000 - 0{\cdot}0369 - 0{\cdot}0011 = 2{\cdot}962$$

Example 16·6. *Using an appropriate formula for interpolation, estimate the number of students who obtained less than 45 marks from the following data :*

Marks	:	*30—40*	*40—50*	*50—60*	*60—70*	*70—80*
No. of students	:	*31*	*42*	*51*	*35*	*31*

[*Punjab Univ. B.Com., 1997; Allahabad Univ. M.Com., 2006*]

Solution. Here we define :

y_x : Number of students who obtained less than x marks, *i.e.*, y_x gives the 'less than' cumulative frequency (*c.f.*).

The 'less than' cumulative frequency and the difference table are given in Table 16·6.

TABLE 16·6 **TABLE OF DIFFERENCES**

x	f	y_x (*less than c.f.*)	Δy_x	$\Delta^2 y_x$	$\Delta^3 y_x$	$\Delta^4 y_x$
40	31	31				
			42			
50	42	73		9		
			51		–25	
60	51	124		–16		37
			35		12	
70	35	159		– 4		
			31			
80	31	190				

We want y_{45}. Since the value to be estimated is in the beginning of the table, we use Newton's forward difference formula given by :

$$y_x = y_0 + u\,\Delta y_0 + \frac{u(u-1)}{2\,!}\Delta^2 y_0 + \frac{u(u-1)(u-2)}{3\,!}\Delta^3 y_0 + \ldots \quad \ldots(*)$$

Here $x = 45,\ \ a = 40,\ \ h = 10 \quad \Rightarrow \quad u = \frac{x-a}{h} = \frac{45-40}{10} = 0{\cdot}5$

Substituting in (*) and using the difference Table 16·6, we get

$$y_{45} = 31 + (0{\cdot}5)(42) + \frac{(0{\cdot}5)(0{\cdot}5-1)}{2}(9) + \frac{(0{\cdot}5)(0{\cdot}5-1)(0{\cdot}5-2)\times(-25)}{6} + \frac{(0{\cdot}5)(0{\cdot}5-1)(0{\cdot}5-2)(0{\cdot}5-3)}{24}\times 37$$

$$= 31 + 21 - 1{\cdot}125 - 1{\cdot}5625 - 1{\cdot}4453 = 47{\cdot}8672 \approx 48$$

Hence, the estimated number of students getting less than 45 marks is 48.

Example 16·7. *From the following table, find the number of workers falling in the earning group of Rs. 2,500 to Rs. 3,500 :*

Earnings in '00 rupees	*No. of workers*
up to 10	50
" " *20*	150
" " *30*	300
" " *40*	500
" " *50*	700
" " *60*	800

Solution. Here the function y_x is defined as :

y_x = Number of workers earning up to x hundred rupees *i.e.*, $\leq x$ hundred rupees.

TABLE 16·7 **TABLE OF DIFFERENCES**

x	y_x	Δy_x	$\Delta^2 y_x$	$\Delta^3 y_x$	$\Delta^4 y_x$	$\Delta^5 y_x$
10	50					
		100				
20	150		50			
		150		0		
30	300		50		−50	
		200		−50		0
40	500		0		−50	
		200		−100		
50	700		−100			
		100				
60	800					

We want to find the value $(y_{35} - y_{25})$.

Since the values to be estimated are in the beginning of the table, we shall use Newton's forward difference formula to estimate y_{25} and y_{35}.

To find y_{25}, we have : $u = \frac{x-a}{h} = \frac{25-10}{10} = 1{\cdot}5$

$$y_{25} = 50 + 1{\cdot}5(100) + \frac{(1{\cdot}5)(1{\cdot}5-1)}{2}\times(50) + \frac{1{\cdot}5(1{\cdot}5-1)(1{\cdot}5-2)}{6}\times(0) + \frac{1{\cdot}5(1{\cdot}5-1)(1{\cdot}5-2)(1{\cdot}5-3)}{24}\times(-50) + \frac{(1{\cdot}5)(1{\cdot}5-1)(1{\cdot}5-2)(1{\cdot}5-3)(1{\cdot}5-4)}{120}\times 0$$

$$= 50 + 150 + 18{\cdot}75 + 0 - 1{\cdot}171875 + 0 = 217{\cdot}57813 \approx 218$$

Hence the number of workers earning up to Rupees 2500 is 218.

Similarly to find y_{35}, we have $u = \frac{35-10}{10} = 2{\cdot}5$

$$\therefore \quad y_{35} = 50 + (2{\cdot}5)\,100 + \frac{2{\cdot}5(2{\cdot}5-1)}{2} \times 50 + \frac{2{\cdot}5(2{\cdot}5-1)(2{\cdot}5-2)}{6} \times 0$$

$$+ \frac{2{\cdot}5(2{\cdot}5-1)(2{\cdot}5-2)(2{\cdot}5-3)}{24} \times (-50) + \frac{2{\cdot}5(2{\cdot}5-1)(2{\cdot}5-2)(2{\cdot}5-3)(2{\cdot}5-4)}{120} \times 0$$

$$= 50 + 250 + 95{\cdot}75 + 0 + 1{\cdot}953125 + 0 = 395{\cdot}70313 \simeq 396$$

Hence the number of workers falling in the earning group of Rs. 2,500 to Rs. 3,500 is :

$$y_{35} - y_{25} = 396 - 218 = 178$$

16·8. NEWTON'S BACKWARD DIFFERENCE FORMULA

This formula is based on the backward differences ∇ and is *specially useful if the estimated value lies towards the end of the difference table*. It uses the leading backward differences of the last entry in the table and is given by the formula :

$$f(x) = f(a+nh) + u\nabla f(a+nh) + \frac{u(u+1)}{2!}\nabla^2 f(a+nh) + \frac{u(u+1)(u+2)}{3!}\nabla^3 f(a+nh) + \dots\dots \qquad \dots(16{\cdot}14)$$

where $a + nh$ is the last argument in the difference table ; $\nabla, \nabla^2, \dots$ are the leading backward differences of the last entry (and are given by the diagonal of the backward difference table) and

$$u = \frac{\text{Period of interpolation} - \text{Last argument}}{\text{Interval of differencing}} \quad \Rightarrow \quad u = \frac{x-(a+nh)}{h} \qquad \dots(16{\cdot}15)$$

Example 16·8. *The following table gives the census population of a town for the years 1961 to 2001. Estimate the population for the year 1995 by using an appropriate interpolation formula.*

Year	:	*1961*	*1971*	*1981*	*1991*	*2001*
Population ('000)	:	*46*	*66*	*81*	*93*	*101*

Solution. Since the value to be interpolated lies towards the end of the given data, we shall use Newton's backward difference interpolation formula.

TABLE 16·8 **TABLE OF BACKWARD DIFFERENCES**

x	$f(x)$	$\nabla f(x)$	$\nabla^2 f(x)$	$\nabla^3 f(x)$	$\nabla^4 f(x)$
1961	46				
		20			
1971	66		–5		
		15		2	
1981	81		–3		–3
		12		–1	
1991	93		– 4		
		8			
2001	101				

In the notations of formulae (16·14) and (16·15), we have $u = \frac{1995-2001}{10} = -0{\cdot}6$

The leading backward differences of last entry are given respectively by 8, – 4, –1 and –3. Substituting in (16·14), we get

$$f(1995) = 101 - (0{\cdot}6) \times 8 + \frac{(-0{\cdot}6)(-0{\cdot}6+1)}{2!} \times (-4)$$

$$+ \frac{(-0{\cdot}6)(-0{\cdot}6+1)(-0{\cdot}6+2)}{3!} \times (-1) + \frac{(-0{\cdot}6)(-0{\cdot}6+1)(-0{\cdot}6+2)(-0{\cdot}6+3)}{4!} \times (-3)$$

$$= 101 - 4{\cdot}8000 + 0{\cdot}4800 + 0{\cdot}0560 + 0{\cdot}1008 = 101{\cdot}6368 - 4{\cdot}8000 = 96{\cdot}837.$$

Hence, the estimated population of the town for the year 1995 is 95·837 thousand.

Example 16·9. *By Newton's or by any other algebraic method find the number of persons who probably will be travelling if rate is 4·2 in the following table :*

Rate	:	*5·0*	*4·5*	*4·0*	*3·5*	*3·0*
Passengers	:	*30,000*	*40,000*	*60,000*	*1,00,000*	*1,50,000*

Solution. Let x : Rate and $f(x)$: Number of passengers in thousands travelling at rate x. Then, we are given (writing in reverse order) :

Rate (x)	:	3·0	3·5	4·0	4·5	5·0
Passengers('000) $f(x)$	:	150	100	60	40	30

We want f (4.2). Since the value to be estimated lies towards the end of the table, we use Newton's Backward Difference Interpolation formula (16·14).

$$u = \frac{x - \text{last argument}}{h} = \frac{4 \cdot 2 - 5 \cdot 0}{0 \cdot 5} = -1 \cdot 6$$

TABLE 16·9. **TABLE OF BACKWARD DIFFERENCES**

x	$f(x)$	$\nabla f(x)$	$\nabla^2 f(x)$	$\nabla^3 f(x)$	$\nabla^4 f(x)$
3·0	150				
		−50			
3·5	100		10		
		−40		10	
4·0	60		20		−20
		−20		−10	
4·5	40		10		
		−10			
5·0	30				

From Table 16·9, the last entry and its successive differences are given by : 30, – 10, 10, –10 and –20. Substituting in Formula (16·14), we get

$$f(4 \cdot 2) = 30 + (-1 \cdot 6) \times (-10) + \frac{(-1 \cdot 6) \times (-0 \cdot 6)}{2} \times 10$$

$$+ \frac{(-1 \cdot 6) \times (-0 \cdot 6) \times 0 \cdot 4}{6} \times (-10) + \frac{(-1 \cdot 6)(-0 \cdot 6) \times 0 \cdot 4 \times 1 \cdot 4}{24} \times (-20)$$

$$= 30 + 16 + 4 \cdot 8 - 0 \cdot 640 - 0 \cdot 448 = 49 \cdot 712 \text{ thousand.}$$

Hence, the number of persons who probably will be travelling if rate is 4·2 is 49712.

EXERCISE 16·1

1. What do you understand by interpolation ? What are the underlying assumptions for the validity of the various methods used for interpolation ?

2. (*a*) What do you understand by 'Interpolation'. Show clearly the necessity of interpolation by taking a few concrete examples.

(*b*) What is interpolation ? What are its uses ? Describe various methods of interpolation and state the conditions under which they are most suitable. (*Punjab Univ. B.Com., Oct. 1999*)

(*c*) What is the utility of interpolation and extrapolation to a businessman ? Mention the chief methods of interpolation, giving the conditions under which they are suitable.

3. Distinguish between interpolation and extrapolation. Explain the requirements and uses of interpolation. (*Punjab Univ. B.Com., April 2000*)

4. (*a*) Discuss the uses of the technique of interpolation in solving most of the economic problems.

(*b*) What are the assumptions on which methods of interpolation are based ?(*Bangalore Univ. B.Com., 1998*)

5. (*a*) Explain the terms 'argument' and 'entry' as used in interpolation.

(*b*) Define the difference operators Δ and E and show that $1 + \Delta = E$.

6. State Newton's interpolation formula for equal intervals and the assumptions underlying it.

7. State Newton's formula for interpolation and discuss some of its uses. Explain why Newton's formula is to be used for interpolating values at the top of the table.

8. Define the difference operators Δ and Δ and state Newton's Forward Difference and Backward Difference formulae. Explain clearly : (*i*) the situations where these formulae can be used, and (*ii*) the assumptions involved.

9. Explain the terms interpolation and extrapolation. Describe

(*i*) Graphic Method, (*ii*) Algebraic Method.

of interpolation and discuss their relative merits and demerits.

10. The following table gives the values of a certain function $y = f(x)$ for some equidistant values of x :

x	:	14	20	26	32	38	44
y	:	110	192	308	464	666	920

Find graphically (*i*) the value of y when $x = 40$ and (*ii*) the value of x when $y = 400$.

Ans. (*i*) $y = 750$ (*ii*) $x = 30$.

11. The following data relate to the amounts of income-tax paid by 600 men during a year :

More than	:	Rs. 500	Rs. 1,000	Rs. 1,500	Rs. 2,000	Rs. 2,500	Rs. 3,000
No. of men	:	600	550	425	275	100	25

Find the number of men who paid more than Rs. 1,200 but not more than Rs. 2,400 as income-tax. Use graphic method.

Ans. 370 (approx.)

12. Explain the 'parabolic curve fitting' method of interpolation.

The following table shows the values of an immediate life annuity for every £ 100 paid :—

Age in years	:	40	50	60	70
Annuity (£)	:	6·2	7·2	9·1	12·0

Interpolate the annuity for the age 42 'by parabolic curve fitting' method.

Ans. £ 6·333.

13. State Newton's formula for interpolation for equal intervals and the assumptions underlying it. Use it to find out the annual net premium payable at the age of 25 from the table given below :

Age	:	20	24	28	32
Annual Net Premium payable	:	0·01427	0·01581	0·01771	0·01996

Ans. 0·01625.

14. Explain the meaning of interpolation. The following table gives the expectation of life at different ages. Find the expectation of life at the age of 49 years.

Age (years)	:	35	45	55	65	75
Expectation of life (years)	:	34	26	18	12	10

Ans. 22·688 years

15. If L_x represents the numbers living at age x in a life table, interpolate by using Newton's method, L_x for the values of $x = 24$ and $x = 29$.

$L_{20} = 512$; $L_{30} = 439$; $L_{40} = 346$; $L_{50} = 243$

Ans. $L_{24} = 486$; $L_{29} = 447$.

16. State Newton's forward interpolation formula and use it to obtain $\sqrt{5 \cdot 5}$, given :

$\sqrt{5} = 2 \cdot 236$, $\sqrt{6} = 2 \cdot 449$, $\sqrt{7} = 2 \cdot 646$, $\sqrt{8} = 2 \cdot 828$.

Ans. 2·345.

17. Given : $\sin 45° = 0 \cdot 7071$, $\sin 50° = 0 \cdot 7660$, $\sin 55° = 0 \cdot 8192$, $\sin 60° = 0 \cdot 8660$,

find sin 52°, by using any method of interpolation.

Ans. 0·7771.

18. Estimate the annual premium payable at the age of 28 years from the following date :

Age (Years)	:	20	25	30	35
Annual (Premium (Rs.)	:	360	390	430	470

Ans. Rs. 413·44 (Using Newton's forward difference formula).

19. From the data given below estimate the number of candidates who get marks more than 48 but not more than 60.

Marks	:	36—45	46—55	56-65	66—75	76—85
No. of candidates	:	8	10	8	6	4

Ans. $27 - 20 = 7$.

20. (*a*) Using Newton's method of interpolation, find from the data given below, the number of persons in the income group between Rs. 20,000 and Rs. 25,000.

Income below rupees :	10,000	20,000	30,000	40,000	50,000
Number of persons :	20	45	115	210	325

Ans. 76 – 45 = 31.

(*b*) Estimate the number of persons whose incomes are between Rs. 400 and Rs. 500 per day from the following data, using Newton's forward difference formula.

Income (Rs.) :	Below 200	200—400	400—600	600—800	800—1000
No. of persons (in '000) :	120	145	200	250	150

[*Mysore Univ. B.Com. 2004*]

Ans. 355 – (120 + 145) = 90

21. From the following data, estimate the number of persons earning between Rs. 60 and Rs. 70 per day.

Wages (in Rs.) :	Below 40	40—60	60—80	80—100	100—120
No. of persons (in '000) :	250	120	100	70	50

(*Bangalore Univ. B.Com., 2005*)

Ans. (423·6 – 370) thousand = 53·6 thousand.

22. Estimate the number of candidates who get more than 48 but not more than 50 marks from the following :

Marks up to :	45	50	55	60	65
No. of candidates :	447	484	505	511	514

Ans. 13.

23. The following are the marks obtained by 492 candidates in a certain examination :

Not more than 40 marks ,	212 candidates	Not more than 60 marks	460 candidates
" " " 45 " ,	296 "	" " 65 " ,	481 "
" " " 50 " ,	368 "	" " 70 " ,	490 "
" " " 55 " ,	429 "	" " 75 " ,	492 "

(*a*) Find the number of candidates who secured more than 42 but not more than 45 marks.

(*b*) Find the number of candidates who secured :

(*i*) more than 48 but not more than 50 marks ; (*ii*) less than 48 but not less than 45 marks.

Ans. (*a*) 296 – 256 = 40 ; (*b*) (*i*) 368 – 331 = 37; (*ii*) 331 – 296 = 35.

24. State Newton's backward difference formula, explaining clearly the assumptions involved. Under what situations do you recommend its use ?

25. What do you understand by interpolation ? Estimate the number of students for 1993 from the data given below.

Year :	1988	1990	1992	1994
No. of students :	50	79	102	113

Ans. (By Newton's Backward formula) : 109.

26. Given the following table, construct a difference table and from it estimate y when $x = 0{\cdot}35$ by using Newton's backward interpolation formula.

x :	0·1	0·2	0·3	0·4
y :	1·095	1·179	1·251	1·310

Ans. 1·282.

27. The population of a district for different years is given below. Find out the population for 2002 :

Year :	1997	1998	1999	2000	2001
Population (in million) :	7	2	36	14	16

Ans. 297 million (Backward difference formula).

28. From the following figures, find the premium payable at the age of 40 :

Age (in years) :	20	25	30	35
Annual Premium (in '00 Rs.) :	28	31·25	35	41

Ans. Rs. 5,100.

29. State Newton's backward interpolation formula with assumptions.

Estimate by Newton's method of interpolation, the expectation of life at age 32 from the following data.

Age (years) :	10	15	20	25	30	35
Expectation of life (years) :	35·3	32·4	29·2	26·1	23·2	20·5

Ans. 22·0948 years.

30. If l_x represents the numbers living at age x in a life table, find as accurately as data will permit, l_x for values of $x = 35$ and 47, given $l_{20} = 512$, $l_{30} = 439$, $l_{40} = 346$ and $l_{50} = 243$.

Ans. $l_{35} = 395$ and $l_{47} = 274$.

31. From the following data, estimate number of persons earning wages between Rs. 25 and 35.

Wages in Rs.	No. of persons
up to 10	50
" 20	150
" 30	300
" 40	500
" 50	700

(Punjab Univ. B.Com., 1999)

Ans. $y_{25} = 218$ (Newton's forward formula) ; $y_{35} = 396$ (Newton's backward formula) ;

$y_{35} - y_{25} = 396 - 218 = 178.$

16·9. BINOMIAL EXPANSION METHOD FOR INTERPOLATING MISSING VALUES

Sometimes we may be given data in which the values of the independent variable x are at equal intervals but one, two or more values of the dependent variable (entries) may be missing. These missing values can be easily interpolated by using the following results of the calculus of finite differences.

(*i*) Suppose we are given $(n + 1)$ equidistant arguments but the entry corresponding to *any one* of them is missing. Thus, we are given n entries and hence we can express the function $y = f(x)$ by a polynomial of $(n - 1)$th degree.

(*ii*) By fundamental theorem of finite differences, since $y = f(x)$ is a polynomial of $(n - 1)$th degree, $(n - 1)$th order differences are constant, and nth and higher order differences are zero.

Symbolically,

$$\Delta^{n-1} f(x) = \text{Constant} \quad \Rightarrow \quad \Delta^n f(x) = 0, \text{ for all } x \qquad ...(16·16)$$

In particular taking $x = a$ (the first argument), we get :

$$\Delta^n f(a) = 0 \quad \Rightarrow \quad (E - 1)^n f(a) = 0 \quad [\text{From } (16·10)] \qquad ...(16·16a)$$

Expanding by binomial theorem, we get

$$[E^n - {^nC_1} E^{n-1} + {^nC_2} E^{n-2} - ... + (-1)^n] f(a) = 0$$

$$\Rightarrow \quad E^n f(a) - {^nC_1} E^{n-1} f(a) + {^nC_2} E^{n-2} f(a) + ... + (-1)^n f(a) = 0$$

Hence, using (16·9) we get

$$f(a + nh) - {^nC_1} f(a + \overline{n-1}\, h) + {^nC_2} f(a + \overline{n-2}\, h) + ... + ... + (-1)^n f(a) = 0 \qquad ...(16·17)$$

From this equation the missing value can be interpolated.

If we are given $(n + 2)$ equidistant arguments and two entries are missing, *i.e.*, as before n entries are given then arguing as above we shall get

$$\Delta^n f(x) = 0, \text{ for all } x \qquad ...(16·18)$$

Since two values are missing, we need two equations to estimate these values. Taking $x = a$ and $a + h$ in (16·18) we get respectively :

$$\Delta^n f(a) - 0 \quad \text{and} \quad \Delta^n f(a + h) = 0 \qquad ...(16·19)$$

$$\Rightarrow \quad (E - 1)^n f(a) = 0 \quad \text{and} \quad (E - 1)^n f(a + h) = 0 \qquad ...(16·19a)$$

Expanding equations (16·19*a*) by binomial theorem and using (16·9), we finally get the estimates of missing values by solving these equations. The following examples will clarify the technique.

Example 16·10. *Estimate u_2 from the following table :*

x	1	2	3	4	5
$u(x)$	2·0000	*	2·0646	2·0954	2·1253

State the necessary assumptions made.

Solution. Since we are given four entries, $u(x)$ may be regarded as a polynomial of 3rd degree so that

$$\Delta^3 u_x = \text{constant} \quad \Rightarrow \quad \Delta^4 u_x = 0, \text{ for all } x \quad \ldots(*)$$

In particular, $\Delta^4 u_1 = 0$ [Taking $x = 1$ in (*)]

$$\Rightarrow \quad (E-1)^4 u_1 = 0$$

$$\Rightarrow \quad (E^4 - 4E^3 + 6E^2 - 4E + 1)\, u_1 = 0$$

$$\Rightarrow \quad u_5 - 4u_4 + 6u_3 - 4u_2 + u_1 = 0 \quad \text{[Using (16·9}a\text{)]}$$

$$2·1253 - 4 \times 2·0954 + 6 \times 2·0646 - 4u_2 + 2·0 = 0$$

$$\Rightarrow \quad 2·1253 - 8·3816 + 12·3876 - 4u_2 + 2·0 = 0$$

$$\Rightarrow \quad 4u_2 = 2·1253 + 12·3876 + 2·0 - 8·3816 = 8·1313 \quad \Rightarrow \quad u_2 = \frac{8·1313}{4} = 2·0328.$$

Example 16·12. *The following table gives the quantity of cement in thousands of tonnes manufactured each year by a company. Find the missing term by a suitable algebraic method of interpolation.*

Year	:	*1992*	*1994*	*1996*	*1998*	*2000*	*2002*
Cement quantity ('000 tonnes)	:	*44*	*90*	*?*	*160*	*270*	*390*

Solution. Taking the year 1992 as origin, we are given :

x	:	0	1	2	3	4	5
y_x	:	$y_0 = 44$	$y_1 = 90$	$y_2 = ?$	$y_3 = 160$	$y_4 = 270$	$y_5 = 390$

Since five entries are given, we can assume y_x to be a polynomial of 4th degree, so that fourth order differences of y_x are constant and fifth order differences are zero, *i.e.*,

$$\Delta^5 y_x = 0 \text{ for all values of } x. \quad \ldots(*)$$

In particular, $\Delta^5 y_0 = 0 \quad \Rightarrow \quad (E-1)^5 y_0 = 0$

$$\Rightarrow \quad (E^5 - 5E^4 + 10E^3 - 10E^2 + 5E - 1)\, y_0 = 0 \quad \Rightarrow \quad y_5 - 5y_4 + 10y_3 - 10y_2 + 5y_1 - y_0 = 0 \quad \ldots(**)$$

Substituting the values of y_5, y_4, y_3, y_1, y_0, in (**), we get

$$390 - 5 \times 270 + 10 \times 160 - 10y_2 + 5 \times 90 - 44 = 0 \quad \Rightarrow \quad 10y_2 = 1046 \quad \Rightarrow \quad y_2 = 104·6$$

Hence the estimated quantity of cement manufactured in 1996 is 104·6 thousand tonnes.

Aliter. Let the missing observation be 'a'. We have the difference table as given in Table 16·10.

TABLE 16·10 **TABLE OF DIFFERENCES**

x	y_x	Δy_x	$\Delta^2 y_x$	$\Delta^3 y_x$	$\Delta^4 y_x$	$\Delta^5 y_x$
1992	44					
		46				
1994	90		$a - 136$			
		$a - 90$		$386 - 3a$		
1996	a		$250 - 2a$		$6a - 686$	
		$160 - a$		$3a - 300$		$1046 - 10a$
1998	160		$a - 50$		$360 - 4a$	
		110		$60 - a$		
2000	270		10			
		120				
2002	390					

Since fifth order differences are zero [See (*)], we have :

$$\Delta^5 y_0 = 0 \quad \Rightarrow \quad 1046 - 10a = 0 \quad \Rightarrow \quad a = \frac{1046}{10} = 104·6$$

Hence missing observation is 104·6 (thousand tonnes).

Example 16·12. *Using any appropriate interpolation formula estimate the percentage number of criminals under 35 years from the data given below :*

Age	*Percentage No. of criminals*
Under 25 years	*32·0*
" *30* "	*47·3*
" *40* "	*64·1*
" *45* "	*69·3*
" *50* "	*74·5*

Solution. We are given :

Age under (years) (x)	:	25	30	35	40	45	50
Perçentage No. of criminals (y_x)	:	32·0	47·3	?	64·1	69·3	74·5

Let the percentage number of criminals under 35 years be a. Since we are given 5 entries, y_x can be approximated by a polynomial of 4th degree so that

$$\Delta^4 y_x = \text{Constant} \quad \Rightarrow \quad \Delta^5 y_x = 0, \text{ for all values of } x \qquad \ldots(*)$$

TABLE 16·11. DIFFERENCE TABLE

x	y_x	Δy_x	$\Delta^2 y_x$	$\Delta^3 y_x$	$\Delta^4 y_x$	$\Delta^5 y_x$
25	32·0					
		15·3				
30	47·3		$a-62·6$			
		$a-47·3$		$174-3a$		
35	a		$111·4-2a$		$6a-344·3$	
		$64·1-a$		$3a-170·3$		$573·5-10a$
40	64·1		$a-58·9$		$229·2-4a$	
		5·2		$58·9-a$		
45	69·3		0			
		5·2				
50	74·5					

Since $\Delta^5 y_x = 0$ [From (*)], we get $573·5 - 10a = 0 \Rightarrow a = \frac{573·5}{10} = 57·35$

Hence the percentage number of criminals under 35 years is 57·35.

Example 16·13. *Estimate* y_3 *from the following data :*

x	:	*0*	*1*	2	3	4
y_x	:	*1*	3	9	–	81

and explain why the value obtained is different from that obtained by putting $x = 3$ *in the expression* 3^x.

Solution. Since we are given four entries we can assume y_x to be a polynomial of 3rd degree so that the fourth order differences of y_x are zero.

$$\therefore \quad \Delta^4 y_x = 0, \text{ for all values of } x \quad \Rightarrow \quad \Delta^4 y_0 = 0 \qquad \ldots(*)$$

Let the missing value be 'a'. Then the difference table is given in Table 16·12.

TABLE 16·12 TABLE OF DIFFERENCES

x	y_x	Δy_x	$\Delta^2 y_x$	$\Delta^3 y_x$	$\Delta^4 y_x$
0	1				
		2			
1	3		4		
		6		$a-19$	
2	9		$a-15$		$124-4a$
		$a-9$		$105-3a$	
3	a		$90-2a$		
		$81-a$			
4	81				

Substituting from this table in (*) we get : $124 - 4a = 0 \Rightarrow a = \frac{124}{4} = 31$

Hence the missing value $y_3 = 31$.

Now putting $x = 3$ in 3^x, we have $y_3 = 3^3 = 27$. Obviously this value differs from the estimated value, *viz.*, 31. The reason for it is that in estimating y_3, we assumed that y_x can be expressed as a polynomial of third degree and hence fourth order differences are zero. But in this case ($y = 3^x$), the function is not a polynomial but is of exponential form. Since the basic assumption of interpolation is violated, we get the difference between actual and estimated values.

Example 16·14. *From the following table, interpolate the missing values.*

Year	:	*0*	*1*	*2*	*3*	*4*	*5*	*6*
Production (in '000 tonnes)	:	*200*	*220*	*260*	*?*	*350*	*?*	*430*

Solution. Taking years as x and production (in '000 tonnes) as y_x we are given :

x	0	1	2	3	4	5	6
y_x	$y_0 = 200$	$y_1 = 220$	$y_2 = 260$	$y_3 = ?$	$y_4 = 350$	$y_5 = ?$	$y_6 = 430$

Since we are given five entries, we can assume that production (y_x) is a polynomial of 4th degree so that fourth order differences of y_x are constant and consequently fifth order differences are zero. *i.e.*,

$$\Delta^5 y_x = 0 \text{ for all values of } x.$$

$$\Rightarrow \quad (E-1)^5 y_x = 0, \quad \text{for all values of } x \qquad \ldots(*)$$

Since we have to estimate two unknowns *viz.*, y_3 and y_5, we need two equations. Hence taking $x = 0$ and $x = 1$ in (*), we get respectively

$$(E-1)^5 y_0 = 0 \quad \text{and} \quad (E-1)^5 y_1 = 0$$

$$(E-1)^5 y_0 = 0$$

$$\Rightarrow \quad (E^5 - 5E^4 + 10E^3 - 10E^2 + 5E - 1)\, y_0 = 0$$

$$\Rightarrow \quad y_5 - 5y_4 + 10y_3 - 10y_2 + 5y_1 - y_0 = 0$$

i.e.,

$$y_5 - 5 \times 350 + 10y_3 - 10 \times 260 + 5 \times 220 - 200 = 0$$

$$\Rightarrow \quad y_5 + 10y_3 = 3450 \qquad \ldots(i)$$

Similarly

$$(E-1)^5 y_1 = 0$$

$$\Rightarrow \quad y_6 - 5y_5 + 10y_4 - 10y_3 + 5y_2 - y_1 = 0$$

$$\Rightarrow \quad 430 - 5y_5 + 3500 - 10y_3 + 260 \times 5 - 220 = 0$$

$$\Rightarrow \quad 5y_5 + 10y_3 = 5010 \qquad \ldots(ii)$$

We have to solve (*i*) and (*ii*) for y_3 and y_5. Substracting (*i*) from (*ii*), we get

$$4y_5 = 5010 - 3450 = 1560 \quad \Rightarrow \quad y_5 = \frac{1560}{4} = 390$$

Substituting the value of y_5 in (*i*), we get

$$390 + 10y_3 = 3450 \quad \Rightarrow \quad y_3 = \frac{3060}{10} = 306$$

Hence the estimated production figures in ('000 tonnes) for years 3 and 5 are 306 and 390 respectively.

Example 16·15. *Given :* $u_{50} = 939$, $u_{52} = 907$, $u_{53} = 841$, $u_{55} = 733$, *estimate* u_{51} *and* u_{54}, *under suitable assumptions.*

Solution. We are given :

x	50	51	52	53	54	55
u_x	939	?	907	841	?	773

Taking $x = 50$ as origin, the above table becomes

x	0	1	2	3	4	5
u_x	$u_0 = 939$	$u_1 = ?$	$u_2 = 907$	$u_3 = 841$	$u_4 = ?$	$u_5 = 773$

Since we are given four entries, u_x may be regarded as a polynomial of 3rd degree so that :

$\Delta^3 u_x$ constant $\Rightarrow$ $\Delta^4 u_x = 0$ $\Rightarrow$ $(E-1)^4 u_x = 0$ for all values of x ...(*)

Since we have to estimate two unknowns, *viz.*, u_1 and u_4 we need two equations. Hence taking $x = 0$ and $x = 1$ in (*) we get respectively :

$$(E-1)^4 u_0 = 0 \quad \text{and} \quad (E-1)^4 u_1 = 0 \qquad ...(**)$$

$$(E-1)^4 u_0 = 0$$
$$\Rightarrow (E^4 - 4E^3 + 6E^2 - 4E + 1)\, u_0 = 0$$
$$\Rightarrow u_4 - 4u_3 + 6u_2 - 4u_1 + u_0 = 0$$
$$\Rightarrow u_4 - 4 \times 841 + 6 \times 907 - 4u_1 + 939 = 0$$
$$\Rightarrow u_4 - 3364 - 5442 - 4u_1 + 939 = 0$$
$$\Rightarrow u_4 - 4u_1 + 6381 - 3364 = 0$$
$$\Rightarrow u_4 - 4u_1 + 3017 = 0 \qquad ...(i)$$

Similarly
$$(E-1)^4 u_1 = 0$$
$$\Rightarrow (E^4 - 4E^3 + 6E^2 - 4E + 1)\, u_1 = 0$$
$$\Rightarrow u_5 - 4u_4 + 6u_3 - 4u_2 + u_1 = 0$$
$$\Rightarrow 773 - 4u_4 + 6 \times 841 - 4 \times 907 + u_1 = 0$$
$$\Rightarrow 773 - 4u_4 + 5046 - 3628 + u_1 = 0$$
$$\Rightarrow u_1 - 4u_4 + 5819 - 3628 = 0$$
$$\Rightarrow u_1 - 4u_4 + 2191 = 0 \qquad ...(ii)$$

We have to solve (*i*) and (*ii*) for u_1 and u_4. From (*ii*), we get

$$u_1 = 4u_4 - 2191 \qquad ...(iii)$$

Substituting the value of u_1 in (*i*), we get

$$u_4 - 4(4u_4 - 2191) + 3017 = 0 \Rightarrow -15u_4 + 11781 = 0 \Rightarrow u_4 = \frac{11781}{15} = 785{\cdot}4 \simeq 785$$

Substituting the value of u_4 in (*iii*), we get $u_1 = 4 \times 785{\cdot}4 - 2191 = 950{\cdot}6 \simeq 951.$

EXERCISE 16·2

1. Explain the Binomial Expansion method for interpolating the missing observations, stating clearly the assumptions involved.

2. Explain the use of the operators Δ and E in estimating (*i*) one and (*ii*) two, missing observations. State clearly the assumptions involved.

3. Interpolate the index number for 2000 from the following table :

Years :	1998	1999	2001	2002
Index Number :	100	107	157	212

(*Punjab Univ. B.Com., II, Sept. 1982*)

Ans. 124.

4. Obtain an estimate of the missing figures in the following table :

x :	4	5	6	7	8
$f(x)$:	3·11	2·96	–	2·77	2·70

Ans. 2·85.

5. Find the missing value in the following : (Use Binomial method)

x :	2	3	4	5	6	7
y :	5·99	7·92	9·49	?	12·59	14·07

Ans. 11·02.

6. Find out the missing value in the following data :

x :	1931	1941	1951	1961	1971
y :	17	25	30	–	100

Ans. 49·25. (*Punjab Univ. B.Com. Oct. 1997*)

7. Using an appropriate formula for interpolation, estimate the average number of children born per mother aged 30—34.

Age of mother in years	*Average number of children born*	*Age of mother in years*	*Average number of children born*
15—19	0·7	30—34	?
20—24	2·1	35—39	5·7
25—29	3·1	40—44	5·8

(*Madras Univ. B.Com., 1998*)

Ans. 4·39.

8. Find the missing value from the following figures by the Binomial Method of interpolation :

Year	:	2002	2003	2004	2005	2006	2007
Value	:	141	131	145	–	149	173

Ans. 150·8 ≃ 151.

9. Estimate the production for the year 2000 with the help of the following table.

Year	:	1975	1980	1985	1990	1995	2000	2005
Production (in tonnes)	:	20	22	26	30	35	?	43

(Bangalore Univ. B.Com., 2006)

Ans. 41 tonnes.

10. By using the most suitable method, estimate the business done in 2000 from the following data :

Years	:	1997	1998	1999	2001	2002
Business done in million Rs.	:	1570	2350	3650	5250	7800

Ans. Rs. 4470 million.

11. Interpolate the two missing figures with the help of a suitable formula.

Years	:	1990	1991	1992	1993	1994	1995	1996
Production (in Millions)	:	76·6	78·7	?	77·7	78·7	?	80·6

Ans. 78·09 (Millions) ; 80·5 (Millions).

12. Interpolate the missing figures from the following data :

x	:	5	10	15	20	25	30	35
y	:	8	?	25	?	40	50	60

Ans. 18, 32.

13. Obtain the estimate of the missing figures in the following table :

x	:	3·0	3·1	3·2	3·3	3·4	3·5	3·6
$f(x)$	:	0·270	–	0·222	0·200	–	0·164	0·148

Ans. 0·246, 0·1808.

14. Estimate the production for the year 1975 and 1985 with the help of following table :

Year	:	1960	1965	1970	1975	1980	1985	1990
Production (in tonnes)	:	20	22	26	–	35	–	43

Ans. 31 tonnes , 39 tonnes.

15. The number of members of International Statistical Society are :

Year	:	1970	1971	1972	1973	1974	1975	1976	1977	1978	1979
No. of Members	:	845	867	–	846	821	772	–	757	761	796

Make the best estimate you can of the members in 1972 and 1976.

Ans. 844, 746.

16. Estimate U_2 from the following table :

X	:	1	2	3	4	5
U_x	:	7	?	13	21	37

and explain why the value obtained is different from that obtained by putting $x = 2$ in the expression $2^x + 5$.

Ans. $U_2 = 9{\cdot}5$; Actual value = 9.

16·10. INTERPOLATION WITH ARGUMENTS AT UNEQUAL INTERVALS

The techniques of interpolation discussed so far are applicable only if the values of the independent variable x are given at equal intervals. In other words, the Binomial Expansion Method and Newton's Difference Formulae (Forward or Backward) can be used if we are given the entries corresponding to equidistant values of the arguments. However, these formulae can not be used if the values of the arguments are given at unequal intervals, since in that case the operators E, Δ and ∇ do not serve our purpose. In such cases when the arguments are not equally spaced, special techniques given below, are used:

(*i*) Newton's Divided Difference Formula

(*ii*) Lagrange's Formula.

Remark. It should be clearly understood that these two methods can be used even if the arguments are equally spaced, though in that case the calculations may be slightly more as compared to Newton's Forward or Backward Difference formula. In practice these methods are usually used when the arguments are not at equal intervals.

16·11. DIVIDED DIFFERENCES

As already pointed out, in case the arguments are not equally spaced the operators Δ, ∇ and E cannot be used. In case of equally spaced arguments, while forming the difference table we considered only the differences between the successive values of the entries, without paying any attention to the corresponding difference between the arguments. *The differences defined on taking into consideration the changes in the values of the arguments are known as divided differences.*

Let the values of the variable x (arguments) be $a_0, a_1, a_2, \ldots, a_n$, which may not necessarily be equally spaced and let $f(a_0), f(a_1), \ldots, f(a_n)$ be the corresponding entries. Then the first order divided difference of $f(x)$ for the arguments a_0 and a_1, usually denoted by $f(a_0, a_1)$ or $\underset{a_1}{\Delta} f(a_0)$ is defined as :

$$\underset{a_1}{\Delta} f(a_0) = f(a_0, a_1) = \frac{f(a_1) - f(a_0)}{a_1 - a_0} \qquad \ldots(16\cdot20)$$

In other words, divided difference $\underset{a_1}{\Delta} U_{a_0}$ is nothing but ordinary difference ΔU_{a_0} divided by the corresponding difference between the arguments. The Table 16·13 gives the divided differences upto 4th order in case of five entries corresponding to the arguments a_0, a_1, a_2, a_3, and a_4.

TABLE 16·13 **DIVIDED DIFFERENCE TABLE**

x	$f(x)$	$\Delta f(x)$	$\Delta^2 f(x)$	$\Delta^3 f(x)$	$\Delta^4 f(x)$
a_0	$f(a_0)$				
		$\frac{f(a_1)-f(a_0)}{a_1-a_0} = \Delta f(a_0)$			
a_1	$f(a_1)$		$\frac{\Delta f(a_1) - \Delta f(a_0)}{a_2-a_0} = \Delta^2 f(a_0)$		
		$\frac{f(a_2)-f(a_1)}{a_2-a_1} = \Delta f(a_1)$		$\frac{\Delta^2 f(a_1) - \Delta^2 f(a_0)}{a_3-a_0} = \Delta^3 f(a_0)$	
a_2	$f(a_2)$		$\frac{\Delta f(a_2) - \Delta f(a_1)}{a_3-a_1} = \Delta^2 f(a_1)$		$\frac{\Delta^3 f(a_1) - \Delta^3 f(a_0)}{a_4-a_0} = \Delta^4 f(a_0)$
		$\frac{f(a_3)-f(a_2)}{a_3-a_2} = \Delta f(a_2)$		$\frac{\Delta^2 f(a_2) - \Delta^2 f(a_1)}{a_4-a_1} = \Delta^3 f(a_1)$	
a_3	$f(a_3)$		$\frac{\Delta f(a_3) - \Delta f(a_2)}{a_4-a_2} = \Delta^2 f(a_2)$		
		$\frac{f(a_4)-f(a_3)}{a_4-a_3} = \Delta f(a_3)$			
a_4	$f(a_4)$				

Remark. If $f(x)$ s a polynomial of nth degree then nth order divided differences of $f(x)$ are constant and higher order differences are zero. Mathematically,

$$\left.\begin{array}{l}\Delta^n f(x) = \text{Constant} \\ \text{and} \quad \Delta^r f(x) = 0,\ r > n\end{array}\right\} \quad \ldots (16·21)$$

provided $f(x)$ is polynomial of degree n.

16·11·1. Newton's Divided Difference Formula. Let $f(a_0)$, $f(a_1)$, ..., $f(a_n)$ be $n + 1$ entries corresponding to the arguments $a_0, a_1, a_2, \ldots, a_n$ not necessarily equally spaced. Then Newton's divided difference (*D. D*) formula gives the form of the function $f(x)$ as :

$$f(x) = f(a_0) + (x - a_0) \,.\, \Delta f(a_0) + (x - a_0)(x - a_1) \,.\, \Delta^2 f(a_0) + (x - a_0)(x - a_1)(x - a_2) \,.\, \Delta^3 f(a_0) + \ldots + (x - a_0)(x - a_1) \ldots (x - a_{n-1}) \,.\, \Delta^n f(a_0) \quad \ldots (16·22)$$

Remarks. 1. The formula (16·22) has also been obtained under the assumptions discussed in § 16·1·1, *viz.*, $f(x)$ can be represented by a polynomial of appropriate degree, depending on the number of entries given.

2. This formula can also be used even if the arguments are at equal intervals, though in practice, it is generally used when arguments are at unequal intervals.

We discuss below some numerical problems to illustrate the use of this formula for interpolation.

Example 16·16. *The observed values of a function are respectively 168, 120, 72, and 63 at the four positions 3, 7, 9 and 10 of the independent variable. What is the best estimate you can give for the value of the function at the position 6 of the independent variable ?*

Solution.

TABLE 16·14. **DIVIDED DIFFERENCE TABLE**

x	$f(x)$	$\Delta f(x)$	$\Delta^2 f(x)$	$\Delta^3 f(x)$
3	168			
		$\frac{120 - 168}{7 - 3} = -12$		
7	120		$\frac{-24 - (-12)}{9 - 3} = -2$	
		$\frac{72 - 120}{9 - 7} = -24$		$\frac{5 - (-2)}{10 - 3} = 1$
9	72		$\frac{-9 - (-24)}{10 - 7} = 5$	
		$\frac{63 - 72}{10 - 9} = -9$		
10	63			

Hence, by Newton's divided difference formula (16·22), we get

$$f(x) = 168 + (x - 3) \times (-12) + (x - 3)(x - 7) \times (-2) + (x - 3)(x - 7)(x - 9) \times 1$$
$$= x^3 - 21x^2 + 119x - 27 \qquad \text{[On simplification]}$$

The estimated value of the function at the point $x = 6$ is given by :

$$f(6) = 6^3 - 21 \times 6^2 + 119 \times 6 - 27 = 216 - 756 + 714 - 27 = 147$$

Example 16·17. *Given the following table, find the function $f(x)$, assuming it to be a polynomial of the third degree in x.*

x :	0	1	2	3
$f(x)$:	1	2	11	34

Solution. We shall do this problem by Newton's D.D. formula.

TABLE 16·15 **DIVIDED DIFFERENCE TABLE**

x	$f(x)$	$\Delta f(x)$	$\Delta^2 f(x)$	$\Delta^3 f(x)$
0	1			
		$\frac{2-1}{1-0}=1$		
1	2		$\frac{9-1}{2-0}=4$	
		$\frac{11-2}{2-1}=9$		$\frac{7-4}{3-0}=1$
2	11		$\frac{23-9}{3-1}=7$	
		$\frac{34-11}{3-2}=23$		
3	34			

Using Newton's D.D. formula, we get

$$f(x)=f(0)+(x-0)\ \Delta f(0)+(x-0)(x-1)\ \Delta^2 f(0)$$
$$+(x-0)(x-1)(x-2)\ \Delta^3 f(0)$$
$$=1+x\times 1+x(x-1)\times 4+x(x-1)(x-2)\times 1$$
$$=1+x+(4x^2-4x)+x(x^2-3x+2)$$
$$=x^3+x^2-x+1$$

which is the required form of function $f(x)$.

Aliter. Here we observe that the arguments are equidistant. Hence, we can also obtain the required polynomial $f(x)$ using Newton's forward difference formula.

TABLE 16·16 **TABLE OF DIFFERENCES (FORWARD)**

x	$f(x)$	$\Delta f(x)$	$\Delta^2 f(x)$	$\Delta^3 f(x)$
0	1			
		1		
1	2		8	
		9		6
2	11		14	
		23		
3	34			

Using Newton's forward difference formula, we have :

$$u=\frac{x-a}{h}=\frac{x-0}{1}=x$$

$$\therefore\ f(x)=1+x\times 1+\frac{x(x-1)}{2\,!}\times 8+\frac{x(x-1)(x-2)}{3\,!}\times 6$$
$$=1+x+4x(x-1)+x(x-1)(x-2)$$
$$=1+x+(4x^2-4x)+x(x^2-3x+2)$$
$$=1+x+(4x^2-4x)+(x^3-3x^2+2x)$$
$$=x^3+(4x^2-3x^2)+(x-4x+2x)+1$$
$$=x^3+x^2-x+1.$$

Remark. This problem could also be done by using *parabolic curve fitting* method.

Example 16·18. *Apply Newton's Divided Difference Method to find the number of persons getting Rs. 600 from the following data.*

Income per day ('00) Rs.	:	*3*	*5*	*7*	*8*	*10*
No. of persons	:	*180*	*154*	*120*	*110*	*90*

Solution.

TABLE 16·17 **DIVIDED DIFFERENCE TABLE**

x	$f(x)$	$\Delta f(x)$	$\Delta^2 f(x)$	$\Delta^3 f(x)$	$\Delta^4 f(x)$
3	180				
		−13			
5	154		−1		
		−17		0·67	
7	120		2·33		− 0·16
		−10		− 0·47	
8	110		0		
		−10			
10	90				

Using Newton's divided difference formula, we have :

$$f(x)=180+(x-3)\times(-13)+(x-3)(x-5)\times(-1)$$
$$+(x-3)(x-5)(x-7)\times 0{\cdot}67+(x-3)(x-5)(x-7)(x-8)\times(-0{\cdot}16)$$

Putting $x=6$, we get :

$$f(6)=180+(6-3)\times(-13)+(6-3)(6-5)\times(-1)$$
$$+(6-3)(6-5)(6-7)\times(0{\cdot}67)+(6-3)(6-5)(6-7)(6-8)\times(-0{\cdot}16)$$
$$=180-39-3-2{\cdot}01-0{\cdot}96=180-44{\cdot}97=135{\cdot}03\simeq 135$$

Hence, the estimated number of persons getting Rs. 600 per day is 135.

16·12. LAGRANGE'S FORMULA

Another formula used to interpolate values when the arguments are not necessarily equally spaced was given by French mathematician Lagrange and is known as Lagrange's interpolation formula.

If $a_0, a_1, a_2, \ldots, a_n$ are $(n+1)$ arguments not necessarily at equal intervals and $f(a_0), f(a_1), \ldots, f(a_n)$ are the corresponding entries, then under the assumptions stated in § 16·1·1, the Lagrange's form of function $f(x)$ is given by :

$$\begin{aligned} f(x) = & \frac{(x-a_1)(x-a_2)\ldots(x-a_n)}{(a_0-a_1)(a_0-a_2)\ldots(a_0-a_n)} \times f(a_0) \\ & + \frac{(x-a_0)(x-a_2)\ldots(x-a_n)}{(a_1-a_0)(a_1-a_2)\ldots(a_1-a_n)} \times f(a_1) \\ & + \quad \ldots \quad \ldots \quad \ldots \quad \ldots \\ & \quad \vdots \quad \vdots \quad \vdots \quad \vdots \\ & + \frac{(x-a_0)(x-a_1)\ldots(x-a_{n-1})}{(a_n-a_0)(a_n-a_1)\ldots(a_n-a_{n-1})} \times f(a_n) \end{aligned} \qquad \ldots(16·23)$$

Remark. While dealing with arguments not equally spaced we can use any of the formulae :

(*i*) Newton's Divided Difference Formula,

(*ii*) Lagrange's Formula,

for determining the form of the function $f(x)$ and hence for estimating the value of $f(x)$ for given value of x. Both these formulae can be used even in the case of equally spaced arguments, though in that case Newton's (forward and backward) difference formulae are much easier to apply.

We discuss below numerical problems to illustrate the use of Lagrange's interpolation formula.

Example 16·19. *Find the polynomial function f (x) given that*

$$f(0) = 2, \quad f(1) = 3, \quad f(2) = 12 \quad \text{and} \quad f(3) = 35. \quad \text{Hence find } f(5).$$

Solution. By Lagrange's formula of interpolation for four arguments 0, 1, 2 and 3, we get :

$$\begin{aligned} f(x) & = \frac{(x-1)(x-2)(x-3)}{(0-1)(0-2)(0-3)} f(0) + \frac{(x-0)(x-2)(x-3)}{(1-0)(1-2)(1-3)} f(1) \\ & \quad + \frac{(x-0)(x-1)(x-3)}{(2-0)(2-1)(2-3)} f(2) + \frac{(x-0)(x-1)(x-2)}{(3-0)(3-1)(3-2)} f(3) \\ & = \frac{(x-1)(x-2)(x-3)}{(-1)\times(-2)\times(-3)} \times 2 + \frac{x(x-2)(x-3)}{1\times(-1)\times(-2)} \times 3 \\ & \quad + \frac{x(x-1)(x-3)}{2\times1\times(-1)} \times 12 + \frac{x(x-1)(x-2)}{3\times2\times1} \times 35 \\ & = -\frac{1}{3}\left(x^3-6x^2+11x-6\right) + \frac{3}{2}\left(x^3-5x^2+6x\right) \\ & \quad - 6\left(x^3-4x^2+3x\right) + \frac{35}{6}\left(x^3-3x^2+2x\right) \\ & = \left(-\frac{1}{3}+\frac{3}{2}-6+\frac{35}{6}\right)x^3 + \left(2-\frac{15}{2}+24-\frac{35}{2}\right)x^2 + \left(-\frac{11}{3}+9-18+\frac{35}{3}\right)x+2 \\ & = \left(\frac{(-2+9-36+35)}{6}\right)x^3 + \left(\frac{4-15+48-35}{2}\right)x^2 + \left(\frac{-11+27-54+35}{3}\right)x+2 \end{aligned}$$

$$\Rightarrow \quad f(x) = x^3 + x^2 - x + 2 \qquad \ldots(*)$$

Taking $x = 5$ in (*) we get : $f(5) = 5^3 + 5^2 - 5 + 2 = 125 + 25 - 5 + 2 = 147.$

Example 16·20. *Given $\log_{10} 654 = 2·8156$, $\log_{10} 658 = 2·8182$, $\log_{10} 659 = 2·8189$, $\log_{10} 661 = 2·8202$, find by Lagrange's interpolation formula $\log_{10} 656$.* [*Retain four decimal places in your answer.*]

Solution. Here $f(x) = \log_{10} x$. The values of arguments and the corresponding entries are as given below :

x	:	$a_0 = 654$	$a_1 = 658$	$a_2 = 659$	$a_3 = 661$
$f(x) = \log_{10} x$	:	2·8156	2·8182	2·8189	2·8202

We want $f(x)$ when $x = 656$, *viz.*, $f(656) = \log_{10} 656$.

Taking $x = 656$ in Lagrange's formula (16·23), and using the above table, we get

$$\log 656 = f(656)$$

$$= \frac{(656-658)(656-659)(656-661)}{(654-658)(654-659)(654-661)} \times 2{\cdot}8156 + \frac{(656-654)(656-659)(656-661)}{(658-654)(658-659)(658-661)} \times 2{\cdot}8182$$

$$+ \frac{(656-654)(656-658)(656-661)}{(659-654)(659-658)(659-661)} \times 2{\cdot}8189 + \frac{(656-654)(656-658)(656-659)}{(661-654)(661-658)(661-659)} \times 2{\cdot}8202$$

$$= \frac{(-2)(-3)(-5)}{(-4)(-5)(-7)} \times 2{\cdot}8156 + \frac{2(-3)(-5)}{4(-1)(-3)} \times 2{\cdot}8182 + \frac{2(-2)(-5)}{5 \times (1)(-2)} \times 2{\cdot}8189 + \frac{2(-2)(-3)}{7(3)(2)} \times 2{\cdot}8202$$

$$= \frac{3}{14} \times 2{\cdot}8156 + \frac{5}{2} \times 2{\cdot}8182 - 2 \times 2{\cdot}8189 + \frac{2}{7} \times 2{\cdot}8202$$

$$= 0{\cdot}6033 + 7{\cdot}0455 - 5{\cdot}6378 + 0{\cdot}8058 = 2{\cdot}8168$$

Remark. If we are asked to find the value of a function $f(x)$ at some point by using Lagrange's formula, then it is not necessary to simplify the function $f(x)$ as a polynomial in x unless we are asked to find the form of the function $f(x)$. The required result is obtained on substituting the value of x in the formula (16·23).

Example 16·21. *By using Lagrange's method, estimate the number of persons whose income is Rs. 1900 and more but less than Rs. 2,500 from the following table :*

Income in ('00) Rs.	*No. of persons*
0—9	*50*
9—19	*70*
19—28	*203*
28—37	*406*
37—46	*304*

Solution. Let us denote the number of persons earning below *Rs. x* hundred by U_x. Then, the given data can be transformed into less than cumulative frequency as follows :

x	$a_0 = 9$	$a_1 = 19$	$a_2 = 28$	$a_3 = 37$	$a_4 = 46$
U_x	$U_{a_0} = 50$	$U_{a_1} = 120$	$U_{a_2} = 323$	$U_{a_3} = 729$	$U_{a_4} = 1033$

Using Lagrange's formula for five arguments a_0, a_1, a_2, a_3, a_4 we get, on taking $x = 25$:

$$U_{25} = \frac{(25-19)(25-28)(25-37)(25-46)}{(9-19)(9-28)(9-37)(9-46)} \times 50 + \frac{(25-9)(25-28)(25-37)(25-46)}{(19-9)(19-28)(19-37)(19-46)} \times 120$$

$$+ \frac{(25-9)(25-19)(25-37)(25-46)}{(28-9)(28-19)(28-37)(28-46)} \times 323 + \frac{(25-9)(25-19)(25-28)(25-46)}{(37-9)(37-19)(37-28)(37-46)} \times 729$$

$$+ \frac{(25-9)(25-19)(25-28)(25-37)}{(46-9)(46-19)(46-28)(46-37)} \times 1033$$

$$= \frac{6.(-3).(-12).(-21)}{(-10).(-19).(-28).(-37)} \times 50 + \frac{16.(-3).(-12).(-21)}{10.(-9).(-18).(-27)} \times 120$$

$$+ \frac{16.6.(-12).(-21)}{19.9.(-9).(-18)} \times 323 + \frac{16{\cdot}6.(-3)(-21)}{28.18.9.(-9)} \times 729 + \frac{16.6.(-3).(-12)}{37.27.18.9} \times 1033$$

$$= -1{\cdot}1522 + 33{\cdot}1852 + 282{\cdot}0741 - 108 + 22{\cdot}0594 = 228{\cdot}1665 \simeq 228.$$

Required number of persons whose income is Rs. 1,900 and more, but less than Rs. 2,500 is given by

$$U_{25} - U_{19} = 228 - 120 = 108$$

Example 16·22. *The mode of a certain frequency curve $y = f(x)$ is attained at $x = 9·1$ and the value of the frequency function $f(x)$ for $x = 8·9$, $9·0$ and $9·3$ are respectively equal to 0·30, 0·35 and 0·25. Calculate the approximate value of $f(x)$ at the mode.*

Solution. We are given :

x :	$a_0 = 8·9$	$a_1 = 9·0$	$a_2 = 9·3$
$f(x)$:	0·30	0·35	0·25

Since mode of the frequency distribution is attained at $x = 9·1$ and we want the value of $f(x)$ at mode, we have to obtain approximate value of $f(9·1)$. Using Lagrange's formula of interpolation we get :

$$f(x) = \frac{(x-9)(x-9·3)}{(8·9-9)(8·9-9·3)}(0·30) + \frac{(x-8·9)(x-9·3)}{(9·0-8·9)(9·0-9·3)}(0·35) + \frac{(x-8·9)(x-9·0)}{(9·3-8·9)(9·3-9·0)}(0·25) \quad \ldots (*)$$

Putting $x = 9·1$ in (*) we get

$$f(9·1) = \frac{(9·1-9·0)(9·1-9·3)}{(8·9-9)(8·9-9·3)} \times 0·30 + \frac{(9·1-8·9)(9·1-9·3)}{(9·0-8·9)(9·0-9·3)} \times 0·35 + \frac{(9·1-8·9)(9·1-9·0)}{(9·3-8·9)(9·3-9·0)} \times 0·25$$

$$= -0·15 + 0·47 + 0·04 = 0·36 \qquad \text{[On simplification]}$$

Remark. Simplifying (*) as a cubic in x, the form of the function $f(x)$ is given as :

$$f(x) = -\frac{25}{12}x^2 + \frac{453·5}{12}x - \frac{3032·3}{12} \quad \ldots (**)$$

Mode of the distribution $f(x)$ is the solution of equations :

$$f'(x) = 0 \quad \text{and} \quad f''(x) < 0,$$

which on simplification give : $\quad \text{Mode} = x = \dfrac{453·5}{50} = 9·07$

$\therefore$ Actual value of mode is 9·07.

16·13. INVERSE INTERPOLATION

So far we were given a set of values of x (arguments) and the corresponding values of $y = f(x)$, (entries) and we were required to estimate $y = f(x)$ for some specified value of x. Let us now consider the reverse problem stated below :

"Given a set of values of x and $y = f(x)$, we are interested to find the value of x for a certain value of y". This is termed as *inverse interpolation.*

The formula for inverse interpolation is obtained from Lagrange's interpolation formula by interchanging the variables x and $y = f(x)$.

Thus, for four arguments a_0, a_1, a_2, and a_3, the value of x for given value of $f(x)$ is given by the formula :

$$x = \frac{[f(x)-f(a_1)]\,[f(x)-f(a_2)]\,[f(x)-f(a_3)]}{[f(a_0)-f(a_1)]\,[f(a_0)-f(a_2)]\,[f(a_0)-f(a_3)]} \times a_0$$
$$+ \frac{[f(x)-f(a_0)]\,[f(x)-f(a_2)]\,[f(x)-f(a_3)]}{[f(a_1)-f(a_0)]\,[f(a_1)-f(a_2)]\,[f(a_1)-f(a_3)]} \times a_1$$
$$+ \frac{[f(x)-f(a_0)]\,[f(x)-f(a_1)]\,[f(x)-f(a_3)]}{[f(a_2)-f(a_0)]\,[f(a_2)-f(a_1)]\,[f(a_2)-f(a_3)]} \times a_2$$
$$+ \frac{[f(x)-f(a_0)]\,[f(x)-f(a_1)]\,[f(x)-f(a_2)]}{[f(a_3)-f(a_0)]\,[f(a_3)-f(a_1)]\,[f(a_3)-f(a_2)]} \times a_3 \quad \ldots (16·24)$$

Example 16·23. *The values of x and $y = f(x)$ are given below :*

x :	5	6	9	11
$f(x)$:	12	13	14	16

Find the value of x when $f(x) = 15$.

Solution. In the usual notations of Lagrange's formula :

x :	$a_0 = 5$	$a_1 = 6$	$a_2 = 9$	$a_3 = 11$
$y = f(x)$:	12	13	14	16

We want x when $f(x) = 15$.

Using inverse interpolation formula (16·24), we get :

$$x = \frac{(15-13)(15-14)(15-16)}{(12-13)(12-14)(12-16)} \times 5 + \frac{(15-12)(15-14)(15-16)}{(13-12)(13-14)(13-16)} \times 6$$

$$+ \frac{(15-12)(15-13)(15-16)}{(14-12)(14-13)(14-16)} \times 9 + \frac{(15-12)(15-13)(15-14)}{(16-12)(16-13)(16-14)} \times 11$$

$$= \frac{2 \times 1 \times (-1)}{(-1)(-2)(-4)} \times 5 + \frac{(3)(1)(-1)}{1(-1)(-3)} \times 6 + \frac{3(2)\ (-1)}{2(1)(-2)} \times 9 + \frac{3(2)(1)}{4(3)(2)} \times 11$$

$$= \frac{5}{4} - 6 + \frac{27}{2} + \frac{11}{4} = \frac{5 - 24 + 54 + 11}{4} = \frac{46}{4} = 11{\cdot}5.$$

EXERCISE 16·3

1. Explain the interpolation methods used for interpolating the values of the dependent variable (entries) when the values of the independent variable (arguments) are not at equal intervals.

2. What do you understand by a divided difference ? Complete the divided difference table for four arguments a_0, a_1, a_2, a_3 and the corresponding entries $f(a_0), f(a_1), f(a_2)$ and $f(a_3)$.

3. State Newton's divided difference formula and give :

(*i*) the assumptions on which it is based ; (*ii*) its uses

4. Find the polynomial of the lowest possible degree which assumes the values 3, 12, 15, –21 when x has the value 3, 2, 1, –1 respectively, by using Newton's divided difference formula.

Ans. $f(x) = x^3 - 9x^2 + 17x + 6$.

5. Construct a divided difference table for the following :

x :	1	2	4	7	12
$f(x)$:	22	30	82	106	216

Ans. Leading D.D. are : 8, 6, –1·6, 0·194.

6. By means of Newton's divided difference formula find the values of $f(8)$ and $f(15)$ from the following table :

x :	4	5	7	10	11	13
$f(x)$:	48	100	294	900	1210	2028

Ans. 448, 3150.

7. State Lagrange's formula of interpolation and give its assumptions and uses.

8. Use Lagrange's interpolation formula to find $f(x)$ when $x = 0$, given the following table.

x :	–1	–2	2	4
$f(x)$:	–1	–9	11	69

Ans. $f(0) = 1$.

9. Determine the percentage of criminals under 35 years of age.

Age	*Percentage of criminals*
Under 25 years	52·0
" 30 "	67·3
" 40 "	84·1
" 50 "	94·4

(*Kashmir Univ. B.Com., 2004*)

Ans. 77·405%.

10. Given $\log_{10} 654 = 2{\cdot}8156$; $\log_{10} 658 = 2{\cdot}8182$; $\log_{10} 659 = 2{\cdot}8189$; $\log_{10} 661 = 2{\cdot}8202$

Find $\log_{10} 656$ using two different interpolation formulae available for observations at unequal intervals, say, Lagrange's formula and Newton's formula for divided differences.

Ans. 2·8168 (By both methods).

11. State Lagrange's interpolation formula. Given the table of values :

x	:	35·0	35·5	39·5	40·5
$f(x)$	:	1175	1280	2180	2020

obtain a value of $f(40)$.

Ans. 2136.

12. State Lagrange's interpolation formula and mention its difference in use from the Newton's interpolation formula.

Given the table of values :

x	:	1·40	1·60	1·70	1·80
$f(x)$	:	0·9855	0·9995	0·9917	0·9737

find $f(1{\cdot}75)$

Ans. 0·9840.

13. Calculate the population in 1976 (estimate) from the population of a country during the four censuses.

Year	:	1941	1951	1961	1971
Population (in crores)	:	29	31	32	35

Ans. 38·1875 crores.

14. The following table gives the normal weight of a baby during the first six months of life :

Age in months	:	0	2	3	5	6
Weight in lbs	:	5	7	8	10	12

Estimate the weight of the baby at the age of 4 months. *(Punjab Univ. B.Com., April 1995)*

Ans. 8·89 lbs [By Lagrange's method].

15. What is interpolation ? Discuss the two methods of studying interpolation.

From the following data interpolate the number of students who secured more than 59 marks. (Use Lagrange's method)

Marks (More than)	:	25	36	45	55	70
No. of Students	:	65	63	40	18	7

(Punjab Univ. B.Com., Oct. 1996)

16. The following are the marks obtained by 65 students in Quantitatives. Estimate the percentage of students who secured first class marks (First Class = 60 marks or more) :

Marks	No. of Students
More than 25	65
More than 36	63
More than 45	40
More than 55	18
More than 70	7

(Punjab Univ. B.Com., 2000)

17. Using the Lagrange's formula of interpolation, find from the data given below the number of workers earning between Rs. 3,000 and Rs. 4,000 :

Earning in ('00) Rs.	:	15—20	20—30	30—45	45—55	55—70
No. of workers	:	73	97	110	180	140

Ans. 53.

18. The observed values of a function are respectively 168, 120, 72 and 63 at the four positions, 3, 7, 9 and 10 of the independent variable. What is the estimate you can give for the value of the function at the position 6 of the independent variable ? Use Lagrange's formula.

Ans. 147.

19. What do you understand by Inverse Interpolation ? Explain how Lagrange's interpolation formula can be used in this respect.

20. A function $f(x)$ takes the values as given in the following table :

x	:	1	3	4
$f(x)$	:	4	12	19

Find the value of x so that $f(x) = 7$.

Ans. 1·86.

17 Interpretation of Data and Statistical Fallacies

17·1. INTRODUCTION

The science of statistics may be broadly classified into the following two headings :

(1) Descriptive Statistics.

(2) Inductive Statistics.

Descriptive Statistics consists in describing some characteristics of the numerical data by finding various measures like averages, dispersion, skewness, correlation coefficient, etc., and may be termed as the *summarization and analysis part of interpretation of data* and have been discussed in details in Chapters 2 to 11.

Inductive Statistics, also known as *Statistical Inference* may be termed as the logic of drawing statistically valid conclusions about the totality of the cases or items termed as *population,* in any statistical investigation :

(*i*) On the basis of the information collected on examining a sample drawn from it in a scientific manner, and

(*ii*) Also on the basis of the various statistical measures calculated.

Statistical inference, which is broadly classified into the following two heads :

(*i*) Estimation Theory, and (*ii*) Testing of hypothesis,

enables us to generalise the results of the sample analysis to the population :

(*a*) To find how far these generalisation are valid.

(*b*) To estimate the population parameters along with the degree of confidence.

(*c*) To make predictions or to take decisions about the future course of action.

A detailed study of the Inductive Statistics or Statistical Inference is however, beyond the scope of the book.

17·2. INTERPRETATION OF DATA AND STATISTICAL FALLACIES – MEANING AND NEED

Interpretation of statistical data involves :

(*i*) Summarisation and analysis of data (See Descriptive Statistics above).

(*ii*) Prediction or Inference (See Inductive Statistics or Statistical Inference above).

Thus, interpretation of data refers to drawing inferences on the basis of the collected data after its statistical analysis (computation of various statistical measures). The utility of collected information, in any field of investigation, lies in its proper interpretation. The conclusions drawn will be accurate and trustworthy if they are based on proper, judicious and careful use of the statistical methods. Improper or inaccurate use of the statistical methods will obviously lead to inaccurate and fallacious conclusions.

Wrong interpretation of the data leads to the so-called *statistical fallacies* which may arise in the collection, presentation, analysis and interpretation of data. *The fallacies committed deliberately or intentionally* (by the use of statistical tools by unscrupulous, dishonest and inexperienced people to fulfill their selfish motives) *refer to abuse of statistics and the fallacies committed unintentionally refer to misuse of statistics.*

17·3. FACTORS LEADING TO MIS-INTERPRETATION OF DATA OR STATISTICAL FALLACIES

We give below some of the factors giving rise to mis-interpretation of data or statistical fallacies.

(*i*) Bias.
(*ii*) Inconsistency in Definitions.
(*iii*) False Generalisations.
(*iv*) Inappropriate Comparisons.
(*v*) Wrong Interpretation of Statistical Measures (like Averages, Dispersion, Skewness, Correlation Coefficient, etc.).
(*vi*) Wrong Interpretation of Index Numbers and Components of Time Series (Trend, Seasonal and Cyclical Variations).
(*vii*) Technical Errors.
(*viii*) Errors in Selection of Units.

We shall now discuss these factors briefly one by one.

Remarks. It may be pointed out that the above list of factors is not exhaustive and complete. As one learns more and more about the subject of Statistics, one can find out numerous other factors leading to mis-interpretation of data or statistical fallacies.

17·3·1. Bias. Bias, conscious or unconscious, is quite common in statistical investigations and analysis and leads to wrong conclusions.

In any statistical investigation *biased errors* creep in because of :

(*i*) Bias on the part of the enumerator or investigator whose personal beliefs and prejudices are likely to affect the results of the enquiry.

(*ii*) Bias in the measuring instrument or the equipment used or in recording the observations.

(*iii*) Bias due to faulty collection of the data and in the statistical techniques and the formulae used for the analysis of the data.

(*iv*) *Respondents' Bias.* An appeal to the pride or prestige of an individual introduces a bias called *prestige bias* by virtue of which he may upgrade his education, occupation, income, etc., or understate his age, thus resulting in wrong answers. Moreover, respondents may furnish wrong information to safeguard their personal interests. For example, for income-tax purposes a person may give an understatement of his salary or income or assets.

(*v*) *Bias due to non-response.* (See item 9, Non-sampling Errors § 15·9·1).

(*vi*) *Bias in the Technique of Approximations.* If, while rounding off, each individual value is either approximated to next highest or lowest number so that all the errors move in the same direction, there is bias for overstatement or understatement respectively. For example, if the figures are to be rounded off to the next highest or lowest hundred then each of the values 305 and 396 will be recorded as 400 and 300 respectively.

It should be ascertained that the collecting agency was unbiased in the sense that it had no personal motives and right from the collection and compilation of the data to the presentation of results in the final form in the selected source, the data was thoroughly scrutinised and edited so as to make it free from errors as far as possible. Moreover, it should also be verified that the data related to normal times free from periods of economic boom or depression or natural calamities like famines, floods, earthquakes, wars, etc., and is still relevant for the purpose in hand.

17·3·2. Inconsistencies in Definitions. In order to make valid comparisons of a phenomenon at two or more periods of time, it is essential that the definitions of the objects being measured or the criteria of classification remain constant (same) throughout. If at all, a change in definition is needed, a footnote at the end should be given so as to make valid comparisons.

For instance, for the construction of cost of living index number, the proper unit of enumeration is household. It should be explained in clear terms whether a household consists of a family comprising blood relations only or people taking food in a common kitchen or all the persons living in the house or the persons enlisted in the ration card only. The concept of the household (to be used in the enquiry) is to be decided in advance and explained clearly to the enumerators so that there are no essential omissions or irrelevant inclusions and should be kept constant throughout.

As another illustration, in order to have meaningful comparisons of the results, the same pattern of classification should be adopted throughout the analysis and also for further enquiries on the same subject. For instance, in the 1961 census, the population was classified *w.r.t.* profession in the four classes *viz.* : (*i*) working as cultivator, (*ii*) working as agricultural labourer, (*iii*) working at household industry, and (*iv*) others. However, in 1971 census, the classification *w.r.t.* profession was as under :

(*a*) *Main Activity.* Worker [Cultivator (*C*), Agricultural Labourer (*AL*), Household Industries (*HHI*), Other Works (*OW*)].

(*b*) *Broad Category.* Non-worker [Household duties (*H*); Student (*ST*); Renteer or Retired person (*R*); Dependent, Beggers, Institutions and Others (*DBIO*)].

Consequently, the results obtained in the two censuses cannot be compared meaningfully.

17·3·3. Faulty Generalisations. Quite often, we commit error in drawing conclusions or making generalisations on the basis of the data which are generally inadequate or incomplete or not representative of the population to which the generalisations are applied. Five such illustrations are discussed in detail in §1·5 – Distrust of Statistics.

17·3·4. Inappropriate Comparisons. In making comparisons between two things, we should keep in mind that the comparisons will be meaningful only if the things are really alike otherwise the conclusions drawn will be wrong.

For example, in order to arrive at meaningful and valid comparisons of two index numbers, it is essential that the commodities selected for construction of the index number are of the same quality or grade in different periods, or in other words, they remain more or less stable in quality for reasonably long periods. Hence, in order to avoid any confusion about the quality of commodities due to time lag, graded or standardised items or commodities should be selected as far as possible.

Moreover, both the index numbers should be calculated by the same formula. If one index number is calculated by Laspeyre's formula and the other by Paasche's formula, then the two indices are not comparable even if the same set of commodities is used in both the cases.

For more illustrations, see Examples 17·1 and 17·2 given below.

Example 17.1. *If the Consumer Price Index (for the same class of people and with same base year) is higher for Delhi than that for Mumbai, does it necessarily mean that Delhi is more expensive (for this class of people) than Mumbai ? Give reasons in support of your answer.*

Solution. If the Consumer Price Index (for the same class of people and with the same base year) is higher for Delhi than that for Mumbai, *generally,* this will imply that Delhi is more expensive (for this class of people) than Mumbai. However, this cannot be the absolute conclusion on the basis of the given information because of the following reasons :

(*i*) It is not necessary that the consumption pattern *viz.,* the basket of goods consumed by the given class of people is same at both the places. Due to the variations in the consumption pattern, even with the same prices, the living at one place may be costlier than the living at the other place.

(*ii*) The sources of obtaining the quotations of prices and quantities consumed of various commodities may be different and this may make all the differences.

Example 17·2. "*The estimated per capita income for India in 1931-32 was Rs. 65. The estimate for 1972-73 was Rs. 650. In 1972-73, every Indian was, therefore, 10 times more prosperous than in 1931-32*". *Comment.*

Solution. "The estimated per capita income of India is 1972-73 in Rs. 650 which is 10 times the estimated income in 1931-32 and hence 10 times more prosperity in 1972-73 *w.r.t.* 1931-32". Using the simple 'unitary rule' of Arithmetic, the given conclusion may seem reasonable. However, from Economics point of view, the conclusion is absolutely wrong, since nothing is said about the cost of living indices at the two periods. Hypothetically, if we assume that the cost of living index in 1972-73 is 10 times the cost of living index in 1931-32 *w.r.t.* same base period, then the average Indian would have been equally prosperous in the two periods. In order to compare the prosperity of people in two different periods, we have to find the real incomes (rather than money incomes) for the two periods *w.r.t.* same fixed base period. Real wages are given by :

$$\text{Real Wages} = \frac{\text{Money Wages}}{\text{Cost of Living Index No.}} \times 100$$

There will be greater prosperity in the period for which real wages are higher.

17·3·5. Wrong Interpretation of Statistical Measures. The various measures like Averages (mean, median, mode, etc.), Dispersion, Skewness, Correlation Coefficient, etc., calculated from the collected data are often misused to present the information in such a manner to suit ones personal selfish motives and thus misguide or deceive the public.

(A) WRONG INTERPRETATION OF AVERAGES (MEAN, MEDIAN, MODE, ETC.)

Let us consider an industrial complex which houses the workers and some big officials like general manager, chief engineer, architect, etc. The average salary of the workers (skilled and unskilled) is, say Rupees 5,500, per week. If the salaries of the few big bosses (who draw very high salaries) are also included, the average wage per worker comes out to be Rs. 7,500, say. Thus, if we say that the average weekly salary of the workers in the factory is Rs. 7,500 p.m., it gives a very good impression and one is tempted to think that the workers are well paid and their standard of living is good. But the real picture is entirely different. Thus, in the case of extreme observations, the arithmetic mean gives a distorted picture and is no longer representative of the distribution and quite often leads to very misleading conclusions.

For more illustrations of mis-interpretation of mean, median and mode, see Examples 17·3 and 17·4 given below.

Example 17·3. *The following data represent travel expenses (other than transportation) for 7 trips made during November by a salesman for a small firm :*

Trip	*Days*	*Expenses (Rs·)*	*Expenses per day (Rs·)*
1	0·5	135	270
2	2·0	120	60
3	3·5	175	50
4	1·0	90	90
5	9·0	270	30
6	0·5	90	180
7	8·5	170	20
Total	25·0	1050	700

An auditor criticised these expenses as excessive, asserting that the average expenses per day is Rs. 100 (Rs. 700 divided by 7). The salesman replied that the average is only Rs. 42 (Rs. 1050 divided by 25) and that in any event the median is the appropriate measure and is only Rs. 30. The auditor rejoined that the arithmetic mean is the appropriate measure, but that the median is Rs. 60.

You are required to :

(i) Explain the proper interpretation of each of the four averages mentioned.

(ii) Which average seems appropriate to you ?

Solution. (*a*) In this problem, we are given four values of the average travel expenses per trip :

(*i*) **Auditor's Assertion of Average**

$$\text{Average expenses per trip} = \text{Rs. } \frac{700}{7} = \text{Rs. } 100$$

This represents the simple arithmetic mean of the 'expenses per day' for the seven trips. This assertion will be true only if the duration of each trip is one day (or same number of days). Here, since the duration of different trips is different (or not 1 day each), the given interpretation of the auditor is wrong.

(*ii*) **Salesman's Assertion of Average**

$$\text{Average expenses per trip} = \text{Rs. } \frac{1050}{25} = \text{Rs. } 42 = \frac{\sum WX}{\sum W}$$

where X : Expenses (in Rs.) per day and W : Duration (in days) of the trip.

This represents the weighted average (A.M.) of the expenses (in Rs.) per day (X), the weights (W) being the corresponding duration (in days) of the different trips.

Of the two averages in (*i*) and (*ii*) above, the salesman's assertion is more appropriate and reasonable.

(*iii*) **Salesman's Assertion of Median.** As in computing the average (A.M.) in (*ii*), the salesman obtained the values of median as Rs. 3 by taking into account the weighted distribution of the expenses per day (*X*), the corresponding weights (frequencies) (*W*) being the number of days in each trip. Thus, we have :

X (Rs.)	270	60	50	90	30	180	20
$f(W)$ (days)	0·5	2·0	3·5	1·0	9·0	0·5	8·5
'Less than' c.f.	0·5	2·5	6·0	7·0	16·0	16·5	25·0 = N

$N/2$ = 12·5. The *c.f.* just greater than 12·5 is 16. Hence, the corresponding value of X, *viz.*, Rs. 30 is the median value.

The salesman's assertion that 'the median expenses per trip is Rs. 30' is more appropriate.

(*iv*) **Auditor's Assertion of Median.** The values of expenses per day (X), arranged in ascending order of magnitude are : 20, 30, 50, 60, 90, 180, 270.

∴ Median = Size of the middle value = Rs. 60.

Hence, the auditor obtained the value of Rs. 60 as the median expenses per trip by taking the simple and not weighted distribution of X. Thus, in computing median also, the auditor committed the same mistake as in computing average (Mean) in (*i*). Hence, auditor's assertion is not correct.

(*b*) From management point of view, of the four averages in (*i*) to (*iv*) in part (*a*) above, the salesman's assertion of the average expenses per trip as obtained in (*ii*) is the most appropriate, since it enables the management to have an idea of the total cost incurred by its salesmen in all the trips undertaken by them in the execution of the business.

Example 17·4. *Atul gets a pocket money allowance of Rs. 12 per day. Thinking that this was rather less, he asked his friends about their allowances and obtained the following data which includes his allowance also – (amounts in Rs.).*

12, 18, 10, 5, 25, 20, 22, 15, 10, 10, 15, 13, 20, 18, 10,
15, 10, 18, 15, 12, 15, 10, 15, 10, 12, 18, 20, 5, 8, 20.

He presented these data to his father and asked for an increase in his allowance as he was getting less than average amount. His father, a statistician, countered pointing out that Atul's allowance was actually more than the average amount.

Reconcile these statements.

Solution. The frequency distribution of the daily allowance (in Rs.) of Atul and his friends is obtained below :

Daily Allowance (in Rs.) (x)	*Tally Bars*	*Frequency (f)*	*f.x*
5	||	2	10
8	|	1	8
10	~~||||~~ ||	7	70
12	|||	3	36
13	|	1	13
15	~~||||~~ |	6	90
18	||||	4	72
20	||||	4	80
22	|	1	22
25	|	1	25
		$N = 30$	$\Sigma fx = 426$

The average (Arithmetic Mean) daily allowance is given by :

$$\bar{x} = \frac{\Sigma fx}{N} = \text{Rs. } \frac{426}{30} = \text{Rs. } 14{\cdot}20$$

Since the maximum frequency is 7, the corresponding value of x *viz.*, 10 gives the mode. Hence, the *modal value* of the daily allowance is Rs. 10.00.

Atul's daily allowance is Rs. 12·00. He asked his father for an increase in his daily allowance as he was getting less than the average amount. In fact, the average allowance, he referred to was the Arithmetic Mean ($\bar{x}$), which in this case is Rs. 14·20.

Atul's father, however, countered his argument pointing that his (Atul's) allowance was, in fact, more than the average amount. He (father) was here referring to Mode as the average, which in this case is Rs. 10·00.

(B) WRONG INTERPRETATION OF MEASURES OF DISPERSION AND SKEWNESS

Suppose we have two series, the first relating to the height in metres and the second relating to the weight in kilograms of a group of 10 individuals. Since the range of observations in the first series (of heights in metres) is obviously less than the range of observations of second series (of weights in kgs.), we may conclude that the second series is more variable than the first series, even without calculating the standard deviation in each case. This conclusion, however, is wrong.

For comparing the variability of two distributions we compute the coefficient of variation (*C.V.*) for each distribution.

$$C.V. = 100 \times \frac{\text{Standard Deviation}}{\text{Mean}} = \frac{100\,\sigma}{\bar{x}},$$

which is a pure number independent of units of measurement. A distribution with smaller *C.V.* is said to be more homogeneous or uniform or less variable than the other and the series with greater *C.V.* is said to be more variable than the other.

For more illustrations regarding interpretation/mis-interpretation of measures of dispersion see Examples 17·5, and 17·6 given below.

Example 17·5. *Comment on the statement "After settlement the average hourly wage in a factory had increased from Rs. 8 to Rs. 12 and the standard deviation had increased from Rs. 2 to Rs. 2·5. After settlement, the wage has become higher and more uniform".*

Solution. It is given that after settlement the average hourly wages of workers have gone up from Rs. 8 to Rs. 12. This implies that the total wages received per hour by all the workers together have increased. However, we cannot conclude that the wage of *each* individual has increased.

Regarding uniformity of the wages we have to calculate the coefficient of variation (*C.V.*) of the wages of workers before the settlement and after the settlement.

$$C.V. \text{ of wages before the settlement } = \frac{100 \text{ S.D.}}{\text{Mean}} = \frac{100 \times 2}{8} = 25$$

$$C.V. \text{ of wages after the settlement } = \frac{100 \text{ S.D.}}{\text{Mean}} = \frac{100 \times 5}{2 \times 12} = 20{\cdot}83$$

Since the latter is less than the former, we may conclude that the wages have become more uniform (less variable) after the settlement.

Example 17·6. *Comment briefly on the following statements :*

(*i*) *A computer obtained the standard deviation of 20 observations whose values ranged from 65 to 85 as 25.*

(*ii*) *A student obtained the mean and variance of a set of 10 observations as 10, – 5 respectively.*

(*iii*) *The range is the perfect measure of variability as it includes all the measurements.*

(*iv*) *For the distribution of 5 observations : 8, 8, 8, 8, 8 ; mean = 8 and variance = 8.*

(*v*) *If the mean and s.d. of distribution A are smaller than the mean and s.d. of distribution B respectively, then the distribution A is more uniform (less variable) than the distribution B.*

Solution. (*i*) Here Range = 85 – 65 = 20 and s.d. (σ) = 25 (Given).

The statement is wrong, since standard deviation of a distribution cannot exceed the range.

(*ii*) The statement is wrong since variance cannot be negative.

(*iii*) The statement is wrong since range is based only on two extreme observations (the largest and the smallest observations) and hence cannot be regarded as a reliable measure of variability.

$$(iv) \text{ Mean} = \frac{8+8+8+8+8}{5} = \frac{40}{5} = 8 \text{ (Correct)}$$

But variance = 8, is wrong because :

x	8	8	8	8	8
$x - \bar{x} = x - 8$	0	0	0	0	0
$(x - \bar{x})^2$	0	0	0	0	0

$\therefore$ Variance $(\sigma^2) = \frac{1}{5} \Sigma (x - \bar{x})^2 = \frac{1}{5} \times 0 = 0$

(*v*) We cannot draw this conclusion from the given information. The conclusion is true if *C.V.* (*A*) < *C.V.* (*B*),

where $\quad C.V. = \text{Coefficient of Variation} = \dfrac{100 \times \text{S.D.}}{\text{Mean}}$

For illustrations of interpretation of measures of dispersion and skewness, see Example 7·3, and Example 17·7 discussed below.

An excellent illustration of the interpretation of mean, median, mode, standard deviation, coefficient of variation and coefficient of skewness is given in Example 7.8.

Example 17·7. *Which group (i) or (ii) is more skewed ?*

(*i*) *Mean* = 22; *Median* = 24; s.d. = 10

(*ii*) *Mean* = 22; *Median* = 25; s.d. = 12

Solution. Karl Pearson's coefficient of skewness is given by :

$$SK = \frac{\text{Mean} - \text{Mode}}{S.D.\ (\sigma)} = \frac{3\ (\text{Mean} - \text{Median})}{\sigma}$$

Hence, Karl Pearson's coefficient of skewness for distributions (*i*) and (*ii*) is given respectively by :

$$Sk\ (i) = \frac{3\ (22 - 24)}{10} = \frac{3 \times (-2)}{10} = -0{\cdot}60$$

$$Sk\ (ii) = \frac{3\ (22 - 25)}{12} = \frac{3 \times (-3)}{12} = -0{\cdot}75$$

Hence both the groups are negatively skewed, *i.e.*, group (*i*) is skewed to the left to the extent 0.60 and group (*ii*) is skewed to the left to the extent 0.75. Since $|Sk\ (ii)| > |Sk\ (i)|$, group (*ii*) is more skewed to the left than group (*i*).

(C) WRONG INTERPRETATION OF CORRELATION COEFFICIENT AND REGRESSION COEFFICIENTS.

Utmost care should be taken in interpreting the values of the correlation coefficient '*r*' (for details see § 8·4·2 and § 8·4·3). It should be kept in mind that *Karl Pearson's coefficient of correlation* $r = r\ (x, y)$, *between two variables is a measure of the intensity of linear relationship only between them* and it fails to reflect any curvi-linear (non-linear) relationships between them. Moreover, correlation does not necessarily mean cause and effect relationship between two variable series. [For detailed discussion see § 8·1·2, "correlation and causation".]

Correlation coefficient may be wrongly used to study the relationship between two series which are really independent of each other. For example, it may be used to study the correlation between

(*a*) the series of heights and income of individuals over a period of time,

(*b*) the series of marriage rate and the rate of agricultural production in a country over a period of time,

(*c*) the series relating to the size of the shoe and intelligence of a group of individuals.

In particular, if we observe a high degree of correlation coefficient, (say, $r = 0{\cdot}8$) between the size of the shoe (x) and the intelligence (y) of a group of persons, we are tempted to conclude that larger the shoe size of an individual, more intelligent he is, a conclusion which sounds absurd. The conclusion is wrong, since the two series are really independent and we should expect $r\ (x, y) = 0$. Such correlation is termed as *chance correlation* or *spurious* or *non-sense correlation.*

Let us take another example, Suppose that the correlation coefficient between the two series of marks of 10 students in Mathematics and Statistics comes out to be 0·9.

Probable Error of Correlation Coefficient is given by :

$$P.E.\ (r) = 0{\cdot}6745\,\frac{1-r^2}{\sqrt{n}} = \frac{0{\cdot}6745 \times 0{\cdot}19}{\sqrt{10}} = \frac{0{\cdot}128155}{3{\cdot}1623} = 0{\cdot}0405$$

Significance of *r*. We have

$r = 0{\cdot}9$ and $6\ P.E.\ (r) = 6 \times 0{\cdot}0405 = 0{\cdot}2430$

Since r is much greater than 6 P.E. (r), the value of r is highly significant.

Remark. Since the value of r is significant, it implies that ordinarily, higher the marks of a candidate in Mathematics, higher is his score in Statistics also and lower the marks of a candidate in Mathematics, lower is his score in Statistics also. However, it does not mean that all the students who are good in Mathematics are also good in Statistics and all those students who are poor in Mathematics are also poor in Statistics. It should be clearly borne in mind that "*the coefficient of correlation expresses the relationship between two series and not between the individual items of the series.*"

For more illustrations regarding the interpretation/mis-interpretation of the values of correlation coefficient (r) and regression coefficients, see Examples 17·8 to 17·14, discussed below :

Example 17·8. *If the coefficient of correlation between the annual value of exports during the last ten years and the annual number of children born during the same period is + 0·9, what inference, if any, would you draw ?*

Solution. The correlation coefficient between x : 'the annual value of exports during the last ten years' and y : 'the annual number of children born during the same period', should be zero since the forces affecting the two variable series are entirely independent of each other. The observed value of $r_{xy} = 0{\cdot}9$ (which reflects a very high degree of positive correlation between x and y) is just by chance and is termed as *chance correlation* or *spurious* or *'non-sense"* *correlation.*

Example 17·9. "*If the correlation coefficient between two variables is zero, then the variables are independent.*" Comment.

Solution. The *statement is wrong since* $r_{xy} = 0$, does not imply that X and Y are independent. $r_{xy} = 0$, simply implies the absence of *linear* (*straight line*) relationship between X and Y. The variables X and Y may, however, be related in some other form (other than straight line), *e.g.*, quadratic, logarithmic, exponential or trigonometric form.

Example 17·10. "*A correlation coefficient of 0·5 does not mean that 50% of the data are explained.*" *Comment.*

Solution. $r = 0{\cdot}5$. This does not mean that 50% of the variation in the dependent variable is due to the variation in the independent variable. But the coefficient of determination in this case is $r^2 = 0.25$, which implies that only 25% of the variation in the dependent variable has been explained by the independent variable.

Example 17·11. *A correlation between two variables has a value r = 0·6 and a correlation between other two variables is 0·3. Does it mean that the first correlation is twice as strong as the second ?*

Solution. It is misleading to conclude that correlation in the first case ($r_1 = 0{\cdot}6$) is twice as high as the correlation in the second case ($r_2 = 0{\cdot}3$) . The coefficient of determination explains this view point since,

$$r_1 = 0{\cdot}6 \ \Rightarrow\ \text{Coefficient of determination} = r_1^{\,2} = 0{\cdot}36$$

and $$r_2 = 0{\cdot}3 \ \Rightarrow\ \text{Coefficient of determination} = r_2^{\,2} = 0{\cdot}09$$

Hence, we conclude that the correlation in the first case ($r_1 = 0{\cdot}6$) is four times as high as the correlation in the second case ($r_2 = 0{\cdot}3$).

Example 17·12. *Comment on the following* :

"The closeness of the relationship between two variables as determined by r, the correlation coefficient between them, is proportional".

Solution. The given statement is wrong, *i.e.*, the closeness of the relationship between two variables, as determined by correlation coefficient r is *not* proportional. This means that a correlation coefficient $r_1 = 0{\cdot}6$ between two variables does not imply twice as strong a correlation as the correlation coefficient $r_2 = 0{\cdot}3$ between two other variables. It is rather, the coefficient of determination (r^2) which is used to study the closeness of the relationship between two variables.

(*For illustration, see Example 17·11.*)

Example 17·13. *Comment on the following statements :*

(*i*) *The correlation coefficient r_{xy} between X and Y is 0·90 and the regression coefficient β_{yx} is – 1.*

(*ii*) *If the two coefficients of regression are negative then their correlation coefficient is positive.*

(*iii*) $r_{xy} = 0{\cdot}9$, $\beta_{yx} = 2{\cdot}04$ *and* $\beta_{xy} = -3{\cdot}2$.

Solution. (*i*) $r = 0{\cdot}9$ and $\beta_{yx} = -1$. The statement is wrong since the sign of the regression coefficients must be same as that of the correlation coefficient and vice versa.

(*ii*) This statement is also wrong since the signs of β_{yx}, β_{xy} and r_{xy} must be same. Thus if two regression coefficient are negative, correlation coefficient must also be negative.

(*iii*) The statement is wrong because of the following reasons :

(*a*) Regression coefficients cannot have different signs. Here β_{yx} is positive and β_{xy} is negative which is not possible.

(*b*) We should have $r^2_{xy} = \beta_{yx} \cdot \beta_{xy}$

But L.H.S. $= (0{\cdot}9)^2 = 0{\cdot}81$; R.H.S. $= (2{\cdot}04) \times (-3{\cdot}2) = -6{\cdot}528$

Thus, L.H.S. $\neq$ R.H.S.

(*c*) r, β_{yx} and β_{xy} must have the same sign.

Example 17·14. *Interpret the following values :*

(*i*) *Product moment coefficient of correlation is 0.*

(*ii*) *Regression coefficient of y on x is – 1·75.*

(*iii*) *Coefficient of rank correlation = 1.*

Solution. (*i*) The product moment correlation coefficient $r_{xy} = 0$, implies that the variables x and y are un-correlated. This does not mean that the variables, x and y are independent. $r_{xy} = 0$, merely implies the absence of linear relationship between the variables x and y. They may, however, be connected by quadratic, polynomial, trigonometric or logarithmic relationship.

If $r_{xy} = 0$, the two lines of regression *viz.*, line of regression of y on x, and x on y are perpendicular to each other.

(*ii*) $b_{yx} = -1{\cdot}75$. This implies that corresponding to a unit change in the value of the independent variable x, the change in the value of the dependent variable y is $-1{\cdot}75$.

(*iii*) Rank correlation coefficient $\rho = 1$, implies that there is perfect positive correlation between the ranks. Spearman's formula gives :

$$\rho = 1 - \frac{6 \sum d_i^2}{n(n^2-1)},$$

where $d_i = x_i - y_i$, $(i = 1, ,2, \ldots, n)$ is the difference of the ranks of ith individual in the two characteristics.

$$\text{Thus, } \rho = 1 \text{ if and only if : } \sum_{i=1}^{n} d_i^2 = 0 \quad \Rightarrow \quad d_i^2 = 0, \text{ for all } i$$

$$\Rightarrow \quad d_i = 0 \text{ for all } i \quad \Rightarrow \quad x_i = y_i, \text{ for all } i = 1, 2, \ldots, n$$

Hence, $\rho = 1$, if and only if the ranks of ith individual in both the characteristics are same, $(i = 1, 2, \ldots, n)$. One case for 5 individuals is given below :

Individual	:	1	2	3	4	5
Rank x	:	3	5	1	2	4
Rank y	:	3	5	1	2	4

17·3·6 (*a*) Wrong Interpretation of Index Numbers

(See § 17·3·4 and Example 17·1 and 17·2.

17·3·6 (*b*) Wrong Interpretation of Components of Time Series – (Trend, Seasonal and Cyclical Variations

The various components of time series may be analysed and interpreted incorrectly.

For example, we may fit a linear trend equation to the given set of data by the principle of least squares and use it to find the corresponding trend values and use this equation to obtain future estimates. These trend values and the future estimates so obtained will be valid only if the data really exhibits a linear trend, *i.e.*, if the time series values increase or decrease by more or less a constant absolute amount, *i.e.*, if the historigram (the graph of the given time series) is approximately a straight line. However, if the given data exhibits a non-linear trend – parabolic trend ($u_t = a + bt + ct^2$) or exponential trend ($u_t = ab^t$), then the trend values and the future projections made on using the linear trend equation will be wrong and misleading.

Remark. Although, in practice, linear trend is commonly used, it is rarely observed in economic and business data. In an economic and business phenomenon, the rate of growth or decline is not of constant nature throughout but varies considerably in different sectors of time. Usually, in the beginning, the growth is slow, then rapid which is further accelerated for quite sometime after which it becomes stationary or stable for some period and finally retards slowly.

As an illustration of interpretation/mis-interpretation of seasonal indices, see Example 17·15, given below.

Example 17·15. *The sales of a company rose from Rs. 40,000 in March to Rs. 48,000 in April 2002. The company's seasonal indices for these two months are 105 and 140 respectively. The owner of the company expressed dissatisfaction with the April sales, but the Sales Manager said that he was quite pleased with the Rs. 8,000 increase. What argument should the owner of the company have used to reply to the Sales Manager ?*

The Sales Manager also predicted on the basis of the April sales that the total 2002 sales were going to be Rs. 5,76,000. Criticise the Sales Manager's estimate and explain how the estimate of Rs. 4,11,000 may be arrived at.

Solution. The Sales Manager did not take into consideration the seasonal indices of March and April. On the basis of March sales, the owner's estimate of sales for April 2002, keeping in view the seasonal indices is :

$$\text{Rs. } \frac{40{,}000}{105} \times 140 = \text{Rs. } 53{,}333{\cdot}33$$

Since company's sales for April *viz.*, Rs. 48,000 are (53,333·33 – 48,000), *i.e.*, Rs. 5,333·33 less than the estimated sales, owner's dissatisfaction is justified.

Sales Manager's estimate of annual sales on the basis of April sales is :

$$\text{Rs. } 48{,}000 \times 12 = \text{Rs. } 5{,}76{,}000$$

Now April's actual sales = Rs. 48,000

and April's seasonal Index = 140 $\Rightarrow$ April's seasonal effect $= \dfrac{140}{100} = 1{\cdot}40$

$\therefore$ April's estimated sales = (April's actual sales) ÷ Seasonal effect

$$= \text{Rs. } (48{,}000 \div 1{\cdot}4)$$

Hence on the basis of April sales, the estimated annual sales for 2002 are :

$$\text{Rs. } \frac{48{,}000}{1{\cdot}4} \times 12 = \text{Rs. } 4{,}11{,}428{\cdot}57 = \text{Rs. } 4{,}11{,}000 \text{ (nearest thousand).}$$

Remark. In the above discussion, we have used multiplicative model of time series.

17·3·7. Technical Errors

Some of the technical errors in statistical work which result in wrong conclusions from the data are :

(*i*) *The error due to improper choice of the statistical formula, e.g.,* we may use median in a situation where mode is more appropriate or we may use arithmetic mean in a situation where geometric mean is more appropriate.

(*ii*) *Wrong choice of the sampling technique for the selection of the sample, e.g.,* we may use random sampling in a situation where stratified random sampling may be more appropriate.

(*iii*) *Inadequate sample size.*

(*iv*) *The error in the use of statistical units* of Enumeration, Recording, Analysis and Interpretation. [For details, see § 2·1·2.]

(*v*) *The error due to bias in the estimation method.* This results due to improper choice of estimation techniques.

(*vi*) *The error committed in the use of ratios and percentages without proper reference to the base.* For example, if the price of a commodity increases from Rs. 25 to Rs. 75 during a particular period, then one generally concludes that there is 300% increase in the price during the given period. However, this is wrong, since the actual increase is 200% as explained below.

Increase on Rs. 25 is Rs. (75 – 25) = Rs. 50

Hence, increase on Rs. 100 is $\frac{50}{25} \times 100$ = Rs. 200.

For another illustration, see Example 17·16.

Example 17·16. *"The increase in the price of a commodity was 20%. Then the price decreased by 15% and again increased by 10%. So the resultant increase in the price was 20 – 15 + 10 = 15%". Comment.*

Solution. Let the price of the commodity be Rs. 100. After an increase of 20%, the increased price becomes Rs. (100 + 20) = Rs. 120. Now the price decreases by 15%. Thus :

Decrease in price = 15% of Rs. 120 = Rs. $\frac{15}{100} \times 120$ = Rs. 18

Hence, the new price is : Rs. (120 – 18) = Rs. 102.

The price further increases by 10%. Thus, the increase in price is :

10% of Rs. 102 = Rs. $\frac{10}{100} \times 102$ = Rs. 10·20.

Hence, the final price of the commodity is Rs. (102 + 10·20) = Rs. 112·20, *i.e.,* there is an over-all increase of (112·20 – 100·00) = 12·20%, in the price of the commodity and not 15% as stated in the problem. Hence, the given statement is wrong.

17·4. EFFECT OF WRONG INTERPRETATION OF DATA – DISTRUST OF STATISTICS

The wrong interpretation of statistical data promotes the distrust of Statistics. For a detailed discussion on 'Distrust of Statistics', see § 1·5.

EXERCISE 17·1

1. What do you understand by interpretation of statistical data ? Write a detailed note on its utility. What precautions should be taken while interpreting the data ? [*Madurai Kamaraj Univ. M.Com. 1996*]

2. What do you understand by statistical fallacies ? What are the mistakes commonly committed in interpretation of data ? What precautions are necessary to avoid them ?

3. (*a*) What are the chief sources from which wrong interpretation of data may emerge ?
[*Madras Univ. B.Com. 1994*]

(*b*) Describe the importance of analysis and interpretation of data in research. What are the mistakes commonly committed in interpretation ? What precautions are necessary to avoid them ?

4. Comment on the following statistical statements, bringing out in detail the fallacies, if any :

(*i*) "A survey revealed that the children of engineers, doctors and lawyers have high intelligence quotients (I.Q.). It further revealed that the grandfathers of these children were also highly intelligent. Hence, the inference is that intelligence is hereditary".

(*ii*) "The number of deaths in military in a recent war in a country was 15 out of 1,000 while the number of deaths in the capital of the country during the same period was 22 per thousand. Hence, it is safe to join military service than to live in the capital city of the country".

(*iii*) "The number of accidents taking place in the middle of the road is much less than the number of accidents taking place on its sides. Hence, it is safer to walk in the middle of the road".

(*iv*) "The frequency of divorce for couples with the children is only about 1/2 of that for childless couples; therefore producing children is an effective check on divorce".

(*v*) "The increase in the price of a commodity was 20%. Then the price decreased by 15% and again increased by 10%. So the resultant increase in the price was 20 – 15 + 10 = 15%".

(*vi*) "Nutritious Bread Company, a private manufacturing concern, charges a lower rate per loaf than that charged by a Government of India undertaking 'Modern Bread'. Thus, private ownership is more efficient than public ownership".

(*vii*) "According to the estimate of an economist, the per capita national income of India for 1931-32 was Rs. 55. The National Income Committee estimated the corresponding figure for 1948-49 as Rs. 225. Hence, in 1948-49 Indians were nearly four times as prosperous as in 1931-32".

5. Point out the ambiguity or mistakes found in the following statements which are made on the basis of the facts given :

(*a*) 80% of the people who die of cancer are found to be smokers and so it may be concluded that smoking causes cancer.

(*b*) The gross profit to sales ratio of a company was 15% in the year 1974 and was 10% in 1975. Hence, the stock must have been undervalued.

(*c*) The average output in a factory was 2,500 units in January 1981 and 2,400 units in February 1981. So workers were more efficient in January 1981.

(*d*) The rate of increase in the number of buffaloes in India is greater than that of the population. Hence, the people of India are now getting more milk per head.

6. Comment on the following :

(*a*) 50 boys and 50 girls took an examination. 30 boys and 40 girls got through the examination. Hence, girls are more intelligent than boys.

(*b*) The average monthly incomes in two cities of Hyderabad and Chennai were found to be Rs. 12,500. Hence, the people of both the cities have the same standard of living.

(*c*) A tutorial college advertised that there was 100 per cent success for the candidates who took the coaching in their institute. Hence, the college has got good faculty.

7. Bring out the fallacy, if any, in the following statements.

(*a*) "An employer lowered the wages of an employee by 20% and later on raised by 50%. The employee is receiving 30% more pay."

(*b*) "The average depth of a river is 3 ft. 8 inches and the average height of the members of a family is 5 feet. The family can safely cross the river".

(*c*) "Two series, quantity of money in circulation and general price index, are found to possess positive correlation of a fairly high order. It is concluded that one is the cause and the other the effect in direct causal relationship".

(*d*) "The population of a city has doubled during the last 20 years. The birth rate has doubled during this period in the city".

(*e*) "The number of accidents in the city of Delhi is much higher in 2002 as compared to 1992. Hence, the arrangement of road signals or alarms or traffic control are not efficient".

(*f*) "The number of deaths in the military in the recent war was 12 out of 1,000 while number of deaths in Chennai in the same period was 20 per 1,000. Hence, it is safe to join military service than to live in the city of Chennai".

(*g*) "The number of deaths (the number of children produced) in the city of Lucknow are more than in Chandigarh in the month of December 2002. Hence, mortality is higher in Lucknow (the women of Lucknow are more fertile than the women of Chandigarh)".

8. The samples, A and B have the same standard deviations but mean of A is greater than that of B. The coefficient of variation of A is :

(*i*) greater than that of B. (*ii*) less than that of B.
(*iii*) equal to that of B. (*iv*) none of these.

9. A frequency distribution is positively skewed.

The mean of the distribution is :

(*i*) greater than the mode. (*ii*) less than the mode.
(*iii*) equal to the mode. (*iv*) none of these.

10. State, giving reasons, whether the following statement is true or false.
"Coefficient of correlation between two variables must be in the same units as the original data".

11. (*a*) Comment on the following :

For a bivariate distribution, the coefficient of regression of y on x is 4.2 and the coefficient of regression of x on y is 0·5.

(*b*) If the two regression coefficients are 0·8 and 0·6, what would be the value of the coefficient of correlation ?

(*c*) A student while studying correlation between smoking and drinking found a value of $r = 2·46$. Discuss.

(*d*) For a bivariate distribution : $b_{yx} = 2·8$; $b_{xy} = -0·3$. Comment.

12. From the following lines of regression data, calculate :

(*i*) Coefficient of correlation,

(*ii*) Standard deviation of y

$$x = 0·854\,y\ ;\ \ y = 0·89\,x\ ;\ \ \sigma_x = 3$$

Ans. $r = 0·87$; $\sigma_y = 3·07$

13. (*a*) Interpret the following values of the correlation coefficient :

(*i*) $r = 0$, (*ii*) $r = +1$, (*iii*) $r = -1$.

(*b*) What conclusions do you draw about the regression lines if :

(*i*) $r = 0$, (*ii*) $r = \pm 1$.

(*c*) What does $b_{yx} = 2·6$, signify ?

(*d*) What can you say about the shape of the curve if :

(*i*) Skewness = 0, (*ii*) Skewness > 0 and (*iii*) Skewness < 0.

(*e*) What can you say about the value of r if :

(*i*) $b_{yx} = 1·6$ and $b_{xy} = 1·2$, (*ii*) $b_{yx} = 2·4$ and $b_{xy} = -0·3$.

14. The linear trend equation for the annual production of sugar (in thousand quintals) in a factory is :

$y = 90 + 2x$ (origin 1996)

(*a*) Estimate the production in 2002.

(*b*) Find the slope of the straight line trend.

(*c*) Do the figures show a rising trend or a falling trend ?

(*d*) What does the difference between the given figures and the trend values indicate ?

Ans. (*a*) 102, ('000 quintals); (*b*) 2; (*c*) Rising trend; (*d*) The difference between the given figures and the trend values indicates the short term fluctuations (seasonal and cyclical) and irregular variations.

15. Comment on the following :

(*a*) In a town, there are two companies A and B. During the year 2002, there was 15% retrenchment in company A. But, in company B, there was 15% increase in the number of persons employed during the year 2002. Hence there is no unemployment problem in the town.

(*b*) "In a random sample of 1000 persons in Delhi, 610 are found to be smokers. Therefore, majority of the people in Delhi are smokers."

(*c*) "Ramesh scored 75% marks in scholastic aptitude test (SAT) in 2001 and his friend Neeraj scored 68% marks in SAT in 2002. Hence Ramesh is more intelligent than Neeraj."

(*d*) It is reported that 20% of the surgical operations by an eminent surgeon are successful. If he is to operate on five persons on any day and four of the operations have proved unsuccessful, the fifth must be a success."

(*e*) "The number of accidents committed by female drivers in Delhi is much less than the number of accidents committed by male drivers. Hence ladies are safe drivers than the men drivers."

(*f*) A student cycles from home to school at 15 km. p.h. and comes back from school to home at 10 km. p.h. His average speed for the entire journey is 12.5 km. p.h.

Ans. Wrong. Average speed = 12 km. p.h.

(*g*) For a group of 20 students, the standard deviation (s.d.) of the distribution of heights is 0·65 metres and the s.d. of the distribution of weights is 15 kg. Hence the distribution of weights is more variable that the distribution of the heights."

Ans. Wrong. We should compute coefficient of variation in each case.

(*h*) "The net profit of an organisation increased from Rs. 125 lakhs in 1995 to Rs. 250 lakhs in 2000. Hence, the organisation has become doubly efficient in 2000, as compared to 1995."

(*i*) The annual salary of an individual increased from Rs. 2·25 lakhs in 1990 to Rs. 4·50 lakhs in 2002. Hence, his standard of living has doubled in 2002 as compared to 1990."

18 Statistical Decision Theory

18·1. INTRODUCTION

The process of decision making consists of making a choice out of two or more alternatives at our disposal. We are faced with the problem of decision making in almost every sphere of human activity, whether it is at the personal level or in business, production, finance, marketing, management, etc. Decisions may be personal or official or at the organisational level.

In our day to day life, we have to make many personal decisions. For example,

(*i*) Every day, a housewife has to decide about how much and which vegetables/fruits to buy for day's consumption ? ; what to cook and how much to cook ? ; what to do buy and from where to do the shopping ?

(*ii*) Where to go for an excursion trip and for how many days ?

(*iii*) Whether to carry an umbrella on a particular day in a rainy season ?

(*iv*) When and whom to marry ?

(*v*) Which career or profession to choose ?

(*vi*) Where and how much to invest ?

(*vii*) Whether to undergo an operation for an ailment or not ?

(*viii*) In a newly set up manufacturing / industrial unit, what to produce and how much to produce, and so on.

Some of these decisions are easy to take and involve little risk *e.g.*, the decisions in (*i*) to (*iii*) above. However, some of the decisions are difficult to make and are very vital and involve good amount of risk *e.g.*, the decisions in (*iv*) to (*viii*).

Earlier, the decisions were taken subjectively based on the skill, experience and intuition of the decision maker. But in today's world of dynamism, the decision making has become very complex, particularly in business, marketing and management because they involve a number of interactive variables (factors) whose values and relationships cannot be determined accurately. In such situations, mere intuition and expertise of the decision maker are inadequate and we require well considered judgment and analysis based on the use of several quantitative techniques and even computers in solving problems. It is in this context that we need a full-fledged decision theory which provides a sound and scientific basis for improved decision making.

SOME DEFINITIONS

1. "*Decision making is a process which results in the selection from a set of alternative courses of action, that course of action which is considered to meet the objectives of the decision problem more satisfactorily than others, as judged by the decision maker.*"

2. "*Solving the decision model consists of finding a strategy for action, the expected relative value of which is at least as great as the expected relative value of any other strategy in a specified set. The prescriptive criterion of a strategy will be maximisation of the decision maker's expected relative value.*"

—Fishburn P.C.

'Decision analysis' is a very vast field. However, in this chapter, we shall confine ourselves to the discussion and development of the elementary ideas and concepts which are common to all the decision problems.

18·2. INGREDIENTS OF DECISION PROBLEM

Decision theory provides a framework which enables us to justify as to how and why a decision maker has selected a particular choice or act or strategy out of the various choices, strategies or courses of action available to him. In this section we will identify and discuss some of the key elements common to all the decision problems.

18·2·1. Acts. The various possible alternatives or the courses of action available to the decision maker, out of which he has to choose one, are termed as *acts or strategies or decisions.* The n acts, say, are usually denoted by A_j, ($j = 1, 2, \dots, n$). The decision maker has control over the choice of these acts or decisions.

18·2·2. States of Nature or Events. The various possible outcomes of any act / strategy on the part of the decision maker are dependent on a number of factors, called the *states of nature* or *events,* say, S_i, ($i = 1, 2, \dots, m$). These are beyond the control of the decision maker.

Illustration 1. If a person is to move out on any day in rainy season, the acts and the states of nature may be as given below :

Acts	*States of Nature*
A_1 : Carry an umbrella	S_1 : Rain on that day
A_2 : Not carry an umbrella	S_2 : No rain on that day

Illustration 2. Suppose a person is suffering from an ailment for which he may need surgery. Then, the various acts and events may be as follows :

Acts	*Events (States of Nature)*
A_1 : Get operated	S_1 : Cured
A_2 : Not get operated	S_2 : Not cured

Illustration 3. Let us consider an industrial unit interested in manufacturing one of the three products, say, A, B or C. Then the various acts and states of nature may be as follows :

Acts	*States of Nature*
A_1 : Manufacture the product A	S_1 : Good demand
A_2 : Manufacture the product B	S_2 : Moderate demand
A_3 : Manufacture the product C	S_3 : Poor demand

18·2·3. Payoff Table. Associated with each combination (S_i, A_j) of the events (states of nature) S_i and the alternative acts (decisions) A_j is a number X_{ij} ; $i = 1, 2, \dots, m$; $j = 1, 2, \dots, n$; called the *payoff,* which reflects the effectiveness of various acts under different states of nature. It is a measure of the net benefit to the decision maker/organisation on taking the decision, A_j under the state of nature S_i. The larger the value of the payoff, the more useful is the strategy (act) to the decision maker.

The set of $m \times n$ payoffs can be represented by $m \times n$ matrix, known as the *payoff matrix* or *payoff table,* as given below.

PAYOFF TABLE OR PAYOFF MATRIX

Event (States of Nature)	*Conditional Payoff (Rs.) Acts (Strategies)*					
	A_1	A_2	…	A_j	…	A_n
E_1 (S_1)	X_{11}	X_{12}	…	X_{1j}	…	X_{1n}
E_2 (S_2)	X_{21}	X_{22}	…	X_{2j}	…	X_{2n}
⋮	⋮	⋮		⋮		⋮
E_i (S_i)	X_{i1}	X_{i2}	…	X_{ij}	…	X_{in}
⋮	⋮	⋮		⋮		⋮
E_m (S_m)	X_{m1}	X_{m2}	…	X_{mj}	…	X_{mn}

In general, the payoffs are measured in terms of monetary units. Larger the value of the payoff, the better is the strategy to the decision maker. Hence, for a given state of nature, the act for which the payoff is maximum is the best act. In other words, for the state of nature S_i, the best act corresponds to the payoff :

$$\underset{1 \le j \le n}{\text{Max}} \ (X_{ij}) = \text{Max}\ (X_{i1}, X_{i2}, \ldots, X_{in}) = M_i, \text{ (say)}.$$

Sometimes, it is not possible to give X_{ij}, a realistic monetary value when the payoff is a measure of something not to be lost by the decision maker *e.g.*, time, material, quality, etc. In such cases, the decision maker/organisation can decide about the effectiveness (worth) of the combination (S_i, A_j) subjectively on the basis of their skill and expertise.

18·2·4. Opportunity Loss (O.L.). *Opportunity Loss (O.L.) may be defined as the loss incurred (or profit not earned) as a consequence of the failure to take the best possible decision.* In other words, opportunity loss is the profit or gain missed for not selecting the best act for any given event. Thus, for any given state of nature (S_i), the opportunity loss for any given act (A_j), is defined as the difference between the highest possible payoff (profit) over different acts/strategies and the actual payoff for the act A_j.

Let
$$M_i = \underset{1 \le j \le n}{\text{Max}} \ (X_{ij}) \qquad \ldots (18·1)$$

Then the opportunity loss (O.L.) for the combination (S_i, A_j) is given by :

$$\text{OL}(S_i, A_j) = \underset{1 \le j \le n}{\text{Max}} \ (X_{ij}) - X_{ij}$$
$$= M_i - X_{ij}\ ; \ (i = 1, 2, \ldots, m \ ; \ j = 1, 2, \ldots, n) \qquad \ldots (18·2)$$

Thus, for any given state of nature, the opportunity losses for different acts are obtained on subtracting from the maximum payoff of that state of nature, the payoffs of different acts or strategies.

The $m \times n$ values of opportunity losses obtained in (18·2) can be arranged in the following matrix, called the *Opportunity Loss Matrix or Table.*

OPPORTUNITY LOSS (REGRET) TABLE

Events *(States of nature)*	*Conditional Opportunity Loss (Rs.)* *Acts (Strategies)*						
	A_1	A_2	...	A_j	...	A_n
$E_1\ (S_1)$	$M_1 - X_{11}$	$M_1 - X_{12}$	...	$M_1 - X_{1j}$	...	$M_1 - X_{1n}$
$E_2\ (S_2)$	$M_2 - X_{21}$	$M_2 - X_{22}$	...	$M_2 - X_{2j}$	...	$M_2 - X_{2n}$
$\vdots$	$\vdots$	$\vdots$		$\vdots$		$\vdots$
$E_i\ (S_i)$	$M_i - X_{i1}$	$M_i - X_{i2}$	...	$M_i - X_{ij}$	...	$M_i - X_{in}$
$\vdots$	$\vdots$	$\vdots$		$\vdots$		$\vdots$
$E_m\ (S_m)$	$M_m - X_{m1}$	$M_m - X_{m2}$	...	$M_m - X_{mj}$	...	$M_m - X_{mn}$

Remarks 1. The expression in (18·2) is also sometimes called the *conditional opportunity loss* for the event S_i, conditional upon selecting the act A_j.

2. Regret Function and Regret Table. The opportunity losses, as a result of not taking the optimal decision, may also be looked upon as *regrets* for the lost opportunities. Hence, the O.L. values defined in (18·2) are also known as *Regret Values* and the O.L. Table given above is also called *Regret Table.*

18·2·5. Decision Making Environment

(*a*) **Decision Maker.** The first and the foremost question that may be asked in any decision problem is: 'Who is the decision maker' ? The decision maker may be an individual or a group of individuals or an organisation.

(*b*) **Objectives.** The decision maker must be very clear about the objectives he wants to achieve. Usually, the objectives are to optimise *i.e.,* maximise profits or returns or minimise the costs or losses.

Sometimes, he may decide to maintain a *status-quo*, which is also a kind of decision not to disturb the existing set up.

(*c*) **Decision Situation**. Next problem is to consider the decision situations. There are two types of decision making situations.

(*i*) *Decision making under certainty.*

(*ii*) *Decision making under uncertainty.*

We shall now briefly explain these concepts.

18·2·6. Decision Making Under Certainty. The process of choosing an act or strategy when the state of nature is completely known, is called *decision making under certainty.* In such a situation, each act will result only in one event and the outcome of the act can be pre-determined with certainty. Hence, such situations are also termed as *deterministic* situations.

Some of the commonly used techniques for decision making under certainty are :

(*i*) Linear programming and simplex method.

(*ii*) Techniques used in assignment and transportation problems.

(*iii*) Input-output analysis and activity analysis and so on.

The discussion on these topics is, however, beyond the scope of the book and the interested reader is referred to any book on Operations Research.

Illustration. Let us suppose that a person has to travel from one place, say, *A* to another place, say, *B*. He can follow any one of the routes, R_1, R_2, R_3, (say), with the following payoff table.

Acts	*States of Nature*		
Routes	*Fuel Saving (litres)* (S_1)	*Time Saving (hours)* (S_2)	*Enjoyment (subjective rating)* (S_3)
R_1	5	0	6
R_2	0	4	3
R_3	8	2	1

The results of each of the acts (routes) are known with certainty. If a person wants to economise on petrol, he will use route R_3 ; if he values time, he would prefer to take route R_2; and if he gives more weight to enjoyment and fun, he would like to take route R_1.

18·2·7. Decision Making Under Uncertainty. The process of choosing an act or strategy out of the various courses of action at hand, when the outcome *i.e.*, the state of nature of any act is unknown, is termed as decision making under uncertainty. Such situations are frequent in business and management. Will the new plant or industrial unit be successful ? Will the new product be able to compete with others in the market ? How much to produce and stock to get maximum returns ? These are some of the problems involving uncertainty.

There are two types of decision making criteria in the face of uncertainty.

(*i*) Non-probabilistic criteria.

(*ii*) Probabilistic criteria.

Non-Probabilistic Criteria. Non-probabilistic criteria are used when the decision maker has the payoff table for various combinations of events and acts (S_i, A_j) ; $i = 1, 2, ..., m$; $j = 1, 2, ..., n$ but cannot assess the probabilities of different states of nature (events). Some of the non-probabilistic criteria used in decision making under uncertainty are :

(*i*) Maximax Criterion.

(*ii*) Maximin Criterion.

(*iii*) Minimax Regret Criterion.

(*iv*) Laplace Criterion of Equal Likelihoods.

(*v*) Hurwicz Criterion.

Probabilistic Criteria. In decision making under uncertainty, though the outcomes of the actions are not known, the probabilities of the various outcomes (states of nature) can be obtained :

(*i*) either subjectively based on the experience, intuition or skill of the decision maker,

(*ii*) or objectively through the use of the past records or prior information pertinent to the problem in the form of some experimental data.

Such criteria are also termed as the *decision criteria under risk.* The fundamental probabilistic criteria used in decision making are :

(*i*) Expected Monetary Value criterion or EMV criterion.

(*ii*) Expected Opportunity Loss criterion or EOL criterion.

Remark. It may be pointed out that in decision making under uncertainty :

(*i*) No single criterion can be regarded as the best criterion; and

(*ii*) Use of different criteria may lead to different optimal (best) strategy.

In the following sections, we shall discuss these criteria in detail.

18·3. OPTIMAL DECISION

A decision maker is interested in selecting that particular act which will maximise his profits or returns or minimise his opportunity losses or costs under all the states of nature. If such a decision exists, it is termed as *uniformly best decision.* However, in practice, such decisions rarely exist. A decision/act which is good under one situation, may not be that good or may even be worse under other states of nature and a decision which is bad under one state of nature may be very good under some other state of nature. In order to obtain the best possible decision in such cases, we have to lay down certain criterion or principle which will enable us to take an optimal action - an action for which the expected payoff (*EMV*) is maximum or the expected opportunity loss (*EOL*) is minimum as determined by the criterion or the principle under consideration.

18·3·1. Maximax Criterion. In maximax criterion, for each act we first locate the maximum possible payoff over different states of nature. Thus, for the *j*th act A_j, we find the maximum of the payoffs $X_{1j}, X_{2j}, \ldots, X_{mj}$.

Let
$$\underset{1 \le i \le m}{\text{Max}} \ (X_{ij}) = P_j \ ; j = 1, 2, \ldots, n \qquad \ldots(18{\cdot}3)$$

be the maximum payoff for the *j*th act A_j, over different states of nature.

Next, we find the maximum of these maxima for different acts *i.e.,* we find the maximum of $P_1, P_2, \ldots, P_n$. Then under the maximax criterion, the act (decision) corresponding to Max. $(P_1, P_2, \ldots, P_n)$ is taken as the optimal act (decision).

In this criterion, since the decision maker is looking for the act with the maximum of maximum payoffs, it is also termed as the *optimistic criterion.* An institution or a firm in sound financial position can afford to adopt this criterion since it can afford to absorb less profits or even loss if it at all occurs.

However, there may be situations where maximax criterion is not suitable because if it is associated with larger risks of loss, then the decision maker, who does not want to undertake risk, will not opt for it. In such a situation maximin criterion, discussed below is suitable.

Remarks 1. For problems in which costs/time, etc., are to be minimised, the maximax criterion is reversed into minimin criterion *i.e.,* we look for the overall minimum of the minimum cost values for each act.

2. If the maximax value is repeated then there are two acts/decisions corresponding to the maximax value. In this case, the choice of the final optimal act is made by looking at the corresponding minima (over different states of nature), for each of these two acts. The act/decision with the higher minimum value will be taken as the optimal act.

18·3·2. Maximin Criterion. In the maximin criterion which was proposed by Abraham Wald, for each act (strategy) we first note the minimum payoff over different states of nature. Thus, for the jth act, we find minimum of the payoffs $(X_{1j}, X_{2j}, \ldots, X_{mj})$.

Let $$\underset{1 \le i \le m}{\text{Min}} \ (X_{ij}) = P_j', \ (j = 1, 2, \ldots, n). \qquad \ldots (18\cdot4)$$

Next, we find the maximum of these minimum payoffs *i.e.*, we find

$$\text{Max}\ (P_1', P_2', \ldots, P_n') \text{ or } \underset{1 \le j \le n}{\text{Max}} \ (P_j'). \qquad \ldots (18\cdot4a)$$

Thus, under the maximin criterion, the act (strategy) corresponding to this maximum of minimum payoffs, is taken as the optimal decision.

In this criterion, since we are looking for the minimum of the payoffs, it is also termed as a *pessimistic criterion,* Caution is the watchword of this criterion and it attempts to avoid the worst. Here, the basic approach is 'self-preservation', rather than looking for huge profits, which is the case in maximax criterion. This criterion is usually adopted by the decision maker who does not want to take undue risks and as such has found favour with firms or institutions which are not in sound financial position or which are in miserable financial position. This criterion is also recommended when the various probabilities for different states of nature are not known or cannot be assessed with reasonable accuracy.

Remark. *In case of the problems for minimising the total cost, etc., the maximin criterion is reversed to minimax criterion i.e.,* we look for minimum of the maximum of the costs for each act *i.e.,*

$$\underset{1 \le j \le n}{\text{Min}} \left[\underset{1 \le i \le m}{\text{Max}} \ (X_{ij}) \right].$$

18·3·3. Minimax Criterion. The minimax criterion is based on the regrets or opportunity losses (discussed in § 18·2·4), costs or damages, instead of profits or gains, and is carried on exactly similarly on interchanging maximum and minimum in max-min principle discussed above.

In minimax criterion, for each act, we first find maximum of regrets (or opportunity losses/damages/costs) over different states of nature. Then we find the minimum of these maxima for different acts (strategies) *i.e.,* we find $$\underset{1 \le j \le n}{\text{Min}} \left[\underset{1 \le i \le m}{\text{Max}} \ (\text{Regrets/O.L.'s}) \right]. \qquad \ldots (18\cdot5)$$

The act corresponding to this minimax value is taken as the optimal decision. This criterion was given by John Von-Neumann and Oskar Morgenstern. This method gives the greatest possible protection against the maximum possible loss.

18·3·4. Laplace Criterion of Equal Likelihoods. This is based on the principle of insufficient reason and is used in the case when the probabilities of different states of nature are not known. It is based on the assumption that for any act, the different states of nature have the same probability.

Under Laplace decision criterion of equal likelihoods, for each act A_j, we compute the expected (average) payoff over different states of nature. Since each of the m states of nature $(S_i\,;\ i = 1, 2, \ldots, m)$ is assigned equal probability, we have :

$$p_i = P(S_i) = \frac{1}{m}\,;\ i = 1, 2, \ldots, m.$$

$$\therefore \quad \text{Average payoff } (A_j) = \sum_{i=1}^{m} p_i X_{ij} = \frac{1}{m} \sum_{i=1}^{m} X_{ij} \qquad \ldots (18\cdot6)$$

(18·6) may also be interpreted as the EMV for the act A_j under the assumption of equal likelihoods for all the states of nature.

The act or strategy with the maximum average value given by (18·6) is the optimal act. In other words, *the strategy with the highest average payoff is the optimal strategy.*

The working steps for Laplace criterion can be summarised as follows.

Steps 1. For each act, compute the average (arithmetic mean) of the payoffs over different states of nature.

2. Choose the maximum of these averages.

3. The act corresponding to the maximum average in Step 2, is taken as the optimal act.

18·3·5. Hurwicz Criterion of Realism. This decision rule developed by Hurwicz is a compromise between the optimistic decision rule (Maximax criterion) and the pessimistic decision rule (Maximin criterion) with an *index of optimism* α and *an index of pessimism* $(1 - \alpha)$, where α is a real number lying between 0 and 1 *i.e.*, $0 < \alpha < 1$ and is also referred to as the *coefficient of realism.* The decision maker has to assign a value to 'α', somewhere between 0 and 1. The value of α close to 1 means that the decision maker is optimistic about the future and the value of α close to '0' reflects that the decision maker is pessimistic about the future.

In the usual notations, for any act A_j $(j = 1, 2, \ldots, n)$, let :

$$\underset{1 \le i \le m}{\text{Max}} (X_{ij}) = \text{Max}(X_{1j}, X_{2j}, \ldots, X_{mj}) = P_j \quad \ldots (18\cdot7)$$

and

$$\underset{1 \le i \le m}{\text{Min}} (X_{ij}) = \text{Min}(X_{1j}, X_{2j}, \ldots, X_{mj}) = P_j' \quad \ldots (18\cdot7a)$$

Then, Hurwicz rule consists in finding the expected value for the act A_j by the formula :

$$\text{Expected Value }(A_j) = \alpha . P_j + (1 - \alpha) P_j' ; (j = 1, 2, \ldots, n) \quad \ldots (18\cdot8)$$

The expression in (18·8) is the weighted sum of both the maximum and minimum payoffs for the jth act, the weights representing the optimism (or pessimism) of the decision maker.

The act with the highest expected value as given by (18·8), is taken as the optimal act (decision).

Example 18·1. *A company is contemplating the introduction of a new product with new packing to replace the existing product at much higher Price* (P_1) *or a moderate change in the composition of the existing product with a new packaging at a small increase in price* (P_2) *or a small change in the composition of the existing product except the word "new" with a very small increase in price* (P_3). *The three possible states of nature are : (i) high increase in sales* (n_1), *(ii) no change in sales* (n_2), *and (iii) decrease in sales* (n_3). *The marketing department of the company calculated the payoffs in terms of yearly net profits from each of the strategies (expected sales). This is represented in the following table :*

Strategies	*States of Nature*		
	n_1	n_2	n_3
P_1	7000	3000	1500
P_2	5000	4500	0
P_3	3000	3000	3000

Which strategy should the concerned executive choose on the basis of :

(i) Maximin criterion, *(ii) Laplace criterion ?* [*I.C.W.A. (Intermedite), Dec. 1999*]

Solution.

PAYOFF TABLE

Strategies	*States of Nature*			*Row Minimum*	*Row Total*
	n_1	n_2	n_3		
(1)	(2)	(3)	(4)	(5)	(6)
P_1	7,000	3,000	1,500	1,500	11,500
P_2	5,000	4,500	0	0	9,500
P_3	3,000	3,000	3,000	3,000	9,000
Probability*	$\frac{1}{3}$	$\frac{1}{3}$	$\frac{1}{3}$	Column Maximum = 3,000	

* Under Laplace criterion of equal likelihood.

1. Maximin Criterion. For each strategy, we find the minimum payoff over all the states of nature, as given in column (5). Next we find the maximum of these minimum payoffs.

Maximum (Minimum payoffs) = 3,000.

Hence, according to the maximin criterion, the strategy corresponding to the row minimum 3,000 in column 5 *i.e.*, the strategy P_3 is the optimal decision.

Laplace Criterion. In this criterion, we assign equal probability viz; $\frac{1}{3}$ to each of the three states of nature. Accordingly, the EMV's for each act are obtained as the arithmetic mean of the payoffs over different states of nature.

$$\therefore \quad EMV\,(P_1) = \frac{11{,}500}{3} = 3{,}833{\cdot}33; \quad EMV\,(P_2) = \frac{9{,}500}{3} = 3{,}166{\cdot}67; \quad EMV\,(P_3) = \frac{9{,}000}{3} = 3000$$

Since $EMV\,(P_1)$ is maximum, according to the Laplace criterion, the strategy P_1 is the best strategy.

Example 18·2. *A person wants to invest in one of three alternative investment plans : stocks, bonds, saving account. It is assumed that the person wishes to invest all of the funds in a plan. The conditional payoffs of the investments are based on three potential economic conditions : accelerated, normal or slow growth. The payoff matrix is given below.*

Alternative Investment	*Economic Conditions*		
	Accelerated Growth	*Normal Growth*	*Slow Growth*
Stocks	*Rs. 10,000*	*Rs. 6,500*	*– Rs. 4,000*
Bonds	*8,000*	*6,000*	*1,000*
Savings Account	*5,000*	*5,000*	*5,000*

Determine the best investment plan using each of the following criteria :

(i) Laplace ; (ii) Maximin ; (iii) Maximax; (iv) Hurwicz with coefficient of optimism $\alpha = 0{\cdot}6$.

[I.C.W.A. (Intermediate), Dec. 1997]

Solution. For Parts (*i*) and (*ii*), proceed as in Example 18·1.

AG : Accelerated Growth ; NG : Normal Growth ; SG : Slow Growth.

PAYOFF TABLE (IN RUPEES)

Act (Investment)	*States of nature*			*Row Minimum*	*Row Maximum*	*Row Total*
	S_1 : AG	S_2 : NG	S_3 : SG			
(1)	(2)	(3)	(4)	(5)	(6)	(7)
A_1 : Stocks	10,000	6,500	– 4,000	– 4,000	10,000	12,500
A_2 : Bonds	8,000	6,000	1,000	1,000	8,000	15,000
A_3 : Savings A/c	5,000	5,000	5,000	5,000	5,000	15,000
Probability*	$\frac{1}{3}$	$\frac{1}{3}$	$\frac{1}{3}$	Column (5) Maximum = 5,000	Column (6) Maximum = 10,000	

* Under Laplace criterion of equal likelihoods.

(*i*) **Laplace Criterion**

$$EMV\,(A_1 : \text{Stocks}) = \text{Rs.}\,\tfrac{1}{3}\,(10{,}000 + 6{,}500 - 4{,}000) = \text{Rs.}\,\frac{12{,}500}{3} = \text{Rs. } 4{,}166{\cdot}67$$

$$EMV\,(A_2 : \text{Bonds}) = \text{Rs.}\,\tfrac{1}{3} \times 15{,}000 = \text{Rs. } 5{,}000$$

$$EMV\,(A_3 : \text{Savings A/c}) = \text{Rs.}\,\tfrac{1}{3} \times 15{,}000 = \text{Rs. } 5{,}000.$$

Max. (*EMV*) = Rs. 5,000, which corresponds to acts A_2 and A_3. Hence, under Laplace criterion, either of A_2 : Bonds and A_3 : Savings Account, can be taken as the optimal act.

(*ii*) **Maximin Criterion.** From column (5) of the above Table, we get :

Maximum (Minimum Payoffs) = Rs. 5,000, which corresponds to act A_3.

Hence, under the Maximin criterion, act A_3 : Savings Account, is the optimal choice.

(*iii*) **Maximax Criterion.** From column (6) of the above Table, we get :

Maximum (Maximum Payoffs) = Rs. 10,000, which corresponds to act A_1.

Hence, according to the maximax criterion, the act A_1 : stock, is the optimal choice.

(*iv*) **Hurwicz Criterion with Coefficient of Optimism $\alpha = 0{\cdot}6$.** Under Hurwicz criterion, the expected value of profit (*EP*) with coefficient of optimism $\alpha = 0{\cdot}6$ is given by :

$$EP \text{ (for any act)} = \alpha . \text{ Maximum Payoff} + (1 - \alpha). \text{ Minimum Payoff} \qquad \ldots(*)$$

With $\alpha = 0{\cdot}6$, using column (5) and (6) of the above Table, we get on using (*) :

EP (A_1 : Stocks) = Rs. $[0{\cdot}6 \times 10{,}000 + 0{\cdot}4 \times (-4{,}000)]$ = Rs. 4,400

EP (A_2 : Bonds) = Rs. $(0{\cdot}6 \times 8{,}000 + 0{\cdot}4 \times 1{,}000)$ = Rs. 5,200

EP (A_3 : Savings) = Rs. $(0{\cdot}6 \times 5000 + 0{\cdot}4 \times 5{,}000)$ = Rs. 5,000

Since $EP(A_2)$ is maximum, hence under Hurwicz criterion with $\alpha = 0{\cdot}6$, the act A_2 : Bonds, is the optimal selection.

Example 18·3. *Suppose that a decision maker is faced with three decision alternatives and four states of nature. Given the following profit payoff table :*

States of Nature → / *Acts* ↓	S_1	S_2	S_3	S_4
a_1	16	10	12	7
a_2	13	12	9	9
a_3	11	14	15	14

Assuming that he has no knowledge of the probabilities of occurrence of the states of nature, find the decisions to be recommended under each of the following criteria :

(i) Maximin, *(ii) Maximax,* *(iii) Minimax Regret.* [*I.C.W.A. (Intermediate), June 1997*]

Solution

PAYOFF TABLE

Act	*States of Nature* S_1	S_2	S_3	S_4	*Row Minimum*	*Row Maximum*
(1)	(2)	(3)	(4)	(5)	(6)	(7)
a_1	16	10	12	7	7	16
a_2	13	12	9	9	9	13
a_3	11	14	15	14	11	15
					Column (6) Maximum = 11	Column (7) Maximum = 16

(*i*) *Maximin Criterion.* For each act, we find the minimum payoff over different states of nature, as given in column (6). Next we find the maximum of these minimum payoffs.

Maximum (Minimum Payoff) = 11, which corresponds to act a_3. Hence, according to the maximin criterion, the act a_3 is the optimal (best) act.

(*ii*) *Maximax Criterion.* For each act, we obtain the maximum payoff over different states of nature, as given in column (7) of the above table. Next, we find the maximum of these maximum payoffs.

Maximum (Maximum Payoffs) = 16, which corresponds to act a_1. Hence, according to the maximax principle, the act a_1 is the optimal act and hence the decision maker should select act a_1.

(*iii*) *Minimax Regret.* This criterion is based on the opportunity losses (or regrets).

For *any given state of nature,* we find the maximum payoff over different acts. Then opportunity losses or regrets are obtained or subtracting from this maximum payoff, the payoffs of each act for that state of nature. Next, for each act we find the maximum of these regrets over different states of nature.

OPPORTUNITY LOSS OR REGRET TABLE

Act	State of Nature				Row Maximum
	S_1	S_2	S_3	S_4	
a_1	16 – 16 = 0	14 – 10 = 4	15 – 12 = 3	14 – 7 = 7	7
a_2	16 – 13 = 3	14 – 12 = 2	15 – 9 = 6	14 – 9 = 5	6
a_3	16 – 11 = 5	14 – 14 = 0	15 – 15 = 0	14 – 14 = 0.	5

∴ Maximum O.L.'s or Regrets for acts a_1, a_2, a_3 are 7, 6 and 5 respectively.

⇒ Minimum (Maximum Regrets) = 5, which corresponds to act a_3. Hence, by the minimax regret criterion, the act a_3 is the optimal solution and decision maker should select act a_3.

Example 18·4. *A decision matrix with cost data is given below :*

Alternatives	States of Nature			
	S_1	S_2	S_3	S_4
a_1	1	3	8	5
a_2	2	5	4	7
a_3	4	6	6	3
a_4	6	8	3	5

Find the best alternative using Minimax Regret Criterion. [C.A. (Foundation), Dec. 1993]

Solution. Since, we are given the cost matrix, the opportunity losses or regret values for any state of nature are obtained on subtracting the minimum cost (over different acts or alternatives) from the cost values for each alternative, as given below.

REGRET TABLE

Alternative	State of nature				Row Maximum Cost
	S_1	S_2	S_3	S_4	
a_1	1 – 1 = 0	3 – 3 = 0	8 – 3 = 5	5 – 3 = 2	5
a_2	2 – 1 = 1	5 – 3 = 2	4 – 3 = 1	7 – 3 = 4	4
a_3	4 – 1 = 3	6 – 3 = 3	6 – 3 = 3	3 – 3 = 0	3
a_4	6 – 1 = 5	8 – 3 = 5	3 – 3 = 0	5 – 3 = 2	5

The maximum costs for the alternatives a_1, a_2, a_3, a_4 are 5, 4, 3 and 5 respectively. The minimum value of these maximum costs is :

Minimum (Maximum Costs) = 3, which corresponds to the alternative a_3.

Hence, by the minimax regret criterion, a_3 is the optimal alternative.

18·3·6. Expected Monetary Value (EMV). Suppose that we know the prior probability p_i of the occurrence of the ith state of nature (event) S_i, $(i = 1, 2, \ldots\ldots, m)$; based on the past data/record or subjective basis so that $\sum_i p_i = 1$. Let there be n possible acts (strategies or decisions) A_j, $(j = 1, 2, \ldots, n)$ available. Let X_{ij} be the conditional payoff corresponding to the combination (S_i, A_j), $(i = 1, 2, \ldots, m; j = 1, 2, \ldots, n)$.

Then for the jth act, we have the adjoining table.

States of Nature	Probability of Occurrence	Conditional Payoff of Act A_j
S_1	p_1	X_{1j}
S_2	p_2	X_{2j}
⋮	⋮	⋮
S_i	p_i	X_{ij}
⋮	⋮	⋮
S_m	p_m	X_{mj}

The expected monetary value (*EMV*) for the jth act A_j $(j = 1, 2, \ldots, n)$ is given by :

$$EMV(A_j) = \sum_{i=1}^{m} p_i X_{ij}\,;\, j = 1, 2, \ldots, n \qquad \ldots(18\cdot9)$$

In other words, the *EMV* for any act is the weighted sum of all the payoffs for that act over different states of nature, the weights being the probabilities of occurrence of the corresponding states of nature.

The expected monetary value (*EMV*) is computed for each act $A_1, A_2, \dots, A_n$ by using the formula (18·9). Next, we find the maximum value of these *EMV's*. Then, under the *EMV* criterion, the act (strategy) which corresponds to the maximum (highest) *EMV* is taken as the optimal act (strategy or decision).

Remarks 1. Generally, the conditional payoffs are given in terms of monetary units and hence in the decision theory, the expected payoff for any act [given by formula (18·9)], is referred to as *expected monetary value* (*EMV*).

2. *EMV* method is adequate only in those cases when the potential losses are not too large and the perspective range of profit is small. However, in problems where large potential losses are involved, some other method of decision making should be recommended.

3. Interpretation of EMV. One should be careful while interpreting the given value of *EMV*. For example, in a given problem, *EMV* of Rs. 500, (say), for an optimal decision, (say), A_j does not mean an assured profit of Rs. 500, on taking the action A_j. It is simply the expected value of making a profit. By this we mean that if the decision maker makes a decision for the *j*th act (A_j) a number of times, then he is expected to make, on the average, a profit of Rs. 500. But, if he makes the decision for the *j*th act A_j only once, he may even lose some money.

If *EMV* criterion results in optimal decision A_j, then the correct interpretation is that there are chances of a greater profit, if the *j*th act is selected.

4. Various steps involved in the EMV criterion of decision making :

1. Identify the various events or states of nature : S_i, $(i = 1, 2, \dots, m)$ and the various acts (strategies or decision) A_j $(j = 1, 2, \dots, n)$.

2. Compute the conditional payoffs (X_{ij}), for various combinations :

$$(S_i, A_j)\ ;\ i = 1, 2, \dots, m\ ;\ j = 1, 2, \dots, n.$$

3. Obtain the probability distribution (p_i, S_i), $i = 1, 2, \dots, m$; for each state of nature so that $p_1 + p_2 + \dots + p_m = 1$. This may be based on the *a*-priori or empirical methods of calculating probabilities.

4. Compute the *EMV* for each act A_j, $(j = 1, 2, \dots, n)$ by the formula (18·9).

5. Choose the act with the maximum value of *EMV*.

This act gives the optimal distribution.

18·3·7. Expected Opportunity Loss (EOL) Criterion. After obtaining the opportunity loss table for various combinations of (S_i, A_j) ; $i = 1, 2, \dots, m$; $j = 1, 2, \dots, n$; the expected opportunity loss (*EOL*) or the expected value of regrets is calculated exactly similarly as the *EMV*.

If p_i in the probability for the *i*th state of nature (S_i), then Expected Opportunity Loss (*EOL*) for the act A_j is given by :

$$EOL\,(A_j) = \text{Regret}\,(A_j) = \sum_{i=1}^{m} p_i \times O.L.\,(A_j) = \sum_{i=1}^{m} p_i\,(M_i - X_{ij});\ j = 1, 2, \dots, n \qquad \dots (18·10)$$

$$\text{where} \quad M_i = \underset{1 \le j \le n}{\text{Max}}\ (X_{ij}) \qquad \dots (18·10a)$$

We compute the *EOL* for each of the acts A_j; $j = 1, 2, \dots, n$. Under the *EOL criterion*, the act with the minimum value of *EOL* is taken as the optimal act (decision).

Remark. Conceptually, although the *EMV*-criterion and the *EOL*-criterion are different, both always lead to the same optimal act (decision). In other words, the act corresponding to the maximum *EMV* is same as the act corresponding to the minimum *EOL* as explained below.

$$EOL(A_j) = \sum_{i=1}^{m} p_i\,(M_i - X_{ij}) = \sum_{i=1}^{m} p_i M_i - \sum_{i=1}^{m} p_i X_{ij}$$

$$\Rightarrow \quad EOL\,(A_j) = k - EMV\,(A_j) \qquad \dots (18·11)$$

where $$k = \sum_{i=1}^{m} p_i M_i = p_1 M_1 + p_2 M_2 + \ldots + p_m M_m,$$

is a constant independent of any act or strategy.

From (18·11), it is obvious that maximising $EMV\ (A_j)$ is equivalent to minimising $EOL\ (A_j)$. In other words, we conclude that *the act corresponding to the highest EMV is same as the act corresponding to the smallest EOL.* Hence, both the *EMV*- criterion and the *EOL*-criterion lead to the same optimal decision.

18·3·8. Expected Value of Perfect Information (EVPI). The expected value of perfect information indicates the expected or the average worth/return in the long run, of the best possible decision, if we have the perfect information before a decision is made. The prior probability distribution (p_i, S_i) ; $i = 1, 2, \ldots, m$ of the different states of nature is not always a perfect predictor, particularly so in business decision problems. In order to maximise his profits or minimise his losses, the decision maker would be interested in basing his decisions on a perfect predictor. In order to look out for perfect predictor, the decision maker will be interested to gather some additional information about the different states of nature. This would involve some expenditure in the form of the cost of conducting some experiment or survey to obtain the perfect information. This perfect information will reduce the opportunity losses due to uncertainty to zero.

By *perfect information* we mean complete and accurate information about the various states of nature in the future. If the businessman, in particular say, the retailer, knows in advance about the exact demand for his daily/weekly/monthly product, he will store the exact number of goods as per demand and consequently will not incur any losses on the unsold stock. The *expected value of perfect information* (EVPI) is the difference between the expected profit with perfect information and without perfect information. In other words, EVPI is the additional profit the businessman (retailer) will earn for having perfect information.

The *expected profit of perfect information (EPPI) or the expected payoff under certainty (EPUC) is the highest expected payoff (profit) in the presence of perfect predictor.*

If (p_i', S_i); $i = 1, 2, \ldots, m$ is the probability distribution of different states of nature under perfect information (predictor), then

$$EPPI = EPUC = \sum_{i=1}^{m} p_i' M_i, \qquad \ldots (18·12)$$

where $$M_i = \underset{1 \le j \le n}{\text{Max}} \ (X_{ij})\ ; i = 1, 2, \ldots, m \qquad \ldots (18·12a)$$

The maximum value of EMV for different acts/strategies is also called the expected payoff or profit (*EP*) of the optimal action in the absence of a perfect predictor. Thus

$$EP = (EMV)_{max} \qquad \ldots (18·13)$$

The expected value of perfect information (*EVPI*) is given :

$$EVPI = EPUC - (EMV)_{max} = \sum_{i=1}^{m} p_i' M_i - (EMV)_{max} \qquad \ldots (18·14)$$

or $$EVPI = EPPI - EP \qquad \ldots (18·14a)$$

Remarks 1. EVPI represents the maximum amount of money, which the decision maker could spend to obtain the additional information (for perfect predictor) about different states of nature. If the expenses incurred by the decision maker in gathering the additional information is more than the *EVPI*, then it is not worth looking for the best predictor.

2. We have from (18·14),

$$EVPI = \sum_{i=1}^{m} p_i' M_i - (EMV)_{max}$$
$$= (EOL) \text{ under optimal decision} \qquad [\text{Using } (18·11)] \qquad \ldots (18·15)$$

Hence, *the Expected Value of Perfect Information (EVPI) is always equal to the Expected Opportunity Loss of selecting the optimal decision under uncertainty.*

Example 18·5. *An umbrella salesman can earn Rs. 400 per day in case of rain but will lose Rs. 100 per day if it does not rain. Find EMV if the probability of rain is 0·4.*

[*Delhi Univ. B.Com. (Hons.) Pt. I, 1996*]

Solution.

CALCULATIONS FOR EMV

States of Nature	*Probability (p)*	*Payoff (Rs.) (X)*	*Expected Payoff (Rs.) (p × X)*
Rain	0·4	400	0·4 × 400 = 160
No Rain	1 – 0·4 = 0·6	– 100	0·6 × (– 100) = – 60
Total			100

$\therefore$ $EMV = \sum pX$ = Rs. (160 – 60) = Rs. 100.

Example 18·6. *A maker of soft-drinks is considering the introduction of a new brand. He expects to sell 50,000 to 1,00,000 bottles of its soft drink in a given period according to the following probability distribution :*

No. of Bottles sold (in '000) :	*50*	*60*	*70*	*80*	*90*	*100*
Probability :	*0·13*	*0·20*	*0·35*	*0·22*	*0·08*	*0·02*

If the product is launched he will have to incur a fixed cost of Rs. 48,000. However, each bottle sold would give him a profit of Rs. 1·25. Should he introduce the new brand ?

[*Delhi Univ. B.Com.(Hons.), 2005*]

Solution. Let the *n* *X* denote the number of bottles sold (in '000). Then we have :

x	50	60	70	80	90	100	
$p(x)$	0·13	0·20	0·35	0·22	0·08	0·02	$\sum p(x) = 1$
$x\,p(x)$	6·5	12·0	24·5	17·6	7·2	2·0	$\sum x\,p(x) = 69{\cdot}8$

Hence, the expected number of bottles solids given by :

$$E(x) = \sum x\,p(x) = 69{\cdot}8 \text{ thousand} = 69{,}800$$

Since the man makes a profit of Rs. 1·25 on each bottle sold, his expected profit (P) is given by

$$P = [\sum x.p(x)] \times \text{Rs. } 1{\cdot}25 = \text{Rs. } 69{,}800 \times 1{\cdot}25 = \text{Rs. } 87{,}250.$$

Further, the fixed cost of launching the product is Rs. 48,000.

Since expected pay-off (P) = Rs. 87,250, is greater than the fixed investment of Rs. 48,000, he should introduce the new brand.

Example 18·7. *The following table gives the payoffs of the acts A, B, C and the states of nature P, Q, R. The probabilities of the states of nature are 0·2, 0·3 and 0·5 respectively. Calculate the Expected Monetary Values (EMV) and select the best act :*

States of Nature	*Acts*		
	A	*B*	*C*
P	*200*	*– 100*	*– 300*
Q	*250*	*300*	*– 500*
R	*300*	*500*	*600*

[*C.A. (Foundation), May 1999*]

Solution.

States of nature	*Probability*	*Payoffs*		
	(p)	*Act A*	*Act B*	*Act C*
P	0·2	200	– 100	– 300
Q	0·3	250	300	– 500
R	0·5	300	500	600

EMV (Act *A*) = 0·2 × 200 + 0·3 × 250 + 0·5 × 300 = 40 + 75 + 150 = 265

EMV (Act *B*) = 0·2 × (– 100) + 0·3 × 300 + 0·5 × 500 = – 20 + 90 + 250 = 320

EMV (Act *C*) = 0·2 × (– 300) + 0·3 × (– 500) + 0·5 × 600 = – 60 – 150 + 300 = 90

Since *EMV* (Act *B*) is maximum, the optimum (best) choice is Act *B*.

Example 18·8. *Following table gives Payoffs for actions A_1, A_2 and A_3 corresponding to states of nature S_1 and S_2 whose chances are 0·6 and 0·4 respectively.*

States of Nature	*Actions*		
	A_1	A_2	A_3
S_1	16	20	18
S_2	19	15	12

Find decisions under :
(i) Maximin criterion
(ii) EMV criterion. [C.A. (Foundation), May 1997]

Solution. (*i*) **Maximin Criterion.**

PAYOFF TABLE

States of Nature	*Probability*	*Actions*		
		A_1	A_2	A_3
S_1	0·6	16	20	18
S_2	0·4	19	15	12
Minimum payoff for each action		16	15	12

Maximum [Minimum payoff] = 16, which corresponds to action A_1. Hence, under the maximin criterion, action A_1 is the optimal decision.

(*ii*) **EMV Criterion**

$$EMV \text{ (Action } A_1) = 16 \times 0{\cdot}6 + 19 \times 0{\cdot}4 = 17{\cdot}20$$
$$EMV \text{ (Action } A_2) = 20 \times 0{\cdot}6 + 15 \times 0{\cdot}4 = 18{\cdot}00$$
$$EMV \text{ (Action } A_3) = 18 \times 0{\cdot}6 + 12 \times 0{\cdot}4 = 15{\cdot}60$$

Since *EMV* (Action A_2) is maximum, by *EMV* criterion, action A_2 is the optimal decision.

Example 18·9. *Mr. Y quite often flies from town A to town B. He can use the airport bus which costs Rs. 13 but if he takes it, there is a 0·08 chance that he will miss the flight. A hotel limousine costs Rs. 27 with a 0·96 chance of being on time for the flight. For Rs. 50 he can use a taxi which will make 99 of 100 flights. If Mr. Y catches the plane on time, he will conclude a business transaction which will produce a profit of Rs. 1,000, otherwise he will lose it. Which mode of transportation should Mr. Y use ? Answer on the basis of EMV criterion.* (C.A., May 1990)

Solution. Let us define the following acts and states of nature.

Acts	*States of Nature*
A_1 : Take airport bus.	S_1 : Reach in time for the flight.
A_2 : Take hotel limousine.	S_2 : Don't reach in time for the flight.
A_3 : Take a taxi.	

Then the above information can be summarised in the following table.

CONDITIONAL PAYOFF

States of nature	*Return (in Rs.) (X)*	*Probability*			*(In Rupees)*		
		Act A_1 (p_1)	*Act* A_2 (p_2)	*Act* A_3 (p_3)	p_1X	p_2X	p_3X
S_1	1,000	$1 - 0{\cdot}08 = 0{\cdot}92$	0·96	$\frac{99}{100} = 0{\cdot}99$	920	960	990
S_2	0	0·08	$1 - 0{\cdot}96 = 0{\cdot}04$	$1 - 0{\cdot}99 = 0{\cdot}01$	0	0	0
Cost (in Rs.)		13	27	50	$\sum p_1 X = 920$	$\sum p_2 X = 960$	$\sum p_3 X = 990$

$$EMV\ (\text{Act } A_1) = \sum p_1X - \text{Cost} = \text{Rs. } (920 - 13) = \text{Rs. } 907$$
$$EMV\ (\text{Act } A_2) = \sum p_2X - \text{Cost} = \text{Rs. } (960 - 27) = \text{Rs. } 933$$
$$EMV\ (\text{Act } A_3) = \sum p_3X - \text{Cost} = \text{Rs. } (990 - 50) = \text{Rs. } 940$$

Since $EMV\ (A_3)$ is maximum, under the EMV criterion, Mr. Y should choose the act A_3 *i.e.,* Mr. Y should take a taxi to reach the airport.

Example 18·10. *A person has the choice of running hot snack stall or an ice cream and cool drink shop at a certain holiday resort during the coming summer season. If the weather during the season is cool and rainy he can expect to make a profit of Rs. 15,000 and if it is warm he can expect to make a profit of only Rs. 3,000 by running a hot snack stall. On the other hand, if his choice is to run an ice cream and cool drink shop, he can expect to make a profit of Rs. 18,000 if the weather is warm and only Rs. 3,000 if the weather is cool and rainy. The meteorological authorities predict that there is 40% chance of the weather being warm during the coming season. You are to advise him as to the choice between the two types of stalls. Base clearly your argument on the expectation of the result of the two courses of action and show the result in a tabular form.*

Solution. The expected profit in each course of action is given in the following table.

TABLE OF EXPECTED PROFITS

Weather	*Probability*	*Hot Snack Stall*		*Ice Cream and Cool Drink Shop*	
	(p)	*Profit* (P_1) *Rs.*	*Expected Profit (Rs.)* $p \times P_1$	*Profit* (P_2) *(Rs.)*	*Expected Profit* $p \times P_2$*(Rs.)*
Cool and Rainy	$1 - 0{\cdot}40 = 0{\cdot}60$	15,000	$15000 \times 0{\cdot}60 = 9{,}000$	3,000	$3000 \times 0{\cdot}60 = 1{,}800$
Warm	$40\% = 0{\cdot}40$	3,000	$3000 \times 0{\cdot}40 = 1{,}200$	18,000	$18{,}000 \times 0{\cdot}40 = 7{,}200$
Total			Rs. 10,200		Rs. 9,000

Since the total expected profit by running a hot snack stall is more than the total expected profit by running an icecream and cool drink stall, the person is advised to run a hot snack stall.

Example 18·11. *An educational entrepreneur is planning to run a computer course. He has narrowed down his options to two courses : CUR and FUT. CUR is based on the existing software packages whereas FUT is based on new packages which are expected to storm the software market in the near future. In consultation with software specialists he has arrived at the following estimates :*

(i) Probability of getting a return of Rs. 5 crore is 0·6 for FUT and 0·2 with CUR.

(ii) FUT's return could be as low as Rs. 40 lakh with a probability 0·4 and the corresponding probability for CUR is 0·8.

(iii) FUT will cost him Rs. 1 crore and CUR only Rs. 30 lakh.

Using EMV obtain the optimum strategy. [*I.C.W.A. (Intermediate), June 1999*]

Solution. The given information can be summarised in the following Table.

Return in (Rs.)	*Probability*			
X	*Course FUT* (p_1)	*Course CUR* (p_2)	p_1X *(Rs.)*	p_2X *(Rs.)*
$+5 \times 10^7$	0·6	0·2	3×10^7	10^7
$+4 \times 10^6$	0·4	0·8	16×10^5	32×10^5
Cost (Rs.)	1×10^7	3×10^6		

EMV for Course FUT

$= \sum p_1X - \text{Cost}$

$= \text{Rs. } 3 \times 10^7 + 16 \times 10^5 - 1 \times 10^7$

$= \text{Rs. } 10^5 (3 \times 10^2 + 16 - 10^2)$

$= \text{Rs. } 10^5 (300 + 16 - 100)$

$= \text{Rs. } 216 \times 10^5$

EMV for Course CUR

$= \sum p_2X - \text{Cost}$

$= \text{Rs. } (10^7 + 32 \times 10^5 - 3 \times 10^6)$

$= \text{Rs. } 10^5 (10^2 + 32 - 3 \times 10)$

$= \text{Rs. } 10^5 (100 + 32 - 30)$

$= \text{Rs. } 102 \times 10^5$

Since $EMV\ (FUT) > EMV\ (CUR)$, the optimal strategy (decision) will be to go for the course FUT.

Example 18·12. *The following table gives the payoffs of three acts A_1, A_2 and A_3 and the states of nature S_1, S_2 and S_3 along with the probability distribution for various combinations $(S_i, A_j); i, j = 1, 2, 3$.*

States of Nature	Acts			Probabilities		
	A_1	A_2	A_3	A_1	A_2	A_3
S_1	10	– 10	60	0·65	0·60	0·35
S_2	20	20	– 20	0·20	0·25	0·45
S_3	30	40	20	0·15	0·15	0·20

Calculate and tabulate the EMV for each act and using the EMV criterion, obtain the best act.

Solution

CALCULATIONS FOR EMV OF VARIOUS ACTS

States of Nature	Act A_1			Act A_2			Act A_3		
	Payoff (X_1)	Prob. (p_1)	p_1X_1	Payoff (X_2)	Prob. (p_2)	p_2X_2	Payoff (X_3)	Prob. (p_3)	p_3X_3
S_1	10	0·65	6·5	– 10	0·60	– 6	60	0·35	21·0
S_2	20	0·20	4·0	20	0·25	5	– 20	0·45	– 9·0
S_3	30	0·15	4·5	40	0·15	6	20	0·20	4·0
EMV			15·0			5·0			16·0

$\therefore$ $EMV(A_1) = 15·0$; $EMV(A_2) = 5·0$; $EMV(A_3) = 16·0$.

Since $EMV(A_3)$ is maximum with highest profit of 16·0 units, by EMV criterion, A_3 is the optimal (best) act.

Example 18·13. *A florist, in order to satisfy the needs of a number of regular and sophisticated customers, stocks highly perishable flowers. A dozen flowers cost Rs. 3 and sell at Rs. 10. Any flowers not sold on the day are worthless.*

Demand distribution in dozens of flowers is as follows :

Demand :	1	2	3	4
Probability :	0·2	0·3	0·3	0·2

How many flowers should he stock daily in order to maximise his expected net profit ?

[*I.C.W.A. (Intermediate), June 2000*]

Solution. Let m be the number of flowers (in dozens) stocked by the florist on any day and n be the number of flowers (in dozens) demanded per day.

Cost of one dozen flowers = Rs. 3

Selling Price of one dozen flowers = Rs. 10

$\therefore$ Profit on one dozen flowers sold = Rs. (10 – 3) = Rs. 7.

Further, it is given that any unsold flowers at the end of the day are worthless. Hence, there is a loss of Rs. 3 per dozen on the unsold flowers.

Case (*i*). $n \geq m$ *i.e.,* demand is ≥ stock. In this case all the m dozen stocked flowers are sold. Hence, florist's conditional profit (P) is given by

$$P = \text{Rs. } 7m, \; n \geq m \qquad \dots (i)$$

Case (*ii*). $n < m$ *i.e.,* the demand is less than the stock. In this case n dozen flowers are sold out and the remaining $(m - n)$ dozen flowers are not sold out. Hence, the conditional profit (P) is given by :

$$\begin{aligned} P &= (\text{Marginal profit}) \times (\text{Units sold}) - (\text{Marginal loss}) \times (\text{Units unsold}) \\ &= \text{Rs. } [7n - 3(m-n)] \\ &= \text{Rs. } (10n - 3m) \; ; \; n < m \qquad \dots (ii) \end{aligned}$$

From (*i*) and (*ii*), we get

$$\left.\begin{aligned} P &= \text{Rs. } 7m \; ; \; n \geq m \\ &= \text{Rs. } (10n - 3m) \; ; \; n < m \end{aligned}\right\} \qquad \dots (iii)$$

Using (*iii*), the florist's payoff table for various combinations of stock (m dozens) and demand (n dozens), each varying from 0 to 4, is as given below.

FLORIST'S PAYOFF TABLE (IN RUPEES)

Stock m (in dozens)	*Demand n (in dozens)*			
	1	2	3	4
1	$7 \times 1 = 7$	7	7	7
2	$10 \times 1 - 3 \times 2 = 4$	$7 \times 2 = 14$	14	14
3	$10 \times 1 - 3 \times 3 = 1$	$10 \times 2 - 3 \times 3 = 11$	$7 \times 3 = 21$	21
4	$10 \times 1 - 3 \times 4 = -2$	$10 \times 2 - 3 \times 4 = 8$	$10 \times 3 - 3 \times 4 = 18$	$7 \times 4 = 28$
Probability of demand	0·2	0·3	0·3	0·2

The expected profit for any stock m (in dozens) is given by :

Expected Profit (stock m) = $\sum$ (Probability × Payoff),

the summation being taken over different states of nature *viz.*, $n = 1, 2, 3$ and 4.

TABLE OF FLORIST'S EXPECTED PROFIT

Stock m (in dozens)	*Expected Profit (in Rupees)*
1	$7 \times 0{\cdot}2 + 7 \times 0{\cdot}3 + 7 \times 0{\cdot}3 + 7 \times 0{\cdot}2 = 7{\cdot}0$
2	$4 \times 0{\cdot}2 + 14 \times 0{\cdot}3 + 14 \times 0{\cdot}3 + 14 \times 0{\cdot}2 = 12{\cdot}0$
3	$1 \times 0{\cdot}2 + 11 \times 0{\cdot}3 + 21 \times 0{\cdot}3 + 21 \times 0{\cdot}2 = 14{\cdot}0$
4	$-2 \times 0{\cdot}2 + 8 \times 0{\cdot}3 + 18 \times 0{\cdot}3 + 28 \times 0{\cdot}2 = 13{\cdot}0$

Since the florist's profit is maximum *viz.*, Rs. 14 if $m = 3$, the florist should stock 3 dozen flowers each day to get the maximum profit.

Example 18·14. *A newspaper agent's experience shows that the daily demand X of newspapers in his area has the following probability distribution :*

Daily demand (x)	:	*300*	*400*	*500*	*600*	*700*
Probability	:	*0·1*	*0·3*	*0·4*	*0·1*	*0·1*

He sells the newspapers for Rs. 2·00 each while he buys each at Re. 1·00. Unsold copies are traded as scrap and each such copy fetches 10 paise. Assuming that he stocks the newspapers in multiple of 100 only, how many should he stock so that his expected profit is maximum ? [*I.C.W.A. (Intermediate), Dec. 1997*]

Solution. Cost price of the newspaper = Re. 1

Selling price of the newspaper = Rs. 2

Hence, the agent makes a profit of Rs. (2 – 1) = Re. 1, on each newspaper sold.

It is further given that each unsold newspaper is treated as scrap and fetches only 10 paise. Hence, on each copy of the unsold newspaper at the end of the day, the agent incurs a loss of Rs. (1 – 0·10) = Re. 0·90 *i.e.*, 90 paise per copy.

Let the newspaper agent stock y (some multiple of 100) copies of the newspaper and let the daily demand of newspapers be x copies.

Case (*i*). $x \geq y$ *i.e., demand is more than the stock.* In this case all the stocked copies (y) of the newspaper are sold out. Hence, at the end of the day, the agent's profit (P) is given by :

$$P = \text{Rs. } 1 \times y = \text{Rs. } y \; ; \; x \geq y \qquad \ldots(*)$$

Case (*ii*). $x < y$ *i.e., demand is less than the stock.*

In this case only x copies of the newspaper are sold out and the remaining $(y - x)$ copies are unsold on each of which the agent loses Re. 0·90. Hence, at the end of the day, the agent's profit (P) is given by :

$$P = (\text{Marginal profit}) \times (\text{Copies sold}) - (\text{Marginal loss} \times (\text{Copies unsold})$$

$$= \text{Rs. } [1 \times x - 0{\cdot}90\,(y - x)]$$

$$= \text{Rs. } (1{\cdot}90x - 0{\cdot}90y) \; ; \; x < y \qquad \ldots(**)$$

From (*) and (**), we get :

$$\therefore\quad P = \text{Rs. } y \quad ; \; x \geq y$$
$$= \text{Rs. } (1{\cdot}90x - 0{\cdot}90y) \quad ; \; x < y \qquad \ldots (1)$$

Using (1), the agent's payoff table, for different combinations of stock (*y*) and demand (*x*), each varying from 300, 400, ... to 700, is as given below.

AGENT'S PAYOFF TABLE (IN RUPEES)

Stock (*y*)	*Demand* (*x*) 300	400	500	600	700
300	300	300	300	300	300
400	210	400	400	400	400
500	120	310	500	500	500
600	30	220	410	600	600
700	− 60	130	320	510	700
Probability of demand	0·1	0·3	0·4	0·1	0·1

Illustration. For $y = 500$ and different values of x, on using (1), $P = P(y, x)$ is :

$P(500, 300) = (1{\cdot}90 \times 300 - 0{\cdot}90 \times 500) = 120$; $P(500, 400) = 1{\cdot}90 \times 400 - 0{\cdot}90 \times 500 = 310$

$P(500, 500) = 500$; $P(500, 600) = 500$; $P(500, 700) = 500$.

and so on.

For any act (stock y),

Expected payoff $(y) = \sum$ Probability × Payoff,

the summation being taken over different states of nature (demand *x*).

AGENT'S EXPECTED PAYOFF TABLE

Stock (*m*)	*Expected Payoff* (*in Rupees*)
300	$300 \times 0{\cdot}1 + 300 \times 0{\cdot}3 + 300 \times 0{\cdot}4 + 300 \times 0{\cdot}1 + 300 \times 0{\cdot}1 = 300$
400	$210 \times 0{\cdot}1 + 400 \times 0{\cdot}3 + 400 \times 0{\cdot}4 + 400 \times 0{\cdot}1 + 400 \times 0{\cdot}1 = 381$
500	$120 \times 0{\cdot}1 + 310 \times 0{\cdot}3 + 500 \times 0{\cdot}4 + 500 \times 0{\cdot}1 + 500 \times 0{\cdot}1 = 405$
600	$30 \times 0{\cdot}1 + 220 \times 0{\cdot}3 + 410 \times 0{\cdot}4 + 600 \times 0{\cdot}1 + 600 \times 0{\cdot}1 = 353$
700	$-60 \times 0{\cdot}1 + 130 \times 0{\cdot}3 + 320 \times 0{\cdot}4 + 510 \times 0{\cdot}1 + 700 \times 0{\cdot}1 = 382$

Since the expected payoff is maximum *viz.*, Rs. 405, when $m = 500$, the newspaper agent should stock 500 copies daily.

Example 18·15. *A physician purchases a particular vaccine on Monday of each week. The vaccine must be used within the week following, otherwise it becomes worthless. The vaccine costs Rs. 2 per dose and the physician charges Rs. 4 per dose. In the past 50 weeks, the physician has administered the vaccine in the following quantities :*

Doses per Week	*Number of Weeks*
20	*5*
25	*15*
50	*25*
60	*5*

On the basis of EMV, find how many doses the physician must purchase each week to maximise his profits ? [*Delhi Univ. B.Com. (Hons.), 2002*]

Solution. Here, the number of doses of the vaccine purchased per week (*m*) is an act and the demand (*n*) for the number of doses of the vaccine per week is an event (*i.e.*, state of nature).

Since the cost price (C.P.) of each dose of the vaccine is Rs. 2 and its selling price (S.P.) is Rs. 4, the physician makes a profit of Rs. (4 − 2) = Rs. 2 on each dose used. However, if the vaccine is not used within the week, it becomes worthless and the physician will incur a loss of Rs. 2 on each dose unused at the end of the week.

Conditional Payoff. (*P*) *n* : Demand ; *m* : Stock.

Case (*i*). $n \geq m$. If demand (*n*) ≥ stock (*m*), then all the *m* doses will be used. Hence,

$$P = 2m \; ; n \geq m \qquad \ldots (i)$$

Case (*ii*). $n < m$. If the demand is less than stock, then only *n* doses of the vaccine are used and the remaining $(m - n)$ doses are not used. Hence,

$$P = 2n + (m - n)(-2) = 4n - 2m \; ; n < m \qquad \ldots (ii)$$

From (*i*) and (*ii*), we get

$$\left.\begin{aligned} P &= 2m \; ; n \geq m \\ &= 4n - 2m \; ; n < m \end{aligned}\right\} \qquad \ldots (iii)$$

Using (*iii*), the conditional payoffs for different combinations of *m* and *n*, each taking the values 20, 25, 50 and 60 can be obtained and are given in the following Payoff Table.

CONDITIONAL PAYOFF (in Rs.) TABLE AND CALCULATIONS FOR EMV

Event	*Act (m)*				*No. of Weeks*	*Probability of Demand*
Demand (n)	A_1 *(20)*	A_2 *(25)*	A_3 *(50)*	A_4 *(60)*	*(f)*	$p = (f/N)$
(S_1) 20	40	30	– 20	– 40	5	0·1
(S_2) 25	40	50	0	– 20	15	0·3
(S_3) 50	40	50	100	80	25	0·5
(S_4) 60	40	50	100	120	5	0·1
					$N = 50$	

$$EMV(A_1) = [40 \times 0{\cdot}1 + 40 \times 0{\cdot}3 + 40 \times 0{\cdot}5 + 40 \times 0{\cdot}1] = \text{Rs. } 40$$
$$EMV(A_2) = [30 \times 0{\cdot}1 + 50\,(0{\cdot}3 + 0{\cdot}5 + 0{\cdot}1)] = 3 + 45 = \text{Rs. } 48$$
$$EMV(A_3) = (-20) \times 0{\cdot}1 + 100 \times (0{\cdot}5 + 0{\cdot}1) = -2 + 60 = \text{Rs. } 58$$
$$EMV(A_4) = (-40) \times 0{\cdot}1 + (-20) \times 0{\cdot}3 + 80 \times 0{\cdot}5 + 120 \times 0{\cdot}1 = -4 - 6 + 40 + 12 = \text{Rs. } 42$$

Since $EMV(A_3)$ = Rs. 58, is maximum *i.e.*, when $m = 50$, A_3 is the optimum act. Hence, the physician should purchase 50 doses of the vaccine each week.

Example 18·16. *Given the following payoff matrix :*

Act	*Payoff (in Rs.) State of Nature*	
	Cold Weather	*Hot Weather*
Sell Cold Drinks	*50*	*100*
Sell Hot Drinks	*120*	*40*

and given the probability of weather being hot is 0·8, set up the opportunity loss table and compute opportunity loss of each action. Select the best act. [C.A. (Foundation), Nov. 1996]

Solution. Maximum payoff for the event S_1 : 'Cold Weather' = Rs. 120

Maximum payoff for the event S_2 : 'Hot weather' = Rs. 100

OPPORTUNITY LOSS (OL) TABLE (in Rs.)

Act	*State of Nature*	
	Cold Weather	*Hot Weather*
Sell Cold Drinks	120 – 50 = 70	100 – 100 = 0
Sell Hot Drinks	120 – 120 = 0	100 – 40 = 60
Probability	1 – 0·8 = 0·2	0·8

Expected Opportunity Loss (EOL)

EOL (Sell Cold Drinks) = Rs. $(0{\cdot}2 \times 70 + 0{\cdot}8 \times 0)$ = Rs. 14

EOL (Sell Hot Drinks) = Rs. $(0{\cdot}2 \times 0 + 0{\cdot}8 \times 60)$ = Rs. 48

Since *EOL* (Sell Cold Drinks) is minimum, by *EOL* criterion, the act : 'Sell Cold Drinks', is the optimal (best) act.

Example 18·17. *A group of students raises money each year by selling souvenirs outside the stadium after a cricket match between teams A and B. They can buy any of the three different types of souvenirs I, II, or III from a supplier. Their sales are mostly dependent on which team wins the match. A conditional payoff table is as given below.*

	I	*II*	*III*
Team A wins	*Rs. 1,200*	*Rs. 800*	*Rs. 300*
Team B wins	*250*	*700*	*1,100*

(i) Construct the opportunity loss table.

(ii) Which type of souvenir should the students buy if probability of team A's winning is 0·6 ?

(iii) Also find the cost of uncertainty. (*C.A. May, 1987*)

Solution. Define the following acts and states of nature :

Acts — A_i : The students buy the souvenir i ; $i = 1, 2, 3$.

States of Nature — S_1 : Team *A* wins. S_2 : Team *B* wins.

PAYOFF TABLE / **REGRET OR O.L. TABLE**

Sources of Nature	*Probability (p)*	*Acts* A_1	A_2	A_3	*Row Maximum*	*Acts* A_1	A_2	A_3
S_1	0·6	1200	800	300	1,200	1200 – 1200 = 0	1200 – 800 = 400	1200 – 300 = 900
S_2	1 – 0·6 = 0·4	250	700	1,100	1,100	1100 – 250 = 850	1100 – 700 = 400	1100 – 1100 = 0

(i) Opportunity Loss (O.L.) Table is given on the right of the above table.

(ii) **EMV Criterion.** Using the above payoff table :

Expected sales (A_1) = Rs. $(0{\cdot}6 \times 1200 + 0{\cdot}4 \times 250)$ = Rs. (720 + 100) = Rs. 820

Expected sales (A_2) = Rs. $(0{\cdot}6 \times 800 + 0{\cdot}4 \times 700)$ = Rs. (480 + 280) = Rs. 760

Expected sales (A_3) = Rs. $(0{\cdot}6 \times 300 + 0{\cdot}4 \times 1100)$ = Rs. (180 + 440) = Rs. 620

Since expected sales (A_1) is maximum, according to *EMV* criterion, the student should buy the souvenir 1.

OR

EOL Criterion

EOL (A_1) = Rs. $(0{\cdot}6 \times 0 + 0{\cdot}4 \times 850)$ = Rs. (0 + 340) = Rs. 340

EOL (A_2) = Rs. $(0{\cdot}6 \times 400 + 0{\cdot}4 \times 400)$ = Rs. (240 + 160) = Rs. 400

EOL (A_3) = Rs. $(0{\cdot}6 \times 900 + 0{\cdot}4 \times 0)$ = Rs. (540 + 0) = Rs. 540.

Since *EOL* (A_1) is minimum, according to *EOL* criterion, A_1 is the optimal act. Hence, the student should buy the souvenir 1.

Remark. *Note that the EMV criterion and the EOL criterion lead to the same optimal decision.*

(iii) Cost of uncertainty = Minimum Value of (*EOL*) = Rs. 340

Example 18·18. *A company is trying to manufacture a new type of toy. The company is attempting to decide whether to bring out a full, partial or minimal product line. The company has three levels of product acceptance and has estimated their probability of occurrence. Management will make the decision on the* *basis of maximising the expected profit from the first year of production. The relevant data are shown in the following table where first year profits in thousand rupees are given :*

	State of Nature →	Good	Fair	Poor
Product Line ↓	*Probability :*	0·2	0·4	0·4
Full		90	60	– 15
Partial		80	65	– 10
Minimal		60	50	0

(i) *What is the optimum product line and its expected profit ?*

(ii) *What is the optimum value of expected opportunity loss and the optimum course of action ?*

[*I.C.W.A. (Intermediate), June 1998*]

Solution. Define the acts :

A_1 : Full product line ; A_2 : Partial product line ; A_3 : Minimal product line

(*i*) **EMV Criterion.**

EMV (for any act) = $\sum$ (Probability × Payoff),

the summation being taken over different states of nature.

$\therefore \quad EMV(A_1) = \text{Rs. } 1{,}000\ [0{\cdot}2 \times 90 + 0{\cdot}4 \times 60 + 0{\cdot}4 \times (-15)]$
$= \text{Rs. } 1000\ (18 + 24 - 6) = \text{Rs. } 36{,}000.$

$EMV(A_2) = \text{Rs. } 1{,}000\ [0{\cdot}2 \times 80 + 0{\cdot}4 \times 65 + 0{\cdot}4 \times (-10)]$
$= \text{Rs. } 1{,}000\ (16 + 26 - 4) = \text{Rs. } 38{,}000.$

$EMV(A_3) = \text{Rs. } 1{,}000\ [0{\cdot}2 \times 60 + 0{\cdot}4 \times 50 + 0{\cdot}4 \times 0]$
$= \text{Rs. } 1{,}000\ (12 + 20) = \text{Rs. } 32{,}000.$

Since *EMV* (A_2) is maximum, by the *EMV* criterion, the act A_2 : '*Partial Product Line*' is the *optimal act* and its expected profit is *EMV* (A_2) = Rs. 38,000.

(*ii*) **Expected Opportunity Loss (EOL) Criterion.**

Maximum Payoffs (*in thousand Rs.*) for different states of nature (over various acts) are :

For S_1 (Good Acceptance) = 90 ; For S_2 (Fair Acceptance) = 65 ; For S_3(Poor Acceptance) = 0

For *any given state of nature,* the Opportunity Losses (*OL*) or *Regrets* for different acts are obtained on subtracting from these maximum payoffs, the corresponding payoffs of different acts, as given in the following table.

OPPORTUNITY LOSS OR REGRET TABLE ('000 Rs.)

Act (*Product Line*)	*State of Nature* S_1 : *Good*	S_2 : *Fair*	S_3 : *Poor*
A_1 (Full)	90 – 90 = 0	65 – 60 = 5	0 – (– 15) = 15
A_2 (Partial)	90 – 80 = 10	65 – 65 = 0	0 – (– 10) = 10
A_3 (Minimal)	90 – 60 = 30	65 – 50 = 15	0
Probability	0·2	0·4	0·4

$\therefore \quad EOL(A_1) = \text{Rs. } 1{,}000\ (0{\cdot}2 \times 0 + 0{\cdot}4 \times 5 + 0{\cdot}4 \times 15) = \text{Rs. } 8{,}000$

$EOL(A_2) = \text{Rs. } 1{,}000\ (0{\cdot}2 \times 10 + 0{\cdot}4 \times 0 + 0{\cdot}4 \times 10) = \text{Rs. } 6{,}000$

$EOL(A_3) = \text{Rs. } 1{,}000\ (0{\cdot}2 \times 30 + 0{\cdot}4 \times 15 + 0{\cdot}4 \times 0) = \text{Rs. } 12{,}000$

Since *EOL* (A_2) is minimum, by *EOL* criterion, the act A_2: '*Partial Product Line*', is the optimal act and

Optimum (Minimum) value of *EOL* = Rs. 6,000.

Remark. Note that the *EMV* criterion and the *EOL* criterion result in the same optimal act.

Example 18·19. *A milk producing co-operative union desires to determine how many kilograms of butter it should produce on daily basis to meet the demand. Past records have shown the following pattern of demand :*

Quantity demanded (Number of kg.)	:	*15*	*20*	*25*	*30*	*35*	*40*	*45*
Number of days on which given level of demand occurred	:	*4*	*16*	*20*	*80*	*40*	*30*	*10*

Assume that the stock levels are restricted to the range 15–45 kg (a multiple of 5 kg) and that butter left unsold at the end of the day must be disposed of due to inadequate storing facilities. Butter costs Rs. 14·00 per kg and is sold at Rs. 20·00 per kg. (a) Construct a conditional profit table. (b) Determine the action alternative associated with the maximisation of expected profit; (c) Determine EVPI.

[*Gujarat Univ. M.B.A., 1996*]

Solution. (*a*) Let : m = Daily production of butter (in kg) by the co-operative union.

n = Daily demand for butter (in kg)

Cost of butter (per kg.) = Rs. 14

Sale price of butter (per kg) = Rs. 20

∴ Profit on sale of 1 kg of butter = Rs. (20 – 14) = Rs. 6 ... (1)

We are further given that any amount of unsold butter left at the end of the day has to be disposed off, resulting in a *dead loss* of Rs. 14 per kg to the union. ... (2)

Conditional Payoff-Case (*i*). $n \geq m$. If demand (n) is ≥ the daily production (m), then all the m kg of butter is sold out. Hence, from (1)

$$P = 6m \; ; n \geq m \qquad \ldots (*)$$

Case (*ii*). $n < m$. If daily demand (n) is less than the production (m), then only n kg. of butter is sold out and ($m - n$) kg. of butter is left unsold. Hence, using (1) and (2), we get

$$P = 6n - 14(m - n) = 20n - 14m \; ; n < m \qquad \ldots (**)$$

From (*) and (**), we get

$$\left.\begin{aligned} P &= 6m \quad &; n \geq m \\ &= 20n - 14m \quad &; n \leq m \end{aligned}\right\} \qquad \ldots (3)$$

Using (3), the conditional payoffs for different combinations of m and n, each ranging from 15 kg to 45 kg (in multiples of 5), can be obtained and are given in the following Payoff Table.

CONDITIONAL PAYOFF TABLE AND CALCULATIONS FOR EPPI

Event (Demand)	*Fre-quency*	*Probability* $p = \frac{f}{N}$	*Conditional payoff (Rs.)* *Act : Production (m)*							*Maximum conditional payoff (Rs.)*	*Expected payoff (Rs.)*
(*n*)	(*f*)	(*p*)	*15*	*20*	*25*	*30*	*35*	*40*	*45*	(*M*)	*p* × *M*
15	4	0·02	**90**	20	– 50	– 120	– 190	– 260	– 330	90	1·80
20	16	0·08	90	**120**	50	– 20	– 90	– 160	– 230	120	9·60
25	20	0·10	90	120	**150**	80	10	– 60	– 130	150	15·00
30	80	0·40	90	120	150	**180**	110	40	– 30	180	72·00
35	40	0·20	90	120	150	180	**210**	140	70	210	42·00
40	30	0·15	90	120	150	180	210	**240**	170	240	36·00
45	10	0·05	90	120	150	180	210	240	**270**	270	13·50
Total	N = 200	1									189·90

Note. Maximum payoff (profit) for each state of nature *i.e.*, demand (n), over different acts *i.e.*, production (m) has been written in bold type in the above table.

(*b*) **Expected Payoffs.** The expected payoff (*EMV*) for *any act* is given by : $\sum$ (Prob.) × (Payoff), the summation being taken over different states' of nature *i.e.*, n.

∴ $EMV\,(m = 15)$ = Rs. 90 (0·02 + 0·08 + 0·10 + 0·40 + 0·20 + 0·15 + 0·05) = Rs. 90 × 1 = Rs. 90

$EMV\ (m = 20)$ = Rs. (20 × 0·02 + 120 × 0·98) = Rs. (0·40 + 117·60) = Rs. 118

$EMV\ (m = 25)$ = Rs. [(– 50) × 0·02 + 50 × 0·08 + 150 × 0·90] = Rs. (–1 + 4 + 135) = Rs. 138

Proceding similarly, we shall get

$EMV\ (m = 30)$ = Rs. (–2·40 – 1·60 + 8 + 72 + 36 + 27 + 9) = Rs. 148

$EMV\ (m = 35)$ = Rs. (–3·80 – 7·20 + 1 + 44 + 42 + 31·50 + 10·50) = Rs. 118

$EMV\ (m = 40)$ = Rs. (–5·20 – 12·80 – 6 + 16 + 28 + 36 + 12) = Rs. 68

$EMV\ (m = 45)$ = Rs. – 6·60 – 18·40 – 13 – 12 + 14 + 25·50 + 13·50) = Rs. 3

Since $EMV\ (m = 30)$ is maximum, by the *EMV* criterion, the Act : $m = 30$, is the optimal act. Hence, the co-operative union should produce $m = 30$ kg of butter daily to maximise its profits.

(*c*) **EVPI.** To compute the Expected Value under Perfect Information (*EVPI*), we shall first compute Expected Profit under Perfect Information (EPPI) which is given by :

$$EPPI = \sum [(\text{Probability}) \times (\text{Max Payoff over different acts})],$$

the summation being taken over different states of nature. Hence, from the Payoff Table, we get

$$EPPI = \Sigma p \times M = \text{Rs. } 189{\cdot}90 \text{ [From Conditional Payoff Table]}$$

$$EVPI = EPPI - (EMV)_{max}$$

$$= \text{Rs. } (189{\cdot}90 - 148{\cdot}00) = \text{Rs. } 41{\cdot}90.$$

Interpretation of EVPI. *EVPI* provides us the upper bound about the amount of money, which the decision maker can spend for obtaining the perfect information about the different states of nature (demand) in this case.

∴ EVPI = Rs. 41·90, implies that the co-operative union will not like to spend more than Rs. 41·90 for obtaining the additional information about the demand of butter.

18·4. DECISION TREE

Decision tree is a network which exhibits graphically the logical relationship between the different parts of the complex decision process. It is a graphic model of each combination of various acts and states of nature $\{S_i, A_j\}$; ($i = 1, 2, \ldots, m$; $j = 1, 2, \ldots, n$) along with their payoffs, the probability distribution of the various states of nature and the *EMV* or *EOL* for each act.

Decision tree is a very effective device in making decisions in various diversified problems relating to personnel, investment, portfolios, project management, new project strategies, etc.

Each combination (S_i, A_j) is depicted by a distinct path through the decision tree. An essential feature of the decision tree is that the flow should be from left to right in a chronological order.

Standard symbols are used in drawing a decision tree.

(*i*) A *square* (☐) is used to represent a *decision point* or *decision node* at which the decision maker has to decide about one of the various acts or alternatives available to him.

(*ii*) Each act or alternative is shown as a line, representing a branch of the tree emanating from the square.

(*iii*) A *circle* (◯) is used to represent a *chance event* or *chance node* at which various events or states of nature are represented by lines, which depict the sub-branches of the tree emanating from the circle.

(*iv*) Each branch of the tree (corresponding to each act or strategy) has as many sub-branches as the number of events or states of nature.

(*v*) Along the branches/sub-branches are also shown the probabilities of various states of nature and the payoffs for each combination (S_i, A_j) ; $i = 1, 2, \ldots, m$; $j = 1, 2, \ldots, n$ along with the EMV or EOL for each act.

(*vi*) As a branch can sub-branch again, we obtain a tree like structure, which represents the various steps in a decision problem.

Illustration. The problem of carrying an umbrella on any day in rainy season can be represented diagrammatically by a decision tree given below.

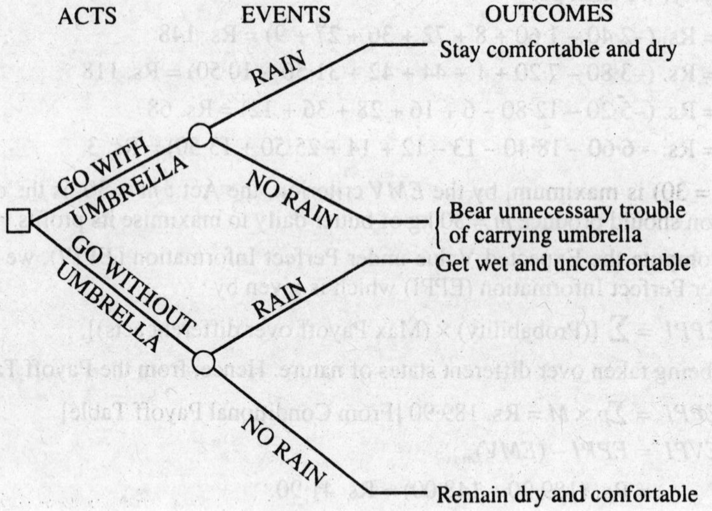

Fig. 18·1. Decision Tree

18·5·1. Roll Back Technique of Analysing a Decision Tree.

A decision tree is extremely useful in multistage situations which involve a number of decisions, each depending on the preceding one. At any stage, to decide about any strategy or act, the decision maker has to take into consideration all future outcomes that may result from choosing the said act. Consequently to analyse a decision tree, we start from the end of the tree (extreme right hand side) *i.e.,* we start from the *last decision/event node, say,* D_l and work backwards. This technique of analysing the decision tree, called the *roll-back technique* is explained in the following steps.

1. (*a*) For each branch of the event node (of D_l) we compute the conditional expected payoffs.

(*b*) Adding these expected payoffs for each event-nodel branch, we obtain the EMV for the given path (act or strategy) emanating from the square (decision node D_l).

(*c*) The optimal act or strategy at D_l is the one which corresponds to the highest EMV.

2. Next we move to the last but one decision mode (D_{l-1}), make the EMV analysis as in steps 1 (*a*), (*b*) and (*c*) and then move back to the preceding decision node (D_{l-2}) and so on.

3. This *roll-back process* is continued till we reach the first decision node (D_1).

Example 18·20. *A manufacturing company has to select one of the two products X or Y for manufacturing. Product X requires investment of Rs. 30,000 and product Y, Rs. 50,000. Market result survey shows high, medium and low demands with corresponding probabilities and return from sales, (in thousand rupees), for the two products, as given in the following table.*

Demand	*Probability*		*Return from Sales ('000 Rs.)*	
	Product X	*Product Y*	*Product X*	*Product Y*
High	*0·4*	*0·3*	*75*	*100*
Medium	*0·4*	*0·4*	*55*	*80*
Low	*0·2*	*0·3*	*35*	*70*

Construct the appropriate decision tree. What decision the company should take ?

Solution. The decision tree based on the above information is given below.

Index. □ : Decision Node ; ○ : Event Node

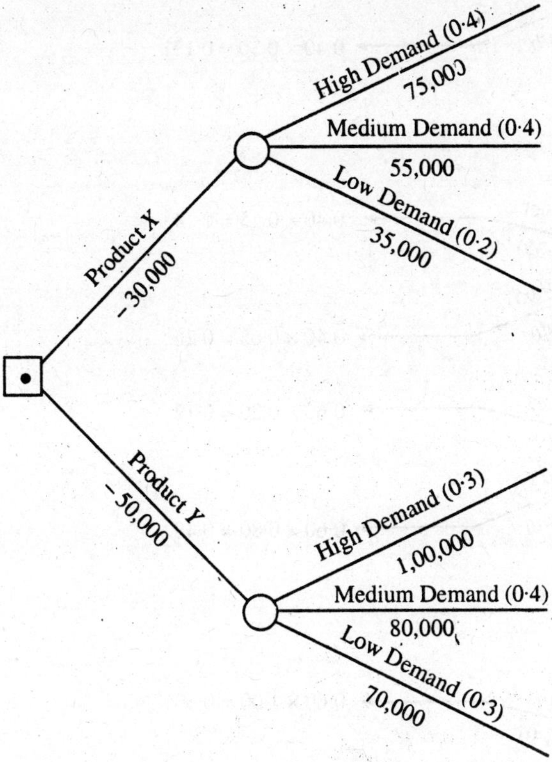

Net Payoff (Rs.)	Expected Payoff (Rs.)
75,000 – 30,000 = 45,000	45,000 × 0·4 = 18,000
55,000 – 30,000 = 25,000	25,000 × 0·4 = 10,000
35,000 – 30,000 = 5,000	5,000 × 0·2 = 1,000
	Total : 29,000 (*EMV*)
1,00,000 – 50,000 = 50,000	50,000 × 0·3 = 15,000
80,000 – 50,000 = 30,000	30,000 × 0·4 = 12,000
70,000 – 50,000 = 20,000	20,000 × 0·3 = 6,000
	Total : 33,000 (*EMV*)

Fig. 18·2. Decision Tree

EMV (Product *X*)
= Rs. (45,000 × 0·4 + 25,000 × 0·4 + 5000 × 0·2)
= Rs (18,000 + 10,000 + 1,000)
= Rs. 29,000.

EMV (Product *Y*)
= Rs. (50,000 × 0·3 + 30,000 × 0·4 + 20,000 × 0·3)
= Rs. (15,000 + 12,000 + 6,000)
= Rs. 33,000

Since *EMV* (Product *Y*) is higher, the company should decide to manufacture product *Y*.

Example 18·21. *There is 40% chance that a patient admitted to the hospital, is suffering from cancer. A doctor has to decide whether a serious operation should be performed or not. If the patient is suffering from cancer and the serious operation is performed, the chance that he will recover, is 70%, otherwise it is 35%. On the other hand, if the patient is not suffering from cancer and the serious operation is performed, the chance that he will recover is 20%, otherwise it is 100%. Assume that recovery and death are the only possible results.*

Construct an appropriate decision tree.

What decision should the doctor take ? [*I.C.W.A. (Intermediate), June 1995*]

Solution. The required decision tree is drawn below.

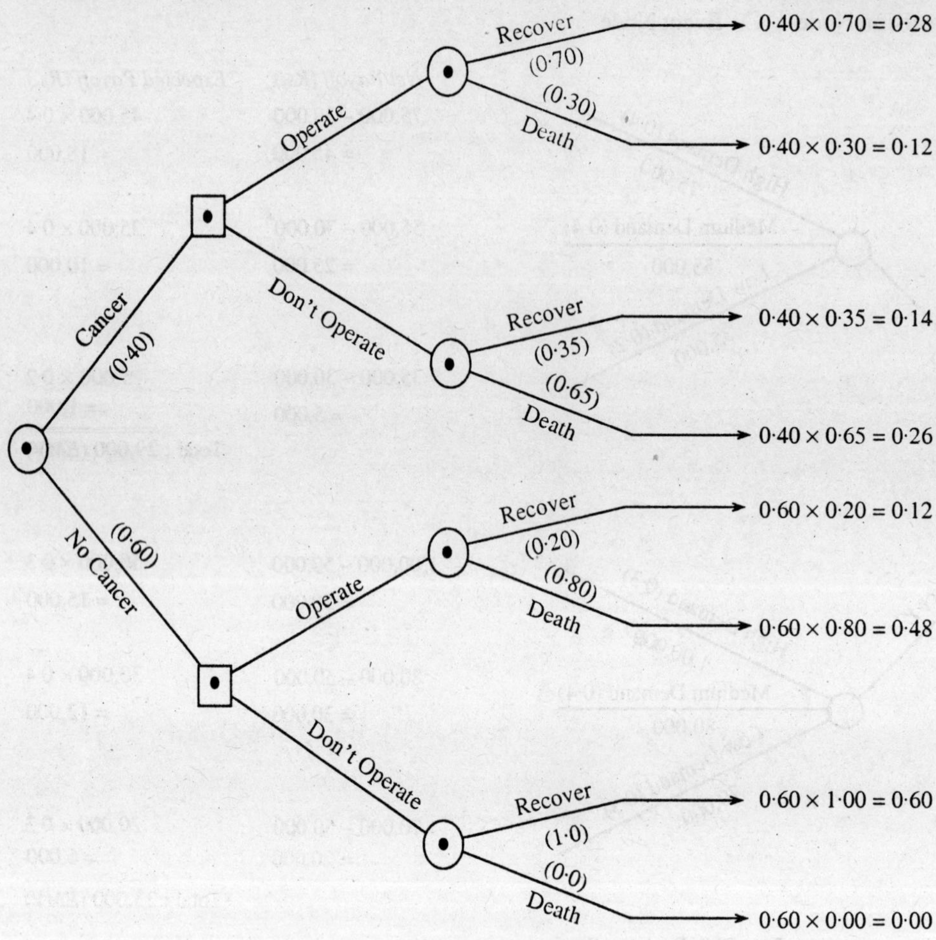

Fig. 18·3. Decision Tree.

Interpretation of Decision Tree

From the decision tree, we find that :

P(Patient recovers when operation is performed) = 0·28 + 0·12 = 0·40 = p_1, (say).

P(Patient recovers when no operation is performed) = 0·14 + 0·60 = 0·74 = p_2, (say).

Since $p_2 > p_1$, we conclude that the doctor should decide not to operate such patients.

Example 18·22. *Amar Company is currently working with a process which after paying for materials, labour, etc., brings a profit of Rs. 12,000. The following alternatives are made available to the company :*

(i) The company can conduct research (R_1) which is expected to cost Rs. 10,000 having 90% chances of success. If it proves a success, the company gets a gross income of Rs. 25,000.

(ii) The company can conduct research (R_2) which is expected to cost Rs. 8,000 having a probability of 60% success, the gross income will be Rs. 25,000.

(iii) The company can pay Rs. 6,000 as royalty for a new process which will bring a gross income of Rs. 20,000.

(iv) The company continues the current process.

Because of limited resources, it is assumed that only one of the two types of research can be carried out at a time.

Use decision tree analysis to locate the optimal strategy for the company.

[*C.A. (Foundation), May 1994*)]

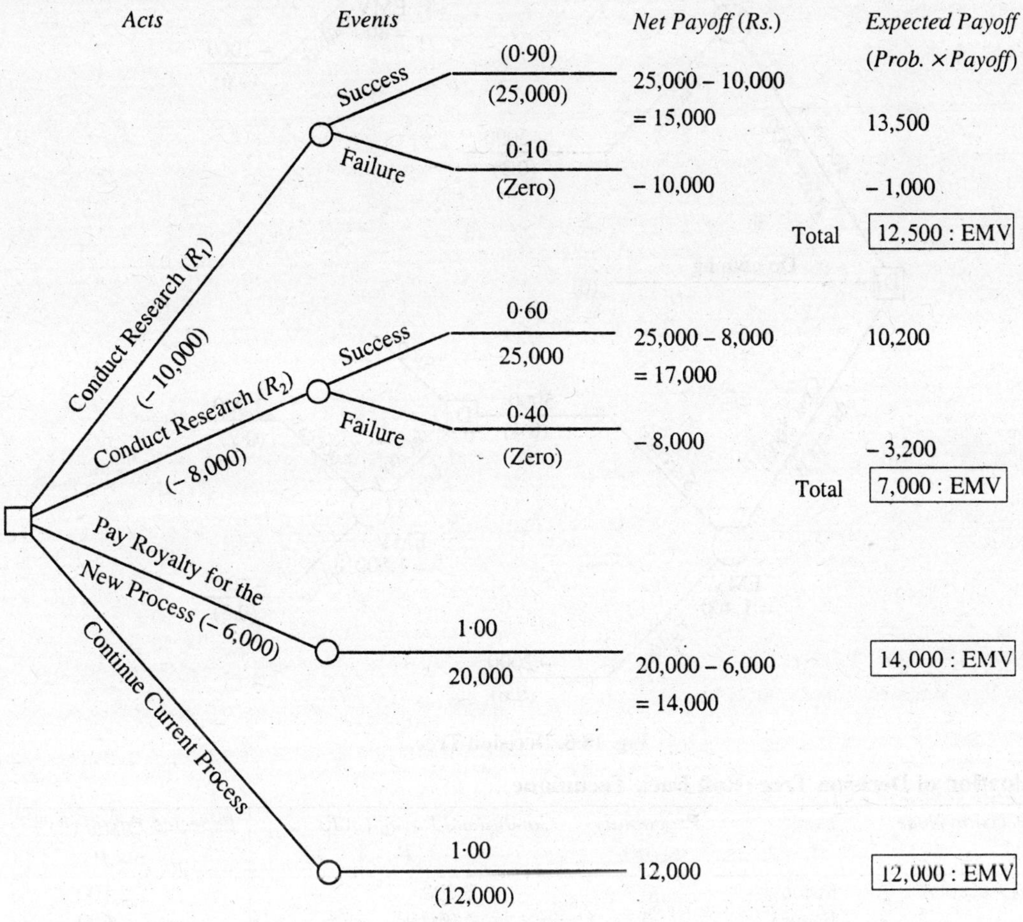

Fig. 18·4. Decision Tree.

Since *EMV* [Pay royalty for the new process], is maximum with highest return of Rs. 14,000; Amar Company's optimal decision would be to go in for "*the new process on royalty basis*".

Example 18·23. *A businessman has two independent investments A and B available to him but he lacks the capital to undertake both of them simultaneously. He can choose to take A first and then stop, or if A is successful then take B, or vice versa. The probability of success for A is 0·7 while for B it is 0·4. Both investments require an initial capital outlay of Rs. 2,000; and both return nothing if the venture is unsuccessful. Successful completion of A will return Rs. 3,000 (over cost), and successful completion of B will return Rs. 5,000 (over cost). Draw and evaluate the decision tree by the roll back technique and determine the best strategy.*

Solution. The decision tree is given in fig. 18·5.

Note. Return of Rs. x (over cost) $\Rightarrow$ Net Profit = Gross Profit – Cost = Rs. x.

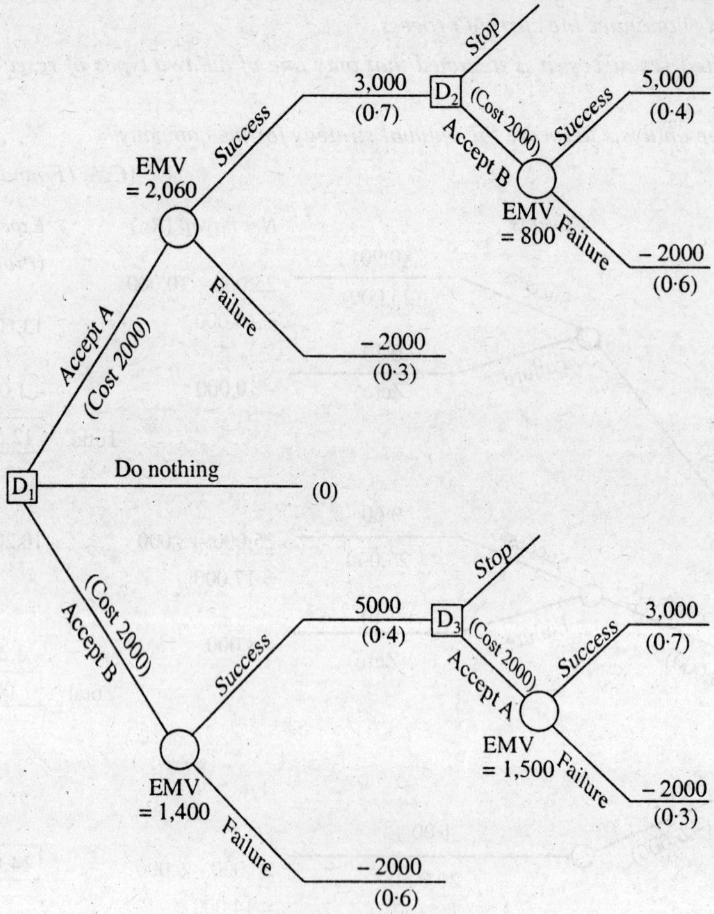

Fig. 18·5. Decision Tree.

Evaluation of Decision Tree (Roll Back Technique),

Decision Node		*Event*	*Probability* (p)	*Conditional Payoff (in Rs.)* P	*Expected Payoff (Rs.)* $p \times P$
D_3	(*i*) Accept *A*	Success	0·7	3,000	2,100
		Failure	0·3	– 2,000	– 600
					1,500 = *EMV*
	(*ii*) Stop				0
D_2	(*i*) Accept *B*	Success	0·4	5,000	2,000
		Failure	0·6	– 2,000	– 1,200
					800 = *EMV*
	(*ii*) Stop				0
D_1	(*i*) Accept *A*	Success	0·7	3,000 + 800 = 3,800	2,660
		Failure	0·3	– 2,000	– 600
					2,060 = *EMV*
	(*ii*) Accept *B*	Success	0·4	5,000 + 1,500 = 6,500	2,600
		Failure	0·6	– 2,000	– 1,200
					1,400 = *EMV*
	(*iii*) Do Nothing				0

From the above table we conclude that the best strategy is to accept investment A first [$\because$ EMV (D_1) > EMV (D_2)] and if it is successful, then accept the investment B.

EXERCISE 18·1.

1. "Statistics is a body of methods for making wise decisions in the face of uncertainty." Examine.

2. What is meant by 'Statistical Decision Theory' ? How is it different from other methods used in decision-making ?

3. Explain briefly statistical decision theory. What are the ingredients of a decision problem.
[*Delhi Univ. B.Com. (Hons.), 2008*]

4. Explain the following terms, as used in decision making, with suitable examples :
(*a*) Payoff Table. (*b*) Opportunity Loss or Regret Table.

5. (*a*) Explain what do you mean by decision making :
(*i*) Under certainty (*ii*) Under uncertainty.
(*b*) "Decision criteria under situation of uncertainty is governed by the attitude of the decision maker". Explain.
(*c*) Explain, how decisions are taken under uncertainty using probabilities. [*C.A. (Foundation), May 2002*]
(*d*) Describe the various methods of decision-making under uncertainty without use of probability.
[*C.A. (Foundation), Nov. 2001*]

6. What is an optimal decision ? How statistical decision theory helps in arriving at such a decision ?

7. (*a*) Explain the difference between the terms "risk" and "uncertainty" as used in statistical decision theory.
(*b*) Describe some methods which are used for decision making under uncertainty using :
(*i*) Non-probabilistic criteria.
(*ii*) Probabilistic criteria.

8. Write notes on the following :
(*a*) Statistical Decision Theory. [*Delhi Univ. B.Com . (Hons.), 1999*]
(*b*) Payoff Table (Matrix) and Regret Table (Matrix), giving suitable examples.
[*Delhi Univ.. B.Com. (Hons.) 1997, 1996*]
(*c*) Criteria of Statistical Decision Making. [*Delhi Univ. B.Com. (Hons.), 1999*]

9. Explain maximin, maximax and minimax regret criterion as used in decision making.
[*C.A. (Foundation), May 1998*]

10. (*a*) Explain EMV and EOL criteria. [*C.A. (Foundation), Nov. 2000; 1997*]
(*b*) Prove that the EMV criterion and EOL criterion lead to the same optimal decision.

11. Explain the difference between (*a*) Expected opportunity loss, (*b*) Expected monetary value, and (*c*) Expected value of perfect information, and their use in decision theory.

12. Describe the following methods for arriving at an optimal decision :
(*a*) Maximax Principle (*b*) Maximin Principle, (*c*) Minimax Regret Criterion,
(*d*) Hurwicz Principle, (*e*) Laplace Criterion of Equal Likelihoods.

13. What do you understand by '*Expected Value of Perfect Information*', ? What does it represent ? Give its significance in decision making.

14. A food products company is contemplating the introduction of a revolutionary new product with new packaging to replace the existing product at much higher price (A_1) or a moderate change in the composition of the existing product with a new packaging at a small increase in price (A_2) or a small change in the composition of the existing product except the word 'New' with a negligible increase in price (A_3).

The three possible states of nature or events are (*i*) high increase in sales (S_1), (*ii*) no change in sales (S_2), and (*iii*) decrease in sales (S_3). The marketing department of the company worked out the payoffs in terms of yearly net profits for each of the strategies of these events (expected sales). This is represented in the adjoining table.

	Payoffs (in '000 Rs.)		
States of Nature	*Act* A_1	*Act* A_2	*Act* A_3
S_1	70	50	30
S_2	30	45	30
S_3	15	0	30

Which strategy should the executive concerned choose on the basis of
(*a*) Maximin Criterion, (*b*) Maximax Criterion, (*c*) Minimax Regret Criterion, (*d*) Laplace Criterion ?
Ans. (*a*) A_2; (*b*) A_1; (*c*) A_1; (*d*) A_1.

15. Consider the following pay off (profit) matrix

		S_1	S_2	S_3	S_4
	a_1	5	10	18	25
Action	a_2	8	7	8	23
	a_3	21	18	12	21
	a_4	30	22	19	15

No probabilities are known for the occurrence of the states of nature. Compare the solutions obtained by each of the following criteria :

(*i*) Laplace, (*ii*) Maximin, (*iii*) Minimax, (*iv*) Hurwicz (assume that $\alpha = 0{\cdot}5$)

[I.C.W.A. (Intermediate), June 2002]

Ans. (*i*) a_2, (*ii*) a_4, (*iii*) a_3, (*iv*) a_4

16. Given below is the pay off (in Rs.) matrix :

Decision

State of nature	*Do not expand*	*Expand 200 units*	*Expand 400 units*
High demand	2500	3500	5000
Medium demand	2500	3500	2500
Low demand	2500	1500	2000

Decide the optimal action by using :

(*i*) the maximin criterion ; (*ii*) Laplace criterion ; and (*iii*) the maximax criterion.

[Delhi Univ. B.Com. (Hons.), (External), 2005]

Ans. (*i*) "Do not Expand." (*ii*) "Expand 400 units." (*iii*) "Do not Expand."

17. A person wants to invest in one of three alternative investment plans ; Stock, Bonds, Debentures. It is assumed that the person wishes to invest all of the funds in a plan. The payoff matrix based on three potential economic conditions is given as under :

	Economic Conditions		
Alternative Investment	*High Growth Rs.*	*Normal Growth Rs.*	*Slow Growth Rs.*
Stock	10,000	7,000	3,000
Bonds	8,000	6,000	1,000
Debentures	6,000	6,000	6,000

Determine the best investment plan using each of the following criteria :

(*i*) Laplace ; (*ii*) Maximin ; (*iii*) Maximax. *[Delhi Univ. B.Com. (Hons.), 2005]*

18. Given is the following pay-off matrix :

		Acts		
States of Nature	*Probability*	*Do not expand*	*Expand 100 units*	*Expand 200 units*
High demand	0·2	3,500	4,500	6,000
Medium demand	0·3	3,500	4,500	3,500
Low demand	0·5	3,500	3,500	2,000

Using EMV criterion, decide the best act. *[C.A. (Foundation), May 2002]*

Ans. The best act is : 'Expand 100 units'.

19. The following table gives the payoff of the acts A_1, A_2 and A_3 and the states of nature E_1, E_2 and E_3 with 0·1, 0·7 and 0·2 as their respective probabilities. Prepare the opportunity loss table and select the best act.

PAYOFF TABLE

States of Nature	*Acts*		
	A_1	A_2	A_3
E_1	25	– 10	– 125
E_2	400	440	400
E_3	650	740	750

[C.A. (Foundation), May 2000]

Ans. $EOL\ (A_1) = 48$; $EOL\ (A_2) = 5{\cdot}5$; $EOL\ (A_3) = 43$. A_2 is the *best act.*

20. A decision maker is faced with three decision alternatives and four states of nature. Given the following profit Pay-off table.

State of Nature →		S_1	S_2	S_3	S_4
	a_1	16	10	12	7
Acts	a_2	13	12	9	9
	a_3	11	14	15	14

Assuming that he has no knowledge of the probabilities of occurrence of the states of nature, find the decisions to be recommended under each of the following criteria :

(*i*) Maximin ; (*ii*) Maximax ; (*iii*) Minimax Regret. [*Delhi Univ. B.Com. (Hons.), (External), 2006*]

Ans. (*i*) α_3, (*ii*) α_1, (*iii*) α_3.

21. A food products company is contemplating the introduction of a new product with new packaging to replace the existing product at a much higher price (S_1) or a moderate change in the composition of the existing product with a new packaging at a small increase in price (S_2) or a small change in the composition of the product with a negligible increase in price (S_3). The three possible states of nature are :

(*i*) high increase in sales (N_1); (*ii*) no change in sales (N_2); and (*iii*) decrease in sales (N_3).

The marketing department of the company worked out the profits for each of the strategies as given in the adjoining table.

Which strategy should the concerned executive choose on the basis of :

Payoff (in Rs.)

Strategies	State of Nature N_1	N_2	N_3
S_1	7,00,000	3,00,000	1,50,000
S_2	5,00,000	4,50,000	0
S_3	3,00,000	3,00,000	3,00,000

(*i*) Maximin criterion; (*ii*) Maximax criterion; (*iii*) Minimax regret criterion; (*iv*) Laplace criterion.

[*Delhi Univ. B.Com. (Hons.), 2008 ; B.Com. (Hons.), (External), 2007*]

Ans. (*i*) S_3, (*ii*) S_1, (*iii*) S_1, (*iv*) S_1.

Hint. For Parts (*i*) and (*iv*), see Example 18·1

(*iii*) **OPPORTUNITY LOSS OR REGRET TABLE (IN Rs.)**

Strategy	N_1	N_2	N_3	Row Maximum
S_1	7,00,000 – 7,00,000 = 0	4,50,000 – 3,00,000 = 1,50,000	3,00,000 – 1,50,000 = 1,50,000	1,50,000
S_2	7,00,000 – 5,00,000 = 2,00,000	4,50,000 – 4,50,000 = 0	3,00,000 – 0 = 3,00,000	3,00,000
S_3	7,00,000 – 3,00,000 = 4,00,000	4,50,000 – 3,00,000 = 1,50,000	3,00,000 – 3,00,000 = 0	4,00,000

Minimum of Maximum Regrets (Loss) is 1,50,000 which corresponds to strategy S_1. Hence, by Minimax Regret criterion, the optimal strategy is S_1.

22. Tabulate the Expected Monetary Values for the data given below and state which act can be chosen as the best :

States of Nature	Probability	Payoffs (in Rs.) Act X	Act Y	Act Z
A	0·3	– 120	– 80	100
B	0·5	200	400	– 300
C	0·2	260	– 260	600

[*Delhi Univ. B.Com. (Hons.) Pt. I, 1998; C.A. (Foundation) June 1998*]

Ans. *EMV* (*X*) = 116 ; *EMV* (*Y*) = 124 ; *EMV* (*Z*) = 0 ; Act *Y* is the optimal act.

23. A cosmetic company is considering the introduction of a new brand. The company estimates that it will be possible for them to sell 50,000 to 1,00,000 pieces in a given period according to the following probability distribution.

No. of pieces sold (in '000)	:	50	60	70	80	90	100
Probability	:	0·13	0·20	0·35	0·25	0·05	0·02

If the company launches the product, it will incur a fixed cost of Rs. 50,000. However, each piece sold would fetch them a profit of Re. 1·00.

Should the company introduce the brand ? [*I.C.W.A. (Intermediate), Dec. 1995*]

Ans. and **Hint.** Expected number of pieces sold = $\sum x \cdot p(x) = 69{\cdot}5 \times 1{,}000 = 69{,}500$.

Net Profit = (69,500 × Re. 1) – Rs. 50,000 = Rs. 19,500.

Hence, the company should introduce the new brand.

24. A manufacturing company is faced with the problem of choosing from four products. The potential demand for each product may turn out to be good, satisfactory and poor. The probabilities estimated for each type of demand are given below in Table A and the estimated profit or loss under different states of demand in respect of each product may be taken in Table B.

TABLE A

PROBABILITY OF TYPE OF DEMAND

Product	*Good*	*Satisfactory*	*Poor*
A	0·60	0·20	0·20
B	0·75	0·15	0·10
C	0·60	0·25	0·15
D	0·50	0·20	0·30

TABLE B

ESTIMATED [PROFIT/LOSS (Rs.)]

Product	*Good*	*Satisfactory*	*Poor*
A	40,000	10,000	1,100
B	40,000	20,000	(–) 7,000
C	50,000	15,000	(–) 8,000
D	40,000	18,000	15,000

Prepare the expected value table and advise the company about the choice of the product to manufacture.

[*Delhi Univ. B.Com. (Hons.), 2009*]

Hint. *EMV (A)* = Rs. [40,000 × 0·60 + 10,000 × 0·20 + 1,100 × 0·20] = Rs. 26,220

Similarly, *EMV (B)* = Rs. 32,300 ; *EMV (C)* = Rs. 32,550 ; *EMV (D)* = Rs. 28,100.

Since *EMV(C)* is maximum, the company should manufacture product '*C*'.

25. Given the following payoff of a factory owner :

States of Nature	*Payoff (in '000 Rs.)* Acts *Do not expand*	*Expand 200 units*	*Expand 400 units*	*Probability*
High demand	300	500	600	0·5
Medium demand	250	300	500	0·3
Low demand	200	– 100	– 300	0·2

Obtain the optimal strategy by using (*a*) *EMV* criterion, and (*b*) *EOL* criterion.

Is the conclusion same in both the cases ? Explain why ?

Ans. (*a*) Act : *Do not expand* *Expand 200 units* *Expand 400 units*

EMV ('000 Rs.) : 265 320 90

Optimal act is to expand the plant by 200 units.

(*b*) Expand the plant by 200 units.

EMV criterion and *EOL* criterion always lead to the same optional decision.

26. A producer of boats has estimated the following distribution of demand for a particular kind of boat :

No. demanded :	0	1	2	3	4	5	6
Probability :	0·14	0·27	0·27	0·18	0·09	0·04	0·01

Each boat cost him Rs. 7,000 and he sells them for Rs. 10,000 each. Any boats that are left unsold at the end of the season must be disposed off for Rs. 6000 each. How many boats should be in stock so as to maximise his expected profit ? [*Punjabi Uiv. M.Com., 2005; Sardar Patel Univ. M.B.A., 1996*]

Ans.

Stock (*m*) :	0	1	2	3	4	5	6
EMV (*m*) (*in Rs.*) :	0	2,440	3,800	4,080	3,640	2,840	1,880

Hence, optimal decision is to stock $m = 3$, boats per season.

27. (*a*) A newspaper distributor assigns probabilities to the demand for a magazine as follows :

Copies demanded	1	2	3	4
Probability	0·4	0·3	0·2	0·1

A copy of the magazine sells for Rs. 7 and costs Rs. 6. What can be the maximum possible expected monetary value (EMV) if the distributor can return unsold copies for Rs. 5 each ?

Ans. Magazines stocked (m) :	1	2	3	4
EMV (m) (in Rs.) :	1	1·2	0·8	0

Hence, the optimal choice is stock $m = 2$ magazines.

(*b*) A magazine vendor has assigned the following probabilities to the demand for a weekly magazine :

Copies Demanded :	10	11	12	13	14
Probability :	0·1	0·3	0·3	0·2	0·1

A copy of the magazine sells for Rs. 10 and costs Rs. 8. An unsold copy can be returned for Rs. 5. How many copies of the magazine should the vendor buy ? Find his expected profits also. [*Delhi Univ. B.Com. (Hons.), 2004*]

Ans. Vendor should buy 11 or 12 copies of the magazine. In each case, expected profit is Rs. 21·50.

28. A shopkeeper of some highly perishable type of fruits sees that the daily demand X of this fruit in his area has the following probability distribution :

Daily demand (in dozen) :	6	7	8	9
Probability :	0·1	0·3	0·4	0·2

He sells fruits for Rs. 10.00 a dozen while he buys each dozen at Rs. 4.00. Unsold fruits in a day are traded on the next day at Rs. 2.00 per dozen. Assuming that he stocks the fruits in dozen, how many should he stock so that his expected profit will be maximum ? [*I.C.W.A. (Intermediate), June 2001*]

Ans. Stock m (in dozens) :	6	7	8	9
EMV(m) in Rs. :	36	41·20	44	43·60

Optimal choice is $m = 8$ dozen fruits.

29. A newspaper distributor assigns probabilities to the demand for a magazine on any day as follows :

Copies demand :	11	12	13	14
Probability :	0·4	0·3	0·2	0·1

A copy of magazine sells for Rs. 7 and costs Rs. 6. The distributor can return the unsold copies of magazine for Rs. 5 each. How many copies of magazine should he order for the next day ? Use *EMV* criterion to answer the question. Also calculate *EVPI*. [*Delhi Univ. B.Com. (Hons.), (External) 2005*]

Ans.

Copies ordered	11	12	13	14
EMV (Rs.)	11	11·20	10·80	10

The distributor should order 12 copies of the magazine.

$E.V.P.I. = E.P.P.I. - (EMV)_{max}$ = Rs. (12 – 11·20) = Re. 0·80.

30. A physician purchases a particular vaccine on Monday of each week. The vaccine must be used within the week following, otherwise it becomes worthless. The vaccine costs Rs. 2 per dose and the physician charges Rs. 4 per dose. In the past 50 weeks the physician has administered the vaccine in the following quantities :

Doses per week :	20	25	40	60
Number of weeks :	5	15	25	5

Determine how many doses the physician should buy every week.

Ans. Optimal decision of the physician will be to buy $m = 40$, doses of the vaccine.

31. Payoff of three acts, A, B and C, and the states of nature X, Y and Z are given below :

States of Nature	*Act A*	*Act B*	*Act C*
X	– 30	– 50	200
Y	200	– 100	– 50
Z	400	600	300

The probabilities of the states of nature are 0·3, 0·4 and 0·3.

Calculate the expected monetary values (*EMV*) for the above data and select the best act.

Also find the expected value of perfect information (*EVPI*). [*I.C.W.A. (Intermediate), Dec. 1996*]

Ans. $EMV(A) = 194$; $EMV(B) = 125$; $EMV(C) = 130$. Therefore, A is the optimal act.

$EVPI = EPPI - \text{Max } (EMV) = 320 - 194 = 126.$

32. A fruit wholeseller buys cases of strawberries for Rs. 200 each and sells them for Rs. 500 each. Any case left, would at the end of the day, have a salvage value of only Rs. 50. An analysis of past sales record, reveals the adjoining probability distribution for the daily number of cases sold :

Daily Sales	*Probability*
10	·15
11	·25
12	·40
13	·20

(*i*) What is the optimum stock action for the fruit seller ?

(*ii*) Also calculate *EVPI* for the same. [*Delhi Univ. B.Com. (Hons.), 2006*]

33. A stockist of a particular commodity makes a profit of Rs. 30 on each sale made within the same week of purchase, otherwise he incurs a loss of Rs. 30 on each item. The data on the past sales are given below :

No. of items sold within the same week	:	5	6	7	8	9	10	11
Frequency	:	0	9	12	24	9	6	0

(*i*) Find out the optimum number of items the stockist should buy every week in order to maximize the profit.

(*ii*) Calculate the expected value of perfect information. [*C.A. (Foundation) May, 1996*]

Ans. (*i*) 8 (*ii*) *EVPI* = Rs. 25·50.

34. What is a *decision tree* ? How is it used in decision theory to arrive at the optimal decision.

35. A person has two independent investments *A* and *B* available to him, but he can undertake only one at a time due to certain constraints. He can choose *A* first and then stop, or if *A* is successful then take *B* or vice-versa. The probability of success of *A* is 0·6 while for *B* it is 0·4. Both investments require an initial capital outlay of Rs. 10,000 and both return nothing if the venture is unsuccessful. Successful completion of *A* will return Rs. 20,000 (over cost) and successful completion of *B* will return Rs. 24,000 (over cost). Draw decision tree and determine the best strategy.

[*Delhi Univ. B.Com. (Hons.) 2007*]

Ans. Accept the investment '*A*' first and then accept the investment *B*.

Hint. Proceed as in Example 18·23.

36. A businessman has two independent investments *A* and *B* available to him but he lacks the capital to undertake both of them simultaneously. Investment *A* requires capital of Rs. 30,000 and investment *B* Rs. 50,000. Market survey shows : High, Medium and Low demands with corresponding probabilities of 0·4, 0·4 and 0·2 respectively in case of investment *A* and 0·3, 0·4 and 0·3 for investment *B*. Returns from investment *A* are Rs. 75,000, Rs. 55,000 and Rs. 35,000 and corresponding figures for investment *B* are likely to be Rs. 1,00,000, Rs. 80,000 and Rs. 70,000 for High, Medium and Low demand respectively. What decision should the company take ? Decide by constructing an appropriate decision tree. [*Delhi Univ. B.Com. (Hons.), (External), 2007*]

Ans. *EMV* (investment *A*) = Rs. 29,000 ; *EMV* (Investment *B*) = Rs. 33,000.

Since *EMV*(*B*) > *EMV* (*A*), the company should go for investment *B*.

Hint. Proceed as in Example 18·20.

37. A manufacturing company has to select one of the two products *A* or *B* for manufacturing. Product *A* requires investment of Rs. 20,000 and product *B*, Rs. 40,000. Market research survey shows high, medium and low demands with corresponding probabilities and returns from sales, in Rs. thousand, for the two products, in the following table :

Market Demand	*Probability*		*Return from sales*	
	A	B	A	B
High	0·4	0·3	50	80
Medium	0·3	0·5	30	60
Low	0·3	0·2	10	50

Construct an appropriate decision tree. What decision the company should take ?

[*I.C.W.A. (Intermediate), Dec. 1995*]

Ans. *EMV* (*A*) = Rs. 12,000 ; *EMV* (*B*) = Rs. 24,000.

∴ Product *B* is the optimal decision.

38. A Finance Manager is considering drilling a well. In the past, only 70% of wells drilled were successful at 20 metres depth in that area. Moreover on finding no water at 20 metres, some persons in that area drilled it further upto 25 metres but only 20% struck water at that level. The prevailing cost of drilling is Rs. 500 per metre. The Finance Manager estimated that in case he does not get water in his own well, he will have to pay Rs. 15,000 to buy water from outside for the same period of getting water from the well. The following decisions are considered :

(*i*) Do not drill any well,

(*ii*) Drill upto 20 metres, and

(*iii*) If no water is found at 20 metres, drill further upto 25 metres.

Draw an appropriate decision tree and determine the Finance Manager's optimal strategy.

[*C.A. May, 1992; I.C.W.A. Dec., 1985*]

Ans. The optimal strategy is *to drill the well up to 20 metres and if no water is struck, then further drill it up to 25 metres.*

39. Each unit of a product produced and sold yields a profit of Rs. 50 but a unit produced but not sold results in a loss of Rs. 30. The probability distribution of the number of units demanded is as follows :

No. of units demanded	:	0	1	2	3	4
Probability	:	0·20	0·20	0·25	0·30	0·05

How many units should be produced to maximise the expected profits ? Also calculate *EVPI.*

[*Delhi Univ., B.Com. (Hons.), 2001*]

Ans. Units produced	:	0	1	2	3	4
EMV (Rs.)	:	0	34	52	50	24

Optimal act is to produce 2 units.

EVPI = *EPPI* – *EMV* = 90 – 52 = Rs. 38

40. The table gives the payoffs of the acts A_1, A_2, A_3 and the states of nature E_1, E_2, E_3 with their respective probabilities. Find the optimum value of the expected opportunity loss and the optimum act.

Act	*States of Nature*		
	E_1	E_2	E_3
A_1	90	60	–15
A_2	80	65	–10
A_3	60	50	0
Probability	0·2	0·4	0·4

[*C.A. (Foundation), May 2001*]

Ans. *EOL* (A_1) = 8; *EOL* (A_2) = 6; *EOL* (A_3) = 12. A_2 is the optimum act.

19 Theory of Attributes

19·1. INTRODUCTION

The dictionary meaning of attribute is quality or characteristic. Some examples of attributes are beauty, honesty, gender (male or female), health, employment, smoking, drinking, blindness, etc. The theory of attributes deals with qualitative characteristics which cannot be measured quantitatively. Hence, the study of attributes requires special statistical treatment which is different from that of the study of variables and has been developed independently.

In the study of attributes, the objects (units of the population/sample) are classified according to the presence or absence of the attribute (quality) in them. For example, a person may be classified as smoker or non-smoker, blind or not blind, male or female, employed or un-employed, healthy or sick, literate or illiterate, and so on. This type of classification in which the units of the population are divided into two exhaustive, mutually exclusive classes *viz*., the one possessing the attribute and the other not possessing the attribute, with respect to one or more of the attributes is called *dichotomous classification.*

On the other hand, if the units of the population are divided into more than two classes with respect to an attribute, the classification may be termed as *manifold classification*. For example, the population, may be divided *w.r.t.* the attribute 'intelligence' into the following classes :

(*i*) Genius, (*ii*) Very intelligent, (*iii*) Average intelligent, (*iv*) Below average intelligent, (*v*) Dull.

19·2. NOTATIONS

The presence of attributes in the units of the population is denoted by the capital letters of the English alphabet, say, A, B, C, D, etc., and their absence is denoted by the corresponding small letters of the Greek alphabet, say, $\alpha, \beta, \gamma, \delta$ respectively. For example,

(*i*) If the attribute A denotes smoking, then α denotes non-smoking.

(*ii*) If the attribute B denotes blindness, then β denotes non-blindness or sight.

(*iii*) If the attribute C denotes males, then γ denotes females and so on.

The combinations of attributes are denoted by grouping together the corresponding letters. Thus, in the above examples, the corresponding attribute AB denotes the simultaneous possession of both the attributes A and B *viz*., blind smokers. Similarly,

	αB	represents	'blind non-smokers'
	$A\beta$	represents	'non-blind smokers'
	BC	represents	'blind males'
	$\beta\gamma$	represents	'non-blind females'
and	ABC	represents	'male blind smokers'.

Similar interpretations can be given to $A\beta C, A\beta\gamma, \alpha BC, \alpha\beta\gamma$ and so on.

Remark. The attribute α used in the sense of not-A is known as the *complementary,* (or *negative*) attribute of A. Similar interpretation can be given to the attributes β, γ, δ, etc.

19·3. CLASSES AND CLASS FREQUENCIES

Different attributes in themselves are called different *classes* and the number of observations assigned to them are called *class frequencies* which are denoted by bracketing the class-symbols. Thus (A) stands for the frequency of A and (AB) for the number of objects possessing the attribute AB.

Remark. The class frequencies of the type (A), (B), (AC), (BC), (ABC), etc., which involve only positive attributes, are called *positive frequencies*. The class frequencies of the type (α), (β), $(\alpha\gamma)$, $(\beta\gamma)$, $(\alpha\beta\gamma)$, etc., which involve only negative attributes, are called *negative frequencies*. The class frequencies of the type $(A\beta)$, (αB), $(AB\gamma)$, (αBC), etc., which involve the mixture of positive and negative attributes, are called *contrary frequencies*.

19·3·1. Order of Classes and Class Frequencies. *A class represented by n attributes is called a class of nth order* and *the corresponding frequency as the frequency of the nth order*. Thus (A), (B), (γ), etc., are class frequencies of order 1 ; (AB), $(A\gamma)$, αC), $(\beta\gamma)$, etc., are class frequencies of second order ; (ABC), $(AB\gamma)$, $(A\beta\gamma)$, $(\alpha\beta C)$ etc., are frequencies of third order and so on. N, the total number of members of the population, without any specification of attributes, is known as a frequency of zero-order.

A class frequency of order r will contain r attributes (symbols). In a dichotomous classification of the population *w.r.t.* n attributes, we can select r attributes out of n in ${}^nC_r$ ways. Further, since each of the r attributes contributes two symbols, [one representing the positive part, say, A and the other representing the negative part, say, α],

$$\text{Total number of class frequencies of order } r = {}^nC_r \cdot 2^r \quad ; \quad r = 0, 1, 2, \ldots, n \qquad \ldots(19\cdot1)$$

Hence, in case of n attributes, the *total number of class frequencies of all orders* is :

$$\sum_{r=0}^{n} {}^nC_r\, 2^r = 1 + {}^nC_1 \cdot 2 + {}^nC_2 \cdot 2^2 + \ldots + {}^nC_n\, 2^n$$

$$= (1+2)^n \qquad \text{[By binomial expansion for positive integer index]}$$

$$= 3^n \qquad \ldots(19\cdot2)$$

Remarks 1. In particular, for n attributes, using (19·1), the total number of class frequencies of different orders are given in Table 19·1.

TABLE 19·1

Order	0	1	2	...	r	...	n
No. of. frequencies	1	$2n$	${}^nC_2\, 2^2$	...	${}^nC_r\, 2^r$	...	2^n

2. In case of 3 attributes A, B and C [from (19·2)], the total number of class frequencies is $3^3 = 27$, as given below :

Order	*Frequencies*				
0			N		
1.	(A), (α)	(B), (β)	(C), (γ)		...(19·3)
2.	(AB), (AC), (BC)	$(A\beta)$, $(A\gamma)$, $(B\gamma)$	(αB), (αC), (βC)	$(\alpha\beta)$, $(\alpha\gamma)$, $(\beta\gamma)$	...(19·3*a*)
3.	(ABC), (αBC)	$(AB\gamma)$, $(\alpha B\gamma)$	$(A\beta C)$, $(\alpha\beta C)$	$(A\beta\gamma)$, $(\alpha\beta\gamma)$	...(19·3*b*)

3. Total Number of Positive Frequencies. The number of positive frequencies in a class of order r is ${}^nC_r$; $r = 0, 1, 2, \ldots, n$. Hence, the total number of positive frequencies is :

$$\sum_{r=0}^{n} {}^nC_r = {}^nC_0 + {}^nC_1 + {}^nC_2 + \ldots + {}^nC_n = (1+1)^n = 2^n \qquad \ldots(19\cdot4)$$

In particular, for 3 attributes, the total number of positive frequencies is $2^3 = 8$, as given below.

$$N, \quad (A), \quad (B), \quad (C), \quad (AB), \quad (AC), \quad (BC), \quad (ABC)$$

19·3·2. Ultimate Class Frequency. In dichotomous classification of the units of the given population with respect to n attributes, the classes of the highest order are known as the *ultimate classes* and their corresponding frequencies are known as the *ultimate class frequencies*.

In case of n attributes, the ultimate class frequencies will be the frequencies of the nth order *i.e.*, each one of them will contain n symbols. Further, since each symbol can be written in two ways, positive or negative *e.g.*, A or α ; B or β, etc.,

$$\text{Total number of ultimate class frequencies} = 2^n \qquad \ldots(19\cdot5)$$

In particular, for two attributes, say, A and B, there are $2^2 = 4$, ultimate class frequencies *viz.*,

$$(AB), \quad (A\beta), \quad (\alpha B) \quad \text{and} \quad (\alpha\beta)$$

For three attributes, say, A, B and C, there are $2^3 = 8$, ultimate class frequencies *viz.*,

$$(ABC), \quad (A\beta C), \quad (\alpha BC), \quad (\alpha\beta C), \quad (AB\gamma), \quad (A\beta\gamma), \quad (\alpha B\gamma) \quad \text{and} \quad (\alpha\beta\gamma)$$

Remark. From (19·4) and (19·5), we observe that :

$$\text{Total number of ultimate frequencies} = \text{Total number of positive frequencies} = 2^n \qquad \ldots(19\cdot6)$$

19·3·3. Relation Between Class Frequencies. All the class frequencies of various orders are not independent of each other and any class frequency can always be expressed in terms of class frequencies of higher order. Thus

$$N = (A) + (\alpha) = (B) + (\beta) = (C) + (\gamma), \textit{etc.}$$

Two Attributes A and B

Also, since each of these A's or α's can either be B's or β's, we have

$$\left.\begin{array}{lll} & (A) = (AB) + (A\beta) \quad \text{and} \quad & (\alpha) = (\alpha B) + (\alpha\beta) \\ \text{Similarly,} & (B) = (AB) + (\alpha B) \quad \text{and} \quad & (\beta) = (A\beta) + (\alpha\beta) \\ \therefore & N = (A) + (\alpha) = (AB) + (A\beta) + (\alpha B) + (\alpha\beta) & \end{array}\right\} \qquad \ldots(19\cdot7)$$

Thus, in the case of two attributes, all the class frequencies can be expressed in terms of the ultimate class frequencies.

Three Attributes A, B and C

$$(C) = (AC) + (\alpha C) = (ABC) + (A\beta C) + (\alpha BC) + (\alpha\beta C)$$

$$\text{Also} \quad (C) = (BC) + (\beta C) = (ABC) + (\alpha BC) + (A\beta C) + (\alpha\beta C) \qquad \ldots(19\cdot8)$$

$$\left.\begin{array}{l} (AB) = (ABC) + (AB\gamma) \quad ; \quad (A\beta) = (A\beta C) + (A\beta\gamma) \\ (\alpha B) = (\alpha BC) + (\alpha B\gamma) \quad ; \quad (\alpha\beta) = (\alpha\beta C) + (\alpha\beta\gamma) \end{array}\right\} \qquad \ldots(19\cdot8a)$$

Substituting in (19·7), we get

$$N = (ABC) + (AB\gamma) + (A\beta C) + (A\beta\gamma) + (\alpha BC) + (\alpha B\gamma) + (\alpha\beta C) + (\alpha\beta\gamma) \qquad \ldots(19\cdot8b)$$

$$\left.\begin{array}{l} (A) = (ABC) + (AB\gamma) + (A\beta C) + (A\beta\gamma) \\ (B) = (ABC) + (AB\gamma) + (\alpha BC) + (\alpha B\gamma) \end{array}\right\} \qquad \ldots(19\cdot8c)$$

Similarly, we can express all other class frequencies in terms of the class frequencies of the third order. The above discussion leads to the following important result.

"Any class frequency can be expressed as the sum of some of the 2^n ultimate class frequencies."

Remarks 1. In dichotomous classification of attributes, the data can be specified completely by :

(*a*) The set of all the ultimate class frequencies.

(*b*) The set of all the positive frequencies.

By this we mean that if we know all the ultimate class frequencies or all the positive class frequencies, then we can obtain the frequencies of all other classes of different orders.

For example, if we are given the set of positive class frequencies for two attributes A and B *viz.*, N, (A), (B) and (AB), then we can obtain all other class frequencies as explained below.

$(A)+(\alpha)=N \Rightarrow (\alpha)=N-(A)$; $(B)+(\beta)=N \Rightarrow (\beta)=N-(B)$ ...(19·9)

$(A)=(AB)+(A\beta) \Rightarrow (A\beta)=(A)-(AB)$; $(B)=(AB)+(\alpha B) \Rightarrow (\alpha B)=(B)-(AB)$ ...(19·9a)

$(\alpha)=(\alpha B)+(\alpha\beta) \Rightarrow (\alpha\beta)=(\alpha)-(\alpha B)=N-(A)-(B)+(AB)$ ...(19·9b)

We give in Table (19·2), a very elegant way of expressing the various class frequencies in terms of

(i) positive class frequencies.

or (ii) ultimate class frequencies.

TABLE 19·2 : **CLASS FREQUENCIES FOR TWO ATTRIBUTES *A* AND *B***

	A	α	*Total*
B	(AB)	(αB)	(B)
β	$(A\beta)$	$(\alpha\beta)$	(β)
Total	(A)	(α)	N

The relations given above in (19·9) to (19·9b) are obvious from this Table.

From Table (19·2), we can easily express the various class frequencies in terms of the ultimate class frequencies. Thus,

$(A)=(AB)+(A\beta)$; $(\alpha)=(\alpha B)+(\alpha\beta)$

$(B)=(AB)+(\alpha B)$; $(\beta)=(A\beta)+(\alpha\beta)$

and $N=(A)+(\alpha)=(AB)+(A\beta)+(\alpha B)+(\alpha\beta)$.

The Table (19·3), enables us to express the class frequencies of various orders in terms of

(i) ultimate class frequencies.

or (ii) positive class frequencies,

for 3 attributes *A*, *B* and *C*.

From this Table we can very conveniently obtain the relations between various class frequencies.

TABLE 19·3 : **CLASS FREQUENCIES FOR THREE ATTRIBUTES *A*, *B* AND *C***

	A		α		*Total*
	B	β	B	β	
C	(ABC)	$(A\beta C)$	(αBC)	$(\alpha\beta C)$	(C)
γ	$(AB\gamma)$	$(A\beta\gamma)$	$(\alpha B\gamma)$	$(\alpha\beta\gamma)$	(γ)
Total	(AB)	$(A\beta)$	(αB)	$(\alpha\beta)$	N

2. Since the class frequencies represent the number of units of the population, which possess the corresponding sets of attributes, none of them can be negative. Hence, *none of the class frequencies should be negative*.

3. Any class frequency of a higher order is always less than or equal to the class frequency of a lower order involving some of the attributes of the class frequency of higher order. Thus,

$(AB) \le (A)$; $(ABC) \le (AB)$; $(ABC) \le (BC)$, and so on.

The above remarks, in fact, are covered in § 19·4, Inconsistency of Data.

4. We have already stated that all the class frequencies can be expressed in terms of

(i) 2^n ultimate class frequencies.

(ii) 2^n positive class frequencies.

Hence, *in dichotomous classification of a population with respect to each of the n attributes, the total number of algebraically independent class frequencies is 2^n.*

Example 19·1. *Given the following ultimate class frequencies, obtain the remaining frequencies :*

$(AB)=471$, $(A\beta)=151$, $(\alpha B)=148$, $(\alpha\beta)=230.$

Solution. We have to find the frequencies : (A), (B), (α), (β) and N.

$(A)=(AB)+(A\beta)=471+151=622$; $(B)=(AB)+(\alpha B)=471+148=619$

$(\alpha)=(\alpha B)+(\alpha\beta)=148+230=378$; $(\beta)=(A\beta)+(\alpha\beta)=151+230=381$

$N=(A)+(\alpha)=622+378=1{,}000$ or $N=(B)+(\beta)=619+381=1{,}000$

Remark. The remaining frequencies can be conveniently obtained on completing the nine square table as given on page 19·5.

Attribute	A	α	Total
B	$(AB) = \mathbf{471}$	$(\alpha B) = \mathbf{148}$	$(B) = 471 + 148 = 619$
β	$(A\beta) = \mathbf{151}$	$(\alpha\beta) = \mathbf{230}$	$(\beta) = 151 + 230 = 381$
Total	$(A) = 471 + 151 = 622$	$(\alpha) = 148 + 230 = 378$	$N = 622 + 378 = 1{,}000$ or $N = 619 + 381 = 1{,}000$

Remark. The figures in the bold are the given figures. The remaining figures are obtained on appropriate additions as explained in the table.

Example 19·2. *From the following set of positive frequencies, obtain all other class frequencies.*

$$N = 64 \quad ; \quad (AB) = 9 \quad ; \quad (A) = 23 \quad ; \quad (B) = 13$$

Solution. We have :

$$(\alpha) = N - (A) = 64 - 23 = 41 \quad ; \quad (\beta) = N - (B) = 64 - 13 = 51$$
$$(A\beta) = (A) - (AB) = 23 - 9 = 14 \quad ; \quad (\alpha B) = (B) - (AB) = 13 - 9 = 4$$
$$(\alpha\beta) = N - (A) - (B) + (AB) = 64 - 23 - 13 + 9 = 37.$$

Aliter. Given the positive class frequencies, the remaining class frequencies can be very conveniently obtained on completing the nine square table, as given below.

Attribute	A	α	Total
B	$(AB) = \mathbf{9}$	$(\alpha B) = 13 - 9 = 4$	$(B) = \mathbf{13}$
β	$(A\beta) = 23 - 9 = 14$	$(\alpha\beta) = 51 - 14 = 37$	$(\beta) = 64 - 13 = 51$
Total	$(A) = \mathbf{23}$	$(\alpha) = 64 - 23 = 41$	$N = \mathbf{64}$

The figures in the bold are the given positive frequencies. The other frequencies are obtained on appropriate subtractions.

Example 19·3. *Given the following ultimate class frequencies, find the frequencies of positive classes.*

$$(ABC) = 156, \quad (AB\gamma) = 431, \quad (A\beta C) = 179, \quad (A\beta\gamma) = 852,$$
$$(\alpha BC) = 272, \quad (\alpha B\gamma) = 1{,}156, \quad (\alpha\beta C) = 163, \quad \text{and } (\alpha\beta\gamma) = 20{,}504,$$

Solution. The frequencies of positive classes are :

$$N, \quad (A), \quad (B), \quad (C), \quad (AB), \quad (AC), \quad (BC), \quad (ABC)$$

$$(A) = (ABC) + (AB\gamma) + (A\beta C) + (A\beta\gamma) = 156 + 431 + 179 + 852 = 1{,}618$$
$$(B) = (ABC) + (AB\gamma) + (\alpha BC) + (\alpha B\gamma) = 156 + 431 + 272 + 1{,}156 = 2{,}015$$
$$(C) = (ABC) + (A\beta C) + (\alpha BC) + (\alpha\beta C) = 156 + 179 + 272 + 163 = 770$$
$$(AB) = (ABC) + (AB\gamma) = 156 + 431 = 587$$
$$(AC) = (ABC) + (A\beta C) = 156 + 179 = 335$$
$$(BC) = (ABC) + (\alpha BC) = 156 + 272 = 428$$

and
$$N = [(ABC) + (AB\gamma) + (A\beta C) + (A\beta\gamma) + (\alpha BC) + (\alpha B\gamma) + (\alpha\beta C) + (\alpha\beta\gamma)]$$
$$= 156 + 431 + 179 + 852 + 272 + 1{,}156 + 163 + 20{,}504 = 23{,}713.$$

Example 19·4. *Given the following set of positive frequencies, find all the remaining class frequencies.*

$$N = 23713 \quad , \quad (A) = 1618 \quad , \quad (B) = 2015 \quad , \quad (C) = 770$$
$$(AB) = 587 \quad , \quad (AC) = 335 \quad , \quad (BC) = 428 \quad , \quad (ABC) = 156$$

Solution. For three attributes there are in all $3^3 = 27$, class frequencies out of which, we are given 8 class frequencies. The remaining $27 - 8 = 19$, class frequencies are obtained below.

Frequencies of Order 1 :

$$(\alpha) = N - (A) = 23713 - 1618 = 22095 \quad ; \quad (\beta) = N - (B) = 23713 - 2015 = 21698$$
$$(\gamma) = N - (C) = 23713 - 770 = 22943$$

Frequencies of Order 2 :

$$(A\beta) = (A) - (AB) = 1618 - 587 = 1031$$
$$(\alpha B) = (B) - (AB) = 2015 - 587 = 1428$$
$$(\alpha\beta) = (\alpha) - (\alpha B) = 22095 - 1428 = 20667$$
$$(A\gamma) = (A) - (AC) = 1618 - 335 = 1283$$
$$(\alpha C) = (C) - (AC) = 770 - 335 = 435$$
$$(\alpha\gamma) = (\alpha) - (\alpha C) = 22095 - 435 = 21660$$
$$(B\gamma) = (B) - (BC) = 2015 - 428 = 1587$$
$$(\beta C) = (C) - (BC) = 770 - 428 = 342$$
$$(\beta\gamma) = (\beta) - (\beta C) = 21698 - 342 = 21356$$

Frequencies of Order 3 :

$$(AB\gamma) = (AB) - (ABC) = 587 - 156 = 431$$
$$(A\beta C) = (AC) - (ABC) = 335 - 156 = 179$$
$$(A\beta\gamma) = (A\beta) - (A\beta C) = 1031 - 179 = 852$$
$$(\alpha BC) = (BC) - (ABC) = 428 - 156 = 272$$
$$(\alpha B\gamma) = (\alpha B) - (\alpha BC) = 1428 - 272 = 1156$$
$$(\alpha\beta C) = (\beta C) - (A\beta C) = 342 - 179 = 163$$
$$(\alpha\beta\gamma) = (\alpha\beta) - (\alpha\beta C) = 20667 - 163 = 20504$$

Example 19·5. *Two different measurements are made on 1,000 husbands and their wives. If measurements of husbands exceed the measurements of wives in 800 cases for the first measure, in 700 cases for the second measure and in 660 cases for both measures, in how many cases will both measures on wives will exceed the measures on husbands ?* *[Delhi Univ. B.A.(Econ. Hons.), 2000]*

Solution. Let us define the attributes :

A : Measurement of the husband exceeds the measurement of the wife for the first measure.

B : Measurement of the husband exceeds the measurement of the wife for the second measure.

Then α and β are the corresponding negative measures.

The given information can be summarised in the Table 19·4.

We are given : $N = 1,000$

TABLE 19·4

	A	α	*Total*
B	**660**	700 − 660 = 40	**700**
β	800 − 660 = 140	200 − 40 = 160	1000 − 700 = 300
Total	**800**	1000 − 800 = 200	**1000**

$(A) = 800, (B) = 700, (AB) = 660$ ...(*)

The number of cases in which both the measures on wives will exceed the measures on the husbands is given by :

$(\alpha\beta) = 160$ [From Table 19·4]

Note. The figures in bold are the given figures.

Hence, in 160 of the cases, both measures on wives will exceed the measures on husbands.

Aliter. *From* (*) *onwards.* The number of cases in which both the measures on wives will exceed the measures on husbands in given by :

$$(\alpha\beta) = N - (A) - (B) + (AB) = 1000 - 800 - 700 + 660 = 160$$

Example 19·6. *Show that for n attributes $A_1, A_2, A_3, \ldots, A_n$*

$$(A_1 A_2 A_3 \ldots A_n) \geq (A_1) + (A_2) + (A_3) + \ldots + (A_n) - (n-1)N \quad \ldots(19\cdot10)$$

Solution. Since the class frequencies must be non-negative, we have for two attributes A_1 and A_2.

$$(\alpha_1 \alpha_2) \geq 0 \Rightarrow N - (A_1) - (A_2) + (A_1 A_2) \geq 0 \Rightarrow (A_1 A_2) \geq (A_1) + (A_2) - N \quad \ldots(i)$$

Hence, the result (19·10) is true for $n = 2$.

Let us now suppose that (19·10) is true for $n = r$, say, so that

$$(A_1 A_2 \ldots A_{r-1} A_r) \geq (A_1) + (A_2) + \ldots + (A_{r-1}) + (A_r) - (r-1)N \quad \ldots(ii)$$

Replacing the attribute A_r by the compound attribute $A_r A_{r+1}$ in (*ii*), we get

$$(A_1 A_2 \ldots A_{r-1} A_r A_{r+1}) \geq (A_1) + (A_2) + \ldots + (A_{r-1}) + (A_r A_{r+1}) - (r-1)N$$

$$\Rightarrow \quad (A_1 A_2 \ldots A_{r-1} A_r A_{r+1}) \geq (A_1) + (A_2) + \ldots + (A_{r-1}) + [(A_r) + (A_{r+1}) - N] - (r-1)N$$

[Using (*i*)]

$$\Rightarrow \quad (A_1 A_2 \ldots A_{r-1} A_r A_{r+1}) \geq (A_1) + (A_2) + \ldots + (A_{r+1}) - rN \quad \ldots(iii)$$

Hence, if (19·10) is true for $n = r$, then it is also true for $n = r + 1$. But, we have proved in (*i*) that (19·10) is true for $n = 2$. Hence, it is true for $n = 2 + 1 = 3$; $n = 3 + 1 = 4$ and so on. Hence, by the principle of mathematical induction, (19·10) is true for all positive integer values of n.

Example 19·7. *In a very hotly fought battle, at least 80% of the combatants lost an eye, at least 70% lost an ear, at least 82% lost a leg and at least 78% lost an arm. At least how many lost all the four ?*

Solution. Let us denote by A, B, C and D the loss of an eye, an ear, a leg and an arm respectively by the combatants in the battle. If we assume that total number of combatants in the battle is 100, then in the usual notations, we are given :

$$N = 100, \quad (A) = 80, \quad (B) = 70, \quad (C) = 82, \quad (D) = 78 \quad \ldots(*)$$

Using the result in Example 19·6, we have :

$$(ABCD) \geq (A) + (B) + (C) + (D) - (4-1)N \Rightarrow (ABCD) \geq 80 + 70 + 82 + 78 - 3 \times 100 = 10$$

Hence, at least 10% of the combatants lost all the four organs.

Example 19·8. *In a war between red and white forces, there are more red soldiers than white, there are more armed white soldiers than unarmed reds; there are fewer armed reds with ammunition than unarmed whites without ammunition. Show that there are more armed reds without ammunition than unarmed whites with ammunition.*

Solution. Let us define the attributes :

A : White soldiers ; B : Armed soldiers ; C : Soldier with ammunition

α : Red soldiers ; β : Unarmed soldiers ; γ : Soldiers without ammunition

Then, in the usual notations, we are given :

$$(\alpha) > (A) \ \ldots(i) \ ; \quad (AB) > (\alpha\beta) \ \ldots(ii) \ ; \quad (\alpha BC) < (A\beta\gamma) \Rightarrow (A\beta\gamma) > (\alpha BC) \ \ldots(iii)$$

We have to show that $(\alpha B\gamma) > (A\beta C)$ ... (*iv*)

We have $(\alpha) > (A)$ [From (*i*)]

$\Rightarrow \quad (\alpha B) + (\alpha\beta) > (AB) + (A\beta)$

$\Rightarrow \quad (\alpha B) + (\alpha\beta) > (\alpha\beta) + (A\beta)$ [From (*ii*)]

$\Rightarrow \quad (\alpha B) > (A\beta)$ [Cancelling $(\alpha\beta)$ on both sides]

$\Rightarrow \quad (\alpha BC) + (\alpha B\gamma) > (A\beta C) + (A\beta\gamma)$

$\Rightarrow \quad (\alpha BC) + (\alpha B\gamma) > (A\beta C) + (\alpha BC)$ [From (*iii*)]

$\Rightarrow \quad (\alpha B\gamma) > (A\beta C)$, [Cancelling (αBC) on both sides]

which is the required result.

Example 19·9. *Show that if A occurs in a larger proportion of cases where B is than where B is not, then B will occur in a larger proportion of cases where A is than where A is not.*

Solution. We are given that $\dfrac{(AB)}{(B)} > \dfrac{(A\beta)}{(\beta)}$ ...(*i*)

and we have to prove $\dfrac{(AB)}{(A)} > \dfrac{(\alpha B)}{(\alpha)}$ ... (*ii*)

From (*i*), we get $\dfrac{(\beta)}{(A\beta)} > \dfrac{(B)}{(AB)}$ [Cross transposing]

Substracting 1 on each side, we get

$$\frac{(\beta)-(A\beta)}{(A\beta)} > \frac{(B)-(AB)}{(AB)} \Rightarrow \frac{(\alpha\beta)}{(A\beta)} > \frac{(\alpha B)}{(AB)} \Rightarrow \frac{(\alpha\beta)}{(\alpha B)} > \frac{(A\beta)}{(AB)} \quad \ldots(iii)$$

Adding 1 to both sides of (*iii*), we get

$$\frac{(\alpha\beta)+(\alpha B)}{(\alpha B)} > \frac{(A\beta)+(AB)}{(AB)} \Rightarrow \frac{(\alpha)}{(\alpha B)} > \frac{(A)}{(AB)} \Rightarrow \frac{(AB)}{(A)} > \frac{(\alpha B)}{(\alpha)}$$

EXERCISE 19·1

1. Define 'attribute' and discuss the importance of study of attributes.

2. Explain the following :

(*a*) Positive and negative attributes.

(*b*) Positive class frequencies.

(*c*) Ultimate class frequencies.

(*d*) Order of a class frequency.

3. What do you mean by class frequency of

(*i*) first order, (*ii*) second order, and (*iii*) third order ?

How would you express a class frequency of first order in terms of

(*a*) class frequencies of second order, and (*b*) class frequencies of third order ?

4. What is dichotomy ? Show that the continued dichotomy according to n attributes gives rise to 3^n classes.

5. In dichotomous classification of three attributes A, B and C, enumerate all the class frequencies of

(*i*) Zero order, (*ii*) First order, (*iii*) Second order, and (*iv*) Third order.

How many class frequencies are there in all ?

6. In dichotomous classification of n attributes, prove that :

(*a*) There are 2^n positive frequencies. ; (*b*) There are 2^n ultimate class frequencies.

7. Given the set of positive frequencies, explain how you will obtain all other class frequencies in dichotomous classification of (*a*) two attributes (*b*) three attributes.

8. Given the set of ultimate class frequencies, explain how you will obtain all other class frequencies in dichotomous classification of :

(*i*) Two attributes , (*ii*) Three attributes.

9. In dichotomous classification of n attributes, prove that the total number of linearly independent class frequencies is 2^n.

10. Given the following positive frequencies, obtain all other class frequencies :

(*i*) $N = 164$, $(A) = 90$, $(B) = 62$, $(AB) = 6$

(*ii*) $N = 200$, $(A) = 160$, $(B) = 79$, $(AB) = 69$

(*iii*) $N = 2500$, $(A) = 800$, $(B) = 1600$, $(AB) = 400$

Ans. (*i*) $(\alpha) = 74$, $(\beta) = 102$, $(A\beta) = 84$, $(\alpha B) = 56$, $(\alpha\beta) = 18$

(*ii*) $(\alpha) = 40$, $(\beta) = 121$, $(A\beta) = 91$, $(\alpha B) = 10$, $(\alpha\beta) = 30$

(*iii*) $(\alpha) = 1700$, $(\beta) = 900$, $(A\beta) = 400$, $(\alpha B) = 1200$, $(\alpha\beta) = 500$

11. Given the following ultimate class frequencies, obtain all other class frequencies.

(*i*) $(AB) = 47$, $(A\beta) = 63$, $(\alpha B) = 53$, $(\alpha\beta) = 77$

(*ii*) $(AB) = 83$, $(\alpha B) = 57$, $(A\beta) = 45$, $(\alpha\beta) = 68$

Ans. (*i*) $(A) = 110$, $(\alpha) = 130$, $(B) = 100$, $(\beta) = 140$, $N = 240$

(*ii*) $(A) = 128$, $(\alpha) = 125$, $(B) = 140$, $(\beta) = 113$, $N = 253$

12. Given the following ultimate frequencies, find the frequencies of the positive classes including the total number of observations N :

$(ABC) = 75$, $(\alpha BC) = 98$, $(AB\gamma) = 310$, $(\alpha B\gamma) = 702$,

$(A\beta C) = 106$, $(\alpha\beta C) = 74$, $(A\beta\gamma) = 489$, $(\alpha\beta\gamma) = 8415$.

Ans. $N = 10269$, $(A) = 980$, $(B) = 1185$, $(C) = 353$,
$(AB) = 385$, $(AC) = 181$, $(BC) = 173$, $(ABC) = 75$.

13. (*a*) Given the following positive frequencies, obtain all the ultimate class frequencies.

$N = 12000$, $(A) = 977$, $(B) = 1185$, $(C) = 596$,
$(AB) = 453$, $(AC) = 284$, $(BC) = 250$, $(ABC) = 127$

Ans. $(ABC) = 127$, $(\alpha BC) = 123$, $(AB\gamma) = 326$, $(\alpha B\gamma) = 609$,
$(A\beta C) = 157$, $(\alpha\beta C) = 189$, $(A\beta\gamma) = 367$, $(\alpha\beta\gamma) = 10102$.

(*b*) From the following given frequencies, find out all the remaining class frequencies:

$N = 1000$, $(A) = 88$, $(B) = 109$, $(C) = 28$
$(AB) = 34$, $(AC) = 14$, $(BC) = 13$, $(ABC) = 6$

[*Punjab Univ. B.Com. Oct. 2000*]

14. At a competitive examination at which 600 graduates appeared, boys outnumbered girls by 96. Those qualifying for interview exceeded in number those failing to qualify by 310. The number of Science graduate boys interviewed was 300 while among the Arts graduate girls there were 25 who failed to qualify for interview. Altogether there were only 135 Arts graduates and 33 among them failed to qualify. Boys who failed to qualify numbered 18.

Find (*i*) the number of boys who qualified for interview,
(*ii*) the total number of Science graduate boys appearing , and
(*iii*) the number of Science graduate girls who qualified. [*Sri Venkateshwara Univ. M.Com., 2005*]

Ans. A : Boys ; B : Qualifying for interview ; C : Offering Science.

(*i*) (AB) = 330 ; (*ii*) (AC) = 310 ; (*iii*) (αBC) = 53

15. 100 children took three examinations *A*, *B* and *C* ; 40 passed the first, 39 passed the second and 48 passed the third, 10 passed all the three, 21 failed all three, 9 passed the first two and failed the third, 19 failed the first two and passed the third. Find how many children passed at least two examinations. Show that for the question asked certain of the given frequencies are not necessary. Which are they ?

Ans. 38. Only frequencies required are (C), $(\alpha\beta C)$, $(AB\gamma)$.

16. A college submitted the following returns to the university office :

Number of students appearing in all the three tests	= 350
Number of students passing the first test	= 125
Number of students passing the second test	= 135
Number of students passing the third test	= 145
Number of students passing all the three tests	= 20
Number of students failing in all the three tests	= 75
Number of students passing the first two but failing in the third	= 25
Number of students failing in the first two but passing in the third	= 60

From the information given above, find out the number of students passing at least two tests.

Ans. 110.

17. (*a*) In a university examination 65% of the candidates passed in English, 90% passed in the second language and 60% passed in the optional subjects. Find how many at least should have passed the whole examination.

Ans. 15%. **Hint.** Use Example 19·6.

(*b*) In a university examination, which was indeed very tough, 50% at least failed in Statistics, 75% at least in Mathematics, 82% at least in Accountancy and 96% at least in Finance. How many at least failed in all the four ?

Hint : (*a*) and (*b*) : Use Example 19·6.

Ans. (*a*) 15%. (*b*) 3%.

18. A social survey in a village revealed that there were more uneducated employed males than educated ones, there were more educated employed males than uneducated unemployed males. There were more educated unemployed under 35 years of age than employed uneducated males over 35 years of age. Show that there are more uneducated employed males under 35 years of age than educated unemployed males over 35 years of age.

19. In a certain class it was found that 60% of the students passed in the terminal examination, 40% passed in the terminal and annual examinations, 25% passed in the annual but failed in the terminal examination. Find. the percentage of students who

(*i*) passed in the annual examination,
(*ii*) passed in the terminal examination but failed in the annual examination,

(*iii*) failed in both the examinations. [*Delhi Univ. B.A. (Econ. Hons.), 2000*]

Ans. (*i*) 65%, (*ii*) 20%, (*iii*) 15%.

20. In a free vote in the House of Commons, 600 members voted. 300 Government members representing English constituencies (including Welsh) voted in favour of the motion. 25 opposition members representing Scottish constituencies voted against the motion. The Government majority among those who voted was 96; 135 of the members voting represented Scottish constituencies. 18 Government members voted against the motion, 102 Scottish members voted in favour of the motion. The motion was carried by 310 votes. Analyse the voting according to the nationality of constituencies and party.

Hint. Define the attributes :

A : Government members ; α : Opposition members

B : Voting for the motion ; β : Voting against the motion

C : English constituencies ; γ : Scottish constituencies

Then we are given : $N = (A) + (\alpha) = (B) + (\beta) = 600$, $(ABC) = 300$, $(\alpha\beta\gamma) = 25$.

$(A) - (\alpha) = 96$; $(\gamma) = 135$, $(A\beta) = 18$, $(B\gamma) = 102$, $(B) - (\beta) = 310$

Ans. $(A) = 348$, $(\alpha) = 252$, $(B) = 455$, $(\beta) = 145$, $(C) = 465$,

$(\gamma) = 135$, $(AB) = 330$, $(AC) = 310$, $(BC) = 353$, $(A\beta) = 18$,

$(A\gamma) = 38$, $(B\gamma) = 102$,

$(\alpha B) = 125$, $(\alpha C) = 155$, $(\beta C) = 112$, $(\alpha\beta) = 127$, $(\alpha\gamma) = 97$,

$(\beta\gamma) = 33$, $(ABC) = 300$, $(AB\gamma) = 30$, $(A\beta C) = 10$, $(A\beta\gamma) = 8$

$(\alpha BC) = 53$, $(\alpha B\gamma) = 72$, $(\alpha\beta C) = 102$, $(\alpha\beta\gamma) = 25$.

19·4. INCONSISTENCY OF DATA

The class frequencies observed within one and the same population are said to be consistent if they are in conformity with each other and do not conflict with each other in any way. *The given set of class frequencies is said to be consistent if none of them is negative, otherwise it is said to be inconsistent.*

Since any class frequency can be expressed as the sum of some of the ultimate class frequencies, it is necessarily non-negative if all the ultimate class frequencies are non-negative. This provides a criterion for testing the consistency of the data, which is stated below.

"*The necessary and sufficient condition for the consistency of a set of independent class frequencies is that no ultimate class frequency is negative.*" ...(19·11)

Hence, the most convenient way of testing the consistency of the given data is to find all the ultimate class frequencies. If any one of them comes out to be negative, the data are said to be inconsistent, otherwise it is said to be consistent.

Remark. It should be clearly understand that the consistency of the data is no proof of the accuracy of counting or calculations. However, inconsistency of the data always implies that threre is some mistake or error in the given information (data) and as such the data are not suitable for further treatment. Such inconsistency may be due to wrong or inaccurate calculations or the error in transcription. Such (inconsistent) information should be rectified if possible, otherwise rejected.

19·4·1. Conditions for Consistency of Data. Criteria for consistency of class frequencies are obtained by using the result in (19·11). For a single attribute A we have conditions of consistency as follows :

$$\left.\begin{array}{l}(i)\ (A) \geq 0\\ (ii)\ (\alpha) \geq 0 \quad \Rightarrow \quad (A) \leq N\end{array}\right\} \qquad \ldots(19\cdot12)$$

For two attributes A and B, the conditions of consistency are :

$$\left.\begin{array}{llll}(i) & (AB) \geq 0 & & \\ (ii) & (A\beta) \geq 0 \Rightarrow & (A) - (AB) \geq 0 & \Rightarrow (AB) \leq (A)\\ (iii) & (\alpha B) \geq 0 \Rightarrow & (B) - (AB) \geq 0 & \Rightarrow (AB) \leq (B)\\ (iv) & (\alpha\beta) \geq 0 \Rightarrow & N + (AB) - (A) - (B) \geq 0 & \Rightarrow (AB) \geq (A) + (B) - N\end{array}\right\} \qquad \ldots(19\cdot13)$$

Conditions of consistency for three attributes *A*, *B* and *C* are :

$$\left.\begin{array}{llll} (i) & (ABC) \geq 0 & & \\ (ii) & (AB\gamma) \geq 0 & \Rightarrow (AB)-(ABC) \geq 0 & \Rightarrow (ABC) \leq (AB) \\ (iii) & (A\beta C) \geq 0 & \Rightarrow (AC)-(ABC) \geq 0 & \Rightarrow (ABC) \leq (AC) \\ (iv) & (\alpha BC) \geq 0 & \Rightarrow (BC)-(ABC) \geq 0 & \Rightarrow (ABC) \leq (BC) \\ (v) & (A\beta\gamma) \geq 0 & \Rightarrow (A)-(AB)-(AC)+(ABC) \geq 0 & \\ & & \Rightarrow & (ABC) \geq (AB)+(AC)-(A) \\ (vi) & (\alpha B\gamma) \geq 0 & \Rightarrow (ABC) \geq (AB)+(BC)-(B) & \\ (vii) & (\alpha\beta C) \geq 0 & \Rightarrow (ABC) \geq (AC)+(BC)-(C) & \\ (viii) & (\alpha\beta\gamma) \geq 0 & \Rightarrow (ABC) \leq (AB)+(BC)+(AC)-(A)-(B)-(C)+N & \end{array}\right\} \quad ...(19\cdot14)$$

(*i*) and (*viii*) in (19·14) give :

$$\left.\begin{array}{ll} & (AB)+(BC)+(AC) \geq (A)+(B)+(C)-(N) \\ \text{Similarly,} & \\ (ii) \text{ and } (vii) & \Rightarrow (AC)+(BC)-(AB) \leq (C) \\ (iii) \text{ and } (vi) & \Rightarrow (AB)+(BC)-(AC) \leq (B) \\ (iv) \text{ and } (v) & \Rightarrow (AB)+(AC)-(BC) \leq (A) \end{array}\right\} \quad ...(19\cdot15)$$

19·4·2. Incomplete Data. We have pointed out in Remark 4 to § 19·3·4 that in dichotomous classification of a population with respect to each of the n attributes, there are 2^n algebraically independent class frequencies.

The remaining ($3^n - 2^n$) class frequencies can be obtained easily from :

(*i*) The set of 2^n ultimate class frequencies or

(*ii*) The set of 2^n positive frequencies.

If the date are incomplete *i.e.*, if one or more of the ultimate class frequencies are not known, or one or more of the positive frequencies are not known, then we cannot determine all the class frequencies. In such cases, (of incomplete data), the conditions of consistency obtained in (19·12) to (19·15), enable us to obtain the maximum or/and minimum limits for the missing class frequencies. For illustration, see Examples 19·12 and 19·14.

Example 19·10. *Given* $N = 2000$, $(A) = 1500$, $(B) = 100$ *and* $(AB) = 350$, *test the consistency of the data.* (*Punjab Univ. B.Com., Oct. 1998*)

Solution. We are given : $N = 2000$, $(A) = 1500$, $(B) = 100$, and $(AB) = 350$

To test the consistency of the data, we will find the ultimate class frequencies *viz*., (αB), $(A\beta)$ and $(\alpha\beta)$.

$$(\alpha B) = (B) - (AB) = 100 - 350 = -250.$$

Since $(\alpha B) < 0$ *i.e.*, negative, the given data are inconsistent.

Example 19·11. *In a report on consumer preference, it was given that out of 500 persons surveyed, 400 preferred variety A, 380 preferred variety B and 270 liked both A and B. Are the data consistent ?*

[*Delhi Univ. B.A. (Econ. Hons.), 1993*]

Solution. In the usual notations, we are given $N = 500$, $(A) = 400$, $(B) = 380$, $(AB) = 270$ ...(*)

$$(\alpha\beta) = N - (A) - (B) + (AB)$$
$$= 500 - 400 - 380 + 270 = 770 - 780 = -10$$

Since each frequency has to be positive, therefore, the given data are inconsistent.

Aliter. *From* (*) *onwards.* Using (*i*), the frequencies of other attributes can be obtained as given in the following table.

	A	α	*Total*
B	270	$380 - 270 = 110$	$(B) = 380$
β	$400 - 270 = 130$	$100 - 110 = -10$	$(\beta) = 500 - 380 = 120$
Total	$(A) = 400$	$(\alpha) = 500 - 400 = 100$	$N = 500$

Since $(\alpha\beta) = -10 < 0$, the given data are inconsistent.

Example 19·12. *In a village actually invaded by anthrax, 65% of the goats were attacked and 90% have been inoculated with vaccine. What is the lowest percentage of the inoculated goats that must have been attacked.*

Solution. Let us define the attributes :

A : Goats attacked by anthrax and B : Goats inoculated with vaccine.

Assuming that there are 100 goats in the village, we have, in the usual notations :

$$N = 100, \quad (A) = 65, \quad \text{and} \quad (B) = 90 \qquad \ldots(*)$$

We want the lower limit for (AB).

Since no class frequency can be negative, we have :

$$(\alpha\beta) \geq 0 \quad \Rightarrow \quad N - (A) - (B) + (AB) \geq 0 \quad \Rightarrow \quad (AB) \geq (A) + (B) - N \qquad \ldots(**)$$

From (*) and (**), we get $\quad (AB) \geq 65 + 90 - 100 = 55$

Hence, the lowest percentage of the inoculated goats that must have been attacked is

$$\frac{(AB)}{(B)} \times 100 = \frac{55}{90} \times 100 = 61{\cdot}11 \quad \textit{i.e.,}\ 61{\cdot}11\%.$$

Example 19·13. *Show that if*

$$\frac{(A)}{N} = x, \quad \frac{(B)}{N} = 2x, \quad \frac{(C)}{N} = 3x \quad \text{and} \quad \frac{(AB)}{N} = \frac{(BC)}{N} = \frac{(CA)}{N} = y,$$

then the value of neither x nor y can exceed 1/4.

Solution. We are given :

$$\frac{(A)}{N} = x, \quad \frac{(B)}{N} = 2x, \quad \frac{(C)}{N} = 3x \quad \Rightarrow \quad (A) = Nx, \quad (B) = 2Nx, \quad (C) = 3Nx \quad \ldots(i)$$

$$\frac{(AB)}{N} = \frac{(BC)}{N} = \frac{(CA)}{N} = y \quad \Rightarrow \quad (AB) = (BC) = (CA) = Ny \qquad \ldots(ii)$$

By the conditions of consistency, we have :

$$(AB) \leq (A) \quad \Rightarrow \quad Ny \leq Nx \quad \Rightarrow \quad y \leq x \qquad \text{[From (i) and (ii)]} \qquad \ldots(iii)$$

Also $(BC) \geq (B) + (C) - N \quad \Rightarrow Ny \geq N(2x + 3x) - N \quad \Rightarrow \quad y \geq 5x - 1$ [From (*i*) and (*ii*)] ...(*iv*)

From (*iv*) and (*iii*), we get $\quad 5x - 1 \leq y \quad \Rightarrow \quad 5x - 1 \leq x \quad \Rightarrow \quad 4x \leq 1 \quad \Rightarrow \quad x \leq \frac{1}{4} \qquad \ldots(v)$

From (*iii*) and (*v*), we get $\; y \leq x \leq \frac{1}{4}$, as required.

Example 19·14. *Given that* $(A) = (B) = (C) = \frac{N}{2}$, *and 80% of A's are B's, 75% of A's are C's, find the limits of the percentage of B's that are C's.*

Solution. We are given :

$$(A) = (B) = (C) = \frac{N}{2} \qquad \ldots(i)$$

$$80\% \text{ of } A\text{'s are } B\text{'s} \quad \Rightarrow \quad (AB) = 80\% \text{ of } (A) = 0.8 \times \frac{N}{2} = 0.4\,N \qquad \ldots(ii)$$

and

$$75\% \text{ of } A\text{'s are } C\text{'s} \quad \Rightarrow \quad (AC) = 75\% \text{ of } (C) = \frac{0.75N}{2} \qquad \ldots(iii)$$

We have to find the limits for the percentage of $\frac{(BC)}{(B)} = \frac{2(BC)}{N}$

Note that $\quad (BC) \le (B) \quad \Rightarrow \quad 0 \le \frac{(BC)}{(B)} = \frac{2(BC)}{N} \le 1$ ...(iv)

The conditions of consistency for three attributes A, B and C are :

$$(AB) + (AC) - (BC) \le (A) \quad ...(v)$$

$$(AB) + (BC) - (AC) \le (B) \quad ...(vi)$$

$$(AC) + (BC) - (AB) \le (C) \quad ...(vii)$$

and $$(AB) + (AC) + (BC) - (A) - (B) - (C) + N \ge 0 \quad ...(viii)$$

On using (*i*), (*ii*) and (*iii*), we get from (*v*) and (*vi*) respectively :

$$0.4N + \frac{0.75}{2}N - (BC) \le \frac{N}{2}$$

$$\Rightarrow \quad 0.80 + 0.75 - \frac{2(BC)}{N} \le 1$$

$$\Rightarrow \quad 0.80 + 0.75 - 1 \le \frac{2(BC)}{N}$$

$$\Rightarrow \quad \frac{2(BC)}{N} \ge 0.55 \quad ...(ix)$$

$$0.4N + (BC) - \frac{0.75}{2}N \le \frac{N}{2}$$

$$\Rightarrow \quad 0.80 + \frac{2(BC)}{N} - 0.75 \le 1$$

$$\Rightarrow \quad \frac{2(BC)}{N} + 0.05 \le 1$$

$$\Rightarrow \quad \frac{2(BC)}{N} \le 0.95 \quad ...(x)$$

Similarly, from (*vii*) and (*viii*), we will get, on simplification (Try it) :

$\frac{2(BC)}{N} \le 1.05$ and $\frac{2(BC)}{N} \ge -0.55$ respectively, both of which give inconsistent results [See (*iv*)].

Hence, from (*ix*) and (*x*), we get

$$\frac{(BC)}{(B)} \ge 0.55 \quad \text{and} \quad \frac{(BC)}{(B)} \le 0.95 \quad \Rightarrow \quad 0.55 \le \frac{(BC)}{(B)} \le 0.95$$

i.e., the percentage of B's that are C's lies between 55% and 95%.

Example 19·15. *Show that if all A's are B's, and no B's are C's, then no A's are C's.*

Solution. We are given :

$$\left.\begin{array}{lll} \text{All } A\text{'s are } B\text{'s} & \Rightarrow & (AB) = (A) \\ \text{No } B\text{'s are } C\text{'s} & \Rightarrow & (BC) = 0 \end{array}\right\} \quad ...(*)$$

We have to prove that $(AC) = 0$

We have $$(AB) + (AC) - (BC) \le (A)$$

$$\Rightarrow \quad (A) + (AC) - 0 \le (A) \quad \text{[From (*)]}$$

$$\Rightarrow \quad (AC) \le 0 \quad ...(**)$$

Since no class frequency can be negative, $\quad (AC) \ge 0$ ...(***)

From (**) and (***), we get $(AC) = 0$, as required.

EXERCISE 19·2

1. What do you understand by consistency of given data ? How do you check it.

2. "A consistent data is always correct". Comment.

3. State the necessary and sufficient condition for the consistency of a given set of class frequencies.

4. In dichotomous classification of two attributes A and B, obtain the conditions for the consistency of class frequencies.

5. In dichotomous classification of three attributes A, B and C, obtain the conditions for the consistency of the class frequencies.

6. Test the consistency of the following data :

(i)	$(A) = 28$,	$(B) = 25$,	$(AB) = 30$,	$N = 50$
(ii)	$(A) = 150$,	$(B) = 300$,	$(AB) = 200$,	$N = 1{,}000$
(iii)	$N = 280$,	$(A) = 250$,	$(B) = 85$,	$(AB) = 35$

Ans. (i) Inconsistent, since $(\alpha B) < 0$; (ii) Inconsistent, since $(A\beta) < 0$; (iii) Inconsistent, since $(\alpha\beta) < 0$.

7. Are the following data consistent :

(i) $N = 100$; $(A) = 60$; $(B) = 42$; $(C) = 50$;
$(ABC) = 10$; $(A\gamma\beta) = 15$; $(AC\beta) = 13$; $(\alpha\gamma B) = 12$.

(ii) $N = 1{,}000$, $(A\beta) = 483$, $(A\gamma) = 378$, $(B\gamma) = 226$
$(A) = 525$, $(B) = 312$, $(C) = 470$ and $(ABC) = 25$.

(iii) $(AB) = 75$, $(BC) = 48$, $(B) = 40$, $(ABC) = 55$

Ans. (i) Inconsistent, since $(\alpha BC) < 0$;
(ii) Inconsistent, since $(\alpha\beta\gamma) < 0$;
(iii) Inconsistent, since $(ABC) > (BC)$ or $(\alpha BC) < 0$.

8. The following summary appears in a report on a survey covering 1,000 fields. Scrutinize the data and point out if there is any mistake or misprint in them.

Manured fields	510
Irrigated fields	490
Fields growing improved varieties	427
Fields both irrigated and manured	189
Fields both manured and growing improved varieties	140
Fields both irrigated and growing improved varieties	85

Hint. Let A : manured fields, B : Irrigated fields, C : Growing improved varieties. Then $(\alpha\beta\gamma) < 0$. Inconsistent.

9. The following information was provided by an investigator who interviewed 1,000 students. 811 read Hindustan Times, 752 read Statesman and 418 read Times of India: 570 read Hindustan Times and Statesman, 356 read Hindustan Times and Times of India, and 348 read Statesman and Times of India, 297 read all the three. Is there any inconsistency in the above information ? *[Utkal Univ. M.Com. 2006]*

Ans. Inconsistent, since $(\alpha\beta\gamma) < 0$.

10. If a report gives the following frequencies as actually observed, show that there must be a misprint or mistake of some sort, and possibly the misprint consists in the dropping of 1 before 85 given as the frequency of (BC).

$N = 1000$, $(A) = 510$, $(B) = 490$, $(C) = 427$, $(AB) = 189$, $(AC) = 140$, $(BC) = 85$.

Hint. $(\alpha\beta\gamma) \ge 0 \Rightarrow N - (A) - (B) - (C) + (AB) + (BC) + (AC) \ge (ABC) \ge 0$

$\Rightarrow (BC) \ge (A) + (B) + (C) - (AB) - (AC) - N = 98.$

11. If $(A) = 50$, $(B) = 60$, $(C) = 50$, $(A\beta) = 5$, $(A\gamma) = 20$, $N = 100$, find the greatest and the least possible values of (BC) so that the data may be consistent.

Ans. $25 \le (BC) \le 45$.

12. Given that $(A) = (B) = (C) = \frac{N}{2}$ and 80 per cent of A's are B's, 75 per cent of A's are C's, find the limits to the percentage of B's that are C's.

Ans. 55% and 95%.

13. A market investigator returns the following data. Of 1,000 people consulted 811 liked chocolates, 752 liked toffees and 418 liked boiled sweets, 570 liked both chocolates and toffees 356 liked chocolates and boiled sweets, and 348 liked toffees and boiled sweets; 297 liked all three. Show that this information as it stands must be incorrect.

Hint. $(\alpha\beta\gamma) = -4$; Inconsistent

14. 1000 persons of *UK* were interviewed by an investigator to find the nationality of the music they liked. The following data were obtained :

570 liked English, 650 liked French, 480 liked German, 440 liked English and French, 360 liked French and German, 240 liked English and German, 125 liked all three.

Show that the information as it stands must be incorrect.

Hint. Let *A, B, C* denote the attributes that persons like music of English, French and German nationality respectively.

Use condition of consistency : $(ABC) \geq (AB) + (BC) - (B)$ or $(\alpha \beta \gamma) \geq 0$.

15. A survey was conducted to study the preference of consumers of cold drinks (Coca-cola, Gold Sport and Pepsi). 50 consumers were contacted in all and the following results obtained : 200 liked Coca-Cola; 145 liked Gold Sport; 240 liked Pepsi; 190 liked Coca-Cola and Gold Spot; 175 liked Coca-Cola and Pepsi; 185 liked Gold Spot and Pepsi.

Show that the information as it standards must be incorrect. [*Panjab Univ. M.A. (Econ.), April 1999*]

16. Three aptitude tests *A, B, C* were given to 200 apprentice trainees. From amongst them 80 passed test *A*, 78 passed test *B* and 96 passed the third test. While 20 passed all the three tests, 42 failed all the three, 18 passed *A* and *B* but failed *C* and 38 failed *A* and *B* but passed the third. Determine how many trainees passed at least two of the three tests.

Ans. 76

17. A coin is tossed three times and the results, heads and tails noted. The process is continued until there are 100 sets of threes. In 69 cases, heads fell first, in 49 cases, heads fell second and in 53 cases heads fell third. In 33 cases heads fell both first and second, and in 21 cases heads fell both second and third. Show that (*i*) there must have been at least five occasions on which heads fell three times and that (*ii*) there could not have been more than 15 occasions on which tails fell three times, though there need not have been any.

Hint. Given : $N = 100$, $(A) = 69$, $(B) = 49$, $(C) = 53$, $(AB) = 33$, $(BC) = 21$

Use : $(ABC) \geq (AB) + (BC) - (B)$ and $(\alpha \beta \gamma) \leq (\alpha \beta) = 15$ or $(\alpha \beta \gamma) \leq (\beta \gamma) = 19$

18. In a school, 50 per cent of the students are boys, 60 per cent are Hindus and 50 per cent are 10 years of age or over. Twenty per cent of the boys are not Hindus and 40 per cent of the boys are under 10. What conclusions can you draw in regard to percentage of Hindu students of 10 years or over ?

Ans. Between 20 and 50.

19. Among the adult population of a certain town 50 per cent are males, 60 per cent are wage-earners and 50 per cent are 45 years of age or over. 10 per cent of the males are not wage-earners and 40 per cent of the males are under 45. Make the best possible inference about the limits within which the percentage of persons (male or female) of 45 years or over are wage-earners.

Ans. Between 25% and 45%.

20. Show that :

(*a*) If all *A*'s are *B*'s and all *B*'s are *C*'s, then all *A*'s are *C*'s.

(*b*) If all *A*'s are *B*'s and no *B*'s are *C*'s, then no *A*'s are *C*'s.

19·5. INDEPENDENCE OF ATTRIBUTES

Two attributes are said to be independent if there does not exist any kind of relationship between them.

19·5·1. Criteria of Independence of Two Attributes.

Criterion 1. Proportion Method. In this method, we compare the presence or absence of a given attribute in the other. If two attributes *A* and *B* are independent, then we would expect :

(*a*) The same proportion of *A*'s amongst *B*'s as amongst β's.

(*b*) The same proportion of *B*'s amongst *A*'s as amongst α's.

For example, if the attributes 'Intelligence' and 'Beauty', are independent, then the proportion of intelligent persons among beautiful and non-beautiful persons must be same or conversely, the proportion of beautiful persons amongst intelligent and un-intelligent persons must be same.

Symbolically, if attributes A and B are independent, the criterion in (a) and (b) respectively imply that :

$$\frac{(AB)}{(B)}=\frac{(A\beta)}{(\beta)} \quad ...(19\cdot16) \qquad\qquad \frac{(AB)}{(A)}=\frac{(\alpha B)}{(\alpha)} \quad ...(19\cdot17)$$

$$\Rightarrow \quad 1-\frac{(AB)}{(B)}=1-\frac{(A\beta)}{(\beta)} \qquad\qquad \Rightarrow \quad 1-\frac{(AB)}{(A)}=1-\frac{(\alpha B)}{(\alpha)}$$

$$\Rightarrow \quad \frac{(B)-(AB)}{(B)}=\frac{(\beta)-(A\beta)}{(\beta)} \qquad\qquad \Rightarrow \quad \frac{(A)-(AB)}{(A)}=\frac{(\alpha)-(\alpha B)}{(\alpha)}$$

$$\Rightarrow \quad \frac{(\alpha B)}{(B)}=\frac{(\alpha\beta)}{(\beta)} \quad ...(19\cdot18) \qquad \Rightarrow \quad \frac{(A\beta)}{(A)}=\frac{(\alpha\beta)}{(\alpha)} \quad ...(19\cdot19)$$

Remarks 1. We know that if $\frac{a}{b}=\frac{c}{d}$, then each of the ratios is equal to $\frac{a+c}{b+d}$ or $\frac{a-c}{b-d}$ *i.e.,*

$$\frac{a}{b}=\frac{c}{d} \quad \Rightarrow \quad \frac{a}{b}=\frac{c}{d}=\frac{a+c}{b+d}=\frac{a-c}{b-d} \quad ...(*)$$

From (19·16) and (*), we get

$$\frac{(AB)}{(B)}=\frac{(A\beta)}{(\beta)}=\frac{(AB)+(A\beta)}{(B)+(\beta)}=\frac{(A)}{N} \quad ...(19\cdot20)$$

which is same as (19·18).

2. In fact (19·16) $\Rightarrow$ (19·17) *i.e.,* the Criterion (a) $\Rightarrow$ Criterion (b), as explained below.

Rewriting (19·20) and using (*), we get :

$$\frac{(AB)}{(A)}=\frac{(B)}{N}=\frac{(B)-(AB)}{N-(A)}=\frac{(\alpha B)}{(\alpha)}, \text{ which is same as (19·17).}$$

3. (19·16) to (19·19) imply that if A and B are independent then (α and B), (A and β), and (α and β) are also independent.

Criterion 2. This criterion of independence of attributes is based on the ultimate class frequencies in terms of the frequencies of the first order.

Rewriting (19·20), we get :

$$(AB)=\frac{(A)\times(B)}{N} \quad \Rightarrow \quad \frac{(AB)}{N}=\frac{(A)}{N}\cdot\frac{(B)}{N} \quad ...(19\cdot21)$$

which leads to the following fundamental rule :

"If the attributes A and B are independent, the proportion of AB's in the population is equal to the product of the proportion of A's and proportion of B's in the population."

Criterion 3. This criterion of independence of two attributes is based on the class frequencies of second order.

If A and B are independent, then by Criterion 1, we have :

$$\frac{(AB)}{(B)}=\frac{(A\beta)}{(\beta)} \quad \text{and} \quad \frac{(\alpha B)}{(B)}=\frac{(\alpha\beta)}{(\beta)} \qquad \text{[From (19·16) and (19·18)]}$$

Dividing these equations, we get

$$\frac{(AB)}{(\alpha B)}=\frac{(A\beta)}{(\alpha\beta)} \quad \Rightarrow \quad (AB)(\alpha\beta)=(A\beta)(\alpha B) \quad ...(19\cdot22)$$

Aliter. If A and B are independent, then (A and β), (α and B), and (α and β) are also independent. Hence, using the Criterion 2 in (19·21), we get

$$(AB).(\alpha\beta)=\frac{(A).(B)}{N}\cdot\frac{(\alpha).(\beta)}{N}=\frac{(A)(\beta)}{N}\cdot\frac{(\alpha).(B)}{N}=(A\beta).(\alpha B),$$

a result obtained in (19·22).

Symbol $(AB)_0$ and (δ). Let $(AB)_0$ denote the expected value of the class frequency (AB) under the hypothesis that the attributes A and B are independent so that

$$(AB)_0 = \frac{(A).(B)}{N} \qquad \ldots(19\cdot23)$$

Let $$\delta = (AB) - (AB)_0 \qquad \ldots(19\cdot24)$$

$$\therefore \quad \delta = (AB) - \frac{(A)(B)}{N} = \frac{1}{N}\left[N(AB) - (A)(B)\right]$$

$$= \frac{1}{N}\left[\left\{(AB) + (A\beta) + (\alpha B) + (\alpha\beta)\right\}(AB) - \left\{(AB) + (A\beta)\right\}\left\{(AB) + (\alpha B)\right\}\right]$$

$$= \frac{1}{N}\left[(AB)(\alpha\beta) - (A\beta)(\alpha B)\right] \quad \text{(On simplification)} \qquad \ldots(19\cdot25)$$

Hence, on using (19·22), we get

$\delta = 0$, *if and only if the attributes A and B are independent.*

Example 19·16. *In a sample of 1,000 individuals, 100 possess the attribute A and 300 possess attribute B. A and B are independent. How many individuals possess both A and B, and how many possess neither ?*

[*Delhi Univ. B.A. (Econ. Hons.), 1999*]

Solution. In the usual notations, we are given : $(A) = 100$; $(B) = 300$; $N = 1{,}000$ ...(*i*)

$\therefore \quad (\alpha) = N - (A) = 1{,}000 - 100 = 900$; $(\beta) = N - (B) = 1{,}000 - 300 = 700$ ...(*ii*)

Since A and B are independent, we have $(AB) = \dfrac{(A)\times(B)}{N} = \dfrac{100\times300}{1{,}000} = 30$ [From (*i*)] ...(*iii*)

Hence, the number of persons who possess both the attributes A and B is 30.

Since A and B are independent, α and β are also independent.

$$\therefore \quad (\alpha\beta) = \frac{(\alpha)\times(\beta)}{N} = \frac{900\times700}{1{,}000} = 630$$

Hence, the number of persons who possess neither of the attributes A and B is 630.

Aliter. From (*iii*) onwards, for $(\alpha\beta)$. $(\alpha\beta) = N - (A) - (B) + (AB) = 1{,}000 - 100 - 300 + 30 = 630.$

OR Using (*i*), (*ii*) and (*iii*), the remaining class frequencies can be obtained as given in the 2 × 2 contingency Table 19·5.

TABLE 19·5

	A	α	
B	30	300 − 30 = 270	$(B) = 300$
β	100 − 30 = 70	700 − 70 = 630	1000 − 300 = 700
	$(A) = 100$	1,000 − 100 = 900	$N = 1{,}000$

$\therefore \quad (\alpha\beta) = 630$

Hence, the number of persons who possess none of the attributes A and B is 630.

Example 19·17. *In an analysis of two attributes, if* :

$N = 160$, $(A) = 96$ and $(B) = 50$, find the frequencies of the remaining classes on the assumption that A and B are independent. [*Delhi Univ. B.A. (Econ.) Hons., 1997*]

Solution. Since the attributes A and B are independent (Given),

$$\therefore \quad (AB) = \frac{(A)\times(B)}{N} = \frac{96\times50}{160} = 30$$

The remaining frequencies can now be obtained on completing the 9-square table as given in Table 19·6.

TABLE 19·6

	A	α	*Total*
B	30	50 − 30 = 20	50
β	96 − 30 = 66	64 − 20 = 44	160 − 50 = 110
Total	96	160 − 96 = 64	$N = 160$

$\therefore \quad (\alpha) = 64, \quad (\beta) = 110, \quad (\alpha B) = 20, \quad (A\beta) = 66, \quad (\alpha\beta) = 44.$

19·6. ASSOCIATION OF ATTRIBUTES

Two attributes are said to be associated if they are not independent but are related in some way or the other. As in the case of independent attributes, we have the following criteria of studying the association between two attributes.

19·6·1. (Criterion 1). Proportion Method. This method consists in comparing the presence or absence of a given attribute in the other.

Two attributes A and B are said to be :

$$\left.\begin{array}{llll} \textit{Positively associated if} & \dfrac{(AB)}{(B)} > \dfrac{(A\beta)}{(\beta)} & \text{or} & \dfrac{(AB)}{(A)} > \dfrac{(\alpha B)}{(\alpha)} \\ \textit{Negatively associated if} & \dfrac{(AB)}{(B)} < \dfrac{(A\beta)}{(\beta)} & \text{or} & \dfrac{(AB)}{(A)} < \dfrac{(\alpha B)}{(\alpha)} \end{array}\right\} \quad \ldots(19\cdot26)$$

However, if $\dfrac{(AB)}{(B)} = \dfrac{(A\beta)}{(\beta)}$ or $\dfrac{(AB)}{(A)} = \dfrac{(\alpha B)}{(\alpha)}$, then A and B are independent.

19·6·2. (Criterion 2). Comparison of Observed and Expected Frequencies. Two attributes A and B are said to be :

$$\left.\begin{array}{llll} \textit{Positively associated if} & (AB) > \dfrac{(A)(B)}{N} & \text{or} & \delta > 0 \\ \textit{Negatively associated if} & (AB) < \dfrac{(A)(B)}{N} & \text{or} & \delta < 0 \\ \text{and} \quad \textit{independent if} & (AB) = \dfrac{(A)(B)}{N} & \text{or} & \delta = 0 \end{array}\right\} \quad \ldots(19\cdot27)$$

Similar expressions can be obtained for other ultimate class frequencies such as $(A\beta)$, (αB), and $(\alpha\beta)$.

Remarks 1. Dis-association. When there is positive association between the two attributes A and B, we quite often, say that they are associated (without adding the adjective positive). If the two attributes are negatively associated, they are said to be *dis-associated*. It should be clearly understood that *dis-association of attributes does not mean the independence of attributes or absence of association between the attributes. It simply means negative association.*

2. In our day to day language, we would say that the two attributes are associated if they occur together in a large number of cases. However, in Statistics, the word association is used in a different sense. *Statistically, two attributes are said to be associated* if they occur together in a large number of cases than expected, if they were independent. From the mere fact that some A's are B's, however great the proportion, we cannot infer that the attributes are associated. For studying association between two attributes, we must be given sufficient information (in terms of class frequencies), for using one of the criteria discussed in this section. For illustration, see Example 19·20.

19·6·3. (Criterion 3) Yule's Coefficient of Association. The main limitation of both the methods (Criterion 1 and Criterion 2), is that each simply gives us an idea if the attributes are positively associated, negatively associated or independent. However, none of these methods gives us any idea about the extent of association between the two attributes. G. Undy Yule's coefficient of association, denoted by Q, is a mathematical measure of the intensity of association between the two attributes, say, A and B. It is based on all the ultimate class frequencies and is given by :

$$Q = \frac{(AB)(\alpha\beta) - (A\beta)(\alpha B)}{(AB)(\alpha\beta) + (A\beta)(\alpha B)} \quad \ldots(19\cdot28)$$

Remarks 1. Limits for Q. Let us write: $a = (AB)(\alpha\beta)$ and $b = (A\beta)(\alpha B)$.

Then obviously, $a > 0$ and $b > 0$, so that

$$|a - b| \leq |a + b| \quad \Rightarrow \quad \left|\frac{a-b}{a+b}\right| \leq 1 \quad \ldots(*)$$

$$\therefore \quad Q = \frac{a-b}{a+b} \quad \Rightarrow \quad |Q| = \left|\frac{a-b}{a+b}\right| \le 1 \quad \text{[From (*)]} \quad \Rightarrow \quad -1 \le Q \le 1 \qquad ...(19{\cdot}29)$$

Hence, Yule's coefficient of association lies between –1 and 1, both inclusive.

(*i*) $Q = 1$, implies that there is perfect positive association between A and B.

(*ii*) $Q = -1 \Rightarrow$ There is perfect negative association or complete dis-association between A and B.

(*iii*) $Q = 0 \Rightarrow$ A and B are independent.

Any other value of Q between –1 and 1 gives us an idea of the intensity of association between A and B. A value of $Q \ge 0.5$ indicates a fairly good degree of positive association and a value of Q lying between 0 and 0.5 indicates a low degree of positive association between A and B. Similar interpretation can be given to negative values of Q.

2. Perfect Positive and Perfect Negative Association. $Q = +1$ *i.e.*, there is perfect positive association between the two attributes A and B if and only if

$$b = (A\beta)\,(\alpha B) = 0 \quad \Rightarrow \quad (A\beta) = 0 \quad \text{or} \quad (\alpha B) = 0$$

$$(A\beta) = 0 \quad \Rightarrow \quad (AB) = (A) \quad [\because (A) = (AB) + (A\beta)]$$

$$\text{or} \quad (\alpha B) = 0 \quad \Rightarrow \quad (AB) = (B) \quad [\because (B) = (AB) + (\alpha B)]$$

Hence, *A and B are completely associated or there is perfect positive association between A and B if and only if* $(AB) = (A)$ *i.e., all A's are B's* or $(AB) = (B)$ *i.e., all B's are A's, whichever is less.*

$Q = -1$, *i.e.*, there is perfect negative association between the two attributes A and B if and only if,

$$a = (AB).\,(\alpha\beta) = 0 \quad \Rightarrow \quad (AB) = 0 \quad \text{or} \quad (\alpha\beta) = 0$$

Hence, *A and B are completely dis-associated or there is perfect negative association between A and B, if and only if.*

$(AB) = 0$ *i.e., none of the A's is B* *or* $(\alpha\beta) = 0$ *i.e., none of the* α*'s is* β.

3. Another *important property of Yule's coefficient Q is that it is independent of the relative proportion of A's or α's in the data.*

Thus, if all the terms containing any attribute, say, A (or B or α or β) in Q are multiplied by a constant, k (say), its value remains unaltered.

19·6·4. (Criterion 4). Coefficient of Colligation. This is another measure of association suggested by Professor Yule and has the same properties as Q. It is denoted by Y and is given by :

$$Y = \frac{1 - \sqrt{\dfrac{(A\beta)\,(\alpha B)}{(AB)\,(\alpha\beta)}}}{1 + \sqrt{\dfrac{(A\beta)\,(\alpha B)}{(AB)\,(\alpha\beta)}}} \qquad ...(19{\cdot}30)$$

Relation Between Q and Y.

$$\text{Let} \quad \frac{(A\beta)\,(\alpha B)}{(AB)\,(\alpha\beta)} = k, \quad \text{so that} \quad Y = \frac{1-\sqrt{k}}{1+\sqrt{k}} \quad \Rightarrow \quad Y^2 = \frac{1+k-2\sqrt{k}}{1+k+2\sqrt{k}}$$

$$\therefore \quad 1 + Y^2 = \frac{(1+k+2\sqrt{k}) + (1+k-2\sqrt{k})}{1+k+2\sqrt{k}} = \frac{2(1+k)}{(1+\sqrt{k})^2}$$

$$\text{and} \quad \frac{2Y}{1+Y^2} = \frac{2(1-\sqrt{k})}{(1+\sqrt{k})} \times \frac{(1+\sqrt{k})^2}{2(1+k)} = \frac{(1-\sqrt{k})\,(1+\sqrt{k})}{(1+k)}$$

$$= \frac{1^2 - (\sqrt{k})^2}{1+k} = \frac{1-k}{1+k} \qquad [\because (a+b)(a-b) = a^2 - b^2]$$

$$= \frac{1 - \dfrac{(A\beta)(\alpha B)}{(AB)(\alpha\beta)}}{1 + \dfrac{(A\beta)(\alpha B)}{(AB)(\alpha\beta)}} = \frac{(AB)(\alpha\beta) - (A\beta)(\alpha B)}{(AB)(\alpha\beta) + (A\beta)(\alpha B)} = Q$$

$$\therefore \quad Q = \frac{2Y}{1 + Y^2} \qquad ...(19·31)$$

Using the relation (19·31), we can obtain the value of Yule's coefficient (Q) from that of coefficient of colligation (Y).

Limits for Y. $\quad -1 \leq Y \leq 1$ ... (19·32)

Proof. The relation (19·31), can be used to establish the limits for Y.

We know that $\quad |Q| \leq 1 \quad \Rightarrow \quad -1 \leq Q \leq 1.$

From (19·31), we get :

Attributes are independent if $Q = 0 \quad \Rightarrow \quad Y = 0$

There is perfect (positive) association between A and B if :

$Q = 1 \quad \Rightarrow \quad 2Y = 1 + Y^2 \quad \Rightarrow \quad 1 + Y^2 - 2Y = 0 \quad \Rightarrow \quad (1 - Y)^2 = 0 \quad \Rightarrow \quad Y = 1$

$Q = -1 \quad \Rightarrow \quad 2Y = -(1 + Y^2) \quad \Rightarrow \quad 1 + Y^2 + 2Y = 0 \quad \Rightarrow \quad (1 + Y)^2 = 0 \quad \Rightarrow \quad Y = -1$

Remark. From the above discussion, it is obvious that both Q and Y possess the same properties. Since Yule's coefficient of association (Q) is much easier to compute, it is more commonly used in practice than the coefficient of colligation (Y).

Example 19·18. *If* $(A) = 450$, $(B) = 650$, $(AB) = 310$ *and* $N = 1000$, *find whether A and B are independent or associated.* *(Punjab Univ. B.Com., April 1999)*

Solution. We are given $(AB) = 310$.

$$\frac{(A) \times (B)}{N} = \frac{450 \times 650}{1000} = 292·5 .$$

Since $(AB) > \dfrac{(A) \times (B)}{N}$, the attributes A and B are positively associated.

Example 19·19. *Out of 715 literates in a particular city of India, number of criminals was 8; while out of 975 illiterates in the same city, 17 were criminals. Find out if illiteracy and criminality are associated or independent by using the Proportion Method.*

Solution. Let us define the attributes :

A : Illiteracy $\qquad$ B : Criminality

so that $\quad \alpha$: Literacy $\qquad$ β : Non-criminality

Then, in the usual notations, we are given :

$(A) = 975, \quad (AB) = 17; \quad (\alpha) = 715, \quad (\alpha B) = 8$

Proportion Method.

$$\text{The proportion of illiterates who are criminals} = \frac{(AB)}{(A)} = \frac{17}{975} = 0·0174 = 1·74\%$$

$$\text{The proportion of literates who are criminals} = \frac{(\alpha B)}{(\alpha)} = \frac{8}{715} = 0·0112 = 1·12\%$$

Since $\quad \dfrac{(AB)}{(A)} > \dfrac{(\alpha B)}{(\alpha)}$, A (illiteracy) and B (criminality) are positively associated.

Example 19·20. *"95% of the people who drink alcohol die before reaching the age of 85 years. Therefore, drinking alcohol is bad for longevity of life". Comment.*

Solution. If we define the attributes :

A : Drinking alcohol and B : Dying before reaching 85 years, then we are given : $\dfrac{(AB)}{(A)} = 95\% = 0·95.$

This information, is insufficient to arrive at any valid conclusion about any association between *A* and *B*. To arrive at any conclusion, we must be given the percentage of persons who do not drink alcohol and die before reaching the age 85 years *i.e.*, we must be given $\frac{(\alpha B)}{(\alpha)}$.

The given statement will be true only if $\frac{(AB)}{(A)} > \frac{(\alpha B)}{(\alpha)}$. Hence, as such, the given statement is wrong.

Note. It might happen that the percentage of persons who do not drink alcohol but die before reaching 85 $\left[i.e., \frac{(\alpha B)}{(\alpha)} \cdot \times 100 \right]$ is, say, 98%. In that case, the given conclusion will be reversed *i.e.*, then drinking alcohol will be regarded good for longevity of life.

Example 19·21. *Given : N = 1482, (A) = 368, (B) = 343 and (AB) = 35, find Yule's coefficient of association.* (*Punjab Univ. B.Com., Oct. 1999*]

Solution. To compute Yule's coefficient of association :

$$Q = \frac{(AB)(\alpha\beta) - (A\beta)(\alpha B)}{(AB)(\alpha\beta) + (A\beta)(\alpha\beta)}, \qquad \ldots(*)$$

we need the ultimate class frequencies.

$(AB) = 35$ (Given)

$(\alpha B) = (B) - (AB) = 343 - 35 = 308$; $(A\beta) = (A) - (AB) = 368 - 35 = 333$

$(\alpha\beta) = N - (A) - (B) + (AB) = 1482 - 368 - 343 + 35 = 1517 - 711 = 806$

Substituting in (*), we get

$$Q = \frac{35 \times 806 - 333 \times 308}{35 \times 806 + 333 \times 308} = \frac{28210 - 102564}{28210 + 102564} = -\frac{74354}{130774} = -0{\cdot}57$$

Since $Q < -0.5$, there is a fairly good degree of negative association between *A* and *B*.

Remark. We can also obtain the ultimate class frequencies by completing the nine square table. This is left as an exercise to the reader.

Example 19·22. *Attributes A and B represent respectively regular morning walk activity and being physically fit. Compute the Yule's coefficient of association between attributes A and B, given :*

N = 100, (A) = 60, (B) = 50 and (AB) = 35

Interpret the result. [*Delhi Univ. B.A. (Econ. Hons.), 1991*]

Solution. The frequencies of other classes, (in the usual notations) are computed as given in the 2 × 2 contingency Table 19·7.

TABLE 19·7

	A	α	*Total*
B	35	50 – 35 = 15	50
β	60 – 35 = 25	40 – 15 = 25	100 – 50 = 50
Total	60	100 – 60 = 40	100

Yule's coefficient of association is given by :

$$Q = \frac{(AB)(\alpha\beta) - (A\beta)(\alpha B)}{(AB)(\alpha\beta) + (A\beta)(\alpha B)} = \frac{35 \times 25 - 25 \times 15}{35 \times 25 + 25 \times 15} = \frac{875 - 375}{875 + 375} = \frac{500}{1250} = 0{\cdot}4$$

Hence, there is a low degree of positive association between the two attributes *A* (morning walk) and *B* (physical fitness).

Example 19·23. *In a population of 1,000 students, the number of married students is 400. Out of 300 students who failed, 120 belonged to the married group. Using Yule's coefficient of association, find out the extent of association between the attributes marriage and failure.* [*Delhi Univ. B.A. (Econ. Hons.), 1995*]

TABLE 19·8

	A	α	Total
B	120	300 – 120 = 180	(B) = 300
β	400 – 120 = 280	600 – 180 = 420	1000 – 300 = 700
Total	(A) = 400	1000 – 400 = 600	N = 1,000

Solution. Let us define the following attributes :

A : Student is married. ;

B : Student failed in the test.

Then, α represents the attribute that student is un-married and β represents the attribute that student passed the test.

In the usual notations, we are given : $N = 1,000$; $(A) = 400$, $(B) = 300$, $(AB) = 120$.

Then the frequencies of various attributes are computed as given in the 2 × 2 Table 19·8.

Yule's coefficient of association between the attributes A and B is given by :

$$Q = \frac{(AB)(\alpha\beta) - (A\beta)(\alpha B)}{(AB)(\alpha\beta) + (A\beta)(\alpha B)} = \frac{120 \times 420 - 280 \times 180}{120 \times 420 + 280 \times 180} = \frac{50{,}400 - 50{,}400}{50{,}400 + 50{,}400} = 0.$$

Hence, the attributes A and B are not associated and we conclude that there is no association between the attributes A (marriage) and B (failure in the test).

Example 19·24. *In a co-education institution, out of 200 students, 150 were boys. In an examinations, 120 boys and 40 girls passed. Apply Yule's coefficient to determine the association between sex and success in the examination. Interpret your result.* [*Delhi Univ. B.A. (Econ. Hons.), 1994*]

Solution. Let us define the following attributes :

A : The student is a boy.

B : The student passed in the examination.

Then α : The student is a girl.

and β : The student failed in the examination.

In the usual notations, were are given :

$N = 200$; $(AB) = 120$, $(\alpha B) = 40$, $(A) = 150$.

The remaining cell frequencies can be obtained as given in the 2 × 2 Table 19·9.

TABLE 19·9

	A	α	Total
B	120	40	120 + 40 = 160
β	150 – 120 = 30	40 – 30 = 10	200 – 160 = 40
Total	(A) = 150	200 – 150 = 50	N = 200

$\therefore$ $(AB) = 120$, $(\alpha\beta) = 10$; $(A\beta) = 30$; $(\alpha B) = 40$

Yule's coefficient of association is given by :

$$Q = \frac{(AB)(\alpha\beta) - (A\beta)(\alpha B)}{(AB)(\alpha\beta) + (A\beta)(\alpha B)} = \frac{120 \times 10 - 40 \times 30}{120 \times 10 + 40 \times 30} = \frac{1200 - 1200}{1200 + 1200} = 0.$$

Hence, the attributes A and B are not associated and we conclude that there is no association between sex and success in the examination.

Example 19·25. *A survey was conducted in respect of marital status and success in examination. Out of 2,000 persons who appeared for an examination, 80% of them were boys, and the rest were girls. Among 300 married boys, 140 were successful. 1100 boys were successful among unmarried boys. In respect of 100 married girls, 40 were successful. 200 unmarried girls were successful. Construct two separate nine square tables, and find out the Yule's coefficient of association to discuss the association between marital status and success in examination.*

Solution. Total number of persons who appeared in the examination = 2000

$$\text{Number of boys} = 80\% \text{ of } 2000 = \frac{80}{100} \times 2000 = 1600$$

$$\therefore \quad \text{Number of girls} = 2000 - 1600 = 400$$

Let us define the attributes :

A : Married person ; B : Success in the examination

α : Unmarried person ; β : Failure in the examination

Then, in the usual notations, we are given :

For Boys : $N = 1600$, $(A) = 300$, $(AB) = 140$, $(\alpha B) = 1100$

For Girls : $N = 400$, $(A) = 100$, $(AB) = 40$, $(\alpha B) = 200$

The above data can be expressed in two separate nine square tables for boys and girls [Table 19·10 (*a*) for boys and Table 19·10(*b*) for girls], as given below.

NINE SQUARE TABLES

TABLE 19·10(*a*) : **FOR BOYS**

Attributes	*A*	*α*	*Total*
B	**140**	**1100**	140 + 1100 = 1240
β	300 – 140 = 160	360 – 160 = 200	1600 – 1240 = 360
Total	**300**	1600 – 300 = 1300	**1600**

Table 19·10(*b*) : **FOR GIRLS**

Attributes	*A*	*α*	*Total*
B	**40**	**200**	40 + 200 = 240
β	100 – 40 = 60	300 – 200 = 100	400 – 240 = 160
Total	**100**	400 – 100 = 300	**400**

In the above Tables, the frequencies in the bold type are the given values. The remaining frequencies can be obtained by appropriate additions or subtractions, as explained in the tables.

Yule's coefficient of association (Q) is given by : $Q = \dfrac{(AB)(\alpha\beta) - (\alpha B)(A\beta)}{(AB)(\alpha\beta) + (\alpha B)(A\beta)}$

FOR BOYS

$$Q = \frac{140 \times 200 - 1100 \times 160}{140 \times 200 + 1100 \times 160}$$

$$= \frac{28000 - 176000}{28000 + 176000} = -\frac{148000}{204000}$$

$$= -0{\cdot}725$$

FOR GIRLS

$$Q = \frac{40 \times 100 - 200 \times 60}{40 \times 100 + 200 \times 60}$$

$$= \frac{4000 - 12000}{4000 + 12000} = -\frac{8000}{16000}$$

$$= -0{\cdot}5$$

Hence, in each case (for boys and for girls) there is a fairly good degree of negative association between marital status and success in the examination, and the degree of association is more in boys.

Example 19·26. *1000 candidates appeared in a certain examination. Boys outnumbered girls by 20% of all candidates who appeared in the examination. Number of passed candidates exceeded the number of failed candidates by 166. Girls failing in the examination numbered 58. Construct the 2 × 2 table and then work out Yule's coefficient of association between male sex and success in the examination. Also interpret the said coefficient.*

Solution. Let us define the attributes :

A : Boys, α : Girls ; B : Passed in the examination, β : Failed in the examination

Then, we are given : $N = 1{,}000$ and $(\alpha\beta) = 58$

$(A) - (\alpha) = 20\%$ of $N = \frac{20}{100} \times 1{,}000 = 200$

Also $(A) + (\alpha) = N = 1000$

$\therefore$ Adding and subtracting, we get respectively :

$2(A) = 1200 \Rightarrow (A) = \frac{1200}{2} = 600$

$2(\alpha) = 800 \Rightarrow (\alpha) = \frac{800}{2} = 400$

$(B) - (\beta) = 166$

Also $(B) + (\beta) = N = 1000$

Adding and subtracting, we get respectively :

$2(B) = 1166 \Rightarrow (B) = \frac{1166}{2} = 583$

$2(\beta) = 834 \Rightarrow (\beta) = \frac{834}{2} = 417$

The above results can be expressed in 2 × 2 contingency Table 19·11 on page 19·24.

From Table 19·11 , we have

$(AB) = 241, \quad (\alpha\beta) = 58$

$(A\beta) = 359, \quad (\alpha B) = 342$

TABLE 19·11

Attribute	A	α	Total
B	583 – 342 = 241	400 – 58 = 342	583
β	417 – 58 = 359	58	417
Total	600	400	1,000

Yule's coefficient of association (Q) is given by :

$$Q = \frac{(AB)(\alpha\beta) - (A\beta)(\alpha B)}{(AB)(\alpha\beta) + (A\beta)(\alpha B)} = \frac{241 \times 58 - 359 \times 342}{241 \times 58 + 359 \times 342} = \frac{13978 - 122778}{13978 + 122778} = -\frac{108800}{136756} = -0{\cdot}7956$$

Since $Q < -0{\cdot}5$, there is a fairly high degree of negative association between the attribute A (boys) and B (success) in the examination.

EXERCISE 19·3

1. What do you mean by independence of attributes ? Give a criterion for the independence of two attributes A and B.

2. Describe :

(*a*) The proportion method and (*b*) Comparison of observed and expected frequencies method, for studying the independence of two attributes.

3. Let $\delta = (AB) - \frac{(A) \times (B)}{N}$; Prove that $\delta = \frac{1}{N}\left[(AB)(\alpha\beta) - (A\beta)(\alpha B)\right]$

Hence, deduce the criteria for independence of two attributes A and B.

4. (*a*) What is meant by Association of two attributes ? Explain briefly the different methods of measuring association between two attributes.

(*b*) What do you understand by 'Association of Attributes'? Differentiate between association, dis-association and independence. Describe the most commonly used methods for determining association between two attributes.

5. (*a*) When are two attributes said to be :

(*i*) independent, (*ii*) positively associated, and (*iii*) negatively associated ?

What are the conditions to be satisfied by class frequencies in each of the above cases ?

(*b*) State the conditions under which two attributes A and B are said to be :

(*i*) independent, (*ii*) positively associated, (*iii*) negatively associated.

[*Delhi Univ. B.A.(Econ. Hons.), 1999*]

6. Write down the conditions under which two attributes A and B are :

(*i*) independent, (*ii*) positively associated, and (*iii*) negatively associated. Explain the conditions.

[*Delhi Univ. B.A. (Econ. Hons.), 1998*]

7. Distinguish between concepts of association and correlation and describe the situations in which each of them should be used. Illustrate your answer with examples.

8. (*a*) Define Yule's coefficient of association (Q) between two attributes A and B.

(*b*) Prove that $-1 \le Q \le 1$.

When are the limits +1 and –1 attained ? Interpret them.

9. Define Yule's coefficient of association (Q) and coefficient of colligation (Y). Establish the following relation between Q and Y :

$$Q = \frac{2Y}{1 + Y^2}$$

Hence, deduce the limits for Y and interpret them.

10. In a study of association of attributes you are given

$(A) = 200, \quad (B) = 400, \quad (AB) = 100, \quad (N) = 1000$

The attributes A and B are :

(*a*) Independent , (*b*) Positively associated , (*c*) Negatively associated.

Ans. Positively associated.

11. Find if A and B are independent, positively associated or negatively associated, in each of the following cases :

(*i*) $N = 1000$, $(A) = 470$, $(B) = 620$, and $(AB) = 320$

[*Punjab Univ. B.Com. Oct., 2002*]

(*ii*) $(A) = 490$, $(AB) = 294$, $(\alpha) = 570$, and $(\alpha B) = 380$

(*iii*) $(AB) = 256$, $(\alpha B) = 768$, $(A\beta) = 48$, and $(\alpha \beta) = 144$

Ans. (*i*) Positively associated, (*ii*) Negatively associated, (*iii*) Independent.

12. The male population of a State in India. is 250 lakhs. The number of literate males is 20 lakhs and the total number of criminals is 26 thousand. The number of literate male criminals is 2 thousand. Do you find any association between literacy and criminality ?

Ans. Negatively associated.

13. Comment on the following statement :

"96% of the people who drink alcohol die before reaching 80 years of age. Therefore, drinking alcohol is bad for longevity."

14. A survey was conducted in respect of marital status and success in examination. Out of 2,000 persons who appeared for an examination, 80% of them were boys, and the rest were girls. Among 300 married boys, 140 were successful, 1100 boys were successful among unmarried boys. In respect of 100 married girls 40 were successful, 200 unmarried girls were successful. Construct two separate nine-square tables, and find out if there is any association between marital status and passing of examination.

Use :

(*i*) Proportion Method.

(*ii*) Comparison of observed and expected frequencies.

(*iii*) Yule's coefficient of association. [*Agra Univ. M.Com. 1997*]

Ans. (*i*) ; (*ii*) : There is negative association between marital status and success in the examination.

(*iii*) Q (Boys) $= -0{\cdot}725$; Q (Girls) $= -0{\cdot}5$.

15. (*a*) Find the Association between Literacy and Unemployment from the following figures :

Total Adults	10,000
Literates	1,290
Unemployed	1,390
Literate Unemployed	820

Comment on the results.

Ans. $Q = 0.923$. Very high positive association.

(*b*) Calculate the coefficient of association between extravagance in fathers and sons from the following data :

Extravagant fathers with extravagant sons	= 327
Extravagant fathers miserly sons	= 545
Miserly fathers with extravagant sons	= 741
Miserly fathers with miserly sons	= 235

[*Punjab Univ. M.A. (Econ.), Oct. 1998*]

16. (*a*) Out of 17,000 literates in a particular district of a country ,number of criminals was 500. Out of 9,30,000 illiterates in the same district, the number of criminals was 15,000. Find out if illiteracy and criminality are associated or independent, by using the Proportion Method. [*Nagpur Univ. M.Com., 2003*]

Ans. A : Illiteracy ; B : Criminality ; $\frac{(AB)}{(A)} > \frac{(\alpha B)}{(\alpha)}$ $\Rightarrow$ A and B are positively associated.

(*b*) Out of 700 literates in a particular taluk, number of criminals was 5. Out of 9,300 illiterates in the same taluk, the number of criminals was 150.

On the basis of these figures, find Yule's coefficient of association between illiteracy and criminality.

Ans. $Q = -0{\cdot}39$.

17. The following table shows the result of inoculation against cholera.

	Attacked	*Not attacked*
Inoculated	6	56
Not-inoculated	84	18

Examine the effect of inoculation in controlling susceptibility to cholera.

Ans. $Q = -0.96$. Inoculation is highly effective in controlling cholera.

18. The following table is reproduced from a memoir written by Karl Pearson :

		Eye colour in son	
		Not light	*Light*
Eye colour in father	Not light	230	148
	Light	151	471

Discuss if the colour of son's eyes is associated with that of father.

Ans. $Q = 0{\cdot}66$. Yes. Positively Associated.

19. Find out association between the intelligence of husbands and the intelligence of wives from the following data :

Intelligent husbands with intelligent wives	40
Intelligent husbands with dull wives	100
Dull husbands with intelligent wives	160
Dull husbands with dull wives	190

Ans. $Q = -0{\cdot}397$. [*Meerut Univ. M.A. Econ., 1994*]

20. In a co-educational institution, out of 200 students 150 were boys. They took an examination and it was found that 120 passed and 10 girls had failed. Is there any association between sex and success in the examination ? [*Jammu Univ. M.Com., 1998*]

Ans. $Q = 0$; Success in the examination is independent of sex.

21. A teacher examined 280 students in Economics and Auditing and found that 160 failed in Economics, 140 failed in Auditing and 80 failed in both the subjects. Is there any association between failure in Economics and Auditing ? [*Himachal Pradesh Univ. M.Com., 1997*)

Ans. $Q = 0$; Failure in Economics and Auditing are independent.

22. The following summary data relate to the adult population of a small village :

Adult population	600
Number of employed	240
Literate adult population employed	80
Number of literates	200

Determine whether literacy and employment are associated or not. [*Madurai-Kamaraj Univ. B.Com., 1997*]

Ans. $Q = 0$. Literacy and employment are independent.

23. Do you find any association between the tempers of brothers and sisters from the following data :

Good natured brothers and good natured sisters	1230
Good natured brothers and sullen sisters	850
Sullen brothers and good natured sisters	530
Sullen brothers and sullen sisters	980

Ans. $Q = 0{\cdot}456$.

24. From the following data, prepare the 2×2 table and using Yule's coefficient, discuss if there is association between literacy and un-employment.

Illiterate unemployed	220 persons
Literate employed	20 persons
Illiterate employed	180 persons
Total number of persons	500

Ans. $Q = 0{\cdot}532$.

25. A survey yielded the following results :

	Boys	*Girls*
Number of candidates appearing at the examination	800	200
Married	150	50
Married and successful	70	20
Unmarried and successful	550	110

Prepare the nine-square tables separately for boys and girls, depicting the marital status and success in the examination. Obtain Yule's coefficient of association in each case and interpret the result.

Ans. Q (Boys) $= -0{\cdot}725$; Q (Girls) $= -0{\cdot}61$.

26. A survey study of 366 students about the performance of matured and fresh certificate holder students admitted in the first year of the Arts Faculty yielded the following information.

$N = 366$, $(A) = 192$, $(B) = 172$, $(\alpha\beta) = 100$, where A denoted maturedness and B, the good performance. Find

(*i*) Yule's Coefficient (Q) and (*ii*) Coefficient of Colligation (Y),

and comment on the value of Q. Also verify the relation : $Q = \frac{2Y}{1+Y^2}$.

Ans. (*i*) $Q = 0{\cdot}17$; (*ii*) $Y = 0{\cdot}087$.

27. In a certain investigation carried on with regard to 500 graduates and 1500 non-graduates, it was found that the number of employed graduates was 450 while the number of unemployed non-graduates was 300. In the second investigation 5000 cases were examined. The number of non-graduates was 3000 and the number of employed non-graduates was 2500. The number of graduates who were found to be employed was 1600.

Calculate the coefficient of association between graduation and employment in both the investigations. Can any definite conclusion be drawn from the coefficients ? [*Jammu Univ. M.Com., 2005*]

Ans. Q (1st Investigation) = + 0·38 , (Second Investigation) = – 0·11

28. 200 candidates appeared for a competitive examination and 60 of them succeeded. 35 received special coaching and out of them 20 candidates succeeded.

Prepare 2 × 2 contingency table and using Yule's Coefficient discuss whether special coaching is effective or not.

Ans. Q [A : Success ; B : Special coaching] = 0·613. Special coaching is effective.

29. In an examination at which 500 candidates appeared, boys out-numbered girls by 14 per cent of all candidates. Number of passed candidates exceeded the number of failed candidates by 300. Boys failing in the examination number 80. Construct the nine-square table and calculate the coefficient of association between boys and success in the examination. [*Meerut Univ. M.A. (Econ.), 1996*]

Hint. Proceed as in Example 19·26.

Ans. A : Boys ; α : Girls ;

B : Success ; β : Failure ;

	A	α	Total
B	205	195	400
β	80	20	100
Total	285	215	500

$Q = -0{\cdot}584 \simeq -0{\cdot}6 < -0{\cdot}5 \Rightarrow$ There is fairly good degrees of negative association between A (boys) and B (success in the examination).

30. With a view to study whether the working condition in a factory had any influence on the frequency of accidents, a researcher collected and tabulated the accident data as follows :

Working Condition	*No. of Accidents*		*Total*
	Less	*More*	
Good	280	80	360
Bad	120	120	240
Total	400	200	600

Using Yule's methodology, calculate the coefficient of association between the number of accidents and the working condition in the factory. What inference would you draw from the result ?

[*Himachal Pradesh Univ. M.Com., 1994*]

Ans. Q [A : Less accidents , B : Working conditions] = 0·56

$\Rightarrow$ Good working conditions in factories should lead to less number of accidents.

31. For a cross-section of 300 students, the information pertaining to their performance in Internal Examination and in the University Final Examination is categorised as given in Table 19·12. Compute the coefficient of association and interpret the result.

TABLE 19·12

		Final Exam. Performance		
		Good	*Bad*	*Total*
Internal Exam. Performance	Good	100	—	120
	Bad	—	—	—
	Total	200	—	300

[*Himachal Pradesh Univ., M.Com. 2004; Delhi Univ. B.A. (Econ. Hons.), 1992*]

Ans. $Q = 0{\cdot}6$; Fairly good positive association between the performance in internal examination and university final examination.

Appendix 1–Numerical Tables

TABLE 1 : LOGARITHMS

	0	1	2	3	4	5	6	7	8	9	1	2	3	4	5	6	7	8	9
10	.0000	0043	0086	0120	0170	0212	0253	0294	0334	0374	4	8	12	17	21	25	29	33	37
11	.0414	0453	0492	0531	0569	0607	0645	0682	0719	0755	4	8	11	15	19	23	26	30	34
12	.0792	0828	0864	0899	0934	0969	1004	1038	1072	1106	3	7	10	14	17	21	24	28	31
13	.1139	1173	1206	1239	1271	1303	1335	1367	1399	1430	3	6	10	13	16	19	23	26	29
14	.1461	1492	1523	1553	1584	1614	1644	1673	1703	1732	3	6	9	12	15	18	21	24	27
15	1761	1790	1818	1847	1875	1903	1931	1959	1987	2014	3	6	8	11	14	17	20	22	25
16	.2041	2068	2095	2122	2148	2175	2201	2227	2253	2279	3	5	8	11	13	16	18	21	24
17	.2304	2330	2355	2380	2405	2430	2455	2480	2504	2529	2	5	7	10	12	15	17	20	22
18	.2553	2577	2601	2625	2648	2672	2695	2718	2742	2765	2	5	7	9	12	14	16	19	21
19	.2788	2810	2833	2856	2878	2900	2923	2945	2967	2989	2	4	7	9	11	13	16	18	20
20	.3010	3032	3054	3075	3096	3118	3139	3160	3181	3201	2	4	6	8	11	13	15	17	19
21	.3222	3243	3263	3284	3304	3324	3345	3365	3385	3404	2	4	6	8	10	12	14	16	18
22	.3424	3444	3464	3483	3502	3522	3541	3562	3579	3598	2	4	6	8	10	12	14	15	17
23	.3617	3636	3655	3674	3692	3711	3729	3747	3766	3784	2	4	6	7	9	11	13	15	17
24	.3802	3820	3838	3856	3874	3892	3909	3927	3945	3962	2	4	5	7	9	11	12	14	16
25	.3979	3997	4014	4031	4048	4065	4082	4099	4116	4133	2	3	5	7	9	10	12	14	15
26	.4150	4166	4183	4200	4216	4232	4249	4265	4281	4298	2	3	5	7	8	10	11	13	15
27	.4314	4330	4346	4362	4378	4393	4409	4425	4440	4456	2	3	5	6	8	9	11	13	14
28	.4472	4487	4502	4518	4533	4548	4564	4579	4594	4609	2	3	5	6	8	9	11	12	14
29	.4624	4639	4654	4669	4683	4698	4713	4728	4742	4757	1	3	4	6	7	9	10	12	13
30	.4771	4786	4800	4814	4829	4843	4857	4871	4886	4900	1	3	4	6	7	9	10	11	13
31	.4914	4928	4942	4955	4969	4983	4997	5011	5024	5038	1	3	4	6	7	8	10	11	12
32	.5051	5065	5079	5092	5105	5119	5132	5145	5159	5172	1	3	4	5	7	8	9	11	12
33	.5185	5198	5211	5224	5237	5250	5263	5276	5289	5302	1	3	4	5	6	8	9	10	12
34	.5315	5315	5340	5353	5366	5378	5391	5403	5416	5428	1	3	4	5	6	8	9	10	11
35	.5441	5453	5465	5478	5490	5502	5514	5527	5539	5551	1	2	4	5	6	7	9	10	11
36	.5563	5575	5587	5599	5611	5623	5635	5647	5658	5670	1	2	4	5	6	7	8	10	11
37	.5682	5694	5705	5717	5729	5740	5752	5763	5775	5786	1	2	3	5	6	7	8	9	10
38	.5798	5809	5821	5832	5843	5855	5866	5877	5888	5899	1	2	3	5	6	7	8	9	10
39	.5911	5922	5933	5944	5955	5966	5977	5988	5999	6010	1	2	3	4	5	7	8	9	10
40	.6021	6031	6042	6053	6065	6075	6085	6096	6107	6117	1	2	3	4	5	6	8	9	10
41	.6128	6138	6149	6160	6170	6180	6191	6201	6212	6222	1	2	3	4	5	6	7	8	9
42	.6232	6243	6253	6263	6274	6284	6294	6304	6314	6325	1	2	3	4	5	6	7	8	9
43	.6335	6345	6355	6365	6375	6385	6395	6405	6415	6425	1	2	3	4	5	6	7	8	9
44	.6435	6444	6454	6465	6474	6484	6493	6503	6513	6522	1	2	3	4	5	6	7	8	9
45	.6532	6542	6551	6561	6571	6580	6590	6599	6609	6618	1	2	3	4	5	6	7	8	9
46	.6628	6637	6646	6656	6665	6675	6684	6693	6702	6712	1	2	3	4	5	6	7	7	8
47	.6721	6730	6739	6749	6758	6767	6776	6785	6794	6803	1	2	3	4	5	5	6	7	8
48	.6812	6821	6830	6839	6848	6857	6866	6875	6884	6893	1	2	3	4	4	5	6	7	8
49	.6902	6911	6920	6928	6937	6946	6955	6964	6972	6981	1	2	3	4	4	5	6	7	8
50	.6990	6993	7007	7016	7024	7033	7042	7050	7059	7067	1	2	3	3	4	5	6	7	8
51	.7076	7084	7093	7101	7110	7118	7126	7135	7143	7152	1	2	3	3	4	5	6	7	8
52	.7160	7168	7177	7185	7193	7202	7210	7218	7226	7235	1	2	2	3	4	5	6	7	7
53	.7243	7251	7259	7267	7275	7284	7292	7300	7308	7316	1	2	2	3	4	5	6	6	7

TABLE 1 : LOGARITHMS

	0	1	2	3	4	5	6	7	8	9	1	2	3	4	5	6	7	8	9
54	.7324	7332	7340	7348	7356	7364	7372	7380	7388	7396	1	2	2	3	4	5	6	6	7
55	.7404	7412	7419	7427	7435	7443	7451	7459	7466	7474	1	2	2	3	4	5	5	6	7
56	.7482	7490	7497	7505	7513	7520	7528	7536	7543	7551	1	2	2	3	4	5	5	6	7
57	.7559	7566	7574	7582	7589	7597	7604	7612	7619	7627	1	2	2	3	4	5	5	6	7
58	.7634	7642	7649	7657	7664	7672	7679	7686	7694	7701	1	1	2	3	4	4	5	6	7
59	.7709	7716	7723	7731	7738	7745	7752	7760	7767	7774	1	1	2	3	4	4	5	6	7
60	.7782	7789	7796	7803	7810	7818	7825	7832	7839	7846	1	1	2	3	4	4	5	6	6
61	.7853	7860	7868	7875	7882	7889	7896	7903	7910	7917	1	1	2	3	4	4	5	6	6
62	.7924	7931	7938	7945	7952	7959	7966	7973	7980	7987	1	1	2	3	3	4	5	6	6
63	.7993	8000	8007	8014	8021	8028	8035	8041	8048	8055	1	1	2	3	3	4	5	5	6
64	.8062	8069	8075	8082	8989	8096	8102	8109	8116	8122	1	1	2	3	3	4	5	5	6
65	.8129	8136	8142	8149	8156	8162	8169	8176	8182	8189	1	1	2	3	3	4	5	5	6
66	.8195	8202	8209	8215	8222	8228	8235	8241	8248	8254	1	1	2	3	3	4	5	5	6
67	.8261	8267	8274	8280	8287	8293	8299	8306	8312	8319	1	1	2	3	3	4	5	5	6
68	.8325	8331	8338	8344	8351	8357	8363	8370	8376	8382	1	1	2	3	3	4	4	5	6
69	.8388	8395	8401	8407	8414	8420	8426	8432	8439	8445	1	1	2	2	3	4	4	5	6
70	.8451	8457	8463	8470	8476	8482	8488	8494	8500	8506	1	1	2	2	3	4	4	5	6
71	.8513	8519	8525	8531	8537	8543	8549	8555	8561	8567	1	1	2	2	3	4	4	5	5
72	.8573	8579	8585	8591	8597	8603	8609	8615	8621	8627	1	1	2	2	3	4	4	5	5
73	.8633	8639	8645	8651	8657	8663	8669	8675	8681	8686	1	1	2	2	3	4	4	5	5
74	.8692	8698	8704	8710	8716	8722	8727	8733	8739	8745	1	1	2	2	3	4	4	5	5
75	.8751	8756	8762	8768	8774	8779	8785	8791	8797	8802	1	1	2	2	3	3	4	5	5
76	.8808	8814	8820	8825	8831	8837	8842	8848	8854	8859	1	1	2	2	3	3	4	5	5
77	.8865	8871	8876	8882	8887	8893	8899	8904	8910	8915	1	1	2	2	3	3	4	4	5
78	.8921	8927	8932	8938	8943	8949	8954	8960	8965	8971	1	1	2	2	3	3	4	4	5
79	.8976	8982	8987	8993	8998	9004	9009	9015	9020	9025	1	1	2	2	3	3	4	4	5
80	.9031	9036	9042	9047	9053	9058	6063	9069	9074	9079	1	1	2	2	3	3	4	4	5
81	.9085	9090	9096	9101	9106	9112	9117	9122	9128	9133	1	1	2	2	3	3	4	4	5
82	.9138	9143	9149	9154	9159	9165	9170	9175	9180	9186	1	1	2	2	3	3	4	4	5
83	.9191	9196	9201	9206	9212	9217	9222	9227	9232	9238	1	1	2	2	3	3	4	4	5
84	.9243	9248	9253	9258	9263	9269	9274	9279	9284	9289	1	1	2	2	3	3	4	4	5
85	.9294	9299	9304	9309	9315	9320	9325	9330	9335	9340	1	1	2	2	3	3	4	4	5
86	.9345	9350	9355	9360	9365	9370	9375	9380	9385	9390	1	1	2	2	3	3	4	4	5
87	.9395	9400	9405	9410	9415	9420	9425	9430	9435	9440	0	1	1	2	2	3	3	4	4
88	.9445	9450	9455	9460	9465	9469	9474	9479	9484	9489	0	1	1	2	2	3	3	4	4
89	.9494	9499	9504	9509	9513	9518	9523	9528	9533	9538	0	1	1	2	2	3	3	4	4
90	.9542	9547	9552	9557	9562	9566	9571	9576	9581	9586	0	1	1	2	2	3	3	4	4
91	.9590	9595	9600	9605	9609	9614	9619	9624	9628	9933	0	1	1	2	2	3	3	4	4
92	.9638	9643	9647	9652	9657	9661	9666	9671	9675	9680	0	1	1	2	2	3	3	4	4
93	.9685	9689	9694	9699	9703	9708	9713	9717	9722	9727	0	1	1	2	2	3	3	4	4
94	.9731	9736	9741	9745	9750	9754	9759	9763	9768	9773	0	1	1	2	2	3	3	4	4
95	.9777	9782	9786	9791	9795	9800	9805	9809	9814	9818	0	1	1	2	2	3	3	4	4
96	.9823	9827	9832	9836	9841	9845	9850	9854	9859	9863	0	1	1	2	2	3	3	4	4
97	.9868	9872	9877	9881	9886	9890	9894	9899	9903	9908	0	1	1	2	2	3	3	4	4
98	.9912	9917	9921	9926	9930	9934	9939	9943	9948	9952	0	1	1	2	2	3	3	4	4
99	.9956	9961	9965	9969	9974	9978	9983	9987	9991	9996	0	1	1	2	2	3	3	3	4

TABLE II : ANTILOGARITHMS

	0	1	2	3	4	5	6	7	8	9	1	2	3	4	5	6	7	8	9
.00	1000	1002	1005	1007	1009	1012	1014	1016	1019	1021	0	0	1	1	1	1	2	2	2
.01	1023	1026	1028	1030	1033	1035	1038	1040	1042	1045	0	0	1	1	1	1	2	2	2
.02	1047	1050	1052	1054	1057	1059	1062	1064	1067	1069	0	0	1	1	1	1	2	2	2
.03	1072	1074	1076	1079	1081	1084	1086	1089	1091	1094	0	0	1	1	1	1	2	2	2
.04	1096	1099	1102	1104	1107	1109	1112	1114	1117	1119	0	1	1	1	1	2	2	2	2
.05	1122	1125	1127	1130	1132	1135	1138	1140	1143	1146	0	1	1	1	1	2	2	2	2
.06	1148	1151	1153	1156	1159	1161	1164	1167	1169	1172	0	1	1	1	1	2	2	2	2
.07	1175	1178	1180	1183	1186	1189	1191	1194	1197	1199	0	1	1	1	1	2	2	2	2
.08	1202	1205	1208	1211	1213	1216	1219	1222	1225	1227	0	1	1	1	1	2	2	2	3
.09	1230	1233	1236	1239	1242	1245	1247	1250	1253	1256	0	1	1	1	1	2	2	2	3
.10	1259	1262	1265	1268	1271	1274	1276	1279	1282	1285	0	1	1	1	1	2	2	2	3
.11	1288	1291	1294	1297	1300	1303	1306	1309	1312	1315	0	1	1	1	2	2	2	2	3
.12	1318	1321	1324	1327	1330	1334	1337	1340	1343	1346	0	1	1	1	2	2	2	2	3
.13	1349	1352	1355	1358	1361	1365	1368	1371	1374	1377	0	1	1	1	2	2	2	3	3
.14	1380	1384	1387	1390	1393	1396	1400	1403	1406	1409	0	1	1	1	2	2	2	3	3
.15	1413	1416	1419	1422	1426	1429	1432	1435	1439	1442	0	1	1	1	2	2	2	3	3
.16	1445	1449	1452	1455	1459	1462	1466	1469	1472	1476	0	1	1	1	2	2	2	3	3
.17	1479	1483	1486	1489	1493	1496	1500	1503	1507	1510	0	1	1	1	2	2	2	3	3
.18	1514	1517	1521	1524	1528	1531	1535	1538	1542	1545	0	1	1	1	2	2	2	3	3
.19	1549	1552	1556	1560	1563	1567	1570	1574	1578	1581	0	1	1	1	2	2	3	3	3
.20	1585	1589	1592	1596	1600	1603	1607	1611	1614	1618	0	1	1	1	2	2	3	3	3
.21	1622	1626	1629	1633	1637	1641	1644	1648	1652	1656	0	1	1	2	2	2	3	3	3
.22	1660	1663	1667	1671	1675	1679	1683	1687	1690	1694	0	1	1	2	2	2	3	3	3
.23	1698	1702	1706	1710	1714	1718	1722	1726	1730	1734	0	1	1	2	2	2	3	3	4
.24	1738	1742	1746	1750	1754	1758	1762	1766	1770	1774	0	1	1	2	2	2	3	3	4
.25	1778	1782	1786	1791	1795	1799	1803	1807	1811	1816	0	1	1	2	2	2	3	3	4
.26	1820	1824	1828	1832	1837	1841	1845	1849	1854	1858	0	1	1	2	2	3	3	3	4
.27	1862	1866	1871	1875	1879	1884	1888	1892	1897	1901	0	1	1	2	2	3	3	3	4
.28	1905	1910	1914	1919	1923	1928	1932	1936	1941	1945	0	1	1	2	2	3	3	4	4
.29	1950	1954	1959	1963	1968	1972	1977	1982	1986	1991	0	1	1	2	2	3	3	4	4
.30	1995	2000	2004	2009	2014	2018	2023	2028	2032	2037	0	1	1	2	2	3	3	4	4
.31	2042	2046	2051	2056	2061	2065	2070	2075	2080	2084	0	1	1	2	2	3	3	4	4
.32	2089	2094	2099	2104	2109	2113	2118	2123	2128	2133	0	1	1	2	2	3	3	4	4
.33	2138	2143	2148	2153	2158	2163	2168	2173	2178	2183	0	1	1	2	2	3	3	4	4
.34	2188	2193	2198	2203	2208	2213	2218	2223	2228	2234	1	1	2	2	3	3	4	4	5
.35	2239	2244	2249	2254	2259	2265	2270	2275	2280	2286	1	1	2	2	3	3	4	4	5
.36	2291	2296	2301	2307	2312	2317	2323	2328	2333	2339	1	1	2	2	3	3	4	4	5
.37	2344	2350	2355	2360	2366	2371	2377	2382	2388	2393	1	1	2	2	3	3	4	4	5
.38	2399	2404	2410	2415	2421	2427	2432	2438	2443	2449	1	1	2	2	3	3	4	4	5
.39	2455	2460	2466	2472	2477	2483	2489	2495	2500	2506	1	1	2	2	3	3	4	5	5
.40	2513	2518	2523	2529	2535	2541	2547	2553	2559	2564	1	1	2	2	3	4	4	5	5
.41	2570	2576	2582	2588	2594	2600	2606	2612	2618	2624	1	1	2	2	3	4	4	5	5
.42	2630	2636	2642	2649	2655	2661	2667	2673	2679	2685	1	1	2	2	3	4	4	5	6
.43	2692	2698	2704	2710	2716	2723	2729	2735	2742	2748	1	1	2	3	3	4	4	5	6
.44	2754	2761	2767	2773	2780	2786	2793	2799	2805	2812	1	1	2	3	3	4	4	5	6
.45	2818	2825	2831	2838	2844	2851	2858	2864	2871	2877	1	1	2	3	3	4	5	5	6
.46	2884	2891	2897	2904	2911	2917	2924	2931	2938	2944	1	1	2	3	3	4	5	5	6
.47	2951	2958	2965	2972	2979	2985	2992	2999	3006	3013	1	1	2	3	3	4	5	5	6
.48	3020	3027	3034	3041	3048	3055	3062	3069	3076	3083	1	1	2	3	4	4	5	6	6
.49	3090	3097	3105	3112	3119	3126	3133	3141	3148	3155	1	1	2	3	4	4	5	6	6

TABLE II : ANTILOGARITHMS

	0	1	2	3	4	5	6	7	8	9	1	2	3	4	5	6	7	8	9
.50	3162	3170	3177	3184	3192	3199	3206	3214	3221	3228	1	1	2	3	4	4	5	6	7
.51	3236	3243	3251	3258	3266	3273	3281	3289	3296	3304	1	2	2	3	4	5	5	6	7
.52	3311	3319	3327	3334	3342	3350	3357	3365	3373	3381	1	2	2	3	4	5	5	6	7
.53	3388	3396	3404	3412	3420	3428	3436	3443	3451	3459	1	2	2	3	4	5	6	6	7
.54	3467	3475	3483	3491	3499	3508	3516	3524	3532	3540	1	2	2	3	4	5	6	6	7
.55	3548	3556	3565	3573	3581	3589	3597	3606	3614	3622	1	2	2	3	4	5	6	7	7
.56	3631	3639	3648	3656	3664	3673	3681	3690	3698	3707	1	2	3	3	4	5	6	7	8
.57	3715	3724	3733	3741	3750	3758	3767	3776	3784	3793	1	2	3	3	4	5	6	7	8
.58	3802	3811	3819	3828	3837	3846	3855	3864	3873	3882	1	2	3	4	4	5	6	7	8
.59	3890	3899	3908	3917	3926	3936	3945	3954	3963	3972	1	2	3	4	5	5	6	7	8
.60	3981	3990	3999	4009	4018	4027	4036	4046	4055	4064	1	2	3	4	5	6	6	7	8
.61	4074	4083	4093	4102	4111	4121	4130	4140	4150	4159	1	2	3	4	5	6	7	8	9
.62	4169	4178	4188	4198	4207	4217	4227	4236	4246	4256	1	2	3	4	5	6	7	8	9
.63	4266	4276	4285	4295	4305	4315	4325	4335	4345	4355	1	2	3	4	5	6	7	8	9
.64	4365	4375	4385	4395	4406	4416	4426	4436	4446	4457	1	2	3	4	5	6	7	8	9
.65	4467	4477	4487	4498	4508	4519	4529	4539	4550	4560	1	2	3	4	5	6	7	8	9
.66	4571	4581	4592	4603	4613	4624	4634	4645	4656	4667	1	2	3	4	5	6	7	8	9
.67	4677	4688	4699	4710	4721	4732	4742	4753	4764	4775	1	2	3	4	5	6	7	9	10
.68	4786	4797	4808	4819	4831	4842	4853	4864	4875	4887	1	2	3	4	5	7	8	9	10
.69	4898	4909	4920	4932	4943	4955	4966	4977	4989	5000	1	2	3	4	6	7	8	9	10
.70	5012	5023	5035	5047	5058	5070	5082	5093	5105	5117	1	2	3	5	6	7	8	9	10
.71	5129	5140	5152	5164	5176	5188	5200	5212	5224	5236	1	2	4	5	6	7	8	9	11
.72	5248	5260	5272	5284	5297	5309	5321	5333	5346	5358	1	2	4	5	6	7	8	10	11
.73	5370	5383	5395	5408	5420	5433	5445	5458	5470	5483	1	2	4	5	6	7	9	10	11
.74	5495	5508	5521	5534	5546	5559	5572	5585	5598	5610	1	3	4	5	6	8	9	10	11
.75	5623	5636	5649	5662	5675	5689	5702	5715	5728	5741	1	3	4	5	6	8	9	10	12
.76	5754	5768	5781	5794	5808	5821	5834	5848	5861	5875	1	3	4	5	7	8	9	10	12
.77	5888	5902	5916	5929	5943	5957	5970	5984	5998	6012	1	3	4	5	7	8	9	11	12
.78	6026	6039	6053	6067	6081	6095	6109	6124	6138	6152	1	3	4	5	7	8	10	11	12
.79	6166	6180	6194	6209	6223	6237	6252	6266	6281	6295	1	3	4	6	7	8	10	11	13
.80	6310	6324	6339	6353	6368	6383	6397	6412	6427	6442	1	3	4	6	7	9	10	11	13
.81	6457	6471	6486	6501	6516	6531	6546	6561	6577	6592	2	3	5	6	8	9	10	12	13
.82	6607	6622	6637	6653	6668	6683	6699	6714	6730	6745	2	3	5	6	8	9	11	12	14
.83	6761	6776	6792	6808	6823	6839	6855	6871	6887	6902	2	3	5	6	8	9	11	13	14
.84	6918	6934	6950	6966	6982	6998	7015	7031	7047	7063	2	3	5	6	8	10	11	13	15
.85	7079	7096	7112	7129	7145	7161	7178	7194	7211	7228	2	3	5	7	8	10	12	13	15
.86	7244	7261	7278	7295	7311	7328	7345	7362	7379	7396	2	3	5	7	8	10	12	13	15
.87	7413	7430	7447	7464	7482	7499	7516	7534	7551	7568	2	3	5	7	9	10	12	14	16
.88	7586	7603	7621	7638	7656	7674	7691	7709	7727	7745	2	4	5	7	9	11	12	14	16
.89	7762	7780	7798	7816	7834	7852	7870	7889	7907	7925	2	4	5	7	9	11	13	14	16
90	7943	7962	7980	7998	8017	8035	8054	8072	8091	8110	2	4	6	7	9	11	13	15	17
.91	8128	8147	8166	8185	8204	8222	8241	8260	8279	8299	2	4	6	8	9	11	13	15	17
.92	8318	8337	8356	8375	8395	8414	8433	8453	8472	8492	2	4	6	8	10	12	14	15	17
.93	8511	8531	8551	8570	8590	8610	8630	8650	8670	8690	2	4	6	8	10	12	14	16	18
.94	8710	8730	8750	8770	8790	8810	8831	8851	8872	8892	2	4	6	8	10	12	14	16	18
.95	8913	8933	8954	8974	8995	9016	9036	9057	9078	9099	2	4	6	8	10	12	15	17	19
.96	9120	9141	9162	9183	9204	9226	9247	9268	9290	9311	2	4	6	8	11	13	15	17	19
.97	9333	9354	9376	9397	9419	9441	9462	9484	9506	9528	2	4	7	9	11	13	15	17	20
.98	9550	9572	9594	9616	9638	9661	9683	9705	9227	9750	2	4	7	9	11	13	16	18	20
.99	9772	9795	9817	9840	9863	9886	9908	9931	9954	9977	2	5	7	9	11	14	16	18	20

TABLE III : POWERS, ROOTS AND RECIPROCALS

n	n^2	n^3	$\sqrt{n}$	$\sqrt[3]{n}$	$\sqrt{10n}$	$\sqrt[3]{10n}$	$\sqrt[3]{100n}$	$\frac{1}{n}$
1	1	1	1	1	3.162	2.154	4.642	1
2	4	8	1.414	1.260	4.772	2.714	5.848	.5000
3	9	27	1.732	1.442	5.477	3.107	6.694	.3333
4	16	64	2	1.587	6.325	3.420	7.368	.2500
5	25	125	2.236	1.710	7.671	3.684	7.937	.2000
6	36	216	2.449	1.817	7.745	3.915	8.434	.1667
7	49	343	2.646	1.913	8.361	4.121	8.879	.1429
8	64	512	2.828	2.000	8.944	4.309	9.283	.1250
9	81	729	3.000	2.080	9.487	4.481	9.655	.1111
10	100	1000	3.162	2.154	10.0	4.642	10.000	.1000
11	121	1331	3.317	2.224	10.488	4.791	10.323	.09091
12	144	1728	3.464	2.289	10.954	4.932	10.627	.08333
13	169	2197	3.606	2.351	11.402	5.066	10.914	.07692
14	196	2744	3.742	2.410	11.832	5.192	11.187	.07143
15	225	3375	3.873	2.466	12.247	5.313	11.447	.06667
16	256	4096	4.000	2.520	12.649	5.429	11.696	.06250
17	289	4913	4.123	2.571	13.038	5.540	11.935	.05882
18	324	5832	4.243	2.621	13.416	5.646	12.164	.05556
19	361	6859	4.359	2.568	13.784	5.749	12.386	.05263
20	400	8000	4.472	2.714	14.142	5.848	12.599	.05000
21	441	9261	4.583	2.759	14.491	5.944	12.806	.04762
22	484	10648	4.690	2.802	14.832	6.037	13.006	.04545
23	529	12167	4.796	2.844	15.166	6.127	13.200	.04348
24	576	13824	4.899	2.884	15.492	6.214	13.389	.04167
25	625	15625	5.000	2.924	15.811	6.300	13.572	.04000
26	676	17576	5.099	2.962	16.125	6.383	13.751	.03846
27	729	19683	5.196	3.000	16.432	6.463	13.925	.03704
28	784	21952	5.292	3.037	16.733	6.542	14.095	.03571
29	841	24389	5.385	3.072	17.029	6.619	14.260	.03448
30	900	27000	5.477	3.107	17.321	6.694	14.422	.03333
31	961	29791	5.568	3.141	17.607	6.768	14.581	.03226
32	1024	32768	5.657	3.175	17.889	6.840	17.736	.03125
33	1089	35937	5.745	3.208	18.166	6.910	14.888	.03030
34	1156	39304	5.831	3.240	18.439	6.980	15.037	.02941
35	1225	42875	5.916	3.271	18.708	7.047	15.183	.02857
36	1296	46656	6.000	3.302	18.974	7.114	15.326	.02778
37	1369	50653	6.083	3.332	19.235	7.179	15.467	.02703
38	1444	54872	6.164	3.362	19.494	7.243	15.605	.02632
39	1521	59319	6.245	3.391	19.748	7.306	15.741	.02504
40	1600	64000	6.325	3.420	20.000	7.368	15.874	.02500
41	1681	68921	6.403	3.448	20.248	7.429	16.005	.02439
42	1764	74088	6.481	3.476	20.494	7.489	16.134	.02381
43	1849	79507	6.557	3.503	20.736	7.548	16.261	.02326
44	1936	85184	6.633	3.530	20.976	7.606	16.386	.02273
45	2025	91125	6.708	3.557	21.213	7.663	16.510	.02222
46	2116	97336	6.782	3.583	21.448	7.719	16.631	.02174
47	2209	103823	6.856	3.609	21.679	7.775	16.751	.02128
48	2304	110592	6.928	3.634	21.909	7.830	16.869	.02083
49	2401	117649	7.000	3.659	22.136	7.884	16.985	.02041
50	2500	125000	7.071	3.684	22.361	7.937	17.100	.02000

TABLE III : POWERS, ROOTS AND RECIPROCALS

n	n^2	n^3	$\sqrt{n}$	$\sqrt[3]{n}$	$\sqrt{10n}$	$\sqrt[3]{10n}$	$\sqrt[3]{100n}$	$\frac{1}{n}$
51	2601	132651	7.141	3.708	22.583	7.990	17.213	.01961
52	2704	140608	7.211	3.733	22.804	8.041	17.325	.01923
53	2809	148877	7.280	3.756	23.022	8.093	17.435	.01887
54	2916	157464	7.348	3.780	23.238	8.143	17.544	.01852
55	3025	166375	7.416	3.803	23.452	8.193	17.652	.01818
56	3136	175616	7.483	3.832	23.664	8.243	17.758	.01786
57	3249	185193	7.550	3.849	23.875	8.291	17.863	.01754
58	3364	195112	7.616	3.871	24.083	8.340	17.967	.01724
59	3481	205379	7.681	3.893	24.290	8.387	18.070	.01695
60	3600	216000	7.746	3.915	24.495	8.334	18.171	.01667
61	3721	226981	7.810	3.936	24.698	8.481	18.272	.01639
62	3844	238328	7.874	3.958	24.900	8.527	18.371	.01613
63	3969	250047	7.937	3.979	25.100	8.573	18.469	.01587
64	4096	262144	8.000	4.000	25.298	8.618	18.566	.01562
65	4225	274625	8.062	4.021	25.495	8.662	18.663	.01538
66	4356	287496	8.124	4.041	25.690	8.707	18.758	.01515
67	4489	300763	8.185	4.062	25.884	8.750	18.852	.01493
68	4624	314432	8.246	4.082	26.077	8.794	18.945	.01471
69	4761	328509	8.307	4.102	26.268	8.837	19.038	.01449
70	4900	343000	8.367	4.121	26.458	8.879	19.129	.01429
71	5041	357911	8.426	4.141	26.646	8.921	19.220	.01408
72	5184	373248	8.485	4.160	26.833	8.963	19.310	.01389
73	5329	389017	8.544	4.179	27.019	9.004	19.399	.01370
74	5476	405224	8.602	4.198	27.203	9.045	19.487	.01351
75	5625	421875	8.660	4.217	27.386	9.086	19.574	.01333
76	5776	438976	8.718	4.236	27.568	9.126	19.661	.01316
77	5929	456533	8.775	4.254	27.740	9.166	19.747	.01299
78	6084	474552	8.832	4.273	27.928	9.205	19.832	.01282
79	6241	493039	8.888	4.291	28.107	9.244	19.916	.01266
80	6400	512000	8.944	4.309	28.284	9.283	20.000	.01250
81	6561	531441	9.000	4.327	28.460	9.322	20.083	.01235
82	6724	551368	9.055	4.344	28.636	9.360	20.165	.01220
83	6889	571787	9.110	4.362	28.810	9.398	20.247	.01205
84	7056	592704	9.165	4.380	28.983	9.435	20.328	.01190
85	7225	614125	9.220	4.397	29.155	9.473	20.408	.01176
86	7396	636056	9.274	4.414	29.326	9.510	20.488	.01163
87	7569	658503	9.327	4.431	29.496	9.546	20.507	.01149
88	7744	681472	9.381	4.448	29.665	9.583	20.646	.01136
89	7921	704969	7.434	4.465	29.833	9.619	20.224	.01124
90	8100	729000	9.487	4.487	30.000	9.655	20.801	.01111
91	8281	753571	9.539	4.498	30.166	9.691	20.878	.01099
92	8464	775688	9.592	4.514	30.332	9.726	20.954	.01087
93	8649	804357	9.644	4.531	30.496	9.761	21.029	.01075
94	8836	830584	9.695	4.547	30.659	9.796	21.105	.01064
95	9025	857375	9.747	4.563	30.822	9.830	21.179	.01053
96	9216	884736	9.798	4.579	30.984	9.865	21.253	.01042
97	9409	912673	9.849	4.595	31.145	9.899	21.327	.01031
98	9604	941192	9.899	4.610	31.305	9.933	21.400	.01020
99	9801	970299	9.900	4.626	31.464	9.697	21.472	.01010
100	10000	1000000	10.000	4.642	31.623	10.000	21.544	.01000

TABLE IV : BINOMIAL COEFFICENTS

n	$\binom{n}{0}$	$\binom{n}{1}$	$\binom{n}{2}$	$\binom{n}{3}$	$\binom{n}{4}$	$\binom{n}{5}$	$\binom{n}{6}$	$\binom{n}{7}$	$\binom{n}{8}$	$\binom{n}{9}$	$\binom{n}{10}$
1	1	1									
2	1	2	1								
3	1	3	3	1							
4	1	4	6	4	1						
5	1	5	10	10	5	1					
6	1	6	15	20	15	6	1				
7	1	7	21	35	35	21	7	1			
8	1	8	28	56	70	56	28	8	1		
9	1	9	36	84	126	126	84	36	9	1	
10	1	10	45	120	210	252	210	120	45	10	1
11	1	11	55	165	330	462	462	330	165	55	11
12	1	12	66	220	495	792	924	792	495	220	66
13	1	13	78	286	715	1287	1716	1716	1287	715	286
14	1	14	91	364	1001	2002	3003	3432	3003	2002	1001
15	1	15	105	455	1365	3003	5005	6435	6435	5005	3003
16	1	16	120	560	1820	4368	8008	11440	12870	11440	8008
17	1	17	136	680	2380	6188	12376	19448	24310	24310	19448
18	1	18	153	816	3060	8568	18564	31824	43758	48620	43758
19	1	19	171	969	3876	11628	27132	50388	75582	92378	92378
20	1	20	190	1140	4845	15504	38760	77520	125970	167960	184756

TABLE V : VALUES OF e^{-m} or exp $(-m)$

$(0 < m < 1)$

m	0	1	2	3	4	5	6	7	8	9
0.0	1.0000	.9900	.9802	.9704	.9608	.9512	.9418	.9324	.9231	.9139
0.1	.9084	.8958	.8869	.8781	.8694	.8607	.8521	.8437	.8353	.8270
0.2	.8187	.8106	.8025	.7945	.7866	.7788	.7711	.7634	.7558	.7483
0.3	.7408	.7334	.7261	.7189	.7118	.7047	.6977	.6907	.6839	.6771
0.4	.6703	.6636	.6570	.6505	.6440	.6376	.6313	.6250	.6188	.6126
0.5	.6065	.6005	.5945	.5886	.5827	.5770	.5712	.5655	.5599	.5543
0.6	.5488	.5434	.5379	.5326	.5273	.5220	.5169	.5117	.5066	.5016
0.7	.4966	.4916	.4868	.4819	.4771	.4724	.4677	.4630	.4584	.4538
0.8	.4493	.4449	.4404	.4360	.4317	.4274	.4232	.4190	.4184	.4107
0.9	.4066	.4025	.3985	.3946	.3906	.3867	.3829	.3791	.3753	.3716

$(m = 1, 2, 3, \ldots 10)$

m	1	2	3	4	5	6	7	8	9	10
e^{-m}	.36788	.13534	.04979	.01832	.00638	.002479	.00091	.000335	.000153	.000045

Note. To obtain values of e^{-m} for other values of m, use the laws of exponents.

Example. $e^{-2.35} = (e^{-2.00})(e^{-0.35}) = (\cdot 13534)(.13534)(.7047) = .095374$

TABLE VI : AREAS UNDER STANDARD NORMAL PROBABILITY CURVE

Normal Probability curve is given by : $f(x) = \frac{1}{\sigma\sqrt{2\pi}} \exp\left\{-\frac{1}{2}\left(\frac{x-\mu}{\sigma}\right)^2\right\}; -\infty < x < \infty$

and standard normal probability curve is given by :

$$f(z) = \frac{1}{\sqrt{2\pi}} \exp\left(-\frac{1}{2}z^2\right), -\infty < z < \infty$$

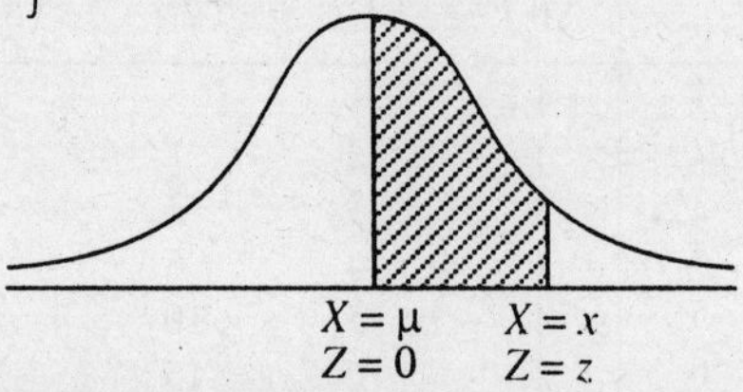

where $$Z = \frac{X - E(X)}{\sigma_x} = \frac{X-\mu}{\sigma} \sim N(0, 1)$$

The following table gives the shaded area in the diagram, *viz.* $P(0 < Z < z)$ for different values of z.

AREAS UNDER STANDARD NORMAL PROBABILITY CURVE

z \ z	0.00	0.01	0.02	0.03	0.04	0.05	0.06	0.07	0.08	0.09
0.0	0.0000	0.0040	0.0080	0.0120	0.0160	0.0199	0.239	0.0279	0.0319	0.0359
0.1	0.0398	0.0438	0.0478	0.0517	0.0557	0.0596	0.0636	0.0675	0.0714	0.0753
0.2	0.0793	0.0832	0.0871	0.0910	0.0948	0.0987	0.1026	0.1064	0.1103	0.1141
0.3	0.1179	0.1217	0.1255	0.1293	0.1331	0.1368	0.1406	0.1443	0.1480	0.1517
0.4	0.1554	0.1591	0.1628	0.1664	0.1700	0.1736	0.1772	0.1808	0.1844	0.1879
0.5	0.1915	0.1950	0.1985	0.2019	0.2054	0.2088	0.2123	0.2157	0.2190	0.2224
0.6	0.2257	0.2291	0.2324	0.2357	0.2389	0.2422	0.2454	0.2486	0.2517	0.2549
0.7	0.2580	0.2611	0.2642	0.2673	0.2704	0.2734	0.2764	0.2794	0.2823	0.2852
0.8	0.2881	0.2910	0.2939	0.2967	0.2995	0.3023	0.3051	0.3078	0.3106	0.3133
0.9	0.3159	0.3186	0.3212	0.3238	0.3264	0.3289	0.3315	0.3340	0.3365	0.3389
1.0	0.3413	0.3438	0.3461	0.3485	0.3508	0.3531	0.3554	0.3577	0.3599	0.3621
1.1	0.3643	0.3665	0.3686	0.3708	0.3729	0.3749	0.3770	0.3790	0.3810	0.3830
1.2	0.3849	0.3869	0.3888	0.3907	0.3925	0.3944	0.3962	0.3980	0.3997	0.4015
1.3	0.4032	0.4049	0.4066	0.4082	0.4099	0.4115	0.4131	0.4147	0.4162	0.4177
1.4	0.4192	0.4207	0.4222	0.4236	0.4251	0.4265	0.4279	0.4292	0.4306	0.4319
1.5	0.4332	0.4345	0.4357	0.4370	0.4382	0.4394	0.4406	0.4418	0.4429	0.4441
1.6	0.4452	0.4463	0.4474	0.4484	0.4495	0.4505	0.4515	0.4525	0.4535	0.4545
1.7	0.4554	0.4564	0.4573	0.4582	0.4591	0.4599	0.4608	0.4616	0.4625	0.4633
1.8	0.4641	0.4649	0.4656	0.4664	0.4671	0.4678	0.4686	0.4693	0.4699	0.4706
1.9	0.4713	0.4719	0.4726	0.4732	0.4738	0.4744	0.4750	0.4756	0.4761	0.4767
2.0	0.4772	0.4778	0.4783	0.4788	0.4793	0.4798	0.4803	0.4808	0.4812	0.4817
2.1	0.4821	0.4826	0.4830	0.4834	0.4838	0.4842	0.4846	0.4850	0.4854	0.4857
2.2	0.4861	0.4864	0.4868	0.4871	0.4875	0.4878	0.4881	0.4884	0.4887	0.4890
2.3	0.4893	0.4896	0.4898	0.4901	0.4904	0.4906	0.4909	0.4911	0.4913	0.4916
2.4	0.4918	0.4920	0.4922	0.4925	0.4927	0.4929	0.4931	0.4932	0.4934	0.4936
2.5	0.4938	0.4940	0.4941	0.4943	0.4945	0.4946	0.4948	0.4949	0.4951	0.4952
2.6	0.4953	0.4955	0.4956	0.4957	0.4959	0.4960	0.4961	0.4962	0.4963	0.4964
2.7	0.4965	0.4966	0.4967	0.4968	0.4969	0.4970	0.4971	0.4972	0.4973	0.4974
2.8	0.4974	0.4975	0.4976	0.4977	0.4977	0.4978	0.4979	0.4979	0.4980	0.4981
2.9	0.4981	0.4982	0.4982	0.4983	0.4984	0.4984	0.4985	0.4985	0.4986	0.4986
3.0	0.4987	0.4987	0.4987	0.4988	0.4988	0.4989	0.4989	0.4989	0.4990	0.4990
3.1	0.4990	0.4991	0.4991	0.4991	0.4992	0.4992	0.4992	0.4992	0.4993	0.4993
3.2	0.4993	0.4993	0.4994	0.4994	0.4994	0.4994	0.4994	0.4995	0.4995	0.4995
3.3	0.4995	0.4995	0.4995	0.4996	0.4996	0.4996	0.4996	0.4996	0.4996	0.4997
3.4	0.4997	0.4997	0.4997	0.4997	0.4997	0.4997	0.4997	0.4997	0.4997	0.4998
3.5	0.4998	0.4998	0.4998	0.4998	0.4998	0.4998	0.4998	0.4998	0.4998	0.4998
3.6	0.4998	0.4998	0.4999	0.4999	0.4999	0.4999	0.4999	0.4999	0.4999	0.4999
3.7	0.4999	0.4999	0.4999	0.4999	0.4999	0.4999	0.4999	0.4999	0.4999	0.4999
3.8	0.4999	0.4999	0.4999	0.4999	0.4999	0.4999	0.4999	0.4999	0.4999	0.4999
3.9	0.5000	0.5000	0.5000	0.5000	0.5000	0.5000	0.5000	0.5000	0.5000	0.5000

TABLE VI A : ORDINATES OF THE NORMAL PROBABILITY CURVE

The following table gives the ordinates of the standard normal probability curve, *i.e.*, it gives the value of

$$\phi(z) = \frac{1}{\sqrt{2\pi}} \exp\left(-\frac{1}{2}z^2\right), -\infty < z < \infty$$

for different valeus of z, where

$$Z = \frac{X - E(X)}{\sigma_X} = \frac{X - \mu}{\sigma} \sim N(0, 1).$$

Obviously $\phi(-z) = \phi(z)$.

↓Z →	.00	.01	.02	.03	.04	.05	.06	.07	.08	.09
0.0	.3989	.3989	.3989	.3988	.3986	.3984	.3982	.3980	.3977	.3973
0.1	.3970	.3965	.3961	.3956	.3951	.3945	.3939	.3932	.3925	.3918
0.2	.3910	.3902	.3894	.3885	.3876	.3867	.3857	.3847	.3836	.3825
0.3	.3814	.3802	.3790	.8778	.3765	.3752	.3739	.3725	.3712	.3697
0.4	.3683	.3668	.3653	.3637	.3621	.3605	.3589	.3572	.3555	.3538
0.5	.3521	.3503	.3485	.3467	.3448	.3429	.3410	.3391	.3372	.3352
0.6	.3332	.3312	.3292	.3271	.3251	.3230	.3209	.3187	.3166	.3144
0.7	.3123	.3101	.3079	.3056	.3034	.3011	.2989	.2966	.2943	.2920
0.8	.2897	.2874	.2850	.2827	.2803	.2780	.2756	.2732	.2709	.2685
0.9	.2661	.2637	.2613	.2589	.2565	.2541	.2516	.2492	.2468	.2444
1.0	.2420	.2396	.2371	.2347	.2323	.2299	.2275	.2251	.2227	.2203
1.1	.2179	.2155	.2131	.2107	.2083	.2059	.2036	.2012	.1989	.1965
1.2	.1942	.1919	.1895	.1872	.1849	.1826	.1804	.1781	.1758	.1736
1.3	.1714	.1691	.1669	.1647	.1626	.1604	.1582	.1561	.1539	.1518
1.4	.1497	.1476	.1456	.1435	.1415	.1394	.1374	.1354	.1334	.1315
1.5	.1295	.1276	.1257	.1238	.1219	.1200	.1182	.1163	.1145	.1127
1.6	.1109	.1092	.1074	.1057	.1040	.1023	.1006	.0989	.0973	.0957
1.7	.0940	.0925	.0909	.0893	.0878	.0863	.0848	.0833	.0818	.0804
1.8	.0790	.0775	.0761	.0748	.0734	.0721	.0707	.0694	.0681	.0669
1.9	.0656	.0644	.0632	.0620	.0608	.0596	.0584	.0573	.0562	.0551
2.0	.0540	.0529	.0519	.0508	.0498	.0488	.0478	.0468	.0459	.0449
2.1	.0440	.0431	.0422	.0413	.0404	.0396	.0387	.0379	.0371	.0363
2.2	.0355	.0347	.0339	.0332	.0325	.0317	.0310	.0303	.0297	.0290
2.3	.0283	.0277	.0270	.0264	.0258	.0252	.0246	.0241	.0235	.0229
2.4	.0224	.0219	.0213	.0208	.0203	.0198	.0194	.0189	.0184	.0180
2.5	.0175	.0171	.0167	.0163	.0158	.0154	.0151	.0147	.0143	.0139
2.6	.0136	.0132	.0129	.0126	.0122	.0119	.0116	.0113	.0110	.0107
2.7	.0104	.0101	.0099	.0096	.0093	.0091	.0088	.0086	.0084	.0081
2.8	.0079	.0077	.0075	.0073	.0071	.0069	.0067	.0065	.0063	.0061
2.9	.0060	.0058	.0056	.0055	.0053	.0051	.0050	.0048	.0047	.0046
3.0	.0044	.0043	.0042	.0040	.0039	.0038	.0037	.0036	.0035	.0034
3.1	.0033	.0032	.0031	.0030	.0029	.0028	.0027	.0026	.0025	.0025
3.2	.0024	.0023	.0022	.0022	.0021	.0020	.0020	.0019	.0018	.0018
3.3	.0017	.0017	.0016	.0016	.0015	.0015	.0014	.0014	.0013	.0013
3.4	.0012	.0012	.0012	.0011	.0011	.0010	.0010	.0010	.0009	.0009
3.5	.0009	.0008	.0008	.0008	.0008	.0007	.0007	.0007	.0007	.0006
3.6	.0006	.0006	.0006	.0005	.0005	.0005	.0005	.0005	.0005	.0004
3.7	.0004	.0004	.0004	.0004	.0004	.0004	.0003	.0003	.0003	.0003
3.8	.0003	.0003	.0003	.0003	.0003	.0002	.0002	.0002	.0002	.0002
3.9	.0002	.0002	.0002	.0002	.0002	.0002	.0002	.0002	.0001	.0001

Appendix 2–Bibliography
(Suggested Further Readings)

Allen, R.G.D., *Statistics for Economics*, Hutchinson & Co. (Publishers) Ltd., London, 1949.

Box and Tiao, *Time Series Analysis, Forecasting and Control,* Holden day.

Charles, A., *Decision-making under Uncertainty : Models and Choices,* Prentice Hall, Englewood Cliffs.

Chou, Ya-Lun. *Statistical Analysis,* Holt, Rinehart and Winston, New York.

Croxton and Cowden, *Applied General Statistics,* Prentice Hall, London and Prentice Hall of India.

Croxton and Cowden, *Practical Business Statistics,* Prentice Hall, London.

Crum, Patton and Tebbutt, *Introduction to Economic Statistics,* McGraw Hill Book Co., New York.

Dixon, W.S. and F.J. Massey, *Introduction to Statistical Analysis,* McGraw Hill Book Company, Inc. New York, 1951.

Fisher, R.A. and **F. Yates,** *Statistical Tables for Biological, Agricultural and Medical Research,* 3rd Ed. Haftner Publishing Company, New York, 1948.

Freund and Williams, *Modern Business Statistics,* Prentice Hall, Englewood.

Gupta, S.C. and **Kapoor, V.K.,** *Fundamentals of Mathematical Statistics,* Sultan Chand and Sons, Delhi, XI edition, 2002.

Gupta, S.C. and **Kapoor, V.K.,** *Fundamentals of Applied Statistics.* Sultan Chand and Sons, Delhi, 4th Edition, January 2007.

Karmel. P.H., *Applied Statistics for Economists,* Sir Issac Pitman and Sons Ltd., London.

King, W.I., *The Elements of Statistical Methods.* The Macmillan Co., New York.

Mills, Richard L., *Statistics for Applied Economics and Business,* McGraw Hill Book Co.

Neiswanger, William A., *Elementary Statistical Methods,* The Macmillian Co., New York.

Richard I. Levin and David S. Rubin. *Statistics for Management.* Seventh Edition. Pearson—Prentice Hall of India, New Delhi.

Riggleman and Frisbee, *Business Statistics,* McGraw Hill Book Co., New York.

Secrist Horace, *An Introduction to Statistical Methods,* The Macmillan Co., New York.

Simpson and Kafka, *Basic Statistics,* Oxford and I.B.H. Publishing Co., Calcutta.

Spurr and Smith, *Business and Economic Statistics,* Richard D. Irwin, Homewood, Illinois.

Tuttle, Alva M., *Elementary Business and Economic Statistics,* McGraw Hill Book Co., New York.

Waugh, A.E., *Elements of Statistical Methods,* 3rd Ed., McGraw Hill Co., New York, 1952.

Wheldon, *Business Statistics and Statistical Methods,* Macdonald and Evans Ltd., London.

Yule and Kendal, *An Introduction to the Theory of Statistics,* Charles Griffin & Co., London.

Index

F

G

H

I

J

K

L

M

R

S

T

U

V

W

Y